Sexuality Now
Embracing Diversity
6e

JANELL L. CARROLL
University of Hartford

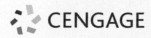
CENGAGE

Australia • Brazil • Mexico • Singapore • United Kingdom • United States

Sexuality Now: Embracing Diversity,
Sixth Edition
Janell L. Carroll

Product Director: Marta E. Lee-Perriard

Product Manager: Andrew Ginsberg

Content Developer: Nedah Rose

Product Assistant: Leah Johnson

Content Project Manager: Tanya Nigh

Art Director: Vernon Boes

Manufacturing Planner: Karen Hunt

Production and Composition Service:
MPS Limited

Photo Researcher: Nisha Bhanu Beegum,
Lumina Datamatics Ltd.

Text Researcher: Priyanga Srinivasan,
Lumina Datamatics Ltd.

Copy Editor: Theresa Kay

Text Designer: Diane Beasley

Cover Designer: Irene Morris

Cover Image: ferrantraite/Vetta/Getty Images;
Backgrounds: Eky Chan/Fotolia LLC, Vladislav
Bashutskyy/Fotolia LLC, Stockphoto-graf/
Shutterstock.com

For product information and technology assistance, contact us at
Cengage Customer & Sales Support, 1-800-354-9706.

For permission to use material from this text or product, submit all requests online at **www.cengage.com/permissions.**
Further permissions questions can be e-mailed to
permissionrequest@cengage.com.

Library of Congress Control Number: 2017938753

Student Edition:
ISBN: 978-1-337-40499-0

Loose-leaf Edition:
ISBN: 978-1-337-56356-7

Cengage
20 Channel Center Street
Boston, MA 02210
USA

Cengage is a leading provider of customized learning solutions with employees residing in nearly 40 different countries and sales in more than 125 countries around the world. Find your local representative at: **www.cengage.com.**

Cengage products are represented in Canada by Nelson Education, Ltd.

To learn more about Cengage platforms and services, visit **www.cengage.com.**

To register or access your online learning solution or purchase materials for your course, visit **www.cengagebrain.com.**

Printed in the United States of America
Print Number: 01   Print Year: 2017

Dedicated to my partner, Greg, and our three
wonderful children, Reagan, MacKenzie, and Samuel.
Thanks to each of you for making me the
luckiest person on earth!

About the Author

Dr. Janell L. Carroll received her PhD in human sexuality education from the University of Pennsylvania. A certified sexuality educator with the American Association of Sexuality Educators, Counselors, and Therapists, Dr. Carroll teaches in the psychology department at the University of Hartford in West Hartford, Connecticut, and has received numerous awards for her teaching and work in the field of human sexuality. The University of Hartford has recognized Dr. Carroll with the Sustained Excellence in Teaching Award and the Gordon Clark Ramsey Award for Creative Excellence, both given to professors who demonstrate outstanding excellence and creativity in the classroom. She has also been recognized by Planned Parenthood as a Sexuality Educator of the Year. Prior to teaching at the University of Hartford, Dr. Carroll was a tenured psychology professor at Baker University in Baldwin City, Kansas, where she was honored with awards for Professor of the Year and Most Outstanding Person on Campus. Dr. Carroll has traveled throughout the world exploring sexuality—from Japan's love hotels to Egypt's sex clinics—and has been actively involved in the development of several television pilots exploring sexuality. She has lectured extensively; has appeared on and has been quoted in several national publications, Internet news media outlets, and cyber-press articles; authored a syndicated sexuality column; and has hosted sexuality-related radio talk shows. She is also the author of a popular press book for young girls about menstruation titled *The Day Aunt Flo Comes to Visit*. She is currently working on a companion puberty book for boys titled *How Did This Frog Get in My Throat?* Dr. Carroll's website (http://www.drjanellcarroll.com) is a popular site for people to learn about sexuality and ask questions.

On a personal level, Dr. Carroll feels it is her mission to educate students and the public at large about sexuality—to help people think and feel through the issues for themselves. Dr. Carroll's success as a teacher comes from the fact that she loves her students as much as she loves what she teaches. She sees students' questions about sex as the foundation for her course and has brought that attitude, together with her enthusiasm for helping them find answers, to the sixth edition of *Sexuality Now*.

Brief Contents

Contents

CHAPTER 1

Exploring Human Sexuality: Past and Present   2

vm/Getty Images

CHAPTER 2

Understanding Human Sexuality: Theory and Research   26

Ryan Pierse/The Image Bank/Getty Images

CHAPTER 3

Communication and Sexuality   54

Tony Freeman/PhotoEdit

CHAPTER **4**

Gender Development, Gender Roles, and Gender Identity 76

Fabrizio Cacciatore/Photolibrary/Getty Images

CHAPTER 5

Female Sexual Anatomy and Physiology 104

From Dr. Carroll's Notebook... 105

The Female Sexual and Reproductive System 106

Laurie Nassif

CHAPTER 6

Male Sexual Anatomy and Physiology   132

Jupiter Images/Creatas/Alamy Stock Photo

CHAPTER 7

Love and Intimacy   154

Kevin Dodge/Getty Images

JGI/Jamie Grill/Blend Images/Getty Images

CHAPTER 8

Childhood and Adolescent Sexuality 176

© Pressmaster/Shutterstock.com

Jim Craigmyle/Getty Images

CHAPTER 9
Adult Sexual Relationships   204

Plush Studios/Blend Images/Getty Images

LStockStudio/Shutterstock.com

CHAPTER **10**

Sexual Expression   232

Pacific Press/Alamy Stock Photo

CHAPTER 11
Sexual Orientation   264

ZUMA Press, Inc./Alamy Stock Photo

DenKuvaiev/Getty Images

CHAPTER 12
Pregnancy and Birth   296

EMMANUEL DUNAND/Getty Images

CHAPTER **13**

Contraception and Abortion   328

Roy McMahon/Getty Images

CHAPTER **14**

Challenges to Sexual Functioning 372

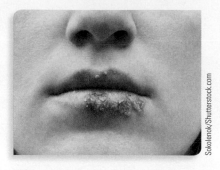
Sokolenok/Shutterstock.com

CHAPTER **15**

Sexually Transmitted Infections   398

From Dr. Carroll's Notebook...   399

Rainer Elstermann/Fancy/Alamy Stock Photo

CHAPTER **16**

Varieties of Sexual Expression   430

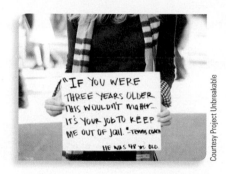

Courtesy Project Unbreakable

CHAPTER 17

Power and Coercion   454

Stefano Paterna/Alamy Stock Photo

CHAPTER **18**

Sexual Images and Selling Sex 488

Preface

Out of all the courses I teach, the human sexuality course is my favorite. Students come to this class with so much interest and enthusiasm; it's hard not to be as excited as they are. My approach to teaching has always been built on the belief that students and teachers have a unique relationship—we teach and learn together. Although it's true that students have much to learn about sexuality, they also are wonderful teachers. I learn a lot in my classes just by listening to my students open up and share their experiences, beliefs, and attitudes about sexuality. It is through these conversations with students that I've learned to appreciate where students are today and what their experiences in college are like. I've had many conversations about what they want to know and what causes problems in their relationships. All that I have learned throughout my many years of teaching I bring to you in this sixth edition of *Sexuality Now: Embracing Diversity*.

For me, the decision to write this book was an easy one. After teaching this course for more than 25 years, I was aware that many textbooks did not address the experience of today's students. Although I realize that authors include information they think students *need* to know, they often miss teaching what the students also *want* to know. I feel strongly that we need to teach students both what they need and want to know. For many years, I have kept files of student questions from my classes, travels, and website. These questions are the foundation of the "On Your Mind" feature. This feature enables students to find answers to the common questions they have about human sexuality.

Students who come to this course often have high levels of interest, but their experience and knowledge levels vary tremendously. Teaching a course with such varied student experience and knowledge levels can be tricky at best. But that is why it is important to have a textbook that is inclusive and speaks to every student, regardless of their experiences, family background, knowledge levels, age, gender, race, ethnicity, sexual orientation, or religion. Students have always been the foundation of *Sexuality Now,* and this is even more evident in the sixth edition of the textbook.

New to This Edition

This new edition of *Sexuality Now: Embracing Diversity* builds on the successes of prior editions and maintains many of the original features. Large-scale changes include a new design, an increased multicultural and multiethnic focus, and completely updated research with hundreds of new reference citations. There are comprehensive changes in the major areas of sexuality, such as gender, sexual expression, sexual orientation, contraception, challenges to sexual functioning, sexually transmitted infections, and sexual violence. Special attention has also been paid to making this new edition more inclusive of gay, lesbian, bisexual, and transgender students.

This sixth edition also includes increased coverage of cultural, ethnic, gender, and sexual orientation research. This is reflected throughout the textbook in new research studies, figures, features, and photos.

Dr. Carroll's Notebook

Throughout my travels around the world, I have met many interesting adults, teens, and children who have graciously shared their personal stories about sexuality with me. At the beginning of each chapter, I discuss a person or persons whose sexual experiences are related to the chapter content. Students will have the opportunity to read these stories and gain a better understanding of unique or difficult experiences. For example, Chapter 5, "Female Sexual Anatomy and Physiology," begins with the story of Stef, a woman fighting breast cancer; Chapter 9, "Adult Sexual Relationships," begins with the story of Dena and Lenny, a newly engaged mixed-race couple; Chapter 14, "Challenges to Sexual Functioning," begins with the story of a Dutch oncosexologist who helps terminally ill patients increase sexual satisfaction; Chapter 15, "Sexually Transmitted Infections and HIV/AIDS," begins with the story of a college student struggling with a recent herpes diagnosis; and Chapter 16, "Varieties of Sexual Expression," begins with one woman's experience with sexual kink. All of these chapter-opening Notebook features help to engage students and motivate them to want to learn more.

Real Research

This sixth edition continues to explore cutting-edge research in sexuality by including a "Real Research" feature. This feature developed out of my experiences in the classroom. I noticed that students love to learn "fun facts" about sexuality, and they would share them with their friends outside the classroom. This feature has been consistently rated highly by students. Following are some examples of "Real Research" features:

- The effects of informal hanging out and relationship satisfaction later in life; the growing practice of *drunkorexia* on college campuses; and celibacy syndrome in Japanese

- young people (Chapter 1, "Exploring Human Sexuality: Past and Present")

- How political ideology, privilege, education, gender, and power norms affect sex research (Chapter 2, "Understanding Human Sexuality: Theory and Research")

- How communication strategies affect stress and cortisol levels; global differences in cell phone usage; and gender differences in parent–teen communication (Chapter 3, "Communication and Sexuality")

- The effects of bisphenol A on the endocrine system; how young men's exposure to mainstream media affects their beliefs about gender roles; and attitudes toward transgender youth (Chapter 4, "Gender Development, Gender Roles, and Gender Identity")

- Pubic hair removal; exposure to bisphenol A and early onset puberty; body image and beliefs about menstruation; tampon use in American women; genital injuries among veterans; and the effects of stress on sperm production (Chapter 5, "Female Sexual Anatomy and Physiology," and Chapter 6, "Male Sexual Anatomy and Physiology")

- The effects of birth order on IQ; gender role expectations in young men; fears of discrimination and legal challenges in parents of transgender youth; declines in sex education among teens; and the effects of "robot babies" on teenage pregnancy (Chapter 8, "Childhood and Adolescent Sexuality")

- Sexual orientations and first impressions; the "anti-fat" bias in gay men; the effects of prenatal hormones on height differences among gay and straight men; self-disclosure and coming out on Facebook; and the effects of anti-gay prejudice on life expectancy (Chapter 11, "Sexual Orientation")

- Morning sickness and breast cancer risk; the use of ADHD medications during pregnancy; ultrasounds and the risk of childhood cancer; the effects of marijuana use on sperm production; and attachment styles and pain during labor (Chapter 12, "Pregnancy and Birth")

- The development of fertility tracking apps; culture and motivations for contraceptive use; the impact of contraceptive use on sexual desire; and ethnicity and contraceptive use (Chapter 13, "Contraception and Abortion")

- Attitudes and sexually transmitted infection (STI) testing; communication about STI risk in college students; condoms that detect STIs; home STI kits; ethnic/racial differences in STI testing; and global HIV prevalence (Chapter 15, "Sexually Transmitted Infections and HIV/AIDS")

- The use of online porn; the effects of Internet pornography on psychosocial functioning; and gender differences in porn use (Chapter 18, "Sexual Images and Selling Sex")

Timelines

Visual representations can often make difficult material easier for students to conceptualize and understand, and for this reason, you will find updated and redesigned Timelines. In this edition, there are Timelines on the following topics:

- Human Sexuality: Past and Present

- A History of Sex on Television

- Important Developments in the History of Sexuality Research

- Same-Sex Relationships Around the Globe

- The History of Assisted Reproduction

- History of Contraceptives in the United States

On Your Mind

Throughout my many years of teaching this course, I have collected thousands of questions that students have about sexuality. I have visited colleges and universities all over the world to better understand what today's college students want to know about sexuality and how it differs between the United States and abroad. My search for these student questions has taken me around the United States as well as to Asia, the Middle East, Latin America, and Europe. I also receive questions about sexuality on my website (http://www.drjanellcarroll.com) and through Twitter (@DrJanellCarroll). Student questions are helpful in understanding what information students want. In each "On Your Mind" feature, I answer a student question related to the nearby chapter content. Examples include the following:

- *Could I get human papillomavirus (HPV) from the HPV vaccine?*

- *Why do men so often wake up with erections?*

- *Can a woman be raped by an ex-boyfriend?*

- *Is it harmful if the sperm do not regularly exit the body?*

- *Is it damaging to children to see their parents naked?*

- *Why do women who live together experience menstruation at the same time?*

- *Can a woman breast-feed if her nipples are pierced?*

- *What are uterine fibroids?*

These types of questions are the backbone of *Sexuality Now* because they reflect what is on students' minds when it comes to sexuality.

Sex in Real Life

In the "Sex in Real Life" features, I present information about sexuality that is relevant to everyday life. These features explore a variety of different topics, such as medications to delay puberty, tampon use, polyamory, social networking, environmental toxins and sperm production, Internet sexual addictions, and media use in teens.

Sexual Diversity in Our World

One way students can challenge their assumptions about sexuality is by understanding how attitudes and practices vary across and among cultures, both within the United States and abroad. In addition to cross-cultural and multicultural information integrated into chapter material, "Sexual Diversity in Our World" features present in-depth accounts of topics such as female genital mutilation, Chinese foot binding, arranged marriage, transsexuality in Iran, AIDS orphans, circumcision, and cultural expressions of sexuality.

Other Important Features

Throughout each chapter, you will find definitions of important terms in the margin and pronunciation guides that help improve student communication about sexuality. Review Questions conclude each major section so that students can test their retention of the material. In addition, a Chapter Review appears at the end of each chapter to help students review important information.

Distinctive Content and Changes by Chapter

Chapter 1: Exploring Human Sexuality: Past and Present

Chapter-Opening Notebook: Dr. Carroll explores how societal, cultural, and family-of-origin factors influence our definition, understanding, and expression of sexuality.

Changes include:

- A revised and updated section on **popular television shows among college students**, including *Shameless, Modern Family, Game of Thrones, Bad Girl's Club,* and *Orange Is the New Black*—and the impact of such shows on personal attitudes about sexuality

- New research on **teens and the use of various media**, including a discussion about the sexual content of various media

- An updated section on the **legal status of same-sex marriage**

- Two redesigned and **updated Timelines**—"Human Sexuality: Past and Present" and "A History of Sex on Television"— helping students to conceptualize and learn material

Chapter 2: Understanding Human Sexuality: Theory and Research

Chapter-Opening Notebook: Dr. Carroll discusses sexuality research and explores the design and implementation of a unique research project done by a student who was taking the human sexuality course.

Changes include:

- Updates from the most recent **Youth Risk Behavior Survey**, the **National College Health Assessment**, and the **National Survey of Family Growth**

- Updates from major research publications including the World Health Organization, United Nations Children's Fund (UNICEF), and Joint United Nations Programme on HIV/AIDS (UNAIDS). Includes most recent statistics from various **global studies focusing on specific issues related to sexuality**

- A revised and updated section on **Internet-based research methods**, including the use of social media in sexuality research

- An updated discussion of **the effects of politics, privilege, education, and power on sexuality research**

- An updated and comprehensive exploration of the future of sexuality research, including a review of **problem-driven**

research and the importance of collaboration between researchers of various disciplines

- A summary table of the major theories and a list of questions that each theorist would ask are included to help students conceptualize theoretical differences; also included is a redesigned and **updated Timeline**—"Important Developments in the History of Sexuality Research"

Chapter 3: Communication and Sexuality

Chapter-Opening Notebook: Dr. Carroll explores the role of communication in intimate relationships and how misuse of these communication technologies can contribute to relationship dissatisfaction.

Changes include:

- A revised and updated section on communication differences and similarities with respect to **gender, culture,** and **sexual orientation**

- An expanded section on **"technoference," computer-mediated communication** and **social networks**, including e-mail, Skype, Facebook, FaceTime, Instagram, and Twitter; information on the **impact of these technologies on communication patterns**, expectations, challenges, and misunderstandings involved with their use; and **cross-cultural research on computer-mediated communication**

- An expanded section on **college students and the use of texting** as a form of communication, including the use of texting on college campuses, texting versus face-to-face communication, gender and age differences in texting, the use of **emojis and emoticons**, the **evolution of technology** adoption and usage, and the **advantages and disadvantages of texting**

- A revised and updated section on **the importance of sexual communication**, including the challenges and obstacles associated with this type of communication, verbal and nonverbal sexual communication, the reciprocal nature of sexual communication, and important components of sexual communication

Chapter 4: Gender Development, Gender Roles, and Gender Identity

Chapter-Opening Notebook: Dr. Carroll discusses one college student's decision to undergo gender transition during her junior year of college.

Changes include:

- An updated introduction exploring the current changes in the **gender landscape**, with information about **transgender rights, gender pronouns**, the effects of **misgendering**, and updated information on gender roles and stereotypes

- A revised and updated section on **intersexuality**, including a feature box dedicated to specific issues involved in the birth of an intersex child

- A revised and updated section on **differences in sex development**, including clarifications about the revised *DSM-5* and a review of chromosomal and hormonal conditions, along with a revised table outlining the various differences of sex development

- An expanded section on the **gender spectrum** that explores the **gender binary** and the richness of gender diversity;

updated discussion of issues concerning the **transgender community**, including gender dysphoria, gender fluidity, and transprejudice

- A revised and updated section on the use of **puberty-delay medications** in transgender children; exploration of the use of these drugs both in the United States and abroad

- A revised and updated section on **medical and surgical gender transitions**, including a discussion about the various paths that transgender people choose from no medical intervention to penectomy, orchiectomy, urethral rerouting, vaginoplasty, scrotoplasty, metoidioplasty, and phalloplasty

- An updated section on **gender-neutral housing** on college and university campuses

Chapter 5: Female Sexual Anatomy and Physiology

Chapter-Opening Notebook: Dr. Carroll discusses breast cancer and explores one woman's journey from diagnosis to remission.
Changes include:

- A new feature box on the **history of tampons**, including controversies, risks associated with use, and updated FDA statements

- A revised and updated section on the popular practice of **pubic hair removal**, including risks and new recommended guidelines

- An updated section on the use of **menstrual suppression in transgender men**

- Revised **recommendations for pelvic examinations** from the American College of Obstetricians and Gynecologists

- An updated section on **vaginal infections**, including risks involved with using various products, such as perfumed body washes, sprays, and talc powders; and common reactions to vaginal infections

- Updates on **female genital mutilation** from a recent World Health Organization report

- A revised and updated section on **polycystic ovarian syndrome, pelvic inflammatory disease**, and **vaccines to prevent urinary tract infections**

- A revised and updated section on **breast, endometrial**, and **cervical cancers** with data from the American Cancer Society; includes guidelines for screening, research on risk factors including smoking and hormonal contraceptive use

- A review of the use of **mammography and the over-diagnosis of breast cancer;** also explores the use of **nipple areola tattooing** in breast reconstruction surgery

- A revised and updated section on the use of **hormone replacement therapy** in menopause

Chapter 6: Male Sexual Anatomy and Physiology

Chapter-Opening Notebook: Dr. Carroll explores masculinity and discusses one man's recollections of growing up male, peer group pressure, and body image issues.
Changes include:

- A revised and updated section on **environmental and dietary causes of decreasing sperm counts**, including BPA and phthalate exposure, stress, laptop computers, smartphones, biking, smoking, stress, and alcohol use on sperm production

- A revised and updated section on the use of **performance-enhancing drugs** including **anabolic-androgenic steroid use** and adverse effects associated with their use

- A revised and updated section on **breast, penile, testicular**, and **prostate cancers in men**, with statistics from the American Cancer Society; includes new research on important risk factors

- A revised and updated section on **male circumcision**; includes cross-cultural research

- Updated information on **HPV infection and penile cancer**

Chapter 7: Love and Intimacy

Chapter-Opening Notebook: Dr. Carroll discusses long-term relationships and explores one couple's strategies for keeping passion alive.
Changes include:

- A revised and updated section on **childhood attachment styles**, including a discussion about the flexible nature of attachment styles and how they are associated with various emotions, including jealousy

- An updated section on **neuroscience**, the **major histocompatibility complex**, pheromones, and brain imaging, and the role these play in the development of love

- A revised and updated section on **relationship breakups** and vulnerability to self-blame, loss of self-esteem, and distrust of others

- An updated section on the **long-term effects of parental divorce**

Chapter 8: Childhood and Adolescent Sexuality

Chapter-Opening Notebook: Dr. Carroll discusses sexuality education and compares America's "sex-negative" approach with Holland's "sex-positive" approach.
Changes include:

- A new feature exploring the use of **puberty delay drugs in children,** along with an introduction to Jazz Jennings

- A revised and updated section with data from the most recent **governmental studies on childhood sexuality**, including the National Survey of Family Growth (NSFG), National Longitudinal Study of Adolescent Males, National Longitudinal Study of Adolescent Health, and the Youth Risk Behavior Surveillance System, with a summary table that shows students the target populations and data methods these four studies used

- Updated statistics on teenage sexual behavior, including masturbation, oral sex, anal sex, sexual intercourse, and same-sex sexual behavior; also includes the latest data on teen contraceptive use, pregnancy, and abortion

- New figures from the Guttmacher Institute on **teenage sexual activity**, timing of **first sexual intercourse in teens**, and **contraceptive use in teens**

Chapter 9: Adult Sexual Relationships

Chapter-Opening Notebook: Dr. Carroll discusses mixed-race relationships and explores some of the challenges that may arise in mixed-race relationships.

Changes include:

- A new section on **non-committed relationships**, exploring hookups, casual sex, **romantic ambiguity, romantic exploitation,** and the use of **social dating apps** such as Tinder, Bumble, Grindr, HER, and FetLife

- A revised and updated section with new data from the U.S. Census on **interracial and intercultural dating, cohabitation,** and **marriage** as well as **living arrangements in older adults**

- An updated section on how communication technologies have increased **long-distance dating** on today's college campuses; includes novel approaches to dating, such as websites and smartphone apps

- A new section on cheating and **Internet Infidelity**; explores the challenges of the Internet

- A revised and updated section on **nonmonogamy** and **polyamory**

- New figures on the **top reasons for marriage**; percentages **of never-married adults in the United States, mixed marriages, and remarriage**

- A redesigned and **updated Timeline**—"Same-Sex Relationships Around the Globe"—on the **legality of same-sex relationships**

Chapter 10: Sexual Expression

Chapter-Opening Notebook: Dr. Carroll discusses the use of online sexual chat rooms and explores one student's experience using this technology and the effects it had on her intimate relationship.

Changes include:

- A revised and updated section on the **important influences on sexuality,** including hormones and neurotransmitters, family background, ethnicity, and religion

- A revised and updated section with updated research on various sexual behaviors, including sexual fantasy, masturbation, manual sex, oral sex, vaginal intercourse, and anal intercourse

- A discussion of the effects of **political orientation on sexual activity**

- A revised and updated section with updated research on **sex in non-committed relationships;** explores sexual behaviors, gender differences, and motivations

- A discussion of how **porn-related masturbation** can affect partnered sex

- A revised and updated section on **safer sex behaviors** and **alcohol use and sexual risk-taking**

Chapter 11: Sexual Orientation

Chapter-Opening Notebook: Dr. Carroll discusses same-sex marriage in the Netherlands and explores one couple's long-term marriage.

Changes include:

- A revised and updated section on **sexual orientation theory,** including new research on biological, developmental, sociological, and interactional theories, including **intersectionality**

- A revised and updated section on the **biological theories of sexual orientation,** including new research on brain, facial shape, and hormones

- A revised and updated section on dating and the use of **LGB social dating apps**

- A revised and updated section on **gay-straight alliances,** clubs, and support groups on college and university campuses

- A new figure on **sexual orientation and earning prospects** around the world

- A new section on legal **same-sex marriage** and the effects of legalized marriage on LGB relationships

- A revised and updated section on **LGBT seniors;** including new information on **LGBT retirement and living communities**

- A revised and updated section on **same-sex parenting** and **adoption**

- A revised and updated section including data from the recently released **Global Study of Attitudes Towards Homosexuality** from the Pew Research Center

- New information from the **International Lesbian, Gay, Bisexual, Trans, and Intersex Association's recent State-Sponsored Homophobia Report** exploring sexual orientation law

- A revised and updated section on **hate crime victimization** with data from the recently released Federal Bureau of Investigation report along with a discussion of the **Pulse Nightclub shooting**

Chapter 12: Pregnancy and Birth

Chapter-Opening Notebook: Dr. Carroll discusses lesbian families and explores one couple's journey to parenthood.

Changes include:

- New figures from the recently released studies by the Centers for Disease Control on **birth rates by age of mother, first-birth rates for older mothers by race and ethnicity,** and **U.S. cesarean rates;** includes a discussion about the American College of Obstetricians and Gynecologists recommendations for choosing cesarean-section delivery

- A revised and updated section on the use of **prescription medications during pregnancy** and the possible link to **autism spectrum disorders;** also includes information on **the use of ADHD medications** during pregnancy

- A revised and updated section on problems during pregnancy, including **ectopic pregnancy, bisphenol A (BPA) and miscarriage;** diagnostic **blood tests for Down syndrome;** and **genetic risk for breech birth**

- A revised and updated section on assisted reproductive technologies; includes updated information on the **Warnock Report on infertility practices** and global **regulations of sperm donation;** updated information on **embryo and ova cryopreservation, preimplantation genetic diagnosis, ovarian tissue removal,** as well as the use of **assisted reproductive techniques in LGB couples**

- A revised and updated section on breast-feeding including **racial/ethnic differences in rates of breast-feeding**

- A redesigned and **updated Timeline:** "The History of Assisted Reproduction"

Chapter 13: Contraception and Abortion

Chapter-Opening Notebook: Dr. Carroll explores illegal abortion and discusses one woman's experience undergoing an abortion procedure prior to the legalization of abortion with *Roe v. Wade*.

Changes include:

- A revised and updated section on **lifestyle, racial/ethnic, educational,** and **religious factors** that influence contraceptive use

- New figures on **contraceptive use in the United States** from the Centers for Disease Control; **median ages at reproductive events and factors associated with unintended pregnancy; global contraceptive use** from the United Nations; the use of emergency contraception in the United States; use of emergency contraception by age, marital status, ethnicity/race, and education; a revised and updated section on **contraceptive use** and **abortion** with recent data and figures from the Centers for Disease Control, Guttmacher Institute, Pew Research Center, and the United Nations

- A revised and updated section on **medications and herbs that may interact with hormonal contraception,** including alcohol and certain antibiotics, antidepressants, anti-inflammatories, and antiretrovirals

- New information about FDA-approved IUDs, including **Kyleena Liletta, Mirena, Paraguard,** and **Skyla,** with a detailed discussion of advantages and disadvantages of each

- A revised and updated section on the relationship between **hormonal contraception and female reproductive cancers**

- A revised and updated section on **emergency contraception (EC)**; includes over-the-counter status and **controversies about the use of EC in women with high BMIs**; also includes information on the use of EC by age, marital status, race/ethnicity, and education; includes new figures on percentages of **women who have used EC**

- New figures on **contraceptive use around the world** and the use of **hormonal contraception for non-contraceptive reasons**

- New table for students to know **what to do if a they forget or are late in using hormonal contraception**

- A revised and updated section on **future directions in contraceptive research,** including injectable implants, reversible vasectomies, implants, plugs, and Vasalgel, long-term hormonal contraceptives, along with **vaccines and immunocontraceptives**

- A revised and updated section on **surgical and medical abortion** procedures, along with advantages and disadvantages of various procedures

- A revised and updated section exploring increasing **state laws restricting abortion,** including physician and hospital requirements, gestational limits, public funding restrictions, state-mandated counseling, waiting periods, and parental involvement/notification/consent laws

- New updates on **threats to *Roe v. Wade*** in the current U.S. political environment

- A redesigned and **updated Timeline:** "The History of Contraceptives in the United States"

Chapter 14: Challenges to Sexual Functioning

Chapter-Opening Notebook: Dr. Carroll discusses sexual pleasure in the terminally ill and explores the work of a Dutch oncosexologist who helps terminally ill patients maintain satisfying sex lives.

Changes include:

- A discussion about *DSM-5* **diagnostic revisions,** including rationale for changes and proposed contributing psychological and relationship factors

- An updated section exploring **differences between desire problems and asexuality**

- A revised and updated section on **treatments for sexual disorders**

- An updated section on **aphrodisiacs,** including risks and side effects

- A revised and updated section with FDA recommendations for the **use of testosterone in erectile disorder**

- A revised and updated section on **vulvodynia** and **vulvar vestibulitis syndrome**

- A revised and updated section on the effects of **cancer diagnosis** and **treatments** on sexual functioning and satisfaction; includes discussion of **minority stress** and the effects of cancer diagnosis on LGB persons

Chapter 15: Sexually Transmitted Infections and HIV/AIDS

Chapter-Opening Notebook: Dr. Carroll discusses sexually transmitted infections and explores one college student's emotional and physical reactions after being diagnosed with herpes.

Changes include:

- New statistics and figures from the recently released **Centers for Disease Control's Sexually Transmitted Disease Surveillance** and **Reported Sexually Transmitted Diseases in the United States,** along with the **UNAIDS Report** on the **Global AIDS Epidemic**

- A revised and updated section on **racial, ethnic,** and **gender disparities in sexually transmitted infection (STI)** rates

- A new feature box on **STIs and sexual assault** discusses the risk for infection, along with recommendations for testing and treatment

- An updated feature box on **safe sex in college** and decreasing the risks for acquiring STIs; includes updated information on **high-risk groups and STIs**

- A revised and updated section on **STIs in same-sex couples**

- A revised and updated section on **STIs in pregnancy** and recommendations for treatment and delivery options

- A new section on the association of **HPV and throat cancer**; also explores the **use of condoms and dental dams** during oral sex

- A revised and updated section on **Gardasil-9,** the only available **vaccine for human papillomavirus,** including recently released recommendations from the Centers for Disease Control

- A revised and updated section on diagnostic testing for **herpes simplex virus**; also includes information on the use of **suppressive therapy** and the **decreased risk of viral shedding** and infections in sexual partners; and the development of a vaccine for herpes simplex virus

- An expanded section on the development and availability of **at-home STI testing**
- Updated recommendations from the Centers for Disease Control for **partners of persons** who have STIs

Chapter 16: Varieties of Sexual Expression

Chapter-Opening Notebook: Dr. Carroll discusses sexual kink and explores one woman's experience in the sexual kink culture.
Changes include:

- An updated discussion about *DSM-5* **diagnostic revisions** to paraphilias and the move to **depathologize unusual sexual behaviors**
- A revised and updated section on **sexual addiction** and **hypersexual disorder**
- A new section on **Internet sexual addictions** as well as a discussion about **video voyeurism** and the illegal practices of **upskirting/downblousing**
- An updated section on **International Megan's Law** and child sex trafficking

Chapter 17: Power and Coercion

Chapter-Opening Notebook: Dr. Carroll discusses sexual violence on college campuses and explores one woman's experience with acquaintance rape.
Changes include:

- Includes data from the recent **National Intimate Partner and Sexual Violence Survey (NISVS)** along with updated statistics from the **CDC's Sexual Violence Surveillance** Program; includes the five types of sexual violence outlined by the NISVS, including **rape, sexual coercion, unwanted sexual contact, forced penetration,** and **non-contact unwanted sexual behavior**
- A revised and updated section on **sexual violence on college campuses**; includes information on the **Campus Sexual Violence Elimination Act (Campus Save Act), Know Your IX campaign,** the **White House Task Force to Protect Students from Sexual Assault**, and the **Not Alone: Together Against Sexual Assault organization**
- Discusses the **Mentors in Violence Prevention program, developed by Jackson Katz**, to reduce sexual violence on college campuses
- A revised and updated section on **sexual violence in transgender persons**
- A revised and updated section on the **link between sexual violence and alcohol use on college campuses**; includes a discussion about the importance of **sexual consent**
- A revised and updated section on **marital rape**
- A revised and updated section on **intimate partner violence** and **intimate partner homicide**, stalking, sexual harassment, and cyber-harassment on college and university campuses; also includes recent events, such as **sexual harassment at major television networks**

Chapter 18: Sexual Images and Selling Sex

Chapter-Opening Notebook: Dr. Carroll explores the impact of reality shows on sexual attitudes and behaviors in today's college students.
Changes include:

- A revised and updated section on sexual content on television and other media
- An updated section on the **Internet and electronic technologies,** including **Pornhub, forums/subreddits, Tumblr, virtual reality porn, web camming,** and image sharing
- A revised and updated section on the **adult entertainment industry** and the use of pornographic websites; also includes updated information about **the use of condoms in pornographic films**
- A revised and updated section on **sex work** that explores the work of sex workers, escorts, phone sex operators, strippers, and porn stars
- A revised and updated section on national and international **sex trafficking** and **sex slavery**; including a review of the work being done to reduce sex trafficking

MindTap for Carroll's *Sexuality Now: Embracing Diversity*

MindTap is a personalized teaching experience with relevant assignments that guide students to analyze, apply, and improve thinking, allowing you to measure skills and outcomes with ease.

- Guide Students: A unique learning path of relevant readings, media, and activities that moves students up the learning taxonomy from basic knowledge and comprehension to analysis and application.
- Personalized Teaching: Becomes yours with a Learning Path that is built with key student objectives. Control what students see and when they see it. Use it as-is or match to your syllabus exactly—hide, rearrange, add, and create your own content.
- Promote Better Outcomes: Empower instructors and motivate students with analytics and reports that provide a snapshot of class progress, time in course, engagement, and completion rates.

In addition to the benefits of the platform, MindTap for Carroll's *Sexuality Now*:

- Integrates videos and animations into the ebook and readings to fully engage students and reinforce important concepts.
- Features "From Dr. Carroll's Notebook" entries, which open every chapter, set the tone for student learning, and often accompanied by video footage of Dr. Carroll's Notebook discussions.
- Includes "Speak Your Mind" videos that allow students to view and respond to intriguing questions about sex, compare their answers with their classmates, and view Dr. Carroll's responses.
- Provides assignments and activities, including gradable matching activities and chapter quizzes.

Supplements to Help Teach the Course

Instructor Resource Center

Everything you need for your course in one place! This collection of book-specific lecture and class tools is available online via www.cengage.com/login. Access and download videos, PowerPoint presentations, images, instructor's manual, and more.

Online PowerPoint for Sexuality Now: Embracing Diversity

PowerPoint slides provide a collection of book-specific Power-Point lecture and class tools to enhance the educational experience.

Online Instructor's Resource Manual

Each chapter of the comprehensive Online Instructor's Resource Manual gives you all you need to teach human sexuality, including:

- A list of "Teaching Tips" to guide your instruction with possible pitfalls and how to address them
- A detailed chapter outline providing quick access to each chapter's content
- A listing of all videos offered only with Carroll's Sexuality Now, as well as discussion questions for each video and suggestions for discussing and directing students to popular and current TV shows, movies, and YouTube videos related to chapter content
- Lecture and discussion tie-ins for the "Real Research" and "On You Mind" features to get students to think critically about sexuality
- Critical thinking questions related to chapter content to help generate classroom discussion
- Suggestions for classroom activities, assessments, and discussions
- A listing of relevant websites related to chapter content

Cognero

Cengage Learning Testing Powered by Cognero is a flexible, online system that allows you to author, edit, and manage test bank content from multiple Cengage Learning solutions, create multiple test versions in an instant, and deliver tests from your LMS, your classroom, or wherever you want.

Acknowledgments

Undertaking a book such as this is a huge task and one that I could never have done without the help of many smart, creative, and fun people. Recognition should first go to all my students who, over the years, have opened themselves up to me and felt comfortable enough to share intimate, and sometimes painful, details of their lives. I know that their voices throughout this book will help students truly understand the complexity of human sexuality.

Second, and of equal importance, a big thank you goes to my family, who helped me pull off this new edition. I couldn't have done it without them. My partner was an endless support, providing around-the-clock statistical and mathematical clarifications. My children have been so patient and helpful and through the process have continued to learn. Having college-aged children has helped me to truly understand the importance of sexuality education in the lives of college students. As in all projects of such magnitude, there are hundreds of others who supported me with friendship, advice, information, laughter, and a focus on the "big picture."

The sixth edition of Sexuality Now is the result of a team effort. Our product team manager, Star Burruto, helped us hit the ground running providing endless support and advice. Andrew Ginsberg, the product manager, joined the team with great visions for this new edition of Sexuality Now and helped support the new cutting-edge video package. Many others deserve thanks, including our content developers, Nedah Rose, and Tangelique Williams-Grayer; Content Project Managers Tanya Nigh, and Samen Iqbal; and Project Manager Lori Hazzard at MPS Limited. Everyone did a superb job of managing all the production details calmly, patiently, and creatively. Vernon Boes, our art director, Diane Beasley (designer), and Irene Morris (cover designer) were instrumental in creating the book's inviting design. I also appreciate the work of our dedicated photo researchers and copy editors, including Theresa Kay. Finally, I am also thankful for the help of Leah Jenson, the product assistant; and Adrienne McCrory in marketing. I look forward to a long and productive relationship with everyone at Cengage Learning.

A special thanks to all the professors who shared feedback and offered suggestions, especially Amy Popillion, Gary Gute, Konnie McCaffree, Carole Mackenzie, and Eli Green. Also thanks to all the students who have used this textbook and took the time to write me with suggestions, questions, and clarifications. I take your feedback very seriously.

I am so grateful to many others who so willingly gave their time or support (or both), especially Lisa Belval, Phyllis Danielson, Lori Nassif, Sheila Kendrick, Susan Rietano Davey, Tucker Davey, Peter Jannuzzi, Michael Carroll, Donna Burke, Barbara Curry, Megan Mahoney, Petra Lambert, Tamara Kanter, Jessica Morrissey, Teo Drake, Kate D'Adamo, Maggie Weisensel, Matt Deiner, Matthew and Noah Blocker-Glynn, and Amy and Nicholas Tsacoyeanes, without whom this would not have been possible.

Reviewers

It is important to acknowledge the contributions of the reviewers who have carefully read my manuscript and offered many helpful suggestions. I would like to thank them all for their time and dedication to this project.

Michael Agopian, Los Angeles Harbor College; Katherine Allen, Virginia Polytechnic Institute and State University; Kristin Anderson, Houston Community College; Veanne Anderson, Indiana State University; Sheryl Attig, University of Arizona; Jim Backlund, Kirtland Community College; Amy Baldwin, Los Angeles City College; Sharon Ballard, East Carolina University; Janice Bass, Plymouth State University; Dorothy Berglund, Mississippi University for Women; Rebecca L. Bosek, University of Alaska–Anchorage; Glenn Carter, Austin Peay State University; Cindi Ceglian, South Dakota State University; Jane Cirillo, Houston Community College–Southeast; Kristen Cole, San Diego City College; Lorry Cology, Owens Community College; Sally Conklin, Northern Illinois University; David Corbin, University of Nebraska–Omaha; Randolf Cornelius, Vassar College; Nancy P. Daley, University of Texas–Austin; Christine deNeveu, National Louis University–Chicago; Michael Devoley, Northern Arizona University; Jim Elias, California State University–Northridge; Edith B. Ellis, College of Charleston; Sussie Eshun, East Stroudsburg University; Linda Evinger, University of Southern Indiana; Joe Fanelli, Syracuse University; Jorge Figueroa, University of North Carolina–Wilmington; Anne Fisher, New College of Florida; Randy Fisher, University of Central Florida; Edward Fliss, Saint Louis Community College; Sue Frantz, Highline Community College; Joyce Frey, Pratt Community College; Irene Frieze, University of Pittsburgh; George Gaither, Ball State University; David Gershaw, Arizona Western College; Lois Goldblatt, Arizona State University; Debra L. Golden, Grossmont College; Anne Goshen, California Polytechnic State University–San Luis Obispo; Kevin Gross, East Carolina University; Gary Gute, University of Northern Iowa; Shelley Hamill, Winthrop University; Michelle Haney, Berry College; Robert Hensley, Iowa State University; Roger Herring, University of Arkansas–Little Rock; Karen Hicks, CAPE; Helen Hoch, New Jersey City University; Lisa Hoffman-Konn, The University of Arizona; Susan Horton, Mesa Community College; Jean Hoth, Rochester Community and Technical College; Karen Howard, Endicott College; Jennifer Hughes, Agnes Scott College; Kathleen Hunter, SUNY College–Brockport; Alicia Huntoon, Washington State University; Bobby Hutchison, Modesto Junior College; Ingrid Johnston-Robledo, SUNY–Fredonia; Ethel Jones, South Carolina State University; Shelli Kane, Nassau Community College; Joanne Karpinen, Hope College; Michael Kelly, Henderson State University; Chrystyna Kosarchyn, Longwood College; Gloria Lawrence, Wayne State College; Holly Lewis, University of Houston–Downtown; Kenneth Locke, University of Idaho; Betsy Lucal, Indiana University–South Bend; Laura Madson, New Mexico State University; Jody Martin de Camilo, St. Louis Community College–Meramec; Genevieve Martinez Garcia, George Washington University; Jennifer McDonald, Washington State University; Sue McKenzie, Dawson College; Mikki Meadows, Eastern Illinois University; Corey Miller, Wright State University; Laura Miller, Edinboro University; Robert Morgan, University of Alaska–Fairbanks; Carol Mukhopadhyay, San Jose State University; Jennifer Musick, Long Beach City College; Robin Musselman, Lehigh Carbon Community College; Shirley Ogletree, Texas State University–San Marcos; Missi Patterson, Austin Community College; Julie Penley, El Paso Community College; Robert Pettit, Manchester College; Grace Pokorny, Long Beach City College; Judy Reitan, University of California–Davis; William Robinson, Purdue University Calumet; Jim Santor, College of Southern Nevada; Lisabeth Searing, University of Illinois at Urbana–Champaign; Peggy Skinner, South Plains College; Kandy Stahl, Stephen F. Austin State University; Dana Stone, Virginia Polytechnic Institute and State University; Cassandra George Sturges, Washtenaw Community College; Silvea Thomas, Kingsborough Community College; Karen Vail-Smith, East Carolina University; Jeff Wachsmuth, Napa Valley College; Laurie M. Wagner, Kent State University; Glenda Walden, University of Colorado–Boulder; Michael Walraven, Jackson Community College; Andrew Walters, Northern Arizona University; Mary Ann Watson, Metropolitan State College of Denver; Tanya Whipple, Missouri State University; Julie Wilgen, University of Delaware; Kelly Wilson, Texas A&M University; Midge Wilson, DePaul University; Amanda Woods, Georgia State University; Patty Woodward, Sacramento State University; Lester Wright, Western Michigan University; Susan Wycoff, California State University–Sacramento; Lynn Yankowski, Maui Community College

Specialist Reviewers

Talia Ben-Zeev, University of California–San Francisco; Thomas Coates, University of California San Francisco AIDS Research Institute; Eli Green, Widener University; Regan A. R. Gurung, University of Washington; Karen M. Hicks, Lehigh University; Linda Koenig, Centers for Disease Control and Prevention; Vicki Mays, University of California–Los Angeles; Konstance McCaffree, Widener University; Robin P. McHaelen, University of Connecticut; Leah Millheiser Ettinger, Stanford University; Cheryl Walker, University of California–Davis

Note to the Student

Campus life is different today from what it was when I was in college. For one thing, you have the Internet, smartphones, e-mail, texting, and Facebook. None of these were around when I was in college. We also didn't have laptops, iPads, or iPhones, so unlike the majority of students today who tell me they've seen online pornography at least once, we never watched any in college. Times were different—we communicated in person or via landline telephones, and we didn't watch reality television, use the morning-after pill, or know what a Brazilian wax was!

College is different today, and college textbooks need to reflect these changes. This textbook is contemporary and fun. I think you'll find it easy to keep up with the reading in this class because I've really worked hard to keep the material fresh and thought-provoking. I've included lots of personal stories from students just like you to help in your exploration and understanding of human sexuality. The chapter-opening Notebook features contain information from many college students who have shared their personal stories about sexuality with me. The result is a book that talks to students like yourself, answering questions you have about sexuality.

As you read through the book, if you have any questions, thoughts, or opinions you'd like to share with me, I'd love to hear from you. Many students e-mail me and ask for clarifications, suggest additions or changes, or just share their thoughts about this book. You can e-mail me at jcarroll@hartford.edu or contact me through Twitter (@DrJanellCarroll) or my website (www.drjanellcarroll.com). You can also send snail mail to Dr. Janell L. Carroll, University of Hartford, Department of Psychology, 200 Bloomfield Avenue, West Hartford, CT 06117.

Enjoy, and remember to always be safe!

Janell Carroll

1 Exploring Human Sexuality: Past and Present

When I went to high school, the health class was all about hygiene and diseases. It was the human sexuality course I took in college that inspired me to pursue sexuality as my graduate specialization. Throughout my studies and work in this field, I have learned that biology is only one component of sexuality. Exactly how we express our sexuality and define what is "normal" is shaped by various societal and cultural influences.

To better understand these influences, I've travelled extensively throughout the United States and around the world, exploring human sexuality. What I've gained through these experiences has been invaluable. All my education, training, and research about the interplay of biology, society, and culture gave me knowledge, but experiencing other cultures gave me understanding. Two important purposes of this textbook are to help you gain knowledge and an understanding about sexuality. Throughout this book I will share many details about my cross-cultural research. I'll help you understand how sexuality is expressed in traditionally conservative countries, such as Japan and Vietnam, and also in more open and liberal countries, such as Holland or France.

I hope this book and its accompanying videos help to broaden your knowledge and understanding of your own sexuality while engaging your interest in the wide spectrum of cultural and individual differences that make human sexuality such a fascinating subject.

Janell Carroll

Laurie Nassif

Welcome to the study of human sexuality! Many students come to this class believing they already know everything they need to know about human sexuality. The truth is, everyone comes to this course with differing levels of knowledge. Some students have parents who provided open and honest conversation about **sexuality**, whereas others had parents who never spoke a word about sex. Some students have had comprehensive levels of sex education in school; others have had none and may bring knowledge about sex gained only from years of watching Netflix and/or conversations with friends. In the end, it doesn't really matter what knowledge level you bring into this class. I guarantee that you will learn plenty more.

Although some people believe that we don't need to be taught about human sexuality, it might surprise you to know that most of sexuality is learned. One of the biggest influences in shaping our values, opinions, and attitudes about human sexuality is our **family of origin**. Our journey begins with our family—which could be our parent(s), stepparents, grandparents, or other caregivers. We learned how to communicate, show affection, deal with emotions, and many more things that contribute to the person we are today. In the end, we learned to be who we are, for better or worse, from our interactions and experiences in our family. We will talk much more about this in the upcoming chapters.

We also learn about sexuality from our friends, partners, religion, culture, society, and many other sources. Our exposure is augmented by the fact that we live in a sex-saturated society that uses sexuality to sell everything from body wash to cars. However, we also live in a time when there is a taboo against honest information about human sexuality. Some people believe that talking to teens about sexuality will increase teenage sexual behavior and lead to skyrocketing teen pregnancy rates, while others believe it will empower teens to make healthy decisions both today and in the future.

Many recent events have profoundly affected the way we view sexuality. From the ongoing debates about sexual assault on college campuses and equal access to public restrooms, the media are full of stories relating to our sexuality and relationships with others. These stories tell us much about how our culture understands, expresses, and limits our sexuality.

In this opening chapter, we define sexuality, examine sexual images in our culture, and explore the effect of the media's preoccupation with sex. A historical exploration of sexuality follows, in which we review the early evolution of human sexuality beginning with the impact of walking erect to ancient civilizations. Following that, we look at religion's role in sexuality and exam-

REAL RESEARCH Informal hanging out, such as watching television or talking to friends, has been found to help adolescents develop and practice supportive communication patterns that are linked to increased relationship satisfaction later in life (TUGGLE ET AL., 2016).

Stephanie Alexandre

Vaccines to protect teens from certain sexually transmitted infections are recommended well before teens become sexually active. Why do you think some parents might not be comfortable getting such vaccines this early?

ine some of the early sexual reform movements. Finally, we take a look at modern developments and influences that continue to shape our sexuality today.

Sexuality Today

Human sexuality is grounded in biological functioning, emerging in each of us as we develop, and is expressed by cultures through rules about sexual contact, attitudes about moral and immoral sexuality, habits of sexual behavior, patterns of relations between the sexes, and more. In this section, let's look at how we define sexuality and discuss how our sexuality is affected by the media and changing technologies.

Only Human: What Is Sexuality?

The sexual nature of human beings is unique in the animal kingdom. Although many of our fellow creatures also display complex sexual behaviors, only human beings have gone beyond instinctual mating rituals to create ideas, laws, customs, fantasies, and art around the sexual act. In other words, although sexual intercourse is common in the animal kingdom, sexuality is a uniquely human trait.

Sexuality is studied by **sexologists**, who specialize in understanding our sexuality, but also by biologists, psychologists,

sexuality
A general term for the feelings and behaviors of human beings concerning sex.

family of origin
The family into which one is born and raised.

sexologist
A person who engages in the scientific study of sexual behavior. Sexologists can be scientists, researchers, or clinicians and can hold a variety of different graduate degrees.

How Do You Decide What Type of Sex You'll Engage In?

Everyone makes decisions about if, when, where, and with whom they will hook up. For most people, at least part of that decision is based on their views of what behaviors are morally acceptable; these views may be derived from their religious beliefs, upbringing, family of origin, or personal decisions about the kind of person they want to be. For example, some people would not have sex with a partner whom they did not love, perhaps because they feel it is meaningless, immoral, or against God's wishes; others find it acceptable if both partners are willing and go into the encounter openly and freely. There are few areas of life in which moral principles are so clearly and commonly debated. Why is it that sexuality evokes such a strong moral response in us?

Human sexual behavior differs from that of all other animals, in part because of our moral, religious, legal, and interpersonal values. How simple it seems for animals, who mate without caring about marriage, pregnancy, or hurting their partner's feelings! Human beings are not (typically) so casual about mating; every culture has developed elaborate rituals, rules, laws, and moral principles that structure sexual relations. The very earliest legal and moral codes archeologists have uncovered discuss sexual behavior at great length, and rules about sexual behavior make up a great part of the legal and ethical codes of the world's great civilizations and religions.

Sexuality is a basic drive, and it is one of the few that involves intimate, one-on-one interaction with another person's basic needs. Conflicts may arise when our own needs, feelings, fears, and concerns are not the same as our partners'. People can be hurt, used, and taken advantage of sexually, or they can be victims of honest miscommunication, especially because sex is so difficult for many people to discuss.

Sexuality is also closely related to the formation of love bonds and to procreation. Every society has a stake in procreation, for without adequate numbers of people, a society can languish, and with too many people, a society can be overwhelmed. Most societies create rules to control the size of their population, such as the outlawing of contraception when childbirth is encouraged or the availability of free contraception during population explosions.

There are certainly other possible explanations for the moral and ethical standards that have developed around sexual behavior. Why do you think morality and sexuality are so closely bound?

---

physicians, anthropologists, historians, sociologists, political scientists, those concerned with public health, and many other people in scholarly disciplines. For example, political scientists may study how sexuality reflects social power; powerful groups may have more access to sexual partners or use their legislative power to restrict the sexual behaviors of less powerful groups.

Few areas of human life seem as contradictory and confusing as sexuality. The United States is often thought of as a sexually "repressed" society, yet images of sexuality are all around us. We tend to think that everyone is "hooking up"; still, we are often uncomfortable talking about sex. Some feel that we should all be free to explore our sexuality; others believe that there should be strong moral restrictions around sexual behavior. To some, only sex between a man and a woman is natural and acceptable; others believe that all kinds of sexual expression are equally "natural" and valid. Although American parents teach their children about safe driving, fire safety, and safety around strangers, many are profoundly uncomfortable talking to their children about sexuality.

Sex Sells: The Impact of the Media

Modern life is full of visual media. Magazines, newspapers, book covers, clothing, and even food packages are adorned with pictures of people, scenes, or products. Advertisements peer at us from billboards, buses, smartphones, computer screens, and anywhere else that advertisers can buy space. Television, movies, computers, and other moving visual images surround us almost everywhere we go, and we will depend on them even more as information technology continues to develop. We live in a visual culture with images we simply cannot escape.

Showtime Networks/Photofest

Shameless, a popular television series, depicts the dysfunctional family of Frank Gallagher, a single father of six children. Storylines have explored topics such as alcohol and drug use, sexual behavior, mixed race and same-sex relationships, as well as stepfamilies and adoption. Television shows can affect our attitudes and beliefs about a variety of issues.

Many of these images are subtly or explicitly sexual. Naked bodies are so common in advertisements that we scarcely notice them anymore. Although we may not immediately recognize it, many of the advertisements we are exposed to use Photoshop to digitally alter the models' bodies and faces—raising beauty standards to unattainable levels. Various countries have proposed legislation that would require warning labels on photos that have been retouched (Sieczkowski, 2012).

Sex is all over television today. The majority of movies, even some of those directed at children, have sexual scenes that would not have been permitted in movie theaters 50 years ago. Popular shows such as *Shameless, Game of Thrones,* or *Bad Girl's Club* often highlight sexual issues, whereas shows such as *16 and Pregnant* and *Teen Mom* explore teenage pregnancy, showcasing the real lives of teen mothers. Critics argue that such shows "glamorize" teen pregnancy and have led to the greater acceptance of teenage pregnancy (Wright et al., 2013).

The Internet has also changed patterns of social communication and relationships. Social networking sites, such as Facebook, Twitter, Snapchat, and Instagram, together with texting, Skype, and FaceTime have changed the way people communicate with one another. Now you can communicate through tweets, snaps, live feeds, photos, video calls, or status updates. You can make your relationship "official" with the click of a button, text a breakup message, and get an app for just about anything you need. We will talk more about these communication technologies in Chapter 3 (Communication).

Countless websites are also available, offering information and advice and providing online visitors with answers to their most personal questions. Vibrators and other sex toys, pornographic pictures and videos, and access to a variety of personal webcam sites can be purchased online, and a variety of blogs cater to just about any conceivable fantasy. The Internet allows for anonymity and provides the freedom to ask questions, seek answers, and talk to others about sexual issues.

All of this information has not been lost on today's teenagers. Teens rate the media as one of their leading sources of sex information (Simon & Daneback, 2013). American teens spend more than 7 hours a day with a variety of different media filled with sexual messages and images (Lenhart, 2015). The majority of this media information, however, is not educational. Although 70% of teen shows in the United States contain sexual content, few of these contain information on risks associated with sexual activity. Even so, many young people accept these sexual portrayals as realistic, even though the information is often inaccurate and misleading.

We now turn our attention to the history of human sexuality, from prehistoric times to the present. Of course, in the space of one chapter, we cannot begin to cover the variety and richness of human sexual experience. However, this overview will give you an idea of how varied human cultures are, while also showing that human beings throughout history have had to grapple with some of the same sexual issues that confront us in American society today. As we begin our review of this material, pay attention to the way that at some points in history, attitudes about sexuality were very conservative, whereas at other times, attitudes became more liberal. The pendulum continues to swing back and forth today as our society debates issues related to human sexuality, such as gender, sex education, and the availability of certain types of contraception.

REAL RESEARCH Eighty percent of college students have engaged in "drunkorexic," which is the practice of skipping meals to get drunk faster or to compensate for the calories in the alcohol (RINKER, 2016).

Review Questions

1 Explain how sexuality can be both contradictory and confusing, and provide one example of how this might be so.

2 Identify some of the ways we learn about sexuality, and give two reasons for questioning the accuracy of these sources.

3 Explain how today's teenagers get messages about sexuality through various media.

The Early Evolution of Human Sexuality

Our ancestors began walking upright more than 3 million years ago, according to recent fossil records. Before that, our ancestors were mostly **quadrupeds** (KWA-drew-peds) who stood only for brief moments—as baboons do now—to survey the terrain. The evolution of an upright posture changed forever the way the human species engaged in sexual intercourse.

Stand Up and Look Around: Walking Erect

In an upright posture, the male genitals are rotated to the front of the body, so merely approaching someone involves displaying the genitals. Because male confrontation often involved acts of aggression, the **phallus**—the male symbol of sex and potency—became associated with displays of aggression. In other words, upright posture may have also contributed to a new tie between sexuality and aggression (Rancour-Laferriere, 1985).

quadruped	phallus
Any animal that walks on four legs.	Symbol of power and aggression.

The upright posture of the female also emphasized her breasts and hips, and the rotation of the female pelvis forward (the vagina faces the rear in most quadrupeds) also resulted in the possibility of face-to-face intercourse. Because more body area is in contact in face-to-face intercourse than in rear entry, the entire sensual aspect of intercourse was enhanced, manipulation of the breasts became possible (the breasts are sexual organs only in humans), and the female clitoris was much more easily stimulated. Only in human females does orgasm seem to be a common part of sexual contact.

Sexuality in the Ancient Mediterranean

It may seem that ancient civilizations were very different from ours, yet some societies had surprisingly modern attitudes about sex. Although the Egyptians condemned adultery, especially among women, it may still have been fairly common. A woman in Egypt had the right to divorce her husband, a privilege, as we will see, that was not allowed to Hebrew women. Egyptians seem to have invented male circumcision, and Egyptian workers left behind thousands of pictures, carvings, and even cartoons of erotic scenes. All told, ancient Egyptians had sexual lives that do not seem all that different from the way humans engage in sex throughout the world today.

From writings and art, we know a bit about ancient accounts of **sexually transmitted infections (STIs)** (some ancient medical texts discuss cures), menstruation (there were a variety of laws surrounding what a woman could do during menstruation), circumcision (which was first performed in Egypt and possibly other parts of Africa), and contraception (heterosexual Egyptian women inserted sponges or other objects in the vagina). Because great value was put on having as many children as possible—especially sons, for inheritance purposes—abortion was usually forbidden. Prostitution was common, and **temple prostitutes** often greeted worshippers.

It is important to remember that throughout history, men dominated public life and women's voices were effectively silenced; we know far more about what men thought, how men lived, and even how men loved than we do about the lives and thoughts of women. In fact, it was only relatively recently in human history that women's voices have begun to be heard on a par with men's in literature, politics, art, and other parts of public life.

Of all the ancient civilizations, modern Western society owes the most to the interaction of three ancient cultures: the Hebrews,

Greeks, and Romans. Each made a contribution to our views of sexuality, so it is worthwhile to examine each culture briefly. At the beginning of each section, we give a date as to when these effects began.

The Hebrews (1000–200 B.C.)

The Hebrew Bible, which was put into written form sometime between 800 and 200 B.C., contains explicit rules about sexual behavior, such as forbidding adultery, homosexuality, and sex with various family members and their spouses. The Bible includes tales of sexual misconduct—for example, incest, sexual betrayal, sex outside of marriage, and sexual jealousy—even by its most admired figures. Yet the Bible also contains tales of marital love and acknowledges the importance of sexuality in marital relationships.

ON YOUR MIND

Do female primates experience orgasm?

Yes, some do, although it is relatively rare compared with human females. Female primates rarely masturbate, although occasionally they stimulate themselves manually during intercourse. Bonobos (pygmy chimpanzees) do have face-to-face intercourse on occasion and may reach orgasm. However, most chimpanzees engage in rear-entry intercourse, a position that does not favor female orgasm (MARGULIS & SAGAN, 1991).

The legacy of the Hebrew attitude toward sexuality has been profound. The focus on marital sexuality and procreation and the prohibition against such things as homosexuality were adopted by Christianity and formed the basis of sexual attitudes in the West for centuries thereafter. The Hebrew Bible sees the marital union and its sexual nature as an expression of love and affection, as a man and woman "become one flesh."

The Greeks (1000–200 B.C.)

The Greeks were more sexually permissive than the Hebrews. Their stories and myths are full of sexual exploits, including incest and rape. The Greeks clearly distinguished between love and sex in their tales, even giving each a separate god: Aphrodite was the goddess of sexual intercourse; Eros (her son) was the god of love.

Greece was one of the few major civilizations in Western history to institutionalize homosexuality successfully. In Greek **pederasty** (ped-er-AST-ee), an older man would befriend a postpubescent boy who had finished his orthodox education and aid in the boy's continuing intellectual, physical, and sexual development. In return, the boy would have sex with his mentor. The mentor was always the active partner, the penetrator; the student was the passive partner. Socrates, for example, was supposed to have enjoyed the sexual attentions of his students (all male), and his students expressed jealousy when he paid too much physical attention to one or another.

In Greece, men and the male form were idealized. When the ancient Greek philosophers spoke of love, they did so almost

---

sexually transmitted infection (STI)
Infection that is transmitted from one person to another through sexual contact. This used to be called sexually transmitted disease (STD) or venereal disease (VD).

temple prostitutes
Women in ancient cultures who would have sex with worshippers at pagan temples to provide money for the temple or to worship the gods.

pederasty
Sexual contact between adult men and (usually) postpubescent boys.

Greek cups, plates, and other pottery often depicted erotic scenes, such as this one from the 5th century B.C.

In Rome, as in Greece, adult males who took the passive sexual position in homosexual encounters were viewed with scorn, whereas the same behavior by youths, foreigners, slaves, or women was seen as an acceptable means to try to please a person who could improve one's place in society. Still, long-term homosexual unions did exist.

Sexuality in Ancient Asia

Indian and Chinese civilizations also had unique views of sexuality. In Indian culture, Hinduism and rebirth give life direction. In Chinese culture, people work to live in harmony with the Tao, which is made up of **yin and yang**.

India (Beginning About 400 B.C.)

Hinduism, the religion of India for most of its history, concentrates on an individual's cycle of birth and rebirth, or **karma**. Karma involves a belief that a person's unjust deeds in this life are punished by suffering in a future life, and suffering in this life is undoubtedly punishment for wrongs committed in previous incarnations. The goal, then, is to live a just life to avoid suffering in the future. One of the responsibilities in this life is to marry and procreate, and because sex is an important part of those responsibilities, it was generally viewed as a positive pursuit, and even a source of power and magic.

There are legends about great women rulers early in India's history, and women had important roles in ceremonies and sacrifices. Still, India's social system, like others we have mentioned, was basically **patriarchal** (PAY-tree-arc-al), and Indian writers (again, mostly male) shared many of the negative views of women that were characteristic of other civilizations. Being born a woman was seen as a punishment for sins committed in previous lives. In fact, murdering a woman was not seen as a particularly serious crime, and **female infanticide** (in-FAN-teh-side) was not uncommon (V. L. Bullough, 1973).

By about 400 B.C., the first and most famous of India's sex manuals, the **Kamasutra** (CAH-mah-SUH-trah), appeared. India

exclusively in **homoerotic** terms. Man's nonsexual love for another man was seen as the ideal love, superior to the sexual love for women. Plato discussed such an ideal love, and so we have come to call friendships without a sexual element **platonic**.

ON YOUR MIND

I've heard that the Greeks believed that sex between men and boys was a "natural" form of human sexuality. Couldn't they see that it was perverted?

One society's perversion may be another society's accepted sexual practice. Every culture sees its own forms of sexuality as natural and obvious—including ours. Not too long ago in our own society, it seemed "obvious" to most people that things such as oral sex and anal sex were perversions (they are still technically illegal in many states), and that masturbation could lead to mental illness. Today, many people see these acts as part of a healthy sexual life. Sexual beliefs and practices are often very different in other cultures and they can change over time within these cultures.

The Romans (500 B.C.–700 A.D.)

Rome had few restrictions about sexuality until late in the history of the empire, so early Romans had very permissive attitudes toward homosexual and bisexual behaviors, which were entirely legal until the 6th century A.D. (Boswell, 1980). Marriage and sexual relations were viewed as a means to improve one's economic and social standing; passionate love almost never appears in the written accounts handed down to us. Bride and groom need not love each other, they believed, for that kind of relationship would grow over the life of the marriage; more important was fair treatment, respect, and mutual consideration. Wives even encouraged their husbands to have slaves (of either sex) for the purposes of sexual release.

homoerotic
The representation of same-sex love or desire.

platonic
Named after Plato's description, a deep, loving friendship that is devoid of sexual contact or desire.

yin and yang
According to a Chinese belief, the universe is run by the interaction of two fundamental principles: yin, which is negative, passive, weak, yielding, and female; and yang, which is positive, assertive, active, strong, and male.

karma
The belief that a person's actions in this and other lives determine their fate in future lives.

patriarchal
A society ruled by the male as the figure of authority, symbolized by the father's absolute authority in the home.

female infanticide
The killing of female infants; this is practiced in some countries that value males more than females.

Kamasutra
Ancient Indian sex manual.

is justifiably famous for this amazing book. The *Kamasutra* discusses not just sex but the nature of love, how to make a good home and family, and moral guidance in sex and love. The *Kamasutra* is obsessive about naming and classifying things. In fact, it categorizes men by the size of their penis (hare, bull, or horse man) and women by the size of their vagina (deer, mare, or cow–elephant woman). A good match in genital size was preferred between heterosexual partners, but barring that, a tight fit was better than a loose one (Tannahill, 1980). The *Kamasutra* recommends that women learn how to please their husbands, and it provides instructions on sexual techniques and illustrations of many sexual positions, some of which are virtually impossible for people who cannot twist their body like a pretzel.

In India, marriage was an economic and religious obligation; families tried to arrange good marriages by betrothing their children at younger and younger ages, although they did not live with or have sex with their future spouses until after puberty. Because childbearing began so young, Indian women were still in the prime of their lives when their children were grown, and they were often able to assert themselves in the household over elderly husbands. However, when a husband died, his wife was forbidden to remarry, and she had to live simply, wear plain clothes, and sleep on the ground. She was to devote her days to prayer and rituals that ensured her remarriage to the same husband in a future life. Many women chose (or were forced) to end their lives as widows by the ritual act of *sati,* which consisted of a woman throwing herself on her husband's burning funeral pyre to die (Jamanadas, 2008).

China (Beginning About 200 B.C.)

Chinese civilization emphasizes the interdependence of all things, unified in the Tao, which represents the basic unity of the universe. The Tao itself is made up of two principles, yin and yang, which represent the opposites of the world: yin is feminine, passive, and receptive; yang is masculine, active, and assertive. Sexuality in Chinese thought is not a matter of moral or allowable behavior but, rather, is a natural procreative process, a joining of the yin and yang, the masculine and feminine principles.

Because sex itself was part of the basic process of following the Tao, sexual instruction and sex manuals were common and openly available in early Chinese society. These texts were explicit, with pictures of sexual positions and instructions on how to stimulate partners, and were often given to brides before their weddings.

Because women's essence, yin, is inexhaustible, whereas man's essence, yang (embodied in semen), is limited, man should feed his yang through prolonged contact with yin. In other words, heterosexual intercourse should be prolonged as long as possible, without the man ejaculating, to release all the woman's accumulated yin energy. (The man may experience orgasm without ejaculation, however, and techniques were developed to teach men how to do so.) Heterosexual men were advised to have sex with many women to prevent the yin energy of any single woman from becoming depleted. It was also important for the man to experience the woman's orgasm, when yin is

Indian sculptors followed the tradition of Tantric art, which is famous for its depictions of eroticism.

REAL RESEARCH The Japanese Family Planning Association identified a condition known as "celibacy syndrome" after revealing that half of 16–49-year-olds had not engaged in sex in the past month (Baer, 2015). Respondents cited fatigue, disinterest, and/or a strong dislike of sex.

at its peak, to maximize his contact with yin energy. The Chinese were unique in stressing the importance of female orgasm (Margolis, 2004).

Same-sex relations were not discouraged, but because semen was seen as precious and primarily for impregnation, male homosexuality was viewed as a wasteful use of sperm (we discuss Chinese views of homosexuality more in Chapter 11). Aphrodisiacs were developed, as were drugs for all kinds of sexual problems. Also common were sexual devices to increase pleasure, such as penis rings, balls and bells that were grafted under the skin of the head of the penis to increase its size, and Ben Wa balls (usually two or three) containing mercury and other substances that were inserted in the vagina and bounced against each other to bring sexual pleasure.

Taoists believed that yin and yang were equally necessary complements of all existence, so one might guess that men and women were treated more equally in China than in the West. Yet, because yin is the passive, inferior principle, women were seen as subservient to men throughout their lives: first to their fathers, then to their husbands, and finally to their sons when their husbands died. **Polygamy** (pah-LIG-ah-mee) was practiced until late in Chinese history, and the average middle-class male had between three and a dozen wives and concubines, with those in nobility having 30 or more.

> **polygamy**
> The practice of marrying more than one partner.

It is often difficult to imagine how sexuality and gender are viewed in other countries. We become accustomed to norms, practices, and behaviors where we live and may not understand how other cultures view the same practices differently. In this chapter, we've looked at images of beauty in U.S. culture. It may seem strange that some people undergo nose jobs, breast implants, liposuction, tattooing, piercing, waxing, or other procedures to look and feel more beautiful or attractive to others. Throughout history, cultures have searched for unique ways to achieve beauty, especially for women. At one point in U.S. history, exceptionally small waists on women were considered beautiful, and many women wore tight-fitting corsets. Women who did so often underwent tremendous pain and broke ribs or damaged internal organs. More disturbing than corsets, however, was the Chinese practice of foot binding, which began in the 10th century and lasted for 1,000 years (Ko, 2007). Foot binding originated out of men's desire for women with small, feminine feet. In fact, many men would refuse to marry women with large feet. One 70-year-old woman who had her feet bound as a child said:

Men would choose or reject you as a prospective wife based on the size of your feet. There was a well-known saying, "If you don't bind, you don't marry. . ." When a girl became eligible for marriage, a matchmaker would find a man for whom the young girl might be suitable. Then she would arrange

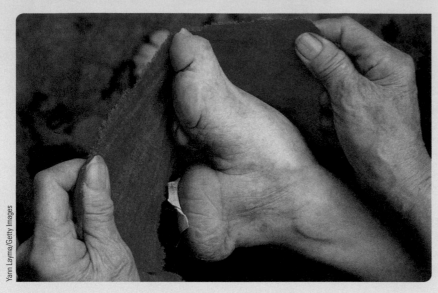

Yann Layma/Getty Images

Review Questions

1 How did prehistoric changes in our posture influence human sexuality?

2 What sources provide information on sexuality in early cultures?

3 Explain how the moral standards of past civilizations influence our own judgments about modern events today.

Sexuality From St. Paul to Martin Luther

Religion has influenced views about sexuality throughout history. Perhaps no single system of thought had as much impact on the Western world as Christianity, and nowhere more so than in its views on sexuality. We explore early Christianity and the Middle Ages, look at the influence of Islam and Islamic law, and consider the views of sexuality that developed during the Renaissance.

Early Christianity: Chastity Becomes a Virtue (Beginning About 50 A.D.)

Christianity began as a small sect following the teachings of Jesus. It was formalized into a religious philosophy by St. Paul and other early leaders who were influenced by the Roman legal structure.

Within a few hundred years, this little sect would become the predominant religion of the Western world, and it has influenced the attitudes of people toward sexuality until the present day.

Jesus himself was mostly silent on sexual issues such as homosexuality and premarital sex. He was born a Jew and was knowledgeable in Jewish tradition, and many of his attitudes were compatible with mainstream Jewish thought of the time. However, he was liberal in his thinking about sexuality, preaching, for example, that men should be held to the same standards as women on issues of adultery, divorce, and remarriage (V. L. Bullough, 1973). The Gospels also show that Jesus was liberal in his recommendations for punishing sexual misadventurers. When confronted with a woman who had committed adultery, a sin for which the Hebrew Bible had mandated stoning, Jesus replied with one of his more famous comments, "Let he who is without sin cast the first stone."

It was St. Paul and later followers, however, who established the Christian view of sexuality that was to dominate Western thought for the next 2,000 years. St. Paul condemned sexuality in a way

a foot viewing. The man would come to the girl's house just to look at her feet. If he thought they were too large, he would turn her down. This was a very embarrassing affair, should it happen, since the whole village would surely hear about it (Rupp, 2007; italics in original).

Foot binding was also sexual in nature—women with bound feet had a sway in their walk that was often viewed as erotic. However, they couldn't walk far, which is why foot binding literally kept women in their place. The ideal foot length was 3 inches, which was referred to as a *Golden Lotus* (*Golden Lotus* feet were often adorned with beautiful silk shoes). Feet that were 3 to 4 inches long were called *Silver Lotuses*. It is estimated that 40% to 50% of Chinese women had their feet bound in the 19th century, although in the upper classes, the percentages were closer to 100% (W. A. Rossi, 1993).

Foot binding was typically done on girls as young as 4 or 5 years because the bones were still flexible. To bind feet, the mother or grandmother would first soak a girl's feet in warm water. She would then cut the toenails very short, massage the feet, and break the four small toes on each foot. These toes would be folded under, leaving the big toe intact. Silk bandages were wrapped tightly around the toes, and the bandages pulled each broken toe closer to the heel. These bandages were changed and tightened every couple of days so that the foot would not be allowed to grow normally. Typically, this process went on for 10 or more years. It was immensely painful, and most girls could not walk for long distances with their feet bound. Most mothers would start the foot-binding process in the winter months so that the cold would help to numb the pain. Although in the beginning only wealthy families bound their daughters' feet because they could afford not to have their children work in the fields, by the 17th century peasants and women from the countryside began foot binding to attract more wealthy suitors for marriage.

Foot binding had several long-term consequences. Many women had difficulties balancing, walking, standing, and squatting (using the toilet was especially difficult). Muscular atrophy and infections were common, and many girls developed a terrible foot smell from the practice. Older women typically developed severe hip and spinal problems.

In the latter part of the Qing Dynasty (1644–1911), the practice of foot binding was outlawed. At that time, women were told to unwrap their feet or face heavy fines. Even so, the practice continued for years, and it wasn't until the formation of the People's Republic of China in 1949 that a strict prohibition was placed on foot binding. This prohibition continues today.

Although it's disturbing to read about this practice, it is interesting to look at how far societies will go for beauty. Foot binding became an integral part of the culture and was much more than a beauty statement. Women whose feet were bound were viewed as more desirable and of a higher social status, making it more likely they would find a husband to provide for them.

SOURCE: The material in this feature was taken from several texts, including *Splendid Slippers: A Thousand Years of an Erotic Tradition* (B. Jackson, 1998), *In Every Step a Lotus: Shoes for Bound Feet* (Ko, 2001), *Cinderella's Sisters: A Revisionist History of Footbinding* (Ko, 2007), *Aching for Beauty: Footbinding in China* (Ping, 2002), and *The Sex Life of the Foot and Shoe* (W. A. Rossi, 1993).

found in neither Hebrew nor Greek thought—nor anywhere in the teachings of Jesus. Paul suggested that the highest love was love of God, and that the ideal was not to allow sexual or human love to compete with that love. Therefore, although sexuality itself was not sinful when performed as part of the marital union, the ideal situation was **celibacy** (SEH-luh-buh-see). **Chastity**, for the first time in history, became a virtue; abstaining from sexual intercourse became a sign of holiness (Bergmann, 1987).

The legacy of early Christianity was a general association of sexuality with sin. All nonprocreative sex was strictly forbidden, as were contraception and masturbation. The result was that the average Christian associated sexual pleasure with guilt (Stark, 1996). Christianity's view of sex has been one of the harshest of any major religious or cultural tradition. You can see how religious views such as these could certainly influence your views on sexuality. It is not uncommon for students to experience **cognitive dissonance** over their disparate views about sexuality and religion.

The Middle Ages: Eve the Temptress and Mary the Virgin (500–1400)

In the early Middle Ages, the church's influence slowly began to increase. Christianity had become the state religion of Rome, and although the church did not have much formal power, its teachings had an influence on law. For example, homosexual relations (even homosexual marriages) had been legal for the first 200 years that Christianity was the state religion of Rome, and the church was very tolerant of homosexuality. Eventually, however, church teachings changed and became much stricter.

Between about 1050 and 1150 (the High Middle Ages), sexuality once again became liberalized. For example, a gay subculture was established in Europe that produced a body of gay literature that had not been seen since the Roman Empire and would not emerge again until the 19th century (Boswell, 1980).

However, the homosexual subculture disappeared in the 13th century when the church cracked down on a variety of groups—including Jews, Muslims, and homosexuals (Boswell, 1980). In 1215, the church instituted **confession**, and soon guides appeared to teach priests about the various sins **penitents** (PENN-ittents) might have committed. The guides seem preoccupied

celibacy
The state of remaining unmarried; often used today to refer to abstaining from sex.

chastity
The quality of being sexually pure, either through abstaining from intercourse or by adhering to strict rules of sexuality.

cognitive dissonance
Uncomfortable tension that comes from holding two conflicting thoughts at the same time.

confession
A Catholic practice of revealing one's sins to a priest.

penitents
Those who come to confess sins (from the word meaning "to repent").

with sexual transgressions and used sexual sins more than any other kind to illustrate their points (Payer, 1991). All sex outside of marriage was considered sinful, and even certain marital acts were forbidden.

European women in the early Middle Ages were only slightly better off than they had been under the ancient Greeks or Romans. By the late Middle Ages, however, new ideas about women were brought back by the Crusaders from Islamic lands (see the section on Islam that follows). Women were elevated to a place of purity and were considered almost perfect (Tannahill, 1980). Woman was no longer a temptress but a model of virtue. The idea of romantic love was first created at this time, and it spread through popular culture as troubadours traveled from place to place, singing songs of pure, spiritual love, untroubled by sex.

At the same time that women were seen to be virtuous, however, they were also said to be the holders of the secrets of sexuality (Thomasset, 1992). Before marriage, men would employ the services of an **entremetteuse** (on-TRAY-meh-toose) to teach them the ways of love. These old women procured young women (prostitutes) for the men and were said to know the secrets of restoring potency, restoring virginity, and concocting potions.

Perhaps no person from the Middle Ages had a stronger impact on subsequent attitudes toward sexuality than Thomas Aquinas (1225–1274). Aquinas established the views of morality and correct sexual behavior that form the basis of the Catholic Church's attitudes toward sexuality even today. Aquinas drew from the idea of "natural law" to suggest that there were "natural" and "unnatural" sex acts. He argued that the sex organs were "naturally" intended for procreation, and using them in other ways was unnatural and immoral; in fact, he argued that semen and ejaculation were intended only to impregnate, and any other use of them was immoral. Aquinas's strong condemnation of sexuality—and especially homosexuality, which he called the worst of all sexual sins—set the tone for Christian attitudes toward sexuality for many centuries.

Islam: A New Religion (About 500 A.D.)

In the 6th century, Muhammad began to preach a religion that drew from Jewish and Christian roots and added Arab tribal beliefs. Islam became a powerful force that conquered the entire Middle East and Persian lands; swept across Asia, and so touched China in the East; and spread through Northern Africa and, from there, north into Christian Europe, particularly Spain. Between about the 8th and 12th centuries, Islamic society was the most advanced in the world, with a newly developed system of mathematics (Arabic

Juanmonino/Getty Images

Many Muslim women wear a hijab, or head-scarf, to cover their head, hair, neck, and/or face. Hijabs are often worn as a symbol of modesty and privacy, but can also be worn as a religious symbol or as an expression of cultural identity.

numbers) to replace the clumsy Roman system and having the world's most sophisticated techniques of medicine, warfare, and science (Wuthnow, 1998).

Many Muslim societies have strong rules of *satr al-'awra,* or modesty, that involve covering the private parts of the body (which for women means almost the entire body). Muhammad had tried to preserve the rights of women. There are examples in the **Koran** (koe-RAN), the Muslim bible, of female saints and intellectuals, and powerful women often hold strong informal powers over their husbands and male children. Still, women in many Islamic lands are subjugated to men, segregated and not permitted to venture out of their homes, and forbidden to interact with men who are not family members.

In Islamic law, as in Christian law, sexuality between a man and a woman is legal only when the couple is married (Coulson, 1979). Sexual intercourse in marriage is a good religious deed for the Muslim male, and the Koran likens wives to fields that men should cultivate as frequently as they want. Islam restricts sex to the marital union exclusively (Shafaat, 2004).

In traditional Islamic communities, women who were married to wealthy men usually lived in secluded areas in their husbands' homes, called **harems**. Harems were not the dens of sex and sensuality that are sometimes portrayed but were self-contained communities where women learned to become self-sufficient in the absence of men. Among the middle and lower classes, men had less wealth to offer potential wives, which gave women more power.

The sultans of the Ottoman Empire, which ruled most of the Islamic world from the 15th to 20th centuries, had between 300 and

---

entremetteuse
Historically, a woman who procures sexual partners for men or one who taught men about lovemaking.

Koran
The holy book of Islam. Also spelled Quran or Qur'an.

harem
Abbreviation of the Turkish word harêmlik (harâm in Arabic), meaning "women's quarters" or "sanctuary."

1,200 women in their harem. The sultan's mother ruled the harem and even sometimes ruled the empire itself if she was strong and her son was weak willed (Tannahill, 1980). Because each woman might sleep with the sultan once or twice a year at most, **eunuchs** (YOU-niks) were employed to guard the women. Eunuchs would not have sex with the women because they often had their testicles or penises (or both) removed.

The Renaissance: The Pursuit of Knowledge (Beginning About 1300)

The Renaissance, which began in Italy in the late 1300s, may be summed up as a time when intellectual and artistic thought turned from a focus on God to a focus on human beings and their place in the world; from the sober and serious theology of the Middle Ages to a renewed sense of joy in life. Part of the cultural shift of the Renaissance was new views of sexuality and, to some degree, the roles of women in society.

During the Renaissance, women made great strides in education and began to become more prominent in political affairs. Lively debates about the worth and value of women took place, and in 1532, it was argued that each of God's creations in the biblical book of Genesis is superior to the one before. Because the human female is the last thing God created, she must be his most perfect creation. In the Bible, a male is the first sinner; men introduce polygamy, drunkenness, and murder into the world; and men are aggressive and tyrannical. Women, on the other hand, are more peaceful, chaste, refined, and faithful.

However, as seems to happen so often in history when women make modest gains, there was a backlash. By the 17th century, witchcraft trials appeared in Europe and the New World, symbols of the fears that men still held of women's sexuality. Thousands of women were killed, and the image of the evil witch became the symbol of men's fear of women for centuries to come.

International outrage and protests about honor killings have increased, especially after high-profile killings of many young women by family members. Here thousands of Turkish women take to the streets to denounce honor crimes.

ON YOUR MIND

I have heard about other countries having "honor crimes" in which women are murdered to maintain family honor. Does this really happen?

The United Nations estimates that about 5,000 honor killings take place every year, although it's impossible to know the exact number (ZOROYA, 2016). Honor crimes occur most frequently in places where female chastity is of utmost importance, including the Middle East and South Asia. These types of crimes target women whose actions—actual or suspected—violate the honor of her family. Crimes might include speaking to someone with whom you should not speak, loss of virginity, wearing inappropriate clothing, extramarital affairs, speaking out about various issues, or even rape. Some reports suggest that some women in these countries have been raped in an attempt to force them to reclaim their honor by serving as suicide bombers (MANDELBAUM, 2010). In Chapters 17 and 18, we explore other forms of gender-based violence, including domestic violence and sex trafficking.

The Reformation: The Protestant Marital Partnership (Beginning About 1500)

In Western Europe in the early 16th century, Martin Luther challenged papal power and founded a movement known as Protestantism. Instead of valuing celibacy, Luther saw in the Bible the obligation to reproduce, saw marital love as blessed, and considered sexuality a natural function. John Calvin, the other great Protestant reformer, suggested that women were not just reproductive vessels but men's partners in all things.

To Luther, marriage was a state blessed by God, and sexual contact was sinful primarily when it occurred out of wedlock, just as any indulgence was sinful (V. L. Bullough, 1973). Because marriage was so important, a bad marriage should not continue, and so Luther broke away from the teachings of the Catholic Church and allowed divorce.

Though sexuality was permissible only in the marital union, it had other justifications besides reproduction, such as to reduce stress, avoid cheating, and increase intimacy—a very different perspective on sex than that preached by the Catholic Church. Calvin, in fact, saw the marital union as primarily a social and sexual relationship. Although procreation was important, companionship was the main goal of marriage.

eunuch
A male who has had his testicles removed (or less often, a man with his penis removed) who guarded a harem. At times, children were also made eunuchs.

Luther did accept the general subjugation of women to men in household affairs and felt that women were weaker than men and should humble themselves before their fathers and husbands. He excluded women from the clergy because of standards of "decency" and because of women's inferior aptitudes for ministry.

Although Calvin and Luther tried to remove from Protestantism the overt disdain of women that they found in some older Christian theologians, they did not firmly establish women's equal place with men.

Review Questions

1 Explain Christianity's impact on our views of human sexuality. Were Islamic views of sexuality more or less conservative than those of Christianity?

2 Explain how views of sexuality changed from the Reformation through the Renaissance.

3 Explain the changes in the church's view of sexuality from St. Paul to Luther.

4 Explain how religious beliefs can lead to cognitive dissonance in college students.

The Enlightenment and the Victorian Era

The Enlightenment, an intellectual movement of the 18th century, influenced most of Europe; it prized rational thought over traditional authority and suggested that human nature was to be understood through a study of human psychology. Enlightenment writers argued that human drives and instincts are part of nature's design, so one must realize the basic wisdom of human urges and not fight them (Porter, 1982).

The Enlightenment (Beginning About 1700)

During the Enlightenment, sexual pleasure was considered natural and desirable. In fact, of all the earthly pleasures, enlightenment thinkers praised sexuality as supreme. Sexuality had become so free that there was an unprecedented rise in premarital pregnancy and births; up to one fifth of all brides in the late 17th century were pregnant when they got married (Trumbach, 1990).

As liberal as the Enlightenment was, many sexual activities, such as homosexuality, were condemned and persecuted. For example, starting in 1730, there was a 2-year "sodomite panic" in the Netherlands; hundreds of men accused of homosexual acts were executed, and hundreds more fled the country. Yet, there were also times of relative tolerance. Napoleon so eased laws against homosexuality that by 1860 it was tolerated, and male prostitutes were common in France (Tannahill, 1980).

The Victorian Era (Early 1800s)

The Victorian era, which refers to Queen Victoria's rule, began in 1837 and lasted until early 1901. It was a time of great prosperity in England. Propriety and public behavior became more important, especially to the upper class, and sexual attitudes became more conservative. Sex was not to be spoken of in polite company and was to be restricted to the marital bed, in the belief that preoccupation with sex interfered with higher achievements. Privately, Victorian England was not as conservative as it has been portrayed, and pornography, extramarital affairs, and prostitution were common. Still, the most important aspect of Victorian society was public propriety, and conservative values were often preached, if not always practiced.

During this period, the idea of male chivalry returned, and women were considered to be virtuous, refined, delicate, fragile, vulnerable, and remote; certainly, no respectable Victorian woman would ever admit to a sexual urge. The prudery of the Victorian era sometimes went to extremes. Victorian women were too embarrassed to talk to a doctor about their "female problems" and so would point out areas of discomfort on dolls (Hellerstein et al., 1981; see "Sex in Real Life" in this section for more information on women who shared their gynecological concerns with their physicians). Women were supposed to be interested in music but were not supposed to play the flute because pursing the lips was unladylike; the cello was unacceptable because it had to be held between the legs; the brass instruments were too difficult for the delicate wind of the female; the violin forced the woman's neck into an uncomfortable position. Therefore, only keyboard instruments were considered "ladylike" (V. L. Bullough, 1973).

Sexuality was repressed in many ways. Physicians and writers of the time often argued that semen was precious and should be conserved; Sylvester Graham, a Presbyterian minister and founder of the American Vegetarian Society, recommended sex only 12 times a year. He argued that sexual indulgence led to all sorts of ailments and infirmities, such as depression, faintness, headaches, and blindness.

The Victorian era had great influence on sexuality in England and the United States. Many of the conservative attitudes that still exist today are holdovers from Victorian standards.

Sex in Real Life   The History of Vibrators

It might surprise you to know that vibrators have a long history dating back to the late 19th century. At that time, many women began voicing complaints to their physicians (who were mostly male) about miscellaneous gynecological problems. Their symptoms typically included fainting, fluid congestion, insomnia, nervousness, abdominal heaviness, loss of appetite for food or sex, and a tendency to cause trouble for others, especially family members (Maines, 1999). Physicians determined that these gynecological complaints were due to "pelvic hyperemia," otherwise known as genital congestion. The condition was diagnosed as "hysteria," a common and chronic complaint in women at the time. In fact, it wasn't until 1952 that the American Psychiatric Association dropped hysteria as a diagnosis (Slavney, 1990).

To relieve the symptoms of hysteria, physicians recommended "intercourse on the marriage bed" or vulvar massage by a physician or midwife (Maines, 1999). Hysteria rates were higher in virgin, unmarried, and widowed women because they did not engage in sexual intercourse. (Notice that there is no mention of lesbian women; physicians believed that hysteria resulted when a woman was not engaging in sexual intercourse with a man.)

Vulvar massage to induce paroxysm (orgasm) was typically painstaking and time-consuming work for a physician, often requiring up to 1 hour of time per woman. It was a strictly medical procedure most commonly prescribed for women diagnosed with hysteria. Because religious mandates prohibited self-masturbation, vulvar massage was the only acceptable solution for women without sexual partners.

The vibrator appeared in the late 1800s in response to physician demands for more rapid therapies to treat hysteria. By the early 1900s, several types of vibrators were available, from low-priced foot-powered models to more expensive battery and electric models. Advertisements began to appear in a variety of women's magazines such as *Needlecraft, Woman's Home Companion*, and *Modern Women* (Maines, 1999). Although the advertisements were primarily directed at women, when they were marketed toward men, they claimed that vibrators made good gifts for women because they could give women a healthy glow with "bright eyes" and "pink cheeks."

Social awareness of vibrators also began to build in the 1920s when the devices made their way into pornographic films. The American Psychiatric Association dropped hysteria as a

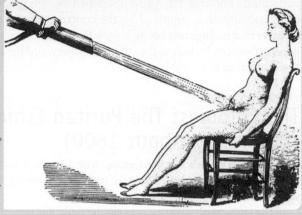

Courtesy of Athena Images

diagnosis in 1952 and soon afterward vibrators were directly marketed for women (Slavney, 1990). Vibrators were the 15th household appliance to be electrified, after the sewing machine, fan, tea kettle, and toaster (Maines, 1999).

In the 1960s, vibrators were openly marketed as sexual aids to improve sexual functioning and satisfaction. This was because of the changing sexual attitudes and increasingly open atmosphere about sexuality. Today, vibrators are often marketed as "massagers" in most stores, with few, if any, references to sexual health. Have you ever seen vibrator packaging that described how the vibrator might improve your sex life? Give you the best orgasm of your life? Help you learn to orgasm? Although sex stores often sell vibrators with sexual images on the packaging, there is typically no discussion of sexual health. Even so, vibrators have come a long way since the beginning of the century!

Boyrcr420/Getty Images

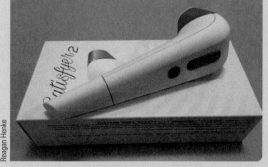

Reagan Henke

Review Questions

1 Explain how sexuality was viewed during the Enlightenment.

2 How did the Victorian era influence the view of sexuality?

3 Explain how sexuality was repressed during the Victorian era.

Sex in American History

American society has been influenced most strongly by Europe, particularly England. Yet, it also developed its own unique mix of ideas and attitudes, tempered by the contributions of the many cultures that immigrants brought with them. Let's look at some of these influences, including the colonies, slavery, and the liberalization of sexuality.

The Colonies: The Puritan Ethic (Beginning About 1600)

The **Puritans** were a religious group who fled England and tried to set up a biblically based society in the New World. They had severe sanctions for sexual transgressions. In New England, for example, the death penalty was applied for sodomy, **bestiality**, adultery, and rape. In Puritan ideology, the entire community was responsible for upholding morality (D'Emilio & Freedman, 1988). However, the Puritans were not as closed-minded about sex as their reputation suggests, and they believed that sexuality was good and proper within marriage. In fact, men were obligated to have intercourse with their wives. The Puritans also tolerated most mild sexual transgressions—such as using non–missionary-style sexual positions or engaging in sexual intercourse during menstruation (J. Watkins, 2003).

As the New World began to grow, it suffered from a lack of women, and the speculation in Europe was that any woman seeking a man should come to America, which offered women greater independence than Europe. On the island of Nantucket, for example, whaling kept the men at sea for months. The women took over the island's businesses, and prestige was granted to those who managed to make the money grow while their husbands were away.

Sexuality was also a bit freer, and courting youths would wander into barns or look for high crops in the field to obscure views of their necking and groping. There was also a custom called **bundling**, in which young couples were allowed to share a bed as long as they were clothed, wrapped in sheets or bags, or had a wooden "bundling board" between them. The large number of premarital pregnancies suggests that couples found ways to get around their bundling impediments, but in most such cases, the couple would quickly marry (D'Emilio & Freedman, 1988).

The United States: Freedom— and Slavery—in the New World

The pendulum swung back to the liberal side after the Revolutionary War in the late 1700s. This was due mostly to the diminishing power of the church in the United States, leading to more liberal sexual attitudes. This liberalization, together with the continuing slave influx from Africa, had powerful effects on U.S. culture's developing sexuality.

The Liberalization of Sex (About the 1700s)

With the diminished power of the church came a new period of practical, utilitarian philosophy (as exemplified in Benjamin Franklin's maxims, such as "Early to bed and early to rise . . ."), which stressed the individual's right to pursue personal happiness. People began to speak more openly about sexuality and romantic love, and women began to pay more attention to appearance and sexual appeal. Children stopped consulting parents about marriage, and some young women simply became pregnant when they wanted to marry. By the late 18th century, as many as one third of all brides in some parts of New England were pregnant (D'Emilio & Freedman, 1988).

This newfound sexual freedom had many implications. In 1720, prostitution was relatively rare, but by the late 18th century, brothels were common in cities and were sometimes attacked by angry mobs. Contraception, such as early condoms, was readily available, and newspapers and almanacs often advertised

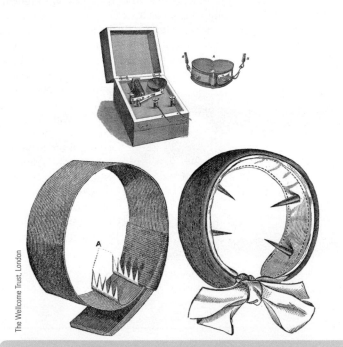

The Wellcome Trust, London

In the late 19th and early 20th centuries, many doctors taught that masturbation was harmful and so devices, such as the two barbed rings and the shock box shown here, were created to keep boys from achieving unwanted erections.

Puritans
Refers to members of a 16th- and 17th-century Protestant group from England who wanted to purge the church of elaborate ceremonies and simplify worship. It has come to mean any person or group that is excessively strict in regard to sexual matters.

bestiality
The act of having intercourse with an animal.

bundling
An American practice of placing a wooden board or hanging sheets in the middle of the bed, or wrapping the body in tight clothes, to allow an unmarried couple to spend the night together without having sex.

contraceptive devices and concoctions to induce abortion. The birth rate dropped, and abortion rates rose through the use of patent medicines, folk remedies, and self-induced abortion by inserting objects into the uterus. Within marriage, sexuality was much celebrated, and in many surviving diaries and letters from that era, couples speak of passion and longing for each other. Extramarital affairs were not uncommon, and some of the diaries quite explicitly record extramarital sexual passion.

Slavery (1600s–1800s)

Before the influx of slaves from Africa, the southern colonies made use of **indentured servants**. Sexual contact with, and even rape of, female indentured servants was fairly common. After 1670, African slaves became common in the South, and many states passed **antimiscegenation** (an-TEE-miss-seg-jen-nay-shun) **laws**. At first the laws were largely ignored. Sexual relations between Whites and Blacks continued, ranging from brutal rape to genuinely affectionate, long-term relationships. By the end of the 18th century, mixed-race children accounted for one fifth of the children born out of wedlock in Virginia (D'Emilio & Freedman, 1988).

The sex lives of slaves were different from those of colonists because of the relative lack of female slaves, the restrictions put on contact with members of the other sex, and the different cultural traditions of Africa. Whites accused African slaves of having loose morals because women tended to have children by different fathers and children slept in the same rooms as their copulating parents. These sexual habits were used as an excuse to rape them, break up their families, and even, at times, kill them. Of course, slave owners did not consider that they were responsible for forcing slaves to live that way. The fear that freed Black men would rape White women (or accusations that they

ON YOUR MIND

How do issues related to race and ethnicity affect sexuality research?

had) was often used as justification to keep Blacks segregated or to lynch them, even though it was far more common for White men to rape Black slaves and servants.

Only recently has there been a growth in areas of sexuality research that explore ethnicity and race. But it's important to ask questions like yours because subjects and populations studied in sexuality research are oftentimes determined by race, which can influence how we perceive the behavior (Andre, 2006). For example, over the last couple of years, there has been a considerable amount of research done on Black men and the *down low*—a term that has been used to refer to heterosexual-identified Black men who engage in secretive sex with other men (Duffin, 2016). This research has led to a perception that only Black men engage in such behaviors, even though this behavior is not new or limited to Black men (Glenn & Spieldenner, 2013). Researchers need to be more cognizant of how race and ethnicity issues can affect sexuality research. We will continue to explore the importance of ethnicity and sexuality throughout this book.

The slaves themselves developed a social system to protect their few freedoms. Adults formed and tried to maintain stable unions when possible, although marriage was officially illegal between slaves. Despite harsh conditions, there was a strong sense of morality within the slave community, and slaves tried to regulate sexual behavior as much as possible, forcing men to take care of the women they impregnated and sanctioning girls who were too promiscuous. The myth of slave sexual looseness is disproved by the lack of prostitution and very low rates of STIs among slaves (D'Emilio & Freedman, 1988). It was difficult, however, to maintain sexual unions when the woman's body was legally owned by the White master or when sexual favors might free one from harsh labor in the cotton fields. Despite the fact that plantation owners often condemned the promiscuity of Blacks (and therefore excused their own sexual exploitation of them), slaves' premarital sexual activity was probably not much different from that of poor Whites (Clinton & Gillespie, 1997).

Settlers throughout early American history used the sexuality of minorities as an excuse to disdain or oppress them. Native Americans had their own cultural system of sexual morality; nonetheless, they were branded as savages for their acceptance of premarital sex and their practice of polygamy, which existed primarily because of the large number of males killed in war. Native American women were freely raped by White men (D'Emilio &

Anti-miscegenation laws criminalizing interracial marriage were first introduced in the late 17th century and remained in force in many U.S. states until 1967.

Stephen Coburn/Shutterstock.com

---

indentured servant
A person who is bound by requirements to work for another person for a specified time in exchange for payment of travel and living expenses.

antimiscegenation laws
Laws forbidding sexuality, marriage, or breeding among members of different races.

Freedman, 1988). Mexicans, who were religious Catholics with strict sexual rules, were considered promiscuous by the Protestants because they did not consider it wrong to dance or show affection in public. The settlers often criticized others for sexual behaviors, such as homosexuality and premarital sex, that were not uncommon in their own communities.

The 19th Century: Polygamy, Celibacy, and the Comstock Laws (Beginning in the 1800s)

The pendulum swung back to the liberal side in the 19th century with the rise of a number of controversial social movements focusing on sexuality. The **free love movement**, which began in the 1820s, preached that love, not marriage, should be the prerequisite to sexual relations. Free love advocates criticized the sexual "slavery" of women in marriage, often condemned the sexual exploitation of slaves, and condemned sexuality without love (although their many critics often claimed that they preached promiscuity).

Another controversial group, the Church of Jesus Christ of Latter-day Saints, or Mormons, announced in 1852 that many of its members practiced polygamy, which almost cost Utah its statehood. As with the free love movement, Americans accused the Mormons of loose morals even though, despite their acceptance of polygamy, they were very sexually conservative (Iverson, 1991). A number of small communities that practiced alternative forms of sexual relations also began during this time. The Oneida community preached group marriage, whereas the Shakers, frustrated with all the arguments over sexuality, practiced strict celibacy (Hillebrand, 2008).

By the close of the 19th century, the medical model of sexuality began to emerge. Americans became obsessed with sexual health, and physicians and reformers began to advocate self-restraint, abstention from masturbation, and eating "nonstimulating" foods (those free from additives and easy to digest). Doctors also argued that women were ruled by their wombs, and many had their ovaries surgically removed to "correct" masturbation or sexual passion. An influential group of physicians even argued that women were biologically designed for procreation and destined only for marriage, for they were too delicate to work or undergo the rigors of higher education. These theories completely ignored the fact that lower-class women often worked difficult labor 12 and 15 hours a day. Male sexuality, however, was viewed as normative.

In the 19th century, homosexuality was underground, although there were some open same-sex relationships that may or may not have been sexual. For example, there are a number of recorded cases in which women dressed and passed as men and even "married" other women (we discuss this more in Chapter 11). There were also men who wrote of intimate and loving relationships with other men, without an explicit admission of sexual contact. The great poet Walt Whitman, now recognized as a same gender loving man, at times confirmed his erotic attraction to men, but at other times denied it. In accordance with the developing medical model of sexuality, physicians began to argue that homosexuality was an illness rather than a sin, a view that lasted until the 1970s.

The movements for more open sexual relationships were countered by strong voices arguing for a return to a more religious and chaste morality, an argument that continues more than a century later. In the 1870s, Anthony Comstock, a dry-goods salesperson, single-handedly lobbied the legislature to outlaw obscenity. The resulting Comstock Act of 1873 prohibited the mailing of obscene, lewd, lascivious, and indecent writing or advertisements, including articles about contraception or abortion. Comstock himself was the act's most vigorous enforcer, and he reported hundreds of people to the authorities, even for such things as selling reprints of famous artwork containing nudity or famous books that mentioned prostitution (M. A. Blanchard & Semoncho, 2006). Literally thousands of books, sexual objects, and contraceptive devices were destroyed, denying many people sophisticated contraceptive devices or information for almost 60 years. It wasn't until 1965 that the U.S. Supreme Court struck down the Comstock laws.

REAL RESEARCH Parents are more likely to tell daughters, rather than sons, when they are old enough to date (KUHLE ET AL., 2015).

The 20th Century: Sexual Crusaders and Sexologists (Beginning in the 1900s)

Even though Comstock laws were in effect at the beginning of the 20th century, one study of 1,000 heterosexual women found that 74% used some form of contraception, most made love at least once a week, and 40% acknowledged masturbating during childhood or adolescence (although others began after marriage; D'Emilio & Freedman, 1988). These statistics reflect the freedom women gradually began to find as they moved to the cities, lived on their own, and began working more outside the home. Yet, the overwhelming majority of heterosexual women still considered reproduction the primary goal of sex.

Moral crusaders were also trying to curb newfound sexual freedoms at this time, and those trying to liberalize sexuality further were in an intense struggle, trying to guide the rapid changes taking place in American sexual behaviors. Crusaders pointed to the spread of prostitution and high rates of STIs. Liberalizers argued that modern industrial society could not sustain the coercive sexual standards of past centuries. In some ways, these battles are still being fought today.

The Social Hygiene Movement (Beginning in 1905)

In response to high STI rates, a New York physician, Prince Morrow, started a movement in 1905 that was a curious mixture of both liberal and traditional attitudes. The social hygiene

---

free love movement
A movement of the early 19th century that preached love should be the factor that determines whether one should have sex (not to be confused with the free love movement of the 1960s).

movement convinced legislators that scores of virtuous women were catching STIs from husbands who frequented prostitutes, and so laws were passed mandating blood tests before marriage, and a number of highly publicized police actions were brought against prostitutes. Although the movement accepted pleasure as an acceptable motivation for sex, followers were against premarital sex and warned that masturbation harmed one's future sex life.

Sexology

Beginning in the early part of the 20th century and increasingly by midcentury, the pioneers of sexual research were beginning to make scientific advances into the understanding of sexuality. Rejecting the religious and moral teachings about how people "should" behave, researchers brought sex out into the open as a subject worthy of medical, scientific, and philosophical debate. We discuss these researchers at length in the following chapter, but here we should note that they had a profound impact on the way people began to talk and think about sexuality.

For example, in the early 1940s, Alfred Kinsey's large-scale surveys of American sexual behavior promised to settle some of the debates and confusion about sexuality by providing scientific answers to questions about how people behaved. Kinsey published his research in two volumes in 1948 and 1953, and both were overnight best sellers. Based on thousands of interviews, Kinsey's findings shocked American culture. His findings revealed that sex was much more important to peoples' lives than originally thought. Masturbation, homosexuality, and infidelity were not uncommon, and women had more sexual interest and desire than society had been led to believe. The popularity of Kinsey's books showed that the American public was hungry for sexual knowledge.

Other researchers, Dr. William Masters and Virginia Johnson, took Kinsey's research a step further and brought sex into a laboratory to study the physiology of sexual response. Their research yielded two important books about sexual functioning that were also overnight best sellers.

The work of these sexologists helped to demystify sex and make it more respectable to publicly discuss the sexual behaviors and problems of real people. Much of this work was condemned by moral crusaders, who criticized its lack of connection to traditional standards of morality.

The Sexual Revolutions (1920s and 1960s)

The phrase **sexual revolution** was coined in the 1920s by Wilhelm Reich, an Austrian psychoanalyst (Allyn, 2000). Reich was one of the leading figures of the sex reform movement in Europe, and he strongly believed in a sexually liberated society. He founded several clinics throughout Europe to educate people about sexuality and disseminate contraceptive information. Unfortunately, Reich's work was cut short by the political turmoil of the 1930s. Even though his dream for liberation never materialized in full, he did set into motion rapid changes in sexual mores throughout Europe and the United States during the first half of the 20th century.

In the mid-1960s a youth movement of "hippies" originated on college campuses. Hippies rejected the Puritanical sexual norms of mainstream American life and advocated nonviolence and love, saying "Make Love, Not War." The movement began to wane in the mid-1970s when a new generation of young people, known as "yuppies," were intent on making careers for themselves.

During this time, the values and attitudes about sexuality that were rooted in the Christian tradition slowly began to change as society became more permissive and accepting of sexual freedom. Advertising and other media became more sexualized, and fashion trends changed as the flapper era was ushered in. Flappers were women who typically wore short skirts, had short bob haircuts, and weren't uncomfortable going against societal expectations for women. They wore more makeup than what was generally accepted and had open attitudes about sexuality (Gourley, 2007). The trend toward more liberal ideas and values about sexuality continued in the late 1920s, but it wasn't until the early 1960s when many would say the real sexual revolution took place.

The modern movement that formed the sexual revolution began in San Francisco, where thousands of young people (who were referred to as "hippies") began to proclaim the power of love and sex. There was also an emerging revolt against the moral code of American society, and movements against the status quo were not uncommon. In fact, the Black Civil Rights Movement and the growing student protests against the Vietnam War in the mid-1960s proved that people could organize and stand up for what they believed in.

The 1960s were a time when the pendulum swung back to the liberal side; Americans went from *No Sex Until Marriage* to *If It Feels Good, Do It!* Some of the biggest sexuality challenges at this time were the reformulation of male gender roles and an examination of the double standard of sexuality (Escoffier, 2003). Two important events helped set the stage for the sexual revolution of the 1960s. One was the discovery of antibiotics in the mid-1930s. This discovery led to decreased fears about STIs, because many

sexual revolution
Changes in sexual morality and sexual behavior that occurred throughout the Western world during the 1960s and 1970s.

Playboy magazine played an important role in the sexual revolution. Founded by Hugh Hefner in 1953, the magazine was the first to contain full frontal nudity of women.

were now curable (we discuss STIs in Chapter 15). Another important event was the development of other media. By the early 1960s, the majority of U.S. homes had a television set (Abramson, 2003). Television, radio, and other mass media began to broadcast more liberal ideas about sexuality to viewers and listeners. Pornography also became more acceptable, and in 1953, Hugh Hefner began publishing *Playboy* magazine.

Nonfiction sex manuals also began to appear, such as Helen Gurley Brown's *Sex and the Single Girl* (1962; Gurley Brown later went on to publish *Cosmopolitan* magazine), Joan Garrity's *The Sensuous Woman* (1969), and David Reuben's *Everything You Always Wanted to Know About Sex (But Were Afraid to Ask)* (1969). There were many others published, and all of them spoke to the changing nature of sexuality. They were all factually written and were best sellers. Mainstream America had been desperate for more information about sexuality. Probably the most important thing these books did was to give readers the opportunity to acknowledge and celebrate their sexuality.

The introduction of the first contraceptive pill was another important event that liberated female sexuality in the early 1960s. For the first time, heterosexual women were free to engage in sexual intercourse without the fear of becoming pregnant. No longer was sexual intercourse associated solely with procreation. Fashions changed once again in the mid-1960s, emphasizing women's bodies and showing more skin. Women wore miniskirts, plunging necklines, and see-through blouses, further emphasizing women's

women's suffrage
The movement to get women the right to vote.

sexuality. Some women began to burn their bras and "free their breasts" as an act of defiance.

Soon, poets, writers, and songwriters began to embrace both sensuality and sexual experimentation. Sexuality began to come out of the closet as repressive attitudes began to lessen. All of these influences led to a generation that was much more sexually liberal than those preceding it. At the end of the 1960s, the gay and lesbian civil rights movement officially started with the Stonewall riots (we discuss this more later in the chapter).

Feminism (Beginning in Early 1900s)

There have always been women who protested against the patriarchy of their day, argued that women were as capable as men in the realms of work and politics, and defied their culture's stereotypes about women. The 20th century, however, saw the most successful feminist movement in history. The **women's suffrage** movement of the early 20th century first put women's agendas on the national scene, but it was Margaret Sanger who most profoundly influenced women's sexuality in the first half of the 20th century.

Sanger, a 30-year-old homemaker, was an early advocate for the rights of women. When her 50-year-old mother died after 18 pregnancies, Sanger was determined to help women learn how to protect themselves from pregnancy. In 1917, she met Katharine Dexter McCormick, who had graduated with a degree in biology from the Massachusetts Institute of Technology (McCormick was only the second woman to do so). In the next few years, Sanger worked with McCormick to build the Birth Control League. Sanger brought her drive, passion, and energy, whereas McCormick provided the knowledge and capital necessary for their project. During the Depression, their movement gained momentum because many families were desperate to limit the size of their families. In fact, while there were 55 contraceptive clinics in the United States in 1930, by 1942, this number grew to more than 800 clinics (Gibbs, 2010). In 1942, Sanger's Birth Control League changed its name to the Planned Parenthood Federation of America.

After Sanger, organized feminism entered a quiet phase, not reemerging until the 1960s. In the middle of the 20th century, women increasingly entered institutions of higher education and entered the labor force in great numbers while men were off fighting World War II. At the same time, divorce rates were rising, many women widowed by war were raising children as single parents, and the postwar baby boom relegated middle-class women to their suburban homes. Social conditions had given women more power just as their roles were being restricted again to wife and mother. A backlash was soon to come, and the pendulum would swing back to the conservative side.

The modern feminist movement can best be summarized by the work of three female authors. In her 1949 book *The Second Sex,* Simone de Beauvoir showed that women were not granted an identity of their own but were considered the objects of men's wishes and anxieties. Betty Friedan followed in 1963 with *The Feminine Mystique,* a 10-year follow-up of the lives of her graduating class from Smith College in which she found that these educated, bright women felt trapped in the role of housewife and wanted careers to have happier,

Same sex marriage has been legal in the United States since 2015 when the U.S. Supreme Court ruled that state-level bans were unconstitutional.

The gay rights movement has been at the forefront in changing sexual attitudes in the United States not only by pressing for recognition of homosexuality, but also by arguing that all sexual minorities have the right to sexual happiness.

more fulfilled lives. Finally, at the height of the Vietnam War, Kate Millett's (1969) *Sexual Politics* argued that patriarchy bred violence and forced men to renounce all that is feminine in them. According to Millett, rape was an act of aggression aimed at controlling women, and men saw homosexuality as a "failure" of patriarchy, so it was violently repressed.

Feminists of the 1960s argued that they were entitled to sexual satisfaction, that the existing relations of the sexes were exploitative, and that women had a right to control their lives and their bodies. Some of the more radical feminists advocated lesbianism as the only relationship not based on male power, but most feminists fought for a transformation of the interpersonal relationship of men and women and of the male-dominated political structure. Part of the freedom women wanted was the freedom to choose when to be mothers, and the right to choose abortion became a firm part of the feminist platform.

Feminism has made great cultural and political strides and has changed the nature of American society and sexual behavior. The pursuit of sexual pleasure is now seen as a woman's legitimate right, and heterosexual men are no longer expected to be the sexual experts relied on by docile, virginal mates. Feminists were at the forefront of the abortion debate and hailed the legalization of abortion as a great step in achieving women's rights over their own bodies. More recently, women have begun entering politics in record numbers, and the Senate, Congress, and governorships are increasingly counting women among their members. Even so, women still have many struggles. Men continue to be paid on average more than women for the same work, poverty is increasingly a problem of single mothers, and rape and spousal abuse are still major social problems in the United States. Still, feminism as a movement has had a major impact on the way America views sexuality.

Gay Liberation (Beginning in Mid-1900s)

The period after World War II was challenging for homosexuals. Senator Joseph McCarthy, who became famous for trying to purge the United States of communists, also relentlessly hunted homosexuals. Homosexuals were portrayed as perverts, lurking in schools and on street corners ready to pounce on unsuspecting youth, and many were thrown out of work or imprisoned in jails and mental hospitals. The news media participated in this view, as in a 1949 *Newsweek* article that identified all homosexuals as "sex murderers." Doctors tinkered with a variety of "cures," including lobotomies and castration. Churches were either silent or encouraged the persecution, and Hollywood purged itself of positive references to homosexuality. Many laws initiated during this period, such as immigration restrictions for homosexuals and policies banning gays from the military, continued for many years (Adam, 1987).

In 1951, an organization for homosexual rights, the Mattachine Society, was founded in the United States by Harry Hay. The Daughters of Bilitis, the first postwar lesbian organization, was founded in 1955 by four lesbian couples in San Francisco. Although these groups began with radical intentions, the vehement antihomosexuality of American authorities forced the groups to lay low throughout the late 1950s.

Although gay activism increased in America with protests and sit-ins throughout the 1960s, modern gay liberation is usually traced to the night in 1969 when New York police raided a Greenwich Village gay bar called Stonewall. For the first time, the gay community erupted in active resistance, and the police were greeted by a hail of debris thrown by the gay patrons of the bar. There had been previous acts of resistance, but the Stonewall riot became a symbol to the gay community and put the police on notice that homosexuals would no longer passively accept arrest and police brutality.

Following Stonewall, gay activism began a strong campaign against prejudice and discrimination all over the country. Groups and businesses hostile to gays were picketed, legislators were lobbied, committees and self-help groups were founded, legal agencies were formed, and educational groups tried to change the image of homosexuality in America. For example, in 1973, strong gay lobbying caused the American Psychiatric Association to remove homosexuality from the *Diagnostic and Statistical Manual of Mental Disorders* (*DSM*), the official reference of psychiatric disorders. The *DSM* change removed the last scientific justification for treating homosexuals any differently from other citizens and demonstrated the new national power of the movement for homosexual rights. Soon the gay movement was a powerful presence in the United States, Canada, Australia, and Western Europe.

The 1970s were, in many ways, the golden age of gay life in America. In cities such as San Francisco and New York, gay bathhouses and bars became open centers of gay social life, and gay theater groups, newspapers, and magazines appeared. In 1979, the National March on Washington for Lesbian and Gay Rights was a symbolic step forward for the gay movement (Ghaziani, 2005). The discovery of the AIDS epidemic in the United States and Europe in the beginning of the 1980s doused the excitement of the 1970s, as thousands of gay men began to die of the disease. Historically, when such fearsome epidemics arise, people have been quick to find a minority group to blame for the disease, and homosexuals were quickly blamed by a large segment of the public (Shilts, 2000).

In 1990, queer theory developed and grew out of lesbian and gay studies (we discuss queer theory in more detail in Chapter 2). The gay rights movement has been at the forefront of trying to

Gender roles have become less restrictive on today's college campuses, allowing for more gender fluidity.

change sexual attitudes in the United States not only by pressing for recognition of homosexuality as a legitimate sexual orientation, but also by arguing that all sexual minorities have a right to sexual happiness. President Obama signed a bill ending the military's "don't ask, don't tell" policy in 2010, which was one of the first moves toward equality for gays and lesbians. In 2011, he reversed his stance on the Defense of Marriage Act (DOMA), concluding that his administration could no longer defend the federal law that defines marriage as between a man and a woman. In 2013, a landmark case, *United States v. Windsor,* held that restricting marriage to only heterosexual couples was unconstitutional under the due process guarantees of the Fifth Amendment. Finally, in 2015, the Supreme Court ruled that same-sex couples could legally marry nationwide. This decision came nearly 46 years to the day after the Stonewall riot.

We are the sum total of our history. Our attitudes and beliefs reflect all of our historical influences, from the ancient Hebrews and Greeks to the Christianity of the Middle Ages to the modern feminist and gay liberation movements. Most of us have a hard time recognizing that our own constellation of beliefs, feelings, and moral positions about sex are a product of our particular time and place, and are in a constant state of evolution. It is important to keep this in mind as we explore the sexual behaviors of other people and other cultures throughout this book.

Review Questions

1 Explain how the Puritans viewed sex. Who did they believe was responsible for upholding morality?

2 Explain some of the influences that led to the liberalization of sex in the 1700s.

3 What was the "free love movement," and what did the movement preach?

4 What are the two most important movements to change sexuality in the latter part of the 20th century? What did each contribute?

Chapter Review

Summary Points

1 Human sexuality is grounded in biological functioning, emerges as we develop, and is expressed by cultures through rules about sexual contact, attitudes about moral and immoral sexuality, habits of sexual behavior, patterns of relations between the sexes, and more.

2 The sexual nature of human beings is unique in the animal kingdom. Humans have created ideas, laws, customs, fantasies, and art around the sexual act. Sexuality is a uniquely human trait.

3 The Internet, through social networking sites such as Facebook, Twitter, Instagram, Snapchat, and FaceTime, has changed patterns of social communication and relationships. Today's teens rate the media as one of their leading sources of sex information.

4 The evolution to an upright posture changed forever the way the human species engages in sexual intercourse.

5 Men dominated public life in early history, and we know far more about men's thoughts than women's. The Hebrew Bible contained explicit rules about sexual behavior. The focus on marital sexuality and procreation formed the basis of sexual attitudes in the West for centuries.

6 The Greeks were more sexually permissive than the Hebrews. In Greek culture, pederasty was considered a natural form of sexuality. Rome had few restrictions about sexuality until late in the history of the empire.

7 Chinese civilization's belief in yin and yang taught people how to maximize their sexuality. A woman's essence, or yin, was viewed as inexhaustible, whereas a man's essence, yang, embodied in semen, was limited. Hinduism concentrates on an individual's cycle of birth and rebirth, also known as karma. India's most famous sex manual, the *Kamasutra*, appeared sometime during the 3rd or 4th century.

8 Perhaps no single system of thought has had as much impact on the Western world as Christianity. According to early forms of the belief system, sexuality itself was not sinful when performed as part of the marital union, but the ideal situation was celibacy. In fact, with the advent of Christianity, chastity became a virtue for the first time in history.

9 In the early Middle Ages, the influence of the church began to increase. Its teachings began to influence laws, which became much stricter. Perhaps no person from the Middle Ages had a stronger impact on attitudes toward sexuality than the theologian Thomas Aquinas.

10 Muhammad began to preach a religion called Islam in the 6th century. Many Muslim societies have strong rules of modesty for women that involve covering private parts of their bodies. According to the Muslim bible, the Koran, marital sexual intercourse was a good religious deed, and men were encouraged to engage frequently in such behavior.

11 The Renaissance witnessed a new view of sexuality and of the roles of women in society. Women made great strides in education and became more prominent in political affairs. Pro-female tracts began to circulate, and lively debates about the value of women ensued. However, by the 17th century, witchcraft trials appeared, symbolizing the fear that men held of women's sexuality.

12 In the early 16th century, Martin Luther started Protestantism. Luther saw in the Bible the obligation to reproduce, considered marital love blessed, and considered sexuality a natural function. Sexuality was permissible only in the marital union, although it had other justifications besides reproduction.

13 Three important movements that influenced modern sexuality were the Renaissance, the Reformation, and the Enlightenment.

14 The Enlightenment (early 1700s) prized rational thought over traditional authority and suggested that human nature was to be understood through a study of human psychology. Sexual pleasure was considered natural and desirable.

15 During the Victorian era (early 1800s), conservative values were often preached, although not always practiced. The idea of male chivalry returned, and women were considered to be virtuous, refined, delicate, fragile, vulnerable, and remote. Sexuality was repressed in many ways for men and women.

16 The Puritans were a religious group who fled England and tried to set up a biblically based society in the New World. Even though they believed that sexuality was good and proper within marriage, they also believed the entire community was responsible for upholding morality.

17 After the Revolutionary War, the church's power began to diminish in the United States. People began to speak more openly about sexuality, and the liberalization of sexual conduct had many results. Prostitution flourished, and contraception became more readily available.

18 Slavery had a profound effect on post-Revolutionary America. Many slaves developed a social system and formed stable unions, although marriage was officially illegal between slaves. There was a strong sense of morality within the slave community, and sexual behavior was regulated as much as possible.

19 During the 19th century, there was an increase in a number of controversial social movements focusing on sexuality. The free love movement preached that love should be the only prerequisite to sexual relations. However, by the end of the 19th century, the medical model of sexuality began to emerge, and physicians and reformers began to advocate self-restraint, abstention from masturbation, and consumption of "nonstimulating" foods. The Comstock Act of 1873 prohibited the mailing of obscene, lewd, and indecent writings, including articles about contraception or abortion.

20 In 1905, the social hygiene movement convinced legislators to pass laws mandating blood tests before marriage. Premarital sex and masturbation were thought to harm one's future sex life. In the early part of the 20th century, pioneers of sexual research began their work, rejecting the religious and moral teachings about how people "should" behave.

21 The sexual revolution brought changes in values and attitudes about sexuality. Society became more permissive and accepting of sexual freedom. Flappers and hippies helped bring more liberal attitudes about sexuality.

22 Feminism and gay liberation also affected society's attitudes about sexuality. Modern gay liberation is usually traced back to the Stonewall riot of 1969. In 1973, strong gay lobbying caused the American Psychiatric Association to remove homosexuality from the *DSM*. In 2015, the U.S. Supreme Court legalized same-sex marriage nationwide.

Critical Thinking Questions

1 Explain your goals for this class and how you developed each of these goals. Do you think this class will help you in the future? If so, in what ways?

2 Why do you think "sex sells" when our culture traditionally has had a problem openly talking about sexuality?

3 The Bible has had a profound impact on our attitudes toward sexuality. Do you think that it is still influential? In what ways?

4 How different do China's and India's sexual histories seem to you today? Are they different from our Western views of sexuality?

5 Provide two examples of how cultural images of beauty affect how men and women feel about themselves. Explain how the Chinese practice of foot binding became so widespread and lasted for 1,000 years.

6 Explore the many influences that led to the sexual revolution of the 1960s. Explain how these events shaped the cultural view of sexuality.

7 Compare and contrast both the role of women and the views of sexuality in modern society and in Islam. How does the practice of honor crimes tie into gender issues in society?

Websites

The Kinsey Institute This official website for the Kinsey Institute is one of only a handful of centers in the world that conducts interdisciplinary research exclusively on sex, and it has a large library that includes books, films, video, fine art, artifacts, photography, archives, and more.

The Journal of the History of Sexuality This journal has a cross-cultural and cross-disciplinary focus that brings together original articles and critical reviews from historians, social scientists, and humanities scholars worldwide. The website offers a look at recently published articles in the journal.

The Sexuality Information and Education Council of the United States (SIECUS) SIECUS is a national organization that promotes comprehensive education about sexuality and advocates the right of individuals to make responsible sexual choices.

2 Understanding Human Sexuality: Theory and Research

It's always interesting for me to talk to students who are taking the human sexuality course. One student I met, Liz, took the course at a small, Midwestern university, and her professor required students to develop a research study exploring human sexuality. Liz had recently met someone on Tinder and was curious about the use of this app on her campus. Tinder lets users find people who might be interested in getting together with them. If a user is interested in someone they swipe right. They "match" if the other person also swipes right for them. Once there is a match they are able to communicate with each other. Liz wanted to know if other students used Tinder and if so, if they were successful in meeting someone. She decided that one-on-one interviews would help her establish rapport with students and explain the nature of her project.

After developing a list of questions, Liz spent a day walking around campus approaching students about their use of Tinder. Several students stopped to talk to her and told her they did use Tinder, mainly because they thought it was fun. Most of the time they used it just to see who was out there. Liz told me that one interesting finding was that male students were more likely than female students to say they used Tinder for casual sex. Only a few of the students she talked with said they had met someone on Tinder they had a relationship with.

All in all, she enjoyed doing the assignment. She liked talking with students and realized that Tinder was more popular on her campus than she thought. But her study also made her realize how much more time she would need to spend on her research design and implementation in order to draw any conclusions. How could she get more students to talk to her? Would they be more honest if she used a different research methodology? She was excited to think about the ways she could improve her study.

Janell Carroll

Stephanie Alexandre

What would you have done if you were approached by Liz? Would you have stopped to talk to her? Do you think the responses she obtained were representative of all students at her university? These questions give us a great introduction into the study of human sexuality. It seems like sexuality studies are everywhere these days—headlines from online news sources, magazines, and newspapers boast findings about sexuality—but how do you know if the research is reliable and accurate? In this chapter, we explore both the major theories and the research methods that underlie the study of sexuality. We also examine some of the most influential sexuality studies that have been done. Theoretical development and ongoing research combine to provide a foundation on which to build further understanding of sexuality.

Before we start, you might wonder why reviewing theory and research in a sexuality textbook is important. Because theories guide our understanding of sexuality, and research helps answer our many questions, learning how theories are formulated and research is pursued will give you insight into the information that is provided in the chapters to come. Let's examine the various theories of sexuality and some of the important sexuality researchers.

The majority of psychological research done in the United States uses undergraduate college students as subjects.

Theories About Sexuality

The study of sexuality is multidisciplinary. Psychologists, sexologists, biologists, theologians, physicians, sociologists, anthropologists, and philosophers all conduct sexuality research. The questions each discipline asks and how its practitioners transform those questions into research projects can differ greatly. However, the insights of these disciplines complement each other, and no single approach to the study of sexuality is better than another.

A **theory** is a set of assumptions, principles, or methods that help a researcher understand the nature of the phenomenon being studied. A theory provides an intellectual structure to help conceptualize, implement, and interpret a topic, such as human sexuality. The majority of researchers begin with theories about human behavior that guide the kind of questions they ask about sexuality. For example, suppose researchers subscribe to the theory that sexuality is innate and biologically determined; they would probably design studies to examine such things as how the hypothalamus in the brain or the monthly cycle of hormones influences our sexual behavior. It is unlikely they would be interested in studying

how society influences sexuality. A person who believes sexuality is determined by environmental influences, in contrast, would be more likely to study how the media influences sexuality rather than genetic patterns of sexual behavior.

Several theories—often clashing—guide much of our thinking about sexuality. These include psychological, biological, sociological, and evolutionary theoretical views of human sexuality. In addition, over the last few years, feminist and queer theories have also become important models for exploring and explaining sexual behavior. We first explore each of these theoretical views and look at how they influence sexuality research. While we do, however, it is important to remember that many theorists borrow from multiple theoretical perspectives, and that these categories often overlap and learn from each other.

Psychoanalytic Theory

Sigmund Freud (1856–1939) was the founder of the psychoanalytic theory. He believed that the sex drive was one of the most important forces in life, and he spent a considerable amount of time studying sexuality. According to Freud, human behavior is motivated by instincts and drives. The two most powerful drives are **libido** (la-BEED-oh), which is sexual motivation, and thanatos (THAN-uh-toes), which is aggressiveness motivation. Of these two, the libido is the more powerful. Two of Freud's most controversial concepts include personality formation and **psychosexual development**.

Freud believed the personality contained the **id**, **ego**, and **superego**. At birth, a child has only the id portion of the personality, which functions as the pleasure center. If the id were the only part of the personality that developed, we would always be seeking pleasure and fulfillment with little concern for others; in other words, we would operate in the way most animals do. As humans get older, however, the id balances its desires with other parts of the personality.

By the second year of life, the ego develops as the child begins to interact with the environment. The ego keeps the id in check by being realistic about what the child can and cannot have. Because the majority of the id's desires may be socially unacceptable, the ego works to restrain the id.

---

theory
A set of assumptions, principles, or methods that helps a researcher understand the nature of a phenomenon being studied.

libido
According to Freud, the energy generated by the sexual instinct.

psychosexual development
The childhood stages of development during which the id's pleasure-seeking energies focus on distinct erogenous zones.

id
The collection of unconscious urges and desires that continually seek expression.

ego
The part of the personality that mediates between environmental demands (reality), conscience (superego), and instinctual needs (id).

superego
The social and parental standards an individual has internalized; the conscience.

Freud believed that the last portion of the personality, the superego, develops by the age of 5 years. The superego contains both societal and parental values, and it puts more restrictions on what a person can and cannot do. It acts as our conscience, and its most effective weapon is guilt. For example, let's say that a woman was raised in a very religious family, and she wants to wait until she's married to have sex. One night she starts hooking up with her partner (an id action). It feels good, and the id is being fulfilled. Soon, reality kicks in (an ego action), and she realizes that she is about to have sex in the backseat of a car! This causes her to reevaluate the situation, and because she has been taught that premarital sex is wrong, she feels guilty (a superego action). Throughout our lives, the id, ego, and superego are in a constant struggle with each other, but it is the ego, or the realistic portion of our personality, that keeps the other two parts balanced. If the ego does not keep things in balance, the superego could take over, and a person could be paralyzed by guilt. The id could also take over, forcing the person to search constantly for pleasure with little concern for others.

One of Freud's most controversial ideas was his theory of psychosexual development, which includes the oral, anal, phallic, and genital stages. Within each stage of development, Freud identified different **erogenous** (uh-RAJ-uh-nus) **zones** in which libido energy was directed. If the stage was not successfully completed, energy would be tied up in that zone, and the child would experience a **fixation**.

The first stage of psychosexual development, known as the **oral stage**, lasts through the first 18 months of life. According to Freud's theory, problems during this stage could result in an oral fixation, leading to behaviors such as cigarette smoking, overeating, fingernail chewing, or alcohol abuse. The next stage, the **anal stage**, begins when a child starts toilet training. Problems during this stage could lead to traits such as stubbornness, orderliness, or cleanliness.

According to Freud, the most important stage was the next one, the **phallic stage**, which occurs between the ages of 3 and 6. Freud believed that during the phallic stage, boys go through the **Oedipus** (ED-uh-puss) **complex**, while girls go through an **Electra complex**. At the end of this stage, children typically identify with the same-sex parent and adopt masculine or feminine characteristics. The superego begins to develop during this time as well, and most children adopt their parents' values.

Before puberty (between the ages of 6 and 12), the child passes through the **latency stage**, and sexual interest goes underground. During this stage, young boys might think girls have "cooties" (and vice versa), and childhood play primarily exists in same-sex groups. Puberty marks the **genital stage**, which is the final stage of psychosexual development. During this stage, sexuality becomes less internally directed and more directed at others as erotic objects.

Freud's ideas were controversial in the Victorian period in which he lived. His claims that children were sexual from birth and lusted for the other-sex parent caused tremendous shock in the conservative community of Vienna. Remember that at the time when Freud came up with his ideas, there was a strong cultural repression of sexuality. Doctors and religious leaders believed that masturbation was physically harmful, and conversations about sex were unheard of.

Among modern psychologists, Freud and the psychoanalytic theory have received a considerable amount of criticism. The predominant criticism is that his theory is unscientific and does not lend itself to testing. How could a researcher study the existence of the phallic stage? If it is indeed unconscious, then it would be impossible to hand out surveys to see when a child was in each stage. Furthermore, because Freud based his theories on his patients, he has been accused of creating his theories around people who were sick; consequently, they may not apply to healthy people (we discuss this further in the "Case Studies" section on research methodology). Finally, Freud has also been heavily criticized because of his unflattering psychological portrait of women.

Behavioral Theory

Behaviorists believe that it is necessary to observe and measure behavior in order to understand it. Psychological states, emotions, the unconscious, and feelings are not measurable and, therefore, are not valid for study. Only overt behavior can be measured, observed, and controlled by scientists. Radical behaviorists (those who believe that we do not actually choose how we behave), such as B. F. Skinner (1953), claim that environmental rewards and punishments determine the types of behaviors in which we engage. This is referred to as **operant conditioning**.

According to behavioral theory, we learn certain behaviors, including most sexual behaviors, through reinforcement and punishment. Reinforcements encourage a person to engage in a behavior by associating it with pleasurable outcomes, whereas punishments make it less likely that a behavior will be repeated, because the behavior becomes associated with unpleasant outcomes. For instance, if a man decided to cheat on his partner with someone in one of his classes, it may be because of the positive reinforcements he receives, such as the increased excitement of going to class. If, in contrast, a man experiences an erection problem the first time he cheats on his partner, it may make it less likely he will try the behavior again. The negative outcomes reduce the likelihood of the behavior.

To help change unwanted behavior, behaviorists use **behavior modification**. For example, if a man wants to rid himself of

---

erogenous zones
Areas of the body that are particularly sensitive to touch and are associated with sexual pleasure.

fixation
The tying up of psychic energy at a particular psychosexual stage, resulting in adult behaviors characteristic of the stage.

oral stage
A psychosexual stage in which the mouth, lips, and tongue are the primary erogenous zone.

anal stage
A psychosexual stage in which the anal area is the primary erogenous zone.

phallic stage
A psychosexual stage in which the genital region is the primary erogenous zone and in which the Oedipus or Electra complex develops.

Oedipus complex
A male child's sexual attraction for his mother and the consequent conflicts.

Electra complex
The incestuous desire of a daughter for her father.

latency stage
A psychosexual stage in which libido and sexual interest are repressed.

genital stage
Final psychosexual stage in which a person develops the ability to engage in adult sexual behavior.

behaviorists
Theorists who believe that behavior is learned and can be altered.

operant conditioning
Learning resulting from the reinforcing response a person receives after a certain behavior.

behavior modification
Therapy based on operant conditioning and classical conditioning principles used to change behaviors.

sexual fantasies about young boys, a behavioral therapist might use **aversion therapy**. To do so, the therapist might show the man slides of young boys; when he has an erection, an electrical shock is administered to his penis. If this pairing of the erection with an electrical shock is repeated several times, behaviorists believe the man will cease getting an erection when looking at the slides. The punishment will have changed the behavior. Contrast this form of therapy with that of a psychoanalytic therapist, who would probably want to study what happened to this man in his early life. A behavior therapist would primarily be concerned with changing the behavior and less concerned with why it's happening.

Learning Theory

Social learning theory actually grew out of behaviorism. Scientists began to question whether behaviorism was too limited in its explanation of human behavior. Many believed that thoughts and feelings had more influence on behaviors than the behaviorists claimed. A noted social learning theorist, Albert Bandura (1969), argued that both external and internal events influence our behavior. Rewards and punishments can influence behavior, but internal events, such as feelings, thoughts, and beliefs, also have an impact. Bandura began to bridge the gap between behaviorism and cognitive theory, which we discuss next.

Social learning theorists believe that imitation and identification are also important in the development of sexuality. For example, we identify with our same-sex parent and begin to imitate him or her, which helps us develop our own gender identity. In turn, we are praised and reinforced for these behaviors. Think for a moment about a young boy who identifies with his mother and begins to dress and act like her. He may be ridiculed or even punished, which may lead him to turn his attention to a socially acceptable figure, most

likely his father. Peer pressure also influences our sexuality. We want to be liked; therefore, we may engage in certain behaviors because our peers encourage it. We also learn what is expected of us from television, our families, and even from the songs we listen to.

ON YOUR MIND
When scientists come up with new theories, how do they know they are true?

They don't. Theories begin as ideas to explain observed phenomena, but they must undergo testing and evaluation. Many early theories of sexuality, such as Sigmund Freud's, were developed out of work with patients, whereas others base their theories on behaviors they observe or the results of experiments they conduct. However, researchers never really know whether their theories are true. Some scientists become so biased by their own theories that they have trouble seeing explanations other than their own for certain behaviors. This is why scientific findings or ideas should always be tested and confirmed by other scientists.

Cognitive Theory

So far, the theories we have discussed emphasize that either internal conflicts or external events control the development of personality. Unlike these, **cognitive theory** holds that people differ in how they process information, and this creates personality differences.

Social learning theorists believe that the clothing teens wear is often influenced by their peers. Most teens want to feel like they fit in.

Stockbroker/Alamy Stock Photo

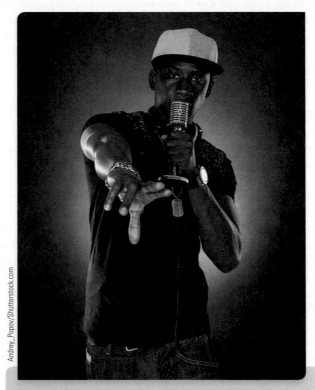

Andrey_Popov/Shutterstock.com

The lyrics in many genres of music, especially hip-hop, have become more explicit in their references to sex, sexual violence, and misogyny. Researchers are exploring how exposure to these messages can affect our behavior and attitudes.

aversion therapy
A technique that reduces the frequency of maladaptive behavior by associating it with aversive stimuli.

cognitive theory
A theory proposing that our thoughts are responsible for our behaviors.

We feel what we think we feel, and our thoughts also affect our behavior. Our behavior does not come from early experiences in childhood or from rewards or punishments; rather, it is a result of how we perceive and conceptualize what is happening around us.

As far as sexuality is concerned, cognitive theorists believe that the biggest sexual organ is the brain. What sexually arouses us is what we *think* sexually arouses us. We pay attention to our physical sensations and label these reactions. For example, if a person doesn't reach orgasm during sex, they could perceive this in one of two ways: it's not a big deal and maybe next time they'll have one; or, there's a problem and they are disappointed. What caused the disappointment, however, is not the lack of an orgasm but their perception of it.

Humanistic Theory

Humanistic (or person centered) psychologists believe that we all strive to develop ourselves to the best of our abilities and to achieve **self-actualization**. This is easier to do if we are raised with **unconditional positive regard**, which involves accepting and caring about another person without any stipulations or conditions. In other words, there are no rules a person must follow to be loved. Let's say a mother walks in on her daughter playing sex games with a group of friends. The mother could respond in a couple of different ways. If she started yelling and sent her daughter to her room, she would be demonstrating **conditional love**. If, however, she calmly told her daughter that she loved her but didn't approve of her behavior, she's demonstrating unconditional positive regard.

Children who grow up with unconditional positive regard learn to accept their faults and weaknesses, whereas children who have experienced conditional love may try to ignore those traits because they know others would not approve. Accepting our faults and weaknesses leads us toward self-actualization.

Self-actualization occurs as we learn our own potential in life. We want to do things that make us feel good about ourselves. Sexual behavior that makes us feel good contributes to our own personal growth and self-actualization.

Biological Theory

The biological theory of human sexuality emphasizes that sexual behavior is primarily biological. Sexual functioning, hormonal release, ovulation, ejaculation, conception, pregnancy, and birth are controlled physiologically. Those who advocate this theory also point out that human sexual behaviors, including gender roles and sexual orientation, are primarily due to inborn, genetic patterns and are not functions of social or psychological forces. Sexual problems are thought to be caused by physiological factors, and intervention often includes medications or surgery.

Evolutionary Theory

Unlike biological theory, which focuses on individual physiology, **evolutionary theory** looks more broadly at the physiological changes of an entire species over time. To understand sexual behavior in humans, evolutionary theorists study animal sexual patterns and look for evolutionary trends. They believe that sexuality exists for the purpose of reproducing the species, and individual sexuality is designed to maximize the chances of passing on one's genes. According to evolutionary theorists, the winners in the game of life are those who are most successful at transmitting their genes to the next generation.

Think about the qualities you look for in a partner. Students often tell me that they are looking for someone who is attractive, intelligent, honest, sensitive, funny, and monogamous. An evolutionary theorist would argue that these qualities have evolved to ensure that a person would be able to provide healthy offspring and care for them well. A physically attractive person is more likely to be fit and healthy. Could this be important to us because of their reproductive capabilities? Evolutionary theorists would say so. They would also argue that qualities such as monogamy, honesty, and sensitivity would help ensure that a partner will be reliable and help raise the offspring.

Evolutionary theorists also believe that some sexual activities have evolved to ensure the survival of the species. For example, orgasms make sexual intercourse pleasurable; this, in turn, increases the frequency that people engage in it, and increases the possibility for reproduction. Differences between the sexes in sexual desire and behavior are also thought to have evolved. The double standard, which states that it's more acceptable for men to hook up, exists because men produce millions of sperm per day and women produce only one viable ovum per month. Males try to "spread their seed" to ensure the reproduction of their family line, whereas females need to protect the one ovum they produce each month.

The evolutionary theory suggests that we are drawn to physically attractive partners because they are likely to be fit and healthy.

self-actualization
Fulfillment of an individual's potentialities, including aptitudes, talents, and the like.

unconditional positive regard
Acceptance of another without restrictions on their behaviors or thoughts.

conditional love
Conditional acceptance of another, with restrictions on their behaviors or thoughts.

evolutionary theory
A theory that incorporates both evolution and sociology, and looks for trends in behaviors.

When women become pregnant, they have a potential lifelong commitment ahead of them.

Evolutionary theory has received a considerable amount of criticism, however, particularly because evolutionary theorists tend to ignore the influence of both prior learning and societal influences on sexuality.

ON YOUR MIND

I am a healthy female college student, but lately I've been having trouble reaching orgasm. How would the biological theory explain this?

A person who adopts a biological theory would explain differences in sexuality as resulting from anatomy, hormones, neurochemicals, or other physical explanations. Therefore, a biological theorist would suggest that trouble reaching orgasm would be due to physical reasons, such as hormonal or neurological causes. Treatment might involve a physical workup and blood work to evaluate hormone levels. However, other theoretical approaches would disagree with this assessment and would look at a variety of other issues, such as stress, internal thought processes, or social pressures.

Sociological Theory

Sociologists are interested in how the society in which we live influences sexual behavior. Even though the basic capacity to be sexual might be biologically programmed, how it is expressed varies greatly across societies, as we saw in Chapter 1. For instance, there are differences in what societies tolerate, gender roles, and how sexuality is viewed. A behavior that may be seen as normal in one society may be considered abnormal in another. For instance, on the island of Mangaia in the South Pacific, women are very sexually assertive and often initiate sexual activity (D. S. Marshall, 1971). From an early age, elders teach them how to have multiple orgasms. However, in Inis Beag, a remote island off the coast of Ireland, sexuality is repressed and is considered appropriate only for procreation (Messenger, 1993). Heterosexual couples engage in sexual intercourse fully clothed with only the genitals exposed, and homosexuality is not tolerated. Each society regulates its sexual behaviors.

Sociologists believe that societal influences, such as the family, religion, economy, medicine, law, and the media, affect a society's rules about sexual expression. Each of these influences dictates certain beliefs about the place of sexuality in one's life and how the culture determines what is considered "normal."

The family is the first factor that influences our values about sexuality. As we discussed in Chapter 1, our family provides strong messages about what is acceptable and unacceptable. Religion also influences how a society views sexuality. Some religions provide strong opinions on issues such as premarital sex, homosexuality, and abortion. Many people within society look to religious institutions and leaders for answers to their questions about sexuality.

The economy also influences the societal view of sexuality. The U.S. economy is based on capitalism, which involves an exchange of services for money (DeLamater, 1987). This influences the availability of sex-related services such as sex work, pornography, and sex shops. These services exist because they are profitable.

In addition to family and the economy, the medical community affects how a society views sexuality. For example, many years ago, physicians taught that masturbation was a disease that could lead to permanent mental illness. This attitude influenced societal opinions of masturbation. Other behaviors that physicians have urged people not to engage in included anal intercourse, extramarital sex, homosexuality, and bisexuality. Society's values about these behaviors were guided by the medical community's attitudes and beliefs.

Laws also influence sexual behavior in the United States by establishing social norms and influencing societal attitudes. For example, some contraceptives, abortion procedures, and even certain sexual behaviors are regulated by existing laws.

Finally, the media are a strong influence on our attitudes about sexuality. The Internet, television, movies, magazines, and music provide valuable information about sexuality. Even though the media have been more inclusive over the past few years, there still exists a biased view that sexuality is more acceptable in young, attractive, able-bodied, heterosexuals (for example, elderly sexuality, homosexuality, and **abstinence** are discussed less frequently). All of these influences impact the social views of sexuality and what behaviors and practices we believe are right and wrong.

Feminist Theory

Feminist theory argues that society has a strong influence on our ideas about sexuality. Many feminists also believe that **sexology** in the United States has been dominated by White, middle-class,

Social influences, such as religion, affect our attitudes about various sexual behaviors, including sex outside of marriage, same-sex marriage, contraceptive use, and abortion.

ColorBlind/Photodisc/Getty Images

abstinence	**sexology**
The practice of refraining from some, or all, sexual behaviors.	The scientific study of sexuality.

Because theorists from various perspectives are interested in different types of studies, they ask different types of questions. Following are a few questions that theorists from different schools of thought might ask.

Psychoanalytic: How are sexual problems later in life related to early childhood experiences? How do children resolve the Oedipal and Electra complexes? Does an overactive superego cause college students to feel guilt about sexual behavior?

Behavioral: What reinforces a person's attraction to same-sex partners? What reinforces a heterosexual college student to use contraception? What are the attractions and hesitancies around the decision to lose one's virginity?

Social Learning: How does peer group pressure influence our sexuality? What effects do the media have on our sexuality? Are children influenced by sexual messages on television?

Cognitive: What is the decision-making process related to contraceptive choice? Do children cognitively understand sexuality? How do men view erectile disorder?

Humanist: How do negative parental reactions to first sexual experience affect teenagers? How does self-actualization affect sexuality?

Biological: How does genetics influence sexuality? What are the effects of hormone levels on sexual desire? Does menstruation affect sexual desire in women?

Evolutionary: Why are women the ones who usually control the level of sexual activity? How has monogamy developed?

Sociological: How does religion influence sexuality? How does the threat of HIV/AIDS affect society? Do laws affect sexual behavior?

Feminist: What is the role of sexual assault in repressing female sexuality? How do the media reinforce a male view of sexuality?

Queer: How do same-sex loving individuals move from a state of identity confusion about their homoerotic feelings to a point at which they accept their sexual orientation? How are same-sex and heterosexual desires interrelated?

As you read through these various questions, which seem of most interest to you? Perhaps these questions can give you insight into which theory makes the most sense to you.

---

heterosexist attitudes that permeate sexuality research. Several feminist researchers have been leaders in the effort to redefine sexual functioning and remove the medical and biological aspects that permeate sexuality today. Leonore Tiefer, a feminist researcher, has written extensively about the overmedicalization of sexuality. Tiefer argues that there may not be any biological sex drive at all—it may be that our culture influences our sexual desire the most (Tiefer, 2012). We talk more about Tiefer's work in Chapter 14.

REAL RESEARCH Negative emotional reactions after sexual interactions typically occur when a person has a lesser or greater perceived commitment than their partner or they worry about their sexual reputation as a result of the interaction (FERNANDES ET AL., 2016).

Overall, feminist scholars believe that the social construction of sexuality is based on power, which has been primarily in the hands of men for centuries (Collins, 1998). They believe there is sexual gender inequality that, for the most part, sees women as submissive and subordinate. This power over women is maintained through acts of sexual aggression such as rape, sexual abuse, sexual harassment, pornography, and prostitution. Catharine MacKinnon (1987) suggests that male-dominated views of sexuality have resulted in a society that believes that "what is sexual gives a man an erection" (p. 75). All of this led to the repression of female sexuality and, as a result, the lack of attention to the female orgasm.

Feminist researchers also believe that there is much to be gained from qualitative research, which uses interviews to gain information. However, they point out that researchers need to be aware of how the questions they ask (and the wording they use) can affect how subjects respond and conceptualize their experiences (Fahs, 2016). For example, a researcher's choice of language (e.g., using the terms *oral sex*, *head*, or *going down on someone*) affects how women understand the question. If a subject says she has engaged in oral sex, there is no way for the researcher to know if the subject is referring to the giving or receiving of oral sex. Studies have found that the majority of women discuss the *giving* of oral sex instead of the *receiving* when asked if they have engaged in oral sex (Fahs, 2016).

Queer Theory

Queer theory shares a common political interest with feminist theory—a concern for women's and gay, lesbian, bisexual, and transgender rights. Growing out of lesbian and gay studies, queer theory developed in the 1990s. This theory focuses on mismatches between sex, gender, and desire and proposes that domination and its related characteristics, such as heterosexism and homophobia, should be resisted (Torkelson, 2012). Queer theorists believe that studies need to examine how a variety of sexualities are constructed and abandon various categorizations (such as homosexual/heterosexual). Categories are cultural constructions that limit and restrain. Overall, queer theorists and some feminists believe that meaningful societal change can come about only through radical change and cannot be introduced into a society in a piecemeal way.

The accompanying "Sex in Real Life" presents examples of studies that researchers with different theoretical backgrounds might be interested in doing. Now let's turn our attention to some of the important sexuality studies that have been done.

1 What is a theory?

2 How does a theory help guide research?

3 Describe the influence of Freud's theories on sexuality.

4 Compare and contrast behavioral, social learning, cognitive, humanistic, biological, evolutionary, and sociological theories.

5 Explain how feminist and queer theories have asked a different set of questions about sexuality.

Sexuality Research: Philosophers, Physicians, and Sexologists

The ancient Greeks, through physicians such as Hippocrates and philosophers such as Aristotle and Plato, may actually be the legitimate forefathers of sexuality research, because they were the first to develop theories regarding sexual responses and dysfunctions, sex legislation, reproduction and contraception, and sexual ethics. It wasn't until the 18th century, however, that there was increased discussion of sexual ethics, and that the first programs of public and private sex education and classifications of sexual behavior were established.

Early Sexuality Research

In the 19th century, researchers from a variety of disciplines (such as Charles Darwin, Heinrich Kaan, Jean-Martin Charcot, and others) laid the foundations of sexuality research in the modern sense. It was during this time that the study of sex began to concentrate more on the bizarre, dangerous, and unhealthy aspects of sex. In 1843, Kaan, a Russian physician, wrote *Psychopathia Sexualis*, which presented a classification of what he termed *sexual mental diseases*. This system was greatly expanded and refined more than 40 years later by Richard von Krafft-Ebing in another book with the same title. Sexuality research during this time almost exclusively focused on people believed to be sick (see the "Important Developments in the History of Sexuality Research" timeline in the Appendix).

During the Victorian period in the 19th century, the majority of sexuality research was thwarted. Some researchers found that they suddenly lost their professional status, were accused of having the very sexual disorders they studied, or were viewed as motivated solely by lust, greed, or fame. However, as interest in medicine in general grew, researchers began to explore how to improve health and peoples' lives, which included researching various aspects of sexuality.

Physicians were the primary sexuality researchers in the late 19th century (keep in mind that at that time nearly all physicians were male). Because physicians were experts in biology and the body, they were also viewed as sexuality experts (V. Bullough, 1994). Interestingly, although the majority of physicians had little or no specialized knowledge of sexual topics, most spoke with authority about human sexuality.

The majority of the early sexuality studies were done in Europe, primarily in Germany. At the time, sexuality research was protected because it was considered part of medical research, even though holding a medical degree did not always offer complete protection. Some researchers used pseudonyms to publish their work, some were verbally attacked, and others had their data destroyed.

At the turn of the 20th century, it was the pioneering work of Sigmund Freud, Havelock Ellis, and Iwan Bloch that established the study of sexual problems as a legitimate endeavor in its own right. It is interesting to note that the overwhelming majority of sexology pioneers were Jewish (Haeberle, 1982). The Jewish roots of much of modern sexology have certainly added to its controversial nature in certain countries. As a result of all the negative reactions and problems with sexuality research in Europe, it gradually moved from Germany to the United States, which has led the way in sexuality research ever since.

In 1921, several prominent European doctors attempted to set up an organization called the Committee for Research in Problems of Sex. After much hard work, the organization established itself but experienced problems in low membership rates and a lack of research and publishing support. However, because of strong beliefs and persistence by the founders, the group continued.

Systematic research into sexuality in the United States began in the early 1920s, motivated by pressures from the social hygiene movement, which was concerned about sexually transmitted infections and their impact on marriage and children. American society was generally conservative and viewed the "sex impulse" as a potential threat to societal stability. Funding for sexuality research was minimal. It took philanthropy from the fortunes of people such as John D. Rockefeller and Andrew Carnegie for researchers to be able to afford to implement large-scale, interdisciplinary projects.

REAL RESEARCH Numerous assumptions having to do with privilege, educational status, and power norms are embedded in the process of collecting qualitative research on sexuality (FAHS, 2016).

Recent Studies on Sexuality

Early sexuality research set the stage for sexuality researchers. We will talk about their specific contributions later in this chapter, but as we take a look at the whole picture of sexuality research, it's interesting to note that the majority of research into human sexuality has been *problem driven*, meaning that most of the research that has been done has focused on a specific problem. Focusing on problems doesn't allow researchers to obtain funding for research on healthy sexuality and answer questions such as, "How does sexual development progress in children?" or "How is sexuality expressed in loving, long-term relationships?"

Many individuals and groups are opposed to sexuality research today, and some believe that the mystery surrounding sexuality will be taken away by increasing scientific knowledge. Many conservative groups believe that research on adolescent sexuality encourages young people to have sex. Sexuality researchers are accustomed to pressure from conservative groups that oppose their work. In fact, after Alfred Kinsey published his two famous studies about male and female sexuality, which were funded by the Rockefeller Foundation, Congress pushed the foundation to withdraw its financial support from Indiana University, which it did (J. H. Jones, 1997). We discuss politics and sexuality research more later in this chapter.

Over the last few decades sexuality research has become very fragmented, with researchers coming from several different disciplines, such as psychology, sociology, medicine, social work, and public health, to name a few. Oftentimes, researchers are unaware of research being published in other disciplines. Journal articles are often inaccessible to a general audience or to researchers outside the discipline from which the research originated (diMauro, 1995). What tends to happen, therefore, is that the popular media become responsible for disseminating information about sexuality, which is often distorted or sensationalistic.

As you may recall from Chapter 1, sexologists—researchers, educators, and clinicians who specialize in sexuality—are scientists who engage in sophisticated research projects and publish their work in scientific journals. Unfortunately, they may not be viewed as "real" scientists or may be accused of studying sexuality because of their own sexual hang-ups. Geer and O'Donohue (1987) claim that, unlike other areas of science, sexuality research is often evaluated as either moral or immoral. We further discuss these issues later in this chapter.

Academic programs that specialize in human sexuality began appearing in the 1970s (for more information about these programs, see the website listings at the end of this chapter). In addition, several groups exist today to promote sexuality research and education, including The Kinsey Institute at Indiana University; the Society for the Scientific Study of Sexuality (SSSS); the American Association for Sexuality Educators, Counselors, and Therapists (AASECT); the Society for Sex Therapy and Research (SSTAR); and the Sexuality Information and Education Council of the United States (SIECUS).

Although sexuality research is still in its early stages, it has begun to help remove the stigma and ignorance associated with discussing human sexual behavior. Ignorance and fear can contribute to irresponsible behavior. Sexuality research has helped sex become a topic of discussion rather than a taboo subject. Today, understanding sexuality has become increasingly important to the work of psychologists, physicians, educators, theologians, and scientists.

Politics and Sexuality Research

In Chapter 1, we discussed how the changing political climate affects attitudes about sexuality. It won't surprise you to learn that the changing political climate also affects sexuality research. When Kinsey's work was published in the 1950s, several politicians claimed that asking people about their sexual lives in a nonjudgmental fashion, like Kinsey did, was immoral (Bancroft, 2004). Some conservative politicians believed that heterosexual families were threatened by liberal values inherent in sexuality research. Negative attitudes such as these affected the public's perception of sexuality research.

Even so, Kinsey's work helped lead to many societal changes associated with sexuality. The changing roles of women and the development of contraceptive pills, along with Kinsey's work, led to decreased acceptance for the double standard of sexuality. In fact, after the publication of Kinsey's second book, the American Law Institute lawyers and judges recommended decriminalizing many forms of sexual behavior (including adultery, cohabitation, and homosexual relationships; Allyn, 1996). As a result, many states revised their laws about certain sexual practices.

Although there is a need for an increased understanding of human sexuality, there are varying levels of resistance to sexuality research. As a result, a lack of federal funding for these kinds of studies may require researchers to seek out private foundations for funding. Many pharmaceutical companies have provided funding for studies on sexual problems, but this has been controversial because the companies have a vested interest in the studies they fund. In fact, pharmaceutical companies have been accused of creating and promoting certain sexual problems to "medicalize" the conditions and create a need for medication (Tiefer, 2006).

REAL RESEARCH Studies have found that sexuality researchers are overwhelmingly liberal in their political values, which potentially could affect the research questions they ask and how they interpret the results (LEY, 2016).

Review Questions

1 Describe the beginnings of sexuality research, and explain how the focus of sexuality research has progressed.

2 Explain how sexuality research has been problem driven, and give two examples.

3 Explain how politics influence sexuality research.

Sexuality Researchers

All of the researchers discussed in this section and their publications helped give credibility to the area of sexuality research. Some of the researchers adopted Freud's psychoanalytic theory, whereas others developed their research without adopting specific theories of sexuality. Although they had introduced scientific principles into the study of sexuality, their influence was mostly limited to the field of medicine.

Early Promoters of Sexology

Several people were responsible for the early promotion of sexology, including Iwan Bloch, Magnus Hirschfeld, Albert Moll, Richard von Krafft-Ebing, Havelock Ellis, Katharine Bement Davis, Clelia Mosher, Alfred Kinsey, Morton Hunt, Alan Bell, Martin Weinberg, William Masters, Evelyn Hooker, and Virginia Johnson. All of these researchers made unique contributions to the study of sexology.

Iwan Bloch: Journal of Sexology

Iwan Bloch (1872–1922), a Berlin dermatologist, believed that the medical view of sexual behavior was shortsighted, and that both historical and anthropological research could help broaden it. He hoped that sexual science would one day have the same structure and objectivity as other sciences. Along with Magnus Hirschfeld, Bloch and several other physicians formed a medical society for sexology research in Berlin. It was the first sexological society, and it exercised considerable influence. Starting in 1914, Bloch published the *Journal of Sexology*, a scientific journal about sexology. For almost two decades, this journal collected and published many important studies. Bloch planned to write a series of sexological studies, but because of World War I and his untimely death at age 50, he never did.

Magnus Hirschfeld: The Institute for Sexology

Magnus Hirschfeld (1868–1935) was a German physician whose work with patients inspired him and convinced him that negative attitudes toward homosexuals were inhumane and unfounded. Using a pseudonym, Hirschfeld wrote his first article on sexology in 1896. In this article, he argued that sexuality was the result of certain genetic patterns that could result in a person being homosexual, bisexual, or heterosexual. He fought for a repeal of the laws that made homosexuality and bisexuality punishable by prison terms and heavy fines. In 1899, he began the *Yearbook for Sexual Intermediate Stages*, which was published for the purpose of educating the public about homosexuality and other sexual "deviations."

Thousands of people came to him for his help and advice about sexual problems, and in 1900, Hirschfeld began distributing questionnaires on sexuality. By this time, he had also become an expert in the field of homosexuality and sexual variations, and he testified as an expert witness in court cases of sexual offenders. Hirschfeld used only a small amount of his data in the books he published because he hoped to write a comprehensive study of sexuality at a later date. Unfortunately, his data were destroyed by the Nazis before they could be published.

In 1919, Hirschfeld founded the *Institut für Sexualwissenschaft* (Institute for Sexology), which contained his libraries, laboratory, and lecture halls. The institute grew in size and influence over the next few years, but as the political climate in Berlin heated up, Hirschfeld was forced to flee Germany in 1933. The Nazis publicly burned the institute, and those who were working there were sent to concentration camps. Hirschfeld never returned to Germany and lived in France until his death in 1935.

Albert Moll: Investigations Concerning the Libido Sexualis

Albert Moll (1862–1939), a Berlin physician, was another big promoter of sexology. He was a very conservative man who disliked both Freud and Hirschfeld and tried to counter their research at every opportunity. Moll formed the International Society for Sex Research in 1913 to counter Bloch and Hirschfeld's Medical Society of Sexology. He also organized an International Congress of Sex Research in Berlin in 1926.

Moll wrote several books on sexology, including *Investigations Concerning the Libido Sexualis* in 1897. Unfortunately, it was probably Moll's disagreements with Freud that caused him to be ignored by the majority of English-speaking sexuality researchers, because Freud's ideas were so dominant during the first half of the 20th century.

Richard von Krafft-Ebing: Psychopathia Sexualis

Richard von Krafft-Ebing (1840–1902) was one of the most significant medical writers on sexology in the late 19th century (V. Bullough, 1994). His primary interest was what he considered "deviant" sexual behavior. Krafft-Ebing believed that deviant sexual behavior was the result of engaging in nonreproductive sexual practices, including masturbation. In 1886, he published an update of a book titled *Psychopathia Sexualis*, which explored approximately 200 case histories of individuals who had experienced **sexual pathology**; the cases included homosexuals and people who engaged in sex with children (pedophiles).

Although Krafft-Ebing was sympathetic to those with sexual "deviations" and he worked to help change discriminatory laws, many believed his work was morally offensive (Kennedy, 2002).

Havelock Ellis: Studies in the Psychology of Sex

Havelock Ellis (1859–1939) was an English citizen who grew up in Victorian society but rebelled against the secrecy surrounding sexuality. In 1875, when he was 16 years old, he decided to make sexuality his life's work. In fact, it is reported that Ellis sought a medical degree primarily so he could legitimately and safely study sexuality (V. Bullough, 1994). On publication of his famous six-volume *Studies in the Psychology of Sex* (1897–1910; H. Ellis, 1910), Ellis established himself as an objective and nonjudgmental researcher.

---

sexual pathology
Sexual disorders.

In his collection of case histories from volunteers, he reported that homosexuality and masturbation were not abnormal and should not be labeled as such. In 1901, *The Lancet*, a prestigious English medical journal, reviewed his early volumes and wrote:

> [Studies in the Psychology of Sex] *must not be sold to the public, for the reading and discussion of such topics are dangerous. The young and the weak would not be fortified in their purity by the knowledge that they would gain from these studies, while they certainly might be more open to temptation after the perusal of more than one of the chapters.* (Grosskurth, 1980, p. 222)

Unfortunately, Ellis's book was fairly dry and boring; as a result, and much to his dismay, Ellis never found the fame and fortune that Freud did.

The rise of behaviorism in the 1920s added new dimensions to sexuality research. The idea of studying specific sexual behaviors became more acceptable, and the formulation of more sophisticated scientific research techniques provided researchers with more precise methods for sexuality research. Many researchers attempted to compile data on sexual behavior, but the results were inconsistent, and the data were poorly organized. This led Alfred Kinsey, an American researcher, to undertake a large-scale study of human sexuality.

Sexuality Research Moves to the United States

Although Alfred Kinsey was mainly responsible for moving sexuality research to the United States, many other American researchers were laying the foundation for sexuality research. These include Clelia Mosher, Katharine Bement Davis, and Evelyn Hooker. Other researchers continued to build on the work of these early researchers, including Morton Hunt, Alan Bell, Martin Weinberg, William Masters, and Virginia Johnson. Here we review their work and contributions to the field of sexuality research.

Alfred Kinsey (1894–1956) implemented the first large-scale survey of adult sexual behavior in the United States.

Clelia Mosher: Important Female Questions

By now you have probably realized that men were doing much of the early research into human sexuality. Male sexuality was viewed as normative, and therefore female sexuality was approached through the lens of male sexuality. Clelia Mosher (1863–1940) was ahead of her time, asking questions about sexuality that were quite different from those of her male predecessors. She was actually the first researcher to ask women about their sexual behavior (Ericksen, 1999).

In 1892, while Mosher was a student at the University of Wisconsin, she began a research project that lasted 28 years. She asked upper-middle-class heterosexual women how often they engaged in sexual intercourse, how often they wanted to engage in it, and whether they enjoyed it (MaHood & Wenburg, 1980). Her main motivation was to help married women have more satisfying sex lives. One of the questions that Mosher asked the women in her study was, "What do you believe to be the true purpose of intercourse?"

(Ericksen, 1999). Although the majority of women said that intercourse was for both sexual pleasure and procreation, many reported feeling guilty for wanting or needing sexual pleasure. Unfortunately, much of Mosher's work was never published and never became part of the sexuality knowledge that circulated during her time.

Katharine Bement Davis: Defending Homosexuality

Katharine Davis (1861–1935) began her sexuality research along a slightly different path. In 1920, Davis was appointed superintendent of a prison, and she became interested in prostitution and sexually transmitted infections. Her survey and analysis were the largest and most comprehensive of her time (Ellison, 2006; Ericksen, 1999).

Davis defended homosexuality as no different from heterosexuality and believed that lesbianism was not pathological. This idea was threatening in the early 1900s because it implied that women did not need men. Her ideas about lesbianism were largely ignored, but the idea that women might have sexual appetites equal to men's worried many male researchers (Ellison, 2006).

Evelyn Hooker: Comparing Gay and Straight Men

Evelyn Hooker (1907–1996), a psychologist, was another important researcher. Her most notable study was on male homosexuality. Hooker compared two groups of men, one gay and the other straight, who were matched for age, education, and IQ levels. She collected information about their life histories, personality profiles, and psychological evaluations, and she asked professionals to try to distinguish between the two groups on the basis of their profiles and evaluations. They could not, demonstrating that there was little fundamental psychological difference between gay and straight men. Hooker's research helped challenge the widely held view that homosexuality was a mental illness.

Alfred Kinsey: Large-Scale Sexuality Research Begins in the United States

As we discussed in Chapter 1, Alfred Kinsey (1894–1956) was probably the most influential sexuality researcher of the 20th century. His work effectively changed many of the existing attitudes about sexuality. In 1938, while he was a professor of zoology at Indiana University, he was asked to coordinate a new course on marriage and the family. Before courses like this appeared on college campuses, human sexuality had been discussed only in hygiene courses, in which the focus was primarily on the dangers of sexually transmitted infections and masturbation (V. L. Bullough, 1998).

Soon after the course began, students came to Kinsey with sexuality questions for which he did not have answers, and the existing literature was of little help. This encouraged him to begin collecting data on his students' sex lives. His study grew and before long included students who were not in his classes, faculty members, friends, and nonfaculty employees. Soon he was able to obtain grant money that enabled him to hire research assistants. By this time, Kinsey's research had become well established in the scientific community.

In his early work, Kinsey claimed to be **atheoretical**. He believed that because sexuality research was so new, it was impossible to construct theories and hypotheses without first having a large body of information on which to base them. Kinsey's procedure involved collecting information on each participant's sexual life history, with an emphasis on specific sexual behaviors. Kinsey chose to interview participants, rather than have them fill out questionnaires, because he believed that questionnaires would not provide accurate responses. He was also unsure about whether participants would lie during an interview, and so he built into the interview many checks to detect false information. Data collected from husbands and wives were compared for consistency, and the interview was done again 2 and 4 years later to see whether the basic answers remained the same.

Kinsey was also worried about **interviewer bias**. To counter interview bias, only Kinsey and three colleagues conducted the interviews. Of the total 18,000 interviews, Kinsey himself conducted 8,000 (Pomeroy, 1972). Participants were asked a minimum of 350 questions, and interviewers memorized each question so that they could more easily build rapport with participants and wouldn't continually have to consult the list of questions. Interviews lasted several hours, and participants were assured that the information they provided would remain confidential.

The sampling procedures Kinsey used were also strengths of his research. He believed that he would have a high refusal rate if he used **probability sampling**. Because of this, he used what he called "quota sampling accompanied by opportunistic collection" (Gebhard & Johnson, 1979, p. 26). In other words, if he saw that a particular group—such as young married women—was not well represented in his sample, he would find organizations with a high percentage of these participants and include them in his research.

Overall, he obtained participants from colleges and universities; hospitals; prisons; mental hospitals; institutions for young delinquents; churches and synagogues; groups of people with sexual problems; settlement houses; homosexual groups throughout the United States; and members of various groups including the YMCA and the YWCA. Within these groups, every member was strongly encouraged to participate in the project to minimize **volunteer bias**. Kinsey referred to this procedure as **100% sampling**.

Kinsey's research found that many practices that had previously been seen as perverse or unacceptable in society (such as homosexuality, masturbation, and oral sex) were found to be widely practiced. As you might guess, such findings were very controversial and created strong reactions from conservative groups and religious organizations. Eventually, controversies about Kinsey's work resulted in the termination of several research grants. Kinsey's research challenged many of the assumptions about sexuality in the United States, and he stirred up antagonism; in this sense, Kinsey was truly a pioneer in the field of sexuality research. (See Table 2.1 for a summary of his early findings.)

Morton Hunt: Playboy *Updates Dr. Kinsey*

Twenty-five years after Kinsey, Morton Hunt (1920–2016) began a large-scale sexuality study in the 1970s. Hunt gathered his sample through random selection from telephone books in 24 U.S. cities and believed it was comparable with Kinsey's research population. A total of approximately 2,000 subjects were included in the study and were given self-administered questionnaires. In addition, Hunt interviewed an additional 200 males and females for qualitative data.

Although Hunt's sampling technique was thought to be an improvement over Kinsey's techniques, there were also drawbacks. People without listed phone numbers, such as college students or institutionalized persons, were left out of the study. Although each person in Hunt's sample was called and asked to participate in a group discussion about sexuality, only 20% agreed to participate. In addition, because his sample was such a small percentage of those he contacted, volunteer bias prevents his results from being **generalizable** to the population as a whole.

Hunt's findings were consistent with Kinsey's—premarital sex was increasing, as was the frequency of other sexual behaviors, such as oral and anal sex. Hunt published his research in a book *Sexual Behavior in the 1970s* (Hunt, 1974). In addition, he reviewed his findings in a series of articles in *Playboy* magazine.

Alan Bell and Martin Weinberg: Homosexualities

Continuing the research on sexual orientation, two colleagues from the Kinsey Institute, Alan Bell (1932–2002) and Martin Weinberg (1939–), began a large-scale study in 1968 on the influences of homosexuality. Bell and Weinberg surveyed thousands of gay and straight men and women to evaluate their mental health and social influences that might have influenced their sexual orientation. Their research supported Evelyn Hooker's previous findings—homosexuals were psychologically well-adjusted and satisfied with their intimate relationships. Bell and

Rich Fury/AP Images

Amateur sex education superstars, such as Laci Green, have become YouTube sensations for their videos about sexuality. Although these "Sexperts" often have no educational training in sexuality, their amateurism is an asset. Green's videos have been viewed over 131 million times.

---

atheoretical
Research that is not influenced by a particular theory.

interviewer bias
The bias of a researcher caused by his or her own opinions, thoughts, and attitudes about the research.

probability sampling
A research strategy that involves acquiring a random sample for inclusion in a study.

volunteer bias
A slanting of research data caused by the characteristics of participants who volunteer to participate.

100% sampling
A research strategy in which all members of a particular group are included in the sample.

generalizable
If findings are generalizable, they can be taken from a particular sample and applied to the general population.

Table 2.1 What Did Kinsey Find in His Early Research?

Kinsey's groundbreaking research and the publication of his 1948 and 1953 books revealed many new findings about sexuality. Following are a few of these statistics. Keep in mind that these statistics are based on people's lives in the middle of the 20th century. For more information, visit the Kinsey Institute online at **http://www.kinseyinstitute.org.**

- Close to 50% of American men engaged in both heterosexual and homosexual activities, or had "reacted to" persons of both sexes in the course of their adult life.

- The majority of men and women masturbated.

- The majority of men and women reached their first orgasm during masturbation.

- Whereas 25% of males had lost their virginity by the age of 16, only 6% of females had.

- The majority of men and women preferred having sex without the lights on (but those who liked the lights on were more likely to be men).

- The majority of couples used the missionary position during sexual intercourse.

- Married couples engaged in sexual intercourse 2.8 times per week in their late teens and only once per week by the age of 50.

- About half of married men had sex outside of marriage, whereas 25% of married women did.

SOURCE: Kinsey et al., 1948; Kinsey et al., 1953.

Weinberg believed their research supported the biological basis for homosexuality, refuting the idea that it was learned or the result of negative experiences (McCoubrey, 2002). Their research was published in two books, *Homosexualities* (1978) and *Sexual Preferences* (1981). Weinberg continued his research and has coauthored several other books based on his research on sexual orientation.

William Masters and Virginia Johnson: Measuring Sex in the Laboratory

William Masters (1915–2001), a gynecologist, and Virginia Johnson (1925–2013), a psychology researcher, began their sexuality research in 1954. They were the first modern scientists to observe and measure the act of sexual intercourse between heterosexual partners in the laboratory. They were primarily interested in the anatomy and physiology of the sexual response and later also explored sexual dysfunction. Masters and Johnson were a dual sex therapy team, representing both male and female opinions, which reduced the chance for **gender bias**. Much of their work was supported by grants, the income from their books, and individual and couples therapy.

Masters and Johnson's first study, published in 1966, was titled *Human Sexual Response.* In an attempt to understand the physiological process that occurs during sexual activity, the researchers brought 700 heterosexual subjects into the laboratory to have their physiological reactions studied during sexual intercourse. The volunteers participated for financial reasons (participants were paid), personal reasons, and even for the release of sexual tension (Masters and Johnson both stated that they believed some volunteers were looking for legitimate and safe sexual outlets). Because Masters and Johnson were studying behaviors they believed were normative (i.e., they happened to most people),

they did not feel they needed to recruit a **random sample**.

When volunteers were accepted as participants in the study, they were first encouraged to engage in sexual activity in the laboratory without the investigators present. It was hoped that this would make them feel more comfortable with the new surroundings. During the study, they were monitored for physiological changes with an electrocardiograph to measure changes in the heart and an electromyograph to measure muscular changes. Measurements were taken of penile erection and vaginal lubrication with **penile strain gauges** and **photoplethysmographs** (FOH-toh-pleth-iss-mo-grafs). Many of the volunteers reported that after a while they did not notice that they were being monitored.

Through their research, Masters and Johnson discovered several interesting aspects of sexual response, including women's potential for multiple orgasms and the fact that sexuality does not disappear in old age. They also proposed a four-stage model for sexual response, which we discuss in more detail in Chapter 10.

In 1970, Masters and Johnson published another important book, *Human Sexual Inadequacy,* which explored sexual dysfunction. Again they brought couples into the laboratory, but this time they

Virginia Johnson (1925–2013) and William Masters (1915–2001) were the first to bring sexuality research into the laboratory.

gender bias
The bias of a researcher caused by their gender.

random sample
A number of people taken from the entire population in such a way to ensure that any one person has as much chance of being selected as any other.

penile strain gauge
A device used to measure penile engorgement.

photoplethysmograph
A device used to measure vaginal lubrication.

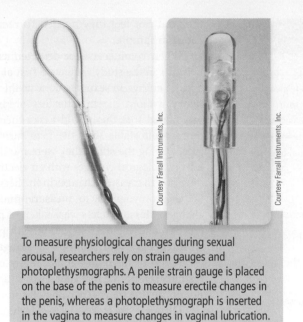

To measure physiological changes during sexual arousal, researchers rely on strain gauges and photoplethysmographs. A penile strain gauge is placed on the base of the penis to measure erectile changes in the penis, whereas a photoplethysmograph is inserted in the vagina to measure changes in vaginal lubrication.

studied only those who were experiencing sexual problems. They evaluated the couples physiologically and psychologically, and they taught them exercises to improve their sexual functioning. Frequent follow-ups were done to measure the therapeutic results—some participants were even contacted 5 years after the study was completed. They found that there is often dual sexual dysfunction in couples (i.e., males who are experiencing erectile problems often have partners who are also experiencing sexual problems). Their studies also refuted Freud's theory that women are capable of both vaginal and clitoral orgasms, and that only vaginal orgasms result from intercourse. According to Masters and Johnson, all female orgasms result from direct or indirect clitoral stimulation.

It is important to point out that Masters and Johnson's books were written from a medical, not a psychological, perspective. They also used clinical language, and many professionals speculate this was a tactic to avoid censorship of the books. However, even with this scientific and medical base, their work was not without controversy. Many people at the time viewed Masters and Johnson's work as both unethical and immoral. In 2013, *Masters of Sex* began airing on Showtime, a popular television show based on the work of Masters and Johnson.

Review Questions

1 Explain the work done by early promoters of sexology.

2 Explore the reasons why there were so few women engaged in the study of human sexuality.

3 Differentiate between Alfred Kinsey's work and that of Masters and Johnson. What did these researchers contribute to our understanding of human sexuality?

Large-Scale Sexuality Research

A variety of large-scale sexuality-related studies have contributed to our knowledge about human sexuality and have impacted how we think about various sexual behaviors. Two of the largest nationally representative studies are the National Health and Social Life Survey (NHSLS) and the National Survey of Sexual Health and Behavior (NSSHB). Another large study, the National College Health Assessment (NCHA), included only college students. These studies were privately funded by a variety of sources such as the Ford, the Robert Wood Johnson, the Rockefeller, and the Henry J. Kaiser Family Foundations. There are also several government-funded studies including the National Survey of Family Growth (NSFG), the Youth Risk Behavior Survey (YRBS), the National Longitudinal Study of Adolescent Health (ADD Health), and the National Survey of Adolescent Males (NSAM). Government-funded studies are typically much broader in scope and include only a few questions about sexuality. For example, the 2017 YRBS, which monitors health-risk behaviors in high school students, contained 89 questions in total, but only 9 related to sexual behaviors (Centers for Disease Control, 2017).

Privately Funded Large-Scale Sexuality Studies

In this section, we discuss privately funded large-scale sexuality studies that have made significant contributions to the field of sexuality research, including the National Health and Social Life Survey, the National Survey of Sexual Health and Behavior, and the National College Health Assessment.

National Health and Social Life Survey

In 1987, facing a devastating AIDS outbreak, the U.S. Department of Health and Human Services called for researchers to study the sexual attitudes and practices of American adults. A group of researchers from the National Opinion Research Center at the University of Chicago—Edward Laumann, John Gagnon, Robert Michael, and Stuart Michaels—were selected to coordinate this national study of more than 20,000 people. Originally, the National Health and Social Life Survey (NHSLS) was to be government funded, but political pressure led to the termination of this funding. Eventually, private funding was acquired from various foundations, but because of limited funds researchers were forced to significantly reduce the sample size. In the end, a representative sample of 3,432 Americans between the ages of 18 and 59 years was used in the final analysis of data (Bancroft, 2004).

The National Health and Social Life Study was sponsored by the Robert Wood Johnson Foundation, the Henry J. Kaiser Family Foundation, the Rockefeller Foundation, the Andrew Mellon Foundation, the John D. and Catherine T. MacArthur Foundation, the New York Community Trust, and the American Foundation for AIDS Research. Above (left to right), researchers Robert Michael, John Gagnon, Stuart Michaels, and Edward Laumann.

All respondents were interviewed face-to-face, supplemented with brief questionnaires. The NHSLS was the most comprehensive study of sexual attitudes and behaviors since Kinsey and is viewed as the most scientifically accurate sexuality study in the United States to date.

Overall, the NHSLS study found that Americans were more sexually conservative than previously thought. The majority of respondents reported engaging in sex a few times a month or less, and women and men reported a median number of two and six sexual partners, respectively. In addition, the majority reported they had not engaged in extramarital sex (75% of married men and 80% of married women reported not engaging in sex outside of their marriages). Findings from the NHSLS were published in two books, *The Social Organization of Sexuality: Sexual Practices in the United States* (Laumann et al., 1994) and *Sex in America: A Definitive Study* (Michael et al., 1994). The former book was directed at an academic audience, while the latter was written for the public. There was an unprecedented wave of national and international publicity after the publication of *Sex in America*.

National Survey of Sexual Health and Behavior

By the time the National Survey of Sexual Health and Behavior (NSSHB) was published in late 2010, it had been 18 years since the last large study of sexual behavior,

the NHSLS. Many societal changes occurred during this time—all potentially impacting the sexual lives of Americans. Policy changes in sexuality education programs and the development of new medications for sexual problems both affected sexual attitudes and behaviors. The NSSHB research was conducted by a team of sexuality researchers from the Center for Sexual Health Promotion at Indiana University. Subjects filled out surveys in the privacy of their own homes, which researchers believe increased participant comfort. The NSSHB study included approximately 6,000 adolescents and adults, ages 14 to 94.

The NSSHB found that masturbation was common throughout the life span and more common than partnered sexual behavior during adolescence and older age. They also reported that young teens were less sexually active than many thought and that fewer than 25% of 14- to 17-year-olds had engaged in vaginal intercourse. Participation in sexual activities was found to gradually increase as teens matured (Rabin, 2010a) (Table 2.2).

Unfortunately, results from the NSSHB could not be generalized to lesbian, gay, and bisexual men and women, because a large sample size can often blur various data points, such as sexual orientation. In addition, although the study included men, women, and a wide age range, it was not representative of all adults, especially because older adults living in hospitals or long-term care facilities were not included. For more information about specific findings, see Table 2.2.

Table 2.2 What Did We Learn from the National Survey of Sexual Health and Behavior?
The National Survey of Sexual Health and Behavior (NSSHB) was a nationally representative study of the sexual health–related behaviors of 5,865 adolescents and adults in the United States, ages 14 to 94. Following are some notable findings from this 2010 study.
• There is great variability in sexual behavior, and adult men and women rarely engage in only one sexual behavior when they engage in sex.
• Vaginal intercourse is the most common sexual behavior reported by adults.
• 25% of acts of sexual intercourse are protected by condoms (1 in 3 among singles).
• 85% of men reported their partner had an orgasm at the most recent sexual interaction, although only 64% of women reported having had an orgasm.
• Many older adults reported active pleasurable sexual lives.
• Men reported being most likely to orgasm during vaginal intercourse, while women reported being more likely to orgasm when they engaged in various sexual behaviors including oral sex.
• 7% to 8% of the respondents identified as lesbian, gay, or bisexual, although a higher percentage reported having experienced same-sex sexual interactions at some point in their lives.
• Rates of insertive anal sex increased in all age groups, with more than 40% of men ages 25 to 59 reported having engaged in insertive anal intercourse in their lifetimes.

SOURCE: Special Issue: Findings from the National Survey of Sexual Health and Behavior (NSSHB), Center for Sexual Health Promotion, Indiana University (2010, October). Journal of Sexual Medicine, 7 (Suppl. 5).

Center for Sexual Health Promotion, Indiana University

The National Survey of Sexual Health and Behavior was conducted by researchers from the Center for Sexual Health Promotion at Indiana University. Above (left to right), researchers Brian Dodge, Debby Herbenick, and Michael Reece (not pictured Vanessa Schick, Stephanie Sanders, and J. Dennis Fortenberry).

National College Health Assessment

The National College Health Assessment (NCHA) is an ongoing privately funded study organized by the American College Health Association. Beginning in 2000, the NCHA examined the habits, behaviors, and perceptions of college students' sexual health, alcohol and tobacco use, weight, nutrition, exercise, violence, and mental health. The NCHA is the largest known comprehensive data on the health of U.S. college students and as of 2016, more than 1.4 million college students at 740 colleges and universities have completed the survey. Important changes to the NCHA questionnaire were instituted in 2016 with the revision of questions about gender identity and sexual orientation. The current questionnaire contains questions about sex assigned at birth, gender identity, and sexual orientation (including options such as asexual, bisexual, pansexual, queer, and questioning).

The NCHA found that although the majority of sexually active heterosexual students reported using contraception, 22% of males and 20% of females reported engaging in unprotected sex after drinking alcohol (American College Health Association, 2016). Figures 2.1–2.4 share some additional findings from the most current NCHA data. Although the results of this study are not generalizable to all college students because the schools that participate in the survey are self-selecting (i.e., they pay to participate), many of the findings are consistent with comparable research studies on college populations.

Government-Funded Large-Scale Studies

In this section, we discuss government-funded large-scale sexuality studies that have made significant contributions to the field of sexuality research, including the National Survey of Family Growth, the Youth Risk Behavior Survey, and the National Longitudinal Study of Adolescent Health.

National Survey of Family Growth

The National Survey of Family Growth (NSFG) is an ongoing government study that gathers data on family life, marriage and divorce, pregnancy, infertility, contraceptive use, and men's and women's health. The study is sponsored by the U.S. National Center for Health Statistics in the Centers for Disease Control and managed by the University of Michigan's Institute for Social Research. Results from the ongoing surveys are used in planning health education interventions and programs.

The NSFG is designed to be nationally representative of U.S. household populations. Data collection began in 1973, and although originally intended to include only women, the NSFG began studying men in 2002 (interestingly, in the first two rounds of data collection only married women were included in the sample because it was unacceptable to ask unmarried women questions relating to sexuality). In 2016, the NSFG expanded its age range from 15–44 to 15–49. Each year an additional 5,000 interviews are completed. In-person interviews are conducted by female researchers through the use of **computer-assisted personal interviewing (CAPI)** and **audio computer-assisted self-interviewing**. Interviews last approximately 60 to 80 minutes and subjects are usually paid a token amount for their participation. Participation is voluntary and the **response rate** is approximately 73%.

Data from the NSFG have been used in various journal articles and book chapters, and we will review the findings from many of these published studies in the upcoming chapters.

REAL RESEARCH Studies have found that some psychological urban legends are often accepted as truth when they are not (FERGUSON ET AL., 2016). For example, the "Mozart Effect," in which listening to Mozart's music can raise IQ scores, is often accepted as truth even though research has not supported this finding.

Youth Risk Behavior Survey

The Youth Risk Behavior Survey (YRBS) is an ongoing national survey that monitors health-risk behaviors among youths and young adults (grades 9–12), including behaviors that contribute to injuries and violence; tobacco, drug, and alcohol use; sexual behaviors; and unhealthy dietary behaviors. The survey began in 1991 and is conducted every 2 years by the Centers for Disease Control and Prevention. From 1991 through 2015, the YRBS has collected data from close to 4 million high school students. The YRBS is believed to be representative of all students in grades 9 to 12 attending public and private schools in the United States.

computer-assisted personal interviewing (CAPI)
An interview technique in which an interview takes place in person but a computer is used to input data.

audio computer-assisted self-interviewing
A private method of data collection in which subjects hear the questions and

response choices through headphones or read them on a computer screen and can enter responses independently.

response rate
The percentage of people who completed the survey, questionnaires, or interviews.

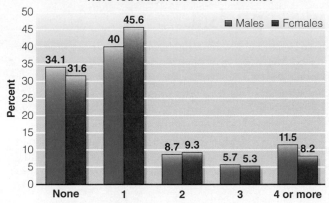

How Many Sexual Partners (Oral, Vaginal, Anal) Have You Had in the Last 12 Months?

FIGURE **2.1** Percentage of college students who reported number of sexual partners in the last 12 months.

SOURCE: Findings from the 2016 National College Health Assessment; American College Health Association – National College Health Assessment II, 2016.

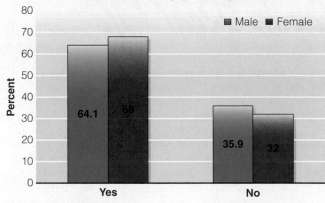

Have You Ever Engaged in Vaginal Sex?

FIGURE **2.2** Percentage of college students who reported engaging in vaginal sex.

SOURCE: Findings from the 2016 National College Health Assessment; American College Health Association – National College Health Assessment II, 2016.

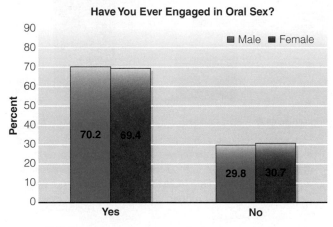

Have You Ever Engaged in Oral Sex?

FIGURE **2.3** Percentage of college students who reported engaging in oral sex.

SOURCE: Findings from the 2016 National College Health Assessment; American College Health Association – National College Health Assessment II, 2016.

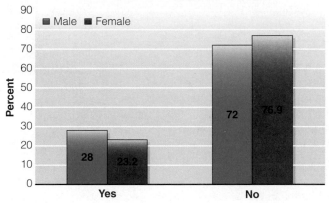

Have You Ever Engaged in Anal Sex?

FIGURE **2.4** Percentage of college students who reported engaging in anal sex.

SOURCE: Findings from the 2016 National College Health Assessment; American College Health Association – National College Health Assessment II, 2016.

Questionnaires are used to collect data and participation is voluntary, although parental permission is required.

The 2015, YRBS study found that 41% of those in grades 9 to 12 had engaged in sexual intercourse and 11.5% had done so with four or more partners during their lifetime (Kann et al., 2016). Among sexually active students, 57% had used a condom the last time they engaged in sexual intercourse. We will discuss more findings from this ongoing study in upcoming chapters.

National Longitudinal Study of Adolescent Health

The National Longitudinal Study of Adolescent Health (ADD Health) is a **longitudinal study** of a nationally representative sample of adolescents in grades 7 to 12 during the 1994–1995 school year. This group of students has been followed into adulthood through the use of four in-home interviews, with the most recent interviews done between 2016 and 2018.

Over the years, data have been collected on each student's family, neighborhood, community, school, friendships, peer groups, romantic relationships, and social, economic, psychological, and physical well-being. ADD Health provides a unique look into adolescent behavior and the health and achievement outcomes in adulthood. The data collected in this study have been used by many researchers and have been analyzed in thousands of research studies. One study done using these data found that the more positive family environment subjects had during adolescence, the more stable intimate relationships they had later in life (Thorsen, 2016). We will discuss many more studies that have used data from ADD Health in the upcoming chapters.

Sexuality research has changed significantly throughout the years, driven mostly by changing societal attitudes and changing data collection methods. The use of the Internet for sexuality research has made it easier to collect data. However, funding for sexuality studies remains difficult, and many studies are

> **longitudinal study**
> A study done over a certain period wherein participants are studied at various intervals.

If the headline in your daily newspaper claimed that eating an orange a day could decrease your risk for sexual problems later in life, would you believe it? How do you know if research studies are accurate? Dr. John Ioannidis, an expert on the credibility of research, believes that 90% of the published medical research is flawed (Freedman, 2010). He points out that flaws can be in several areas, such as:

1. The questions asked

2. The methodologies used

3. The participants recruited

4. How the data are analyzed

Although Dr. Ioannidis primarily discusses medical research, similar issues affect sexuality research. Methodological issues are important, especially because a major problem in sexuality research is getting participants to respond honestly about very personal and sensitive issues. Embarrassment, social pressures, and/or a lack of an ability to discuss such issues can interfere with honest responses. In an attempt to increase honesty, sexuality researchers have used a variety of data collection methodologies.

In the National Survey of Sexual Health and Behavior (NSSHB), online polling was used in hopes that participants would be more comfortable and honest in their responses. The research supports this idea: One study found that when self-administered questionnaire results were compared with online polling results, significant differences were found (see Figure 2.5; Turner et al., 1998).

However, even with the best data collection methods, the numbers in sexuality research don't always add up. For example:

- Whereas 14- to 17-year-old males reported using condoms 79% of the time during sexual intercourse, the females in the same age group reported their male partners using condoms 58% of the time.

- Whereas 85% of heterosexual men reported their partners having an orgasm at the most recent sexual event, only 64% of heterosexual women

reported having had an orgasm at their most recent sexual event.

Another example has to do with the reported number of sexual partners. In one study, males reported a median of seven female sexual partners, whereas females reported a median of four male sexual partners (Kolata, 2007). Another study found males had an average of 12.7 lifetime sexual

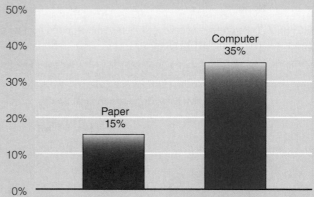

FIGURE **2.5** Computer-assisted self-interviews have been found to elicit greater responses on sensitive questions than questionnaire methods. For example, the above graph illustrates the percentage of affirmative responses to the question, "*Were you or your partner drunk or high the last time you had sex?*" Little difference was found on questions that concerned less sensitive behaviors.

threatened by political pressure, especially if researchers want to study issues beyond fertility and sexual health issues. As we look ahead to sexuality research in the future, private funding will continue to be an important avenue for sexuality research. Next, we take a closer look at some of the contemporary sexuality research methods.

Review Questions

1 Compare and contrast the methodology and participants involved in the NHSLS, the NSSHB, and the NCHA studies.

2 Compare and contrast the methodology and participants involved in the NSFG, the YRBS, and the ADD Health studies.

3 Differentiate between privately funded and government-funded sexuality research, and explain which studies often yield more comprehensive information about sexuality.

Sexuality Research Methods and Considerations

Now that we have explored some of the studies done on sexuality, let us look at the specifics of how these studies are conducted. Each study that we have discussed in this chapter was scientific,

yet researchers used different experimental methods depending on the kind of information they were trying to gather. For example, Freud relied on a **case study** methodology, whereas Kinsey used interviews to gather data. There are other ways that

case study
A research methodology that involves an in-depth examination of one participant or a small number of participants.

partners, whereas females reported an average of 6.5 (Johnson et al., 2001). Why the differences? It's too simple to assume that the participants are dishonest or exaggerating. There are a multitude of reasons for the differences. Here are some possible reasons:

1. Sampling differences—There are inherent group differences within the male participant group that contribute to the differences.

2. Sexual orientation issues—Some of the males were engaging in same-sex behavior, which could result in gender differences (however, the difference in number of partners is too large to be accounted for simply by this factor).

3. Societal norms and dishonesty—Societal pressures contributed to male overexaggeration and female underexaggeration, and/or participants provided false information.

4. Open populations—Because participants can have sex with partners outside the study population, this can lead to a "potential mismatch" between sexual encounters.

5. Greater number of available females—More available females would give men more potential partners.

Numbers are more likely to add up equally if a study is done on a *closed population*.

Think about it this way: If we were to do a study on the average number of partners of the other sex that students dance with at the prom, do you think the male and female average would be similar? Probably. Because it is a closed population, they can only dance with each other (see Figure 2.6). However, most large sexuality studies have open populations, which means that participants have sexual partners outside the study population.

The bottom line is that it is important to critically analyze sexuality research. Although great care is taken to ensure that results are valid and generalizable, the sensitive nature of this area of research brings up many issues that could potentially interfere with the questions that are asked, data collection, participant populations, and the interpretation of the data. Sometimes research can raise more questions than it answers.

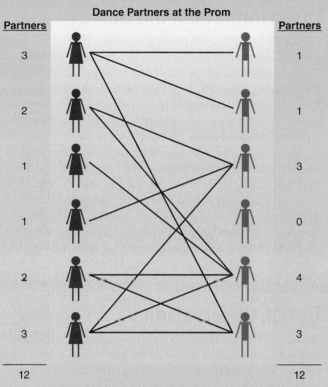

Dance Partners at the Prom

FIGURE **2.6** Let's say we did a study on the average number of partners of the other sex that males and females danced with at the prom. Because the prom is a closed event, we would expect there to be consistent answers for both groups. In this example, each male and female danced with an average of two partners.

researchers collect information, such as questionnaires, laboratory experiments, direct observation, participant observation, correlations, and Internet-based research methods.

Whatever techniques they use, researchers must be certain that their experiment passes standards of validity, reliability, and generalizability. Tests of **validity** determine whether a question or other method actually measures what it is designed to measure. For example, the people who read the question need to interpret it the same way as the researcher who wrote it. **Reliability** refers to the consistency of the measure. If we ask a question today, we would hope to get a similar answer if we ask it again in 2 months. Finally, generalizability refers to the ability of samples in a study to have wide applicability to the general population. A study can be generalized only if a random sample is used. All of the methods we review here must fit these three criteria.

Case Studies

When researchers describe a case study, they attempt to explore individual cases to formulate general hypotheses. Freud was famous for his use of this methodology. He would study hysteria in only one patient, because he didn't have several patients with

similar complaints. Using this method, however, does not allow researchers to generalize to the wider public because the sample is small. Even so, the case study method may generate hypotheses that can lead to larger, generalizable studies.

Interviews

We began this chapter with an exploration of a student's research study in which she used interviews to collect data about the use of Tinder. Interviews can be useful research tools because they allow the researcher to establish a rapport with each participant and emphasize the importance of honesty in the study. In addition, the researcher can vary the order of questions and skip questions that are irrelevant. However, they can be time-consuming and expensive. In addition to this, as we pointed out earlier, researchers have to be aware of how the questions they ask can influence the responses they get.

validity	reliability
The property of a device measuring what it is intended to measure.	The dependability of a test as reflected in the consistency of its scores on repeated measurements of the same group.

Questionnaires and Surveys

Questionnaire or survey research is generally used to identify the attitudes, knowledge, or behavior of large samples. For instance, Kinsey used this method to obtain information about his many participants, although questions have since been raised about Kinsey's validity and reliability. Kinsey recognized these problems and tried to increase the validity by using interviews to supplement the questionnaires.

Some researchers believe that questionnaires provide more honesty than interviews because the participant may be embarrassed to admit things to another person that they would be more likely to share with the anonymity of a questionnaire. However, despite the anonymous nature of questionnaires, research has revealed that when people answer sexuality questionnaires, they are likely to leave out the questions that cause the most anxiety, especially questions about masturbation (Catania et al., 1986). We discuss using online questionnaires later in this section.

Direct Observation

Masters and Johnson used direct observation for their research on sexual response and physiology. This method is the least frequently used because it is difficult to find participants who are willing to come into the laboratory to have sex while researchers monitor their bodily functions. However, if direct observation can be done, it does provide information that cannot be obtained elsewhere. Researchers can monitor behavior as it happens, giving the results more credibility. For example, a man may exaggerate the number of erections per sexual episode in a self-report, but he cannot exaggerate in a laboratory.

Direct observation is expensive and may not be as generalizable, because it would be impossible to gather a random sample. In addition, direct observation focuses on behaviors and, as a result, ignores feelings, attitudes, or personal history.

Participant Observation

Participant observation research involves researchers going into an environment and monitoring what is happening naturally. For instance, a researcher who wants to explore the impact of alcohol on flirting patterns might monitor interactions between and among college students in bars. This would entail several visits and specific note taking on all that occurs. However, it is difficult to generalize from this type of research because the researcher could subtly, or not so subtly, influence the research findings. Also, this method has limited use in the area of sexuality research because much of sexual behavior occurs in private.

Experimental Methods

Experiments are the only research method that allows us to isolate cause and effect. This is because in an experiment, strict control is maintained over all variables so that one variable can be isolated and examined.

For example, let's say you want to teach high school students about chlamydia, but you don't know which teaching methodology would be most effective. You could design an experiment to examine this more closely. First, you choose a high school and randomly assign all the students to one of three groups. You might start by giving them a questionnaire about chlamydia to establish baseline data about what they know or believe. Group A then listens to a lecture about chlamydia, Group B is shown a video, and Group C listens to people with chlamydia talk about their experiences. Strict care is taken to make sure that all of the information that is presented in these classes is identical. The only thing that differs is the teaching method. In scientific terms, the type of teaching method is the **independent variable**, which is manipulated by the researcher. After each class, the students are given a test to determine what knowledge they have gained about chlamydia. This measurement is to determine the effect of the independent variable on the **dependent variable**, which in this case is knowledge about chlamydia. If one group shows more learning after one particular method was used, we might be able to attribute the learning to the type of methodology that was used.

Experiments can be more costly than any of the other methods discussed, in terms of both finances and time commitment. It is also possible that in an attempt to control the experiments, a researcher may cause the study to become too sterile or artificial (nothing like what conditions would be outside of the laboratory), and the results may be faulty or inapplicable to the real world. Finally, experiments are not always possible in certain areas of research, especially in the field of sexuality. For instance, what if we wanted to examine whether early sexual abuse contributed to adult difficulties with intimate relationships? It would be entirely unethical to abuse children sexually to examine whether they develop these problems later in life.

Correlational Methods

Correlations are often used when it is not possible to do an experiment. For example, because it is unethical to do a controlled experiment in a sexual abuse study, we would study a given population to see whether there is any correlation between past sexual abuse and later difficulties with intimate relationships. The limitation of a **correlational study** is that it does not provide any information about cause. We would not learn whether past sexual abuse causes intimacy difficulties, even though we may learn that these factors are related. The intimacy difficulties could occur for several other reasons, including factors such as low self-esteem or a personality disorder.

Internet-Based Research Methods

Internet-based research methods have become more commonplace over the last few years. Earlier in this chapter, we discussed the use of computer-assisted personal interviewing and audio

participant observation
A research methodology that involves actual participation in the event being researched.

independent variable
The variable controlled by the experimenter and applied to the participant to determine its effect on the participant's reaction.

dependent variable
The measured results of an experiment that are believed to be a function of the independent variable.

correlation
A statistical measure of the relationship between two variables.

correlational study
A type of research that examines the relationship between two or more variables.

computer-assisted self-interviewing, both of which are Internet-based research techniques. The accessibility and sense of anonymity of the Internet provide researchers access to larger samples that can include difficult-to-reach populations. In addition, these methods can increase participant comfort and convenience while at the same time decreasing survey costs.

However, there are also some drawbacks to this type of research. In 2014, a large-scale research study was published using data collected from Facebook (Kramer et al., 2014). The study explored whether exposure to emotions in friends' Newsfeeds affected users' status updates. Subjects included approximately 160,000 randomly selected Facebook users in the one-week study period. The subjects were unaware that their Newsfeeds were being manipulated or that they were participating in a research study. Not surprisingly, there was public outcry and protests in reaction to this Internet-based study (Booth, 2014). There were multiple issues associated with the study, which we will explore in the following section. Before we do, though, how do you think you'd feel if something like this happened to you? Would it be OK that a researcher purposely manipulated your online information to see how you'd respond to it? I'm guessing you probably wouldn't like this, and you wouldn't be alone.

Anyone who participates in research has the right to know they are doing so, but in the above study they did not. However, the researchers who did the study pointed out that when someone signs up to use Facebook they consent to a "Data Use Policy," which states that information posted on Facebook may be used for multiple purposes, including research.

Although there are advantages and disadvantages to internet-based sexuality research, many researchers believe that subjects who participate online may be more representative of the general population than the typical college student.

There are other drawbacks to this type of research, including the fact that these methods limit the sample to those who have Internet access. Even so, some researchers claim that the participant pool available online may be more representative of the general population than a group of typical college students—who are most commonly used in psychological research (Mustanski, 2001; Reips & Bachtiger, 2000). It is likely that more researchers will turn to the Internet and social media for data collection in the future.

Review Questions

1 Differentiate between validity and reliability, and give one example of each.

2 What makes a study generalizable?

3 Identify the advantages and disadvantages of using interviews and questionnaires.

4 Explain how direct observation and participant observation are used in research studies.

5 Explain how the Internet can be used in sexuality research. What are some of the benefits and drawbacks of this method?

Problems and Issues in Sexuality Research

Many problems in sexuality research are more difficult to contend with than they are in other types of research (see the accompanying "Sex in Real Life"). These include ethical issues, volunteer bias, sampling problems, and reliability.

Ethical Issues

Ethical issues affect all social science—and sexuality research in particular. Before people participate in a study of sexuality, researchers must obtain their **informed consent**. This is especially important in an area such as sexuality because it is such a personal subject. Informed consent means that the subjects know what to expect from the questions and procedures, how the information will be used, that their **confidentiality** will be assured, and to whom they can address questions. Some things that people reveal in a study, such as their acknowledgment of an affair or a sexual problem, can cause harm or embarrassment if confidentiality is not maintained. In the controversial Facebook study we discussed

informed consent
Informing participants about what will be expected of them before they agree to participate in a research study.

confidentiality
Assurance that all materials collected in a research study will be kept private and confidential.

IN OUR WORLD

A few global studies have shed some light on cross-cultural sexuality. Global studies are expensive to conduct, and because of this, usually pharmaceutical or contraceptive companies fund them.

The Global Study of Sexual Attitudes and Behaviors (GSSAB) was the first large, multi-country survey to study sexual attitudes, beliefs, and health in middle-age and older adults. The study was funded by Pfizer Pharmaceuticals (the maker of Viagra). Interviews and surveys were conducted in 29 countries representing all world regions (Africa/Middle East, Asia, Australasia, Europe, Latin America, and North America). A total of 13,882 women and 13,618 men, aged 40 to 80 years old, were included in the study.

Various countries required specific data collection methods. For example, random-digit telephone dialing was used in Europe, Israel, North America, Brazil, Australia, and New Zealand, and interviews were conducted by phone. However, a bias against telephone interviews in certain populations in Mexico required using in-person interviews. Mail surveys were used in Japan, but in other Asian countries, questionnaires were handed out in public locations. Finally, door-to-door methods using questionnaires were used in the Middle East and South Africa. Cross-cultural research requires flexibility in the use of data collection methods.

Despite wide cultural variations, there are several predictors of sexual well-being—such as physical and mental health and relationship satisfaction—that are consistent throughout the regions of the world. In addition, ratings of sexual satisfaction throughout the world are correlated with overall happiness in both men and women (Laumann et al., 2006). However, there were some limitations to this study. First of all, there was a relatively low response rate of 19%, which means that those who did agree to participate may have been more interested or comfortable in discussing sexual issues. In addition, since a variety of data collection methods were used, the results may not be generalizable in those countries where the data collection didn't enable researchers to collect a random sample, such as the Middle East, South Africa, and certain Asian countries.

Another global study of sexuality, the Durex Sexual Wellbeing Global Survey, was conducted in 2006 and was financed by the Durex Corporation. The study included more than 26,000 adults in 26 countries. Internet-based research methodologies were used in every country except Nigeria, where face-to-face interviews were done because of low Internet usage. The Durex study found that the frequency of sexual activity varies by country (see Figure 2.7). Although 60% of respondents said that sex is an enjoyable part of their lives, only 44% said they were fully satisfied with their sex lives.

The study also found the average age for engaging in first vaginal intercourse worldwide was 17.3 (Durex.com, 2007). The age at first vaginal intercourse was 15.6 (youngest) in Iceland and 19.8 (oldest) in India. Finally, the study also reported that heterosexual couples in Greece are the most sexually active, whereas heterosexual couples in Japan are the least. Data from the Durex study have been used in a variety of studies, which we will talk about in upcoming chapters.

The London School of Hygiene also conducted a global study and used meta-analysis to analyze 200 studies on demographic sexual behaviors published between 1996 and 2006 from 59 countries (Wellings et al., 2006). This was an interesting idea for a study that compared data on published articles around the world instead of collecting new data. The study found that a shift toward later marriage around the world has led to an increase in sex outside of marriage. It also revealed that monogamy is the dominant sexual pattern, and that around the world, men report more sexual partners than women.

The Center for Health Promotion at Indiana University, which authored the National Survey of Sexual Behavior and Health study, has also been actively collecting data on global studies of sexuality. The center

---

earlier, many users did not feel they gave informed consent to be in the study. Do you think this was ethical? Overall, it is standard procedure in sexuality research to obtain informed consent from all participants.

ON YOUR MIND

How do researchers know that what people tell them is true?

The fact is that they don't know, and they hope that people are being honest. Sometimes researchers build into studies little tricks that can catch someone who is lying, such as asking the same questions in different wording again later in a survey. Researchers also anticipate that participants will understand the questions asked and be able to provide the answers. In actuality, researchers may take many things for granted.

Volunteer Bias

Think back to the student's research project we discussed at the beginning of this chapter. Do you think that the students who didn't stop to talk to her were different from those who stopped to answer her questions? Or, do you think her results are generalizable to all the students at her university? If the volunteers could potentially differ from those who didn't volunteer, there is volunteer bias at work. Volunteer bias prevents the results of her study from being generalizable to the population as a whole.

As early as 1969, Rosenthal and Rosnow (1975) claimed that those who volunteer for psychological studies often have a special interest in the studies in which they participate. Studies that have examined volunteer bias in sexuality research conducted with college students generally support the finding that volunteers

works with various research partners in Africa, Europe, Latin America, and Asia. Global studies can help us learn more about societal and cultural factors that influence sexuality. Unfortunately, these studies are expensive, and funding can be difficult to come by. To reduce cost, many global studies rely on Internet data collection and self-reporting, which also raise several reliability and validity concerns.

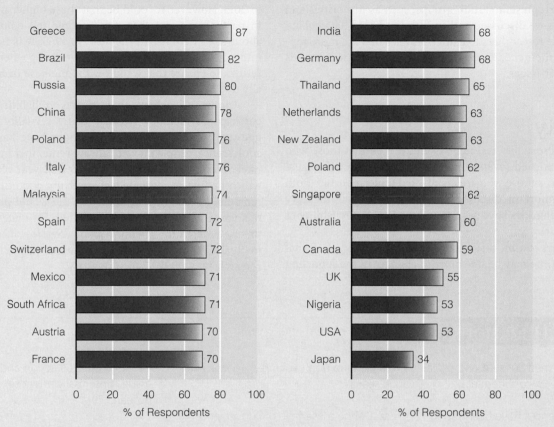

Frequency of Having Sex Varies Considerably by Country

Country	% of Respondents
Greece	87
Brazil	82
Russia	80
China	78
Poland	76
Italy	76
Malaysia	74
Spain	72
Switzerland	72
Mexico	71
South Africa	71
Austria	70
France	70

Country	% of Respondents
India	68
Germany	68
Thailand	65
Netherlands	63
New Zealand	63
Poland	62
Singapore	62
Australia	60
Canada	59
UK	55
Nigeria	53
USA	53
Japan	34

FIGURE **2.7** Percentage of respondents who report engaging in sex at least once a week.

differ from nonvolunteers (Catania et al., 1995; Gaither et al., 2003). Volunteers have been found to be more sexually liberal, more sexually experienced, and more interested in sexual variety, and they report less traditional sexual attitudes than nonvolunteers (Bogaert, 1996; Gaither, 2000; Plaud et al., 1999; Wiederman, 1999). You might be wondering how researchers would know whether their volunteer sample is different from the nonvolunteer sample. After all, how can researchers know anything about the nonvolunteers who are not in the study? Researchers have designed ways to overcome this problem. Before asking for volunteers to take part in a sexuality study, researchers ask all participants to fill out a questionnaire that contains personality measures and sexuality questions. Participants are then asked whether they would volunteer for a sexuality study. Because the researchers already have information from both volunteers and nonvolunteers, they simply compare these data. Because volunteers appear to differ from nonvolunteers, it is impossible to generalize the findings of a study that used a volunteer sample. The Kinsey studies attempted to decrease volunteer bias by obtaining full participation from each member of the groups they studied.

Sampling Problems

Like most psychological research, sexuality studies routinely involve the use of college-age populations. Brecher and Brecher (1986) refer to these populations as **samples of convenience**, because the participants used are convenient for researchers

samples of convenience
A research methodology that involves using samples that are easy to collect and acquire.

who tend to work at universities. Kinsey used such samples in his initial research at Indiana University. The question is, can these studies be generalized to the rest of the population? Are college students similar to noncollege students of the same age, or people who are older or younger? Probably not. These samples also underrepresent certain groups, such as minorities and the disabled. As we discussed earlier, Internet-based data collection may enable researchers to gather samples that are more representative of the general population, although these methods often have other issues.

Reliability

How reliable is sexuality research? Couldn't it be that those who are sexually satisfied overestimate their frequency of sexual behavior, whereas those who are dissatisfied underreport it? Both participant comfort in discussing sexuality and their memory about sexual behaviors have been found to affect the reliability of the study.

Some critics claim that changes in frequency of sexual behavior over time may be due more to changes in the reporting of behavior than to actual changes in frequency (Kaats & Davis, 1971). For instance, if we had done a study in 2015 about the number of college students who had sex before marriage and compared this with data collected in 1963, we would undoubtedly find more people reporting having sex outside of marriage in 2015. However, it could be that these higher numbers are due, in part, to the fact that more people felt comfortable talking about sex in 2015 than they did in 1963. It is necessary to take into account the time period of the study when evaluating the results, to ensure that we know the increase in numbers is actually due to an increase in behavior.

Another problem that affects reliability involves the participant's memory. Because many sexuality researchers ask questions about behaviors that might have happened in one's adolescence, people may not always remember information accurately. For instance, if we were to ask a 52-year-old man the age at which he first masturbated, chances are good that he would not remember exactly how old he was. He would probably estimate the age at which he first masturbated. Estimates are not always precise enough for scientific study. (See the accompanying "Sex in Real Life" for more information on skepticism in sexuality research.)

Review Questions

1 Define informed consent and explain the importance of confidentiality.

2 What differences have been found between those who volunteer and those who don't volunteer for sexuality research?

3 Define a "sample of convenience" and explain how it is used.

4 How do satisfaction and memory issues potentially affect sexuality research?

Sexuality Research Across Cultures

Many studies examine sexuality in cultures outside the United States. Some have been general studies that examine knowledge levels and attitudes in different populations; others have evaluated specific areas such as pregnancy, rape, homosexuality, or sex education. These studies are done by both international and U.S. researchers.

Of all the topics that have been studied cross-culturally, we have probably learned the most about how societies' values and culture influence sexuality. Every culture develops its own rules about which sexual behaviors are encouraged and which will not be tolerated. In 1971, Donald Marshall and Robert Suggs published a classic anthropological study, *Human Sexual Behavior: Variations in the Ethnographic Spectrum*, which examined how sexuality was expressed in several different cultures. This study remains one of the largest cultural studies ever done on sexuality, and some of its interesting findings include:

- Masturbation is rare in preliterate cultures (those without a written language).
- Foreplay is usually initiated by males in heterosexual couples.
- Heterosexuals engage in sexual intercourse most commonly at night before falling asleep.
- Female orgasmic ability varies greatly from culture to culture.

More recent studies on cross-cultural sexuality have yielded other interesting results. In the nearby Sexual Diversity feature we discussed Pfizer's comprehensive global study of sexuality, called The Global Study of Sexual Attitudes and Behaviors. This study was the first global survey of sexuality, and surveys assessed the importance of sex and intimacy in relationships, attitudes and beliefs about sexual health and treatment-seeking behaviors for sexual dysfunctions. This survey provided an international baseline regarding sexual attitudes to compare various countries and also monitor cultural changes over time. Another global study of sexuality done by the Durex corporation, called the Durex Sexual Wellbeing Global Survey, explored sexual attitudes and behaviors around the world (see Figure 2.7). The study included 26,000 people who responded to a web survey (see "Sexual Diversity in Our World: Global Sexuality Research" for more information about both of these studies).

ON YOUR MIND

How could an entire culture's attitudes about sex differ from those of another culture?

It makes more sense when you think about two very different types of cultures. A collectivist culture (e.g., India, Pakistan, Thailand, or the Philippines) emphasizes the cultural group as a whole and thinks less about the individuals within that society. In contrast, an individualistic culture (e.g., the United States, Australia, or England) stresses the goals of individuals over the cultural group as a whole. This cultural difference can affect the way that sexuality is viewed. For example, a culture such as India may value marriage because it is good for the social standing of members of the society, whereas a marriage in the United States is valued because the two people love each other and want to spend their lives together.

Global studies that focus on specific issues related to sexuality are also done by various organizations, such as the World Health Organization (WHO), the Joint United Nations Programme on HIV/AIDS (UNAIDS), and the United Nations Children's Fund (UNICEF). In 2016, WHO and UNAIDS released the Global AIDS Update exploring treatments for HIV/AIDS in 160 countries as well as global studies on adolescent contraceptive use and violence against women. UNICEF's research is done in 192 countries on issues such as adolescent development, gender equality, and HIV/AIDS. Wide-scale studies like these are important in our understanding of global public health problems and can help promote global change. We will discuss the findings of many of these studies in upcoming chapters.

Societal influences affect all aspects of sexuality. Throughout this book, we explore more details from cross-cultural studies on sexuality and examine how cultures vary from each other.

Review Questions

1 Of all the cross-cultural topics that have been studied, what have we learned the most about?

2 Identify two findings from Marshall and Suggs's large-scale cross-cultural study of sexuality.

3 Explain why global research studies from world organizations can help us understand various issues related to sexuality.

Sexuality Research in the Future: Beyond Problem-Driven Research

Many view America as a country "obsessed with sex." As we discussed in Chapter 1, sex is used to sell everything from jeans to smartphones and is oozing from television sitcoms, advertising, music videos, and song lyrics. However, even with this openness and sex all around us, there is a painful lack of solid sexuality research.

Our problem-driven approach has resulted in a lack of information in several key areas in human sexuality. We know little about sexual desire and arousal and what makes couples happy long term, or about childhood and adolescent sexuality, which has long been a taboo area of research. Although we are learning more about the development of sexual identity, sexual risk taking, and how the increase in sexual material on the Internet affects people's sexual behaviors, there is still a lack of solid research about sexuality.

In the future, it is hoped that sexuality research will help us understand the emotional and relational aspects of human sexuality. Instead of focusing primarily on what does not work in sexual relationships, such as problems with erections or orgasms, it will help us understand what does work and what keeps couples happy and satisfied. An increased willingness on the part of the federal government to consider sexuality-related research will also help improve our knowledge about sexuality and will aid in bringing sexuality researchers together. Some collaboration between researchers of various disciplines would help us more fully understand the influences that affect our sexuality and, in turn, help build the field of sexual science.

In the following chapters of this book, keep in mind the importance of theory and how it guides the questions we have about sexuality. The scientific method helps sexologists find answers to the varied questions we have about human sexual behavior. Throughout the upcoming chapters, we will be reviewing the data collected in several of the research studies we have reviewed in this chapter.

Review Questions

1 Explain how our "problem-driven" approach to sexuality research has limited what we know about sexuality.

2 What direction does sexuality research need to go in the future and why?

3 Identify one way in which research collaboration might be increased.

Chapter Review

Summary Points

1 A theory is a set of assumptions, principles, or methods that help a researcher understand the nature of a phenomenon being studied. The psychoanalytic theory was developed by Sigmund Freud. He believed the sex drive was one of the most important forces in life. Two of Freud's most controversial concepts included personality formation (the development of the id, ego, and superego) and psychosexual development (oral, anal, phallic, latency, and genital stages).

2 Behavioral theory argues that only overt behavior can be measured, observed, and controlled by scientists. Behaviorists use rewards and punishments to control behavior. A treatment method called *behavior modification* is used to help change unwanted behaviors.

3 Social learning theory looks at reward and punishment in controlling behavior but also believes that internal events, such as feelings, thoughts, and beliefs, can influence behavior. Another theory, cognitive theory, holds that people differ in how they process information, and this creates personality differences. Our behavior is a result of how we perceive and conceptualize what is happening around us.

4 Humanistic theory purports that we all strive to develop ourselves to the best of our abilities and to become self-actualized. Biological theory claims that sexual behavior is primarily a biological process, whereas evolutionary theory incorporates both evolution and sociology to understand sexual behavior. Sociological theory is interested in how the society in which we live influences sexual behavior.

5 Feminist theory looks at how the social construction of sexuality is based on power and the view that women are submissive and subordinate to men. Queer theory, another politically charged theory, asserts that domination, such as heterosexism and homophobia, should be resisted.

6 The legitimate forefathers of sexuality research may be Aristotle and Plato, because they were the first to develop theories regarding sexual responses and dysfunctions, sex legislation, reproduction, contraception, and sexual ethics. The majority of the early sexuality research was done in Europe, primarily in Germany. It wasn't until the 1900s that sexuality research moved to the United States, which has led sexuality research ever since.

7 The majority of sexuality research has been problem driven, and because of this, we know little about what constitutes healthy sexuality. The research has also become fragmented, with researchers coming from several disciplines, many unaware of the work being done by others.

8 The changing political climate affects attitudes about sexuality, as well as sexuality research. Negative attitudes can affect the public perception of sexuality research. Politics also can influence what sexuality research gets funded.

9 The most influential early promoters of sexology were Iwan Bloch, Magnus Hirschfeld, Albert Moll, Richard von Krafft-Ebing, and Havelock Ellis. Clelia Mosher did a great deal of sexuality research in the 1800s, but most of her work was never published. Katharine Bement Davis found that homosexuals were no different from heterosexuals, but her work was ignored because it caused fear among male researchers. The focus of sexuality research began to change after her research.

10 Alfred Kinsey was probably the most influential sexuality researcher of the 20th century. He was the first to take the study of sexuality away from the medical model. Kinsey established the Institute for Sex Research at Indiana University. Morton Hunt updated Kinsey's earlier work on human sexuality.

11 William Masters and Virginia Johnson were the first scientists to observe and measure sexual acts in the laboratory. They discovered several interesting aspects of sexuality, including a model called the *sexual response cycle*.

12 Two of the largest nationally representative studies are the NHSLS and the NSSHB, both of which were funded by private organizations. In addition to these studies, several governmental studies have contributed to our understanding of sexual behavior, including the NSFG, the YRBS, the NCHA, and the ADD Health study.

13 Researchers can use several methods to study sexuality, including case study, questionnaire, interview, participant observation, experimental methods, and correlations.

14 Researchers must be certain that their experiment passes standards of validity, reliability, and generalizability. Several problems can affect sexuality research, such as ethical issues, volunteer bias, sampling, and reliability problems. Of all the topics that have been studied cross-culturally, we have learned the most about how societies' values and culture influence sexuality.

15 Our problem-driven approach to sexuality research has interfered with what we really know and understand about relationships, love, and human development.

Critical Thinking Questions

1 Is sexuality research as valid and reliable as other areas of research? Explain.

2 Do you think that people would be more honest about their sex lives if they were completing an online survey or if they were being interviewed by a researcher? Which method of research do you think yields the highest degree of honesty? With which method would you feel most comfortable?

3 Why do you think couples might have volunteered to be in Masters and Johnson's study? Would you have volunteered for this study? Why or why not?

4 If you could do a study on sexuality, what area would you choose? What methods of data collection would you use? Why? How would you avoid the problems that many sexuality researchers face?

American Association of Sexuality Educators, Counselors, and Therapists (AASECT) AASECT is devoted to the promotion of sexual health through the development and advancement of the fields of sex therapy, counseling, and education.

Sexuality Information and Education Council of the United States (SIECUS) SIECUS is a national, private, nonprofit advocacy organization that promotes comprehensive sexuality education and HIV/AIDS prevention education in the schools.

Society for the Scientific Study of Sexuality (SSSS) SSSS is an interdisciplinary, international organization for sexuality researchers, clinicians, educators, and other professionals in related fields.

3 Communication and Sexuality

Over the years I've had the opportunity to talk with my students about their relationships. Many have had interesting experiences that help illustrate the importance of communication in close relationships. One student, Corelle, learned the importance of communication when she painfully realized how much it was lacking in her relationship with her boyfriend. She had been dating him for a little over 3 years but they had recently broken up—mostly because of communication problems. Since they were long-distance dating they had to rely on texting, e-mail, and phone and video calls to communicate. She found that being able to stay in touch made their relationship work, even though they were so far apart. Unfortunately, one day her boyfriend just stopped communicating. He didn't respond to her texts or e-mails and wouldn't pick up phone calls. She knew he was under a lot of stress, and she tried to get him to talk to her about it. The more she tried to get him to talk, the more he pulled away. She felt exhausted and finally couldn't take it anymore. She texted him one final message: "I'm done. Enjoy being single." Although they talked a few more times after this, the long-term lack of communication had irreparably damaged their relationship. In the end, as sad as she was, she told me that she learned many things about the importance of communication. She believes that dating couples really need to know how they want to communicate early in the relationship. Do they want to talk in person? Text? FaceTime? Skype? She wished that she and her boyfriend had talked about these issues because it might have saved their relationship.

Corelle is right—good communication is a key ingredient in happy relationships. But navigating all the communication technologies can be a major source of frustration in close relationships. Although texting has become a central part of many couples' relationships today, it can contribute to disagreements and relationship dissatisfaction. The key to using communication technologies is finding the right balance you can both agree on.

Janell Carroll

Communication has changed drastically over the last few years. In the past, if you wanted to talk to people, you went to see them, picked up the phone, or wrote them a letter. Today's college students rely on smartphones, text messaging, e-mail, and social media to communicate with friends and family on a daily basis. Although these communication technologies have allowed for increased communication, they have also created many new communication challenges. In this chapter, we talk about the importance of communication, how we learn to communicate, changing communication technologies, how people differ in the ways they communicate, and ways to improve interpersonal communication, including the ability to communicate about sexual issues. Improving communication has been found to enrich personal sexuality. We discuss other ways to enrich your personal sexuality by learning to feel good about yourself and about your sexual skills, and by improving your relationships with others.

The Importance of Communication

Imagine meeting someone new tonight. Your eyes find each other across the room, and slowly you make your way over to talk to each other. What would you talk about? How do you decide? Most likely you'll keep it simple with something like, "Pretty loud in here, huh?" or "I can't believe how crowded it is!" The first unwritten rule about communication early in a relationship is that you talk about something relevant but impersonal. You wouldn't walk up to someone you don't know and say, "Do you get along with your parents?" or "Do you ever cry?" No, these questions are too personal to discuss with someone you just met.

When do people start to talk about personal things in relationships? Social psychologists talk about the "onion" theory of communication. We all are onions with many, many layers, and when we first meet someone, we are careful about what we say—our onion layers stay in place. As more and more time goes by (and the amount of time differs from person to person), we begin to peel back our layers. At first we might talk about the weather ("I can't believe it's still so humid out!") and then progress to certain classes or professors ("I really enjoyed my psychology class last semester"). These comments are low risk and really don't involve sharing too much personal information. However, the next layer may include information about politics or family relationships, and the information gets more personal. The key to the onion theory is that as you begin to reveal your layers, so, too, does your partner. If you share something personal about yourself, your partner is likely to do the same.

Some people make the mistake of prematurely disclosing too much. Have you ever met someone who shared really personal information early, maybe within the first few days of meeting you? Some people talk about personal issues very early in the relationship, which may make others feel uncomfortable. Why do you think this would make people uncomfortable?

Good communication is one of the most important factors in a satisfying relationship (Benson et al., 2012; Lavner & Bradbury, 2012; Ledermann et al., 2010; Moore, 2010). Communication skills can be applied to all aspects of life, such as improving family relationships, being more effective in relationships at school or work, or developing an intimate relationship. Communication fosters mutual understanding, increases emotional intimacy, and can help deepen feelings of love.

Relationships between two people inevitably run into difficulties. It's nearly impossible not to experience difficulties when you are sharing your space with another person. This is precisely why many forms of therapy emphasize learning communication skills and why communication self-help books overflow from bookstore shelves. Communication problems usually occur when partners have poor communication skills, are unable to self-disclose, have trouble listening, or cannot agree on how to use various communication technologies (Gordon & Chen, 2016; Hiew et al., 2016; McDaniel & Coyne, 2016).

Misunderstandings, anger, and frustration are common reactions to communication problems, and these can lead to a downward spiral in which communication becomes less and less effective. Poor communication skills can contribute to many serious relationship problems, including physical and emotional abuse (Cornelius et al., 2010). Although smartphones can help couples stay connected, they can also lead to uncertainty and conflict in relationships when partners have different expectations about how much and when they should be used (McDaniel & Coyne, 2016).

It is important to point out, however, that not all relationship problems are caused by a lack of communication or poor communication. Studies have also found that certain discussion topics, such as money or sex, may be harder for couples to communicate about (Williamson et al., 2013). Problems may occur if the couple is unwilling to acknowledge a problem or issue that needs to be discussed. In other cases, issues such as poor health or economic stresses can create problems that hinder communication and intimacy.

Partners who can talk to each other have a better chance of their relationship working out.

Rob Bartee/Alamy Stock Photo

What we do know is that couples who know how to communicate with each other are happier, more satisfied, and have a greater likelihood of making their relationship last (Gordon & Chen, 2016; Hiew et al., 2016). But learning to communicate effectively isn't easy. Why can it be so difficult to talk to your partner? How can you share yourself physically with someone but feel unable to talk about things that are important to you? How do the various communication technologies affect your relationships?

Learning to Communicate

Are we born with the ability to communicate? If you've ever been around babies, you know that even though they don't have the ability to speak, they certainly know how to communicate with their caregivers. When they are hungry, tired, or just want to be held, they cry. Crying communicates to their caregiver that they need something. As children acquire language, they learn more effective ways of communicating.

Have you ever heard someone use the idiom "out of the mouths of babes"? Typically we use this saying when a child says something that is very intelligent or truthful. My friend Lisanne told me a story about taking her 5-year-old daughter to try on shoes at a store where one of the salespeople had acne. Lisanne's daughter couldn't take her eyes off the salesperson's acne and eventually

blurted out, "How did you get those nipples all over your face?" This story illustrates an important point—kids are notorious for saying exactly what they're thinking. As we grow up, we learn what is socially acceptable in conversation as various issues surface and interfere with our ability to talk to others. We begin to worry about what others might think, we feel selfish for asking for things we want and need, and we don't know how to talk about ourselves and our needs.

Goals of Communication

When we communicate with other people, we have three competing goals (Vanfossen, 1996). The first is to "get the job done"—we have a message for someone, and we want to communicate that message. Second, we also have a "relational goal"—we want to maintain the relationship and not hurt or offend the person with our message. Finally, we have an "identity management goal"—that is, we want our communication to project a certain image of ourselves.

All of these goals compete with one another (we want to tell someone something, not hurt the relationship, and maintain our image), making the job of communicating our thoughts, needs, or desires even that much tougher. Let's now explore the impact of our families on our ability to communicate, and perhaps we can uncover the mystery of good communication.

Family communication helps children develop a social and emotional understanding of the world around them.

Families and Communication

In Chapter 1, we introduced the important influence that our *family of origin* has on our personal development. Our ability to communicate, and the strategies we use to do so, were often learned through our interactions within our families (Buckner et al., 2013; Isaacs, 2013; Odenweller et al., 2013). Family members use language and communication strategies to negotiate, inform, reinforce values and beliefs, share stories, manage a household, and maintain relationships, among other things (Howe et al., 2010; Tannen et al., 2007). Throughout these processes, interactions and experiences in our families teach us important aspects of communication, such as negotiation, conflict avoidance, arguing, and interpersonal skills in romantic relationships (Isaacs, 2013; Ledbetter, 2010; Schrodt et al., 2009). Family communication also helps children develop a social and emotional understanding of the world around them and can affect a child's self-esteem, mental well-being, and potential for depression (Howe et al., 2010; Koerner & Fitzpatrick, 1997; Schrodt & Ledbetter, 2007).

If children learn positive ways of communicating, they will develop healthy strategies of communicating with others. But if they learn negative ways of communicating, they may encounter

difficulties in their later relationships. One of my students, Cherie, had a pattern of always walking away when she and her boyfriend got in an argument. She found it easier to avoid conversations. Her boyfriend was frustrated by this and tried to get her to talk things out. Cherie told me that she's "just like her parents" because they always gave each other the *silent treatment* when they disagreed. Did Cherie learn to avoid conflict by watching and interacting with her parents? It's possible.

Review Questions

1 Explain why good communication is the hallmark of a healthy relationship, and give three examples of how poor communication could lead to relationship problems.

2 Identify and describe the three competing goals for good communication.

3 Explain the influence that our family of origin can have on our ability to communicate.

Types of Communication

We have been talking about communicating through the use of words. There is, however, much more to communication than verbal words alone. We use nonverbal communication to get our message across, and we also communicate with others remotely through smartphones, computers, e-mail, texting, or various social networks. All of these methods of communication raise other important issues.

Nonverbal Communication

The majority of our face-to-face communication is done nonverbally, and nonverbal cues are an important and influential part of our communication (Knapp & Hall, 2005). Although

nonverbal communication includes facial expressions, hand and arm gestures, postures, and body positioning, it can also include many of the specifics of how verbal communication is used, including speech rates, durations, and intensities (Boomer, 1963; Ekman & Friesen, 1969; Mehrabian, 2009; Sauter et al., 2010). Research has found that nonverbal information helps fill in the gaps in verbal communication and may have a stronger impact when there is a conflict between verbal and nonverbal information (Jacob et al., 2013). As humans, we are uniquely designed to read these nonverbal cues and respond accordingly.

nonverbal communication
Communication without words (includes eye contact, head nodding, touching, and the like).

Using the nonverbal cues in this photo, what would you guess is going on with this couple and why?

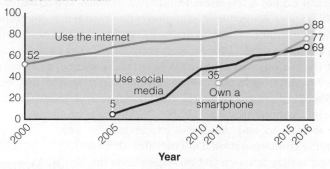

The Evolution of Technology Adoption and Usage
% of U.S. Adults Who...

FIGURE **3.1** **The Growing Popularity of Technology in the United States**
The Pew Research Center has found that approximately three-quarters of Americans own smartphones today, with large increases in lower-income Americans and those over the age of 50. The use of social media also has climbed, with 70% of Americans using it today. While social media use is more popular among 18–29-year-olds (86%), it is also popular among 30–49-years-olds (80%) and 50–64-year-olds (64%).

SOURCE: The Pew Research Center, Smith, 2016

Although we get better at recognizing nonverbal cues as the intensity of the emotional expressions increases, we also improve our ability to recognize these cues as we grow up. Young children in the United States can identify emotional expressions of anger, fear, happiness, and sadness, but their ability to identify these emotions increases as they age (Glenwright & Pexman, 2010; Montirosso et al., 2010). Most children do not learn to identify sarcasm until much later in childhood. However, even though adults are better at recognizing emotional expressions, as we age we lose the ability to recognize basic emotions in facial, vocal, and bodily expressions (Ruffman et al., 2009).

Culture is also important to consider here, because nonverbal communication differs widely from culture to culture. Many of the primarily negative emotions, such as anger or disgust, can be recognized across cultures, but several of the positive emotions, such as joy and happiness, may be communicated with culture-specific signals (Crivelli et al., 2016). These signals may include certain vocalizations, facial expressions, and/or posturing. In most Western cultures, nonverbal communication can completely change the meaning of a verbal expression. When a friend tells you "You're the best" with a smile on their face and a relaxed body posture, you'll probably believe them. However, the same statement coming from a person who has arms crossed, teeth clenched, and eyebrows furrowed has a completely different message.

Computer-Mediated Communication

When I was in college we didn't have smartphones or computers, so all of our communication was accomplished via face-to-face conversation, landline phone calls, or handwritten letters. Today, an estimated 95% of Americans own cell phones, and with the availability of **computer-mediated communication (CMC)** they have a variety of communication technologies at their disposal, including e-mail, text messaging, video calls, and various social

media sites such as Facebook, Instagram, or Twitter (see Figure 3.1; Pew Research Center, 2017). College students use such CMC methods daily in their communication with their friends and families, with texting and Facebook being the most popular communication technologies (Ehrenreich & Underwood, 2016; Nielsen Mobile Netview, 2016; Steers et al., 2016). Texting continues to grow in popularity especially among young people. In fact, when Millennials were given the choice between being able to call or text on their phones, the overwhelming majority said they'd rather lose the ability to call rather than text (Adotas, 2016).

College students view texting as a useful, intimate, and valuable form of communication that enables them to stay connected with friends, lovers, and family members (Luo & Tuney, 2015; Schade et al., 2013; Wise & Rodriguez, 2013). Interestingly, the ability to stay continuously connected is often rated as one of the best, and worst, aspects of texting. In intimate relationships, texting is most commonly used to express affection, but it can also be used to communicate about difficult topics, clarify misunderstandings, or apologize. Although some use texting for negative purposes (e.g., to hurt someone), studies have found this is uncommon (Coyne et al., 2011). Gender differences have been found in texting, with females more likely to see it as a positive connection with others and males viewing it as restricting their freedom (Ling et al., 2014).

REAL RESEARCH With the advent of predictive messaging and auto-correction, there is much less use of "textese" (a texting language that uses abbreviations and slang; e.g., u r nice) in text messaging today (Ouellette & Michaud, 2016).

computer-mediated communication (CMC)
Communication produced when people interact with one another by transmitting messages via networked computers.

Unlike video calls through Skype or FaceTime, texting and e-mail do not allow users to monitor physical nonverbal cues. This lack of nonverbal information is one reason that communication misunderstandings are more common using these methods (Coyne et al., 2011; Kelly et al., 2012). This is probably one of the reasons why **emoticons** (e-MOTE-ick-cons) and **emojis** (e-MO-jeez) have become so popular. It's estimated that over 75% of Americans regularly use emoticons and emojis in their online communications (Seiter, 2015). Both of these enable us to add emotional expressions to our online communication. Do you think that seeing a smiley face in a text message affects the way you think about the message? It might. Studies have found that when we view a smiley face emoticon, our brains respond as if we are looking at a happy human face (Churches et al., 2013).

ON YOUR MIND

My boyfriend spends a lot of time on the Internet. The other night, I discovered that he was obsessed with another girl's Facebook page. He had left her several messages and was checking out her photos from a weekend party. I was heartbroken. Do you think this constitutes cheating? It sure feels that way to me.

This is an interesting question. Many people believe that if their partner is having an intimate relationship with someone on the Internet, this is indeed cheating, but this really depends on how you define "intimate." Online relationships often involve sharing personal information about yourself and learning personal information about the person with whom you are communicating, which can increase emotional connections. Studies have found that emotional online infidelity elicits significant distress in dating and married partners (Dijkstra et al., 2013; Guadagno & Sagarin, 2010; Henline et al., 2007; Hertlein & Piercy, 2012; Whitty & Quigley, 2008). Both online and conventional infidelity cause anger, jealousy, and reduce relationship satisfaction (Cravens et al., 2013). Communication is key here—see whether your boyfriend can help you understand why he was drawn to engaging in such conversations on Facebook. We will explore issues related to cybersex and cheating in Chapter 10.

message without having to engage in a long, drawn-out conversation (Kelly et al., 2012). Texting also enables users to engage in multiple conversations at one time, take their time articulating responses, and have private conversations in public places. Since it can be done almost anywhere and at any time, it can increase productivity (you can text while on the toilet or even during class—but you shouldn't!). Texting also provides a private record of conversations that users can review and analyze at a later time (and researchers suggest that this is one reason why users are often reluctant to send negative texts; Wise & Rodriguez, 2013).

Texting, like e-mailing, has also been found to reduce inhibitions and anxieties that might surface during face-to-face communication, leading to higher rates of self-disclosure and direct questioning (Jiang & Hancock, 2013). This is probably why texting is easier than face-to-face communication for people who are shy or uncomfortable talking in public.

However, there are also some disadvantages to texting, include misunderstandings and confusion that can result from the lack of nonverbal cues and use of abbreviations or texting shortcuts. Many students have disagreements about how quickly texts should be responded to (Schade et al., 2013). If a sender expects an immediate reply (and is notified the message has been read), they might feel ignored and get upset. One of my students told me:

I once dated a woman who took forever to respond to my texts and it became a constant stressor because I would keep checking to see if she responded. It would make me anxious and insecure throughout the whole day sometimes since I couldn't gauge what she was thinking or if she even was interested in talking in the first place.

Emoticons and emojis may also make us more likely to accept negative feedback. Let's say your friend sends you a text message criticizing something you've done but includes a winking face emoji 😉. Studies have found that the presence of the emoji makes us more likely to accept what our friend is saying (Wang et al., 2014). See Figure 3.2 for more information about popular emojis around the world.

Texting is one of the most popular forms of communication on college campuses today because it is convenient, efficient, and fairly discreet. Users report preferring texting over face-to-face communication because it enables them to quickly send a

emoticons
Typographic symbols used in online communication to convey emotion; an example would be :-).

emojis
Graphic symbols used to represent concepts in electronic messages.

© Janell Carroll

Today's college students use computer-mediated communication methods daily in their conversations with friends and families.

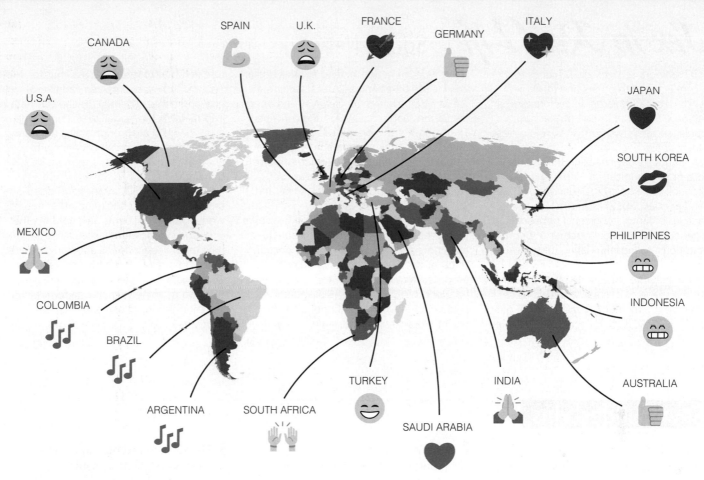

FIGURE **3.2 Top-Tweeted Emojis by Country**
TWITTER celebrates World Emoji Day in July of every year, and above are the top emojis tweeted in 20 countries in 2016. In the United States, Canada, and the United Kingdom, this was the weary face, while in South America it was musical notes. Romance won out in France, Italy, Japan, and South Korea with hearts and kissy lips most popular.

SOURCE: TWITTER; Lips, 2016

Some users believe that text messages from intimate partners should be responded to immediately. Research has found the amount of time between the receipt of a text message and the response serves as a barometer of relationship health (Kelly et al., 2012). It's important talk about your expectations with your partner (and even friends) so that you know how they would like you to respond. Talking about these issues can help decrease any potential problems.

Finally, it's important to point out that the use of technology can be problematic, especially if a person has a difficult time resisting the urge to constantly check their phone or struggles to disconnect from it. Studies have found that "technoference," or the interference of technological devices during personal interactions, can increase conflict and decrease relationship satisfaction (McDaniel & Coyne, 2016). Walk into any restaurant today and I bet you can find people eating a meal together while all on their phones. Since we depend on our technological devices for so many things today, we often develop strong relationships with them, which can interfere with our real-time relationships. In fact, studies have found that technology interferes in people's leisure time at least once a day (McDaniel & Coyne, 2016).

Although there is limited research on the risks associated with an overreliance on CMC technologies, some experts warn that decreased face-to-face communication may lead to emotional atrophy (Nass, 2012). Our brains are wired to respond to both verbal and nonverbal cues (including facial movements, gestures, vocal pitch, intonation, speech rate, and/or body posture) during communication (Kotlyar & Ariely, 2013). Healthy emotional development is fostered during face-to-face communication with others, and since these CMC technologies reduce nonverbal cues, they can negatively affect emotional development and growth. This is certainly an interesting area of research that is sure to grow in the next few years.

REAL RESEARCH Female students who were "stressed out" became more relaxed when they could talk to their mother on the phone and hear her voice as opposed to texting her (SELTZER ET AL., 2012). Researchers believe this has to do with the fact that hearing their mothers' voices decreased stress hormone levels, including cortisol.

Social network services allow friends to be connected with others and make new friends, facilitating large, impersonal social networks. Facebook is one of the most popular social networking sites, and college students have been found to spend more than an hour a day checking their news-feeds or communicating with friends on Facebook (Ehrenreich & Underwood, 2016; Manago et al., 2012). Social networks are made up of large, impersonal networks of people who are tied together through institutions, friendship, dating, or special interests.

Research into social networks has found that the shape of a network affects its use-fulness to the member. Smaller, tighter networks can be less useful because friends in these types of networks tend to have similar knowledge bases and attitudes. Larger networks often allow more creativity and open discussions about new ideas and concepts. Think about it this way: If you only had friends with similar interests to yours, there would be less chance for learning something new. With a larger, looser network, people are often introduced to new ideas and thoughts.

Early work in the field of social networks found that the average person is able to form only a limited number of connections to other people. "Dunbar's number" proposed that the typical size of a social network is 150 members (Bialik, 2007; Dunbar, 1998). This number originated out of cross-cultural and evolutionary research that found there is a limit to how many friends a person can recognize and about whom he or she can track information. The "small-world phenomenon" claims that through social networks, one random person can connect with another random person anywhere in the world.

What are the advantages and disadvantages to using Facebook and other networking sites? Students have told me that although social network sites are great to help them keep in touch and know what's going on, they can also be a distraction. Once again, balance is the key here—make sure you're not relying on one form of communication, or else you're sure to feel overwhelmed.

Review Questions

1 What is nonverbal communication? What can you learn from your partner's nonverbal cues? Provide one example.

2 What is computer-mediated communication? Explain some of the advantages and disadvantages of using CMC technologies.

3 Explain how texting might increase or decrease relationship satisfaction and provide examples of each.

Communication Differences and Similarities

Many factors, in addition to the family, can influence our communication. Various aspects of who we are, such as our gender, sexual orientation, ethnic and cultural background, and even our mood, health, age, and/or educational background can all affect our communication strategies and skills (Coyne et al., 2011; Ling et al., 2011). Let's review the impact of gender, culture, and sexual orientation on communication.

genderlect	**tag question**
Coined by Deborah Tannen, this term refers to the fundamental differences between the way men and women communicate.	A way of speaking in which speakers renounce or deny the validity of what they are saying by adding a questioning statement at the end of their statement.

Communication and Gender

Do men and women have different styles or ways of communicating? Gender differences in communication have long been a topic of scientific interest (Burleson et al., 1996; Holmstrom, 2009; Litosseliti, 2006; Tannen, 1990).

Research Studies of Gender Differences

Linguist Deborah Tannen (1990) has done a great deal of research in the area of face-to-face communication and gender differences. She has termed the fundamental differences between the way men and women communicate as **genderlects** (JEN-der-lecks). Women have been found to use more rapport-talk, which establishes relationships and connections, whereas men use more report-talk, which imparts knowledge. Tannen (1990) asserts that women use conversations to establish and maintain intimacy, whereas men use conversations to establish status.

Tannen also found that women use less assertiveness in their communication. For example, when stating an opinion, women often end their statement with **tag questions** (e.g., "It's really

A female mode of communication uses more rapport-talk, which establishes relationships and maintains intimacy.

A male mode of communication uses more report-talk, which imparts knowledge and helps to establish status.

There have been criticisms of Tannen's genderlect theory. One of the biggest criticisms has been in her unidimensional approach of studying gender differences in communication. To Tannen, gender is based on *biological* sex. Therefore, all women communicate one way and all men another way. However, it could be that an individual's communication skills, rather than his or her gender, could contribute to communication differences.

Other communication experts have identified two categories of communication skills, affective and instrumental (Burleson, 2003; Burleson et al., 1996). Affectively-oriented communication skills are comforting and involve a significant amount of listening, whereas instrumentally-oriented communication skills are more persuasive and narrative. Think about friends you know and consider for a moment their communication skills. Some might be more comforting and great listeners (an affective style), while others might talk a lot and give lots of advice (an instrumental style).

We value different types of communication skills in our relationships with others. For example, when we need social support or want to "vent," we are more likely to prefer the company of our friends with affectively-oriented communication skills; but if we want to discuss strategies or learn more about a particular topic, we are more likely to prefer the company of our friends with instrumentally-oriented communication skills (Kunkel & Burleson, 1998). Overall, women are more likely than men to value affectively-oriented communication skills, whereas men are more likely to value instrumentally-oriented skills (Burleson et al., 1996; Samter & Burleson, 2005).

Another interesting area of research on face-to-face communication involves speech quantity. The stereotype is that women talk more than men. This stereotype was supported by the research of neuropsychiatrist Louann Brizendine, who reported that women used 20,000 words per day, whereas men used only 7,000 (Brizendine, 2006). Brizendine claimed these differences were due to hormones during fetal development (Brizendine & Allen, 2010). However, when a group of researchers tried to replicate Brizendine's study using electronically activated recorders, they found that men and women both used about 16,000 words a day (Mehl et al., 2007). The subjects in this study were college students, which may limit the results, but the researchers point out that if the differences were biologically based, they would have appeared in this sample regardless.

Keep in mind that numerous studies on gender and face-to-face communication have found that overall differences in many areas of communication are small (Hyde, 2014; Leaper & Robnett, 2011). Many other factors contribute to our ability to communicate, such as social philosophies, gender roles,

cold in here, isn't it?" or "That's an interesting idea, isn't it?") to invite discussion and minimize disagreements. They also use **disclaimers** (e.g., "I may be wrong, but. . ."), **question statements** "Am I off base here?"; Vanfossen, 1996), and **hedge words** such as "sort of," "kind of," "aren't you?" or "would you mind?" All of these tend to decrease the speaker's perceived assertiveness of speech (Mithun, 2012). Although tag questions are frequently used in English, they are not used as often in other languages. In fact, the French and Swedish languages lack an equivalent feature (Cheng & Warren, 2001).

disclaimer
A way of speaking in which speakers renounce or deny the validity of what they are saying by including a negative statement.

question statement
A way of speaking in which speakers renounce or deny the validity of what they are saying by adding a question at the end of their statement.

hedge word
A way of speaking in which speakers renounce or deny the validity of what they are saying by using certain words to decrease their perceived assertiveness.

dominance, power, and as we talked about earlier, our family of origin. Many of the studies on gender differences in communication have studied only young, well-educated, middle-class Americans (Mortenson, 2002), and as you remember from our discussion in Chapter 2, we do not know whether these findings are generalizable to different groups and cultures within and outside of the United States.

Earlier we discussed how our ability to read nonverbal cues is an important ingredient in successful interpersonal relationships. Researchers have found a few gender differences in nonverbal communication. Overall, women use more nonverbal communication techniques including eye contact and head nods than men, and they are more likely to smile, lean forward, touch, and gaze more in face-to-face conversations (Mast & Sczesny, 2010; Wood, 1999). Men tend to use less eye contact, fewer head nods, and minimal "encouragers" (nonverbal cues to let their partner know they are listening). Women also tend to be better at decoding and translating nonverbal communication (DeLange, 1995; Schubert, 2004; Wolfe, 2005).

What about gender differences in texting, e-mailing, or the use of social networks? While both men and women quickly adopted these methods of communication when they first became available, there have been some differences found in use and preferences. Overall, women rely on communication technologies more than men for relational maintenance and use texting, social media, and online video calls more than men (Kimbrough et al., 2013; Tufekci, 2010, 2014). Men are more likely to rely on communication technologies for establishing new relationships and finding job leads. Finally, since many CMC technologies reduce the constraining gender roles that occur in face-to-face conversations, women have been found to have an easier time making their voices heard online than in a face-to-face conversation.

ON YOUR MIND

I am really confused about my relationship with my girlfriend. I thought we had good communication, but now I don't know what to think. She told me about a problem she is having with another friend. I listened for hours and tried to offer some solutions to help her improve the situation. To my surprise, she became angry with me! What's going on?

If you're a heterosexual man, it could be that there are some gender issues interfering with your ability to communicate here. Research has found that men tend to view conversations as ways to exchange information or fix problems, whereas women tend to try to confirm the other person's feelings and empathize (GARD, 2000). These are tendencies, however, and not all men and women respond the same way. In your case, it sounds as if you listened to your girlfriend and moved on to trying to fix the problem. Perhaps she was looking for your emotional support and some TLC, instead of potential solutions. Unfortunately, women often feel frustrated by men's tendencies to try to fix their problems, whereas men often complain that women refuse to take action to solve their problems. These communication issues can also affect the relationships of same-sex couples, and it really depends on the person's individual communication style.

Theories About Gender Differences

In the preceding section, we discussed some of the research on gender differences in both face-to-face and computer-mediated communication. Scholars often disagree about whether gender differences exist, but those who agree that there are differences often disagree on the reasons for them. There may be a biological basis—physically innate differences between men and women that cause gender differences in communication. There may be psychological reasons—men and women have experienced different reinforcements for communicating, and these have shaped their patterns of communication. There may also be societal reasons for the differences. Social role theory explains the differences in terms of role expectations about masculinity and femininity in society, whereas societal development theories focus on male dominance in society and its effects on communication patterns.

Although it's true that all of these theories can explain some of the gender differences in communication, gender communication can often be best understood as a form of cross-cultural communication. If you were suddenly in a conversation with a person from another country who had no experience with your culture, you might find this conversation difficult. You wouldn't know the subtleties of that person's communication style, and they wouldn't know yours. It's hypothesized that even though men and women grow up in similar environments, they learn different ways of communicating, which results in male–female communication being a form of cross-cultural communication.

Maltz and Borker (1982) believe that American men and women come from different "sociolinguistic subcultures" and learn different communication rules, especially in face-to-face communication. They interpret conversations and use language differently. This all begins with children in same-sex play groups, which are often organized very differently. Most young girls play in small groups and have "best friends." Reaching higher levels of intimacy is the goal, and their games, such as playing house, less often have winners and losers. Boys, on the other hand, learn to use speech to express dominance and play in hierarchically organized groups that focus on directing and winning. Boys often jockey for status by telling jokes, showing off, or claiming they are the best at things.

According to Maltz and Borker (1982), during same-sex conversations, girls and boys learn the rules and assumptions about communication, and these rules follow them through life. As adolescents, they begin to communicate in mixed-sex groups with the rules they learned from same-sex communication, which can cause problems. Earlier we discussed how women use more nonverbal communication techniques. Girls learn to nod their head during face-to-face conversations with other girls. This lets the talker know that she is being listened to. When a woman nods her head during a conversation with a

Sex in Real Life   Gossiping and Complaining

I asked a group of students what it would be like to spend 24 hours with their partner if they could use only nonverbal communication. Many students didn't know what to make of the question. Would it really be possible for them to be alone with their partner but not (verbally) speak to each other for 24 hours?

Several of the heterosexual women who were asked this question said that although they'd be willing to try, they didn't think it would work out well. They weren't sure they could be with their partner without using verbal communication. The heterosexual men, on the other hand, were enthusiastically up for the challenge. When pressed for their reasoning, several said, "I wouldn't have to listen to her complain!" This made me think—what exactly is "complaining," and do women do this more than men? The answer depends on your definition. Many women say that it's not really "complaining" but rather "discussing" important issues.

Women have been found to complain more than men and are more likely to commiserate with each other about their complaints (Boxer, 1996; Jaworski & Coupland, 2005; Rose et al., 2016). Many women say this helps them cope with disappointment and that they enjoy engaging in this type of communication with other women. Studies have found that women bond with other women through complaining, whereas men are more likely to bond with other men through the process of generating potential solutions (Goodwin, 2007; Sotirin, 2000) or the use of humor (Rose et al., 2016).

Women's informal talk includes gossip, complaining, "troubles talk," and "bitching" (Sotirin, 2000). Although at first glance these types of talk might seem similar, each appears to have its own structure and function. The focus of gossip is on an absent target and includes contributions from several participants. Gossiping may also have an aggressive component to it, wherein the gossip is meant to hurt or harm a particular relationship (Conway, 2005; Feinberg et al., 2012; Ferguson, 2004; Melwani, 2013). Complaining is usually brief and to the point. "Bitching," in contrast, relates an in-depth account of events, usually about an injustice or something negative that has happened to the speaker, allowing her to express her dissatisfaction (Sotirin, 2000). In "troubles talk," there is one "troubles teller," and the focus of the conversation stays on the teller the entire length of the conversation. Men have been found to engage in gossip, too, although they are more likely to gossip to a romantic partner, whereas women were equally likely to share gossip with their romantic partners and their same-sex friends (Hambaugh, 2012; McAndrew et al., 2007).

Next time you stroll through the mall or even your student union, take a look around you. Do you notice any complaining or gossiping? What do you think the purpose of these forms of communication are?

man, he thinks she agrees with him (when she might not agree or disagree—her head nod may simply be showing him that she is listening). When a man doesn't nod his head when a woman is talking to him, she may think he isn't listening to her. All of this can lead to feeling misunderstood and to poor communication. Understanding the differences in communication styles won't automatically prevent disagreements, but it will help keep the disagreements manageable.

Weestock Images/Dambrosia/Alamy Stock Photo

Purestock/Getty Images

Communication patterns begin when children play in same-sex groups.

Communication and Culture

Cultures differ in many ways, and these differences affect communication patterns. One important dimension that has been extensively studied is the degree to which a culture encourages individual versus group needs. Individualistic cultures encourage their members to have personal goals and values, and an independent sense of self, whereas collectivist cultures encourage members to value group needs over their individual needs (Cai et al., 2000; Matsumoto, 1996; Xia, 2011, 2012). The United States is among the more individualistic countries, together with Canada, Australia, and Great Britain, whereas Asian and Latin cultures tend to be more collectivistic (Adler et al., 2007). This individualistic approach is probably why people from the United States are more comfortable disclosing personal information to a variety of people than members of collectivistic cultures. Persons from collectivistic cultures, such as Japan or Korea, rarely disclose personal information to those outside of their immediate family because it is thought to be inappropriate to do so (Chen & Danish, 2010; Seki et al., 2002).

In addition, anthropologists have identified two distinct ways in which individuals from various cultures deliver messages to one another (Adler et al., 2007). A "low-context culture," such as the Scandinavian, German, Swiss, and North American countries, uses language to express thoughts, feelings, and ideas as directly as possible (Hall, 1976, 1990). Statements are simple, and the meaning of the statement is in the words that are spoken. A "high-context" culture, which is typical of Asian and Arab cultures, relies heavily on subtle and nonverbal cues in its communication (Ambady et al., 1996; Hall, 1990). Communication is not direct, and a listener's understanding depends on the context of the conversation, nonverbal behavior, relationship history, and social rules. Communicators from high-context cultures may often beat around the bush in their conversations and expect listeners to know what they mean.

The Pew Research Center found that smartphones outnumber landlines three to one around the globe (McPhillips, 2016). Like in the United States, texting and e-mail are popular and used worldwide for relational maintenance, social networking, emotional support, and social and business scheduling. One interesting area of research has explored international workplace communication via CMC technologies. In fact, in 2017, French laws established the "right to disconnect" law, which required companies with more than 50 workers to establish hours when staff should not send or receive e-mails (Morris, 2017). The use of texting and e-mailing in the workplace has become more popular over the last few years, but since these communication technologies eliminate nonverbal cues, they can increase misunderstandings between people from different cultures (Bazarova & Yuan, 2013; Vignovic & Thompson, 2010). The use of emojis in these conversations can also be confusing, as cultures may use emojis differently (see Figure 3.2 for more information). Recipients of international texts or e-mails are more likely to attribute misunderstandings to a sender's personal characteristics, such as intelligence or abilities, rather than to cultural differences in communication.

When our partner listens to us, we feel worthy and cared about, which, in turn, strengthens our relationship.

Ryan Pierse/The Image Bank/Getty Images

REAL RESEARCH Nearly all smartphones in Japan are waterproof mostly because the Japanese like to talk on their phones while they are bathing or showering (Ramirez, 2016; Sharma, 2016).

Communication and Sexual Orientation

Although the majority of research on communication has used heterosexual couples, we do have limited information about communication patterns and strategies in same-sex couples. As we discussed earlier, many issues are at play when a couple communicates—gender, dominance, gender role, social philosophy, and power. Like heterosexual couples, conversational styles in same-sex relationships have been found to reflect power differences in the relationship more than the biological sex of the communicator (Steen & Schwartz, 1995). Overall, few communication differences have been found in gay, lesbian, and heterosexual intimate relationships (Julien et al., 2003).

Differences in same-sex communication may also have to do with gender roles. Men who are higher in nurturance engage in more cooperative speech, whereas women who are lower in nurturance engage less in such speech (Edwards & Hamilton, 2004). In addition, stereotypically "feminine" men and women have been found to use more submissive speech patterns, whereas stereotypically "masculine" men and women have been found to use more dominance language than stereotypically "feminine" or androgynous men and women (Ellis & McCallister, 1980). It may be that gay men and lesbian women are more flexible in their gender roles, and their communication patterns could reflect this comfort. An interesting study done by John Gottman and colleagues found that same-sex couples were more positive than heterosexual couples when discussing areas of conflict in their relationships (Gottman et al., 2003). Gottman believed this could be due to the fact that same-sex couples tend to value equality more than heterosexual couples.

When compared with heterosexual men's speech, gay men's speech more commonly includes the use of "qualifying adjectives" (such as "adorable" or "marvelous"), a wider pitch range than used by heterosexual men, extended vowel length speech (e.g., "maarvelous"), a tendency to avoid reduced forms of speech (e.g., contractions such as "can't" and "won't"), and a greater likelihood of arm and hand gestures (Knöfler & Imhof, 2007; Salzmann, 2007).

In the future, more research is needed to examine the speech and communication patterns of gay men and lesbian women. Research addressing communication strengths and weaknesses in gay and lesbian couples would be helpful to further our understanding of these relationships. Remember that sexual orientation, culture, ethnicity, and communication styles are all interconnected, and it may be impossible to look at one variable without also looking at these other influences.

Review Questions

1 What do we know about the impact of gender on communication? Describe the theories that have been proposed to explain gender differences in communication styles.

2 What do we know about the impact of culture on communication? Differentiate between individualistic and collectivistic cultures and high- and low-context cultures and explain how these issues can affect communication.

3 What do we know about the impact of sexual orientation on communication?

Sexual Communication

Sexual communication involves discussing aspects of one's sex life with a partner. These types of conversations are often more challenging because sexuality tends to magnify all the communication problems that exist in any close relationship (Brogan et al., 2009; Rehman et al., 2011). We grow up in a society instilled with a sense of shame about our sexuality and are taught at an early age that talking about sex is "dirty." Approaching the subject of sex for the first time in a relationship implies moving on to a new level of intimacy, which can be scary. It also opens the way for judgment and possible rejection. Because of this, many couples avoid conversations about sex altogether.

Sexual communication can involve talking *about* sex with a partner or talking about sex *during* sex with a partner (Babin, 2013; Faulkner & Lannutti, 2010). Although most of the research in this area has explored communication *about* sex with a partner, we do know that conversations about sexual pleasure are more likely to happen during sex with a partner (Brogan et al., 2009; Faulkner & Lannutti, 2010). There is also a reciprocal nature of sexual communication—the more a couple communicates *during* sex, the more they will be able to talk about sex with their partner and vice versa. Couples who can communicate about sex report higher relationship satisfaction than those who cannot talk about these issues (Babin, 2013; Brogan et al., 2009; Faulkner & Lannutti, 2010; Mark & Jozkowski, 2013).

Important Components in Sexual Communication

Several important components contribute to healthy sexual communication. We will discuss the importance of a positive self-image, self-disclosure, trust, and nonverbal communication.

Positive Self-Images and Feeling Good About Yourself

Healthy sexuality depends on feeling good about yourself. If you have a negative self-image or do not like certain aspects of your body or personality, how can you demonstrate your attractiveness to an intimate partner? Imagine a person who is overly concerned about their body while in bed with a partner. Maybe a woman is worried that her partner will not be attracted to the size or shape of her chest, thighs, or stomach. Perhaps a man is consumed with anxiety about penis size or body hair and worries his partner won't find it attractive. Fears, worry, and anxiety can interfere with our ability to let go, relax, open up, and enjoy our sexual experiences.

Talking about our fears, worries, anxieties, and concerns with our partners can help them to understand, and it may even be the first step to coming to terms with these issues ourselves. We all have parts of our bodies we wish we could change. In fact, most of

ImagesBazaar/Alamy Stock Photo

Good lovers are not mind readers. They learn about their partner's needs through listening and communication.

us are much more critical of our bodies than our partners would ever be. Self-esteem also has a powerful effect on how we communicate with others (Adler et al., 2007). A person with positive self-esteem will often expect to be accepted by their partners, whereas someone with negative self-esteem will often expect to be rejected by their partners (Hamachek, 1982). It's not difficult to see how negative self-images and fears of rejection can inhibit healthy sexual communication.

In American society, learning to like our bodies is often difficult. We discussed in Chapter 1 how magazines, television, and advertisers all play into our insecurities about our bodies. The beauty images that the media present to us are often impossible to live up to and leave many of us feeling unattractive by comparison. To sell products, advertisers must first convince us that we are not OK the way we are—that we need to change our looks, our smells, or our habits. In the United States in particular, we put a high value on physical attractiveness throughout the life cycle, and our body image greatly affects how attractive we feel. It's true that before anyone else can accept us, we need to accept ourselves.

Self-Disclosure and Asking for What You Need

Opening up and talking with your partner and sharing feelings, or **self-disclosure**, helps deepen intimacy and sexual satisfaction (Macneil, 2004; Posey et al., 2010; Schiffrin et al., 2010). It is critical to maintaining healthy and satisfying sexual relationships. Self-disclosure lets your partner know what is wrong and how you feel about it, and it enables you to ask for specific change. When you open up and share, your partner will be more likely to reciprocate by opening up and sharing as well.

Too often, we assume that being good in bed also means being a mind reader. Somehow, our partner should just know what turns us on. In reality, nothing could be further from the truth. Good lovers are not mind readers—they are able and willing to listen and communicate with their partners. Doing so helps ensure you are both on the same page when it comes to various sexual activities and behaviors. One man recounts an early sexual experience:

I'll never forget the first time. She was lying on her parents' bed with the lamplight shining on her, naked and suntanned all over… I climbed on that bed and I lifted her up onto my thighs—she was so light I could always pick her right up—and I opened up her [vagina] with one hand and I rammed my [penis] up there like it was a Polaris missile. Do you know, she screamed out loud, and she dug her nails in my back, and without being too crude about it, I [screwed] her until she didn't know what the hell was happening… She loved it. She screamed out loud every single time. I mean I was an active, aggressive lover. (Masterton, 1987, p. 70)

self-disclosure
Opening up, talking with your partner, and sharing feelings.

Yet his partner viewed the sex very differently:

What did I think about it?… I don't know. I think the only word you could use would be "flabbergasted." He threw me on the bed as if he were Tarzan, and tugged off all of my clothes, and then he took off his own clothes so fast it was almost like he was trying to beat the world record… He took hold of me and virtually lifted me right up in the air as if I were a child, and then he pushed himself right up me, with hardly any foreplay or any preliminaries or anything. (Masterton, 1987, p. 73)

Communication is key here, because whereas the man thinks he is doing exactly what his partner wants, the woman can't figure out why he's doing what he's doing! Studies have found that men who watch online pornography often have a very distorted view of what their partners want in bed, which can decrease a couple's sexual satisfaction (Adams, 2015; Kühn & Gallinat, 2014; Wright & Bae, 2015). Unfortunately, this couple's relationship eventually ended, mainly because they were unable to talk about what they needed and wanted in the sexual relationship, which left both feeling confused and frustrated. If this couple could have self-disclosed more, they might have been able to work through these issues. We will discuss the use of pornography more in Chapter 18.

As we discussed earlier, talking about sexual issues in intimate relationships can increase relationship satisfaction. But this isn't always easy. Telling your partner what you really want and need during sex can be difficult. Many of us feel insecure about our sexuality and may worry about our sexual skills. At the same time, however, we may be hesitant to make suggestions to improve our partner's techniques because we worry they will be insulted and think that their sexual skills are being criticized. Anxieties like these do not foster a sense of open and mutual communication. Ultimately, not being open about your likes or dislikes is self-defeating because you may end up feeling resentful of your partner or unhappy in your relationship.

ON YOUR MIND

I have been in a relationship with my boyfriend for almost 1 year. We love each other very much, but most of the time we don't communicate well, mainly because I'm just too afraid to talk about things like sex. I love him very much and want our relationship to last. How can we learn to communicate better?

Communicating our thoughts, needs, wants, hopes, and desires isn't always easy. Intimate or personal information is usually difficult to share. It's natural to worry about what your boyfriend might think or say. It's best to start slowly. Don't try to tell him everything at one time. You might try sharing a few small details about what you're thinking and what you like about your sex life. Remember that asking for what you need involves self-disclosure. If you can open up, share your thoughts, and listen to what your boyfriend is saying, this can help you grow together as a couple.

Trusting Your Partner

Trusting your partner means that you have confidence in them and feel secure in the relationship. One of the most important ingredients in any happy and satisfying sexual relationship is trust (Luchies et al., 2013; Sprecher et al., 2013). Earlier we discussed the importance of our family of origin in learning to communicate. Our family also contributes to our ability to trust an intimate partner. Having more trusting relationships early in life lays the foundation for happier and healthier sexual relationships later in life (Campbell et al., 2010). If we trust our partner and feel confident and secure in our relationship, self-disclosure will be much easier.

Building trust takes time, and it is typically a process of *uncertainty reduction* (Holmes & Rempel, 1989). Our prior relationships influence our ability to trust, but the level of trust in any new sexual relationship depends in large part on various aspects of our current partner (Campell et al., 2010). Being hurt by someone in a previous relationship, experiencing a loss, or being fearful about rejection can all interfere with the ability to trust an intimate partner, but over time trust can grow.

People who report being more trusting of their partners also tend to be more optimistic about the relationship and think more positive thoughts about their partner's negative behaviors (e.g., trusting partners are less likely to take things personally if their partner is late to meet them; Simpson et al., 2007). However, nontrusting partners would have many doubts and concerns and might think their partner doesn't love them anymore.

Nonverbal Communication

Although verbal communication about your likes and needs is far more effective than nonverbal communication, nonverbal communication can help increase sexual satisfaction (Babin, 2013). It's important to keep in mind that everyone expresses nonverbal communication in a unique and individual way. As we get to know our partner better, we also get better at understanding their nonverbal communication. Some gender differences in nonverbal communication have been found, with men more likely to initiate touch in casual relationships and women more likely to do so in serious relationships (Prinsen & Punyanunt-Carter, 2009).

Couples use both verbal and nonverbal communication to initiate sexual activity. Nonverbal communication can help partners express sexual desires and also reinforce verbal messages. For example, if you wanted your partner to kiss your neck more during foreplay, you could show this by demonstrating more pleasure when they are kissing your neck. You can moan or shift positions to communicate your pleasure to your partner. You might also try performing the behavior on your partner that you wish they would do to you. Keep in mind, however, that exclusive use of nonverbal communication may lead to misunderstandings, as demonstrated by this couple:

> One woman attempted to communicate her preference for being kissed on the ears by kissing her partner's ears. However, she found that the more she kissed her partner's ears, the less he seemed to kiss hers. Over a period of time her kissing of his ears continued to increase, while his kissing of her ears stopped

altogether. Finally she asked him why he never kissed her ears anymore, only to discover that he hated having his ears kissed and was trying to communicate this by not kissing hers. After their discussion, he began to kiss her ears, she stopped kissing his, and both were happier for the exchange. (Barbach, 1982, p. 105)

Using nonverbal communication to share your sexual needs during sexual activity can be easier and less disruptive than verbal communication. For example, moving a partner's hand to your breast during sex can be less threatening than saying, "Could you please touch my breast?" Either way, couples who communicate their needs and desires to their sexual partner have higher levels of sexual satisfaction than those who do not communicate their needs (Babin, 2013).

Obstacles to Sexual Communication

Several factors can interfere with our ability to talk about sex with our partners, such as embarrassment and concerns about sexual terminology.

Embarrassment

Earlier we discussed how we live in a society that tends to instill a sense of shame about our sexuality. Many of us have learned that sex is "dirty" or "bad," and we feel uncomfortable talking about it. This is natural and understandable. But how can we learn to reduce our embarrassment and feel more comfortable talking about sex?

The answer: Relax and take it slow.

Many young adults are embarrassed to talk about sexual issues (van Teijlingen et al., 2007). Embarrassment can inhibit our ability to open up and talk with our partners. We may worry that our partner will judge us or think differently about us. The good news is that it gets easier over time. The more comfortable you get in a relationship, the less embarrassing it often is. For some, using humor and being able to laugh can help reduce the tension.

Sexual Terminology

Lastly, to have a meaningful conversation about sex with your partner, you need to know the correct terminology and have a sexual vocabulary. Throughout this course you will learn the correct terminology for various sexual organs, behaviors, and activities, but you will also need to learn which type of sexual vocabulary you are comfortable using. You can use scientific and anatomical words (such as *vagina, penis,* or *sexual intercourse*), or you can use sexual slang (such as *vajayjay, dick,* or *doin' it*). Sometimes scientific terminology can seem unromantic and awkward, whereas sexual slang may not really let you accurately describe what you want to say. Talking about these language and vocabulary issues with your partner can help lessen the anxiety and make you more comfortable with sexual communication.

Although many couples avoid communication about sex because it can be difficult to talk about, learning to communicate your sexual desires and needs can strengthen your relationship.

Michael Goldman/Photographer's Choice/Getty Images

1 Why is it difficult to talk about sexual issues?

2 Why is a positive self-image important in sexual relationships, and how can it affect communication?

3 Explain how self-disclosure and trust can increase satisfaction in sexual relationships.

4 How can nonverbal communication be used to help express sexual likes and dislikes?

5 Identify and explain some of the obstacles to sexual communication.

Listening, Expressing Criticism, and Nonconstructive Communication

The majority of couples spend too much time criticizing each other and not enough time really listening and making affectionate comments (P. Coleman, 2002). One partner often becomes defensive and angry when the other says something that they don't want to hear. For example, if your partner told you that they felt you weren't giving enough time to your relationship, you could hear this message with an open mind, or you could get angry and think, "What do you know about my time?" Let's now talk about the importance of listening, constructive and nonconstructive communication, and verbal disagreements.

The Importance of Listening

Listening is one of the most important communication skills. Adults spend nearly 70% of their waking time communicating and 45% of this time listening (Adler et al., 2007; Rankin, 1952). **Active listening** involves using nonverbal communication to let your partner know that you are attentive and present in the conversation (Floyd, 2014; Weger et al., 2014). For example, as your partner talks, you can maintain eye contact to let them know you are actively listening.

Another important skill is **nondefensive listening**, which involves focusing your attention on what your partner is saying without being defensive (Gottman, 1994). Nondefensive listening relies on self-restraint, which is often absent in distressed couples, who have a difficult time hearing and listening to each other. It can be difficult to listen fully, but this skill reduces your inclination to interrupt or to defend yourself.

---

active listening
Communication and listening technique in which the listener uses nonverbal communication, such as nodding or eye contact, to signal that they are attentive to the speaker.

nondefensive listening
Listening strategy in which the listener focuses attention on what their partner is saying without being defensive.

Poor listeners often think that they understand what their partner is trying to say, but they rarely do. Instead, they try to find a way to circumvent the discussion and talk about something else. It is difficult to really listen to someone when you are angry or defensive. Good listening allows you to understand and retain information while building and maintaining your relationships.

Being a More Effective Listener

Many things interfere with our ability to be an effective listener. These include information overload, preoccupation with personal concerns, rapid thoughts, and noise. It is easy to reach information overload today. We hear so much during the course of our day that it can be difficult to listen carefully to everything going on. As a result, we must choose what information we will listen to and pay attention to. A preoccupation with personal concerns may also interfere with our ability to listen. If we are wrapped up in our own thoughts and issues, it's difficult to listen to someone else. Consider this: We are capable of understanding speech at rates of up to 600 words per minute (Versfeld & Dreschler, 2002); however, the average person speaks between 100 and 140 words per minute. This gives your brain time to think about other things, such as what you'll say to your professor this afternoon, what you'll have for dinner tonight, or when you'll study for the exam tomorrow. In addition to this there are often other conversations going on around us, music playing, or other noise. This can make it very difficult to focus on what is being said and really listen to our partner.

Listening and really paying attention can also help you learn important things about your partner. John Gottman, a relationship expert, gives couples a relationship quiz to determine whether they have been paying attention to each other's likes and dislikes (Gottman, 1999). His questions include the following:

- What is the name of your partner's best friend?
- Who has been irritating your partner lately?
- What are some of your partner's life dreams?
- What are three of your partner's favorite movies?
- What are your partner's major current worries?
- What would your partner want to do if he or she suddenly won the lottery?

When others listen to us, we often feel cared about, worthy, and protected. Sometimes being listened to can also help us understand what upsets us. As we mentioned earlier, encouraging your partner through active listening, such as eye contact, nodding, or saying "um-hum" (Fowers, 1998; Weger et al., 2014), shows your partner that you are "tuned in." It also encourages your partner to continue talking.

When your partner is finished talking, it is important to summarize what your partner has told you as accurately as possible. This lets your partner know that you heard what they were saying, and also enables your partner to correct any misunderstandings. Finally, it is also important when listening to validate your partner's statement. Saying "I can understand why you might feel that way" or "I know what you mean" can help you show your partner that you think what they are saying is valid. This doesn't necessarily mean that you agree, but you can accept your partner's point of view.

Message Interpretation

In all face-to-face conversations, the recipient of the message must interpret the intended meaning of the message (R. Edwards, 1998). This is dependent on several factors, such as the nature of the relationship with the person and your mood at the time. For example, if you tripped and fell as you and your partner were walking across campus and your partner says "Be careful!" how do you interpret this? Did they think you were being clumsy and not paying attention? Or was your partner genuinely worried you might hurt yourself?

Our feelings can also influence message interpretation. For example, if you're angry or upset you'll probably perceive more hostility in ambiguous or benign comments than someone who is not angry or upset (Epps & Kendall, 1995). Being worried or preoccupied with something can affect how you interpret what someone says to you. In one study, women who were preoccupied with their weight were more likely to interpret ambiguous sentences with negative or "fat" meanings, whereas women who were not preoccupied with their weight did not (Jackman et al., 1995).

Negative Feelings and Criticism

It's inevitable that at some point we'll get upset or angry in our conversations with others. Unfortunately, not all conversations have happy, peaceful endings. However, the key is in managing the tension. When we disagree with our partner, the opening minutes of a disagreement can indicate whether the conversation will turn angry or simply be a quiet discussion (P. Coleman, 2002). If harsh words are used, chances are the disagreement will build, and the tension will escalate. However, if softer words are used, there is a better chance the disagreement can be resolved.

Negative feelings may also involve sharing or accepting criticism. Accepting criticism isn't an easy thing to do—we are all defensive at times. Although it would be impossible to eliminate all defensiveness, it's important to reduce defensiveness to resolve disagreements. If you are defensive while listening to your partner's criticism, chances are good that you will not be able to hear their message. Common defensive techniques are to deny the criticism (e.g., "That is just NOT TRUE!"), make excuses without taking any responsibility (e.g., "I was just exhausted!"), deflecting responsibility (e.g., "Me? What about your behavior?"), and

righteous indignation (e.g., "How could you possibly say such a hurtful thing?") (P. Coleman, 2002). All of these techniques interfere with our ability to really understand what our partner is trying to tell us. Keeping our defensiveness in check is another important aspect of good communication.

John Gottman, the relationship expert we discussed earlier, found that happy couples experienced 20 positive interactions for every negative one (Nelson, 2005). Couples who were in conflict experienced only 5 positive interactions for every negative one, and those couples soon to be divorced experienced only 0.8 positive interactions for every negative one. This research suggests that positive and negative interactions can shine light on a couple's relationship happiness.

Nonconstructive Communication

Couples often make many mistakes in their communication patterns that can lead to arguments, misunderstandings, and conflicts. **Overgeneralizations**, or making statements such as "Why do you always. . .?" or "You never. . .," generally exaggerate an issue. Telling your partner that they "always" (or "never") do something can cause defensiveness and will often lead to complete communication shutdown. Try to be specific about your complaints and help your partner to see what it is that is frustrating you. For example, if you find yourself frustrated by the amount of time your partner spends with friends, find a time when you can discuss your concerns. Try not to be defensive or overgeneralizing and share your thoughts (say, "I feel like I would like to spend more time together," rather than "You always seem to want to be with your friends more than me!").

Try to stay away from **name-calling** or stereotyping words, such as calling your partner a "selfish bastard" or a "nag." These derogatory terms will only help escalate anger and frustration, and they will not lead to healthy communication. Digging up the past is another nonconstructive communication pattern that accomplishes nothing. It is also important to stay away from old arguments and accusations. The past is just that—the past. So try to leave it there and move forward. Dwelling on past events won't help to resolve them.

Another common mistake that couples make in conversations is to use **overkill**. When you are frustrated with your partner and threaten the worst (e.g., "If you don't do that, I will leave you!"), even when you know it is not true, you reduce all communication. Don't make threats if you don't intend to follow through with them. In the same vein, it is important to focus on your frustration in conversation.

Try not to get overwhelmed and throw too many issues in the conversation at once (e.g., the fact that your partner didn't take the trash out last night, forgot to kiss you good-bye, and ignored you when they were with friends). This approach makes it really

---

overgeneralization
Making statements that tend to exaggerate a particular issue.

name-calling
Using negative or stereotyping words when in disagreement.

overkill
A common mistake that couples make during arguments, in which one person threatens the worst but doesn't mean what they say.

difficult to focus on resolving any one issue because there is just too much happening. Also, avoid yelling or screaming, which can cause your partner to be defensive and angry, and less likely to be rational and understand what you are saying. Even though it's not easy, it's important to stay calm during conversation.

Clinging to any of these communication patterns can interfere with the resolution of problems and concerns. If you recognize any of these patterns in your own relationship, try talking to your partner about it and try to catch yourself before you engage in them.

REAL RESEARCH Older adults in the United States overwhelming prefer face-to-face communication although their most commonly used method is the telephone (YUAN ET AL., 2016).

Fighting

Verbal disagreements are a common part of intimate relationships and are much more likely during times of stress (Bodenmann et al., 2010). Couples may disagree about public issues (concerns outside of their relationship) or personal issues (concerns related to their relationship) (Johnson, 2009). Generally, public issue arguments are engaged in to provide new knowledge or pass the time, whereas personal issue arguments are typically engaged in to help portray oneself in a more positive light. Regardless of the type of argument, however, couples who disagree are usually happier than those who say, "We never, ever fight!" (It's important to point out, however, that verbal disagreements are different from physical disagreements. We will discuss domestic violence in Chapter 17.)

Happy couples have been found to think more positive thoughts about each other during their disagreements, whereas unhappy couples are inundated with negative thoughts about each other (P. Coleman, 2002). Even though a happy couple is disagreeing about an issue, the two partners still feel positively about each other, which is important. Forgiveness is another important aspect of healthy couples. Couples who positively rate their relationships are more likely to forgive their partners for transgressions, whereas those who are less invested in a relationship are more likely to withhold forgiveness and believe their partner hurt them intentionally (Guerrero & Bachman, 2010).

Some couples avoid conflict by ignoring problems or avoiding communicating about certain issues. Studies have found that although conflict avoidance can cause relationship problems, women are more likely than men to say that conflict avoidance decreases their overall relationship satisfaction (Afifi et al., 2009; Dillow et al., 2009).

What happens after an argument? Generally, women are more likely to demand a reestablishment of closeness, whereas men are more likely to withdraw (Noller, 1993). Remember that your family of origin also influences your communication strategies. Do you recall what used to happen after your parents had an argument? Do you see any similarities in the way that you behave after arguments in your relationships?

Taking a time-out and finishing a discussion later, learning to compromise, or validating each other's differences in opinions are important ways to resolve a disagreement. Also remember that in every relationship, some issues may simply be unresolvable. It is important to know which issues can be worked out and which cannot. The question is, can you live with the irresolvable issues? How can you work on improving these issues?

Sometimes arguments continue long after both partners have said everything they want to say because neither wants to be the one to call for a truce. Calling for a truce can also be tricky to do. One couple told me that when they want to stop arguing, they have agreed that whoever is ready first holds up a pinky finger. This signals to the other that they are ready to end the fight. The other partner must touch their pinky to the partner's pinky to acknowledge that the fight is over. This isn't always easy, but it has helped this couple to end arguments amicably.

Throughout this chapter, we have discussed the importance of communication and its role in the development of healthy, satisfying relationships. As communication technologies continue to grow and change, it will be important to consider the impact of these technologies on intimate relationships. Good communication skills are vital to healthy relationships and can help strengthen your overall relationship. It's important to be honest and open and ask for what you need.

Review Questions

1 Why is listening one of the most important communication skills? What is nondefensive listening?

2 Explain how information overload, personal concerns, rapid thoughts, and noise interfere with our ability to listen.

3 Describe two nonconstructive communication strategies, and explain why they could lead to a communication shutdown.

Chapter Review

1 Communication has changed drastically over the last few years. College students today rely on smartphones, text messaging, e-mail, and social media to communicate with others. Communication fosters mutual understanding, increases emotional intimacy, and helps deepen feelings of love and intimacy.

2 Communication problems can occur when partners have poor communication skills, are unable to disclose, have trouble listening, or cannot agree on how to use various communication technologies. Good communication skills are an integral part of all healthy relationships, and couples who know how to communicate with each other are happier, more satisfied, and have a better chance of making their relationship last.

3 The three goals of communication include getting the job done, maintaining the relationship, and managing our identity. All of these three goals compete with each other, making communication difficult.

4 Our ability to communicate and the strategies we use to do so were learned in our interactions within our families. We learn many communication skills such as negotiation, conflict avoidance, arguing, and interpersonal communication skills. Children also develop a social and emotional understanding of the world around them. All of this learning can affect a child's self-esteem, mental well-being, and the potential for depression. If children learn positive ways of communicating, they will develop healthy strategies of communicating with others.

5 The majority of our face-to-face communication is done nonverbally, and nonverbal cues are an important and influential part of our communication. This form of communication is often done through eye contact, smiling, or touching. Nonverbal information may have a stronger impact when there is a conflict between verbal and nonverbal information. As we get older, we get better at recognizing nonverbal cues, but at a certain age our abilities to recognize these cues begin to decrease again. Nonverbal communication differs from culture to culture, and some positive emotion may be communicated with culture-specific signals.

6 Today's college students use computer-mediated communication (CMC) methods daily in their communication with their friends and families, with texting and Facebook being the most popular. Texting allows users to stay connected with others and communicate when apart, which can increase relationship satisfaction. Gender differences have been found with women more likely to view texting as a positive connection with others and men more likely to view it as restricting their freedom.

7 The lack of nonverbal information in texting and e-mailing makes communication misunderstandings more common with these CMC technologies. This may be one reason why emoticon and emoji use has increased over the last few years.

8 Advantages to texting include convenience, efficiency, the ability to engage in multiple conversations at one time, time to articulate responses, private conversations in public places, higher rates of self-disclosure, and private records for later review. Disadvantages include the addictive nature of texting, disagreements about texting expectations, safety hazards, and the possibility of private conversations being shared with others.

9 The use of technology can be problematic, especially if a person has difficulty resisting the urge to check their phone or struggles to disconnect from it. "Technoference," or the interference of technological devices during personal interactions, can increase conflict and decrease relationship satisfaction.

10 Many factors, such as gender, culture, and sexual orientation, can influence communication patterns. Deborah Tannen proposed the idea of *genderlects* and believed that women engaged in more rapport-talk and used less assertiveness in their communication, whereas men engaged in more report-talk. There have been criticisms of Tannen's theory and other experts have differentiated between affective and instrumental communication skills. Although many theories have been proposed to explain gender differences in communication, numerous studies on gender and face-to-face communication have found that overall gender differences in many areas of communication are small.

11 Gender differences have been found in CMC with women more likely to rely on these technologies for relational maintenance than men and using texting, social media, and online video calls more than men. Men were more likely to rely on CMC for establishing new relationships and finding job leads.

12 Communication patterns have been found to vary depending on cultural orientation. Individualistic cultures encourage their members to have individual goals and values, and an independent sense of self. Collectivist cultures emphasize the needs of the whole group over individual needs. In addition, anthropologists have identified low- and high-context cultures. Low-context cultures use language to express thoughts and feelings directly, whereas high-context cultures rely more on subtle and nonverbal cues. Preliminary research indicates that the cross-cultural use of CMC technologies can lead to communication misunderstandings.

13 The majority of communication research has been done on heterosexual couples, although there is limited information on communication in gay and lesbian relationships. We do know that power, gender role, and social philosophies all affect communication patterns. Research has found differences between the speech patterns of gay and heterosexual men.

14 Sexual communication can be challenging because sexuality often magnifies communication that exists in any close relationship. We are often taught that talking about sex is "dirty" and, therefore, learn to avoid it. Research has examined both communication *about* sex and communication about sex *during* sex and has found that couples who communicate with each other about sexual issues report more relationship satisfaction. Heterosexual men who watch online pornography often have a distorted view of what their partners want in bed, which can decrease sexual satisfaction.

15 Those with a positive self-esteem often expect their partners to accept them, whereas those with a negative self-esteem often expect rejection. Although verbal communication about sex is preferable, nonverbal communication can also be used.

16 Self-disclosure is critical in maintaining healthy and satisfying sexual relationships. It helps partners know each other's needs and wants. Trust is also important, and self-disclosure is easier if we trust our partner. Those who trust their sexual partners feel more optimistic about their relationships. Both embarrassment and sexual terminology issues can interfere with our ability to communicate about sex.

17 Several things can interfere with our ability to listen, including information overload, personal concerns, rapid thoughts, and noise. The majority of couples spend too much time criticizing each other and not enough time really listening and making affectionate comments. Active and nondefensive listening are important.

18 When we express negative feelings, it's important not to use harsh words, because tension will escalate. It is also important to learn how to accept criticism without becoming defensive. Mistakes in communication patterns that can get couples into trouble include overgeneralizations, name-calling, and overkill. Verbal disagreements are a common part of intimate relationships and are more common during times of stress. Happy couples think more positive thoughts during disagreements than do unhappy couples.

Critical Thinking Questions

1 The research shows that couples who know how to communicate have a greater likelihood of making their relationship last. Apply this to a relationship that didn't work out for you, and explain how poor or absent communication may have affected your relationship.

2 Do you think that men and women have different communication styles and may, in fact, have "cross-cultural" styles of communication? Explain why or why not and give examples.

3 Do you agree with findings claiming that women use texting, social media, and online video calls more than men? How might expectations about texting in intimate relationships cause disagreements, and what do you think could be done to avoid any problems?

4 Have you ever communicated with someone online and then met later face-to-face? If so, how did your online communication affect your face-to-face communication? What was your online impression of them before you met in person?

5 Identify issues that make it difficult to talk to a sexual partner about your sex life. What can you do to improve the communication?

6 Can you think of any incidence in which a lack of self-esteem on your part negatively affected a relationship? Explain.

7 How have computer-mediated communication technologies, such as texting, e-mailing, and Facebook, changed communication patterns on today's college campuses? What do you see as the advantages and disadvantages of these communication technologies?

Websites

The American Communication Association   The American Communication Association (ACA) has links to the *American Communication Journal* and the Communication Studies Center, which contains a collection of online resources.

Journal of Communication   *The Journal of Communication* is an interdisciplinary journal with an extensive online offering that focuses on communication research, practice, policy, and theory, and includes the most up-to-date and important findings in the communication field.

4 Gender Development, Gender Roles, and Gender Identity

Most college students don't spend a lot of time thinking about what gender they are. But what if you thought about it every single second? And, what if, for as long as you could remember, you felt uncomfortable with your gender? That's exactly what had been happening to Sophie, a student I met from the University of Nebraska. She was smart, outgoing, and passionate about life, hoping to one day find a job as a video game journalist. Twenty-two years ago Sophie was assigned a male gender at birth and given a male name. Despite going through male puberty and the development of male body parts, she knew early on that she wasn't a boy. Growing up in a small, Midwestern town, Sophie couldn't easily put a finger on what didn't feel right as a child, but she knew she was different. She didn't feel she fit in with the boys and men in her hometown and felt more comfortable being around girls and women. After graduating from high school, Sophie was excited to begin a new chapter of life in college. During the summer after freshman year, Sophie began to undergo a medical transition so that her body would be in line with her mind.

Sophie's parents were supportive of her decision to transition, although they would have preferred she waited until after graduation. They were worried about the process and the potential impact on her college career if she medically transitioned while she was still a student. But when Sophie decided she was ready, she started her transition and came out to the whole campus at her school. Although she had support, she also received plenty of hate mail. Looking back, she told me there were many difficult days. Yet, she said she would still go through it again today if she had to.

She told me that while many people might look at her and get caught up in gender issues, the bottom line is that she's just like any other college student—she likes Subway, Coke, and video games. Talking with her made me realize how many assumptions we have about gender.

Janell Carroll

© Aletha Crews

The **gender** landscape has been slowly changing over the last decade. Conventional **gender roles** have typically defined males as tough, dominant, non-emotional, and ambitious, and females as weak, emotional, intuitive, and nurturing. There were only two options: you were male or female. Today many experts conceptualize gender more as a spectrum and less as a binary. With more people coming out as transgender today, this has led to some changes in American culture that have affected a variety of institutions, including schools, college campuses, and workplaces. Although **transgender** individuals and advocates have been fighting for equal rights for decades, many recent events have begun to reshape our understanding of gender in American culture. Standardized college application forms, including the Common Application and the Universal College Application, along with Facebook, now offer multiple gender options, including male, female, transgender male, transgender female, **genderqueer**, gender non-conforming, and **non-binary**. The English language has also expanded to reflect less rigid gender norms, with the Oxford English Dictionary adding **gender fluid** and Dictionary.com adding **cisgender**, genderqueer, and **misgender** (Gutierrez-Morfin, 2016). Various television shows containing transgender characters, such as *Transparent*, have won multiple Emmys, while Oregon became the first state to rule that "non-binary" is a legal gender (Segal, 2016). Some colleges today encourage professors to ask their students what pronouns they use. All of these recent events influence our own thoughts, behaviors, and actions regarding gender identity, expression, and roles. Yet, even with all of this change, strong support remains for gender stereotyping (Haines et al., 2016).

Gender raises many issues. Beginning in 1970, many U.S. colleges began offering coeducational residence halls in addition to single-sex dorms—typically putting males and females on separate floors or wings. Soon afterward, coeducational hallways were available. By 2008, gender-neutral housing, which allows students to share rooms regardless of gender, became available on a few campuses as a strategy to provide safe housing options for transgender students. As of late 2017, more than 200 universities offered gender-neutral housing including Boston, Carnegie-Mellon, Cornell, Columbia, Dartmouth, Duke, George Washington, Harvard, Stanford, and New York Universities (Human Rights Campaign, 2017).

Before we go any further, let's talk about how the words *sex* and *gender* are often used synonymously, even though they have different meanings. When you fill out a questionnaire that asks you "What is your sex?" how do you answer? When you apply for a driver's license and are asked, "What gender are you?" how do you respond? Although your answers here might be the same, researchers usually use the word *sex* to refer to the biological aspects of being male or female, and *gender* to refer to the behavioral, psychological, and social characteristics of men and women (Pryzgoda & Chrisler, 2000).

It is important to explore gender to more fully understand sexuality. Gender stereotypes shape our opinions about how men and women act sexually. For example, if we believe that men are more aggressive than women, we might believe that these gender stereotypes carry over into the bedroom as well. Traditionally, men are viewed as the initiators in sexual activity, and they are the ones who are supposed to make all the "moves." Stereotypes about women, on the other hand, hold that women are more emotional and connected when it comes to sex—more into "making love" than "having sex." Do gender stereotypes really affect how people act and interact sexually? Do they affect gay and lesbian couples? What about those who are transgender or non-binary? We explore the relationship between gender and sexuality later in this chapter.

For many years, scientists have debated whether gender is more genetics and biology ("nature") or social environment and upbringing ("nurture"). Or is it a combination of the two? The story of Bruce and Brenda discussed in the accompanying "Sex in Real Life" feature illustrates the fact that both nature and nurture are important in the development of gender. In Chapter 2, we discussed evolutionary theory, which argues that many behaviors in

---

gender
The behavioral, psychological, and social characteristics associated with being male or female.

gender roles
A set of societal norms dictating the types of behaviors that are generally acceptable for people based on their actual or perceived sex.

transgender
An umbrella term for a person whose gender identity or gender expression is incongruent with (or does not "match") the sex they were assigned at birth.

non-binary
An umbrella term that refers to a continuum of gender identities and expressions often based on the rejection of the gender binary.

gender fluid
A person whose gender identity shifts between masculine and feminine or moves across the gender spectrum.

cisgender
A person whose gender identity is congruent (or "matches") with the sex they were assigned at birth.

genderqueer
A gender identity label often used by people who do not identify with the gender binary.

misgender
The act of referring to someone using a word or pronoun that does not correctly reflect the gender with which they identify.

Over the last few years, gender lines have been blurring in fashion with a widening acceptance of androgynous styles.

Sex in Real Life A Case of a Boy Being Raised as a Girl

In 1967, a young Canadian couple brought their two identical twin boys (Bruce and Brian) to the hospital for routine circumcisions; the boys were 8 months old. A surgical mistake during one twin's circumcisions resulted in the destruction of his penis. The couple met with Dr. John Money, a well-known medical psychologist from Johns Hopkins University, who believed that gender was learned and could be changed through child rearing. He did not believe gender was contingent on **chromosomes**, genitals, or even sex hormones (Money, 1975). After meeting with Dr. Money and discussing their options, the couple decided to have their son, Bruce, undergo castration (removal of the testicles) and have surgery to transform his genitals into those of an anatomically correct female. Bruce became Brenda and was put on hormone treatment beginning in adolescence to maintain her feminine appearance. For many years, this Brenda/Bruce case stood as "proof" that children were psychosexually "neutral" at birth, and that gender could be assigned, no matter what the genetics or biology indicated. This

case had a profound effect on how children who were born with ambiguous genitalia or who had experienced genital trauma were raised (Colapinto, 2001).

However, even though Money paraded the Brenda/Bruce story as a success and around the globe intersex children began sex reassignments, no one paid much attention to the fact that Brenda was struggling with her gender identity. In 1997, a study published by Milton Diamond, a reproductive biologist at the University of Hawaii, exposed the case and discussed how Brenda had struggled against her

str old/Reuters

girlhood from the beginning (Diamond & Sigmundson, 1997). Once Brenda reached puberty, despite her hormone treatments, her misery increased. She became depressed and suicidal. She never felt that she was a girl, and she was relentlessly teased by peers. Her parents finally told her the truth, and at 15 years old, she stopped hormonal treatments and changed her name to David.

Soon afterward, David Reimer went public with his medical story in hopes of discouraging similar sex reassignment surgeries. In 2001, John Colapinto wrote the details of this real-life story in a book called *As Nature Made Him: The Boy Who Was Raised as a Girl* (Colapinto, 2001). This book, in conjunction with interviews with David, influenced medical understandings about the biology of gender. Today, the Intersex Society of North America opposes the use of sex reassignment surgery for nonconsenting minors.

Although David Reimer eventually married and adopted children, sadly he took his own life at the age of 38 (Burkeman & Younge, 2005).

men and women have evolved in the survival of the species, and that gender differences between men and women may be at least partially a result of heredity.

In this chapter, we explore the nature versus nurture debate as it relates to gender. We start by reviewing prenatal development and sexual differentiation. We also look at atypical sexual differentiation and chromosomal and hormonal disorders. Although these disorders are not exceedingly common, their existence and how scientists have dealt with them help us learn more about gender. Our biological exploration of sex will help set the foundation on which we can understand how complex sex and gender really are. We also explore gender roles, theories about gender, and socialization throughout the life cycle.

REAL RESEARCH Young men's exposure to mainstream media, which endorses a view of masculinity centered on power, aggression, and the objectification of women, is associated with more traditional beliefs about the male role (GIACCARDI ET AL., 2016).

Prenatal Development: X and Y Make the Difference

Human beings have a biological urge to reproduce and thus are in some sense "designed" to be sexual beings; any species that does not have good reproductive equipment and a strong desire to use it will not last very long. Simpler organisms, such as amoebas, split in two, creating a pair genetically identical to the parent amoeba. More complex organisms, however, reproduce through **sexual reproduction**, in which two parents each donate a **gamete** (GAM-meet), or **germ cell**, the two of which combine to create a new organism.

---

chromosome
A threadlike structure in the nucleus of a cell that carries genetic information.

sexual reproduction
The production of offspring from the union of two parents.

gamete
A reproductive cell—the spermatozoon or ovum; also referred to as a germ cell.

germ cell
A reproductive cell—the spermatozoon or ovum; also referred to as a gamete.

Gender Development, Gender Roles, and Gender Identity **79**

The tiny germ cells from the male (sperm) and the much larger but also microscopic cell from the female (egg, or ovum) each contain half of the new person's genes and determine their sex, hair and eye color, general body shape, the likely age at which they will reach puberty, and literally millions of other aspects of the developing fetus's physiology, development, and emotional nature. The genes direct the development of the genitals and the reproductive organs, and they set the biological clock running to trigger puberty and female **menopause** or male **andropause**. We discuss both of these topics in Chapters 5 and 6.

Most cells in the human body contain 46 chromosomes: 23 inherited from the mother and 23 from the father, arranged in 23 pairs. Twenty-two of the pairs look almost identical and are referred to as **autosomes**; the exception is the 23rd pair, the **sex chromosomes**. The two sex chromosomes, which determine whether a person is biologically male or female, are made up of an X chromosome donated by the mother through the ovum and either an X or a Y chromosome donated by the father's sperm. If the male contributes an X chromosome, the child will be female (XX); if he contributes a Y chromosome, the child will be male (XY).

All the cells of the body (somatic cells), except gametes, contain all 23 pairs of chromosomes (46 total) and are called *diploid* (meaning "double"). However, if a merging sperm and egg also had 23 pairs each, they would create a child with 46 pairs, which is too many (remember that most cells contain only 23 pairs of chromosomes). So gametes are *haploid*, meaning they contain half the number of chromosomes (23) of a somatic cell (46). During **fertilization**, a haploid sperm and a haploid egg join to produce a diploid **zygote** (ZIE-goat) containing 46 chromosomes, half from each parent. The zygote can now undergo **mitosis**, reproducing its 46 chromosomes as it grows.

Since male and female babies look so similar, many American parents feel the need to dress their babies in blue or pink to identify their gender.

The 46 chromosomes are threadlike bodies made up of somewhere between 20,000 and 25,000 genes, each of which contains **deoxyribonucleic** (dee-OCK-see-rye-bow-new-KLEE-ik) **acid (DNA)**. DNA acts as a blueprint for how every cell in the organism will develop. At first, the zygote reproduces exact copies of itself. Soon, however, the cells begin a process of differentiation. Differentiation is one of the great mysteries of human biology—suddenly, identical cells begin splitting into liver cells, brain cells, skin cells, and all the thousands of different kinds of cells in the body. The DNA determines the order in which cells differentiate, and a cell's position may determine to some degree which type of cell it will become. Researchers in evolutionary developmental biology explore how and when cells differentiate.

ON YOUR MIND

Does the father's sperm really determine the sex of the child?

Yes, it is the sperm that determines the sex of the child, but the woman's body does have a role to play; there are differences between X and Y sperm (Xs are heavier and slower but live longer; Ys are faster but die more quickly), and a woman's vaginal environment or ovulation cycle may favor one or the other. However, the biological sex of the child does depend on whether an X chromosome sperm or a Y chromosome sperm, donated by the father, joins with the ovum (which is always an X). The irony is that for many years, in many cultures, men routinely blamed and even divorced women who did not produce a child of a certain sex (usually a boy), when, in fact, the man's sperm had much more to do with it.

Whether the zygote will develop into a male or female is determined at the moment of conception, and part of the process of differentiation includes the development of our sexual characteristics. If sexual differentiation proceeds without a problem, the zygote will develop into a fetus with typically male or typically female sexual characteristics. However, a variety of things can happen during development that can later influence the person's own sense of gender.

menopause
A period in a woman's life, usually during her 40s or 50s, when estrogen decreases, causing the eventual cessation of menstruation.

andropause
A period in a man's life, usually during his 70s or 80s, when testosterone decreases, causing changes in spermatogenesis, muscle strength, and libido.

autosome
Any chromosome that is not a sex chromosome.

sex chromosomes
Rod-shaped bodies in the nucleus of a cell at the time of cell division that contain information about whether the fetus will become male or female.

fertilization
The union of two gametes, which occurs when a haploid sperm and a haploid egg join to produce a diploid zygote, containing 46 chromosomes.

zygote
The single cell resulting from the union of sperm and egg cells.

mitosis
The division of the nucleus of a cell into two new cells such that each new daughter cell has the same number and kind of chromosomes as the original parent.

deoxyribonucleic acid (DNA)
A nucleic acid in the shape of a double helix in which all genetic information in the organism is encoded.

Sexual Differentiation in the Womb

A human embryo normally undergoes about 9 months of **gestation**. At about 4 to 6 weeks, the first tissues that will become the embryo's gonads begin to develop. Sexual differentiation begins a week or two later and is initiated by the sex chromosomes, which control at least four important aspects of sexual development: (1) the internal sexual organs (e.g., whether the fetus develops ovaries or testicles); (2) the external sex organs (such as the penis or clitoris); (3) the hormonal environment of the embryo;

and (4) the sexual differentiation of the brain (which includes a cyclic or noncyclic hormonal pattern; Wilson & Davies, 2007). The timing of all these events varies, however. Although sexual differentiation of the genitals begins within the first 2 months of pregnancy, sexual differentiation of the brain does not occur until sometime after the 5th month of pregnancy (Savic et al., 2010).

gestation
The period of intrauterine fetal development.

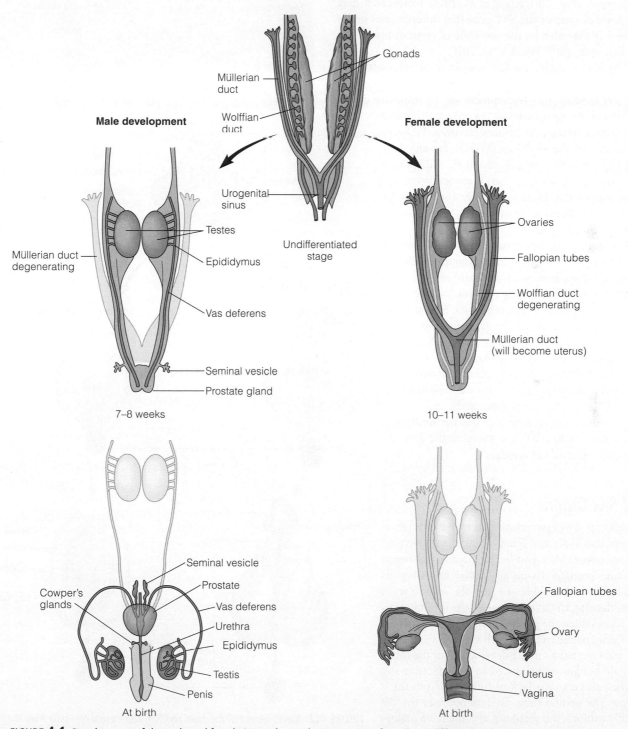

FIGURE **4.1** Development of the male and female internal reproductive systems from the undifferentiated stage.

Internal Sex Organs

In the first few weeks of development, XX (female) and XY (male) embryos are identical. Around the 5th to 6th week, the primitive gonads form; at this point, they can potentially develop into either **testes** or **ovaries**. Traditional developmental models claim that the "default" development is female; without the specific masculinizing signals sent by the Y chromosome and the SRY (sex-determining region Y) gene, the gonads will develop as female. The SRY is a Y chromosome–specific gene that plays a central role in sexual differentiation and development in males (DiNapoli & Capel, 2008; Ngun et al., 2011; Xiang et al., 2013). However, it may not be only **testosterone** or the SRY gene that differentiates males from females—it may also be the presence of ovarian hormones (Blecher & Erickson, 2007; Wu & Shah, 2011).

In most biological males, the testes begin to differentiate from the primitive gonad by the 7th to 8th week after conception. In most biological females, the development of the primitive gonad begins to differentiate into ovaries by the 10th or 11th week. The primitive duct system, the **Müllerian** (myul-EAR-ee-an) **duct** (female) or the **Wolffian** (WOOL-fee-an) **duct** (male), also appears at this time (Krone et al., 2007). Once the gonads have developed, they then hormonally control the development of the ducts into either the female or male reproductive system (we discuss these specific structures further in Chapters 5 and 6).

In female embryos, the lack of male hormones results in the disappearance of the Wolffian ducts, and the Müllerian duct fuses to form the uterus and inner third of the vagina. The unfused portion of the duct remains and develops into the two oviducts or Fallopian tubes (see Figure 4.1 on page 81.). In the presence of a Y chromosome, the gonads develop into testes, which soon begin producing **Müllerian inhibiting factor** and testosterone. Müllerian inhibiting factor causes the Müllerian ducts to disappear during the 3rd month, and testosterone stimulates the Wolffian duct to develop into the structures surrounding the testicles. The body converts some testosterone into another **androgen**, called *dihydrotestosterone* (DHT), to stimulate the development of the male external sex organs.

External Sex Organs

External genitals follow a pattern similar to that of internal organs, except that male and female genitalia all develop from the same tissue. Male and female organs that began from the same prenatal tissue are called **homologous** (HOE-mol-lig-gus; see Table 4.1 for an overview of homologous tissues). Until the 8th week, the undifferentiated tissue from which the genitalia will develop exists as a mound of skin, or tubercle, beneath the umbilical cord. In females, the external genitalia develop under the influence of female hormones produced by the placenta and by the mother, and also the lack of influence from the Y chromosome. The genital tubercle develops into the clitoris, the labia minora, the vestibule, and the labia majora (see Figure 4.2).

Table 4.1	Homologous Tissues
	Male and female organs that began from the same prenatal tissue are called homologous. Below are some of the homologous tissues.
Female	**Male**
Clitoral glans	Glans penis
Clitoral hood	Foreskin
Labia minora	Penile shaft
Labia majora	Scrotum
Ovaries	Testes

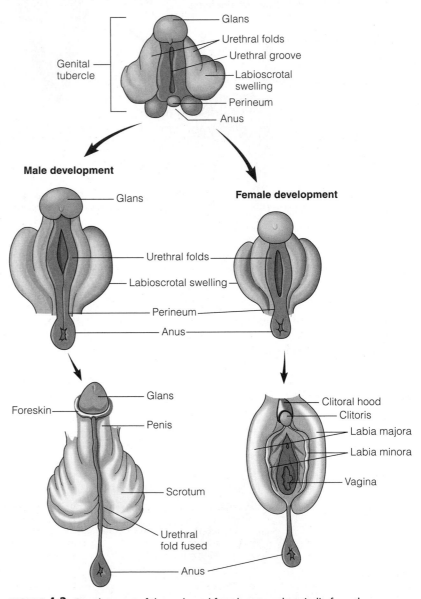

FIGURE **4.2** Development of the male and female external genitalia from the undifferentiated genital tubercle.

Table 4.2 The Sex Hormones

Hormone	Purposes
Androgens	A group of hormones that control male sexual development and include testosterone. Androgens stimulate the development of male sex organs and secondary sex characteristics such as beard growth and a deepening voice. Testosterone also plays an important part in stimulating sexual desire and is secreted by the testes in men and the ovaries in women. A small amount is also produced by the adrenal glands in both men and women.
Estrogens	A group of hormones that control female sexual development. Estrogen controls development of the female sex organs, the menstrual cycle, parts of pregnancy, and secondary sex characteristics such as breast development. The ovaries produce most of the estrogen in women, although the adrenal glands and the placenta also produce small amounts. Men also produce a small amount of estrogen in the testes.
Progesterone	A female hormone secreted by the ovaries. Progesterone helps to prepare the lining of the uterus for the implantation of the fertilized ovum, to stimulate milk production in the breasts, and to maintain the placenta. Progesterone works in conjunction with estrogen to prepare the female reproductive system for pregnancy.
Gonadotropin-releasing hormone (GnRH)	A hormone that affects the nervous system. It is produced in the hypothalamus of the brain. Gonadotropin means "gonad stimulating," and GnRH stimulates the release of hormones, which induce the ovaries and testes (as well as other glands) to secrete hormones.
Follicle-stimulating hormone (FSH)	A hormone released by the pituitary gland that stimulates the follicular development in females and the formation of sperm in males.
Luteinizing hormone (LH)	A hormone released by the pituitary gland that stimulates ovulation and the release of other hormones, notably progesterone in the female and testosterone in the male. It also stimulates the cells in the testes to produce testosterone.
Prolactin	A pituitary hormone that stimulates milk production after childbirth and also the production of progesterone.
Oxytocin	A pituitary hormone that stimulates the ejection of milk from the breasts and causes increased contractions of the uterus during labor.
Inhibin	A hormone produced by the cells of the testes that signals the anterior pituitary to decrease FSH production if the sperm count gets too high.

In males, by the 8th or 9th week, the testes begin androgen secretion, which begins to stimulate the development of male genitalia. The genital tubercle elongates to form the penis, in which lies the urethra, culminating in an external opening called the *urethral meatus*. Part of the tubercle also fuses together to form the scrotum, where the testicles will ultimately rest when they descend.

Hormonal Development and Influences

Hormones play an important role in human development. Table 4.2 lists the various sex hormones and the roles they play.

Endocrine glands, such as the gonads, secrete hormones directly into the bloodstream to be carried to the target organs. The ovaries, for example, produce the two major female hormones, estrogen and progesterone. **Estrogen** is an important influence in the development of female sexual characteristics throughout fetal development and later life, whereas **progesterone** regulates the menstrual cycle and prepares the uterus for pregnancy. The testicles produce androgens, which are quite important to the male, because even a genetically male embryo will develop female characteristics if androgens are not secreted at the right time or if the fetus is insensitive to androgens.

testes
Male gonads inside the scrotum that produce sperm and sex hormones.

ovaries
Female gonads that produce ova and sex hormones.

testosterone
A male sex hormone that is secreted by the Leydig cells of mature testes and produces

secondary sex characteristics in men.

Müllerian duct
One of a pair of ducts that develops in female embryos into the female reproductive system and regresses in male embryos.

Wolffian duct
One of a pair of ducts that develops in male embryos into the

male reproductive system and regresses in female embryos.

Müllerian inhibiting factor
A hormone secreted in male embryos that prevents the Müllerian duct from developing into female reproductive organs.

androgen
A hormone that promotes the development of male genitals and secondary sex

characteristics. It is produced by the testes in men and by the adrenal glands in both men and women.

homologous
Corresponding in structure, position, or origin but not necessarily in function.

endocrine gland
A gland that secretes hormones into the blood.

estrogen
A hormone that produces female secondary sex characteristics and affects the menstrual cycle. Men also produce a small amount of estrogen in the testes.

progesterone
A hormone that is produced by the ovaries and helps to regulate the menstrual cycle.

Brain Differentiation

Most hormonal secretions are regulated by the brain—in particular, by the hypothalamus, which is the body's single most important control center. Yet, hormones also affect the development of the brain itself, both in the uterus and after birth (Berenbaum & Beltz, 2011; Savic et al., 2010). Male and female brains have different tasks and thus undergo different development. For example, female brains control menstruation and, therefore, must signal the release of hormones in a monthly cycle, whereas male brains signal release continuously. With the brain, as with sexual organs, the presence of androgens during the appropriate critical stage of development may be the factor that programs the central nervous system to develop male sexual behaviors (Bocklandt & Vilain, 2007; Garcia-Falgueras & Swaab, 2010; Juntti et al., 2010). As we discussed earlier, sexual differentiation of the genitals begins early in a pregnancy, whereas sexual differentiation of the brain occurs much later in pregnancy.

Review Questions

1 Differentiate between sex and gender, and explain how the Bruce/Brenda case shed light on the nature versus nurture debate.

2 Describe sexual reproduction, and explain what happens after a sperm fertilizes an ovum.

3 Describe sexual differentiation in a developing fetus.

4 Explain the role that hormones and brain differentiation play in human development.

Differences in Sex Development

Prenatal development depends on carefully orchestrated developmental stages. At any stage, sex chromosome or hormone conditions can result in **disorders of sex development (DSD)**. There has been some controversy over the use of the DSD term, since it implies something is broken and/or in need of repair (González & Ludwikowski, 2016; Viloria, 2014). For this reason, we will refer to these conditions as *differences* in sex development. They are sometimes referred to as **intersex** (see the nearby "Sex in Real Life" for more information about intersex). It's likely discussions about terminology will continue in the future.

Children who are born with differences in sex development may have a variety of physical conditions, such as the **gonads** (testes or ovaries) of one sex but ambiguous external genitalia or the external genitals of one sex and the genetic makeup of the other sex. Although assigning a new term for these differences in the DSM has improved our understanding, it has also led to more questions (González & Ludwikowski, 2016; Topp, 2013; Viloria, 2014). Below we'll explore both chromosomal and hormones conditions that can contribute to DSD. Table 4.3 provides an overview of various DSD.

Chromosomal Conditions

Some differences in sex development can be caused by chromosomal conditions. Although medical researchers have identified more than 70 such conditions, we discuss here the three most common.

Klinefelter syndrome, the most common chromosomal condition in males, occurs when an ovum containing an extra X chromosome is fertilized by a Y sperm (designated XXY), giving a child 47 chromosomes (Herlihy & McLachlan, 2015). It is estimated that 1 in 500–600 males is born with an extra X chromosome (Defendi, 2016). In Klinefelter syndrome, the Y chromosome triggers the development of male genitalia, but the extra X prevents them from developing fully. As adults, men with Klinefelter syndrome typically have small testes, low levels of testosterone, **gynecomastia**, and possible learning disabilities (Skakkebaek et al., 2015). **Testosterone therapy**, especially if it is begun during adolescence, can enhance the development of **secondary sexual characteristics**. Although two thirds of men with Klinefelter syndrome are never diagnosed, those who are diagnosed are typically identified when they present during an evaluation for infertility (Herlihy & McLachlan, 2015). Men with Klinefelter syndrome

---

disorders of sex development (DSD)
DSM-5 term that refers to conditions that can result in a body that often cannot be easily categorized as male or female; in the past has been referred to as intersex, hermaphroditism, or pseudohermaphroditism. Often referred to as differences in sex development.

intersex
A term that is used for a variety of conditions that can lead to the development of reproductive or sexual anatomy that doesn't fit the typical definitions of female or male.

gonads
The male and female sex glands—ovaries and testes.

Klinefelter syndrome
A genetic condition in men in which there are three sex chromosomes, XXY, instead of two; characterized by small testes, low sperm production, breast enlargement, and absence of facial and body hair.

gynecomastia
Abnormal breast development in the male.

testosterone therapy
The use of testosterone to replace missing hormones in males with hormonal conditions.

secondary sexual characteristics
The physical characteristics, other than the genitalia, that distinguish males from females.

Table 4.3 Differences in Sex Development

Syndrome	Chromosomal Pattern	External Genitals	Internal Structures	Description	Possible Intervention
CHROMOSOMAL					
Klinefelter syndrome	47, XXY	Male	Male	Testes are small; breasts may develop; low testosterone levels, erectile dysfunction, and mental retardation are common; people with this disorder have unusual body proportions and are usually infertile.	Testosterone therapy during adolescence may enhance development of secondary sexual characteristics.
Turner syndrome	45, XO	Female	Uterus and oviducts	There is no menstruation or breast development; a broad chest with widely spaced nipples, loose skin around the neck, nonfunctioning ovaries, and infertility.	Androgens during puberty can help increase height, and estrogen and progesterone can enhance development of secondary sexual characteristics.
XYY syndrome	47, XYY	Male	Male	There is likelihood of slight mental retardation, some genital irregularities, and decreased fertility or infertility.	None.
Triple X syndrome	47, XXX	Female	Female	There is likelihood of slight mental retardation and decreased fertility or infertility.	None.
HORMONAL					
Congenital adrenal hyperplasia (CAH)	46, XX, XY	Some male and some female traits	Internal organs are consistent with biological gender	Little effect on developing male fetus and small effect on developing female fetus (such as an enlarged clitoris).	None.
Androgen-insensitivity syndrome (AIS)	46, XY	Female	Male gonads in the abdomen	Breasts develop at puberty, but menstruation does not begin. No internal reproductive organs except two testes, which remain in the abdomen.	Surgery can lengthen vagina to accommodate a penis for intercourse if necessary.

may still be able to father children through sperm retrieval (we will discuss assisted reproductive techniques in more detail in Chapter 12).

Turner syndrome is the most common chromosomal condition in women (Grynberg et al., 2016). It results from an ovum without any sex chromosome being fertilized by an X sperm (designated XO), which gives the child only 45 chromosomes altogether (if an ovum without a chromosome is fertilized by a Y sperm, and thus contains no X sex chromosome, it will not continue to develop). It is relatively rare, occurring in 1 out of 2,500 female births (Smith, 2016). The median age at which a young girl is diagnosed with Turner syndrome is about 6 to 7 years old, although some are not diagnosed until much later (Massa et al., 2005).

Although the external genitalia develop to look like a biological female's, the woman's ovaries do not develop fully, causing **amenorrhea** (aye-men-uh-REE-uh) and probable infertility. In addition, Turner syndrome is characterized by short stature, a relatively high-pitched voice, immature breast development, and abnormalities of certain internal organs (Fiot et al., 2016; Marques & Aires, 2015; Nadeem & Roche, 2014). Early diagnosis is important

Turner syndrome
A genetic condition in females in which there is only one X sex chromosome instead of two, characterized by lack of internal female sex organs, infertility, short stature, and mental retardation.

amenorrhea
The absence of menstruation.

because therapeutic administration of estrogen and progesterone during puberty can help enhance secondary sex characteristics and slightly increase height (Grynberg et al., 2016). Although the majority of girls with Turner syndrome will never undergo puberty, those who do may be capable of pregnancy. However, pregnancies in women with Turner syndrome have a high risk for chromosomal abnormalities and fetal loss. In adulthood, many women with Turner syndrome may experience diabetes, hypertension, bone thinning, and/or thyroid problems (Aversa et al., 2015; Folsom & Fuqua, 2015).

XYY syndrome and **triple X syndrome** are also rare conditions, affecting approximately 1 in 1,000 males and females. As the names imply, these conditions occur when a normal ovum is fertilized by a sperm that has two Y chromosomes or two X chromosomes, or when an ovum with two X chromosomes is fertilized by a normal X sperm. Although many individuals with XYY and XXX are often taller than average, there are few outwardly physical symptoms. As a result, their unusual genetic status is often not detected. Although they often have normal fertility, occasionally they experience communication problems and learning difficulties. A small percentage of XYY individuals develop autism spectrum disorders (Margari et al., 2014; Ross et al., 2015).

Hormonal Conditions

Differences in sex development can also be caused by hormonal conditions. In this section, we discuss two of the most common hormonal conditions, **congenital adrenal hyperplasia (CAH)** and **androgen-insensitivity syndrome (AIS)**.

Congenital adrenal hyperplasia (CAH) can occur in both males and females when they lack an enzyme in the adrenal gland, forcing the body to produce higher amounts of androgen. The excess androgens often have little effect on a developing male fetus and may have only a small effect, such as an enlarged clitoris, on a developing female fetus (Johannsen et al., 2010; Roan, 2010). Although CAH girls often have female internal gonads (uterus and ovaries), some experience menstrual irregularities and difficulties with vaginal penetration and/or maintaining pregnancies later in life (González & Ludwikowski, 2016). A similar

syndrome can also develop if the mother takes androgens or drugs with effects that mimic male hormones (a number of pregnant women were prescribed such drugs in the 1950s, resulting in a group of CAH infants born during that time). CAH is a rare condition, occurring in 1 in 15,000 infants, but it is one of the most common causes of ambiguous genitals in females (González & Ludwikowski, 2016). Because newborn screening for CAH is common today, most infants are diagnosed at birth (Auchus & Arlt, 2013).

Early androgen concentrations in CAH girls may affect childhood play and adult sexual orientation. Studies have found that CAH girls exhibit more tomboyism and have higher rates of bisexuality and homosexuality than non-CAH girls (González & Ludwikowski, 2016; Meyer-Bahlburg et al., 2008; Pasterski et al., 2005, 2007).

Androgen-insensitivity syndrome (AIS), also known as testicular feminization, is another hormonal condition that can cause DSD. AIS occurs when a genetic male (XY) is resistant to male hormones. Although a newborn child with AIS may be identified at birth as female based on external genitalia, usually the condition is first detected when a teenage girl fails to menstruate and chromosomal analysis reveals that she is XY. Approximately 1 in 20,000 infants are born each year with AIS (Mendoza & Motos, 2013; Oakes et al., 2008). In this syndrome, although the gonads develop into testes and produce testosterone normally, for some reason, the AIS individual's cells cannot absorb it; in other words, the testosterone is there but has no effect on the body. Because the Wolffian ducts did not respond to testosterone during the sexual differentiation phase, no male genitalia developed; however, because the gonads, which are male, did produce Müllerian inhibiting factor, the Müllerian ducts did not develop into normal female internal organs either. The AIS individual ends up with no internal reproductive organs except two testes, which remain in the abdomen producing testosterone that the body cannot use.

> **REAL RESEARCH** Bisphenol A (BPA), an endocrine-interrupting chemical found in certain plastics and resins that line food and beverage containers, has been found to disrupt the endocrine system and affect reproductive and sexual development in mice (CHRISTIANSEN ET AL., 2013). Since the Centers for Disease Control have found BPA in the urine of nearly all Americans tested for it, research is ongoing to evaluate the effects of BPA exposure in humans.

XYY syndrome
A genetic abnormality in which a male has an extra Y sex chromosome; characterized by decreased fertility, some genital abnormality, and slight mental retardation.

triple X syndrome
A genetic abnormality in which a female has an extra X sex chromosome; characterized by decreased fertility, some genital abnormality, and slight mental retardation.

congenital adrenal hyperplasia (CAH)
A condition involving overproduction of androgen in the adrenal glands that

can affect males and females. Females born with this condition frequently have masculinized genitals because of excess prenatal androgen exposure, whereas males typically experience early pubertal changes.

androgen-insensitivity syndrome (AIS)
A condition in which a male's cells are insensitive to androgens, resulting in the development of female external genitalia (but no internal reproductive organs).

The AIS infant has the "default" female genitals, but because the Müllerian ducts also form the last third of the vagina, the infant has only a very shallow vagina. Because males do produce a small amount of estrogen, the breasts develop at puberty but menstruation does not. As with the other DSD, experts agree that an AIS child and their family should decide the path they will take after diagnosis. Many continue to live as females and undergo hormone therapy or reconstructive surgery (Chen et al., 2015).

Now that we have discussed the various chromosomal and hormonal conditions that may affect sexual development, the important question becomes, What can a parent do after a child is born with a DSD? For many years, parents opted for immediate surgery to quickly assign their child's gender when they were

Sex in Real Life — What Is Intersex?

Intersex is a term used to refer to a variety of conditions in which a person is born with a reproductive or sexual anatomy that doesn't appear to fit the typical definition of male or female (these conditions are also referred to as disorders of sex development). Our biological sex is determined by several factors, including our sex chromosomes, sex hormones, gonads (ovaries or testes), and our internal and external reproductive anatomy. Most of the time these are congruent, for example, an XX female has estrogen, ovaries, a uterus, and a vagina. But it's possible that a person could be XX and have male gonads or be XY with a scrotum that has an opening that resembles female labia. Studies have found that approximately 1% of the human population is intersex (Joel, 2012).

Typically, medical doctors assign the sex of a child by the appearance of the child's genitals at birth. The presence of a penis indicates the baby is male and the absence of a penis indicates the baby is female. But these decisions are often arbitrary and medical decisions vary considerably. Some professionals believe that having "ambiguous" genitalia (genitals that don't clearly fit the male or female pattern, such as a very small penis or a large clitoris) qualifies for a diagnosis of intersex, while others believe the brain has to be exposed to a certain level of hormones in the womb before a child should receive a diagnosis of intersex. While many children are identified as having an intersex condition at birth, others aren't aware of the condition until they are older. Examples include a female teen who doesn't undergo the physical changes of puberty and finds out she lacks the necessary hormones, or a couple undergoing an infertility workup who find out the male partner has an extra X chromosome.

Intersex conditions include children born with genitals that cannot be classified as male or female or those who have an incomplete development of the internal or external reproductive organs. In addition, injuries caused by medical treatments, such as the case you read about in an earlier feature involving David Reimer, can also lead to intersex conditions.

In the past, doctors determined the best form of treatment for intersex children and parents were counseled on how to raise their children. Typically this involved concealing any information about gender from the child. Today many experts believe in the *patient-centered model,* which focuses on removing the shame and secrecy that surrounds intersex conditions. This model advocates a shame-free, open, and honest approach in which intersex children are assigned a gender after diagnostic workups without genital "normalizing" surgeries until the child is mature enough to make a decision for themselves (Intersexual Society of North America [ISNA], 2014).

born. However, medical experts today recommend, if there is no medical emergency, to wait until a child is old enough to consent to treatment (Mason, 2013; Wiesemann et al., 2010).

Gender Roles and Gender Traits

Gender stereotypes are fundamental to our ways of thinking, which makes it difficult to realize how thoroughly our conceptions of the world are shaped by gender issues. Today many parents have "gender reveal" parties to announce the sex of their fetus prior to their birth. When they are born, often the very first question asked is, "Is it a boy or a girl?" The parents proudly display a sign in their yard or send a card to friends, proclaiming "It's a girl!" or "It's a boy!" as the sole identifying trait of the child. The card does not state "It's a redhead!" From the moment of birth onward, the child is thought of first as male or female, and all other characteristics—whether the child is tall, bright, an artist, Irish, disabled, or gay—are seen in light of the person's gender.

We are so used to gender stereotypes that we may become uncomfortable when we aren't able to identify a person's gender. If you walked into class today and sat next to someone who you couldn't tell their gender, how would you feel? Most likely you'd search for gender clues. Often our need to categorize people by gender is taken for granted because it is something that our brains do automatically. Even our language is constructed around gender. Until recently, English had no neutral pronoun (neither do many other languages, including French, Spanish, German, and Italian), meaning that every time you refer to a person, you must write either "he" or "she." Today it is acceptable to use the singular "they" in place of "he" and "she."

Many of our basic assumptions about gender are open to dispute. Gender research has been growing explosively since the 1980s, and many of the results challenge long-held beliefs

ON YOUR MIND

It seems that the majority of heterosexual women want a guy who is tough, and they don't give the nice guys a chance. Straight guys, on the other hand, tend to look for attractive girls instead of thinking about how nice or intelligent the girls are. Why is this?

Men and women always seem to wonder why people of the other sex behave the way they do. Yet, society itself supports those kinds of behaviors. Is it really any surprise that men often seem to pursue appearance over substance in women when advertising, television, and women's and men's magazines all emphasize women's appearance? Is it surprising, conversely, that some women pursue the "tough guys" when society teaches them to admire male power? In the end, it is society that determines the way we view gender relationships, and each of us is responsible to some degree for continuing those attitudes.

about gender differences and gender roles. Gender roles are culturally defined behaviors that are seen as appropriate for men and women, including the attitudes, personality traits, emotions, and even postures and body language that are considered fundamental to being a man or a woman in this culture. Gender roles also extend into social behaviors, such as the occupations we choose, how we dress and wear our hair, how we talk (as we discussed in Chapter 3), and the ways in which we interact with others.

Note that by saying gender roles are culturally defined, we are suggesting that such differences are not primarily due to biological, physiological, or even psychological differences between men and women but, rather, to the ways in which we are taught to behave. Yet, many people believe that various gender differences in behavior may be biologically programmed. Who is correct?

Another way to ask the question is this: Which of our gender-specific behaviors are gender roles (i.e., culturally determined), and which are **gender traits** (innate or biologically determined)? If gender-specific behaviors are biologically determined, then they should remain constant in different societies; if they are social, then we should see very different gender roles in different societies. The majority of gender-specific behaviors, however, differ widely throughout the world and are determined primarily by culture.

Masculinity and Femininity

What is masculine? What is feminine? Not too long ago, the answers would have seemed quite obvious: Men naturally have masculine traits, meaning they are strong, stable, aggressive, competitive, self-reliant, and emotionally undemonstrative; women are naturally feminine, meaning they are intuitive, loving, nurturing, emotionally expressive, and gentle. Even today, many would agree that such traits describe the differences between the sexes. These gender stereotypes, however, are becoming less acceptable as our culture changes. **Masculinity** and **femininity** refer to the cluster of traits that society attributes to each gender.

Models of masculinity and femininity are changing rapidly in modern American society. It is not uncommon to see men sporting "man buns" or wearing eye liner or mascara, and to see women wearing buzzed haircuts on today's college campuses. Occupations have become less gender segregated, more women contribute the primary income in the household, and more men are stay-at-home dads. Yet, gender role change can also result in confusion, especially among older Americans. I'm sure your grandparents might not understand why a man might want to wear his hair in a bun or a woman would want to shave her hair off. Gender roles exist for many reasons, in part because they allow comfortable interaction between the sexes but also because they

It is common for young children to wear a variety of clothing types—including traditional feminine or masculine outfits. Dressing up is fun for many children and a healthy way for them to learn about and think about the world they live in.

establish power differences. If you know how you are expected to behave and what personality traits you are expected to assume in relation to the other sex, interactions between the sexes may go more smoothly.

We also learn about masculinity and femininity from our ethnic group's cultural heritage (M. Crawford, 2006). In the United States, studies have documented less gender role stereotyping among Blacks than among Whites. Overall, Blacks are less sex-role restricted than Whites and believe that they possess both masculine and feminine traits (Carter et al., 2009; Dade & Sloan, 2000; Hill, 2002; Leaper, 2000; Redway & Miville, 2013). In fact, Blacks often view others through a lens of age and competency before gender.

Are Gender Roles Innate?

As gender stereotypes evolve, a trait may no longer be seen as the exclusive domain of a single gender. For example, many people have been trying to change our current stereotypes of men as "unemotional" and women as "emotional." The constellation of traits that has been traditionally seen as masculine and feminine may be becoming less rigid. For many centuries, these types of gender traits were seen as innate, immutable, and part of the biological makeup of the sexes. Few scientists suggested

gender traits
Innate or biologically determined gender-specific behaviors.

masculinity
The traits of gender expression that society attributes to males.

femininity
The traits of gender expression that society attributes to females.

that the differences between men and women were primarily social; most believed that women and men were fundamentally different.

Not only did scientists believe that the differences in the sexes were innate, but they also believed that men were superior—having developed past the "emotional" nature of women (Gould, 1981). While science has moved forward, these outdated attitudes still exist, both subtly in cultures like our own and overtly in cultures where women are allowed few of the rights granted to men.

How many of our gender behaviors are innate, and how many are socially transmitted? The truth is that the world may not split that cleanly into innate versus social causes of behavior. Behaviors are complex and are almost always interactions between one's innate biological capacities and the environment in which one lives and acts. Behaviors that are considered innately "male" in one culture may be assumed to be innately "female" in another. Even when modern science suggests that a certain gender trait seems to be based on innate differences between the sexes, culture can contradict that trait or even deny it.

For example, most researchers accept the principle that males display more aggressive behavior than females; adult males certainly demonstrate this tendency, which may be the result, in part, of higher levels of testosterone. When female bodybuilders, for example, take steroids, they often find themselves acquiring male traits, including losing breast tissue, growing more body hair, and increased aggression. However, the difference is also demonstrated in early childhood, when boys are socialized to be more aggressive in play, whereas girls are socialized to be less aggressive.

Yet, Margaret Mead's (1935/1988/2001) famous discussion of the Tchambuli tribe of New Guinea shows that such traits need not determine gender roles. Among the Tchambulis, the women performed the "aggressive" occupations such as fishing, commerce, and politics, whereas the men were more sedentary and artistic and took more care of domestic life. The women assumed the dress appropriate for their activities—plain clothes and short hair—whereas the men dressed in bright colors. So even if we accept biological gender differences, societies such as the Tchambuli show that human culture can transcend biology.

Despite these cases, some gender differences are considered innate. Physically, males tend to be larger and stronger, with more of their body weight in muscle and less in body fat than females (Angier, 1999). Females, however, are born more neurologically advanced than males, and they mature faster. Females are also biologically heartier than males; more male fetuses miscarry, more males are stillborn, the male infant mortality rate is higher, males acquire more hereditary diseases and remain more susceptible to disease throughout life, and men die at younger ages than women (although the gender gap in mortality is smaller among the educated and economically advantaged segments of the U.S. population). Males are also more likely to have developmental conditions such as learning disabilities or autism (Baron-Cohen et al., 2011; Beacher et al., 2012; Bloom et al., 2012; Lai et al., 2013), whereas females have a higher prevalence of depression (Bjornelv et al., 2011; Silverstein et al., 2013). It has long been believed that males are better at mathematics and spatial problems, whereas females are better at verbal tasks; for example, female children learn language skills earlier than

males. Yet, many of these differences may be the result of socialization rather than biology (Hyde, 2014; Hyde & Mertz, 2008).

Boys and girls do show some behavioral differences that appear to be universal. For example, in a study of six cultures, Bea and John Whiting and their colleagues (Whiting & Edwards, 1988; Whiting & Whiting, 1975) discovered that certain traits seemed to characterize masculine and feminine behavior in 3- to 6-year-olds. In almost all countries, boys engaged in more rough-and-tumble play, and boys "dominated egoistically" (tried to control the situation through commands), whereas girls more often sought or offered physical contact, sought help, and "suggested responsibly" (dominated socially by invoking rules or appealing to greater good).

Interestingly, although their strategies are different, both boys and girls often pursue the same ends; for example, rough-and-tumble play among boys and initiation of physical contact among girls are both strategies for touching and being touched. However, the Whitings suggest that even these behaviors might be the result of different kinds of pressures put on boys and girls; for example, in their sample, older girls were expected to take care of young children more often than boys, and younger girls were given more responsibility than younger boys. These different expectations from each gender may explain later differences in their behaviors. Thus, even gender behaviors that are spread across cultures may not prove to be innate differences.

There is some evidence that biological men's and women's brains are different; autopsies have shown that men's brains are more asymmetrical than women's, and women seem to recover better from damage to the left hemisphere of the brain (as in strokes), where language is situated. In addition, studies on sex differences in human brain structure found differences in brain volume and connectivity (Ingalhalikar et al., 2013; Ruigrok et al., 2013). Yet, it has always been unclear what causes this and what facts such as these mean. Newer techniques in brain imaging have provided evidence that women's and men's brains not only differ in size, but that women and men use their brains differently during certain activities (DeBellis et al., 2001; Menzler et al., 2011; Sánchez & Vilain, 2010). For example, male brains tend to perform tasks predominantly using the left side, while female brains tend to use both sides.

However, a recent meta-analysis (a statistical procedure that combines data from multiple research studies) done at the Rosalind Franklin University of Medicine and Science in Chicago found no significant differences between male and female brains ("Mounting Challenge to Brain Differences," 2017). This large study supports the idea that there are more gender similarities in the human brain than differences.

Almost no differences between the sexes are universally accepted by researchers and, in fact, the majority of gender differences that have been found are small or very close to zero (Hyde, 2014). This does not mean that there are not other innate gender differences; we simply do not know for sure. Even if it turns out, for example, that female infants recognize faces earlier than males, as has been suggested, or that male children are more active than females, would that really account for the enormous gender role differences that have developed over time? Although biologists and other researchers still study innate differences between the sexes, today more attention is being paid to gender similarities.

Review Questions

1 Identify the chromosomal conditions that may result in differences of sex development.

2 Identify the hormonal conditions that may result in differences of sex development.

3 Differentiate between gender roles and gender traits, and explain how cross-cultural research helps us identify each.

4 Compare masculinity and femininity and explain how our ethnic groups' cultural heritage may affect these concepts.

5 Which gender behaviors/traits are considered to be innate?

6 Are any gender differences universal?

Gender Role Theory

In Chapter 2, we reviewed general theories of sexuality, and the debates there centered on how much of human sexuality is programmed through our genes and physiology, and how much is influenced by culture and environment. Gender role theory struggles with the same issues, and different theorists take different positions. Social learning theorists believe that we learn gender roles almost entirely from our environment, whereas cognitive development theorists believe that children go through a set series of stages that correspond to certain beliefs and attitudes about gender. In this section, we talk about evolutionary, social learning, cognitive development, and gender schema theories.

When babies are born, they possess no knowledge and few instinctual behaviors. However, by the time children are about age 3 or 4 years, they can usually talk, feed themselves, interact with adults, describe objects, and use correct facial expressions and body language. This process, whereby an infant who knows nothing becomes a preschooler who has the basic skills for functioning in society, is called **socialization**.

Socialization occurs at every age and level of development, and the same is true of gender role socialization. Many boys dress and act like other boys and play with traditionally male toys (guns, trucks), whereas many girls insist on wearing dresses and express a desire to do traditionally "female" things, such as playing with dolls and toy kitchens. Is this behavior innate, or are gender stereotypes still getting through to these children through television and in playing with their peers? Below are some theories on gender role development.

Evolutionary Theory: Adapting to Our Environment

Recently, we began to understand more about the innate differences between men and women through the field of evolutionary theory. Gender differences are seen as ways in which we have developed in our adaptation to our environment. For example, later in this book we explore how the double standard in sexual behavior developed, in which a man who hooks up with several partners was viewed as a "player," whereas a woman who does the same was viewed as a "slut." An evolutionary theorist would explain this gender difference in terms of the innate differences between men and women. A man can impregnate several women at any given time, but a woman, once pregnant, cannot become pregnant again until she gives birth. The time investment of these activities varies tremendously; the man has much less to lose. If evolutionary success is determined by how many offspring we have, then biological men have the advantage.

Social Learning Theory: Learning from Our Environment

Social learning theory suggests that we learn gender roles from our environment, from the same system of rewards and punishments that we learn our other social roles. For example, research shows that many parents commonly reward gender-appropriate behavior and disapprove of gender-inappropriate behavior. Telling a boy sternly not to cry "like a girl," approving a girl's use of makeup, taking a Barbie away from a boy and handing him Spider-Man, making girls help with cooking and cleaning and boys take out the trash—these little, everyday actions build into powerful messages about gender.

Children also learn to model their behavior after the same-gender parent to win parental approval. They may learn about gender-appropriate behavior from parents even if they are too young to perform the actions themselves; for example, they may see that their mom is more likely to make dinner, whereas their dad is more likely to pay the bills. Children also see models of the "appropriate" ways for their genders to behave in their books, on television, and when interacting with others. Even the structure of our language conveys gender attitudes about things, such as the dominant position of the male; for example, the use of male words to include men and women (using "freshman," "chairman," or "mankind" to refer to men and women), or the differentiation between Miss and Mrs. to indicate whether a woman is married. However, people are trying to amend these inequalities today, as evidenced by the growing acceptance of words such as "chairperson" and "humankind," along with the gender neutral option of "Mx."

---

socialization
The process in which an infant is taught the basic skills for functioning in society.

Cognitive Development Theory: Age-Stage Learning

Cognitive development theory assumes that all children go through a universal pattern of development, and there really is not much parents can do to alter it. As children's brains mature and grow, they develop new abilities and concerns; at each stage, their understanding of gender changes in predictable ways. This theory follows the ideas of Piaget (1951), the child development theorist who suggested that social attitudes in children are mediated through their processes of cognitive development. In other words, children can process only a certain kind and amount of information at each developmental stage.

As children begin to be able to recognize the physical differences between girls and boys, and then to categorize themselves as one or the other, they look for information about their genders. Around the ages of 2 to 5, they form strict stereotypes of gender based on their observed differences: Men are often bigger and stronger and are seen in more aggressive roles such as policeman and superhero; women tend to be associated with motherhood through their roles of nurturing and emotional expressiveness. These "physicalistic" thought patterns are universal in young children and are organized around ideas of gender.

As children mature, they become more aware that gender roles are, to some degree, social and arbitrary, and cognitive development theory predicts, therefore, that rigid gender role behavior should decrease after about the age of 7 or 8. So cognitive development theory predicts what set of gender attitudes should appear at different ages; however, the research is still contradictory on whether its predictions are correct (see Albert & Porter, 1988).

Newer theories of gender role development try to combine social learning theory and cognitive development theory to address weaknesses in both. Cognitive development theory neglects social factors and differences in the ways different groups raise children. On the other hand, social learning theory neglects a child's age-related ability to understand and assimilate gender models, and portrays children as too passive. In social learning theory, children seem to accept whatever models of behavior are offered without passing them through their own thought processes.

Gender Schema Theory: Our Cultural Maps

Sandra Bem's (1974, 1977, 1981) theory is a good example of a theory that tries to overcome the difficulties posed by the other theories. According to Bem, children (and, for that matter, all of us) think according to **schemas** (SKI-muz), which are cognitive mechanisms that organize our world. These schemas develop over time and are universal, like the stages in cognitive development theory; the difference lies in Bem's assertion that the contents of schemas are determined by the culture. Schemas are like maps in our heads that direct our thought processes.

Bem suggests that one schema we all have is a **gender schema**, which organizes our thinking about gender. From the moment we are born, information about gender is continuously presented to us by our parents, relatives, teachers, peers, television, movies, advertising, and the like. We absorb the more obvious information about sexual anatomy, "male" and "female" types of work and activities, and gender-linked personality traits. However, society also attributes gender to things as abstract as shapes (rounded, soft shapes are often described as "feminine," and sharp, angular shapes as "masculine") and even our drinks (wine is seen as more feminine, whereas beer is seen as more masculine; Crawford et al., 2004).

Gender schemas are powerful in our culture. When we first meet a man, we immediately use our masculine gender schema and begin our relationship with an already established series of beliefs about him. For example, we may believe that men are strong or assertive. Our gender schema is more powerful than other schemas and is used more often, Bem argues, because our culture puts so much emphasis on gender and gender differences. This is where she parts company with cognitive development theorists, who argue that gender is important to children because of their naturally physicalistic ways of thinking.

The gender schema becomes so ingrained that we do not even realize its power. For example, some people so stereotype gender concepts that it would never occur to them to say, "My, how strong you are becoming!" to a little girl, whereas they say it easily to a little boy. Bem argues that "strong" as a feminine trait does not exist in the female schema for many people, so they rarely invoke the term to refer to women.

---

schemas
Cognitive mechanisms that help to organize information.

gender schema
A cognitive mechanism that helps us to understand gender roles.

Review Questions

1 Explain how gender role socialization occurs in children.

2 Describe the differences among the evolutionary, social learning, and cognitive development theories.

3 Explain how one's development of a "gender schema" influences their view of gender. Give examples to support your answer.

Varieties of Gender

Culture and social structure interact to create **sex typing**, a way of thinking that splits the world into two basic categories—male and female—and suggests that most behaviors, thoughts, actions, professions, emotions, and so on fit one gender more than the other (Eliot, 2009; Liben & Bigler, 2002; Maccoby, 2002). This relates to the earlier discussion about the traditional view of gender as a binary rather than a spectrum, which we will explore more in the next section. Although there are fewer sex-typed assignments and attitudes today than there were years ago, sex typing still exists.

These stereotypes become so basic to our way of thinking that we do not even realize the powerful hold they have over our conceptions of the world. Many cultures build their entire worldviews around masculinity and femininity. Some cultures have taken these ideas and created models of the universe based on masculine and feminine traits, such as the Chinese concept of yin and yang, which we discussed in Chapter 1.

Because gender is socially constructed, societies decide how gender will be defined and what it will mean. J. E. Williams and Best (1994) collected data about masculinity and femininity in 30 countries and found that throughout the world, people largely agree on gender role stereotypes. In a study of 37 countries, Buss (1994) found that women and men value different qualities in each other. Women place a higher value on the qualities of being "good financial prospects" and "ambitious and industrious" for their mates, whereas men place a higher value on physical attractiveness.

In American society, conceptions of "masculinity" and "femininity" have been seen as mutually exclusive; that is, a person who is feminine cannot also be masculine and vice versa (Spence, 1984). However, research has shown that masculinity and femininity are independent traits that can exist in people separately (Bem, 1977; Spence, 1984). Bem (1974) suggests that this can lead to four types of personalities: those high in masculinity and low in femininity, those high in femininity and low in masculinity, those low in both ("undifferentiated"), and those high in both ("androgynous," a topic we will discuss later in this chapter). Such categories may challenge traditional thinking about gender. In fact, the more one examines the categories of gender that really exist in the social world, the clearer it becomes that gender is more complicated than just splitting the world into male and female.

Masculinity: The Hunter

From the moment of a baby's birth, almost every society has different expectations of its males and females. In many societies, men must go through trials or rites of passage in which they earn their right to be men; few societies have such trials for women. For example, the !Kung bushmen have a "rite of the first kill" that is performed twice for each boy—once after he kills his first large male animal and once after he kills his first large female animal (Collier & Rosaldo, 1981). During the ceremony, a gash is cut in the boy's chest and filled with a magical substance that is supposed to keep the boy from being lazy. Hunting prowess is ritually connected with marriage, and men acquire wives by demonstrating their ability at the hunt (Lewin, 1988). For example, a boy may not marry until he goes through the rite of first kill, and at the wedding, he must present to his bride's parents a large animal he has killed. Even the language of killing and marrying is linked; !Kung myths and games equate marriage with hunting and talk of men "chasing," "killing," and "eating" women just as they do animals.

In American society, men are often judged by their "prowess" in business, with successful men receiving society's admiration. Although in many societies men tend to have privileges that women do not, and despite the fact that male traits in many societies are valued more than female traits (which we discuss in further detail soon), it is not easy for men to live up to the strong social demands of being male in a changing society.

Great contradictions are inherent in the contemporary masculine role: The man is supposed to be the provider and yet is not supposed to live entirely for his work; he is supposed to be a strong, stable force, yet not cut his emotions off from his loved ones; and he is never supposed to be scared, inadequate, sexually inexperienced, or financially dependent on a woman. Men in all societies live with these types of gender role contradictions. In some cases, men simplify their lives by exaggerating the "macho" side of society's expectations and becoming hypermasculine males (Ben-Zeev et al., 2012). To these macho men, violence is manly, danger is exciting, and sexuality must be pursued callously.

David Gilmore (1990) believes there is an evolutionary purpose behind masculine socialization. In most societies, masculine socialization prepares men to adopt the role of safeguarding the group's survival, to be willing to give their own lives in the hunt or in war to ensure the group's future by protecting women's ability to reproduce. Gilmore's point is that men are not concerned with being macho as an end in itself, but are concerned with the ultimate welfare of society. In fact, Gilmore argues, men are as much nurturers as women, concerned with society's weaker and more helpless members, willing to give their energy and even their lives for the greater social good.

Although masculinity has its privileges, it has its downside, too. Men do not live as long as women, in part because of the demands of the male role. For example, men are more likely to die of stress-related illnesses, including lung cancer (men smoke more than women), motor vehicle accidents, suicide (women attempt suicide more often, but men are more successful at actually killing themselves), other accidents, and cirrhosis of the liver (there are more male alcoholics and drug addicts; Courtenay, 2000; Crosby et al., 2011; D. R. Nicholas, 2000).

In fact, with all the attention on how gender stereotypes harm women, men are equally the victims of society's expectations. Male stereotypes tend to be narrower than female stereotypes, and men who want to conform to society's ideas of gender have less flexibility in their behavior than women (Lips, 2008). For example, it is still unacceptable for men to cry in public except in the most extreme circumstances. Crying is the body's natural response to being upset. Boys are taught not to cry, but that is difficult when they are emotionally moved; so they stop allowing themselves to be moved

---

sex typing
A cognitive thinking pattern that divides the world into male and female categories and suggests the appropriate behaviors, thoughts, actions, professions, and emotions for each.

emotionally—and then are criticized for not letting their emotions show (Chaplin & Aldao, 2013; Jellesma & Vingerhoets, 2012).

Femininity: The Nurturer

When someone says, "She is very feminine," what image comes to mind? A beautiful woman wearing a pink dress? A mother caring for her child? In American culture, we associate femininity with qualities such as beauty, softness, empathy, concern, and modesty. In fact, in almost every culture, femininity is defined by being the opposite of masculinity.

On the other hand, ideas of femininity are not static. Sheila Rothman (1978) has argued that American society has gone through a number of basic conceptions of what "womanhood" (and, by extension, femininity) should be. For example, the 19th century emphasized the value of "virtuous womanhood," whereby women instilled "morality" in society by starting women's clubs that brought women together and eventually led to the battling of perceived social ills. The Women's Christian Temperance Union, for example, started a movement to ban alcohol that eventually succeeded.

By the early part of the 20th century, the concept of the ideal woman shifted to what Rothman calls "educated motherhood," whereby the woman was supposed to learn all the new, sophisticated theories of child rearing and was to shift her attention to the needs of children and family. Over the next few decades, the woman's role was redefined as a "wife–companion," and she was supposed to redirect her energy away from her children and toward being a sexual companion for her husband. Finally, Rothman argues, the 1960s began the era of "woman as person," in which a woman began to be seen as autonomous and competent, and able to decide the nature of her own role in life independent of gender expectations.

Among feminist scholars, ideological battles rage about the meaning of being a woman in today's society. For example, many have faulted feminism for its attitude, at least until recently, that women who choose to stay in the home and raise children are not fulfilling their potential. Yet, women with young children who do

work often report feelings of guilt about not being with their children (Bingham, 2014). Many argue that the idea of femininity itself is an attempt to mold women in ways that are determined by men. The media reinforce the ideals of feminine beauty, and the pressures on women to conform to these ideals lead to eating disorders and the surge in cosmetic surgery, especially among White women (Miller et al., 2000). We further discuss the powerful influences of the media in Chapter 18.

Androgyny: Feminine and Masculine

Up until the 1970s, masculinity and femininity were thought to be on the same continuum. The more masculine you were, the less feminine you were, and vice versa. However, in the 1970s, researchers challenged this notion by suggesting that masculinity and femininity were two separate dimensions and a person could be high or low on both dimensions.

The breakdown of traditional stereotypes about gender has refocused attention on the idea of **androgyny**. Bem (1977), as we mentioned earlier, suggested that people have different combinations of masculine and feminine traits. She considered those who had a high score on both masculinity and femininity to be androgynous. Androgyny, according to Bem, allows greater flexibility in behavior because people have a greater repertoire of possible reactions to a situation. Bem (1974, 1977, 1981) has tried to show that androgynous individuals can display "masculine" traits (such as independence) and "feminine" traits (such as gentleness) when situations call for them.

Because of Bem's early research on masculinity, femininity, and androgyny, some have suggested that androgyny was a desirable state and androgynous attitudes were a solution to the tension between the sexes. There has been more research on gender roles and androgyny since, and androgyny may not be the answer to the world's gender problems. Suggesting that people should combine aspects of masculinity and femininity may simply reinforce and retain outdated ideas of gender. It's also important to point out that although androgyny is often favored for women, men are often viewed as feminine, rather than androgynous, and punished accordingly (Green, 2017).

Later research questioned whether the masculine and feminine traits that Bem used were still valid nearly 30 years later. One study found that, although 18 of 20 feminine traits still qualified as feminine, only 8 of 20 masculine traits qualified as strictly masculine (Auster & Ohm, 2000). Traits originally associated with masculinity, such as analytical, individualistic, competitive, self-sufficient, risk taking, and defends own beliefs, were no longer viewed as only masculine traits. These findings reflect recent societal changes that render some masculine traits desirable for both men and women.

The Gender Spectrum

In Western culture, the **gender binary** has traditionally divided people into two categories—male and female. As we discussed in the earlier "Sex in Real Life" feature, genital anatomy is often

Traditional gender roles often contribute to men being judged by how well they do at work, whereas women are judged by how attractive and thin they are.

androgyny
A gender expression that has high levels of both traditionally masculine and feminine behaviors.

gender binary
The classification of sex and gender into two distinct, opposite, and disconnected forms of male and female.

used at birth (and even before birth) to determine biological sex. John Money, whom we discussed earlier in this chapter, suggested that the majority of people are "gender congruent," which means that their biological sex, gender identity, and gender expression all "match" and their sexual orientation is heterosexual (Money, 1955). In his view, an XY male is a man; he acts masculine, and he is sexually attracted to women.

Today, we know that gender is much more complicated than Money proposed. The sex that we are assigned at birth, our gender identity and gender expression all intersect, creating a multidimensional **gender spectrum**. One person can be born female (XX), identify as a woman, act feminine, and be sexually attracted to men, whereas another can be born female (XX), identify as a woman, act masculine, and be sexually attracted to both men and women. Although the term **transsexualism** has been used in the past to describe a person whose experiences an incongruence between their sex assigned at birth and their gender identity, this is considered an outdated term today.

A person is considered cisgender when their gender identity is congruent with their sex assigned at birth. It's estimated that 99% of the population is cisgender. A transgender person has a gender identity that does not match their sex assigned at birth. Current statistics indicate that about .6% (or 1.4 million) people identify as transgender, though due to the limitations in research, it is likely this number is much higher.

Transgender is an adjective that is used to describe an individual or group of people who have a different personal history with gender than someone whose gender identity matches their sex assigned at birth (i.e., cisgender; may also be referred to as **gender diverse**). In some ways, the term *transgender* is used as an umbrella term to refer to anyone whose gender identity does not match their sex assigned at birth. The most commonly used terms under this umbrella are **transgender woman** (which refers to a woman who was assigned male at birth) and **transgender man** (which refers to a man who was assigned female at birth).

There are other transgender people whose gender identities do not easily fall into the distinct categories of "man" or "woman." This

Several colleges and universities offer pronoun buttons on their campuses today to create a more welcoming and inclusive environment. Wearing these buttons reduces the chances of being disrespectful and misgendering someone.

is referred to as having a non-binary gender identity. *Non-binary* is also an umbrella term, and there are many terms that fall under this category, for example, **agender**, **bigender**, **pangender**, and gender fluid. The terms **queer** and genderqueer have become umbrella terms that refer to a range of different sexual orientations, gender behaviors, or ideologies. Typically, individuals who identify as queer or genderqueer reject traditional gender roles and believe that gender fluidity allows them a more flexible range of gender expression. It's important to point out that transgender terminology is complex and changes relatively quickly (Green & Maurer, 2015).

Today experts may recommend the use of reversible hormone-blocking intervention to delay puberty in children who are experiencing **gender dysphoria** (dis-FOR-ee-uh; Vrouenraets et al., 2016). These medications enable a child to continue growing without developing the irreversible physical characteristics of a specific biological gender (such as breasts, facial hair, or Adam's apple). When the child is ready, they can elect to either stop the medications and resume natural pubertal development or begin **medical transition** by taking cross-sex hormones. We will discuss puberty delay drugs more in Chapter 8.

---

gender spectrum
The continuum of possibilities of biological gender, gender identity, gender expression, and sexual orientation.

transsexualism
An older term that used to refer to a transgender person who has had hormonal or surgical interventions to change their bodies to be more aligned with their gender identity than the sex that they were assigned at birth.

gender diverse
An individual whose gender identity or gender expression lies outside of the socially accepted gender norms.

transgender woman
A woman who was assigned male at birth.

transgender man
A man who was assigned female at birth.

agender
Not having a gender identity.

bigender
Identifying as both a man and a woman.

pangender
Identifying as a person instead of a gender.

gender dysphoria
A formal diagnosis in the *DSM-5* used by psychologists and medical personnel to indicate that a person feels extreme confusion and/or discomfort between their sex assigned at birth and their gender identity. This diagnosis often meets the criteria to pursue medical transition.

medical transition
The process of using hormones or surgeries to bring one's body in line with their gender identity.

Transparent is an award-winning comedy-drama television show that explores one family's reaction to the discovery that their father is transgender. Shows like this increase transgender visibility in the media.

Sexual Diversity
IN OUR WORLD

Transgender People in Iran[1]

Homosexual relationships were banned in Iran for many years, and since transgender people were thought to be homosexual, they were not accepted. They were imprisoned, beaten, and even stoned to death. However, in 2008 Iran had one of the highest rates of sex change operations in the world (Barford, 2008). It took the bravery of one woman to change things.

For most of Maryann Khatoon Molkara's life, she knew she was a woman, even though she was born male and given a male name. Maryann had experienced years of bullying and harassment and was fired from her job, injected with male hormones, and institutionalized. Knowing the only way to begin to change attitudes about transgenderism and sexual reassignment surgery was to get the Ayatollah Khomeini to issue a statement, Maryann began writing him letters in 1975. She never received a response. Her luck changed during the mid-1980s when she was a volunteer helping to care for wounded soldiers during the Iran–Iraq war. One of her pa-

Kaveh Kazemi/Getty Images

tients was a high-ranking government worker who helped her secure a meeting with top officials. However, getting to Khomeini required her to break into a heavily guarded compound. She did this wearing a man's suit

and carrying a copy of the Quran, but she was quickly surrounded by guards and severely beaten. Hassan Pasandide, Khomeini's brother, intervened and brought her to see the Ayatollah. At first the guards and officers were fearful that Maryann was carrying explosives because they could tell she had tape around her chest. When she removed the tape, she revealed female breasts. After a long talk with the Ayatollah, a *fatwa* (a religious or legal decree) was issued in support of sexual reassignment surgery. The *fatwa* gave her religious authorization to undergo sexual reassignment surgery.

Sexual reassignment surgery has been legal in Iran since 1983. Today, many transgender people travel to Iran from Eastern European and Arab countries for medical transitions. Maryann continues her work fighting for transgender rights and today runs Iran's leading transgender campaign group.

[1]The information in this feature was gathered from Barford (2008), Kamali (2010), McDowall and Kahn (2004), and Tait (2005).

As we have been discussing, there has been growing acceptance for transgender people in the United States in the past few years. Television shows such as *Doubt, Orange Is the New Black, Transparent,* and *I Am Jazz* have all had transgender characters or people in their shows. Even with this increased acceptance, however, many transgender people experience extensive discrimination or prejudice, known as anti-transgender prejudice, which is also sometimes referred to as **transphobia.**

Transgender People in History

In 1952, after a lifetime of desiring to be a woman, Christine Jorgensen, a retired Marine, went to Denmark to have her genitals surgically altered to be more congruent with her identity as a woman (Jorgensen, 1967). In doing so, Christine was one of the first transgender women to undergo medical transition (although this has been referred to as **sex reassignment surgery [SRS]** in the past, today this medical term is less popular in the United States mostly because it overemphasizes the physical transition instead of affirming a person's gender identity; Green & Mauer, 2015). The United States and international media quickly found out about Jorgensen's story, and she was **outed** and soon became the subject of intense scrutiny and fascination. Christine was regularly denied employment because she was transgender, and she was forced to sell her story to the media to make money to survive.

Another famous case was that of Renée Richards, a transgender woman who was an eye doctor and tennis player. After her

medical transition in the 1970s, she tried to play in a professional women's tennis tournament, but when it was discovered that she was a born a male, Richards was barred from playing on the women's tennis tour. She later disputed the ban and the New York Supreme Court ruled in her favor, allowing her to play. You might also remember the tragic story of Brandon Teena, a transgender man, who was raped and murdered in Nebraska in 1993. His life and death were the subject of the 1999 film, *Boys Don't Cry.*

Medical Transition

A transgender person may seek out hormonal or **gender affirmation** or **confirmation surgery** to align their physical body with their gender identity. As we have been discussing, many transgender men and women feel confident and comfortable about their biological sex and gender identity without medical interventions.

---

transphobia
Negative attitudes, behaviors, or discrimination against transgender people (also referred to as anti-transgender prejudice).

sex reassignment surgery (SRS)
Used by some medical professionals to refer to a group of surgical options that alter a person's biological sex; also referred to as *gender-affirmation* or *gender-confirmation surgery.*

outed
Being found out and exposed, usually with respect to gender or sexual orientation, against one's will.

gender affirmation or gender confirmation surgery
Medical gender transition; used to be called sexual reassignment surgery.

Although in the United States state laws govern the requirements for changing gender, some states may require surgery or medical interventions in order to amend a birth certificate. In 2014, the American Medical Association adopted a new policy supporting the elimination of surgery to change a birth certificate ("AMA Calls for Modernizing," 2014). The World Professional Association for Transgender Health (WPATH) also opposes surgery as a prerequisite to changing gender. WPATH has proposed "Standards of Care" that outline protocols and treatments for those seeking gender reassignment. Around the world, these guidelines have helped transgender people obtain access to safe and legal care.

Transgender men have been assigned female at birth but identify as male, whereas transgender women are assigned male at birth but identify as female. A variety of medical options are available, and although some transgender people proceed through all the stages to eventual surgery, many do not. Treatment often begins with psychotherapy, which helps explore options, establish realistic life goals, and identify points of conflict that have been interfering with life happiness. They may be encouraged to take on the role of the desired gender, through cross-dressing, hair removal, body padding, vocal training, or various other behaviors. A "real-life test" enables them to live as the desired gender and understand the effects that changing gender will have on their work, home, and personal relationships.

For some transgender people, the next step typically involves cross-sex hormone therapy, in which androgens are given to transgender men and estrogens (and possibly testosterone-blockers) are given to transgender women. Taking these drugs significantly changes the physical appearance of a man or woman, typically within about 2 years. However, there are several risks to these drugs, especially for those with chronic health problems or those who are obese or smoke cigarettes.

Transgender women who take estrogens (and possibly testosterone-blockers) will develop breasts, a redistribution of body fat, decreased upper body strength, a softening of the skin, a decrease in body hair, a slowing or stopping of hair loss in the scalp, decreased testicular size, and fewer erections (World Professional Association for Transgender Health, 2001). However, if the drugs were stopped, most of these effects would be reversible, with the exception of the breast tissue. Transgender men who take testosterone will develop several permanent changes, including a deeper voice, clitoral enlargement, increased facial and body hair, and possible baldness (World Professional Association for Transgender Health, 2001). They may also experience several reversible changes including increased sexual interest, upper body strength,

weight gain, and a redistribution of body fat (World Professional Association for Transgender Health, 2001). For some transgender people, these changes are enough and they do not feel the need to undergo additional medical interventions.

Although hormonal therapy may produce adequate breast tissue in some transgender women, others may desire additional breast augmentation surgery. Transgender men often undergo breast reduction or chest surgery. Although many different genital surgical options are available, it is important to point out that not every transgender person desires genital surgery. Some might not be able to afford it, others might not be happy with the options available, and still others might be content with the results of hormonal treatments.

If a person proceeds to genital surgeries, transgender women's genital surgeries include **penectomy**, **orchiectomy**, urethral rerouting (to allow for urination through the shorter urethra), or **vaginoplasty**. Transgender men's genital surgeries include **hysterectomy**, urethral rerouting (to allow for urination through the end of the reconstructed penis), **scrotoplasty**, **metoidioplasty**, or **phalloplasty**.

For transgender men, the most popular option today is a clitoral release procedure called metoidioplasty (Djordjevic et al., 2009; Gibson, 2010). Transgender men who undergo testosterone therapy

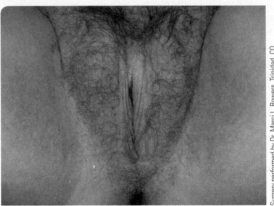

Surgery performed by Dr. Marci L. Bowers, Trinidad, CO.

Surgery performed by Dr. Toby R. Meltzer, Scottsdale, AZ

Some transgender people undergo gender affirmation/confirmation surgery. Above is a completed vaginoplasty on a transwoman and a completed phalloplasty on a transman.

penectomy
Removal of the penis.

orchiectomy
Removal of the testes.

vaginoplasty
Reconstructive surgery procedure used for the construction of the labia and vaginal canal.

hysterectomy
A surgical operation to remove all or part of the uterus.

scrotoplasty
Reconstructive surgery procedure in which a scrotum is made; silicone implants may be placed in the scrotum.

metoidioplasty
A clitoral release procedure used in medical transition in which the enlarged clitoris is released from its position and moved forward to more closely resemble the position of a penis.

phalloplasty
Reconstructive surgical procedure used for the construction of a penis.

typically experience clitoris elongation anywhere from 1 to 3 inches in length. A metoidioplasty releases the enlarged clitoris, allowing it to hang like a natural penis. Another surgical option, phalloplasty, involves constructing an artificial penis from abdominal skin. Phalloplasty is a difficult procedure and, as a result, is much less popular today. Penises made from phalloplasty cannot achieve a natural erection, so penile implants of some kind are usually used (we will discuss these implants in more detail in Chapter 14). Overall, metoidioplasty is a simpler procedure than phalloplasty, which explains its popularity. It also has fewer complications, takes less time, and is less expensive (e.g., a metoidioplasty takes about 1 to 2 hours and can cost around $15,000 to $20,000, whereas a phalloplasty can take about 8 hours and cost more than $65,000).

Over the years, gender affirmation/confirmation surgery has been relatively controversial, with some studies showing healthy postoperative functioning (DeCuypere et al., 2005; Johansson et al., 2010; Klein & Gorzalka, 2009; Lawrence, 2006) and other studies showing no alleviation of the psychological suffering (Dhejne et al., 2011; Newfield et al., 2006; Olsson & Möller, 2006). Even so, some transgender people seeking medical intervention have longed for years to bring their bodies into line with their sense of gender identity, and gender affirmation/confirmation surgery is their ultimate goal.

Gender Diversity in Other Cultures

Outside the United States, transgender people experience varying degrees of acceptance. Whereas Iran officially recognized transsexualism in the mid-1980s and began allowing medical transition shortly after (Harrison, 2005; see accompanying "Sexual Diversity in Our World"), Japan has been more reluctant to deal with transgender issues. Although sexual reassignment surgery was approved in Japan in 1997 and the first surgery was done in 1998, there are few institutions offering it today (Ako et al., 2001; Masumori, 2012; Matsubara, 2001; Nagai, 2013). In many Caribbean islands, transgender people are often ridiculed, assaulted, and forced to pretend they are cisgender (Bellot, 2015). For safety, many leave their countries and live elsewhere.

Some cultures challenge our notions of gender and even have a gender category that encompasses both aspects of gender. **Two-spirits** have been found in many cultures throughout the world, including American Indian, Indian, and Filipino cultures.

A two-spirit was usually (but not always) a biological male who was effeminate or androgynous in behavior and who took on the social role of a female (Blackwood, 1984; Jacobs et al., 1997; W. L. Williams, 1986). Being a two-spirit was considered a vocation, like being a hunter or warrior, which was communicated to certain boys in their first adult vision. In all social functions, the two-spirit was treated as a female. The two-spirit held a respected, sacred position in society and was believed to have special powers.

Two-spirits
A person who adopts some combination of gender identity, dress, and social roles in some cultures.

Biologically female two-spirits also lived in Native American tribes. Female two-spirits began showing interest in boys' activities and games during childhood (Blackwood, 1984; Jacobs et al., 1997). Adults, recognizing this desire, would teach the girls the same skills the boys were learning. (In one tribe, a family with all girl children might select one daughter to be their "son," tying dried bear ovaries to her belt to prevent conception!)

These females were initiated into puberty as men, and thereafter they were essentially considered men. They hunted and trapped, fought in battle, and performed male ceremonial tasks. Among the Alaskan Ingalik, for example, these biological women would even participate in nude, men-only sweat baths, and the men would ignore the female genitalia and treat the two-spirit as a man. The female two-spirit could marry a woman, although the unions remained childless, and the two-spirit would perform the appropriate rituals when her partner menstruated but would ignore her own menses. Female two-spirits became prominent members of some Native American societies.

Other cultures have similar roles. The Persian Gulf country of Oman has a class of biological males called the *xani-th* (Wikan, 1977). The *xani-th* are exempt from the strict Islamic rules that restrict men's interaction with women because they are not considered men. They sit with females at weddings and may see the bride's face; they may not sit with men in public or do tasks reserved for men. Yet, the *xani-th* are not considered females either; for example, they retain men's names.

Another important example is the *hijra* of India. The *hijra* are men who undergo ritual castration in which all or part of their genitals are removed, and they are believed to have special powers to curse or bless male children. *Hijra* dress as women, although they do not really try to "pass" as women; their mannerisms are exaggerated, and some even sport facial hair. In India, the *hijra* are considered neither men nor women but inhabit a unique third social gender (Nanda, 2001).

In Thailand, there is a group of people called the *kathoey,* who are similar to Oman's *xani-th.* Two other examples are the *aikane* of native Hawaii, who were attached to the court of the chiefs and served sexual, social, and political functions (Morris, 1990), and the *mahu* of Tahiti (Herdt & Stoller, 1990). The belief in these societies that it is neither obvious nor natural that there are only two genders should make us carefully reconsider our own assumptions about gender.

ON YOUR MIND

I don't think there is anything wrong with letting kids act like boys and girls! Why try to discourage boys from playing with guns and girls with dolls? Everyone I know grew up that way, and they are OK.

Perhaps we should not forbid boys from ever playing with toy guns (anyway, they would probably just make other toys into guns) or forbid girls to play with dolls, but trying to encourage children to appreciate the activities of the other sex can only help matters. Research has found that parents allow their girls more flexibility in toy choices, whereas they limit the toys that boys play with mainly to masculine toys (FREEMAN, 2007; WOOD ET AL., 2002).

Review Questions

1 Describe the stereotypic views of masculinity, and identify the risks associated with these stereotypes.

2 Describe the stereotypic views of femininity, and identify the risks associated with these stereotypes.

3 Define androgyny, and give one example of androgynous behavior.

4 Discuss the options available to transgender people who desire medical transition. Explain why gender affirmation/confirmation surgery has been controversial.

5 Explain how gender diversity can be experienced differently in other cultures.

Gender Role Socialization Throughout the Life Span

Socialization into gender roles begins at birth and nowadays may begin even before. Parents can now know months before birth whether the fetus is male or female and can begin to prepare accordingly. Parents even speak to the unborn child—a mother simply by talking and her partner by putting their mouth close to the mother's belly—and communicate ideas about their "little boy" or "little girl." In a real sense, then, these parents may begin trying to communicate gender-specific messages before the child is even born (whether the child actually is influenced by these sounds diffusing into the womb is, of course, another question). Parents awaiting the birth of a child are filled with gender expectations, stereotypes, and desires.

Children learn much of their gender role behavior from modeling those around them.

Childhood: Learning by Playing

From the moment parents find out the sex of their baby, a child's life is largely defined by their gender. From the baby's name, to how they are dressed, to how their room is decorated, gender suffuses the newborn's life. Not only do parents construct different environments for children from birth, they tend to treat them differently as well.

Parents also serve as gender role models. As early as age 2, children begin to identify with their same-sex parent, and by observing and imitating that parent's behavior, they learn that objects and activities are attributed to specific genders. The cognitive schema that children develop at this point are not flexible but universal; to the children, only women can wear skirts, and only men can shave their faces. In fact, cross-gender humor is very funny to young children; a television program that shows a man dressed up in a woman's clothes or a woman sporting a mustache will elicit bursts of laughter. As children begin to show more complex behaviors,

they realize that there are often societal restrictions on acceptable behaviors.

Early in childhood, gender segregation in play, also known as homosocial play, begins. Children tend to gravitate to same-sex friends, and as early as 2 to 3 years old, children play more actively and more interactively with same-sex playmates (Maccoby & Jacklin, 1987). This tendency is universal. Researchers have tried rewarding children for playing with the other sex, but as soon as the reward is discontinued, play reverts back to same-sex groupings. This gender segregation may be because of the different playing and communication styles of boys and girls, the attraction of children to others like themselves, or to learned social roles; most probably, it involves a combination of all these factors.

During the school years, gender roles become the measure by which children are judged by their peers. Children receive strong messages about acceptable clothing choices (including colors and styles), haircuts (long or short), and participation in sports. While girls have been finding increasing support for a variety of sports, such as lacrosse or ice hockey, boys who are interested in pursuing ballet or figure skating are often ridiculed (Chemaly, 2013).

Overall, boys are treated more harshly than girls when they adopt cross-gender characteristics (Chemaly, 2013; Mustich, 2013; Sandnabba & Ahlberg, 1999).

The classroom itself can also strongly reinforce gender stereotypes. Even though teachers believe they show equal attention to boys and girls, research shows that teachers spend more time with boys, give them more attention, both praise and criticize boys more, direct more follow-up questions to boys, and tolerate more bad behavior among boys than girls (Duffy et al., 2001; McClowry et al., 2013).

Adolescence: Practice Being Female or Male

By adolescence, gender roles are firmly established, and they guide adolescents through their exploration of peer relationships and different "love styles" with potential partners. Part of the task of adolescence is to figure out what it means to be a "man" or a "woman" and to try to adopt that role. Boys quickly learn that to be accepted, they should be interested in and good at sports, should express interest in sex and women, should not be overly emotional, and should not display interests that are seen as feminine or girlish (recall Sophie's struggle in my chapter-opening Notebook feature). Girls, in some ways, seem to have more latitude in their behavior but are supposed to express interest in boys and men, show concern with their appearance, and exercise a certain amount of sexual restraint. As we said earlier, the consequences for boys deviating from gender role behavior are more severe than they are for girls deviating. However, when girls deviate from gender stereotypes of sexuality (and have multiple sexual partners, for example), they experience more severe consequences.

Although there has been an increased acceptance of lesbian, gay, bisexual, and transgender (LGBT) youth in many schools, adolescence can potentially be a difficult time for those who are gender-nonconforming, gay, lesbian, bisexual, and transgender. There can be limited tolerance for these behaviors in adolescence because they are viewed as the opposite of what teenagers are "supposed" to do. Teenage boys are supposed to be striving for genuine "masculinity." Gender-nonconforming, gay, lesbian, bisexual, and transgender youth are often at elevated risk for victimization (Kosciw et al., 2008).

The life of an emerging gender-nonconforming, gay, lesbian, bisexual, or transgender adolescent may be fraught with tension, which contributes to the increased risk for depression among these adolescents. Many survive the adolescent years by limiting the sharing of their sexual orientation or gender identity and making compromises between their identities and their safety. We further discuss the physical and emotional harassment of LGBTQ students in Chapter 11.

When it comes to sexuality, teenage gender roles have been changing since the 1970s. For example, it is more common for heterosexual girls today to assert themselves and initiate hanging out with boys than they were 25 years ago, when they may have been considered a "slut." Yet, such changing roles are also confusing; adolescent girls and boys still receive contradictory messages. Traditional male attitudes value sexual achievement, control of the sexual

relationship, and suppression of emotions. However, today, as heterosexual teenage boys are being approached by girls, they are not necessarily more sexually experienced than the girls they date, and they are expected to be sensitive to issues of female equality. Heterosexual teenage girls, on the other hand, have often been taught to assert their independence but also must be aware of existing social pressures that contribute to feelings of guilt and shame for girls who seek to fulfill their sexual needs. So even with all the changes that have leveled the playing field between the sexes, it is still not easy for adolescents to negotiate their way into sexual adulthood.

Adulthood: Careers and Families

As men and women grow into adulthood, they tend to derive their gender identity primarily from two realms—their careers and their family lives. Although many believe that ideas about gender are firmly established by the time we reach adulthood, recent social changes in sex roles show that adults do have the capacity to revise their thoughts about gender. One of the biggest transformations in career and family life in the United States over the last few years involves the movement of women out of the home and into paid employment (Haines et al., 2016). These changes have caused a major shift in family gender roles.

Decades ago, the most common family system consisted of a working father and a stay-at-home mother (see Figure 4.3). With high unemployment, more women have been returning to

jpb/imageBROKER/Alamy Stock Photo

The traditional family structure of a stay-at-home mom and a working dad has been changing over the last few years. These changes have led to shifts in household responsibilities with men taking on more traditionally female household responsibilities, such as child care and meal preparations. How do you think these became gendered jobs in the first place?

Female Breadwinners and Co-Breadwinners by Race/Ethnicity, 1970–2015.

White — 37.4% / 24.7%
Black — 14.7% / 70.7%
Latina — 18.6% / 40.5%

■ Breadwinner ■ Co-Breadwinner

FIGURE **4.3** Share of mothers who are breadwinners or co-breadwinners, by race and ethnicity, 1970 to 2015.

SOURCE: Center for American Progress; Glynn, 2016

work or working longer hours. In both of these cases, their heterosexual partners are taking on more of the household duties. Women make up half of the U.S. labor force today and 42% are either the sole or primary breadwinner (Glynn, 2016). In Figure 4.3 we present information about female breadwinners by race and ethnicity.

The Senior Years

Because American culture values youthfulness and holds many negative stereotypes toward aging, it can often be a difficult time for seniors. There are gender differences, especially because of a double standard of aging in which aging men are viewed as "distinguished," whereas aging women are viewed as "old" (Sontag, 1979; Teuscher & Teuscher, 2006). Because women have historically been valued for their reproductive ability, they may be viewed as old once they lose the ability to reproduce, whereas men are valued for their achievements and are not viewed as old until they are physically incapacitated or unable to work. Overall, although both men and women have been found to value physical appearance, women have been found to be more concerned about the effects of aging on their physical appearance (Slevin, 2010).

American media helps foster negative attitudes toward women by pushing advertising for anti-aging products, such as creams, lotions, and cosmetic surgeries to help women stay healthy and look younger (Gilleard & Higgs, 2000). One study found that the majority of older women equated gray hair with ugliness and poorer health, and because of this, the majority of women in the sample reported dying their hair in later life (Clarke & Korotchenko, 2010).

However, it is important to keep in mind that attitudes about aging vary by race, ethnicity, and sexual orientation. Black and Latina women have less rigid aging stereotypes than White women, as do lesbian women, who are more positive about aging and looking old compared with heterosexual women (Schuler et al., 2008; Slevin, 2010; Wolf, 1991). Gay men, on the other hand, tend to have more negative attitudes about aging, because American gay culture places more emphasis on young and youthful bodies (Slevin, 2010).

The changing economic climate has also contributed to increased stresses in later life. With high levels of unemployment and men and women working at lower paying jobs than they might otherwise would have, men and women who derive a large sense of their identity from their work may be particularly at risk adjusting to such changes. In families with children, the parents can experience either a great sense of loneliness or a newfound freedom as their children grow and leave the home. A few women, especially those with traditional roles as wife and mother, become depressed about losing their primary roles as caretakers and mothers. The phrase "empty nest syndrome" identifies the feelings of sadness and loss that many women experience when their children leave home or no longer need day-to-day care (McBride, 2007). Significant changes are common in the senior years that may involve difficult adjustments.

REAL RESEARCH Emotional expression, including crying, has only been considered socially acceptable for men in the context of sports (MacArthur & Shields, 2015).

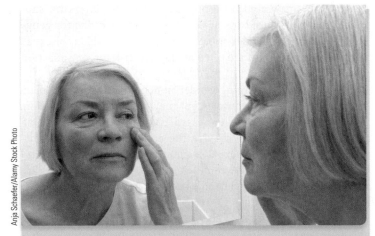

Anja Schaefer/Alamy Stock Photo

Women are surrounded by images of youth and beauty in the media and constantly bombarded by a multitude of products that promise to erase the signs of aging from their faces. These products have been popular because of the double standard of aging in American society, which views aging men as distinguished but aging women as tired and old.

100   CHAPTER 4

Review Questions

1 How are children and teenagers socialized about gender roles throughout childhood and adolescence?

2 How are adults socialized about gender roles throughout adulthood, and how does this socialization affect career choice?

3 Describe the conflicting messages that women receive about career and family life.

4 How has the role of the husband/ father in the family changed over the past few decades?

5 Explain how gender roles change as people enter later life.

Toward Gender Equality

Many religious and cultural systems clearly define gender roles. Advocates of such systems deny that differentiating gender roles means that one gender is subordinate to the other. For example, Susan Rogers (1978) has argued that we cannot apply Western notions of gender equality to countries with fundamentally different systems. She argues that equality can exist in society only when women and men are seen in that society as fundamentally similar.

In Oman, for example, women are subject to strict social rules that we in the West would clearly see as subordination. Rogers argues, though, that women in Oman see themselves as quite different from men and are uninterested in the male role and male definitions of power. Is it appropriate for us to impose our categories on their society and suggest that women in Oman are exploited and subordinate even though they themselves do not think so? Such questions go to the heart of the discussion of power in society.

The goal for many is not a society without gender distinctions; a world without differences is boring. Yet a world that restricts people's ability to express difference because of the color of their skin, their religious beliefs, the type of genitalia they happen to have (or not have!), or their sexual attractions is unjust. It is the content of gender roles, not their existence, that societies can alter to provide each person an opportunity to live without being judged by stereotypes of gender.

Review Questions

1 Do you think there could ever be a society without gender distinctions? Why or why not?

2 Explain how dichotomous thinking can exaggerate gender differences.

Chapter Review

Summary Points

1 The gender landscape has been slowly changing over the last decade, and many experts today conceptualize gender more as a spectrum. Some recent events have begun to reshape our concept of gender in American culture.

2 Human beings use sexual reproduction to combine 23 chromosomes in the mother's gamete with the 23 in the father's. The zygote then begins to undergo cell differentiation. If the 23rd chromosome pair is XX, the fetus will develop typically female sexual characteristics.

3 Female genitalia develop from the Müllerian duct, whereas male genitalia develop from the Wolffian duct. Both male and female external genitalia develop from the same tubercle, so many male and female genital structures are homologous.

4 Endocrine glands secrete hormones directly into the bloodstream to be carried to the target organs. The ovaries produce estrogen and progesterone, and the testicles produce androgens. The hypothalamus is the body's single most important control center.

5 *Intersex* is a general term used to refer to a variety of conditions in which a person is born with a reproductive or sexual anatomy that doesn't appear to fit the typical definition of male or female. Although the DSM-5 refers to these conditions as disorders of sex development (DSD), we prefer to call them *differences* in sex development.

6 Differences of sex development include sex chromosome and hormone conditions. Chromosomal conditions include Klinefelter syndrome when an ovum containing an extra X chromosome is fertilized by a Y sperm (XXY); Turner syndrome when an ovum without any sex chromosome is fertilized by an X sperm (XO); XYY syndrome when a normal ovum is fertilized by a sperm with two Y chromosomes; and XXX syndrome when two X chromosomes are fertilized by a normal X sperm. Hormonal conditions include congenital adrenal hyperplasia (CAH), which occurs when a child produces higher amounts of androgen, and androgen-insensitivity syndrome (AIS), in which a chromosomal male's body does not respond to testosterone.

7 Gender roles are the culturally determined pattern of behaviors that societies prescribe to the sexes. Gender traits are the biologically determined characteristics of gender. Little agreement exists on which gender characteristics are innate and which are learned.

8 The terms *masculinity* and *femininity* are used in three ways in society: first, a masculine or feminine person is said to exemplify characteristics that differentiate the sexes; second, the terms refer to the extent to which adults adhere to socially prescribed gender roles; and third, masculinity and femininity refer to sexual characteristics.

9 Most people agree that males are larger, stronger, and more aggressive, whereas females are neurologically more advanced than males, mature faster, and are biologically heartier. Some also cite evidence that males have better spatial abilities, whereas females have better verbal abilities. However, aside from these behaviors and physical attributes, almost no differences between the sexes are universally accepted by researchers. In fact, a recent meta-analysis found that gender differences were small or very close to zero.

10 Three types of theories about gender role development have been offered: social learning theories, which postulate that almost all gender knowledge is dependent on what children are taught; cognitive development theories, which suggest that children go through a universal set of stages during which they can learn only certain types of information about gender; and newer theories, such as Bem's gender schema theory, which suggests that children do go through developmental stages, and that the kinds of things they learn at each stage are largely culturally determined.

11 Gender is socially constructed, and societies decide how it will be defined and what it will mean. In American society, masculinity and femininity have been viewed as mutually exclusive. Masculine traits include being a good provider, strong, stable, unemotional, fearless, sexually experienced, and financially independent. Feminine traits include being beautiful, soft, empathetic, modest, and emotional. Many traits of femininity are considered to be the opposite of masculinity.

12 Masculinity and femininity were thought to be on the same continuum—the more masculine you were, the less feminine you were, and vice versa. However, in the 1970s, researchers challenged this notion by suggesting that masculinity and femininity were two separate dimensions and a person could be high or low on both dimensions. Androgyny is high levels of both masculine and feminine characteristics, and some advocate it as a way to transcend gender stereotypes.

13 The gender binary divides people into two groups—male and female. We are typically put into either of these groups at birth. Societal expectations are that biological sex, gender identity, and gender expression are all congruent. However, all these variables interact to create a multidimensional gender spectrum. When behaviors fall outside of gender norms, they may be referred to as gender diverse or transgender.

14 Individuals who identify as queer or genderqueer often reject traditional gender roles and believe that gender fluidity allows them a more flexible range of gender expression. Transgender terminology is complex and changes relatively quickly.

15 Transexual and sexual reassignment surgery are both outdated terms. Gender dysphoria involves confusion and/or discomfort about sex assigned at birth and gender identity. Some transgender people may seek out medical interventions to align their gender identity with their physical body. Many transgender men and women feel confident and comfortable about their biological sex and gender identity without medical interventions.

16 Transgender men are assigned female at birth but identify as male, whereas transgender women are assigned male at birth but identify as female. A variety of medical options are available, and although some transgender people proceed through all the stages to eventual surgery, many do not.

17 Young children experiencing gender dysphoria may be prescribed reversible hormone-blocking intervention to delay puberty. Individuals who identify as queer or genderqueer reject traditional gender roles and believe in the fluidity of gender. Many transgender people experience discrimination or prejudice, known as anti-transgender prejudice, or transphobia.

18 The World Professional Association for Transgender Health has proposed Standards of Care, which outline treatments for those seeking gender affirmation/confirmation surgery. Treatment usually begins with psychotherapy and then proceeds to medical interventions.

19 Some cultures challenge our notions about gender by proposing categories that are neither male nor female. Native Americans have the two-spirit, whereas other cultures have similar roles, such as the *xani-th* or the *hijra*.

20 Infants are socialized into gender roles early through the way they are dressed and treated, and through the environment in which they are brought up. They are reinforced for appropriate gender activity through ridiculing of children who violate gender boundaries. Adolescents "try on" adult gender roles and attitudes.

21 As people grow into adulthood, they tend to derive their gender identity from two realms—careers and family lives. Social changes in sex roles show that adults do have the capacity to revise their thoughts about gender roles. One of the biggest transformations in career and family life in the United States over the last few years involves the movement of women out of the home and into paid employment.

22 Because American culture values youthfulness and holds many negative stereotypes toward aging, life can often be difficult for seniors. However, attitudes about aging vary by race, ethnicity, and sexual orientation. With high levels of unemployment and people working at lower paying jobs than they should be, men and women who derive a large sense of their identity from their work may be particularly at risk adjusting to such changes. Some parents can experience either a great sense of loneliness or a newfound freedom as their children grow and leave the home.

23 To build a society that avoids gender stereotyping and encourages gender equality, we would need to change our basic, human, dichotomous thinking and the splitting of the world into opposites, such as good and bad. Maintaining this way of thinking only exaggerates differences and invests energy into keeping things separate.

Critical Thinking Questions

1 What questions does the case study example on Brenda/Bruce raise about the nature of gender? Do you feel that gender is innate, socially learned, or a combination of both?

2 How are definitions of masculinity and femininity changing in society? Are many of the old stereotypes still powerful?

3 Why do you think a woman considers the phrase "She's one of the guys" to be a compliment, whereas a man considers the phrase "He's one of the girls" to be a put-down?

4 Which theory of gender development do you favor? Can you relate this theory to your own gender development? What are the theory's strengths and weaknesses?

5 If you met someone at a party tonight who was transgender, what kind of emotions or thoughts do you think you would have? Would you be interested in pursuing a relationship with them? Why or why not?

6 Why do you think the gender binary has traditionally divided people into only two groups in Western Culture? Does the gender spectrum make more sense to you? Why or why not?

Websites

World Professional Association for Transgender Health (WPATH) WPATH is an interdisciplinary professional and educational organization devoted to transgender health. Publishes the *Standards of Care and Ethical Guidelines*, which provide a professional consensus about the psychiatric, psychological, medical, and surgical management of gender dysphoria.

The Accord Alliance The Accord Alliance promotes comprehensive and integrated approaches to care that enhance the health and well-being of people and families affected by disorders of sex development. Offers partnership with patients and families and educational and informational materials.

AskANonBinary A comprehensive online pronoun guide that provides information on pronouns used in general, non-English, animals, nature, creature, etc.

5 Female Sexual Anatomy and Physiology

Many years ago I lost a good friend, Anne, to breast cancer. Prior to her diagnosis I didn't know a lot about breast cancer. Anne was a mom with three young children at home. She fought hard for her life, but in the end the cancer won. The main issue that worked against her was the fact that the cancer was not discovered until it was at a very advanced stage. From this painful experience I learned about the importance of screening in the detection of early stage breast cancer. Breast self-examination (BSE) is important because it enables you to familiarize yourself with your breasts so you have a baseline understanding of what is normal for you. This will enable you to more readily detect any change, such as a lump, dimpling, or skin irritation.

Steven Belcher

When I met Stef Woods I realized just how important BSE really is. Stef had been diagnosed with breast cancer months before we met and had already been through countless rounds of chemotherapy.

What makes Stef's story so important for you to hear is that she found the first lump in her breast when she was 25 years old. Stef had always been vigilant about breast self-exams, mostly because her mother had died of cancer 13 years earlier. Thankfully, the lump she found the first time was not cancerous. A few years later another lump was found on a yearly mammogram but once again, it was not cancerous. However, the third time a lump was found she knew her luck might not hold out. Her doctor called to share her test results and as she put the phone to her ear, she was keenly aware of her heart racing. She remembered her doctor telling her, "Your test is positive. You have breast cancer." Stef told me that although this was the hardest thing she could imagine, she knew something was wrong before the call. She had found the lump, but in addition to that, her dog, Flake, had recently begun sleeping by her right breast (instead of her feet, like usual). Stef had heard stories about dogs being able to detect cancer. Stef is an amazing woman and her story helps us realize the importance of friendship and positive thinking.

Janell Carroll

For many years, only physicians were thought to be privileged enough to know about the human body. Today, we realize how important it is for all of us to understand how our bodies function. Considering the number of sex manuals and guides that line the shelves of American bookstores, it may seem surprising that the majority of questions that students ask about human sexuality are fundamental, biological questions.[1] It becomes less surprising, though, when we realize that many parents are still uncomfortable discussing sexual biology with their children, and younger people often do not know whom to approach or are embarrassed about the questions they have (we discuss this further in Chapter 8). Questions about sexual biology are natural, however, for the reproductive system is complex, and there are probably more myths and misinformation about sexual biology than any other single part of human functioning.

Children are naturally curious about their genitals and spend a good deal of time touching and exploring them. However, they are often taught that this exploration is something to be ashamed of. Because girls' genitals are more hidden and recessed, and girls are often discouraged from making a thorough self-examination, they tend to be less familiar with their genitals than are boys. This may be reinforced as females mature and are taught that menstruation is "dirty." These attitudes are reflected in ads for "feminine hygiene" products, which suggest that the vagina is unclean and has an unpleasant smell.

In this chapter, we will explore the anatomy and physiology of biological females. Although there are many similarities to biological male anatomy and physiology, as you will soon learn, female anatomy and physiology are a bit more complicated. Unlike males, females have fluctuating hormone levels, monthly menstruation cycles, and experience menopause. In Chapter 6, we will explore male sexual anatomy and physiology.

The Female Sexual and Reproductive System

It is important for all of us to understand the structure of the female reproductive system, which is really a marvel of biological engineering. Women who have not done a thorough genital self-examination should do so, not only because it is an important part of the body to learn to appreciate but because any changes in genital appearance should be brought to the attention of a **gynecologist** or other health care provider. See the accompanying "Sex in Real Life" for instructions on performing a genital self-examination.

External Sex Organs

Although many people refer to the female's external sex organs collectively as the "vagina," this is technically incorrect; the more accurate term for the whole region is **vulva**. The vulva, as we will see, is made up of the mons veneris, the labia majora and labia minora, the vestibule, the perineum, and the **clitoris** (see Figure 5.1). Although the vagina does open into the vulva, the vagina is mainly an internal sex organ and is discussed in the next section.

---

gynecologist
A physician who specializes in the study and treatment of disorders of the female reproductive system.

vulva
The collective designation for the external genitalia of the female.

clitoris
An erectile organ of the female located under the prepuce; an organ of sexual pleasure.

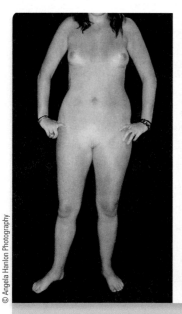
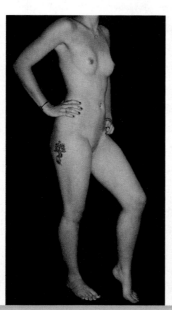
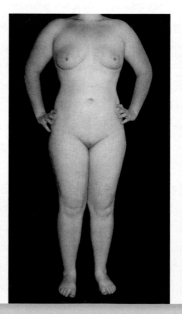
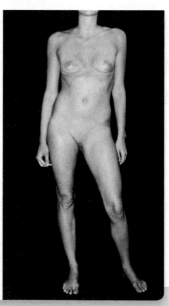

© Angela Hanlon Photography

All of the women in these photos have "normal" bodies. Individual differences in weight; size and shape of hips, breasts, and thighs; and even pubic hair are normal.

---

[1]Consider the questions two students asked during a lecture on human sexual biology: *Can a woman pee with a tampon in?* (Yes.) *Can a man pee with an erection?* (Not that well.) If you didn't know the answers to these questions, this chapter and Chapter 6 can help.

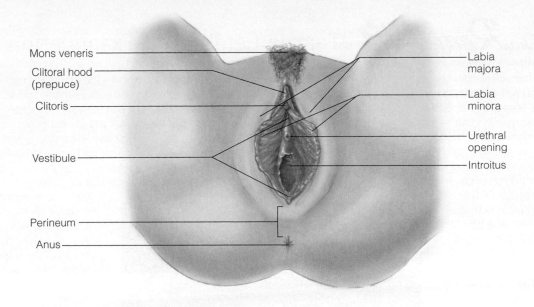

FIGURE **5.1** The external genital structures of the mature female.

The Mons Veneris

The fatty cushion resting over the front surface of the pubic bone is called the **mons veneris** or **mons pubis**. The mons veneris becomes covered with pubic hair after puberty and serves largely as a protective cushion for the genitals, especially during sexual activity.

The Labia Majora

The **labia majora** (LAY-bee-uh muh-JOR-uh) (outer lips) are two longitudinal folds of fatty tissue that extend from the mons, frame the rest of the female genitalia, and meet at the perineum (the tissue between the vagina and the anus). The skin of the outer labia majora is pigmented and covered with hair, whereas the inner surface is hairless and contains sebaceous (oil) glands. During sexual excitement, the labia majora fill with blood and engorge, which makes the entire pubic region seem to swell.

The Labia Minora

The **labia minora** (LAY-bee-uh muh-NOR-uh) (inner lips) are two smaller pink skin folds situated inside the labia majora. They are generally more delicate, shorter, and thinner than the labia majora and join at the clitoris to form the **prepuce** (PREE-peus), the "hood" over the clitoris. The labia minora contain no hair follicles, although they are rich in sebaceous glands. They also contain some erectile tissue and serve to protect the vagina and urethra. During sexual arousal, the labia minora will darken, although the appearance can differ considerably among women.

The Clitoris

For a long time, people believed that the clitoris (KLIT-uh-rus) was only a small knob of erectile tissue located under the prepuce. The invisibility of the clitoris led many to believe that this was so.

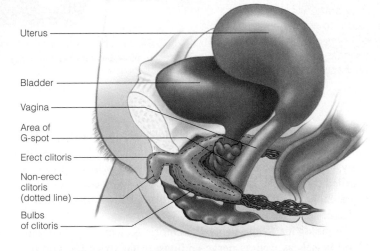

FIGURE **5.2** Side inner view of the erect clitoris.

SOURCE: Based on Cass, Vivienne, The Elusive Orgasm, Marlowe & Company, 2007.

However, in 1991, a group of female researchers, using historical and modern anatomical descriptions, created a new definition of the clitoris that encompasses all of the clitoral structures (see Figure 5.2). This group identified 18 structures of the clitoris—some of which are readily visible and others that are not (Federation of Feminist Women's Health Centers, 1991). In addition to the glans,

mons veneris or mons pubis
The mound of fatty tissue over the female pubic bone, also referred to as mons pubis, meaning "pubic mound."

labia majora
Two longitudinal folds of skin extending downward and backward from the mons pubis of the female.

labia minora
Two small folds of mucous membrane lying within the labia majora of the female.

prepuce
A loose fold of skin that covers the clitoris.

Many female health problems can be identified when changes are detected in the internal or external sexual organs; therefore, self-examination has an important health function. It is important to understand why females should examine their genitals regularly.

Begin by examining the outside of your genitals; using a hand mirror can help. Using your fingers to spread open the labia majora, try to identify the other external structures—the labia minora, the prepuce, the vaginal and urethral openings. Look at the way your genitals look while sitting, lying down, standing up, squatting. Feel the different textures of each part of the vagina, and look carefully at the coloration and size of the tissues you can see. Both coloration and size can change with sexual arousal, but such changes are temporary, and the genitals should return to normal within a couple of hours after sexual activity. Any changes over time in color, firmness, or shape of the genitals should be

brought to the attention of a health care provider.

If it is not uncomfortable, you may want to move back the prepuce, or hood, over the clitoris and try to see the clitoral glans. Although the clitoris is easier to see when erect, note how it fits beneath the prepuce. Note also whether there is any smegma be-

Thomas Michael Corcoran/PhotoEdit

Genital self-examination can help a woman become more comfortable with her own body.

neath the prepuce; fluids can accumulate and solidify there, and so you should gently clean beneath the prepuce regularly.

If you place a finger inside your vagina, you should be able to feel the pubic bone in the front inside part of your vagina. It is slightly behind the pubic bone that the **G-spot** is supposed to be, but it is difficult for most women to stimulate the G-spot with their own fingers. Squat and press down with your stomach muscles as you push your fingers deeply in the vagina, and at the top of the vagina you may be able to feel your cervix, which feels a little like the tip of your nose. Note how it feels to touch the cervix (some women have a slightly uncomfortable feeling when their cervix is touched). Feeling comfortable inserting your fingers into your vagina will also help you if you choose a barrier method of contraception, such as the contraceptive sponge, which must be inserted deep within the vagina at the cervix (see Chapter 13).

the clitoris is composed of a body and paired crura (legs). The bulbs of the clitoris lie under the labia. These bulbs, the glans, the body, and crura form an erectile tissue cluster, which altogether is called the clitoris. Magnetic resonance imaging confirmed this more expansive definition of the clitoris in 2005 (O'Connell & DeLancey, 2005).

Homologous to the penis, the clitoris is richly supplied with blood vessels as well as nerve endings; it has twice the number of nerve endings (8,000) as the penis (4,000; Angier, 1999). The clitoral glans is a particularly sensitive receptor and transmitter of sexual stimuli. The body, bulbs, and crura enlarge and engorge with blood in much the same way as the penis does during physical arousal. The clitoris is the only human organ for which the sole function is to bring sexual pleasure (we discuss the clitoris and sexual pleasure in more detail in Chapter 10).

The clitoral glans is difficult to see in many women unless the prepuce is pulled back, although in some women the glans may swell enough during sexual arousal to emerge from under the prepuce (see the accompanying "Sex in Real Life"). It is easy to feel the clitoral glans, however, by gently grasping the prepuce and rolling it between the fingers. In fact, most women do not enjoy direct stimulation of the glans and prefer stimulation through the prepuce. It is important to clean under the prepuce, for secretions can accumulate underneath as a material known as **smegma**. Smegma can also accumulate in the skin folds of the labia and if left unclean, can cause pain and irritation.

REAL RESEARCH   The clitoris is the center for orgasmic response and is homologous to the male penis (PAULS, 2015). Although smaller than the penis, the clitoris has twice the number of nerve endings and a higher concentration of nerve fibers than anywhere else on the body, including the tongue or fingertips (ANGIER, 1999).

In some cultures, the clitoris is removed surgically in a ritual **circumcision**, often referred to as a **clitorectomy**. Other parts of the vulva can also be removed in a procedure known as **infibulation** (in-fib-you-LAY-shun) (see accompanying "Sexual Diversity in Our World").

smegma
A natural lubricating residue made up of shedded skin cells, skin oil secretions, and moisture, including sweat. Typically gathers in skin folds, such as between the labia and under the clitoral hood.

circumcision
Surgical removal of the clitoris in women; also referred to as clitorectomy.

clitorectomy
Surgical removal of the clitoris; also referred to as circumcision.

infibulation
The ritual removal of the clitoris, prepuce, and labia, and the sewing together of the vestibule.

Gräfenberg spot (G-spot)
A structure that is said to lie on the anterior (front) wall of the vagina and is reputed to be a seat of sexual pleasure when stimulated.

IN OUR WORLD

Female genital mutilation (FGM) is a cultural tradition in more than 30 countries in Africa, Asia, and the Middle East. The United Nations estimates that 200 million living girls and women have undergone various forms of FGM worldwide (World Health Organization, 2016). FGM involves partial or total removal of the external female genitalia for nonmedical reasons. Throughout history, FGM has been performed to distinguish "respectable" women and to ensure and preserve a girl's virginity (Gruenbaum, 2006; Harris, 2013; O'Connor, 2008). The most common reason given for undergoing such procedures is culture and tradition. The World Health Organization has proposed four classifications of FGM:

- Type I: Partial or total removal of the clitoris and/or prepuce (referred to as a clitorectomy)

- Type II: Partial or total removal of the clitoris and the labia minora with or without excision of the labia majora (referred to as an excision)

- Type III: Narrowing of the vaginal orifice by cutting the labia minora and labia majora with or without excision of clitoris (referred to as infibulation)

- Type IV: All other harmful procedures to female genitalia for nonmedical purposes including piercing, pricking, scraping, and cauterization

FGM procedures are usually done on girls from infancy to the age of 15, although in some cultures, it is performed later. Procedures are often done without anesthesia or antiseptic, and the majority of procedures are performed by medically untrained personnel (Iavazzo et al., 2013). The most severe type of circumcision involves the complete removal of the clitoris and labia minora, and also the scraping of the labia majora with knives, broken bottles, or razor blades. The remaining tissue is sewn together, leaving a matchstick-sized hole to allow for the passing of urine and menstrual blood. The young girl's legs are then bound together with rope, and she is immobilized for anywhere from 14 to 40 days for the circumcision to heal. In some instances, the tighter the girl's infibulation, the higher her bride price.

FGM can cause extreme pain, urinary complications or dysfunction, shock, hemorrhage, infection, scarring, recurrent urinary infections, retention of menses at menarche, vulval cysts, and pelvic inflammatory disease (Bazi, 2016; World Health Organization, 2016). Of these symptoms, severe pain and bleeding are most common.

There is ongoing controversy about what Americans and others should do to try to discourage this practice. The United States has been strongly opposed to the practice of FGM and views it as a violation of the human rights of girls and women. In 2015, a global resolve was made to end FGM by 2030 (UNICEF, 2016).

Ton Koene/age fotostock/Superstock

The Vestibule

The **vestibule** is the name for the entire region between the labia minora and can be clearly seen when the labia are held apart. The vestibule contains the opening of the urethra and the vagina and the ducts of Bartholin's glands.

THE URETHRAL MEATUS The opening, or meatus (mee-AYE-tuss), to the urethra (yoo-REE-thruh) lies between the vagina and the clitoris. The urethra, which brings urine from the bladder to be excreted, is much shorter in women than in men, in whom it goes through the penis. A shorter urethra allows bacteria greater access into the urinary tract, making women much more susceptible to **urinary tract infections (UTIs)**. One in five women will develop a UTI in her lifetime, and 20% of these women will experience a recurrence of the UTI after treatment (Hooton, 2003). Common symptoms for UTI include pain or burning in the urethra or bladder and an increased urge to urinate. Over-the-counter medication can help decrease pain, but antibiotics are necessary to cure the infection. Consuming cranberry products (i.e., drinks, breads) can

be effective in decreasing UTI recurrence (Maki et al., 2016; Occhipinti et al., 2016). Although scientists have been working on a vaccine to prevent UTIs, it is unlikely one will be available within the next few years.

THE INTROITUS AND THE HYMEN The entrance, or **introitus** (in-TROID-us), of the vagina also lies in the vestibule. The introitus is usually covered at birth by a fold of tissue known as the **hymen** (HIGH-men). The hymen varies in thickness and extent, and is sometimes absent. The center of the hymen is usually perforated,

---

vestibule
The entire region between the labia minora, including the urethra and introitus.

urinary tract infection (UTI)
Infection of the urinary tract, often resulting in a frequent urge to urinate,

painful burning in the bladder or urethra during urination, and fatigue.

introitus
Entrance to the vagina.

hymen
A thin fold of vascularized mucous membrane at the vaginal opening.

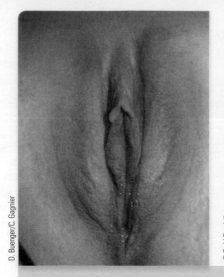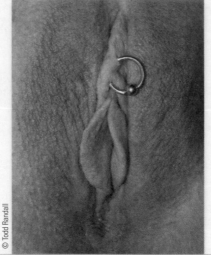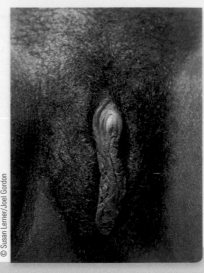

The female external genitals are referred to collectively as the vulva. While some women may worry that their vulvas aren't "normal," there is enormous variation in the size, shape, and color of the vulva, and also in the size and symmetry of the vaginal lips.

and it is through this perforation that the menstrual flow leaves the vagina and that a tampon is inserted. If the hymen is intact, it will usually rupture easily and tear at several points during the first penetrative sexual event, accompanied by a small amount of blood. If the woman is sexually aroused and well lubricated, the rupture of the hymen usually does not cause more than a brief moment's discomfort. In rare cases, a woman has an **imperforate hymen**, which is usually detected because her menstrual flow is blocked. A simple surgical procedure can open the imperforate hymen.

An intact hymen has been a symbol of "purity" throughout history, a sign that a woman had not engaged in sexual intercourse. In reality, many activities can tear the hymen, including vigorous exercise, horseback or bike riding, masturbation, or the insertion of tampons or other objects into the vagina (Cook & Dickens, 2009). Still, in many cultures during many historical eras, the absence of bloodstained sheets on the wedding night was enough to condemn a woman as "wanton" (promiscuous), and some knowing mothers encouraged their newlywed daughters to have a little vial of blood from a chicken or other animal to pour on the sheet of their bridal bed, just in case. Although virginity "testing" (to check for an intact hymen) is against the law in many parts of the world, including Turkey, Indonesia, and parts of South Africa, illegal virginity tests are still performed. Reconstructive surgery to repair a ruptured hymen, called *hymenoplasty* or *revirgination*,

ON YOUR MIND

I've always been worried about the size and shape of my vaginal lips. They just seem too big and floppy. At this point, I'm so embarrassed about them that I can't imagine ever being comfortable showing them to anyone. Is there anything I can do to fix them?

is available in many countries, with high demand from Middle Eastern, Korean, and Latina women (Ahmadi, 2016; Wei et al., 2015; Wynn, 2016).

BARTHOLIN'S GLANDS The "greater vestibular glands," or **Bartholin's** (BAR-tha-lenz) **glands**, are bean-shaped glands with ducts that empty into the vestibule in the middle of the labia minora. Historically, Bartholin's glands have been presumed to provide vaginal lubrication during sexual arousal; however, research by Masters and Johnson found that the vagina is capable of lubrication (we will discuss this

The size, length, shape, color, texture, and symmetry of the labia and clitoris vary greatly among women. Some women have long labial lips, whereas others have shorter ones. With the introduction of smaller swimsuits, bikini waxes, and exposure to various pornographic images, many women today are feeling increased pressure to undergo genital plastic surgery in search of a "designer vagina" (GOODMAN, 2009; GOODMAN ET AL., 2010). However, there are several potential risks to these procedures, including pain, decreased sensitivity, and changes in sexual pleasure (LIAO ET AL., 2010). Our cultural fixation with perfection has also led some women to undergo G-spot enhancement (injecting collagen into the area to increase sensitivity) and even anal bleaching (using bleach to restore the anus to a pinkish hue). Because of medical risks and possible complications, the American College of Obstetricians and Gynecologists (2007) recommends against these procedures.

imperforate hymen
An abnormally closed hymen that usually does not allow the exit of menstrual fluid.

Bartholin's glands
A pair of glands on either side of the vaginal opening that open by a duct into the space between the hymen and the labia minora; also referred to as the greater vestibular glands.

more in Chapter 10). The Bartholin's glands can become infected and form a cyst or abscess, causing pain and swelling in the labial and vaginal areas. Bartholin gland cysts are most common in women of reproductive age and are typically treated with antibiotics, laser treatment, and/or surgery (Kessous et al., 2013; Speck et al., 2016).

The Anus and Perineum

The anus is the external opening of the rectum through which feces are expelled. The area of tissue between the vagina and the anus is called the **perineum** (pear-uh-NEE-um), and research has found this area is twice as long in men as in women (McEwen & Renner, 2006). The perineum is rich with nerve endings, and some men and women find it arousing to have this area stroked during sexual activity. During childbirth, however, care must be taken so that this tissue does not tear, which we will discuss further in Chapter 12.

Internal Sex Organs

Now that we've covered the female's external sex organs, let's move inside and explore the internal sex organs. The internal female sex organs include the vagina, uterus, cervix, Fallopian tubes, and ovaries (see Figure 5.3).

The Vagina

The **vagina** is a thin-walled tube extending from the cervix of the uterus to the external genitalia; it serves as the female organ for penetration, a passageway for sperm, and a canal through which menstrual fluid and babies can pass from the uterus. It is tilted toward the back in most women and thus forms a 90-degree angle with the uterus, which is commonly tilted forward (see Figure 5.3). The vagina is approximately 4 inches in length when relaxed but contains numerous folds that help it expand somewhat like an accordion. The vagina can expand during sexual activity and can stretch four to five times its normal size during childbirth.

The vagina does not contain glands but lubricates through small openings on the vaginal walls during engorgement (almost as if the vagina is sweating) and by mucus produced from glands on the cervix. Although the first third of the vaginal tube is well endowed with nerve endings, the inner two thirds are practically without tactile sensation; in fact, minor surgery can be done on the inner part of the vagina without anesthesia.

A spot about the size of a dime or quarter in the lower third of the front part of the vagina, the Gräfenberg spot (G-spot), was first described by Ernest Gräfenberg in 1950. The G-spot is found about 2 or 3 inches up the anterior (front or stomach) side of the vagina, just past the pubic bone (see Figure 5.4; Whipple, 2000). The existence of the G-spot has been a controversial issue in the

perineum Area between the vagina and the anus. **vagina** A thin-walled muscular tube that leads from the uterus to the vestibule and is	used for penetrative sex and as a passageway for menstrual fluid, sperm, and a newborn baby.

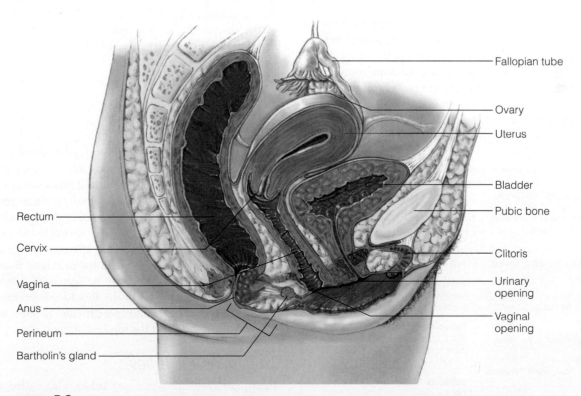

FIGURE **5.3** The female internal reproductive system (side view).

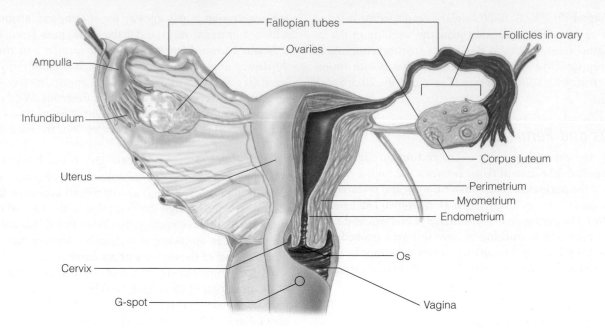

FIGURE 5.4 The female internal reproductive system (front view).

field of human sexuality for many years. Although some women report pleasurable sensations when this area is stimulated, there has never been any scientific proof of its existence (Pan et al., 2015; Puppo & Puppo, 2015). Growing research on clitoral structures indicates that increased sensitivity in the G-spot area may be caused by stimulation of the bulbs of the clitoris (Emhardt et al., 2016).

The Uterus

The **uterus** is a thick-walled, hollow, muscular organ in the pelvis sandwiched between the bladder in front and the rectum behind. It is approximately the shape of an inverted pear, with a dome-shaped top (fundus), a hollow body, and the doughnut-shaped cervix at the bottom. The uterus is about 3 inches long and flares to about 2 inches wide, but it increases greatly in size and weight during and after a pregnancy, and it atrophies after menopause.

The uterus has several functions: it undergoes a cycle of change every month that leads to menstruation, and it provides a path for sperm to reach the **ovum**, which returns to the uterus after it is fertilized and implants itself in the uterine wall. The uterus also nourishes and protects the developing fetus during gestation and provides the contractions for expulsion of the mature fetus during labor.

The uterine wall is about 1 inch thick and made up of three layers (see Figure 5.4). The outer layer, or **perimetrium**, is part of the tissue that covers most abdominal organs. The muscular layer of the uterus, the **myometrium**, contracts to expel menstrual fluid and to push the fetus out of the womb during delivery. The inner layer of the uterus, the **endometrium**, responds to fluctuating hormone levels, and its outer portion is shed with each menstrual cycle.

The Cervix

The **cervix** (SERV-ix) is the lower portion of the uterus that contains the opening, or **os**, leading into the body of the uterus. It is through the os that menstrual fluid flows out of the uterus and that sperm gain entrance. Glands of the cervix secrete mucus with varying properties during the monthly cycle; during **ovulation**, the mucus helps sperm transport through the os, and during infertile periods, it can block the sperm from entering. During childbirth, the cervix softens and the os dilates to allow the baby to pass through. The cervix can be seen with a mirror during a pelvic examination, and women should not hesitate to ask their gynecologist or other health care provider to show it to them. The cervix can also be felt at the top end of the vagina.

The Fallopian Tubes

Fallopian (fuh-LOH-pee-un) **tubes**, also called **oviducts**, are 4-inch-long, trumpet-shaped tubes that extend laterally from

---

uterus
The hollow muscular organ in females that is the site of menstruation, implantation of the fertilized ovum, and labor; also referred to as the womb.

ovum
The female reproductive cell or gamete; plural is ova.

perimetrium
The outer wall of the uterus.

myometrium
The smooth muscle layer of the uterus.

endometrium
The mucous membrane lining the uterus.

cervix
The doughnut-shaped bottom part of the uterus that protrudes into the top of the vagina.

os
The opening of the cervix that allows passage between the vagina and the uterus.

ovulation
The phase of the menstrual cycle in which an ovum is released.

Fallopian tubes
Two ducts that transport ova from the ovary to the uterus; also referred to as oviducts.

oviducts
Another name for the Fallopian tubes.

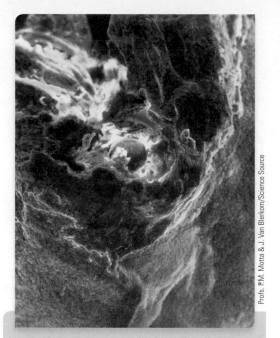

The release of a mature ovum at ovulation is shown. The ovum (red) is surrounded by remnants of cells and liquid from the ruptured ovarian follicle. Mature ova develop in the ovaries from follicles that remained dormant until sexual maturity.

the sides of the uterus. From the side of the uterus, the tube expands into an ampulla, which curves around to a trumpet-shaped end, the **infundibulum** (in-fun-DIB-bue-lum). At the end of the infundibulum are finger-like projections that curl around the ovary, poised to accept **ova** when they are released (see Figure 5.4).

Once a month, an ovary releases an ovum that is swept into the Fallopian tube by the waving action of the **fimbriae** (FIM-bree-ee). The fimbriae sense the chemical messages released from the ovary that signal the release of the ovum and begin a series of muscular contractions to help move the ovum down the tube. If the Fallopian tube is long and flexible, it may even be able to catch the released ovum from the opposite ovary; some women with a single active ovary on one side and a single functioning Fallopian tube on the other have become pregnant (Nilsson, 1990).

The inner surfaces of the Fallopian tubes are covered by cilia (hairlike projections); the constant beating action of the cilia creates a current along which the ovum is moved toward the uterus. Fertilization of the ovum usually takes place in the ampulla region

infundibulum The funnel- or trumpet-shaped open end of the Fallopian tubes.	**fimbriae** The branched, fingerlike border at the end of each Fallopian tube.
ova Two or more ovum; singular is ovum.	**oocyte** A cell from which an ovum develops.

of the Fallopian tube, and the entire transit time from ovulation until arrival inside the uterus is normally about 3 days.

The Ovaries

The mature ovary is a light gray structure most commonly described as the size and shape of a large almond shell. With age, the ovaries become smaller and firmer, and after menopause, they may become difficult for gynecologists to feel during an examination. The ovaries have dual responsibilities: to produce ova and to secrete hormones.

The ovary is the repository of **oocytes** (OH-oh-sites), also known as ova, or eggs, in the female. A woman is born with approximately 250,000 ova in each ovary, each sitting in its own primary follicle (Rome, 1998). Approximately 300 to 500 of these will develop into mature eggs during a woman's reproductive years. The primary follicle contains an immature ovum surrounded by a thin layer of follicular cells. Follicle-stimulating hormone (FSH) and luteinizing hormone (LH) are released in sequence by the pituitary gland during each menstrual cycle, causing about 20 primary follicles at a time to begin maturing. Usually only one follicle finishes maturing each month, which is then termed a *secondary follicle,* containing a secondary oocyte. At ovulation, the secondary follicle bursts, and the ovum begins its journey down the Fallopian tube. The surface of a mature ovary is thus usually pitted and dimpled at sites of previous ovulations.

Ovulation can occur each month from either the right or left ovary. No one knows why one or the other ovary releases an ovum any given month; sometimes they take turns, and sometimes they do not. It seems to be mostly a matter of chance. If one ovary is removed, however, the other ovary will often ovulate every month (Nilsson, 1990). The ovaries are also the female's most important producer of female sex hormones, such as estrogen, which we discuss later in this chapter.

ON YOUR MIND

I had my nipples pierced, but now I'm wondering whether I'll be able to breast-feed later on. Is there any research on nipple piercing and breast-feeding?

The Breasts

Breasts, or mammary glands, are modified sweat glands that produce milk to nourish a newborn child. The breasts contain fatty

Body art, including nipple and genital piercing, is more popular today than ever. If you are going to have your nipples pierced, it is important to seek out a reputable technician to do the piercing and be sure to maintain good after-care to minimize the risk for infection. Most nipple piercings are done horizontally, which decreases the risk for scarring. An improperly pierced nipple, or frequent re-piercings, can lead to blocked milk ducts (GARBIN ET AL., 2009). Because each nipple has several milk ducts, if there were scarring in one area of the nipple, it is possible that other areas may be able to make up for it. Even so, a small percentage of women with breast piercings experience problems breast-feeding, including duct obstruction and/or impaired lactation (GOLLAPALLI ET AL., 2010; KAPSIMALAKOU ET AL., 2010; KLUGER, 2010).

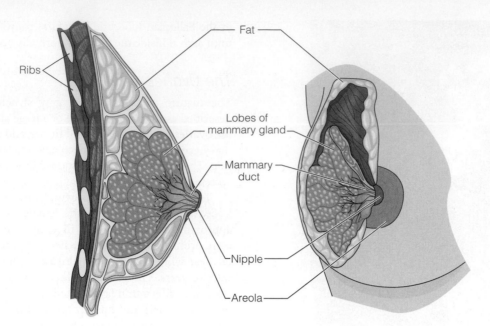

FIGURE **5.5** The female breast.

tissue and milk-producing glands, and they are capped by a **nipple** surrounded by a round, pigmented area called the **areola** (ah-REE-oh-luh) (Figure 5.5). Each breast contains between 15 and 20 lobes, made up of a number of compartments that contain alveoli, the milk-secreting glands. Alveoli empty into secondary tubules, which, in turn, pass the milk into the mammary ducts and then into the lactiferous sinuses, where the milk is stored until the lactiferous ducts release it from the nipple. When **lactation** begins, infant suckling stimulates the posterior pituitary gland to release **prolactin**, which signals milk synthesis, and **oxytocin**, which allows the milk to be released.

Most people see the breasts as an erogenous zone and include stimulation of the breasts in sexual activity. Some women can even experience orgasm from breast and nipple stimulation alone. However, many women in American society are uncomfortable about the appearance of their breasts. Because breasts are a constant source of attention in our society and are considered an important part of a woman's attractiveness, many women are dissatisfied with the size of their breasts (Frederick et al., 2008). Although breast augmentation has been one of the most popular cosmetic surgery procedures in the United States since 2006, there has been a surge in procedures to remove implants (Gold, 2015; Mooney, 2016).

REAL RESEARCH A recent study on pubic hair grooming found that 84% of women reported a history of grooming, while 62% said they have completely removed all of their pubic hair at least once in their lifetime (ROWEN ET AL., 2016).

The female breast is mostly fatty tissue and can take various shapes and sizes.

nipple
A pigmented, wrinkled protuberance on the surface of the breast that contains ducts for the release of milk.

areola
The pigmented ring around the nipple of the breast.

lactation
The collective name for milk creation, secretion, and ejection from the nipple.

prolactin
A hormone secreted by the pituitary gland that initiates and maintains milk secretion.

oxytocin
A hormone secreted by the hypothalamus that stimulates contraction of both the uterus for delivery of the newborn and the mammary gland ducts for lactation.

1 Identify and discuss the functions of the external female sexual organs.

2 Identify and discuss the functions of the internal female sexual organs.

3 Explain what breasts are composed of and the various structures contained in them.

The Female Maturation Cycle

Now that we've discussed the female sexual and reproductive system, let's explore female maturation. The female reproductive system undergoes cyclic hormonal events that lead to pubertal changes, menstruation, and, eventually, menopause.

Female Puberty

After birth, the female's sexual development progresses slowly until puberty. In the past, the first stirrings of puberty began somewhere between 10 and 14 years old, but research has found that girls are beginning puberty earlier than ever before (Biro et al., 2010; Chen et al., 2013; Weil, 2012). The proportion of girls who experience the physical changes of puberty (such as breast and pubic hair development) at ages 7 and 8 years old is greater today than was reported on girls born 10 to 30 years ago. Experts are studying various factors that may be contributing to this trend, such as diet, exposure to environmental chemicals, genetic mutations, insecure attachments in early childhood, and stressful home environments (Belsky et al., 2010; Bianco, 2012; Mouritsen et al., 2010; Schoelwer et al., 2015). Girls whose parents divorced when they were young, as well as girls who grew up in difficult homes, often go through puberty earlier than girls who grew up in intact homes (Ellis, 2013; Ellis et al., 2011). Research is ongoing to explore these possible links.

No one really knows how the body senses it is time for puberty to begin. Although research has found that the onset of puberty varies by race and ethnicity (with Black girls having the first signs of puberty at a median age of 8.8 years old and White and Asian girls experiencing puberty at a median age of 9.7 years old; Biro et al., 2013), we know that the onset of puberty is often related to weight. Girls with a higher body mass index typically begin puberty earlier than those who are average weight or underweight (Biro et al., 2013; Loucks & Nattiv, 2005; Terasawa et al., 2012).

When puberty begins, a girl's internal clock signals the pituitary gland to begin secreting the hormones FSH and LH, which stimulate the ovaries to produce estrogen while the girl sleeps. As puberty continues, the ovaries, in response to stimulation by the pituitary gland, begin to release increasing amounts of estrogen into the circulatory system. Estrogen is responsible for the development and maturation of female primary and secondary sexual characteristics. Under its influence, the Fallopian tubes, uterus, and vagina all mature and increase in size. The breasts also begin to develop, as fat deposits increase and the elaborate duct system develops. The pelvis broadens and changes from a narrow, funnel-like outlet to a broad oval outlet, flaring the hips. The skin remains soft and smooth under estrogen's influence, fat cells increase in number in the buttocks and thighs, and pubic hair develops. Certain bones in the body, which are responsible for height, fuse with the bone shaft, and growth stops. However, if there was a delay or absence of estrogen, females usually grow several inches taller than average.

The changes that accompany puberty prepare the woman for mature sexuality, pregnancy, and childbirth. At some point during puberty, usually at about the age of 11 or 12, the woman will begin to ovulate. Most women are unable to feel any internal signs during ovulation. In a few women, however, a slight pain or sensation, referred to as **mittelschmerz**, accompanies ovulation. The pain may result from a transitory irritation caused by the small amount of blood and fluid released at the site of the ruptured follicle.

For most girls, the beginning of ovulation often closely corresponds to **menarche** (MEN-are-kee), the first menstrual period. However, some may begin menstruating a few months before their first ovulation, whereas others may ovulate a few times before their first full menstrual cycle. In the first year after menarche, **anovulation** is common (Basaran et al., 2013).

The majority of girls reach menarche at approximately the same age that their biological mothers did (Towne et al., 2005). With minor variations, the average age of menarche in most developed countries is 12 to 13 years, but the age of menarche (like the age of puberty) has been decreasing. One hundred years ago, the average age of first menstruation was about 16 years (Patton & Viner, 2007; Remsberg et al., 2005). On average, menarche age is significantly earlier in Black than White or Hispanic girls, and significantly later in Asian girls (Chumlea et al., 2003; Demerath et al., 2013; Freedman et al., 2002). Like puberty, menarche can be influenced by various factors, including genetics, nutrition, and environment.

REAL RESEARCH Exposure to bisphenol A (BPA), found in a variety of common consumer goods, is related to an early onset of female puberty (SUPORNSILCHAI, 2016).

mittelschmerz
German for "middle pain." A pain in the abdomen or pelvis that some women feel at ovulation.

menarche
The start of menstrual cycling, usually during early puberty.

anovulation
A menstrual cycle during which the ovaries do not release an ovum.

In some cultures in the past, as soon as a girl reached menarche, she was considered ready to marry and begin bearing children. In American culture, most people believe that there is a difference between being physiologically capable of bearing children and being psychologically ready for sexual intercourse and childbearing. In Chapter 8, we will discuss the psychological and emotional changes of female puberty.

ON YOUR MIND

Someone once told me that women who live together often experience menstruation at the same time. Is this true, and if it is, why does this happen?

Menstrual synchronicity, as this phenomenon is called, is common, and women who live in the same apartment or house often notice that they begin to cycle together (however, this will happen only if the women are not using hormonal forms of contraception). Menstrual synchronicity occurs because of pheromones, chemicals that are produced by females (more powerfully in animals) during their fertile periods that signal their reproductive readiness. Women who live together detect each other's pheromones (unconsciously), and slowly their fertile periods begin to converge.

Menstruation

Menstruation (also referred to as a "period") is the name for the monthly bleeding that the majority of healthy women of reproductive age experience. The menstrual cycle lasts from 24 to 35 days, but the average is 28 (meaning there are 28 days from the first day of bleeding to the next first day of bleeding). During the cycle, the lining of the uterus builds up and prepares for a pregnancy. When there is no pregnancy, menstruation occurs, and the lining of the uterus is released in the form of blood and tissue. A cycle of hormones controls the buildup and the release. The biological purpose of menstrual cycles is to enable a woman to become pregnant.

The menstrual cycle can be divided into four general phases: follicular, ovulatory, luteal, and menstrual (see Figure 5.6). The **follicular phase** begins after the last menstruation has been completed and lasts anywhere from 6 to 13 days. Only a thin layer of endometrial cells remains from the last menstruation. As the follicles in the ovaries begin to ripen with the next cycle's ova, estrogen released by the ovaries stimulates regrowth of the endometrium's outer layer, to about 2 to 5 millimeters thick.

During the **ovulatory phase**, an ovum is released, usually about the 14th day of the cycle. The particulars of ovulation were described in the preceding section on the ovaries and Fallopian tubes. The third phase is the **luteal phase**. Immediately after ovulation, a small, pouchlike gland, the **corpus luteum**, forms on the ovary. The corpus luteum secretes additional progesterone and estrogen for 10 to 12 days, which causes further growth of the cells in the endometrium and increases the blood supply to the lining of the uterus. The endometrium reaches a thickness of 4 to 6 millimeters during this stage (about a quarter of an inch) in preparation to receive and nourish a fertilized egg. If fertilization does not occur, however, the high levels of progesterone and estrogen signal the hypothalamus to decrease LH and other hormone production. The corpus luteum begins to degenerate as LH levels decline. Approximately 2 days before the end of the normal cycle, the secretion of estrogen and progesterone decreases sharply as the corpus luteum becomes inactive, and the menstrual phase begins.

In the **menstrual phase**, the endometrial cells shrink and slough off (this flow is referred to as **menses** [MEN-seez]). The uterus begins to contract in an effort to expel the dead tissue along with a small quantity of blood. During menstruation, approximately 35 milliliters of blood, 35 milliliters of fluid, some mucus, and the lining of the uterus (about 2 to 4 tablespoons of fluid in all) are expelled from the uterine cavity through the cervical os and ultimately the vagina (this amount may be significantly reduced if a woman is using hormonal contraception; see Chapter 13). If a woman loses too much blood during her period she may develop **anemia**. For most women, menstrual flow stops about 3 to 7 days after the onset of menstruation.

This monthly cyclical process involves a **negative feedback loop**, in which one set of hormones controls the production of another set, which, in turn, controls the first (see Figure 5.7). In the menstrual cycle, the negative feedback loop works like this: estrogen and progesterone are produced by the ovaries at different levels during different parts of the cycle; as these levels increase, the hypothalamus is stimulated to decrease its production of **gonadotropin-releasing hormone (GnRH)**, which sends a message to the pituitary to decrease levels of FSH and LH; the decrease in FSH and LH signals the ovaries to decrease their production of estrogen and progesterone, which signals the hypothalamus to increase its level of GnRH; and it all begins again. This process is similar to a thermostat; when temperature goes down, the thermostat kicks on and raises the temperature, until the rising heat turns off the thermostat and the heat begins slowly to fall.

---

follicular phase
Phase of the menstrual cycle in which the follicles in the ovaries begin to mature.

ovulatory phase
Phase of the menstrual cycle when the the ovum is released.

luteal phase
Phase of the menstrual cycle when the corpus luteum begins to form on the ovary.

corpus luteum
A yellowish endocrine gland in the ovary formed when a follicle has discharged its secondary oocyte.

menstrual phase
Phase of the menstrual cycle when the endometrial cells shrink and slough off.

menses
The blood and tissue discharged from the uterus during menstruation.

anemia
A deficiency in the oxygen-carrying material of the blood, often causing symptoms of fatigue, irritability, dizziness, memory problems, shortness of breath, and headaches.

negative feedback loop
When one set of hormones controls the production of another set, which, in turn, controls the first, thus regulating the monthly cycle of hormones.

gonadotropin-releasing hormone (GnRH)
A hormone produced in the hypothalamus that triggers the onset of puberty and sexual development, and is responsible for the release of FSH and LH from the pituitary.

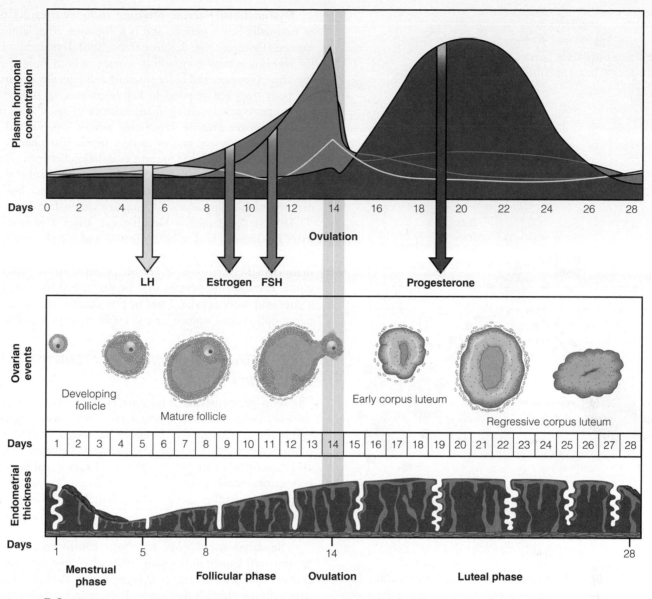

FIGURE **5.6** The menstrual cycle and its relation to the ovarian cycle.

Variations in Menstruation

Amenorrhea (aye-men-oh-REE-uh), the absence of menstruation, can take two forms. In **primary amenorrhea**, a woman never even begins menstruation, whereas in **secondary amenorrhea**, previously normal menses stop before the woman has gone through menopause. Primary amenorrhea may result from malformed or underdeveloped female reproductive organs, glandular disorders, general poor health, emotional factors, or excessive exercise. The most common cause of secondary amenorrhea is pregnancy, although a woman can also stop menstruating because of emotional factors, certain diseases, surgical removal of the ovaries or uterus, hormonal imbalance caused naturally or through the ingestion of steroids, excessive exercise, or eating disorders. For example, almost all women with anorexia nervosa will experience amenorrhea (Pinheiro et al., 2007). When a woman with an eating disorder regains weight, she may not begin ovulating and

menstruating and may need medications to induce ovulation and menstruation (Allaway et al., 2016; Andrisani et al., 2016). If amenorrhea persists, a health care provider should be consulted.

Menstrual cramps are caused by prostaglandins, which stimulate the uterus to contract and expel the endometrial lining during menstruation. The uterine muscles are powerful (remember that the muscles help push an infant out at birth), and the menstrual contractions can be strong and sometimes quite painful. Although the majority of women experience mild-to-moderate cramping during menstruation, some experience **dysmenorrhea**

primary amenorrhea
The lifelong absence of menstruation.

secondary amenorrhea
The absence of menstruation after a period of normal menses.

dysmenorrhea
Painful menstruation.

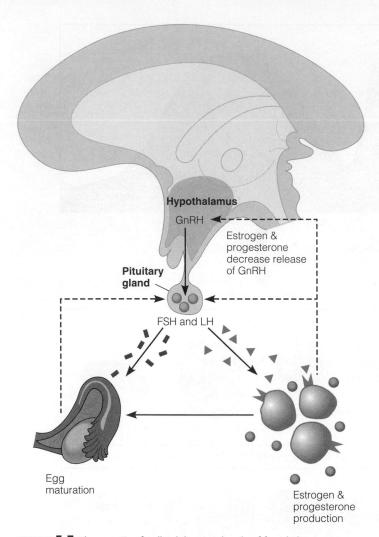

Hypothalamus

GnRH

Estrogen &
progesterone
decrease release
of GnRH

**Pituitary
gland**

FSH and LH

Egg
maturation

Estrogen &
progesterone
production

FIGURE **5.7** The negative feedback loop and cycle of female hormones.

(dis-men-uh-REE-uh), or extremely painful menstruation. Dysmenorrhea may be caused by a variety of inflammations, constipation, or even psychological stress. Poor eating habits, an increase in stress, alcohol use, insufficient sleep, and a lack of exercise can also aggravate the problem. Reducing salt, sugar, and caffeine intake; increased consumption of green leafy vegetables, nuts, seeds, and whole grains, along with omega-3 dietary supplements; moderate exercise; relaxation; warm baths; yoga; and gentle massage of the lower back can decrease dysmenorrhea, as can antiprostaglandin pain relievers, such as ibuprofen (Liu et al., 2011; Rahbar et al., 2012).

dysfunctional uterine bleeding
Menstrual bleeding for long periods of time or intermittent bleeding throughout a cycle.

menorrhagia
Excessive menstrual flow.

intrauterine devices
Devices that are inserted into the uterus for contraception. Progesterone IUDs often inhibit menstruation.

premenstrual syndrome (PMS)
A group of physiological and psychological symptoms related to the postovulation phase of the menstrual cycle.

premenstrual dysphoric disorder (PMDD)
The most debilitating and severe cases of premenstrual syndrome.

Dysfunctional uterine bleeding includes irregular periods or unusually heavy periods and is a common complaint among women (Deligeoroglou & Karountzos, 2016). Dysfunctional uterine bleeding is most common in women at both ends of the age spectrum (younger and older women) and typically occurs when the body does not respond to key hormones, such as estrogen and progesterone, resulting in anovulatory cycles. Causes include stress, excessive exercise, significant weight loss, vaginal injury, hormonal imbalances, and/or chronic illness (Estephan & Sinert, 2010). Newer research has found a correlation between celiac disease and abnormal uterine bleeding (Ehsani-Ardakani et al., 2014). Women with celiac disease were found to experience less abnormal uterine bleeding after switching to a gluten-free diet.

Dysfunctional uterine bleeding can affect a woman's quality of life and can lead to both medical and social complications. Some women suffer from excessive menstrual flow, known as **menorrhagia** (men-or-RAY-gee-uh). Contraceptive pills or hormonal **intrauterine devices** may be prescribed to make menses lighter and more regular. Later in this chapter, we discuss some newer options that women have to avoid menstruation altogether.

Premenstrual Syndrome and Premenstrual Dysphoric Disorder

The term **premenstrual syndrome (PMS)** refers to physical or emotional symptoms that appear in some women during the latter half of the menstrual cycle. Research has found that the majority of women experience at least one emotional, behavioral, or physical premenstrual symptom (Rapkin & Mikacich, 2013). Common complaints include feelings of bloating, fatigue, breast tenderness, food cravings, sadness, mood swings, irritability, restlessness, poor concentration, and sleep problems (including both trouble falling asleep and excessive sleepiness).

The diagnosis of PMS has been controversial. The term became well known in the early 1980s when two separate British courts reduced the sentences of women who had killed their husbands on the grounds that severe PMS reduced their capacity to control their behavior (Rittenhouse, 1991). Although this defense never succeeded in a U.S. trial, publicity over the British trials led to much discussion about this syndrome. Some women objected to the idea of PMS, suggesting that it would reinforce the idea that women were "out of control" once a month and were slaves to their biology, whereas others supported it as an important biological justification of the symptoms they were experiencing each month. The extreme views of PMS have been tempered somewhat, and women who suffer from it can now find sympathetic health care providers and a number of suggestions for coping strategies. Although many women experience premenstrual changes in a positive way, the process has been pathologized for many years (King & Ussher, 2012).

In 2013, the American Psychiatric Association included the diagnosis of **premenstrual dysphoric disorder (PMDD)** in the *Diagnostic and Statistical Manual of Mental Disorders* (*DSM-5*). PMDD is used to identify the most debilitating cases of PMS and it is estimated that approximately 2% to 5% of women meet the criteria for PMDD (Epperson et al., 2012; Rapkin & Winer, 2008). However, Black women are less likely than White women to experience either PMS or PMDD (Gold et al., 2007; Pilver et al., 2010, 2011).

There are four main groups of PMDD symptoms: mood, behavioral, somatic, and cognitive. Mood symptoms include depression, irritability, mood swings, sadness, and hostility. Behavioral symptoms include becoming argumentative, increased eating, and a decreased interest in activities. Somatic symptoms include abdominal bloating, fatigue, headaches, **hot flashes**, insomnia, backache, constipation, breast tenderness, and a craving for carbohydrates (Yen et al., 2010). Cognitive symptoms include confusion and poor concentration. PMDD symptoms seem to have both biological and lifestyle components, and so both medication and lifestyle changes can help.

Although the exact causes for PMDD remain unclear, it is often blamed on physiological factors, such as hormones, neurotransmitters, and brain mechanisms (Shulman, 2010). Hormonal fluctuations are related to mood disorders associated with PMDD, such as depression and hopelessness, whereas neurotransmitters, such as serotonin, have been found to be involved in the expression of irritability, anger, depression, and specific food cravings (Rapkin & Winer, 2008; Zukov et al., 2010). Brain imaging has revealed that increased activity in certain areas of the brain may also contribute to PMDD (Epperson, 2013; Rapkin et al., 2014).

Once documented, the first treatment for PMS or PMDD usually involves lifestyle changes. Dietary and vitamin/nutritional changes such as decreasing caffeine, salt, and alcohol intake; maintaining a low-fat diet; increasing calcium, magnesium, and vitamin E (to decrease negative mood and fluid retention); and various alternative medical interventions, such as herbal remedies and acupuncture, have been found to be helpful. Stress management, increased regular exercise, light therapy, and cognitive behavioral therapy have also shown promising effects (Jang et al., 2014; Sepede et al., 2016; Sohrabi et al., 2013).

Women who have a history of major depression, **posttraumatic stress disorder**, or sexual abuse, or those who smoke cigarettes, tend to be more at risk for development of PMS or PMDD (Forrester-Knauss et al., 2011; Pang et al., 2016). One of the most promising pharmacological treatments has been the use of selective serotonin reuptake inhibitors (antidepressants; Panay & Fenton, 2015; Sepede et al., 2016). Overall, the majority of women who suffer from PMS and PMDD do respond well to treatment.

Menstrual Manipulation and Suppression

Many years ago, women had fewer periods than they do today. Because of poorer health and nutrition, shorter life spans, more pregnancies, and longer periods spent breast-feeding, women had 50 to 150 periods during their lifetime (Ginty, 2005; Thomas & Ellertson, 2000), whereas today they have up to 450.

Over the last few years, **menstrual manipulation** has become more popular, and in the future it is likely that **menstrual suppression** will make periods optional (McMillan & Jenkins, 2016). Continuous-use contraceptive pills (in which a woman takes contraceptive pills with no break), progesterone intrauterine devices, and injections have been used to eliminate and/or reduce menstrual bleeding. Many women report a desire to reduce the number of menstrual periods or schedule their periods around certain events in their lives (e.g., athletic events, dates, or vacations; Steinauer & Autry, 2007). The first continuous-use contraceptive pill became available in 2007 and allows users to stop menstruating altogether. We will discuss these forms of contraception in more detail in Chapter 13. Many transmen who have not undergone surgery to remove their uterus also use menstrual suppression to reduce or eliminate menstrual periods (Chrisler et al., 2016).

Continuous contraceptive pills suppress the growth of the uterine lining, leaving little or nothing to be expelled during menstruation. This treatment has been used for years to treat a menstrual condition known as **endometriosis** (en-doe-mee-tree-OH-sus), which can cause severe menstrual cramping and irregular periods. We will discuss endometriosis more later in this chapter. Overall, there is no medical evidence that women need to have a monthly menstrual period, and studies conclude that continuous use of Food and Drug Administration–approved pills to stop periods is a safe and effective option for preventing pregnancy and reducing menstrual-related symptoms (Strandjord & Rome, 2015).

Women with painful periods, intense cramps, heavy menses, migraines, PMS, epilepsy, asthma, rheumatoid arthritis, irritable

© Todd Randall

While regular exercise is a good thing, it's important for female athletes to maintain a healthy weight. Females who significantly reduce their body fat may stop menstruating.

hot flashes
A symptom of menopause or premenstrual dysphoric disorder in which a woman feels sudden heat, often accompanied by a flush.

posttraumatic stress disorder
A stress disorder that follows a traumatic event, causing flashbacks, heightened anxiety, and sleeplessness.

menstrual manipulation
The ability to plan and schedule the arrival of menstruation.

menstrual suppression
The elimination of menstrual periods.

endometriosis
The growth of endometrial tissue outside the uterus.

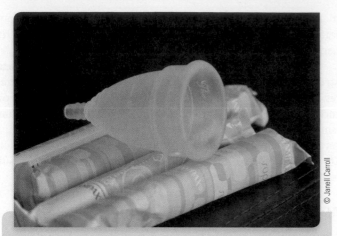

The Diva Cup is a silicone menstrual cup that can be used as an alternative to disposable menstrual products such as tampons.

bowel syndrome, and diabetes can benefit from menstrual suppression (Freeman, 2008; Merki-Feld et al., 2008; Stacey, 2008). In addition, some experts suggest that menstrual suppression may be more beneficial than monthly periods because it allows women to avoid the sharp hormonal changes that occur throughout the menstrual cycle.

Originally, contraceptive pills were designed to mimic the normal menstrual cycle, which is why they allowed a period of time for a woman to bleed. This bleeding, called *withdrawal bleeding,* is a result of stopping contraceptive pills or taking placebo pills for one week each month (Stacey, 2008). Withdrawal bleeding itself bears little biological resemblance to a menstrual period because there is little built-up endometrium to be shed. Even so, most women link having their period with health and fertility. Bleeding has psychological importance to many women; many report it lets them know that their bodies are working the way they should. In fact, abnormal bleeding (spotting or clotting) or an absence of bleeding is an important event that should be reported to a health care provider promptly.

REAL RESEARCH Women with healthy body images are more likely to have positive attitudes toward and beliefs about menstruation (CHRISLER ET AL., 2015).

Menstruation and Sexual Behavior

Many cultures have taboos about engaging in sexual behavior during menstruation. Orthodox Jewish women are required to abstain from sexual intercourse for 1 week after their menstrual period. After this time, they engage in a mikvah bath, after which sexual activity can be resumed.

Although some heterosexual couples report avoiding sexual intercourse during menstruation (often referred to as *menstrual sex*), this might have to do more with personal comfort than anything else. Overall, couples who are more comfortable with their sexuality report higher levels of menstrual sex than couples who are less comfortable (Allen & Goldberg, 2009). Couples should

discuss these issues and decide what they are comfortable with. As mentioned earlier, however, menstrual suppression might make this question obsolete.

Menopause

Menopause refers to the time in a woman's life in which the ovaries become less responsive to hormonal stimulation from the anterior pituitary, resulting in decreased hormone production. Decreased hormone production can lead to irregular cycles or a lack of menstruation. Amenorrhea may occur for 2 or 3 months, followed by a menstrual flow. Women may begin to experience these symptoms during **perimenopause** (pear-ee-MEN-oh-pawz), which occurs anywhere from 2 to 8 years before menopause (Brinton et al., 2015; McNamara et al., 2015). In most cases, menstruation does not stop suddenly. Periods become irregular and intervals between periods become longer. Once menopause has occurred and a woman has not had a period in 1 year, she is considered postmenopausal and is no longer considered at risk for pregnancy. Menopause typically occurs sometime between the ages of 40 and 58; women whose mother gave birth after the age of 35 tend to experience menopause at the later end of that range (Steiner et al., 2010).

Decreasing estrogen can lead to several possible adverse effects, including hot flashes, forgetfulness, mood swings, sleep disorders, bone loss, menstrual irregularities, vaginal dryness, decreased sexual interest, and joint aches (Davis & Jane, 2011; Lloyd et al., 2012; Pinkerton & Stovall, 2010; Timur & Sahin, 2010; Tom et al., 2010). Changes in estrogen can also lead to atrophy of the genitalia. The clitoris and labia become smaller, and degenerative changes occur in the vaginal wall. At the same time, the ovaries and uterus also begin to shrink. Other possible changes include thinning of head hair, growth of hair on the upper lip and chin, drooping of the breasts and wrinkling of skin because of loss of elasticity, and **osteoporosis** (ah-stee-oh-po-ROW-sus), resulting in brittle bones.

Estrogen is important for bone formation and growth in women, and decreased exposure to estrogen can cause osteoporosis. Women with fewer than 25 years of menstruation have an increased incidence of osteoporosis (Parker et al., 2014). Incidentally, *osteopenia* (a thinning of the bones) also can occur in younger women and is a precursor to osteoporosis. To maintain bone strength, women over the age of 20 are advised to get at least 1,000 milligrams of calcium each day and to engage in frequent exercise. Women who smoke, use Depo-Provera, or have an eating disorder or a family history of osteoporosis might consider asking their health care provider for a bone density test.

Most American women go through menopause with few problems, and many find it to be a liberating time, signaling the end of their childbearing years and a newfound freedom from

perimenopause
Transition period in a woman's life, just before menopause.

osteoporosis
An age-related disorder characterized by decreased bone mass and increased susceptibility to fractures as a result of decreased levels of estrogens.

contraception. In fact, the most prevalent sexual problems of older women are not the classic complaints but rather the lack of tenderness and sexual contact with a partner (von Sydow, 2000). In fact, for many menopausal women, life satisfaction is more closely related to relationship with a partner, stress, and lifestyle than menopause status or hormone levels. Keep in mind, however, that a woman's experience of menopause is also shaped by the culture in which she lives. In Chapter 4, we discussed how American media help foster negative attitudes toward aging, especially in women. Cultural issues have an enormous impact on our attitudes about aging, fertility, health, and sexuality.

Hormone Replacement Therapy

In the past, **hormone replacement therapy (HRT)** was used to help maintain vaginal elasticity and lubrication, restore regular sleep patterns, and reduce hot flashes and depression in menopausal women. It was also used to decrease the risks for osteoporosis, cardiovascular disease, and colorectal and lung cancers (Beshay et al., 2015; Sullivan et al., 2016; Whayne & Mukherjee, 2015). However, in 2002, after the publication of results from the Women's Health Initiative that linked HRT to an increased rate of breast cancer, the use of HRT declined significantly (Lobo et al., 2016).

Today, the use of HRT remains controversial. Although some health care providers continue to prescribe it for some patients, others have stopped prescribing it altogether; some prescribe hormone replacement only for those women with severe menopausal symptoms. Newer therapies containing lower levels of hormones have recently become available, and an increasing number of physicians and health care providers are prescribing these newer options to their menopausal patients (Lobo et al., 2016). Some women use nutritional or vitamin therapy or use herbal remedies that contain natural estrogens, such as black cohosh, ginseng, or soy products, instead of hormones to help lessen symptoms (although the use of these products is controversial and may lead to a variety of adverse effects).

Menopausal women need to weigh the risks and benefits of menopausal treatments and HRT. It is important to discuss these issues with a trusted health care provider. No single treatment option is best for everyone.

Review Questions

1 Identify and explain the physiological changes that signal the onset of puberty.

2 Identify and explain the four phases of the menstrual cycle.

3 Explain the variations in menstruation and define amenorrhea, dysmenorrhea, dysfunctional uterine bleeding, and menorrhagia.

4 Explain what is known about the existence of PMS/PMDD. What treatments are available?

5 Differentiate between menstrual manipulation and menstrual suppression.

6 Explain what causes the physical and emotional changes of perimenopause and menopause, and describe the available treatment options.

Female Reproductive and Sexual Health

It is a good idea for every woman to examine and explore her own sexual anatomy. A genital self-examination (see the "Sex in Real Life" feature earlier in the chapter) can help increase a woman's comfort with her genitals. In addition, to maintain reproductive health, it has been recommended that women undergo routine gynecological examinations with **Papanicolaou (Pap) tests** beginning at age 21 (Moyer, 2012). Routine gynecological examinations include a general medical history and checkup, a pelvic examination, and a breast examination. During the pelvic examination, the health care provider inspects the genitals, both internally and externally, and manually examines the internal organs.

In a pelvic exam, the health professional will often use a **speculum** to hold open the vagina to examine the cervix (although there is a sense of stretching, this is not generally painful). Many women report discomfort with speculums, and research is currently being done to find alternatives that would allow health care providers access to the cervix. During a pelvic exam, a Pap test is taken from the cervix (see the discussion on cervical cancer that follows). The practitioner will then insert two fingers in the vagina and press down on the lower abdomen to feel the ovaries and uterus for abnormal lumps or pain. A rectovaginal exam may also be performed, in which the practitioner inserts one finger into the rectum and one into the vagina to feel the membranes in between and also check for blood in the stool.

In 2015, the Well-Woman Task Force of the American College of Obstetricians and Gynecologists reported that women without specific symptoms or complaints might not need annual internal speculum and bimanual exams (U.S. Preventive Services Task Force, 2016). They recommended women talk to their health care providers about this.

---

hormone replacement therapy (HRT)
Medication containing one or more female hormones, often used to treat symptoms of menopause.

Papanicolaou (Pap) test
A microscopic examination of cells scraped from the cervix.

speculum
An instrument for dilating the vagina to examine the cervix and other internal structures.

It is important to choose a health care provider with care, for this person should be a resource for sexual and contraceptive information as well. Referrals from friends or family members, college health services, women's health centers, and Planned Parenthood centers can direct you to competent professionals. Do not be afraid to change practitioners if you are not completely comfortable.

Gynecological Health Concerns

Several conditions can interfere with gynecological health. We discuss some of the most prevalent, including endometriosis, menstrual toxic shock syndrome, polycystic ovarian syndrome, uterine fibroids, vulvodynia, and infections.

Endometriosis

Earlier we discussed how contraceptive pills have been used to treat a condition known as endometriosis. Endometriosis occurs when endometrial cells begin to migrate to places other than the uterus. Endometrial cells may implant on any of the reproductive organs or other abdominal organs and then engorge and atrophy every month with the menstrual cycle, just like the endometrium does in the uterus. The disease ranges from mild to severe, and women may experience a range of symptoms or none at all.

Endometriosis is one of the most common gynecological health problems for women; it affects 6% to 10% of reproductive-age women (Liu et al., 2015). In women who have never given birth, prevalence increases to 30% to 40% (Meuleman et al., 2009). Endometriosis can affect any woman with menstrual periods but is most common in women in their 30s and 40s. Women who experience heavy menstrual cycles and those who have a mother, aunt, or sister with endometriosis are at higher risk for the disease (Audebert et al., 2015; Saha et al., 2015).

The cause of endometriosis is still unknown, although some have suggested that it is due to retrograde menstrual flow (a process in which parts of the uterine lining are carried backward during the menstrual period into the Fallopian tubes and abdomen;

During a pelvic examination, a woman lies on her back with her feet in stirrups. A speculum is used during the pelvic exam to view the cervix.

Frackiewicz, 2000; Leyendecker et al., 2004). The symptoms of endometriosis depend on where the endometrial tissue has invaded but commonly include painful menstrual periods, pelvic or lower back pain, and pain during penetrative sex; some women also experience pain on defecation. Symptoms often wax and wane with the menstrual cycle, starting a day or two before menstruation, becoming worse during the period, and gradually decreasing for a day or two afterward. The pain is often sharp and can be mistaken for menstrual cramping. Many women discover their endometriosis when they have trouble becoming pregnant. The endometrial cells can affect fertility by infiltrating the ovaries or Fallopian tubes and interfering with ovulation or ovum transport through the Fallopian tubes.

Traditionally, endometriosis is diagnosed through ultrasound, magnetic resonance imaging (MRI), biopsy, or the use of a **laparoscope**. Researchers are working on a urine test to aid in diagnosing endometriosis (Liu et al., 2015). Treatment consists of hormone therapy, surgery, or laser therapy to try to remove endometrial patches from the organs (Brown et al., 2010). Endometriosis declines during pregnancy and typically disappears after menopause.

Menstrual Toxic Shock Syndrome

Menstrual toxic shock syndrome (mTSS) is an acute inflammatory disease that develops when *Staphylococcus aureus* bacteria are allowed to grow in the vagina. It is most commonly associated with the use of high-absorbency tampons and forgetting to remove a tampon, which becomes a breeding ground for bacteria. mTSS is a fast-developing disease that can cause multiple organ failure. Symptoms of mTSS usually include fever, sore throat, diarrhea, vomiting, muscle aches, and a scarlet-colored rash. It may progress rapidly from dizziness or fainting to respiratory distress, kidney failure, shock, and heart failure, and it can be fatal if medical attention is not received immediately. (See "Sex in Real Life.")

REAL RESEARCH Eighty percent of American women use tampons, and it's estimated that the average woman uses more than 16,000 tampons in her lifetime (FETTERS, 2015).

Despite the risks, it is estimated that more than 80% of women in the United States use tampons during their periods (Fetters, 2015). Although any woman who uses tampons is at risk for development of mTSS, Black women have been found to be more susceptible than White women (Parsonnet et al., 2005). Regularly removing tampons and using less absorbent tampons reduces the risk for development of mTSS. Research continues to evaluate whether adding various fibers to tampons can decrease the risk for development of mTSS.

laparoscope
A small instrument through which structures within the abdomen and pelvis can be viewed.

menstrual toxic shock syndrome (mTSS)
A bacteria-caused illness, associated with tampon use, that can lead to high fever, vomiting, diarrhea, sore throat and shock, loss of limbs, and death if left untreated.

Women have always tried to find ways to contain menstrual blood without using bulky, external pads. Throughout history there are accounts of women using wads of cotton, wool, sponges, vegetable fibers, or paper to internally absorb menstrual fluids. It wasn't until 1930 that the first tampon, manufactured by Tampax, became available in the United States. Controversy ensued, however, with some arguing that tampon use could damage a woman's hymen or even lead to sexual pleasure. To decrease fears surrounding the need for self-touching while inserting a tampon, Tampax developed a cardboard applicator in the 1940s. By 1944, 25% of American women—mostly young and educated—were using tampons.

Manufacturers continued to tweak the design in an attempt to build a better tampon. In 1971, Playtex developed deodorant tampons infused with a "fresh, clean scent," even though developers knew that menstrual blood didn't smell until it was exposed to air. Tampon use continued to grow, and by 1973 approximately 70% of American women were using them.

In 1975, Procter & Gamble began manufacturing Rely, a super-absorbent tampon. Rely was made of synthetic materials, such as carbonmethylcellulose (CMC). Users could insert a Rely for hours without having to worry about leakage. These tampons were very successful and by 1980, 25% of American women were using this particular brand of tampons. Competitors raced to include similar super-absorbent materials in their products.

By late 1980, over 80% of American women were using tampons. Reports of toxic shock syndrome occurring in tampon users began surfacing, and a link was found between super-absorbent materials, such as CMC, and menstrual toxic shock syndrome (mTSS). Since the majority of cases occurred in women who had been using Rely tampons, Procter & Gamble was forced to take them off the market. By this time, 812 mTSS cases had been reported, with 38 deaths. Every major tampon manufacturer faced multiple lawsuits. Moving forward, the Food and Drug Association required all tampon boxes to contain warning labels on the box about tampon use and the risk of mTSS. In addition, they developed a standard method for designating absorbency (including junior, regular, super, and super-plus) and required tampon manufacturers to label their products. Fears about mTSS had led many women to stop using tampons and resort to the use of pads exclusively. As cases of mTSS declined, many women began using tampons again.

Controversy has surrounded how tampons are made and what ingredients are used. Chemicals such as BPA and phthalates can be harmful and may lead to multiple health problems as we discussed in Chapter 4. However, since tampons are considered "medical devices," the FDA does not require ingredients to be listed on the label. Tampon manufacturers claim that tampons are made from rayon, a synthetic fiber that is made from bleached wood pulp. At one time when the wood pulp was bleached it released dioxin, which is a potential carcinogen. Although today chlorine-free bleach-

Daniela Staerk/Shutterstock.com

ing processes are used, they still release trace amounts of dioxin. In 2013, the FDA released a statement claiming that trace amounts of dioxin did not pose a serious health risk to women (Food and Drug Association, 2013). However, others claim dioxin is stored in fat cells and can accumulate over time. This led to the development of the Robin Danielson Feminine Hygiene Product Safety Act, named after a woman who died from mTSS. This bill would provide women with accurate information about the safety of menstrual products and the risk of mTSS. Although it's been introduced multiple times in Congress, it has never passed (Giordano, 2015).

Today's tampons are safe to use, but it's important for women to always use the lowest absorbency necessary for their menstrual flow and to regularly change them. Most tampon manufacturers recommend frequent changing and never leaving them in for longer than 8 hours. Longer wear can lead to irritation and possible infections. Some women choose to use natural, organic, chemical-free tampons and pads or menstrual cups, such as the Diva Cup (see the nearby photo). These products are often free from chemical dyes or fragrances and have applicators made with biodegradable or sustainable materials. Each brand has its own way of making its products, so it's important to read labels. If you notice negative symptoms (such as itching or burning) after using traditional tampons, it might be worth switching to an organic one that is free from chemicals and fragrances. But remember, organic tampons aren't any safer when it comes to mTSS. Tampon use increases your risk of mTSS no matter what type of tampon you use.

SOURCE: Material in this feature was taken from several sources, including Fetters (2015) and Vostral (2008).

Polycystic Ovarian Syndrome

Polycystic ovarian syndrome (PCOS) is an endocrine disorder that affects approximately 4% to 8% of women worldwide and is a leading cause of female infertility (Daan et al., 2016; Krishnan & Muthusami, 2017). PCOS causes cyst formation on the ovaries during puberty, which causes estrogen levels to decrease and androgen levels (including testosterone) to increase. A girl with PCOS typically experiences irregular or absent menstruation; a lack of ovulation; excessive body and facial hair or hair loss; obesity; acne, oily skin, or dandruff; infertility; or any combination of these.

---

polycystic ovarian syndrome (PCOS)
An endocrine disorder in women that can affect the menstrual cycle, fertility, hormones, a woman's appearance, and long-term health.

Because many of the symptoms, including increased body and facial hair, acne, and weight gain, affect a woman's sense of self, many young women with PCOS experience emotional side effects, including mild depression or self-esteem issues. Getting adequate medical care, education, and support are crucial factors in managing PCOS. There are many possible long-term health concerns associated with PCOS, such as an increased risk for diabetes, high blood pressure, and increased cholesterol levels (Chen & Shi, 2010; Vrbikova et al., 2011). A variety of treatment options are available, including contraceptive pills to regulate the menstrual period and inhibit testosterone production. Many women find that some of the symptoms associated with PCOS decrease with weight loss (Ravn et al., 2013).

ON YOUR MIND

My gynecologist told me I have uterine fibroids and I'm scared to death. Could fibroids turn into cancer? Will I ever be able to have a baby?

The majority of fibroids are **benign**. It is rare for a uterine fibroid to turn into a cancer. The majority of women who have uterine fibroids have normal pregnancies and deliveries. However, in some cases, there may be some issues related to delivery, especially if the fibroids are large when it is time to deliver. If so, a cesarean section may be indicated. Finding a health care provider you trust and educating yourself about uterine fibroids will lessen your fears.

Although the actual cause of PCOS is unknown, researchers continue to explore possible causes. In Chapter 4, we discussed bisphenol A (BPA), a chemical used in various plastics that can disrupt the endocrine system. Recent research has found greater levels of BPA in women with PCOS, which indicates that BPA may play a role in the development of PCOS (Kandaraki et al., 2011; Rutkowska & Rachoń, 2014). In addition, there is some evidence that high levels of androgens during a woman's pregnancy may contribute to the development of PCOS in her offspring (Puttabyatappa et al., 2016).

Uterine Fibroids

Uterine fibroids are noncancerous growths that occur in the myometrium layer of the uterus (see Figure 5.4). It's estimated that 80% of Black women and 70% of White women will develop uterine fibroids by the age of 50 (Upson et al., 2016). However, many women are unaware of them because of the lack of symptoms. If there are symptoms, a woman might experience bleeding between periods, prolonged or heavy bleeding, heavy cramping, pelvic pain and pressure, constipation, abdominal tenderness or bloating, frequent urination, and/or painful penetrative sex. Of all of these symptoms, excessive menstrual bleeding is the most common complaint. It is important to point out that the majority of uterine fibroids are not cancerous and do not cause any problems. However, left untreated, they may cause fertility problems (Quinn & Gedroyc, 2015).

Overall, overweight women and women with a genetic risk for development of uterine fibroids (i.e., a mother or sister with fibroids) are at greater risk for the development of fibroids (Ciebiera et al., 2016). Research has found that an early life hormonal exposure (such as being fed soy formula during infancy), having a mother with pre-pregnancy diabetes, or being born at least 1 month early may be related to the development of uterine fibroids later in life (Upson et al., 2016). More research is needed to explore these links.

Various treatments are used to treat uterine fibroids, including hormone or drug therapy and the use of progesterone intrauterine devices to decrease endometrial buildup, laser therapy, and/or surgery (Donnez et al., 2016; Quinn & Gedroyc, 2015). For many years, **hysterectomy**, the surgical removal of the uterus, was the leading treatment for uterine fibroids, although today it is used only in extreme cases in which the fibroids are very large. Various herbs, such as *curcumin* (a component of turmeric), have been found to decrease uterine fibroids.

Vulvodynia

At the beginning of the 21st century, many physicians were unaware that a condition known as **vulvodynia** (vull-voe-DY-nia) existed. Vulvodynia refers to chronic vulval pain and soreness, and it is estimated that 16% of women experience such pain (Ben-Aroya & Edwards, 2015). Although a burning sensation is the most common symptom, women also report itching, rawness, stinging, or stabbing vaginal/vulval pain. Pain can be either intermittent or constant and can range from mildly disturbing to completely disabling. Over the years, many women experiencing vulval pain were undiagnosed and left untreated because of a lack of knowledge and understanding about the condition. Because of this, women who suffer from vulvodynia experienced high levels of psychological distress and depression (Goldstein et al., 2016). Overall, women with understanding and supportive partners have fewer psychological side effects than those with unsupportive partners (Rosen et al., 2013).

No one really knows what causes vulvodynia, but there have been several speculations, including injury or irritation of the vulval nerves, hypersensitivity to vaginal yeast, allergic reaction to environmental irritants, or pelvic floor muscle spasms (Bohm-Starke, 2010; Murina et al., 2008, 2010; Tommola et al., 2010). Treatment options include biofeedback, diet modification, drug therapy, oral and topical medications, nerve blocks, vulvar injections, surgery, and pelvic floor muscle strengthening (Goldstein et al., 2016). Women experiencing vulvar pain should speak to their health care providers about individualized treatment plans.

benign A nonmalignant, mild case of a disease that is favorable for recovery.	develops within, or is attached to, the uterine wall.
uterine fibroid A (usually noncancerous) tumor of muscle and connective tissue that	**hysterectomy** The surgical removal of the uterus. **vulvodynia** Chronic vulvar pain and soreness.

Infections

Numerous kinds of infections can afflict the female genital system, and not all are necessarily sexually transmitted (we will discuss those that are sexually transmitted in Chapter 15). For example, as we discussed earlier in this chapter, the Bartholin's glands and the urinary tract can become infected, just as any area of the body can become infected when bacteria get inside and multiply. Common vaginal infections include **vaginitis**, **vulvovaginal candidiasis** (can-DID-i-ass-sis; yeast infections) and **bacterial vaginosis (BV)**. We will also discuss **pelvic inflammatory disease (PID)**.

Every woman will experience an irritation of the vulva or vagina at some point in her life, and some women may experience it multiple times. Vaginitis and **yeast infections** are two of the most common reasons why women seek medical attention. Vaginitis can occur when the vaginal tissue becomes irritated by certain products, such as feminine hygiene soaps, powders, scented tampons, panty liners, perfumed soaps, bubble baths, scented or colored toilet paper, or inexpensive sex toys. Horseback riding, hot tubs, or wearing tight pants or underwear without a cotton crotch can also contribute to vaginitis. Vaginitis causes the vaginal tissue to become irritated and red, and there may be pain and burning as well.

Yeast infections (vulvovaginal candidiasis) are usually caused by an overgrowth of *C. albicans* or other *Candida* (or yeast) in the vagina. It's estimated that 75% of women will experience a yeast infection in their lifetime, and about 40% to 45% will have two or more episodes in their lifetime (Workowski & Berman, 2010). Typically, the yeast organism multiplies when the pH balance of the vagina is disturbed because of antibiotics, **douching**, pregnancy, contraceptive pill use, diabetes, or careless wiping after defecation (yeast is present in fecal material, and so it is important to make sure it does not come into contact with the vulva). Although yeast infections are usually not sexually transmitted, if a woman experiences multiple infections, her partner should be evaluated and treated with topical antifungal creams (C. Wilson, 2005). Although male partners are less likely to transmit yeast because the penis does not provide the right environment for the growth of the yeast, female partners can transmit yeast infections during sexual activity (R. Bailey et al., 2008).

Symptoms of a yeast infection include burning, itching, and an increase in vaginal discharge. The discharge may be white, thin, and watery and may include thick white chunks. Treatment includes either an antifungal prescription or over-the-counter drugs (such as Monistat or Gyne-Lotrimin), which are applied topically on the vulva and can be inserted into the vagina. Probiotics that contain "good" bacteria, such as *lactobacillus,* have been found to help regulate bacteria and yeast in the body and have been helpful in controlling yeast infections (Falagas et al., 2006; Watson & Calabretto, 2007). Taking probiotics or eating one cup of yogurt daily may decrease yeast infection recurrences.

Bacterial vaginosis is also caused by an overgrowth of various types of bacteria in the vagina, and it is the most common cause of vaginal discharge, although some women might be asymptomatic (Workowski & Berman, 2010). If there are symptoms, they may include an increase in vaginal discharge (usually a thin, white discharge) accompanied by a strong "fishy" odor. Although it's unclear whether BV is sexually transmitted, research has shown that risk factors include multiple sex partners, inconsistent condom use, and/or douching (Workowski & Berman, 2010). Women who have sex with women may be at increased risk for BV because they have more exposure to vaginal secretions (Evans et al., 2007; Marrazzo et al., 2008, 2010). Recurrent BV can negatively affect women's self-esteem, and embarrassment often causes many women to avoid sexual activity, in particular oral sex (Bilardi et al., 2013).

Treatment for BV involves the use of antibiotics, most commonly oral or vaginal metronidazole or clindamycin (van Schalkwyk et al., 2015). Research has also found that oral probiotics can lengthen remission in women with recurrent BV (Heczko et al., 2015).

Concern about vaginal odor and cleanliness is typically what drives women to use a variety of feminine hygiene products, such as sprays, powders, vaginal soaps, or scented tampons and/or panty liners. However, many of these products may put a woman at risk for vaginal infections because they can irritate vaginal tissue and potentially destroy healthy bacteria necessary to maintain proper pH balance in the vagina.

Some vaginal infections may lead to pelvic inflammatory disease (PID), an infection of the uterus, Fallopian tubes, and/or the ovaries. PID is caused by certain types of bacteria in the vagina and cervix. It is more likely in women who have had multiple sexual partners or have had sex with a partner who has had several sexual partners. Women who douche may also be at increased risk of developing PID. Although many women have no symptoms, those who do may experience abdominal pain, fever, unusual discharge, pain or bleeding during sexual intercourse, and/or burning during urination. Untreated PID may result in the development of scar tissue in the Fallopian tubes, which can cause fertility problems later on. In fact, untreated PID is the leading cause of female infertility. Since some contraceptive devices and sexually transmitted infections can affect the development of PID, we will discuss it more in Chapters 13 and 15.

Cancer of the Female Reproductive Organs

Cancer is a disease in which certain cells in the body do not function properly—they divide too quickly or produce excessive tissue that forms a tumor (or both). A number of cancers can affect the female reproductive organs. In this section, we discuss breast, uterine, cervical, endometrial, and ovarian cancers. We will also review preventive measures for detecting or avoiding common female health problems. In Chapter 14, we will discuss how these illnesses affect women's lives and sexuality.

---

vaginitis
An irritation of the vulva or vagina.

vulvovaginal candidiasis
An infection of the vagina that involves an overgrowth of yeast; also called a yeast infection.

bacterial vaginosis (BV)
Bacterial infection that can cause vaginal discharge and odor, but it often does not have any symptoms.

pelvic inflammatory disease (PID)
Infection of the female reproductive organs.

yeast infection
An infection of the vagina that involves an overgrowth of yeast; also called vulvovaginal candidiasis.

douching
A method of vaginal rinsing or cleaning that involves squirting water or other solutions into the vagina.

Breast Cancer

In my chapter-opening Notebook feature, you read about my friend Stef, who had been battling breast cancer. Breast cancer is one of the most common cancers among American women and the second leading cause of cancer death in women (after skin cancer). The American Cancer Society estimated there would be approximately 255,000 new cases of breast cancer and 41,000 deaths caused by the disease in 2017 (American Cancer Society, 2017a).

There is no known way to prevent breast cancer; however, as Stef's story showed, early detection improves the chances that it can be successfully treated. Women should have their breasts examined during routine gynecological checkups and can perform monthly breast self-examinations. Another important preventive measure is **mammography**, which can detect cancer at early stages when treatment is more effective and cures are more likely. The American Cancer Society released new guidelines for breast cancer screening in 2015 that advise most women to start having regular mammograms at the age of 45 and then every other year beginning at age 55 (Simon, 2015). Women who are at higher risk because of a family history, or another reason, should begin screening earlier and more often. Women should discuss their risk of breast cancer with health care providers to find out whether mammography is appropriate for them.

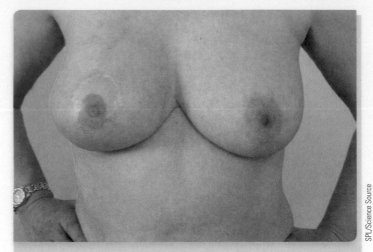

After a mastectomy and breast reconstruction, the new breast does not have a nipple. In the photo above, the woman has undergone nipple areola tattooing on her right breast.

Partial or modified mastectomies are more common today than radical mastectomies.

The earliest sign of breast cancer is either a lump felt on physical exam or an abnormality seen on a mammogram. However, sometimes there are symptoms, including nipple discharge, changes in nipple shape, and skin dimpling. It should be noted here that the discovery of a lump or mass in your breast does not mean you have cancer; most masses are benign, and many do not even need treatment. If it is **malignant** and left untreated, however, breast cancer usually spreads throughout the body, which is why it is important that any lump be immediately brought to the attention of your physician or other health care provider.

RISK FACTORS Being female, older, and having a family history of breast cancer (or ovarian cancer) in a first-degree relative (mother, sister, daughter, father, or brother) are risk factors for developing breast cancer (American Cancer Society, 2015). However, it's important to keep in mind that the majority of women who develop breast cancer do not have a family history of the disease. Breast cancer rates are highest in non-Hispanic White women followed by Black women, and lowest in Asian/ Pacific Islander women. The risk of breast cancer increases with age, with the median age at the time of diagnosis being 61 for White women and 58 for Black women (American Cancer Society, 2017a). Pathogenic genetic mutations related to breast cancer risk were found to be highest in women over the age of 35 who were of Ashkenazi (Eastern European) Jewish ancestry (American Cancer Society, 2017a).

Other risk factors for breast cancer include experiencing menarche before the age of 12 and menopause after the age of 55 (both of which potentially expose a woman to higher levels of reproductive hormones); delayed or absent childbearing; a lack of breast-feeding; obesity; alcohol consumption; cigarette smoking; and the

---

mammography
A procedure for internal imaging of the breasts to evaluate breast disease or screen for breast cancer.

malignant
A cancerous growth that tends to spread into nearby normal tissue and travel to other parts of the body.

use of hormone replacement therapy (American Cancer Society, 2017a). Like Angelina Jolie, some women who have been found to have a high risk for development of breast cancer choose to undergo prophylactic (preventive) mastectomies before breast cancer can develop.

There has been some controversy over the effect of contraceptive pills on breast cancer rates, with many contradictory studies; some studies report an increased risk while others report no increased risk. Studies have found the use of contraceptive pills slightly increases a woman's risk of breast cancer, particularly among women who started taking the pill before the age of 20 (Bassuk & Manson, 2015; Beaber et al., 2014; Nelson et al., 2012), but the risk depends on many factors, such as the type of contraceptive pill used (contraceptive pills have different levels of hormones). A comprehensive study conducted by the U.S. Food and Drug Administration (FDA) concluded that there is no concrete evidence that the pill causes or influences the development of breast cancer; however, the long-term effects of using contraceptive pills are not yet certain, and those with a family history of breast cancer might want to consider using other forms of contraception.

Finally, many rumors and myths about things that cause breast cancer circulate from time to time, such as the idea that using antiperspirant, wearing bras, undergoing elective abortion, having breast implants, or engaging in night work increases a woman's risk for breast cancer. Currently, none of these factors has been associated with an increased risk for breast cancer (American Cancer Society, 2017a).

TREATMENT In the past, women with breast cancer usually had a **radical mastectomy**. Today, few women need such drastic surgery. More often, if necessary, a partial or modified mastectomy is performed, which leaves many of the underlying muscles and lymph nodes in place (see photo accompanying this section). If the breast must be removed, many women choose to undergo breast reconstruction, in which a new breast is formed from existing skin and fat or breast implants (Bellino et al., 2010). While breast reconstruction surgery can re-create a woman's breast by using implants or her own body tissue, her nipples and areolas are usually completely removed. While some women undergo skin grafts and other procedures in search of realistic looking nipples after a mastectomy, others have turned to nipple areola tattoos (Kiernan, 2014). Nipple areola tattoos can also be done in 3D to give the illusion of protrusion. See the nearby photo of nipple areola tattooing.

If it appears that the tumor has not spread, a **lumpectomy** may be considered. A lumpectomy involves the removal of the tumor, together with some surrounding tissue, but the breast is left intact. Survival rates from lumpectomies are similar to, or better than, rates for mastectomies (Hwang et al., 2013). **Radiation**, **chemotherapy**, or both are often used in conjunction with these surgeries.

Uterine Cancer

Different types of cancer can affect the uterus. In this section, we discuss cervical, endometrial, and ovarian cancers.

CERVICAL CANCER The American Cancer Society estimated there would be approximately 13,000 new cases of cervical cancer and 4,200 deaths caused by the disease in 2017 (American Cancer Society, 2017b). At one time cervical cancer was one of the most common causes of death from cancer for American women. However, the death rate from cervical cancer has decreased by more than 50% over the last 40 years (American Cancer Society, 2017b). The main reason for this is the development and use of the Pap test. Although we briefly discussed Pap tests earlier in this chapter, it's important to realize the role they play in the detection of cervical cancer. Pap tests can detect early changes in the cervical cells, which could lead to cervical cancer. Early diagnosis can lead to more effective treatment and higher cure rates. During a Pap test, a few cells are painlessly scraped from the cervix and are examined under a microscope for abnormalities. The majority of cervical cancers develop slowly, so if a woman has regular Pap tests, nearly all cases can be successfully treated (American Cancer Society, 2017b). Unfortunately, studies have found that the majority of women do not understand the importance of regular Pap tests (Daley et al., 2013).

The main cause of cervical cancer is an infection with certain types of human papillomavirus (HPV), which we will discuss further in Chapter 15. Women who begin having sex at a young age or who have multiple sex partners are at an increased risk for HPV infection and cervical cancer. Long-term use of contraceptive pills (5 years or more) and cigarette smoking are also associated with an increased risk for cervical cancer (Franceschi, 2005; Lamb et al., 2013). Unfortunately, few symptoms are associated with cervical cancer until the later stages of the disease. When the cervical cells become cancerous and invade nearby cells, a woman may experience abnormal bleeding during the month, or after penetrative sex or a pelvic exam.

Cervical cancer has high cure rates because it starts as an easily identifiable lesion, called a **cervical intraepithelial neoplasia**, which usually progresses slowly into cervical cancer. Better early detection of cervical cancer has led to a sharp decrease in the number of serious cervical cancer cases. For some poor or uninsured women in the United States and for many women abroad, routine pelvic examinations and Pap tests may not be available. It is for this reason that approximately 80% of the 500,000 new cases of cervical cancer diagnosed every year are in poor countries such as sub-Saharan Africa and Latin America (Catarino et al., 2015).

---

radical mastectomy
A surgical procedure that involves removal of the breast, its surrounding tissue, the muscles supporting the breast, and underarm lymph nodes.

lumpectomy
A modern surgical procedure for breast cancer in which only the tumorous lump and a small amount of surrounding tissue are removed.

radiation
A procedure that uses high-energy radiation to kill cancer cells by damaging their DNA.

chemotherapy
A procedure that uses chemicals to kill rapidly dividing cancer cells.

cervical intraepithelial neoplasia
A change in the cells on the surface of the cervix that may signal early beginnings of cervical cancer; sometimes referred to as cervical dysplasia.

Cervical lesions can be treated with surgery, radiation, chemotherapy, or a combination of these treatments, which has resulted in cure rates up to 90% in early stage disease and a dramatic decline in mortality rate for cervical cancer. If the disease has progressed, treatment commonly includes a hysterectomy followed by radiation and chemotherapy. The FDA has approved vaccines for the prevention of most types of HPV that cause cervical cancer. We discuss these vaccines more in Chapter 15.

ENDOMETRIAL CANCER   The American Cancer Society estimated there would be approximately 61,000 new cases of uterine cancer and 11,000 deaths caused by the disease in 2017 (American Cancer Society, 2017c), most of which involved the endometrial lining. Endometrial cancer affects mainly postmenopausal women and is rare in women under the age of 45. Symptoms include abnormal uterine bleeding or spotting and pain during urination or penetrative sex. Because a Pap test is rarely effective in detecting early endometrial cancer, a **D&C (dilation and curettage)** is more reliable. Endometrial cancer is typically treated with surgery, radiation, hormones, and chemotherapy, depending on the stage of the disease.

Like other cancers of the female reproductive system, women who experienced early menarche and late menopause; delayed or absent childbearing; or who have a history of PCOS or PID are at increased risk for endometrial cancer (American Cancer Society, 2017c). Because unexpected and heavy bleeding are possible indications of endometrial cancer, women who experience changes in menstrual bleeding should inform their health care providers. The earlier endometrial cancer is detected, the higher the survival rates. Unlike other forms of cancer in women, the use of contraceptive pills has been found to lower the risk for endometrial cancer, and this protection remains for at least 10 years after a woman stops taking contraceptive pills (Gierisch et al., 2013; Ruana et al., 2015).

Table 5.1 Reproductive Cancers in Women

Type of Cancer	Diagnosed Cases in 2017	Deaths in 2017	Deaths per Case
Breast	255,000	41,000	16%
Uterine	61,000	11,000	18%
Ovarian	22,000	14,000	64%
Cervical	13,000	4,200	32%

Above is the estimated number of reproductive cancer cases and deaths for 2017. Ovarian cancer accounts for more deaths than any other cancer of the female reproductive system. Deaths from both breast and cervical cancer have been dropping, mostly due to increased screening and improved treatments. The development of the Pap test has contributed to decreased death rates from cervical cancer.

SOURCE: American Cancer Society, 2017.

OVARIAN CANCER   The American Cancer Society estimated there would be approximately 22,000 new cases of ovarian cancer and 14,000 deaths caused by the disease in 2017 (American Cancer Society, 2017d). Although not as common as uterine or breast cancer, ovarian cancer causes more deaths than any other gynecological cancer because it invades the body silently, with few warning signs or symptoms until it reaches an advanced stage. Because the ovary floats freely in the pelvic cavity, a tumor can grow undetected without producing many noticeable symptoms (i.e., there is little pressure on other organs; see Figure 5.4).

Although there are usually few symptoms of ovarian cancer, some women experience abdominal bloating, pelvic pain, difficulty eating or feeling full quickly, and an increased need to urinate (Devlin et al., 2010). Because these symptoms are similar to other conditions (such as irritable bowel syndrome), it is important for a woman to check with her health care provider should she experience such symptoms for more than a week or two. The most important factor in the survival rate from ovarian cancer is early detection and diagnosis. It is estimated that over 70% of ovarian cancer cases are diagnosed late (Chen et al., 2013).

The cause of ovarian cancer is unknown. Like other cancers, an increased incidence is found in women who have not had children, undergo early menopause, have pelvic inflammatory disease, or eat a high-fat diet. Women who are lactose-intolerant or who use talc powder (especially on the vulva) have also been found to have higher rates of ovarian cancer. In 2016, a Missouri jury awarded $72 million to the family of a woman who died of ovarian cancer found to be caused by using Johnson & Johnson's baby powder and other products that contained talc (Yu, 2016). A reduced risk of ovarian cancer has been found in women who use contraceptive pills for an extended time period, undergo tubal ligation (have their Fallopian tubes "tied" to prevent pregnancy), or have had a hysterectomy (Havrilesky et al., 2013; Rice et al., 2012; Rice et al., 2013).

Although there is no 100% accurate test for ovarian cancer, health care providers can use blood tests, pelvic examinations, and ultrasound to screen for the cancer. Women who are at high risk for ovarian cancer may be given an ultrasound and pelvic exam, together with a CA-125 blood test (Lenhard et al., 2009). However, there is some controversy over the usefulness of these tests, because they have fairly high **false negatives** (Rettenmaier et al., 2010). This is why many women with ovarian cancer are diagnosed after the cancer has spread beyond the ovary.

The main treatment options for ovarian cancer include surgery, chemotherapy, hormone therapy, and/or radiation. The type of treatment often depends on how advanced the cancer is. Surgery is the most common treatment, and the ovaries, Fallopian tubes, and uterus could be surgically removed. In women who have not yet had children, the uterus may be spared, although chemotherapy is more successful after the uterus has been removed (American Cancer Society, 2010).

---

dilation and curettage (D&C)
The surgical scraping of the uterine wall with a spoon-shaped instrument.

false negatives
Incorrect result of a medical test that wrongly shows the lack of a finding, condition, or disease.

As you have learned throughout this chapter, understanding anatomy and physiology is an important piece in learning about human sexual behavior. It is important to understand all of the physiological and hormonal influences and how they affect the female body before we can move on to the emotional and psychological issues involved in human sexuality. Anatomy and physiology, therefore, are really the foundations of any human sexuality class. We continue to lay this foundation in the next chapter.

Review Questions

1 Explain what is done in a yearly pelvic exam and why. At what age should women start having pelvic exams?

2 Name and explain three gynecological health concerns.

3 Identify and explain common vaginal infections, including vaginitis, vulvovaginal candidiasis, and bacterial vaginosis.

4 Identify and explain the risk factors that have been identified for breast cancer.

5 Explain how Pap tests and an HPV vaccine can decrease the incidence of cervical cancer.

6 Identify and describe the two most common forms of uterine cancer.

7 Explain why ovarian cancer is the most deadly gynecologic cancer.

Chapter Review

Summary Points

1 A woman's external sex organs, collectively called the vulva, include a number of separate structures, including the mons veneris, labia majora, labia minora, and clitoris. The clitoris is composed of a glans, body, and paired crura (legs). It is richly supplied with both blood vessels and nerve endings and becomes erect during sexual excitement. The introitus, or the opening of the vagina, is usually covered at birth by a fold of tissue known as the hymen.

2 The female's internal sexual organs include the vagina, uterus, cervix, Fallopian tubes, and ovaries. The vagina serves as the female organ of penetration and the passageway to and from the uterus. The inner two thirds of the vagina have very little tactile sensation. The existence of the G-spot has been a controversial issue in the field of human sexuality for many years, and there has never been any scientific proof of its existence.

3 The uterus is a thick-walled, hollow, muscular organ that provides a path for sperm to reach the ovum and provides a home for the developing fetus. The uterine wall is made up of three layers: perimetrium, myometrium, and endometrium. The mature ovaries contain a woman's oocytes and are the major producers of female reproductive hormones.

4 The breasts are modified sweat glands that contain fatty tissue and produce milk to nourish a newborn. Milk creation, secretion, and ejection from the nipple are referred to as breast-feeding, or lactation.

5 Female puberty occurs when the ovaries begin to release estrogen, which stimulates growth of the woman's sexual organs and menstruation. Puberty may be influenced by diet, exposure to environmental chemicals, genetic mutations, insecure attachments in early childhood, and stressful home environments. The onset of puberty varies with race and ethnicity. For most girls, the beginning of ovulation often closely corresponds to menarche. Menstruation is the name for the monthly bleeding that the majority of healthy women of reproductive age experience, and the biological purpose of menstrual cycles is to enable a woman to become pregnant.

6 Menstruation can be divided into four general phases: the follicular phase, the ovulatory phase, the luteal phase, and the menstrual phase. A number of menstrual problems are possible, including amenorrhea, which involves a lack of menstruation; menorrhagia, which involves excessive menstrual flow; and dysmenorrhea, which is painful menstruation. The physical and emotional symptoms that may occur late in the menstrual cycle are called premenstrual syndrome (PMS). The most debilitating and severe cases of PMS are referred to as premenstrual dysphoric disorder (PMDD).

7 Menstrual manipulation, the ability to schedule menstrual periods, and menstrual suppression, the ability to completely eliminate menses, are becoming more popular. There are cultural taboos against sex during menstruation; however, engaging in menstrual sex is a personal decision. Couples who are more comfortable with their sexuality report higher levels of menstrual sex.

8 As women age, hormone or estrogen production wanes, leading to perimenopause and then menopause, or the cessation of menstruation. Menopause typically occurs sometime between the ages of 40 and 58; women whose mother gave birth after the age of 35 tend to experience menopause at the later end of that age range. Most American women go through menopause with few problems, and many find it to be a liberating time. Some women use nutritional therapy to help lessen menopausal symptoms, whereas others use HRT, which has its advantages and disadvantages.

9 A regular gynecological examination is recommended for all women to help detect uterine, ovarian, and cervical cancers. Women should undergo routine gynecological examinations with Pap tests beginning at age 21. Routine gynecological examinations include a general medical history and checkup, a pelvic examination, and a breast examination. During the pelvic examination, the health care provider inspects the genitals, both internally and externally, and manually examines the internal organs.

10 Several conditions can interfere with gynecological health, including endometriosis, menstrual toxic shock syndrome, polycystic ovarian syndrome, uterine fibroids, vulvodynia, and vaginal infections. Common vaginal infections include vaginitis, vulvovaginal candidiasis, and bacterial vaginosis. Concern about vaginal odor and cleanliness often drive women to use a variety of feminine hygiene products, such as sprays, powders, vaginal soaps, or scented tampons and/or panty liners. However, these products may put a woman at risk for vaginal infections.

11 A number of cancers can affect the female reproductive organs, including breast, uterine, cervical, endometrial, and ovarian cancers.

12 Breast cancer is one of the most common cancers among American women, but early detection improves the chances that it can be successfully treated. Risk factors for breast cancer include being female, older, and having a family history of breast cancer (or ovarian cancer) in a first-degree relative. Other risk factors include experiencing early menarche and late menopause; delayed or absent childbearing; a lack of breast-feeding; obesity; alcohol consumption; cigarette smoking; and the use of hormone replacement therapy. Studies have found the use of contraceptive pills slightly increases a woman's risk of breast cancer.

13 Rates of cervical cancer have decreased over the past several decades mostly due to the development and use of Pap tests. Pap tests can detect early changes in the cervical cells, which could lead to cervical cancer. Early diagnosis can lead to more effective treatment and higher cure rates. The majority of women do not understand the importance of regular Pap tests. The main cause of cervical cancer is an infection with certain types of HPV.

14 Endometrial cancer is rare in women under the age of 45, and symptoms include abnormal uterine bleeding or spotting and pain during urination or penetrative sex. Endometrial cancer is typically treated with surgery, radiation, hormones, and chemotherapy depending on how far along it is.

15 Ovarian cancer causes more deaths than any other gynecological cancer. Because the ovary floats freely in the pelvic cavity, cancer can grow undetected without symptoms. The main treatment options for ovarian cancer include surgery, chemotherapy, hormone therapy, and/or radiation. The type of treatment often depends on how advanced the cancer is.

Critical Thinking Questions

1 What were the early messages that you received about menstruation? Did you receive any information about it when you were growing up? What do you wish would have been done differently?

2 Do you think that PMS really exists? Provide a rationale for your answer.

3 How would you feel about engaging in menstrual sex? Why do you think you feel this way?

4 If you are a woman, have you ever done a breast self-exam? If so, what made you decide to perform one? If you have never done a breast self-exam, why not?

Websites

Museum of Menstruation & Women's Health (MUM) An online museum that illustrates the rich history of menstruation and women's health. It contains information on menstruation's history and various aspects of menstruation.

The American College of Obstetricians and Gynecologists (ACOG) ACOG is the nation's leading group of professionals providing health care for women. This site contains information on recent news releases relevant to women's health, educational materials, and links to various other health-related websites.

Office on Women's Health, U.S. Department of Health and Human Services This website, operated by the Department of Health and Human Services, provides a gateway to women's health information services. Information is available on pregnancy, cancers, menstruation, breast-feeding, polycystic ovary syndrome, urinary tract infections, pregnancy, and menopause, as well as many other health-related areas.

National Vulvodynia Association (NVA) The National Vulvodynia Association (NVA) is a nonprofit organization created to educate and provide support. NVA coordinates a central source of information and encourages further research.

Cancer.net This site contains material for health professionals, including cancer treatments, prevention, and CANCERLIT, a bibliographic database.

6 Male Sexual Anatomy and Physiology

Over the years, I've given many lectures on sexual anatomy and physiology. Students are always interested in learning more about both male and female reproductive anatomy. I usually ask students to submit anonymous questions about anatomy and then have a class discussion about these issues. One particular topic always gets a lot of questions: penises. Students are always curious about them and have lots of questions. How long is the average penis? How do men feel about them? Do guys check out other guys' penises?

While I've had lots of conversations with groups of students about how men feel about penises in general, I have not had many opportunities to sit down with one man and talk about how he came to know his penis. What did he remember thinking about it when he was young? How did he feel he compared to other boys and men? Was there pressure to compare himself with others?

Lucky for me, I met Vic, a very funny guy who just so happened to want to talk about his penis. He grew up in a neighborhood surrounded by older kids, which is why he knew more about sex and anatomy than most kids his age. He talked about being exposed to Playboy magazines and listening to guys talk in the locker room. He thought the locker rooms were fairly reserved in high school and that most guys were pretty modest. In college, though, guys became much more open and walked around naked. While most guys were fairly undemonstrative, there were some who felt the need to show their penis to everyone (and it wasn't always the biggest guys).

Vic believes that all guys check each other out, even though most might not admit it. He told me how he used to think that the huge soft penises in the locker room got enormous when they were hard. But he soon learned that if a guy is huge when he's soft, he probably doesn't get much bigger when he's hard. My conversation with Vic was refreshing, honest, and a lot of fun.

Janell Carroll

Mark Golembeski

In this chapter, we explore the anatomy and physiology of biological males. In the previous chapter, we discussed the anatomy and physiology of biological females, and although there are many similarities between the two, there are also many important differences. One obvious difference is the fact that the male gonads (the testes) lie outside of the body, whereas the female gonads (ovaries) are located deep within the abdomen. Because of the location of the male genitalia, boys are often more comfortable and familiar with their genitalia compared with girls. In this chapter, we explore the male reproductive system, maturation, and sexual health issues.

The Male Sexual and Reproductive System

Most men are fairly familiar with their penis and scrotum. Boys learn to hold their penises while urinating, certainly notice them when they become erect, and generally talk more freely about their genitals among themselves than girls do. Yet, the male reproductive system is a complex series of glands and ducts, and few men have a full understanding of how the system operates physiologically.

External Sex Organs

The external sex organs of the male include the penis (which consists of the glans and root) and the scrotum. In this section, we discuss these organs and the process of penile erection.

REAL RESEARCH A recent U.S. Army report revealed that from 2001 to 2013, 1,400 male soldiers who fought in Iraq or Afghanistan suffered injuries to their penis and/or testicles, mostly from bomb blasts (JANAK ET AL., 2016). These injuries can impair sexual functioning, fertility, and/or urinary functions.

penis
The male copulatory and urinary organ, used both to urinate and move spermatozoa out of the urethra through ejaculation; it is the major organ of male sexual pleasure and is homologous to the female clitoris.

semen
A thick, whitish secretion of the male reproductive organs, containing spermatozoa and secretions from the seminal vesicles, prostate, and Cowper's glands.

erection
The hardening of the penis caused by blood engorging the erectile tissue.

corpora cavernosa
Plural of corpus cavernosum (cavernous body); areas in the penis that fill with blood during erection.

corpus spongiosum
Meaning "spongy body," the erectile tissue in the penis that contains the urethra.

glans penis
The flaring, enlarged region at the end of the penis.

corona
The ridge of the glans penis.

frenulum
Fold of skin on the underside of the penis.

urethral opening or meatus
The opening of the penis through which urine and semen are expelled.

foreskin
The fold of skin that covers the glans penis; also called the prepuce.

The Penis

The **penis** is the male sexual organ. It contains the urethra, which carries urine and semen to the outside of the body. The penis has the ability to engorge with blood and stiffen, which evolutionary theorists would tell us allows for easier penetration of the vagina to deposit sperm near the cervical os for its journey toward the ovum. Although there is no bone and little muscle in the human penis, the root of the penis is attached to a number of muscles that help eject **semen** and allow men to move the penis slightly when erect. Throughout history, men have experienced anxiety about penis size. In the accompanying "Sex in Real Life," we discuss this anxiety.

The penis is composed of three cylinders, each containing erectile tissue—spongelike tissue that fills with blood to cause **erection**. Two lateral **corpora cavernosa** (CORE-purr-uh cav-er-NO-suh) lie on the upper sides of the penis, and the central **corpus spongiosum** (CORE-pus spon-gee-OH-sum) lies on the bottom and contains the urethra. The three are bound together with connective tissue to give the outward appearance of a single cylinder and are permeated by blood vessels and spongy tissues that fill with blood when the penis is erect.

THE GLANS PENIS The corpus spongiosum ends in a conelike expansion called the **glans penis**. The glans penis is made up of the **corona**, the **frenulum** (FREN-yu-lum), and the **urethral opening**, or **meatus** (mee-ATE-us; see Figures 6.1 and 6.2). The glans is very sensitive to stimulation, and some males find direct or continuous stimulation of the glans irritating.

The prepuce of the glans penis is a circular fold of skin usually called the **foreskin**. The foreskin is a continuation of the loose skin that covers the penis as a whole to allow it to grow during erection. The foreskin can cover part or all of the glans and retracts back over the corona when the penis is erect. In many cultures, the foreskin is removed surgically through a procedure called a circumcision (sir-kum-SI-zhun; see the "Sexual Diversity in Our World" feature in this chapter for more information about circumcision).

THE ROOT The root of the penis enters the body just below the pubic bone and is attached to internal pelvic muscles (see Figure 6.2). The root of the penis goes farther into the body than most men realize; it can be felt in the perineum (between the scrotum and anus), particularly when the penis is erect.

ERECTION During an erection the penis becomes engorged and firm. This can be the result of any form of stimulation the individual perceives as sexual—visual, tactile, auditory, olfactory, or cognitive. The shape and angle of an erection varies considerably in men. Although many penises point upward when erect, it's possible for them to point horizontally or downward. Erections are not always entirely under conscious control, meaning they can occur spontaneously. In fact, involuntary sleep-related erections

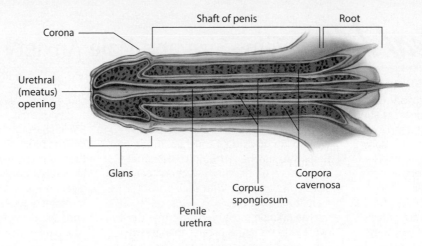

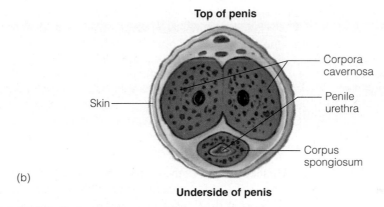

FIGURE **6.1** The internal structure of the penis.

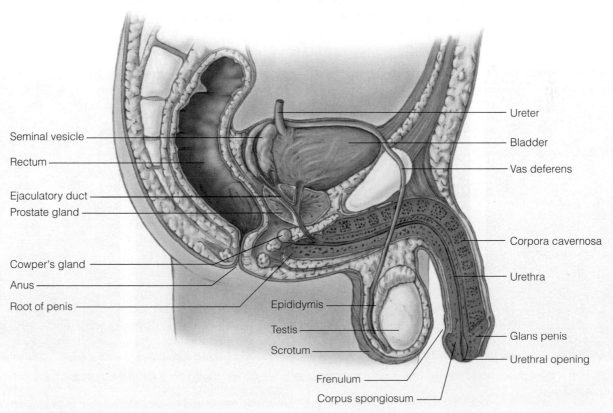

FIGURE **6.2** The male reproductive organs.

Sex in Real Life — Penis Size and Male Anxiety

The penis has been defined as the symbol of male sexuality throughout history. Men have often been plagued by concerns about penis function and size. As discussed in my chapter-opening Notebook feature, many men worry about the size of their penis. Some men assume there is a correlation between penis size and masculinity, or sexual prowess, and many men assume that their partners prefer a large penis. Others worry about their size and fear that they are not "normal." Although there may be a psychological preference for large penises among some partners (just as some partners desire women with large breasts), penis size has no correlation with the ability to excite a partner sexually.

The average flaccid penis is between 3 and 4 inches long, and the average erect penis is 6 inches. Gary Griffen, author of *Penis Size and Enlargement* (1995), has found that only 15% of men have an erect penis measuring more than 7 inches, and fewer than 5,000 erect penises worldwide measure 12 inches. In the end, penis size has been found to be largely dependent on heredity—fathers' penis sizes correlate well with their sons' (T. Hamilton, 2002).

The opinion most men have that the average penis size is greater than it really is comes from pornographic films (which tend to use the largest men they can find), from men's perspective on their own penis (which, from the top, looks smaller than from the sides), and from overestimates of actual penis size (researchers consistently find that people's estimation of the size of penises they have just seen is exaggerated; Shamloul, 2005).

It is erroneous beliefs such as these that cause some men to be anxious and dissatisfied with their penis size (Cranney, 2015). Some succumb to the advertisements for devices promising to enlarge their penises. Men who purchase these devices are bound to be disappointed, for there is no nonsurgical way to enlarge the penis, and many of these techniques (most of which use suction) can do significant damage to the delicate penile tissue (D. Bagley, 2005; Ghanem et al., 2013). Other men with size anxiety refrain from sex altogether, fearing they cannot please a partner or will be laughed at when their partner sees them naked. Despite the self-doubts that perceived penis size inspire in some men, the vast majority of women and men report that penis size is not a significant factor in the quality of a sex partner.

occur several times each night in healthy men (Hirshkowitz & Schmidt, 2005).

Erection is triggered by the parasympathetic division of the autonomic nervous system causing nerve fibers to swell the arteries of the penis, allowing blood to rush into the corpora cavernosa and corpus spongiosum. Nearby muscles compress the veins of the corpora cavernosa, restricting the blood from escaping. The erectile tissues fill with blood, causing the penis to become erect. The penis returns to its flaccid state when the arteries constrict, the pressure closing off the veins is released, and the sequestered blood is allowed to drain. Drugs for erectile dysfunction, such as Viagra, work in a similar way by regulating blood flow in the penis

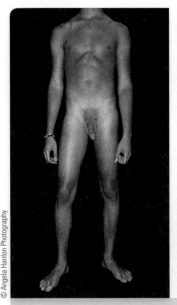 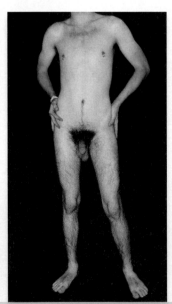 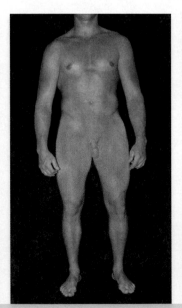 

© Angela Hanlon Photography

All of the men in these photos have "normal" bodies. Individual differences in weight, the size and the shape of the torso, and fullness of pubic hair are normal.

and inhibiting the release of blood (we will discuss these drugs more in Chapter 14).

The Scrotum

The **scrotum** (SKROH-tum) is a loose, wrinkled pouch beneath the penis, covered with sparse pubic hair. The scrotum contains the testicles, each in a sac, separated by a thin layer of tissue. The production and survival of sperm require a temperature that is a few degrees lower than the body's temperature, so the scrotum is actually a kind of cooling tank for the testicles.

When the testicles become too warm, sperm production is halted; in fact, soaking the testicles in hot water has been used as a form of contraception. (Of course, such a technique is highly unreliable, and it takes only a few hardy sperm to undo an hour of uncomfortable soaking. I do not recommend you try it!) Likewise, after a prolonged fever, sperm production may be reduced for as long as 2 months. It has also been suggested that men who are trying to impregnate their partner should wear loose-fitting underwear, because tight underwear has been shown to reduce sperm counts somewhat. In the nearby "Sex in Real Life" feature, we explore factors that have been found to decrease sperm concentrations and quality.

The scrotum is designed to regulate testicular temperature using two mechanisms. First, the skin overlying the scrotum contains many sweat glands and sweats freely, which cools the testicles when they become too warm. Second, the **cremaster muscle** of the scrotum contracts and expands: When the testicles become too cool, they are drawn closer to the body to increase their temperature; when they become too warm, they are lowered away from the body to reduce their temperature. Men often experience the phenomenon of having the scrotum relax and hang low when taking a warm shower, only to tighten up when cold air hits it after exiting the shower. The scrotum also contracts and elevates the testicles in response to sexual arousal, which may be to protect the testicles from injury during sexual activity.

When a boy or man jumps into cold water, muscles in the scrotum pull the testicles up closer to the body in an attempt to keep them at the correct temperature.

Laurie Nassif

ON YOUR MIND

Why do men so often wake up with erections?

Men's penises (and women's clitoral glans) become erect during a part of sleep known as the REM (rapid eye movement) cycle. Some physiologists have suggested that nighttime erections help keep the cells of the penis supplied with blood. Both men and women typically enter REM sleep many times each night, and often we are in a REM cycle right before we wake up. That is why men often awaken with an erection. Some men believe that having a full bladder makes the morning erection firmer and longer lasting, although there is little medical evidence to support this. Because men have no control over nighttime erections, physicians often ask men who have problems getting erections if they experience erections in their sleep, which can indicate whether their erectile problem is physiological or psychological. We discuss this further in Chapter 14.

Internal Sex Organs

The internal sex organs of the male include the testicles, epididymis, vas deferens, seminal vesicles, prostate gland, and Cowper's glands. All of these organs play important roles in spermatogenesis, testosterone production, and the process of ejaculation.

The Testicles

The testicles (also referred to as the testes [TEST-eez]) are egg-shaped glands that rest in the scrotum, each about 2 inches long and 1 inch in diameter. The left testicle usually hangs lower than the right in most men, although this can be reversed in left-handed men (T. Hamilton, 2002). Having one testicle lower than the other helps one slide over the other instead of crushing together when compressed. The testicles serve two main functions: **spermatogenesis** and testosterone production (see Figures 6.3 and 6.4).

SPERMATOGENESIS Sperm are produced and stored in some 300 microscopic tubes located in the testes, known as **seminiferous** (sem-uh-NIF-uh-rus) **tubules**. Uncoiled, this network of tubes would extend over a mile! Figure 6.4 shows the development of the **spermatozoon** in the seminiferous tubules.

scrotum
External pouch of skin that contains the testicles.

cremaster muscle
The "suspender" muscle that raises and lowers the scrotum to control scrotal temperature.

spermatogenesis
The production of sperm in the testes.

seminiferous tubules
The tightly coiled ducts located in the testes where spermatozoa are produced.

spermatozoon
A mature sperm cell.

First, a **spermatogonium** (sper-MAT-oh-go-nee-um) develops in the cells lining the outer wall of the seminiferous tubules and progressively moves toward the center of the tubules. Sertoli cells located in the seminiferous tubules secrete nutritional substances for the developing sperm.

As the spermatogonium grows, it becomes a primary **spermatocyte** (sper-MAT-oh-site) and then divides to form two

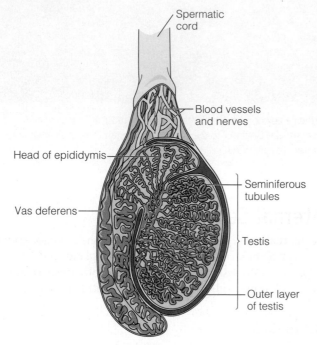

Spermatic cord

Blood vessels and nerves

Head of epididymis

Seminiferous tubules

Vas deferens

Testis

Outer layer of testis

FIGURE **6.3** The internal structure of the testicle.

secondary spermatocytes. As the developing sperm approach the center of the seminiferous tubules, the secondary spermatocytes divide into two **spermatids**. The spermatid then reorganizes its nucleus to form a compact head, topped by an acrosome, which contains enzymes to help the sperm penetrate the ovum. The sperm also develops a midpiece, which generates energy, and a **flagellum** (flah-GEL-lum), which propels the mature spermatozoon. Human sperm formation requires approximately 72 days; yet because sperm is in constant production, the human male produces about 300 million sperm per day (for more information on sperm production, see the nearby "Sex in Real Life" feature).

TESTOSTERONE PRODUCTION Testosterone is produced in the testicles in **interstitial** (in-ter-STIH-shul) or **Leydig** (LIE-dig) **cells**. Testosterone is the most important male hormone; we discuss its role in puberty later in this chapter.

The Epididymis

Once formed, immature sperm enter the seminiferous tubule and migrate to the **epididymis** (ep-uh-DID-uh-mus; see Figure 6.3),

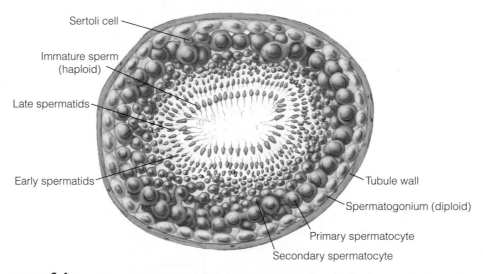

Sertoli cell

Immature sperm (haploid)

Late spermatids

Early spermatids

Tubule wall

Spermatogonium (diploid)

Primary spermatocyte

Secondary spermatocyte

FIGURE **6.4** Spermatogenesis is continually taking place with various levels of sperm development throughout the testis.

spermatogonium An immature sperm cell that will develop into a spermatocyte.	**spermatids** The cells that make up the final intermediate stage in the production of sperm.	**interstitial cells** Cells responsible for the production of testosterone; also referred to as Leydig cells.	**epididymis** A comma-shaped organ that sits atop the testicle and holds sperm during maturation.
spermatocyte The intermediate stage in the growth of a spermatozoon.	**flagellum** The tail-like end of a spermatozoon that propels it forward.	**Leydig cells** The cells in the testes that produce testosterone; also referred to as interstitial cells.	

Sperm, Toxins, Cell Phones, and Tofu: What's the Relationship?

Spermatogenesis occurs throughout a man's life, although sperm morphology (sperm form and structure) and motility (sperm's ability to swim), together with semen volume, have been found to decline continuously between the ages of 22 and 80 years (Eskenazi et al., 2003). Researchers have been evaluating changes in total sperm counts, quality, morphology, and motility and have found that sperm counts have been declining in men throughout the world (Huang et al., 2010; Merzenich et al., 2010; Muratori et al., 2011). Although declines in sperm counts and quality are a normal function of aging, researchers have begun to look at occupational, environmental, and lifestyle factors, such as radiation, heat, cigarette smoke, pollutants, sexually transmitted infections, cell phone usage, diet, and obesity.

Environmental toxins, such as dioxins, bisphenol A (BPA), and phthalates, have also been found to reduce sperm quality (Kalb et al., 2015; Othman et al., 2016). Dioxins are petroleum-derived chemicals that are in herbicides, pesticides, and industrial waste, but they are also commonly found in fish and cow milk products. An analysis of research on pesticide exposure and human sperm found reduced semen quality in areas where pesticides are commonly used (Noorimotlagh et al., 2016). Phthalates have also been found to decrease sperm counts and quality (Ho et al., 2016).

Cell phones have also been identified as a possible factor in the decreasing quality of sperm, although the research is controversial (Agarwal et al., 2011; Harkinson, 2016). Cell phones emit radiofrequency electromagnetic waves, which have been found to affect sperm quality. High cell phone usage may reduce semen quality in men by decreasing sperm counts, motility, and morphology (Agarwal et al., 2008). A strong

Cell phones emit radiofrequency electromagnetic waves, which have been found to potentially affect sperm quality.

association was found between the length of cell phone use and sperm count: Men who talked more than 4 hours a day had lower sperm quality. In addition, because of the heat generated by cell phones, there may be some risks associated with carrying them too close to the body, such as in a pants pocket (Harkinson, 2016).

Several other factors have been found to affect sperm production, such as stress, laptop computer use, biking 5 or more hours a week, and cigarette, alcohol, and marijuana use (Avendaño et al., 2012; Pacey et al., 2014; Wise et al., 2011; Young, 2014). Researchers have also explored soy food intake and sperm concentrations and have found possible links between diets high in soy and male infertility (Giahi et al., 2016). Soy products, such as tofu, contain high levels of isoflavones, which mimic estrogen in the body, causing hormonal changes in a man's body. Research in all these areas will continue to explore the effects of these behaviors on sperm production and quality.

Decreasing sperm counts and quality may contribute to male infertility—in fact, 7% of infertility cases are due to defects in the quality, concentration, and/or motility of sperm (Muratori et al., 2011). There are no known treatments to help a man produce more or higher quality sperm. We will discuss male infertility in more detail in Chapter 12.

---

where they mature for about 10 to 14 days and where some faulty or old sperm are reabsorbed. The epididymis is a comma-shaped organ that sits atop the testicle and can be easily felt if the testicle is gently rolled between the fingers. If uncoiled, the epididymis would be about 20 feet in length. After sperm have matured, the epididymis pushes them into the vas deferens, where they can be stored for several months.

The Ejaculatory Pathway

The **vas deferens** (vass DEH-fuh-renz), or ductus deferens, is an 18-inch tube that carries the sperm from the testicles, mixes it with fluids from other glands, and propels the sperm toward the urethra during ejaculation (see Figure 6.2). **Ejaculation** is the physiological process whereby the seminal fluid is forcefully ejected from the penis. During ejaculation, sperm pass successively through the epididymis, the vas deferens, the ejaculatory duct, and the urethra, picking up fluid along the way from three glands—the seminal vesicles, the prostate gland, and the Cowper's glands.

Colored scan of seminiferous tubules, each containing a swirl of forming sperm cells (in blue).

vas deferens
One of two long tubes that convey the sperm from the testes and in which other fluids are mixed to create semen.

ejaculation
The reflex ejection or expulsion of semen from the penis.

THE SEMINAL VESICLES The vas deferens hooks up over the ureter of the bladder and ends in an **ampulla**. Adjacent to the ampulla are the **seminal vesicles**. The seminal vesicles contribute rich secretions, which provide nutrition for the traveling sperm and make up about 60% to 70% of the volume of the ejaculate. The vas deferens and the duct from the seminal vesicles merge into a common **ejaculatory duct**, a short straight tube that passes into the prostate gland and opens into the urethra.

> ## ON YOUR MIND
> *I've heard people say that what a man eats can influence the taste of his semen. Is this really true?*

Yes. The flavor and taste of the ejaculate varies from man to man and is strongly influenced by what a man eats (T. Hamilton, 2002). For example, the ejaculate of a man who smokes cigarettes or marijuana and drinks coffee or alcohol is often bitter. A man who eats red meat, certain vegetables (such as spinach, asparagus, or broccoli), chocolate, garlic, or greasy foods often has a very sharp flavor to his ejaculate. And a mild to sweet ejaculate is often due to a vegetarian diet or one high in fruits (especially pineapple) and herbs such as peppermint, parsley, or spearmint.

THE PROSTATE GLAND The **prostate** (PROSS-tayt) **gland**, a walnut-sized gland at the base of the bladder, produces several substances that are thought to aid sperm in their attempt to fertilize an ovum. The vagina maintains an acidic pH to protect against bacteria, yet an acidic environment slows down and eventually kills sperm. Prostatic secretions, which comprise about 25% to 30% of the ejaculate, effectively neutralize vaginal acidity almost immediately after ejaculation.

The prostate is close to the rectum, so a doctor can feel the prostate during a rectal examination. The prostate gland can cause a number of physical problems in men, especially older men, including prostate enlargement and the development of prostate cancer. There are various screening methods available to detect prostate cancer (see the Male Reproductive and Sexual Health section later in this chapter).

THE COWPER'S GLANDS The **Cowper's** or **bulbourethral** (bul-bow-you-REE-thral) **glands** are two pea-sized glands that flank the urethra just beneath the prostate gland. The glands have ducts that open right into the urethra and produce a fluid that cleans and lubricates the urethra for the passage of sperm, neutralizing any acidic urine that may remain in the urethra. The drop or more of pre-ejaculatory fluid (often referred to as *pre-cum*) that many men experience during arousal is the fluid from the Cowper's glands. The presence of sperm in this fluid is debated, with some researchers claiming it could have sperm in it and other researchers disagreeing (Killick et al., 2010, 2011; Rogow & Horowitz, 1995; Zukerman et al., 2003). Although fluid produced in the Cowper's glands does not have sperm in it, if sperm was left behind in the urethra after a recent ejaculation, it's possible it could get into the pre-ejaculatory fluid.

EJACULATION Ejaculation, like erection, begins in the spinal column; however, unlike erection, there is seldom a "partial" ejaculation. Once the stimulation builds to the threshold, ejaculation usually continues until its conclusion. When the threshold is reached, the first stage of ejaculation begins: the epididymis, seminal vesicles, and prostate all empty their contents into the urethral bulb, which swells up to accommodate the semen. The bladder is closed off by an internal sphincter so that no urine is expelled with the semen. Once these stages begin, some men report feeling that ejaculation is imminent, that they are going to ejaculate and nothing can stop it; however, others report that this feeling of inevitability can be stopped by immediately ceasing all sensation.

If stimulation continues, strong, rhythmic contractions of the muscles at the base of the penis squeeze the urethral bulb, and the ejaculate is propelled from the body, usually

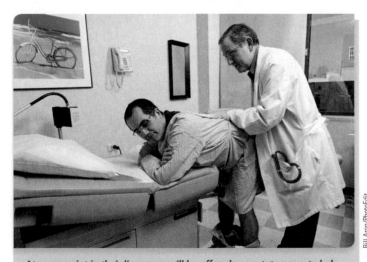

Bill Aron/PhotoEdit

At some point in their lives men will be offered a prostate exam to help detect prostate cancer in its early stages. A man may be asked to either lean over or lie on his side while the health care provider inserts a gloved finger into a man's rectum to check the size of the prostate gland.

---

ampulla
Base of the vas deferens, where the vas hooks up over the ureter of the bladder.

seminal vesicles
The pair of pouchlike structures lying next to the urinary bladder that secrete a component of semen into the ejaculatory ducts.

ejaculatory duct
A tube that transports spermatozoa from the vas deferens to the urethra.

prostate gland
A walnut-sized gland that wraps around the urethra as it comes out of the bladder, contributing fluid to the semen.

Cowper's (or bulbourethral) gland
One of a pair of glands located under the prostate gland on either side of the urethra that secretes a fluid into the urethra.

accompanied by the pleasurable sensation of orgasm. Most men have between 5 and 15 contractions during orgasm, and many report enjoying strong pressure at the base of the penis during orgasm. From an evolutionary standpoint, this may be a way of encouraging deep thrusting at the moment of ejaculation to deposit semen as deeply as possible within the woman's vagina.

Once orgasm subsides, the arteries supplying the blood to the penis narrow, the veins taking the blood out enlarge, and the penis usually becomes flaccid again. Depending on the level of excitement, the person's age, the length of time since the previous ejaculation, and his individual physiology, a new erection can occur anywhere from a few minutes to an hour or so later. In older men, however, a second erection can take hours or even a day or so (we will discuss aging and sexual function further in Chapter 10).

EJACULATE The male ejaculate, or semen, averages about 2 to 5 milliliters—about 1 or 2 teaspoons. Semen normally contains secretions from the seminal vesicles and the prostate gland and about 50 to 150 million sperm per milliliter. If there are fewer than 20 million sperm per milliliter, the male is likely to be infertile—even though the ejaculate can have up to 500 million sperm altogether! Sperm is required in such large numbers because during procreation only a small fraction ever reach the ovum. Also, the sperm work together to achieve fertilization; for example, many die to plug up the os of the cervix for the other sperm, and the combined enzyme production of all sperm is necessary for a single spermatozoon to fertilize the ovum.

Directly after ejaculation, the semen initially coagulates into a thick, mucus-like liquid, probably an evolutionary development to aid in procreation by decreasing the chances it would leak back out of the vagina. After 5 to 20 minutes, the prostatic enzymes contained in the semen cause it to thin out and liquefy. If it does not liquefy normally, coagulated semen in heterosexual men may be unable to complete its movement through the cervix and into the uterus.

> **ON YOUR MIND**
>
> *If a man's testicles produce so much sperm every day, is it harmful if the sperm do not regularly exit the body? Can sperm build up and cause a problem?*

The testicles will not explode if a man doesn't reach orgasm. Sperm are so tiny that even 300 million of them would form a mere drop or two of fluid; most male ejaculate is fluid from other glands, not sperm. Also, sperm are regularly reabsorbed by the body as they sit in the epididymis and vas deferens, and Sertoli cells secrete a hormone to signal the pituitary to decrease follicle-stimulating hormone (FSH) production if the sperm count is getting too high (see Figure 6.5). Many men go days, weeks, months, perhaps even years without ejaculating at all without any physiological damage, and if the body really "needs" to ejaculate, **nocturnal emissions** (also referred to as a wet dream) relieve that pressure.

The Breasts

Men's breasts are mostly muscle, and although they do have nipples, they seem to serve no functional purpose. Some men experience sexual pleasure from having their nipples stimulated, especially during periods of high excitement, whereas others do not.

Gynecomastia, or breast enlargement, is a common problem in boys and men and can occur in newborns, during adolescence, and/or in old age. Most of the time it is caused by hormonal issues, such as increased estrogen or decreased testosterone, the use of various medications, excessive weight, marijuana use, and/or certain diseases (Maseroli et al., 2014; Morcos & Kizy, 2012; Nuttall et al., 2015). Environmental toxins, such as BPA, have also been found to contribute to the development of gynecomastia (Vandenberg et al., 2013). In Chapter 4 we discussed Klinefelter syndrome in which men have an extra X chromosome. Research has shown that this condition may increase a man's risk for gynecomastia (Brinton, 2011; National Cancer Institute, 2014).

REAL RESEARCH Stress can affect sperm production—semen samples from male college students who were experiencing acute lifestyle changes found decreases in sperm quality (Cruz et al., 2015).

Other Sex Organs

Like women, men have other erogenous zones, or areas of the body that may be responsive to sexual touch. This is often an individual preference, but it can include the breasts and other erogenous zones, including the scrotum, testicles, and anus.

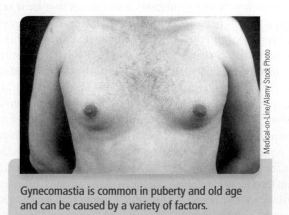

Gynecomastia is common in puberty and old age and can be caused by a variety of factors.

Medical-on-Line/Alamy Stock Photo

nocturnal emissions
Involuntary ejaculation during sleep, also referred to as wet dreams.

Although gynecomastia can make men feel self-conscious, most cases resolve without treatment within about a year (Ladizinski et al., 2014). It is typically a benign condition, but if there is pain or psychological distress, treatment options include pharmacological intervention and surgery, including liposuction (Kim et al., 2016).

It is possible for men to get breast cancer, although it is much more common in women. We will discuss breast cancer further later in this chapter.

Other Erogenous Zones

Besides the penis, many men experience pleasure from stimulation of the scrotum, testicles (usually through gentle squeezing), and anus. As with women's erogenous zones, there is no part of the male body that is not erogenous if caressed in the right way and at the right time during sex. When the body is sexually stimulated, almost all moderate sensation can enhance excitement.

Review Questions

1 Identify the external male sex organs and discuss the functions of each.

2 Explain the process of penile erection.

3 Explain why the male gonads are located outside of the body.

4 Identify and discuss the functions of the internal male sexual organs.

5 Describe the ejaculatory pathway and discuss the path taken by a sperm from the moment it is a spermatogonium until it is ejaculated. What other internal male organs contribute to semen along the way?

The Male Maturation Cycle

Now that we've discussed the male sexual and reproductive system, let's explore male maturation. In the following section, we discuss the physical changes that accompany male puberty. Many of these changes are controlled by hormonal changes that occur and contribute to physical changes in a young boy's body. In Chapter 8, we discuss the psychosexual changes of male puberty.

Male Puberty

During a boy's early life, the two major functions of the testes—to produce male sex hormones and to produce sperm—remain dormant. No one knows exactly what triggers the onset of puberty or how a boy's internal clock knows that he is reaching the age at which these functions of the testes will be needed. Still, at an average of 10 years of age, the hypothalamus begins releasing gonadotropin-releasing hormone (GnRH), which stimulates the anterior pituitary gland to send out follicle-stimulating hormone (FSH) and luteinizing hormone (LH; see Table 4.2).

These hormones flow through the circulatory system to the testes, where LH stimulates the production of the male sex hormone, testosterone, which, together with FSH, stimulates sperm production. A negative feedback system regulates hormone production; when the concentration of testosterone in the blood increases to a certain level, GnRH release from the hypothalamus is inhibited, causing inhibition of LH and FSH production and resulting in decreased testosterone and sperm production (see Figure 6.5 for more information about the negative feedback loop). Alternately, when testosterone levels decrease below a certain level, this stimulates GnRH production by the hypothalamus, which increases the pituitary's LH and FSH production, and testosterone production goes up.

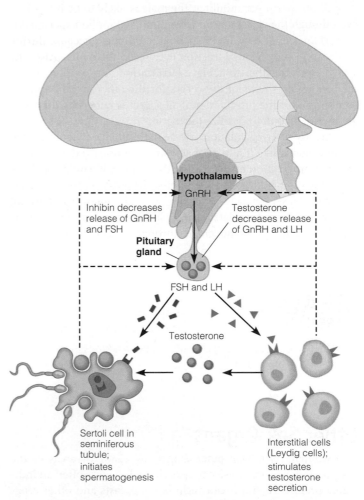

FIGURE **6.5** The negative feedback loop and cycle of male hormones.

Sexual Diversity IN OUR WORLD

Ethnicity, Religion, and Circumcision

Male circumcision is practiced in many parts of the world. It's estimated that approximately 1.5 billion—or 38%—of the world's men are circumcised (Morris et al., 2016). Reasons for circumcision vary around the world but include religious, cultural, social, and/or medical reasons. Nonreligious circumcision became popular in the 1870s because it was thought to promote hygiene, reduce "unnatural" sexual behaviors, prevent syphilis and gonorrhea, and reduce masturbation (G. Kaplan, 1977; Wallerstein, 1980). An article published in 1947 supporting circumcision reported that cancer was more common in laboratory mice who were not circumcised (Plaut & Kohn-Speyer, 1947). All of these medical reports and social considerations have influenced the incidence of male circumcision.

Circumcision can be done at any age, but it is most commonly done at birth up until the mid-20s. Infant circumcision is commonly done in the United States, Canada, Australia, New Zealand, the Middle East, Central Asia, and West Africa. Many parents cite hygiene and health reasons for circumcising their infants at birth. In other areas of the world, such as East and southern Africa, male circumcisions are viewed as rites of passage for boys and a transition from child to man (Brown, 2017). In western Kenya, circumcision represents a transition from boy to man. Prior to circumcision a boy is seen as his mother's child, but afterwards he is his father's son (Brown, 2017). As a result, he is exempt from household chores and moves into his own hut.

Various ethnic groups have different preferences concerning circumcising their male children. If circumcision is common in a particular ethnic group, parents may be inclined to circumcise their male children so their sons will look like other boys (Centers for Disease Control and Prevention, 2008). In addition, fathers who are circumcised often have their sons circumcised (Goldman, 1999). These social considerations have been found to outweigh the medical facts when parents are deciding whether to circumcise their sons.

The practice of male circumcision has elicited more controversy than any other surgical procedure in history. Most of the controversy revolves around the risks and potential benefits of circumcision. However, many studies have found that male circumcision offers protection from HIV infection in men who had sex with women and/or men (Kaufman et al., 2016; Tobian et al., 2015; Weiss et al., 2010).

Circumcised men have also been found to have lower rates of infant urinary tract infections and other sexually transmitted infections, such as herpes and human papillomavirus (see Chapter 15; Morris & Wiswell, 2013; Weiss et al., 2010). Female partners of circumcised men also have lower rates of certain types of vaginal infections and cervical cancer (Chelimo et al., 2013; Hayashi & Kohri, 2013).

A Samburu youth is circumcised in Kenya while his sponsors attend to him—one holding his leg, while the other turns his face away from the circumciser. Boys are not allowed to show any signs of fear or pain during the procedure. Even the blink of an eyelid is frowned upon.

In 2007, the American Academy of Pediatrics released a statement that current evidence of health benefits of newborn male circumcision outweighed the risks (American Academy of Pediatrics, 2012). Benefits of male circumcision included the prevention of urinary tract infections, penile cancer, and the transmission of certain sexually transmitted infections, including HIV.

As puberty progresses, the testicles grow, and the penis begins to grow about a year later. The epididymis, prostate, seminal vesicles, and Cowper's glands also grow over the next several years. Increased testosterone stimulates an overall growth spurt in puberty, as bones and muscles rapidly develop. This spurt can be dramatic; teenage boys can grow 3 or 4 inches within a few months. The elevation of testosterone affects a number of male traits: The boy develops longer and heavier bones, larger muscles, thicker and tougher skin, a deepening voice because of growth of the voice box, pubic hair, facial and chest hair, increased sex drive, and increased metabolism.

Spermatogenesis begins at about 12 years of age, but ejaculation of mature sperm usually does not occur for about another 1 to 1½ years. At puberty, FSH begins to stimulate sperm production in the seminiferous tubules, and the increased testosterone induces the testes to mature fully. The development of spermatogenesis and the sexual fluid glands allow the boy to begin to experience his first nocturnal emissions, although at the beginning, they tend to contain a very low live sperm count.

REAL RESEARCH Women who smoke cigarettes during pregnancy are more likely to have sons with smaller testes and impaired semen quality (VIRTANEN ET AL., 2012).

Andropause

As men age, their blood testosterone concentrations decrease. In fact, it's estimated that testosterone begins decreasing in a man's early 30s at a rate of 1% to 2% a year (Varner, 2013). While a man in his 20s may have a testosterone level of 1,000 to 1,200 ng/dL (nanogram per deciliter), a man in his 80s might have a level of only 200 ng/dL. Unlike women during menopause, men do not go through an obvious set of stages, but some experience a less well-defined set of symptoms called andropause. Although men's ability to ejaculate viable sperm is often retained past age 80 or 90, spermatogenesis does decrease, the ejaculate becomes thinner, and ejaculatory pressure decreases. The reduction in testosterone production can result in decreased muscle strength, decreased libido, easy fatigue, and mood fluctuations. It may also contribute to osteoporosis (Mohamad et al., 2016).

During andropause some men undergo testosterone replacement therapy. Benefits to testosterone replacement therapy include increased sexual interest and functioning, increased bone density and muscle mass, and improved mood (Guth, 2015). However, the use of testosterone replacement therapy is controversial due to possible risks, including the increased risk for prostate cancer, and limited long-term studies of its use (Cunningham & Toma, 2011; Lang et al., 2012; Varner, 2013). Even so, testosterone replacement therapy is commonly used in the United States today.

Review Questions

1 Describe the two major functions of the testes, and explain the hormonal negative feedback loop in males.

2 Identify the age at which spermatogenesis typically begins. At what age does the ejaculate contain mature sperm?

3 What effect do decreasing levels of testosterone have on men? How has testosterone replacement therapy been found to help?

Male Reproductive and Sexual Health

It is a good idea for every man to examine and explore his own sexual anatomy. A regular genital self-examination can help increase a man's comfort with his genitals (see the accompanying "Sex in Real Life" feature). It can also help a man know what his testicles feel like just in case something were to change. We will first discuss various disorders that may affect the male reproductive organs; then we turn to cancer of the male reproductive organs, its diagnosis, and its treatment.

Male Reproductive Health Concerns

Several conditions can affect the male reproductive organs, including cryptorchidism, testicular torsion, priapism, Peyronie's disease, inguinal hernia, and hydroceles. It is important for everyone to have a good understanding of what these conditions are and what symptoms they might cause.

Cryptorchidism

Cryptorchidism (krip-TOR-kuh-diz-um), or undescended testes, is the most common genital condition in boys. The testicles of a male fetus begin high in the abdomen near the kidneys and descend into the scrotum through the inguinal canal during fetal development (see Figure 6.6 for more information). It's estimated that up to 33% of male infants who are born prematurely have cryptorchidism, whereas 2% to 5% of full-term male infants have at least one undescended testicle (Mathers et al., 2011).

There are no clear reasons why cryptorchidism occurs, although research has explored several risks including genetics, hormones, placental abnormalities, and maternal smoking during pregnancy (Massart & Saggese, 2010; Thorup et al., 2010; Virtanen et al., 2012). Studies have found geographic variations

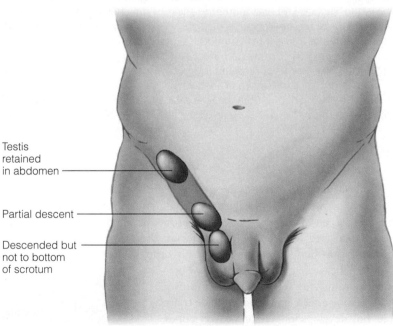

Testis retained in abdomen

Partial descent

Descended but not to bottom of scrotum

FIGURE **6.6** Although the testicles of a fetus begin high in the abdomen, they must descend into the scrotum during fetal development. If they do not, the male may be permanently infertile.

cryptorchidism
A condition in which the testes fail to descend into the scrotum.

Although there are no obvious symptoms of testicular cancer, when detected early, it

© Joel Gordon

is treatable. The only early detection system for testicular cancer is testicular self-examination. In the most recent analysis of data collected by the National College Health Assessment (see Chapter 2), 31% of college men reported they had done a testicular self-exam in the last 30 days (American College Health Association, 2016). Men should examine their testicles at least once a month. This will enable them to have an understanding of what things feel like under normal condi-

tions, which will help them to find any lumps or abnormal growths, should they appear.

To do a testicular examination, compare both testicles simultaneously by grasping one with each hand, using thumb and forefinger. This may be best done while taking a warm shower, which causes the scrotum to relax and the testicles to hang lower. Determine their size, shape, and sensitivity to pressure.

As you get to know the exact shape and feel of the testicles, you will be able to notice any swelling, lumps, or unusual pain. Report any such occurrence to your physician without delay, but do not panic; most lumps are benign and nothing to worry about.

and increasing trends in several countries, which may indicate environmental effects and exposure to certain chemicals (Skakkebaek, 2016; Skakkebaek et al., 2016). Research in these areas is ongoing.

Newborn boys with cryptorchidism may be given testosterone to help with testicular descent. However, surgery may be required to relocate the undescended testis to the scrotum, and it is usually recommended that this be done before the age of 1 (Lee & Houk, 2013). As many as 90% of untreated men with cryptorchidism will be infertile, because excessive heat in the abdomen impairs the ability to produce viable sperm (Fawzy et al., 2015). Men with a history of cryptorchidism also have an increased risk for testicular cancer (Komarowska et al., 2015).

Testicular Torsion

Testicular torsion occurs when a testicle rotates and twists on the spermatic cord (see Figure 6.7). This can happen after vigorous activity, an injury, and even while sleeping. It is fairly rare, affecting approximately 1 in 4,000 males younger than age 25 (Ringdahl & Teague, 2006; Sharp et al., 2013). However, it is most common between the ages of 12 and 16.

Severe scrotal pain and swelling are two of the most common symptoms of testicular torsion, although there can also be abdominal pain, nausea, and vomiting (Sharp et al., 2013). Such pain should be considered a medical emergency, and any man who experiences a rapid onset of scrotal pain should immediately have this checked out. An ultrasound may be used to help diagnose this condition, although oftentimes there is not enough time for an ultrasound because the twisted cord can immediately cut off blood supply to the testicle. Restoration of blood flow to the testicle, through manipulation of the spermatic cord or surgery, must be made within 4 to 8 hours or permanent damage to the testicle may

occur (Sharp et al., 2013). Although we don't know exactly what causes testicular torsion, research indicates men with a family history of the condition are more at risk (Shteynshlyuger & Yu, 2013).

Priapism

Priapism (PRY-uh-pizm) is an abnormally prolonged and painful erection that is unrelated to sexual interest or stimulation. It is primarily a vascular condition that causes blood to become trapped in the erectile tissue of the penis. Although researchers don't know exactly what causes priapism, men with certain conditions, such as sickle cell disease, leukemia, and/or spinal cord injuries, are at greater risk for development of priapism (Salonia et al., 2014; Serjeant &

ON YOUR MIND

Can a male have an orgasm without an ejaculation?

Yes. Before puberty, boys are capable of orgasm without ejaculation. In adulthood, some men report feeling several small orgasms before a larger one that includes ejaculation, whereas other men report that if they have stimulated to orgasm a second or third time, they experience an orgasm without ejaculatory fluid. There are also some Eastern sexual disciplines, such as Tantra, that teach men to develop ejaculatory control and achieve orgasm without ejaculation. Such practices are thought to preserve vital fluids and energy, enabling a man to increase his experience of orgasm and prolong his erection.

testicular torsion	**priapism**
The twisting of a testis on its spermatic cord, which can cause severe pain and swelling.	A condition in which erections are long-lasting and often painful.

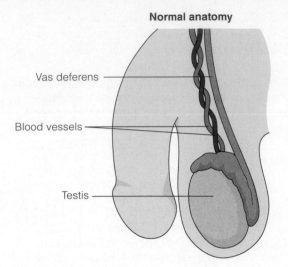
Normal anatomy

Vas deferens

Blood vessels

Testis

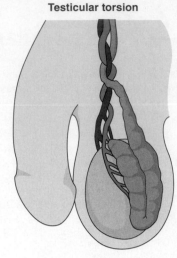
Testicular torsion

FIGURE **6.7** Testicular torsion can occur after injury, exercise, sexual activity, and even while sleeping.

with the disease develop plaques (areas of hardened tissue), which can cause severe erectile pain (Gelbard, 1988). It can be caused by a minor injury to the penis that results in the buildup of scar tissue, but it can also occur in men with a genetic risk or who have certain medical conditions, such as high blood sugar, wound healing problems, or in those who use tobacco. Peyronie's can be treated in a variety of ways, including medication, surgery, or a combination of the two (Heidari et al., 2010; Perovic & Djinovic, 2010; Seveso et al., 2010). The first Food and Drug Administration–approved medication to treat men with Peyronie's disease became available in 2013 (Talib et al., 2016). Penile curvature can often be successfully reduced with treatment, and many men find they are able to engage in penetrative sex again. Smartphone applications to assess penile curvature associated with Peyronie's are being evaluated (Hsi et al., 2013).

Hambleton, 2015). In some cases, drug use (erectile drugs, cocaine, marijuana, or anticoagulants) is to blame. Scientists have been using penile tissue from various animals, such as dogs, cats, rabbits, and mice, to study priapism, which has enhanced researchers' understanding of this condition (Dong et al., 2011).

Like testicular torsion, priapism is considered a medical emergency because it can damage erectile tissue if left untreated. Treatment may involve pharmaceutical agents to reduce blood flow or stents to remove the built-up blood. If there is a neurological or other physiological cause for the priapism, surgery may be necessary (Shrewsberry et al., 2010).

REAL RESEARCH During vigorous vaginal or anal penetration, it is possible for the penis to slide out and slam into the perineum, resulting in a penile bruising (BAR-YOSEF ET AL., 2007). Researchers have found such injuries can lead to pain during erection, penile curvature, and potential hardening of the penile arteries. Seeking immediate medical attention may be necessary, especially if the pain increases.

Peyronie's Disease

Every male has unique curves to his penis when it becomes erect. However, in approximately 1% of men, abnormal penile curvature can cause a painful erection, leading to a condition known as **Peyronie's** (pay-row-NEEZ) **disease**. While it is quite normal for the penis to curve to the right or left, men with Peyronie's experience significant curvature that often makes them unable to engage in penetrative sex. Typically, this is more common in older men, although younger men can also experience Peyronie's disease.

Peyronie's disease occurs in the connective tissue of the penis, and although some cases are asymptomatic, some men

Inguinal Hernia

An **inguinal hernia** (ING-gwuh-nul HER-nee-uh) is caused when the intestine pushes through the opening in the abdominal wall into the **inguinal canal** (the inguinal canal was originally used by the testes when they descended into the scrotum shortly before birth). This can happen during heavy lifting or straining. When it does, the intestine pushes down onto the testicles and causes a bulge or lump in the groin or scrotum. The bulge may change shape and size depending on what the man is doing, because it can slide back and forth within the testicle. Other symptoms include pain and possible blockage of the intestine. Depending on the size and the pain associated with the bulge, surgery may be necessary to push the protruding intestines back into the abdomen, and mesh reinforcement may be used to hold the intestines in place (Hussain et al., 2010; Yeh & Alam, 2014).

Hydrocele

A **hydrocele** (HI-druh-seal) is a condition in which there is an excessive accumulation of fluid within the tissue surrounding the testicle, which causes a scrotal mass (making the scrotum look and feel like a water balloon). This accumulation could be caused

---

Peyronie's disease
Abnormal calcifications or fibrous tissue buildup in the penis, which may cause painful curvature, often making sexual penetration impossible.

inguinal hernia
A condition in which the intestines bulge through a hole in the abdominal muscles of the groin.

inguinal canal
Canal through which the testes descend into the scrotum.

hydrocele
A condition in which there is an excessive accumulation of fluid within the tissue surrounding the testicle, which causes a scrotal mass.

by an overproduction of fluid or poor reabsorption of the fluid, and it can also be caused by a leak through the inguinal canal. Hydroceles are common in newborn males and typically go away on their own after a few months. Although they are relatively painless, some men experience pain and swelling within the testicle. Health care providers often use ultrasound to diagnose a hydrocele, and treatment involves removing the built-up fluid through needle aspiration.

Performance-Enhancing Drug Abuse

Performance-enhancing drugs (PED) include substances that are used to improve any activity in humans, especially in competitive and recreational sports. In professional sports, the use of these substances is often called "doping." Anabolic-androgenic steroids (AAS) and human growth hormone are performance-enhancing drugs, and they have been banned by the International Olympic Committee since 1975. They were also banned by many major sports organizations, including Major League Baseball, the National Football League, and Major League Soccer. The National Collegiate Athletic Association also bans the use of performance-enhancing drugs in college sports.

During puberty in males, the release of androgens increases weight and muscle size and can also increase endurance and aggressiveness. AAS mimic testosterone in the body and are used to gain muscle mass, lose body fat, and enhance athletic performance. Their effects are both anabolic (they build muscle) and androgenic (they increase male characteristics). AAS have been used by elite athletes since the 1950s but became more popular in the athletic community and general population after 1980. In the early 2000s steroids became very controversial as more and more athletes disclosed past steroid use.

> ## ON YOUR MIND
> *If a right-handed man's penis curves to the right when he gets an erection, does this mean he masturbated too much as a child?*

No, although many men worry about this during their adolescent years. The fact is that erect penises are rarely straight or smooth—some curve left or right, and some go up or down on erection. All of these variations are normal. A man may be able to influence the angle of his erect penis by the way he places his penis in his underwear. Pointing the flaccid penis up, down, or sideways in one's underwear can affect the penis's tendency to point in a certain direction when erect (T. HAMILTON, 2002).

The use of AAS has been associated with many damaging changes in the physiological characteristics of organs and body systems. The best documented effects are to the liver, serum lipids, and the reproductive system, including shrinkage of the testicles (and menstrual cycle changes in women; Kovac et al., 2015; Nieschlag & Vorona, 2015). Other areas of concern include cerebrovascular accidents (strokes), prostate gland changes, and impaired immune function (El Scheich et al., 2013; Wysoczanski et al., 2008). In younger athletes, steroids can cause early fusion of the bone-growth plates, resulting in permanently shortened stature. Use of steroids has also been associated with changes in mood and behavior. Schizophrenia and increases in irritability, hostility, anger, aggression (sometimes referred to as "roid rage"), depression, hypomania, psychotic episodes, and guilt have all been reported among users (Piacentino et al., 2015). It may be difficult for some to stop using steroids since many users go through withdrawal when attempting to quit them.

A 2012 study found that 1 in 20 teenagers have used steroids to increase their muscle mass (Eisenberg et al., 2012). In addition to this, one-third of boys also reported using nutritional supplements and/or protein shakes to increase muscle mass. Researchers believe that increased pressure on boys to be muscular and do well in sports has fueled the increased use of these substances. Many well-known athletes have been found guilty of using PEDs, including Lance Armstrong, who was stripped of his seven Tour de France titles and banned from cycling for life after his team was found guilty of using PEDs (Macur, 2012).

Cancer of the Male Reproductive Organs

As we discussed in Chapter 5, cancer is a disease in which certain cells in the body do not function properly—they divide too fast or produce excessive tissue that forms a tumor, or both. A number of cancers can affect the male reproductive organs. Let's now look at prostate, testicular, breast, and penile cancer. In this section, we also review preventive measures for detecting or avoiding common male health problems. In Chapter 14, we will discuss how these illnesses affect men's lives and sexuality.

Prostate Cancer

The American Cancer Society estimates that 1 in 7 men will be diagnosed with prostate cancer in their lifetimes, but that most men who are diagnosed do not die from it. In addition, they reported there would be approximately 161,000 new cases of prostate cancer and 27,000 deaths caused by the disease in 2017

The World Anti-Doping Agency revealed that more than 1,000 Russian athletes, including Olympians, had participated in a state-sponsored doping program from 2011 to 2015.

(American Cancer Society, 2017h). As men age, their prostate glands enlarge. In most cases, this natural occurrence, **benign prostatic hypertrophy (BPH)**, causes few problems. Because of its anatomical position surrounding the urethra, BPH may block urination, and surgeons may need to remove the prostate if the condition becomes bad enough. Of far more concern than BPH is prostate cancer, which is the second-most-common cancer in men (behind skin cancer).

Although men of all ages can experience development of prostate cancer, it is found most often in men over 65. For reasons not clearly understood, prostate cancer is about twice as common among Black men as it is among other ethnicities and races (Lloyd et al., 2015). In addition, Black men are more likely to die of prostate cancer than men from any other racial/ethnic group. Worldwide, the incidence of prostate cancer varies, and it is less common in Asia, Africa, and Central and South America (American Cancer Society, 2017h).

We don't know exactly what causes prostate cancer, but we do know there are several risk factors. Men with a first-degree relative, such as a father or brother, with prostate cancer are two to three times more likely to experience development of prostate cancer, whereas men with more than one first-degree relative are three to five times more likely to experience development of the cancer (American Cancer Society, 2017h). Other risk factors include obesity, along with a diet high in red meat and/or high-fat dairy products.

Early signs of prostate cancer may include problems urinating (including slow stream or an increased need to urinate); blood in the urine or semen; lower back, chest, pelvic, or upper thigh pain; or weakness in the legs or feet. These are also the early signs of BPH, but it is important to talk to a health care provider about any changes. Prostate cancer can often be found early through a **prostate-specific antigen (PSA)** blood test or a digital rectal exam. A PSA measures levels of molecules that are overproduced by prostate cancer cells, allowing health care providers to identify prostate cancer. In the past, a yearly PSA was recommended for men older than 50, but today the American Cancer Society recommends men talk to their health care providers about whether they should be tested. Men with high risk factors should consider getting testing. The PSA test has been one of the most important advances in the area of prostate cancer (Lakhey et al., 2010; Madan & Gulley, 2010). A digital rectal exam is also used to detect prostate cancer early, although it is less effective than the PSA. During a digital rectal exam a health care provider inserts a gloved finger into a man's rectum to feel for lumps or masses on the prostate gland. This test is recommended for men each year beginning at the age of 50 (or earlier for men with a history of prostate cancer).

There are many treatments for prostate cancer. Some argue that, in older men especially, the best thing is "watchful waiting" in which the cancer is simply left alone, because this type of cancer is slow growing and most men will die of other causes before the prostate cancer becomes life-threatening. Men who have a history of poor health or are older than 80 years often opt for watchful waiting (McCarthy, 2015).

Others choose **radical prostatectomy** or radiation treatment, or **cryosurgery** (K. Cohen et al., 2008c; Guo et al., 2015). Two of the most common adverse effects of surgical treatment for prostate cancer include erectile disorder and the inability to hold one's urine. However, the likelihood of these problems depends on several things, including the extent and severity of the cancer and a man's age at the time of surgery (Froehner et al., 2005). Although younger men who experienced satisfactory erections before any prostate cancer treatments have fewer erectile problems after surgery, for most men, erections will improve over time. Difficulty holding urine or urinary leakage may also occur; however, treatments are available to lessen these symptoms. Cryosurgery, which uses a probe to freeze parts of the prostate, has been found to reduce the occurrence of postsurgical erectile disorder and incontinence (Guo et al., 2015).

Prostate cancer may also be treated with hormone therapy or chemotherapy. Newer treatments include drugs that attack only cells with cancer, unlike radiation and chemotherapy, which kill both healthy cells and cancerous cells. Research has found that these drugs hold much promise in the treatment of prostate cancer (Simondsen & Kolesar, 2013). Research into vaccines for prostate cancer also continues. In 2010, the U.S. Food and Drug Administration approved the first vaccine for prostate cancer. Prostate cancer vaccines boost the ability of the immune system to attack prostate cancer cells in the body.

Testicular Cancer

Testicular cancer is fairly rare, with 1 in every 263 males developing it at some point in their lives. It is more common in young and middle-aged men, with the average age of diagnosis being 33 years old. The American Cancer Society estimated there would

ON YOUR MIND

Can a man who has been treated for testicular cancer still have children?

Many men with testicular cancer also have fertility problems. Cancer treatments can cause scarring or ejaculation problems that will interfere with later fertility. During radiation or chemotherapy, sperm production does decline significantly, and some men have no sperm in their semen. However, for the majority of men, sperm production generally returns to normal within 2 to 3 years. Because many men with testicular cancer are in their reproductive prime, waiting 2 or more years might not be an option. For this reason, many health care providers recommend sperm banking before cancer treatment.

---

benign prostatic hypertrophy (BPH)
The common enlargement of the prostate that occurs in most men after about age 50.

prostate-specific antigen (PSA)
Blood test that measures levels of molecules that are overproduced by prostate cancer cells, enabling physicians to identify prostate cancer early.

radical prostatectomy
The surgical removal of the prostate.

cryosurgery
Surgery that uses freezing techniques to destroy part of an organ.

be approximately 9,000 new cases of testicular cancer and 410 caused by the disease in 2017 (American Cancer Society, 2017g).

Testicular cancer has few symptoms until it is advanced, which is why early detection is so important. Most men first develop testicular cancer as a painless testicular mass or a harder consistency of the testes. If there is pain or a sudden increase in testicular size, it is usually due to bleeding into the tumor. Sometimes lower back pain, gynecomastia, shortness of breath, or urethral obstruction may also be found. Blood tests, ultrasound, and biopsy may be used to diagnose testicular cancer.

Risk factors for testicular cancer include a family history of the disease, undescended testicles (cryptorchidism), body size, age, and race/ethnicity. The highest risks are in White males who are tall and between the ages of 20 and 34. Frequent marijuana use has also been found to increase the risk for developing testicular cancer (Huang et al., 2015). Although the incidence of testicular cancer has continuously increased during the last few decades, cure rates have significantly improved. In fact, testicular cancer is one of the most curable forms of cancer (Shanmugalingam et al., 2013). Treatment may involve radiation, chemotherapy, and/or surgery (although radiation and chemotherapy can affect future fertility, the removal of a testicle may not since the remaining testicle produces sperm). Some men with testicular cancer opt to preserve sperm in a sperm bank for future use. If removal of the testicle is necessary, many men opt to get a prosthetic testicle implanted, which gives the appearance of having two natural testicles.

Early diagnosis is very important, because the treatment is less severe early on, and one's chance of being cured is greater.

Lance Armstrong was diagnosed with testicular cancer when he was 25, by which time the cancer had spread to his lungs and brain. Had he known about the importance of early detection, he would have never ignored the swelling and pain in his testicle. Armstrong underwent aggressive surgery and chemotherapy. Sperm banking enabled him to father five children.

Because testicular cancer primarily affects younger men, educational programs targeting college students have been increasing on college campuses. Studies have found that males who attend educational programs are more likely to conduct testicular self-examinations than men who didn't attend the programs (Wanzer et al., 2013).

Male Breast Cancer

Although breast cancer is uncommon among men, approximately 1% of individuals diagnosed with breast cancer are male (Van Der Pol et al., 2016). The American Cancer Society estimated there would be approximately 2,500 new cases of male breast cancer in men and 460 deaths caused by the disease in 2017 (American Cancer Society, 2017e). Even though breast cancer is rare in men, it has a higher mortality rate in men than in women, mainly because it is often diagnosed at a more advanced stage in men compared with women (Rabbee & Grogan, 2016). A national study on gender differences in breast cancer found that men with breast cancer were more likely to be older than women with breast cancer (Greif et al., 2012). Ethnic/racial differences have also been found, with more non-Hispanic Black men diagnosed with breast cancer than White men (Chavez-Macgregor et al., 2013).

Risk factors for breast cancer in men are similar to some of the risk factors for women, including heredity, obesity, hormonal issues, heavy alcohol use, liver disease, and physical inactivity. As it is in women, breast cancer risk in men is increased if other family members have been diagnosed with the disease. There is also an increased risk in men who have gynecomastia or Klinefelter syndrome (see Chapter 4; Brinton, 2011; National Cancer Institute, 2014). As do some women, some men opt for genetic testing to learn whether they are at increased risk, and many experience strong emotional reactions to positive test results. However, men are less likely than women to disclose this information to others (Rabbee & Grogan, 2016). If they do talk to friends about it, most men report females as their main source of support and find it difficult to talk to other men about their diagnosis.

Treatment for breast cancer for men can involve surgery, radiation, chemotherapy, and/or hormone therapy. Studies have found that men with breast cancer are more likely to receive mastectomies (rather than lumpectomies) than women with breast cancer (Fields et al., 2013). Researchers continue to explore differences in surgical options.

Penile Cancer

A wide variety of cancers involving the skin and soft tissues of the penis can occur, although cancer of the penis is rare (Mosconi et al., 2005). The American Cancer Society estimated that in 2014 there were approximately 1,640 new cases of penile cancer, along with 320 deaths from the disease. Any lesion on the penis must be examined by a health care provider, for benign and malignant conditions can be very similar in appearance, and sexually transmitted infections can appear as lesions. Even though most men handle and observe their penis daily, there is often significant

Table 6.1 Reproductive Cancers in Men

Type of Cancer	Diagnosed Cases in 2017	Deaths in 2017	Deaths per Case
Prostate	161,000	27,000	16%
Testicular	9,000	410	4.5%
Breast	2,500	460	18%
Penile	1,640	320	19%

Above is the estimated number of reproductive cancer cases and deaths for 2017. While prostate cancer is one of the most common cancers in men, most men who are diagnosed with prostate cancer do not die from it. Testicular cancer can usually be successfully treated as well. Breast and penile cancers are fairly rare in men. In fact, breast cancer is about 100 times less common among men than women.

SOURCE: American Cancer Society, 2017, e, f, g, h.

delay between a person's recognition of a lesion and seeking medical attention. Fear and embarrassment may contribute most to this problem, yet almost all of these lesions are treatable if caught early.

Newer research is exploring the link between exposure to human papillomavirus (HPV) and penile cancer. HPV is found in 50% of men with penile cancer and may be an important risk factor for penile cancer (Flaherty et al., 2014; Hernandez et al., 2014). We will discuss HPV more in Chapter 15.

As you have learned throughout this chapter and the last one on female anatomy, understanding anatomy and physiology is an important part of learning about human sexual behavior. We must understand all of the physiological and hormonal influences, and how they affect both the female and male body, before we can move on to the emotional and psychological issues involved in human sexuality. Anatomy and physiology, therefore, are really the foundations of any human sexuality class. Now we can turn our attention to other important aspects of human sexuality. In Chapter 7, we discuss love and intimacy.

Review Questions

1 Differentiate between cryptorchidism, testicular torsion, priapism, and Peyronie's disease. Explain what these conditions are and what symptoms they might cause. What are some treatments for these conditions?

2 Explain how anabolic-androgenic steroids work, why they are often abused, and some of the adverse side effects.

3 Identify the various types of cancers of the male reproductive organs, and discuss the most and least common cancers in men.

4 Identify the most common cancer in men between the ages of 25 and 34, and explain the early symptoms and treatment.

5 Identify the most frequently diagnosed cancer in the male reproductive organs overall, and describe early symptoms and treatment.

Chapter Review

Summary Points

1 Because the male genitalia sit outside the body, unlike female gonads, boys are often more comfortable with their genitalia. The external male sex organs include the penis and the scrotum. The penis contains the urethra and three cylinders—two corpora cavernosa and one corpus spongiosum. These cylinders are bound together with connective tissue and allow the penis to fill with blood during sexual arousal.

2 In many cultures, the foreskin of the penis is removed during circumcision. Benefits of male circumcision include the prevention of urinary tract infections, penile cancer, and the

transmission of certain sexually transmitted infections, including HIV. In addition, female partners of circumcised men have lower rates of certain types of vaginal infections and cervical cancer. Recently, the American Academy of Pediatrics said the health benefits of newborn male circumcision outweigh the risks.

3 An erection is a spinal reflex, and many types of sexual stimulation can lead to this response. Erectile shape and angle varies considerably in men. Although many penises point upward when erect, they may point horizontally or downward. Erections are not

always entirely under conscious control and can occur spontaneously. Erection is caused by parasympathetic division of the autonomic nervous system causing nerve fibers to swell the arteries of the penis, allowing blood into the corpora cavernosa and corpus spongiosum. Muscles compress the veins of the corpora cavernosa, restricting the blood from escaping.

4 The scrotum sits outside the man's body and contains the testicles. Sperm survival requires a temperature that is a few degrees lower than the body's temperature. The scrotum is designed to regulate testicular temperature using two mechanisms—sweat glands and the cremaster muscle. The cremaster muscle pulls the testicles closer to the body to increase their temperature when it is cold and lowers them away from the body to decrease their temperature when it is warm. The muscle also contracts and elevates the testicles in response to sexual arousal, which may be to protect the testicles during sexual activity.

5 The internal male sex organs include the testes, epididymis, vas deferens, seminal vesicles, prostate gland, and Cowper's glands. All of these organs play important roles in spermatogenesis, testosterone production, and the process of ejaculation. The testicles have two main functions: spermatogenesis and testosterone production. One testicle usually hangs lower (or higher) than the other so that they do not hit each other when compressed. Testosterone, the most important male hormone, is produced in the Leydig cells.

6 The ejaculatory pathway is the route the sperm and semen take to exit the body. Ejaculation is the physiological process whereby the seminal fluid is ejected from the penis. The vas deferens, seminal vesicles, prostate, and Cowper's glands all work together during ejaculation. The seminal vesicles contribute 60% to 70% of the semen; the prostate gland contributes 25% to 30%; and the Cowper's glands contribute the rest. An average ejaculate is approximately 1 to 2 teaspoons. After orgasm, the blood that has been trapped in the penis is released, and the penis becomes flaccid.

7 Gynecomastia, or breast enlargement, is a common problem in boys and men and can occur in newborns, during adolescence, and/ or in old age. It can be caused by hormonal imbalance, drug therapy, drug abuse, excessive weight, and/or certain diseases, such as Klinefelter syndrome. Some environmental toxins have also been found to possibly contribute to the development of gynecomastia. Although it can make men feel self-conscious, most cases resolve without treatment within about a year.

8 At about the age of 10, a boy enters the first stages of puberty. A negative feedback system regulates hormone production. As puberty progresses, the testicles increase in size, and the penis begins to grow. Increased testosterone stimulates an overall growth spurt in puberty, and the bones and muscles grow rapidly. Spermatogenesis usually begins about the age of 12, but it takes another year or so for an ejaculation to contain mature sperm.

9 Blood testosterone levels decrease as a man ages, and men experience a condition known as andropause. During this time, testosterone levels decrease, sperm production slows down, the ejaculate becomes thinner, and ejaculatory pressure decreases. Decreased testosterone may lead to decreased muscle strength, decreased libido, easy fatigue, mood fluctuations, and osteoporosis. Some men undergo testosterone replacement therapy for andropause, and benefits include increased sexual interest and functioning, increased bone density and muscle mass, and improved mood. However, one of the largest risks involves the increased risk for prostate cancer. Even so, testosterone replacement therapy is commonly used in the United States today.

10 There are several diseases of the male reproductive organs, including cryptorchidism, testicular torsion, priapism, and Peyronie's disease. Cryptorchidism is the most common genital disorder in boys. Because of the risk of infertility, surgery may be required to relocate the undescended testis to the scrotum. Testicular torsion refers to a twisting of a testis on its spermatic cord. This can happen after injury, exercise, sexual activity, or while sleeping. Acute scrotal pain and swelling are common symptoms, although there can also be abdominal pain, nausea, and vomiting. Restoration of blood flow to the testicle must be made within 4 to 8 hours or permanent damage to the testicle may occur.

11 Priapism is an abnormally prolonged and painful erection that is unrelated to sexual interest or stimulation. It is primarily a vascular condition that causes blood to become trapped in the erectile tissue of the penis. Like testicular torsion, priapism is considered a medical emergency because it can damage erectile tissue if left untreated. Peyronie's disease involves abnormal penile curvature that can lead to painful erections. It is often caused by scar tissue that develops under the skin of the penis.

12 An inguinal hernia is caused when the intestine pushes through the opening in the abdominal wall into the inguinal canal. This can happen during heavy lifting or straining and can cause a bulge or lump in the groin or scrotum. A hydrocele is a condition in which there is an excessive accumulation of fluid within the tissue surrounding the testicle, which causes a scrotal mass. Fortunately, these are treatable conditions.

13 Performance-enhancing drug use involves using substances to improve certain activities, such as athleticism. Anabolic-androgenic steroids (AAS) are performance-enhancing drugs that mimic testosterone in the body. Typically, they are used to gain muscle mass, lose body fat, and enhance athletic performance. They have been used by elite athletes but recently they became more popular in the athletic community and general population. Steroid use can cause liver and prostate gland changes, testicular shrinkage, and impaired immune function. Research has also found an increased risk for cerebrovascular accidents and, for young people, early fusion of bone growth plates.

14 Men can be at risk for the development of prostate, testicular, breast, and penile cancers. As men age, their prostate gland enlarges. Prostate cancer is the second leading cause of cancer death in men behind skin cancer. The American Cancer Society estimates that 1 in 7 men will be diagnosed with prostate cancer in their lifetime. Prostate cancer is more common in men older than 65. For unknown reasons, this type of cancer is twice as common in Black men as in men of other ethnicities and races. Risk factors include genetics and diets high in red meat and/or high-fat dairy products.

15 Early signs of prostate cancer include lower back, pelvic, or upper thigh pain; inability to urinate; loss of force in the urinary stream; urinary dribbling; pain or burning during urination; blood in the urine; and frequent urination, especially at night. Today, PSA and digital rectal exams are used to detect prostate cancer as early as possible. Most men are encouraged to have PSA and digital rectal exams beginning around the age of 50 or earlier if they have risk factors for prostate cancer. Treatment includes watchful waiting, medications, surgery, radiation, chemotherapy, or hormone therapy. The FDA approved the first vaccine for prostate cancer in 2010; vaccines boost the ability of the immune system to attack prostate cancer cells in the body.

16 Testicular cancer is the most common malignancy among young men. Most men have few, if any, symptoms until the cancer is advanced, which is why early detection is so important. A painless testicular mass or a harder consistency of the testes, pain, or a sudden increase in testicular size may be early indications of testicular cancer. Risk factors include a family history, cryptorchidism, body size, age, and race/ethnicity. White men, tall men, and those who frequently use marijuana may also be at increased risk. Testicular cancer is one of the most curable forms of cancer.

17 Even though breast cancer is rare in men, it has a higher mortality rate in men than in women, mostly because it is diagnosed at a more advanced stage. Risk factors include heredity, obesity, hormonal issues, heavy alcohol use, liver disease, and physical inactivity. Men with gynecomastia or Klinefelter syndrome may also have an increased risk. Treatment can involve surgery, radiation, chemotherapy, and/or hormone therapy.

18 Penile cancer is relatively uncommon, but it usually appears as a noticeable change on the penis, such as swelling, skin or color changes, lumps, sores, or growths. Newer research is exploring the link between exposure to HPV and penile cancer. HPV is found in 50% of men with penile cancer.

Critical Thinking Questions

1 We don't seem to need to know how the digestive system works to eat. Why is detailed knowledge of the sexual functioning of men important in human sexuality?

2 Why do you think most men have anxiety about penis size? Do you think most men you know are happy with the size of their penis today? Why or why not?

3 If you have a baby boy in the future, would you have him circumcised? Why or why not?

4 Why do you think men are uncomfortable talking about their own body image issues? Why aren't men encouraged to explore these issues?

Websites

Testicular Cancer Resource Center   The Testicular Cancer Resource Center provides accurate information about testicular self-examination and the diagnosis and treatment of testicular cancer. Links are also provided for other cancers and additional websites.

MedlinePlus Health Information: Men's Health Topics   MedlinePlus contains information on issues such as prostate cancer, circumcision, reproductive health concerns, gay and bisexual health, and male genital disorders.

Lance Armstrong Foundation   The Lance Armstrong Foundation focuses on cancer information and education. It provides services and support and strives to help cancer patients through diagnosis and treatment, encouraging each to adopt the same positive attitude that Lance Armstrong adopted in his own battle with cancer.

National Organization of Circumcision Information Resource Centers (NOCIRC)   NOCIRC is the first national clearinghouse for information about circumcision. It claims that it owns one of the largest collections of information about circumcision in the world.

7 | Love and Intimacy

I've always been a "people watcher," and nothing interests me more than watching couples in love. I watch how couples look at each other when they talk and how they interact with each other. I recently met Neil and Joan, a couple who have been married for 34 years. They met when Neil was 21 and Joan was 16. Although it was "love at first sight" for Neil, it took Joan a bit longer. They married three years later and today they have three grown children. We talked about their relationship and how they think their marriage has survived the test of time. I could tell how much Joan and Neil cared about each other. As they sat together on the couch for our talk they constantly smiled at each other, laughed, and even finished each other's sentences. They shared their advice for making love last, and here are some key thoughts:

1. In any relationship, it's important to be nice to each other, respect each other, and always treat each other the way you want to be treated.

2. Relationships really take a lot of work and compromise to succeed.

3. Finding common interests can help strengthen a relationship. One example that Joan shared with me had to do with camping. She never liked camping but since Neil did, she agreed to go on family camping trips. Doing so helped her realize that she enjoyed it as well.

4. Always find time for each other. At the beginning of their marriage it was tough to keep the focus on themselves because most of their time was spent on their children. They worked hard to find time for each other. Sometimes one of their parents would come stay with the kids so that they could have a weekend together.

5. Know that relationships aren't always perfect. Joan and Neil said they always find a way to work problems out. They believe that the key to staying in love is being willing to work at it.

Janell Carroll

Love and the ability to form loving, caring, and intimate relationships with others are important for both our physical and emotional health. In his 1999 best-selling book *Love and Survival: The Scientific Basis for the Healing Power of Intimacy*, Dean Ornish (1999) discusses the importance of love and intimacy. He points to a variety of research studies that support the fact that physical health is strengthened when people feel loved and can open up and talk to each other. Many studies support Ornish's findings and have found that social support and love decrease **allostatic load** and are related to stronger immune systems and lower levels of illnesses (Brooks et al., 2014; Tomfohr et al., 2016). Following are some other interesting findings from Ornish's (1999) longitudinal research:

- College students who had distant and non-emotional relationships with their parents had significantly higher rates of hypertension and heart disease years later than did students who reported close and emotionally connected relationships.

- Heart patients who felt "loved" had 50% less arterial damage than those who said they did not feel "loved."

In this chapter, we talk about the forms and measures of love, where love comes from, love throughout the life cycle, and building intimate relationships. Before we begin, try answering this question: What is love?

When people love each other, they experience less stress in their lives, stronger immune systems, and better overall health.

REAL RESEARCH College students who believe in "love at first sight" may have greater levels of relationship satisfaction and commitment than those who do not believe in such romantic ideas (Vannier & O'Sullivan, 2016).

What Is Love?

One of the great mysteries of humankind is the capacity to love, to make attachments with others that involve deep feeling, selflessness, and commitment. Throughout history, literature and art have portrayed the saving powers of love. How many songs have been written about its passion, and how many films have depicted its power to change people's lives? Yet after centuries of writers discussing love, philosophers musing over its hold on people, and religious leaders teaching of the necessity to love one another, how much do we really know about love? Are there different, separate kinds of love, or are they all simply variations on one fundamental emotion? Does love really "grow"? Is love different at age 15 than at 50? What is the relationship between love and sexuality?

We go through life trying to come to terms with loving, trying to figure out why we are attracted to certain types or why we fall in love with the people we do. The mystery of love is part of its attraction. We are surrounded with images of love in the media and are taught from the time we first listen to fairy tales that love is the answer to most of life's problems. The majority of songs played on popular radio stations are about love—wanting it, having it, and/or losing it. In fact, music, movies, and television inundate us with stories of what love is, and these stories have a powerful impact on us.

Love in Other Times and Places

The desire for love is as old as humanity. Each new generation somehow imagines that it is the first, the inventor of "true love," but look at this poem from the late Egyptian empire, written more than 3,000 years ago:

> *I found my lover on his bed, and my heart was sweet to excess.*
> *I shall never be far away (from) you while my hand is in*
> *your hand, and I shall stroll with you in every favorite place.*
> (Quoted in Bergmann, 1987, p. 5)

The Middle Ages glorified the modern idea of **romantic love**, including loving from afar, or loving those one could not have (**unrequited** [un-ree-KWI-ted] **love**). Not until the 19th century did people begin to believe that romantic love was the most desirable form of loving relations. Through most of Western history, marriage was an economic union, arranged by the parents. Once wed, husbands and wives were encouraged to learn love for one another, to develop love. How different that is from the modern romantic ideal of love preceding marriage.

---

allostatic load
The biological effects, including the production of adrenaline, cortisol, and other chemical messengers, of stress on the human body.

romantic love
Idealized love, based on romance and perfection.

unrequited love
Loving another when the love will never be returned.

Review Questions

1 Discuss the research on the effects of love and intimacy on physical health.

2 Explain how images of love in the media influence our concept of what love is.

3 Explain how love today may be different from love that was experienced through most of Western history.

Forms and Measures of Love

We must admire those researchers who are willing to tackle a difficult subject such as the origins of love or the different forms of love. We all love, and one of the characteristics of love is that we often believe that the intensity of the emotion is unique to us, that no one else has ever loved as we have loved. We also feel many different kinds of love, such as love of a friend, love of a parent, love of a child, love of a celebrity, or love of a pet. Philosophers, historians, social scientists, and other scholars have made attempts to untangle these types of love.

Romantic Versus Companionate Love

Romantic love is the all-encompassing, passionate love of romantic songs and poetry, of tearjerker movies and romance novels, and has become the prevailing model of sexual relationships and marriage in the Western world. Romantic love is also sometimes called passionate love, infatuation, obsessive love, and even lovesickness, and with it comes a sense of ecstasy and anxiety, physical attraction, and sexual desire. We tend to idealize the partner, ignoring

ON YOUR MIND

Why is love so confusing?

faults in the newfound joy of the attachment. Passionate love blooms in the initial euphoria of a new attachment to a sexual partner, and it often seems as if we're swept away by it; that is why we say we "fall" in love or fall "head over heels" in love.

Love is confusing because it often evokes a host of other emotions and personal issues, such as self-worth and self-esteem, fears of rejection, passion and sexuality, jealousy and possessiveness, great joy and great sadness. Dealing with those emotions is confusing enough, but in love, we try to communicate and share intimacies with another person who is going through the same kinds of confused feelings that we are. When so many emotions are fighting for attention, it comes as no surprise that the mind doesn't seem to work that well!

Few feelings are as joyous or exciting as romantic love. The explosion of emotion is often so intense that people talk about being unable to contain it; it feels as if it spills out of us onto everything we see. Some people joke that there is nothing quite as intolerable as those in love; they are just so annoyingly happy all the time! It is not surprising that such a powerful emotion is celebrated in poetry, story, and song. It is also not surprising that such a powerful emotion seems as though it will last forever. After all, isn't that what we learn when the couples in fairy tales "live happily ever after" and when the couples in movies ride off into the sunset?

Unfortunately, perhaps, passion of that intensity fades after a time. If the relationship is to continue, romantic love usually develops into **companionate love**, or **conjugal** (CONN-jew-gull) **love**. Companionate love involves feelings of deep affection, attachment, intimacy, and ease with the partner, as well as the development of trust, loyalty, acceptance, and a willingness to sacrifice for the partner (Shaver & Hazan, 1987). Although companionate love does not have the passionate high and low swings of romantic love, passion is certainly present for many companionate lovers. Companionate love may even be a deeper, more intimate love than romantic love.

Jupiter Images

Companionate love involves deep affection, trust, loyalty, attachment, and intimacy; although passion is often present, companionate love lacks the high and low swings of romantic love.

companionate love
An intimate form of love that involves friendly affection and deep attachment based on a familiarity with the loved one. Also referred to as conjugal love.

conjugal love
An intimate form of love that involves friendly affection and deep attachment based on familiarity with the loved one. Also referred to as companionate love.

It can be difficult for couples to switch from passionate love to the deeper, more mature companionate love (Peck, 1978). Because the model of love we see on television and in movies is the highly sexual, swept-off-your-feet passion of romantic love, some may see the mellowing of that passion as a loss of love rather than a development of a different kind of love. Yet the mutual commitment to develop a new, more mature kind of love is, in fact, what we should mean by "true love."

The Colors of Love: John Alan Lee

Psychologist John Alan Lee (1974, 1988, 1998) suggests that in romantic relationships, there are more forms of love than just romantic and companionate love. Lee collected statements about love from hundreds of works of fiction and nonfiction, starting with the Bible and including both ancient and modern authors. He gathered a panel of professionals in literature, philosophy, and the social sciences and had them sort into categories the thousands of statements he found. Lee's research identified six basic ways to love, which he calls "colors" of love, to which he gave Greek and Latin names. Lee's categories are described in Table 7.1.

Lee's colors of love have generated a substantial body of research, much of which shows that his love styles are independent from one another, and that each can be measured to some degree (Hendrick & Hendrick, 1989). Lee points out that two lovers with compatible styles are probably going to be happier and more content with each other than two with incompatible styles.

Table 7.1 Lee's Colors of Love	
1. **Eros: The Romantic Lover**	Eros is like romantic love. Erotic lovers speak of their immediate attraction to their lover, to their eyes, skin, fragrance, or body. Most have the picture of an ideal partner in their mind, which a real partner cannot fulfill; that is why purely erotic love does not last. In childhood, erotic lovers often had a secure attachment style with their caregivers.
2. **Ludus (LOO-diss): The Game-Playing Lover**	Ludic lovers play the "game" of love, enjoying the act of seduction. Commitment, dependency, and intimacy are not valued, and ludic lovers will often juggle several relationships at the same time. In childhood, ludic lovers often had an avoidant attachment style with their caregivers.
3. **Storge (STOR-gay): The Quiet, Calm Lover**	Storgic love is a quiet, calm love that builds over time, similar to companionate love. Storgic lovers don't suddenly "fall in love" and do not dream of some idealized, romantic lover; marriage, stability, and comfort within love are the goal. Should the relationship break up, the storgic partners would probably remain friends, a status unthinkable to erotic lovers who have split.
4. **Mania: The Crazy Lover**	Manic lovers are possessive and dependent, consumed by thoughts of the beloved, and are often on a roller-coaster of highs and lows. Each encouraging sign from the lover brings joy; each little slight brings heartache, which makes their lives dramatic and painful. Manic lovers fear separation; they may sit by the phone waiting for the beloved to call, or they may call their beloved incessantly. They tend to wonder why all their relationships ultimately fail. In childhood, manic lovers often had an anxious/ambivalent attachment style with their caregivers.
5. **Pragma: The Practical Lover**	Pragmatic lovers have a "shopping list" of qualities they are looking for in a relationship. They are very practical about their relationship and lovers. Pragmatic lovers want a deep, lasting love but believe the best way to get it is to assess their own qualities and make the best "deal" in the romantic marketplace. They tend to be planners—planning the best time to get married, have children, and even when to divorce ("Well, in two years the house will be paid for and Billy will be in high school, so that would be a good time to get divorced.").
6. **Agape (AH-ga-pay): The Selfless Lover**	Altruistic, selfless, never demanding, patient, and true is agapic love. Never jealous, not needing reciprocity, agapic love tends to happen in brief episodes. Lee found very few long-term agapic lovers. Lee gives the example of a man whose lover was faced with a distressing choice between him and another man, and so he gracefully bowed out.

As you read through these descriptions, where do you think your love style fits in? Are you a pragmatic lover, planning all the details of who you'll fall in love with? Do you feel stir-crazy in a relationship and end up juggling lovers and playing games? Or do you have a romantic and sensitive love style? It is possible that more than one style will fit you, and also that your love style may change throughout your lifetime. What influences in your life do you think contributed to your love style today?

SOURCE: Based on John Alan Lee, "The Styles of Loving," Psychology Today, 8, 43–51.

Couples who approach loving differently often cannot understand why their partners react the way they do or how they can hurt their partners unintentionally. Imagine how bored an erotic lover would be with a pragmatic lover, or how much a ludic lover would hurt a manic lover. Each would consider the other callous or even cruel, suggests Lee, when people simply tend to love differently. Higher levels of manic and ludic love styles are associated with poorer psychological health, whereas higher levels of storge and eros love styles are associated with higher levels of psychological health (Blair, 2000).

Triangles: Robert Sternberg

Robert Sternberg (1998, 1999), a researcher and academician, has suggested that different strategies of loving are really different ways of combining the basic building blocks of love. He proposed that love is made up of three elements—passion, intimacy, and commitment—that can be combined in different ways. Sternberg refers to a total absence of all three components as nonlove.

Passion is sparked by physical attraction and sexual desire, and it drives a person to pursue a romantic relationship. Passion instills a deep desire for union, and although it is often expressed sexually, self-esteem, nurturing, domination, submission, and self-actualization may also contribute to the experience. Passion is the element that identifies romantic forms of love; it is absent in the love of a parent for a child. Passion fires up quickly in a romantic relationship but is also the first element to fade (Ahmetoglu et al., 2010).

Intimacy involves feelings of closeness, connectedness, and bondedness in a loving relationship. It is the emotional investment one has in the relationship and includes such things as the desire to support and help the other, happiness, mutual understanding, emotional support, and communication. The intimacy component of love is experienced in many loving relationships, such as parent–child, sibling, and friendship relationships.

Commitment, in the short term, is the decision to love someone; in the long term, it is the determination to maintain that love. This element can sustain a relationship that is temporarily (or even permanently) going through a period without passion or intimacy. The marriage ceremony, for example, is a public display of a couple's commitment to each other. Unlike passion, which is quick to fire up and die out, commitment builds slowly and is often related to relationship length (Ahmetoglu et al., 2010).

Sternberg combines these elements into seven forms of love, which are described in Table 7.2. A person may experience

different forms of love at different times; romantic love may give way to companionate love, or the infatuated lover may find a person to whom he or she is willing to commit and settle down. In the emotionally healthy person, as we shall see, love evolves and changes as we mature (Sternberg, 1998).

Can We Measure Love?

Based on these types of theories, theorists have tried to come up with scales that measure love. However, you can't just ask people, *"How deeply do you love [your partner]?"* Participants will interpret love in their own way. One strategy is to create a scale that measures love by measuring something strongly associated with love. Zick Rubin (1970, 1973) was one of the first to try to scientifically measure love. Rubin thought of love as a form of attachment to another person and created a "love scale" that measured what he believed to be the three components of attachment: degrees of needing (*"If I could never be with _____, I would feel miserable."*), caring (*"I would do almost anything for _____."*), and trusting (*"I feel very possessive about _____."*). Rubin's scale proved to be an extraordinarily powerful tool to measure love. For example, how a couple scores on the "love scale" is correlated not only with their rating of the probability that they will get married, but their score even predicts how often they will gaze at each other!

ON YOUR MIND

What is the difference between love and lust? How do I know if it's love or just physical attraction?

Everyone struggles with these questions as they mature, particularly in the teenage and early adulthood years, before gaining much experience with romantic love. There is no easy answer, but there are some indications that a relationship may be infatuation rather than love when it involves a compulsion (rather than a desire) to be with the person, a feeling of lack of trust (such as a need to check up on the partner), extremes of emotions (ecstatic highs followed by depressing lows), and a willingness to take abuse or behave in destructive ways that one would not have before the relationship. Some questions to ask yourself about your love relationship are: Would I want this person as a friend if they were not my partner? Do my friends and family dislike this person or think they are not right for me? (Friends and family are often more level-headed judges of character than the infatuated individual.) Do I really know this person, or am I fantasizing about how they are with little confirmation by their actual behavior? It's not always easy to tell the difference between infatuation and love—many people have a hard time differentiating between the two (Aloni & Bernieri, 2004)!

Others have since tried to create their own scales. Keith Davis and his colleagues (K. E. Davis & Latty-Mann, 1987) created the

Table 7.2   Sternberg's Triangular Theory of Love

Robert Sternberg believes that love is made up of three elements: passion, intimacy, and commitment, each of which may be present or absent in a relationship. The presence or absence of these components produces eight triangles (seven of these involve at least one component; the eighth represents the absence of any components, referred to as nonlove). Problems can occur in a relationship if one person's triangle differs significantly from their partner's triangle. This can happen when one person has more or less of one of the three elements of love. Following are the various types of love proposed by Sternberg.

	Nonlove	In most of our casual daily relationships, there is no sense of intimacy, passion, or commitment.
	Liking	When there is intimacy without (sexual) passion and without strong personal commitment, we are friends. Friends can separate for long periods of time and resume the relationship as if it had never ended.
	Infatuation	Passion alone leads to infatuation. Infatuation refers to physiological arousal and a sexual desire for another person. Casual hookups and one-night stands would fall into this category. Typically, infatuation quickly fades, often to be replaced with infatuation for someone else!
	Empty love	Empty love involves only commitment, as in a couple who stays together even though their relationship long ago lost its passion and intimacy. However, relationships can begin with commitment alone and develop intimacy and passion.
	Romantic love	Passion and intimacy lead to romantic love, which is often the first phase of a relationship. Romantic love is often an intense, joyful experience.
	Companionate love	Companionate love ranges from long-term, deeply committed friendships to married or long-term couples who have experienced a decrease in the passionate aspect of their love.
	Fatuous (FAT-you-us) love	Love is fatuous (which means silly or foolish) when one does not really know the person to whom one is making a commitment. Hollywood often portrays two people who meet, become infatuated, and make a commitment by the end of the movie. However, a committed relationship continues even after passion fades, so it makes sense to know one's partner before making a commitment.
	Consummate love	Consummate, or complete, love has all three elements in balance. Even after achieving consummate love, we can lose it: passion can fade, intimacy can stagnate, and commitment can be undermined by attraction to another. But it is consummate love we all strive for.

SOURCE: Based on Sternberg, Robert J. (1986). "A Triangle Theory of Love," Psychological Review, 93, 119–135.

Relationship Rating Scale (RRS), which measures various aspects of relationships, such as intimacy, passion, and conflict. Hatfield and Sprecher (1986) created the Passionate Love Scale (PLS), which tries to measure the degree of intense passion or "longing for union."

Will measures of love eventually tell us what love is made of? Well, as you can imagine, many problems are inherent in trying to measure love. Most love scales really focus on romantic love and are not as good at trying to measure the degree of companionate love (Sternberg, 1987). Also, measuring degrees of love, or types of love, is different from saying what love actually is. Finally, when you ask people questions about love, they can answer only with their conscious attitudes toward love. Many theorists suggest that we don't consciously know why we love, how we love, or even how much we love. Other theorists argue that people do not realize to what degree love is physiological (see the section on physiological arousal theories later in this chapter). So we may be measuring only how people *think* they love.

Review Questions

1 What is the difference between romantic and companionate love?

2 Identify and describe John Alan Lee's six colors of love.

3 Identify and describe the three elements of love according to Robert Sternberg. Explain how these elements combine to make different forms of love.

4 Is it possible to measure love? What problems have researchers run into when attempting to do so?

Origins of Love

Why do we love in the first place? What purpose does love serve? After all, most animals mate successfully without experiencing "love." Researchers' theories on why we form emotional bonds in the first place can be grouped into five general categories: behavioral reinforcement, cognitive, evolutionary, physiological arousal, and biological.

Behavioral Reinforcement Theories

One group of theories suggests that we love because another person reinforces positive feelings in ourselves. Lott and Lott (1961) suggested that a rewarding or positive feeling in the presence of another person makes us like them, even when the reward has nothing to do with the other person. For example, they found that children who were rewarded continually by their teachers came to like their classmates more than children who were not equally rewarded. The opposite is also true. Griffitt and Veitch (1971) found that people tend to dislike people they meet in a hot, crowded room, no matter what those people's personalities are

The behavioral reinforcement theory suggests that we love people we associate with feeling good. Our love for them grows out of doing things together that are mutually reinforcing.

like. Behavioral reinforcement theory suggests that we like people we associate with feeling good and love people if the association is very good. Love develops through a series of mutually reinforcing activities.

Cognitive Theories

Cognitive theories of liking and loving are based on an interesting paradox: The less people are paid for a task, the more they tend to like it. In other words, a person tends to think, "*Here I am washing this car, and I'm not even getting paid for it. Why am I doing this? I must like to wash cars!*" The same goes for relationships. If we are with a person often and find ourselves doing things for them, we ask, "*Why am I with them so often? Why am I doing their laundry? I must like them—I must even love them!*" This theory suggests the action comes first and the interpretation comes later (Tzeng, 1992). Studies have also found that when we think certain people like us, we're more likely to be attracted to them (Ridge & Reber, 2002).

Evolutionary Theory

We introduced evolutionary theory in Chapter 2 and explained how this theory looks at the evolutionary advantages of human behaviors. Evolutionary theorists believe that love is a strategy that helps us form the bonds we need to reproduce and pass our genes on to the next generation (Gonzaga et al., 2008). We love to propagate the species.

To evolutionary theorists, that would explain why we tend to fall in love with people whom we think have positive traits; we want to pass those traits along to our children. Heterosexual men want a fit, healthy woman to carry their offspring, and heterosexual women want a man with the resources to protect them and help care for the infant in the long period they devote to reproduction. In support of this theory, evolutionary theorists point out that attractive men have been found to have higher quality sperm while attractive women have been found to be more fertile (Gallup & Frederick, 2010). Love creates the union that maximizes each partner's chance of passing on their genes to the next generation.

While it's true that evolutionary theory has primarily explored love between heterosexual couples, the theory has also

IS885/Image Source Plus/Alamy Stock Photo

been applied to same-sex couples. Although same-sex couples cannot pass all their genes on to their offspring, loving relationships between same-sex couples provide a solid foundation in which to raise a family (whether the children are adopted or conceived artificially). Other research has explored how mothers and maternal aunts of gay men have significantly more offspring than the maternal relatives of straight men, indicating evolutionary benefits to maternal reproduction (Iemmola & Camperio Ciani, 2009).

Physiological Arousal Theory

How does love feel? Most people describe physiological sensations: "*I felt so excited I couldn't breathe*"; "*My throat choked up*"; "*I felt tingling all over.*" If you look at those descriptions, couldn't they also be descriptions of fear, anger, or excitement? Is there a difference between being in love and being on a roller-coaster?

Perhaps not. In a famous experiment, Schachter and Singer (1962) gave students a shot of epinephrine (adrenaline), which causes general arousal, including sweaty palms, increased heart rate, increased breathing, and so on. They split the students into four groups: one was told exactly what was happening and what to expect; another was told the wrong set of symptoms to expect (itching, numbness, a slight headache); a third group was told nothing; and a fourth group got an injection of saline solution (saltwater) rather than epinephrine.

Each group was put into a waiting room with a student who was actually part of the study. In half the cases, the confederate acted happy, and in half, angry. The interesting result was that the students in the informed group, when they felt aroused, assumed they were feeling the effects of the epinephrine. However, the uninformed groups tended to believe they were experiencing the same emotion as the other person in the room. They thought they were happy, or they thought they were angry. Schachter and Singer (2001) concluded that an emotion happens when there is general physiological arousal for whatever reason and a label is attached to it—and that label might be any emotion. In other words, people tend to be vulnerable to experiencing love (or another emotion) when they are physiologically aroused for whatever reason. More recent studies confirm the physiological arousal theory (Aron et al., 2005; H. Fisher, 2004). For example, couples who met during a crisis (such as during an emergency plane landing) were found to be more likely to feel strongly about one another (Aron et al., 2005; Kluger, 2008). They often incorrectly attributed their high levels of arousal to feelings for the other person.

So, is love just a label we give to a racing heart? The idea may explain why we tend to associate love and sex so closely; sexual excitement is a state of intense physiological arousal. Certainly arousal of some sort is a necessary component of love. Would you want to be in love with someone who wasn't the least bit excited when you entered the room? Love, however, is almost certainly more than arousal alone. Perhaps arousal has a stronger connection to initial attraction than to love. Maybe that is why lust is so often confused with love.

Other Biological Factors

There are many other biological factors that can influence who we fall in love with. We register the "smells" of people through their **pheromones** (FAIR-oh-moans)—odorless chemicals secreted by both humans and animals. These pheromones are processed in the hypothalamus, and they influence attraction, mating, and bonding (Crawford et al., 2011; Rodriguez, 2004; Savic et al., 2005; Thorne & Amrein, 2003; Wright, 1994). Research on pheromones and sexual orientation has found that gay and straight men respond differently to odors that are involved in sexual attraction, with gay men responding in similar ways as straight women (Savic et al., 2005). Other studies have found that pheromones released during women's ovulation may contribute to increased loving and jealous behaviors in their male partners (Hasleton et al., 2007). Pheromones have also been found to promote the love bond between a mother and her infant (Kohl & Francoeur, 2002).

Our odor preferences are influenced by our major histocompatibility complex (MHC), a group of genes that helps the body recognize invaders such as bacteria and viruses (Herz, 2007; Santos et al., 2005). To pass a more complete MHC along to our offspring and protect them with the broadest array of disease resistance, heterosexual men and women may be programmed to mate with a partner whose MHC differs from their own (Crawford et al., 2011; Garver-Apgar et al., 2006; Roberts & Roiser, 2010). We are more likely to be attracted and fall in love with someone whose MHC is different from our own. Research has been exploring how the use of hormonal contraceptives, such as birth control pills, may alter MHC and odor preferences in women (Crawford et al., 2011; Larson, 2015; Roberts & Roiser, 2010).

Finally, researchers have also been looking for love in neurotransmitters and various areas of the brain. Using magnetic resonance imaging, researchers have found that certain areas of the brain are stimulated when couples are in love (Aron et al., 2005; Fisher et al., 2010; Ortigue et al., 2010; Seshadri, 2016). In addition, when these areas of the brain are stimulated, neurotransmitters, such as dopamine, create motivation and cravings to be with a particular partner (see "Sex in Real Life: Love—It's All in Your Head," later in the chapter). So it appears there may be more to love and attraction than we thought. Certainly more research is needed in these areas.

---

pheromones
Chemical substances that are secreted by humans and animals and facilitate communication.

What does our brain have to do with our feelings of love and romance? It might be more involved than you think. Magnetic resonance imaging of brain functioning shows that certain areas of the brain experience increases in blood flow when a newly in love person looks at a photograph of their romantic partner (Aron et al., 2005; Ortigue et al., 2010; Sukel, 2012). More than 2,500 brain images from people who rated themselves as "intensely in love" were analyzed and showed strong activity in the motivation areas of the brain, where an overabundance of cells produces or receives the neurotransmitter dopamine. Other studies have found that when a person falls in love, multiple areas of the brain are stimulated to release neurotransmitters, including dopamine, oxytocin, adrenaline, and vasopressin. All of these neurotransmitters contribute to feelings of euphoria and happiness, but dopamine is critical for motivation. In fact, neuroscientists have found that people who gamble have increased dopamine when they are winning (Carey, 2005). The researchers concluded that romantic love serves as a motivation for a person to reach a goal. In this case, the goal is to spend time with the love interest.

The area of our brain responsible for sexual arousal is also activated in newly in love people, but the motivation area receives the most stimulation. Researchers hypothesize that when the motivation area is stimulated, a person is motivated to get rewards with their love interest above all else. Think about it for a minute. When we are hungry, thirsty, or tired, the motivation area of our brain is stimulated, motivating us to find food, water, or a place to sleep. When we are in love, this same area motivates us to make the connection and seek out the person we want to be with.

This may also explain why new love can feel so crazy. Feelings of euphoria, sleeplessness, a preoccupation of thoughts of the partner, and an inability to concentrate are all common when a person is newly in love.

Some people describe new love as a "drug," one that often leads them to do things they wouldn't normally do. Perhaps it is a result of the increased blood flow to our motivation center—and the increases in dopamine—that motivate us to get more of what we desire.

Although more research is needed on neuroscience, brain activity, and emotions, it has been suggested that this research might help us understand why people with autism often are indifferent to romantic relationships (Strunz et al., 2017). It's possible that atypical brain development in the motivational areas of the brain contribute to the difficulties with intimacy in those with autism. This research may also help us understand why love changes over the years. The strength of activity in the motivation section of the brain decreases as the length of the relationship increases. In the future, research into brain physiology will continue to teach us more about the biology of love.

SOURCE: Aron et al., 2005.

Review Questions

1 How does the behavioral reinforcement theory explain love?

2 How do cognitive theories explain love?

3 How does evolutionary theory explain love?

4 How does the physiological arousal theory explain love?

5 What other biological factors influence love?

Love from Childhood to Maturity

Throughout our lives, we love others. First, we love our parents or caretakers, and then siblings, friends, and romantic partners. At each stage of life, we learn lessons about love that help us mature into the next stage. Love gets more complex as we get older. Let us walk through the different stages of individual development and look at the various ways love manifests itself as we grow.

Childhood

In infancy, the nature and quality of the bond with the caregiver can have profound effects on the ability of a person to form attachments throughout life. Our parents, or the adults who raised us, are our first teachers of love and intimacy. Children are keenly aware of parental love, and those who feel loved report feeling safe and protected (D'Cruz & Stagnitti, 2010; Rauer & Volling, 2007). Loving, attentive caregivers tend to produce secure, happy children.

Attachment theory grew out of the work of John Bowlby in the 1940s. Bowlby, a psychoanalyst, believed that children had an innate motivational system to attach to their primary caregiver, which helped ensure their safety and survival. This theory grew out of Bowlby's work with teenage criminals who experienced difficulties forming relationships with others. He believed these difficulties were caused by their early, insufficient bonds with caregivers. Bowlby proposed that infants developed an attachment, or an emotional bond, with their mother. (Although Bowlby wrote about attachment as a mother–child bond, we know today that children can develop this bond with a mother, father, nanny, grandparent, or primary caregiver. However, it was the mother's response to her child that Bowlby [1969] believed was

A strong and secure bond with a caregiver can have profound effects on the ability of the person to form attachments throughout life.

their caregivers, adults like to be close to their romantic partners and are often comforted by their presence, especially during times of stress. Hazen and Shaver (1987a,b) suggested that childhood attachment styles may influence the type of intimate relationships we form as adults. They believe that we tend to relate to others in our love relationships much as we did with our primary caregiver when we were young.

Adults who had anxious/ambivalent attachments with their caregivers often have a negative view of others as adults and tend to have a difficult time with trust. They may worry that their partner doesn't really love them or will leave them. Finally, those with an avoidant attachment often have a negative view of others and are uncomfortable with intimacy. If you grew up in a family in which your caregiver was inconsistent or distant, you learn that love is emotionally risky. In fact, those who do not experience intimacy growing up may have a harder time establishing intimate relationships as adults (Brumbaugh & Fraley, 2010; Dorr, 2001). This doesn't mean it's not possible to love someone if you didn't experience intimacy as a child, but it can be more challenging to allow yourself to love and be loved.

While many researchers believe that attachment styles are stable and unchanging throughout a person's life, some "revisionist" theorists believe that our attachment styles are relatively flexible and can be revised and modified throughout our lives (Fraley, 2002; Kagan, 1996; Lewis, 1997, 1999). Certain negative experiences, such as the loss of a parent or abusive relationships, can modify one's attachments with others. For example, children with divorced parents have decreased psychological, social, and physical well-being after their parents' divorce, are less trusting of their partners in intimate relationships, and are more likely to experience a divorce in their own lives (Braithwaite et al., 2016; Schaan & Vögele, 2016). But keep in mind that having divorced parents does not put children at an overall disadvantage in the development of

most important.) Children whose mothers were attentive and responded in sensitive, patient, and kind manners were more likely to form secure attachments. These children were often playful, social, uninhibited, and confident in exploring the world around them. However, children whose mothers were unavailable or responded in inconsistent, angry, or dismissive manners were more likely to form insecure attachments. These children were more likely to feel threatened when alone and exhibited crying or clinging behaviors to reestablish contact with their caregivers. Consistent and sensitive caregiving makes children feel protected and safe, which sets the foundation for regulating emotions later in life (Wellisch, 2010).

Ainsworth and her colleagues (Ainsworth et al., 1978) built on Bowlby's research and suggested that infants form one of three types of attachment behaviors that follow them throughout life. Secure infants tolerate caregivers being out of their sight because they believe the caregiver will respond if they cry out or need care. Inconsistent caregiving results in anxious/ambivalent babies who cry more than secure babies and panic when the caregiver leaves them. Avoidant babies often have caregivers who are uncomfortable with hugging and holding them and tend to force separation on the child at an early age. A child's attachment style is established by the age of 9 months (Prior & Glaser, 2006).

Adults who had a secure attachment in childhood report more positive childhood experiences, higher levels of self-esteem, better health, more advanced language development, as well as less anxiety, shame, guilt, and loneliness (Akbag & Imamoglu, 2010; Diamond & Fagundes, 2010; Feeney & Noller, 1990; Gentzler et al., 2010; Maunder & Hunter, 2008; Prior & Glaser, 2006). In addition, they also have a fairly easy time trusting and establishing intimate relationships (Bartholomew & Horowitz, 1991; Neal & Frick-Horbury, 2001).

In the 1980s, Cindy Hazen and Phillip Shaver applied attachment theory to adult intimate relationships. They suggested that relationships between adult romantic partners were similar to those between children and primary caregivers. Like children and

Young love lays the groundwork for adult intimacy.

love relationships. The most important factor is the quality of the relationships with the parents after the divorce. If children have a good relationship with at least one of their parents, the negative effects from the divorce may be reduced (Ensign et al., 1998). Our initial expectations about relationships may or may not be confirmed as we grow, and it's possible our thoughts and ideas about attachment may be modified to incorporate updated experiences and information.

Adolescence

There is something attractive about young love, which is why it is celebrated so prominently in novels and movies. The love relationship seems so important, so earnest, and so passionate at the time, and yet so innocent in retrospect. Why are the dips and rises of our loves so important to us in adolescence? Adolescent love teaches us how to react to love, to manage our emotions, and to handle the pain of love. It also lays the groundwork for adult intimacy. Adolescents must learn to establish a strong personal identity separate from their family. Experimentation with different approaches to others is natural, and during adolescence, we develop the **role repertoire** that follows us into adulthood. Similarly, we experiment with different intimacy styles (J. Johnson &

Alford, 1987) and develop an **intimacy repertoire**, a set of behaviors that we use to forge close relationships throughout our lives.

Establishing our repertoires can be a difficult task. This helps explain why adolescent relationships can be so intense and fraught with jealousy, and why adolescents often are unable to see beyond the relationship (J. Johnson & Alford, 1987). Our first relationships often take the form of a "crush" or infatuation and are often directed toward unattainable partners such as teachers or movie stars. In fact, studies have found that movie stars provide adolescents with safe outlets for developing romantic love before dating and sexual activity begin (Bui, 2017; Karniol, 2001).

Sometimes the first lessons of love are painful, as we learn that love may not be returned or that feelings of passion fade. Yet managing such feelings helps us develop a mature love style. Many factors have been found to be associated with the ability to find romantic love in adolescence, such as marital status of the parents, the quality of the parental relationship, and comfort with one's body (Cecchetti, 2007; Coordt, 2005; Seiffge-Krenke et al., 2001).

The emotions of adolescent love are so powerful that adolescents may think that they are the only ones to have gone through such joy, pain, and confusion. They may gain some comfort in knowing that almost everyone goes through the same process to some degree. Confusion about love certainly does not end with adolescence.

Review Questions

1 Explain how the nature and quality of our bond with caregivers can affect our ability to form relationships later in life.

2 Identify the various attachment styles. Which of these styles is most like yours?

3 What makes love relationships so difficult and unstable for many adolescents? Why do you think those highs and lows even out as we get older?

Adult Love and Intimacy

Love relationships can last many years. As time goes by, love and relationships grow and change, and trying to maintain a sense of stability and continuity while still allowing for change and growth is probably the single greatest challenge of long-term love relationships.

Attaining intimacy is different from loving. We can love our cat, our favorite musician, or a great leader, but intimacy requires reciprocity—it takes two. Intimacy is a dance of two souls, each of whom must reveal a little, risk a little, and try a lot. In some ways, therefore, true intimacy is more difficult to achieve than true love because the emotion of love may be effortless, whereas the establishment of intimacy always requires effort.

Does fate determine whom you will fall in love with, or are there other factors at work? We now talk about some of the factors that contribute to adult love and intimacy.

Attraction

Why are we attracted to certain people but not others? We've already discussed the role of pheromones, and you'll probably

agree that smell is an important component of attraction. But researchers also talk about the **field of eligibles** (Kerckhoff, 1964). Although we are surrounded by hundreds of people, we are only attracted to a handful of them. Our culture helps determine who is in our field of eligibles through social rules about acceptable and unacceptable partners. Because of these rules, we are more likely to be attracted to those who are similar to us in race, ethnicity, religion, socioeconomic group, and even age. Think about an older person who dates a much younger person. Many people might criticize them or dismiss the relationship. In this way, society teaches us to whom we should, and shouldn't, be attracted.

---

role repertoire
A set of behaviors that we use in our interactions with others. Once we find what works, we develop patterns of interacting with others.

intimacy repertoire
A set of behaviors that we use to forge intimate relationships throughout our lives.

field of eligibles
The group of people from which it is socially acceptable to choose an intimate partner.

One of the most reliable predictors of attraction is proximity. Although we might want to believe that we could meet a complete stranger at a bar and fall madly in love, the research tells us this scenario is rare. People are most likely to find lovers among the people they know or meet through the people they know. We are much more likely to meet our romantic partners at a party, religious institution, or friend's house, where the people are likely to come from backgrounds very similar to our own.

We also tend to be attracted to partners who are similar to ourselves—in ethnicity, race, social class, religion, education, and even in attitudes and personality (Byrne & Murnen, 1988; Hitsch et al., 2010). Although folklore tells us both that "birds of a feather flock together" and that "opposites attract," the research supports only the first saying. We are also more likely to be attracted to someone who has a similar family history and political views (Michael et al., 1994; Z. Rubin, 1973). The "matching hypothesis" claims that we are even drawn to others with similar levels of attractiveness.

Although we are typically first attracted to another person based on physical factors, such as their hair, eyes, or smile, physical appearance tends to fade in importance over the life of the relationship. Physically attractive people are assumed by others to have more socially desirable personalities and to be happier and more successful (Maestripieri et al., 2016). Interestingly, the correlation between levels of attractiveness is highest for couples who meet and start dating within a month or so. Couples who were friends before they started dating are more likely to have different levels of attractiveness (Hunt et al., 2015). This is due to the fact that the longer a couple knows each other, the more they get to know unique and interesting aspects about each other, and the less focused they are on looks.

We are attracted to people who are open, receptive, social, emotionally stable, and who have a good sense of humor. It also wouldn't hurt if they are financially stable. In the past, research found that heterosexual women rated financial stability in a partner higher than heterosexual men did (Buss, 1989). This was consistent across cultures. However, over the years these gender differences have decreased, and more recently people report being attracted to partners with financial resources (Buss et al., 2001; Sheldon, 2007).

What is it, finally, that we really look for in a partner? Although physical attractiveness is important, people around the world also report that mutual attraction, kindness, and reciprocal love are important factors (Buss et al., 2001; Pearce et al., 2010). In addition to this, people are in surprising agreement on what factors they want in an ideal partner. A study of LGBTQ individuals showed that, no matter what their sexual orientation, gender, or cultural background, all really wanted the same thing: They wanted partners who had similar interests, values, and religious beliefs, who were physically attractive, honest, trustworthy, intelligent, affectionate, warm, kind, funny, financially independent, and dependable (Amador et al., 2005; Toro-Morn & Sprecher, 2003). Now that doesn't seem to be too much to ask, does it?

Attraction in Different Cultures

Do men and women in every culture look for the same traits? For example, are more males than females looking for physically attractive mates in Nigeria? Is earning potential more important in males than females in China? David Buss (1989) did an ambitious study comparing the importance of, among other things, physical attractiveness, earning potential, and age difference to men and women in 37 cultures. His results confirmed the nature of mate attraction (although Buss assumed all his respondents were heterosexual and, therefore, assumed they were all talking about the other sex). He found that across all 37 cultures, men valued "good looks" in a partner more than women did, whereas women valued "good financial prospect" in a partner more than men did. Also interesting is that men preferred mates who were younger than they were, whereas women preferred mates who were older. See the nearby "Sexual Diversity in Our World" feature for more information about this study.

Intimate Relationships

What exactly is intimacy? Think about the word; what does it imply to you? The word *intimacy* is derived from the Latin word *intimus*, meaning "inner" or "innermost" (Hatfield, 1988). Keeping our innermost selves hidden is easy; revealing our deepest desires, longings, and insecurities can be scary. As we discussed in Chapter 3, intimate partners reveal beliefs and ideas to each other, disclose personal facts, share opinions, and admit to their fears and hopes. In fact, self-disclosure is so important to intimacy that early researchers thought that willingness to self-disclose was itself the definition of intimacy (M. S. Clark & Reis, 1988). True self-disclosure is a two-way street, and it involves both partners sharing feelings, fears, and dreams, not just facts and opinions. As we discussed in Chapter 3, individuals who can self-disclose have higher levels of self-esteem and confidence in their relationships, and rate their relationships as more satisfying (Gordon & Chen, 2016; Hiew et al., 2016).

A Vietnamese ritual of "lacquering" involves blackening a young woman's teeth when she is ready for marriage. Once stained, the teeth remain blackened for the rest of her life. Lacquered teeth are considered attractive in many parts of Vietnam.

Laurie Nassif

Intimacy involves a sense of closeness, bondedness, and connectedness. People who value intimacy tend to express greater trust in their friends; are more concerned for them; tend to disclose more emotional, personal, and relational content; and have more positive thoughts about others. They also tend to be seen as more likable and noncompetitive by peers and to smile, laugh, and make eye contact more often (M. S. Clark & Reis, 1988).

However, all types of disclosures are risky; the other person may not understand or accept the information offered or may not reciprocate. Thus, risk taking and trust are crucial to the development of intimacy. Because intimacy makes us vulnerable and because we invest so much in the other person, intimacy can also lead to betrayal and disappointment, anger, and jealousy. We explore the dark side of intimacy later in this chapter.

Gender Differences in Styles of Intimacy

If any area of research in love and intimacy has yielded conflicting findings, it is the question of gender differences. Overall, the research has found that heterosexual women tend to give more importance to the hope of having an intimate relationship in their future than heterosexual men do (Lassche & Martinez, 2010; Oner, 2001). However, M. S. Clark and Reis (1988) suggest that the subject remains murky because many other variables are at work, such as culturally determined gender roles.

For example, men and women report equally desiring and valuing intimacy, but many men grow up with behavioral inhibitions to expressing intimacy. Although this has been slowly changing, traditionally boys are discouraged from displaying vulnerability or doubt about intimacy. As one man's experience reveals in the accompanying "Sex in Real Life," it is acceptable for men to talk about sex, but talk of intimacy is often taboo. Although this man's experience may have been extreme, exaggerated by the all-male atmosphere of the athletic team, such attitudes are often communicated in subtle ways to most men. Therefore, men may remain unexpressive about intimacy, however strongly they may desire it. It could also be that men simply express intimacy differently—perhaps more through action than words.

However, some evidence indicates that the differences in attitudes between the genders may be changing. Although in the past women were more comfortable with intimate encounters and men were more comfortable taking independent action, now men and women are more comfortable in both roles (Choi, 2004). If so, maybe we can expect greater ease in intimacy between and among the sexes in the upcoming generations of men and women.

The importance of accepting traditional gender roles is also reflected in comparisons of gay and straight men. Although both agree on the ideal characteristics of love partners and express the same amounts and kinds of love, gay men are more likely to believe that "you should share your most intimate thoughts and feelings with the person you love" (Engel & Saracino, 1986, p. 242). This may be because gay men tend to adopt fewer stereotyped beliefs about gender roles than straight men.

REAL RESEARCH Research has found that because of the difficulties involved in managing close relationships, individuals who begin a new romance are at risk for losing two close friends (SAMPLE, 2010).

Intimacy in Different Cultures

Love seems to be a basic human emotion. Aren't "basic human emotions" the same everywhere? Isn't anger the same in Chicago and Timbuktu, and sadness the same in Paris and Bombay? Although there is evidence that the majority of worldwide cultures experience romantic love (see this chapter's "Sexual Diversity in Our World" feature), we do know that one's culture has been found to have a more powerful impact on love beliefs than one's gender (Sprecher & Toro-Morn, 2002). Culture affects how a person defines love, how easily they fall in love, whom they fall in love with, and how the relationship proceeds (Hatfield et al., 2015; Rohmann et al., 2016).

As we discussed in Chapter 3, cultural differences in individual versus group needs can affect communication patterns. It should come as no surprise that these cultural differences can also affect patterns of intimacy. Passionate love is typically emphasized in individualistic cultures, but in collectivist cultures, passionate relationships are often viewed negatively because they may disrupt family traditions (Cao et al., 2015; Hiew et al., 2015; Kim & Hatfield, 2004). For example, although Americans often equate love with happiness, the Chinese have equated love with sadness and jealousy (Shaver et al., 1992). This is because collectivist cultures, such as that of China or Japan, traditionally marry for reasons other than love. Passionate love dies and is not viewed as stable enough to base a marriage on. In a study of France, Japan, and the United States, intimacy style was directly related to whether the culture was individualistic, collectivistic, or mixed (France), and also to how much the culture had adopted stereotypical views of gender roles (that is, how much it tended to see men as assertive and women as nurturing; Ting-Toomey et al., 1991). The Japanese, with a collectivistic culture and highly stereotypical gender roles, had lower scores in measures of attachment and commitment and were less likely to value self-disclosure than the French or Americans (Kito, 2005). Americans have traditionally had stereotypical gender roles, but because of the highly individualistic culture in the United States, Americans tend to have high levels of confusion and ambivalence about relationships. Interestingly, the French, who have a culture with high individual motivation yet with a strong group orientation, and who also have a more balanced view of masculine and feminine gender roles, had the lowest degree of conflict in intimate relationships.

Culture also affects one's sense of self. For example, in China, people's sense of self is entirely translated through their relationships with others. A Chinese man would consider his roles as a son, brother, husband, or a father before he would think of himself as an individual (Dion & Dion, 2010). In China, love is thought of in terms of how a mate would be received by family and community, not in terms of one's sense of romance. Because of this, the

Sexual Diversity
IN OUR WORLD
What Do You Want in a Partner?

In a classic study on cultural differences in what heterosexual men and women look for in a mate, David Buss (1989) found that, almost universally, men value good looks more in a mate, and women value good financial prospects. More recent research has found that in the United States, good looks and financial stability are important partner qualities for both men and women (Amador et al., 2005; Lacey et al., 2004). Buss (1989) also found that men preferred women younger than themselves, while women preferred men older than themselves. These preferences have been found to be nearly universal (Gustafson & Fransson, 2015). A more recent study by Schwarz and Hasse-brauck (2012) found that while men were willing to accept a partner who was any-where from 4 years older to 10 year younger,

the preference in women was reversed. Buss (1989) believed that these mate preferences were due to reproductive trends—men prefer younger women because they have a higher reproductive capacity, while women prefer older men because they offer more financial resources.

In the accompanying graph, participants rated the importance of age difference in potential mates. A negative number refers to a desire for a mate who is younger by a certain number of years, whereas a higher number refers to a desire for a mate who is older by a certain number of years.

SOURCE: Based on David Buss, Sex Differences in Human Mate Preferences: Evolutionary Hypotheses Tested in 37 Cultures. *Behavioral and Brain Sciences*, 12, 149, 1989.

There is more social acceptance for older man/younger woman relationships than there is for older woman/younger man relationships. Here Jeff Goldblum and his wife, Emilie Livingston, who is 30 years younger.

How many years older/younger do you want your partner to be?

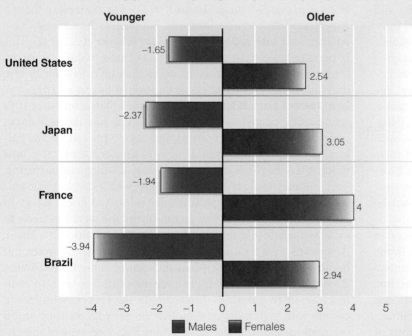

In this graph, heterosexual respondents from different countries rated the importance of age difference in potential mates. A negative number refers to a desire for a mate who is younger by a certain number of years, whereas a positive number refers to a desire for a mate who is older by a certain number of years.

Chinese have a more practical approach to love than do Americans (Cao et al., 2015; Sprecher & Toro-Morn, 2002).

Finally, a cross-cultural study of Brazil, Russia, and Central Africa found several differences in how love is conceptualized (Pilishvili & Koyanongo, 2016). While participants from all cultures agreed that love included friendship, patience, and passion, Brazilians were more likely to view love as sensual, interpersonal, and intimate while Africans were more likely to view it as God-given and divine. Russians, on the other hand, viewed love as an obstacle that must be overcome. Researchers have found that

Sex in Real Life   Gender Roles and Expressions of Love

Following is a story written by a heterosexual man who was reflecting about his experiences growing up as a young boy. As you read through it, consider the impact of gender roles on our expressions of love and intimacy. Do you think today's men are more comfortable expressing their emotions? Why or why not?

I played organized sports for 15 years, and they were as much a part of my growing up as Cheerios, television, and homework. My sexuality unfolded within this all-male social world of sport, where sex was always a major focus. I remember, for example, when we as prepubertal boys used the old "buying baseball cards" routine as a cover to sneak peeks at Playboy and Swank magazines at the newsstand. We would talk endlessly after practices about "boobs" and what it must feel like to kiss and neck. Later, in junior high, we teased one another in the locker room about "jerking off" or being virgins, and there were endless interrogations about "how far" everybody was getting with their girlfriends.

Eventually, boyish anticipation spilled into real sexual relationships with girls, which, to my delight and confusion, turned out to be a lot more complex than I ever imagined. While sex (kissing, necking, and petting) got more exciting, it also got more difficult to figure out and talk about. Inside, most of the boys, like myself, needed to love and be loved. We were awkwardly reaching out for intimacy. Yet publicly, the message that got imparted was to "catch feels," be cool, and connect with girls but don't allow yourself to depend on them. Once when I was a high school junior, the gang in the weight room accused me of being wrapped around my girlfriend's finger. Nothing could be further from the truth. I assured them; to prove it, I broke up with her. I felt miserable about this at the time, and I still feel bad about it.*

Within the college jock subculture, men's public protests against intimacy sometimes became exaggerated and ugly. I remember two teammates, drunk and rowdy, ripping girls' blouses off at a mixer and crawling on their bellies across the dance floor to look up skirts. Then there were the Sunday morning late breakfasts in the dorm. We jocks would usually all sit at one table and be forced to listen to one braggart or another describe his sexual exploits of the night before. Although a lot of us were turned off by such kiss-and-tell, ego-boosting tactics, we never openly criticized them. Real or fabricated, displays of raunchy sex were also assumed to "win points."*

When sexual relationships were "serious," that is, tempered by love and commitment, the unspoken rule was silence. It was rare when we young men shared our feelings about women, misgivings about sexual performance, or disdain for the crudeness and insensitivity of some of our teammates. I now see the tragic irony in this: We could talk about superficial sex and anything that used, trivialized, or debased women, but frank discussions about sexuality that unfolded within a loving relationship were taboo. Within the locker room subculture, sex and love were seldom allowed to mix. There was a terrible split between inner needs and outer appearances, between our desire for the love of women and our feigned indifference toward them.

SOURCE: Adapted from Sabo and Runfola (1980).

---

love is given highest importance in Westernized nations and the lowest importance in the less developed Asian nations (R. Levine et al., 1995). Thus, culture plays a role in how we experience and express both love and intimacy.

Long-Term Love and Commitment

The ability to maintain love over time is the hallmark of maturity. Many people regard love as something that happens to them, almost like catching the flu. In my chapter-opening Notebook feature, I discussed how it takes effort and commitment to maintain love—not only commitment to the other person but also commitment to continually build on and improve the quality of the relationship. Most long-term relationships that end do so not because the couple "fell out of love" but because, somewhere down the line, they stopped working together on their relationship. In this sense, the old saying is true: The opposite of love is not hate, but indifference.

R. J. Sternberg (1985), you may recall, claimed that passion, intimacy, and commitment are the three elements of love; in consummate love, he says, all three are present. Research has found that age and relationship length are both positively related to intimacy and commitment; that is, the older the couple and the longer the relationship, typically the stronger the intimacy and commitment in the relationship (Ahmetoglu et al., 2010). Nonetheless, one tends to hear very little talk of commitment in our culture, with its great emphasis on passionate love. Couples going through hard times can persevere and build even stronger and more intimate relationships when their commitment reflects such a deep sense of trust.

The ability to maintain love over time is the hallmark of maturity. Couples who have been together a long time often have a sense of ease with each other.

Couples who continue to communicate with each other, remain committed to each other and the relationship, and remain interested in and intimate with each other build a lasting bond of trust. Those who don't may feel isolated and lonely in relationships that nevertheless endure for many years. Although passionate love may fade over time, love itself does not necessarily diminish. The decline of passion can allow the other components of love to flourish in the relationship.

Loss of Love

Popular songs are often about the loss of love; the blues is a whole genre of music built on the experience of losing love, and country music is well known for its songs of lost love. Most of us will experience the loss of love at some point in our lifetimes. In fact, it's not uncommon today to experience multiple relationship breakups (Morris et al., 2015).

ON YOUR MIND

I've always wondered, how can a person stay with only one person their whole life and not get bored?

Although it might be hard to believe you could do this, it's also important to remember that love grows and changes when two people commit themselves to work on a relationship. Are you the person you were 10 years ago? What makes you think you'll be the same 10 years from now? When two people allow each other to grow and develop, they find new experiences and new forms of love all the time. People get bored primarily when they lose interest, not because the other person has no mysteries left.

The loss of love can cause deep sadness and a profound sense of loss for most people. Many are vulnerable to self-blame, loss of self-esteem, and distrust of others, and they may rush into another relationship to replace the lost partner (Luciano & Orth, 2017). Research on brain physiology has found that a relationship breakup stimulates areas of the brain that are related to motivation, reward, and addiction, which sheds some light on the excessive alcohol consumption or drug use in those who have been rejected (Fisher et al., 2010).

As difficult as a breakup can be, several factors may lower the level of distress. One of these is high self-esteem, which can help people continue to feel hopeful and think more positive thoughts about themselves after a breakup (Luciano & Orth, 2017). Those with low self-esteem tend to blame themselves and worry that no one will ever love them. Earlier, we discussed the importance of attachment styles, and it probably won't surprise you to learn that those with secure attachment styles often have the easiest time with breakups, whereas those with anxious attachment styles have the most difficulties (Luciano & Orth, 2017). They may desperately try to get the relationship back or refuse to let go.

There is no easy way to decrease the pain of a breakup. Time helps, mostly because as time goes by there is less activity in the area of the brain related to attachment (Fisher et al., 2010). When this activity slows down, a person is better able to reappraise the breakup and assess what was learned in the relationship. The good news is that most people do bounce back after the loss of love and realize they learned important lessons that may be useful in future relationships (Luciano & Orth, 2017). We will discuss relationship breakups more in Chapter 9.

Review Questions

1 What do we know about why we are attracted to certain people? Explain what factors might be involved.

2 Explain what we know about cross-cultural attraction, and identify some of the qualities that people may find attractive in other cultures.

3 Explain the importance of self-disclosure on the development of intimacy.

4 Explain what the research has found with respect to gender differences in intimacy styles.

5 Provide three ways in which cultural differences may affect patterns of intimacy.

6 Explain how the ability to maintain love over time is the hallmark of maturity.

Love, Sex, and How We Build Intimate Relationships

One way to express deep love and intimacy is through sexual behavior, but sexual behavior itself is not necessarily an expression of love or intimacy. How do we make the decision to have sex? There are many levels of relationships that can lead to sex. Casual sex and "hooking up" can happen between people who barely know each other, generated by excitement, novelty, and/or pure physical pleasure.

Love and Sex

Sex can be an expression of affection and intimacy without including passionate love; sex can also be engaged in purely for sexual pleasure or for procreation; or sex can be an expression of love within a loving relationship. Problems can develop when one partner has one view of the developing sexual relationship and the other partner takes a different perspective.

Because the decision to engage in sexual behavior involves the feelings and desires of two people, examining your own motivations, as well as your partner's, is important. When making the decision to initiate a sexual relationship with another person, consider the following:

1. Clarify your values. At some point, each of us needs to make value decisions regarding intimacy, sex, and love. What role does love play in your sexual decisions? How will you reconcile these values with those you have learned from your family, friends, and religion?

2. Be honest with yourself which is often more difficult than being honest with others. Entering a relationship with another person takes close self-examination. What do you really want out of the experience? From this person? Are you hoping the sexual contact will lead to something deeper, or are you in it simply for the physical pleasure? What will you do if you find that you (or your partner) have a sexually transmitted infection? Are you in this because you want to be or because you feel some kind of pressure to be sexual—from yourself or from your partner? Could you say "no" comfortably? Are you ready for a sexual relationship with this person?

3. Be honest with your partner. Another person's feelings and needs are always at issue in any relationship, and part of our responsibility as caring human beings is not to hurt or exploit others. Why is your partner interested in sex with you? Do their expectations differ from yours? Will they be hurt if your relationship does not develop further? Have you discussed your feelings?

The decision to engage in sex may or may not be related to feelings of love. Casual sex has become much more common and accepted than it was before the 1970s, when young people (especially women) were strongly advised to save their "greatest asset," their virginity, for marriage. Overall, the importance of love as an essential condition for sexual relations has diminished.

Studies have found that when we do begin to feel attracted to someone, we act intimate; we gaze longer at each other, lean on each other, and touch more (Hatfield, 1988). People meeting each other for the first time tend to reveal their levels of attraction by their body language. Perper (1985) observed heterosexual strangers approaching each other in bars. The first stage he called the initial contact and conversation. If two people are mutually attracted, they will begin to turn their bodies more and more toward each other, until they are facing one another. The first tentative touches begin, a hand briefly on a hand or a forearm, for example, and an increase in duration and intimacy as the evening progresses. Finally, the couple shows "full body synchronization"; their facial expressions, posture, and even breathing begin to mirror their partner's. As we discussed in Chapter 3, women smile, gaze, lean forward, and touch more often than men do in conversation. Women also "flirt" with their nonverbal cues (such as hair flipping and head nodding) to encourage their partner to reveal more about themselves, which would, in turn, allow the women to formulate an impression of the person (W. E. Martin, 2001).

REAL RESEARCH Although "hooking up" is common on many college campuses today, one study exploring ethnic/racial differences in casual sex and dating behaviors found a higher proportion of White students engaged in casual sex, while a higher proportion of Hispanic students went on dates (EATON ET AL., 2016).

Developing Intimacy Skills

There are many ways to improve our intimacy skills. Developing intimacy often begins with understanding and liking ourselves—self-love. Other important skills we can develop to enhance our ability to form relationships include receptivity, listening, showing affection, trust, and respect.

Self-Love

Self-love is different from conceit or **narcissism**; it is not a process of promoting ourselves but of being at ease with our positive qualities and forgiving ourselves for our faults. If you are not willing to get to know yourself and to accept your own faults, why would others think you are any more interested in them or that you would judge them any less harshly? Many people look to others for indications of their own self-worth. We must first take responsibility to know ourselves (self-intimacy) and then to accept ourselves as we are. Once we like ourselves, we can reach out to others.

ON YOUR MIND

How can I tell the difference between being in love and just deeply liking someone?

Unfortunately, no one has come up with a foolproof way of making that distinction. Being "in love" can feel a lot like being "in deep like." One would hope we deeply like those whom we love, and in fact, we probably love those we deeply like. The element that may be missing from those we deeply like is sexual passion, but sometimes we don't realize that we are not in love with them until after we develop a sexual relationship. The discovery can be painful to both parties, which is why it is advisable to think it through before initiating a sexual relationship with a friend.

self-love	narcissism
Love for oneself; the instinct or desire to promote one's own well-being.	Excessive admiration of oneself.

Receptivity

Many of us think we are receptive to others when actually we are sending subtle signals that we do not want to be bothered. Receptivity can be communicated through eye contact and smiling. This allows the other person to feel comfortable and makes us approachable. Taking 5 minutes a day to sit and reconnect with your partner may improve your relationship and help preserve intimacy and passion.

Listening

We discussed in Chapter 3 how true communication begins with listening. Nothing shows you care about another person quite as much as your full attention. It can be very difficult to listen to people talk only of themselves or to people who see any comment made by another person primarily in terms of how it relates to them. Learning to truly listen enhances intimacy.

Affection

How do we show affection to another person? If you watch loving parents with their child, it is easy to see how affection is displayed. Parents attend to their children, smile at them, touch them in affectionate ways, look in their eyes, and hug and kiss them. Most people want the same things from their intimate friends and lovers. Affection shows that you feel a sense of warmth and security with your partner.

Trust

To trust another is an act of courage because it grants that person the power to hurt or disappoint you. However, intimacy requires trust. Usually trust develops slowly. You trust your partner a little bit at the beginning of your relationship and begin to trust them more and more as they prove to be dependable and predictable. Having trust in our partner leads to more confidence that the relationship will last. When a couple trusts each other, each expects the partner to care and respond to the other's needs, now and in the future (Zak et al., 1998).

Remember earlier we talked about children from divorced families being less able to trust in intimate relationships? Perhaps it is because they have seen firsthand what happens in unsuccessful marriages, and they fear intimate relationships just don't work. It can be tough to trust when one is ambivalent or scared. The important thing to remember is that often the longer a relationship lasts, the more trust builds between the partners (Jacquet & Surra, 2001).

Forgiveness is another important part of trust. It's possible that a partner may do something to make us question our trust in them. Knowing how and when to forgive are important aspects of a healthy relationship (Kato, 2016).

Respect

We enter into relationships with our own needs and desires, which sometimes cloud the fact that the other person is different from us and has their own special needs.

Respect is the process of acknowledging and understanding that person's needs, even if you don't share them.

The Dark Side of Love

Love evokes powerful emotions; this is both its strength and its weakness. Many of the emotions that can come from strong feelings about another person can also be destructive to a relationship and may require great maturity or a strong act of will to overcome. Let's now examine three of the dark sides of love: jealousy, compulsiveness, and possessiveness.

Jealousy: The Green-Eyed Monster

Imagine you are at a party with a person with whom you are in an exclusive sexual relationship. You notice that person standing close to someone else, talking and laughing, and occasionally putting their hand on the other person's arm. At one point, you notice your partner whispering in the other person's ear, and they both laugh. How does that make you feel? Are you jealous? But wait, I forgot to tell you: The person your partner was talking to is their cousin. Are you still jealous?

Jealousy is an emotional reaction to a relationship that is being threatened (Knox et al., 1999, 2007; Sharpsteen & Kirkpatrick, 1997). A threat is a matter of interpretation; people who deeply trust their partners may not be able to imagine a situation in which the relationship is really threatened. We are most jealous in a situation in which the person flirting with our partner has traits we ourselves want (or we fantasize that they do). Maybe we imagine our partner will find the other person more desirable than us, sexier, or funnier. We imagine that the partner sees in the other person all those traits we believe that we lack.

Men and women experience similar levels of jealousy in intimate relationships, yet there is controversy over what triggers jealousy. Some research supports the fact that men are more jealous when they believe that their partner had a sexual encounter with another person, whereas women are often more focused on the emotional or relationship aspects of infidelity (Zandbergen & Brown, 2015). However, it may have to do with whether the relationship is short or long term. In short-term relationships, both men and women are more threatened by sexual infidelity, whereas emotional infidelity is often more threatening in a long-term relationship (Mathes, 2005; Penke & Asendorpf, 2008). Cheating, either emotional or sexual, can lead to jealousy in both men and women. Although the majority of research on infidelity has been done on heterosexual couples, limited studies on same-sex couples have found that reactions to infidelity in lesbian and gay couples are similar to those in heterosexual couples, with emotional pain and jealousy the most common responses (Harris, 2012; LaSala, 2004; Shernoff, 2007). We will discuss infidelity more in Chapter 9.

REAL RESEARCH Couples who post their relationship status on Facebook may be more jealous than those who do not post such statuses (Orosz et al., 2015). Researchers believe that becoming "Facebook Official" is akin to a "digital wedding ring," letting others know about one's unavailability.

We are often jealous when we think, fantasize, or imagine that another person has traits we ourselves want.

Although many people think that jealousy shows that they really care for a person, in fact, it shows a lack of trust in the partner and low self-esteem (Redlick, 2016). One study on levels of distrust of men among women of different ethnicities found that heterosexual Hispanic women had more distrust of men with whom they had intimate relationships than either Black or White women (levels were highest in Dominican women, followed by Puerto Rican and Mexican; Estacion & Cherlin, 2010). Jealousy is also related to attachment styles, with anxious and avoidant attachment styles experiencing more jealousy (Lassri et al., 2016; Luo & Jiang, 2016). People who do not experience jealousy are often more secure, and this security in intimate relationships tends to increase as the couple's relationship grows. That is, the longer we are in a relationship with someone, the more our vulnerability to jealousy decreases.

Jealousy can also be a self-fulfilling prophecy; jealous individuals can drive their mates away, which convinces them that they were right to be jealous in the first place. Jealousy can be contained by trying to improve one's own self-image, by turning it around into a compliment (not "*she's flirting with other guys*" but "*look at how lucky I am—other guys also find her attractive*"), and by trust of one's partner. Communicating with your partner about your jealous feelings can often help to maintain your relationship. Opening up and talking about your uncertainty about the relationship or reassessing the relationship can help restore and strengthen the relationship.

Finally, in a nearby Real Research feature we discuss jealousy and the use of Facebook. Overall, couples who report higher levels of "love" report fewer Facebook maintenance behaviors (e.g., checking, revising, posting on partner's page; Northrup & Smith, 2016).

Compulsiveness: Addicted to Love

Being in love can produce a sense of ecstasy, euphoria, and a feeling of well-being, much like a powerful drug (see "Sex in Real Life: Love—It's All in Your Head," earlier in the chapter). In fact, when a person is in love, their body releases the drug phenylethylamine, which produces these feelings (Sabelli et al., 1996; by the way, phenylethylamine

is an ingredient in chocolate, which may be why it can make us feel better, especially during a breakup!). Some people do move from relationship to relationship as if they were love addicted, trying to continually re-create that feeling, or else they obsessively hang on to a love partner long after their interest has waned.

Love addiction is reinforced by the popular media's portrayals (even as far back as Shakespeare's *Romeo and Juliet*) of passionate love as all-consuming. It fosters the belief that only one person is fated to be your "soul mate," that love is always mutual, and that you'll live "happily ever after." Some people feel the need to be in love because society teaches that only then are they really whole, happy, and fulfilled in their role as a human being. Yet love based solely on need can never be truly fulfilling. In Peele and Brodsky's (1991) book *Love and Addiction*, they argue that love addiction is more common than most believe, and that it is based on a continuation of an adolescent view of love that is never replaced as the person matures. Counseling or psychotherapy may help people come to terms with their addiction to love.

Possessiveness: Every Move You Make, I'll Be Watching You

Because love also entails risk, dependency to some degree, and a strong connection between people, there is always the danger that the strength of the bond can be used by one partner to manipulate the other. Abusive love relationships exist when one partner tries to increase their own sense of self-worth or to control the other's behavior by withdrawing or manipulating love.

For intimacy to grow, partners must nurture each other. Controlling behavior may have short-term benefits (you might get the person to do what you want for a while), but long term, it smothers the relationship. No one likes the feeling of being manipulated, whether it is subtle, through the use of guilt, or overt, through physical force. Part of love is the joy of seeing the partner free to pursue their desires and appreciating the differences between partners. Although every relationship has its boundaries, freedom within those agreed-on constraints is what encourages the growth and maturation of both partners.

Possessiveness indicates a problem of self-esteem and personal boundaries and can eventually lead to **stalking**. Stalking can involve intimidation, verbal, and/or physical abuse (Sinclair & Frieze, 2015). Federal laws prohibit stalking, and police can arrest a person who constantly shadows someone or makes threatening gestures or claims. Studies have found that stalking can have both psychological and physiological causes (Marazziti et al., 2015). We will discuss power and coercion more in Chapter 17.

We started this chapter talking about the importance of love in our lives. The ability to form loving, caring, and intimate relationships with others is important for our emotional health and also our physical health. Love and intimacy are two of the most powerful factors in well-being. Love might not always be easy to understand, but it is a powerful force in our lives, and intimacy is an important component of mature love in our culture.

stalking
Relentlessly pursuing someone, shadowing them, or making threatening gestures or claims toward the person when the relationship is unwanted.

1 What factors might a couple consider when making the decision to initiate a sexual relationship?

2 Why do people feel jealous, and how are jealousy and self-esteem related?

3 Compare and contrast compulsiveness and possessiveness.

Chapter Review

Summary Points

1 Love and the ability to form loving, caring, and intimate relationships with others are important for both our physical and emotional health. Social support and love are related to stronger immune systems and lower allostatic load. We go through life trying to come to terms with loving, trying to figure out why we are attracted to certain types or why we fall in love with all the wrong people. The mystery of love is part of its attraction.

2 Not until the 19th century did people begin to believe that romantic love was the most desirable form of loving relationships. Through most of Western history, marriage was an economic union arranged by the parents. Once wed, husbands and wives were encouraged to learn to love one another, to develop love.

3 Romantic love comes with a sense of ecstasy and anxiety, physical attraction, and sexual desire. We tend to idealize the partner, ignoring faults in the newfound joy of the attachment. Passionate love blooms in the initial euphoria of a new attachment to a sexual partner. If a relationship is to continue, romantic love must develop into companionate love.

4 Romantic love is the passionate, highly sexual part of loving. Companionate love involves feelings of affection, intimacy, and attachment to another person. In many cultures, marriages are based on companionate love, assuming that passion will grow as the couple does.

5 John Alan Lee suggests that there are six basic "colors" of love, including eros, ludus, storge, mania, pragma, and agape. Lovers with compatible styles are often happier and more content with the relationship than those with incompatible styles.

6 Robert Sternberg proposed that love is made up of three elements: passion, intimacy, and

commitment. Passion is the physical aspect of love and is the first to fire up in a romantic relationship. Intimacy involves closeness, connectedness, and bondedness. Commitment is the long-term determination to maintain love. These elements can combine in different ways, creating seven basic ways to love.

7 Researchers suggest that there are five general categories that help explain why we form emotional bonds. These include behavioral reinforcement, cognitive, evolutionary, physiological arousal, and biological theories. The behavioral reinforcement theories suggest that we love because the other person reinforces positive feelings in ourselves. Positive feelings in the presence of another person make us like them, even when the reward has nothing to do with the other person.

8 The cognitive theories propose that we love because we think we love. This theory suggests that the action comes first and the interpretation comes later. In the physiological arousal theory, people are vulnerable to experiencing love (or another emotion) when they are physiologically aroused for whatever reason. An emotion happens when there is general physiological arousal and a label is attached to it—and that label might be any emotion.

9 Evolutionary perspectives of love believe that love developed out of our need to be protected from outside threats, to protect children, and from our sexual drive; love is an evolutionary strategy that helps us form the bonds we need to reproduce and pass our genes on to the next generation. Biological theories believe that pheromones may contribute to feelings of love. Our odor preferences are influenced by our major histocompatibility complex (MHC). Neurotransmitters and the brain also have been found to affect our feelings of love.

10 Love develops over the life cycle. In infancy, we develop attachments to our caregivers; receiving love in return has an influence on our capacity to love later in life. In adolescence, we deal with issues of separation from our parents and begin to explore adult ways of loving. Adolescents tend to experience romantic love. Attachment styles we learn in infancy, such as secure, avoidant, and ambivalent styles, may last through life and influence how we begin to form adult attachments in adolescence.

11 As we mature and enter adulthood, forming intimate relationships becomes important. Developing intimacy is risky, and individuals have different styles of intimacy, but intimacy is seen as an important component of mature love in our culture. As we grow older, commitment in love becomes more important, and passion may decrease in importance.

12 Relationships take effort, and when a couple stops working on the relationship, both partners can become very lonely, love can fade, and intimacy can evaporate. When love is lost, for whatever reason, it is a time of pain and mourning. The support of family and friends can help us let go of the lost love and try to form new attachments.

13 Gender differences have been found in intimacy styles. For example, traditionally men have been taught to suppress communication about intimacy as they grow, or they may learn to express it in different ways. Overall, heterosexual women tend to give more importance to the hope of having an intimate relationship in their future than heterosexual men do.

14 Although there is evidence that the majority of world cultures experience romantic love, we do know that one's culture has been found to have a more powerful impact on love beliefs than one's gender. Culture affects how a person defines love, how easily they fall in love, with whom they fall in love, and how the relationship proceeds.

15 Couples who continue to communicate with each other, remain committed to each other and the relationship, and remain interested in and intimate with each other build a lasting bond of trust. Those who don't may feel isolated and lonely in relationships that nevertheless endure for many years. Although passionate love may fade over time, love itself does not necessarily diminish. The decline of passion can allow the other components of love to flourish in the relationship.

16 Most people will experience the loss of love at some point in their lifetimes. This can cause deep sadness and a profound sense of loss. After a breakup, many people are vulnerable to self-blame, loss of self-esteem, and distrust of others, and they may rush into another relationship to replace the lost partner. Most people do bounce back after the loss of love and realize they learned important lessons for future relationships.

17 Sex can be an expression of affection and intimacy without including passionate love; sex can also be engaged in purely for sexual pleasure or for procreation; or sex can be an expression of love within a loving relationship. Problems can develop when one partner has one view of the developing sexual relationship and the other partner takes a different perspective. The decision to be sexual is often confused with the decision to love. Values need to be clarified before a sexual relationship is begun.

18 Developing intimacy begins with understanding ourselves and liking ourselves. Receptivity, listening, showing affection, trusting in your partner, and respecting them are important in the development of intimacy.

19 Love also has its negative side. Jealousy plagues many people in their love relationships, whereas others seem addicted to love, going in and out of love relationships. Some people also use love as a means to manipulate and control others.

20 Possessiveness indicates a problem of self-esteem and personal boundaries and can eventually lead to stalking. Most states have passed stalking laws, which enable the police to arrest a person who constantly shadows someone or makes threatening gestures or claims.

Critical Thinking Questions

1 Using John Alan Lee's colors of love, examine a relationship that you are in (or were in) and analyze the styles of love that you and your partner use(d). Which love style do you think would be hardest for you to deal with in a partner and why?

2 Think of a love relationship that you have been in. Describe how each of the theories proposed in this chapter would explain why you loved your partner. Which theory do you think does the best job? Why?

3 Do you think the research on pheromones fits with your own experiences? Are you attracted (or not attracted) to people by their smell?

4 Explain what gender differences have been found in love, and tie this research to an example from one of your past relationships.

5 How long do you think is appropriate to wait in a relationship before engaging in sex? Why?

6 Have you ever been involved with a partner who was jealous? What was the hardest part of this relationship? How did you handle the jealousy?

Websites

Loving You   This website contains advice, love poems, and free romantic love notes and quotes. There are also links to dating services, love libraries, and gift shops.

Love Test   A nonscientific but fun website that offers a multitude of different "love" tests. Compatibility analysis, astrology reports, fortune tellers, and relationship rating tests are available.

Queendom   This site offers the largest online battery of professionally developed and validated psychological assessments. This website is a fun place to find a variety of different quizzes.

8 Childhood and Adolescent Sexuality

Sexuality education can help teens develop a positive view of sexuality, protect their sexual health, and make good decisions. However, there is an ongoing debate in the United States about the form that sexuality education should take. Should teens be taught to abstain? Should they be taught about STIs and contraception? Should they be taught about sexual pleasure? Historically the United States has been very "sex negative" when it comes to sexuality education, teaching students mainly why sex should be avoided (e.g., loss of reputation, diseases, pregnancy). It's very different in the Netherlands, where comprehensive sexuality education is mandatory. To learn more about the Dutch approach to sexuality education I met with Ruud Winkel at the Amsterdam Lyceum, a Dutch secondary school. Ruud teaches human sexuality to 13- to 18-year-olds and strongly believes that students should be knowledgeable about how their bodies work. He teaches them about sexual pleasure, including masturbation and orgasmic response. Equally important, he believes, is teaching students about contraception and sexually transmitted infections. At the beginning of every class he lets students ask any questions they have about sexuality, and some of the most common questions include, How much sperm have you got? What does an orgasm feel like? What's a wet dream? or How long does it take to get a baby out? During the yearlong course, he has students watch many educational videos, including one of a couple engaging in sexual intercourse. He does this because he believes that students should understand what making love is all about. He explained it would be difficult to teach students about making babies if he couldn't teach them first about making love. At the end of the day, Ruud wants his students to understand that sex is good and it should be enjoyed. I bet this wasn't something you heard from your high school sexuality education teacher!

It's interesting to note that the Netherlands has the world's lowest rates of teenage pregnancy, birth, and abortion. While we can't say that comprehensive programs are directly responsible for these lower rates, we do know that sexuality education programs in the Netherlands focus on responsibility, respect, and pleasure and don't shy away from the tough questions. I find this approach refreshing and hope that one day the United States will do something similar.

Janell Carroll

Today's adolescents have grown up with conflicting messages about sexuality. Although they have lived during a time of relative political and social conservatism and their school health programs concentrate on abstinence and the risks of sexual behavior (such as sexually transmitted infections [STIs] or unintended pregnancy), they have also had unlimited exposure to sexual information and images through the Internet. Nightly news stories focus on a variety of issues related to sexuality, including gender-inclusive bathrooms, erectile drugs, new contraceptive methods, and increasing global rates of HIV and AIDS, while popular reality television shows such as *16 and Pregnant* and *Teen Mom* tell stories about teen pregnancy. All of these events and influences have shaped this generation of adolescents.

We think of children today as undergoing their own, exclusive stage of development. Children are not just "little adults," and though they can be sexual, childhood sexuality is not adult sexuality (Gordon & Schroeder, 1995). Children want love, appreciate sensuality, and engage in behaviors that set the stage for the adult sexuality to come. Nonetheless, we must be careful not to attribute adult motives to childhood behaviors. When a 5-year-old boy and a 5-year-old girl sharing a bath reach out to touch each other's genitals, the meaning that they ascribe to

that action cannot be considered "sexual" as adults use the term. As Plummer (1991) notes, a little boy having an erection shows simply that his physiology functions normally; seeing the erection as "sexual" is to overlay an adult social meaning onto the physiology. The child is probably not even aware of the "sexual" nature of his erection and, indeed, may not even be aware that his penis is erect.

Every society distinguishes between young and old; every society also creates rules around the sexuality of the young. Sexual growth involves a host of factors—physical maturation of the sexual organs, psychological dynamics, familial relations, and peer relations, all within the social and cultural beliefs about gender roles and sexuality. In this chapter, we'll begin with the special challenges faced by researchers who study childhood and adolescent sexuality. Then we'll take a look at sexuality from infancy through adolescence. Finally, we'll discuss the importance of sexuality education and the controversies surrounding it.

Studying Childhood and Adolescent Sexuality

Many people oppose questioning children about sexuality, often believing that research on child sexuality will somehow encourage promiscuity. Others seem to believe that if we do not talk about children's sexuality, it will just go away. Despite the opposition, many researchers have been forging ahead in their study of children's sexual behavior. We will discuss the research on child and adolescent sexuality throughout this chapter. We will also discuss findings from the National Survey of Sexual Health and Behavior, as well as findings from several of the ongoing, large-scale governmental studies, including the National Longitudinal Study of Adolescent Health, the National Survey of Family Growth, the National Longitudinal Study of Adolescent Males, and the Youth Risk Behavior Surveillance System (see Chapter 2 for more information about these studies).

Although methodologies and populations varied for each of the aforementioned governmental studies, adolescents between the ages of 14 and 17 were a common subpopulation. As we discussed in Chapter 2, sexuality research is often problem driven—that is, many studies are aimed at decreasing "problems," such as STI rates or teenage pregnancy—and nowhere is this more apparent than the research on adolescent sexuality. In the future, more research is needed on a variety of aspects of adolescent sexuality, including frequency of sexual behaviors; differences in gender, ethnicity, race, religion, and social class; same-sex attraction and behavior; transgender identities and behavior; cross-cultural research; and the meaning of eroticism and sexuality in young people's lives.

Throughout most of history, children were treated as miniature adults, and concepts such as "childhood" and "adolescence" did not exist. Most children worked, dressed, and were expected to behave (as much as they were capable) like adults.

Oscar Gustav Rejlander/Otto Herschan/Getty Images

Review Questions

1 Explain how today's adolescents are being exposed to sexuality in different ways than the generations before them.

2 Explain why there has been opposition to childhood sexuality research.

3 Identify the large-scale studies on adolescent sexual behavior and explain their study populations.

4 Give one example of how research into childhood sexuality has been problem driven.

Beginnings: Birth to Age 2

Let's first take a look at physical and psychosexual changes from birth to age 2. We would not label behavior as "sexual" during this time; however, many behaviors arise out of curiosity.

Physical Development: Fully Equipped at Birth

Our sexual anatomy becomes functional even before we are born; ultrasound has shown male fetuses with erections in the uterus, and some infants develop erections shortly after birth—even before the umbilical cord is cut (Masters et al., 1982). Female infants are capable of vaginal lubrication from birth (Martinson, 1981). Infant girls produce some estrogen from the adrenal glands before puberty, whereas infant boys have small testes that produce very small amounts of testosterone. Young children are even capable of orgasm!

Kinsey and his colleagues (1948, 1953) established that 50% of boys between the ages of 3 and 4 could achieve the urogenital muscle spasms of orgasm (although no fluid is ejaculated), and almost all boys could do it 3 to 5 years before puberty. Kinsey did not collect systematic data on the abilities of young girls to reach orgasm, although he did include some anecdotal material on the subject. Still, since we know there are significant similarities in the biological male and female genital systems, it's logical to assume that young girls have the capacity for orgasm, just like boys.

Psychosexual Development: Bonding and Gender

Throughout this textbook we have discussed the importance of early relationships and the development of an attachment to a primary caregiver. Infants can develop many attachment styles, including secure, anxious/ambivalent, or avoidant (see Chapter 7). Infants are helpless creatures, incapable of obtaining nourishment or warmth or relieving pain or distress. In fact, the bond between a biological mother and child is more than psychological; a baby's crying actually helps stimulate the secretion of the hormone oxytocin in the mother, which releases her milk for breast-feeding (Rossi, 1978; we'll discuss breast-feeding more in Chapter 12).

Fabrizio Cacciatore/Photolibrary/Getty Images

Young children are curious about their bodies and bodily functions.

In Chapter 7, we also discussed the importance of pheromones, which promote the bond between a mother and her infant. Equally important as the infant's need for nourishment is the need for holding, cuddling, and close contact with caregivers. An infant's need for warmth and contact was demonstrated in Harlow's (1959) famous experiment, in which rhesus monkeys were separated at birth from their mothers. When offered two surrogate mothers, one a wire figure of a monkey equipped with milk bottles and one a terry-cloth–covered figure, the monkeys clung to the terry-cloth figure for warmth and security and ventured over to the wire figure only when desperate for nourishment. The need for a sense of warmth and security in infancy overwhelms even the desire to eat.

In Chapter 4, we discussed how infants between 1 and 2 years of age begin to develop their gender identity. For most children, gender identity is congruent with their sex assigned at birth. After about age 2, it becomes increasingly difficult to change the child's gender identity (which is occasionally done when, for example, a child is mistakenly identified at birth). It takes a little longer to achieve gender constancy, whereby young children come to understand that they will not become a member of the other sex sometime in the future. Most children develop **gender constancy** by about age 6, and a strong identification with one gender typically develops that becomes a fundamental part of a child's self-concept (Warin, 2000).

> **gender constancy**
> The realization in the young child that one's gender does not normally change over the life span.

Many young children engage in cross-gender behavior, but some children are insistent they are not the sex they were assigned at birth (Zucker & Lawrence, 2009). Expressing a wish to be another gender can be temporary or it can be a permanent desire that leads a person to live as a transgender adult. It's estimated that about 0.3% of U.S. adults are transgender, although because of underreporting the prevalence is probably closer to 1% (Gates, 2011). Studies have found that children who are persistent, consistent, and insistent about their gender identity are likely to be transgender (Green & Mauer, 2015). Later in this chapter we will discuss options for transgender children.

Sexual Behavior: Curiosity

In infancy, children's bodies are busy making sure all of their organs work and learning to control them. The sexual system is no exception. Male infants sometimes have erections during breast-feeding (which may be disconcerting to the mother), whereas females have clitoral erections and lubrication (although this is unlikely to be noticed). The baby's body (and mind) has not yet differentiated sexual functions from other functions, and the pleasure of breast-feeding, as well as the stimulation from the lips, mouth, and tongue, create a generalized neurological response that stimulates the genital response.

Genital touching is common in infancy, and many infants touch their genitals as soon as their hands are coordinated enough to do so (Casteels et al., 2004; Kellogg, 2009). Some babies only occasionally or rarely touch themselves, whereas others do it more regularly. Although babies clearly derive pleasure from this activity, it is not orgasm based. In fact, it is soothing to the baby and may serve as a means of tension reduction and distraction. Overall, genital touching is normal at this age, and parents should not be concerned about it.

Review Questions

1 Explain how infants have functional sexual anatomy, perhaps even before birth.

2 Identify the single most important aspect of infant development, and explain the importance of pheromones, warmth, and contact with caregivers.

3 Differentiate between gender identity and gender constancy.

4 Discuss genital touching in infancy and possible parental concerns about this behavior.

Early Childhood: Ages 2 to 5

Children continue to develop physically, and in early childhood they begin to understand what it means to be a boy or girl. Curiosity is still the basis for their sexuality during this time. Children also learn that their genitals are private during these years, and they often begin to associate sexuality with secrecy.

Physical Development: Mastering Coordination

Early childhood is a crucial period for physical development. Children of this age must learn to master the basic physical actions, such as eye–hand coordination, walking, talking, and generally learning to control their bodies. Think of all the new things a child must learn—all the rules of speaking and communicating; extremely complex physical skills such as self-feeding, walking, and running; how to interact with other children and adults; control of bodily wastes through toilet training; and handling all the frustrations of not being able to do most of the things they want to do when they want to do them. Although this period of childhood is not a particularly active one in terms of physical sexual development, children may learn more in the first few years of childhood about the nature of their bodies than they learn in the entire remainder of their lives. It is truly a time of profound change and growth.

Psychosexual Development: Who Am I?

In early childhood, children begin serious exploration of their bodies. It is usually during this period that children are toilet trained, and they go through a period of intense interest in their genitals and bodily wastes. They begin to ask the first, basic questions about sex, usually about why some people have different genitals and what they are for. They begin to explore what it means to be "boys" or "girls" and turn to their parents, siblings, or television for models of gender behavior. Sometimes children at this age will appear flirtatious or engage in sexual behaviors such as kissing in an attempt to understand gender roles.

REAL RESEARCH First-born children score higher than their siblings on IQ tests primarily because their parents offer them the most mental stimulation, including reading books, arts and crafts, and music lessons (LEHMANN ET AL., 2016).

Sexual Behavior: Curiosity and Responsibility

Toddlers are not yet aware of the idea of sexuality or genital sexual relations. Like infants, toddlers and young children engage in many behaviors that involve exploring their bodies and doing things that feel good. Both girls and boys at this age continue to engage in genital touching.

Genital touching is more common in early childhood than later childhood, although it picks up again after puberty (Friedrich et al., 1991; Friedrich et al., 1998; Kellogg, 2009). The act may be deliberate and obvious, and may even become a preoccupation. As discussed, boys at this age are capable of erection, and some proudly show it off to visitors. Parental reaction at this stage is important; strong disapproval may teach their children to hide the behavior and to be secretive and even ashamed of their bodies, whereas parents who are tolerant of their children's emerging sexuality can teach them to respect and take pride in their bodies. It is perfectly appropriate to make rules about the times and places that such behavior is acceptable, just as one makes rules about other childhood actions, such as the correct time and place to eat or to urinate.

Child sex play often begins with games exposing the genitals ("I'll show you mine if you show me yours. . . ."), and by the age of 4, may move on to undressing and touching, followed by asking questions about sex around age 5. Sometimes young children will rub their bodies against each other, often with members of the same sex, which seems to provide general tactile pleasure.

Sexual Knowledge and Attitudes

During this period of early childhood, children learn that the genitals are different from the rest of the body. They remain covered up, at least in public, and touching or playing with them is either discouraged or to be done only in private. This is the beginning of the sense of secrecy surrounding sexuality.

As we discussed in Chapters 5 and 6, children this age, especially girls, rarely learn the anatomically correct names for their genitals. Why is it that some parents teach their children the correct names for all the body parts except their genitalia? What message do you think it might send children when we use cute play words such as "weiner" or "piddlewiddle" for their genital organs?

In our culture, boys are often taught about the penis, but girls rarely are taught about the vagina or clitoris. This tends to discourage girls from learning more about their sexuality (Ogletree & Ginsburg, 2000). Although girls are quite interested in boys' genitalia at these ages, boys tend to be relatively uninterested in girls' genitalia (Gundersen et al., 1981).

ON YOUR MIND

Is it damaging to children to see their parents naked? What about accidentally seeing them having sex?

For many years in Western society, it has been thought that children would be somehow traumatized by seeing their parents naked. In fact, nudity is natural and common in many cultures, such as European countries, which have a reputation for physical health and beauty. Parents' casual nudity, openness to sexual questions, and willingness to let their children sleep at times in their beds has been found to be correlated with generally positive overall effects on the well-being of children (Lewis & Janda, 1988; Okami et al., 1998). If children walk in on their parents having sex, the parents' best tactic is not to be upset, but to tell the children calmly that the parents are showing each other how much they love each other. Most children are scared when they walk in on their parents having sex and talking about it can help the children understand. More significant trauma can come from the parents' overreaction than from the sight of parents having sex.

Review Questions

1 Explain how curiosity is still the basis for sexuality in early childhood.

2 What does the research show about genital touching during this age range?

3 Explain how a lack of knowledge about proper anatomical terms for the genitals may affect children.

4 What is the impact of learning in childhood that the genitals are different from the rest of the body? Explain.

Middle Childhood to Preteen: Ages 6 to 12

Between ages 6 and 12, the first outward signs of puberty often occur, and children become more private about their bodies. They begin building a larger knowledge base about sexual information—and acquire information from many sources, including their parents/caregivers, peers, and siblings. During the middle childhood to preteen years, children often play in same-sex groups.

Physical Development: Puberty

Until a child's body starts the enormous changes involved in puberty, the sexual organs grow in size only to keep up with general body growth and change very little in their physiological

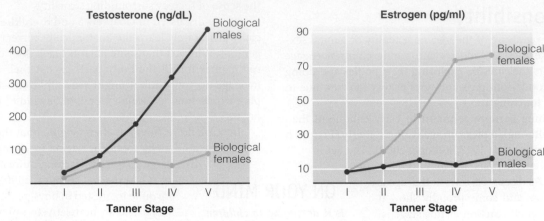

Changes in Sex Hormones During Puberty

FIGURE **8.1** The changes that occur during puberty are driven by changes in hormone production

activity. Puberty marks the transition from sexual immaturity to maturity and the start of reproductive ability. In Chapters 5 and 6, we discussed the physiological and hormonal changes that accompany puberty, so in this chapter we review only those physical changes that have an effect on the nature of adolescent sexuality.

Pubertal changes can be frightening for children who are not prepared for them, and even if prepared, the onset of puberty can be emotionally, psychologically, and physically difficult for some children. Transgender children, who believe they are not the sex they were assigned at birth, often have a difficult time with the onset of puberty. Studies have found alarming rates of depression, anxiety, self-injury, and suicide in transgender youth (Katz-Wise et al., 2017; Shiffman et al., 2016; Tebbe & Moradi, 2016). In fact, studies have found they are 2–3 times more likely than cisgender youth to attempt suicide (Reisner et al., 2015). In the nearby Sex in Real Life we discuss reversible hormone-blocking drugs to delay the onset of puberty in transgender children.

Although the body begins internal changes to prepare for puberty as early as age 6 or 7, the first outward signs of puberty begin at 9 or 10. The physiological changes of puberty begin anywhere between the ages of 8 and 13 in most girls and 9 and 14 in most boys (see Figure 8.1 for hormonal changes that occur during puberty and Figure 8.2 for more information about signs of puberty in boys and girls). As we discussed in Chapter 5, research has found that girls are beginning puberty earlier than ever before (Buttke et al., 2012; Chen et al., 2013; Weil, 2012). Overall, girls' maturation is about 1.5 to 2 years ahead of boys. Below we will explore the physical changes that occur during puberty.

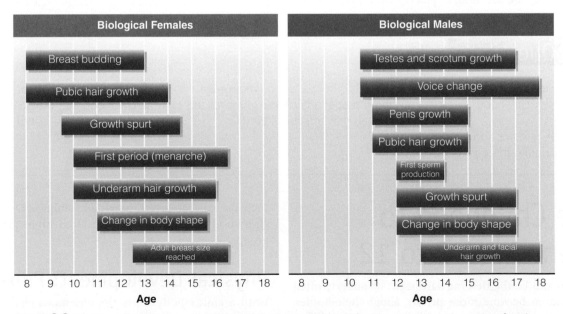

FIGURE **8.2** Above are the average ages of pubertal changes in biological females and males. On average, females begin these changes earlier than males

Sex in Real Life   Puberty on Hold

Puberty causes many physical changes, some of which are permanent. A biological male develops facial and body hair, an Adam's apple along with a deepening of the voice, a growth spurt, and spontaneous erections, while a biological female experiences an increase in fat deposits in the buttocks and thighs and breasts, a stop in bone growth, and the beginning of menstruation. All of these changes can be disconcerting for a transgender child who does not identify with the sex they were assigned at birth. Since the World Professional Association for Transgender Health recommends that children experiencing gender dysphoria do not begin cross-sex hormonal treatments before the age of 16 (or surgical interventions before the age of 18), some health care providers recommend the use of puberty-delay drugs to put a hold on irreversible body changes that would occur during puberty. These drugs can buy time for a child to make an informed decision about whether they want to move forward with a gender transition and, if so, how best to do this. If they do decide to transition, the medications decrease the need for interventions later in life (WPATH, 2012). For example, by putting puberty on hold an adolescent undergoing a male-to-female transition wouldn't have to undergo electrolysis later in life to remove facial hair.

Puberty-delay drugs also have psychological and emotional benefits because they enable a transgender child to keep their body in an androgynous state. The drugs are administered through monthly injections or implants in the upper arm, which last for 2–3 years (Tishelman et al., 2015). Some transgender children begin a social transition while taking the medications, in which they change their name, dress, and/or pronouns. They can stay on the puberty-delay drugs for as long as necessary, but when the medications are stopped the physical changes of puberty begin. If a child, with family support, decides they do want to transition, the puberty-delay drugs are stopped and cross-sex hormones are begun to bring their physical body in line with their gender identity.

There has been controversy related to the use of puberty-delay drugs. Some health providers believe that gender dysphoria is a phase that children will grow out of and drugs are unnecessary (Wallien & Cohen-Kettenis, 2008), while others believe puberty-delay drugs are an invaluable part of the treatment process (Spack et al., 2012; Vance et al., 2014). The American Academy of Pediatrics supports the use of puberty-delay drugs.

In 2016, the U.S. National Institutes of Health launched the largest-ever study of transgender youth: the Transgender Youth Project. This study will evaluate the long-term outcomes of the use of both puberty-delay medications and cross-sex hormones.

Researchers hope to follow 300 transgender children and adolescents for at least five years to track the effects of delayed puberty and the use of cross-sex hormones. Research will continue to explore the best practices for transgender youth.

Jazz Jennings, a YouTube personality and LGBTQ rights activist, was assigned male at birth but began taking puberty delay drugs when she was 11. Today she is living happily as a young woman.

Females

The first signs of puberty in biological females are typically the appearance of **breast buds** and pubic hair growth. As we discussed in Chapter 5, menarche is the hallmark of female puberty and is often viewed as one of the most important events in a woman's life (Ersoy et al., 2005; we discussed the physiology of menarche in Chapter 5). This can be a scary time for a girl who is uninformed about what to expect and an embarrassing time if she is not taught how to use pads or tampons correctly. Overall, on average, girls experience menarche before boys experience their first ejaculation (often referred to as a wet dream or **semenarche** [SEM-min-ark]).

The beginning of menstruation can mean different things to an adolescent girl depending on how her family or her culture explains it to her. It can signify the exciting beginning of adulthood, sexuality, and the ability to have babies—but with all the potential problems that brings as well. Girls who are prepared for menstruation and who are recognized for their intellectual or creative capabilities are more likely to describe pleasurable reactions to the onset of menstruation, whereas girls who are not recognized for other abilities often experience more fear and embarrassment associated with first menstruation (Ruble & Brooks-Gunn, 1982; Teitelman, 2004).

Although boys' first sign of sexual maturity—ejaculation—is generally a pleasurable experience that is overtly associated with sexuality, girls' sign of maturity is not associated with sexual pleasure and may be accompanied by cramps and discomfort, as well as embarrassment if the onset is at an inopportune time (such as during school). Some girls begin menstruation

breast buds	**semenarche**
The first swelling of the area around the nipple that indicates the beginning of breast development.	The experience of first ejaculation.

with little idea of what is happening or with myths about it being bad to bathe, swim, exercise, or engage in sexual activities. Many are unfamiliar with their genital anatomy, making tasks such as inserting tampons difficult and frustrating (Carroll, 2009; M. Diamond & Diamond, 1986).

Males

In biological boys, the first signs of puberty also involve pubic hair growth, but this generally starts a couple of years later than in girls. Boys will experience semenarche and common reactions include surprise, curiosity, confusion, and pleasure—and typically most boys don't tell anyone about this event (Frankel, 2002; J. H. Stein & Reiser, 1994). Preadolescent boys experience frequent erections as they progress through puberty, which can occur at random times and can be embarrassing. Increased erections during puberty are due to rising levels of testosterone.

Adolescent development in males differs in many ways from the development in girls. Boys' voices change more drastically than girls', and their growth spurts tend to be more extreme and dramatic, usually accompanied by an increase in appetite. Because boys' adolescent growth tends to be more uneven and sporadic than girls', the adolescent boy will often appear gangly or awkward. As boys continue to develop, the larynx enlarges, bones grow, and the frame takes on a more adult appearance.

Psychosexual Development: Becoming More Private

As children mature, sexual behaviors, such as public genital touching or sex games, decrease. However, this may be because such behaviors are less tolerated by parents and adults as the child grows older. For example, although it may be acceptable for a 3-year-old to put his hand down his pants, such behavior would not be as acceptable for a 9-year-old.

Typically, children engage in more sexual exploration behavior up until age 5; then this behavior decreases. One study found that 2-year-old children of both sexes engaged in more natural sexual exploration than did children in the 10- to

12-year-old range (Friedrich, 1998). This may simply be because children get better at hiding such behaviors.

Sexual Behavior: Learning About the Birds and Bees

Children through the middle and late childhood years continue to engage in genital touching and may explore both same- and other-sex contact. Curiosity drives some to display their genitals and seek out the genitals of other children. Prepubescence is the age of sexual discovery; most children learn about adult sexual behaviors such as sexual intercourse at this age and assimilate cultural taboos and prejudices concerning unconventional sexual behavior. For example, it is at this age that children (especially boys) first begin to use sexual insults with each other (using taunts like "That's so gay!"), questioning their friends' sexual orientation. Over the last few years, educators have developed many resources to help children and adolescents understand the negativity of such phrases and the potential consequences of the words they use.

Masturbation

Generally, by the end of this period, most children are capable of stimulating themselves to orgasm. Although orgasm is possible, not all children in this age range engage in genital touching for the purpose of orgasm. When masturbation does begin, both boys and girls may stimulate themselves by rubbing their penis or clitoris against soft objects such as blankets, pillows, or stuffed animals. Some girls experience pleasure and even orgasm by rhythmically rubbing their legs together. Most boys and girls learn about masturbation from the media or peers and not their parents or teachers (Kaestle & Allen, 2011).

Sexual Contact

Children from age 6 to puberty engage in a variety of same- and other-sex play. Sex games, such as "spin the bottle" (spinning a bottle in a circle while asking a question such as, "Who is going to kiss Marie?" and then the person whom the bottle points to must perform the task), are common and allow children to make sexual contact under the guise of a game. Play, in a sense, is the "work" of childhood, teaching interpersonal and physical skills that will be developed as we mature. Children at this age have some knowledge about sex and are curious about it, but they often have incomplete or erroneous ideas. Children exhibit a range of same-sex sexual behaviors as they move through childhood, from casual rubbing and contact during horseplay to more focused attention on the genitals.

Rates of sexual contact among school-age children are difficult to come by, and most experts still cite Kinsey's data of 1948 and 1953. Kinsey found that 57% of men and 46% of women remembered engaging in some kind of sex play in the preadolescent years. However, the problem with research in this area is that many studies are retrospective (i.e., they asked older adults to remember what they did when they were young), and there are many reasons to think people's recollections of childhood sexuality may not be entirely accurate.

Sexuality and Relationships: What We Learn

As we grow up, all of our experiences influence our sexuality in one way or another. We learn different aspects of sexuality from these varied influences; for example, we may learn values and taboos from our parents, information from our siblings, and techniques and behavior from our peers, television, and the Internet. All of these influences contribute to our developing sexuality.

Relationships with Parents and Caretakers

In Chapter 7, we discussed how our parents, or the adults who raised us, are the very first teachers of love and intimacy. As we grow and find relationships of our own, we tend to relate to others in our love relationships much as we did when we were young.

When it comes to childhood sexual behaviors, many American parents feel conflicted. They may want their children to have a positive attitude toward sexuality, but many do not know how to go about fostering this attitude. Children have a natural curiosity about sexuality, and when parents avoid children's questions, they reinforce children's ideas that sex is secret, mysterious, and/or bad. As adolescents' bodies continue to change, they may feel anxious about these changes or their relationships with other people. Accurate knowledge about sexuality may lead to a more positive self-image and self-acceptance. We discuss the importance of sexuality education later in this chapter.

Parents may get upset and confused when they discover that their child engages in sexual or cross-gender play. As we discussed earlier, cross-gender play is normal in children. Parents should probably be more concerned if their children show no interest in their own or other children's bodies than if they want to find out what other children have "down there." Family support is

critical for children who question their gender or sexual orientation. Studies have shown that family rejection at a young age can increase the risk of depression, isolation, and loneliness (Baiocco et al., 2014). In addition, teens who are rejected by their families are more likely to engage in risky behaviors (such as drug/alcohol use or early sexual behavior). Overall, LGBTQ students who were accepted by their family have more secure attachments, higher levels of self-esteem, and less risky behavior (Dickenson & Huebner, 2016; McConnell et al., 2016; Rosario, 2015; we discuss this further in Chapter 11).

Relationships with Peers

As children age and try to determine how they will fare in the world outside the family, their peer groups increase in importance. Friendships are an essential part of adolescent social development (Ojanen et al., 2010). Studies have found that friendships

Young boys develop strong relationships with same-sex and other-sex friends and relatives, and these relationships set the stage for adult intimate relationships.

JGI/Jamie Grill/Blend Images/Getty Images

among adolescents from marginalized groups in the United States (including Mexican, Central/South American, Puerto Rican, and Cuban adolescents) increase feelings of belongingness as well as academic achievement (Delgado et al., 2016). Learning acceptable peer-group sexual standards is as important as learning all the other attitudes and behaviors. Children learn acceptable attitudes and behaviors for common games, sports, and even the latest media trends.

SAME-SEX PEERS During middle childhood, adolescents overwhelmingly prefer same-sex to other-sex friends (Hendrick & Hendrick, 2000; Mehta & Strough, 2010). Although other-sex friendships do develop, the majority of early play is done in same-sex groupings. Early on these friendships tend to be activity-based (friends are made because of shared interests or proximity), but by early adolescence, affective qualities (such as trust, loyalty, honesty) replace the activity-based interests (Bigelow, 1977; Ojanen et al., 2010). With these qualities in place, friendships can tolerate differences in interests or activities and reasonable distance separations (such as not being in the same classroom). As a result, friendships in adolescence become more stable, supportive, and intimate than they were before this time.

Peers are a major catalyst in the decision to partake in voluntary sexual experimentation with others. Often initial sexual experimentation takes place among preadolescents of the same sex. Same-sex experimentation is quite common in childhood, even among people who grow up to be predominantly heterosexual.

OTHER-SEX PEERS For most American children, preadolescence is when they begin to recognize their sexual nature and to see peers as potential boyfriends or girlfriends. Although this does not happen until the very end of this period, children as young as 11 begin to develop interest in others and may begin pairing off within larger groups of friends or at parties. Preadolescence has traditionally been a time of early sexual contact, such as kissing and affectionate touching, but for many this does not occur until later.

SIBLINGS Another fairly common childhood experience is sexual contact with siblings or close relatives, such as cousins. Most of the time, this occurs in sex games or fondling, but it can also occur as abuse, with an older sibling or relative coercing a younger one into unwanted sexual activity. Greenwald and Leitenberg (1989) found that among a sample of college students, 17% reported having sibling sexual contact before age 13. Only a small percentage involved force or threat, and penetration was rare. Research on sexual contact between siblings suggests that it can be psychologically damaging when there is a large difference between the ages of siblings or coercive force is used (Finkelhor, 1980; Rudd & Herzberger, 1999).

REAL RESEARCH Gender role expectations that encourage boys to experiment sexually to be "real men" reinforce the view of girls as sex objects (IGRAS ET AL., 2014).

Review Questions

1 Explain physical and psychosexual development in middle childhood through the preteen years.

2 Identify and discuss the types of sexual behaviors that are common in middle childhood through the preteen years.

3 Discuss the importance of relationships with parents, peers, and siblings in childhood through preadolescence.

Adolescence: Ages 12 to 18

Adolescence begins after the onset of puberty and is, in part, our emotional and cognitive reactions to puberty. Adolescence ends when the person achieves "adulthood," signified by a sense of individual identity and an ability to cope independently with internal and external problems (Lovejoy & Estridge, 1987). People reach adulthood at different times; adolescence can end at around age 17 or 18, or it can stretch into a person's 20s. It is recognized the world over as a time of transition, as the entrance into the responsibilities and privileges of adulthood. Most societies throughout history have developed rites of passage around puberty; the Jewish Bar or Bat Mitzvah, Christian confirmation, and the Hispanic Quinceañera come to mind, and other cultures have other rites. The Quinceañera—a 15th birthday celebration for Latina girls—has traditionally been used as an opportunity to discuss female adolescent developmental tasks and challenges, including teenage pregnancy and sexuality (H. Stewart, 2005).

We know the most about this developmental period because of ongoing research studies on adolescent sexual behavior. Overall, we know there is no other time in the life cycle that so many things happen at once: the body undergoes rapid change; the individual begins a psychological separation from the parents; peer relationships, dating, and sexuality increase in importance; and attention turns to job, career, or college choices.

Many young people have their first experience with partnered sex during this time. It is no wonder that many adults look back on their adolescence as both a time of confusion and difficulty and a time of fond memories.

Physical Development: Big Changes

During early adolescence, parents are often shocked at the extreme changes that occur in their children; children can add 5 or 6 inches in height and gain 10 to 20 pounds in less than a year.

In their relationships with each other, children in middle childhood often imitate adults.

Many cultures have rites of passage that signify the entry of the child into adulthood. Here a young Jewish boy practices reading from the Torah for his Bar Mitzvah.

Boys may develop a lower voice and a more decidedly adult physique, whereas girls develop breasts and a more female physique. Biological changes take place in virtually every system of the body and include changes in the brain, cardiovascular status, energy levels, sexual desire, mood, and personality characteristics (Hamburg, 1986; Herting & Sowell, 2017; Juraska & Willing, 2017).

Maturing early or late can also be awkward for adolescents. Because girls' growth spurts happen earlier than boys', there is a period when girls will be at least equal in height and often taller than boys; this reversal of the cultural expectation of male height often causes both sexes to be embarrassed at dances. Girls who consider themselves to be "on time" in developing feel more attractive and positive about their bodies than those who consider themselves "early" or "late" (Ellis et al., 2011; Natsuaki et al., 2011). Studies have found that early maturing girls may be at increased risk for sexual harassment and depression (Skoog & Özdemir, 2016; Wang et al., 2016).

Being the last boy (or the first) in the locker room to develop pubic hair and have the penis develop can be a humiliating experience that many remember well into adulthood. Similarly, girls who are the first or last to develop breasts often suffer the cruel taunts of classmates, although the messages can be mixed. It may be this combination of beginning of sexual exploration, changing bodies, and peer pressure that results in the average adolescent having a negative **body image** (Brumberg, 1997).

For the most part, early development in boys is usually not as embarrassing as it is in girls; beginning to shave may be seen as a sign of maturity and adulthood. However, as we discussed earlier, adolescent boys do experience frequent spontaneous erections, which can be quite embarrassing. Their increased sexual desire is often released through nocturnal emissions and more frequent masturbation.

Psychosexual Development: Emotional Self-Awareness

Adolescence can be the most psychologically and socially difficult of the life cycle changes. Adolescents struggle with a number of tasks: achieving comfort with their bodies, developing an

identity separate from their parents', trying to prove their capacity to establish meaningful intimate and sexual relationships, beginning to think abstractly and futuristically, and establishing emotional self-awareness (Gemelli, 1996). We now examine these life cycle changes.

In early adolescence, preteens begin to shift their role from child to adolescent, trying to forge an identity separate from their family by establishing stronger relationships with peers. Same-sex friendships are common by the eighth grade and may develop into first same-sex sexual contacts as well (L. M. Diamond, 2000). The importance of a best friend grows as an adolescent matures. In fact, by the end of high school, adolescents rated their relationship with their best friend as their most important relationship (B. B. Brown et al., 1997; see Figure 8.3).

Early adolescence, as most of us remember, is often filled with "cliques," as people look to peers for validation and standards of behavior. Dating also often begins at this age, which drives many adolescents to become preoccupied with their bodily appearance and to experiment with different "looks." Young adolescents are often very concerned with body image at this time. Many young girls, in an attempt to achieve the perfect "model" figure, will endlessly diet, sometimes to the point of serious eating disorders. The Youth Risk Behavior Survey (YRBS) found that many young boys and girls are developing eating disorders and may turn to drugs

body image
A person's feelings and mental picture of their own body's beauty.

Relationship Importance in Adolescence

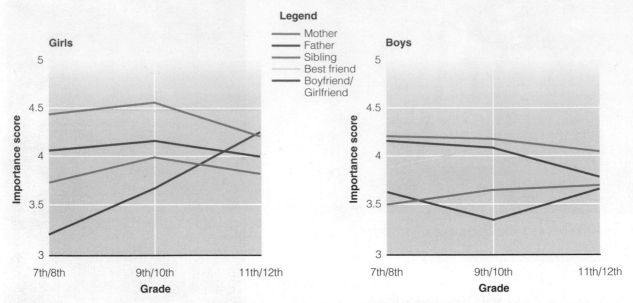

Legend
- Mother
- Father
- Sibling
- Best friend
- Boyfriend/Girlfriend

Girls

Importance score (y-axis: 3, 3.5, 4, 4.5, 5)
Grade (x-axis: 7th/8th, 9th/10th, 11th/12th)

Boys

Importance score (y-axis: 3, 3.5, 4, 4.5, 5)
Grade (x-axis: 7th/8th, 9th/10th, 11th/12th)

FIGURE **8.3** This graph shows the age differences in mean ratings of the importance of each type of relationship to one's life during adolescence (1 = not at all important; 5 = extremely important).

SOURCE: Brown et al., 1997.

such as steroids to achieve the perfect body (Pisetsky et al., 2008; see Chapter 2 for more information about the YRBS). Studies have found that girls who go through puberty early may be at an increased risk for developing eating disorders (Harden et al., 2012; Rohde et al., 2016).

By about age 14, most adolescents experience an increasing interest in intimate relationships. The social environment also helps build this interest through school-sponsored dances and private parties (B. B. Brown et al., 1997). Adolescents who have not yet reached puberty or those who might be questioning their sexual orientation may feel pressure to express interest in other-sex relationships at this time (K. M. Cohen & Savin-Williams, 1996). Many adolescents increase the frequency of dating as they try to integrate sexuality into their growing capacity for adult-to-adult intimacy.

For the average middle adolescent, dating consists of texting or spending time together after school or on weekends. Early dating is often quite informal, and going out in mixed groups is very popular. During this period, couples develop longer term and more exclusive relationships, and early sexual experimentation (including deep kissing and/or erotic touching) may also begin.

Because developing the adolescent sense of self is a delicate process, adolescents may be very sensitive to perceived threats to their emerging ideas of masculinity or femininity. There is an unfortunate tendency among adolescents to portray certain partners as "desirable" and others as undesirable or outcast, which as you can imagine (or remember) can be extremely painful if you are on the wrong side of that judgment. The development of a LGBTQ identity may challenge long-held or socially taught images of the acceptable way to be a man or a woman. Oftentimes, the pattern for LGBTQ adolescents may be quite different from that of their heterosexual and cisgender counterparts. Rates of depression, loneliness, drug and alcohol abuse, and suicide are significantly

In early and middle adolescence, teens try on different looks, from trendy to rebellious, as they develop an identity separate from their parents.

higher in these youth (Blosnich et al., 2016; Mueller et al., 2015; Smith et al., 2016).

There is no clear line between adolescence and adulthood. Almost all cultures allow marriage and other adult privileges in late adolescence, although there still may be certain restrictions (such as needing parental permission to marry). Late adolescence was, until recently, the stage during which people in Western cultures were expected to begin their search for marital partners through serious dating. As we discuss in Chapter 9, many of today's adults wait longer to establish permanent relationships and perhaps marry.

Sexual Behavior: Abstinence and Experimentation

Although many television reports and news headlines about adolescent sexual behavior seem to imply that adolescents are reckless and becoming sexually active at young ages, the National Survey of Sexual Health and Behavior (NSSHB) found that today's adolescents are more likely to act responsibly about sexual behavior (Fortenberry et al., 2010). By studying a variety of teenage sexual behaviors, including masturbation, oral sex, penile-vaginal intercourse, anal intercourse, and the use of condoms, the NSSHB was able to compare data on adolescent sex behaviors with other national surveys (such as the National Survey of Family Growth and the Youth Risk Behavior Survey); see Chapter 2 for more information about these studies.

Masturbation

As boys and girls enter adolescence, masturbation may increase, and the activity is often more directed toward achieving orgasm than simply producing pleasurable sensations. Kinsey and his colleagues (1953) found a sharp increase between the ages of 13 and 15 in boys, with 82% of boys having masturbated by age 15. The girls' pattern was more gradual, with 20% having masturbated by age 15 and no sharp increase at any point. More recent research has found that while more males than females report masturbating, there were similarities in attitudes about masturbation, sexual fantasies, sexual functioning, and the use of objects (Driemeyer et al., 2016). The NSSHB found that masturbation increases during adolescence and then decreases as partnered sex increases later in life (Herbenick et al., 2010a).

Abstinence

Sexual **abstinence**, the practice of refraining from sexual activity, can be voluntary (motivated by an individual's personal or religious beliefs) or involuntary (when there are no available sexual partners). One study found that close to 30% of sexually active adolescents chose to refrain from sexual activity at some point (Byers et al., 2016). Reasons for refraining included personal values, lack of sexual pleasure, relationship concerns, and/or negative emotional or physical experiences. But what does it mean to *refrain* from

ON YOUR MIND

I am 19 years old, and I masturbate at least twice a week, but not as much if I am having good sex with my girlfriend. But she tells me that she doesn't masturbate as much as I do. Why do teenage males masturbate so much more than teenage females?

sexual activity? Does it mean a person doesn't engage in any sexual activities? Do they engage in only certain activities? Adolescents who abstain from sexual activity typically avoid penetrative sex, but they may engage in other activities. The Sexuality Information and Education Council of the United States promotes abstinence and encourages adolescents to delay sexual activity until they are physically, cognitively, and emotionally ready for mature sexual relationships.

While research has found that many adolescents and young adults in the United States masturbate, masturbation rates in males are generally higher than in females (HERBENICK ET AL., 2010a). This could be because of several things. First of all, females may underreport their masturbation in surveys because they are less comfortable discussing it. Boys tend to reinforce the social acceptability of masturbation by talking about it more freely among themselves. There may also be biophysical reasons for more frequent male masturbation, such as the obvious nature of the male erection and higher levels of testosterone.

Adolescents often think about many factors when deciding to be sexual. Perceived family and peer attitudes about sexuality are key factors in the decision to become sexual (Akers et al., 2011). Teens who delay sexual activity are more likely to live with both biological parents, feel a personal connection to their family, have discussed sex and abstinence with their parents, and have higher intelligence levels (C. J. Halpern et al., 2000; Maguen & Armistead, 2006; Meschke et al., 2000). Some teens decide they are not ready because they haven't met the "right" person or want to wait for marriage, whereas others delay for other reasons (such as STI or pregnancy fears; Morrison-Beedy et al., 2008).

REAL RESEARCH Fears about issues such as discrimination, difficulties navigating the health care system, and legal challenges create unique barriers for the parents of transgender or gender nonconforming youth, which can interfere with their ability to envision a positive future for their children (KATZ-WISE ET AL., 2017).

Sexual Contact

Adolescents may engage in a variety of sexual behaviors, including kissing, affectionate touching, oral sex, anal sex, or vaginal intercourse. Like cisgender adolescents, transgender adolescents engage in a variety of sexual behaviors and may identify as

abstinence
Refraining from intercourse and often other forms of sexual contact.

straight, lesbian, gay, or bisexual. Below we'll explore a variety of sexual behaviors (see Figure 8.4 for more information on selected sexual behaviors in adolescence).

ORAL SEX Kinsey and his colleagues (1948, 1953) reported that 17% of adolescents reported engaging in **fellatio** (fil-LAY-she-oh) and 11% in **cunnilingus** (kun-nah-LING-gus). However, more recent studies, including the National Survey of Family Growth and the National Survey of Sexual Health and Behavior, found that oral sex has increased in all age groups (Herbenick et al., 2010a; see Figure 8.4). Approximately half of teenagers between the ages of 15 and 19 have engaged in oral sex, with 47% of male teens and 41% of female teens reporting they have received oral sex (Chandra et al., 2013). Although female teens are as likely to

give oral sex as they are to receive it (41% and 43%, respectively), male teens are more likely to receive oral sex than to give it (47% and 35%, respectively; Copen et al., 2012).

Many heterosexual teens engage in oral sex before progressing to sexual intercourse. In fact, an analysis of the sexual practices of 2,271 15- to 19-year-olds found that oral sex was more common in heterosexual teen couples who had already initiated sexual intercourse—87% of nonvirgin teens reported engaging in oral sex, whereas only 27% of virgins reported engaging in oral sex (Lindberg et al., 2008). It's estimated that 50% of all heterosexual teens who engage in oral sex during 9th grade will engage in sexual intercourse by the end of 11th grade (Song & Halpern-Felsher, 2011).

Gender, ethnic/racial, and socioeconomic differences have been found in the rates of oral sex in teens. Female teens are significantly more likely than male teens to indicate they have given oral sex, while White females were significantly more likely to have given oral sex to a male than Hispanic and Black females (Lefkowitz et al., 2016; Lindberg et al., 2008). Studies have also found that teens from higher socioeconomic classes are more likely to report engaging in oral sex.

ANAL SEX The National Survey of Family Growth found that approximately 17% of males and 15% of females aged 18 to 19 years have engaged in anal sex (Chandra et al., 2011). The NSSHB also collected information on prevalence of anal sex in adolescence and found that same-sex receptive anal sex was the least common sexual behavior reported in men (see Figure 8.4; Herbenick et al., 2010a). Some studies find a higher number of individuals report engaging in anal sex. For example, a study of 15–24-year-olds in Baltimore City, Maryland, found that 29% of males and 15% of females reported engaging in anal sex in the last six months (Hebert et al., 2015). Overall, heterosexual adolescents who had engaged in sexual intercourse were more likely to have engaged in anal sex (Lindberg et al., 2008). Although the overall likelihood of engaging in heterosexual anal sex was not found to differ significantly by ethnic or racial group, Hispanic males were more likely than non-Hispanic White males to report ever having engaged in anal intercourse (Lindberg et al., 2008).

MASTURBATION		
AGE	MALE	FEMALE
14–15	67.5%	43%
16–17	79%	52%
18–19	86%	66%
20–24	92%	77%

(a)

VAGINAL INTERCOURSE		
AGE	MALE	FEMALE
14–15	10%	12%
16–17	30%	32%
18–19	62.5%	64%
20–24	70%	86%

(b)

ANAL SEX			
AGE	MALE		FEMALE
	GAVE	RECEIVED	
14–15	4%	1%	4%
16–17	6%	1%	7%
18–19	10%	4%	20%
20–24	24%	11%	40%

(c)

fellatio
The act of sexually stimulating the male genitals with the mouth.

cunnilingus
The act of sexually stimulating the female genitals with the mouth.

ORAL SEX								
AGE	MALE				FEMALE			
	WITH A MALE		WITH A FEMALE		WITH A FEMALE		WITH A MALE	
	GAVE	RECEIVED	GAVE	RECEIVED	GAVE	RECEIVED	GAVE	RECEIVED
14–15	2%	2%	8.5%	13%	5%	4%	13%	10%
16–17	3%	3%	20%	34%	9%	7%	29%	26%
18–19	10%	9%	61%	60%	8%	8%	61%	62%
20–24	9%	9%	71%	73.5%	14%	17%	78%	77%

(d)

FIGURE **8.4** Average percentage of men and women by age who have engaged in specific sexual behaviors.

SOURCE: National Survey of Sexual Health and Behavior (NSSHB) results in Herbenick et al. (2010a).

HETEROSEXUAL INTERCOURSE Although the number of high school students engaging in sexual intercourse has decreased since 1988, the most recent Youth Risk Behavior Survey (YRBS) found that the majority of high school students report engaging in sex (Kann et al., 2016). In fact, by the time students are seniors, 59% of males and 57% of females report having engaged in sexual intercourse (Kann et al., 2016). The YRBS data also showed an increase in the use of contraception among high school students, decreases in condom use and HIV testing, and increases in forced sexual activity. The National Survey of Family Growth found slightly lower numbers, with 44% and 47% of female and male teenagers, respectively, having engaged in sexual intercourse (Martinez & Abma, 2015). The National Survey of Family Growth found that the most common reason given for abstaining from sexual intercourse was religion (Martinez et al., 2011).

Although 4% of students experience sexual intercourse before the age of 13, the average age for first engaging in sexual intercourse is approximately 17.1 years (Finer & Philbin, 2014; Kann et al., 2016; see Figure 8.5). However, there are some ethnic differences; on average, Black males are younger, and Asian American males are older at the time of first sexual intercourse. Studies have found that female teens who engage in sexual intercourse at a young age are more likely to experience decreased self-worth and higher levels of substance abuse (Golden et al., 2016).

Most studies find that females have sex later than males throughout the teen years in all racial groups (Kann et al., 2016). In most of the developed countries, the majority of heterosexual men and women engage in sexual intercourse during their teen years. In fact, the age at which heterosexual teenagers become sexually active is similar across comparable developed countries, such as Canada, France, Sweden, and the United States. Contrast this with Japan, where the majority of heterosexual men and women wait until they are in their 20s (Althaus, 1997; Haworth, 2013).

The majority of heterosexual teens experience first sexual intercourse with someone they are in a relationship with, rather than someone they just met (Martinez et al., 2011). However, males and females tend to react differently to their first sexual intercourse. The National Health and Social Life Survey found that more than 90% of men said they wanted to have sexual intercourse the first time they did it; more than half were motivated by curiosity, whereas only a quarter said they had sexual intercourse out of affection for their partner. Although 70% of women reported wanting to have sexual intercourse, nearly half said they had sex the first time out of affection for their partner, whereas a quarter cited curiosity as their primary motivation. Approximately 25% of female teens said they just went along with it the first time, and 4% reported being forced to have sex the first time. Only 8% of male teens report just going along with it, and 0.3% reported being forced to have sex the first time. For many, the first sexual intercourse was a monumental occasion. Many believe this experience contributes to the redefining of self and the reconfiguration of relationships with friends, family members, and sexual partners (Upchurch et al., 1998).

Although the majority of female teens have first sex partners who are 1 to 3 years older, approximately 25% of female teens have partners who are 4 or more years older (Abma et al., 2010). Other research has found that age differences between sex partners are more common in Latinas' relationships than among non-Latinas (Frost & Driscoll, 2006). In fact, these age differences can put younger heterosexual Latinas at an increased risk for early initiation into sexual behavior, unprotected sex, pregnancy, and STIs. First sex with a partner who is older has been found to be associated with higher percentages of females saying they didn't want the sex to happen (Abma et al., 2010).

SAME-SEX SEXUAL BEHAVIOR We know that same-sex sexual behavior is common in adolescence, both for those who will go on to have predominantly heterosexual relationships and those who will have predominantly same-sex relationships. Some gay and lesbian adolescents experience sexual intercourse during their teenage years, before they identify as lesbian or gay (Saewyc et al., 1998). Although 3% of 18–19-year-old males and 8% of females report their sexual orientation as lesbian, gay, or bisexual, a higher percentage report having engaged in same-sex sexual behaviors (12% of females and 4% of males; Chandra et al., 2011; Martinez et al., 2011).

The first nationally representative study on the health behaviors among lesbian, gay, bisexual, and questioning high school students found that more than 11% of high school students nationwide identified as LGB, or unsure about their sexual orientation (Kann et al., 2016a). This study also found that rates of sexual assault, dating violence, and bullying were three times the rates of heterosexual students.

The Youth Risk Behavior Survey included questions on sexual identity (heterosexual, gay or lesbian, bisexual, or unsure), the sex of sexual contacts (same sex only, other sex only, or both sexes), and whether students were currently sexually active. The prevalence of being currently sexually active ranged from 19% to 42% (median = 32%)

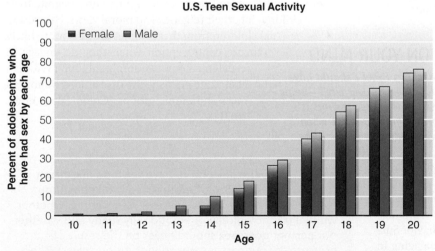

U.S. Teen Sexual Activity

FIGURE **8.5** On average, young people in the U.S. experience sexual intercourse for the first time at about the age of 17. The proportion of young people who have engaged in sexual intercourse increases rapidly with age.

SOURCE: Guttmacher Institute, 2016.

in students who identified as heterosexual; 25% to 63% (median = 53%) in students who identified as gay or lesbian; 44% to 61% (median = 52%) in students who identified as bisexual; and 14% to 36% (median = 32%) in students who identified as unsure (Centers for Disease Control, 2011b; see Figure 8.4 for more information about specific same-sex sexual behaviors).

REAL RESEARCH Teenage girls who take contraceptive pills are more likely to be prescribed antidepressants than teens who do not take contraceptive pills (SKOVLUND ET AL., 2016).

OTHER SEXUAL SITUATIONS There are many other types of sexual situations that adolescents can experience, including sexual assault and participation in sex work. It's estimated that 7% of all 9th- through 12th-grade students report being forced to engage in sexual intercourse; however, the prevalence of forced sex was higher in LGB (18%) and questioning (13%) students, compared to heterosexual (5%) students (Kann et al., 2016a). When these rates are broken down by gender, rates were higher among lesbian and female bisexuals (21%) and female questioning students (10%), compared to female heterosexual students (9%). Rates were also higher among gay and male bisexuals (8%) and male questioning students (13.5%), compared to male heterosexual students (2.5%; Kann et al., 2016a). It's not surprising that nationwide 43% of LGB students and 32% of questioning students reported seriously considering attempting suicide, compared to 15% of heterosexual students. Clearly much more work needs to be done to help LGBTQ students in U.S. schools.

Some teenagers, especially runaways—engage in sex work for money to buy food (Popkin et al., 2016). Others become involved in child pornography, posing nude for pictures, or performing sexual acts. Although there are few comprehensive studies of the results of engaging in sex work or pornography as an adolescent (or younger), there is every clinical indication that it results in many sexual and psychological difficulties later on (we discuss this more in Chapter 18).

Ethnic and Racial Differences in Sexual Activity

An adolescent's ethnicity, race, and culture affect their sexual attitudes, which sexual behaviors they engage in, and the frequency of these behaviors. Several ethnic and racial differences have been found in participation in certain sexual behaviors, such as oral and anal sex, age of first sexual intercourse, and age differences between sexual partners. The Youth Risk Behavior Survey we discussed earlier found that the prevalence of engaging in sexual intercourse was higher among Black and Hispanic students than White students (Cabral et al., 2017; Kann et al., 2016). As you will soon see, ethnic and racial differences have also been found in contraceptive use, teen pregnancy, birth rates, abortion, and rates of STIs. We explore these issues in more detail in upcoming chapters.

Influences: Peers, Family, and Religion

The decision to engage in sexual contact with another person is a personal one, yet it is influenced by many social factors, including peers, family, and religion. A number of other social factors influence sexual behavior as well, and we discuss here a few of the more important ones.

Peer Influences

Peer pressure is often cited as the most important influence on teen sexual behavior, and adolescence is certainly a time when the influence of one's friends and peers is at a peak (Busse et al., 2010). Even among preadolescents, peer influences are strong; among sixth graders who have engaged in sexual intercourse, students were more likely to initiate sexual intercourse if they thought that peers were engaging in it and that it would bring them some kind of social gain. Those who did not initiate sexual intercourse were more likely to believe that their behavior would be stigmatized or disapproved of by their peers (Grunbaum et al., 2002).

Remember, though, that a person's perceptions of what their peers are doing have a greater influence than peers' actual behavior. Among those subject to and applying peer pressure, many heterosexual adolescent males feel the need to "prove" their masculinity, leading to early sexual activity. Peer pressure is often rated as one of the top reasons that adolescents give for engaging in sexual intercourse.

Relationship with Parents

Good parental communication, an atmosphere of honesty and openness in the home, a two-parent home, and reasonable rules about dating and relationships are among the most important factors associated with teens' delay of sexual activity (Grossman et al., 2016). This may be attributed to the fact that close families are more likely to transmit their sexual values and integrate their children into their religious and moral views. Heterosexual children from these homes are also more likely to use contraception when they do engage in sexual intercourse (Cabral et al., 2017; Widman et al., 2016). This is the case among almost all races and ethnic groups (Colón-López et al., 2017).

ON YOUR MIND

Sometimes I feel I should have sex just to get it over with—being a virgin is embarrassing! It's pretty hard to resist when everybody else seems to be doing it.

The decision to have sex is an important one. Too often this step is taken without consideration of its consequences—for example, whether we feel psychologically or emotionally ready and whether our partner does. Sex should never be the result of pressure (by our partner, our friends, or ourselves). There may be many reasons that we want to delay sexual experimentation—including moral or religious reasons. Teens also often overestimate the numbers of their friends who are sexually active.

As we discussed earlier, LGBTQ youth who are accepted by their family have higher self-esteem and lower levels of depression and substance abuse. Overall, studies have found that Latino, immigrant, religious, and low socioeconomic status families are often less accepting of LGBTQ teens.

Research has found that many American parents do not discuss sex before an adolescent's first sexual experience (Beckett et al., 2010). If a parent does talk about sex, it is generally the mother who tends to be the primary communicator about sexuality to children; in one study of Latino youths, mothers did the majority of all communication about sexuality to their teenagers (L. M. Baumeister et al., 1995; Raffaelli & Green, 2003). Even though mothers do the majority of communication, they also are likely to talk more to daughters about sexuality than to sons (Kuhle et al., 2015; Widman et al., 2016).

The National Longitudinal Study of Adolescent Health (see Chapter 2) has also found that there is a maternal influence on the timing of first sexual intercourse for heterosexual adolescents, especially for females. A mother's satisfaction with her relationship with her daughter, disapproval of her daughter having sex, and frequent communication about sex is related to a delay of first sexual intercourse (Lam et al., 2008; Tsui-Sui et al., 2010). Fathers are also important—in fact, girls who have a close relationship with their father are more likely to delay sex (Day & Padilla-Walker, 2009; Regnerus & Luchies, 2006; Wilson et al., 2010).

Religion

Although the relationship between religiosity and sexual activity is complex, in general, more religious youths tend to delay sexual behavior and have fewer sexual partners (Hawley et al., 2015: Schmitt & Fuller, 2015). This correlation may be because young people who attend church frequently and who value religion in their lives are less sexually experienced overall. Not only do major Western religions and many other world religions discourage early sexual activity, but religious adolescents also tend to develop friendships and relationships within their religious institutions, and thus have strong ties to people who are more likely to disapprove of early sexual activity. However, once teens begin engaging in sexual behaviors, religious affiliation and frequency of religious attendance have been found to have little impact on frequency of sexual behaviors (R. Jones et al., 2005).

Contraception, Pregnancy, and Abortion: Complex Issues

Although we discuss pregnancy, contraception, and abortion more in Chapters 12 and 13, we introduce these concepts here. In 2011–2013, approximately 80% of female teenagers reported using a contraceptive method the first time they engaged in sexual intercourse, while 84% of male teens did (Martinez & Abma, 2015). Not surprisingly, teens who are 14 years old and younger are less likely to use birth control than older teens (Finer & Philbin, 2014). The most common methods of birth control were condoms, withdrawal, and birth control pills.

Higher contraceptive usage rates are in non-Hispanic White teens (66%) and lower in Hispanic (54%) and non-Hispanic Black teens (46%; Martinez et al., 2011). The use of emergency contraception continues to increase in teens from 8% in 2002 to 22% in 2011–2013 (Martinez & Abma, 2015).

Of all the areas of adolescent sexual behavior, we probably know the most about teenage pregnancy because of its many impacts on the life of the teenager, the teenager's family, and society as a whole. Overall, the national teen pregnancy rate has continued to decrease over the last two decades. While there were approximately 709,000 teen pregnancies in 2009, this decreased to 250,000 pregnancies in 2014 (Hamilton et al., 2016). Pregnancy rates were highest among non-Hispanic Black and Hispanic teens and lowest among non-Hispanic White teens (Cabral et al., 2017). Although the teen pregnancy rate in the United States has declined significantly since 1991, U.S. rates are still higher than in other developed countries. For comparison, the teen pregnancy rate in the United States was 52 pregnancies per 1,000 females teens in 2011, which was nearly double the rates in Sweden (29 per 1,000) and France (25 per 1,000; Ahern & Bramlett, 2016; Sedgh et al., 2015). Interestingly, although the majority of U.S. teens want to avoid a pregnancy, 13% of teens report they would be a little or very pleased if they found out they were pregnant (Abma et al., 2010).

The long-term consequences of teenage pregnancy may be difficult for the mother, child, and extended family. Teenage mothers are more likely to drop out of school, have poorer physical and mental health, and be on welfare than their non-childbearing peers, and their children often have lower birth weights, poorer health and cognitive abilities, more behavioral problems, and fewer educational opportunities (Goossens et al., 2015; Perper et al., 2010). Teen parenting also has an impact on others, such as the parents of the teens (who may end up having to take care of their children's children), and on society in general, because these parents are more likely to need government assistance. Unfortunately, the popularity of shows such as *16 and Pregnant* and *Teen Mom* have led to a perception that the benefits of teen pregnancy outweigh the risks (Aubrey et al., 2014). In addition, these shows often inaccurately portray the effects of teen pregnancy. For example, the teen mothers portrayed in these shows are more likely to get help from the babies' fathers and go on to graduate from high school (Martins et al., 2016).

REAL RESEARCH Nationally representative data from the National Survey of Family Growth found significant declines in sex education among teens (Lindberg et al., 2016). Thirty-five percent of males and 21% of females did not receive any information about birth control methods from either their parents or schools.

However, it's also important to point out that teen pregnancies do not always preclude teen mothers from living healthy, fulfilling lives. In fact, there are examples of teenagers who become pregnant and raise healthy babies while pursuing their own interests.

However, the problems a teenage mother faces are many, especially if there is no partner participating in the child's care. A teen who has support from her partner, family, and friends, and who is able to stay in school, has a better chance of living a fulfilling life.

In studies of teen pregnancy and birth, most of the focus has been on the mothers, who often bear the brunt of the emotional, personal, and financial costs of childbearing (Wei, 2000). Adolescent fathers are more difficult to study. Teenage fathers may not support their partners and become uninvolved soon after, and thus the problem of single mothers raising children can be traced, in part, to the lack of responsibility of teen fathers. Society asks little of the teenage male, and there are few social pressures on him to take responsibility for his offspring.

However, some adolescent fathers do accept their role in both pregnancy and parenthood, and realistically assess their responsibilities toward the mother and child. Ideally, teenage fathers should be integrated into the lives of their children and should be expected to take equal responsibility for them.

What is it about American society that seems to foster such high rates of teenage pregnancy? A complex series of factors is at work. American society is extremely conflicted about the issue of sexuality in general. Our teens are exposed to sexual scenes in movies and television, yet we hesitate to discuss sexuality frankly with them. We allow advertising to use blatantly sexual messages and half-dressed models, yet we will not permit advertising for birth control; there is also significant resistance to sexuality education in the schools.

Today, when teenagers do become pregnant, opportunities may be limited; it is difficult to have a baby and attend high school all day or work at a job. The United States is far behind most other Western countries in providing day-care services that would help single or young parents care for their children. Better counseling, birth control, day-care services, and hope for the future can help ensure that the teenagers who are at risk for unwanted pregnancies and the children of those unwanted pregnancies are cared for by our society.

Sexually Transmitted Infections: Education and Prevention

Although we discuss STIs in great detail in Chapter 15, here we briefly talk about adolescent STI rates. Sexually active teens are at greater risk for acquiring some STIs for behavioral, cultural, and biological reasons (Abma et al., 2010). Teens have less access to information about how to protect themselves from STIs, and adolescent females are also physiologically more susceptible to infection because of the immature development of the cervix. Half of the 20 million new cases of sexually transmitted infections occur in people between the ages of 15 and 24 years old (Centers for Disease Control and Prevention, 2016a). In fact, chlamydia and gonorrhea are higher in 15- to 19-year-old females than in any other age group (Centers for Disease Control, 2014). Although rates of other STIs are lower, they have been steadily increasing every year.

Although LGBTQ youth may not need contraception for birth control purposes, they do need it for protection from STIs. We know that condom use has been declining in men who have sex with men over the last few years (Centers for Disease Control and Prevention, 2016b). Increasing condom use in all teens, regardless of sexual orientation, is imperative to decrease STIs.

Preventing STIs and teenage pregnancy are both important goals of sex education programs. In the following section, we discuss the importance of sexuality education and what is being taught in schools today.

Review Questions

1 Explain physical and psychosexual development in adolescence.

2 Explain what we know about the specific sexual behaviors that often occur during adolescence.

3 Identify and explain the influences on adolescent sexuality.

4 Identify and discuss the reasons that adolescents may be erratic users of contraception.

5 Explain how ethnicity, race, and culture are all important influences on adolescent sexual behavior.

What Children Need to Know: Sexuality Education

In my chapter-opening Notebook feature, I discussed the importance of sexuality education. Sexuality education inspires powerful emotions and a considerable amount of controversy. In fact, it may be one of the most heated topics in the field of sexuality, as different sides debate whether and how sexuality education programs should be implemented in the schools.

Why Sexuality Education Is Important

Although many people claim that knowledge about sexuality may be harmful, studies have found that it is the lack of sexuality education, ignorance about sexual issues, or unresolved curiosity that is harmful (S. Gordon, 1986). Students who participate in comprehensive sexuality education programs are less permissive about premarital sex than students who do not take these courses. Accurate knowledge about sexuality may also lead to a more positive self-image and self-acceptance.

Sexuality affects almost all aspects of human behavior and relationships with other persons. Therefore, if we understand and accept our own sexuality and the sexuality of others, we will have more satisfying relationships. Some experts believe that not talking to children about sex before adolescence is a primary cause of sexual problems later in life (Calderone, 1983).

Today's children receive a great deal of information about sexuality from the media, and much of it is not based on fact (Lenhart, 2015; Rideout et al., 2010). The media and peers are often primary sources of information about sexuality. Sex is present in many of the songs children listen to, the magazines they look at, the Internet sites they visit, and the shows they watch on television.

Proponents of sexuality education believe that sexual learning occurs even when there are no formalized sexuality education programs. When teachers or parents avoid children's questions or appear embarrassed or evasive, they reinforce children's ideas that sex is secret, mysterious, and bad (Walker & Milton, 2006). As adolescents approach puberty, they may feel anxious about their bodily changes or their relationships with other people. Many teenagers feel uncomfortable asking questions and may be pressured by their peers to engage in sexual activity when they do not feel ready. Giving teenagers information about sex can help them deal with the changes they are going through at this time of their lives.

> **REAL RESEARCH** Students who participated in carrying around "robot babies" in an attempt to discourage teenage pregnancy were found to be more likely to get pregnant than those who didn't participate in such programs (BRINKMAN ET AL., 2016). Researchers believe this may be due to the fact that that the students who carried the dolls received more attention from their peers and families, reinforcing the positive aspects of teen parenting.

History of Sexuality Education in the United States

People have always been curious about sexuality. However, it was only in the 20th century that the movement to develop formal and effective sexuality education programs began. Public discussion of sexuality was due, in part, to the moral purity movement of the late 19th century and the medicalization of sex movement in the early 20th century.

Several developments in the United States set the stage for sexuality education. Concern over skyrocketing rates of venereal diseases (what we now refer to as STIs) in the early 1900s resulted in the formation of two groups, the American Society of Sanitary and Moral Prophylaxis and the American Federation for Sex Hygiene. Although these groups helped to further the cause of sexuality education, they concentrated their attention on STIs. Their approach was to use sexuality education to explain biology and anatomy and to address adolescents' natural sexual curiosity. School sexuality education was very scientific and avoided all discussions of interpersonal sexuality.

Starting in the early 1900s, sexuality education was implemented by various national youth groups, including the YMCA, YWCA, Girl Scouts, Boy Scouts, and 4-H Clubs. These programs were developed mainly to demonstrate to young people the responsibilities required in parenting and to discourage early childbearing. More controversial, however, has been whether to include sexuality education as part of the public school curriculum.

In the United States, for example, the opposition to sexuality education has often been due to two attitudes: first, that sexuality is private, should be discouraged in children, and is best discussed in the context of a person's moral and religious beliefs; and second, that public schools are by their nature public, cannot discuss sex without giving children implicit permission to be sexual, and should not promote the moral or religious beliefs of any particular group. The result of these conflicting attitudes was the belief that sexuality education was best performed by parents in the home.

Attitudes toward sexuality, however, began to change, and sexuality education was seen as more important, not only because of the increasing rates of teenage pregnancy (which shatters the illusion that kids are not actually having sex) but also because of the increasing rates of STIs and AIDS. Television and other media contributed by being so sex-saturated that sexuality was no longer a private topic. Yet even with all these changes, many still believe that public educational institutions will present a view of sexuality that they object to, and so many still oppose sexuality education in the United States.

Early sexuality education programs focused primarily on increasing knowledge levels and educating students about the risks of pregnancy. The belief was that if knowledge levels were increased, then students would understand why it was important for them to avoid unprotected sexual intercourse (Kirby, 1992). Soon sexuality education programs added values clarification and skills, including communication and decision-making skills. These second-generation sexuality education programs were based on the idea that if knowledge levels were increased and if students became more aware of their own values and had better decision-making abilities, they would have an easier time talking to their partners and evaluating their own behavior.

Sexuality Education Today

In the United States, each individual state is responsible for developing its own sexuality education programs in conjunction with nationally recommended topics. However, a study by the Centers for Disease Control and Prevention found that less than half of all high schools in the United States, and only a fifth of middle schools, included all the recommended topics (Demissie et al., 2015). This study also found that many schools did not provide relevant sex education to LGBTQ students. The Alan Guttmacher Institute published a report on sexuality education programs and found the following:

- 24 states and the District of Columbia required sex education
- 37 states required that sex education programs include abstinence (with 26 requiring abstinence be stressed)

Sex in Real Life
What Do Children Want to Know and What Are They Ready For?

Because developmental differences influence children's ability to comprehend sexuality education, educators often evaluate what types of questions students ask to develop programs that can meet the needs of differ-ent age levels. Many proponents of sexuality education programs believe that these programs should be sequential (i.e., there should be a logical order in the curriculum) and comprehensive (i.e., they should include information on biological, psychological, social, and spiritual components). Following are some typical questions students ask at various ages and suggestions for what to include in sexuality education programs at these levels.

Age Range	Developmental Issues	Questions Children Might Ask	Focus of Sexuality Education
3 to 5 years	Shorter attention spans	*What is that?* (referring to specific body parts) *What do mommies do? What do daddies do? Where do babies come from?*	At this level, sexuality education can focus on the roles of family members, the development of a positive self-image, and an understanding that living things grow, reproduce, and die.
6 to 8 years	Very curious about how the body works	*Where was I before I was born? How does my mommy get a baby? Did I come from an egg?*	Sexuality education can include information on plant and animal reproduction, gender similarities and differences, growth and development, and self-esteem.
9 to 12 years	Curiosity about their bodies contin-ues, and heterosexual children are often interested in the other sex and reproduction; gay, lesbian, and bisexual children may experience same-sex interests at this time	*How does the reproductive system work? Why do some girls have larger breasts than others? Do boys menstruate? Why don't some women have babies?*	Sexuality education can include focus on biological topics such as the endocrine system, menstruation, masturbation and wet dreams, sexual intercourse, birth control, abortion, self-esteem, and interpersonal relationships.
12 to 14 years	Preteens may be concerned or confused about the physical changes of puberty, including changes in body shape, body control, reproductive ability, men-struation, breast and penis devel-opment, and voice changes	*How can you keep yourself looking attractive? Should your parents know if you're going steady? Why are some people homosexual? Does a girl ever have a wet dream? Does sexual intercourse hurt? Why do people get married?*	Sexuality education can focus on increasing knowledge of contracep-tion, intimate sexual behavior (why people do what they do), dating, and variations in sexual behaviors (homosexuality, transvestism, transsexualism).
15 to 17 years	Increased interest in sexual topics and curiosity about relationships with others, families, reproduc-tion, and various sexual activity patterns; many teenagers begin dating at this time	*What is prostitution? What do girls really want in a good date? How far should you go on a date? Is it good to have sexual intercourse before marriage? Why is sex considered a dirty word?*	Sexuality education can include more information on birth control, abortion, dating, premarital sexual behavior, communication, marriage patterns, sexual myths, moral decisions, parent-hood, sexuality research, sexual dys-function, and the history of sexuality.

SOURCE: Based on Breuss & Greenberg (1981, pp. 223–231).

- 19 states required schools to teach about the importance of being married before engaging in sexual activity

- 18 states and the District of Columbia required schools to include information about contraception

- 13 states required schools to include information about sexual orientation (with 4 requiring only negative informa-tion be included)

- 11 states required that sex education include tools on how to talk to one's parents about sex (Alan Guttmacher Institute, 2017)

Overall, sex education programs are typically either comprehen-sive or abstinence-based. In the United States, most schools teach programs that might have components of both of these, and they are often called a variety of names. Let's review these various types of programs in more detail.

Comprehensive Sexuality Education Programs

Comprehensive sexuality education programs are those that begin in kindergarten and continue through 12th grade; they include a wide variety of topics and help students to develop their own skills and learn factual information. Today, comprehensive sexuality education programs try to help students develop a positive view of sexuality. The Guidelines for Comprehensive Sexuality Education (Sexuality Information and Education Council of the United States, 2004) are a framework designed to help promote the development of comprehensive sexuality education programs nationwide. Originally developed in 1990, the guidelines include four main goals for sexuality education:

1. To provide accurate information about human sexuality.

2. To provide an opportunity for young people to develop and understand their values, attitudes, and insights about sexuality.

3. To help young people develop relationships and interpersonal skills.

4. To help young people exercise responsibility regarding sexual relationships, which includes addressing abstinence, pressures to become prematurely involved in sexual intercourse, and the use of contraception and other health measures.

The guidelines have also been adapted for use outside the United States and are being used in many countries to help design and implement a variety of sexuality education programs.

Abstinence-Only Sexuality Education Programs

Abstinence-only programs emphasize abstinence from all sexual behaviors, and they typically do not provide information about contraception or disease prevention. These programs began in the early 1990s when there was a proliferation of sexuality education programs that used fear to discourage students from engaging in sexual behavior. These programs include mottos such as "Do the right thing—wait for the ring," or "Pet your dog—not your date." Important information about topics such as anatomy or STIs is often omitted from these programs, and there is an overreliance on the negative consequences of sexual behavior. These negative consequences are often exaggerated, portraying sexual behavior as dangerous and harmful. In 1996, the federal government also passed a law outlining the federal definition of abstinence education. These programs teach:

- Abstinence from sexual activity outside marriage as the expected standard for all school-age children

- Sexual activity outside of the context of marriage is likely to have harmful psychological and physical effects

- Bearing children out of wedlock is likely to have harmful consequences for the child, the child's parents, and society

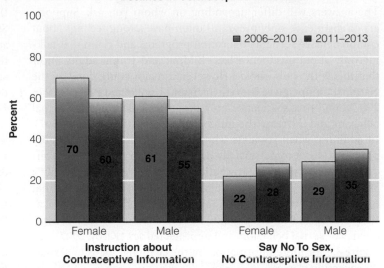

Declines in Contraceptive Education

FIGURE **8.6** Sexuality education classes today are less likely to include contraceptive information and more likely to focus on abstinence and how to say no to sex

SOURCE: Guttmacher Institute, 2016.

From 1996 to 2010, federal funding for abstinence-based sexuality education grew significantly. In fact, during this time, the federal government spent more than $1.5 billion promoting abstinence-based programs (Alan Guttmacher Institute, 2010; Waxman, 2004). Federal funds could be used for sexuality education only if programs taught abstinence-only-until-marriage, which often excluded information about contraception (see Figure 8.6 for more information on the changing focus of sexuality education classes).

While the majority of Americans believe abstinence should be taught in sexuality education programs, the question is how it should be included. Some of the abstinence-only programs use fear tactics to encourage abstinence by claiming the consequences of premarital sexual behavior to include things such as:

[L]oss of reputation; limitations in dating/marriage choices; negative effects on sexual adjustment; negative effects on happiness (premarital sex, especially with more than one person, has been linked to the development of emotional illness [and the] loss of self-esteem); family conflict and possible premature separation from the family; confusion regarding personal value (e.g., "Am I loved because I am me, because of my personality and looks, or because I am a sex object?"); and loss of goals. (Kantor, 1992, p. 4)

---

comprehensive sexuality education programs
Programs that often begin in kindergarten and continue through 12th grade, presenting a wide variety of topics to help students develop their own skills while learning factual information.

abstinence-only programs
Sexuality education programs that emphasize abstinence from all sexual behaviors.

The important question is: Do abstinence-only programs work? The answers will differ depending on whom you ask. Supporters of abstinence-only programs often have strong feelings about comprehensive sexuality education programs and claim that talking only about abstinence lets children and young adults know that this is the only choice. However, a major study done by the National Campaign to Prevent Teen and Unplanned Pregnancy in 2007 found that abstinence-only programs failed to delay sexual behavior and decrease the number of sex partners (Kirby, 2007). In addition, when students who had abstinence-based sexuality programs do become sexually active, they often fail to use condoms or any type of contraception (Brückner & Bearman, 2005; Walters, 2005). Comprehensive sexuality education programs that included abstinence education together with contraceptive education were found to delay sexual behavior and to reduce the frequency of sexual behaviors and unprotected sex (Kirby, 2007). See Figure 8.6 for more information on the changing focus of sexuality education classes.

Effects and Results of Sexuality Education Programs

The main way that researchers determine whether a sexuality program is successful is by measuring behavioral changes after a program has been presented. The standard measures include sexual behavior, pregnancy, and contraceptive use (Remez, 2000). If the rates of sexual behavior increase after sexuality education, a program is judged to be ineffective. If these rates decrease, a program is successful. So what are the effects of sex education programs? Do sexuality education courses change people's actual sexual behavior? It is difficult to measure and evaluate these behavioral changes after a sexuality education program, but it appears that there are some limited changes.

Comprehensive sexuality programs have been found to be the most successful at helping adolescents delay their involvement in sexual intercourse and help protect adolescents from STIs and unintended pregnancies (Kirby, 2001, 2007; Kohler et al., 2008; Starkman & Rajani, 2002). In addition, sexuality education programs that teach contraception and communication skills have been found to delay the onset of sexual intercourse or reduce the frequency of sexual intercourse, reduce the number of sexual partners, and increase the use of contraception (Kirby, 2007; Kohler et al., 2008).

Abstinence-only programs, in contrast, have not yielded successful results in delaying the onset of intercourse (Kirby, 2007; Weed, 2008). In 2007, a federally funded study of abstinence-only programs, conducted by Mathematica Policy Research, found these programs had no effects on sexual abstinence (Trenholm et al., 2007). Overall, there have been no published reports of abstinence-based programs providing significant effects on delaying sexual intercourse. Although many who teach abstinence-only classes claim that these programs are successful, outside experts have found the programs to be ineffective and methodologically unsound (Kirby, 2007; Kohler et al., 2008; Weed, 2008).

Some abstinence-only programs involved teens taking virginity or chastity pledges, in which they signed pledge cards and promised to remain virgins until marriage. A recent study found that approximately 12% of girls and young women in the United States take such pledges (Paik et al., 2016). The ADD Health study, which we discussed earlier in this chapter, found that teenagers who made virginity pledges were less likely to become sexually active in the months that followed the pledge than students who did not take the pledge (Bearman & Bruckner, 2001). However, the majority of them broke their pledges and engaged in sexual intercourse before marriage (Paik et al., 2016). They were also at higher risk for pregnancy and STIs since they often would not use protection when they broke the pledge (Brückner & Bearman, 2005).

Why do you think this was? Researchers believe that signing the pledge may make teenagers unable to accept the responsibilities of using contraception when they decide to become sexually active. Overall, 88% of students who pledged virginity engaged in premarital sex, and they were less likely to use contraception than peers who didn't take a virginity pledge (Brückner & Bearman, 2005; Planned Parenthood Federation of America, 2005).

The United States has one of the highest rates of teen pregnancy in the developed world.

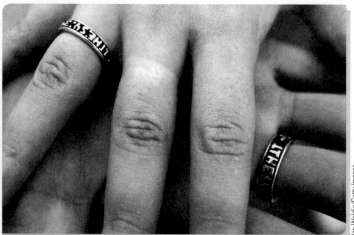

Celibacy rings are often worn by those who pledge to not engage in sexual intercourse until marriage.

Sexual Diversity

Sexuality Education Around the World

IN OUR WORLD

In 2010, the World Health Organization (WHO) published the first detailed European guidelines to help develop curricula for sexuality education programs, *Standards for Sexuality Education in Europe: A Framework for Policy Makers, Educational and Health Authorities and Specialists* (World Health Organization, 2010). The guidelines were developed by a group of 20 experts from nine European countries, along with the WHO and the Federal Centre for Health Education In Germany. The focus of sexuality education in Europe has shifted from the risks associated with sex to a more holistic approach that asserts that children and teens need unbiased, scientifically correct information about sexuality in order to develop the skills necessary to protect themselves in the future (World Health Organization, 2010).

Around the world, the European countries have the longest history of sexuality education. Sweden made sexuality education a mandatory subject in schools in 1955. From there, it became mandatory in Germany (1968), Austria (1970), the Netherlands (1970), France, the United Kingdom, Portugal, Spain (2001), and Ireland (2003; World Health Organization, 2010). Today, Swedish children receive a portion of sexuality education in youth health centers in addition to schools, since this helps them to learn where to seek out services should they need them. As we

discussed in the chapter opening story, the Netherlands has the world's lowest rates of teenage pregnancy, abortion, and childbearing (see Figure 8.7). It is the best example of the value of high-quality sex education. The Dutch government supports a variety of sexuality organizations and finances mass-media campaigns aimed at educating the public about sexuality.

The majority of European sexuality education programs are "personal-growth" oriented, unlike the United States, which tends to be "prevention" oriented or "problem-solving" oriented (World Health Organization, 2010). In fact, educators point out:

In Western Europe, sexuality, as it emerges and develops during adolescence, is not primarily perceived as a problem and a threat, but as a valuable source of personal enrichment (World Health Organization, 2010:15).

In many other countries around the world, the focus of sex education has also been "prevention" oriented, focusing specifically on HIV and AIDS education, especially in those countries that are significantly affected by HIV and AIDS (United Nations Scientific and Cultural Organization [UNESCO], 2008). In Japan, the Japanese Association for Sexuality Education was established in 1974 to help

design comprehensive sexuality education in the schools, although abstinence education has always been very popular in Japan. In 1986, a new sexuality education curriculum was distributed to all middle schools and high schools in Japan (Kitazawa, 1994). This was again revised in 1992, and the Japanese Ministry of Education approved the discussion of secondary sex characteristics in coeducational fifth-grade classes and also mandated that sexuality education be taught in schools. Before this time, there was no discussion of sexuality in elementary schools (Hatano & Shimazaki, 2004).

We know that around the world, few young adults receive adequate sex education and, as a result, are at risk for negative consequences (UNESCO, 2009). Today, there is overwhelming evidence to support the need for sex education. Sex education can increase knowledge levels and reduce the risk for teen pregnancy and STIs. Yet, debates and controversies will continue throughout the world about the necessity of these programs; how best to implement the programs; who should teach them; and how success should be measured (UNESCO, 2009). Experts are hopeful that continued research on global sex education will increase support for global sex education.

Dr. Carroll visits with students from Amsterdam's Lyceum, a Dutch secondary school.

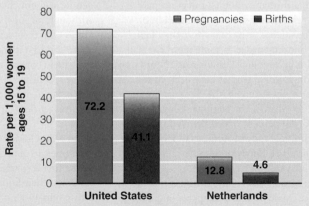

FIGURE **8.7** Pregnancy and birth rates per 1,000 women ages 15 to 19, United States and the Netherlands.

SOURCE: Advocates for Youth, Feijoo (2008).

Measuring attitudes or changes in attitudes and values is difficult at best. Overall, we do know that comprehensive sex education programs can increase knowledge levels, affect attitudes, and change behaviors (Kirby, 2007; Kohler et al., 2008). The most successful programs are those in which schools and parents worked together to develop the programs. However, we also have to keep in mind that many of the effects of sexuality education programs may not be quantifiable. Programs may help students to feel more confident, be more responsible, improve their mental health, and increase their communication skills. We rarely measure for these changes.

Politics often pushes the pendulum in one direction or another in support for sexuality education. In 2010, in a sharp departure from the abstinence-only model of sex education, the federal government approved a health law that put $375 million into grants available to schools that provided teens with comprehensive sexuality education programs (Rabin, 2010b). At the same time, however, $50 million was available to schools that taught abstinence-only education. President Obama completely cut funding for all abstinence-only sexuality education in his proposed federal budget for 2017, but we have yet to see what President Trump and his administration will do. Although the federal government does control much of the funding for sexuality education, individual states also have a role. Many are hopeful that states, along with their local school boards, will continue to determine what types of programs their schools will adopt.

In summary, childhood sexuality is an evolving phenomenon. Sexual knowledge and sexual behavior are common among children in today's society, in which sexuality is so much a part of our culture. However, knowledge does not necessarily mean that children must act on it; there are still very good reasons to encourage children and teenagers to think carefully about sexuality and to advise them to refrain from expressing their sexual feelings physically until the time is right for them and they are ready to do so.

What we do know is that a close and respectful parent–adolescent relationship that allows for open communication about sexuality has been found to decrease adolescent sexual behaviors and reduce the influence of peers with regard to sexual issues. This is an important finding and is partially responsible for delaying first intercourse, fewer teenage pregnancies, and fewer numbers of sexual partners. Open communication about sexuality, along with good, solid sexuality education, encourages this kind of responsible sexual behavior.

Review Questions

1 Explain both sides of the sexuality education debate.

2 Identify and discuss the various types of sexuality education programs.

3 Discuss research findings on the effects of sexuality education.

Chapter Review

Summary Points

1 Throughout most of history, children were treated as miniature adults, and concepts such as childhood did not exist. Children were considered presexual. More than half of all children engage in some type of sexual behavior before their 13th birthday. Four large-scale longitudinal studies have been conducted on adolescent sexuality: the National Survey of Family Growth, the National Longitudinal Study of Adolescent Males, the National Longitudinal Study of Adolescent Health, and the Youth Risk Behavior Survey.

2 Sexual anatomy is functional even before we are born. Male infants are capable of erection, and female infants are capable of vaginal lubrication. The single most important aspect of infant development is children's relationship with their caretakers. Gender identity develops between the ages of 1 and 2 years. It takes a little longer for children to develop gender constancy, which is the realization that their gender will not change during their lifetime. Although for most children gender identity aligns with their sex assigned at birth, in some children it does not. Children who are persistent, consistent, and insistent about their gender identity being incongruent with their sex assigned at birth are usually more likely to be transgender.

3 In early childhood, physical development continues. In fact, children may learn more in the first few years of childhood about the nature of their bodies than they learn in the entire remainder of their lives. Child sex play is common at this age, and many parents or caregivers need to teach that this behavior is private. Children learn that their genitals are private and must be covered up in public. Boys are often taught about the penis, yet it is rare for girls to be taught about the clitoris.

4 Sometime between the ages of 6 and 12, a child experiences the first outward signs of puberty. This can be emotionally, psychologically, and physically difficult for some children. Transgender children may have a difficult time with the onset of puberty, and studies have found alarming rates of depression, anxiety, self-injury, and suicide in transgender youth. Reversible hormone-blocking drugs can be used to delay the onset of puberty in transgender children.

5 Puberty prepares the body for adult sexuality and reproduction. Adolescence often includes our emotional and cognitive reactions to puberty. There are many physical, emotional, and cognitive changes during this time. Some of the first signs of female puberty include the development of breast buds, the appearance of pubic hair, a widening of the hips, a rounding of the physique, and the onset of menstruation.

Girls who are "on time" in developing feel more positive about their bodies.

6 Menarche is the hallmark of female puberty and is often viewed as one of the most important events in a woman's life. The beginning of menstruation can mean different things to an adolescent girl depending on how her family or her culture explains it to her.

7 Adolescent development in males differs in many ways from the development in girls. In boys, the first signs of puberty also involve pubic hair growth, but this generally starts a couple of years later than in girls. Common reactions to semenarche include surprise, curiosity, confusion, and pleasure—and typically most boys don't tell anyone about this event.

8 During preadolescence, genital touching continues, and both sexual fantasies and sex games may begin. A sexual script is the sum total of a person's internalized knowledge about sexuality, and it can have different themes. All of our intimate relationships influence our sexuality. We learn from our parents and our peers.

9 Sexual contact with siblings, or close relatives, is common at this age. Most of the time this occurs in sex games, but it can also occur as abuse when an older sibling or relative coerces a younger one into unwanted sexual activity. Psychological damage can occur when there is a large age difference between siblings or coercive force is used.

10 Children typically engage in more sexual exploration behavior up until the age of five when the behaviors decrease. Prepubescence is the age of sexual discovery, and most children learn about adult sexual behaviors during this time. Family support is critical for children who question their gender or sexual orientation. Teens who are accepted by their families have more secure attachments and higher levels of self-esteem.

11 We know the most about the developmental period of adolescence because of ongoing research studies. In early adolescence, preteens must forge an identity separate from their family by establishing stronger relationships with peers. By about age 14, most adolescents experience an increasing interest in intimate relationships.

12 The development of a gay or transgender identity may challenge long-held or socially taught images of the acceptable way to be a man or a woman. Family reactions to a LGBTQ identity and self-expectations may result in depression or confusion.

13 Mature sexual experimentation often begins in adolescence. Cliques are common and people look to peers for validation and standards of behavior. Girls' body image tends to improve as they progress through adolescence, whereas boys' tends to worsen. However, girls' general self-image tends to worsen as they grow older, whereas boys' tends to improve. Girls who go through puberty early are at increased risk for eating disorders. LGBTQ adolescents often have different experiences than heterosexual teens and have higher rates of depression, loneliness, drug and alcohol abuse, and suicide.

14 The National Survey of Sexual Health and Behavior (NSSHB) explored several sexual behaviors in teens. Masturbation was found to increase during adolescence and then decrease as partnered sex increases later in life. Oral sex has increased in all age groups and is usually engaged in after sexual intercourse. An adolescent's ethnicity, race, and culture affect their sexual attitudes, and which sexual behaviors they engage in.

15 Although the number of high school students engaging in sexual intercourse has decreased, the majority of high school students report engaging in sex. Most studies find that females have sex later than males throughout the teen years in all racial groups. The YRBS data showed an increase in the use of birth control among high school students, decreases in condom use and HIV testing, and increases in forced sexual activity.

16 Same-sex sexual behavior is common in adolescence, both for those who go on to have heterosexual relationships and for those who go on to have same-sex relationships. The first nationally representative study on the health behaviors among LGBTQ high school students found that more than 11% of high school students nationwide identified as LGB or unsure about their sexual orientation. This study also found that rates of sexual assault, dating violence, and bullying were three times the rates for heterosexual students.

17 It's estimated that 7% of all 9th through 12th grade students report being forced to engage in sexual intercourse; however, the prevalence of forced sex was higher in LGBTQ students. Rates were higher among lesbian and female bisexual and female questioning students compared to female heterosexual students. Rates were also higher among gay and male bisexual and male questioning students, compared to male heterosexual students.

18 Peer pressure is often cited as the most important influence on teen sexual behavior, but a teen's perceptions of what his or her peers are doing often has a greater influence than peers' actual behaviors.

19 More religious youths delay sexual behavior and have fewer sexual partners. Good parental communication, an atmosphere of honesty and openness in the home, a two-parent home, and reasonable rules about dating and relationships are among the most important factors associated with teens' delay of sexual activity. LGBTQ teens who have family acceptance have higher self-esteem and lower levels of depression and substance abuse than teens who are not accepted by their families. There is a maternal influence on the timing of first sexual intercourse for heterosexual adolescents, especially for females.

20 Today's adolescents have high contraceptive use, although the United States has the highest rates of teen pregnancy, abortion, and childbearing of any Western country. There are higher contraceptive usage rates for non-Hispanic White teens and lower for Hispanic and non-Hispanic Black teens. Long-term consequences of teenage pregnancy include increased risk of dropping out of school, poorer physical and mental health, lower birth weights in children, poorer health and cognitive abilities, more behavioral problems, and fewer educational opportunities.

21 Opposition to sexuality education has often been due to two attitudes: One says that sexuality is private, and the second says that public schools cannot discuss sexuality without giving children implicit permission to be sexual and should not promote certain values. Individual states can mandate that schools provide sexuality education. Attitudes toward sexuality began to change because of the increasing rates of teenage pregnancy and the increasing rates of STIs and AIDS.

22 Comprehensive sexuality education programs include a wide variety of topics and help students to develop their own skills and learn factual information. Abstinence-only programs emphasize abstinence from all sexual behaviors, and they typically do not provide information about contraception or disease prevention. There have been significant declines in the number of U.S. students who receive formal sex education in their schools.

23 Although many Americans believe that abstinence should be included in sexuality education, they also believe that information on contraception and STIs should be included. The most successful programs are those in which schools and parents worked together to develop the programs.

24 Researchers measure behavioral changes in sexual activity, pregnancy, and contraceptive use after a program to find out if the sexuality education programs were successful. Comprehensive sexuality programs have been found to be the most successful at helping adolescents delay their involvement in sexual intercourse, help protect adolescents from STIs and unintended pregnancies, delay the onset of sexual intercourse or reduce the frequency of sexual intercourse, reduce the number of sexual partners, and increase the use of contraception. Abstinence-only programs have not yielded successful results in delaying the onset of intercourse.

25 Politics often affects sex education policies. Although President Obama's administration cut funding for abstinence-only sexuality education in his proposed federal budget, we have yet to see what the new administration will do. Although the federal government does control much of the funding for sexuality education, individual states also have a role.

26 A close and respectful parent–adolescent relationship that allows for open communication about sexuality has been found to decrease adolescent sexual behaviors and reduce the influence of peers with regard to sexual issues.

Critical Thinking Questions

1 Should genital touching in young children be encouraged, ignored, or discouraged? What message do you think it sends to a child when parents encourage their child to discover and play with toes, ears, and fingers but pull the child's hands away when they discover their genitals?

2 Young children often play sex games, such as "doctor," with each other. What age differences do you think pose the biggest problems? Are sex games acceptable? Why or why not? How should a parent respond?

3 Where should children get their sexual knowledge? Should children learn everything from their parents, school, or church? Is it better to learn about some things from a particular place? Explain.

4 If you had a transgender child do you think you would consider using puberty-delay drugs? Why or why not?

5 People today are engaging in sex relatively early in life, often in their middle or early teens. Do you think this is a good time to experiment with sex, or do you think it is too early? What do you think is the "ideal" age to begin experimenting with sex?

Websites

Sexuality Information and Education Council of the United States The Sexuality Information and Education Council of the United States (SIECUS) is a national nonprofit organization that develops, collects, and disseminates information; promotes comprehensive education about sexuality; and advocates the right of individuals to make responsible sexual choices.

National Survey of Sexual Health and Behavior Findings from the largest nationally representative study of sexual and sexual health behaviors ever fielded, conducted by Indiana University sexual health researchers, provide an updated and much needed snapshot of contemporary Americans' sexual behaviors, including adolescent and teen sexual behaviors.

Alan Guttmacher Institute The mission of the Alan Guttmacher Institute (AGI) is to provide information and services about issues of sexuality. The institute conducts important research on adolescent and child sexual issues.

Society for Research on Adolescence The Society for Research on Adolescence's goal is to promote the understanding of adolescence through research and dissemination. Members conduct theoretical studies, basic and applied research, and policy analyses to understand and enhance adolescent development.

9 Adult Sexual Relationships

Our first relationship is with our primary caregiver—our mother, father, or whomever was responsible for our care. The attachment bond we formed with that person profoundly influenced our ability to develop and maintain successful relationships in the future. As we grow up, we learn many things about relationships from watching those around us. Many of us learn what type of partners our parents have in mind for us. Some parents want their children to have partners of the same race, ethnicity, religion, or even age, while others have no preferences. I recently met an engaged couple, Dena and Lenny, who have been dating for more than 2 years. Although Dena and Lenny are a mixed-race couple, they told me this has never been an issue in their relationship. They were both raised in open-minded families that stressed the importance of hard work, dedication, and education. Lenny's father told him that as long as he was a good man and got a good education, he could date whomever he wanted to. In fact, Lenny remembered his father telling him, "You can date an alien or a purple person—I don't care." Dena's and Lenny's families have been incredibly supportive of their relationship.

Dena and Lenny couldn't take their eyes off each other the whole time I talked to them—they held hands, giggled, and finished each other's sentences as they told me about the first time they met, dating, and how they got engaged (she found the hidden ring before he could ask the question!). They are excited about their future and having children together one day. Although they sometimes worry about whether their children might be bullied or teased about their mixed-race background, they are determined to raise their children to be self-confident and strong, just as their parents raised them. Dena and Lenny have a wonderful relationship that is based on honesty, communication, and trust. I'm sure they have a bright future ahead of them!

Janell Carroll

Throughout this book, we've talked about the importance of family and the impact that your family has on your feelings about love, intimacy, and relationships. We also know that other factors, such as society, culture, ethnicity, race, religion, and age, also influence our connections with others. By late adolescence, the majority of teens have attained the ability to become involved in intimate relationships (Shulman et al., 2010). However, every society has rules to control the ways that people develop sexual bonds with others. In many parts of the world, parents or other family members arrange for their children to meet members of the other sex, marry them, and begin their sexual lives together. The expectation was that couples would remain sexually faithful and that marital unions would end only in death. In such societies, adult sexual relationships were clearly defined, and deviating from the norm was frowned upon.

In our society today, people openly engage in a variety of adult sexual relationships, including same-sex, other-sex, non-committed, premarital, marital, extramarital, and polyamorous relationships. (Note that a term such as *premarital sex* assumes eventual marriage; for people who never marry, their sexual relationships for their entire lives are considered "premarital"!) Our relationships can change and evolve over the course of a lifetime, and at different times a person might live alone and date, cohabit with a partner or partners, marry, divorce, or remarry. In this chapter, we look at adults' intimate sexual relationships with others.

Dating and Committed Relationships

In traditional heterosexual dating, before the 1970s, the boy would pick up the girl at her house, the father and mother would meet or chat with the boy, and then the boy and girl would go to a well-defined event (e.g., a "mixer"—a chaperoned, school-sponsored dance—or a movie), and she would be brought home by the curfew her parents imposed (Benokraitis, 1993). Today, however, formal dating has given

The dating years, especially for heterosexual teens, usually begin in high school in the United States.

In the 1950s, traditional heterosexual dating involved going out together to share a fountain drink.

way to more casual dating, in part because of teenagers' almost universal access to cars and parents' more permissive attitudes toward exploring romantic relationships. Teenagers still go to movies and dances, but just as often they will get together at someone's house. Because of the risk of rejection, today's teens often use friend and social networks to find out if someone might be interested in them before asking them out. The Internet and various smartphone apps also provide many novel ways to meet interested partners today.

REAL RESEARCH There has long existed a prejudice against couples that are visibly different from each other (in race, religion, and age) and this may also include mixed-weight couples. One study found that couples with different body weights (one significantly heavier than the other) had the lowest couple acceptability ratings (COLLISSON ET AL., 2016).

In Chapter 7, we discussed the physical benefits of love and intimacy. Dating has been found to provide similar benefits. Relationships provide companionship, emotional support, and even, at times, economic support. Of course, the key may be the kind of people who are in the relationship. For example, people with a strong sense of self have been found to be more satisfied and happy with their dating relationships (Fruth, 2007; Fuller-Fricke, 2007). Not surprisingly, those without a strong sense of self have been found to experience more relationship conflict (Longua, 2010).

"Dating" has changed on college campuses; today, it is much more common for groups of students to "hang out" rather than go out on dates. One study found that half of heterosexual female seniors reported being asked out on six or more dates while at college; one third said they had been on only two or fewer dates while at college (Glenn & Marquardt, 2001). Typically, college students go out with friends and meet up with partners at campus parties, rather than prearranging dates. The sexual revolution has changed society's attitudes about sexuality, making hooking up and casual sex more acceptable.

In Chapter 3 we talked about how communication technologies have increased long-distance (LD) dating and relationships. It's estimated that 25% to 50% of college students are currently in a LD relationship and nearly 75% of college students have engaged in a LD relationship at some point in their lives (Stafford & Merolla, 2005). Couples in LD romantic relationships often have more constant and deeper communication than couples in non-LD relationships. This may be the reason for the high levels of relationship satisfaction and trust in LD relationships, which often equals or exceeds the relationship satisfaction and trust in non-LD relationships (Bloom, 2016; Carter et al., 2016; Jiang & Hancock, 2013). As our society becomes more mobile, it's likely that LD relationships will continue to increase in popularity.

Interracial and Intercultural Dating

Today's college students include the largest group of mixed-race students in the history of the United States (Saulny, 2010). It's estimated that by midcentury, multiracial Americans will represent a majority of the U.S. population (Colby & Ortman, 2015). This has led to increases in interracial and intercultural (usually grouped together as "mixed race") dating. In Chapter 1 we discussed antimiscegenation laws that enforced racial segregation and criminalized interracial marriage. These laws were struck down by the Supreme Court in 1967.

Since that time, attitudes about interracial relationships have been changing. While 73% of Americans disapproved of interracial marriage in 1968, by 2007 only 17% disapproved (Carroll, 2007). These changes were due to many things, including the increased media exposure to mixed-race relationships. Shows such as *Modern Family* or *Shameless,* which showcased mixed partnerships, helped to change attitudes about these relationships. In fact, studies have found that media exposure positively influences attitudes toward interracial relationships (Lienemann & Stopp, 2013).

Although mixed-race dating was not always societally acceptable, today many college students are open to the idea of dating someone of a different race or ethnicity.

Those who are more open to dating someone from a different race or ethnic group are younger and are often more politically liberal and less religious (Perry, 2013; Tsunokai et al., 2009). Overall, Blacks, non-White women with higher educations, and White women with lower educations are more likely to be open to having a relationship with someone of a different race or ethnicity (Fu, 2010; Mendelsohn et al., 2014). In addition, gay men and lesbian women are twice as likely as straight men and women to be in a mixed-race relationship (Oswald & Clausell, 2005).

Race and ethnicity are not the only criteria on which a person's suitability is judged; there are also issues of different religions, social classes, disabilities, and ages. Think about your preferences for the age of someone you'd date—would you date someone a few years older or younger? We discussed the importance of age differences in dating couples in Chapter 7. Studies have found that couples with large age differences may face some of the same challenges that mixed-race couples do. In Figure 9.1, we explore the "half-age-plus-seven rule," which is a rule of thumb about the social acceptability of dating a younger partner.

Sexuality in Dating Relationships

Although we discuss specific sexual behaviors in Chapter 10, here we introduce sexuality in dating relationships. One of my students told me she remembered rules at her high school dictating when it was appropriate to engage in sexual behaviors with a partner.

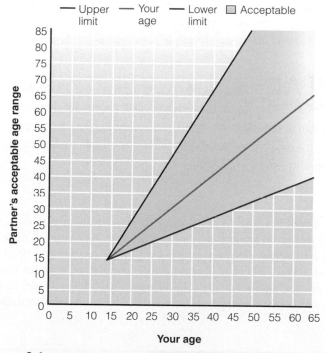

FIGURE **9.1 Half-Age-Plus-Seven Relationship Rule**
The "half-age-plus-seven" rule is a mathematical guide to judge the socially acceptable age differences in dating couples. A person takes their age, divides it in half, and adds seven to arrive at the lowest socially acceptable age of a person they should date (for example, a 20-year-old divides their age in half = 10, plus 7 = 17, which means they should not date anyone younger than 17 years old).

Kissing was allowed from day one, but touching each other's genitals required a month of dating. After 4 months of dating couples could engage in oral sex, but they should date for at least 6 months before they have sexual intercourse. Do you remember hearing similar rules when you were in high school? Actually, studies do support the fact that couples who wait to have sex in their relationship experience better relationship outcomes (Busby et al., 2010). Researchers suggest that waiting allows a couple to develop other aspects of their relationship. However, every couple has to determine what works best for them. Sexuality has been found to be a key element that helps shape the quality of romantic relationships (Muise et al., 2016).

ON YOUR MIND

I have a female friend whom I hook up with at least once a week, sometimes more. We don't ever talk about our relationship, but the sex is great. I'd like to take this to the next level and become a couple, but I just don't know how.

Overall, couples report less relationship satisfaction in hookups compared with long-term dating relationships (Armstrong et al., 2012; Owen & Fincham, 2011). Moving from a hookup into a more serious dating situation can be difficult primarily because of this dissatisfaction, but also because there is often a significant lack of communication between the partners. Although it is possible for a serious relationship to develop out of a hookup, it's estimated that fewer than 10% of hookups progress into committed relationships (Bisson & Levine, 2009; Owen & Fincham, 2011). Your best bet would be to find a time when the two of you can talk about your feelings and hope for a more committed relationship. Students have different motivations for hooking up and engaging in casual sex, and you won't know your partner's motivations unless you ask.

REAL RESEARCH Race has been found to be a more important factor than religion when people are choosing whom to date (Stillwell, 2010). This may be because a person from a different religion would be more physically similar, creating less societal stigma.

Levels of sexual satisfaction are similar in lesbian, gay, bisexual, and straight relationships, and couples with higher levels of sexual satisfaction are more satisfied with their relationship (Peplau et al., 2009). There is also a positive correlation between good health and sexual activity (Holmberg & Blair, 2009; Trudel et al., 2010). Like their younger counterparts, older adults who are dating also value sexuality. A healthy sex life in the later years may keep aging adults happy and vibrant. However, when we picture people engaging in sex, we rarely think of two people older than 60 years. In fact, when I show a film on older adult sexuality in my class, many of my students cover their eyes and feel repulsed. Why is this? Why are we so averse to the idea that older people have healthy and satisfying sex lives? It is probably because we live in a society that equates sexuality with youth. Although there are physical changes associated with aging that may affect a person's sex life, we know that the majority of older adults maintain an interest in sexuality and often continue to be sexually active (Arena & Wallace, 2008; de Vries, 2009; Waite et al., 2009). We discuss sexuality and the physical and psychological changes of aging in Chapter 10.

Breaking Up

As we discussed in Chapter 7, most of us will experience a relationship breakup at some point in our lifetimes. Research suggests there are five stages to a relationship breakup: dissatisfaction with the relationship, exposure and awareness of the problems in the relationship, negotiation of possible solutions, resolution and transformation of the relationship, and possible termination of the relationship (Lee, 1984). If a couple recognizes and communicates potential issues, they may be able to negotiate solutions and improve the relationship. However, it's possible these solutions may not successfully resolve the issues, in which case they may decide to end the relationship. The Social Exchange Theory proposes that we evaluate our relationships with a cost-benefit analysis. If the benefits outweigh the costs, we're generally content in the relationship. However, if the costs outweigh the benefits, we may want out.

Intimate relationships that are formed before the age of 25 years old are significantly more likely to break up than transition to a more committed relationship (Sassler et al., 2016). As we discussed in Chapter 7, how a person reacts to a breakup really depends on several factors, including attachment styles, levels of self-esteem, who initiated the breakup, how much social support is available, and the amount of contact with the ex-partner after the breakup. Those who were broken up with often feel rejection and experience more depression and a loss of self-esteem, while those that initiated the breakup feel less distress but are more at risk for guilt (Locker et al., 2010; Perilloux & Buss, 2008). Social support is important—those who have friends to lean on and talk to have an easier time moving on after a breakup. Minimizing contact with an ex-partner can make it easier to recover from the breakup.

Review Questions

1 Explain how dating has changed on college campuses today.

2 Identify some of the reasons why there have been increases in mixed-race dating on college campuses.

3 What factors are associated with an easier recovery after a breakup?

Non-Committed Relationships

Despite the belief that sexuality is most satisfying within the context of a committed intimate relationship, there has been increasing acceptance over the last few years of sex in non-committed relationships (often referred to as hookups, casual sex, friends with benefits, or booty calls; Kuperberg & Padgett, 2016; Mark et al., 2015; Napper et al., 2016). Although a hookup can be a one-time occurrence, sometimes they develop into non-committed relationships in which partners regularly hook up with no expectations of romantic or emotional intimacy. Although many students say they engage in these types of relationships mainly for physical reasons, the research isn't so clear-cut. Heterosexual women are more likely than heterosexual men to have emotional feelings, desire a committed relationship, and feel disappointed when feelings aren't reciprocated in non-committed relationships (Bisson & Levine, 2009; Eshbaugh & Gute, 2008; Garcia & Reiber, 2008; Hamilton & Armstrong, 2009; Lovejoy, 2015). An example of this is an experience I had in my class a few years ago. I had two students who sat on opposite sides of the classroom. Since I never saw them interact, I assumed they were strangers. However, midway through the semester they handed in autobiographical papers, and I was surprised to learn they had been hooking up for many months. Even so, there were differences in how they described their relationship. Jildy said she was sure that Len wanted a relationship because they hooked up every weekend. Len said that although he liked the sex, he was relieved that Jildy accepted that their relationship would never be anything more than a hookup.

It's not just men who seek out non-committed sexual relationships (see the nearby On Your Mind feature). There are women who find such relationships to be easier and less time-consuming, allowing them more time to focus on academics or future goals (Lovejoy, 2015). In addition, they find that such relationships increase self-growth, sexual freedom, and empowerment without the constraints of emotional commitment or peer approval (Lyons et al., 2014; Reid et al., 2011; Snapp et al., 2015; Vrangalova, 2015).

Sexuality in Non-Committed Relationships

There is tremendous variation in the types of sexual behaviors that couples engage in during casual or non-committed sex. This can include kissing, mutual masturbation, oral or anal sex, or sexual intercourse. Although some studies have found that people who engage in these types of casual sexual interactions are emotionally and sexually satisfied (Reiber & Garcia, 2010; Vrangalova, 2015), other studies have found that participants are often less attentive and interested in the sexual satisfaction of their partners (Armstrong et al., 2012). Among heterosexual couples, men report being more sexually satisfied than women during non-committed sex (Bogle, 2008; Bradshaw et al., 2010; Mark et al., 2015; Regnerus & Uecker, 2011). This may be due to a double standard in expectations for sexual enjoyment in such interactions, wherein men are viewed as more entitled to sexual pleasure than women (Armstrong et al., 2012). Other researchers believe this is due to the "male in the head" phenomena in which sexual satisfaction is determined by the presence of male orgasm and not based on female sexual pleasure (Holland et al., 2004; McClelland, 2011).

Sexual and emotional satisfaction in non-committed relationships is significantly different among gay men and lesbian women. While gay men report the most sexual and emotional satisfaction in such interactions, lesbian women report the least (Mark et al., 2015). Some gay men also experience the phenomena of "male in the head" and base their sexual satisfaction off the presence of their partner's orgasm (Holland et al., 2004; McCelland, 2011).

Romantic Ambiguity in Non-Committed Relationships

Long-term non-committed relationships may lead to romantic ambiguity, wherein one partner begins to have feelings for the other and starts to see the relationship differently than their partner. They may expect partner loyalty and get jealous when their partner doesn't feel the same way. Romantic exploitation, in which one person takes advantage of the other's romantic interest for their own sexual benefit, can also occur. Studies have found that heterosexual women are twice as likely as men to be victims of sexual exploitation in non-committed relationships (Lovejoy, 2015).

Interestingly, many college students report that although they might be open to engaging in non-committed relationships with men and women from other ethnic and racial groups, they would prefer someone from their own race or ethnic group for a committed relationship (McClintock, 2010).

Review Questions

1 Explain the reasons why a person might engage in non-committed sexual relationships and what the research has found about sexual satisfaction in these types of relationships.

2 What is romantic ambiguity and romantic exploitation?

Cohabitation

It's probably hard for you to believe that there was little research on **cohabitation**, or living together, until fairly recently. Researchers documented no increase in cohabitation rates between 1880 and 1970. In the mid-1990s, the Census and the Current Population Survey started allowing couples to identify themselves as "unmarried partner" of the homeowner (instead of a roommate), which allowed researchers to get more accurate statistics about cohabitation (Stevenson & Wolfers, 2007). Even so, researchers today believe that statistical data on cohabitation is skewed because of inadequate relationship labels. Some heterosexual couples who live together might not think of themselves as "unmarried partners" but rather "boyfriend and girlfriend"; gay and lesbian couples might describe themselves as "roommates." You can see how terminology issues can make it difficult to adequately measure certain behaviors.

Statistics and Current Trends

Many young couples today live together first before entering into marriage. In fact, close to half of all couples live together without marriage (Aleccia, 2013). Ongoing data from the National Survey of Family Growth reveal that the number of cohabiting couples continues to increase.

Many factors have been suggested to explain this trend. They include, but are not limited to, shifts in cultural attitudes about cohabitation and marriage, delays in the age at which people are marrying, and economic and financial issues. Couples have many reasons for living together. One study found that 60% of couples moved in together to spend more time together; 14% did so to "test" the relationship, and 19% did so for financial reasons (Rhoades et al., 2009). The U.S. Census found a connection between partners' employment status and cohabitation. Since the late 2000s, the percentage of couples who moved in together in which one was unemployed increased, whereas the percentage of couples who moved in together who were both employed decreased (Pew Research Center, 2010).

Although the increases in cohabitation have led to decreases in marriage (which we will discuss further later in this chapter), many heterosexual couples who live together transition to marriage within 3 years (Copen et al., 2013; Goodwin et al., 2010). Not all couples marry, however; some couples live together, break up, and live with someone else, referred to as **serial cohabitation**. White women and foreign-born Hispanic women were more likely to marry their partners, while Black women and Hispanic women born in the United States were less likely to do so.

cohabitation
Living together in a sexual relationship when not legally married.

serial cohabitation
A series of cohabitating relationships with a person living with one partner, breaking up, and living with a new partner.

The National Survey of Family Growth recently outlined a new trend in increased cohabitation in unwed couples experiencing an unplanned pregnancy. Although years ago unwed pregnant couples were encouraged to quickly marry (often referred to as "shotgun weddings"), today pregnant couples are encouraged to move in together (referred to as "shotgun cohabitation"; Crossland, 2014; Yen, 2014). Although this trend is a result of the increased social acceptance of cohabitation, some experts warn that higher rates of relationship breakups in cohabiting relationships will have detrimental effects on the well-being of the offspring (Crossland, 2014).

The meaning and significance of cohabitation in same-sex couples may be different from other-sex couples (Hass & Whitton, 2015). Before same-sex marriage was legalized in 2015, cohabitation was viewed as a serious commitment in gay and lesbian relationships. Living together indicated long-term commitment and enabled a couple to share a life together. Overall, studies have found that levels of stability and satisfaction are similar in same-sex and other-sex couples who live together (Manning et al., 2016).

Advantages and Disadvantages of Cohabitation

There are advantages and disadvantages to cohabitation. Although the link between living together and emotional health is not as established as the link between marriage and emotional health, studies have found that couples who live together do experience improved emotional health (Musick & Bumpass, 2012). They also are able to learn more about each other's habits and idiosyncrasies, share finances, and mature in their relationship. However, there are also potential disadvantages: parents and relatives may not support the union, and society as a whole tends not to recognize people who live together for purposes of health care or taxes. Also, the partners may want different things out of living together: One partner may view it as a stronger commitment to the relationship, whereas the other sees it as a way to save money. Overall, other-sex couples who live together are less invested in their relationship than married couples (Poortman & Mills, 2012).

Some couples believe that living together can help them smooth out the rough spots in their relationship and determine whether they would be able to take their relationship to the next level. Research indicates, however, that this may not be true. Other-sex couples who live together before marriage have been found to be more likely to experience marital distress and divorce (Jose et al., 2010). This may be due to the development of inertia in the relationship, which makes it difficult to end a relationship and increases the chances it progresses into marriage (Rhoades et al., 2009). Couples who live together with the intention to marry have higher levels of stability in their relationship and are similar to married couples in their relationship quality (Guzzo, 2009; Poortman & Mills, 2012; Rhoades et al., 2009). These committed couples have the same chance of divorce as couples who marry without living together first (Goodwin et al., 2010).

Review Questions

1 Explain the relationship between cohabitation and divorce.

2 Identify and explain the various advantages and disadvantages of cohabitation.

Marriage

In the United States, the most common reason for getting married is love (see Figure 9.2). In this section, we discuss marriage statistics and trends, mixed marriages, marriages in later life, marital satisfaction, sex within marriage, and sex outside of marriage.

Statistics and Current Trends

In the mid-1960s, heterosexual marriage was nearly universal among 24- to 34-year-olds, with more than 80% of men and women marrying (Mather & Lavery, 2010). However, in the 1970s, many societal issues, such as the economy, an increased number of women in higher education and the labor force, and increasing rates of cohabitation, led to decreases in marriage rates. The proportion of married heterosexuals older than 18 decreased from 72% in 1960 to 50% in 2015 (Livingston & Caumont, 2017).

The average age at which a heterosexual man and woman marry today in the United States is the highest in recorded history. While the median age for first marriage in the United States in 1970 was 23 for men and 21 for women, this increased to 29 for men and 27 for women in 2016 (Livingston & Caumont, 2017). Research has found that many factors, such as education, ethnicity, and race, affect heterosexual marital rates (see Figure 9.3). Although before 1990 marriage rates for those with a high school education were higher than for those with a college degree, today college graduates are more likely to marry than those with less education (Mather & Lavery, 2010). From 1980 to 2008, female high school dropouts went from "most likely to marry" to "least likely to marry" (Stevenson & Isen, 2010). Racial differences have also been found, with Blacks less likely to marry than any other racial/ethnic group. In 2012, 29% of Blacks, 43% of Hispanics, 52% of Whites, and 58% of Asians were married (Lamidi & Payne, 2012).

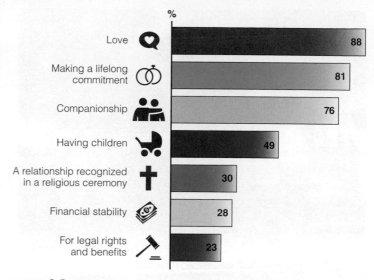

FIGURE **9.2 Top Reasons for Getting Married in the U.S.**
An online poll done by the Pew Research Center found that love remains one of American's top reasons for marriage.

SOURCE: Pew Research Center (http://www.pewresearch.org/fact-tank/2017/02/13/5 -facts-about-love-and-marriage/)

Same-sex marriage has been legal in the United States since 2015 when the Supreme Court ruled that state-level bans were unconstitutional. Although several individual states did offer legal marriage for same-sex couples before 2015, these unions were not recognized by the federal government (and were not often recognized by other states). Although **civil unions** and **domestic partnerships** were available in some states before this time, they offered limited rights and benefits to same-sex couples. It wasn't until the legalization of same-sex marriage in 2015 that the federal rights, privileges, and benefits of marriage were available to same-sex couples.

Although the U.S. Census Bureau began collecting data on same-sex marriages in 2010, it is estimated that 1 in 7 same-sex couples were not identified as such in the Census data collection. Some couples neglected to identify themselves or their partners as spouse or unmarried partner because they didn't view the relationship in this way, because of confidentiality concerns, or because they were offended by the Census options that were presented (Gates & Renna, 2010). Same-sex couples who were married and lived in a state that legally recognized their marriage were more likely to report being married. It's estimated there are close to one million same-sex couples in the United States, 40% of whom are married (Gates & Newport, 2015).

Mixed Marriages

There has been a tremendous increase in the number of marriages between people of different races or ethnicities in the United States. Whereas less than 1 in 1,000 new marriages were between

---

ON YOUR MIND

What is a prenuptial agreement?

If a couple divorces, their marriage contract is governed by state law, which determines how assets are divided. However, some couples decide to implement nuptial agreements, or financial plans that couples agree on in marriage, that supersede state laws (Kaslow, 2000). These agreements can be either prenuptial (drawn up before a marriage) or postnuptial (drawn up after a couple has wed). Since 2005, there has been an increase in prenuptial agreements (Strickler, 2010). An increase in prenuptials is mainly because of societal changes, including the delay in the age at which couples marry, as well as increases in divorce and remarriages.

Proponents of prenuptial agreements believe that because many couples have a hard time talking about financial issues, a prenuptial agreement can help them to sort through these important issues before marriage (Daragahi & Dubin, 2001). However, these types of agreements can also cause problems because they are often initiated by the financially stronger partner and may involve issues of power (Margulies, 2003).

---

civil union	**domestic partnership**
A legal union sanctioned by a civil authority.	Persons other than spouses who cohabit. Domestic partners can be either same-sex or other-sex.

Married couples are more likely to enjoy better emotional and physical health compared to their non-married friends.

Black and White spouses in 1961, this number increased to 1 in 150 in 1980, and in 2013, 1 in 8 new marriages were between spouses of different races or ethnicities (Wang, 2015; Figure 9.4). Of the almost 4 million other-sex couples in the United States who married in 2013, 58% of American Indians, 28% of Asians, 19% of Blacks, and 7% of Whites married someone whose race or ethnicity was different from their own (Wang, 2015).

Among Blacks and Asians, there are significant gender differences in marrying outside of one's race or ethnicity. Black females are less likely to marry outside their race than Black males (25% of Black male newlyweds married outside their race in 2013 but only 12% of Black females did; Wang, 2015). Gender differences were found in the opposite direction for Asians. Asian males are less likely to marry outside their race than Asian females (37% of

Asian female newlyweds married outside their race but only 16% of Asian males did; see Figure 9.4c).

Geographically, mixed marriages are more common in Western states, where 1 in 5 newlyweds married someone of a different race or ethnicity in 2010 (Wang, 2015). The U.S. Census Bureau reported that Hawaii had the highest percentage of mixed-race marriages (42%), followed by Nevada, Oregon, Oklahoma, and California.

The loosening up of relationship conventions has also led to mixed-age marriages. Historically, the majority of heterosexual men married younger women, which was probably related to the fact that a younger woman could produce more offspring (Biello, 2007; Kershaw, 2009). Between 2008 and 2010, men were on average about 2.5 years older than their wives (Wang, 2012). The highest age differences were found in mixed-race couples, with White men and Asian women having the largest age difference (with an age difference of more than five years).

Although there has been growing acceptance for mixed-race relationships in the United States, bias against such relationships persists. One study found that even when respondents claimed to accept mixed-race relationships, neural disgust responses recorded in their brains were found while viewing photos of mixed-race couples (Skinner & Hudac, 2017). Researchers believe that although some people may report being accepting of such relationships, they may still experience conflict in their attitudes.

Marriages in Later Life

Marriage has a positive impact on the lives of both aging men and aging women. It decreases loneliness, especially because older adults often have few nonspousal places to turn for emotional support. Those with single or divorced children often get additional emotional, financial, and practical help compared to those with children who are married. Married children are less likely to stay in touch and give emotional, financial, and practical help to their parents (Sarkisian & Gerstel, 2008). Overall, we know that older adults who are married are happier and have lower rates of disease than their non-married counterparts (Dupre & Meadows, 2007). In fact, married older adults who have been diagnosed with cancer live longer than widowed older adults diagnosed with cancer (Ortiz et al., 2007).

However, there is a higher percentage of married men than women; women live longer than men and widowhood is more common for them. Seventy-nine percent of men between the ages of 65 to 74 were married in 2004, whereas only 57% of women in the same age group were married. Although an estimated 500,000 people older than 65 remarry in the United States every year (M. Coleman et al., 2000), more and more older couples decide to live together in place of marriage (S. L. Brown et al., 2006).

Percentage of Never-Married Adults in the U.S.

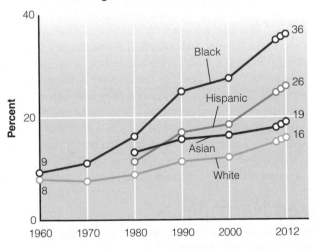

Note: Data on Hispanics and Asians prior to 1980 are not plotted given the small sample sizes.

FIGURE **9.3** **Percent of Never-Married Adults in the U.S.**
The number of never-married adults has increased for all racial and ethnic groups in the U.S. but the rate of increase has been most dramatic among Blacks.

SOURCE: Pew Research Center; Wang & Parker, 2014 (http://www.pewsocialtrends .org/2014/09/24/record-share-of-americans-have-never-married/)

REAL RESEARCH A study using magnetic resonance imaging (MRI) found that the brain works differently in married and cohabitating couples (COAN, 2014). The brains of married couples reacted less to stress than the brains of couples who were living together. Researchers claim that the increased trust in marital relationships was one of the main reasons for their findings.

Mixed Marriage Trend, United States, 1980–2010

(a)

Above are percentages of mixed marriages, for both new marriages and the overall married population.

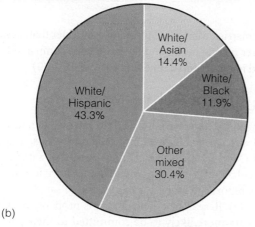

Newly Married Mixed Couples, United States, 2010

(b)

Since Whites are currently the largest racial group in the U.S., marriages between Whites and minority groups are the most common type of mixed marriage.

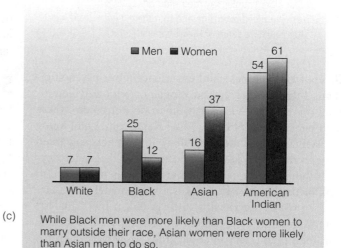

Percentages of Newlyweds Marrying Someone of Different Race, by Sex and Race, 2013

(c)

While Black men were more likely than Black women to marry outside their race, Asian women were more likely than Asian men to do so.

SOURCE (a–b): Pew Research Center; Wang, 2012 (http://www.pewsocialtrends.org/2012/02/16/chapter-1-overview/; (c) Pew Research Center, 2015. Retrieved from http://www.pewresearch.org/fact-tank/2015/06/12/interracial-marriage-who-is-marrying-out/

FIGURE **9.4** Mixed Marriages in the United States

Many older adults who experience the death of a spouse will remarry. While older men are often more likely to remarry than older women, this gap has been narrowing. Among adults whose first marriage ended in divorce or widowhood, 64% of men remarried in 2013, while 52% of women did (Livingston, 2014). Marriages that follow the death of a spouse tend to be more successful if the couple had the opportunity to get to know each other fairly well before the marriage, if their children and peers approve of the marriage, and if they are in good health, financially stable, and have adequate living conditions. One 73-year-old man describes his experience:

I can't begin to tell you how happy I am. I am married to a wonderful woman who loves me as much as I love her. My children gave me a hard time of it at first, especially because she is a bit younger than me, but they finally accepted the relationship and came to our wedding. In fact, they gave me away at the ceremony. That's a switch, isn't it? (Janus & Janus, 1993, p. 8)

Marital Satisfaction

The quality of the friendship with one's spouse and the ability to resolve conflict are two of the most important factors in marital satisfaction (Gottman & Silver, 2000). Other important variables, including being able to talk to each other and self-disclose, physical and emotional intimacy, and personality similarities, are instrumental in achieving greater marital satisfaction. Earlier we discussed the Social Exchange Theory, and this theory applies here as well. High rewards, such as emotional support and a satisfying sex life, and low costs, such as arguing, conflicts, and financial burdens, are also key to marital satisfaction (Impett et al., 2001). If a marriage has high costs but low rewards, a person might end the relationship or look outside the marriage for alternative rewards.

There has been an ongoing debate about gender differences in marital happiness and satisfaction. Studies have shown that married heterosexual men have better physical and mental health,

Most older couples say their marriages have improved over time and that the later years are some of their happiest.

Sexuality remains an essential part of many marriages, even though many couples experience changes in their sex lives over time.

more self-reported happiness, and experience fewer psychological problems than either divorced, single, or widowed heterosexual men; married heterosexual women do not receive these same health benefits (Forry et al., 2007; Hemstrom, 1996; Joung et al., 1995; Williams & Umberson, 2004). Researchers suggested this was due to the multiple role responsibilities that heterosexual women often have; for example, married women still tend to do the bulk of the housework and disproportionately take care of the children (Baxter & Hewitt, 2010). A recent meta-analysis found that, on average, heterosexual women report less marital satisfaction than men (Jackson et al., 2014). However, when the researchers looked more closely at the data and sampling procedures, they found that many studies on marital satisfaction used clinical populations (couples who were in marital therapy). Since women in marital therapy are less likely to be satisfied with their marriages than their husbands, this could bias the results. When the data were analyzed using only nonclinical populations, no significant gender differences were found (Jackson et al., 2014). Researchers also point out that dissatisfied wives could be more likely to participate in marital surveys, further biasing the results. Today the majority of couples say that sharing household responsibilities is the key to a happy marriage (Geiger, 2016).

People who are married tend to be happier and healthier and have longer lives than either widowed or divorced persons of the same age (Dush & Amato, 2005; Mernitz & Dush, 2016; Waldinger & Schulz, 2010). In fact, in a study of various types of relationships, married couples had the highest level of well-being, followed by (in order) cohabitating couples, steady dating relationships, casual dating relationships, and individuals who dated infrequently or not at all (Dush & Amato, 2005). Marriage has also been found to reduce the impact of several potentially traumatic events, including job loss, retirement, and illness (Waldinger & Schulz, 2010) and in younger couples reduced episodes of "drunkenness" (Uecker, 2012). However, more recent studies have found that the benefits of marriage may depend on the age at which a person marries. Marrying both earlier and later than desired resulted in poorer mental health and fewer benefits compared to those who married in their desired time frame (Carlson, 2012).

Sexuality Within Marriage

Sexual satisfaction is often based on factors such as communication, desire, compatibility, emotional awareness, and personality factors (Mark et al., 2015). Studies on sexual satisfaction among single, cohabitating, and married couples have found that married couples report the highest levels of sexual satisfaction (Laumann et al., 1994). Researchers believe this is probably because married couples are more likely to be committed to their partner's sexual satisfaction. Other studies have found higher levels of emotional satisfaction in relationships in which partners are exclusive to each other (Waite & Joyner, 2001).

Sexuality is an essential part of marriage, although men often report higher sexual needs than women (Elliott & Umberson, 2008). The National Survey of Sexual Health and Behavior found that the majority of married other-sex couples have sex weekly or a few times per month, and that younger married couples engage in more frequent sex (Herbenick et al., 2010a). Laumann et al. (1994) found that 40% of married other-sex couples engage in sexual intercourse two or more times a week, whereas 50% engage in it a few times each month. The frequency of sexual activity and satisfaction with a couple's sex life have been found to be positively correlated (Blumstein & Schwartz, 1983; that is, the more frequent the sexual behavior, the greater the relationship satisfaction. However, it is not known whether increased sexual frequency causes more satisfaction or whether increased relationship satisfaction causes increased sexual behavior.

As we discussed in Chapter 7, most long-term relationships often start out high on passion, but this decreases as time passes. Over time, many couples report decreased sexual frequency. This is consistent with cross-cultural studies that have found that a declining frequency of sexual behavior over time is a common feature of human populations (Brewis & Meyer, 2005). Typically, the reason sex decreases in long-term relationships has less to do

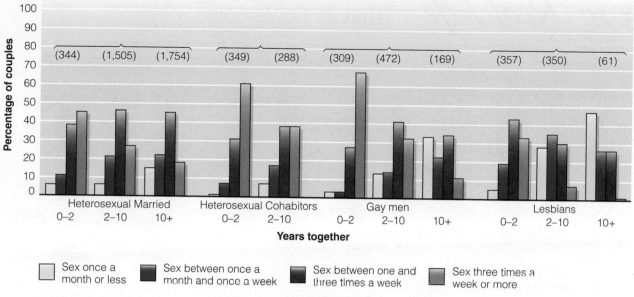

The Frequency (in Percentage) of Sexual Behavior

Note: Very few of the cohabitors had been together more than 10 years.
Numbers in parentheses are the number of couples on which the percentages are based.

FIGURE **9.5** Frequency of sexual behavior in various types of relationships by years. The numbers above each category represent the total number of respondents.

SOURCE: Based on Blumstein, P., & Schwartz, P. (1983). Frequency of sex in marriage from American couples (p. 196). New York: HarperCollins Publishers.

with getting bored with one's partner than it has to do with the pressures of children, jobs, commuting, housework, and finances.

Some marriages are **asexual relationships**, which means that the partners do not engage in sexual behavior. This may be because of sexual problems, including erection or desire disorders, or it may be a mutual decision not to have sex (Chasin, 2011; Donnelly & Burgess, 2008). In either case, most asexual married couples are in stable and satisfying relationships.

Sexuality Outside of Marriage

The majority of couples, whether dating, living together, or married, expect sexual exclusivity, or monogamy, from each other. Some experts suggest that our cultural ideals of romantic love have shaped the concept of monogamy (Conley et al., 2013; Croydon, 2014). Although some married couples might discuss their expectations for monogamy prior to marriage, the majority of couples simply assume their partner will be monogamous.

Infidelity

Although extramarital sex refers to sex outside of marriage, cheating and infidelity can also occur in dating relationships (sometimes known as extra-relationship sex). Not surprisingly, adults in the United States are more likely to cheat while living together than while married (Treas & Giesen, 2000). Those who cheat in intimate relationships have been found to have stronger sexual interests, more permissive sexual values, less satisfaction in their intimate relationship, and more opportunities for sex outside the relationship. Typically, religiosity and church attendance are associated with lower odds of extramarital affairs (Burdette et al., 2007).

It's estimated that 20% to 40% of married other-sex couples have engaged in extramarital affairs (Laumann et al., 1994; Marín et al., 2014). Variations in these percentages are probably due to both the definitions of extramarital affairs and the populations studied.

How does an extramarital affair typically begin? In the first stage, a person might become emotionally close to someone at school, work, a party, or even on the Internet. As they get to know each other, there is chemistry and a powerful attraction. This moves into the second stage, in which the couple decides to keep the relationship secret. They don't tell their closest friends about their attraction. This secret, in turn, adds fuel to the passion. In the third stage, the couple starts doing things together, even though they would not refer to it as "dating." Each still believes that the relationship is all about friendship. Finally, in the fourth stage, the relationship becomes sexual, leading to an intense emotional and sexual affair (Layton-Tholl, 1998).

Although many people think that sexual desire drives an extramarital affair, research has found that more than 90% of extramarital affairs occur because of unmet emotional needs within the marital relationship (Previti & Amato, 2004). Laumann and colleagues (1994) found that, overall, couples are faithful to each other as long as the marriage is intact and satisfying. A. P. Thompson (1984) found three types of extramarital affairs: sexual but not emotional, sexual and emotional, and emotional but not sexual. Twenty-one percent of respondents having extramarital sex were involved in predominantly sexual affairs; 19% in both sexual and emotional affairs; and 18% in affairs that were emotional but not sexual (the remaining affairs did not fit clearly into

asexual relationship
A type of intimate relationship in which the partners do not engage in sexual behavior.

Sex in Real Life   What Is Polyamory?

The dominant construction of sexuality in Western culture asserts that sexual relationships should be monogamous. We live in a society that expects monogamy from sexual partners. If you are in a relationship, do you expect monogamy from your partner? Many of us would answer this question with a resounding "Yes!" But have you talked to your partner about it? Studies have found that while many gay couples make agreements about whether to be monogamous, the majority of heterosexual couples neither discuss it, nor come to an agreement about it (Hoff et al., 2010; Martell & Prince, 2005; Parsons et al., 2012).

Polyamory is a nonpossessive, honest, and nonmonogamous philosophy and practice that involves loving several people at the same time. In these "ethically nonmonogamous" relationships, partners engage in loving, sexual relationships with multiple partners simultaneously (Bennett, 2009). Polyamorous couples can be old, young, gay, or straight, and the key to the relationship is honesty. It's estimated there are more than half a million openly polyamorous families living in many major cities in the United States (Bennett, 2009).

Polyamorous relationships can take many varied and complex forms. Nearby are some

examples (primary relationships are indicated by double arrows, secondary relationships by single arrows):

(a) "V" : One person is the focal point of the relationship and is involved with two partners. The partners are not involved with each other

(b) Triad: Three people involved in a committed intimate relationship. All three relationships are equal, and there is no primary relationship

(c) Quad: Four partners in a relationship. Can be open or closed

One of the most difficult things for most people to understand is how polyamorists don't feel jealous about their partner's other partners. One woman who had been married for several years and recently started dating a friend from work explained it this way: "jealousy is born from a fear of losing a partner, if you believe that love and intimacy can be shared, and are not diminished by sharing, then that fear loses a lot of its power" (Stevens, 2014). Her boyfriend has since moved in with her family and she is currently living with both partners, along with her teenage daughter, in a loving relationship based on honesty, trust, respect, and communication.

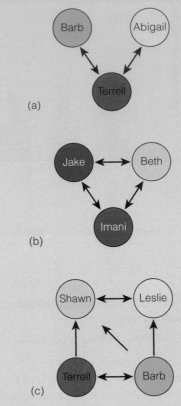

FIGURE **9.6** Types of Polyamorous Relationships

---

any of these categories). Affairs that are both emotional and sexual appear to affect the marital relationship the most, whereas affairs that are primarily sexual affect it the least.

Gender plays a role in both the types of extramarital affairs in which a person engages and a partner's acceptance of these affairs. Heterosexual women are more likely than heterosexual men to have emotional affairs, whereas heterosexual men are more likely to have sexual affairs. When it comes to accepting a partner's extramarital affair, although both men and women experience emotional distress when they find out their partner has cheated on them, heterosexual women have been found to experience higher levels of distress than men (Leeker & Carlozzi, 2014; see Chapter 7 for more information about gender differences in jealousy).

Emotional reactions to a partner's infidelity include jealousy, anger, rejection, insecurity, fear, sadness, depression, confusion, resentment, and loneliness (Buss, 2000; Dijkstra et al., 2013; Leeker & Carlozzi, 2014). Infidelity can often destroy the trust between partners, which is why couples who experience affairs are twice as likely to divorce (Gordon et al., 2005).

The increasing popularity of the Internet has also created new challenges for today's couples. The proliferation of pornographic websites and sexual chatrooms has increased the opportunity for people in committed relationships to engage in Internet infidelity or cybersex affairs (Cravens et al., 2013; Dijkstra et al., 2013; Hertlein & Piercy, 2012; Wright et al., 2014). Internet infidelity is a romantic or sexual relationship that is initiated and maintained via online communication. The majority of Americans agree that these types of online sexual interactions constitute cheating (Randall & Byers, 2003). Like traditional infidelity, Internet infidelity can negatively affect a relationship, causing feelings of betrayal, a loss of trust, anger, and decreased desire for sexual interactions. Inappropriate use of social networks, such as Facebook, can also lead to online infidelity (Carter, 2016; Cravens & Whiting, 2016; McDaniel et al., 2017). Early warning signs of Facebook infidelity include secretiveness, changing passwords, and/or quickly exiting Facebook when a partner approaches. Research has shown that the majority of couples do not communicate their rules about appropriate Internet use with their partners (Carter, 2016; Cravens et al., 2013).

Nonexclusive Marriages

In 1972, George and Nena O'Neill published a book titled *Open Marriage* (O'Neill & O'Neill, 1972). In this book, they explained

---

polyamory
The practice of having more than one intimate relationship at a time with the knowledge and consent of everyone involved.

that "sexual adventuring" was fine, as long as both spouses knew about it. In open marriages, each partner is free to seek out sexual partners outside of the marriage. Partners were often referred to as **swingers** and they engaged in "safe-sex circles" in which they would only have **comarital sex** with people who have tested negative for sexually transmitted infections.

The majority of swingers are White, middle class, middle-aged, and churchgoing (Bergstrand & Williams, 2000). The North American Swing Club Association claims there are organized swing clubs in almost every U.S. state, as well as in Japan, Canada, England, Germany, and France (Bergstrand & Williams, 2000). While swingers typically engage in recreational sexual activity outside the marriage to enhance their married sexual lives, polyamory (pah-lee-AM-more-ee; "many loves") involves having more than one intimate relationship at a time with the knowledge and consent of all partners.

It's estimated there are at least 265 polyamory groups across 158 countries today (Manley et al., 2015). Polyamorous individuals often reject the idea that monogamy is the only acceptable form of romantic pairing and do not believe that sexual exclusivity is necessary for satisfying, committed, and long-term relationships. Since all participants are aware of the nonmonogamous bonds they have with each other, polyamory is often described as "responsible nonmonogamy" (see "Sex in Real Life" for more information about polyamory). Research has found that jealousy increased sexual excitement and arousal in swinging couples, particularly in men (deVisser & McDonald, 2007). However, for some couples, jealousy can be detrimental to the relationship (Bergstrand & Williams, 2000).

Review Questions

1 Explain current trends in heterosexual marriage.

2 Define "mixed marriage" and explain how it has changed over the years.

3 Explain what we know about marital happiness, gender, and race.

4 Explore the importance of sexuality in marriage.

5 What do we know about sex outside of marriage? Explain extramarital affairs, polyamory, and nonexclusive marriages.

Same-Sex Relationships

Although we have been talking about same-sex relationships throughout this chapter, it's important to realize that in many ways, gay and lesbian relationships have changed more than heterosexual relationships over the last few decades. First, these relationships came "out of the closet" in the 1960s and 1970s, when there was a blossoming and acceptance of a gay subculture. Then the advent of AIDS resulted in fewer sexual partners and more long-term, monogamous relationships, especially in the gay community.

Heterosexual, gay, and lesbian men and women all hold similarly positive views of their intimate relationships (Roisman et al., 2008). Even so, there has been considerable debate throughout the years about what type of intimate relationships promote the healthiest psychological adjustment. One study by Blumstein and Schwartz (1983) compared same- and other-sex couples using interviews and questionnaires. Although this study is dated, it remains a classic, because no other studies have undertaken such a large sample population comparing couples in a variety of different relationships (see Figure 9.5 for more information about this study).

Differences and Similarities in Same-Sex and Other-Sex Relationships

For many years, researchers suggested that same-sex relationships were less stable in adulthood because of negative early life experiences and the challenges of accepting one's sexual orientation (Savin-Williams, 2001). Others claimed that societal pressures on same-sex couples, such as the struggle to manage a gay or lesbian identity in a heterosexist culture, led to weaker intimate relationships (Pachankis & Goldfried, 2004). However, although it may be true that same-sex couples face more relationship challenges than do other-sex couples, theories that describe gay or lesbian intimate relationships as weaker than those of heterosexual couples have not been supported by research (Herek, 2006; Roisman et al., 2008). The majority of gay men and lesbian women were found to be secure in both their sexual orientation and childhood experiences, and able to connect fully in intimate relationships.

Same-sex couples are more likely to have equal sharing of household responsibilities, less emphasis on attractiveness, increased intimacy, and better communication than other-sex couples (Balsam et al., 2008; Cohen et al., 2008; R. J. Green, 2008a; Soloman et al., 2005). As in other-sex relationships, the partner in gay relationships with more resources or power has been found to perform fewer household chores (Sutphin, 2010). Gay and lesbian couples have higher levels of relationship satisfaction; share more affection, humor, and joy in their relationships; have less conflict; and have less fear and negative feelings about their relationship than other-sex couples (Gottman et al., 2003; Herek, 2006; Roisman et al., 2008).

Although many same-sex couples report that they have more challenges dealing with societal discrimination and negative attitudes about homosexuality, they may be more satisfied with their intimate relationships because they are forced to work harder at them (R. J. Green et al., 1996). Same-sex couples may not have as much family or societal support as other-sex couples do, which tends to put more focus on their intimate relationships. Studies evaluating the importance of family and friend support in intimate relationships have found that although family support is related to

swinger	comarital sex
A person or couple who openly exchanges sexual partners.	The consenting of married couples to exchange partners sexually.

relationship quality in other-sex couples, this is often not the case in same-sex couples. Friend support is often more valuable in same-sex couples. In fact, the more friend support a same-sex couple has, the higher the relationship satisfaction (Graham & Barnow, 2013).

Research on emotional closeness in same-sex relationships has found that lesbian relationships are emotionally closer than relationships between gay male couples (R. J. Green, 2008b; Mock & Cornelius, 2007). Lesbian couples report higher levels of intimate communication in their relationships compared with other couple types (Henderson et al., 2009; Julien et al., 2003). In Chapter 3 we discussed the role of communication in relationship satisfaction.

Sexuality in Same-Sex Relationships

Like heterosexual couples, gay men and lesbian women report many positive aspects of sexuality in their relationships. Some of the most important benefits cited by gay men and lesbian women are emotional and physical intimacy, feeling accepted and supported, increased communication, and a positive view of self (Cohen et al., 2008). Yet, to gain these benefits, they report it is necessary to be vulnerable and take risks. The stigma of social and cultural attitudes about same-sex relationships can interfere with healthy sexual functioning.

Earlier in this chapter, we discussed gender differences in initiating sexual activity in heterosexual relationships: Men often do more of the initiating. Does this mean that lesbians may be uncomfortable initiating sex or that gay men don't have problems doing so? According to a classic study done by Blumstein and Schwartz (1983), this may be the case. They found that some lesbians do have difficulty initiating or balancing sex in their relationships. Problems with initiating sex in lesbian relationships may be because of the social pressures women have while growing up. In lesbian couples, it is often the more emotionally expressive partner who is responsible for maintaining the couple's sex life.

Similarly, in relationships between gay men, the more emotionally expressive partner is usually the one who initiates sexual activity. However, gay men are much less bothered by their role of initiator. This may lead to other problems if one partner feels he is always the initiator.

Gay men engage in sexual behavior more often than both lesbian and heterosexual couples (Kurdek, 2006). Lower rates of sexual behavior in lesbian couples have been explained in many ways. It could be that the biological nature of the sex drive is lower in women, that females typically do not initiate sexual activity and may not be comfortable doing so, or that women are less likely than men to express their feelings through sex. Finally, it also must be pointed out that perhaps lesbian lovemaking lasts longer than heterosexual lovemaking (focusing more on foreplay), and a longer duration of lovemaking could lead to a decrease in the actual number of occurrences. We discuss same-sex sexual behavior more in Chapter 10.

Although the majority of same-sex couples are monogamous, arrangements about nonmonogamy, or sex outside of the primary relationship, are common among some gay couples (Martell & Prince, 2005; Parsons et al., 2012). However, these sexual arrangements have not been found to decrease sexual satisfaction, communication, or sexual frequency. For other same-sex couples, monogamy is expected in their relationships. Like in monogamous heterosexual couples, infidelity and cheating does occur. Overall, studies have found that gay men are more likely to cheat than lesbian women (Roisman et al., 2008), but that same-sex couples experience less emotional distress in response to infidelity than heterosexual couples (Dijkstra et al., 2013; Leeker & Carlozzi, 2014). Experts suggest this may be due to the fact that there is no evolutionary threat (e.g., pregnancy risk) when lesbian or gay men cheat, which reduces emotional distress. When cheating does occur, studies have found that lesbian women have similar reactions to heterosexual men confronted with cheating. Common responses include increased verbal and physical possession signals (such as talking more about the partner, increased kissing and/or hand holding, or increased online posts about the relationship; Brewer & Hamilton, 2014).

Review Questions

1 Explain how same-sex relationships have changed more than other-sex relationships over the last few decades.

2 Identify some of the differences and similarities in same-sex and other-sex relationships.

3 Explain why same-sex relationships may experience fewer power imbalances and greater equality and satisfaction than other-sex relationships.

Having Children or Remaining Childless

Although we discuss pregnancy and childbirth in Chapter 12, here we'll examine the impact of parenting on adult relationships. We know that in heterosexual relationships, children can be conceived and born at any time—while a couple is hooking up, dating, living together, or married. Some couples decide to have children without a formal commitment to each other, some get married to have children, and others get married because the woman is pregnant. Although unplanned pregnancies can occur, ambivalence and uncertainty are common in couples making decisions about parenthood (Pinquart et al., 2008). Unlike other-sex couples, same-sex couples can't get pregnant by accident, but many do decide to become parents in a variety of ways, including surrogacy, adoption, foster care, arrangements with friends and family, or through a partner's biological children. They may decide to have children while dating, living together, or married. In any case, the decision to have or raise children is one that most people face at one time or another, and research shows that the timing of parenthood can affect a couple's relationship quality.

REAL RESEARCH The "parenting happiness gap," in which parents report being unhappier than nonparents, is highest in the United States (GLASS ET AL., 2016). However, in eight countries—Portugal, Hungary, Spain, Norway, Sweden, Finland, France, and Russia—parents reported being happier than nonparents.

Statistics and Current Trends

Today's parents are more likely to be older, more educated, and ethnically diverse (Koropeckyj-Cox et al., 2007; Livingston & Cohn, 2010). While there were high rates of teenage births in 1990, by 2008 birth rates increased among older women. In fact, between 1990 and 2008, births to women older than 35 years increased 64%, increasing in all ethnic and racial groups (Livingston & Cohn, 2010). Births among unmarried and cohabiting women also increased. Whereas 28% of births were to unmarried women in 1990, by 2008, 40% of births were to unmarried women (Hamilton et al., 2015). Unmarried births were highest in Black women (72%) and lowest in Asians (18%; Livingston &

Cohn, 2010). Although rates are lower in Hispanics (53%) and Whites (29%) than in Blacks, unmarried births among White women have increased 69% since the 1990s. All of these changing trends are because of demographic and behavioral changes, such as population changes, delays in marriage, increases in education, and changing attitudes about marriage, pregnancy, and birth. Whereas several years ago having a child outside of wedlock might have seemed odd, today most Americans know at least one woman who has had a baby without being married and at least one man who fathered a baby without being married (Livingston & Cohn, 2010).

Same-sex couples are less likely than other-sex couples to be raising children, although this has been changing. In 2010, 19% of same-sex couples had children under the age of 18, compared with 43% of other-sex couples (Gates, 2013). Even so, many gay men and lesbian women express a desire to have and raise children (Balsam et al., 2008; Riskind et al., 2013; Riskind & Patterson, 2010). In the United States more than 1 in 3 lesbian women have given birth, while 1 in 6 gay men have fathered or adopted a child (Gates et al., 2007).

Same-sex couples with children are more likely to be female than male (Umberson et al., 2015). Most gay men over the age of 50 with children had their children within the context of an other-sex marriage, whereas most gay men under the age of 50 had their children through adoption or some other means.

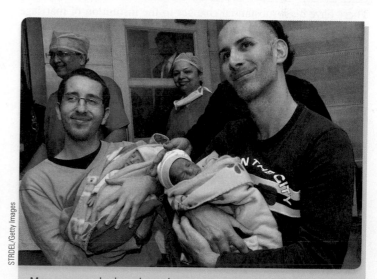

Many gay couples have been drawn to surrogacy in India, since it is legal and less expensive than surrogacy options in the United States. Here a Spanish couple poses with their newborn twin girls in New Delhi after an Indian surrogate mother gave birth to the children.

STRDEL/Getty Images

Parenting and Relationship Satisfaction

Longitudinal research on same-sex and other-sex couples has found the quality of intimate relationships declines when couples become parents (Bergman et al., 2010; Campos et al., 2009; Claxton & Perry-Jenkins, 2008; Goldberg et al., 2010; Huebner et al., 2012). Parents with children often experience decreases in leisure time and time to work on their relationship, which is why they often report lower relationship satisfaction than those without children. Relationship satisfaction continues to decline as the number of children increases. In fact, relationship happiness is higher before the children come, declines steadily until it hits a low when the children are in their teens, and then begins to increase once the children leave the house. This may be due to several factors, including reduced time for the relationship or disagreements about child-care responsibilities.

Many gay and lesbian parents also have to contend with societal attitudes and increased scrutiny about their parenting ability (Herbstrith et al., 2013; Lavner et al., 2014). Couples who live in areas

Having children decreases a couple's quality time together, which can lower relationship satisfaction.

where there is little acceptance of gay and lesbian families have higher levels of depression and negativity after becoming parents (Goldberg et al., 2010). Living in a gay-friendly area can make the transition to parenthood easier for gay and lesbian couples.

Review Questions

1 Identify one way in which having children affects adult relationships.

2 Explore similarities and differences in having children in same-sex and other-sex couples.

3 Identify a current trend in parenting, and give one reason for this trend.

4 Give two examples of how relationship satisfaction might decline when a couple becomes parents.

Divorce

There have been substantial changes in the institution of marriage since the early 1980s. During most of U.S. history, a married couple was viewed as a single, legal entity (M. A. Mason et al., 2001). Today, however, marriage is viewed more as a partnership between two people. This shift in perception of marriage brought with it a shift in how marriage was dissolved. The liberalization of divorce laws made it easier to obtain a divorce and made it a less expensive process.

Divorce laws vary from state to state, but **no-fault divorce** has been available since 2010. In a no-fault divorce neither partner needs to be found guilty of a transgression to dissolve the marriage. Although all states allow "no fault" divorces, many states may look at the behavior of the individuals in determining such things as child custody and support, and the division of property and debts. The availability of no-fault divorce contributed to skyrocketing divorce rates (Stevenson & Wolfers, 2007). In an attempt to reduce divorce rates, three states (Arizona, Arkansas, and Louisiana) instituted **covenant marriages**,

which revolve around restrictive agreed-on rules and regulations for ending a marriage and also involve premarital counseling and an agreement to pursue additional counseling if marital problems develop. Several other states have introduced legislation for covenant marriages, although they have not yet been approved. Covenant marriages also discourage divorce and extend the wait time for a divorce, in some cases to 2 years or more, unless there is domestic violence involved. We will talk more about covenant marriages later in this chapter.

Because same-sex marriage has been legalized for a short time in the United States, there is not a great deal of research on same-sex divorce. We do know that many long-term same-sex couples typically dissolve their relationships privately, married or not. Oftentimes, couples that divorce in states that did not previously recognize same-sex marriage often have a difficult time navigating the legal system. This can be especially difficult when it comes to child custody issues. One lesbian couple living in Mississippi had been legally married in Massachusetts and had two children together. Since same-sex marriage was not legal in Mississippi, only one woman's name was listed on the children's birth certificates. This was not a problem until their marriage fell apart 15 years later and one partner was not allowed access to her children (Compton, 2016). The couple is currently involved in a bitter legal battle. Other gay and lesbian couples have also experienced difficulties with federal and state laws. There is much more work to be done in this area.

---

no-fault divorce
A divorce law that allows for the dissolution of a marriage without placing blame on either of the partners.

covenant marriage
A marriage that is preceded by premarital counseling and has strict rules about divorce.

Statistics and Current Trends

Divorce rates for married heterosexuals increased sharply between 1970 and 1975, in part because of the liberalization of divorce laws (Kreider, 2005). Rates stabilized after this and began to decrease. By 2005, divorce rates were at the lowest level since 1970 (Stevenson & Wolfers, 2007). The U.S. Census Bureau reports that 50% of marriages end in divorce, with 20% of marriages ending within the first five years of the marriage (Copen et al., 2012). However, research has found that marital stability has increased over the years. Whereas 23% of couples who married in the 1970s split within 10 years, only 16% of those who wed in the 1990s divorced (Parker-Pope, 2010). Ethnic/racial differences have been found in divorce rates with Black couples experiencing higher divorce rates and Asian couples experiencing lower divorce rates (Raley et al., 2015). Mixed-race couples also have higher divorce rates compared with same-race couples (Wang, 2015).

The changing economic conditions in the United States have led to some couples delaying or avoiding divorce and staying together for financial reasons (Paul, 2010). For example, legal fees and health insurance costs may make it necessary for couples to stay together, either in the same home or different homes. However, these couples are still legally and economically married and responsible for joint finances and expenses.

Earlier in this chapter we talked about long-distance dating relationships. It's important to point out that some married couples live apart for reasons other than marital discord. Dual-career pursuits, military deployment, and many other factors have led to increased LD marital relationships, wherein married couples live in different places during the week. It's estimated that more than 3 million married couples live apart for reasons other than divorce or relationship discord (Bergen et al., 2007). It's anticipated that LD marital relationships will continue to increase in popularity as our society becomes more mobile.

Gwyneth Paltrow and Chris Martin "consciously uncoupled" in 2014. Conscious Uncoupling is a process for amicably ending an intimate relationship that relies on learning more about oneself and the reasons for the breakup, rather than on blame and finger-pointing. Many experts believe that this type of uncoupling can lead to positive changes in a person's life and help children and family members heal after the breakup.

wants a divorce often comes as a shock to his or her spouse. In heterosexual divorce, when one partner is the initiator, it is usually the female. One study found that heterosexual women initiated two thirds of all divorces (Brinig & Allen, 2000). The individual who wants their marriage to end is likely to view the marriage totally differently from the individual who wants the marriage to continue. In addition, the partner who initiated the divorce has often completed the mourning of the relationship by the time the divorce is complete, unlike the partner, whose mourning begins once the divorce is finalized. We now explore some of the social, predisposing, and relationship factors that may contribute to divorce.

Reasons for Divorce

What causes a couple to end their marriage? The question is complicated because not all unstable or unhappy marriages end in divorce. Couples stay together for many reasons—for the children, because of lack of initiative, because of religious prohibitions against divorce, or for financial reasons—even though they have problems in their marriages. Similarly, couples with seemingly happy marriages separate and divorce, sometimes to the surprise of one of the partners who did not even know the marriage was in trouble.

REAL RESEARCH Researchers often point out that divorces are more common in the seventh year of marriage because of a "seven-year itch" (Feiler, 2010). Interestingly, the "seven-year itch" originally referred to an infection with scabies, an untreatable skin condition at the time that took 7 years to go away.

The most common reasons given for divorce include a lack of communication or commitment, infidelity, financial problems, substance abuse, and conflict/arguing (Lavner & Bradbury, 2012; Scott et al., 2013). But it's difficult to determine why some marriages fail; every couple has their own story. Sometimes the spouses themselves are at a loss to understand why their marriage failed. A mutually shared decision to divorce is actually uncommon. Usually, one partner wants to terminate a relationship more than the other partner, who is still strongly attached to the marriage and who is more distraught at its termination. In fact, the declaration that a partner

Social Factors That Affect Divorce

Divorce rates in the United States are influenced by changes in legal, political, religious, and familial patterns. For example, as we discussed earlier, no-fault divorce laws have made it easier for couples to dissolve a marriage. The growth of low-cost legal clinics and the availability of lawyers have made divorce cheaper and thus more accessible. In addition, the more equitable distribution of marital assets has made some people less apprehensive about losing everything to their spouses. Changing social issues, such as more women entering the workforce and earning advanced degrees, have also had an impact on divorce rates. Research has found that divorce is more common in other-sex couples in which the woman has a professional degree (Wilson, 2008).

Predisposing Factors for Divorce

Certain situations may predispose a couple to divorce. People who have been divorced before or whose parents have divorced have more accepting attitudes toward divorce than those who grew up in happy, intact families (Amato & Hohmann-Marriott, 2007; Eldar-Avidan et al., 2009; Sassler et al., 2009; Wolfinger, 2000). In addition, people who have divorced parents are significantly more likely to report marital problems in their own relationships than people from intact families, and they also tend to be more skeptical about marriage, feeling insecure about the permanence of these relationships (Gähler et al., 2009; Jacquet & Surra, 2001; Weigel, 2007; Wolfinger, 2000).

Other factors that may contribute to divorce are marrying at a young age (Scott et al., 2013), marrying because of an unplanned pregnancy (Copen et al., 2012), alcohol or drug abuse (R. L. Collins et al., 2007), and having children quickly after getting married (S. P. Morgan & Rindfuss, 1985). The interval between marriage and the arrival of children is an important factor; waiting longer promotes marital stability by giving couples time to get accustomed to being a married couple before the arrival of children and may also allow them to become more financially secure. Religion is also important: those who are Catholic or Jewish are less likely to divorce than those who are Protestant, and divorce rates tend to be higher for marriages of mixed religions. However, overall, the more religious a person is, the more conservative his or her views are about divorce (Stokes & Ellison, 2010).

Relationship Factors in Divorce

In general, couples who divorce have known for a long time that there were difficulties in their marriage, although they may not have contemplated divorce. These problems are made worse, in most cases, by communication problems. Some warning signs are communication avoidance (not talking about problems in the relationship); **demand and withdrawal patterns of communication**, whereby one partner demands that they address the problem and the other partner pulls away; and little mutually constructive communication (Thompson, 2008).

Some couples make poor assessments of their partner or believe that the little annoyances or character traits that they dislike in their potential spouses will disappear or change after marriage (Neff & Karney, 2005). Marrying a person with the intention to change their personality or bad habits is not a good idea.

Adjusting to Divorce

How a person will adjust to a divorce depends on several factors, including who initiated the divorce, personal attitudes about divorce, income levels, and the onset of a new relationship (Wang & Amato, 2000). Social connectedness and support is also an important factor in a person's adjustment. Although most divorces are emotionally painful for both partners, after 10 years, 80% of the

---

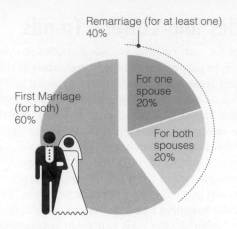

Note: "New marriages" are marriages that began in the past 12 months. A first marriage is one in which neither spouse has been previously married. A remarriage includes at least one spouse who has been married before. Based on couples, not individuals, where at least one spouse is age 18 or older.

FIGURE **9.7** **Percent of New Marriages in the U.S., 2013**
While 60% of marriages in 2013 were first marriages for both partners, 40% involved a remarriage for one or both of the spouses.

SOURCE: Pew Research Center; Livingston & Caumont, 2017

---

heterosexual women and 50% of the heterosexual men said that their divorce was the right decision (Faludi, 1991).

Depression and sadness can surface when divorced couples find that they have less in common with married friends as many friends separate into "yours" and "mine." Older individuals experience more psychological problems because there are fewer options for forming new relationships in older age (H. Wang & Amato, 2000). Older divorced heterosexual women are more likely to feel anger and loneliness than are younger divorced heterosexual women.

There are some gender differences in the consequences of divorce. In heterosexual marriages, financial adjustment after divorce is often harder for women, because in many cases a woman's standard of living declines more than a man's after divorce (Leopold, 2016; Wallerstein et al., 2013). Studies have found that after a divorce a man's income increases by around one third, whereas a woman's income falls more than a fifth and remains low for years after the divorce (Jenkins, 2009). Many women who previously lived in a middle-class family find themselves slipping below the poverty line after divorce. However, when it comes to emotional health and well-being, women have been found to do better after a divorce than men (Leopold, 2016).

Dating after a divorce can be difficult for some. People may have been involved in committed relationships for many years; consequently, they may find that the dating environment has changed drastically since they were younger. It is not uncommon for newly single people to feel frustrated or confused about this unfamiliar environment. The majority of divorced men and women remarry, and some remarry, divorce, and remarry again (often referred to as **serial divorce**). In fact, the median time between heterosexual divorce and a second marriage is about 3.5 years (see Figure 9.7 for more information about remarriages). Men remarry at higher rates than women, and Hispanics and Blacks remarry at lower rates than Whites (Livingston, 2014).

---

demand and withdrawal pattern of communication
A pattern of communication in which one partner is a "demander," seeking change or discussion, while the other is a "withdrawer," seeking to end or avoid discussions.

serial divorce
The practice of divorce and remarriage, followed by divorce and remarriage.

Review Questions

1 Explain what makes a no-fault marriage different from a covenant marriage.

2 Identify some of the factors that research has found might predispose a couple to divorce.

3 Explain some of the legal difficulties associated with divorce among same-sex couples.

4 Explain how people adjust to divorce.

Adult Sexual Relationships in Other Cultures

Dating, marriage, cohabitation extramarital sex, divorce, and same-sex relationships are often viewed differently outside the United States. Let's now take a look at some of these institutions, customs, and practices in various cultures around the world.

Dating and Marriages in Other Cultures

In most industrialized countries, partner selection through dating is the norm. However, some countries have no dating systems. For example, in Sweden, there is no Swedish term for what Americans call "dating"—couples meet at dance clubs, bars, schools, or through friends (Trost, 2004).

There are still a few industrialized cultures in which **arranged marriages** take place. In Iran, many marriages are arranged, even those that are based on love (Drew, 2004). A young man will visit the home of the woman he wishes to marry accompanied by three members of his family. The woman is not allowed to speak unless directly questioned. A contract is signed, and although the couple is not formally married, this contract is legally binding. A formal marriage ceremony usually takes place a year later. (For more information about arranged marriage, see the accompanying "Sexual Diversity in Our World.")

In some cultures, courtship is a highly ritualized process in which every step is defined by one's kin group or tribe (Hutter, 1981). For example, the marriages of the Yaruros of Venezuela are arranged and highly specified; a man must marry his "cross-cousin"—that is, the daughter of either his father's sister or his mother's brother. The marriages are arranged by the shaman or religious leader in consultation with one of the boy's uncles.

The Hottentots of South Africa also marry their cross-cousins, but here the boy can choose which cousin he wants to marry; once he does, he informs his parents, who send someone to seek permission from the girl's parents. Tradition dictates that they must refuse. The youth then approaches the girl, going to her house late at night once everyone is asleep and lying down next to her. She then gets up and moves to the other side of the house. The next night he returns, and if he finds her back on the side where he first lay next

In India, where arranged marriage is common, divorce rates are among the lowest in the world.

Plush Studios/Blend Images/Getty Images

to her, he lies down again with her, and the marriage is consummated (Hutter, 1981).

For 2,000 years, marriages in China were arranged by parents and elders, and emotional involvement between prospective marriage partners was frowned upon; if a couple appeared to like having their marriage arranged, the marriage was called off! In China, the primary responsibility of each person was supposed to be to his or her extended family. If there was a marriage bond that was very strong outside of that extended family, it could jeopardize the cohesiveness of the group.

This all began to change with the Communist Revolution of 1949. Through contact with the West, these customs began to erode. Only 8 months after coming to power, the Communist

arranged marriage
Marriage that is arranged by parents or relatives and is often not based on love.

Sexual Diversity IN OUR WORLD
First Comes Marriage, Then Comes Love

How would you feel about your mother or father choosing a person for you to marry? Don't they know you better than anyone else? While you might not think this is a great idea, consider what type of person they might choose for you. Although arranged marriages aren't common in the United States today, they are popular in large parts of Africa, Asia, Latin America, and the Middle East. Typically, marriage partners are chosen by parents, relatives, friends, and matchmakers based on the prospective partner's finances, family values, status, and perceived compatibility (Batabyal, 2001). Parents or relatives are thought to know their children the best and to be capable of not being blinded by emotion in choosing a partner for their sons and daughters. Although the relationship does not begin with "love," couples in arranged marriages are thought to fall more in love with their partners because they are from similar families, religions, cultures, and socioeconomic groups (Xiaohe & Whyte, 1990).

Some of the women who are offered as brides come with cash or gifts for the groom or the groom's family at the time of the marriage (called a *dowry*). Although giving and accepting a dowry is illegal in many countries, it is widely practiced. In fact, despite the changing roles of women in many countries that have a dowry system, the practice and value of the dowry has increased over the years (Srinivasan & Lee, 2004).

The Manhattan-based *India Abroad*, which can be accessed online, runs about 125 classified ads every week for families or others searching for Indian brides and grooms. The ads are very specific about what qualities the potential bride or groom has to offer. For example, a recent search yielded the following results:

[male] Affluent Hindu Panjabi parents invite correspondence for son, 31, 5'10", owning successful Financial Services business, settled in NY Metro area.

[female] Exceptionally beautiful, caring spiritual daughter. Family values. Studying Ivy League university. U.S. born, 24, 5'7" 125 pounds. Seek very handsome boy with similar background.

[male] Alliance invited for clean shaven Jat Sikh engineer, 44, 5'8" educated in India and U.K.

[female] Hindu parents looking for reasonable Hindu, Christian etc. husband for American born daughter, 29, 5' beautiful, clear complexion, socially conservative.

[male] North Indian parents invite alliance for their U.S. educated, well-settled handsome son, 34, from beautiful educated girls with good family values.

[female] Punjabi parents seek match for 5'4", 1979, beautiful, slim, hotel professional daughter from accomplished grooms.

SOURCE: Retrieved March 7, 2017, from http://www.indiaabroad-digital.com/indiaabroad/20170310?pg=46#pg46

---

leaders established the Marriage Law of the People's Republic of China, in which, among other things, they tried to end arranged marriages and establish people's right to choose their spouse freely. Today in China, although arranged marriages still take place in the rural areas, people date and meet each other in public places—a condition that was virtually unknown a few generations before.

In many parts of Africa, too, parents used to be involved in mate selection (Kayongo-Male & Onyango, 1984). Marriages were arranged between families, not individuals, and each family had a set of expectations about the other's role. Courtship was highly ritualized, with the groom's family paying a "bride wealth" to the bride's family. The rituals that preceded marriage were intended to teach the couple what their particular tribe or culture believed married couples needed to know to keep their marriage successful. However, young people did have some say in whom they were to marry; in many cases, young people would reject their parents' choices or meet someone they liked and ask their parents to arrange a marriage. One Egyptian boy commented:

> We all know the girls of our village. After all, we played together as kids, and we see them going back and forth on errands as they get older. One favorite place for us to get a glimpse of girls is at the village water source. The girls know that and like to linger there. If we see one we like and think she might be suitable, we ask our parents to try to arrange a marriage, but usually not before we have some sign from the girl that she might be interested. (Rugh, 1984, p. 137)

Today, however, mate selection in most places is a much more individual affair. However much we in the West believe in the right of individuals to choose their own mates, there were some advantages to parental participation in mate selection, and the transition to individual mate selection in traditional societies is often difficult.

Forced marriages, where families force their daughters into early marriage or sell them to make money, have been on the rise in countries such as Afghanistan, Bangladesh, and Vietnam. Girls between the ages of 8 and 12 years old are sold for anywhere from $300 to $800. It's estimated that one in every three girls is married before the age of 18 in developing countries (United Nations Population Fund, 2017). Between 2011 and 2020, the United Nations Population Fund estimates there will be more than 140 million girls forced into marriage.

Girls who are forced to marry early are less educated, experience more domestic violence, have partners who are significantly older, and have more children (United Nations Population Fund, 2012). Another practice, **sex trafficking**, in which young girls are sold for prostitution, is discussed in Chapter 18. Today, many groups in the West are working to stop these practices.

sex trafficking
A form of modern-day slavery in which people are forced or coerced into the commercial sex trade against their will.

Cohabitation in Other Cultures

There has been a delay of entry into marriage in all countries around the world, which is mainly the result of an earlier entry into cohabitation. Instead of these changes being viewed as shifts in moral attitudes, however, they are often seen as simply cultural changes.

The most acceptance comes from Western European nations where there have been substantial increases in unmarried cohabitation among heterosexual partners. Couples who live together in Norway for a minimum of 2 years are given similar rights as married couples, including obligations to social security, pensions, and joint taxation. Cohabitation is also common in Sweden, where the majority of heterosexual couples live together before marriage (Trost, 2004). In France, although cohabiting couples (other-sex and same-sex) can apply for legal recognition of their relationship, a legal battle was waged by a cohabiting other-sex couple in 2017 who was denied legal recognition of their civil partnership (Sanghani, 2017). We will discuss the legal recognition of these relationships later in this chapter.

However, cohabitation among heterosexual couples in Spain and Italy is not as popular as it is in most other European countries, mainly because many young adults remain in their family home at least until their 30s (Lanz & Tagliabue, 2007). Cohabitation is also rarer in more traditional societies where, even if a couple has sex before or outside of marriage, social customs would never tolerate an unmarried heterosexual couple living together openly. For example, Asian societies still frown on it, although it is sometimes allowed, and it is severely discouraged in Islamic societies.

Marital Customs and Practices in Other Cultures

Marriage ceremonies take place in every society, but marriage customs vary widely from culture to culture. In some cultures, girls can be married very young, whereas other cultures mandate marriages between certain relatives, and still others allow multiple spouses. Most cultures celebrate marriage as a time of rejoicing and have rituals or ceremonies that accompany the wedding process.

Among various Berber tribes in Morocco, for example, wedding rituals can include performing a sacrifice, painting the heels of the couple's feet with goat's blood, having a feast, having fish cast at the feet of the bride, or feeding bread to the family dog (Westermarck, 1972). In Iranian culture, a "temporary marriage" allows a Muslim man an opportunity for female companionship outside of legal marriage when he travels or is employed by the military (Drew, 2004). Temporary marriages were formally approved by the Iranian government in 1990.

In many preliterate cultures (and in some literate ones, too), there is a tendency to believe that the main purpose of being female is to get married and have babies. Among the Tiwi, a group of Australian aborigines, this was taken to its logical conclusion; a woman was to get married, and there was no word in their language for a single woman, for there was, in fact, no female—of any age—without at least a nominal husband. The Tiwi believed that pregnancy happens because a spirit entered the body of a female,

but one could never be sure exactly when that happened; the best thing to do was to make sure that the woman was married at all times. Therefore, all Tiwi babies were betrothed before or as soon as they were born, and widows were required to remarry at the gravesides of their husbands, no matter how old they were (Hart & Pilling, 1960). Many of these traditions still continue today in some Australian aborigine groups.

Earlier in this chapter we discussed arranged marriages. For some, the concept of "loving" one's partner is not a relevant aspect of marriage. In Japan, for example, "love" marriages are often frowned upon because a couple can fall out of love and split up (Kristof, 1996). Some would argue that Japanese men and women actually love each other less than American couples do. Yet the secret to a strong family, claim the Japanese, is low expectations and patience (Kristof, 1996). These factors lead to couples staying together through thick or thin, rather than splitting up when the going gets rough. When one Japanese man, married for 33 years, was asked whether he loved his wife, he replied, "Yeah, so-so, I guess. She's like air or water. You couldn't live without it, but most of the time, you're not conscious of its existence" (Kristof, 1996). This is probably why Japanese couples scored the lowest on what they have in common with each other, compared with couples in 37 other countries (Figure 9.8).

Some countries allow the practice of polygamy (pah-LIGG-uh-mee). Usually, this takes the form of **polygyny** (pah-LIDGE-uh-nee), or having more than one wife, which is a common practice in many areas of Africa and the Middle East, among other places. Most commonly, a polygynous marriage involves two or three wives, although in Islam a man is allowed up to four.

Some have suggested that polygyny began as a strategy to increase fertility, but the suggestion is controversial. In fact, the majority of studies have found that polygyny is associated with lower fertility among wives (Anderton & Emigh, 1989),

José Nicolas/Getty Images

The practice of polygyny is common in many areas of Africa and the Middle East. In this photo, an Afghan man stops at a roadside vendor with his three wives and child.

---

polygyny
The condition or practice of having more than one wife at one time.

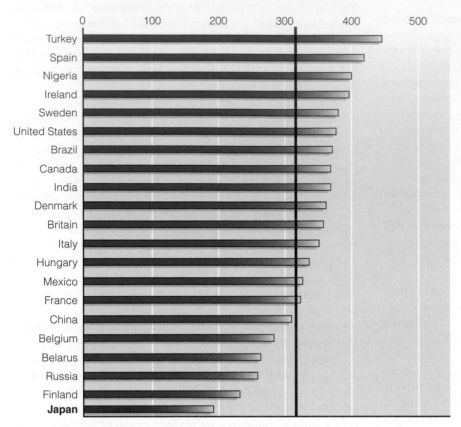

Compatibility of Spouses Index (Average = 316)

FIGURE **9.8** In a survey by the Dentsu Research Institutes and Leisure Development Center in Japan, spouses answered questions about politics, sex, social issues, religion, and ethics. A score of 500 would indicate perfect compatibility.

SOURCE: Based on Who needs love! In Japan, many couples don't. New York Times, February 11, 1996, p. A1.

although a few studies have found no differences and a few have even found higher rates of fertility (Ahmed, 1986). This is because husbands in polygynous marriages must divide their time between each of their wives, which decreases the chance of impregnation for each individual wife. Therefore, it may be more likely that polygyny developed as a strategy for men to gain prestige and power by having many wives, whereas women could gain the protection of a man in countries where there was a scarcity of men (Barber, 2008).

In Islam, a woman may have sex with only one man, but a man may marry up to four wives. Al-Ghazali, the great Islamic thinker and writer of the 11th century, believed that polygyny was permitted because of the desires of men. What determines whether a Muslim man has multiple wives in most Islamic countries today is his wealth more than anything else, for he usually sets up a different household for each wife. Another reason for polygyny in many Muslim countries is the desire for a male child; if one wife does not deliver a male heir, the man may choose a second and third wife in hopes of having a male child (Donnan, 1988).

One woman commented on the negative aspects of polygyny:

You hear everything, your husband and the other wives. You hear how he behaves with his favorite, usually the new one. The women end up hating the man. Everyone feels bad inside. (M. Simons, 1996, p. A1)

However, polygynous husbands have a different view. One polygynous husband says:

My father did it, my grandfather did, so why shouldn't I? When my wife is sick and I don't have another, who will care for me? Besides, one wife on her own is trouble. When there are several, they are forced to be polite and well behaved. If they misbehave, you threaten that you'll take another wife. (M. Simons, 1996, p. A1)

Polyandry (PAH-lee-ann-dree), in which a woman has more than one husband, is much less common than polygyny, and it is usually used to consolidate inheritance. For example, in Tibet, a woman may marry several brothers to avoid dividing up the inherited property. The same rationale is used in many **consanguineous** (con-san-GWIN-ee-us) **marriages**, in which a woman marries her own relative to maintain the integrity of family property.

Marriage between certain blood relatives is illegal in all U.S. states and has been since the late 19th century. However, in many Muslim countries in northern Africa; western and southern Asia; north, east, and central India; and the middle Asian republics of the former Soviet Union, marriages take place between relatives between 20% and 55% of the time (Bittles et al., 1991). In Islamic societies, marriages between first cousins are most common, whereas in Hindu states of south India, uncle–niece and first cousin marriages are equally common. Incidentally, marriages between certain cousins are legal in many U.S. states.

Extramarital Sex in Other Cultures

Extramarital sex is forbidden in many cultures but often tolerated—even in cultures in which it is technically not allowed. For example, it is considered a grave transgression in Islam and, according to the Koran, is punishable by 100 lashes for both partners (Farah, 1984). However, there are a number of Muslim societies in areas such as Africa and Pakistan where adultery is tacitly accepted as a fact of life (Donnan, 1988; Kayongo-Male & Onyango, 1984).

Those countries that tolerate extramarital sex often find it more acceptable for men than for women. In Zimbabwe, for example, women were asked what they would do if they found out their partners were engaging in extramarital sex: 80% reported they would confront their partners, 15% said they would caution their husbands,

---

polyandry
The condition or practice of having more than one husband at one time.

consanguineous marriage
A type of marriage between blood relatives, usually to maintain the integrity of family property.

and 5% were indifferent. However, when men were asked the same question, 60% replied they would divorce their wives, 20% would severely beat their wives, 18% would severely caution her, and 2% would express disappointment and ask their partner to change (Mhloyi, 1990). Although extramarital affairs are relatively common in China, they are seldom discussed. Elderly neighborhood women often keep watch in "neighborhood committees" and report suspicious extramarital activities (Ruan & Lau, 2004).

Divorce in Other Cultures

Divorce is common in almost all societies, but cultural views are changing as societies develop. In societies such as the United States, Sweden, Russia, and most European countries, divorce is relatively simple and has little stigma. In Chapter 3 we discussed the differences between individualistic and collectivist cultures, and it probably won't surprise you to learn that individualist cultures tend to have more favorable attitudes toward divorce than collectivist cultures (Toth & Kemmelmeier, 2009).

Another important issue that can affect attitudes toward divorce is religiosity. It can be difficult to obtain a divorce in Roman Catholic countries because Catholicism does not allow divorce. Ireland legalized divorce in 1995; before this, it was the only country in the Western world to *constitutionally* ban divorce (Pogatchnik, 1995). In South America, a heavily Roman Catholic continent, Chile was the last country to legalize divorce in late 2004.

Traditional laws about divorce can still be enforced, especially in more patriarchal cultures. Islamic law, like traditional Jewish law, allows a man to divorce his wife simply by repudiating her publicly three times. A wife, on the other hand, must go to court to dissolve a marriage (Rugh, 1984). In Egypt, it is far easier for men to divorce than for women, and because of this only about 33% of divorces in Egypt are initiated by females. In Israel, women need their husband's permission for a divorce, and councils have been set up to try to convince men to let their wives have a divorce.

In 2001, China's government revised its 20-year-old marriage law and included the concept of fault in marriage (Dorgan, 2001; Ruan & Lau, 2004). Before this law was implemented, Chinese couples had an equal division of family property regardless of the reasons for the divorce. Under this new law, however, if a partner is caught engaging in extramarital sex, he can lose everything (research has found that it is mostly men who cheat in China).

The reasons that people get divorced are numerous, although different patterns emerge in various societies. In Egypt, the most common reason given for divorce is infidelity by the husband, whereas among the Hindus of India, the most common reason is cruelty (either physical or mental) from their partner (Pothen, 1989). Arab women's main reasons for divorce include the husband's physical, sexual, or verbal abuse; alcoholism; mental illness; and in-law interference (Savaya & Cohen, 2003). In China, more than 70% of divorces are initiated by women, and the main reason given is an extramarital affair of the husband (Ruan & Lau, 2004). This is also the main reason for divorce in Brazil and many other countries (de Freitas, 2004).

Overall, divorce rates seem to be increasing worldwide as countries modernize and as traditional forms of control over the family lose their power. Only time will tell, however, whether a backlash will stabilize marriage rates, as they seem to be doing in the United States.

Same-Sex Relationships in Other Cultures

Same-sex relationships outside the United States are supported in some countries and ignored in others. As of 2017, 24 countries allowed same-sex marriage, including Argentina (2010), Belgium (2003), Brazil (2013), Canada (2005), Columbia (2016), Denmark (2012), England/Wales (2013), Finland (2015), France (2013), Germany (2017), Greenland (2016), Iceland (2010), Ireland (2015), Luxembourg (2014), The Netherlands (2000), New Zealand (2013), Norway (2009), Portugal (2010), Scotland (2014), South Africa (2006), Spain (2005), Sweden (2009), Uruguay (2013), and the United States (2015; Pew Research Center, 2017; Cameron & Berkowitz, 2016). In Mexico, same-sex marriage is allowed in some jurisdictions but not others (see the accompanying Timeline "Same-Sex Relationships Around the Globe" in the Appendix for more information).

The Netherlands was the first country to legalize same-sex marriage in 2000, giving same-sex couples the right to marry, divorce, and adopt children. Although several religions in the Netherlands opposed this law, individual congregations were given the authority to decide whether or not to conduct marriage ceremonies. In 2003, Belgium legalized same-sex marriage and recognized the marriages of couples who were married in countries where same-sex marriage was legal. In 2005, both Spain and Canada legalized same-sex marriage, providing same-sex couples with the same rights as married other-sex couples.

Although South Africa legalized same-sex marriage in 2006, anti-gay attitudes are prevalent in Africa (Sigamoney & Epprecht, 2013). In 2014, the Nigerian president imposed anti-gay laws that mandated 14-year prison terms for participating in same-sex relationships. A few months later, Uganda's president signed similar laws into effect and called homosexuality a "disgusting" and "learned" behavior (Okeowo, 2014). Ugandans were pressured to report any homosexual behavior, since failing to do so is a crime. The president of Zimbabwe claimed that homosexuality was a "Western invention" that disrupted the moral fiber of Africa, while the president of Gambia said homosexuals were "satanic." Many other African countries have enforced long-ignored anti-gay laws. While there are some African countries where same-sex relationships are legal (including Mali, Togo, Ivory Coast, both Congos, and Chad), the greatest protection of same-sex rights is in South Africa, which prohibits discrimination based on sexual orientation. However, although South Africa legalized same-sex marriage in 2006, there are still high levels of prejudice against same-sex relationships, with more than 80% of citizens 16 and older reporting these types of relationships are always wrong (Roberts & Reddy, 2008).

In 2009, both Norway and Sweden legalized same-sex marriage, and in 2010, Iceland, Portugal, and Argentina followed suit. Argentina was the first Latin American country to legalize same-sex marriage, in 2010, despite strong opposition from the Catholic Church. In 2012, Denmark legalized same-sex marriage (Denmark was the first country to allow domestic partnerships for same-sex couples, in 1989). In 2013, Uruguay became the second Latin American country to legalize same-sex marriage, following Argentina. Also in 2013, New Zealand, France, Brazil, England, and Wales legalized same-sex marriage. Scotland voted to legalize same-sex marriage in 2014, and the United States followed suit in 2015. It's possible that Taiwan may be the first country in Asia to allow same-sex marriage in the near future.

As we have discussed, religion is a key issue in many countries. Many religious countries, such as Italy, do not formally acknowledge same-sex partnerships. Interestingly, a gay couple who married in New York had their marriage formally recognized by an Italian court in 2014 (Grindley, 2014). They were the first same-sex couple to have their marriage from a foreign country recognized in Italy.

Throughout this chapter, we have explored various aspects of adult sexual relationships. Relationships hold a central place in our lives. When people are asked what makes them happy, most say their close relationships and feeling loved and needed (Perlman, 2007). In the next chapter, we turn our attention to adult sexual behaviors.

Review Questions

1 Explain how marital quality typically changes throughout the life cycle.

2 How does marriage affect a person's health?

3 Explain how sexuality changes throughout marriage and the reasons this might be so.

4 Explain what we know about marital satisfaction in older couples.

5 Explain what is known about dating, marriage, cohabitation, divorce, and same-sex relationships outside the United States.

Chapter Review

Summary Points

1 Every society has rules to control the ways in which people develop sexual bonds with other people. People openly engage in a variety of adult sexual relationships, including same-sex, other-sex, non-committed, premarital, marital, extramarital, and polyamorous. On college campuses, there have been many recent changes in dating practices.

2 In traditional dating, the boy would pick up the girl at her house, giving her father and mother time to meet with the boy, and then they would go to a well-defined event. Formal dating has given way to more casual dating. Dating provides companionship, emotional support, and economic support, all of which can improve physical health.

3 Communication technologies have increased long-distance (LD) dating, which has been found to have high levels of relationship satisfaction. Today's college students are also more likely to consider dating someone of a different race, religion, or culture. Those who are more open to mixed-race dating are younger, politically liberal, and less religious than those who wouldn't date someone of a mixed race.

4 Sexuality has been found to be a key element that helps shape the quality of romantic relationships, and sexual satisfaction levels are similar in gay, lesbian, bisexual, and heterosexual couples. As people age, sexuality often changes, and this can affect their relationships. Sexual inactivity has been found to be a major cause of decreases in sexual functioning.

5 Relationships formed before the age of 25 are significantly more likely to break up than transition to a more committed relationship. There are five stages to relationship breakups: dissatisfaction in the relationship, exposure and awareness of the problems, negotiation of solutions, resolution, and transformation of the relationship or possible termination of the relationship. Individuals in relationships often do a cost-benefit analysis to see if the relationship is worth continuing.

6 Over the last few years there has been an increase in sex in non-committed relationships. Although a hookup can be a one-time occurrence, sometimes they do develop into long-term sexual relationships in which partners regularly hook up with no expectations of emotional intimacy. Men are more likely to be sexually satisfied than women in these types of relationships due to a double standard in expectations for sexual enjoyment in casual sex interactions. Romantic ambiguity and sexual exploitation can occur in non-committed relationships.

7 In recent years, cohabitation has increased dramatically. In the United States, the typical pattern is to live together before marriage and not in place of marriage. Advantages of cohabitation are that it allows couples to learn more about each other, share finances, and mature in their relationship. Cohabitating couples tend to either marry or separate after just a few years. The meaning and significance of living together may be different in same-sex couples since marriage was not an option prior to 2015 in the majority of states.

8 The majority of young people say they are planning and expecting to marry at some point in their lives. The median age for first marriage has been increasing, and in 2016, the age at first marriage was 29 for men and 27 for women. Many factors affect marital rates, including education, ethnicity, and race. College graduates are more likely to marry today than those with less education, and Blacks are less likely to marry than Whites.

9 Same-sex marriage has been legal in the United States since 2015 when the Supreme Court ruled that state-level bans were unconstitutional. Although several individual states did offer legal marriage for same-sex couples before 2015, these unions were not recognized by the federal government and were not often recognized by other states.

10 Mixed marriages have become more popular, with 1 in 8 new marriages between spouses of different races or ethnicities in 2013. Black females are less likely to marry outside their race than Black males, and Asian males are less likely to marry outside their race than Asian females.

11 Marital satisfaction has been found to be related to the quality of the friendship, frequency of pleasurable activities, being able to talk to each other and offer self-disclosure, physical and emotional intimacy, and personality similarities. High rewards–low costs are also important. Although married women report lower levels of marital satisfaction than men, this might be a result of sampling issues. When data are analyzed using nonclinical samples, no significant gender differences in marital satisfaction are found.

12 Marital quality tends to peak in the first few years of a marriage and then declines until midlife, when it rises again. Marital happiness is higher before having children, declines steadily until it hits a low when the children are in their teens, and then begins to increase once the children leave the house. The majority of married couples report that their marriages are happy and satisfying.

13 Married couples report the highest levels of sexual satisfaction probably because married couples are more likely to be committed to their partner's sexual satisfaction. Almost all couples, whether dating, living together, or married, expect sexual exclusivity from each other. Cheating occurs in 20% to 40% of American married couples. Those who cheat have stronger sexual interests, more permissive sexual values, less satisfaction in their intimate relationship,

and more opportunities for sex outside the relationship. The increasing popularity of the Internet has created new challenges for today's couples, and some might engage in Internet infidelity.

14 Women experience more emotional distress about infidelity than men do. A woman is also more likely to be upset about emotional infidelity, whereas a man is more likely to be upset about his partner's sexual infidelity.

15 Some couples engage in comarital sex, but the sex is viewed as separate from the marriage. Polyamory involves having more than one intimate relationship at a time with the knowledge and consent of all partners. Polyamorous individuals often reject the idea that monogamy is necessary for satisfying long-term relationships.

16 In many ways, same-sex relationships have changed more than other-sex relationships over the past few decades. Compared with heterosexual couples, gay and lesbian couples have higher levels of relationship satisfaction; share more affection, humor, and joy; and have less fear and negative feelings about the relationship. These relationships often have more equality as well. Friend support is more important in same-sex relationships than family support, whereas family support is more important in other-sex relationships.

17 Although the majority of same-sex couples are monogamous, arrangements about nonmonogamy are common among gay couples. However, these arrangements have not been found to decrease sexual satisfaction, communication, or sexual frequency.

18 In other-sex relationships, pregnancies can be experienced as unplanned events, but same-sex couples can't get pregnant by accident. Many same-sex couples decide to become parents through surrogacy, adoption, foster care, or through arrangements with friends and family. Research shows that the timing of parenthood can affect a couple's relationship quality.

19 The liberalization of divorce laws has made it easier and less expensive to obtain a divorce. The current U.S. divorce rate remains high compared with earlier times and with other countries. Certain factors increase the

likelihood of divorce. These include marrying at a young age, marrying because of an unplanned pregnancy, having no religious affiliation, being Protestant or a mixed-religion couple, having many communication problems, having divorced before, or having parents who have divorced. Women often have an increase in depression after a divorce, whereas men experience poorer physical and mental health.

20 In most industrialized countries, dating is the norm. However, there are still a few industrialized cultures in which arranged marriages take place. Mate selection in most places is a much more individual affair. However, although many in the West believe in the right of individuals to choose their own mates, there were some advantages to parental participation in mate selection, and the transition to individual mate selection in traditional societies is often difficult.

21 Cohabitation is rarer in more traditional societies in which, even if a couple has sex before or instead of marriage, social customs would never tolerate an unmarried heterosexual couple living together openly. In some countries, cohabitation is often a step toward marriage or is seen as a "lower form" of marriage.

22 Marriage ceremonies take place in every society on Earth, but marriage customs vary widely from culture to culture. Some cultures mandate marriages between certain relatives, whereas other cultures allow multiple spouses. Usually, this takes the form of polygyny, or having more than one wife, which is a common practice in many areas of Africa and the Middle East. Same-sex marriages are legal in some countries outside of the United States. The Netherlands was the first country to allow same-sex marriages. Extramarital sex is forbidden in many cultures, but it is often tolerated even in cultures in which it is technically not allowed.

23 Divorce is common in almost all societies, but cultural views about it are changing as societies develop. In societies such as the United States, Japan, Sweden, Russia, and most European countries, divorce is relatively simple and has little stigma. The exceptions are countries that are largely Roman Catholic, because Catholicism has negative attitudes toward divorce.

Critical Thinking Questions

1 What are the qualities you look for in a partner? Why do you think these qualities are important to you? Which could you live without? Which are nonnegotiable?

2 Do you ever want to settle down in a lifelong, committed relationship? Why or why not? If so, how long do you think you would want to date someone before settling down for life?

3 How would you feel if your partner cheated on you and engaged in sex outside of your relationship without your knowledge? What would you say to them? Have you ever had a conversation with a partner about monogamy?

4 Suppose this morning when you woke up, you realized your roommate had another "hookup" last night. How do you feel about their frequent hooking up activity? What do you think encourages or discourages hookups on your campus?

5 Pretend you live in a country that practices arranged marriage, and write an informational paragraph about yourself to give to a matchmaker. What would you want the matchmaker to look for in your marriage partner?

6 There have been many changes in the liberalization of divorce laws. Do you think that this has made divorce too easy today? Explain.

Websites

The Gottman Institute This website provides information on the work of John Gottman and Julie Schwartz Gottman. The Gottman Institute provides information and training workshops on relationships and parenting for couples.

Divorce Service Center CompleteCase.com is an online uncontested divorce service center. This site offers assistance with divorce documents without the expenses of a personal lawyer. This is an interesting website that illustrates the changing attitudes about divorce today.

Queendom Tests This Internet magazine includes interactive tests to explore personality, relationships, intelligence, and health. Tests appear in four formats—for lesbians, gay men, heterosexual women, and heterosexual men. Although these tests allow you to explore important issues related to relationships, they are not scholarly or scientific.

The Polyamory Society A nonprofit organization that promotes and supports the interest of individuals of multi-partner relationships and families.

Romance 101 This website contains humorous information about relationships, including information about men's and women's views on dating, romance, and the "dating bill of rights." This is a fun place to visit for a lighthearted look at romance.

10 Sexual Expression

232

The popularity of the Internet has raised some interesting issues related to sexual behaviors and intimate relationships. Endless sex-related websites, subreddits, social networks, and sexual chat rooms lure many of us, often causing problems in our personal relationships. Students often ask me if I think "virtual sex" constitutes cheating—if people have "sex" with a person online, are they cheating on their partner? Heidi's story really made me think about this question. Heidi had dated Jason throughout high school and they became a "long distance" couple when she left for college. Being separated was difficult for both of them, especially because neither had many friends. Jason didn't have access to the Internet or a smartphone so they couldn't Facetime or Skype, but they did talk on a landline phone a few times each week. They also tried to see each other once or twice a month. Heidi had a single room her first year in college, but without Jason around she was very lonely. Her loneliness eventually led her into an online sexual chat room. Although she felt guilty at first, she figured it wouldn't hurt anything just to talk to some of the people in the chat room. She blocked her video, but several of the men begged her to turn on her video so they could see how beautiful she was. Over the next couple of weeks she found herself becoming more and more consumed with her online chat sessions, and her behavior began to change. She turned on her video and began taking off her clothes and touching herself while talking with some of the men in the chat room. This eventually led to private online masturbation sessions with men she didn't know. It all left her feeling desirable and beautiful. A few months later she decided it was time to tell Jason about what she was doing. She hoped he would think it was good for her, but his reaction shocked her. He was angry and hurt and told her she had cheated on him. They spent months trying to repair their relationship. Heidi's story helped me realize the impact that virtual sex can have on an intimate relationship.

Janell Carroll

Human sexuality is a complex part of life, with cultural, psychological, and biological influences shaping how people choose to express their sexuality. Some adults choose not to engage in sexual behavior, whereas others may choose to experiment with various sexual behaviors. Celibacy, or abstinence, occurs when a person chooses not to engage in sexual behaviors. Some people remain abstinent their whole lives and have no sexual partners, whereas others may go through life with one or more partners. Throughout this chapter we will explore findings from the National Survey of Sexual Health and Behavior (NSSHB), which was the largest nationally representative and comprehensive study on sexual behavior ever conducted (see Chapter 2). This study found that our sexual repertoire varies with age, health, and ethnicity (Herbenick et al., 2010a).

In this chapter, we explore influences on sexuality, review the human sexual response cycle, and explore various ways that adults express their sexuality.

Influences on Sexuality

Our sexual attitudes and behaviors are shaped by many factors, including hormones, culture, ethnicity, religion, and the media. As we grow, we learn strong messages about acceptable and unacceptable sexual behaviors from the culture at large, our family, social classes, and even our language. In this section, we discuss four of the biggest influences: hormones and neurotransmitters, family background, ethnicity, and religion.

Hormones and Neurotransmitters

Hormones and **neurotransmitters** both have powerful effects on our bodies. In most animals, the brain controls and regulates sexual behavior chiefly through hormones and neurotransmitters, and these have an enormous effect on sexual behavior in humans as well (Krüger et al., 2006). We discussed hormones in Chapters 5 and 6 and reviewed the various endocrine glands that secrete hormones into the bloodstream, carrying them throughout the body. Sexologists believe that testosterone is the most influential hormone in sexual behavior, but estrogen also plays a role. The majority of people produce these hormones, although in differing quantities. For example, in biological men, testosterone is produced in the testes and adrenal glands, and in biological women, testosterone is produced in the adrenal glands and ovaries. Even so, men produce much more testosterone than women: Men produce 260 to 1,000 nanograms per deciliter (ng/dL) of blood plasma (a nanogram is one billionth of a gram), whereas women produce about 15 to 70 ng/dL. Testosterone levels typically decrease with age.

In Chapter 5 we discussed how women's estrogen levels decline during menopause, often resulting in thinner vaginal walls, vaginal dryness, and decreased vaginal sensitivity. Despite this decrease

in estrogen, testosterone levels often remain constant, which may result in an increase in sexual desire even though the physical changes of menopause can negatively affect sexual functioning. In men, decreases in testosterone can lead to lessening sexual desire and decreases in the quality and quantity of erections. We discuss aging and sexuality in more detail later in this chapter.

Neurotransmitters, chemical messengers that transmit messages from one nerve cell to another, also have a powerful effect on our bodies. Various neurotransmitters, including oxytocin, serotonin, dopamine, and vasopressin, have been found to affect sexual desire, arousal, orgasm, and our desire to couple with certain partners (Ishak et al., 2008; K. A. Young et al., 2008). Directly after orgasm, levels of serotonin, oxytocin, and vasopressin increase, which can lead to feelings of pleasure, relaxation, and attachment (Fisher, 2004).

Transgender men who are put on testosterone often experience what is called a "second puberty" that may lead to a period of sexual experimentation (Wylie et al., 2016). This may result in shifts in what they find sexually attractive and/or arousing. Although hormones and neurotransmitters are important, our social experiences also affect our sexual attitudes and behaviors. Unlike animals, humans are strongly influenced by learned experiences and their social, cultural, and ethnic environment.

Family Background

We have discussed the importance of family throughout this textbook. Our family of origin is our first reference group, and throughout our interactions with them we internalize norms about sexual attitudes and behaviors (Davidson et al., 2008; Garneau et al., 2013). Although the influence of our family is tied into our culture and religion, there have been some interesting studies about the influences of family. Students who come from households with married parents and traditional family backgrounds have been found to have more conservative attitudes about sexual behavior (Davidson et al., 2008). They are more likely to have witnessed displays of affection between their parents and to have talked to one or both parents about sex. Overall, people from such homes have fewer lifetime sexual partners (see Figure 10.1).

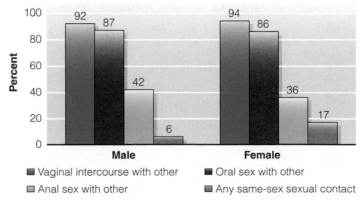

FIGURE **10.1** Sexual behavior among men and women aged 18–44, United States, 2011–2013.

SOURCE: Copen et al., 2016.

---

neurotransmitters
Specialized chemical messengers in the body that transmit messages from one nerve cell to another.

Ethnic differences in family composition reveal that Black college students are more likely than students of other ethnicities to have divorced, separated, or never-married parents (Davidson et al., 2008). Studies have found that Black teens engage in vaginal intercourse earlier than other racial/ethnic groups, have the highest rates of adult sexual behavior and have lower rates of contraceptive use (Herbenick et al., 2010a; Sharp & Ispa, 2009). Although experts in family systems would say that these events are closely tied to family background, there are several other potential issues to consider, such as poverty, discrimination, and racism.

Ethnicity

Ethnicity is one of the most influential variables that affects both sexual attitudes and sexual behaviors (Davidson et al., 2008). Our ethnicity forms a barrier, a "sexualized perimeter," that helps us decide who we have sex with (Nagel, 2003). It also affects our sexual attitudes, our ability to communicate about sex, which sexual behaviors we engage in, and the frequency of these behaviors. Many studies have explored ethnic and racial differences in sexual behavior (Davidson et al., 2008; Dodge et al., 2010; Laumann et al., 1994; Maestripieri et al., 2014; Voisin et al., 2015).

We will explore ethnic and racial differences throughout this chapter, but as we discussed, the highest levels of sexual behavior are among Blacks, followed by Whites, Hispanic Americans, and Asian Americans (Davidson et al., 2008; Eisenberg, 2001; Fryar et al., 2007; see Figure 10.2 for more information about ethnicity/race, gender, and sexual behavior). Asian American men have been found to have the lowest number of sexual partners (Maestipieri et al., 2014).

Keep in mind that many racial and ethnic identities are closely tied to religious affiliation. For example, although studies have found that Hispanic college students are more conservative and less permissive about sexual behaviors than many other students, this may also be because a large number of Hispanics are Catholic (Davidson et al., 2008). Let's discuss the impact of religion on sexual behavior.

Religion

Sexual behavior is one aspect of social life that is commonly targeted for regulation by religious beliefs (Li & Cohen, 2014). Religions try to regulate various aspects of sexuality, such as participation

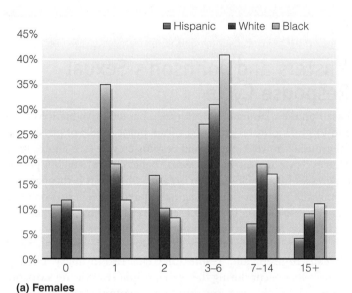

(a) Females

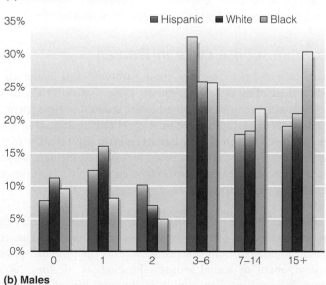

(b) Males

FIGURE **10.2** Number of other-sex partners in lifetime for females (a) and males (b) 15 to 44 years old in the United States by ethnicity/race, 2006–2008.

SOURCE: Chandra et al., 2011.

In early 2011, Brandon Davies, a Brigham Young University starting basketball player, was suspended from the team for engaging in consensual sex with his girlfriend. The school's honor code prohibits premarital sex.

in certain sexual behaviors, motives for sexual behavior, and the use of contraception. We know that religiosity and strength of religious beliefs influence sexual attitudes and behavior (Hobern, 2014; Laumann et al., 1994; Schmitt & Fuller, 2015; Turner & Stayton, 2014). Typically, the more religious people are, the more conservative their sexual behavior tends to be. For example, men and women with high levels of religiosity are more likely to have conservative attitudes about sex; less likely to engage in risky sexual behavior; less approving of certain types of sexual behaviors (such as oral sex); have fewer sexual partners; and experience more guilt about sexual behavior (Daniluk & Browne, 2008; Moore et al., 2013). A meta-analysis of 40 studies found a negative correlation between religiosity and premarital sex—those with higher levels of religiosity engaged in less premarital sexual activity.

Review Questions

1 Identify the most influential hormones and neurotransmitters in sexual behavior and explain their roles in sexual behavior.

2 Explain how our family background can affect sexual behavior.

3 Explain how ethnicity and culture can affect sexual behavior.

4 Explain how religion can affect sexual behavior.

Studying Sexual Response

A series of physiological and psychological changes occur in the body during sexual behavior, referred to collectively as our **sexual response**. Over the years, several models of these changes have been proposed to explain the exact progression and nature of the human sexual response. These models are beneficial in helping physicians and therapists identify how disorders, disease, illness, and disability affect sexual functioning. The most well-known model has been Masters and Johnson's sexual response cycle. Throughout the years several other sex therapists and sexologists have criticized and suggested changes to Masters and Johnson's model; we discuss these later in the chapter.

sexual response
Series of physiological and psychological changes that occur in the body during sexual behavior.

sexual response cycle
Four-stage model of sexual arousal proposed by Masters and Johnson.

excitement
The first stage of Masters and Johnson's sexual response cycle, in which there is an increase in blood concentrated in the genitals, breasts, or both.

plateau
The second stage of Masters and Johnson's sexual response cycle, occurring before orgasm, in which vasocongestion builds up.

orgasm
The third stage of Masters and Johnson's sexual response cycle, which

involves an intense sensation during the peak of sexual arousal and results in a release of sexual tension.

resolution
The fourth stage of Masters and Johnson's sexual response cycle, in which the body returns to the prearoused state.

vasocongestion
An increase in the blood concentrated in the genitals, breasts, or both.

myotonia
Involuntary contractions of the muscles.

transudation
The lubrication of the vagina during sexual arousal.

Masters and Johnson's Sexual Response Cycle

Based on their laboratory work (see Chapter 2), William Masters and Virginia Johnson proposed a four-phase model of physiological arousal known as the **sexual response cycle** (see Figure 10.3). This cycle occurs during all sexual behaviors in which a person progresses from excitement to orgasm, whether it is through oral or anal sex, masturbation, or vaginal intercourse. These physiological processes are similar for all sexual relationships, whether they are between heterosexual or homosexual partners.

The four phases of the sexual response cycle are **excitement**, **plateau**, **orgasm**, and **resolution**. The two primary physical changes that occur during the sexual response cycle are **vasocongestion** (VAZ-oh-conn-jest-shun) and **myotonia** (my-uh-TONE-ee-uh), which we will discuss in greater detail shortly.

Sexual Response Cycle in Women

Sexual response patterns vary among women (and in the same woman depending on her menstrual cycle; Caruso et al., 2014). These variations can be attributed to the amount of time spent in each phase. For example, more time spent during arousal in foreplay may result in a greater orgasmic response. The intensity of the response may also be affected by factors such as menstrual cycle and previous childbearing. However, even with these differences, the basic physical response is always the same.

EXCITEMENT PHASE The first phase, excitement, begins with vasocongestion, an increase in the blood concentrated in the genitals, breasts, or both. Vasocongestion is the principal physical component of sexual arousal (Frohlich & Meston, 2000). Many circumstances can induce excitement, including hearing your partner's voice, seeing an erotic picture, having a fantasy, or being touched a certain way. Within 30 seconds, vasocongestion causes the vaginal walls to begin lubricating, a process called **transudation** (trans-SUE-day-shun). If a woman is lying down

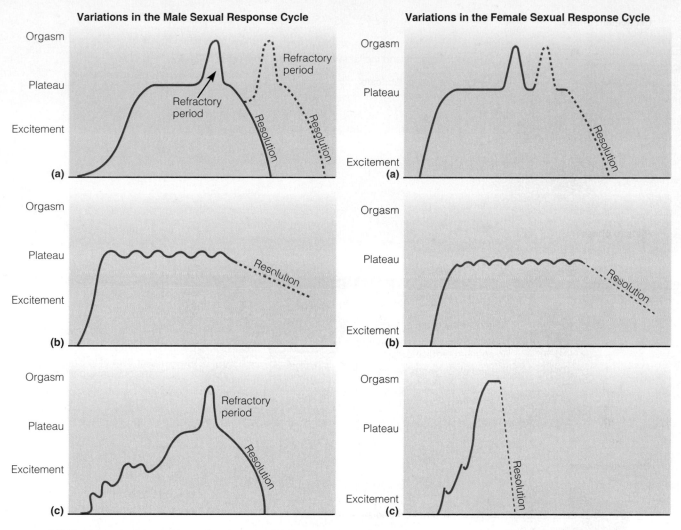

Variations in the Male Sexual Response Cycle

Variations in the Female Sexual Response Cycle

FIGURE **10.3** Variations within male and female response cycles.

SOURCE: Masters, W., Johnson, V., & Kolodny, R. (1994). Heterosexuality (pp. 51–52). New York: HarperCollins Publishers.

(which is common during foreplay), the process of lubricating the vaginal walls may take a little longer than if she is standing up. This may help explain why it takes most women longer than men to feel physically ready for penetration. During the excitement phase, the walls of the vagina, which usually lie flat together, expand. This has also been called the **tenting effect** (see Figure 10.4).

During sexual arousal in women who have not had children, the labia majora thin out and become flattened, and may pull slightly away from the introitus. The labia minora often turn bright pink and begin to increase in size. The increase in size of the vaginal lips adds an average of 0.5 to 1 inch of length to the vaginal canal.

The breasts also experience changes during this phase. Nipple erections may occur in one or both breasts, and the areolae enlarge (Figure 10.5). The breasts enlarge, which may cause an increased definition of the veins in the breasts, especially if a woman has fair skin and large breasts.

Because of the increased vascularity (blood flow) to the genitals during pregnancy and childbirth, women who have had children have a more rapid increase in vasocongestion and enlargement of both the labia majora and minora, which may become two

to three times larger by the end of the excitement phase. Vasocongestion may also cause the clitoral glans to become erect, depending on the type and intensity of stimulation. Generally, the more direct the stimulation, the more engorged the entire clitoral organ will become. Sexual arousal may also be facilitated by the neurotransmitter serotonin, which we discussed earlier in this chapter (Frohlich & Meston, 2000).

The excitement phase can last anywhere from a few minutes to hours. Women report varied sensations during the excitement phase, which are often felt all over the body, rather than being concentrated in one area. Toward the end of the excitement phase, a woman may experience a **sex flush**, which resembles a rash. This usually begins on the chest and, during the plateau stage, spreads from the breasts to the neck and face, shoulders, arms, abdomen, thighs, buttocks, and back.

tenting effect
The pulling up of the cervix, uterus, and ballooning of the upper third of the vagina which occurs during sexual arousal in women.

sex flush
A temporary reddish color change of the skin that sometimes develops during sexual excitement.

Sexual Expression   **237**

Excitement phase

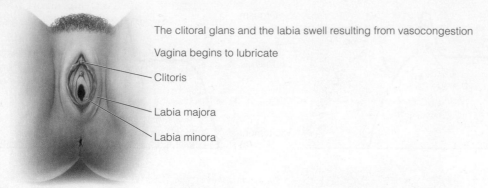

The clitoral glans and the labia swell resulting from vasocongestion

Vagina begins to lubricate

Clitoris

Labia majora

Labia minora

Plateau phase

Clitoris retracts under hood

Labia minora increase in size and turn reddish purple

Bartholin's glands secrete fluid

Uterus elevates and increases in size

Inner two thirds of vagina expands and lengthens

Outer third of vagina forms orgasmic platform

Orgasmic phase

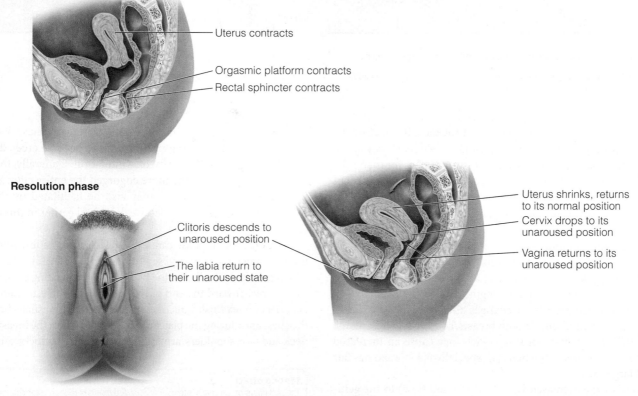

Uterus contracts

Orgasmic platform contracts

Rectal sphincter contracts

Resolution phase

Clitoris descends to unaroused position

The labia return to their unaroused state

Uterus shrinks, returns to its normal position

Cervix drops to its unaroused position

Vagina returns to its unaroused position

FIGURE **10.4** Internal and external changes in the female sexual response cycle.

SOURCE: Masters, W., Johnson, V., & Kolodny, R. (1994). Heterosexuality. New York: HarperCollins Publishers. Copyright © 1994 by William H. Masters, Virginia E. Johnson, and Robert C. Kolodny. Reprinted by permission of HarperCollins Publishers, Inc.

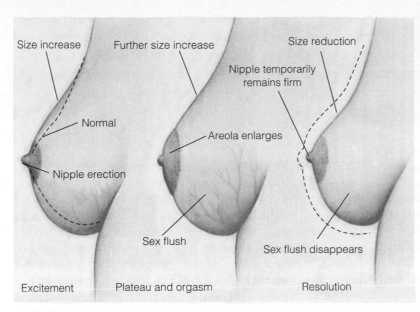

FIGURE **10.5** Breast changes in the female sexual response cycle.

SOURCE: Masters, W., Johnson, V., & Kolodny, R. (1994). Heterosexuality (p. 59). New York: HarperCollins Publishers.

Labels in figure:
Size increase — Further size increase — Size reduction — Nipple temporarily remains firm — Normal — Areola enlarges — Nipple erection — Sex flush — Sex flush disappears — Excitement — Plateau and orgasm — Resolution

PLATEAU PHASE   Women often need more time than men to reach the plateau phase, because they have a larger and more vascular pelvic area, requiring more intense vasocongestion. Once they reach this stage, breast size continues to increase, and the nipples may remain erect. The clitoral glans retracts behind the clitoral hood anywhere from 1 to 3 minutes before orgasm, and it may not be visible at all just before orgasm.

During sexual arousal in women who have not had children, the labia majora are difficult to detect, because of the flattened-out appearance. The labia minora, in contrast, often turn a brilliant red. In women who have had children, the labia majora become very engorged with blood and turn a darker red, almost burgundy. At this point, if sexual stimulation were to stop, the swelling of the clitoris and labia, which can continue for anywhere from a few minutes to hours, can be very uncomfortable. Orgasm helps to relieve this pressure, whether through masturbation or sexual activity with another person. Overall, the plateau stage may last anywhere from 30 seconds to 3 minutes.

REAL RESEARCH   Political ideologies have been found to affect sexual practices. Political conservatives have fewer sexual partners and engage in more traditional sexual behaviors, including kissing and missionary position sex, while political liberals have more sexual partners and engage in more masturbation and sex toy use (HATEMI ET AL., 2017).

orgasmic platform
The thickening of the walls of the lower third of the vagina.

ORGASM PHASE   At the end of the plateau phase, vasocongestion in the pelvis creates an **orgasmic platform** in the lower third of the vagina, labia minora (and labia majora in women who have had children), and uterus (see Figure 10.4). When this pressure reaches a certain point, a reflex in the surrounding muscles is set off, causing vigorous contractions. These contractions expel the blood that is trapped in the surrounding tissues and, in doing so, cause pleasurable orgasmic sensations. Myotonia of the pelvic muscles is primarily responsible for these contractions; without these muscles (as in the case of a woman who has had a hysterectomy, the surgical removal of the uterus), the orgasmic response may be significantly reduced.

Muscular contractions occur about every 0.8 seconds during orgasm. In total, there are about 8 to 15 contractions, and the first 5 or 6 are felt most strongly. Women often experience longer orgasmic contractions than men. A possible explanation for this is that vasocongestion occurs in the entire pelvic region in women (the internal clitoral organ fills the pelvic region), whereas it is localized in men (mainly in the penis and testicles). Because of this, women need more muscle contractions to remove the built-up blood supply. In Chapter 2, we discussed Freud's two types of orgasms, the clitoral and the vaginal. Today, we know that all orgasms in women are thought to be the result of direct or indirect clitoral stimulation, even though orgasms might feel different. Masters and Johnson

ON YOUR MIND

I've heard that many women fake orgasm. Why would they do that?

It might surprise you, but lots of people report having faked orgasms at some point in their lives (KNOX ET AL., 2008; MUEHLENHARD & SHIPPEE, 2010). The National Survey of Sexual Health and Behavior found that although 85% of men said their female partner reached orgasm the last time they had sex, only 64% of women said they did (HERBENICK ET AL., 2010a). While there are several potential reasons for this difference (see the "Sex in Real Life" feature on "Research and Skepticism" in Chapter 2), it is possible that some of the partners of the men who responded to the survey were faking. Women fake orgasm for several reasons—they might not know how to reach orgasm, want to end a sexual encounter, or want to avoid hurting a partner's feelings (because we live in a culture that often expects men to provide women's orgasms, a woman might fake to minimize any negative feelings in her partner; MUEHLENHARD & SHIPPEE, 2010). Men have also been known to fake orgasms, and although the majority report doing so during sexual intercourse, some men report faking orgasm during oral sex, manual stimulation, and/or phone sex (MUEHLENHARD & SHIPPEE, 2010). Men's reasons for faking are similar to women's, but common reasons are because they are tired or don't feel that orgasm is possible. In all of these instances, partners are giving false information, and even though they are probably doing it under the guise of good intentions, open, honest communication about sexual needs and feelings is a far better strategy.

believed that the clitoral hood rubbing and pulling over the clitoral glans contributed to female orgasm during penetrative sex.

During orgasm, there is a release of vasocongestion and muscle tension. The body may shudder, jerk uncontrollably, or spasm. In addition, orgasms may involve facial grimacing, groans, spasms in the hands and feet, contractions of the gluteal and abdominal muscles, and contractions of the orgasmic platform. Peaks in blood pressure and respiration patterns have been found during both male and female orgasms.

Kinsey reported that 14% of women regularly experienced **multiple orgasms**, and although Masters and Johnson believed all women were capable of such orgasms, the majority of women they studied did not experience them. Multiple orgasms are more likely to occur from direct stimulation of the clitoris, rather than from thrusting during penetrative sex. In Chapter 5 we discussed the Gräfenberg spot (G-spot), and some women claim when this area is stimulated it leads to intense orgasms and female ejaculation of fluid (see Chapter 5).

RESOLUTION PHASE   During the last phase of the sexual response cycle, resolution, a woman's body returns to pre-excitement conditions. The extra blood leaves the genitals, erections disappear, muscles relax, and heart and breathing rates return to normal. After orgasm, the skin is often sweaty, and the sex flush slowly disappears. The breasts begin to decrease in size, although many women experience nipple erections after an orgasm because the breast as a whole quickly decreases in size while the areolae remain engorged for a few minutes. The clitoris returns to its original size but remains extremely sensitive for several minutes. Some women may not like their clitoris to be touched during this time because of the increased sensitivity.

In women who are not on hormonal contraception, menstrual cycles may influence sexual responsiveness (Brown et al., 2008; Suschinsky et al., 2014). In fact, sexual excitement occurs more frequently during the last 14 days of a woman's menstrual cycle (Sherfey, 1972). During this time, more lubrication is produced during the excitement phase, which may be because of the increased vasocongestion. Orgasms can be very helpful in reducing cramps during menstruation, presumably because they help to relieve the buildup of pelvic vasocongestion that may occur as a side effect of menstruation (Ellison, 2000; Herbenick, 2008).

Sexual Response Cycle in Men

The sexual response cycle in males is similar to that of females, with vasocongestion and myotonia leading to physiological changes in the body (see Figure 10.6). However, in men, the four phases are less well defined.

multiple orgasms	detumescence
More than one orgasm experienced within a short period.	The loss of tumescence, which causes an erect penis to become flaccid.
tumescence	ejaculatory inevitability
Vasocongestive swelling of the penis, which creates an erection.	The inability to control an impending ejaculation.

EXCITEMENT PHASE   During the excitement phase, the penis, like the clitoris in women, begins to fill with blood and become erect. Erection, or **tumescence** (too-MESS-cents), begins quickly during excitement, generally within 3 to 5 seconds (although the speed of this response lengthens with age). The excitement phase of the sexual response cycle in men is often very short, unless a man uses deliberate attempts to lengthen it. Often this causes **detumescence** (dee-too-MESS-cents), a gradual loss of tumescence. Distractions during the excitement phase (such as a roommate walking into the room) may also cause detumescence. However, once the plateau stage is reached, an erection is often more stable and less sensitive to outside influences.

During the excitement phase, the testicles also increase in size, becoming up to 50% larger. This is both a vasocongestive and myotonic response. The cremaster muscle pulls the testicles closer to the body to avoid injury during thrusting (see Chapter 6 for more information about this muscle). If sexual stimulation were to stop at this point, the swelling in the testicles may be uncomfortable.

PLATEAU PHASE   All of these physical changes continue during the plateau phase. Some men may experience a sex flush, which is identical to the sex flush women experience. In addition, it is not uncommon for men to have nipple erections. Just before orgasm, the glans penis becomes engorged (this is comparable with the engorgement of the clitoral glans in women). At this point, a few drops of pre-ejaculatory fluid from the Cowper's gland may appear on the glans of the penis.

ORGASM PHASE   Although we often think of orgasm and ejaculation as always occurring together (see Figure 10.6), some men can experience orgasm without ejaculation (Chia & Abrams, 1997; J. Johnson, 2001). Although uncommon, some men can teach themselves to experience multiple orgasms before ejaculating (Benzer, 2009; Chia & Abrams, 1997; J. Johnson, 2001). The Chinese were the first to learn how to achieve multiple orgasms by delaying and withholding ejaculation. The average number of orgasms a multiorgasmic man can have varies between two and nine orgasms per sexual interaction.

Ejaculation usually occurs in two stages, and during the first stage, which lasts only a few seconds, there are contractions in the vas deferens, seminal vesicles, and prostate gland. These contractions lead to **ejaculatory inevitability**, whereby just before orgasm there is a feeling that ejaculation can no longer be controlled. In the second stage, the semen is forced out of the urethra by muscle contractions (the same set of muscles that contract in female orgasm).

The first three or four orgasmic contractions are the most pleasurable and tend to be the most forceful (various herbal and

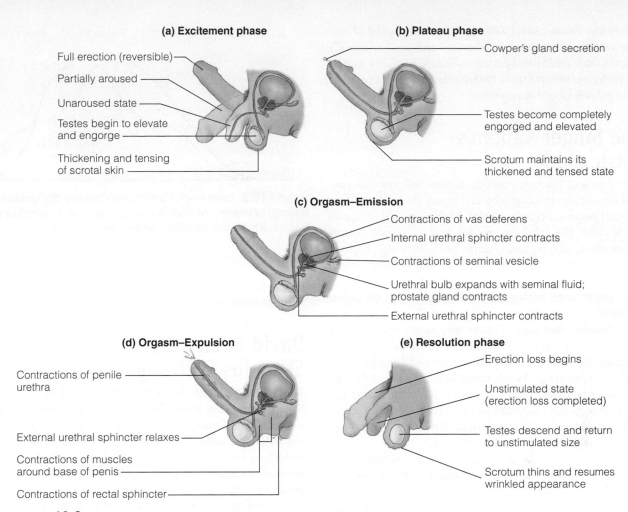

(a) Excitement phase

- Full erection (reversible)
- Partially aroused
- Unaroused state
- Testes begin to elevate and engorge
- Thickening and tensing of scrotal skin

(b) Plateau phase

- Cowper's gland secretion
- Testes become completely engorged and elevated
- Scrotum maintains its thickened and tensed state

(c) Orgasm–Emission

- Contractions of vas deferens
- Internal urethral sphincter contracts
- Contractions of seminal vesicle
- Urethral bulb expands with seminal fluid; prostate gland contracts
- External urethral sphincter contracts

(d) Orgasm–Expulsion

- Contractions of penile urethra
- External urethral sphincter relaxes
- Contractions of muscles around base of penis
- Contractions of rectal sphincter

(e) Resolution phase

- Erection loss begins
- Unstimulated state (erection loss completed)
- Testes descend and return to unstimulated size
- Scrotum thins and resumes wrinkled appearance

FIGURE **10.6** External and internal changes in the male sexual response cycle.

SOURCE: Masters, W., Johnson, V., & Kolodny, R. (1994). Heterosexuality (p. 60). New York: HarperCollins Publishers.

drug products have recently appeared on the market claiming to increase male orgasmic contractions; see the accompanying "Sex in Real Life"). The force of the ejaculation can propel semen up to 24 inches, although this distance is considerably shorter in older men. After these major contractions, minor ones usually follow, even if stimulation stops. As with women, the muscular contractions during orgasm occur about every 0.8 seconds.

RESOLUTION PHASE Directly after ejaculation, the glans of the penis decreases in size, even before general penile detumescence. During the resolution phase of sexual response, when the body is returning to its prearousal state, men go into a **refractory stage**, during which they cannot be re-stimulated to orgasm for a certain time period. The refractory period gets longer as men get older (we discuss this further later in this chapter). Younger men, in contrast, may experience another erection soon after an ejaculation.

refractory stage
The period after an ejaculation in which men cannot be stimulated to another erection or orgasm.

ON YOUR MIND

Does the condition "blue balls" really exist?

Masters and Johnson's model of sexual response is one of the most comprehensive models proposed. However, it has not been without controversy. Many feminist therapists believe that Masters and Johnson's sexual response cycle should not be used universally for classification and diagnosis of sexual disorders. Some experts argue that the definition of healthy sexuality has traditionally focused on orgasm and given less importance to emotions

The concept of blue balls refers to a pain in the testicles that is experienced by men if sexual arousal is maintained for a significant period but is not followed by an orgasm. It is true that the pressure felt in the genitals, which is caused by vasocongestion, can be uncomfortable (CHALETT & NERENBERG, 2000). This discomfort can be relieved through masturbation. Women also experience a similar condition if they are sexually aroused and do not reach orgasm (some of my students refer to such pain as "pink ovaries"). There can be pressure, pain, or a bloating feeling in the pelvic region, which can also be relieved through masturbation.

Sexual Expression **241**

and relationships (Tiefer, 2001). Others claim that a model of sexuality that values performance, penetration, and orgasm is really a male model of sexuality since it views female sexuality as passive and even nonexistent (Burch, 1998; Kaplan, 1974). Let's explore some other models of sexual response.

Helene Singer Kaplan's Triphasic Model

Unlike Masters and Johnson's model, Kaplan believes that psychological, emotional, and cognitive factors are also an important part of sexual response (Kaplan, 1974). Kaplan's model of sexual response is called the **triphasic model**, and it includes sexual desire, excitement, and orgasm (Figure 10.7). Although Kaplan's second and third stages are physiological and involve genital vasocongestion and muscular contractions, sexual desire is of paramount importance, because without sexual desire, the physiological functions cannot occur.

Kaplan believes that many factors may block sexual desire, such as depression, pain, fear, medications, or past sexual abuse. We discuss the importance of the desire phase and disorders associated with it in Chapter 14. An advantage to Kaplan's model is that it is easier to conceptualize than Masters and Johnson's model. For example, most of us can recognize and differentiate desire, excitement, and orgasm but may have a difficult time recognizing when we are in Masters and Johnson's plateau phase.

However, there has been criticism of Kaplan's model claiming it is based on the male linear model of sexual function (Sugrue & Whipple, 2001). Critics point out that women can experience sexual arousal, orgasm, and satisfaction without

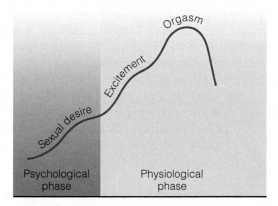

FIGURE **10.7** Helen Singer Kaplan's three-stage model of sexual response includes the psychological phase of sexual desire and two physiological stages of excitement and orgasm.

triphasic model	Dual Control Model of Sexual Response
A model of sexual response, proposed by Helen Singer Kaplan, which includes three phases.	A model of sexual response, proposed by John Bancroft and colleagues, which views sexual response as a neurobiological two-part process involving both sexual excitation and inhibition.

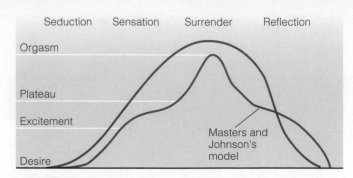

FIGURE **10.8** David Reed's Erotic Stimulus Pathway (ESP) model blends features of Masters and Johnson's and Kaplan's models using four phases: seduction, sensation, surrender, and reflection.

sexual desire and can experience desire, arousal, and satisfaction without orgasm.

David Reed's Erotic Stimulus Pathway

The Erotic Stimulus Pathway (ESP) model was proposed by David Reed. This model blends features of both Masters and Johnson's and Kaplan's models and includes four phases, including seduction, sensation, surrender, and reflection (Figure 10.8). Seduction includes all those things that we might do to entice someone to have sex with us—what we wear, what we say, and so on. In the next stage of sensation, our senses take over. What we hear, smell, taste, touch, and fantasize about all have the potential to turn us on and enhance our excitement. Both the seduction and sensation phase are psychosocial, and they contribute to our physiological response.

In the third phase, surrender—orgasm—occurs. Reed believes that we need to be able to let go and allow ourselves to reach orgasm. Too much control or not enough may interfere with this response. The final phase of Reed's model is the reflection phase, in which we reflect on the sexual experience. Whether the experience was positive or negative will affect future sexual functioning.

Beverly Whipple, who researched and reported on the G-spot in women, expanded Reed's Erotic Stimulus Pathway to demonstrate that if the sexual experience was pleasant and produced satisfaction, then it could lead to the seduction phase of the next sexual experience (Whipple & Brash-McGreer, 1997).

The Kinsey Institute's Dual Control Model of Sexual Response

The **Dual Control Model of Sexual Response**, developed by John Bancroft and colleagues at the Kinsey Institute, views sexual response as a neurobiological two-part process involving sexual excitation and inhibition (Bancroft et al., 2009; Bancroft et al., 2005). A person's ability to become sexually aroused involves an interaction between sexual excitation and inhibition. Sexual excitation can be triggered by a variety of things, such as thoughts,

Is it possible to take an over-the-counter drug to improve your sex drive, erections, or orgasms? Will $59.95 buy you a 1-month supply of awesome orgasms? How much would you pay to find out? Although we discuss the use of aphrodisiacs in Chapter 14, here we consider those advertisements that clog our e-mail accounts and appear in many magazines, promoting better sex.

Over the last few years, I've had many male students ask me about a drug called

Mioplex. This "male orgasm intensifier" has intrigued many college students, a group the company tends to target. The Europe-based producers of Mioplex claim that it can increase a man's "ropes," or number of physical ejaculatory contractions during orgasm. It also claims that increasing a man's ejaculatory contractions will help female partners to have better and longer orgasms. Mioplex is a flower seed extract, which has been unavailable in the United States but can be ordered online.

These vitamins or health food supplements are considered "food" items and not drugs—as such, they don't have to be approved by the U.S. Food and Drug Administration. There is no guarantee that they work, and they may cause adverse effects. The bottom line on products like this is that many are ineffective. But an interesting question remains: Why would so many people be so willing to pay for such products?

feelings, and sensations, and there are variations in individual levels of sexual excitation and inhibition. While some people are easily stimulated and excited, others may not be.

Sexual inhibition reduces the likelihood of sexual response and is the opposite of sexual excitation. Two main aspects can inhibit physiological sexual arousal—performance anxieties and fears about negative consequences. Fears and worries about performing or about acquiring a sexually transmitted infection (STI) can decrease the likelihood of sexual response. While individuals vary in their propensity for sexual excitement and inhibition, this model proposes that a person is more likely to experience problems with sexual response when he or she is low in sexual excitability and high in sexual inhibition (Bancroft et al., 2009).

Unlike other models, this neurobiological model conceptualizes sexual excitation and sexual inhibition as two distinct systems, rather than as two ends of a spectrum. Ongoing research is exploring the application of this model to sexual problems.

Future Directions in Sexual Response Models

One of the chief critics of medically based sexual response models is Leonore Tiefer, a noted feminist sexologist. Tiefer suggests that Masters and Johnson's model leaves out important aspects of sexual functioning because it focuses exclusively on adequate genital functioning—vasocongestion, myotonia, physical excitement, and orgasm (Tiefer, 2001). Tiefer believes that pleasure, emotionality, sensuality, cultural differences, power issues, and communication are important components of sexual response, and that women's sexual experiences do not fit neatly into Masters and Johnson's four stages. This is how Tiefer characterizes the perspective of the medical model: "If it's wet and hard and works, it's normal; if it's not, it's not" (Tiefer, 2001).

Rosemary Basson (2000a) also believes women's motivations for sex are more complex than men's motivations. Although many men experience sexual arousal with a genital response, sexual

arousal in women is often dependent on various thoughts and feelings (Basson, 2005). She believes that the decision to be sexual for many women is driven by the desire for intimacy. A woman might agree to sex for a variety of reasons: to express feelings for her partner, to feel emotionally closer to her partner, to feel wanted and needed, or to receive and share pleasure (Basson, 2005). These motivations lead to a conscious decision to focus on sexual stimuli, which can lead to sexual arousal. Like Tiefer, Basson believes that nonsexual distractions of everyday life (such as work and home responsibilities) in addition to sexual distractions (such as worries about arousal or the ability to orgasm) interfere with a woman's ability to feel sexual arousal. If a woman can overcome these distractions, Basson suggests that continued sexual stimulation could lead to sexual pleasure, which will eventually trigger desire for sex itself (Figure 10.9). Tiefer's and Basson's work has begun a much-needed dialogue about the relationship between gender and sexual functioning.

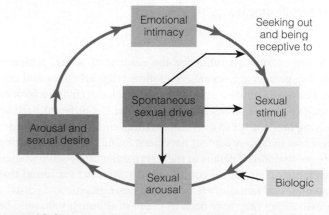

Basson's Non-Linear Model

FIGURE **10.9** Basson believes that many women do not feel spontaneous sexual desire. Instead, a desire for intimacy may lead a woman to seek out, and be receptive to, sexual stimuli, which then may lead to sexual arousal.

SOURCE: Basson, 2001.

Review Questions

1 Identify and describe the four phases of Masters and Johnson's female sexual response cycle and explain what happens in women.

2 Identify and describe the four phases of Masters and Johnson's male sexual response cycle, noting any differences between the male and female cycles.

3 Compare and contrast the various models of sexual response that have been proposed.

Solitary Sexual Behavior

We began this chapter with a story about a woman who engaged in online sexual behavior. Would you consider her behavior to be solitary or partnered? Below we will discuss typical solitary sexual behavior, sexual fantasy and masturbation. Although these behaviors can be practiced alone, they are often used during partnered sexual behavior as well.

Sexual Fantasy

Sexual fantasies are erotic thoughts about sex that can create or enhance sexual arousal. They exist in a person's mind and imagination and may originate from past experience or something that was read or seen. Although some people might wish to act out a sexual fantasy, many have no desire to engage in the behaviors they fantasize about. Even though men have more sexual cognitions, or thoughts about sex, than women (Laumann et al., 1994; Nelson, 2013; Renaud & Byers, 1999), both men and women use sexual fantasy to heighten sexual arousal, both when alone and with a partner. Although Sigmund Freud believed that only sexually unsatisfied people fantasized about sex, today many researchers believe that not only are sexual fantasies normal and healthy, but they may be a driving force behind human sexuality (Frostino, 2007; Hicks & Leitenberg, 2001).

REAL RESEARCH Women's sexual fantasies include more themes related to their own romantic and sexual desirability in another's eyes than men's sexual fantasies (BOGAERT ET AL., 2015).

Many factors can influence the content of sexual fantasies, including gender, age, sexual orientation, religious views, and culture. The most common sexual fantasies include reliving a favorite sexual experience, fantasizing about sex with a different partner, receiving oral sex, sex in a certain location, and forced sex. Gender differences in fantasy content have been found, with men focusing more on anatomical details in their sexual fantasies, while women focus more on emotional connectedness. Studies have found that women's sexual fantasies are becoming more graphic and sexually aggressive than they have been in the past, although this could be due to increased comfort in reporting (Shulman & Horne, 2006). The majority of people have a select few fantasies that they use over and over again for arousal purposes. Sexual fantasies are used for a variety of reasons, including to help enhance masturbation, increase sexual arousal, help a person reach orgasm, and allow a person to explore various sexual activities that he or she might find taboo or too threatening to actually engage in. Overall, the sexual fantasies of lesbians, gays, and heterosexuals are more similar than different, except for the sex of the fantasized partner (Leitenberg & Henning, 1995). Sexual fantasy is common in transgender adolescents and adults who may fantasize about having a physical body that is congruent with their gender identity (Doorduin & Van Burlo, 2014).

Earlier we discussed the impact of religiosity on sexuality, and we bring it up here because the use of sexual fantasies is often related to a person's religion. For example, agnostics and atheists report a significantly wider variety of sexual fantasies than Christians, Jews, and Hindus; significantly more sex-positive fantasies than Christians or Hindus; and significantly more intercourse fantasies than Hindus (Ahrold et al., 2011). Overall, liberal attitudes and more sexual experience have been found to be associated with longer and more explicit sexual fantasies (Kahr, 2008).

Women's Sexual Fantasies

Many women report using sexual fantasy on a regular basis to increase their arousal, self-esteem, and sexual interest, or to relieve stress (Maltz & Boss, 2001; Shulman & Horne, 2006). In fact, an absence of sexual fantasies in women may be an indication of a sexual desire problem (McCabe & Goldhammer, 2013; we will discuss this more in Chapter 14).

Overall, women's sexual fantasies tend to be more emotional than men's and include more touching, feeling, partner response, and ambiance (Zurbriggen & Yost, 2004). The five most common sexual fantasies for women include sex with their current partner, reliving a past sexual experience, engaging in different sexual positions, having sex in rooms other than the bedroom, and sex on a carpeted floor (Maltz & Boss, 2001). Female sexual fantasies tend to be romantic, as illustrated by this 21-year-old woman's fantasy:

My ultimate fantasy would be with a tall, strong man. We would spend a whole day together—going to a beach on a motorcycle, riding horses in the sand, and making love on the beach. Then we'd ride the motorcycle back to town, get dressed up, and go out to dinner. After dinner we'd come home and make love by the fire. Or we could make love in a big field of tall grass while it is raining softly. (Author's files)

Sexual fantasies are used by heterosexual, lesbian, and bisexual women. One 20-year-old lesbian shared her favorite sexual fantasy:

She has black hair and I stop the car and motion her to get in. She walks quickly, with a slight attitude. She gets in with silence—her hands and eyes speak for her. I take her home, and she pulls me in. I undress her, and she is ready for me. Down on the bed she goes, and down on her I go. With legs spread, her clitoris is swollen and erect, hungry for my touch. I give her what she wants. She moans as orgasm courses through her body. (Author's files)

Older women also use sexual fantasies, and using them later in life may help women experience arousal and orgasm (Maltz & Boss, 2001). One 50-year-old woman reveals her fantasies at this point in her life:

One big change in my imaginary sex life since I was a young woman: I no longer have those fluffy romantic fantasies where most of the story is about pursuit and the sex at the end is NG, no genitals, in view. Now I picture the genitals, mine and his, and I watch them connect in full juicy color. I see a big penis, always a big penis, and every detail, including the little drops of pre-ejaculate like dew on the head. (Block, 1999, p. 100)

Studies have found that some women use sexual fantasies involving forced sex (Bivona & Critelli, 2009; Brown-James, 2017; Critelli & Bivona, 2008). The most common forced sex fantasy involves being overpowered or forced to surrender sexually to a partner. Women who have such fantasies report using them anywhere from once a week to once a month and are often more open to sexual variety and have lower levels of sexual guilt than women who didn't use such fantasies (Bivona et al., 2012; Shulman & Horne, 2006). It's important to keep in mind that fantasizing about forced sexual behavior does not mean a woman wants to be forced to have sex in real life. In a sexual fantasy, the woman is in control and able to transform something fearful into something pleasurable (Maltz & Boss, 2001).

Men's Sexual Fantasies

Men's sexual fantasies tend to be more active and aggressive than women's (Zurbriggen & Yost, 2004). They are often more frequent and impersonal, dominated by visual images. These fantasies move quickly to explicit sexual acts and often focus on the imagined partner as a sex object. They generally include visualizing body parts, specific sexual acts, group sex, a great deal of partner variety, and less romance.

The five most common sexual fantasies for men include engaging in different sexual positions, having an aggressive partner, getting oral sex, having sex with a new partner, and having sex on the beach (Maltz & Boss, 2001). Following is a sexual fantasy from a 20-year-old man:

benis arapovic/Alamy Stock Photo

Sexual fantasies, such as engaging in sex with multiple partners, play a role in many people's lives, and may or may not be shared with a partner.

My sexual fantasy is to be stranded on an island with beautiful women from different countries (all of them horny, of course). I'm the only male. I would make all of them have multiple orgasms, and I would like to have an everlasting erection so I could please them all nonstop. (Author's files)

Sexual fantasies are used by heterosexual, gay, and bisexual men. For gay and bisexual men, common sexual fantasies are receiving oral sex from another man, being manually stimulated by another man, engaging in anal intercourse, and kissing (Kahr, 2008). When asked about his favorite sexual fantasy, one 21-year-old gay man shared:

My favorite sexual fantasy consists of a purely coincidental meeting between myself and an old friend from high school, Jason. We would eventually end up at my house and talk for hours about what each of us had been up to for the last few years. Eventually, the conversation would become one of his talking about trouble with a girlfriend or something of that nature. Jason tells me that he was always aware that I was gay and that he had been thinking about that a lot lately. He tells me that he has always wondered what it would be like to have sex with another man. I offer to have sex with him. He agrees and we engage in passionate, loving sex. (Author's files)

ON YOUR MIND

I've always had a fantasy about having sex in a very public place, with lots of people watching. I don't really want to try this, but the thought turns me on. Am I weird?

Fantasies are private mental experiences that involve sexually arousing thoughts or images. They are used for many reasons, but primarily to heighten sexual arousal. Having sexual fantasies does not mean you want certain events to happen. It can be a turn-on to think about having sex with a lot of people watching, even though you would never do it in real life. Researchers today have found that sexual fantasies are a concern only if they interfere with healthy sexual expression or the development of partner intimacy (BLOCK, 1999).

Masturbation

Health experts have had a major role in shaping public opinion about masturbation. In the 18th and 19th centuries, masturbation was viewed as a disease that could lead to hairy palms, insanity, sterility, or death. Parents would go to extremes to protect their children from the sins of masturbation. In fact, aluminum gloves were sold to parents for the purpose of covering children's hands at bedtime so that children wouldn't be able to masturbate (Laqueur, 2003; Stengers & Van Neck, 2001). In 1994, the U.S. surgeon general Jocelyn Elders was asked to step down after a speech in which she suggested that masturbation should be taught in public schools. More recently, masturbation has been viewed as a strategy to improve sexual health, reduce stress and unwanted pregnancy, and avoid STIs (Kaestle & Allen, 2011).

The majority of men and women report learning about masturbation from peers and the media, rather than from their parents or teachers (Kaestle & Allen, 2011). Masturbation is common throughout the life span for both men and women (Herbenick et al., 2010a). However, although the majority of men in all age groups reported masturbating during the past year, only 40% of women reported doing so. Experts believe this may be because women may be less comfortable with masturbation, which can decrease their masturbatory behavior as well as their ability to talk about it (Kaestle & Allen, 2011). Asexual women are significantly less likely to masturbate than sexual women, sexual men, and asexual men (Yule et al., 2016). In addition, both asexual women and men were less likely to report masturbating for sexual pleasure.

Overall, the majority of American boys experience their first ejaculation through masturbation, and it is often the main sexual outlet for both boys and girls during adolescence (see Chapter 8). Masturbation is a common and frequent component of male sexual behaviors, regardless of age or relationship status. Rates of masturbation were greatest in those who were 25 to 39 years old and lowest among married men older than 70 (Dodge et al., 2010; Reece et al., 2010d). Whereas men who were in a relationship reported less masturbation than men who were not in a relationship, 60% of men in a relationship reported masturbating (Reece et al., 2010d). Men report masturbating more than twice a week on average, up until the age of 50, when frequency begins to decrease (Reece et al., 2010d).

Masturbation is also common in women, although rates are highest in the 25- to 29-year age group (Herbenick et al., 2010a). Like men, the frequency of masturbation decreases with age in women. At age 50, 40% of women report masturbating, 33% at age 60, and 16% at age 70 (Dodge et al., 2010; Herbenick et al., 2010a). Unlike other sexual behaviors, masturbation is unrelated to a person's health or relationship status. For some, masturbation complements an active sex life, whereas for others, it compensates for a lack of partnered sex or satisfaction with sex (Das, 2007). Masturbation fulfills a variety of needs for people at different ages, and it can decrease sexual tension and anxiety and provide an outlet for sexual fantasy. It allows people the opportunity to experiment with their bodies to see what feels good and where they like to be touched (see Figures 10.10 and 10.11).

Some men and women use vibrators or dildos during masturbation (Herbenick et al., 2009; Reece et al., 2009). A vibrator uses batteries and can vibrate at different speeds. Vibrators may be used directly on the genitals, or they may be inserted into a vagina or anus. A dildo, which can be made of silicone, rubber, or jelly, and comes in a variety of shapes and sizes, can also be inserted into the vagina or anus but does not use batteries.

REAL RESEARCH Among men who masturbate frequently, 70% use pornography at least once a week, referred to as "pornography-related masturbation" (CARVALHEIRA ET AL., 2015). This practice is typically related to sexual boredom and low relationship intimacy.

FIGURE **10.10** Female masturbation.

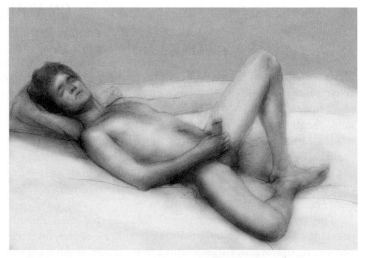

FIGURE **10.11** Male masturbation.

Cultural and religious taboos against masturbation can increase sex guilt. These cultural taboos are related to whether masturbation is perceived to be "normal" in a particular culture. Conservative cultures are less accepting of masturbation, which may decrease the actual practice of masturbation. For example, Asian American women have been found to masturbate significantly less than non-Asian women (Chi et al., 2015; Meston et al., 1996). A study on masturbation in 20- to 59-year-old Chinese men and women found that 35% of men and 13% of women engaged in masturbation (Das et al., 2009; Tao & Brody, 2011).

Review Questions

1 Describe the research on sexual fantasy.

2 How has masturbation been viewed throughout history? Are there cultural differences in masturbation attitudes?

3 Explain the differences in frequency of male versus female masturbation.

Partnered Sexual Behavior

Partnered sexual behaviors peak in a person's 20s and decrease with age (Herbenick et al., 2010a; Table 10.1). People have many motives for engaging in sexual behavior—they might want to reproduce, experience sexual pleasure, and/or reduce stress. But they might also engage in sexual behaviors to feel love or get revenge, out of duty or curiosity, or even for exercise (Meston & Buss, 2007; Stephenson et al., 2011). In a longitudinal study on sexual satisfaction in intimate relationships, researchers found that the majority of individuals reported their sex lives remained as passionate as they were in the beginning of their relationships (Frederick et al., 2017). However, couples who engaged in more frequent sex, received more oral sex, reached orgasm more consistently, and had more variety in their sex lives had higher levels of sexual satisfaction.

As we discussed in Chapter 9, studies have found that women are more likely than men to prefer sexual behavior within the context of a committed relationship (Bradshaw et al., 2010; Carroll et al., 1985; Meston & Buss, 2007). People who engage in sexual intercourse during a hookup are more likely to do it again in the future. In fact, one study found that college students who have engaged in sexual intercourse during a hookup in the last year were six times more likely to do it again within the year, compared to those who didn't engage in intercourse during their hookups (Owen et al., 2011).

Next, we will discuss various sexual behaviors including foreplay, manual sex, oral sex, vaginal intercourse, anal intercourse, and same-sex sexual behaviors (for more information about the practice of certain sexual behaviors by various age groups, see Table 10.1). Partnered sexual behavior can occur in **monogamous** or **nonmonogamous relationships** (see Chapter 9 for more information about monogamy).

Foreplay

It is interesting to consider how people define "foreplay." Is foreplay all of the sexual behaviors that take place before penetration? What if penetration does not occur? For the majority of heterosexuals, foreplay is often defined as everything that happens before sexual intercourse. In fact, many people view foreplay as something a man has to do to get a woman ready for sexual intercourse.

Foreplay can include behaviors such as erotic massage, deep tongue kissing, dry humping (no actual skin-on-skin contact), and oral sex. Kissing releases certain neurotransmitters, including dopamine, oxytocin, and serotonin, which can increase arousal and motivation (Kirshenbaum, 2011). Hugging can also be an important foreplay activity but it is often neglected. In fact, one study found that married couples had deeper, more relaxed hugs with their young children than they did with each other (Schnarch, 1997). Touchless foreplay, techniques that stimulate the brain rather than the body, can also be used and include talking dirty, reading an erotic story together, or sending your partner a intimate text message or e-mail.

Manual Sex

Manual sex (also referred to as a "hand job") refers to the physical caressing of the genitals, and it can be done individually or during **mutual masturbation** (also called partnered masturbation). Generally, people think of manual sex as something that happens before penetrative sex, but it has become more popular over the years as a form of safer sex. This is because during manual sex, there is no exchange of body fluids (we will discuss safer sex later in this chapter).

Men and women in the 25- to 39-year-old age group are most likely to engage in mutual masturbation (Herbenick et al., 2010a). Although the National Health and Social Life Survey (NHSLS) did not collect data on mutual masturbation, the

monogamous relationship	manual sex
A relationship in which a person has only one sexual partner.	The physical caressing of the genitals during solo or partner masturbation.
nonmonogamous relationship	**mutual masturbation**
A relationship in which a person has multiple sexual partners.	Simultaneous masturbation of sexual partners by each other.

Table 10.1 Percentage of Americans Performing Certain Sexual Behaviors in the Past Year Based on the 2010 National Survey of Sexual Health and Behavior (N = 5,865)

	Age Groups									
	14–15		16–17		18–19		20–24		25–29	
Sexual Behaviors	Men	Women	Men	Women	Men	Women	Men	Women	Men	Women
Masturbated Alone	62%	40%	75%	45%	81%	60%	83%	64%	84%	72%
Masturbated with Partner	5%	8%	16%	19%	42%	36%	44%	36%	49%	48%
Received Oral Sex from a Woman	12%	1%	31%	5%	54%	4%	63%	9%	77%	3%
Received Oral Sex from a Man	1%	10%	3%	24%	6%	58%	6%	70%	5%	72%
Gave Oral Sex to a Woman	8%	2%	18%	7%	51%	2%	55%	9%	74%	3%
Gave Oral Sex to a Man	1%	12%	2%	22%	4%	59%	7%	74%	5%	76%
Vaginal Intercourse	9%	11%	30%	30%	53%	62%	63%	80%	86%	87%
Received Penis in Anus	1%	4%	1%	5%	4%	18%	5%	23%	4%	21%
Inserted Penis into Anus	3%		6%		6%		11%		27%	

	Age Groups									
	30–39		40–49		50–59		60–69		70+	
Sexual Behaviors	Men	Women	Men	Women	Men	Women	Men	Women	Men	Women
Masturbated Alone	80%	63%	76%	65%	72%	54%	61%	47%	46%	33%
Masturbated with Partner	45%	43%	38%	35%	28%	18%	17%	13%	13%	5%
Received Oral Sex from a Woman	78%	5%	62%	2%	49%	1%	38%	1%	19%	2%
Received Oral Sex from a Man	6%	59%	6%	52%	8%	34%	3%	25%	2%	8%
Gave Oral Sex to a Woman	69%	4%	57%	3%	44%	1%	34%	1%	24%	2%
Gave Oral Sex to a Man	5%	59%	7%	53%	8%	36%	3%	23%	3%	7%
Vaginal Intercourse	85%	74%	74%	70%	58%	51%	54%	42%	43%	22%
Received Penis in Anus	3%	22%	4%	12%	5%	6%	1%	4%	2%	1%
Inserted Penis into Anus	24%		21%		11%		6%		2%	

National Survey of Sexual Health and Behavior (NSSHB) found that mutual masturbation was less common than solo masturbation (Dodge et al., 2010; Reece et al., 2010d). Among Black men and women, mutual masturbation was much less common than solo masturbation, with 24% of men and 28% of women reporting engaging in this behavior (Dodge et al., 2010). Decreased rates of mutual masturbation were also found in Hispanic men and women, with 41% of men and 34% of women reporting engaging in this behavior.

Manual Sex on Women

Many people may not know exactly what to do with the female genitals. What feels good? Can rubbing hurt? When does a woman like to have her clitoris touched? Where do women like to be touched? People who worry about these questions may become overly cautious or eager in touching a woman's clitoris and vulva.

Because each woman differs in how she likes her clitoris stroked or rubbed, it is important that partners communicate

Caressing and snuggling are common during foreplay.

their preferences. A water-based lubricant, such as Astroglide or K-Y Jelly, can make manual sex more comfortable. The majority of women enjoy a light caressing of the shaft of the clitoris, together with an occasional circling of the clitoris, and maybe digital (finger) penetration of the vagina. Other women dislike direct stimulation and prefer to have the clitoris rolled between the lips of the labia. Some women like to have the entire area of the vulva caressed, whereas others like the caressing to be focused on the clitoris. As a woman gets more aroused, she may breathe more deeply or moan, and her muscles may become tense.

Manual Sex on Men

Many people may not know exactly what to do with the male genitals either. Does rubbing feel good? How do men like to have their genitals stroked? When do men like to have their penis touched? To reach orgasm, many men like to have the penis stimulated with strong and consistent strokes.

However, at the beginning of sexual stimulation, most men like soft, light stroking of the penis and testicles. The testicles can be very responsive to sexual touch, although out of fear of hurting them, oftentimes partners avoid touching them at all. It is true that the testicles can be badly hurt by rough handling, but a light stroking can be pleasurable. Remember, also, that the friction of a dry hand can cause irritation, so hand lotion, baby oil, or a lubricant can be used while manually stimulating the penis. However, if manual stimulation leads to vaginal or anal penetration, any lotion or oil should be washed off, because these products may cause vaginal problems in women and can weaken the strength of latex condoms or diaphragms.

The most sensitive parts of the male penis are the glans and tip, which are very responsive to touch. In fact, some men can masturbate by rubbing only the glans of the penis. For others, stimulation at the base may help bring on orgasm because it mimics deep thrusting. Switching positions, pressures, and techniques often can be frustrating for a man who feels almost at the brink of an orgasm.

All men have their own individual preferences for what feels good during manual sex. However, the most common techniques involve a quick up-and-down motion that is applied without a great deal of pressure. To enhance the effectiveness of this motion, partners should try varying the pressure every once in a while (harder and then softer). At the point of orgasm, firm stroking on the top and sides of the penis can continue but not on the underside. Firm pressure on the underside (the underside is the part of the penis that is "under" when the penis is not erect) of the penis during orgasm can restrict the urethra, which can be uncomfortable during ejaculation.

Oral Sex

Oral sex involves using the lips, tongue, or teeth to stimulate the genitals of a partner. **Cunnilingus** is oral sex performed on a woman, while **fellatio** is oral sex performed on a man. Oral sex has been practiced throughout history. Tenth-century temples in India, 19th-century playing cards, and even ancient Greek and Chinese art all portrayed couples engaging in different types of oral sex (see the nearby photo).

Over the years, however, there have been many taboos associated with oral sex. Although some people do not engage in oral sex because they find it unappealing, for many others it is an important part of their sexual behavior. Some couples use oral sex as a form of foreplay, whereas others engage in oral sex as their main form of sexual behavior. Couples may also engage in **sixty-nine** (Figure 10.12), which can be challenging and may not provide the best stimulation for either of them. **Anilingus** (ain-uh-LING-gus; also called *rimming*), another form of oral sex, involves oral stimulation of the anus.

Oral sex is a common sexual behavior that is typically first experienced sometime during adolescence and becomes increasingly prevalent throughout adulthood (Holway, 2015; see Table 10.1). In recent years, it has become more common among young people than vaginal sex (Brewster & Tillman, 2008). The National Survey of Family Growth found that most adults have engaged in oral sex at some point in their lives, both giving and receiving (86% of women and 87% of men; Copen et al., 2016). However, there are ethnic/racial variations in rates of oral sex. It is more common among Whites (92%) than Blacks (83%) or Hispanics (78%; Copen et al., 2016).

Younger people often engage in more oral sex than older people. While only 7% of women older than 70 years reported giving

cunnilingus	sixty-nine
Oral sex performed on a woman.	Oral sex that is performed simultaneously by two partners.
fellatio	
Oral sex performed on a man.	**anilingus**
	Oral stimulation of the anus.

Depictions of oral sex were not uncommon in ancient Chinese art, such as this woodcut.

FIGURE **10.12** The sixty-nine position.

Some couples view oral sex as less intimate than other sexual behaviors and may not like it for this reason. Because there is little face-to-face contact during cunnilingus or fellatio, it may make partners feel emotionally distant. Others report that engaging in oral sex is one of the most intimate behaviors that a couple can engage in because it requires total trust and vulnerability. Not surprisingly, the majority of people are more interested in receiving oral sex than giving it (Brewster & Tillman, 2008; Laumann et al., 1994).

Cunnilingus

In the United States, women have historically been inundated with negative messages about their vaginas. Many makers of feminine powders, douches, creams, jellies, and other scented items try to persuade women that they need to buy such products to eliminate any vaginal odors. For this reason, some women express concern about the cleanliness of their vaginas during cunnilingus. When their partners try to have oral sex with them, fears and anxieties may prevent them from enjoying it. This, coupled with many women's lack of familiarity with their own genitals, contributes to many women's discomfort with oral sex. In fact, researchers have found that many female college students feel less comfortable receiving oral sex than engaging in vaginal sex (Lefkowitz et al., 2016).

Overall, many heterosexual men and lesbian women find cunnilingus to be erotic (we will discuss oral sex among lesbian women later in this chapter). They report that the taste of the vaginal secretions is arousing to them, and they find the female vulva beautiful and sexy, including its smell and taste. Generally, when we are sexually aroused we are less alert to sensory impressions. This means that when we are aroused, the flavor of the vagina or of semen may be more appealing than it would be if we were not aroused.

Women report that they like oral sex to begin in a slow and gradual way. They dislike an immediate concentration on the clitoris. Before cunnilingus, many women like to be kissed and have their neck and shoulders, breasts, stomach, and finally their vulva

oral sex to a man in the last year, 43% said they had done so at some point in their lives (Herbenick et al., 2010a). Overall, older men and women in better health have more oral sex than those in poor or failing health (Herbenick et al., 2010). Rates of oral sex are also related to education level. Those with a bachelor's degree or higher are more likely to engage in oral sex compared to those who have not finished high school or have a GED (Copen et al., 2016).

ON YOUR MIND

I have heard that you can get genital herpes if your partner performs oral sex on you and has a cold sore on his or her lip. Is this true?

It appears that even though oral herpes (a cold sore) is caused by a different strain of the herpes virus than genital herpes, oral herpes can be passed on during oral sex and lead to a herpes infection on the genitals. It is best to avoid oral sex when either partner has a cold sore. We discuss the herpes simplex virus in more depth in Chapter 15.

REAL RESEARCH Although there is an expectation of reciprocity of oral sex in heterosexual interactions, oral sex performed on a female partner is often viewed as a "bigger deal" than oral sex performed on a male partner (LEWIS & MARSTON, 2016).

massaged. A persistent rhythmic caressing of the tongue on the clitoris will cause many women to reach orgasm. During cunnilingus, some women enjoy a finger being inserted into their vagina or anus for extra stimulation. Because pregnant women have an increased vascularity of the vagina and uterus, care should be taken to never blow air into a woman's vagina during cunnilingus. This can force air into her uterine veins, which can cause a fatal condition known as an air embolism, in which an air bubble travels through the bloodstream and can obstruct the vessel (Hill & Jones, 1993; Sánchez et al., 2008).

Fellatio

The majority of men enjoy oral sex, and many are displeased if their partners do not like to perform fellatio (Blumstein & Schwartz, 1983). Before fellatio, many men enjoy having their partners stroke and kiss various parts of their bodies, gradually getting closer to their penis and testicles. Some men like to have their testicles orally stimulated as well. They may also like to have the head of the penis gently sucked while their partner's hand is slowly moving up and down the shaft. When performing fellatio, partners must be sure to keep their teeth covered with their lips, because exposed teeth can cause pain. Some men like the sensation of being gently scratched with teeth during oral sex, but this must be done very carefully.

Pornographic movies tend to show a sex partner who takes the entire penis into their mouth, but this is often uncomfortable for many people because of the gagging response. It is often helpful to place a hand around the base of the penis while performing fellatio to avoid a gagging response. By placing a hand there, the penis will be kept from entering the back of the mouth, thus reducing the urge to gag. In addition, the hand can be used to provide more stimulation to the penis.

Some partners are concerned about having their partners' ejaculate in their mouths after fellatio. If your partner is free from STIs, swallowing the ejaculate is harmless. Some people enjoy the taste, feel, and idea of tasting and swallowing ejaculate, but others do not. If swallowing is unacceptable, another option may be to spit out the ejaculate after orgasm or not allow your partner to ejaculate in your mouth.

How much semen a man ejaculates often depends on how long it has been since his last ejaculation. If a long period has gone by, generally the ejaculate will be larger. An average ejaculation is approximately 1 to 2 teaspoons; consists mainly of fructose, enzymes, and different vitamins; and contains approximately 5 calories. The taste of the ejaculate can vary, depending on a man's use of drugs or alcohol, stress level, and diet (Tarkovsky, 2006). Coffee and alcohol can cause the semen to have a bitter taste, whereas fruits (pineapple in particular) can result in sweet-tasting semen. Men who eat lots of red meat often have very acid-tasting semen. The taste of semen also varies from day to day.

Some people dislike performing fellatio. There have been some ethnic differences found as well. For example, in Gail Wyatt's study of Black female sexuality, more than 50% of the hundreds of women in her sample had never engaged in fellatio and had no

ON YOUR MIND

Do women like their partners to kiss them right after they have performed cunnilingus on them?

desire to do so (Wyatt, 1998). If you dislike performing fellatio on your partner, try talking about it. Find out if there are things that you can do differently (using your hands more) or that your partner can vary (ejaculating outside of your mouth).

Some women do; some do not. For some women, sharing a kiss after cunnilingus can be very erotic and sensual. However, other women feel uncomfortable with the taste of their own genitals. It would be best to ask your partner to see what her individual pleasure is.

Vaginal Intercourse

Vaginal intercourse (also referred to as sexual intercourse) involves inserting the penis into the vagina. The National Survey of Family Growth found that 94% of women and 92% of men reported engaging in vaginal intercourse (Copen et al., 2016), and most heterosexual couples engage in vaginal intercourse almost every time they have sex (Sanders & Reinisch, 1999).

Heterosexual Americans fall into three groups: those who engage in vaginal intercourse at least twice a week (one third of Americans), those who engage in it a few times a month (another one third), and those who engage in it a few times a year or have no sexual partners (Laumann et al., 1994). Vaginal intercourse is the most prevalent sexual behavior among heterosexuals of all ages and ethnicities (Herbenick et al., 2010a). Like other partnered sexual behaviors, people in better health were more likely to report engaging in this behavior. As they age, the frequency of vaginal intercourse decreases. In fact, 18- to 29-year-olds engage in vaginal intercourse 112 times per year on average, whereas 30- to 39-year-olds engage in it 86 times per year on average, and 40- to 49-year-olds engage in it 69 times per year on average (Piccinino & Mosher, 1998; see Figure 10.13 for more information about the frequency of sexual intercourse by age group).

Couples use a variety of techniques and positions in their lovemaking.

We discussed the sexual response cycle earlier in this chapter, and how, during arousal, the vagina becomes lubricated, making penetration easier and providing more pleasure for both partners. It is important for couples to delay vaginal penetration until after lubrication has begun. Penetrating a dry vagina, forcefully or not, can be very uncomfortable for both partners. If the woman is aroused but more lubrication is needed, a water-based lubricant can be used.

During vaginal intercourse, many women like a slower pace for penetration and thrusting. It can be intimate and erotic to make love very slowly, circling the hips, varying pressure and sensations, while maintaining eye contact. Unfortunately, pornography has helped reinforce the idea that women want thrusting to be fast and rough during intercourse. Porn often showcases hard and fast thrusting with women begging for more (we discuss pornography in more detail in Chapter 18). Both nonverbal and verbal communication can help ensure that both partners are happy with the timing and pace of intercourse.

ON YOUR MIND

Do men want their partners to swallow the ejaculate after their orgasms?

Some men do; some don't care. Men who like their partners to swallow after fellatio say that it increases the stimulation, leading to a better orgasm. Others say that swallowing shows their partner is totally into them (they believe that spitting the ejaculate is a rejection). Some men differentiated between casual and long-term partners and believe that partners should "swallow when dining, but spit when sampling." It's important to remember that communication is key here. Partners should talk about their desires and decide what would work best for them.

more than 13 minutes was "too long." "Adequate" vaginal intercourse lasts 3 to 7 minutes, and "desirable" intercourse lasts 7 to 13 minutes (Corty & Guardiani, 2008). If intercourse lasts too long the vagina may become dry, causing pain and discomfort.

Most couples close their eyes during vaginal intercourse (Schnarch, 1997). Maintaining eye contact can intensify intimacy but can be difficult for many couples. To increase the intensity during vaginal intercourse, try keeping your eyes open (it's not as easy as you might think).

REAL RESEARCH

Close to 50% of female college students reported experiencing negative emotions after sex, including tearfulness, anxiety, agitation, and/or sadness (Schweitzer et al., 2015). Researchers referred to this as "post-sex blues" and concluded that such feelings were probably triggered by hormonal shifts that occur after orgasm rather than sexual dissatisfaction.

Although many men try to delay ejaculation until their partners are satisfied with the length of thrusting, longer thrusting does not always ensure female orgasm. Sex therapists report that heterosexual intercourse typically lasts anywhere from 3 to 13 minutes (Corty & Guardiani, 2008). Intercourse that lasts only 1 to 2 minutes was viewed as "too short," whereas intercourse that lasts

Positions for Vaginal Intercourse

According to the *Complete Manual of Sexual Positions* (J. Stewart, 1990), there are 116 vaginal entry positions, and in *The New Joy of Sex* (Comfort & Rubenstein, 1992), 112 positions are illustrated. Of course, we don't have enough room to describe all of these positions, so we will limit this discussion to the four main positions for vaginal intercourse: male-on-top, female-on-top, rear entry, and side by side. There are advantages and disadvantages to each of these positions, and couples must choose the sexual positions that are best for them. Keep in mind that although we are discussing positions for heterosexual vaginal intercourse here, many gay and lesbian couples use similar positions (with or without dildos) in their sexual activity.

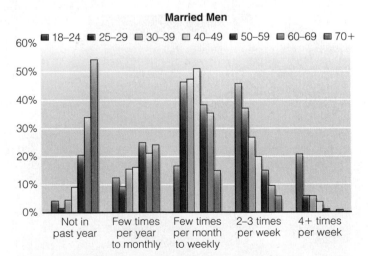

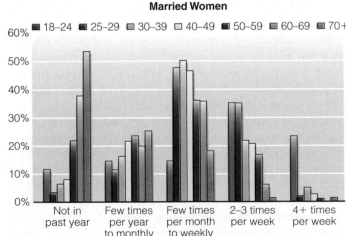

FIGURE **10.13** Frequency of vaginal intercourse by age for married men and women in the United States based on findings from the 2010 National Survey of Sexual Health and Behavior.

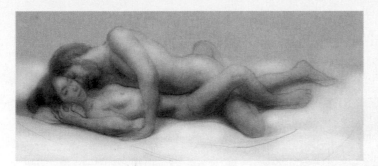

FIGURE **10.14** The male-on-top position.

MALE-ON-TOP   The male-on-top (also called the "missionary" or "male superior") position is one of the most common positions for vaginal intercourse. In this position, the woman lies on her back and spreads her legs, often bending her knees to make penetration easier. The man positions himself on top of the woman, between her legs (Figure 10.14). Because his full weight might be uncomfortable for the woman, he should support himself on his arms or elbows and knees.

The male-on-top position allows the male to control the thrusting and permits deep penetration for the man during intercourse. It enables the partners to look at each other, kiss, and hug during vaginal intercourse. The woman can move her legs up around her partner or even put them on his shoulders. She can also use a pillow under her hips to increase clitoral stimulation. For some couples, this position is the most comfortable because the male is more active than the female. This position may also be the most effective for procreation, because the penis can be thrust deep into the vagina, which allows the semen to be deposited as deeply as possible; furthermore, because the woman is lying on her back, the semen does not leak out as easily.

However, there are also some disadvantages to the male-on-top position. If either partner is overweight, or if the female is in the advanced stages of pregnancy, this position can be very uncomfortable. Also, the deep penetration that is possible in this position may be uncomfortable for the woman, especially if her partner has a large penis, which can bump the cervix. This position also makes it difficult to provide clitoral stimulation for the female and may prevent the woman from moving her hips or controlling the strength or frequency of thrusting. Finally, in the male-on-top position, it may be difficult for the man to support his weight, because his arms and knees may get tired.

FEMALE-ON-TOP   In the female-on-top position (also called "female superior"), the man lies on his back while his partner positions herself above him (Figure 10.15). She can either put her knees on either side of him or lie between his legs. By leaning forward, she has greater control over the angle and degree of thrusting and can get more clitoral stimulation. Other variations of this position include the woman sitting astride the man facing his feet or the woman sitting on top of her partner while he sits in a chair.

In the female-on-top position, the female can control clitoral stimulation either by manual stimulation or through friction on her partner's body. She can also control the depth and rhythm of thrusting. Her partner's hands are also free so that he can caress her body

FIGURE **10.15** The female-on-top position.

during sexual intercourse. Because this position is face-to-face, the partners are able to see each other, kiss, and have eye contact.

Sex therapists often recommend this position for couples who are experiencing difficulties with early ejaculation or a lack of orgasms, because the female-on-top position can extend the length of erection for men and facilitates female orgasm. It also doesn't require a man to support his weight. For women who are in the advanced stages of pregnancy, the female-on-top position may be a very good position.

There are, however, some drawbacks to the female-on-top position. This position puts the primary responsibility on the female, and some women may not feel comfortable taking an active role in vaginal intercourse. Some men may feel uncomfortable having their partners be on top and may not receive enough penile stimulation in this position to maintain an erection.

SIDE BY SIDE   The side-by-side position takes the primary responsibility off both partners and allows them to relax during vaginal intercourse. In this position, the partners lie on their sides, and the woman lifts one leg to facilitate penile penetration (Figure 10.16). This is a good position for couples who want to take

FIGURE **10.16** The side-by-side position.

Sexual Diversity
IN OUR WORLD

Meet Me in the Love Hotel

A "love hotel" is a short-stay hotel room that is commonly found in many Asian countries, such as Japan, Hong Kong, or South Korea. Typically rooms are rented for several hours (a "rest") or for the night (a "stay"). Reservations are not accepted; a "rest" typically costs anywhere from 3,000 to 7,000 yen ($30–$70), whereas a "stay" costs approximately 10,000 yen ($100). It is estimated that 1.4 million couples visit a love hotel every day in Japan (Chaplin, 2007). I had the opportunity to explore love hotels on my recent trip to Shibuya, a district of Tokyo, Japan.

Because Japanese homes and apartments are very small and often have paper-thin walls, they offer little privacy to couples wanting to have sex. Many Japanese couples say they have a hard time getting "in the mood" in their traditional homes (Keasler, 2006). A love hotel offers couples privacy, and the sexual décor can often help increase sexual interest and desire. Entrances to love hotels are discreet, and there is limited contact with hotel staff. Rooms are selected from an electronic display board posted in the entranceway—if the room is lit up, it is available. Payment is often automated or done through pneumatic tubes, but some hotels offer small windows through which payment can be made discreetly without exposing a customer's face. Identification

© Janell Carroll

is not required, and there are no age limits to enter a love hotel. Some love hotels offer specific themes, such as samurai, jungle, pirate, S&M, or even cartoon character themes ("Hello Kitty" is popular).

The rooms in most love hotels are small; in fact, they are usually a little bigger than a queen-sized bed. Many rooms come with various amenities, including large flat screen televisions with DVD players, slot or karaoke machines, video consoles, refrigerators, or microwaves. The room I saw even had a costume rental option offering maid, nurse, stewardess, schoolgirl, or cheerleader costumes (I found it interesting there were only costumes for women). There was also a large electric vibrator attached to the head of the bed, with a sign that said "disinfected." Many rooms also have vending machines that offer a full line of skin care and sex-related products (condoms, lubricants, and sex toys). Couples often talk for a while, play games, have sex, and take a bath (love hotel bathrooms are often fully stocked—mine even offered peppermint bath crystals; Keasler, 2006).

Starting in 2008, Japan began to consider laws that would regulate these hotels. One main issue revolves around collecting personal information from customers. Although Japanese inns and hotels are required to collect personal information from guests, including name and address, love hotels are not (Shimanaka, 2008). As you could probably guess, many love hotel guests are reluctant to share such information. Lawmakers are also trying to reduce the amount of sexual content both outside and within the love hotels, in an attempt to improve the overall concept of the hotels. Interestingly, many Japanese believe that American motels are like Japanese love hotels—illustrating how commonly we believe our cultural traditions and values are shared (Keasler, 2006).

---

it slow and extend vaginal intercourse. Both partners have their hands free and can caress each other's bodies. In addition, they can see each other, kiss, and talk during intercourse.

Disadvantages include the fact that sometimes couples in this position have difficulties with penetration. It can also be difficult to get a momentum going, and even more difficult to achieve deep penetration. Women may also have a difficult time maintaining contact with the male's pubic bone during intercourse, which often increases the chances of orgasm.

REAR ENTRY There are many variations to the rear-entry position of vaginal intercourse. Intercourse can be fast or slow depending on the variation chosen. One variation involves a woman on her hands and knees (often referred to as "doggie style") (Figure 10.17), while her partner is on his knees behind her. The female can also be lying on her stomach with a pillow under her hips while the male enters her from behind. Another variation is to use the side-by-side position, in which the male lies behind his partner and introduces his penis from behind.

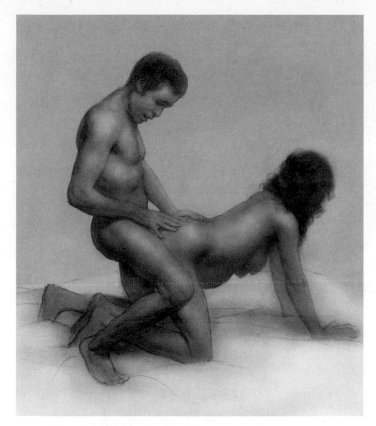

FIGURE **10.17** The rear-entry position.

The rear-entry positions provide an opportunity for clitoral stimulation, either by the male or the female. It may also provide direct stimulation of the G-spot. The rear-entry position also can be good for women who are in the later stages of pregnancy or who are overweight.

Anal Intercourse

During anal intercourse, either a man's penis enters his partner's anus (Figure 10.18) or a strap-on dildo is used. There are many nerve endings in the anus, and it is frequently involved in sexual response, even if it is not directly stimulated. Some people experience orgasm during anal intercourse, especially with simultaneous penile or clitoral stimulation (Maynard et al., 2009). The landmark University of Chicago study found that only 1 in 10 heterosexual couples had engaged in anal sex (Laumann et al., 1994); however, more recent studies have found that anal sex is increasing in heterosexuals (O'Leary et al., 2017).

Although fewer women report engaging in anal intercourse than other partnered sexual behaviors, the National Survey of

anal sphincter
A ringlike muscle that surrounds the anus; it usually relaxes during normal physiological functioning.

FIGURE **10.18** Anal intercourse.

Family Growth found that 36% of women and 42% of men had engaged in anal sex (Copen et al., 2016). Some differences were found with educational levels—those with a bachelor's degree or higher are more likely to have engaged in anal sex compared to those who have not finished high school or have a GED (Copen et al., 2016).

Because the anus is not capable of producing lubrication and the tissue is so fragile, it is important that additional water-based lubricants be used. An oil-based lubricant (such as Vaseline) may cause problems later because the body cannot easily get rid of it, and it can damage latex condoms. Without lubrication, there may be pain, discomfort, and possibly tearing of the tissue in the anus. It's also important to use a condom with sex toys, which we will discuss more later in this chapter.

During anal intercourse, the **anal sphincter** muscle must be relaxed or intercourse can

ON YOUR MIND

My girlfriend told me that my penis is too large for her vagina and that it causes her pain during intercourse. How far can the vagina expand?

Although it is true that the vagina expands and lengthens during sexual arousal, not every vagina expands to the same degree. If a man's penis is very large, it can bump against the woman's cervix during thrusting, which can cause discomfort. In such cases it is particularly important to make sure the woman is fully aroused before attempting penetration and to try a variety of positions to find which is most comfortable for her. The female-superior position or the rear-entry position may help her control the depth of penetration. Either partner's hand around the base of the penis (depending on the position) may also prevent full penetration, as will some devices such as "cock rings," which are sold through adult catalogs or in adult stores. If the woman's pain continues, she should consult with her gynecologist to rule out a physiological problem and to get more advice and information.

be painful. If a couple decides to engage in anal intercourse, it is important to take it slowly. Unless partners are absolutely sure that both are free of STIs and HIV-negative, a condom is a must. Anal intercourse is one of the riskiest of all sexual behaviors and has been implicated in the transmission of HIV. Research has shown that the risk for contracting HIV through unprotected anal intercourse is greater than the risk for contracting HIV through unprotected vaginal intercourse (Mumba, 2010; Silverman & Gross, 1997; we discuss this further in Chapter 15).

In addition, any couple who decides to engage in anal intercourse should never transfer the penis from the anus to the vagina or mouth without changing the condom or washing the penis (dildos should also be washed with antibacterial soap). The bacteria in the anus can cause vaginal infections in women.

Same-Sex Sexual Behaviors

The National Survey of Family Growth found that 17.4% of women and 6.2% of men reported engaging in same-sex behavior in their lifetimes (Copen et al., 2016). Although the percentage of men engaging in same-sex behavior didn't vary by ethnic/racial groups, there were differences among women. Hispanic women (11.2%) were less likely than White women (20%) or Black women (19%) to have engaged in same-sex behavior (Copen et al., 2016). A comparison of data from the 2006–2010 and 2011–2013 NSFG found higher percentages of women and men who identified as bisexual and a lower percentage of women who identified as lesbian or gay (Copen et al., 2016).

There are many similarities in the sexual behaviors of heterosexuals, lesbians, and gays. Lesbian and gay couples report engaging in sexual behavior to increase emotional and physical intimacy, feel accepted and supported, and increase the positive view of self (Cohen et al., 2008). In the following sections we discuss sexual behaviors in same-sex couples.

Gay Men

Gay men use a variety of sexual techniques, including hugging, kissing, oral sex, mutual masturbation, and anal intercourse (see Figure 10.19). Overall, gay and bisexual men engage in oral sex more often than heterosexual or lesbian couples. This is not surprising, given the fact that research has shown that, overall, men are more likely than women to have received oral sex (Brewster & Tillman, 2008). Gay couples who engage in frequent oral sex report higher levels of sexual satisfaction (Blumstein & Schwartz, 1983).

Studies have found that between 4% and 8% of men have performed oral sex on another man in the previous year and among men in the 40- to 59-year-old age group 10% had (Herbenick et al., 2010a). However, 14% of 40- to 49-year-old men and 15% of 50- to

FIGURE **10.19** Gay men use a variety of sexual techniques in their lovemaking.

59-year-old men have received oral sex from a man in their lifetimes. Rates of oral sex among Black and Hispanic men are lower than rates of oral sex with other sex partners—7% of Black men and 11% to 13% of Hispanic men said they had given or received oral sex from a man (Dodge et al., 2010).

Although many gay men report engaging in anal intercourse, not all gay men do. The NHSLS study found that although the majority of gay men reported engaging in anal intercourse, 20% of gay men did not (Laumann et al., 1994.).). Some gay couples (and other couples, too) engage in **fisting** (also called "hand-balling"), which involves the insertion of the fist and even part of the forearm into the anus or vagina. The use of rubber gloves during fisting can decrease the risk of STIs and has become more common since the early 2000s (Richters et al., 2003).

Like many other couples, gay men enjoy hugging, kissing, and body caressing; **interfemoral** (in-ter-fem-OR-ull) **intercourse** (thrusting the penis between the thighs of a partner); and **buttockry** (BUT-ock-ree; rubbing of the penis in the cleft of the buttocks).

Gay male sexual behavior changed significantly in the 1980s after the arrival of AIDS. Undoubtedly because of the massive education efforts initiated in the gay community, in the early 1990s, safe sex practices increased (at least in the major cities) among gay men (Catania et al., 1989). However, researchers believe that STI increases among sexually active gay men since the mid-2000s are due to a decreased fear of acquiring HIV, an increase in high-risk sexual behaviors (e.g., oral sex without a condom), a lack of knowledge about diseases, and increased Internet access to sexual partners (Hughes, 2006; Zablotska et al., 2012).

fisting
Sexual technique that involves inserting the fist and even part of the forearm into the anus or vagina.

interfemoral intercourse
Thrusting the penis between the thighs of a partner.

buttockry
Rubbing of the penis in the cleft of the buttocks.

Lesbians

Lesbians enjoy a wide range of sexual behaviors, including kissing, hugging, body rubbing, manual stimulation, oral sex, and the use of sex toys such as dildos or vibrators. Manual stimulation of the genitals is the most common sexual practice among lesbians, although they tend to use a variety of techniques in their lovemaking. Two-women couples have been found to kiss more than heterosexual couples, and two-men couples kiss least of all.

After manual stimulation, the next most common practice is cunnilingus, which many lesbian and bisexual women report is their favorite sexual activity. In fact, Blumstein and Schwartz's classic study (1983) found that like gay men, the more oral sex a lesbian couple had, the higher their levels of sexual satisfaction. Lesbian women often have fewer worries about their vaginas than heterosexual women. As one woman said, "Gay women are very much into each other's genitals. . . . Not only accepting, but truly appreciative of women's genitals and bodies. . . . Lesbians are really into women's bodies, all parts" (Blumstein & Schwartz, 1983, p. 238). Rates of oral sex are highest among 18- to 24 year old lesbian women (Herbenick et al., 2010a). Among Black and Hispanic women, rates of oral sex with same-sex partners are lower than rates of oral sex with other-sex partners—between 12% and 13% of Black women and 10% and 12% of Hispanic women said they had given or received oral sex from a woman (Dodge et al., 2010).

Another common practice is **tribadism** (TRY-bad-iz-um), also called *scissoring,* in which the women rub their vulvas together (Figure 10.20). Some lesbians engage in fisting and also may use dildos or vibrators, often accompanied by manual or oral stimulation.

Although it is rather dated, a nonscientific survey was conducted of more than 100 members of a lesbian social organization in Colorado (Munson, 1987). When asked what sexual techniques they had used in their last 10 lovemaking sessions, 100% reported kissing, sucking on breasts, and manual stimulation of the clitoris; more than 90% reported French kissing, oral sex, and fingers inserted into the vagina; and 80% reported scissoring. Lesbians in their 30s

Some couples use sex toys, such as vibrators or dildos, to enhance their sex lives. Strap-on dildos may also be used by both partners.

were twice as likely as other age groups to engage in anal stimulation (with a finger or dildo). Approximately one third of women used vibrators, and there were a small number who reported using a variety of other sex toys, such as dildo harnesses, leather restraints, and handcuffs. Sexual play and orgasm are important aspects of lesbian sexuality (Bolso, 2005; Tomassilli et al., 2009).

Lesbian women also report frequently thinking about sex and the use of sexual fantasy. One woman said:

> I think about sex during the day, staring at my computer screen, while I'm supposed to be writing. Sometimes I call Dana up at work, she picks up the phone, I say, "I'll meet you at home in fifteen minutes, and I'm going to rip off your clothes and throw you down on the couch, and I'm going to eat your pussy. That's what I'm having for lunch." (S. E. Johnson, 1996, p. i)

There has been some preliminary research done on the existence of **lesbian erotic role identification** (or the roles of "butch" [masculine] and "femme" [feminine] in lesbian relationships). Some scholars believe that such roles are simply social contracts, whereas others believe they are natural expressions of lesbian sexuality (D. Singh et al., 1999; Vidaurri et al., 1999). One study examined physiological and behavioral differences of women in these self-identified roles and found that "butch" lesbians had higher saliva testosterone levels (D. Singh et al., 1999). However, just like heterosexual and gay couples, there is no "typical" lesbian couple. Some lesbian couples may engage in role identification, but many others do not.

Overall, lesbians have been found to be more sexually responsive, more satisfied with their sexual relationships, and to have lower rates of sexual problems than heterosexual women (Henderson et al., 2009; Kurdek, 2008). Some studies have suggested that the frequency of sexual contact among lesbians declines dramatically in their long-term, committed relationships

FIGURE **10.20** Lesbians have been found to be more sexually responsive and more satisfied in their sexual relationships than heterosexual women.

tribadism
A form of non-penetrative sex that involves a woman rubbing her vulva against her partner's vulva.

lesbian erotic role identification
The roles of "butch" and "femme" in lesbian relationships.

(Blumstein & Schwartz, 1983; Cohen & Byers, 2013; Nichols, 1990; Rosmalen-Noojjens et al., 2008). By the beginning of the 1990s, the decreasing sexual interest among lesbian women had become well established and was referred to as "lesbian bed death" (Nichols, 2004). Although decreased sexual behavior in lesbian couples has been a controversial topic, it's possible that genital sexual activity is not important to overall sexual satisfaction among lesbian couples (Cohen & Byers, 2013).

Review Questions

1 Explain why manual sex can be a form of safer sex.

2 Describe the differences that have been found in how men and women view oral sex.

3 Identify any gender differences that have been found in the experience of sexual intercourse.

4 Identify various positions for sexual intercourse. Name some advantages and disadvantages of each.

5 Identify the risks of engaging in anal sex.

6 Compare and contrast lesbian and gay sexual behavior.

Sexual Behavior Later in Life

Today, older men and women are healthier and more active than previous generations. Although the prevalence of sexual activity often declines with age (73% among those 57–64 years old to 53% among those 65–74 years old; Lindau et al., 2007), many older individuals remain interested in sexuality and engage in several sexual behaviors (see Figure 10.21). The NSSHB found that 20% to 30% of men and women remain sexually active well into their 80s (Schick et al., 2010).

Continued sexual activity in older adults has been found to improve both physical and emotional health in older adults. Sexual activity involves stretching of the muscles and tendons, flexing of the joints, and hormone fluctuations, which have been found to improve cardiovascular health (Frappier et al., 2013; Levin, 2007; Liu et al., 2016). In addition, sexual intimacy provides both emotional and social support, reducing stress. Let's explore the physical changes of aging and their effect on sexual behavior (we discuss more of the challenges of aging and health concerns in Chapter 14).

Physical Changes

As we age, there are inevitable changes to our physical health, some of which can affect normal sexual functioning (Table 10.2). Changes in sexual functioning are exacerbated by sexual inactivity. In fact, research clearly indicates that older adults who stay sexually active throughout their aging years have a greater potential for a more satisfying sex life later in life (Dimah & Dimah, 2004; Lindau & Gavrilova, 2010). Better knowledge of these changes would help older adults anticipate changes in their sexual activity.

Changes in Sexual Behavior

Frequent complaints among older adult women are decreases in sexual desire and pain during vaginal intercourse (Lindau et al., 2007; Schick et al., 2010). Older men are more likely to report problems with erectile functioning, and many turn to erectile drugs to enhance sexual functioning. It's estimated that about 14% of older men use medications to improve erectile functioning (Lindau et al., 2007).

The majority of older men and women report continued masturbation (63% of men and 47% of women; Schick et al., 2010).

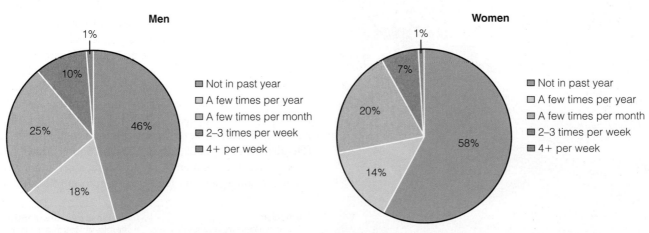

FIGURE **10.21** Percentage of men and women 50 to 80 years old who reported engaging in vaginal intercourse within the past year.

SOURCE: National Survey of Sexual Health and Behavior, 2010.

Table 10.2 Physical Changes in Older Men and Women

In men:
- Delayed and less firm erection
- More direct stimulation needed for erection
- Extended refractory period (12–24 hours before rearousal can occur)
- Reduced elevation of the testicles
- Reduced vasocongestive response to the testicles and scrotum
- Fewer expulsive contractions during orgasm
- Less forceful expulsion of seminal fluid and a reduced volume of ejaculate
- Rapid loss of erection after ejaculation
- Ability to maintain an erection for a longer period
- Less ejaculatory urgency
- Decrease in size and firmness of the testes, changes in testicle elevation, less sex flush, and decreased swelling and erection of the nipples

In women:
- Reduced or increased sexual interest
- Possible painful intercourse because of menopausal changes
- Decreased volume of vaginal lubrication
- Decreased expansive ability of the vagina
- Possible pain during orgasm because of less flexibility
- Thinning of the vaginal walls
- Shortening of vaginal width and length
- Decreased sex flush, reduced increase in breast volume, and longer postorgasmic nipple erection

FIGURE **10.22** The majority of older adults maintain an interest in sex and sexual activity.

Masturbation may fulfill a variety of needs. If older adults find that their partners are no longer interested in sexual activity, masturbation often becomes an important outlet. This can also be an important activity for older people who have lost their sexual partners, because it offers a sexual release that may help decrease depression, hostility, or frustration. Studies have found that many widowed individuals experience "sexual bereavement" and mourn the loss of sexual intimacy after their partner dies (Radosh & Sinkin, 2016).

Many older couples continue to engage in vaginal intercourse (67% of men and 68% of women; Schick et al., 2010). Research on older gay men has found that they continue to be sexually active; however, they tend to engage in less anal intercourse than younger gay men (Van de Ven et al., 1997). Physical problems, such as arthritis, diabetes, and osteoporosis, can interfere with sexual functioning. We discuss many other physical problems, such as illness, surgery, and injuries that can affect sexual functioning, in Chapter 14.

The stereotype that sex worsens with age is not inevitably true. Many older adults are very interested in maintaining an active sex life (Schick et al., 2010; Thomas et al., 2014). A key to sexual enjoyment later in life is for partners to be patient and understanding with each other. Physical fitness, good nutrition, adequate rest and sleep, a reduction in alcohol intake, and positive self-esteem can all enhance sexuality throughout the life span.

Review Questions

1 Identify the most frequent sexual complaints among older men and women.

2 Identify and explain some of the physiological changes that occur with aging.

3 Explain how the physical changes of aging might affect the sexual response cycle.

Safer Sex Behaviors

The term **safe sex** was coined in 1983, two years after the start of the AIDS epidemic. It referred to sexual behaviors that reduce the risk of acquiring a sexually transmitted infection. We know that the only 100% effective way to avoid becoming infected with a sexually transmitted infection is abstaining from sex altogether.

Although there are few safe sex behaviors, engaging in **safer sex** reduces the chances of contracting an STI (see accompanying "Sex in Real Life"). All sexually active people should be aware of

safe sex
Sexual behaviors that do not pose a risk for the transmission of sexually transmitted infections.

safer sex
Sexual behaviors that reduce the risk of acquiring sexually transmitted infections.

Sex in Real Life   Safer Sex Behavior Guidelines

Following are some sexual behaviors that are rated for safety. Remember that engaging in non-committed sexual relationships, such as hooking up, and alcohol use are two activities that can increase your risk for acquiring a sexually transmitted infection. Typically, unsafe behaviors involve contact with semen, blood, or other body fluids. Those behaviors that are considered safe include activities that involve no exchange of bodily fluids. Sex toys, including dildos, vibrators, strap-ons, and butt plugs, should be thoroughly washed after use (and when used on different body parts) since they can be made of porous materials that can retain bacteria. They should also be used with condoms, which should be changed when used by different partners.

Remember that many people might not know whether or not they are infected with a sexually transmitted infection (STI) or might not be honest about their status.

Contact your local health clinic or Planned Parenthood organization for more information.

Safe

- Sexual behaviors with a partner who has no STIs

- Massage
- Hugging
- Kissing without sharing saliva
- Body rubbing, dry humping
- Sexual fantasy
- Masturbation; mutual masturbation
- Watching porn or erotica
- Online or cybersex
- Sex toys (provided they are clean and condoms are used if toys are shared)
- Taking a bath together

Possibly Safe

- French kissing
- Vaginal intercourse with condom
- Anal intercourse with condom
- Cunnilingus with dental dam
- Fellatio with condom
- Anal rimming or anilingus with dental dam

- Vaginal or anal stimulation with fingers using latex glove

Possibly Unsafe

- Cunnilingus without a dental dam
- Vaginal or anal stimulation with fingers without latex glove
- Fellatio without a condom
- Sharing sex toys without cleaning or changing condoms in between uses
- Anal rimming or anilingus without a dental dam

Unsafe

- Anal intercourse without condom
- Vaginal intercourse without condom
- Blood contact
- Cunnilingus without a dental dam during menstruation

SOURCE: Adapted from "Safer Sex" (2017).

the risks associated with various sexual behaviors. Overall, safer sex practices involve communicating with your partner about their sexual history, avoiding unprotected vaginal and anal intercourse and other risky activities, using condoms, and reducing the number of sexual partners. People are more likely to engage in high-risk sexual behaviors when they have a high propensity for sexual excitation and low propensity for sexual inhibition (Bancroft et al., 2009; see the prior section on the Dual Control Model of Sexual Response).

Communication is key to safer sex relationships (see Chapter 3 for more information on the importance of communication). It is important for couples to talk about each other's past sexual relationships before engaging in sexual activity. Such openness will result not only in safer sex but also healthier relationships.

Although condom use has become more commonplace over the last few years, behavior that has been clearly linked to sexual risk-taking is alcohol and drug use, which can impair judgment. Alcohol use is one of the most important factors repeatedly linked to engaging in risky sexual behaviors (Hipwell et al., 2012; Newcomb, 2013). In one study, 75% of college students had made decisions about sexual activity that they later regretted while under the influence of alcohol (Poulson et al., 1998). Alcohol use is common during non-committed sex, such as hooking up (Lewis et al., 2012; Olmstead et al., 2013). Although many students say they are worried about the possibility of acquiring an STI during hookups, condom use is inconsistent (Owen et al., 2011; Uecker & Regnerus, 2010).

Throughout this chapter you have learned that human sexuality is shaped by a multitude of factors, including cultural, ethnic, religious, psychological, and biological. All of these factors influence our attitudes about sexuality and our decisions to engage in certain sexual behaviors.

Review Questions

1 Define "safe sex" and differentiate it from "safer sex."

2 Give some guidelines for safer sex behaviors.

3 Explain how alcohol use is linked to sexual risk-taking.

Chapter Review

1 Our hormones have a powerful effect on our bodies. The endocrine glands secrete hormones into the bloodstream. The most influential hormones in sexual behavior are estrogen and testosterone. In most animals, the brain controls and regulates sexual behavior chiefly through hormones, although in humans, learned experiences and social, cultural, and ethnic influences are also important. Hormone levels decrease as we age, and this can cause a variety of physical changes, such as vaginal dryness and decreased vaginal sensitivity in women, and slower and less frequent erections in men.

2 We internalize norms about sexual attitudes and behaviors from our families. Our ethnic/racial groups also affect the types of sexual behaviors we engage in, our sexual attitudes, and our ability to communicate about sexuality. Differences have been found between Blacks, Hispanics, Whites, and Asian Americans. Religiosity also influences sexual behavior. The more religious people are, the more conservative their sexual behavior tends to be.

3 A series of physiological and psychological changes occur during sexual behavior. Masters and Johnson's sexual response cycle involves four physiological phases, including excitement, plateau, orgasm, and resolution. During these phases, there are changes in both vasocongestion and myotonia. In men, there is a refractory period during resolution, and generally the stages are less well defined. In women, the menstrual cycle may affect the sexual response cycle.

4 Kaplan's model of sexual response has three stages: desire, excitement, and orgasm. It is easier to recognize when a person is going through Kaplan's stages. Reed's Erotic Stimulus Pathway (ESP) model encompasses features of both Kaplan's and Masters and Johnson's models. Phases include seduction, sensation, surrender, and reflection. Tiefer argues that these models are all based on the medical model, and because of this, they leave out important aspects of sexual functioning.

5 The Dual Control Model of Sexual Response, developed by the Kinsey Institute, views sexual response as a neurobiological two-part process involving both sexual excitation and inhibition. A person's ability to become sexually aroused involves an interaction between sexual excitation and inhibition.

6 Solitary sexual behaviors can include sexual fantasy and masturbation, although both of these can be used during partnered sex as well. Sexual fantasies are erotic thoughts about sex that can create or enhance sexual arousal. Although some people want to act out sexual fantasies, many have no desire to engage in the behaviors they fantasize about. Both men and women use sexual fantasy to heighten sexual arousal. Many factors can influence the content of sexual fantasies, including gender, age, sexual orientation, religious views, and culture.

7 Health experts have had a major role in shaping public opinion about masturbation. Masturbation has been viewed as a strategy to improve sexual health, reduce stress and unwanted pregnancy, and avoid STIs. Masturbation is common throughout the life span for both men and women.

8 People engage in sexual behavior for many reasons—to reproduce, experience sexual pleasure, and/or reduce stress. But there are many other motives for engaging in sexual behavior, such as love, social status, revenge, duty, curiosity, or even for exercise. Non-committed sexual interactions, or hookups, have increased on college campuses and can occur between friends, acquaintances, and strangers. Sexual behaviors during a hookup range from kissing to sexual intercourse.

9 The majority of individuals in long-term relationships say their sex lives are still as passionate as they were in the beginning of their relationships. Couples who engaged in more frequent sex, received more oral sex, reached orgasm more consistently, and had more variety in their sex lives had higher levels of sexual satisfaction.

10 The majority of heterosexuals define foreplay as "anything that happens before penetration" or something a man does to get a woman in the mood. It often includes behaviors such as erotic massage, deep tongue kissing, dry humping, and oral sex. Touchless foreplay, techniques that stimulate the brain rather than the body, can also be used.

11 Manual sex refers to the physical caressing of the genitals, and it can be done individually or during mutual masturbation. No exchange of bodily fluids occurs. Men and women both have concerns about how best to stimulate their partners manually.

12 Oral sex involves using the lips, tongue, or teeth to stimulate the genitals. Cunnilingus refers to oral sex performed on a woman, while fellatio refers to oral sex performed on a man. Oral sex typically is first experienced sometime during adolescence and becomes increasingly prevalent throughout adulthood. Rates of oral sex are related to both age and education level.

13 The majority of heterosexual couples engage in sexual intercourse almost every time they have sex, and when most people think of sex, they assume it includes sexual intercourse. It is important to delay intercourse until after a woman's vaginal lubrication has begun. If a woman needs more lubrication, a water-based lubricant can be used.

14 There are a variety of positions for sexual intercourse. The male-on-top position is one of the most common positions. This position allows the male to control the thrusting and permits deep penetration during intercourse. The female-on-top and rear-entry positions both allow for increased clitoral stimulation.

15 Anal intercourse involves penile penetration of the anus. The anus is frequently involved in sexual response, even if it is not directly stimulated. Some men and women experience orgasm during anal intercourse, especially with simultaneous penile or clitoral stimulation. After anal intercourse, the penis should never be transferred from the anus to the vagina because of the risk for infection.

16 Hispanic women are less likely than White or Black women to have engaged in same-sex behavior. The 2011–2013 NSFG found higher percentages of women and men who identified as bisexual and a lower percentage of women who identified as gay or lesbian. There are more similarities than differences between same-sex and other-sex sexual behavior. Overall, lesbians tend to be more sexually satisfied than heterosexual women and have lower rates of sexual problems. Both same- and other-sex couples engage in anal sex, and some experience orgasm during anal sex.

17 The majority of elderly persons maintain an interest in sex and sexual activity, even though society often views them as asexual. There are inevitable changes to our physical health as we age, some of which can affect normal sexual functioning. A lack of education about the physiological effects of aging on sexual functioning may cause elderly adults to think their sex lives are over when a sexual problem is experienced. Older women frequently complain about decreases in sexual desire and pain during vaginal intercourse, while older men complain about problems with erectile functioning.

18 The term *safe sex* was coined in 1983 and refers to sexual behaviors that reduce the risk of acquiring a sexually transmitted infection. The only 100% effective way to avoid becoming infected with an STI is abstaining from sex altogether. All sexually active people should be aware of the risks associated with various sexual behaviors. Safer sex practices involve communicating about sexual history, avoiding unprotected vaginal and anal intercourse and other risky activities, using condoms, and reducing the number of sexual partners. Alcohol use is one of the most important factors repeatedly linked to engaging in risky sexual behaviors. Although many students worried about STIs, condom use is inconsistent during casual sex and hookups.

Critical Thinking Questions

1 Why do you think so many people are hesitant to talk about sexual pleasure? There is no doubt that you talk about sex with friends, but why has it become so taboo and so difficult to talk about what brings you sexual pleasure?

2 Do you think your ethnicity affects your sexuality? In what ways? Why do you think this is?

3 Suppose that your sexual partner shares with you that they have been engaging in sexual fantasies during sexual activity with you. How would this make you feel? Would you be comfortable hearing about these fantasies and sharing your own with your partner? Why or why not?

4 Susan has been masturbating regularly since age 15, although she feels very guilty about it because she has always been taught it's wrong and sinful. Recently she started engaging in partnered sex but is unable to reach orgasm with her partner. After reading this chapter, explain to Susan what you've learned about masturbation, and offer her some advice.

5 Think about what your life might look like in 30 years. What type of relationship do you imagine yourself in? What do you hope your sex life will be? What factors might contribute to any problems you might experience?

6 Suppose you are in a new relationship and have just begun engaging in sexual activity. How can you communicate your desires to keep the sex safe? What problems might come up in this discussion?

Websites

Electronic Journal of Human Sexuality This online publication of the Institute for Advanced Study of Human Sexuality in San Francisco disseminates information about all aspects of human sexuality. The site offers a database of research articles, book reviews, and posters from various conference presentations.

San Francisco Sex Information Organization San Francisco Sex Information (SFSI) is a free information and referral switchboard that provides anonymous, accurate, nonjudgmental information about sex. If you have a question about sex, they will answer it or refer you to someone who can.

Healthy Sex HealthySex.com is an educational site, designed by Wendy Maltz, to promote healthy sexuality based on caring, respect, and safety. The site contains information on sexual health, intimacy, communication, sexual abuse and addiction, sexual fantasies, and midlife sex, and it links to a variety of sexuality sites.

Go Ask Alice! Go Ask Alice! is a question-and-answer format website produced by Columbia University's Health Education Program. It provides factual, in-depth, straightforward, and nonjudgmental information to improve sexual health. You can visit recently asked questions or search the database.

11 | Sexual Orientation

In 2001, the Netherlands became the first country in the world to legalize same-sex marriage. Legal marriage provided same-sex couples with all the rights and benefits associated with heterosexual marriage. Prior to this legalization, couples lived together in registered partnerships that had limited benefits. One Dutch couple I met, Peter and Stephan, had been together for 22 years when they wed in 2001. They had been together for so long that they had recently ordered new rings (the original ones they got when they first committed to each other had worn out). Their wedding was a big event, and they invited friends and family from around the world to celebrate their marriage. I spoke with them about how they met, why they married, and same-sex relationships in the Netherlands.

Peter remembered the first time he saw Stephan, at a party when he was 20 years old. It was definitely love at first sight, but he was sure that Stephan was out of his league. At the same time, Stephan was looking for a guy with the same ideas about life and was excited to find these qualities in Peter. Thinking back, they remembered how in the mid-1990s, the Netherlands became more accepting of same-sex relationships but how excited they were to marry in 2001 when same-sex marriage was legalized. They had worried about what would happen if they got sick because they had a friend who wasn't allowed to be with her partner when she was dying in the hospital. They married in 2001 and although it hasn't been easy, Peter told me that when he thought back to the hard times in his life, he was still happy to be gay. In fact, he said, if he were ever born again, he'd wish to be gay all over again! Talking to Peter and Stephan was interesting, funny, and at times heartbreaking. They helped me understand the depth of love, respect, and commitment inherent in many same-sex relationships.

Janell Carroll

Sexual orientation refers to an emotional, physical, sexual, and romantic attraction to persons of the same, other, or both sexes. Heterosexuals are predominantly attracted to members of the other sex; homosexuals to members of the same sex (the word *gay* is often used to refer to a male homosexual, whereas *lesbian* is often used to refer to a female homosexual); and bisexuals are attracted to both sexes.

Although such distinctions may seem simple, human sexual behavior does not always fit easily into such neat boxes. Today, many people use the acronym **LGBTQ** to refer to people who identify as lesbian, gay, bisexual, transgender, or questioning (or queer). Because we discussed transgender issues in Chapter 4 and we focus on lesbian, gay, bisexual issues in this discussion, we will predominantly use the acronym LGB throughout this chapter.

Before the 1980s, most of published research on homosexuality focused on causes or on associated mental disorders (because homosexuality was classified as such until 1973; see Chapter 1), whereas in the 1990s, HIV and AIDS dominated the research studies (Boehmer, 2002). Today, we are learning more about the development of lesbian, gay, and bisexual identities, coming-out issues, aging, and health care, to name a few areas. We discuss this research throughout this chapter.

What Determines Sexual Orientation?

How should we categorize a person's **sexual orientation**? The simplest way to categorize a person's sexual orientation seems to be through sexual behavior; that is, with whom does the person have sex? However, there are many other factors to consider. What about a person's sexual fantasies? If a man sometimes fantasizes about sex with men, even though he considers himself **straight** and has sex only with women, what is his sexual orientation?

> **REAL RESEARCH** Although sexual orientation is a perceptually ambiguous category, we often use indirect cues such as gait, speech, and facial features to determine whether a person is gay or lesbian. First impressions about a person's sexual orientation are so powerful that they can override what we learn about people later (STERN ET AL., 2013).

Perhaps we should consider romantic love instead of sex to determine a person's sexual orientation. Whom does the person love, or whom could the person love? If a married man has sex with men but loves his wife romantically and would never consider an emotional attachment to the men he has sex with, would you consider him **heterosexual** because he loves only his wife? Maybe we should just let people decide for themselves; if they believe they are heterosexual or homosexual, they are, no matter how they behave. Yet when people's behavior and beliefs about themselves are in conflict, social scientists usually define them by their behavior.

Courtesy Janell Carroll

Same-sex marriage is now legal in the entire United States after a Supreme Court ruling in 2015 struck down state marriage bans.

The problem may be that we tend to think of sexual orientation in discrete categories: People are either **homosexual** or heterosexual (or, occasionally, **bisexual**). The full variety and richness of human sexual experience, however, cannot be easily captured in such restrictive categories. People can show enormous variety in their sexual behavior, sexual fantasies, emotional attachments, and sexual self-concept, and each contributes to a person's sexual orientation. Various other terms have been used to provide more clarification about sexual orientation, including **androsexual, asexual, gynesexual, pansexual**, and **skoliosexual**.

In this chapter, we explore the nature of sexual orientation and the ways researchers and scholars think about it. Heterosexuality is a sexual orientation, and the question "Why is a person heterosexual?" is no less valid than "Why is a person homosexual?" or "Why is a person bisexual?" Let's explore the research and writing about homosexuality and bisexuality.

LGBTQ
Acronym for lesbian, gay, bisexual, transgendered, or questioning (or queer) adults or youth.

sexual orientation
The gender(s) that a person is attracted to emotionally, physically, sexually, and romantically.

straight
Slang term for heterosexual.

heterosexual
People who are erotically attracted to members of the other sex.

homosexual
People who are erotically attracted to members of the same sex.

bisexual
People who are erotically attracted to members of either sex (may also be referred to as pansexual).

androsexual
Being primarily emotionally, physically, sexually, and/or romantically attracted to some men, males, and/or masculinity.

asexual
A person who experiences little or no sexual attraction to others and/or a lack of interest in sexual relationships/behavior. Some researchers have proposed that asexuality is a sexual orientation.

gynesexual
Being primarily emotionally, physically, sexually, and/or romantically attracted to some women, females, and/or femininity.

pansexual
A person who experiences emotional, physical, sexual, and/or romantic attraction for members of all gender identities/expressions.

skoliosexual
Being primarily emotionally, physically, sexually, and/or romantically attracted to some genderqueer, transgender, and non-binary people.

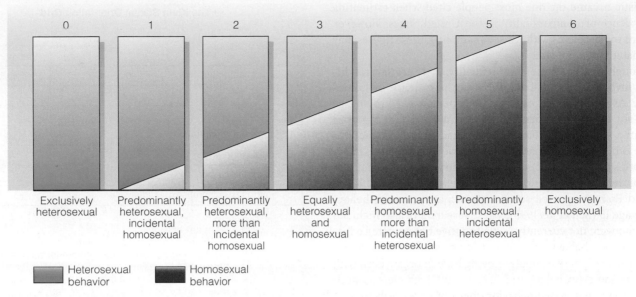

FIGURE **11.1** The Kinsey continuum. The seven-point scale is based on behaviors ranging from exclusively heterosexual behavior to exclusively homosexual behavior.

SOURCE: From Kinsey, A., Pomeroy, W. B., & Martin, C. E. (1948). Sexual Behavior in the Human Male. Philadelphia, PA: Saunders. The Kinsey Institute for Research in Sex, Gender, and Reproduction, Inc.

Models of Sexual Orientation: Who Is Homosexual?

Kinsey and his colleagues (1948) believed that relying on the categories "homosexual" and "heterosexual" to describe sexual orientation was inadequate. They also suggested that using a category such as "homosexual" was not as helpful as talking about homosexual behavior. Trying to decide who is homosexual is difficult; trying to compare amounts or types of homosexual behavior (including fantasies and emotions) is easier.

So Kinsey introduced a seven-point scale ranging from exclusively heterosexual behavior (0) to exclusively homosexual behavior (6; see Figure 11.1). The Kinsey continuum was the first scale to suggest that people engage in complex sexual behaviors that cannot be reduced simply to "homosexual" and "heterosexual." Many theorists agree that sexual orientation is a continuous variable rather than a categorical variable; that is, there are no natural cutoff points that would easily separate people into categories such as "heterosexual" or "homosexual" (Berkey et al., 1990; L. Ellis et al., 1987).

Although Kinsey's hypothesis that sexual orientation lies on a continuum has been supported by research (Drucker, 2012; Epstein et al., 2012), the Kinsey scale is not without its problems. First, Kinsey primarily emphasized people's behavior, but some researchers suggest that people's emotions and fantasies are the most important determinants of sexual orientation (Bell et al., 1981; F. Klein, 1993; Storms, 1980, 1981). Second, the Kinsey scale is static in time; how recently must one have had same-sex contact to qualify for "incidents" of homosexual behavior? If a man had sex with six men over the last year but had sex with his wife once a week, is he in category 5 (because he had sex with 6 men and

only 1 woman) or category 2 (because he had 52 experiences with a woman, but only 6 with men; F. Klein, 1990)?

Other models, such as the Klein Sexual Orientation Grid (KSOG), try to take the Kinsey continuum further by including seven dimensions—attraction, behavior, fantasy, emotional preference, social preference, self-identification, and lifestyle (Klein et al., 1985; see Figure 11.2). Since this model proposes that sexual orientation identity is fluid over time, each of these dimensions is measured for the past, the present, and the ideal. Take the KSOG to create a profile of your sexual orientation.

ON YOUR MIND

If I played sex games with a friend of the same sex when I was 15, am I gay?

Sexual experimentation and sexual orientation are two different things. It is very common, especially in the teenage years and before, to experiment with same-sex contact (and for people who are predominantly lesbian or gay to experiment with the other sex). Yet only a fairly small percentage of people who experiment are lesbian, gay, or bisexual (FAY ET AL., 1989).

Measuring Sexual Orientation: How Prevalent?

How prevalent are homosexuality, heterosexuality, and bisexuality in society? Kinsey and his colleagues (1948) found that 37% of men and 13% of women reported that they had had at least one adult sexual experience with a member of the same sex that resulted in orgasm, and that about 4% of men and 3% of women were lifelong homosexuals. He also reported that 10% of White men had been mostly gay for at least 3 years between the ages of 16 and 55, and this statistic became the one most people cited when estimating the prevalence of homosexuality in the United States. However, because of the problems with Kinsey's sampling, these figures may be unreliable (see Chapter 2).

Although we can define homosexuality, there are several difficulties involved in measuring the exact prevalence of homosexuality. As we discussed earlier, does a person need to engage in same-sex behavior to identify as LGB? What if they fantasize about same-sex behavior but have only had sexual interactions with the other sex? One national population-based study measured both same-sex attraction and behavior and found that 16% to 20% of the adult population of the United States, United Kingdom, and France reported some same-sex attraction or behavior since age 15 (Sell et al., 1995). These researchers also included people who were not currently sexually active but reported a history of same-sex behavior in the past (many studies often do not count nonsexually active people as being lesbian or gay, even with a history of same-sex behavior; Sell et al., 1995). Numerous studies have shown that sexual behavior does not necessarily predict self-identified sexual orientation (Copen et al., 2016; Hill et al., 2016; Pathela et al., 2006).

Although there is much work to be done in determining the prevalence of homosexuality, the most recent National Health Interview Survey (an annual survey done by the Centers for Disease Control and Prevention) found that 1.6% of respondents identified as gay or lesbian, while 0.8% identified as bisexual (National Center for Health Statistics, 2015). Overall, we know that from 2012 to 2016 there was an increase in the number of Americans that identified as LGBT (from 3.5%, or 8.25 million, in 2012, to 4.1%, or 10 million, in 2016; Gates, 2017).

The Klein Sexual Orientation Grid

	Past	Present	Ideal
A. Sexual attraction			
B. Sexual behavior			
C. Sexual fantasies			
D. Emotional preference			
E. Social preference			
F. Self-identification			
G. Heterosexual/homosexual lifestyle			

0 = other sex only
1 = mostly other sex, incidental same sex
2 = mostly other sex, more than incidental same sex
3 = both sexes equally
4 = mostly same sex, more than incidental other sex
5 = mostly same sex, incidental other sex
6 = same sex only

FIGURE **11.2** The Klein Sexual Orientation Grid (KSOG) was designed to examine seven dimensions of an individual's sexual orientation to determine whether these dimensions have changed over time and to look at a person's fantasy of his or her "ideal" sexual orientation. The KSOG gives a set of numbers that can be compared to determine rates of different sexual orientations.

SOURCE: From Klein, F. (1990). The need to view sexual orientation as a multivariable dynamic process: A theoretical perspective. In D. P. McWhirter, S. A. Sanders, & J. M. Reinisch (Eds.), Homosexuality/heterosexuality: Concepts of sexual orientation (p. 280). New York, NY: Oxford University Press. The Kinsey Institute for Research in Sex, Gender, and Reproduction, Inc.

Review Questions

1 Describe the difficulties involved in our attempts to categorize sexual behavior.

2 Outline the Kinsey model of sexual orientation, and compare and contrast it with the KSOG.

3 Describe the research on the prevalence of LGB orientations. Explain why this research is difficult and may be controversial.

Why Are There Different Sexual Orientations?

In the 1930s and 1940s, a group of scientists tried to explain homosexuality by looking for "masculine" traits in lesbians and "feminine" traits in homosexual men. They claimed that gay men had broad shoulders and narrow hips (indicating "immature skeletal development"), and lesbians had abnormal genitalia, including larger-than-average vulvas, longer labia minora, a larger glans on the clitoris, a smaller uterus, and higher eroticism, shown by their tendency to become sexually aroused when being examined (Terry, 1990)! Modern research has failed to find any significant physiological differences between homosexuals and heterosexuals, although attempts to examine physical differences continue.

Today's theories can be divided into five basic types: biological, developmental, behavioral, sociological, and interactional theories. Biological theories suggest that homosexuals are physically different from heterosexuals. Developmental theories, in contrast, suggest that homosexuality develops in response to a person's upbringing and personal history, and therefore nothing is physically different between the two. Behavioral theory explores how homosexuality is a learned behavior, whereas sociological theories look at how social forces produce homosexuality in a society. Finally, interactional theories look at the interaction between biology, development, and societal factors.

Scholars in different fields tend to take different approaches to explain why some people are lesbian, gay, or bisexual. Note, however, that almost all the researchers we will discuss assume there are two exclusive, nonoverlapping categories: homosexual and heterosexual. Most theories on sexual orientation ignore bisexuality or do not offer enough research to explain why bisexuality exists. We discuss bisexuality throughout this chapter.

Biological Theories

Early biological theories implied that homosexuality was an abnormality in development, which contributed to the argument that homosexuality was a sickness. More recently, lesbian and gay scholars, in an attempt to prove that homosexuality is not a "lifestyle choice" as antihomosexual forces have argued, have themselves been arguing that homosexuality is a biologically based sexual variation. Biological theories claim that differing sexual orientations are due to differences in physiology. These differences can be due to genetics, hormones, birth order, or physiology.

Genetics

In 1952, Franz Kallman, a German-born psychiatrist, tried to show that there was a genetic component to homosexuality. Kallman compared identical twins (who come from one zygote and have the same genes) with fraternal twins (who come from two zygotes; we talk more about twins in Chapter 12). Although Kallman found a strong genetic component to homosexuality, his study had a number of problems and was unreliable.

Bailey and his colleagues have performed a number of studies of twins to determine the genetic basis of homosexuality. They reported 52% of identical twin brothers of gay men were also gay compared to 22% of fraternal twins (J. M. Bailey & Pillard, 1995). In genetically unrelated brothers (those who were adopted) the rate was 11%, showing that the more closely genetically related two siblings were, the higher the likelihood that if one is gay, the other will also be gay. Among females, 48% of identical twins, 16% of fraternal twins, and 6% of adoptive siblings of lesbians were found to also be lesbians (J. M. Bailey et al., 1995). However, identical twins share much more than genetics. They also share many more experiences than do other kinds of siblings. So the studies cannot tell how much of the concordance is due to genetic factors and how much is due to the identical twins having grown up under similar environmental influences. More recent research on twins has found DNA differences that may contribute to the genetic expression of homosexuality (Ngun et al., 2015). Using data gleaned from 57 pairs of twins, researchers developed an algorithm that could successfully predict sexual orientation with 70% accuracy in men. It is likely this will continue to be an important area of research in the future.

Some studies have found that sexual orientation is familial (runs in the family; Francis, 2008; Schwartz et al., 2010). Hamer and colleagues (1993) found that gay males tended to have more gay relatives on their mother's side, and he traced that to the existence of a gene that he found in 33 of 40 gay brothers. This gene is inherited from the mother's, but not the father's, side (Keller, 2005). Studies have also found that lesbians have more lesbian relatives (Bogaert, 2005; Pattatucci, 1998). Other studies support the familial link but have found that male sexual orientation is inherited from the father's, and not the mother's, side (Schwartz et al., 2010). In this study, gay men were found to have more homosexual male relatives than heterosexual men, and sisters of gay men were more likely to be lesbians than sisters of heterosexual men (Schwartz et al., 2010).

From an evolutionary perspective, if homosexuality were solely a genetic trait, it should have disappeared long ago. Because homosexuals have been less likely than heterosexuals to have children, each successive generation of homosexuals should have become smaller, until genes for homosexuality disappeared from the gene pool. However, since homosexual men tend to come from larger families, their female relatives also carry the genes that may predispose their offspring to homosexuality (Chaladze, 2016).

Concordance rates for siblings, twins, and adoptees reveal that genes account for at least half of the variance in sexual orientation (Pillard & Bailey, 1998). Even so, Bailey and his colleagues agree that environmental factors are also important.

ON YOUR MIND

Why are men often turned on by watching two females having sex but turned off by watching two males?

Heterosexual men's magazines often feature two women together in sexual positions but almost never two men. In the United States, watching women interact sexually is much more socially acceptable. These pictorials always imply that the women are still attracted to men, waiting for them, just biding their time until a man arrives. An internalized fear of homosexuality in men also makes it difficult for many men to see two men being sexual with each other. It is much less threatening to watch two women. In Chapter 18, we discuss gender and the use of pornography.

Hormones

Hormonal theories about homosexuality can concentrate either on hormonal imbalances before birth or on hormone levels in adults. In this section, we examine both prenatal and adult hormonal levels.

PRENATAL FACTORS When certain hormones are injected into pregnant animals, such as rats or guinea pigs, at critical periods of fetal development, the offspring can be made to exhibit homosexual behavior (Dorner, 1983; for more information about hormones, see Chapter 4). Some researchers have found evidence that sexual orientation may be influenced by levels of prenatal hormones in human beings as well (Cohen-Bendahan et al., 2005; Jenkins, 2010; Skorska & Bogaert, 2016). Hormonal levels can be affected by stress during pregnancy, and research has explored how this stress can influence the sexual orientation of a fetus (L. Ellis, 1988; Hall & Schaeff, 2008).

Although many of the hormonal studies have focused on deficiencies in certain hormones, there is also research indicating that excess hormonal exposure during prenatal development may be related to sexual orientation. For example, females who were exposed to diethylstilbestrol (DES; synthetic estrogen) in the womb are more likely to identify as bisexual or lesbian compared with those females not exposed to DES (Meyer-Bahlburg et al., 1985).

Overall, the evidence for the effect of prenatal hormones on both male and female homosexuality is weak (Gooren, 2006; Hall

& Schaeff, 2008). In other words, even if prenatal hormones are a factor in sexual orientation, environmental factors may be equally important. The one area of research in prenatal hormones that has yielded the most interesting research has been on finger lengths, which we will discuss in the upcoming physiology section.

ADULT HORMONE LEVELS Many studies have compared blood androgen levels in adult male homosexuals with those in adult male heterosexuals, and most have found no significant differences (Green, 1988; Mbügua, 2006). Of five studies comparing hormone levels in lesbians and straight women, three found no differences between the two groups in testosterone, estrogen, or other hormones, and the other two found higher levels of testosterone in lesbians (and one found lower levels of estrogen; Dancey, 1990). However, a more recent study did find that lesbian and bisexual women had higher overall testosterone and progesterone levels than heterosexual women, while no hormonal differences were found among gay, bisexual, and heterosexual men (Juster et al., 2016).

Birth Order

Studies have found that in families with multiple brothers, later born brothers from the same mother are more likely to be gay (Blanchard, 2004; Bogaert & Skorska, 2011; Breedlove, 2017). Each older brother increases a man's chance of being gay by about 33%. This is often explained by the **maternal immune hypothesis**, which proposes there is a progressive immunization to male-specific antigens after the birth of successive sons in some mothers, which increases the effects of anti-male antibodies on the sexual differentiation of the brain in the developing fetus (this has also been referred to as the *fraternal birth order effect;* Bogaert & Skorska, 2011; Valenzuela, 2010).

Although most of the research on birth order has been done on men, limited research on women has found that having an older brother or any sisters decreases the likelihood of homosexuality in women (Francis, 2008). This research is controversial, but nonetheless research in this direction continues to look for possible interactions.

Physiology

Two articles in the early 1990s reported differences between the brains of homosexual and heterosexual men (S. LeVay, 1991; Swaab & Hofman, 1990). Both studies found that certain areas of the hypothalamus, known to play a strong role in

maternal immune hypothesis
Theory of sexual orientation that proposes that the fraternal birth order effect of gay brothers reflects the progressive immunization of some mothers to male-specific antigens by each succeeding male fetus.

sexual motivation, were either larger or smaller in gay men than in straight men. More recent studies have also found brain differences—specifically in the cerebral hemispheres—between heterosexual and homosexual subjects (Hu et al., 2008; Ponseti et al., 2006, 2009; Savic & Lindström, 2008). Homosexual men's brains were similar to heterosexual women's, while heterosexual men's brains were similar to homosexual women's. Other brain research has found that gay men use both sides of their brain, a pattern similar to heterosexual women (Brewster et al., 2010). However, it has not yet been determined whether brain differences were there from birth or developed later in life, and the research cannot prove that the differences were primarily due to sexual orientation.

Physiological studies have also looked at differences between heterosexuals and homosexuals for a variety of factors, such as the amount of facial hair, size of external genitalia, ear structure, hair whorls (a cowlick in the back of a hair part), hearing, body and facial shape, eye-blink startle responses, and spatial ability (Bailey & Hurd, 2005; Beaton & Mellor, 2007; Hall & Schaeff, 2008; McFadden, 2011; Valentova et al., 2014). Various findings have come out of this research. For example, studies on spatial ability have found similarities in the spatial learning and memory abilities of gay men and heterosexual women, which differ from heterosexual men (Rahman & Koerting, 2008). Studies on handedness have found that gay men are more likely than straight men to be left-handed (Blanchard, 2008; Schwartz et al., 2010), while other studies have found that gay men have more masculine facial structures, with wider jaws and smaller noses, than heterosexual men (Valentova et al., 2014).

However, the area with the most physiological research is finger length. Some experts suggest that the ratio of the index and ring fingers is affected by prenatal exposure to testosterone, especially in the right hand (McFadden et al., 2005; Rizwan et al., 2007; Schwartz et al., 2010). The typical male-type finger pattern is a longer ring finger than index finger, whereas the typical female-type pattern is similar index and ring finger lengths, or a longer index finger. Lesbian women are more commonly found to have a typical male-type finger length pattern, whereas gay men are more likely to have a typical female-type finger length pattern (Galis et al., 2010; Grimbos et al., 2010; Hall & Schaeff, 2008). These studies indicate that male-type finger length patterns in lesbians indicate more prenatal exposure to testosterone, while female-type finger length patterns in gay men indicate less prenatal exposure to testosterone (Rizwan et al., 2007).

In summary, although there have been some physiological differences found among homosexuals, heterosexuals, and bisexuals, the findings are inconsistent, and in many cases, the evidence is weak. Given the complexity of physiological factors, it is impossible to make accurate individual predications because of the randomness of neural connections during development (Pillard, 1998). Because of this, it appears that sexual orientation is the result of an interaction of genetic, physiological, and social influences (Schüklenk et al., 1997). We now examine some of the developmental, behaviorist, sociological, and interactional theories of sexual orientation.

Developmental Theories

Developmental theories focus on a person's upbringing and personal history to find the origins of homosexuality. First, we discuss the most influential development theory, psychoanalytic theory; then we examine gender-role nonconformity and peer group interaction theories of homosexuality.

Freud and the Psychoanalytic School

Sigmund Freud (1953) seemed to be of two minds about homosexuality. On the one hand, he believed that the infant was "polymorphous perverse"—that is, the infant sees all kinds of things as potentially sexual. Because both males and females are potentially attractive to the infant, thought Freud, all of us are inherently bisexual.

On the other hand, Freud saw male heterosexuality as the result of normal maturation and male homosexuality as the result of an unresolved Oedipal complex (see Chapter 2 for a more complete discussion of this topic). An intense attachment to the mother coupled with a distant father could lead the boy to fear revenge by the father through castration. Female genitalia, lacking a penis, could then represent this castration and evoke fear throughout his life. After puberty, the child might shift from desire for the mother to identification with her and begin to look for the love objects she would look for—men.

Like Freud's view of female sexuality in general, his theories on lesbianism were less coherent: he basically argued that the young girl becomes angry when she discovers she lacks a penis and blames her mother (we discussed the Electra complex in Chapter 2). Unable to have her father, she defensively rejects him and all men, and minimizes her anger at her mother by eliminating the competition between them for male affection.

Freud viewed homosexuality as partly narcissistic; by making love to a body like one's own, one is really making love to a mirror of oneself. Freud's generally tolerant attitude toward homosexuality was rejected by some later psychoanalysts, especially Sandor Rado (1949). Rado claimed that humans were not innately bisexual and that homosexuality was a mental illness. This view (not Freud's) became standard for the psychiatric profession until at least the 1970s.

Another influential researcher who followed Rado's perspective was Irving Bieber. Bieber and colleagues (1962) studied 106 homosexual men and 100 heterosexual men who were in psychoanalysis. He claimed that all boys had a normal, erotic attraction to women. However, some had overly close and possessive mothers who were also overintimate and sexually seductive. Their fathers, in contrast, were hostile or absent, and this drove the boy to the arms of his mother, who inhibited his normal masculine development. Bieber thus blamed homosexuality on a seductive mother who puts the fear of heterosexuality in her son. However, Bieber's participants were all in psychoanalysis and thus might have had other issues. Also, fewer than two thirds of the homosexual participants fit his model, and almost a third of heterosexual participants came from the same type of family and yet did not engage in homosexual behavior.

> **REAL RESEARCH** Studies on physical development have found that although there are no differences in the height of lesbian and heterosexual women, gay men are shorter, on average, than heterosexual men (SKORSKA & BOGAERT, 2016). Researchers believe these differences may be due to variations in exposure to prenatal hormones.

The psychoanalytic views of homosexuality dominated for many years. Evelyn Hooker, a clinical psychologist, was a pioneer in gay studies who tried to combat the psychoanalytic view that homosexuality was an illness (see Chapter 2). Hooker (1957) used psychological tests, personal histories, and psychological evaluations to show that homosexuals were as well-adjusted as heterosexuals, and that no real evidence existed that homosexuality was a psychological disorder. Although it took many years for her ideas to take hold, many modern psychoanalysts eventually shifted away from the pathological view of homosexuality. Lewes (1988) demonstrated that psychoanalytic theory itself could easily portray homosexuality as a result of healthy development, and that previous psychoanalytic interpretations of homosexuality were based more on prejudice than on science.

Gender-Role Nonconformity

One group of studies that has begun to fuel debate about the role of early childhood in the development of homosexuality is **gender-role nonconformity** research. The studies are based on the observation that boys who exhibit cross-gender traits—that is, who behave in ways more characteristic of girls of that

> **ON YOUR MIND**
>
> *Is homosexuality found only in humans, or do some animals also exhibit homosexual behavior?*
>
> Same-sex activity has been found in 450 species of birds and mammals, although some scientists believe this number may be as high as 1,500 (BAGEMIHL, 1999; MOSKOWITZ, 2008). In the summer months, killer whales spend one tenth of their time engaging in same-sex activity (MACKAY, 2000). Many mammal species, from rats to lions to cows to monkeys, exhibit same-sex mounting behavior. Males mount other males, and females mount other females (although they rarely do it when a male is present). In some penguin species, males have been found to form lifelong same-sex partnerships (BAGEMIHL, 1999). Bonobo chimpanzees have been found to engage in all types of sexual behaviors, including same- and other-sex behaviors (WAAL, 1995). Even so, no one has reliably reported on cases in which individual animals display exclusively same-sex behavior; animal bisexuality is more common (BAGEMIHL, 1999).

> **gender-role nonconformity**
> Theory that looks at the role of early childhood in the development of homosexuality and explores cross-gendered traits in childhood.

age—are more likely to grow up to be gay, whereas girls who behave in typically masculine ways are more likely to grow up to be lesbian. As children, gay men, on average, have been found to be more feminine than straight men, whereas lesbians have been found to be more masculine (Bailey & Pillard, 1995; Calzo et al., 2014; Pillard, 1991; Rieger et al., 2016; Steensma et al., 2013). In childhood, both gays and lesbians recall more gender-atypical behavior than heterosexual individuals and similar findings have been found in different cultural groups (Lippa & Tan, 2001). Remember, though, that these findings are correlational, meaning that cross-gender traits and later homosexuality appear to be related but do not have a cause-and-effect relationship.

ON YOUR MIND

Is there any therapy that can change a person's sexual orientation?

Some people believe that sexual orientation is determined by social and environmental factors, and that homosexuals can change their sexual orientation through therapy or religious faith. Since the early 1980s, the ex-gay movement (persons who once identified as gay or lesbian but now identify as straight) has claimed that homosexuals can be changed into heterosexuals through **reparative** (rep-PEAR-at-tiv) **therapy** (also known as sexual reorientation or conversion therapy). These types of therapies are based on the premise that homosexuality is an illness that needs to be cured. LGB individuals who have actual or expected negative family reactions to their sexual orientation and are highly religious are significantly more likely to participate in reparative or sexual reorientation therapy (MACCIO, 2010).

These therapies are not supported by any reliable research, and the majority of professional organizations are opposed to the use of such therapies (BYNE, 2016; CIANCIOTTO & CAHILL, 2006; CRAMER ET AL., 2008; KANTOR, 2015). In 2009, after an extensive review of the literature in this area, the American Psychiatric Association (APA) reported that the research failed to show any changes in sexual orientation. As a result, the APA passed a resolution to stop advising clients about such therapies (MUNSEY, 2009). Several states have specific bans against conversion therapy for minors, including California, Illinois, New Jersey, New Mexico, Oregon, Vermont, and the District of Columbia. Several additional states have pending legislation to ban it as well.

Overall, cross-gender boys are viewed more negatively than cross-gender girls in U.S. society (Sandnabba & Ahlberg, 1999). In addition, cross-gender boys are more often thought to be gay than cross-gender girls are thought to be lesbian. R. Green (1987) did a prospective study by comparing 66 pervasively feminine boys with 56 conventionally masculine boys as they matured. Green

---

reparative therapy
Therapy to change sexual orientation; also called sexual reorientation or conversion therapy.

---

calls the feminine boys "sissy-boys," an unfortunate term. However, he found that these boys cross-dressed, were interested in female clothing, played with dolls, avoided rough play, wished to be girls, and did not desire to be like their fathers from a young age. Three fourths of them grew up to be homosexual or bisexual, whereas only one of the masculine boys became bisexual. The "sissy-boys," however, also tended to be harassed, rejected, and ignored more by their peers, and they had higher rates of physical and psychological disorders (Zucker, 1990).

One cannot tell from these types of studies whether these boys are physiologically or developmentally different, or whether society's reaction to their unconventional play encouraged them to develop a particular sexual orientation. Whether right or wrong, gender-role nonconformity theory cannot be the sole explanation of homosexuality, because not all effeminate boys grow up to be gay, and not all "tomboy" girls grow up to be lesbians.

Peer Group Interaction

Storms (1981) suggests a purely developmental theory of homosexuality. Noting that a person's sex drive begins to develop in adolescence, Storms suggests that those who develop early begin to become sexually aroused before they have significant contact with the other sex. Because dating usually begins around age 15, boys who mature at age 12 still play and interact in predominantly same-sex groupings, and thus their emerging erotic feelings are more likely to focus on boys.

Storms's theory is supported by the fact that homosexuals do tend to report earlier sexual contacts than heterosexuals. Also, men's sex drive may emerge at a younger age than women's, if such things as frequency of masturbation are any measure, which may explain why there are fewer lesbians than gay men.

Yet Storms's theory also has its problems. Later in this chapter, we will discuss the example of Sambian boys who live communally and have sex with other boys from an early age until they are ready to marry. If Storms is right and a male becomes homosexual because only males are available at the time of sexual awakening, then all male Sambians should be gay. However, almost all go on to lead heterosexual lives.

Behavioral Theories

Behaviorists consider homosexuality a learned behavior, brought about by the reinforcement of homosexual behaviors or the punishing of heterosexual behavior (Masters & Johnson, 1979). For example, a person may have a same-sex encounter that is pleasurable, coupled with an encounter with the other sex that is frightening; in their fantasies, that person may focus on the same-sex encounter, reinforcing its pleasure with masturbation. Masters and Johnson (1979) believed that even in adulthood, some people move toward same-sex behaviors if they have bad heterosexual encounters and pleasant same-sex ones.

It is interesting to point out, however, that in a society like ours that tends to view heterosexuality as the norm, it would seem that ongoing discrimination and prejudice would discourage homosexual behavior. Yet homosexuality exists even without positive reinforcement from society.

Sociological Theories

Sociological theories look at how social forces produce homosexuality in a society. They suggest that concepts such as homosexuality, bisexuality, and heterosexuality are products of our social fabric and are dependent on how we as a society decide to define things. In other words, we learn our culture's way of thinking about sexuality, and then we apply it to ourselves.

The idea of "homosexuality" is a product of a particular culture at a particular time; the idea did not even exist before the 19th century (although the behavior did). Some have argued that the use of the term *homosexuality* as a way to think about same-sex behavior arose only after the Industrial Revolution freed people economically from the family unit and urbanization allowed them to choose new lifestyles in the cities (Adam, 1987). Thus, the idea that people are either "heterosexual" or "homosexual" is not a biological fact but simply a way of thinking that evolves as social conditions change. In many other countries, as we note later, these terms are not used, and a person's sexuality is not defined by the gender of their partners.

Sociologists are interested in the models of sexuality that society offers its members and how individuals come to identify with one model or another. For example, maybe feminine young boys begin to act "gay" because they are ridiculed by their peers. If American society did not split the sexual world into "homosexual" and "heterosexual" categories, perhaps these boys would move fluidly through same-sex and other-sex contacts without being forced to choose between the "gay" and "straight" communities.

Interactional Theory

Finally, interactional theory proposes that homosexuality results from a complex interaction of biological, psychological, and social factors. Perhaps a child is born after being exposed to prenatal hormones that could predispose them toward a particular sexual orientation, but this predisposition, in conjunction with social experiences, either facilitates or inhibits a particular sexual orientation.

Social psychologist Daryl Bem (2000) has proposed an interactional theory that combines both biology and sociological issues. Bem suggests that biological variables, such as genetics, hormones, and brain neuroanatomy, do not cause certain sexual orientations, but rather they contribute to childhood temperaments that influence a child's preferences for sex-typical or sex-atypical activities and peers.

Bem believes that males who engage in "male-typical activities," such as rough-and-tumble play or competitive team sports, prefer to spend time with other boys who also like these activities. Similarly, girls who prefer "female-typical activities," such as socializing quietly or playing jacks, prefer the company of other girls who like to do the same activities. Gender-conforming children (those who engage in activities typical for their gender) prefer the other gender for romantic interests, whereas nonconforming children prefer the same gender. Bem's "exotic-becomes-erotic" theory suggests that sexual feelings evolve from experiencing heightened arousal in situations in which one gender is viewed as more exotic, or different from oneself (Bem, 2000). Bem asserts that lesbian and gay children had playmates of the other sex while growing up, and this led them to see the same sex as more "exotic" and appealing. However, his research has been contradictory and hasn't been supported by other research (Peplau et al., 1998). Many gay and lesbian children report playmates of both the same sex and the other sex while growing up.

Review Questions

1 Identify and describe the various areas of research within the biological theory of homosexuality.

2 Identify and describe the various developmental theories of homosexuality.

3 Explain the behavioral theory of homosexuality.

4 Explain the sociological theory of homosexuality.

5 Explain the interactional theory of homosexuality.

6 Differentiate the various theories that have been proposed to explain homosexuality.

Homosexuality in Other Times and Places

When the American Psychological Association (APA) removed homosexuality from its list of official mental diseases in 1973, many psychiatrists were outraged. Homosexuality had been considered a mental illness for more than 100 years, and they demanded a vote of the full APA membership (Bayer, 1981). Only when scientists dropped the assumption that homosexuality was a disorder

did they make real progress in understanding homosexuality. The enormous complexity of the human brain allows highly flexible human behavior patterns in almost every aspect of life, and human sexuality is not an exception to that rule.

Homosexuality remains controversial in the United States. Some people see it as a sin and others argue that homosexuals are a "bad influence" on society and children (and, for example, believe homosexuals should not be allowed to become parents, teachers, Boy Scout leaders, or fight in the military). Still others defend homosexual rights and attack America's view of sexuality.

Western history has included many periods when homosexuality was generally accepted. In fact, Gilbert Herdt (1988), a prominent scholar of homosexuality, states that the modern American attitude toward homosexuality is much harsher than attitudes in the majority of other countries throughout most of history. The history of social attitudes toward homosexuality can teach us something about our own views today.

Homosexuality in History

Homosexuality has been viewed differently throughout history. Although there have been times when homosexuality has been accepted, there have also been times it has been scorned. The influence of the Church has greatly affected societal tolerance and acceptance of homosexuality.

The Classical Era

Before the 19th century, men who engaged in homosexual acts were accused of **sodomy** (SA-duh-mee), or **buggery**, which were simply seen as crimes and not considered part of a person's fundamental nature. Even so, homosexual activity was common, homosexual prostitution was taxed by the state, and the writers of the time seemed to consider men loving men as natural as men loving women. Even after Rome became Christian, there was no antihomosexual legislation for more than 200 years.

Lesbian love seems to have puzzled ancient writers (who were almost all men). The word *lesbian* itself comes from the island

Ancient societies left evidence to show that same-sex behavior was not uncommon, as in this illustration from a 19th century book depicting anal sex between two men.

Paul Fearn/Alamy Stock Photo

sodomy
Any of various forms of sexual intercourse held to be unnatural or abnormal, especially anal intercourse or bestiality (also called buggery).

buggery
Any of various forms of sexual intercourse held to be unnatural or abnormal, especially anal intercourse or bestiality (also called sodomy).

passing woman
Woman who disguises herself as a man.

of Lesbos, in Greece, where the poet Sappho lived about 600 B.C. Lesbianism was rarely explicitly against the law in most ancient societies (in fact, two or more unmarried women living together has usually been seen as proper, whereas a woman living alone was viewed with suspicion; Bullough, 1979).

Contrary to popular belief, homosexuality was not treated with concern or much interest by early Christians (Boswell, 1980). Neither ancient Greek nor Hebrew had a word for homosexual; it was rarely mentioned in the Bible; Saint Paul never explicitly condemned homosexuality; and Jesus made few pronouncements on proper or improper sexuality (except fidelity) and never mentioned homosexuality. Why, then, did Christianity become so antihomosexual?

The Middle Ages

By the 9th century, almost every part of Europe had some sort of local law code based on Church teachings, and although these codes included strong sanctions for sexual transgressions, including rape, adultery, incest, and fornication, homosexual relations were not forbidden in any of them (Boswell, 1980). Church indifference to homosexuality lasted well through the 13th century; in other words, for the first 1,000 years of Christianity, the Church showed little interest in homosexuality and did not generally condemn the behavior (Boswell, 1980; Kuefler, 2006; Siker, 1994). Male brothels appeared, defenses of homosexual relations began to appear in print, and homosexuality became a fairly accepted part of the general culture until the late Middle Ages.

Homosexuality was completely legal in most countries in Europe in the year 1250 (Boswell, 1980). By 1300, however, there was a new intolerance of differences, and homosexuality was punishable by death almost everywhere (Boswell, 1980; Kuefler, 2006). This view from the late Middle Ages has influenced the Western world's view of homosexuality for the last 700 years.

The Modern Era

From the 16th century on, homosexuals were subject to periods of tolerance and periods of severe repression. In the American colonies, for example, homosexuality was a serious offense. In 1656, the New Haven Colony prescribed death for both males and females who engaged in homosexual acts (Boswell, 1980). The severe attitude toward homosexuality in America reflects its Puritan origins, and America remains, even today, more disapproving of homosexuality than Europe is.

Even in times when homosexual acts were condemned, however, homoerotic poems, writings, and art were created. Openly homosexual communities appeared now and then. Other cultures also had periods of relative tolerance of homosexuality. In Japan, for example, the Edo period (1600–1868) saw a flourishing homosexual subculture, with openly gay clubs, geisha houses, and a substantial gay literature (Hirayama & Hirayama, 1986).

During the 19th and early 20th centuries in the United States, it was not uncommon for single, upper-middle-class women to live together in committed, lifelong relationships, although they may not all have engaged in genital sexuality (Nichols, 1990). At the same time, **passing women** disguised themselves as men, entered the workforce,

Being Young and Lesbian, Gay, or Bisexual in Different Cultures

It is important to remember that although we have been exploring the lesbian, gay, and bisexual experiences in the United States, in different parts of the world, LGB adolescents may have very different experiences. Here we take a look at LGB adolescents in a variety of places around the globe.

English (male): Between the ages of 13 and 15 I closed myself off from the outside world. I would rarely go out and would never dare to go places where other people of my own age would be. The only thing I knew was that homosexuality was bad. (Plummer, 1989, p. 204)

East Indian (female): My family holds Western culture somehow responsible for offbeat youth. They think my being a lesbian is my being young, and confused, and rebellious. They feel it has something to do with trying to fit into White culture. . . . They're waiting for me to stop rebelling and go heterosexual, go out on dates, and come home early. (Tremble et al., 1989, p. 260)

Mexican (male): I thought myself very bad, and many times I was at the point of suicide. I don't know if I really might have killed myself, but many times I thought about it and believed it was the only alternative. That caused me many problems with my friends. I felt they thought me to be different, homosexual, and really sick. It made me separate from them. I felt myself inferior and thought I was the only one these things happened to. (Carrier, 1989, p. 238)

Chinese (male): I am longing to love others and to be loved. I have met some other homosexuals, but I have doubt about this type of love. With all the pressure I was afraid to reveal myself and ruined everything. As a result, we departed without showing each other homosexual love. As I am growing older my homosexual desire increases. This is too troubling and depressing for anyone. I thought about death many times. When you are young you cannot fall in love and when you are old you will be alone.

Thinking of this makes the future absolutely hopeless. (Ruan & Tsai, 1988, p. 194)

Canadian (female): I feel like I am the terrific person I am today because I'm a lesbian. I decided I was gay when I was very young. After making that decision, which was the hardest thing I could ever face, I feel like I can do anything. (Schneider, 1989, p. 123)

Scottish (male): I don't like being gay. I wouldn't choose to be gay, and I don't like the gay scene. It's too superficial. I've got high moral standards. Lust is a sin but love isn't. In the gay scene people use other people and throw them away again. (Burbidge & Walters, 1981, p. 41)

Asian American (gender not identified): I wish I could tell my parents—they are the only ones who do not know about my gay identity, but I am sure they would reject me. There is no frame of reference to understand homosexuality in Asian American culture. (Chan, 1989, p. 19)

and even married women—who sometimes never knew their husbands were female. In most cases, the wife knew, and the couple probably lived as lesbians in a disguised heterosexual marriage. Some of these passing women held offices of great power, and their biological sex was not discovered until their death (Nichols, 1990).

In the 19th and early 20th centuries, physicians and scientists began to suggest that homosexuality was not a sin but an illness, which, if left "untreated," would spread like a contagious disease (Hansen, 1989). The dangers of this perspective were realized in Nazi Germany, where homosexuals were imprisoned and murdered along with Jews, Gypsies, epileptics, and others as part of the program to purify the "Aryan race" (Adam, 1987). In America, psychiatry continued to view homosexuality as a mental illness into the 1970s.

Ironically, the medical model's view of homosexuality, which influenced modern ideas of sexual orientation, changed the politics of homosexuality. Because physicians saw homosexuality not as just a behavior but as a built-in trait, it became a primary part of the way people looked at each other (Risman & Schwartz, 1988). Homosexuals began to argue: "If homosexuality is something I am, not just something I do, then I should have a right to be 'who I am' just as Blacks, women, and other groups have a right to be who they are." The new view of homosexuality encouraged homosexuals to band together and press for recognition of their civil rights

as a minority group, which led to the modern gay and lesbian liberation movement we discussed in Chapter 1.

Same-Sex Behavior in Other Cultures

We all have a natural tendency to believe that others see the world the way we do. Yet what we call "homosexuality" is viewed so differently in other cultures that the word itself might not apply. In many societies, individuals have same-sex sexual relations as a normal part of their lives. This can be minor, as in Cairo, Egypt, where heterosexual men casually kiss and hold hands, or it can be fully sexual, as in the sequential homosexuality of Papua New Guinea, where young males have sexual contact exclusively with other males until getting married at age 18, after which they have sexual contact only with women (see the subsequent discussion on the Sambian tribe).

Same-sex behavior is found in every culture, and its prevalence remains about the same no matter how permissive or repressive that culture's attitude is toward it (Mihalik, 1988). A classic study by Broude and Greene (1976) examined 42 societies for which there were good data on attitudes toward homosexuality. They found that a substantial number of the cultures in the sample have an accepting or only mildly disapproving view of same-sex behavior, and less than half punished homosexuals for their sexual activities.

Many international organizations, such as the International Gay and Lesbian Human Rights Commission and the International Lesbian, Gay, Bisexual, Trans and Intersex Association, work to protect the rights of lesbians, gays, and bisexuals around the world. In many parts of the world, LGBTQ people experience discrimination, harassment, physical and emotional abuse, and violence. Many are forbidden to live with a same-sex partner, and some are forced into heterosexual marriages, raped, imprisoned, beaten, or killed because of their sexual orientation. Cultural factors play an important role in acceptance of homosexuality.

A 2013 Pew Research Center study found significant variations in acceptance by region. While some countries have laws protecting LGB individuals and allow civil unions and same-sex marriages, other countries have laws criminalizing homosexuality and will even sentence homosexuals to death (Pew Research Center, 2013a; see Figure 11.3). Overall, acceptance of homosexuality is higher in countries in which religion is less central to individuals' lives. It is also more acceptable in younger generations. In this section, we explore some country-specific information on how LGB individuals are treated around the world.

Latin American Countries

Rights for same-sex couples have been increasing in the last few years throughout Latin America even though many countries are under the control of the Roman Catholic Church, which strongly opposes same-sex unions. While Argentina became the first Latin American country to legalize same-sex marriage in 2010, since that time, Brazil, Colombia, Uruguay, and parts of Mexico have also legalized same-sex marriage.

In Brazil, same-sex behavior has been legal since 1830, while same-sex marriage was legalized in 2013. There are many LGBT organizations, and the São Paulo Gay Pride Parade, one of the world's largest LGBT celebrations, takes place in Brazil every year.

In many Central and South American countries, people do not tend to think in terms of homosexuality and heterosexuality, but rather in terms of masculinity and femininity. Male gender roles, for example, are defined by one's *machismo*, which, in terms of

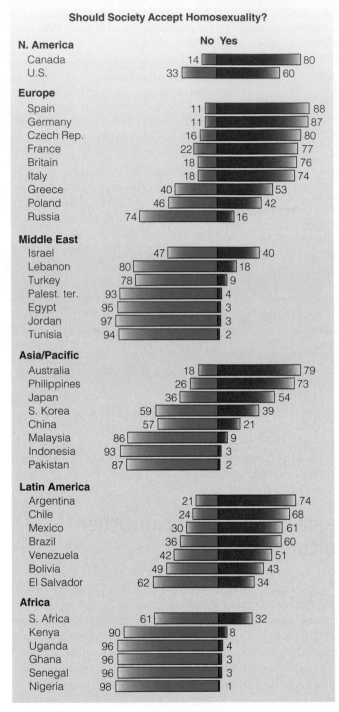

Should Society Accept Homosexuality?

	No	Yes
N. America		
Canada	14	80
U.S.	33	60
Europe		
Spain	11	88
Germany	11	87
Czech Rep.	16	80
France	22	77
Britain	18	76
Italy	18	74
Greece	40	53
Poland	46	42
Russia	74	16
Middle East		
Israel	47	40
Lebanon	80	18
Turkey	78	9
Palest. ter.	93	4
Egypt	95	3
Jordan	97	3
Tunisia	94	2
Asia/Pacific		
Australia	18	79
Philippines	26	73
Japan	36	54
S. Korea	59	39
China	57	21
Malaysia	86	9
Indonesia	93	3
Pakistan	87	2
Latin America		
Argentina	21	74
Chile	24	68
Mexico	30	61
Brazil	36	60
Venezuela	42	51
Bolivia	49	43
El Salvador	62	34
Africa		
S. Africa	61	32
Kenya	90	8
Uganda	96	4
Ghana	96	3
Senegal	96	3
Nigeria	98	1

FIGURE **11.3** Percentage of people answering "yes" or "no" to the question, "Should society accept homosexuality?"

SOURCE: Pew Research Center, 2013a (http://www.pewglobal.org/files/2013/06 /Pew-Global-Attitudes-Homosexuality-Report-FINAL-JUNE-4-2013.pdf).

machismo
Characterized or motivated by stereotypical masculine behavior or actions.

The São Paulo LGBT Pride Parade takes place every year in São Paulo, Brazil, and is one of the largest gay pride parades in the world. In 2015, the parade theme was "*I was born this way. I grew up so I will always be like this: Respect me.*"

Pacific Press/Alamy Stock Photo

sexual behavior, is determined by being the active partner, or penetrator. Therefore, a man is not considered homosexual for taking the active, penetrating role in intercourse, even if he is penetrating other men. As long as he is penetrating, he is masculine.

This is similar in Nicaragua where a man who is the active partner in same-sex anal intercourse is called *machista* or *hombre-hombre* ("manly man"), a term used for any masculine male (Murray & Dynes, 1999). In fact, penetrating other men is seen as a sign of manliness and prestige, whereas feminine men allow themselves to be penetrated and are generally scorned.

Note that the implicit message of such cultures is that to mimic female behavior is disgraceful and shameful in a male. This attitude reflects the general nature of these societies, which tend to be patriarchal, with women lacking political and social power. Because women are, in general, considered inferior to men, men who mimic women are to be ridiculed.

Arabic Cultures

Although classic works of Arabic poetry use homoerotic imagery, and young boys were often used as the standard of beauty and sexuality in Arabic writing (Boswell, 1980), homosexuality in Arab countries, like sexuality in general, is usually not discussed. It is not uncommon to see men holding hands or walking down the street arm in arm, but for the most part, male homosexuality is taboo. Sexual relations in the Middle East are often about power and are based on dominant and subordinate positions. Because of this,

similar to some Latin American countries, being the penetrating partner with another man does not make a man gay (Sati, 1998).

In many Middle Eastern countries, homosexuality is a crime punishable by death. Although same-sex behavior in Iraq is not prohibited, there are high levels of persecution of lesbians and gays made worse by constant war. Although attitudes about homosexuality are slowly changing in Arabic cultures, many countries still hold negative views about homosexuality. Many Middle Eastern countries criminalize private homosexual acts and, in fact, four countries—Sudan, Saudi Arabia, Yemen, and Iran—permit the state to impose death penalties for same-sex behavior.

Asian and Pacific Countries

Although there is little support for homosexuality in Arabic cultures, LGB rights in Asia are also very limited. Same-sex behavior is banned in several Asian countries, including Bangladesh, India, Malaysia, Pakistan, Singapore, and Sri Lanka (International Gay and Lesbian Human Rights Commission, 2010; Misra, 2009). As we discussed earlier, in some countries same-sex behavior is punishable by death. (See Figure 11.4.) In 2001, the Chinese Psychiatric Association removed homosexuality from its list of mental disorders (Gallagher, 2001). This is a significant change for China, which has openly opposed homosexuality as recently as 1994. Homosexuality was seen as a result of Western influences, and it was considered a "Western social disease" (Ruan & Lau, 2004). In India, although homosexual sex is punishable by up to 10 years in jail, several gay

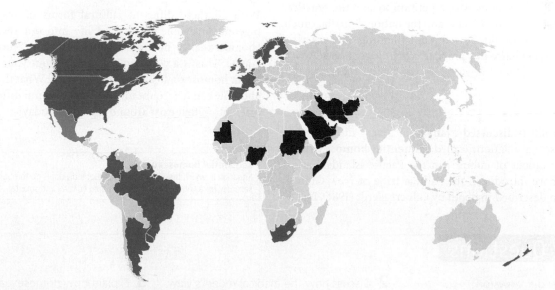

Punishment for homosexual acts
■ Homosexual acts can be punished by death
☐ Homosexual acts are illegal

Relatively neutral
☐ Homosexual acts are legal

Recognition of same-sex unions
■ Same-sex marriage is allowed
■ Same-sex marriage is allowed in some jurisdictions
☐ Civil unions are legal

FIGURE **11.4** **Same-Sex Rights Around the World**
Above are where various countries stand on same-sex rights (see graphic https://www.washingtonpost.com/graphics/world/gay-rights/).

SOURCE: International Lesbian, Gay, Bisexual, Trans and Intersex Association's June 2016 survey, Cameron & Berkowitz, 2016.

couples have made headlines by publicly declaring themselves married in an attempt to overturn an existing law from 1861 (Predrag, 2005). In 2016, a marriage bureau was established in India to help LGB persons find prospective life partners both within and outside the country (Agnihotri, 2016). In Chapter 9 we discussed the popularity of arranged marriage in India, and the development of an LGB marriage bureau will enable family members to find suitable partners for their lesbian, gay, and bisexual children (see "Sexual Diversity in Our World").

There is much more support for same-sex couples in countries such as Hong Kong, Israel, Japan, Taiwan, and Vietnam. It is likely that Taiwan will become the first Asian country to legalize same-sex marriage (Cheng & Chien, 2017). However, while there has been increasing pressure to change the island's civil code legalizing same-sex marriage, this could still take years to accomplish.

African Countries

More than two thirds of African countries have laws against same-sex behavior (Law Library of Congress, 2014). Homosexuality is illegal and punishable by death in countries such as Nigeria, Sudan, and Mauritania, and punishable by imprisonment in many other countries. For example, those found guilty of homosexual contact can get up to 5 years of jail time in Cameroon and Libya; 14 years in Kenya and the Seychelles; and 30 years to life in Tanzania and Uganda (Law Library of Congress, 2014). In many African countries, those who challenge existing laws are arrested, punished, jailed, and/or discriminated against in work, education, and/or health care.

Although South Africa legalized same-sex activity in 1998 and recognizes gay marriage, the practice of "corrective rape" to change South African lesbians into heterosexuals began circulating on the Internet in 2010 (Huff-Hannon, 2011). To call attention to the practice, a group in Capetown, South Africa, named *Luleki Sizwe* (named after two South African women who died after "corrective rape") began posting photographs of women who had been beaten and raped, along with a petition to stop the practice. This got the attention of politicians and the national media, which supporters believed would be helpful in ending the practice. However, there is evidence this practice continues in South Africa (Strudwick, 2014).

Sambia

A famous and much discussed example of a very different cultural form of sexual relations, called **sequential homosexuality**, is found in a number of cultures in the Pacific islands. Earlier in this chapter we introduced the Sambia tribe of New Guinea, which has been described in depth by Gilbert Herdt (1981). Life in

In 2016, Colombia became the fourth country in Catholic-majority South America to legalize same-sex marriage, following Argentina, Uruguay, and Brazil.

Fernando Vergara/AP Images

Sambia is difficult because food is scarce and war is common; warriors, hunters, and many children are needed to survive. Sambians believe that mother's milk must be replaced by man's milk (semen) for a boy to reach puberty, and so, at age 7, all Sambian boys move to a central hut where they must fellate the postpubescent Sambian boys and drink their semen. After a boy reaches puberty, he no longer fellates others but is himself sucked by the prepubescent boys until he reaches the age of marriage at about 18. Despite his long period of same-sex activity, he will live as a heterosexual for the rest of his life.

The Lesson of Cross-Cultural Studies of Homosexuality

With all these different cultural forms of sexuality, trying to pigeonhole people or ways of life into our restrictive, Western "homosexuality–heterosexuality–bisexuality" model seems inadequate. This is a good time to think about your personal theory about homosexuality and to ask yourself: What theory do I believe, and how can it account for the cross-cultural differences in sexual orientation that exist around the world today?

---

sequential homosexuality
Situation in which heterosexual or bisexual individuals go through a period of homosexuality for a variety of reasons, including cultural and societal.

Review Questions

1 Explain how our views on homosexuality have changed from ancient times through the Middle Ages.

2 Discuss how the medical model's view of homosexuality during the modern era influenced modern ideas of sexual orientation.

3 Explain how homosexuality has been viewed in other cultures, citing as many examples as possible.

Lesbians, Gays, and Bisexuals Throughout the Life Cycle

Lesbians, gays, and bisexuals in America face particular problems that are not faced by most heterosexuals. Many struggle with families and friends who reject them, discrimination, prejudice, and/or lack of benefits for their partners. Even so, many couples live together in stable, happy unions, leading lives not really that much different from the heterosexual couple next door. LGB lifestyles are as varied and different as those of the rest of society. In this section, we examine the special challenges and circumstances that face LGB individuals.

Growing Up Lesbian, Gay, or Bisexual

Imagine what it must be like to be an adolescent and either to believe or to know that you are lesbian, gay, or bisexual (a number of you reading this book do not have to imagine it). All your life, from the time you were a toddler, you were presented with a single model of sexual life: You were expected to be attracted to the other sex, to go on dates, and eventually to marry. No other scenario was seriously considered; if you are heterosexual, you probably have never even reflected on how powerfully this "presumption of heterosexuality" (Herdt, 1989) was transmitted by your parents, your friends, television and movies, newspapers and magazines, even the government. Advertisements on TV and in magazines always highlighted heterosexual couples; your friends played house, doctor, or spin the bottle, assuming everyone was attracted to the other sex; your grade school, parties, and social activities were organized around this presumption of heterosexuality. There were open questions about many things in your life—what career you would pursue, where you might live, what college you would attend. However, one thing was considered certain: You were going to marry (or at least date) someone of the other sex.

Imagine that while all your friends were talking about the other sex, dating, and sex, you were experiencing a completely different set of emotions. Why, you wondered, can't I join in on these conversations? Why can't I feel the attractions that all my friends feel? Then, at some point in your early teens, you began to realize why you felt differently from your friends. All of a sudden you understood that all the models you had taken for granted your whole life did not apply to you. You began to look for other models that described your life and your feelings—and they weren't there. In fact, in hundreds of subtle and not-so-subtle ways, society taught you that you were different. Now what do you do? Who can you talk to?

The experiences of many lesbians, gays, and bisexuals, at least until recently, followed this scenario, although the timing and intensity varied with individual cases. For example, many gay men grew up with close male friends, enjoyed sports, and differed only in their secret attraction to other boys, whereas others remember

Many major advertising campaigns, including travel, financial services, alcoholic beverages, automotive, entertainment, fashion, hair, and skincare, have been using same-sex couples to promote their products. These advertisements can draw attention to the LBGT community in a positive and welcoming way.

feeling and acting differently from their friends as early as 4 or 5 years old (Martin, 1991).

Today, many schools and universities have clubs, support groups, and meeting areas for LGBTQ students. Whereas in the mid-1990s, there were only a handful of gay–straight alliance (GSA) clubs in U.S. schools, these clubs are more common today. LGBT teens who attend schools with GSAs have more positive school experiences, higher GPAs, less bullying based on sexual orientation or gender expression, and lower rates of depression and substance abuse (Coulter et al., 2016; Goldbach & Gibbs, 2015; Ioverno et al., 2016; Marx & Kettrey, 2016). Recent studies have found that GSAs can also offer prevention benefits to heterosexual boys who experience bullying (Saewyc et al., 2014).

Coming Out to Self and Others

One of the most important tasks of adolescence is to develop and integrate a positive adult identity. This task is an even greater challenge for LGB youth because they learn from a very young age the stigma of being different from the heterosexual norm (Ryan & Futterman, 2001). Special challenges confront the person who believes they are lesbian, gay, or bisexual, including the need to establish a personal self-identity and communicate it to others, known as **coming out** (see the accompanying "Sex in Real Life" feature). A number of models have been offered to explain how

coming out
The process of establishing a personal self-identity and communicating it to others.

A number of authors have created models of the process of coming out. For example, Vivienne Cass (1979, 1984) has proposed one of the leading models, which encompasses six stages of lesbian and gay identity formation. Not all lesbians and gays reach the sixth stage; it depends how comfortable one is at each stage with one's sexual orientation.

Stage 1: Identity confusion. The individual begins to believe that their behavior may be defined as gay or lesbian. There may be a need to redefine one's own concept of lesbian and gay behavior, with all the biases and misinformation that most people have. The person may accept that role and seek information, may repress it and inhibit all lesbian and gay behaviors (and even perhaps become an antihomosexual crusader), or may deny its relevance at all to their identity (like a man who has same-sex behavior in prison but doesn't believe he is "really" gay).

Stage 2: Identity comparison. The individual accepts potential lesbian and gay identity; they reject the heterosexual model but have no substitute. The person may feel different and even lost. If willing to even consider a lesbian and gay self-definition, they may begin to look for appropriate models.

Stage 3: Identity tolerance. Here the person shifts to the belief that they are probably lesbian or gay and begins to seek out the homosexual community for social, sexual, and emotional needs. Confusion declines, but self-identity is still more tolerated than truly accepted. Usually, the person still does not reveal new identity to the heterosexual world but maintains a double lifestyle.

Stage 4: Identity acceptance. A positive view of self-identity is forged, and a network of lesbian and gay friends is developed. Selective disclosure to friends and family is made, and the person often immerses themselves in homosexual culture.

Stage 5: Identity pride. Homosexual pride is developed, and anger over treatment may lead to rejecting heterosexuality as bad. One feels validated in the new lifestyle.

Stage 6: Identity synthesis. As the individual truly becomes comfortable with their lifestyle and as nonhomosexual contacts increase, they realize the inaccuracy of dividing the world into "good lesbians and gays" and "bad heterosexuals." No longer is sexual orientation seen as the sole identity by which an individual can be characterized. The person lives an open, gay lifestyle so that disclosure is no longer an issue and realizes that there are many sides and aspects to personality, of which sexual orientation is only one. The process of identity formation is complete.

SOURCE: From Cass (1979, 1984).

this process proceeds (see, for example, Cass, 1979, 1984; Coleman, 1982; Martin, 1991; Schneider, 1989; Troiden, 1989).

Coming out refers, first, to acknowledging one's sexual identity to oneself, and many LGB persons have their own negative feelings about homosexuality to overcome. The often difficult and anxiety-ridden process of disclosing the truth to family, friends, and eventually the public at large comes later. Disclosure of identity plays an important role in identity development and psychological adjustment for LGB individuals.

Although first awareness of sexual orientation typically occurs between the ages of 8 and 9, people vary in when they share this information with others. Some may come out early in their lives, whereas others remain closeted into adulthood (Savin-Williams & Diamond, 2000; Taylor, 2000). Coming out does not happen overnight; being homosexual for some may mean a lifetime of disclosing different amounts of information to family, friends, and strangers in different contexts (Hofman, 2005). Deciding whether and how to tell friends and family can be difficult. To minimize the risk for rejection, LGB adolescents choose whom they come out to very carefully.

Although years ago many LGB persons worked hard to hide their sexual orientation for fear of discrimination, harassment, and violence, today's teens are coming out earlier than any other time in history. In the 1970s, many teens waited until adulthood to come out; in the 1980s and 1990s, they began coming out in their teens (Ryan et al., 2009). By 2007, teens began coming out as early as middle school (Denizet-Lewis, 2009; Elias, 2007). A more accepting social climate and increased acceptance of homosexuality are responsible for these changes. In addition, support groups such as GSAs, along with a more positive portrayal of LGB role models in the media, have contributed to early ages in coming out. The continually changing social climate has also lessened the pressure to "fit in" and as a result, many more people today live openly as lesbian, gay, or bisexual.

In Chapter 7, we discussed attachment styles that form in our childhood and stay with us as we grow up. These attachment styles can influence many aspects of our adult development, including the coming-out process for LGB people. Research has found strong correlations between shame and negativity about being gay and anxious/ambivalent and avoidant attachment styles (Cook & Calebs, 2016).

Family Reactions to Coming Out

Lesbian, gay, and bisexual youth who have positive coming-out experiences have higher self-confidence, lower rates of depression, and better psychological adjustment than those who have negative coming-out experiences (Needham & Austin, 2010; Shpigel et al., 2015). Research has found that more than 50% of parents of LGB youth initially react with some degree of negativity, including disappointment, shame, and shock when they learn about a child's homosexuality (D'Augelli, 2010; LaSala, 2000). They may feel responsible and believe they did something to "cause" their child's sexual orientation. Other parents are accepting of their LGB children right away. The following story was written by a student of mine who had a positive coming-out experience:

I was worried about coming out to my mom since we were so close. I wondered what she would think of me and if she would still love me. One day she picked me up from school early, and asked me if everything was OK. I assured her it was, but she knew something was up. She stopped the car and told me I needed to talk to her. I looked at her concerned face and started to give in. "It is something about me. . ." I said slowly. "What is it?" she said, looking as if she was about to cry. "It's something that you may not like about me. . ." I said as I started to get teary eyed. "I'm. . . I'm. . ." and tears began rolling down my face. "You're. . . gay. . .?" I nodded my head and started to cry. My mother unbuckled her seatbelt and hugged me. "Did you think that would change our relationship? You're still my son and I still love you," she said as she wiped the tears away from my eyes. (Author's files)

It's estimated that more than 70% of LGB youth experience some degree of parental rejection related to their sexual orientation, with Black and Hispanic LGB youth experiencing greater rejection than White or non-Hispanic LGB youth (Richter et al., 2017). Parental rejection during the coming-out process is a major health risk for LGB youth. Children who are rejected by their parents have been found to have increased levels of isolation, loneliness, depression, and thoughts of suicide, as well as higher rates of sexually transmitted infections and homelessness (Baiocco et al., 2014; Puckett et al., 2015; Skerrett et al., 2016). Compared with LGB teens with no or low levels of family rejection, LGB teens who reported high levels of family rejection were:

- 8.4 times more likely to attempt suicide
- 6 times more likely to report high levels of depression
- 3.4 times more likely to use illegal drugs
- 3.4 times more likely to report engaging in unprotected sexual behavior (Ryan et al., 2009)

Families with high levels of religiosity have been found to use religion as a tool to defend their positions against homosexuality. Studies have found that in religious families, Christian families use more religious tools to mediate conflict over coming out issues than do Jewish families (Etengoff & Daiute, 2014).

Studies have found that more than 25% of LGB teens were kicked out of their homes after coming out to their parents (Brown & Trevethan, 2010; Martin et al., 2010). In fact, the number one cause for homelessness for LGB teens is family conflict (Durso & Gates, 2012; Keuroghlian et al., 2014). It's estimated that between 20% and 40% of homeless teens are LGB, although the exact number is unknown (Rice et al., 2013; Rosario at al., 2012). Homeless LGB youth are also more at risk than homeless heterosexual youth to abuse drugs and alcohol and experience physical and sexual abuse (Chakraborty et al., 2011; Needham & Austin, 2010). Today, homeless shelters that cater specifically to LGB youth have been set up across the United States.

Oftentimes the family must go through its own "coming out," as parents and siblings slowly try to accept the idea and then tell their own friends (in fact, it's been said that when LGB children come out of the closet, the family members go in; Strommen, 1993). The importance of positive resolution in the family has prompted the formation of a national organization, Parents, Families, & Friends of Lesbians and Gays (PFLAG), which helps parents and family members learn to accept their children's sexual orientation and gain support from other families experiencing similar events.

REAL RESEARCH Studies have found there are three groups of gay men on Facebook: "Out & Proud," "Out & Discreet," and "Facebook Closeted" (Owens, 2017). Those who are "Out & Proud" use Facebook as a way to celebrate their sexual identity while those who are "Out & Discreet" come out to some friends on Facebook but not others. Finally, those who are "Facebook Closeted" actively manage their online presentation and work hard to make sure their sexual orientation is not exposed.

Effects of Stigma

A nationally representative survey of LGB adults found that 4 in 10 were rejected by a family member or close friend because of their sexual orientation; 58% were the target of slurs or jokes; 30% were physically attacked or threatened; 29% were made to feel unwelcome in a church or synagogue; and 21% were treated unfairly by an employer (Pew Research Center, 2013b). Many lesbian, gay, and bisexual youth also experience high levels of stigmatization and discrimination (Chakraborty et al., 2011; Cox et al., 2010). Gay male youth often report a history of feeling unattached and alienated—most probably because heterosexual dating is often a focal point in male peer group bonds (Bauermeister et al., 2010; Herdt, 1989). The same is true of young lesbians and female bisexuals, although the pressure and alienation may be felt slightly later in life because same-sex affection and touching are more accepted for girls and because lesbians often tend to determine their sexual orientation later than gay men.

For many years, psychiatrists and other therapists argued that LGB youth and adults had a greater risk for health problems than heterosexuals. This has been supported by various studies that have found a higher risk of chronic disease, depression, insomnia, substance abuse, and suicide in LGB youth (Chen & Shiu, 2016; Dirkes et al., 2016; McCay et al., 2017; Smith et al., 2016). These risks are highest among those who identify as bisexual as well as those who are ethnic/racial minorities (Li et al., 2016; Silva et al., 2015). As public acceptance has grown for same-sex relationships, there have been decreases in depression among LGB youth. For example, after the legalization of same-sex marriage in the United States in 2015, there was a significant decrease in the incidence of suicide among LGB high school students (Raifman et al., 2017).

The problems of LGB life may not be because of psychopathology but rather the enormous pressures of living in a society that discriminates against them. Vulnerable and stigmatized groups in general have higher rates of these types of behaviors, and these problems often result from coping with stigma-related stress. Workplace discrimination also adds stress to the lives of

Relationship satisfaction is very similar across couple types (same- and other-sex). However, same-sex couples may be more upbeat in the face of conflict and remain more positive after disagreements.

men. Gay and bisexual men earn 10% to 32% less than similarly qualified heterosexual men (Badgett et al., 2007; Klawitter, 2014). Lesbian women, on the other hand, tend to earn more money than heterosexual women (Kurtzleben, 2013; Mize, 2016; see Figure 11.5 for more information). Experts believe that lesbians might earn more than their heterosexual female peers because they are perceived as more career-oriented and less likely to leave the workforce to raise children.

Life Issues: Partnering, Sexuality, Parenthood, and Aging

Although growing up and coming out can be difficult for many lesbian, gay, and bisexual youth, the next step is establishing intimate relationships. Let's now explore same-sex coupling, sexuality, parenting, and aging.

Looking for Partners

In Chapter 9, we discussed some of the difficulties lesbians and gays face in meeting others. Meeting other same-sex partners in the heterosexual world can be difficult, so the gay community has developed its own social institutions to help people meet one another and socialize. Adults can meet others at gay bars or clubs that cater primarily to lesbian, gay, and bisexual individuals at mainstream bars that offer LGB nights; through LGB support or discussion groups; at churches and synagogues; and through LGB organizations. Groups and meeting areas in schools also offer LGB students a place to meet potential partners.

Gay magazines such as *The Advocate* carry personal ads and ads for dating services, travel clubs, resorts, bed and breakfasts, theaters, businesses, pay phone lines, sexual products, and other services to help LGBs meet others. And many LGB people are introduced to

LGB individuals. Although there are federal laws that protect people from workplace discrimination on the basis of race, religion, sex, age, and disability, there is no federal law that outlaws workplace discrimination on the basis of sexual orientation in private workplaces (federal government workers are protected from this type of discrimination). The Employment Non-Discrimination Act, which would provide protections to all LGBTQ employees throughout the United States, has been included in almost every session of the U.S. Congress since 1994 but has not been passed. At the state level close to half of all U.S. states and the District of Columbia having laws prohibiting workplace discrimination based on sexual orientation in both private and public workplaces.

Research on workplace discrimination has also revealed a significant pay gap for gay men when compared to heterosexual

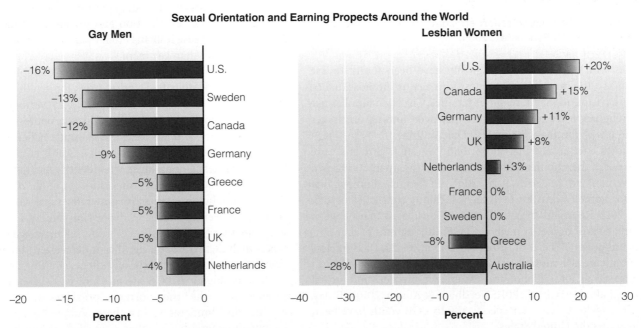

FIGURE **11.5** While gay men in many countries often earn less than heterosexual men with comparable education, skills, and experience, lesbian women in many countries often earn more than heterosexual women with comparable education, skills, and experiences.

SOURCE: Drydakis, 2014: IZA World of Labor.

While Tinder and Bumble allow users to "prefer" a certain sex, several apps have been developed specifically with LGB individuals in mind, such as such as HER, Scruff, Hornet, and Grindr.

partners through gay and straight friends. Like heterosexuals, LGB individuals use various apps on their smartphones to meet people, such as HER, Hornet, Grindr, and U2nite. LGB individuals in committed or legally recognized relationships have been found to experience less sadness, lower levels of stress, and an increased sense of well-being compared with LGB singles (Riggle et al., 2010).

Lesbian and Gay Parenting

Lesbian and gay individuals can become parents in a variety of different ways, including artificial insemination, adoption, or surrogacy (we discuss these options in more detail in Chapter 12). Over the last few years, same-sex parenting has become more mainstream, as popular gay and lesbian celebrities, such as Dan Savage, Jane Lynch, Cynthia Nixon, Ricky Martin, Elton John, Neil Patrick Harris, and Wanda Sykes, have all become parents. Many same-sex couples become parents, and they cite most of the same reasons for wanting to be parents that straight parents do. Although fewer lesbian women have children than heterosexual women (see Chapter 9), it is estimated that more than 1 in 3 lesbians has given birth and 1 in 6 gay men has fathered or adopted a child (Gates et al., 2007).

Same-sex couples who wish to be parents often encounter problems that heterosexual couples do not face. Parenting is seldom an individual or couple decision for them and often involves several negotiations with others. In addition, because same-sex marriage was recently legalized in the United States, unmarried gay couples may have trouble gaining joint custody of a child, and employers may not grant nonbiological parents parental leave or benefits for the child. For the most part, our society assumes a heterosexist view of parenting. However, things have been slowly changing, and the majority of Americans today say that their definition of a family includes same-sex couples with children (Roberts, 2010).

Adoption may be another option for same-sex couples. When a federal judge ruled in 2016 that Mississippi's ban on same-sex couples adopting a child was unconstitutional, adoption became legal for same-sex couples in all 50 states (Reilly, 2016). Florida had laws against same-sex couple adoption up until 2010, even though a single gay or lesbian person in Florida could legally adopt (or foster a child). Throughout the United States, organizations such as PFLAG and Lambda (a national organization committed to the civil rights of lesbians, gays, and bisexuals) support same-sex parenting and are working to make adoption an easier option for same-sex couples.

Children who grow up with same-sex parents do as well emotionally, cognitively, socially, and sexually as children from heterosexual parents, and no significant differences have been found in the psychological adjustment and social relationships between the

REAL RESEARCH Lesbian, gay, and bisexual individuals who live in communities with high levels of anti-gay prejudice have a life expectancy that's shorter by 12 years, on average, compared with their peers in less prejudiced communities (HATZENBUEHLER ET AL., 2014).

children of same-sex and heterosexual couples (Adams & Light, 2015; Bos et al., 2016; Manning et al., 2014; Patterson, 2005, 2013). In fact, some studies suggest that children of same-sex parents are psychologically healthier than their peers raised by heterosexual parents (Gartrell & Bos, 2010; Golombok et al., 2014).

Same-sex couples in all states can adopt children today, although couples may be required to be in a legally recognized relationship.

Pop singer Ricky Martin is the proud father of two sons who were born via a surrogate mother.

Some critics of same-sex parenting have suggested that lesbian and gay parents will raise homosexual children (Cameron, 2006; Morrison, 2007). Although the research does not support the idea that lesbian and gay parents are more likely to raise homosexual children (Gato & Fontaine, 2013; Golombok et al., 2014; Haney-Caron & Heilbrun, 2014), one study found that social and parental factors may influence the expression of nonheterosexual sexual orientations, especially in females (Schumm, 2010). However, controversy surrounds these studies for many reasons, including researcher bias (one researcher works at a conservative family institute) and statistical errors in analysis.

Overall, the majority of the research on same-sex parenting has focused on lesbian mothers with less attention paid toward gay fathers. A meta-analysis on the psychological adjustment of children by the sexual orientation of their parent found that children of gay fathers had significantly better psychological outcomes than did children of heterosexual parents (Miller et al., 2017). Researchers attributed this to more egalitarian parenting roles, dual earner households, and a commitment to parenthood. This will be an important area of research in the future.

Lesbian, Gay, and Bisexual Seniors

Lesbian, gay, and bisexual seniors make up a significant, and growing, share of the over-50-year-old population. It's estimated that there are more than 2.7 million adults that identify as LGBT aged 50 and over in the United States, and this number is expected to more than double by 2030 (Fredriksen-Goldsen & Kim, 2017). Researchers have identified three generations of LGBT older adults living in the United States, including the Invisible, Silenced, and Pride generations (Fredriksen-Goldsen & Kim, 2017). The Invisible Generation includes the oldest LGBT adults, who lived through the Great Depression and World War II and grew up surrounded by an absence of any discussions about sexual minorities. The Silenced Generation include those who grew up surrounded by shame and negativity and the classification of homosexuality as a pathological condition. The Pride Generation includes the youngest of the older generation, that came of age during a period of significant social changes, including the Stonewall riots.

While older LGBT adults are confronted with the same challenges that heterosexual older adults face as they age, they also face various inequalities and difficulties that can interfere with a healthy and satisfying life in later years. Coming out before the senior years often helps an LGB senior to feel more comfortable with their life and sexuality. Lesbian, gay, or bisexual seniors who were in the Invisible and/or Silenced Generations may never have felt comfortable coming out and feel alone as they continue to age. In addition, they may experience depression from the years of internalized homophobia (Altman, 2000; Gross, 2007). For some, hiding their sexual orientation when they are ready for a nursing home is their only choice (often referred to as "re-closeting"). One gay man who had been in a relationship with his partner for more than 20 years said, "When I'm at the gate of the nursing home, the closet door is going to slam shut behind me" (Gross, 2007, p. 2).

Studies have found that LGB older adults, compared with heterosexuals of the same age, experience higher rates of chronic conditions, including low back pain, neck pain, and weakened immune systems (Fredriksen-Goldsen & Kim, 2017). They are also more likely to report poor health and increased risk of stroke, heart attacks, and arthritis. Compared to their heterosexual peers, they are less likely to be married and have adequate support networks. They may not have adult children to help or support them and may be estranged from their families. In addition, they are 20% less likely than their heterosexual peers to seek preventative health care and access various governmental services, such as senior centers, food stamps, or housing assistance (Czaja et al., 2015). Historical prejudice against LGB seniors can disrupt their lives, relationships with family members, and planning for retirement and assisted living. A 2011 national survey by the National Senior Citizens Law Center found that less than 25% of LGB seniors felt they could be open about their sexuality in their long-term care facility. In 2010, the National Resource Center on LGBT Aging was launched by Services and Advocacy for Gay, Lesbian, Bisexual & Transgender Elders (SAGE) with the help of a federal grant from the U.S. Department of Health and Human Services. This organization will help connect aging providers and LGBTQ organizations around the country to provide better services to aging gay, lesbian, bisexual, and transgender individuals. Retirement communities for LGBTQ residents currently exist in various states, including California, Florida, Massachusetts, New Mexico, North Carolina, Ohio, and Oregon. In addition, many retirement apartments are available for LGBTQ seniors in several large cities throughout the United States.

Lesbian, Gay, and Bisexual Organizations

Over the last few years, many organizations have formed to help lesbian, gay, and bisexual individuals obtain medical, social, and legal services. In addition, local LGB organizations that provide information on counseling centers, hotlines, legal aid, and AIDS information have been established in almost every reasonably sized city in the United States. For example, the National Gay and Lesbian Task Force (NGLTF) and its associated Policy Institute advocate for gay civil rights and lobby Congress for such things as a Federal Gay and Lesbian Civil Rights Act, health care reform, AIDS policy reform, and hate-crime laws. In 1987, they helped establish the Hate Crimes Statistics Act, which identifies and records **hate crimes**. Also well-known are the Lambda Legal Defense and Education Fund (for more information, see the list of websites at the end of this chapter), which pursues litigation issues for the LGB community, and the Human Rights Campaign Fund, which lobbies Capitol Hill on LGB rights, HIV/AIDS, and privacy issues.

The first and largest accredited public school in the world devoted to the educational needs of lesbian, gay, bisexual, transgender, and questioning youth, the Harvey Milk School, was opened in New York City in 1985. The school was named for a gay elected official from San Francisco who was murdered in 1978. Fourteen- to 18-year-old students from across the country come to the Harvey Milk School to study in an environment in which their sexual orientation is accepted and where they will not be ridiculed, ostracized, or assaulted, as many were in the schools they came from. Universities and colleges have also begun to offer LGB students separate housing, and as we discussed earlier, many high schools provide gay–straight alliances that help encourage tolerance and provide a place for students to meet.

Since the early 1980s, LGB media, including countless magazines and newspapers across the country, have been published. The largest and best-known magazine, *The Advocate,* is a national publication that covers news of interest, entertainment reviews, commentaries, LGB-oriented products and services, and hundreds of personal ads. Many other specialty magazines are available for LGB individuals including parenting magazines (such as *Gay Parent* and *Proud Parenting*), travel magazines (such as *Out and About*), and religious magazines (such as *Whosoever*).

Most major cities now have their own gay newspaper, some of which get national exposure; some noteworthy examples are New York's *Gay City News,* Philadelphia's *Gay News,* and the *Seattle Gay News.* These newspapers are often the best first sources for young LGB people who are looking for the resources available in their community.

Review Questions

1 Identify the need for LGB youth to establish a personal self-identity, and describe the task of coming out.

2 Explain some of the tasks involved in living a LGB life, including looking for partners, sexuality, parenting, aging, and specific problems encountered by LGB individuals.

3 Identify and explain the three generations of older LGBT adults.

4 Explain why many LGB groups have set up their own organizations, and give one example of such an organization.

Homophobia and Heterosexism

Lesbians, gays, and bisexuals have long been stigmatized. When homosexuality as an illness was removed from the *Diagnostic and Statistical Manual of Mental Disorders* in 1973, negative attitudes toward homosexuality persisted. It was at this time that researchers began to study these negative attitudes and behaviors.

What Is Homophobia?

Many terms have been proposed to describe the negative, often violent, reactions of many people toward homosexuality—*antihomosexualism, homoerotophobia, homosexism, homonegativism,* and **homophobia**. The popularity of the term *homophobia* is unfortunate, for *phobia* is a medical term describing an extreme, anxiety-provoking, uncontrollable fear accompanied by obsessive avoidance. We use this term here to refer to strongly negative attitudes toward homosexuals and homosexuality.

Are people really homophobic? Some might accept homosexuality intellectually and yet still dislike being in the presence of homosexuals, whereas others might object to homosexuality as a practice and yet have personal relationships with individual homosexuals whom they accept (Forstein, 1988). When compared with people who hold positive views of LGB individuals, people with negative views are less likely to have had contact with homosexuals and bisexuals, and they are more likely to be older and less well educated; be religious and subscribe to a conservative religious ideology; have more traditional attitudes

---

hate crime
A criminal offense, usually involving violence, intimidation, or vandalism, in which the victim is targeted because of their affiliation with a particular group.

homophobia
Irrational fear, negativity, or prejudice against homosexuals and homosexuality.

toward sex roles and less support for equality of the sexes; be less permissive sexually; and be authoritarian (Herek, 1984). Overall, heterosexual men, compared with heterosexual women, have been found to have significantly more negative attitudes toward gay men (McDermott et al., 2014; Verweij et al., 2008).

It is important to point out that heterosexuals aren't the only people to experience homophobia. Homosexuals who harbor negative feelings about homosexuality experience internalized homophobia (or negative feelings based on sexual orientation directed at oneself). This is especially true in older generations in which there has been less overall acceptance of homosexuality. Overall, older gay men have been found to experience more internalized homophobia than older lesbian women (Barnes & Meyer, 2012; D'Augelli et al., 2001; Wight et al., 2015). Homosexuals with internalized homophobia have been found to have decreased levels of self-esteem and increased levels of shame and psychological distress (Puckett et al., 2017).

An even bigger problem for most lesbians and gay men is **heterosexism**. Heterosexism describes the "presumption of heterosexuality" discussed earlier and the social power used to promote it (Neisen, 1990). Because heterosexual relationships are seen as "normal," a heterosexist person feels justified in suppressing or ignoring those who do not follow that model.

For example, even those with no ill feelings toward homosexuality are often unaware that businesses will not provide health care and other benefits to the partners of homosexuals. In other words, heterosexism can be passive rather than active, involving a lack of awareness rather than active discrimination. One of my students told me about an experience she had that made her painfully aware of her heterosexism:

> I remember there was a really cute guy in my psychology class. It took me all semester to walk up to him and talk. I was hoping to ask him out for coffee or something. As I walked up behind him to say hello I became aware of a button pinned to the back of his backpack. I was horrified when I read what it said, "How dare you assume I'm heterosexual!!" I nearly tripped and fell over backwards. (Author's files)

The gay rights movement has been successful at changing some of these assumptions, especially in larger cities, but today heterosexism still dictates a large part of the way the average American considers their world. Heterosexism can lead to a lack of awareness of issues that can harm LGB individuals today. Let's now turn our attention to hate crimes against LGB individuals.

Hate Crimes Against Lesbian, Gay, and Bisexual Individuals

Throughout history, persecution of minorities has been based on philosophies that portrayed those minorities as illegitimate, subhuman, or evil. Likewise, homophobia is not just a set of attitudes; it creates an atmosphere in which people feel they are permitted to

harass, assault, and even kill homosexuals. Earlier we talked about hate crimes, or those crimes that are motivated by hatred of someone's religion, sex, race, sexual orientation, disability, gender identity, or ethnic group (Parrott & Peterson, 2008). They are known as "message crimes" because they send a message to the victim's affiliated group (American Psychiatric Association, 1998).

One of the deadliest incidents of violence against lesbian, gay, bisexual, and transgender people in the history of the United States occurred in June of 2016, when an armed man entered a gay nightclub in Orlando, Florida, and killed 49 people and wounded 53. The FBI claimed that since the nightclub wasn't targeted because it was an LGBTQ venue, it was not officially a hate crime (Goldman, 2016). However, many experts disagreed and have called it one of the deadliest homophobic hate crime attacks in history. This was further evidenced by the fact that various hate groups around the country celebrated the massacre by tweeting hateful comments about the victims (Solis, 2016). Shortly after the attack, Equality Florida, one of Florida's largest LGBTQ rights groups, started a fundraising campaign to aid the victims and their families. By late 2016, the group had raised more than $9 million (a GoFundMe record; Evans, 2016).

It was estimated that nearly 20% of all single-bias hate crimes reported to the FBI in 2014 were due to a person's sexual orientation (or perceived sexual orientation; Park & Mykhyalyshyn, 2016). Hate crimes based on sexual orientation were the third

The Pulse Nightclub shooting in 2016 was one of the deadliest incidents of violence against LGBT people in the history of the United States.

---

heterosexism
The "presumption of heterosexuality" that has sociological implications.

most common type of hate crime in 2015 (behind race and religion), with gay men being targeted more than lesbians or bisexuals (Uniform Crime Report, 2015). According to the American Psychological Association, hate crimes against homosexuals are the most socially acceptable form of hate crimes. Some experts believe that the violence against LGB people may be due to the increased societal acceptance of same-sex relationships since those who are opposed to them often become more radical in their hatred.

The majority of LGBTQ youth report having experienced bullying or hate crimes, with higher victimization rates among boys. Victimization typically begins around age 13, although some verbal attacks began as early as age 6. In fact, one study found that close to 80% of LGB youth experienced verbal victimization, while 11% reported physical victimization and 9% reported sexual victimization (D'Augelli et al., 2006). Victims often suffer a variety of symptoms including anger, depression, acute stress, fear, and anxiety (Herek, 1993; Taylor, 2007).

ON YOUR MIND

Are people really homophobic because they fear that they themselves are homosexuals?

This question is difficult to answer, but many psychologists believe that fear of one's own sexual desires is a factor in homophobia. The best evidence is the level of brutality of gay hate crimes; the degree of violence suggests that there is a deep fear and hatred at work. Why such hatred of somebody you don't even know? The answer must lie within oneself.

Why Are People Homophobic?

What motivates people to be homophobic? A number of theories have been suggested. Because rigid, authoritarian personalities are more likely to be homophobic, it may be a function of personality type; for such people, anything that deviates from their view of "correct" behavior elicits disdain (Smith, 1971). Another common suggestion is that heterosexual people fear their own suppressed homosexual desires or are insecure in their own masculinity or femininity (Adams et al., 1996). Others believe that this explanation is too simplistic (Rosser, 1999). Perhaps people are simply ignorant about homosexuality and would change their attitudes with education. Most likely, all of these are true to some degree in different people.

How Can We Combat Homophobia and Heterosexism?

Heterosexism is widespread and subtle, and therefore difficult to combat. The late Adrienne Rich (1983), a prominent poet and scholar of lesbian studies, used the term *heterocentrism* to describe the neglect of homosexual existence, even among feminists. Perhaps we can learn from the history of a similar term: *ethnocentrism*. Ethnocentrism refers to the belief that all standards of correct behavior are determined by one's own cultural background, leading to racism, ethnic bigotry, and even sexism and heterosexism. Although ethnocentrism is still rampant in American society, it is slowly being eroded by the passage of new laws, the media's

spotlight on abuses, and improved education. Perhaps a similar strategy can be used to combat heterosexism.

Legislating Against Hate Crimes

Hate crimes legislation targets violence that is committed in response to a victim's identity, including sexual orientation. The Hate Crimes Statistics Act was enacted by Congress in 1990. This law requires the compilation of data on hate crimes so that there is a comprehensive picture of these crimes. In 1997, the Hate Crimes Right to Know Act was passed, which requires college campuses to report all hate crimes. In 2009, the Matthew Shepard and James Byrd, Jr. Hate Crimes Prevention Act was signed into law, which provided the Justice Department with jurisdiction over hate crimes and enabled the department to help in the investigation of such crimes (Cramer et al., 2013).

Promoting Positive Change Through the Media

The representation of the lesbian, gay, and bisexual community has been increasing in the media over the last few years. Shows such as *Orange Is the New Black, Shameless,* and *Modern Family* continue to pave the way for LGBTQs on television, resulting in vastly different programming from just a few years ago. A focus on LGBTQ issues has also increased in other forms of media. For example, you might recall the comic book character

Brandi Carlile, a popular lesbian American folk rock singer/songwriter, says that since she was influenced by many gay artists and celebrities, she believes it's an honor to be a role model for LGB teens today. In 2012, Carlile married her long-term partner, Catherine Shepherd.

Archie, from the series *Life with Archie*. In 2014, Archie died when he took a bullet meant for his friend who was being targeted for being gay (Putterman, 2014). Although these are difficult issues, having them in the mainstream media can translate into a greater acceptance of the LGBTQ community.

Another important development in the media is the explosion of music, fiction, nonfiction, plays, and movies that portray lesbian and gay life in America more realistically. Whereas once these types of media were shocking and hidden, now they appear on television and radio stations as well as in mainstream bookstores and movie theaters.

Promoting Positive Change Through Education

Another important step to stopping heterosexism is education. Homosexuality remains a taboo subject in many schools, and most proposals to teach sexuality in general—never mind homosexuality in particular—encounter strong opposition by certain parent groups. When sexuality education is taught in schools, there is often little information included about sexual orientation. Educating today's students about homophobia and heterosexism can help reduce negative attitudes, gay bashing, and hate crimes.

Review Questions

1 Define homophobia and explain what factors have been found to be related to the development of homophobia. Explain how homosexuals can be homophobic.

2 Define heterosexism and heterocentrism, and give one example of each.

3 Explain how hate crimes are known as "message crimes" and give one example.

4 Explain how laws, the media, and education have all helped to reduce homophobia and hate crimes.

Differences Among Homosexual Groups

Because homosexuality exists in almost every ethnic, racial, socio-economic, and religious group, many lesbians, gays, and bisexuals also belong to other minority groups. We now discuss the unique situations of some of these groups.

Lesbianism

Many women do not fall neatly into homosexual–heterosexual categories. Maybe this is because society is less threatened by lesbian sexuality than by gay sexuality. The research on lesbianism suggests that women's sexual identity is more fluid than men's (see the accompanying "Sex in Real Life" feature; Diamond, 2005; Gallo, 2000; Notman, 2002). For some women, an early same-sex relationship is temporarily or permanently replaced by a heterosexual one, or a heterosexual relationship may be replaced by a lesbian relationship later in life (Notman, 2002).

The lesbian community is a vibrant one. Bars, coffeehouses, bookstores, sports teams, political organizations, living cooperatives, media, and lesbian-run and -owned businesses often represent a political statement about the ways in which women can live and work together. A number of lesbian musicians—including Chely Wright, Brandi Carlile, Melissa Etheridge, and the Indigo Girls—sing of issues important to the lesbian community and yet have strong crossover appeal to the heterosexual community. Many lesbian magazines are dedicated to lesbian fiction, erotica, current events, and photography.

Studies have found that lesbians who feel supported and accepted have higher levels of self-esteem and well-being (Beals & Peplau, 2005). However, compared to heterosexual women, they have an increased risk for health problems, including higher levels of depression and antidepressant use, obesity, and cigarette and alcohol use (Fredriksen-Goldsen & Kim, 2017; Johns et al., 2017). Lesbians have also been found to have lower rates of preventive care (yearly physical examinations) than heterosexual women (Agénor et al., 2015; Kerr et al., 2013).

Bisexuality

Although we have been discussing bisexuality throughout this chapter, bisexuality has emerged more recently as a separate identity from lesbian, gay, or heterosexual identities. Notably, for many years, few people noticed the absence of research on bisexuality. This absence stemmed from the fact that researchers believed that sexuality was composed of only two opposing forms of sexuality: heterosexuality and homosexuality (Herek, 2002). Social and political bisexual groups began forming in the 1970s, but it wasn't until the late 1980s that an organized bisexual movement achieved visibility in the United States.

We do know that people who identify as bisexual often first identified as heterosexuals, and their self-labeling generally occurs later in life than either lesbian or gay self-labeling (Weinberg et al., 1994). Bisexual individuals may constitute the majority of the LGB community (Gates, 2011; Hill et al., 2016; Weinrich, 2014). In addition, studies have found that women are significantly more likely than men to identify as bisexual (Chandra & Febo-Vasquez, 2016; Copen et al., 2016).

Homosexuals have tended to see bisexuals either as on their way to becoming homosexual or as people who want to be able to "play both sides of the fence" by being homosexual in the gay community and heterosexual in straight society. Heterosexuals have tended to lump bisexuals in with homosexuals. Some scholars have suggested that bisexuality is a myth, or an attempt to deny one's homosexuality; identity confusion; or an attempt to be "chic" or "trendy" (Alarie & Gaudet, 2013; Rust, 2000). Some studies claim that bisexuals are people who are ambivalent about their homosexual behavior (Carey,

Let's imagine you go to a party on campus tonight and while you are there, two heterosexual girls kiss each other deeply. Why do they do it? What would the reaction of the other partygoers be? What if two straight men kissed in the same way? Chances are there would be less support for the two men, but why? Overall, sexual behavior between women is more acceptable than sexual behavior between men (Turner et al., 2005). Same-sex sexual contact does occur between heterosexual women on college campuses, and it typically occurs in front of friends in public places where people have been drinking alcohol (Hegna & Rossow, 2007). The women might kiss to see what it feels like, to show off, or to feel more attractive and sexy.

Attitudes about same-sex sexual behavior have become more liberal in the past few decades. The percentage of women responding that sexual behavior between two women is "not wrong at all" increased from 5.6% (for women born before 1970) to 45% (for women born after 1970; men showed a similar increase from 7.5%

Paula Eureka

to 32%; Turner et al., 2005). Data from the 2011–2013 National Survey of Family Growth found that three times as many women (17.4%) reported engaging in same-sex behavior in their lifetimes compared with men (6.2%; Copen et al., 2016).

Researchers believe that there is more stigmatization of sexual contact between males, and perhaps this is one reason why young heterosexual women who engage in sexual contact with other women experience fewer negative reactions from others (Hegna & Rossow, 2007; Otis & Skinner, 1996). An interesting question would be to consider what the partygoers' responses would be if the two girls who were kissing in front of the crowd were lesbians and not straight. Would it still garner attention?

2005; Rieger et al., 2005). Bisexuals themselves have begun to call attention to **biphobia** (also referred to as **monosexism**), which they suggest exists in both the straight and lesbian and gay communities (Galupo, 2006; Mulick & Wright, 2002; Ross et al., 2010). Bisexuals may experience internalized biphobia or monosexism.

Many bisexuals see themselves as having the best of both worlds. As one bisexual put it, "The more I talk and think about it, and listen to people, I realize that there are no fences, no walls, no heterosexuality or homosexuality. There are just people and the electricity between them" (quoted in Spolan, 1991, p. 7). In our society, fear of intimacy is expressed through either homophobia if you are heterosexual or **heterophobia** if you are lesbian or gay; no matter what your sexual orientation, one gender or another is always taboo—restricting your sexual intimacy (Klein, 1978). From that perspective, bisexuality is a full acceptance of all partners.

More people in American society exhibit bisexual behavior than exclusively homosexual behavior (Klein, 1990). In **sequential bisexuality**, the person has sex exclusively with one gender, followed by sex exclusively with the other; **contemporaneous bisexuality** refers to having male and female sexual partners during the same period (Paul, 1984). Numbers are hard to come by because bisexuality itself is so hard to define. How many encounters with both sexes are needed for a person to be considered bisexual? One? Fifty? And what of fantasies? It is difficult to determine what percentage of people is bisexual because many who engage in bisexual behavior do not self-identify as bisexual (Weinberg et al., 1994).

Some people experience bisexuality through intimate involvement with a close friend of the same sex, even if they have not had same-sex attractions before. The new bisexual movement may succeed in breaking through the artificial split of the sexual world into homosexuals and heterosexuals. Perhaps we fear the fluid model of sexuality offered by bisexuality because we fear our own cross-preference encounter fantasies and do not want to admit that most of us, even if hidden deep in our fantasies, are to some degree attracted to both sexes. Pansexuality is also sometimes included under the definition of bisexuality, since it rejects the gender binary and encompasses romantic or sexual attractions to all gender identities. Bisexuals, pansexuals, and skoliosexuals may be attracted to non-binary and transgender people.

Like lesbians and gays, bisexuals experience hostility, discrimination, and violence in response to their sexual orientation (Herek, 2002). Some researchers suggest that bisexuals experience "double discrimination," because they may experience discrimination from both the heterosexual and homosexual communities (Ross et al., 2010). Compared with lesbians and gays, bisexuals have decreased social well-being, more barriers to health care, and increased risks of heart disease, obesity, depression, substance abuse, and suicide (Hill et al., 2016; Ross et al., 2016).

Minority Homosexuality

Many lesbian, gay, or bisexual people who are members of racial or ethnic minorities in the United States often have to simultaneously negotiate other stigmatized identities (Ross et al., 2010).

biphobia
Irrational fear, negativity, or prejudice against bisexuals and bisexuality.

monosexism
The belief that a person can only be attracted to one gender.

heterophobia
Irrational fear, negativity, or prejudice against heterosexuals and heterosexuality.

sequential bisexuality
Engaging in sexual behavior exclusively with a member of one sex followed by an exclusive sexual relationship with a member of the other sex.

contemporaneous bisexuality
Having sexual partners of both sexes during the same period.

Lesbians, gays, and bisexuals who belong to other minority groups must deal with the prejudices of society toward both groups, as well as each group's prejudices toward the other.

Homosexuality is less accepted by many ethnic groups, and yet the gay community has historically had some difficulties accommodating expressions of ethnic identity. Intersectionality theory helps us examine LGBTQ lives in the context of other social identities, including ethnic and racial groups (McCall, 2005). Social identities intersect to create a unique personal identity that may differ from each individual component.

Being in two stigmatized minority groups provides a "double jeopardy" for minority LGB individuals (Eaton & Rios, 2017). This contributes to increased psychological distress and often makes individuals feel torn between multiple communities (Fredriksen-Goldsen & Kim, 2017). As one gay Asian American put it, "While the Asian-American community supports my Asian identity, the gay community only supports my being a gay man; as a result I find it difficult to identify with either" (Chan, 1989, p. 18).

Cultural norms in Latino communities can make added stress for gay and bisexual men. For example, Latino men who are gay often struggle with cultural expectations about gender norms such as *machismo*, which endorses hypermasculinity (Eaton & Rios, 2017). As a result, Latino men who are gay often experience high levels of prejudice and stress (Balsam et al., 2011). One study found that the majority of gay Latino men in college reported negative responses to their sexual identity disclosures (Eaton & Rios, 2017).

Black lesbians and gays can also have difficulties because they often have to deal with the heterosexism of the Black community and the racism of the homosexual and straight communities (Tye, 2006). Studies have found that Black lesbians are one of the most vulnerable groups, with an increased risk for physical and emotional health issues, shorter life expectancies, and poverty rates of 21% (compared with poverty rates of 4% for White lesbians and 14% for gay Black men; Ramsey et al., 2010). Unfortunately, Black lesbians are also less likely than other groups to seek out mental or physical health services (Agénor et al., 2015; Ramsey et al., 2010; Seelman et al., 2016). It is also worth pointing out that research has found that although many

Black lesbians report positive relationships and pleasant feelings about their sexual relationships, more than half also report feeling guilty about these relationships (Wyatt, 1998). This is consistent with the aforementioned research noting the prevalence of psychological distress in homosexual minorities.

Studies have found that conflicts in allegiances between identities are most complicated when a minority LGB person has high levels of racial/ethnic group identity but low levels of sexual orientation group identity (Sarno et al., 2015). For example, a Latino man would have the most conflict when he has a strong identity to the Latino culture but not does identify with the gay male culture. Researchers believe fewer conflicts may arise when minority LGB persons have high levels of involvement in both racial/ethnic and sexual orientation group identities, mainly because they would find more support and resources available to them (Sarno et al., 2015).

Same-Sex Sexual Behavior in Prison

Homosexual behavior varies greatly in prisons. Sexual contact between inmates, although prohibited, still occurs in prisons today. Researchers who study prison rape have had difficulties defining it. If a man is scared for his life and provides sex to a more powerful man for protection, is this rape? Sexual behaviors in prison are governed by a hierarchy of roles and relationships that define an inmate's position within the prison system (Hensley, 2002). Although forced sex does occur in prisons, overall it is less common in women's prisons than in men's.

Many individuals who engage in same-sex sexual behavior in prison claim that they are not homosexual and that their sexual behavior is an adaptation to their all-male or all-female environments (Girshick, 1999; Ricciardelli et al., 2016). Some claim they plan to return to heterosexual relationships exclusively once they are released. One female prisoner said:

I think a lot of [the motivation for gay relationships] is loneliness, despair, and in some cases I know for a fact that it's for financial purposes. I have seen women have relationships with women, leave this dorm hugging and kissing this woman, then go out to visitation and hug and kiss their husband. (Girshick, 1999, p. 87)

This **situational homosexuality** is also found in other places where people must spend long periods of time together, such as on ships at sea.

Same-sex relationships in prison can be strong and jealously guarded (Girshick, 1999; Nacci & Kane, 1983). Inmates speak of loving their inmate partners, and relations can become extremely intimate, even among those who return to a heterosexual life on release.

ON YOUR MIND

Are bisexuals really equally attracted to both sexes?

It depends on the bisexual. Some are more attracted to one sex than the other, whereas others say that they have no preference. Masters and Johnson (1979) found that both heterosexuals and homosexuals have at least some "cross-preference" fantasies; perhaps if social pressures were not as strong as they are, many more people would be bisexual to some degree.

1 Explain how women's sexual identity may be more fluid than men's sexual identity, and give one example.

2 Differentiate between sequential and contemporaneous bisexuality.

3 Describe intersectionality theory and explain the importance of examining LGBTQ lives in the context of other social identities, including ethnic and racial groups.

4 Explain what is known about same-sex sexual behavior in prisons.

Homosexuality in Religion and the Law

Religion has generally been considered a bastion of antihomosexual teachings and beliefs, and these beliefs have often helped shape laws that prohibit homosexual behaviors. We now discuss both of these powerful influences.

Homosexuality and Religion

There has been a great deal of negativity surrounding homosexuality in religion, and changes in social attitudes toward homosexuality beginning in the early 1980s have provoked conflict over homosexual policies in many religious denominations. Traditionally, both Judaism and Christianity have strongly opposed homosexual behavior.

Some Christian religions are more tolerant, such as the United Church of Christ. This church and its members have welcomed lesbian, gay, bisexual, and transgender members, worked for equal rights, and ordained LGBTQ clergy. They generally view homosexuality as neither a sin nor a choice, and they believe that it is unchangeable. One of the most accepting churches, the Metropolitan Community Churches, promotes itself as the world's largest organization with a primary, affirming ministry to LGBTQ persons (Metropolitan Community Churches, 2005).

More conflict about sexual orientation exists in other Christian religions, such as Presbyterian, Methodist, Lutheran, and Episcopalian, resulting in both liberal and conservative views. Even so, in recent years, a number of these denominations have voted to allow openly gay and lesbian women to serve as clergy. This includes the Evangelical Lutheran Church in America, the U.S. Episcopal Church, the Presbyterian Church, and the United Church of Christ.

In many churches and synagogues, most of the more conservative views, including the idea that homosexuality can be changed through prayer and counseling, come from older members and those living in the southern part of the United States. The conservative Christian faiths, such as Catholics, Southern Baptists, and the Assemblies of God, may view homosexuality as a sin and work to restrict LGB rights.

There is also controversy over sexual orientation in many synagogues throughout the United States. Although Orthodox Jews traditionally have believed that homosexuality was an abomination forbidden by the Torah, today there is more acceptance in Orthodox as well as Reform congregations. A Reform movement in 1990 allowed the ordaining of gay rabbis (Albert et al., 2001). In 2010, a Statement of Principles was signed and released by a group of Orthodox rabbis that supports the acceptance of homosexual members (Nahshoni, 2010).

Around the world, Muslims overwhelmingly believe that homosexuality is morally wrong (Pew Research Center, 2013). Like many conservative Christians and Jews, conservative Muslims often consider homosexual acts sinful (Van der Krogt, 2016). However, American Muslims are often more liberal about homosexuality and have a broader interpretation of the Qur'an based on compassion and empathy for those who are homosexual (Shackford, 2016).

Among various Buddhist sects in the United States, there is also no real consensus about lesbian and gay relationships. Buddhism differs from Christianity in that it views behaviors as helpful or nonhelpful (whereas Christianity views behaviors as good/evil) and looks at whether there was intent to help. As a result of this, Buddhism encourages relationships that are mutually loving and supportive. While there are no rules prohibiting LGBTQ people from serving as Buddhist monks or nuns, some temples and monasteries may not allow the ordination of LGBTQ people.

Religious scholars have begun promoting arguments based on religious law and even scripture for a more liberal attitude toward homosexuality. For example, some Jewish scholars have argued that because homosexual orientation is not a free choice but an unalterable feature of the personality, it is immoral to punish someone for it (Kahn 1989-1990). (See Figure 11.6 for statistics about public support for same-sex marriage.)

Homosexuality and the Law

Throughout history, laws have existed in the Western world that prohibited same-sex sexual behavior. In the United States, sodomy

---

situational homosexuality
Homosexuality that occurs because of the lack of heterosexual partners.

AP Images/David Zalubowski

Although there is still hostility toward homosexuality within many major religions, religious scholars have begun to promote a more liberal attitude, including ordination of lesbian and gay clergy and marriage or commitment ceremonies.

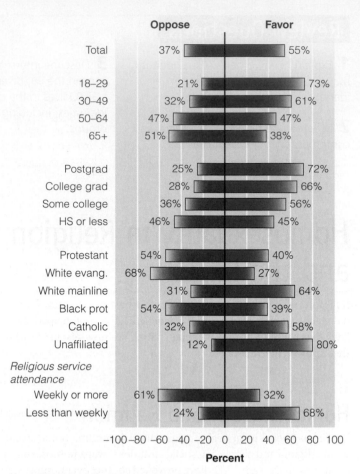

Note: "Don't know" responses not shown.

FIGURE 11.6 Public Support for Same-Sex Marriage
For more information about graph, go to: http://www.pewresearch
.org/fact-tank/2016/05/12/support-steady-for-same-sex-marriage-and
-acceptance-of-homosexuality/

SOURCE: Fingerhut, 2016: Pew Research Center.

has been illegal since colonial days, and it was punishable by death until the late 18th century (Boswell, 1980). Fellatio was technically legal until the early 20th century, although it was considered to be "loathsome and revolting" (Murphy, 1990). Up until 1961, all 50 states outlawed homosexual sexual behaviors.

In 2003, the Supreme Court overturned the Texas antisodomy law, which made consensual sex between same-sex couples illegal. Before 2003, under Texas homosexual conduct law, for example, individuals who engaged in "deviate sexual intercourse" with a person of the same sex (even if the partner was consenting) could be charged with a misdemeanor punishable by up to $500 in fines (Lambda, 2001).

Over the last few years, the legal landscape for lesbian and gay rights has been changing in the United States. In 2010, President Obama signed a bill ending the military's "don't ask, don't tell" policy, which was one of the first moves toward equality for lesbians and gays. In 2011, he rescinded his support for the Defense of Marriage Act (DOMA), concluding that his administration could no longer defend the federal law that defines marriage as between a man and a woman. The dismantling of DOMA was a major victory for gay rights advocates. A variety of legal cases that challenged the federal government's denial of same-sex marriage and marriage-related benefits made their way to the Supreme Court, and in 2015 the Court ruled that state-level bans on same-sex marriage were unconstitutional. This legalized same-sex marriage in all states, the District of Columbia, and all U.S. territories (except American Samoa).

Review Questions

1 Explain how changes in social attitudes toward homosexuality have provoked conflict over LGB policies in many religious denominations.

2 Identify some of the more liberal and conservative religions and explain how each religion views homosexuality.

3 Explain how the legal landscape has been changing for lesbian and gay rights in the United States.

Chapter Review

1 Sexual orientation refers to an emotional, physical, sexual, and romantic attraction to persons of the same, other, or both sexes. Heterosexuals are predominantly attracted to members of the other sex, homosexuals to members of the same sex, and bisexuals are attracted to both. Other sexual orientations include androsexual, asexual, gynesexual, pansexual, and skoliosexual.

2 Alfred Kinsey introduced a seven-point sexual orientation scale based mostly on people's sexual behaviors. The Kinsey continuum was the first scale to suggest that people engage in complex sexual behaviors that cannot be reduced simply to "homosexual" and "heterosexual." Other researchers suggest that people's emotions and fantasies, more than their behaviors, are the most important determinants of sexual orientation. The Klein Sexual Orientation Grid (KSOG) includes the elements of time, fantasy, social and lifestyle behavior, and self-identification.

3 The frequency of lesbian, gay, and bisexual (LGB) behavior in the United States has remained constant over the years. Scholars generally agree that between 2% and 4% of males are gay, 1% to 3% of women are predominantly lesbian, and about 3% of people are bisexual. However, many of these studies have methodological flaws and have not taken into account feelings of attraction or fantasies.

4 Numerous studies have shown that sexual behavior does not necessarily predict self-identified sexual orientation. From 2012 to 2016, there was an increase in the number of Americans that identified as LGBTQ.

5 Several theories have been proposed to explain homosexuality. These include the biological, developmental, behavioral, sociological, and interactional theories.

6 Biological theories claim that differences in sexual orientation are caused by genetics, hormones, birth order, or simple physical traits. Developmental theories focus on a person's upbringing and personal history to find the origins of homosexuality. Developmental theories include psychoanalytic, gender-role nonconformity, and peer-group interaction. Behaviorist theories view homosexuality as a learned behavior, whereas the sociological theories explain how social forces produce homosexuality in a society. The interactional theories explore the combined impact of biology and sociology.

7 Same-sex activity was common before the 19th century, and homosexual prostitution was taxed by the state. Homosexuality was not treated with concern or much interest by either early Jews or early Christians. The church's indifference to homosexuality lasted well through the 13th century. By 1300, however, the new intolerance of differences resulted in homosexuality being punishable by death almost everywhere. This view, from the late Middle Ages, has influenced the Western world's view of homosexuality for the past 700 years. In the 19th and early 20th centuries, physicians and scientists began to suggest that homosexuality was not a sin but an illness.

8 Same-sex sexual behavior is found in every culture, and its prevalence remains about the same no matter how permissive or repressive that culture's attitude is toward it. Many homosexuals and bisexuals struggle with discrimination, prejudice, laws that do not recognize their same-sex unions, lack of benefits for their partners, and families who may reject them. A recent Pew Research Center study found significant variations in acceptance by region. While some countries have laws protecting LGB individuals and allow civil unions and same-sex marriages, other countries have laws criminalizing homosexuality and will even sentence homosexuals to death.

9 Someone who is lesbian or gay must first acknowledge their sexual identity to themselves, and undergo a process known as coming out. Today's teens are coming out earlier than at any other time in history. A changing social climate has lessened the pressure to "fit in." However, there are still some youth who remain closeted into late adolescence and even adulthood. LGB youth who have positive coming-out experiences have higher self-confidence, lower rates of depression, and better psychological adjustment than those who have negative coming-out experiences.

10 Studies have found that more than half of parents of LGB youth initially react with some degree of negativity, including disappointment, shame, and shock, when they learn about a child's homosexuality. More than 70% of LGB youth experience some degree of parental rejection related to their sexual orientation, with Black and Hispanic LGB youth experiencing greater rejection than White or non-Hispanic LGB youth.

11 LGB youth are more likely than heterosexuals to experience stress and tension and are at greater risk for the development of chronic diseases and mental health issues. They have higher rates of substance abuse, and higher rates of truancy, homelessness, and sexual abuse compared with heterosexual youth and adults.

12 Risks for LGB youth are highest among those who identify as bisexual, as well as those who are ethnic/racial minorities. These issues may all be related to the pressures of living in a society that discriminates against LGB individuals.

13 Children who grow up with same-sex parents do as well emotionally, cognitively, socially, and sexually as children from heterosexual parents, and no significant differences have been found in the psychological adjustment and social relationships between the children of same-sex and heterosexual couples. In fact, some studies suggest that children of same-sex parents are psychologically healthier than their peers raised by heterosexual parents.

14 Much of the research on same-sex parenting has focused on lesbian mothers with less attention paid toward gay men as parents. However, children of gay fathers have been found to have significantly better psychological outcomes compared to children of heterosexual parents. As of 2016, same-sex adoption is legal in all 50 states. Florida had laws against same-sex couple adoption up until 2010, even though a single gay man or lesbian woman in Florida could legally adopt.

15 Lesbian, gay, and bisexual older adults make up a significant, and growing, share of the over-50-year-old population. Researchers have identified three generations of LGBT older adults living in the United States, including the Invisible, Silenced, and Pride generations. While older LGBT adults are confronted with the same challenges that heterosexual older adults face as they age, they also face various inequalities and difficulties that can interfere with a healthy and satisfying life in the later years.

16 Studies have found that LGB older adults, compared with heterosexuals of the same age, experience higher rates of chronic conditions, including low back pain, neck pain, and weakened immune systems. They are also more likely to report poor health and increased risk stroke, heart attacks, and arthritis.

17 LGB seniors who have not come out may feel alone as they continue to age. In addition, they may experience depression from the years of internalized homophobia. Retirement communities for LGBT residents currently exist in various states, including California, Florida, Massachusetts, New Mexico, North Carolina, Ohio, and Oregon. Retirement apartments are available for LGBTQ seniors in several large cities throughout the United States.

18 Many terms have been proposed to describe the negative, often violent, reactions of many people toward homosexuality. *Homophobia* is a medical term describing an extreme, anxiety-provoking, uncontrollable fear accompanied by obsessive avoidance. We use this term here to refer to strongly negative attitudes toward homosexuals and homosexuality.

19 Hate crimes, also known as "message crimes," are motivated by hatred of someone's religion, sex, race, sexual orientation, disability, or ethnic group. One of the deadliest incidents of violence against LGBTQ people in U.S. history occurred in 2016 at a gay nightclub in Orlando, Florida, when 49 people were killed and many more were wounded.

20 The majority of LGB youth report having experienced bullying or hate crimes, and rates of victimization are higher for boys. Victimization typically begins around age 13, although some verbal attacks began as early as age 6. Some experts believe that the violence against LGBTQ people may be due to the increased societal acceptance of same-sex relationships since those who are opposed to them often become more radical in their hatred.

21 Society is less threatened by lesbian sexuality, and perhaps this is the reason that women's sexual identity is more fluid than men's. Studies have found that lesbians who feel supported and accepted have higher levels of self-esteem and well-being. Overall, lesbian and bisexual women have been found to have lower rates of preventive care than heterosexual women.

22 Bisexual men and women may constitute the majority of the LGB community, and studies have found that women are significantly more likely than men to identify as bisexual. Bisexuals often identify first as heterosexuals, and their self-labeling generally occurs later in life than either gay or lesbian self-labeling. Pansexuality also rejects the gender binary and encompasses romantic or sexual attractions to all gender identities. Both bisexuals and pansexuals may be attracted to intersexed and transgender people who may identify as male, female, or neither. Biphobia is a fear of bisexuals.

23 Intersectionality theory can help us examine LGBTQ lives in the context of other social identities and understand how all these identities intersect to create a unique personal identity that may differ from each individual component. Studies have found that the added stresses of being in multiple stigmatized minority groups can provide a "double jeopardy" for minority LGB individuals, creating increased psychological distress

24 Some religions have become more accepting of homosexuals. Some Christian religions, such as Presbyterian, Methodist, Lutheran, and Episcopalian, have more conflict over the issue of sexual orientation, resulting in both liberal and conservative views. Laws that prohibited homosexual behavior have existed throughout history in the Western world, even on pain of death. In the United States before new legislation, sodomy had been illegal since colonial days.

25 Over the last few years the legal landscape for gay rights has been changing. The military's "don't ask, don't tell" policy ended in 2010, and in 2011, the Defense of Marriage Act (DOMA) was challenged. In 2015 the Supreme Court ruled that state-level bans on same-sex marriage were unconstitutional, legalizing same-sex marriage throughout the United States.

Critical Thinking Questions

1 If you are not lesbian, gay, or bisexual, imagine for a moment discovering that you are. Whom do you think you would approach first to talk about the issues surrounding this discovery? Would you feel comfortable talking with your friends? Parents? Siblings? Teachers? Why or why not?

2 Suppose that one of your good friends, Tim, comes to you tomorrow and tells you that he thinks he is bisexual. You have seen Tim date only women and had no idea he was interested in men. What kinds of questions do you ask him? After reading this chapter, what can you tell him about the current research on bisexuality?

3 If a person only fantasizes about engaging in same-sex behavior but never has actually done so, would they be homosexual? Why or why not?

4 Where do you fall on Kinsey's continuum? What experiences in your life contribute to your Kinsey ranking? Why?

5 What theory do you think best explains the development of sexual orientation? What features do you feel add to the theory's credibility?

Websites

GLBTQ   An encyclopedia of gay, lesbian, bisexual, transgender, and queer culture. Contains information about culture, history, and current rulings on same-sex marriage, civil unions, and domestic partnerships.

National Gay and Lesbian Task Force   The National Gay and Lesbian Task Force (NGLTF) works for the civil rights of gay, lesbian, bisexual, and transgender people. The website contains press releases and information on many issues, including affirmative action, domestic partnerships, and same-sex marriage.

Gay and Lesbian Association of Retiring Persons   The Gay and Lesbian Association of Retiring Persons (GLARP) is an international, nonprofit membership organization that was launched to enhance the aging experience of gays and lesbians. This website provides retirement-related information and services and also works to establish same-sex retirement communities in the United States and abroad.

Lambda Legal   Lambda Legal is the oldest and largest national legal organization whose mission is to achieve full recognition of the civil rights of lesbians, gay men, bisexuals, transgender people, and those with HIV. Their website contains information on a variety of issues related to LGBTQ individuals.

Parents, Families, & Friends of Lesbians and Gays   Parents, Families, Friends, and Allies United with LGBT People (PFLAG) is the nation's largest family and ally organization supporting parents, families, friends, and straight allies united with people who are lesbian, gay, bisexual, and transgender. Through education, support, and dialogue, PFLAG provides opportunities to learn more about sexual orientation and helps to create a society that is respectful of human diversity.

12 Pregnancy and Birth

Laura and Ozlem are a lesbian couple who have been together for close to 18 years. Spending time with them made me realize how much their relationship is based on love, shared values, common interests, and a strong commitment to each other. Both of them had always wanted children and had talked about it early on in their relationship. Unlike fertile heterosexual couples, however, they had to talk about how they were going to make this happen. They felt fortunate to have a large circle of lesbian couples and friends who were also making similar decisions.

© Janell Carroll

After years of discussing their options, they finally decided to use a known donor who was a family friend. They chose their donor because he was kind, thoughtful, athletic, and intelligent. He had tremendous visual-spatial skills and was a carpenter by trade. He understood that although he would be able to have a relationship with the children, he would not parent them. He had not fathered any children and he knew this might be his only opportunity to do so. In the end, he agreed to donate sperm to father two children but relinquished all parental rights and responsibilities. After all the agreements were made, Ozlem was inseminated first and gave birth to a healthy baby boy, Deniz. Laura was inseminated a few years later and gave birth to a healthy baby girl, Isabelle. Today, Deniz and Isabelle see their father on a regular basis and are thrilled he is in their lives.

It was really fun to talk to Deniz and Isabelle about their two-mom family. They told me about all the fun things they do and the other two-mom families they know. They also told me how they handle it when kids at school ask about their family. Their mom, Laura, summed it up the best when she said, "We're just like any other family. In fact, our similarities are far greater than our differences."

Janell Carroll

We tend to think of a family as consisting of a father, mother, and their biological children. However, increasing divorce, adoption, teenage pregnancy, and single and same-sex parenting, together with advances in assisted reproductive technologies (ARTs), have led to a new view of the family. Whereas at one time vaginal intercourse was required for pregnancy, this is no longer true—donor sperm, ova, embryos, and surrogate uteruses can be used today. In this chapter, we begin to explore issues related to fertility, pregnancy, and childbearing.

Fertility

Most parents, sooner or later, must confront the moment when their child asks, "Where did I come from?" The answer they give depends on the parent, the child, the situation, and the culture. Every culture has its own traditional explanations for where babies come from. The Australian Aborigines, for instance, believe that babies are created by the mother earth and, therefore, are products of the land. The spirits of children rest in certain areas of the land, and these spirits enter a young woman as she passes by (Dunham et al., 1992). Women who do not want to become pregnant either avoid these areas or dress up like old women to fool the spirits. In Malaysia, the Malay people believe that because man is the more rational of the two sexes, babies come from men. Babies are formulated in the man's brain for 40 days before moving down to his penis for eventual ejaculation into a woman's womb.

In American culture, we take a more scientific view of where babies come from, and so it is important to understand the biological processes involved in conceiving a child, being pregnant, and giving birth. Most students have a pretty good idea about how babies are made, but there are many gaps in knowledge about reproduction and birth. For example, a study of 18- to 40-year-old women found multiple misconceptions about fertility, conception, pregnancy, and basic reproductive health–related concepts (Lundsberg et al., 2014). The biological answer to the question "Where did I come from?" is that we are created from the union of an ovum and a spermatozoon. You may recall from the sexual anatomy and physiology chapters that fertilization and conception are dynamic processes that result in the creation of new life, a process so complex it is often referred to as "the incredible journey."

Statistics and Current Trends

There were close to 4 million registered births in the United States in 2015, which was slightly lower than the prior year (Martin et al., 2016). Most interesting about these numbers, however, is that while birth rates dropped to record lows among women under the age of 30, they rose in women 30–44 (see Figures 12.1 and 12.2 for more information; Martins et al., 2015). In fact, birth rates to teenagers has decreased 46% since 2007, while birth rates to women

> **mucus plug**
> A collection of thick mucus in the cervix that prevents bacteria from entering the uterus.

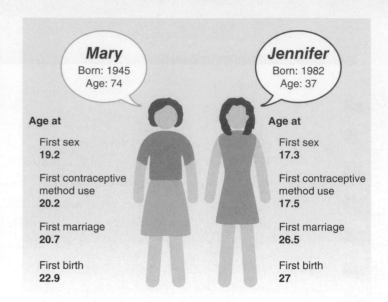

FIGURE **12.1** Although the age at which an American woman has sex has changed little over time, today she is getting married and having children later.

SOURCE: Alan Guttmacher Institute, 2014.

aged 40–44 increased 15% (Martins et al., 2015) (See Figure 12.3.). Overall, birth rates have fallen in all ethnical/racial groups (see Figure 12.4 for more information).

Conception

Our bodies are biologically programmed in many ways to help pregnancy occur. For instance, a woman's sexual desire is usually at its peak during her ovulation until just before her menstruation (Bullivant et al., 2004). In addition, the **mucus plug** that usually blocks the cervix disappears during ovulation and the cervical mucus becomes thinner. Both of these changes make it easier for sperm to move through the cervix. The consistency of the cervical mucus also helps to quickly move healthy sperm and detain any abnormal sperm. The female orgasm may also help pull semen

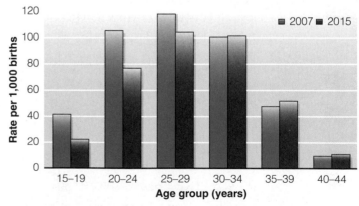

FIGURE **12.2** While birth rates have been declining in women under the age of 30, they continue to increase in 30–44-year-old women.

SOURCE: Martin et al., 2016; Centers for Disease Control, National Center for Health Statistics. Hamilton et al., 2013.

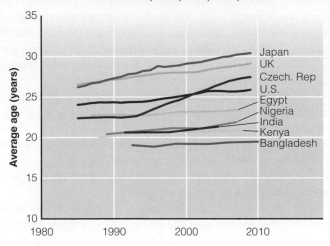

Mean Age at First Birth in Selected Countries, 1980, 1990, 2000, 2010

FIGURE **12.3** While there were modest increases in age at birth in many countries, the mean ages for the United States, United Kingdom, Japan, and the Czech Republic have been rising at a more rapid pace.

SOURCES: Bongaarts & Blanc, 2015; Demographic and Health Surveys.

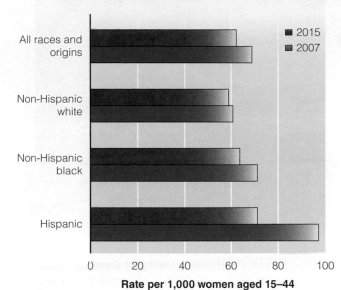

U.S. Birth rates by Ethnicity and Race, 2007 and 2015

FIGURE **12.4** From 2007 to 2015, birth rates have decreased in all ethnic/racial groups.

SOURCES: Centers for Disease Control and Prevention; Martin et al., 2016.

into the uterus and help push the sperm up toward the Fallopian tubes (even though we know that pregnancy does occur without female orgasm). Finally, the changes in the consistency of the ejaculated semen can also help pregnancy occur. Almost immediately after ejaculation, semen thickens to help it stay in the vagina, but it liquefies again after about 20 minutes.

With all the help our bodies are programmed to give, the process of getting pregnant may appear rather easy; however, this is not always the case. The process of becoming pregnant is complex, and there are several potential problems. For example, the female's immune system itself begins to attack the sperm immediately after ejaculation, thinking it is unwanted bacteria. Although many sperm are killed by the woman's immune system, this process is usually not a threat to conception. A fertile woman who doesn't use any contraception will become pregnant approximately 30% of the time (Zinaman et al., 1996).

Because the ovum can live for up to 24 hours and the majority of sperm can live for up to 72 hours in the female reproductive tract, pregnancy may occur if intercourse takes place either a few days before or after ovulation (Wilcox et al., 1995). Although most sperm die within 72 hours, fewer than 1% can survive up to 7 days in the female reproductive tract (Ferreira-Poblete, 1997). Throughout their trip in the Fallopian tubes, the sperm haphazardly swim around, bumping into various structures and each other. When (and if) they reach the jelly-like substance that surrounds the ovum, they begin wriggling violently. Although it is not clear how the sperm locate the ovum, research indicates that the ovum releases chemical signals that indicate its location (Palca, 1991).

Several sperm may reach the ovum, but only one will fertilize it. The sperm secretes a chemical that bores a hole

through the outer layer of the ovum, allowing it to penetrate the ovum for fertilization. The outer layer of the ovum immediately undergoes a physical change, making it impossible for any other sperm to enter. This entire process takes about 24 hours. Fertilization usually occurs in the ampulla (the funnel-shaped open end of the Fallopian tube; Figure 12.5); after fertilization, the fertilized ovum is referred to as a zygote.

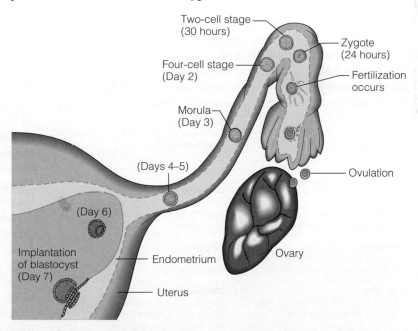

FIGURE **12.5** After ovulation, the follicle moves through the Fallopian tube until it meets the spermatozoon. Fertilization takes place in the wide outer part of the tube. Approximately 24 hours later, the first cell division begins. For some 3 or 4 days, the fertilized ovum remains in the Fallopian tube, dividing again and again. When the fertilized ovum enters the uterus, it sheds its outer covering to be able to implant in the wall of the uterus.

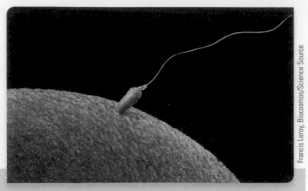
As the head of the spermatozoon enters the ovum, the ovum prevents penetration by another spermatozoon.

The sperm carry the genetic material from the male. Each sperm contains 23 chromosomes, including the X or Y sex chromosome, which will determine whether the fetus is male or female. Other information is determined by both the male and female genes, including eye and hair color, skin color, height, and weight.

The first cell division begins approximately 12 hours after the genetic material from the sperm and ovum join together. At this point, the collection of cells is referred to as a **blastocyst**. The blastocyst will divide in two every 12 to 15 hours, doubling in size. As this goes on, the cilia in the Fallopian tube gently push the blastocyst toward the uterus. Fallopian tube muscles also help to move the blastocyst by occasionally contracting.

The blastocyst enters the uterus anywhere from 3 to 4 days after conception. Once there, it absorbs nutrients secreted by the endometrial glands. On about the sixth day after fertilization, the uterus secretes a chemical that dissolves the hard covering around the blastocyst, allowing it to implant in the uterine wall (Jones, 1984). Implantation involves a series of complex interactions between the lining of the uterus and the developing embryo, and usually occurs 5 to 8 days after fertilization. The endometrium must have been exposed to the appropriate levels of estrogen and progesterone to facilitate implantation. Most of the time, implantation takes place in the upper portion of the uterus, and after this occurs, the woman's body and the developing embryo begin to exchange chemical information. Hormones are released into the woman's bloodstream (these can be detected through pregnancy tests). If implantation does not occur, the blastocyst will degenerate and the potential pregnancy will be terminated.

It is fascinating that a woman's body allows the blastocyst to implant when so many of her body's defenses are designed to eliminate foreign substances. Apparently there is some weakening of the immune system that allows for an acceptance of the fertilized ovum (Nilsson, 1990). Some women do continually reject the fertilized ovum and experience repeat **miscarriages**. We will discuss this in greater detail later in this chapter.

After implantation, the blastocyst divides into two layers of cells—the ectoderm and the endoderm. A middle layer, the mesoderm, soon follows. These three layers will develop into all the bodily tissues. From the second through the eighth weeks, the developing human is referred to as an **embryo** (EMM-bree-oh). Soon a membrane called the **amnion** begins to grow over the developing embryo, and the amniotic cavity begins to fill with **amniotic fluid**. This fluid supports the fetus, protects it from shock, and also assists in fetal lung development. The **placenta**, which is the portion that is attached to the uterine wall, supplies nutrients to the developing fetus, aids in respiratory and excretory functions, and secretes hormones necessary for the continuation of the pregnancy. The **umbilical cord** connects the fetus to the placenta. By the fourth week of pregnancy, the placenta covers 20% of the wall of the uterus, and at 5 months, the placenta covers 50% of the uterine wall (Jones, 1984). Toward the end of pregnancy, approximately 75 gallons of blood will pass through the placenta each day.

The majority of pregnant women deliver a single fetus. However, in approximately 2 of every 100 pregnancies there is a multiple birth. This can happen in two ways. Sometimes two ova are released by the ovaries, and if both are fertilized by sperm, **fraternal twins** (nonidentical) result. These twins are **dizygotic**, and they can be either of the same or different sexes. Two thirds of all twins are fraternal and are no more closely genetically related than any two siblings. The tendency to have fraternal twins may be inherited from the mother, and older women (over the age of 30) seem to have fraternal twins more often than younger women (because of erratic ovulation and an increased possibility of releasing more than one ovum).

Identical twins occur when a single zygote completely divides into two separate zygotes. This process produces twins who are genetically identical and are referred to as **monozygotic** twins. They often look alike and are always of the same sex. In rare cases, the zygote fails to divide completely, and two babies may be joined together at some point in their bodies; these are known as conjoined twins, once referred to as Siamese twins. In some instances, many ova are released and fertilized, and triplets (three offspring) or quadruplets (four offspring) may result. Over the past four decades there has been a substantial rise in the rate of multiple births, mainly due to the increased use of fertility treatments in the United States (Kulkarni et al., 2013; Sunderam et al., 2013). We will talk more about fertility treatments later in this chapter.

blastocyst
The hollow ball of embryonic cells that enters the uterus from the Fallopian tube and eventually implants.

miscarriage
A pregnancy that terminates on its own; also referred to as a spontaneous abortion.

embryo
The developing organism from the second to the eighth week of gestation.

amnion
A thin, tough, membranous sac that encloses the embryo or fetus.

amniotic fluid
The fluid in the amniotic cavity.

placenta
The structure through which the exchange of materials between fetal and maternal circulations occurs.

umbilical cord
The long, ropelike structure that connects the fetus to the placenta.

fraternal twins
Two offspring developed from two separate ova fertilized by different spermatozoa.

dizygotic
Pertaining to or derived from two separate zygotes.

identical twins
Two offspring developed from a single zygote that completely divides into two separate, genetically identical zygotes.

monozygotic
Pertaining to or derived from one zygote.

Early Signs of Pregnancy

If the zygote does implant, most women experience physical signs very early that alert them to their pregnancy. The most common early indicator is missing a period, although some women notice some light spotting (vaginal bleeding) during the pregnancy. More than light spotting can indicate possible problems, such as an impending miscarriage. Other physical signs include breast tenderness, frequent urination, and **morning sickness** (see Table 12.1).

It is estimated that between 70% and 90% of all pregnant women experience some form of nausea, vomiting, or both during pregnancy (Cardwell & Center, 2012; Matthews et al., 2010; Piwko et al., 2013). This sickness is due to the increase in estrogen and progesterone during pregnancy, which may irritate the stomach lining. It is often worse in the morning because there is no food in the stomach to counter its effects, although it can happen at any point during the day. Researchers believe that morning sickness may protect the fetus from food-borne illness and chemicals in certain foods during the first trimester, which is the most critical time in development (Boyd, 2000; Cardwell & Center, 2012). The lowest rates of morning sickness are found in cultures without animal products as a food staple. Some women also develop food aversions, the most common of which are to meat, fish, poultry, and eggs—all foods that can carry harmful bacteria.

In rare cases, **pseudocyesis** (sue-doe-sigh-EE-sis), or false pregnancy, occurs. This is a condition in which a woman believes she is pregnant when she is not. Her belief is so strong that she begins to experience several of the signs of pregnancy, including missed periods, morning sickness, and weight gain (Kenner & Nicolson, 2015; Tarin et al., 2013).

Although the majority of cases of pseudocyesis have a psychological basis, some have physical causes. For instance, a tumor on the pituitary gland may cause

Table 12.1 Pregnancy Signs

Physical Sign	Time of Appearance	Other Possible Reasons
Period late/absent	Entire pregnancy	Excessive weight gain or loss, fatigue, hormonal problems, stress, breast-feeding, going off contraceptive pills
Breast tenderness	1–2 weeks after conception	Use of contraceptive pills, hormonal imbalance, period onset
Increased fatigue	1–6 weeks after conception	Stress, depression, thyroid disorder, cold or flu
Morning sickness	2–8 weeks after conception	Stress, stomach disorders, food poisoning
Increased urination	6–8 weeks after conception	Urinary tract infection, excessive use of diuretics, diabetes
Fetal heartbeat	10–20 weeks and then throughout entire pregnancy	None
Backaches	Entire pregnancy	Back problems
Frequent headaches	May be entire pregnancy	Caffeine withdrawal, dehydration, eyestrain, birth control pills
Food cravings	Entire pregnancy	Poor diet, stress, depression, period onset
Darkening of nipples	Entire pregnancy	Hormonal imbalance
Fetal movement	16–22 weeks after conception	Bowel contractions, gas

ON YOUR MIND

Will guys ever be able to become "pregnant"?

As of 2017, there have not been any documented pregnancies in a biological man. However, it is possible that newer techniques will enable a biological man to carry a pregnancy to term in the future. An embryo would have to be implanted into a man's abdomen with the placenta and attached to an internal organ. Hormonal treatment would be necessary to sustain the pregnancy. In addition, the father would have to undergo a **cesarean section (C-section)** birth. There may not be many men standing in line to carry a pregnancy, however, because the hormones needed to maintain the pregnancy can cause breast enlargement and penile shrinkage. A transgender man may be able to carry a pregnancy to term if he retained his ovaries and uterus.

an oversecretion of prolactin, which, in turn, can cause symptoms such as breast fullness and morning sickness. Pseudocyesis has been found to be more common in women who believe childbearing is central to their identity, have a history of infertility or depression (or both), or have had a miscarriage (Gaskin, 2012). Although rare, there have been a few cases in which men experienced pseudocyesis, although this is typically due to psychological impairment (Shutty & Leadbetter, 1993). Male and female partners of pregnant

---

morning sickness
The nausea and vomiting that some women have when they become pregnant; typically caused by the increase in hormones. Can occur at any point in the day.

pseudocyesis
A condition in which a woman experiences signs of pregnancy, even though she is not pregnant.

cesarean section (C-section)
A surgical procedure in which the woman's abdomen and uterus are surgically opened and a newborn is removed.

Sexual Diversity Is It a Boy or a Girl?

IN OUR WORLD

Throughout the world, people have relied on folk wisdom to predict the sex of their baby. Here are some examples:

It's a Girl!

- Baby sits on the left side of the womb (Nyinba, Nepal)
- Mother puts her left foot first crossing the threshold (Bihar, India)
- Baby sits low in the belly (Lepchas, Himalayas, and Bedouin tribes)
- Mother is grumpy with women (Dinka, Africa)
- Fetus moves slowly and gently (Dustin, North Borneo, and Egypt)
- Mother first feels the baby when she is outside (Serbia)

- Mother dreams of human skulls (Maori, New Zealand)
- Mother dreams of a headkerchief (Egypt)
- Mother craves spicy foods (Nyinba, Nepal)
- Mother's face has yellow spots (Poland)
- Baby "plays in stomach" before sixth month (Nyinba, Nepal)

It's a Boy!

- Baby sits on the right side of the womb (Nyinba, Nepal)
- Mother puts her right foot first crossing the threshold (Bihar, India)
- Baby sits high in the belly (Lepchas, Himalayas, and Bedouin tribes)

- Mother is grumpy with men (Dinka, Africa)
- Fetus moves fast and roughly (Dustin, North Borneo, and Egypt)
- Mother first feels baby move when at home (Serbia)
- Mother dreams of huia feathers (Maori, New Zealand)
- Mother dreams of a handkerchief (Egypt)
- Mother craves bland foods (Nyinba, Nepal)
- Mother looks well (Poland)
- Baby first "plays in stomach" after sixth month (Nyinba, Nepal)

SOURCE: Dunham et al., 1992.

women may experience a related condition called **couvade** (coo-VAHD) syndrome. Partners with this condition experience the symptoms of pregnancy, including nausea, vomiting, increased or decreased appetite, diarrhea, or abdominal bloating (Brennan et al., 2007; Kazmierczak et al., 2013).

Pregnancy Testing

Pregnancy tests determine whether a woman is pregnant by looking for certain pregnancy markers in her urine or blood. One of these markers is **human chorionic gonadotropin (hCG**; corr-ee-ON-ick go-nadoh-TRO-pin), which is a hormone produced by the placenta shortly after the embryo attaches to the uterine lining. This hormone builds up rapidly in the first few days of pregnancy and can be identified in the blood or urine after ovulation. The presence of hCG helps build and maintain a thick endometrial layer,

and thus prevents menstruation. Peak levels of hCG are reached in the second and third months of pregnancy and then drop off.

Urine pregnancy tests are the most commonly used pregnancy tests, and every brand has a unique way of indicating a positive or negative test result. Some test strips change color, while others might develop a line or symbol (such as + or −). Digital tests may show the phrases "pregnant/not pregnant" or "yes/no" after testing. All pregnancy tests come with specific instructions that should be carefully followed for accurate results. Most tests recommend waiting until the first day of a missed period, but digital tests can often provide results before a period is missed. If a urine pregnancy test is done too early (or too late) it may be inaccurate. A pregnant woman who uses a urine pregnancy test after the 12th week of pregnancy may have a **false-negative** result, since hCG levels drop and will be too low to be detected by the test at that point. **False-positive** test results may occur in the presence of a kidney disease or infection, an overactive thyroid gland, or large doses of aspirin, tranquilizers, antidepressants, or anticonvulsant medications (Hatcher et al., 2007).

Although used less often, blood tests are the most accurate. These tests can detect hCG at about 7–12 days from conception and can be useful for monitoring the progress of an early pregnancy that may be in jeopardy. The levels of hCG increase early in pregnancy, and if a woman's hormones do not follow this pattern, a miscarriage or an **ectopic pregnancy** may have occurred. We will discuss both of these later in this chapter.

If a woman plans on continuing the pregnancy, her health care provider helps her to calculate a **due date**. Most physicians date the pregnancy from the first day of the last menstrual period rather than the day of ovulation or fertilization. The standard for due date

---

couvade
A condition in which a partner experiences the symptoms of the pregnant woman.

human chorionic gonadotropin (hCG)
The hormone that stimulates production of estrogen and progesterone to maintain pregnancy.

false negative
Incorrect result of a pregnancy test that indicates a negative result.

false positive
Incorrect result of a pregnancy test that indicates a positive result.

ectopic pregnancy
The implantation of the fertilized egg outside the uterus, such as in the Fallopian tubes or abdomen.

due date
The projected birth date of a baby.

calculation is called the **Naegele's** (nay-GEL-lays) **rule**—subtract 3 months from the first day of the last period and add 7 days for a single birth (Mittendorf et al., 1990; for example, if the last period began on August 1, subtract 3 months and add 7 days, which means that the due date would be May 8). This rule works most effectively with women who have standard 28-day menstrual cycles.

Sex Selection: Myth and Modern Methods

Throughout time, many couples have searched for ways to choose the sex of their child. A variety of techniques have been proposed by different cultures. Aristotle believed that if a couple had sexual intercourse in the north wind, they would have a male child, and if intercourse took place in the south wind, they would have a female child. Hippocrates believed that males formed on the right side of the uterus and females on the left; so, to conceive a daughter, a woman was advised to lie on her left side directly after intercourse. The ancient Greeks thought that if a man cut or tied his left testicle, a couple would not have girls because male sperm were thought to be produced in the right testicle (Dunham et al., 1992). Although some of these suggestions sound absurd today, people in many cultures still hold on to myths of how to choose and how to know the gender of their child (see accompanying "Sexual Diversity in Our World").

Reasons for wanting to choose a child's sex vary; although some couples simply prefer a male or female child, others desire to choose the sex of their children for medical reasons. For example, certain inherited diseases are more likely to affect one sex (such as hemophilia, which affects more males).

Modern-day methods of gender selection were popularized by Shettles and Rorvik (1970) in their groundbreaking book *Your Baby's Sex: Now You Can Choose*. According to these authors, by taking into account the characteristics of the female (X) and male (Y) sperm, couples can use timing and pH-level adjustments to the vaginal environment (douches) to increase the concentration of X or Y sperm.

Because Y sperm swim faster and thrive in an alkaline environment, Shettles and Rorvik recommend that to have a boy, a couple should have intercourse close to ovulation (to allow the faster-swimming Y sperm to get there first) and douche with a mixture of baking soda and water. Because X sperm tend to live longer and thrive in an acidic environment, for a girl, a couple should time intercourse 2 to 3 days before ovulation and douche with a mixture of vinegar and water.

Medical procedures for sex selection include "microsorting" (also known as "spinning"—separating the X and Y sperm followed by artificial insemination). When using these methods, the reported likelihood of conceiving a male is between 50% and 70%, and the likelihood of conceiving a female is between 50% and 90% (Pozniak, 2002). **Preimplantation genetic diagnosis (PGD)** is another procedure that can identify chromosomal sex after conception, although it is used during assisted reproduction to identify chromosomal or genetic abnormalities in an embryo. An **amniocentesis** (am-nee-oh-sent-TEE-sis) can also determine, among other things,

Gender "reveal" parties, in which expectant parents invite friends over to find out the sex of their baby, have been a hot trend in the last few years. The "reveal" part of the party can be done in a variety of different ways, such as putting blue or pink filling into cupcakes.

the chromosomal sex of the fetus. These tests raise many moral, sociological, and ethical issues about sex selection. The controversies revolve around multiple issues, such as women undergoing unnecessary testing, destroying embryos of the unwanted sex, and the long-term psychological harm that might develop in the offspring.

In several countries around the world, such as India, China, and Taiwan, parents go to extremes to ensure the birth of a male baby. In some Indian states, for example, males are valued more than females because of their ability to care for aging parents. Female offspring, in contrast, move into a husband's home after marriage and are unavailable to help care for their parents. An old Indian saying claims that having a girl is like "watering your neighbor's lawn" (Sharma & Haub, 2008). The increasing availability of inexpensive blood tests in several

ON YOUR MIND

I have missed my period now for 2 months in a row. Does this mean that I am pregnant? What should I do?

If you have been engaging in vaginal intercourse, there is certainly a chance that you are pregnant. However, there are several other reasons for missing your period, including stress, weight changes, active participation in sports, or changes in eating patterns, as well as certain diseases. In any case, it is a good idea to see a health care provider, gynecologist, or the student health center for an evaluation.

Naegele's rule
A means of figuring the due date by subtracting 3 months from the first day of the last menstrual period and adding 7 days.

preimplantation genetic diagnosis (PGD)
Genetic testing used during assisted reproductive technologies that screens

for various genetic or chromosomal diseases in embryos prior to implantation. Can also be used to identify the prenatal sex of the embryo.

amniocentesis
A procedure in which a small sample of amniotic fluid is analyzed to detect chromosomal abnormalities in the fetus.

countries has led to an increase in the ratio of male to female births, which has resulted in gender imbalances in many countries (Brink, 2015). For example, it's estimated that by 2020, 15% to 20% of heterosexual men in some parts of India will not be able to find female partners (Arsenault, 2011). This, in turn, can lead to many other potential problems, including increased violence in men.

Review Questions

1 Explain the process of conception, and describe how the human body is programmed to help pregnancy occur.

2 Identify four signs of pregnancy and explain why they occur.

3 Explain how pregnancy tests work.

4 Explain the methods for sex selection.

Infertility

Infertility is defined as the inability to conceive (or impregnate) after 1 year of regular vaginal intercourse without the use of any form of contraception (if a woman is older than 35, usually infertility is diagnosed after 6 months of not being able to conceive). Infertility typically affects 15% to 20% of couples worldwide (Varshini et al., 2012). Rates of infertility have been decreasing among women of childbearing age in the United States. There were 2.4 million women who were infertile in 1982; this number fell to 1.5 million between 2006 and 2010 (Chandra et al., 2013). Overall, non-Hispanic Black women were more likely to experience infertility than non-Hispanic White women, while Asian women had the lowest rates of infertility (Chandra et al., 2013).

Women and men who delay pregnancy may experience infertility because of the decreasing quality of their ova and sperm (Coccia & Rizzello, 2008; Girsh et al., 2008). Infertility and problems carrying a pregnancy to term are more common in women as they age (see Figure 12.6; Chandra et al., 2013). In Chapter 6, we discussed the worldwide declines in sperm counts and quality because of occupational, environmental, and lifestyle factors. Studies have found that male infertility can be caused by exposure to many environmental toxins, including bisphenol A (BPA), mercury, paint solvents, lead, video display terminals, and computers (Harkinson, 2016; Kalb et al., 2015; Othman et al., 2016). In addition, shift work and work-related stress can significantly increase the risk for male infertility.

Infertility has a strong impact on a couple's well-being. Emotional reactions can include depression, anxiety, anger, self-blame, guilt, frustration, and fear. Because the majority of people have no experience dealing with infertility, many of those who find out they are infertile isolate themselves and try not to think about it. Overall, women tend to have more emotional reactions to infertility and are more willing to confide in someone about their infertility than are men (Darwiche et al., 2013). Childbearing in the United States is part of what defines being female, and so women who are infertile often feel less valued than fertile women. The term **motherhood mandate** refers to the idea that something is wrong with a woman if she does not play a central role in caregiving and child care (Riggs, 2005).

The most common causes of female infertility include ovulation disorders, blocked Fallopian tubes, endometriosis, structural uterine problems, or excessive uterine fibroids (see Chapter 5). The majority of male infertility is due to problems with sperm production, including low sperm counts, poor sperm quality, or both. Traditional semen analysis may not accurately identify fertility issues, and as a result, multiple tests are often used today (Leushuis et al., 2014).

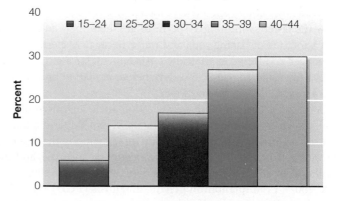

FIGURE 12.6 Infertility and problems carrying a pregnancy to term are more common as women age.

SOURCE: Chandra et al., 2013; National Survey of Family Growth, 2006.

---

infertility
The inability to conceive or impregnate after 1 year of regular vaginal intercourse without the use of any form of contraception.

motherhood mandate
The idea that motherhood should be a central aspect of being a woman and that something is wrong with a woman who does not have children.

Infertility can also be caused by past infections with gonorrhea, chlamydia, or pelvic inflammatory disease (Hafner, 2015; Kidd & Workowski, 2015; Menon et al., 2015; Peterman et al., 2016), which is one of the reasons college students are encouraged to have regular medical checkups and women are encouraged to have regular Pap tests. If a sexually transmitted infection is treated early, there is less chance that it will interfere with future fertility. For some men and women who experience reproductive problems, changing lifestyle patterns, reducing stress, avoiding rigorous exercise, and maintaining a recommended weight may restore fertility (Chavarro et al., 2007b). For other couples, new medical interventions offer additional possibilities.

Fertility problems can be traced to a single partner 55% of the time (35% of the time to the female and 20% of the time to the male). In 20% of cases there is a combined problem and in 25% the reason is unknown (Leaver, 2016). Historically, women have been blamed for infertility problems, and until recently, men were not even considered a possible part of the problem.

Assisted Reproductive Technologies

Today, many couples—married, unmarried, straight, gay, lesbian, transgender, young, and old—use assisted reproductive technologies (ARTs). Some couples use these techniques because they have infertility issues, whereas others use them to get pregnant without a partner or with a same-sex partner. Although in the past single women and gay, lesbian, and bisexual couples were denied access to ARTs, this has been changing. In 2006, the Ethics Committee of the American Society for Reproductive Medicine released a statement supporting access to fertility treatment by unmarried, lesbian, and gay persons (Ethics Committee Report, 2006). Unique issues face lesbians and gay men who want to be pregnant. Lesbian and bisexual women who use infertility services often find that because these centers primarily cater to infertile heterosexual women, they are required to undergo significant infertility workups (even though they are not "infertile") before any reproductive procedures (Priddle, 2015; Toadvine, 2016). Like Laura and Ozlem in my chapter-opening Notebook feature, some lesbian couples both use ART and carry a pregnancy. However, in the majority of lesbian couples (76%) only one partner uses ARTs (Carpinello et al., 2016). This may be due to financial or age issues.

Gay men also face unique issues, as assisted reproduction is often more complicated and expensive because they need a surrogate to carry the pregnancy (Friedman, 2007). Although some gay couples seek out coparenting arrangements with female friends or adoption, many prefer surrogacy since other options may be less accessible to them (Blake et al., 2017). Surrogacy raises additional issues for gay couples because they must choose whose sperm will be used. Some gay men mix their sperm so they don't know which one of them is the biological father.

Like LGB individuals, many transgender or gender nonconforming persons who are interested in becoming parents experience discrimination in trying to create a family (Dickey et al., 2016). They may not be able to find trans-affirming medical providers to provide fertility workups, or they might find that a prior

medical procedure has left them unable to have children (Eyler et al., 2014). Transgender individuals often need to consider whether they want to become parents prior to beginning any gender affirming medical interventions, such as hormonal therapy (DeRoo et al., 2016). It is possible for transgender people to cryopreserve sperm or ova prior to beginning hormone therapy or surgeries (deRoo et al., 2016; Dickey et al., 2016). Transgender individuals (or people) who are already taking hormones need to discontinue doing so to allow their bodies to return to its reproductive cycle (Light et al., 2014; Wierckx et al., 2014). However, doing so can have medical and emotional consequences, such as increased anxiety and/or depression (Dickey et al., 2016). Even so, many transgender people do hope to become parents. One study found the majority of transgender men wanted to have children at some point (Wierckx et al., 2014) and studies have found it is possible for them to successfully experience pregnancy after having socially or medically transitioned (Light et al., 2014).

The National Survey of Family Growth found that 17% of women and 9.4% of men ages 25–44 had ever used infertility services from 2006 to 2010 (Chandra et al., 2014). The use of infertility services was highest among older, non-Hispanic white women who were married, with higher levels of education and income. It's estimated that 5% of all infants born in the United States in 2012 were conceived through ART (Sunderam et al., 2015).

Although many technologies are available to people today, deciding which treatment to use depends on factors such as cost, a woman's age, duration of infertility, and chances of conceiving without treatment. Many of these options are very time-consuming and expensive, and they do not guarantee success. Now we'll discuss several of the available ARTs.

Fertility Drugs

Some couples may use fertility drugs to help achieve a pregnancy. As we discussed in Chapters 5 and 6, ovulation and sperm production are a result of a well-balanced endocrine system (pituitary, hypothalamus, and gonads). Some women and men have hormonal irregularities that may interfere with the process of ovulation or sperm production. Although we do not always know why these hormonal problems develop, many problems can be treated with fertility drugs.

A major risk of the use of fertility drugs has been the development of **ovarian hyperstimulation syndrome** because the drugs stimulate the ovaries to produce more ova. This has raised concern about the possible correlation between the use of fertility drugs and the development of breast or ovarian cancer. Whereas some studies have found a possible increased risk in women who have never been pregnant, older women, those with extensive fertility workups, and those with a history of cancer, many studies have found no increased risk (Brinton et al., 2013; Diergaarde & Kurta, 2014; LoRusso et al., 2015). While infertile women may

---

ovarian hyperstimulation syndrome Adverse effects of excessive hormonal stimulation of the ovaries through fertility drugs, including abdominal bloating, nausea, diarrhea, weight gain, and abdominal, chest, and leg pain.

be at an increased risk of various reproductive cancers, the use of fertility drugs has not been found to increase this risk (Practice Committee of the American Society for Reproductive Medicine, 2016). However, fertility drugs do increase the likelihood of multiple births, since they overstimulate ovarian production (Kulkarni et al., 2013).

Surgery

Cervical, vaginal, or endometrial abnormalities that prevent conception may be corrected surgically. Scar tissue, cysts, tumors, or adhesions, as well as blockages inside the Fallopian tubes, may be surgically removed. The use of diagnostic techniques such as **laparoscopy** (la-puh-RAH-ske-pee) and **hysteroscopy** (hissstare-oh-OSK-coe-pee) are also common. In men, surgery may be required to remove any blockage in the vas deferens or epididymis, or to repair a **varicocele** (VA-ruh-coe-seal).

Artificial Insemination

Artificial insemination is the process of introducing sperm into a woman's reproductive tract without vaginal intercourse. This is a popular option for both heterosexual and same-sex couples. Ejaculated sperm, collected through masturbation, can come from a partner or from a sperm donor.[1] Several samples may be collected from men with a low sperm count to increase the number of healthy sperm. Once medically washed, sperm can be deposited in the vagina, cervix, uterus (intrauterine), or Fallopian tubes (intratubal).

Men who decide to undergo sterilization or who may become sterile because of surgery or chemotherapy can collect sperm before the procedure. Sperm can be frozen indefinitely in a **sperm bank**. Some couples who don't produce sperm (including men who don't produce viable sperm, lesbian and/or single women) can use donor sperm. Although the cost of donor sperm varies among sperm banks, typically donor sperm costs between $200 and $600 per insemination. Many sperm banks charge more for more information about the donor, such as a handwriting sample, photographs, or a video. Some couples buy several vials from the same donor so that offspring can have the same donor father. Recall that in my chapter-opening Notebook feature, Laura and Ozlem's children were conceived with sperm from the same known donor so their children would be genetically related.

A donor may be found through one of the many sperm banks throughout the United States and abroad, usually from an online donor catalog (see the Websites section at the end of this chapter for more information). After a donor is chosen, the sperm bank will typically send sperm to the health care provider who will be performing the insemination procedure, but in some cases, the donor sperm is sent directly to the buyer. Fertility drugs are often used in conjunction with artificial insemination to increase the chances that there will be healthy ova present when the sperm is introduced.

In Vitro Fertilization

Another reproductive technology is **in vitro fertilization (IVF)**, or the creation of a test-tube baby. In 1978, Louise Brown, the first **test-tube baby**, was born in England. Since that time, thousands of babies have been conceived in this fashion. The name is a bit deceiving, however, because these babies are not born in a test tube; rather, they are *conceived* in a petri dish, which is a shallow circular dish with a loose-fitting cover. In 2010, Robert Edwards, a British scientist who developed IVF, won the Nobel Prize in medicine (Jha, 2010).

Heterosexual and lesbian women with infertility problems may use IVF because of blocked or damaged Fallopian tubes or endometriosis (see Chapter 5). Like other artificial reproductive technologies, fertility drugs are typically used before IVF to help stimulate the ovaries. When the ova have matured, 4 to 6 are retrieved with the use of microscopic needles and inserted into the abdominal cavity. The ova are put into a petri dish and mixed with washed sperm. Once fertilization has occurred (usually anywhere from 3 to 6 days), the zygotes are either transferred to the woman's uterus or frozen for use at another time (we will discuss this further later in the chapter). Improved understanding of human reproduction has led to many improvements in IVF, such as increased success rates and decreased multiple births.

Earlier we discussed how preimplantation genetic diagnosis (PGD) can be used to screen for chromosomal and genetic abnormalities prior to implantation and pregnancy. A PGD screening costs between $3,000 and $5,000.

Gamete and Zygote Intra–Fallopian Tube Transfer

Gamete intra–Fallopian tube transfer (GIFT) is similar to IVF in that ova and sperm are prepared in an artificial environment. However, after this occurs, both the ova and sperm are placed in the Fallopian tube, before fertilization. Fertilization is allowed

---

laparoscopy
A procedure that allows a direct view of all the pelvic organs, including the uterus, Fallopian tubes, and ovaries; also refers to a number of important surgeries (such as tubal ligation or gall bladder removal) involving a laparoscope.

hysteroscopy
Visual inspection of the uterine cavity with an endoscope.

varicocele
An unnatural swelling of the veins in the scrotum.

artificial insemination
Artificially introducing sperm into a woman's reproductive tract.

sperm bank
A storage facility that holds supplies of sperm for future use.

in vitro fertilization (IVF)
A procedure in which a woman's ova are removed from her body, fertilized with sperm in a laboratory, and then surgically implanted back into her uterus.

test-tube baby
A slang term for any zygote created by mixing sperm and egg outside a woman's body.

gamete intra–Fallopian tube transfer (GIFT)
A reproductive technique in which the sperm and ova are collected and injected into the Fallopian tube before fertilization.

---

[1] In 2013, the movie *Delivery Man,* starring Vince Vaughn, told the story of a man who fathered 533 children through sperm donations. Many countries, including Britain, France, and Sweden, follow recommendations from the Warnock Report, which limits the number of children a donor can father to 10 (Warnock, 1988). However, the United States has not imposed any limits to the number of children a donor can father.

to occur naturally rather than in an artificial environment. **Zygote intra–Fallopian tube transfer (ZIFT)** is similar to IVF in that the sperm and ova are allowed to fertilize outside the body. However, after fertilization the zygote is placed into the Fallopian tube (similar to GIFT), which allows it to travel to the uterus and implant naturally. These two procedures are closer to natural conception and success rates are similar to IVF, which is typically the preferred choice for most couples and health care providers.

Intracellular Sperm Injections

Couples who experience sperm problems or ova that are resistant to fertilization may use **intracytoplasmic sperm injection (ICSI)**. ICSI involves injecting a single sperm into the center of an ovum under a microscope. Usually, fresh, ejaculated sperm are used, but sperm can also be removed from the epididymis or the testes, or frozen sperm can be used (Karacan et al., 2013; Yanagimachi, 2011).

Overall, ICSI results have been controversial—with some studies showing no adverse outcomes compared with natural conception (Knoester et al., 2008; Nauru et al., 2008) and other studies showing increased risks for genetic defects (Qin et al., 2017; Xiong et al, 2017). This may be due to the fact that ICSI eliminates many of the natural barriers to conception, which increases the transmission of abnormal genes. Scientists do not know how nature chooses one sperm for fertilization, and choosing one randomly may not be appropriate, although physicians usually try to pick one that appears vigorous and healthy.

Oocyte and Embryo Transplants

Women who are not able to produce healthy ova because of ovarian failure or age-related infertility, and same-sex couples, may use oocyte (egg) and embryo donation. Oocyte donation involves using a donor ova, whereas embryo donation can involve using frozen embryos donated by a couple or the creation of an embryo with a donated ova and sperm. Younger women are more likely to use their own ova, whereas older women use donor ova. This is mainly because the risk of miscarriage is higher in women in older age groups who use their own ova. The mean age of donor ova recipients has remained constant at 41 years old (Kawwass et al., 2013).

Surrogate Parenting

Surrogate parenting is a popular option both for heterosexual couples who cannot carry a pregnancy to term and for same-sex couples. There are two types of surrogate parenting: gestational surrogacy and traditional surrogacy. In gestational surrogacy, an embryo is created through IVF and is transferred into another woman, called a **surrogate mother** or gestational carrier. The resulting child is genetically unrelated to the surrogate. In traditional surrogacy, the surrogate is artificially or naturally impregnated, and the resulting child is genetically related to the surrogate. In the United States, gestational surrogacy is more common than traditional surrogacy.

U.S. laws regulating surrogacy vary state by state. However, many states have ambiguous laws or do not directly address surrogacy issues. States also vary with respect to whether the surrogacy is traditional or gestational, since gestational surrogacy is less legally complex. Some states, such as New York, refuse to recognize surrogacy contracts, whereas others, such as California, have legalized it and fully support it (Human Rights Campaign, 2010; Klimkiewicz, 2008). Outside the United States, surrogacy has been popular in countries such as India, Thailand, Nepal, and Mexico. In India, clinics would match U.S. couples with local women who were willing to serve as surrogates (Dolnick, 2007; see photo on p. 219). These women are impregnated with embryos of couples who are unable to carry a pregnancy to term. Over the last few years, however, many countries have begun enforcing laws to ban commercial surrogacy (Preiss & Shahi, 2016). In 2013, several wealthy Chinese couples were hiring American women to serve as surrogates to avoid restrictive family planning policies in China, but also to ensure that the resulting children would be legal U.S. citizens (Harney, 2013).

REAL RESEARCH Although the majority of women who are taking attention deficit hyperactivity disorder (ADHD) medications can safely discontinue using them during pregnancy, there are some cases in which the benefits of using the medications during pregnancy might outweigh the potential risks (FREEMAN, 2014).

In this enlarged image, a single sperm is injected into the center of an ovum during an intracellular sperm injection procedure.

ISM/Phototake

zygote intra–Fallopian tube transfer (ZIFT)
A reproductive technique in which the sperm and ova are collected and fertilized outside the body, and the fertilized zygote is then placed into the Fallopian tube.

intracytoplasmic sperm injection (ICSI)
Fertility procedure that involves mechanically injecting a sperm into the center of an ovum.

surrogate parenting
Use of a woman who, through artificial insemination or in vitro fertilization, gestates a fetus for another person or a couple who will raise the child.

surrogate mother
A woman who is hired to carry a pregnancy for a couple who may not be able to do so.

Other Options

Other options involve freezing embryos, sperm, and ova for later fertilization. **Embryo cryopreservation** involves freezing embryos to use at a later date in IVF procedures. One case involving frozen embryos involved a couple who created 18 embryos after fertility treatments (Buckwalter-Poza, 2014). Four of the embryos were transferred to the woman's uterus and when a pair of twins, a girl and boy, was born their family was complete. However, they had to decide what to do with the remaining 14 embryos. Did they want to keep them frozen for use at a later time? Donate them to science? Put them up for adoption? Destroy them? This raised multiple ethical, legal, and religious questions. In the end, the embryos were adopted and four additional children (two more sets of twins) were carried to term in two pregnancies by two sets of parents. All three sets of twins are genetically related and being raised by three sets of parents. Embryo adoption and transfer typically costs anywhere from $2,500 to $6,000, much less than IVF. This will be an ongoing area of research in the future as more and more infertile couples freeze their embryos for later use.

Sperm cryopreservation is also available and enables men to freeze sperm for later use. This can be beneficial for men who are diagnosed with illnesses (such as cancer) whose treatments might interfere with their ability to manufacture healthy sperm. The sperm can be collected from the testis, the epididymis, or an ejaculate, and can be frozen and stored in liquid nitrogen for many years. The effectiveness of the sperm, once thawed, is variable, and sometimes the sperm do not survive the thawing process (Borini et al., 2008; Leibo, 2008; Youssry et al., 2008).

A growing number of women have been undergoing **ova cryopreservation** (also called *vitrification;* Hodes-Wertz et al., 2013; see the Extend Fertility website detailed in the Websites section later in this chapter). Typically, a woman uses fertility drugs to stimulate the ovulation of several ova, which are surgically extracted, frozen, and stored. Ova cryopreservation can be beneficial for women who want to delay childbearing to pursue educational, career, or other personal goals; women diagnosed with cancer; women who have religious objections to storing frozen embryos; and/or women with a family history of early menopause. The average age at which women freeze their ova is 37 and many report doing so because of career concerns and/or workplace inflexibility (Hodes-Wertz et al., 2013; Rosenblum, 2014). Although embryos and sperm are easily frozen, ova are the largest cell in the human body and as such have a higher water concentration. This increases the risk of chromosomal damage in ova during the freezing and thawing processes (Martínez-Burgos et al., 2011). Immature ova, which are less developed and fragile, do better in the thawing and freezing process. Many physicians are hopeful that ova cryopreservation will become a routine part of women's health within the next 30 years (Rosenblum, 2014).

An experimental area of research has evaluated the use partial removal of ovarian tissue for cryobanking (ovarian tissue freezing) prior to cancer treatment (Beckmann et al., 2016). The tissue is cut into small pieces and frozen until after cancer treatment when it is placed back inside the body in hopes of regenerating and producing hormones.

ON YOUR MIND

Do physicians ever mix up ova or embryos during embryo transplants? How do they know whose is whose?

Embryos are rarely mixed up because collection requirements are strictly followed. However, even using these methods, accidents can happen. When mistakes are made, clinics have a responsibility to inform patients about potential errors. In 2006, the American Society for Reproductive Medicine released a statement claiming that although these errors were rare, clinics should offer full disclosure to patients (Ethics Committee Report, 2006).

Review Questions

1 Define infertility, and identify some of the most common causes of both male and female infertility.

2 Explain how same-sex couples, older women, and single women who seek assisted reproduction have been treated unfairly, and identify some of the unique issues that confront these groups.

3 Identify and describe the various assisted reproductive options.

4 Differentiate between embryo, sperm, and ova cryopreservation. What are the risks associated with each?

---

embryo cryopreservation
The freezing of embryos for later use.

sperm cryopreservation
The freezing of sperm for later use.

ova cryopreservation
The freezing of ova for later use.

trimester
Three periods of 12 to 15 weeks each; typically refers to the division of the 9 months of pregnancy.

A Healthy Pregnancy

Pregnancy is divided into three periods called **trimesters**. Throughout these trimesters, important fetal development occurs as a pregnant woman's body changes and adjusts to these developments. We now explore these changes.

Prenatal Period

Although you would think a trimester would be a 3-month period, because pregnancies are dated from the woman's last menstrual period, a full-term pregnancy is actually 40 weeks; therefore, each trimester is approximately 12 to 15 weeks long. Throughout the pregnancy, physicians can use electronic monitoring and **sonography**, or **ultrasound**, to check on the status of the fetus. We now discuss the physical development of the typical, healthy mother and child in each of these trimesters.

> **REAL RESEARCH** Although the use of ultrasound during pregnancy has become more popular over the last few years, research has found ultrasound scans of the fetus may increase the risks for childhood cancer (Rajaraman et al., 2011). Researchers suggest cautious use of diagnostic radiation imaging of a woman's abdomen and pelvis during pregnancy.

First Trimester

The first trimester includes the first 13 weeks of pregnancy (weeks 1–13). It is the trimester in which the most important embryonic development takes place. When a woman becomes pregnant, her entire system adjusts. Her heart pumps more blood, her weight increases, her lungs and digestive system work harder, and her thyroid gland grows. All of these changes occur to encourage the growth of the developing fetus.

PRENATAL DEVELOPMENT By the end of the first month of pregnancy, the fetal heart is formed and begins to pump blood. In fact, the circulatory system is the first organ system to function in the embryo (Rischer & Easton, 1992). In addition, many of the other major systems develop, including the digestive system, beginnings of the brain, spinal cord, nervous system, muscles, arms, legs, eyes, fingers, and toes. By 14 weeks, the liver, kidneys, intestines, and lungs have begun to develop. In addition, the circulatory and urinary systems are operating, and the reproductive organs have developed. By the end of the first trimester, the fetus weighs 0.5 ounce and is approximately 3 inches long.

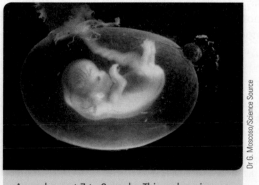

An embryo at 7 to 8 weeks. This embryo is approximately 1 inch long.

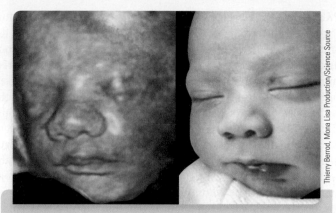

A 3D ultrasound provides a three-dimensional image of the fetus which can give parents a fairly accurate idea of what their baby will look like. In this photo, the left 3D ultrasound image was taken at approximately 34 weeks and the right image was taken shortly after birth.

CHANGES IN THE PREGNANT MOTHER During the first few weeks of pregnancy, a woman's body adjusts to increased levels of estrogen and progesterone. This can cause fatigue, breast tenderness, constipation, increased urination, and nausea or vomiting (see Table 12.1). Some women experience nausea and vomiting so severe during pregnancy that they must be hospitalized because of weight loss and malnutrition (Sheehan, 2007). Specific food cravings are normal, as is an increased sensitivity to smells and odors.

Although some women feel physically uncomfortable because of all these changes, many also feel excited and happy about the life growing within them. The final, confirming sign of pregnancy—a fetal heartbeat—can be a joyous moment that offsets all the discomforts of pregnancy. The fetal heartbeat can usually be heard through ultrasound by the end of the first trimester.

Since its introduction in 1950, ultrasound has become a useful tool in obstetrics. It can capture images of the embryo for measurement as early as 5.5 weeks into the pregnancy, and a heartbeat can be seen by 6 weeks. Fetal heartbeat can also be heard through a stethoscope at approximately 9 to 10 weeks, and after a heartbeat is either seen or heard, the probability of miscarriage declines significantly. Ultrasounds help to confirm a pregnancy, rule out abnormalities, indicate gestational age, and confirm multiple pregnancies (we further discuss its use as a prenatal screening device later in this chapter). Newer three-dimensional and even four-dimensional ultrasounds (that include real-time fetal movement) allow parents to view almost lifelike fetal images, including yawns and facial expressions (see the nearby photo).

Second Trimester

The second trimester includes the second 15 weeks of pregnancy (weeks 14–28). The fetus looks noticeably more human.

sonography	ultrasound
Electronic monitoring; also called ultrasound.	The use of ultrasonic waves to monitor a developing fetus; also called sonography.

PRENATAL DEVELOPMENT The fetus grows dramatically during the second trimester and is 13 inches long by the end of the trimester. The fetus has developed tooth buds and reflexes, such as sucking and swallowing. Although the sex of the fetus is determined at conception, it is not immediately apparent during development. If the fetus is positioned correctly during ultrasound, the sex may be determined as early as 16 weeks, although most of the time it is not possible until 20 to 22 weeks.

During the second trimester, soft hair, called **lanugo** (lan-NEW-go), and a waxy substance, known as **vernix**, cover the fetus's body. These may develop to protect the fetus from the constant exposure to the amniotic fluid. By the end of the second trimester, the fetus will weigh about 1.75 pounds. If birth takes place at the end of the second trimester, the baby may be able to survive with intensive medical care. We discuss premature birth later in this chapter.

CHANGES IN THE PREGNANT MOTHER During the second trimester, nausea begins to subside as the body adjusts to the increased hormonal levels. Breast sensitivity also tends to decrease. However, fatigue may continue, as well as an increase in appetite, heartburn, edema (ankle or leg swelling), and a noticeable vaginal discharge. Skin pigmentation changes can occur on the face. As the uterus grows larger and the blood circulation slows down, constipation and muscle cramps bother some women. Internally, the cervix turns a deep red, almost violet color because of increased blood supply.

As the pregnancy progresses, the increasing size of the uterus and the restriction of the pelvic veins can cause more swelling of the ankles. Increased problems with varicose veins and hemorrhoids may also occur. Fetal movement is often felt in the second trimester, sometimes as early as the 16th week. Usually women can feel movement earlier in their second or subsequent pregnancies because they know what fetal movement feels like.

The second trimester of pregnancy is usually the most positive time for the mother. The early physiological signs of pregnancy such as morning sickness and fatigue lessen, and the mother-to-be finally feels better physically. Feeling better physically often leads to positive psychological feelings including excitement, happiness, and a sense of well-being. Many women report an increased sex drive during the second trimester, and for many couples, it is a period of high sexual satisfaction.

As the developing fetus begins to move around, many women feel reassured after anxiously wondering whether the fetus was developing at all. In fact, many women report that the kicking and moving about of the developing fetus are very comforting. Additionally, many women are happy to finally make the transition to maternity clothes because they are more comfortable and enable women to publicly share their pregnancies.

Third Trimester

The third trimester includes the final weeks of pregnancy (weeks 29–40) and ends with the birth of a child. The fetus gains both fat deposits and muscle mass during this period.

PRENATAL DEVELOPMENT By the end of the seventh month, the fetus begins to develop fat deposits. The fetus can react to pain, light, and sounds. Some fetuses develop occasional hiccups or begin to suck their thumb. If a baby is born at the end of the seventh month, there is a good chance of survival. In the eighth month, the majority of the organ systems are well developed, although the brain continues to grow. By the end of the eighth month, the fetus is 15 inches long and weighs about 3 pounds. During the third trimester, there is often stronger and more frequent fetal movement, which will slow down toward the ninth month (because the fetus has less room to move around). At birth, an infant, on average, weighs 7.5 pounds and is 20 inches long.

CHANGES IN THE PREGNANT MOTHER Many of the symptoms from the second trimester continue, with constipation and heartburn increasing in frequency. Backaches, leg cramps, increases in varicose veins, hemorrhoids, sleep problems, shortness of breath, and **Braxton–Hicks contractions** often occur. At first these contractions are scattered and relatively painless (the uterus hardens for a moment and then returns to normal). In the eighth and ninth months, the Braxton–Hicks contractions become stronger. A thin, yellowish liquid called **colostrum** (kuh-LAHS-trum) may

At 5 months, the fetus is becoming more and more lively. It can turn its head, move its face, and make breathing movements. This 5-month fetus is approximately 9 inches long.

Neil Bromhall/Science Source

lanugo
The downy covering of hair over a fetus.

vernix
Cheeselike substance that coats the fetus in the uterus.

Braxton–Hicks contractions
Intermittent contractions of the uterus.

colostrum
A thin, yellowish fluid, high in protein and antibodies, secreted from the nipples at the end of pregnancy and during the first few days after delivery.

be secreted from the nipples as the breasts prepare to produce milk for breast-feeding. Toward the end of the third trimester, many women feel an increase in apprehension about labor and delivery; impatience and restlessness are common.

The Partner's Experience

In the United States today, partners are allowed and encouraged to participate in the birth. However, this was not always the case. For many years, fathers were told to go to the waiting room and sit until the baby was born. In some other cultures, such as in Bang Chan, Thailand, the father aids in the actual birth of his child (Dunham et al., 1992). The role of the father in pregnancy varies among cultures. Some fathers are required to remain on a strict diet during the course of the pregnancy or to cater to their partner's food cravings at all times.

Pregnancy can be a time of joy and anticipation for the partner of a pregnant woman, but it can also be a time of stress and

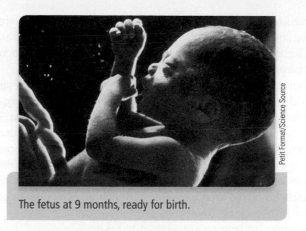

The fetus at 9 months, ready for birth.

anxiety. Feelings about parenting in combination with the many changes their partners are undergoing can all add to increased vulnerability.

Review Questions

1 How many weeks is a typical pregnancy, and how are trimesters determined?

2 Trace prenatal development and changes in the pregnant mother throughout the three trimesters of pregnancy.

3 Explain the changes in a pregnant mother, and identify the trimester in which a woman generally feels the most positive and explain why.

Health Care During Pregnancy

A pregnant woman can do many things to be healthy during her pregnancy, including participating in physical exercise, getting good nutrition, and avoiding drugs and alcohol. Women often maintain sexual interest during pregnancy, although it may begin to decrease during the third trimester.

Exercise and Nutrition

How much exercise should a woman get during pregnancy? Many physicians strongly advise light exercise during pregnancy; it has been found to result in a greater sense of well-being, enhanced mood, shorter labor, and fewer obstetric problems (Perales et al., 2016; Ward-Ritacco et al., 2016). In addition, studies have found that maternal exercise may improve the brain and memory functioning in unborn children (Labonte-Lemoyne et al., 2017). Most health care providers agree that a woman's exercise routine should not exceed pre-pregnancy levels. Although a woman should always discuss exercise with her health care provider, if she exercised before her pregnancy, keeping up with a moderate amount of exercise during the pregnancy is usually fine.

Although it is true that pregnant women are "cardiovascularly challenged" early in pregnancy, it is a myth that too much exercise

may cause a miscarriage or harm the developing fetus. Hundreds of pregnant women learned this before the legalization of abortion when they tried to exercise excessively or punch their abdomens in an unsuccessful attempt to dislodge the fertilized ovum. The implanted embryo is difficult to dislodge.

However, certain sports should be avoided during pregnancy, such as waterskiing, scuba diving, vigorous racquet sports, contact sports, and horseback riding, because these may cause injuries in both the mother and her fetus. Aquatic exercise may be the best choice for a pregnant woman because it is non–weight bearing, low impact, and reduces the risk for injury. In addition, aquatic exercise has been found to decrease maternal discomfort and improve body image (Smith & Michel, 2006). Physical stresses, such as prolonged standing, long work hours, and heavy lifting, can also affect a pregnancy. These stresses can reduce blood flow to the uterus, resulting in lower birth weights and prematurity (Clapp, 1996). It is also important to drink lots of water during pregnancy because water is an essential nutrient and is important for all bodily functions.

Nutritional requirements during pregnancy call for extra protein, iron, calcium, folic acid, and vitamin B6 (found in foods such as milk, yogurt, beef, vegetables, beans, and dried fruits). In addition, it is important for a woman to increase her caloric intake during pregnancy. Pregnant women who do not follow nutritional requirements may have low-birth-weight babies or an increased risk for miscarriage. Poor nutrition during pregnancy may also have long-term consequences and affect the infant's risk for cardiovascular disease, hypertension, and diabetes (Clapp & Lopez, 2007; Godfrey et al., 1996). Fetuses who are forced to adapt to a limited supply of nutrients may permanently "reprogram" their physiology and metabolism (Barker, 1997).

During the second trimester, an average-weight woman is advised to increase her caloric intake by 300 calories per day, and protein requirements increase. For vegetarians and vegans, it is necessary to increase consumption of vegetables, whole grains, nuts, and seeds, and also to include a protein supplement to ensure adequate protein intake. An increase in calcium is also necessary to help with bone calcification of the growing fetus. Because a woman's blood volume increases as much as 50% during pregnancy, iron may be diluted in the blood; thus, many pregnant women are advised to take prenatal vitamins, which include iron supplements.

Drugs and Alcohol

Physicians recommend avoiding several substances during pregnancy, including caffeine, nicotine, alcohol, marijuana, and other drugs. All of these substances are teratogens that can cross the placenta, enter into the developing fetus's bloodstream, and cause physical or mental deficiencies. **Fetal alcohol syndrome (FAS)**, the most severe condition associated with alcohol intake, occurs when a woman drinks heavily during pregnancy, producing an infant with irreversible physical and mental disabilities.

The National Survey on Drug Use and Health (2013) found that 18% of pregnant women ages 15–44 reported using alcohol in 2012. Another study found that worldwide, approximately 119,000 children are born with FAS each year (Popova et al., 2017). Smoking during pregnancy has been associated with spontaneous abortion, low birth weight, prematurity, and low iron levels (Tong et al., 2013). It has also been found to increase the risk for vascular damage to the developing fetus's brain and potentially interfere with a male's future ability to manufacture sperm. It is estimated that 16% of pregnant women ages 15–44 reported smoking cigarettes during pregnancy (Witt et al., 2015). Children whose mothers smoked during pregnancy have been found to experience an increased aging of the lungs and a higher risk for lung damage later in life (Maritz, 2008). Secondhand smoke has negative effects, too, and partners, fathers, friends, relatives, and strangers who smoke around a pregnant woman jeopardize the future health of a developing baby. Experts agree that there is no safe level of alcohol or tobacco use during pregnancy.

Prescription and nonprescription medications may also cause problems in the developing fetus. A study on common medications used during pregnancy found that women self-reported using medications such as oral contraceptives, antidepressants, amoxicillin, acetaminophen, ibuprofen, and aspirin (Stergiakouli et al., 2016; Thorpe et al., 2013). Although there is insufficient data to determine fetal risk of many of these medications, some studies have found that antidepressant use during pregnancy may be associated with an increased risk of birth defects, autism spectrum disorders, and/or stillbirth (Boukhris et al., 2016; Gentile, 2015; Jordan et al., 2016).

Widespread legalization of marijuana has raised many concerns about its use among pregnant women (Leemaqz et al., 2016). In fact, marijuana is the most commonly used illicit drug during pregnancy, being used by 3–30% of pregnant women (Mark et al., 2016; Metz & Stickrath, 2015). There are potential risks associated with marijuana use during pregnancy, including cognitive impairment, low birth weight, delivery problems, and stillbirth (Metz & Stickrath, 2015; Roth et al., 2015). These risks are higher in women who also smoke cigarettes, which is troubling since marijuana use during pregnancy is strongly correlated with cigarette use (Chabarria et al., 2016; Mark et al., 2016).

ON YOUR MIND

I've heard women say that if the average baby weighs about 7 pounds, then they will gain no more than 10 pounds during pregnancy. Is that safe? How small a weight gain is considered healthy? What about women with eating disorders?

It is estimated that a pregnant woman of average size should gain between 15 and 40 pounds throughout a pregnancy, and weight loss or weight maintenance is not recommended (Bish et al., 2008). Pregnancy weight gain accounts for the fetus, amniotic fluid, placenta, and breast, muscle, and fat increases. Gaining less than this is not healthy for either the developing fetus or the mother—and may actually predispose a baby to obesity later in life (because fetuses learn to restrict calories in the womb, but when nutrition is readily available, overeating is likely; Barker, 1997). In addition, too little weight gain during pregnancy has also been found to be related to a higher blood pressure in offspring once they reach early childhood (Clark et al., 1998). Although women with eating disorders often experience an improvement in symptoms during a pregnancy (Crow et al., 2008), it's important that anyone with an eating disorder consult with their health care provider before getting pregnant to determine an appropriate weight gain.

Pregnancy in Women Older Than 30

Earlier in this chapter, we discussed how fertility decreases with age—both ova and sperm quality are affected by age. As we discussed earlier, today many women are postponing their first pregnancies (see Figures 12.2 and 12.3). Declines in fertility in older women also make it more difficult for them to become pregnant (see Figure 12.6).

Success rates for artificial reproductive technologies (ARTs) in older women are low (MacArthur et al., 2016). Although older women who do get pregnant are more likely to take better care of themselves and eat healthier than younger women, there are increased risks to the pregnancies, including spontaneous abortion, first-trimester bleeding, low birth weight, increased labor

---

fetal alcohol syndrome (FAS)
A disorder involving physical and mental deficiencies, nervous system damage, and facial abnormalities found in the offspring of mothers who consumed large quantities of alcohol during pregnancy.

Throughout this chapter we have been discussing trends in pregnancy and birth. Although birth rates have been decreasing in every ethnicity, race, and age group, birth rates in single women older than 40 are increasing. Following is a story written by a woman who had a child on her own at the age of 43.

My life is not according to plan. I expected that after college, I would get a good job, find a great guy, fall in love, get married, and have three kids while establishing a rewarding career—all before the age of 30. In the real world, I have a successful career that I truly enjoy; I've been in love more than once but never married and never had children. At 43 years old, I was faced with the biggest decision of my life—having a child on my own. This is something I have discussed with friends and family over the years as a possibility but always hoped it wouldn't be necessary. Although I felt nervous, I also was really excited about my decision.

Anonymous sperm donation did not appeal to me. I really wanted to know the father: his personality, sense of humor, looks, intelligence, athleticism, and medical history. I did some research into sperm banks and sperm donation, and was actually pleasantly surprised at the amount of information each sperm bank provides (such as height, weight, hair color, eye color, ethnicity, education, occupation, family medical history). In many ways, it felt like an online dating service—but still wasn't the route I wanted to take.

Over the years, I have floated the idea of fathering a child for me to numerous male friends of mine. The man I chose has been a friend for a long time (we dated briefly

many years ago); he is married with children of his own and is a good father. We have agreed to keep his identity secret, and that he will not play a role in the child's life—emotionally or financially. We will remain good long-distance friends, and I will always be thankful for his generosity.

I went through a battery of fertility tests, and the test results were favorable for a woman my age. The entire process took about a year, and the year was full of excitement, as well as anguish and disappointment. I estimate that the treatments cost about $30,000 altogether, and my insurance company covered about half these costs, which is pretty good.

© Janell Carroll

After a comprehensive workup, I started fertility drugs in preparation for in vitro fertilization (IVF). I was put on a series of drugs that produced several ova, and when the time was right, I was scheduled for ova retrieval. The doctor used a needle through my vagina to retrieve the four ova that were available. The lab took the ova and immediately attempted to fertilize them. Four embryos resulted, but only three survived to be

frozen. I was unable to complete the transfer on that cycle, so we decided to do a new full IVF cycle the following month.

The next month, everything seemed to be going perfectly—the ova retrieval and fertilization resulted in three embryos, and all three were transferred to my uterus (the transfer happened 3 days after the ova retrieval). I was sure I was pregnant, and when my period started again I was devastated. Afterward the doctor counseled me that it was highly unlikely my eggs would work and that I should consider egg donation or adoption unless I had unlimited funds and the stamina to keep trying. I said I would look into both options but wanted to transfer my frozen embryos as soon as possible.

The transfer took place that cycle. This time my optimism took a negative turn. In fact, I was so certain it failed that I didn't even bother with a home pregnancy test before going to the doctor for testing on the 12th day. To my surprise, while the nurse was drawing my blood, the urine test showed positive. My doctor said I was his oldest patient to get pregnant with her own eggs. As happy and relieved as I was, I tried to keep my joy in check—knowing that miscarriage and genetic abnormalities were not uncommon for someone my age. So I viewed each checkup and test as clearing a hurdle. Even so, the smile didn't leave my face for 9 months.

My daughter, Tessa, was born healthy, after a grueling 22-hour labor. All in all, I feel like I hit the jackpot. Even though life is very different for me today, it is better than I could have ever imagined.

SOURCE: Author's files.

---

time and rate of C-section, and chromosomal abnormalities (see Table 12.2). Advancing paternal age can also contribute to potential problems. Studies have found that advancing paternal age was associated with an increased risk of genetic problems in offspring, including autism spectrum disorders (Quinlan et al., 2015; Smith, 2015; Vierck & Silverman, 2015).

REAL RESEARCH Research has found that regular marijuana use can negatively affect sperm production, leading to potential fertility problems (GUNDERSEN ET AL., 2015). Marijuana use of more than once per week was found to reduce sperm concentration by 52% and total sperm count by 55%.

Sex During Pregnancy

In some cultures, sex during pregnancy is strongly recommended because it is believed that a father's semen is necessary for proper development of the fetus (Dunham et al., 1992). While we know this isn't true, we do know that in an uncomplicated pregnancy, sexual behavior during pregnancy is safe for most mothers and the developing fetus up until the last several weeks of pregnancy. Orgasm during pregnancy is also safe in an uncomplicated pregnancy, but occasionally it may cause painful uterine contractions, especially toward the end of pregnancy.

Table 12.2 Risk for Down Syndrome in Live Birth Infants Based on Maternal Age

Age of Mother	Risk for Down Syndrome
20	1 in 1,667
25	1 in 1,250
30	1 in 952
35	1 in 385
40	1 in 106
45	1 in 30
49	1 in 11

SOURCES: Hook, E. B. (1981). Rate of chromosome abnormalities at different maternal ages. Obstetrics and Gynecology, 58(3), 282–285; Newberger, D. (2000). Down syndrome: Prenatal risk assessment and diagnosis. American Family Physician, 62(4), 825–832.

Cunnilingus can also be safely engaged in during pregnancy; however, as we discussed in Chapter 10, air should never be blown into the vagina of a pregnant woman because it could cause an air embolism, which could be fatal to both the mother and baby (Hill & Jones, 1993; Kaufman et al., 1987; Nicoll & Skupski, 2008; Sánchez et al., 2008).

During a woman's first trimester, sexual interest is often decreased because of physical changes, including nausea and fatigue. Sexual interest and satisfaction often increases during the second trimester and then begins to decrease again as the woman and fetus grow during the third trimester (Gokyildiz & Beji, 2005). The increasing size of the abdomen puts pressure on many of the internal organs and also makes certain positions for sexual behavior difficult. During the first and part of the second trimester, heterosexual women are more likely to use the male-on-top position during vaginal intercourse. However, later in pregnancy, the side-by-side, rear-entry, and female-on-top positions are used more frequently because they are more comfortable since they take the weight and pressure off the uterus.

REAL RESEARCH An ancient custom on the Indonesian island of Bali forbids a newborn's feet from touching the ground for 105 days (ROUSSEAU, 2017). After 105 days have passed, a child is given a name and their feet are allowed to touch the ground.

Review Questions

1 Explain the benefits of exercise in pregnancy, and describe some of the issues that must be considered when exercising during pregnancy.

2 Explain the importance of avoiding drugs and alcohol during pregnancy.

3 Discuss the reasons women are delaying pregnancy more often these days. What are the risks of delayed pregnancy?

4 Discuss the changes in women's sexual interest during pregnancy.

Problems During Pregnancy

The majority of women go through their pregnancy without any problems. However, understanding how complex the process of pregnancy is, it should not come as a surprise that occasionally things go wrong.

Ectopic Pregnancy

Most zygotes travel through the Fallopian tubes and end up in the uterus. However, in an ectopic pregnancy, the zygote implants outside of the uterus (Figure 12.7). Ninety-five percent of ectopic pregnancies occur when the fertilized ovum implants in the Fallopian tube (Hankins, 1995). These are called *tubal pregnancies*. Ectopic pregnancies can also occur in the abdomen, cervix, or ovaries. Approximately 2% (1 in 50) of all U.S. pregnancies are ectopic, and this number has been steadily increasing primarily because of increases in the incidence of pelvic inflammatory disease caused by chlamydia infections (Alkatout et al., 2013; Bugg & Taira, 2016; Shao et al., 2012).

Before the 19th century, 50% of all women with an ectopic pregnancy died. The development of surgical intervention to treat ectopic pregnancy in the 20th century significantly decreased morbidity rates. By the end of the 20th century, fewer than 5% of women with ectopic pregnancies died (Sepilian & Wood, 2004). The effects of ectopic pregnancy can be serious. The Fallopian tubes, cervix, and abdomen are not designed to support a growing fetus, and when one implants in these places, it could lead to a rupture and internal bleeding. Possible symptoms include abdominal pain (usually on the side of the body that has the tubal pregnancy), cramping, pelvic pain, vaginal bleeding, nausea, dizziness, and fainting (Levine, 2007; Seeber & Barnhart, 2006; Tay et al., 2000). Survival rates are improving, even though ectopic pregnancy remains the leading cause of maternal mortality in the first trimester (Tenore, 2000).

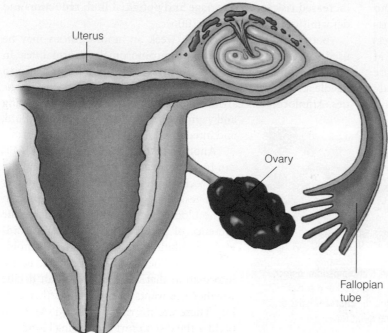

Uterus

Ovary

Fallopian tube

FIGURE **12.7** In an ectopic pregnancy, the zygote implants outside the uterus. In the majority of cases, it remains in the Fallopian tube.

What contributes to the likelihood of an ectopic pregnancy? Although many women without risk factors can experience one, there are some factors that may put a woman at greater risk. Daughters of mothers who experienced an ectopic pregnancy have a 50% higher risk of developing an ectopic pregnancy themselves (Kårhus et al., 2014). In addition, a woman who has experienced an ectopic pregnancy is at greater risk for development of another in future pregnancies. Other risk factors include smoking, since smoking cigarettes has been found to change the tubal contractions and muscular tone of the Fallopian tubes, which may lead to tubal inactivity, delayed ovum entry into the uterus, and changes in the tubes' ability to transport the ovum (Albers, 2007; Handler et al., 1989; Seeber & Barnhart, 2006).

A woman's future reproductive potential may be affected by ectopic pregnancy. Since the 1980s, treatment of ectopic pregnancy has shifted away from surgery toward medical treatments. Medical treatments include the use of medications and is preferred over surgery because of decreased tubal damage and lower morbidity rates (Hoover et al., 2010).

Spontaneous Abortion

A spontaneous abortion, or miscarriage, is a natural termination of a pregnancy before the time that the fetus can live on its own. Miscarriages can occur anytime during a pregnancy, although the percentage declines dramatically after the first trimester. It is estimated that there are more than 1 million miscarriages each year in the United States, with the majority occurring before 20 weeks of pregnancy (MacDorman & Gregory, 2015). The miscarriage rates for non-Hispanic Black women are more than twice the rate for non-Hispanic White and Asian or Pacific Islander women.

In a significant number of miscarriages, there is some chromosomal abnormality (Christiansen, 1996; Vorsanova et al., 2010). In other cases, in which there are no chromosomal problems, the uterus may be too small, too weak, or abnormally shaped, or the miscarriage may be caused by maternal stress, nutritional deficiencies, drug exposure, or pelvic infection. Recent studies have found that high levels of bisphenol A (BPA), a chemical in many plastics and canned food linings, may increase the risk of miscarriage (Lathi et al., 2014; Li et al., 2016; see Chapter 4 for more information about BPA).

Common symptoms of miscarriage include vaginal bleeding, cramps, and lower back pain. Usually a normal menstrual period returns within 3 months after a miscarriage, and future pregnancies may be perfectly normal. However, some women experience repeated miscarriages, often caused by anatomic, endocrine, hormonal, genetic, or chromosomal abnormalities (Bick et al., 1998; Carrell et al., 2003). Tests are being developed to try to predict when a miscarriage will occur.

A miscarriage can be emotionally difficult for both a woman and her partner, although research has found that male partners experience less intense emotional symptoms than female partners for a shorter period (Abboud & Liamputtong, 2003; Musters et al., 2011). Lesbian couples have been found to have an especially difficult time with miscarriage, probably because the complexity of planning and achieving a pregnancy are often much more difficult for lesbian couples (Wojnar, 2007). Although historically health care providers have recommended women wait between 6 and 24 months before trying to get pregnant again after a miscarriage, studies have found that women who started trying to conceive within 3 months of a miscarriage were more likely to become pregnant and experienced fewer complication rates in their pregnancies than those who waited longer to become pregnant (Love et al., 2010; Schliep et al., 2016). Even so, some women (and their partners) need time to emotionally heal after the loss of a pregnancy and choose to wait longer to try to conceive again.

Birth Defects

It is estimated that 1 of every 33 babies is born with a birth defect (Morbidity and Mortality Weekly Report [MMWR], 2014). There are many different types of birth defects that may be present at birth and they range from minor to serious. Although many can be treated or cured, they are also the number one cause of infant death (Matthews et al., 2015). Prenatal diagnostic testing can be used to determine whether there are chromosomal or genetic abnormalities in the fetus. The most common tests include blood work, ultrasound, **chorionic villus sampling (CVS)**, **maternal-serum alpha-fetoprotein screening (MSAFP)**, amniocentesis, and

---

chorionic villus sampling (CVS)
The sampling and testing of the chorion for fetal abnormalities.

maternal-serum alpha-fetoprotein screening (MSAFP)
A blood test used during early pregnancy to determine neural tube defects such as spina bifida or anencephaly.

cord blood sampling. Most of these tests are used by couples who have an increased risk for birth defects, although, as we have discussed, some couples may also use them to determine fetal sex. Because the ova and sperm of older women and men are more at risk for chromosomal and genetic abnormalities, these tests are often recommended for women older than 35. As we've already discussed, women who have undergone artificial reproductive technologies may choose to use PGD to identify any abnormalities in an embryo before implantation in the uterus.

Genetic abnormalities include **spina bifida** (SPY-na BIF-id-uh), **anencephaly** (an-en-SEH-fuh-lee), sex chromosome conditions (such as Turner and Klinefelter syndromes; see Chapter 4), and many other diseases, such as cystic fibrosis or sickle cell disease. The most common chromosomal abnormality appears on the 21st chromosome and is known as **Down syndrome**.

In Down syndrome, an extra chromosome has been added to the 21st chromosome; while most of us have 46 chromosomes (23 from each parent), a person with Down syndrome has 47. A child with Down syndrome often exhibits low muscle tone, a flat facial profile, slanted eyes, delayed mental and social development, and an enlarged tongue. A prenatal *screening* test can reveal higher risk for Down syndrome, but a prenatal *diagnostic* test is necessary to determine with certainty that Down syndrome is present. Down syndrome occurs in 1 of every 700 live births (Irving et al., 2008; Parker et al., 2010).

Screening tests for Down syndrome, including ultrasound and blood tests, can be done in the first trimester (Bianchi et al., 2014). An ultrasound can evaluate the fetal neck thickness, which may indicate an increased risk for Down syndrome. Another more invasive test, a chorionic villus sampling (CVS), is available between the 10th and 12th weeks of pregnancy. In this procedure, a sliver of tissue from the chorion (the tissue that develops into the placenta) is removed and checked for abnormalities. CVS testing has more risks than ultrasound, including

Down syndrome, a chromosomal defect, can cause delayed mental and social development and the characteristics of slanted eyes and a flat face.

DenKuvaiev/Getty Images

increased risk for miscarriage and potential limb reduction and deformities (Caughey et al., 2006).

Between the 15th and 20th week an amniocentesis may be used to detect either genetic or chromosomal abnormalities. In this procedure, amniotic fluid is extracted from the womb using a needle and is evaluated for genetic and chromosomal abnormalities. Amniocentesis carries a slight risk of miscarriage, cramping and vaginal bleeding, leaking amniotic fluid, and infection.

Another second trimester test, MSAFP, can be performed between the 15th and the 20th weeks of pregnancy. MSAFP is a simple blood test that evaluates levels of protein in the blood. High levels may indicate the presence of potential birth defects, including spinal bifida or anencephaly (Reynolds et al., 2008). The MSAFP can provide useful information that can help a woman decide whether she wants to undergo further testing. There are no risks to the MSAFP test besides the discomfort of drawing blood.

Finally, **cordocentesis**, or cord blood sampling, involves collecting blood from the umbilical cord anytime after the 18th week of pregnancy for a chromosome analysis. Cordocentesis is an invasive test, and although it can slightly increase the risk for miscarriage, it is considered a safe and reliable procedure for prenatal diagnosis (Ghidini & Bocchi, 2007; Liao et al., 2006; Piyamongkol et al., 2012). Keep in mind that if a woman does decide to undergo such testing, she and her partner must decide what to do with the information these tests provide.

Rh Incompatibility

The Rh factor naturally exists on some people's red blood cells. If your blood type is followed by "+," you are "Rh positive," and if not, you are "Rh negative." This is important when you are having a blood transfusion or when pregnant.

A father or donor who is Rh positive often passes on his blood type to the baby. If the baby's mother is Rh negative, any of the fetal blood that comes into contact with hers (which happens during delivery, not pregnancy) will cause her to begin to manufacture antibodies against the fetal blood. This may be very dangerous for any future pregnancies. Because the mother has made antibodies to Rh-positive blood, she will reject the fetal Rh-positive blood, which can lead to fetal death. After an Rh-negative woman has delivered, she is given **RhoGAM** (row-GAM), which prevents antibodies from forming and ensures that her future pregnancies will be healthy. RhoGAM is also given if an Rh-negative pregnant woman has an amniocentesis, miscarriage, or abortion.

Toxemia

In the last 2 to 3 months of pregnancy, 6% to 7% of women experience **toxemia** (tock-SEE-mee-uh), or **preeclampsia** (pre-ee-CLAMP-see-uh). Symptoms include rapid weight gain, fluid retention, an increase in blood pressure, and protein in the urine. If toxemia is allowed to progress, it can result in **eclampsia**, which

---

cord blood sampling
A prenatal test that removes fetal blood from the umbilical cord to detect fetal abnormalities (also called cordocentesis).

spina bifida
Congenital defect of the vertebral column in which the halves of the neural arch of a vertebra fail to fuse in the midline.

anencephaly
Congenital absence of most of the brain and spinal cord.

Down syndrome
A problem occurring on the 21st chromosome of the developing fetus that can cause mental retardation and physical challenges.

cordocentesis
A prenatal test that removes fetal blood from the umbilical cord to detect fetal

abnormalities (also called cord blood sampling).

RhoGAM
Drug given to mothers whose Rh is incompatible with the fetus; prevents the formation of antibodies that can imperil future pregnancies.

toxemia
A form of blood poisoning caused by kidney disturbances.

preeclampsia
A condition of hypertension during pregnancy, typically accompanied by leg swelling and other symptoms.

eclampsia
A progression of toxemia with similar, but worsening, conditions.

involves convulsions, coma, and in approximately 15% of cases, death. Even though preeclampsia typically occurs at the end of pregnancy, research indicates that it may actually be caused by defective implantation or placental problems at the beginning of pregnancy (Urato & Norwitz, 2011).

Preeclampsia is a complication that occurs in approximately 3% of pregnancies (Hutcheon et al., 2011). Women who have experienced preeclampsia in a previous pregnancy are at an increased risk of recurrence in future pregnancies, while women whose mothers experienced it are also at increased risk (Groom et al., 2017). Male offspring from mothers who experienced preeclampsia are twice as likely to father daughters who will undergo preeclampsia compared to men whose mothers did not experience preeclampsia (Seppa, 2001; Urato & Norwitz, 2011). Overall, Black women are at greater risk for preeclampsia than non-Hispanic White or Hispanic women (Ghosh et al., 2014; Mbah et al., 2011). Early screening for preeclampsia, along with ultrasound and blood tests, can identify women at risk for developing preeclampsia.

Review Questions

1 Define ectopic pregnancy and spontaneous abortion, and discuss what we know about these conditions.

2 Define prenatal diagnostic testing, identify some of the tests, and explain how they can be used to determine whether there are fetal abnormalities.

3 What is Down syndrome and what testing is available to detect it?

4 What is RhoGAM and why would a woman use it?

Childbirth

The average length of a pregnancy is 9 months, but a normal birth can occur 3 weeks before or 2 weeks after the due date. It is estimated that only 4% of American babies are born exactly on the due date predicted (Dunham et al., 1992). Early delivery may occur in cases in which the mother has exercised throughout the pregnancy, the fetus is female, or the mother has shorter menstrual cycles (Jones, 1984).

No one knows why, but there is also a seasonal variation in human birth. More babies are conceived in the summer months and in late December (Macdowall et al., 2008). There are also more babies born between the hours of 1 and 7 a.m., and again this is thought to have evolved because of the increased protection and decreased chances of predator attacks (Jones, 1984).

We do not know exactly what starts the birth process. It appears that in fetal sheep, a chemical in the brain signals that it is time for birth (Palca, 1991). Perhaps this may also be true in humans, but the research remains incomplete.

Preparing for Birth

As the birth day comes closer, many women (and their partners!) become anxious, nervous, and excited about what is to come. This is probably why the tradition of baby showers started. These gatherings enable women (and more recently, men) to gather and discuss the impending birth. People often share their personal experiences and helpful hints. This ritual may help couples to prepare themselves emotionally and to feel more comfortable.

engagement
When the fetus moves down toward the birth canal before delivery.

Increasing knowledge and alleviating anxiety about the birth process are the main concepts behind childbirth classes. In these classes, women and their partners are taught what to expect during labor and delivery, and how to control the pain through breathing and massage. Tension and anxiety during labor have been found to increase pain, discomfort, and fatigue. Many couples feel more prepared and focused after taking these courses. However, some same-sex couples report feeling uncomfortable with childbirth classes that cater primarily to heterosexual couples (Ross et al., 2006a). Having other same-sex couples in the class often makes it a more positive experience.

A few weeks before delivery, the fetus usually moves into a "head-down" position in the uterus (Figure 12.8). This is referred to as **engagement**. Ninety-seven percent of fetuses are in this position at birth (Nilsson, 1990). If a baby's feet or

ON YOUR MIND

What determines how long a woman will be in labor? Why do they say a woman's first baby is hardest? A friend of mine was in labor for 36 hours!

Usually, first labors are the longest and most difficult labors. Second and subsequent labors are usually easier and shorter because there is less resistance from the birth canal and the surrounding muscles. Overall, the biggest differences are in the amount of time it takes for the cervix to fully dilate and the amount of pushing necessary to move the baby from the birth canal. We do not know why some women have easier labors than others. It could be the result of diet or exercise during the pregnancy. Ethnic, racial, and maternal age differences have been found in the length of labor. Black women have been found to experience shorter second-stage labors than White, Asian, and Hispanic women (Greenberg et al., 2006). In addition, younger women often experience shorter labors than older women (Greenberg et al., 2007).

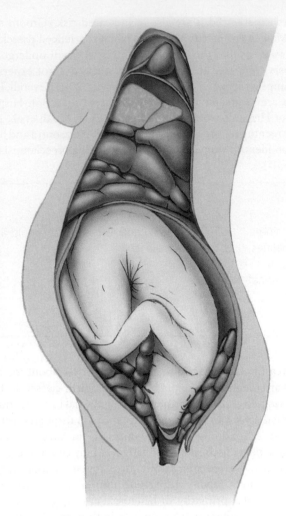

FIGURE **12.8** A full-term fetus in the head-down position in the uterus.

There are some increased risks for home births, including problems during labor and delivery, infections, and fetal malformations (Grünebaum et al., 2016). While the American College of Obstetricians and Gynecologists believes the risks associated with home births are low, women need to make medically informed decisions about birthplace choices.

The majority of home births are done with the help of a **midwife** (Macdorman et al., 2011; Martin et al., 2013). Same-sex couples are more likely to use midwives in their birthing experience, even if they deliver in a hospital setting. This is primarily because many same-sex couples feel that midwives are more accepting of nontraditional families (Ross et al., 2006b).

Inducing the Birth

Inducing birth involves using techniques to start the birth process artificially. Usually this is in the form of drugs given in increasing doses to mimic the natural contractions of labor, although induced contractions can be more painful and prolonged than natural labor. Birth can occur anywhere from a few hours to several days after induction begins, depending on a woman's prior birth history. Since the early 2000s, there has been a tremendous increase in childbirth induction. After nearly 20 years of consecutive increases in labor inductions, this medical procedure reached its highest point in 2010 and then began to decline slightly (Osterman & Martin, 2014).

Labor induction may be done in cases in which labor is slow to progress (see below), pregnancy has lasted beyond 42 weeks, the baby is large, preeclampsia exists, or in cases of fetal death. Unless there is a medical reason for it, most women are advised to avoid labor induction (Amis, 2007; Durham et al., 2008). Some women elect to have inductions for nonmedical reasons, including anything from wanting to avoid birth on a certain day (such as a holiday) or to accommodate a woman's or her partner's work schedule.

buttocks are first (**breech position**), the physician may either try to rotate the baby before birth or recommend a C-section. We discuss this later in the chapter.

Birthplace Choices

In the United States, the majority of babies today are born in hospitals (Martin et al., 2013). In 2012, only 1.4% of births took place outside of a hospital; of these, most occurred in a residence. Many hospitals now offer the use of birthing centers, which include comfortable rooms with a bed for a woman's partner, music, a television, a shower, and perhaps even a Jacuzzi (to help ease labor pains).

In nonindustrialized countries, nearly all babies are born at home; worldwide, approximately 80% of babies are (Dunham et al., 1992).

breech position	midwife
An abnormal and often dangerous birthing position in which the baby's feet, knees, or buttocks emerge before the head.	A person trained to assist women during childbirth.

ON YOUR MIND

Is it safe to use drugs to lessen the pain of labor and birth?

Although some women believe in a "natural" childbirth (one without pain medications), other women want to use medication to lessen the pain. The search for a perfect drug to relieve pain, one that is safe for both the mother and her child, has been a long one. Every year, more and more progress is made. Medication is often recommended when labor is long and complicated, the pain is more than the mother can tolerate or interferes with her ability to push, forceps are required during the delivery, or when a mother is so restless and agitated that it inhibits labor progress. In all cases, the risks of drug use must be weighed against the benefits.

How well a pain medication works depends on the mother, the dosage, and other factors. We do know that the use of some drugs, including epidurals, can increase labor time and may be associated with other risk factors. However, newer lower dosage epidurals have been found to produce fewer adverse effects and are better tolerated by women (NERUDA, 2005).

Birthing Positions

Although women can assume a variety of positions during childbirth, the dominant position in Westernized countries is the semi-reclined position with a woman's feet up in stirrups (DeJonge et al., 2008). Some feminist health professionals claim that this position is easier for the doctor than for the pregnant woman, and that it is the most ineffective and dangerous position for labor. Recently, women have been given more freedom in deciding how to position themselves for childbirth in the United States. A woman on her hands and knees or in the squatting position allows her pelvis and cervix to be at their widest. In addition, the force of gravity can be used to help in the birth process. Health care providers today recommend that women use whatever birthing position feels most comfortable for them (DeJonge et al., 2008; Gupta & Nikodem, 2000).

Positions for birth vary in different parts of the world. Rope midwives in rural areas of the Sudan hang a rope from the ceiling and have the mother grasp the rope and bear down in a squatting position. In Bang Chan, Thailand, a husband cradles his pregnant wife between his legs and digs his toes into her thighs. This toe pressure is thought to provide relief from her pain (Dunham et al., 1992).

Stages of Childbirth

Birth itself begins with **cervical effacement** and **dilation**, which leads to expulsion of the fetus and, soon afterward, expulsion of the placenta. The beginning of birth is usually marked by an expulsion of the mucus plug from the cervix. This plug protects the fetus from any harmful bacteria that might enter the vagina during pregnancy. Sometimes women experience false labor, in which contractions are irregular and do not dilate the cervix. In real labor, contractions will be regular and get closer together over time. In a typical birth process, the process is divided into three stages.

Stage One

In the United States, if the birth process is taking too long, physicians may administer the drug Pitocin to speed up labor. In Bolivia, however, certain groups of people believe that nipple stimulation helps the birth move quicker. So if a birth is moving too slowly, a woman's nipples may be massaged. Biologically, nipple stimulation leads to a release of oxytocin, which is a natural form of Pitocin. This is why many midwives in the United States also practice nipple stimulation during childbirth.

In some Guatemalan societies, long and difficult labors are believed to be due to a woman's sins, and so she is asked to confess her sins. If this does not help speed up labor, her husband is asked to confess. If neither of these confessions helps, the father's loincloth is wrapped around the woman's stomach to assure her that he will not leave her once the baby is born (Dunham et al., 1992).

The first stage of labor can last anywhere from 20 minutes to 24 hours and is longer in first births. When true labor begins, the Braxton–Hicks contractions increase. The cervix begins dilation (opening up) and effacement (thinning out) to allow for fetal passage (this phase is called *early labor*). Throughout the first stage of labor, the entrance to the cervix (the os) increases from 0 to 10 centimeters to allow for the passage of the fetus.

Toward the end of this stage, the amniotic sac usually ruptures (however, this may happen earlier or not at all in some women). Contractions may last for about 30 to 60 seconds at intervals of between 5 and 20 minutes, and the cervix usually dilates to 4 to 5 centimeters. Couples are advised to time the contractions and the interval between contractions and report these to their health care provider.

The contractions will eventually begin to last longer (1 minute or more), become more intense, and increase in frequency (every 1 to 3 minutes). Dilation of the cervix continues from 4 to 8 centimeters (this phase is called *active labor*). The contractions that open the os can be very painful, and health care providers will usually monitor the progress of cervical dilation.

The last phase in stage one is called **transition**, which for most women is the most difficult part of the birth process. Contractions are very intense and long and have shorter periods in between, and the cervix dilates from 8 to 10 centimeters. The fetus moves into the base of the pelvis, creating an urge to push; however, the woman is advised not to push until her cervix is fully dilated. Many women feel exhausted by this point.

The woman's body produces pain-reducing hormones called **endorphins**, which may dull the intensity of the contractions. Should a woman feel the need for more pain relief, she can also be given various pain medications. The most commonly used pain medications include analgesics (pain relievers) and anesthetics (which produce a loss of sensation). Which drug is used depends on the mother's preference, health history, and present condition and the baby's condition. An epidural block (an anesthetic) is very popular for the relief of severe labor pain. Although there has been an increased use of drugs to reduce the pain of labor in recent years, advances in medical technology allow physicians to customize pain-relieving drugs for each woman (Leo & Sia, 2008; Moen & Irestedt, 2008).

The fetus is monitored for signs of distress, such as slowed heart rate or lack of oxygen. This is done either through the woman's abdomen with a sensor or by accessing the fetus's scalp through the cervix. Fetal monitoring can determine whether the fetus is in any danger that would require a quicker delivery or a C-section.

REAL RESEARCH Women with secure attachment styles report significantly less pain and lower use of pain medications during labor than insecurely attached women (Costa-Martins et al., 2014).

---

cervical effacement
The stretching and thinning of the cervix in preparation for birth.

dilation
The expansion of the opening of the cervix in preparation for birth.

transition
The last period in labor, in which contractions are strongest and the time between contractions the shortest.

endorphins
Neurotransmitters, concentrated in the pituitary gland and parts of the brain, that inhibit physical pain.

Stage Two

After the cervix has fully dilated, the second stage of birth, the expulsion of the fetus, begins. Contractions are somewhat less intense, lasting about 60 seconds and spaced at 1- to 3-minute intervals.

Toward the end of this stage of labor, the doctor may perform an **episiotomy** (ee-pee-zee-AH-tuh-mee) to reduce the risk for a tearing of the tissue between the vaginal opening and anus as the fetus emerges. There has been an ongoing debate about the usefulness of episiotomy (Lurie et al., 2013). Those who support the practice argue that it can speed up labor, prevent tearing during a delivery, protect against future incontinence, and promote quicker healing. Those who argue against the practice claim that it increases infection, pain, and healing times and may increase discomfort when penetrative sex is resumed (Chang et al., 2011; McDonald & Brown, 2013; Radestad et al., 2008). The American College of Obstetricians and Gynecologists recommends against the routine use of episiotomy and suggests its use only in limited cases.

As the woman pushes during contractions, the top of the head of the baby soon appears at the vagina, which is known as **crowning**. Once the face emerges, the mucus and fluid in the mouth and nostrils are removed by suction. The baby emerges and, after the first breath, usually lets out a cry. After the baby's first breath, the umbilical cord, which supplies the fetus with oxygen, is cut; this is painless for the mother and child. Eye drops are put into the baby's eyes to prevent bacterial infection.

Directly after birth, many physicians and midwives place the newborn directly on the mother's chest to begin the bonding process. However, sometimes the woman's partner may be the first to hold the child, or the nurses will perform an **Apgar test**. This test evaluates a newborn on five components, including heart rate, respiratory effort, muscle tone, reflex irritability, and color. A newborn score of 1 to 2 is assigned to each component, and the sum of all individual scores makes up the total score. A total score of 7 or higher suggests a good to excellent condition. A newborn with a low Apgar score may require intensive care after delivery.

Stage Three

During the third stage of labor, the placenta (sometimes referred to as the "afterbirth") is expelled from the uterus. Strong contractions continue after the baby is born to push the placenta out of the uterus and through the vagina. Most women are not aware of this process because of the excitement of giving birth. The placenta must be checked to make sure all of it has been expelled. If there was any tearing or an episiotomy was performed, this will

Women who have lumbar tattoos may have increased risks with an epidural injection during labor. Studies have found that the injection may push pigmented tissue into the spinal canal (Kuczkowski, 2006). If the tattoo is large, an anesthesiologist either needs to find a pigment-free area or make a small incision into the tattoo before administering the epidural.

Seth Resnick/Seth Resnick

need to be sewn up after the placenta is removed. Usually this stage lasts about 30 minutes or so. In the United States, placentas are usually disposed of after birth, although some women are able to take them home if they wish.

In parts of Kenya, the placenta of a female baby is buried under the fireplace, and the placenta of a male baby is buried by the stalls of baby camels. This practice is thought to forever connect the children's future to these locations. Some cultures bury their placentas, whereas others hang the placentas outside the home to show that a baby indeed arrived!

episiotomy
A cut made with surgical scissors to avoid tearing of the perineum at the end of the second stage of labor.

crowning
The emergence of a baby's head at the opening of the vagina at birth.

Apgar test
Developed by Virginia Apgar, MD, this system assesses the general physical condition of a newborn infant for five criteria.

Review Questions

1 Describe the emotional and physical preparation necessary for the birth of a child, childbirth induction, and the various birthing positions.

2 Identify the three stages of birth and explain what happens at each stage. Generally, how long does each stage last?

3 Which phase of the birthing process is the most difficult for most women and why?

4 What is an episiotomy and why might it be used?

Problems During Birthing

For most women, the birth of a newborn baby proceeds without problems. However, a number of problems can arise, including premature birth, breech birth, C-section delivery, and stillbirth. Earlier we discuss seasonal variations in birth, and research has found there are also seasonal variations in birthing problems around the world (Strand et al., 2011). Low birth weights, premature births, and stillbirths peak in the winter and summer. Experts believe this may be because of extreme temperature changes.

Premature Birth

Most babies are born late rather than early. Birth that takes place before the 37th week of pregnancy is considered **premature (or preterm) birth**. Although the incidence of premature birth has been declining since 2007, it began increasing in again in 2015 (Hamilton et al., 2016). In 2015, premature birth occurred in 1 out of every 10 deliveries (Centers for Disease Control, 2016). Ethnic/racial disparities exist, with Black women and Hispanic women experiencing more premature births than White women (Borrell et al., 2016).

Premature birth increases the risk for birth-related defects and infant mortality. In fact, premature birth accounts for 28% of infant deaths worldwide (Menon, 2008). Research into pediatrics has led to tremendous improvements in the survival rates of premature infants. Infants born at 24 weeks' gestation have a greater than 50% chance of survival (Welty, 2005). Unfortunately, more than half of these infants who survive develop complications and long-term effects of prematurity.

Birth may occur prematurely for several reasons, including early labor or early rupture of the amniotic membranes or because of a maternal or fetal problem. It is common for women who have had one premature birth to have subsequent premature births. Approximately 50% of all twin births are premature, and delivery of multiple fetuses occurs about 3 weeks earlier, on average, than single births (Croft et al., 2010). In 2004, the world's smallest surviving premature baby was born, weighing in at 8.6 ounces (her twin sister weighed 1 pound, 4 ounces; Huffstutter, 2004). These twins were delivered via C-section in the 26th week of pregnancy because of medical problems experienced by their mother. Other factors that may be related to premature birth include smoking during pregnancy, alcohol or drug use, inadequate weight gain or nutrition, heavy physical labor during the pregnancy, infections, and teenage pregnancy. Eating or drinking artificial sweeteners may also increase a woman's risk for premature birth. Pregnant women who drank one or more artificially sweetened soft drinks a day had higher rates of premature birth than women who either drank sugar-sweetened soft drinks or didn't drink soft drinks at all (Englund-Ögge et al., 2012).

Breech Birth

In 97% of all births, the fetus emerges in the head-down position. However, in approximately 3% of cases, the fetus is in the breech position, with the feet and buttocks against the cervix (Figure 12.9).

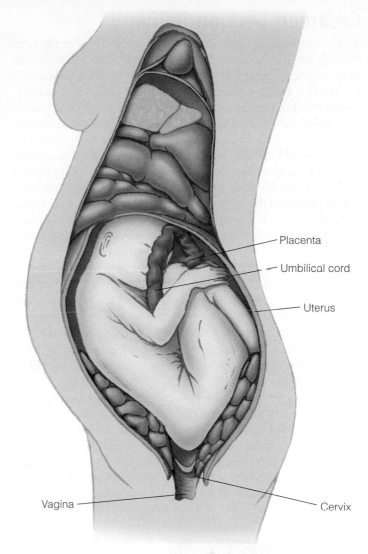

FIGURE **12.9** A full-term fetus in the breech position, with feet and buttocks against the cervix.

Interestingly, about half of all fetuses are in this position before the seventh month of pregnancy, but most rotate before birth (Jones, 1984). Studies have found that risk factors associated with breech birth include lower birth weight or preterm fetuses, increased age of mother, past C-sections, congenital malformations, or a parent who was born breech (Cammu et al., 2014; Nordtveit et al., 2008; Vendittelli et al., 2008).

Sometimes doctors are aware of the position of the fetus before delivery and can try to change the fetus's position for normal vaginal delivery. However, if this is not possible, or if it is discovered too late into delivery, labor may take an unusually long time. A skilled midwife or physician often can flip the baby or deliver it safely even in the breech position. However, in the United States today, a C-section will often be performed to ensure the health and well-being of both the mother and her child.

---

premature birth
Any infant born before the 37th week of pregnancy. Also referred to as preterm birth.

Cesarean-Section Delivery

A cesarean section (C-section) involves the delivery of the fetus through an incision in the abdominal wall. Elective C-sections were more popular a few years ago and were often chosen if a woman had a prior C-section birth, wanted to choose her delivery date, and/or to reduce the risk of potential pelvic floor trauma that could occur during vaginal delivery (Dietz, 2006; Herbruck, 2008). C-section births are most commonly done for medical reasons that could include the baby being too large for a woman to deliver vaginally, the inability of a woman to push the baby out the birth canal, the blocking of the cervix by the placenta (**placenta previa**), failure of the cervix to dilate to 10 centimeters, twin births, or **fetal distress**. If a health care provider decides that an emergency C-section is necessary, the woman is moved to an operating room and given either a general anesthetic or an epidural. The operation usually lasts between 20 and 90 minutes from start to finish (although the baby can be out within minutes if necessary). Women who have C-sections usually stay in the hospital longer than those who have vaginal deliveries. While the incidence of C-section births peaked in 2009, rates have declined every year since then (Hamilton et al., 2016). Overall, older women are more likely than younger women to undergo a C-section delivery (Richards et al., 2016).

Women who have had a C-section birth may be at greater risk for small fetal size, placental separation from the uterine wall, and uterine rupture in subsequent pregnancies (Daltveit et al., 2008). Even so, some women deliver their next babies vaginally after a C-section (referred to as a VBAC, or vaginal birth after C-section), whereas others choose another C-section for a variety of reasons, including to avoid the pain or the increased risks of vaginal labor.

Stillbirth

A fetus that dies after 20 weeks of pregnancy is called a **stillbirth** (before 20 weeks, it is called a miscarriage). There are many possible causes for a stillbirth, including umbilical cord accidents, problems with the placenta, birth defects, infections, and maternal diabetes or high blood pressure. Oftentimes the fetal loss is completely unexpected, because 50% of all stillbirths occur in pregnancies that appeared to be without problems (Pasupathy & Smith, 2005). Approximately 86% of fetal deaths occur before labor even begins, whereas 14% occur during labor and delivery (Fretts et al., 1992). In most cases, a woman goes into labor approximately 2 weeks after the fetus has died; if not, her labor will be induced. Some ethnic differences have been noted, with higher rates of stillbirth in Black and mixed-race couples (Getahun et al., 2005).

Improved treatments of certain maternal medical conditions have decreased the frequency of stillbirths in the United States. To decrease the risk of stillbirth, many women are advised to monitor fetal movement beginning in the 28th week of pregnancy. While there are many ways to check fetal movement, most experts recommend "kick counts," in which women time how long it takes to feel 10 fetal kicks or movements. If a woman notices decreased movement, fetal monitoring can be performed to check on the status of the fetus. Research has shown that women who have experienced a stillbirth often have a live birth in their next pregnancy, even though they are often viewed as high-risk patients (Black et al., 2008; Ofir et al., 2013).

In the 1970s, a perinatal bereavement movement began in the United States, which offered parents a way to deal with the death of a newborn. The International Stillbirth Alliance, an organization that works to prevent stillbirth and improve bereavement care worldwide, was founded in 2002. These groups help families deal with issues related to stillbirth and infant death.

Review Questions

1 Define preterm birth, and discuss some of the causes and risks associated with preterm birth.

2 Define breech birth and identify some of the factors that have been associated with breech birth.

3 Explain some of the reasons for a C-section birth.

4 Differentiate between a miscarriage and a stillbirth.

Postpartum Parenthood

The majority of people are excited about being parents. However, many couples are not prepared for the many physical and emotional changes that occur after the child is born. They may also find changes in their sex lives because of the responsibility and exhaustion that often accompany parenthood.

More Physical Changes for the Mother

Many women report painful contractions for a few days after birth. These contractions are caused by the secretion of oxytocin, which is produced when a woman breast-feeds and is responsible for the shrinking of the uterus. The uterus returns to its original size about 6 weeks postpartum; in breast-feeding women, the uterus returns to its original size quicker than in non–breast-feeding women. A bloody vaginal discharge can persist for anywhere from a week to several weeks after delivery. After the bleeding stops, the discharge is often yellow–white and can last for a couple of weeks in mothers who breast-feed and up to a month or so in women who do not.

---

placenta previa
A condition in which the placenta is abnormally positioned in the uterus so that it partially or completely covers the opening of the cervix.

fetal distress
Condition in which a fetus has an abnormal heart rate or rhythm.

stillbirth
An infant who is born dead.

Women may experience an increase in frequency of urination, which can be painful if an episiotomy was performed or natural tearing occurred. Women may be advised to take sitz baths, in which the vagina and perineum are soaked in warm water to reduce the pain and to quicken the healing process. Until the cervix returns to its closed position, full baths are generally not advised.

Postpartum Psychological Changes

Many women experience an onset of intense emotions after the birth of a baby. One study found that 52% of new mothers felt excited and elated, 48% reported feeling like they did not need sleep, 37% reported feeling energetic, and 31% reported being more chatty (Heron et al., 2008). At the same time, many women report feeling overwhelmed and exhausted. Although minor sadness and feelings of being overwhelmed are common emotions after the birth of a baby, for some women it can be a difficult time with tearfulness and anxiety.

Research has found that 10–15% of women experience **postpartum depression** (Brummelte & Galea, 2016). Symptoms include low energy, sadness, anxiety, and irritability, along with changes in sleep, eating, and sexual desire. Physical exhaustion, physiological changes, and an increased responsibility of child rearing all contribute to these feelings, coupled with postpartum hormonal changes (including a sudden decline in hormones). Women with a history of depression are at higher risk of developing postpartum depression (Becker et al., 2016). As we discussed earlier, there are risks associated with taking antidepressants during pregnancy, but it is important for women and their health care providers to weigh these risks against the risk of untreated depression. Women with premature infants are at greater risk for postpartum depression because of the increased stress involved in these births. In addition, women whose pregnancies were unintended also have an increased risk of postpartum depression (Gauthreaux et al., 2017). Finally, partner violence has also been found to be related to postpartum depression (Ludermir et al., 2010). We discuss intimate partner violence in more detail in Chapter 17.

Some ethnic and racial differences have been found in the rates of postpartum depression, with Black and Hispanic mothers reporting more postpartum depression than White mothers (Howell et al., 2005). Limited research on postpartum depression among lesbian and bisexual women has found that it may be more common than in heterosexual women, but more research is needed in this area (Flanders et al., 2015; Ross et al., 2007). Male partners may also experience postpartum depression after the birth of a baby (Davé et al., 2010).

Overall, partner support has been found to decrease postpartum depression in both heterosexual and same-sex couples (Misri et al., 2000; Ross, 2005; Storm, 2011). Postpartum depression in a mother has been found to have a negative impact on the offspring and may lead to cognitive and emotional problems (Drury et al., 2016). Studies have found that although postpartum depression is treatable with medications, it is often underdiagnosed and untreated (Ko et al., 2017).

In the most severe cases, mental disturbances, called **postpartum psychosis**, occur; in rare cases, women have killed or neglected their babies after delivery (Rammouz et al., 2008). Symptoms of postpartum psychosis can include depression, paranoia, hallucinations, and delusions.

Sexuality for New Parents

Although most health care providers advise their patients to wait 6 weeks postpartum before resuming sexual activity, in an uncomplicated vaginal delivery (with no tears or episiotomy), sexual activity can safely be engaged in 2 weeks after delivery. This period is usually necessary to ensure that no infection occurs and that the cervix has returned to its original position. If an episiotomy was performed, it may take up to 3 weeks for the stitches to dissolve. Health care providers generally advise women who have had a C-section birth to wait 4 to 6 weeks to resume sexual activity. In an uncomplicated delivery, 90% of women report resuming sexual activity by 6 months after the baby is born, although those with a complicated labor often wait longer to resume sexual activity (Brubaker et al., 2008). Immediately after delivery, many women report slower and less intense excitement stages of the sexual response cycle and a decrease in vaginal lubrication (Masters & Johnson, 1966). However, at 3 months postpartum, the majority of women return to their original levels of sexual desire and excitement.

Breast-Feeding the Baby

Within an hour after birth, the newborn baby usually begins a rooting reflex, which signals hunger. The baby's sucking triggers the flow of milk from the breast. This is done through receptors in the nipples, which signal the pituitary to produce prolactin, a chemical necessary for milk production. Another chemical, oxytocin, is also produced, which helps increase contractions in the uterus to shrink it to its original size. In the first few days of breast-feeding, the breasts release a fluid called colostrum, which is very important in strengthening the baby's immune system. This is one of the reasons that breast-feeding is recommended to new mothers.

Breast-feeding has many benefits, including strengthening of the infant's immune system and cognitive development, and a reduction in infant allergies, asthma, diarrhea, tooth decay, and ear, urinary tract, and respiratory infections (Daniels & Adair, 2005; Duijts et al., 2010; Khadivzadeh & Parsai, 2005). While there has been controversy about whether or not breast-fed children have higher IQ scores than non–breast-fed children, this research is ongoing (Caspi et al., 2007; Girard et al., 2017; Horta et al., 2015; Luby et al., 2016). Benefits to the mother include an earlier return to pre-pregnancy weight and a lower risk for breast cancer and osteoporosis (Stuebe et al., 2009). In addition, the body-to-body contact during breast-feeding has been found to decrease stress and improve mood for both mother and child (Groer, 2005).

---

postpartum depression
A woman's clinical depression that occurs after childbirth.

postpartum psychosis
The rare occurrence of severe, debilitating depression or psychotic symptoms in the mother after childbirth.

The American Academy of Pediatrics (2012) recommends babies be exclusively breast-fed for at least the first 6 months of life and to continue for another 6 months or longer after solid foods are introduced. The Centers for Disease Control found 81% of newborn infants began breast-feeding, over half were still breast-feeding by 6 months, and close to one-third were doing so at 12 months (Breastfeeding Report Card, 2016). There have been some ethnic/racial differences found in breast-feeding, with the highest rates in Hispanic women, followed by White and Black women ("Progress in Increasing Breastfeeding," 2013).

Some women are not able to breast-feed because of time constraints and/or work pressures. A study on sleep loss in new mothers found that a baby's primary caregiver loses between 450 and 700 hours of sleep in the first year of the baby's life, with breast-feeding mothers losing the most sleep (Brizendine, 2006; Maas, 1998).

Women who want to continue breast-feeding when they return to work can use a breast pump. This allows a woman to express milk from her breasts that can be given to her child through a bottle at a later time. Breast milk can be kept in the refrigerator or freezer, but it must be heated before feeding. In 2011, the Internal Revenue Service (IRS) announced that breast pumps and other breast-feeding supplies were tax deductible (Belkin, 2011). This reversed an earlier decision by the IRS that stated that breast-feeding did not contribute sufficient medical benefits to qualify for such a deduction. The Affordable Health Care Act requires employers with more than 50 employees to provide break time for their female employees to express breast milk for one year after birth and must also provide a place, other than a bathroom, to express breast milk ("Breastfeeding State Laws," 2016).

Some transgender men might choose to become pregnant, birth a baby, and/or **chestfeed** (MacDonald et al., 2016). Transgender men who use this term tend to appreciate it since they

Research has found that body contact during breast-feeding can decrease stress and improve mood for both the mother and her infant.

Mary Kent/Alamy Stock Photo

prefer to call their upper torso their "chest." While some may argue that everyone has breasts so the practice should be referred to as breastfeeding, others claim that such terms are more inclusive to all parents.

Throughout this chapter, we have explored many issues related to fertility, infertility, pregnancy, and childbearing. In the next chapter, we begin to look at limiting fertility through contraception and abortion.

> **chestfeed**
> A term used to refer to transgender men who nurse their babies.

Review Questions

1 Describe the physical and emotional changes that women experience after the birth of a child.

2 Differentiate between postpartum depression and postpartum psychosis.

3 How might a woman's sexuality change after the birth of a baby?

4 Identify and explain some of the benefits of breast-feeding.

Chapter Review

Summary Points

1 There were close to 4 million registered births in the United States in 2015, which was slightly lower than the prior year. Birth rates dropped to record lows among women under the age of 30 and rose in women 30–44. Birth rates have fallen in all ethnical/racial groups.

2 Our bodies are biologically programmed to help pregnancy occur: A woman's sexual desire peaks at ovulation, female orgasm helps push semen into the uterus, and semen thickens after ejaculation. The ovum can live for up to 24 hours and sperm can live up to 72 hours in the female reproductive tract.

3 Pregnancy can happen when intercourse takes place a few days before or after ovulation, and the entire process of fertilization takes about 24 hours. The fertilized ovum is referred to as a *zygote*. After the first cell division, it is referred to as a *blastocyst*. From the second to the eighth week, the developing human is called an *embryo*. The majority of women deliver a single fetus, but some women have fraternal (nonidentical) or identical twins. Over the past four decades there has been a substantial rise in the rate of multiple births, mainly due to the increased use of fertility treatments in the United States.

4 Early signs of pregnancy include missing a period, breast tenderness, frequent urination, and morning sickness. Pregnancy tests determine whether a woman is pregnant by looking for certain pregnancy markers in her urine or blood. One of these markers is human chorionic gonadotropin (hCG). Urine pregnancy tests are the most commonly used pregnancy test. Although used less often, radioimmunoassay blood tests are the most accurate.

5 Some couples try to choose the sex of their children by using sex-selection methods. Shettles and Rorvik popularized their gender selection techniques, which took into account the characteristics of the X and Y sperm, along with pH-level adjustments to the vaginal environment.

6 Microsorting, preimplantation genetic diagnosis, and amniocentesis can be performed to evaluate the fetus for chromosomal abnormalities, and identify the sex of the fetus. Increased pregnancy terminations have been noted in areas where females are less valued in society and where there are governmental regulations on family size.

7 Many couples, including married, unmarried, straight, gay, lesbian, transgender, young, and old, use assisted reproductive technologies. Although all couples use ARTs in hopes of achieving a pregnancy, same-sex couples and single women often use these methods to create a pregnancy. Although some lesbian couples decide to both use ART to conceive and carry a baby, the majority of lesbian couples have only one partner carry a pregnancy.

8 Infertility is the inability to conceive (or impregnate) after 1 year of regular vaginal intercourse without the use of any form of contraception. Although unmarried individuals, gay men, and lesbian women have historically been denied access to ARTs, this has been changing. An increasing number of singles and same-sex couples are using assisted reproduction today.

9 Couples interested in assisted reproduction have many options: fertility drugs; surgery to correct cervical, vaginal, or endometrial abnormalities and blockage in the vas deferens or epididymis; artificial insemination; in vitro fertilization (IVF); gamete intra–Fallopian tube transfer (GIFT); zygote intra–Fallopian tube transfer (ZIFT); zonal dissection; intracellular sperm injections; oocyte or embryo transplants; surrogate parenting; and cryopreservation.

10 There are two types of surrogate parenting: gestational surrogacy and traditional surrogacy. In gestational surrogacy, an embryo is created through IVF and is transferred into a surrogate mother. The resulting child is genetically unrelated to the surrogate. In traditional surrogacy, the surrogate is artificially or naturally impregnated, and the resulting child is genetically related to the surrogate. In the United States, gestational surrogacy is more common than traditional surrogacy.

11 Other options involve freezing embryos, sperm, and ova for later fertilization. Embryo cryopreservation involves freezing embryos to use at a later date in IVF procedures. Sperm cryopreservation is also available and enables men to freeze sperm for later use. A growing number of women have been undergoing ova cryopreservation. An experimental area of research has evaluated the use of partial removal of ovarian tissue for cryobanking.

12 Pregnancy is divided into three 3-month periods called *trimesters*. In the first trimester, the most important embryonic development takes place. At this time, the fetus grows dramatically and is 3 inches long by the end of this trimester. The mother often feels the fetus moving around inside her uterus during the second trimester. By the end of the second trimester, the fetus is approximately 13 inches long and weighs about 2 pounds. The second trimester of pregnancy is usually the most positive time for the mother.

13 By the end of the eighth month, the fetus is 15 inches long and weighs about 3 pounds. Braxton–Hicks contractions begin, and colostrum may be secreted from the nipples. Pregnancy can be a time of joy and anticipation for the partner of a pregnant woman, but it can also be a time of stress and anxiety. Feelings about parenting in combination with the many changes their partners are undergoing can all add to increased vulnerability.

14 A woman's exercise routine should not exceed pre-pregnancy levels. Exercise has been found to result in a greater sense of well-being, shorter labor, and fewer obstetric problems. Certain sports should be avoided during pregnancy, such as waterskiing, scuba diving, vigorous racquet sports, contact sports, and horseback riding.

15 Underweight and overweight women are at greater risk for impaired pregnancy outcome, and they are advised to gain or lose weight before pregnancy.

16 Drugs and alcohol can cross the placenta, enter into the developing fetus's bloodstream, and cause physical or mental deficiencies. Fetal alcohol syndrome occurs when a woman drinks heavily during pregnancy, producing an infant with irreversible physical and mental disabilities. Studies have found that some women use alcohol, tobacco, or illicit drugs during pregnancy.

17 Widespread legalization of marijuana has raised many concerns about its use among pregnant women. Marijuana is the most commonly used illicit drug during pregnancy. There are potential risks associated with marijuana use during pregnancy, including cognitive impairment, low birth weight, delivery problems, and stillbirth.

18 Success rates for artificial reproductive technologies in older women are low. Although older women who do get pregnant are more likely to take better care of themselves and eat healthier than younger women, there are increased risks to the pregnancies, including spontaneous abortion, first-trimester bleeding, low birth weight, increased labor time and rate of C-section, and chromosomal abnormalities.

19 Sexual behavior during pregnancy is safe for most mothers and the developing child up until the last several weeks of pregnancy in an uncomplicated pregnancy; orgasm is safe but occasionally may cause painful uterine contractions.

20 In an ectopic pregnancy, the zygote implants outside the uterus, usually in the Fallopian tube. Although many women without risk factors can develop an ectopic pregnancy, some factors may put a woman at increased risk. Daughters of mothers who experienced an ectopic pregnancy have an increased risk of developing an ectopic pregnancy themselves. Other risk factors include smoking and a history of sexually transmitted infections.

21 A spontaneous abortion, or miscarriage, is a natural termination of a pregnancy before the time that the fetus can live on its own. The majority of miscarriages occur during the first trimester of pregnancy. The most common reason for miscarriage is a fetal chromosomal abnormality. Prenatal diagnostic testing can be used to determine whether there are chromosomal or genetic abnormalities in the fetus.

22 One of every 33 babies is born with a birth defect. Prenatal diagnostic testing can be used to determine whether there are chromosomal or genetic abnormalities in the fetus. The risk for chromosomal abnormality increases as maternal age increases. The most common chromosomal abnormality is Down syndrome.

23 An Rh-negative woman must be given RhoGAM immediately after childbirth, abortion, or miscarriage so that she will not produce antibodies and to ensure that her future pregnancies are healthy. Toxemia is a form of blood poisoning that can develop in pregnant women; symptoms include weight gain, fluid retention, an increase in blood pressure, and protein in the urine.

24 Increasing knowledge and alleviating anxiety about the birth process are the main concepts behind childbirth classes. Worldwide, the majority of babies are born at home, although most U.S. babies are born in hospitals.

25 Birth itself takes place in three stages: cervical effacement and dilation, expulsion of the fetus, and expulsion of the placenta. The first stage of labor can last anywhere from 20 minutes to 24 hours and is longer in first births. Transition, the last part of stage one, is the most difficult part of the birth process. The second stage of birth involves the expulsion of the fetus. In the third stage of labor, strong contractions continue and push the placenta out of the uterus and through the vagina.

26 The majority of babies are born late, but if birth takes place before the 37th week of pregnancy, it is considered premature. Premature birth may occur early for several reasons, including early labor, early rupture of the amniotic membranes, or a maternal or fetal problem.

27 Problems during birthing include premature or breech birth and stillbirth. A birth that takes place before the 37th week of pregnancy is considered premature and may occur for various reasons. The amniotic membranes may have ruptured, or there may be a maternal or fetal problem. Multiple births also occur earlier than single births. In a breech birth, the fetus has his or her feet and buttocks against the cervix, and either the baby is rotated or a C-section must be performed.

28 A C-section involves the delivery of the fetus through an incision in the abdominal wall. Some women also choose to have an elective C-section for a variety of reasons. C-sections are most commonly done for medical reasons when the baby is too large for a woman to deliver vaginally, the woman is unable to push the baby out the birth canal, there is placenta previa or placental separation from the baby before birth, or the baby is in fetal distress.

29 A fetus that dies after 20 weeks of pregnancy is called a stillbirth. The most common cause of stillbirth is a failure in the baby's oxygen supply, heart, or lungs. To decrease the risk of stillbirth many women are advised to monitor fetal movement beginning in the 28th week of pregnancy.

30 After delivery, the uterus returns to its original size in about 6 weeks. Many women report painful contractions, caused by the hormone oxytocin, for a few days after birth. Uteruses of breast-feeding women return to the original size quicker than those of non–breast-feeding women.

31 The majority of women feel both excitement and exhaustion after the birth of a child. However, for some, it is a very difficult time of depression, crying spells, and anxiety. Research has found that 10–15% of women experience postpartum depression. In the most severe cases, a woman might experience postpartum psychosis and experience depression, along with paranoia, hallucinations, and delusions.

32 Although most physicians advise their heterosexual patients to wait 6 weeks postpartum before resuming sexual behavior, in an uncomplicated vaginal delivery (with no tears or episiotomy), intercourse can safely be engaged in 2 weeks after delivery. Many women report slower and less intense excitement stages of the sexual response cycle and a decrease in vaginal lubrication immediately after delivery; however, at 3 months postpartum, most women return to their original levels of desire and excitement.

33 In the first few days of breast-feeding, the breasts release a fluid called colostrum, which is very important in strengthening the baby's immune system. The American Academy of Pediatrics recommends breast-feeding for at least 1 year. The Affordable Health Care Act requires employers to provide break time for their female employees to express breast milk and must also provide a place, other than a bathroom, to express breast milk.

Critical Thinking Questions

1 If sex preselection were possible, would you want to determine the sex of your children? Why or why not? If you did choose, what would you choose? Why?

2 Do you think assisted reproductive techniques should be used in women older than 50? Older than 60? How do you think age affects parenting?

3 If women can safely deliver at home, should they be encouraged to do so with the help of a midwife, or should they be encouraged to have children in the hospital? If you have children, where do you think you would want them to be born?

4 At what age do you think a child should be weaned? Should a woman breast-feed a child until they are 6 months old? Two years old? Four years old? How old?

5 In 2001, a woman ran an ad in a school newspaper at Stanford University offering $15,000 for a sperm donation from the right guy. She required the guy be intelligent, physically attractive, and over 6 feet tall. The year before, an ad ran in the same newspaper from a couple who offered $100,000 for eggs from an athletically gifted female student. Would you have answered either of these ads? Why or why not?

American Society for Reproductive Medicine (ASRM) The ASRM is an organization devoted to advancing knowledge and expertise in reproductive medicine, infertility, and ARTs. Links to a variety of helpful websites are available.

BirthDiaries This interesting website contains true birth stories from a variety of women, including first-time moms, veteran moms, and births after a pregnancy loss. It also has information on birthing, breast-feeding, and newborns.

International Council on Infertility Information Dissemination (INCIID) This website provides detailed information on the diagnosis and treatment of infertility, pregnancy loss, family-building options, and helpful fact sheets on various types of fertility treatments and assisted reproductive techniques. Information on adoption and child-free lifestyles is also included.

Extend Fertility Extend Fertility is the nation's first firm devoted solely to getting the word out about egg freezing. This website, started by a woman who froze her eggs, provides a guide for women and the names of clinics offering such services.

Resolve The National Infertility Association was established in 1974. It works to promote reproductive health, ensure equal access to fertility options for men and women experiencing infertility or other reproductive disorders, and provide support services and physician referral and education.

Sperm Bank Directory A national directory of sperm cryobanks. Provides information on cryopreservation, sperm donation, and donor sperm. There are also links to sperm banks throughout the country, some of which include online donor catalogs.

Storknet This website provides a week-by-week guide to a woman's pregnancy. For each of the 40 weeks of pregnancy, there is information about fetal development, what types of changes occur within the pregnant body, and suggested readings and links for more information.

13 Contraception and Abortion

From Dr. Carroll's Notebook...

Joan was 18 years old when she realized she was pregnant. She and her boyfriend had been dating for a few months, but they never discussed contraception. They were both still in college, and neither one of them was ready to have a baby. It was 1972 and abortion was illegal in the United States. A few of Joan's friends had heard about a gynecologist who performed abortions after hours. Joan called his office the next day. When the doctor confirmed her pregnancy, she told him that she didn't want to be pregnant and she needed his help.

She remembers how his demeanor quickly changed—in a hushed, business-like tone he told her that it would cost her $500—cash only. He told her to come back to the office early Saturday morning by herself and not to tell anyone where she was going. She remembers thinking she could have died having the procedure, but that didn't stop her. She knew she couldn't have a baby at that time. The building was dark when she arrived for the procedure, and the doctor was the only person there. He instructed her to go to the exam room, remove her clothes, and wait for him. When he came in the room he told her she had to be completely quiet and could not scream or make any sounds. The procedure was incredibly painful and Joan remembers silently weeping throughout. When it was over, the doctor told her to lie still. He reached over to massage her breasts, explaining that it was necessary to get them back to "normal." She gathered the strength to push him away and quickly got dressed. Thinking back, she's amazed she did what he told her to, but she felt so desperate and alone and didn't know what else to do. In 1973, when abortion was legalized, she remembered being so thankful that women wouldn't have to experience what she did in that office. Today, Joan is a firm supporter of women's rights and works in reproductive health.

Janell Carroll

© Kari Mutscheller

329

The typical heterosexual American woman spends about 30 years trying *not* to get pregnant and only a couple of years trying to become pregnant (Figure 13.1). In response to the negative health effects of repeated pregnancies on women's health, the **contraception** (also called **birth control**) movement began in 1912. The first available contraceptive methods included condoms and withdrawal, but it wasn't until 1960 that more modern methods, such as contraceptive pills, became available. Since that time, many newer and highly effective methods have been introduced. Contraceptive use continues to increase in the United States, and today more than 99% of sexually active women aged 15 to 44 years old have used at least one contraceptive method (Daniels et al., 2013a). Male condoms are the most common contraceptive method used in the United States, followed by contraceptive pills (Daniels et al., 2013a). Many personal characteristics interact with contraceptive use, such as age, ethnicity, race, marital status, past pregnancies, education, and income. In addition, several factors put women at greater risk for unintended pregnancies, such as being young, unmarried, or poor.

College students take risks when it comes to contraception, even though they are intelligent and educated about it. There are many factors that increase a person's motivation to use contraception, including the ability to communicate with a partner, cost of the method, effectiveness rates, frequency of vaginal intercourse, motivation to avoid pregnancy, the contraceptive method's side effects, and one's openness about sexuality (Frost et al., 2008; Hatcher et al., 2011). Contraceptive use is further complicated by the fact that an ideal method for one person may not be an ideal method for another, and an ideal method for one person at one time in their life may not be an ideal method as they enter into different life stages. Having a wide variety of choices available is important to allow couples to choose and change methods as their contraceptive needs change.

As we begin our exploration into contraception and **abortion**, consider this: Have you thought about whether you ever want to have a child? Maybe you have an exact plan about when you'd like to experience a pregnancy in your life. Or perhaps you have already decided you won't have any children. For many heterosexual couples, deciding how to plan and also how to avoid pregnancies are important issues in their lives. In this chapter, we explore the array of contraceptive methods available today, investigate their advantages and disadvantages, and also discuss emergency contraception and abortion.

Contraception: History and Method Considerations

Although many people believe that contraception is a modern invention, its origins actually extend back to ancient times. We now explore contraception throughout history, both within and outside of the United States.

Contraception in Ancient Times

People have always tried to invent ways to control fertility. The ancient Greeks used magic, superstition, herbs, and drugs to try and control their fertility. The Egyptians tried fumigating the female genitalia with certain mixtures, inserting a tampon soaked in herbal liquid and honey into the vagina, and inserting a mixture of crocodile feces, sour milk, and honey (Dunham et al., 1992). Another strategy was to insert objects into the vagina that could entrap or block the sperm. Such objects included vegetable seed pods (South Africa), a cervical plug of grass (Africa), sponges soaked with alcohol (Iran), and empty pomegranate halves (Greece). These methods may sound far-fetched to us today, but they worked on many of the same principles as modern methods. In the accompanying "Sexual Diversity in Our World" feature, we discuss some of these methods.

Contraception in the United States: 1800s and Early 1900s

In the early 1800s, several groups in the United States wanted to control fertility to reduce poverty. However, contraception was considered a private affair, to be discussed only between partners in a relationship. As we learned in Chapter 1, Anthony Comstock worked with Congress in 1873 to pass the Comstock laws, which prohibited the distribution of all obscene material; this included contraceptive information and devices. Even medical doctors were not allowed to provide information about contraception (although a few still did). Margaret Sanger, the founder of Planned Parenthood, was one of the first people to publicly advocate the importance of contraception in the United States.

---

contraception
The deliberate use of artificial methods or other techniques to prevent pregnancy.

abortion
Induced termination of a pregnancy before fetal viability.

birth control
Another term for contraception.

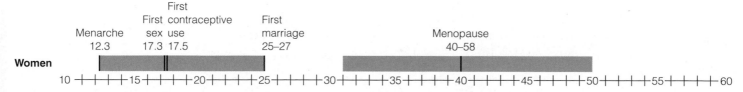

FIGURE **13.1** The Alan Guttmacher Institute has found that the average woman spends 5 years pregnant, postpartum, or trying to get pregnant, and 30 years avoiding pregnancy. Above is a timeline of reproductive events for the typical American woman. Shaded area represents when a typical American woman is trying to avoid unintended pregnancy.

SOURCE: Copen et al., 2012; Finer & Philbin, 2014; the Guttmacher Institute (http://www.guttmacher.org/pubs/fulfill.pdf); Steiner et al., 2010.

Contraception Outside the United States

Worldwide, contraception is used by the majority of sexually active women; however, it is much more common in developed countries ("Trends in Contraceptive Use Worldwide," 2015; in Figure 13.2 we present the use of contraceptive methods worldwide). Social and economic issues, knowledge levels, and gender roles affect contraceptive use around the world. A woman might not use contraception because she is uneducated about it or doesn't have access to methods; she may also worry about adverse effects, not understand she is at risk for pregnancy, or believe that she needs to be married to use contraception (Sedgh et al., 2007a). Gender roles and power differentials also contribute to a country's contraceptive use. In many countries women may not be involved in contraceptive decision making, and men might refuse to use contraception because of cultural views that it decreases masculinity.

Religious views can also affect contraceptive use. The Catholic Church's position on contraception was formally presented in 1968 with the publication of the *Humanae Vitae* (the document that prohibits Catholics from using artificial contraception). Since this time there have been several exceptions to the Catholic Church's ban on contraception. In 2010 Pope Benedict suggested condoms could be used to prevent the spread of HIV/AIDS, and then in 2016 Pope Francis condoned them in the fight to prevent the spread of the Zika virus (Aran, 2016; Burke & Cohen, 2016). In fact, many predominantly Catholic regions and countries have limited contraceptive devices available. In the Philippines, where more than half of all pregnancies are unintended (Finer & Hussain, 2013), there has been an ongoing battle between the country's president and Catholic leadership over access to contraception. In 2017, the Philippine president ordered government agencies to expand contraceptive availability, especially to poor women, and demanded all contraceptive needs be met by 2018 (Domonoske, 2017). Increased contraceptive availability has led experts to suggest that Southern Asia will have one of the highest growth rates of contraceptive use by 2030.

Even though the Catholic Church prohibits contraceptive use, many residents of predominately Catholic countries do support the use of contraception. One survey found that 88% of Mexicans, 91% of Colombians, and 93% of Brazilians supported the use of contraceptives (Burke & Cohen, 2016; de Freitas, 2004; Tomaso, 2008).

In Brazil, one of the largest predominately Catholic countries, close to 80% of sexually active women use contraception, mostly female sterilization, oral contraceptives, and condoms (Ford & Holder, 2016).

Scandinavian countries are regarded as some of the most progressive with respect to contraceptive usage. Contraceptive use is high in Denmark, Sweden, and Finland (Lindh et al., 2016). In many of these countries contraceptive methods are free and easily available. Many students can obtain contraception from school health services. Contraceptive use was over 70% in 13 countries in Europe ("Trends in Contraceptive Use Worldwide," 2015).

In Asia, there are significant variations in contraceptive use between countries. For example, while more than 80% of women use contraception in China, less than 30% do in Afghanistan (Ford & Holder, 2016). In Japan, men are primarily responsible for contraceptive decisions, and Japanese women express shock over

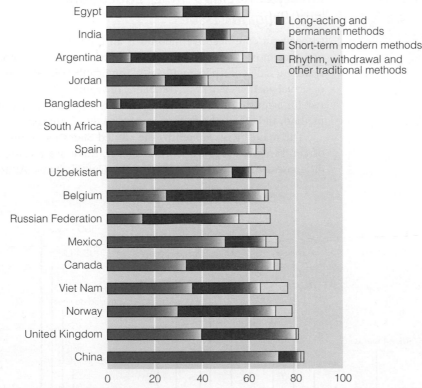

Contraceptive Use Around the World

Legend:
- Long-acting and permanent methods
- Short-term modern methods
- Rhythm, withdrawal and other traditional methods

Countries (top to bottom): Egypt, India, Argentina, Jordan, Bangladesh, South Africa, Spain, Uzbekistan, Belgium, Russian Federation, Mexico, Canada, Viet Nam, Norway, United Kingdom, China

x-axis: 0, 20, 40, 60, 80, 100

Note: Estimates are from annex table III.

FIGURE **13.2** Contraceptive prevalence by method among married/coupled women in countries with 60% or higher contraceptive prevalence, 2015.

SOURCE: "Trends in Contraceptive Use Worldwide," 2015; United Nations.

the liberal views that many American women hold about using oral contraceptives (Hatano & Shimazaki, 2004).

Overall, Africa has the lowest percentage of women using contraception and the highest unmet contraceptive use in the world (Ford & Holder, 2016). Condoms are often popular, although in certain areas, such as Kenya, married couples have low condom usage because it signifies unfaithfulness on the part of the husband (Brockman, 2004). More recent studies have found that today, 65% of women in Kenya use a variety of contraceptive methods (Tumlinson et al., 2015). We will discuss cross-cultural use of individual methods later in this chapter.

Contraception in the United States Today

Before the availability of any medical contraceptive method in the United States, the **U.S. Food and Drug Administration (FDA)** must formally approve the method. The FDA is responsible for promoting and protecting public health in the United States, and it regulates and supervises the safety of medical supplies. Let's explore the FDA approval process and individual lifestyle issues that may affect contraceptive method choice.

> **REAL RESEARCH** Motivations for contraceptive use are often influenced by cultural factors. In some areas of eastern Africa, condom use is extremely low because of the cultural significance of semen (COAST, 2007). Strongly held beliefs about wasting semen have led to low condom use, even when knowledge levels about contraception and STIs are high.

U.S. Food and Drug Administration (FDA)
The agency in the U.S. federal government that has the power to approve and disapprove new drugs.

intrauterine devices (IUDs)
A small device made of flexible plastic that is placed in the uterus to prevent pregnancy.

FDA Approval Process

The FDA is responsible for approving all prescription medications and medical devices in the United States. To get approval for a new medication, a pharmaceutical company must first submit a new drug application to the FDA showing that the drug is safe in animal tests and that it is reasonably safe to proceed with human trials of the drug. After this, there are a total of three phases to evaluate the safety of the medication. In Phase 1, the drug is introduced to approximately 20 to 80 healthy volunteers to collect information on the drug's effectiveness. In Phase 2, several hundred people take the drug to evaluate how it works and determine adverse effects and risks. In Phase 3 trials, the study is expanded, and hundreds to thousands of people are enrolled in the study. Like drugs, medical devices, such as **intrauterine devices (IUDs)**, are also subject to strict evaluation and regulation. It is estimated that it takes 10 to 14 years to develop a new contraceptive method (Hatcher et al., 2007; Stewart & Gabelnick, 2004). See Figure 13.3 and the "The History of Contraception" Timeline in the Appendix for more information.

Choosing a Method of Contraception

As we discussed earlier, no single method of contraception is best for everyone; the best one for you is one that you and your partner will use correctly every time you have vaginal intercourse.

Lifestyle, Racial/Ethnic, Educational, and Religious Issues

Choosing a contraceptive method is an important decision and one that must be made with your lifestyle in mind. Important issues include your personal health and health risks, the number of sexual partners you have, frequency of vaginal intercourse, your risk for acquiring an STI, how responsible you are, the cost of the method, and the method's advantages and disadvantages.

The majority of women in the United States use some form of contraception (Figure 13.4). However, there are racial/ethnic differences in contraceptive use in the United States. Although

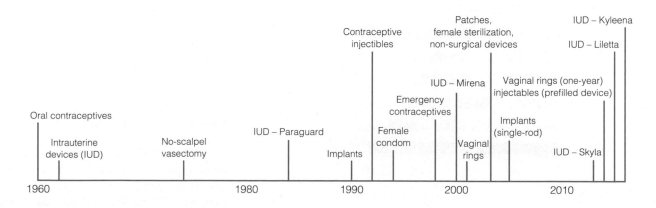

FIGURE **13.3 Selected Developments of Contraceptive Methods**

SOURCE: Hatcher et al., 2011; "Trends in Contraceptive Use Worldwide," 2015.

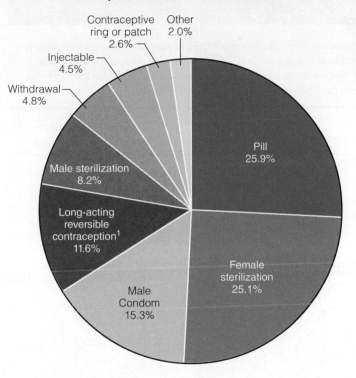

Contraceptive Use in the United States, 2011–2013

- Other 2.0%
- Contraceptive ring or patch 2.6%
- Injectable 4.5%
- Withdrawal 4.8%
- Male sterilization 8.2%
- Long-acting reversible contraception[1] 11.6%
- Male Condom 15.3%
- Female sterilization 25.1%
- Pill 25.9%

[1]Includes intrauterine devices and implants.

FIGURE **13.4** Percent Distribution of Women Aged 15–44 who are Using Contraception, by type of Contraceptive Method Used; U.S., 2011–2013.

SOURCE: Daniels et al., 2015; Centers for Disease Control and Prevention.

contraceptive pills and condoms are the most widely used methods, White women are more likely to use highly effective, reversible methods, compared with Hispanic and Asian women (Daniels et al., 2013a). More White women have used contraceptive pills than any other racial and ethnic group (Daniels & Mosher, 2014). Black and Hispanic women are more likely than White women to use injectables or hormonal methods other than the pill, such as the patch or vaginal ring. While 63% of Asian women use highly effective and reversible methods, only 19% report using hormonal methods other than the pill, and 10% have used injectables. See Figure 13.5 for more information about contraceptive use in various ethnic/racial groups.

While the use of contraceptive pills is high among all educational levels, there are variations in the user rates of other methods. For example, women with higher levels of education are more likely to use contraceptive pills, while women with a high school diploma or less are more likely to use injectables (Daniels & Mosher, 2014). As for the association of the use of contraceptive pills and religious affiliation, studies have found while many religious women report using contraceptive pills, the usage is lower in Catholic women compared to women who are members of other religious groups (Daniels et al., 2013a).

Unreliable Contraception

Unfortunately, many people rely on myths and false information when it comes to contraception. They may keep their fingers crossed in hopes of not getting pregnant, have sex standing

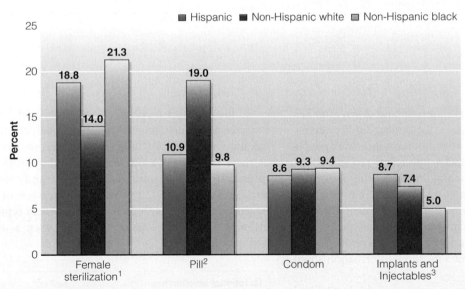

Contraceptive Use in Women by Race/Ethnicity, United States, 2011–2013

Legend: ■ Hispanic ■ Non-Hispanic white ■ Non-Hispanic black

	Hispanic	Non-Hispanic white	Non-Hispanic black
Female sterilization[1]	18.8	14.0	21.3
Pill[2]	10.9	19.0	9.8
Condom	8.6	9.3	9.4
Implants and Injectables[3]	8.7	7.4	5.0

[1]Percentage for non-Hispanic white women is significantly different from non-Hispanic black women.
[2]Percentage for Hispanic and non-Hispanic black women is significantly different from non-Hispanic white women.
[3]Percentage for Hispanic and non-Hispanic white women is significantly different from non-Hispanic black women.

NOTES: Women currently using more than one method were classified according to the most effective method they were using.

FIGURE **13.5** Percentage of women aged 15–44 using various methods of contraception by Hispanic origin and race, United States, 2011–2013.

SOURCE: Daniels et al., 2014; Centers for Disease Control and Prevention.

Table 13.1 Overview of Contraceptive Methods

Following is an overview of contraceptive methods, including effectiveness rates, required health care provider visit(s), and partner involvement. Even though both typical and perfect effectiveness rates are provided here, remember that a method's effectiveness depends on the user's ability to use a method correctly and to continue using it. For many methods, user failures are more common than method failures. Also keep in mind that although partner involvement is not required for many methods, partners can be involved by helping purchase methods.

Contraceptive Method	Perfect/Typical Use Effectiveness Rates	Required Health Care Provider Visit(s)	Partner Involvement
Male Sterilization	99%–99.9%	Yes	Yes
Female Sterilization	99%–99.9%	Yes	No
Subdermal Implant (Nexplanon)	99%–99%	Yes	No
Intrauterine Devices	99.2%–99.9%	Yes	No
Hormonal Injectibles (Depo-Provera)	97%–99.7%	Yes	No
Hormonal Ring (NuvaRing)	92%–99.7%	Yes	No
Hormonal Patch	92%–99.7%	Yes	No
Combination Contraceptive Pill	92%–99.7%	Yes	No
Progestin-Only Contraceptive Pill	92%–99.7%	Yes	No
Male Condoms	85%–98%	No	Yes
Fertility Awareness Methods	88%–97%	No	No
Female Condoms	79%–95%	No	No
Cervical Barrier	84%–94%	Yes	No
Contraceptive Sponge	84%–91%	No	No
Withdrawal	73%–96%	No	Yes
Spermicides	71%–82%	No	No

up to try to invoke gravity, or even jump up and down after sex in an attempt to dislodge sperm from swimming up the vagina. We know these techniques won't work, but for many years people thought they would. In the mid-1800s, physicians recommended douching as a contraceptive. Douching involves using a syringe-type instrument to inject a stream of water (which may be mixed with other chemicals) into the vagina. Today, health care providers strongly recommend against douching because it can increase the risk for pelvic infections and STIs. In addition, it is an ineffective contraceptive method (see Chapter 5 for more information about douching).

Another ineffective contraceptive method is the **lactational amenorrhea method (LAM)**, which is based on the postpartum infertility that many women experience when they are breast-feeding. During breast-feeding, the cyclic ovarian hormones are typically suspended, which may inhibit ovulation. However, this is an ineffective contraceptive method because ovulation may still occur (Hatcher et al., 2011; see Chapter 12 for more information about breast-feeding).

In the following sections, we will discuss effective methods of contraception, including barrier, hormonal, chemical, intrauterine, natural, permanent, and emergency contraception. For each of these methods, we will cover how they work, **effectiveness rates**, cost, advantages and disadvantages, and cross-cultural patterns of usage. Table 13.1 provides an overview of available contraceptive methods with their effectiveness in **typical use** (which includes user error) and **perfect use** (when a method is used without error).

lactational amenorrhea method (LAM)
A method of avoiding pregnancies based on the postpartum infertility that many women experience when they are breast-feeding.

effectiveness rates
Estimated rates of the number of women who do not become pregnant each year using each method of contraception.

typical use
Refers to the probability of contraceptive failure for less than perfect use of the method.

perfect use
Refers to the probability of contraceptive failure for use of the method without error.

Review Questions

1 Explain what we know about contraception in ancient times.

2 How was contraception viewed in the United States in the early 1900s?

3 What factors have been found to be related to contraceptive nonuse outside the United States?

4 Identify two important lifestyle issues to consider when choosing a contraceptive method.

5 Identify and discuss ineffective contraceptive methods.

Barrier Methods

Barrier methods of contraception work by preventing the sperm from entering the uterus. These methods include condoms, cervical barriers, and the contraceptive sponge.

Male Condoms

Penile coverings have been used as a method of contraception since the beginning of recorded history. In 1350 B.C., Egyptian men wore decorative sheaths over their penises. Eventually, sheaths of linen and animal intestines were developed. The Goodyear Company improved the strength and resiliency of rubber through vulcanization, and by the mid-1800s, rubber (latex) **condoms** were available in the United States (McLaren, 1990). Polyurethane (paul-lee-YUR-ith-ain; nonlatex) condoms were launched in the United States in 1994 and can be used by those with latex allergies. However, if a person does not have a latex allergy, health care providers generally recommend using latex condoms because they have lower rates of slippage and breakage.

Male condoms are one of the most inexpensive and cost-effective contraceptive methods, providing not only high effectiveness rates but also added protection from STIs and HIV (Hatcher et al., 2011). They typically cost about $1 each but may be free at health clinics. Condom use is highest among unmarried adults and higher in adolescents than adults (see Figure 13.6 for more information on condom use by age). It is estimated that there were close to 6 million American women using male condoms for contraception in 2012 ("Contraceptive Use in the United States," 2016; see Table 13.2).

How They Work

The male condom ("rubber" or "prophylactic") is placed on an erect penis before vaginal penetration. Condoms must be put on before there is any vaginal contact by the penis because sperm may be present in the urethra. Some condom manufacturers recommend leaving space at the tip of the condom to allow room for the ejaculation, but others do not. To prevent tearing the condom, the vagina should be well lubricated. Although some condoms

---

condom
A latex or polyurethane sheath that fits over the penis and is used for protection against pregnancy and sexually transmitted infections; female condoms made of either polyurethane or polymer, which protect the vaginal walls, are also available.

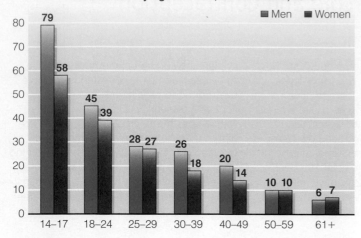

Condom Use by Age and Sex, United States, 2010

■ Men ■ Women

Age	Men	Women
14–17	79	58
18–24	45	39
25–29	28	27
30–39	26	18
40–49	20	14
50–59	10	10
61+	6	7

FIGURE **13.6** Percent of the past 10 acts of vaginal intercourse protected by condoms by age and sex.

SOURCE: National Survey of Sexual Health and Behavior; Reece et al., 2010c.

come prelubricated, if extra lubrication is needed, water, contraceptive jelly or cream, or a water-based lubricant such as K-Y Jelly should be used. Oil-based lubricants such as hand or body lotion, petroleum jelly (e.g., Vaseline), baby oil, massage oil, or creams for

vaginal infections (e.g., Monistat and Vagisil) should not be used because they may damage the latex and cause the condom to break (polyurethane condoms are not damaged by these products; see Table 13.3).

To avoid the possibility of semen leaking out of the condom, withdrawal must take place immediately after ejaculation, while the penis is still erect, and the condom should be grasped firmly at the base to prevent its slipping off into the vagina during

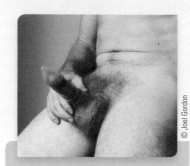

Consistent and correct use of condoms has been widely recommended to reduce the risk of sexually transmitted infections. A condom should be placed on an erect penis prior to penetration.

Table 13.2 Contraceptive Method Use Among U.S. Women Who Use Contraception, 2012			
Method	**No. of users**	**% of all women 15–44 (%)**	**% of all contraceptive users**
Pill (combined estrogen and progestin)	9,720,000	16	25.6
Tubal (female) sterilization	9,443,000	15.5	25.1
Male condom	5,739,000	9.4	15.3
Intrauterine device (IUD)	3,884,000	6.4	10.3
Vasectomy (male sterilization)	3,084,000	5.1	8.2
Withdrawal	1,817,000	3.0	4.8
Injectable	1,697,000	2.8	4.5
Vaginal ring (NuvaRing)	759,000	1.2	2.0
Fertility awareness–based methods	509,000	0.8	1.4
Implant	492,000	0.8	1.3
Hormonal Patch	217,000	0.4	0.6
Emergency Contraception	91,000	0.2	0.2
Other methods*	133,000	0.2	0.4
No method, at risk of unintended pregnancy	4,175,000	6.9	—
Total number of women 15–44	60,887,000	100.0	100.00

Includes emergency contraception, female condom, spermicides, diaphragm, and contraceptive sponges.

SOURCE: Guttmacher Institute, 2016; https://www.guttmacher.org/fact-sheet/contraceptive-use-united-states

Table 13.3 What to Use with Condoms

Male condoms can be made out of latex or polyurethane. All types of lubricants, including oil-based lubricants, can be safely used with polyurethane condoms. However, latex condoms should be used with only a water-based lubricant. Following is a list of products that can be used with all condoms and products that should never be used with latex condoms.

Use with All Condoms

- Water-based lubricants (including products such as AquaLube, AstroGlide, or K-Y Jelly)
- Glycerine
- Spermicides
- Saliva
- Water
- Silicone lubricant

Do Not Use with Latex Condoms

- Baby oil
- Cold creams
- Edible oils (such as olive, peanut, or canola oil)
- Massage oil
- Petroleum jelly
- Rubbing alcohol
- Suntan oil and lotions
- Vegetable or mineral oil
- Vaginal infection medications in cream or suppository form

SOURCE: Hatcher et al. (2011).

withdrawal. Although condoms can last a long time, it's always good to check expiration dates before using them.

When used correctly, condoms offer both pregnancy and STI protection. Spermicidal condoms are lubricated with a small amount of **nonoxynol-9**, but there are risks to using this **spermicide** (Hatcher et al., 2011; see the accompanying "Sex in Real Life"). There are many types of male condoms on the market, including lubricated, non-lubricated, colored, glow-in-the-dark, flavored, and studded or textured. It's important that whatever type of condom you choose, make sure it is FDA approved and offers pregnancy and STI protection (for example, "novelty" types of condoms do not provide this protection).

Effectiveness

Effectiveness rates for male condoms range from 85% to 98%. Studies have demonstrated that when used correctly, the overall risk for condom breakage is very low (Hatcher et al., 2011). Using a condom after the expiration date is the leading cause of breakage.

Advantages

Male condoms can be discreetly carried in a pocket or purse, offer some protection from many STIs, allow men to help prevent pregnancy, can be purchased without a prescription, are relatively inexpensive, have minimal adverse effects, may reduce the incidence of premature ejaculation, can reduce **postcoital drip**, can be used in conjunction with other contraceptive methods, and

can be used during oral or anal sex to reduce the risk for STIs (we discuss this further in Chapter 15). Polyurethane condoms have a longer shelf life and can be used with both oil- and water-based lubricants (Hatcher et al., 2011).

Disadvantages

The male condom decreases spontaneity, may pose sizing and erection problems, and may reduce male sensation. In one study, men wearing condoms reported decreased penile sensitivity (Hill et al., 2014). Condoms may not be comfortable for all men, and some who use polyurethane condoms report slipping or bunching up during use (Hollander, 2001). Finally, some men may be embarrassed to use condoms or feel uncomfortable interrupting foreplay to put one on.

Cross-Cultural Use

Worldwide, male condoms are the fourth most popular contraceptive method (behind female sterilization, IUDs, and oral contraceptives with 8% of couples reporting relying on this method ("Trends in Contraceptive Use Worldwide," 2015). Condoms are popular in more developed regions of the world, such as Europe and North America (Figure 13.7). In many other countries, however, male condoms are not widely used. Low condom use may be due to a lack of availability but can also be due to embarrassment or religious prohibition. In Botswana, for example, many couples are embarrassed to purchase condoms (Mookodi et al., 2004), and a similar attitude is found in Brazil, especially among women (de Freitas, 2004). A lack of information, myths, or misconceptions about condom use can also decrease condom usage. Many international organizations, including UNICEF and the World Health Organization (WHO), are working to educate people around the world about condom use.

Female Condoms

The original version of the female condom, the Reality Vaginal Pouch (often referred to as "FC"), became available in the United States in the early 1990s and was made of polyurethane. A newer female condom (the "FC2") made of a softer and more flexible material was approved by the FDA in 2009. It

---

nonoxynol-9
A spermicide that has been used to prevent pregnancy and protect against sexually transmitted infections.

spermicide
Chemical method of contraception, including creams, gels, foams, suppositories, and films, that works to reduce the survival of sperm in the vagina.

postcoital drip
A vaginal discharge (dripping) that occurs after sexual intercourse.

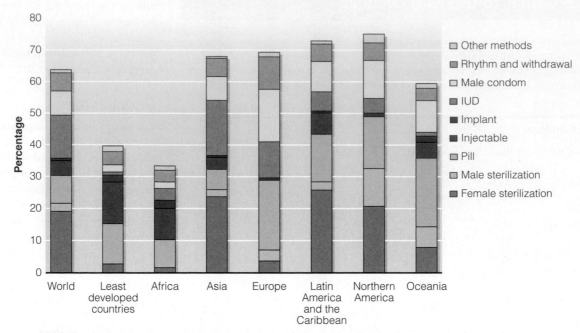

FIGURE **13.7** Contraceptive prevalence among married/coupled women aged 15–49 by contraceptive method and region, 2015.

SOURCE: "Trends in Contraceptive Use Worldwide," 2015; United Nations (2013).

is about 7 inches long with two flexible polyurethane rings. The inner ring serves as an insertion device, and the outer ring stays on the outside of the vagina. A third female condom made of latex with an inner sponge to hold the condom in place (called the Reddy or VA w.o.w. Feminine Condom) is available outside the United States but is not approved by the FDA. Female condoms are more expensive than male condoms and cost approximately $3.50 each, but they may be free in many health clinics. Female condoms are less popular than male condoms in the United States.

REAL RESEARCH College students view condoms primarily as a means of preventing pregnancy; few describe disease prevention as a main motivation for condom use (O'SULLIVAN ET AL., 2010).

How They Work

A female condom is inserted into the vagina before penile penetration. The inner ring (or sponge, depending on which type of female condom is used) is squeezed between the thumb and middle finger, making it long and thin, and then inserted into the vagina. Once this is done, an index finger inside the condom

ON YOUR MIND

Do some men have problems maintaining an erection when they use a condom?

A female condom is inserted deep into the vagina prior to vaginal intercourse. The ring at the closed end holds the condom in the vagina, while the ring at the open end stays outside the vaginal opening during intercourse. The female condom can also be used during anal intercourse.

© Joel Gordon

Some men do report that they have more difficulties maintaining an erection when they use a latex condom. Some couples complain that wearing a condom is like "taking a shower with a raincoat on," or that it decreases sensitivity during vaginal intercourse. Adding two or three drops of a lubricant, such as K-Y Jelly, into the condom before rolling it on to the penis can improve penile sensitivity. Many women also report that putting a small amount of a lubricant into their vagina before intercourse helps increase their pleasure and sensitivity while using a condom. Lubricated and polyurethane condoms may help maintain erections by increasing sensitivity. It is also important to note that men who experience problems with premature ejaculation often find that condoms can help maintain erections.

AVAHAN, an AIDS-prevention initiative in India funded by the Bill and Melinda Gates Foundation, teaches sex workers to use condoms. Here an Indian sex worker teaches other women about condoms while her son watches her from behind.

Advantages

Like male condoms, female condoms can be discreetly carried in a purse, offer some STI protection, can be purchased without a prescription, reduce postcoital drip, can be used by those with latex allergies, can be used with oil-based lubricants, can be used by breast-feeding women, and have minimal adverse effects. Unlike male condoms, female condoms do not require a male erection to put on and will stay in place if a man loses his erection. Female condoms can also be used in the anus during anal sex. Finally, the external ring of the female condom may provide extra clitoral stimulation during vaginal intercourse, enhancing female sexual pleasure.

Disadvantages

Female condoms can be difficult to insert, uncomfortable to wear, and expensive, and they may decrease sensations and slip during vaginal intercourse. One study found that 57% of women and 30% of men reported difficulties with insertion, discomfort during sex, and/or excess lubrication with use (Kerrigan et al., 2000). Although some users reported that female condoms were "noisy" to use and uncomfortable because they hung outside the vagina during use, the newest FC2 version is less "noisy." Finally, some women may feel uncomfortable interrupting foreplay to put one in, although they can be put in prior to sexual activity.

can push the inner ring/sponge up close to the cervix. The outer ring sits on the outside of the vulva (Figure 13.8). During intercourse, the penis is placed within the female condom, and care should be taken to make sure it does not slip between the condom and the vaginal wall. It is important that the vagina is well lubricated so that the female condom stays in place. Female and male condoms should never be used together, because they can adhere to each other and slip or break.

Cross-Cultural Use

Female condoms have not been popular in developing countries. Several issues may contribute to this, including the fact that many women in other countries are not comfortable touching the vagina or inserting anything into it (in fact, tampon use is also much lower in countries outside the United States). In addition, female condoms are expensive and difficult to insert. However, there are signs that female condom use is increasing in some countries. For example, in Zimbabwe, although acceptance of the female condom was low when they were first introduced in 1997, after a creative media campaign using billboards, television, and radio commercials about female condoms, use increased sixfold (Helmore, 2010). The media campaign helped increase knowledge levels and broke down the stigma associated with female condoms. Studies from around the world have found that the use of female condoms is increasing since it makes women feel more protected and safe (Koster et al., 2015; Schuyler et al., 2016).

Many female sex workers around the world use female condoms since they enable women to use them without involving a male and they do not involve hormones (Dunn et al., 2016). In many countries in Africa, sex workers have been known to wash and reuse FCs because of the low availability and high cost, although they are not made to be used this way (Mathenjwa & Maharaj, 2012).

Effectiveness

Effectiveness rates for female condoms range from 79% to 95%.

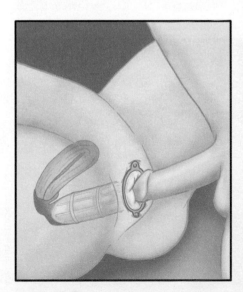
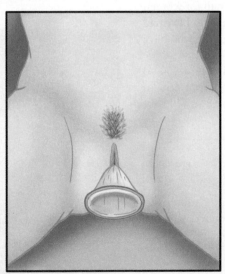

FIGURE **13.8** Female condoms are inserted into the vagina like a tampon. The inner ring is pushed up inside the vagina until it reaches the cervix, while the outer ring hangs about an inch outside of the vagina.

Over the years, public health experts have recommended using condoms that contain the spermicide nonoxynol-9 (N9) to decrease the risk of pregnancy. Although N9 is an effective spermicide, several studies have raised concerns about its safety and protection effects for sexually transmitted infections (STIs). Frequent use of N9 may create rectal and vaginal irritation that can increase HIV risk. In addition to this, N9 does not offer protection from gonorrhea, chlamydia, or HIV. In 2007, the U.S. Food and Drug Administration released a statement requiring all over-the-counter spermicidal products that contained N9 to include a warning that N9 does not protect against STIs and HIV (U.S. Food and Drug Administration, 2007a,b). In addition, the revised labeling included the warning that spermicides can cause vaginal and anal irritation, which may increase STI transmission. The required label on vaginal contraceptives and spermicidal products now states:

Sexually Transmitted Infection Alert: This product does not protect against HIV/AIDS or other STIs and may increase your risk of getting HIV from an infected partner.

Do not use if you or your partner has HIV/AIDS.

Concern over the use of N9 has spurred development of new products, **microbicides**, which can reduce the risk for STIs. Ongoing trials are evaluating a variety of safer spermicides and/or microbicides (McGregor et al., 2013). We discuss microbicides further in Chapter 15.

Cervical Barriers: Diaphragms and Cervical Caps

Cervical barriers include **diaphragms** (DIE-uh-frams) and **cervical caps**. The diaphragm is one of the oldest contraceptive methods, and it was the most frequently prescribed contraceptive method in the United States in 1930 (Harvey et al., 2004). Cervical barriers are inserted into the vagina before intercourse and fit over the cervix, creating a barrier so that sperm and ova cannot meet. We will discuss traditional diaphragms and the **FemCap**, which is the only brand of cervical cap available in the United States today.

The diaphragm is a dome-shaped cup, made of either latex or silicone, with a flexible rim. It comes in several sizes and shapes and must be fitted by a health care provider. Like latex condoms, latex diaphragms should not be used with oil-based lubricants because these can damage the latex (see Table 13.3). The FemCap is made of silicone and is available in three sizes: small for women who have never been pregnant; medium for women who have had a cesarean delivery or an abortion; and large for women who have had a vaginal birth.

Diaphragms and cervical caps cost approximately $60 to $75, a medical examination may cost anywhere from $50 to $200, and spermicidal cream or jelly costs about $8 to $10 (but

Diaphragms come in a variety of different shapes and sizes and must be fitted by a health care practitioner.

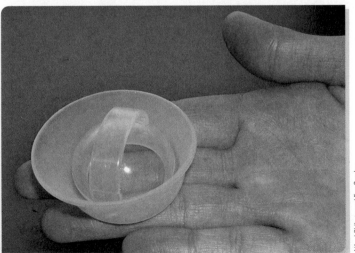

The FemCap is a silicone cup shaped like a sailor's hat that fits securely over the cervix.

---

microbicide
Chemical that works by inhibiting sperm function; effective against HIV and other STIs, and not harmful to the vaginal or cervical cells.

cervical barrier
A plastic or rubber cover for the cervix that provides a contraceptive barrier to sperm.

diaphragm
A contraceptive device consisting of a latex dome on a flexible spring rim; used with spermicidal cream or jelly.

cervical cap
A contraceptive device similar to a diaphragm, but smaller.

FemCap
Reusable silicone barrier vaginal contraceptive that comes in three sizes.

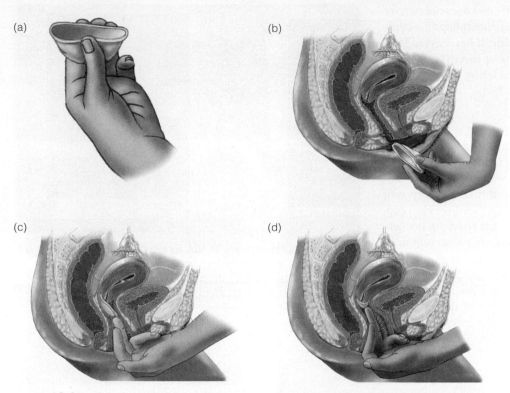

FIGURE **13.9** Insertion of diaphragm (and other cervical barriers): (a) after placing the spermicide, the diaphragm is folded in half, rim to rim and (b) inserted into the vagina (c) as far as it will go; then (d) check to feel the cervix is covered by the diaphragm.

diaphragm or FemCap must be refitted by her health care provider.

Effectiveness

Effectiveness rates for these devices range from 84% to 94%. Women who have not had children have higher effectiveness rates than women who have given birth.

Advantages

Cervical barriers can be discreetly carried in a purse, are immediately effective, do not affect spontaneity or hormonal levels, can be used by breast-feeding women, and allow couples to engage in intercourse multiple times. Research has also found that diaphragm use may reduce the risk for cervical dysplasia and cancer (Hatcher et al., 2011).

Disadvantages

Cervical barriers do not offer protection from STIs, may be difficult to insert and/or remove, require genital touching, increase postcoital drip, may shift during vaginal intercourse, cannot be used during menstruation, may develop a foul odor if left in place too long, and require a prescription in the United States. In addition, some women experience vaginal irritation from the spermicidal cream or jelly.

Cross-Cultural Use

Cervical barriers are widely used in England, and in some countries—including Germany, Austria, Switzerland, and Canada—they have been available without a prescription since 1993 (Long, 2003). However, they are used less frequently in less-developed countries. This is possibly related to a shortage of health care providers, limited availability of spermicidal cream or jelly, high cost, and required genital touching.

may be less at many health clinics). Cervical barriers are one of the least common methods of contraception in the United States today.

How They Work

Cervical barriers work by blocking the entrance to the uterus and deactivating sperm through the use of spermicidal cream or jelly. Before insertion, spermicidal cream or jelly should be placed inside the device and rubbed on the rim. They are folded and inserted into the vagina while a woman is standing with one leg propped up, squatting, or lying on her back (Figure 13.9). The device should be pushed downward toward the back of the vagina, while the front rim or lip is tucked under the pubic bone. After insertion, a woman must check to see that the device is covering her cervix. Once in place, a woman should not be able to feel the device; if she does, it is improperly inserted.

These methods can be inserted before intercourse but must be left in place for either 6 hours (FemCap) or 8 hours (diaphragm) after intercourse. If intercourse is repeated, more spermicide should be inserted in the vagina, without removing the device. The diaphragm should not be left in place for longer than 24 hours, whereas the FemCap should not be left in place for longer than 48 hours. After use, all the devices should be washed with soap and water and allowed to air-dry.

With proper care, these devices can be used for up to 2 years, depending on usage. If a woman loses or gains more than 10 pounds or experiences a pregnancy (regardless of how the pregnancy was resolved—through birth, miscarriage, or abortion), the

Contraceptive Sponge

The Today **contraceptive sponge** was approved by the FDA in 1983; however, it was withdrawn from the market from 1994 to 2005 because of stringent new government safety rules that had to do with the manufacturing plant. It became available for a few years starting in 2005 but was later taken off the market when the manufacturer was sold. The contraceptive sponge has been

---

contraceptive sponge
Polyurethane sponge impregnated with spermicide, inserted into the vagina for contraception.

available in the United States since mid-2009 and does not require a prescription. The one-size-fits-all polyurethane sponge is a combination of a cervical barrier and spermicide. It has a nylon loop on the bottom to help with removal. A box of three sponges can cost approximately $13 to $17, depending on where it is purchased (and may be less at health clinics).

How They Work

A contraceptive sponge works by blocking the entrance to the uterus and by absorbing and deactivating sperm. Before vaginal insertion, the sponge is moistened with water, which activates the spermicide. It is then folded in half and inserted deep into the vagina (Figure 13.10). Like the diaphragm and cervical cap, the sponge must be checked to make sure it is covering the cervix. Intercourse can take place immediately after insertion or at any time during the next 24 hours and can occur as many times as desired without adding additional spermicidal jelly or cream. However, the sponge must be left in place for 6 hours after intercourse. For removal, the loop on the bottom of the sponge is

The contraceptive sponge is an FDA-approved contraceptive device that prevents sperm from entering the uterus. It is inserted deep into the vagina prior to sexual intercourse and is held in place by vaginal muscles. The strap is used to remove the sponge.

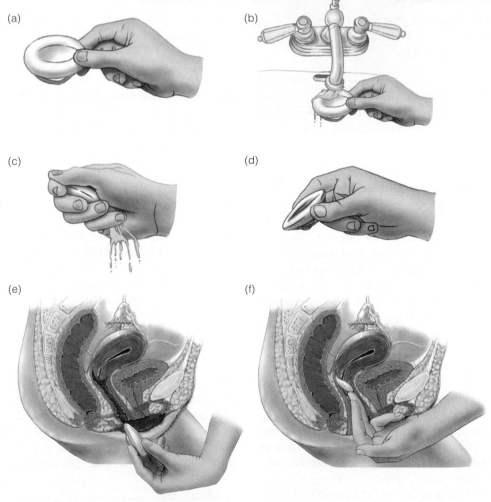

FIGURE **13.10** Insertion of a contraceptive sponge: (a) take it out of the packaging, (b) moisten with water, (c) wring out extra water, (d) fold in half, (e) insert the sponge into the vagina as far as it will go, (f) check to feel the cervix is covered by the sponge.

grasped to gently pull the sponge out of the vagina. The sponge should not be left in place for more than 30 hours.

Effectiveness

Effectiveness rates for the contraceptive sponge range from 84% to 91%. Women who have not had children have higher effectiveness rates than women who have given birth.

Advantages

Like cervical barriers, a contraceptive sponge can be discreetly carried in a purse, is immediately effective, does not affect spontaneity or hormonal levels, allows couples to engage in intercourse multiple times during a 24-hour period, and can be used during breast-feeding. Unlike the cervical barriers, the contraceptive sponge can be purchased without a prescription.

Disadvantages

The contraceptive sponge does not offer protection from STIs, may be difficult to insert and/or remove, requires genital touching, increases postcoital drip, cannot be used during menstruation, may cause a foul odor if left in place too long, and may increase the risk for toxic shock syndrome and urinary tract infections (Hatcher et al., 2011). In addition, some women experience vaginal irritation from the spermicide.

Cross-Cultural Use

Contraceptive sponges have been fairly popular in European countries. In fact, women in France have used vaginal sponges dipped in various chemicals to avoid pregnancy for years. These sponges are washed and used over and over. This practice is not recommended, however, because of the risk for infection and toxic shock syndrome. They are not widely used in other parts of the world.

Review Questions

1 Explain how barrier methods of contraception work, and identify four barrier contraceptive methods in order of their effectiveness rates.

2 How do male and female condoms work, and what are some of the advantages and disadvantages of these barrier methods?

3 Differentiate between the various cervical barriers. How do these methods work, and what are some of the advantages and disadvantages of these methods?

4 How does the contraceptive sponge work, and what are some of the advantages and disadvantages of this method?

Combined Hormone Methods for Women

Combined hormone methods use a blend of hormones to suppress ovulation and thicken the cervical mucus to prevent sperm from joining the ovum. We will discuss oral contraceptive pills, vaginal rings, and patches. Combined hormone methods have been found to be effective, safe, reversible, and acceptable to most women. However, for protection against STIs, condoms must also be used.

Oral Contraceptive Pills

Margaret Sanger was the first to envision **oral contraceptives** (the birth control pill, or simply "the pill"). Many researchers had been working with chemical methods to inhibit pregnancy in animals, but they were reluctant to try these methods on humans because they feared that increasing hormones could cause cancer. The complexity of a woman's body chemistry and the expense involved

Ted Morrison/Getty Images

Many types of contraceptive pills are available and a health care provider can prescribe the one that's best for an individual.

oral contraceptive
The "pill"; a preparation of synthetic female hormones that blocks ovulation.

in developing the pill inhibited its progress. The birth control pill was approved as a contraceptive method in the United States in 1960 (see "The History of Contraception" Timeline in the Appendix for more information).

At first, the pill was much stronger than it needed to be. In the search for the most effective contraception, researchers believed that higher levels of estrogen were more effective. Today's contraceptive pills have less than half the dose of estrogen the first pills had. After more than 50 years on the market, oral contraceptives are one of the most popular contraceptive methods not only in the United States but also around the world (see Figure 13.7).

Combination oral contraceptives, which contain synthetic estrogen and progestin (a type of progesterone), are the most commonly used contraceptive method in the United States (see Figure 13.4). They require a prescription and a medical office visit, and they typically cost between $30 and $60 per month. Most oral contraceptives come in 28-day or 21-day packs and have been designed to mimic an average menstrual cycle, which is why a woman takes them for 21 days and then has 1 week off, when she usually starts her period. Originally, this 3-week-on/1-week-off regimen was developed to convince women that the pill was "natural," which pill makers believed would make the product more acceptable to potential users and reassure them that they were not pregnant every month (Clarke & Miller, 2001; Thomas & Ellertson, 2000). As we discussed in Chapter 5, the bleeding that women experience while on the pill is medically induced and has no physiological benefit.

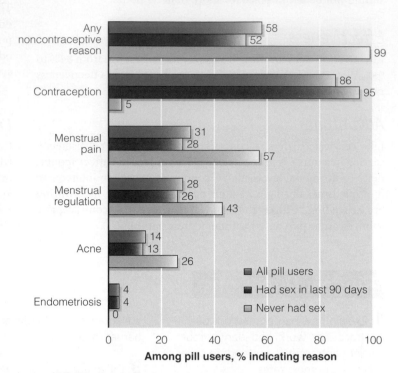

Use of Oral Contraceptive Pills for Non-Contraceptive Reasons, United States

FIGURE **13.11** Many women use contraceptive pills for non-contraceptive reasons, including those who have never engaged in vaginal intercourse.

SOURCE: "Contraceptive Use in the United States," 2016; Guttmacher Institute.

REAL RESEARCH Some brands of oral contraceptive pills may decrease sexual desire and vaginal lubrication, and these effects may last after a woman has stopped taking the pill (Hatcher et al., 2011; Roberts et al., 2013). However, if a woman is less sensitive to hormonal changes, she may not notice these adverse effects. If she does, changing pill brands may restore sexual desire.

Extended-cycle oral contraceptives (also called continuous cycle combined oral contraceptives) became available in 2003 with the FDA approval of Seasonale, which uses a continuous 84-day active pill with a 7-day placebo pill (an 84/7 pill). Seasonale enabled women to have only four periods per year. In 2006, Seasonique, a similar extended-cycle pill, was approved by the FDA. The difference between these brands has to do with the placebo pills—although they are inactive in Seasonale, Seasonique placebo pills contain a low dose of estrogen that has been found to cause less spotting during the active pills. Another

continuous oral contraceptive pill that completely stops menstrual periods, Lybrel, was approved by the FDA in 2007. Lybrel contains lower levels of estrogen than other pills but is taken daily for 365 days a year.

Continuous-use oral contraceptives are not new. In fact, before FDA approval of these methods, some health care providers were known to "bicycle" contraceptive pills (back-to-back use of two packs of active pills with placebo pills at the end of the second pack) or "tricycle" (back-to-back-back use of three packs of active pills with placebo pills at the end of the third pack; Hatcher et al., 2011). In addition, some health care providers have used short-term, continuous-use contraceptive pills for scheduling convenience (i.e., to eliminate the chance of having a period during an athletic event, vacation, or important event). Oral contraceptive pills are also prescribed for noncontraceptive reasons, such as heavy or dysfunctional menstrual bleeding, irregular periods, recurrent ovarian cysts, polycystic ovary syndrome, or acne (see Chapter 5; see Figure 13.11).

Today, more than 100 brands of oral contraceptives are on the market in the United States. They vary with the amount of estrogen (low, regular, high, or varied levels) and the type of progestin (there are a variety of progestin hormones). Recent studies have

combination oral contraceptives A contraceptive pill that contains synthetic estrogen and progesterone.	**monophasic pill** A type of oral contraceptive that contains one level of hormones in all the active pills.	**biphasic pill** A type of oral contraceptive that contains two different doses of hormones in the active pills.	**triphasic pill** A type of oral contraceptive that contains three different doses of hormones in the active pills.

found that one type of progestin, drospirenone, may increase the risk for cardiovascular problems (Jick & Hernandez, 2011; Karabay et al., 2013). It is important to talk to a health care provider to determine which pills are right for you. It is estimated that there were close to 10 million American women using oral contraception in 2012 ("Contraceptive Use in the United States," 2016; see Table 13.2).

How They Work

The hormones estrogen, progesterone, luteinizing hormone (LH), and follicle-stimulating hormone (FSH) fluctuate during a woman's menstrual cycle. These fluctuations control the maturation of an ovum, ovulation, the development of the endometrium, and menstruation. The synthetic hormones replace a woman's natural hormones but in different amounts. The increase in estrogen and progesterone prevent the pituitary gland from sending hormones to cause the ovaries to begin maturation of an ovum. Hormone levels while taking the pill are similar to when a woman is pregnant, and this is what interferes with ovulation. Oral contraceptive pills also work by thickening the cervical mucus (which inhibits the mobility of sperm) and by reducing the buildup of the endometrium.

Combination oral contraceptives pills can be **monophasic**, **biphasic**, or **triphasic** (try-FAY-sic). Monophasic pills contain the same amount of hormones in each pill, whereas biphasic and triphasic pills vary the hormonal amount. Biphasic pills change the level of hormones once during the menstrual cycle, whereas triphasic pills contain three sets of pills for each week during the cycle. Each week, the hormonal dosage is increased, rather than keeping the hormonal level consistent, as with monophasic pills. **Breakthrough bleeding** is more common in pills that have fluctuating hormone levels.

Traditionally, oral contraceptives been used on a monthly cycling plan that involved either a 21- or 28-day regimen and started on the first or fifth day of menstruation or on the first Sunday after menstruation. **Start days** vary depending on the pill manufacturer. The majority of manufacturers recommend a Sunday start day, which enables a woman to avoid menstruating during a weekend. Each pill must be taken every day at approximately the same time. This is important because they work by maintaining a certain hormonal level in the bloodstream. If this level drops, ovulation may occur (see Table 13.4 for more information).

In most 28-day oral contraceptive packs, the last seven pills are **placebo pills**. The placebo pills do not contain hormones, and because of this, a woman usually starts menstruating while taking them. In fact, some low-dose pill brands extended usage to 24 days with a reduced 2- or 4-day placebo pill regimen (a 24/2 or 24/4 pill; Hatcher et al., 2011). Women on these extended cycle regimens report higher levels of satisfaction than women on traditional 21/7 regimens (Caruso et al., 2011; Cremer et al., 2010; Dinger et al., 2011). Overall, women who take oral contraceptives usually have lighter menstrual periods and less menstrual discomfort because the pills decrease the buildup of the endometrium.

Before starting on oral contraceptives, a woman must have a full medical examination. Women with a history of circulatory problems, strokes, heart disease, breast or uterine cancer, hypertension, diabetes, and undiagnosed vaginal bleeding are generally advised not to take oral contraceptives (Hatcher et al., 2011). Although migraine headaches have typically been a reason for not using oral contraceptives, some women may experience fewer migraines while taking them, especially if used continuously without placebo pills. If a woman can use oral contraceptives, health care providers usually begin by prescribing a low-dose estrogen pill, and they increase the dosage if breakthrough bleeding or other symptoms occur.

If a woman taking the pill experiences abdominal pain, chest pain, severe headaches, vision or eye problems, or severe leg or calf pain, she should contact her health care provider immediately. In addition, a woman who takes oral contraceptives should always inform her health care provider of her oral contraceptive use, especially if she is prescribed other medications or undergoes any type of surgery. Certain drugs may have negative interactions with oral contraceptives (see the accompanying "Sex in Real Life" feature). Women are advised not to smoke cigarettes while taking them, because smoking may increase the risk for cardiovascular disease (Hatcher et al., 2011; Raval et al., 2011; Ryan et al., 2014).

Finally, as we discussed in Chapter 5, there has been a vocal debate in recent years about the relationship between oral contraceptive use and cancer. The debate has focused on whether or not oral contraceptives increase the risk of various cancers, including ovarian, endometrial, cervical, and breast cancers. The results of research studies can be inconsistent, confusing, and not always clear-cut. Overall, we know that the risk of

ON YOUR MIND

I usually take my birth control pill at 7 a.m. each morning. When we switch to daylight savings time, what should I do? Should I continue to take my pill at 7 a.m. (the normal time I take it), or should I take it at 8 a.m. (what would have been 7 a.m.) now?

It is important to take oral contraceptives at about the same time each day. Making sure you pick a time that works for you and allows you to regularly remember is the most important thing. Typically, most pills have about a 1- to 2-hour window in which effectiveness is not compromised. Although an hour in each direction probably wouldn't matter, it is probably better to take it 1 hour earlier than later (especially if you are taking a low-dose pill). So, take the pill at your normal time when the clock springs forward (and you'll probably be fine taking it at the same time in the fall when the time changes back, but check with your health care provider to be sure).

---

breakthrough bleeding
Slight blood loss from the uterus that may occur when a woman is using oral contraceptives.

start day
The actual day that the first pill is taken in a pack of oral contraceptives.

placebo pills
In a pack of 28-day oral contraceptives, the seven pills at the end; these pills are sugar pills and do not contain any hormones.

Table 13.4 What to Do If You Forget a Pill, the Patch, or a Ring

Many women who use hormonal contraception might forget to take, apply, or insert it. As we've discussed throughout this chapter, these methods need to be used consistently. Below are some recommendations from the Centers for Disease Control outlining what do to if you forget.

Recommended Actions After Late or Missed Combined Oral Contraceptives

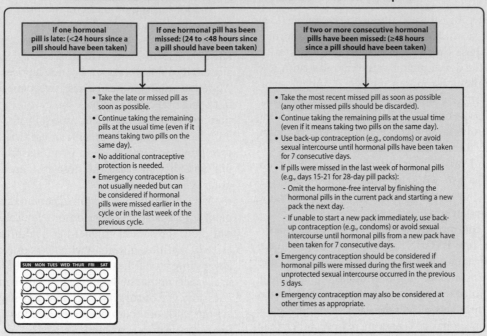

If one hormonal pill is late: (<24 hours since a pill should have been taken)

If one hormonal pill has been missed: (24 to <48 hours since a pill should have been taken)

- Take the late or missed pill as soon as possible.
- Continue taking the remaining pills at the usual time (even if it means taking two pills on the same day).
- No additional contraceptive protection is needed.
- Emergency contraception is not usually needed but can be considered if hormonal pills were missed earlier in the cycle or in the last week of the previous cycle.

If two or more consecutive hormonal pills have been missed: (≥48 hours since a pill should have been taken)

- Take the most recent missed pill as soon as possible (any other missed pills should be discarded).
- Continue taking the remaining pills at the usual time (even if it means taking two pills on the same day).
- Use back-up contraception (e.g., condoms) or avoid sexual intercourse until hormonal pills have been taken for 7 consecutive days.
- If pills were missed in the last week of hormonal pills (e.g., days 15-21 for 28-day pill packs):
  - Omit the hormone-free interval by finishing the hormonal pills in the current pack and starting a new pack the next day.
  - If unable to start a new pack immediately, use back-up contraception (e.g., condoms) or avoid sexual intercourse until hormonal pills from a new pack have been taken for 7 consecutive days.
- Emergency contraception should be considered if hormonal pills were missed during the first week and unprotected sexual intercourse occurred in the previous 5 days.
- Emergency contraception may also be considered at other times as appropriate.

Recommended Actions After Delayed Application or Detachment of Contraceptive Patch

Delayed application or detachment* for <48 hours since a patch should have been applied or reattached

- Apply a new patch as soon as possible. (If detachment occurred <24 hours since the patch was applied, try to reapply the patch or replace with a new patch.)
- Keep the same patch change day.
- No additional contraceptive protection is needed.
- Emergency contraception is not usually needed but can be considered if delayed application or detachment occurred earlier in the cycle or in the last week of the previous cycle.

*If detachment takes place but the woman is unsure when detachment occurred, consider the patch to have been detached for ≥48 hours since a patch should have been applied or reattached.

Delayed application or detachment* for ≥48 hours since a patch should have been applied or reattached

- Apply a new patch as soon as possible.
- Keep the same patch change day.
- Use back-up contraception (e.g., condoms) or avoid sexual intercourse until a patch has been worn for 7 consecutive days.
- If the delayed application or detachment occurred in the third patch week:
  - Omit the hormone-free week by finishing the third week of patch use (keeping the same patch change day) and starting a new patch immediately.
  - If unable to start a new patch immediately, use back-up contraception (e.g., condoms) or avoid sexual intercourse until a new patch has been worn for 7 consecutive days.
- Emergency contraception should be considered if the delayed application or detachment occurred within the first week of patch use and unprotected sexual intercourse occurred in the previous 5 days.
- Emergency contraception may also be considered at other times as appropriate.

Recommended Actions After Delayed Insertion or Reinsertion of Contraceptive Ring

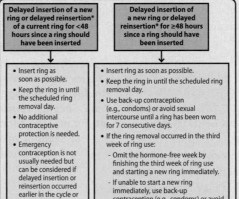

Delayed insertion of a new ring or delayed reinsertion* of a current ring for <48 hours since a ring should have been inserted

- Insert ring as soon as possible.
- Keep the ring in until the scheduled ring removal day.
- No additional contraceptive protection is needed.
- Emergency contraception is not usually needed but can be considered if delayed insertion or reinsertion occurred earlier in the cycle or in the last week of the previous cycle.

*If removal takes place but the woman is unsure of how long the ring has been removed, consider the ring to have been removed for ≥48 hours since a ring should have been inserted or reinserted.

Delayed insertion of a new ring or delayed reinsertion* for ≥48 hours since a ring should have been inserted

- Insert ring as soon as possible.
- Keep the ring in until the scheduled ring removal day.
- Use back-up contraception (e.g., condoms) or avoid sexual intercourse until a ring has been worn for 7 consecutive days.
- If the ring removal occurred in the third week of ring use:
  - Omit the hormone-free week by finishing the third week of ring use and starting a new ring immediately.
  - If unable to start a new ring immediately, use back-up contraception (e.g., condoms) or avoid sexual intercourse until a new ring has been worn for 7 consecutive days.
- Emergency contraception should be considered if the delayed insertion or reinsertion occurred within the first week of ring use and unprotected sexual intercourse occurred in the previous 5 days.
- Emergency contraception may also be considered at other times as appropriate.

SOURCE: Centers for Disease Control. https://www.cdc.gov/reproductivehealth/unintendedpregnancy/pdf/248124_fig_2_3_4_final_tag508.pdf

Sex in Real Life — Medications and Herbs That May Interact with Hormonal Contraceptives

Many over-the-counter (nonprescription) drugs, prescription medications, and herbal supplements may interact with the hormones in oral contraceptive pills, hormonal patches, and hormonal rings. Although progestin emergency contraception is typically not affected by these medications, ulipristal acetate (brand name ella) may be. You should always let your health care provider know that you are using hormonal methods of contraception. There are many other contraceptive methods that are not affected by these medications, including IUDs, contraceptive implants, and contraceptive shots. Below is a list of medications and herbs that may interact with hormonal contraception.

Drug	Effect
Alcohol (beer, wine, mixed drinks, etc.)	Hormonal contraception can increase the effects of alcohol.
Antibacterial medications (including erythromycin)	When used with hormonal contraception, these medications can increase estrogen levels and could increase risk of estrogen-related adverse events.
Antibiotics (including rifampicin or rifabutin, which are typically prescribed for lung infections)	Certain types of antibiotics can decrease the effectiveness of hormonal contraception.
Anticoagulants	Hormonal contraception can decrease the effects of anticoagulant medication.
Anticonvulsants (antiepilepsy drugs)	Certain types of anticonvulsants may decrease effectiveness of hormonal contraception.
Antidiabetics	Hormonal contraception can decrease the effects of antidiabetic medications.
Antifungal medications	The use of antifungal medications along with hormonal contraception may cause breakthrough bleeding and spotting.
Antihypertensives	Hormonal contraception can increase the hypotensive effect of antihypertensive medication.
Antiretrovirals (used to treat HIV)	Certain types of antiretrovirals may decrease effectiveness of hormonal contraception.
Mood stabilizers (includes medications to treat bipolar and depression disorders)	May decrease effectiveness of hormonal contraception; also may decrease the effectiveness of mood medications.
Muscle relaxants	Hormonal contraception can increase the effects of muscle relaxants.
Nonsteroidal anti-inflammatory medications	When used with hormonal contraception, these medications can increase estrogen levels and could increase risk of estrogen-related adverse events.
Statins	When used with hormonal contraception, these medications can increase estrogen and progesterone; unknown clinical significance, but likely to be small.
St. John's wort (an herb often used to treat depression, anxiety, or insomnia)	May decrease effectiveness of hormonal contraception.
Thyroid medications	Hormonal contraception can decrease the effects of thyroid medications.
Vitamin C	When used with hormonal contraception, large doses of vitamin C (1,000 mg or more) can increase estrogen levels and could increase risk of estrogen-related adverse events.

SOURCE: Hatcher et al., 2007; Faculty of Sexual and Reproductive Healthcare, 2011.

developing cancer is highest in women who took oral contraceptives before 1975 because hormonal levels were much higher than the types of pills available today (Gaffield et al., 2009).

Studies have found that the use of oral contraceptives may provide significant protection from both ovarian and endometrial cancers, and protection may increase the longer the pills are taken (Huang et al., 2015; Iversen et al., 2017; Ruan & Mueck, 2015). One study found the risk for ovarian cancer decreased 20% for each 5 years of oral contraceptive use (Cibula et al., 2010).

However, studies have also found that women who take oral contraceptives may have an increased risk of developing cervical cancer, which increases the longer they take the pills (Gierisch et al., 2013). Experts point out that this increased risk may be due to infections with the human papillomavirus (HPV), which causes almost all cases of cervical cancer (Chagas et al., 2013; we will discuss HPV more in Chapter 15).

As for the risk of breast cancer, studies have found that using oral contraceptives slightly increases the risk of developing breast cancer, but that the risk goes back to normal 10 years after discontinuing the pill (Beaber et al., 2014; Gierisch et al., 2013; Iatrakis et al., 2011). One study found that women who had used oral contraceptives in the last year had a 50% increased risk of developing breast cancer compared with former users and nonusers (Beaber et al., 2014a). However, this risk was dependent on the level of estrogen in the pills—pills with high levels of estrogen increased the risk for breast cancer the most, those with moderate levels of estrogen had minimal risk, and those with low estrogen levels did not increase the risk of breast cancer (Beaber et al., 2014a).

Overall, it appears that taking oral contraceptives decreases the risks of ovarian and endometrial cancers but may increase the risks of cervical and breast cancers. The risks are lower with low-dose estrogen pills and oftentimes the risk goes back to normal after discontinuing the pill. It is important for women to talk to their health care providers about any factors that may increase their risk for cancers. Overall, we know that women who have used oral contraceptives have significantly lower rates of death from all cancers, compared with nonusers (Geraghty, 2010; Hannaford et al., 2010).

Effectiveness

Effectiveness rates for oral contraceptives range from 92% to 99.7%. However, women who are significantly overweight may experience lower effectiveness rates (Brunner-Huber & Toth, 2007; Gardner, 2004; Hatcher et al., 2011).

Advantages

Oral contraceptives offer one of the highest effectiveness rates, do not interfere with spontaneity, increase menstrual regularity

and reduce the flow of menstruation, menstrual cramps, premenstrual syndrome, and facial acne (Hatcher et al., 2011). They also provide important degrees of protection against ovarian cysts, uterine and breast fibroids, certain cancers, and **pelvic inflammatory disease**. They may increase sexual enjoyment because fear of pregnancy is reduced, and they have rapid reversibility (the majority of women who stop taking the pill return to ovulation within 2 weeks; Hatcher et al., 2011).

REAL RESEARCH Studies have found that the majority of adverse effects from oral contraceptive use, such as headaches, breast tenderness, or bloating, occur during the week when women take their placebo pills and not when they are taking their hormone pills (HATCHER ET AL., 2007; SULAK ET AL., 2000). This is one of the reasons pharmaceutical companies developed continuous-use oral contraceptives that reduce or eliminate menstrual periods.

Disadvantages

Oral contraceptives require a prescription, must be taken every day, provide no protection from STIs, can be expensive, may increase a woman's risk of breast cancer, and have several possible side effects, including nausea, increase in breast size, breast tenderness, water retention, increased appetite, fatigue, weight gain, and high blood pressure (Hatcher et al., 2011; these are similar to early signs of pregnancy but they usually disappear within a couple of months after a woman's body becomes used to the increased hormones; see Chapter 12). More serious side effects could include migraines, depression, changes in sexual desire and bone density, blood clots, strokes, and/or heart attacks (Hatcher et al., 2011; Skovlund et al., 2016; Trémollieres, 2013).

Cross-Cultural Use

Worldwide, oral contraceptives are the third most popular contraceptive method (behind female sterilization and IUDs), and it's estimated that 10% of women in 70 countries around the world use them (see Figure 13.7). Usage is higher in developed countries, such as Europe, Latin America, and the Caribbean, but lower in underdeveloped countries, such as Africa ("Trends in Contraceptive Use Worldwide," 2015). In some countries, oral contraceptives are available without a prescription (Arroba, 2004; Ng & Ma, 2004). A lack of advertising also affects usage rates. For example, although oral contraceptives were not approved for use in Japan until 1999, they have remained unpopular because of safety concerns, negative side effects, required daily pill taking, countrywide conservatism, and lack of advertising (Hayashi, 2004; Kon, 2004).

Hormonal Ring

NuvaRing is a hormonal contraceptive method that was approved by the FDA in 2001. It is a one-size-fits-all plastic ring that is inserted into the vagina once a month and releases a constant dose

pelvic inflammatory disease
Widespread infection of the female pelvic organs.

NuvaRing
A small plastic contraceptive ring that is inserted into the vagina once a month and releases a constant dose of estrogen and progestin.

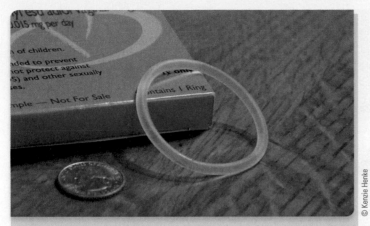

The NuvaRing is inserted deep into the vagina; moisture and heat cause it to time-release hormones that inhibit ovulation.

© Kenzie Henke

of estrogen and progestin. The amount of hormones released into the bloodstream with the NuvaRing is lower than in both oral contraceptives and the patch (Roumen & Mishell, 2012; we will talk more about the patch later in this chapter). The hormonal ring costs approximately $15 to $70 per month to use. It is estimated that there were close to 800,000 American women using NuvaRing for contraception in 2012 ("Contraceptive Use in the United States," 2016; see Table 13.2).

How They Work

Like oral contraceptives, NuvaRing works chiefly by inhibiting ovulation, but it is also likely to increase cervical mucus and changes the uterine lining (Hatcher et al., 2011). The ring is inserted deep inside the vagina, where the vaginal muscles hold it in place, and moisture and body heat activate the release of hormones. Each ring is left in place for 3 weeks and then taken out for 1 week, during which a woman typically has her period. The used ring is disposed of and a new ring is put back in after the week break.

Although rare, the NuvaRing may fall out of the vagina during a bowel movement, tampon use, or vaginal intercourse. If this happens and the ring has been out less than 3 hours, it should be washed and immediately reinserted. If the ring falls out for more than 3 hours, a backup method of contraception should be used, because contraceptive effectiveness may be reduced.

Like oral contraceptives, NuvaRing may be used continuously, without a monthly break, to eliminate monthly periods (although it is important to discuss this with your health care provider). A longer-use vaginal ring that is continuously inserted after being removed for 1 week every month (unlike the shorter-use one that is disposed of after the 1-week break) is currently available outside the United States (Hatcher et al., 2011).

Effectiveness

Effectiveness rates for the NuvaRing range from 92% to 99.7%. Effectiveness rates may be lower when other medications are taken, when the unopened package is exposed to high temperatures or direct sunlight, or when the ring is left in the vagina for more than 3 weeks.

Advantages

The NuvaRing is highly effective, does not interfere with spontaneity, increases menstrual regularity, and reduces the flow of menstruation, menstrual cramps, and premenstrual syndrome (Hatcher et al., 2011). It is easy to use and provides lower levels of hormones than some of the other combined hormone methods. In addition, NuvaRing may also offer some protection from pelvic inflammatory disease and various cancers.

Disadvantages

A prescription is necessary to use NuvaRing, and it offers no protection against STIs. In addition, it requires genital touching and like oral contraceptives may cause a variety of adverse effects, including breakthrough bleeding, weight gain or loss, breast tenderness, nausea, mood changes, headaches, and decreased sexual desire (Hatcher et al., 2011; Lopez et al., 2008). It may increase a woman's risk for toxic shock syndrome, as well as vaginal irritation and discharge. After discontinuing usage, it may take longer for a woman's period to return to a normal cycle.

Like other hormonal methods of contraception, NuvaRing has serious, but rare, risks, which can be increased if a woman has other health problems. Any woman with a history of or risk for blood clots should fully discuss her medical history with health care providers before using any hormonal contraceptives.

Cross-Cultural Use

NuvaRing is marketed in more than 50 countries today, which makes it a popular form of contraception. It is estimated that 1.5 million women use NuvaRing throughout the world (Siddiqui, 2013). In some countries, usage levels may be low because the NuvaRing requires genital touching. Even so, cross-cultural research has found that the NuvaRing is highly effective, and users report high levels of satisfaction with this method (Brucker et al., 2008; Bruni et al., 2008; Merki-Feld & Hund, 2007).

Hormonal Patch

The **Ortho Evra patch** is a hormonal contraceptive method that was approved by the FDA in 2001, but it was taken off the market by the manufacturer in 2015. Today a generic version of the patch is available. It is a thin, peach-colored patch that sticks to the skin and time-releases hormones into the bloodstream. The hormonal patch costs approximately $15 to $75 per month to use.

> **Ortho Evra patch**
> A thin, peach-colored patch that sticks to the skin and time-releases synthetic estrogen and progestin into the bloodstream to inhibit ovulation, increase cervical mucus, and render the uterus inhospitable; also referred to as the "patch."

It is estimated that there were close to 220,000 American women using the hormonal patch for contraception in 2012 ("Contraceptive Use in the United States," 2016; see Table 13.2).

How They Work

Like other hormonal methods, the patch uses synthetic estrogen and progestin to inhibit ovulation, increase cervical mucus, and render the uterus inhospitable to implantation. The patch is placed on the buttock, stomach, upper arm, or torso (excluding the breast area) once a week for 3 weeks, followed by a patch-free week (break week), which usually causes a woman to have her period. A woman can maintain an active lifestyle with the patch in place—she can swim, shower, use saunas, and exercise without the patch falling off.

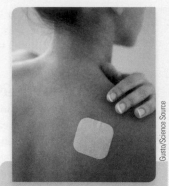
Gusto/Science Source

The contraceptive patch can be placed on the upper outer arm, abdomen, buttock, or back. It should not be placed on the breasts, on cut or irritated skin, or in the same location as the last patch.

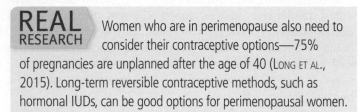

REAL RESEARCH Women who are in perimenopause also need to consider their contraceptive options—75% of pregnancies are unplanned after the age of 40 (LONG ET AL., 2015). Long-term reversible contraceptive methods, such as hormonal IUDs, can be good options for perimenopausal women.

Effectiveness

Effectiveness rates for the hormonal patch range from 92% to 99.7%. It may be less effective in women who are significantly overweight and as with other hormonal methods, certain medications can decrease effectiveness (Hatcher et al., 2011; Zieman et al., 2002).

Advantages

The hormonal patch is highly effective, does not interfere with spontaneity, increases menstrual regularity, and reduces menstrual flow, menstrual cramps, and premenstrual syndrome (Hatcher et al., 2011). Unlike other hormonal methods, the patch has a more than 90% perfect dosing level because it is applied directly to the skin (Roumen & Mishell, 2012).

Disadvantages

The hormonal patch offers no protection from STIs, and because the patch is worn on the skin, it is nearly impossible to conceal. It is peach-colored and is readily apparent on darker skin and can collect fuzz and lint from the user's clothing. Possible side effects include breakthrough bleeding, breast tenderness, nausea, mood changes, changes in sexual desire, skin reactions, or headaches (Hatcher et al., 2011). Some users have found that it can take longer for their period to return to a normal cycle after they stop using the hormonal patch. Like NuvaRing users, users of the hormonal patch may be more at risk for the development of blood clots (Food and Drug Administration, 2008; Hitti, 2008). Finally, the hormonal patch has been found to expose women to higher levels of estrogen than typical oral contraceptives (Hitti, 2008; Nelson, 2015).

Cross-Cultural Use

We do not know a lot about the use of this method outside the United States. However, early estimates found that approximately 2 million women worldwide use the contraceptive patch (Bestic, 2005).

Review Questions

1 Explain how combination hormonal methods of contraception work.

2 Identify three combined hormone contraceptive methods in order of their effectiveness rates.

3 What are extended-cycle oral contraceptives? How do they work?

4 How have health care providers been using regular oral contraceptives for extended-cycle use?

5 Identify the advantages and disadvantages of combined hormone contraceptive methods.

6 What do we know about the cross-cultural usage of combined hormone contraceptive methods?

Progestin-Only Hormone Methods for Women

Progestin-only hormone methods are contraceptive methods that do not contain estrogen. The methods can be used by women who cannot take estrogen or by women who are breast-feeding, because the hormones do not affect the production of breast milk. Progestin-only contraception works by changing a woman's menstrual cycle, which may result in changes in menstrual flow and frequency of periods, as well as an increase in breakthrough bleeding. Over time, many users of progestin-only methods report having no periods at all.

progestin-only hormone method A hormonal contraceptive method that does not contain estrogen and works by changing a woman's menstrual cycle.

Progestin-Only Pills

Progestin-only pills (**minipills**) are similar to combination birth oral contraceptives, except they do not contain any estrogen and have lower levels of progestin. Minipills are taken every day with no hormone-free days. They are less popular than combined-hormonal oral contraceptives.

How They Work

Minipills work by inhibiting ovulation, thickening cervical mucus, and decreasing endometrial buildup.

Effectiveness

Effectiveness rates for minipills range from 92% to 99.7%.

Advantages

Minipills do not contain estrogen and also have a lower level of progestin than combination oral contraceptives. They can be safely used by almost all women, including those who are older than 35, are overweight, smoke, have high blood pressure, have a history of blood clots, or women who are breast-feeding (Hatcher et al., 2011). They also reduce menstrual symptoms and may eliminate periods altogether. Once discontinued, fertility is quickly restored.

Disadvantages

Because minipills contain lower hormone levels, they require obsessive regularity in pill taking (Hatcher et al., 2011). They offer no protection from STIs and may cause several side effects such as breakthrough bleeding or spotting, headaches, nausea, weight gain or loss, breast tenderness, decreased sexual desire, and an increased risk for ovarian cysts. Because progestin affects cilia movement in the Fallopian tubes, women who get pregnant while taking minipills have a higher rate of ectopic pregnancy compared with women taking combination oral contraceptives (see Chapter 12 for more information about ectopic pregnancy). Finally, many pharmacies do not stock minipills, so they may be more difficult to find.

Subdermal Implants

Subdermal contraceptive implants involve surgically inserting a matchstick-sized rod that time-releases progestin under the skin. **Norplant** was the first such method introduced in the United States in 1990. As of 2017, the only implant available in the United States is Nexplanon (and a slightly older version called Implanon), which was approved by the FDA in 2006. Several other versions are currently in development both within and outside the United States. Nexplanon and Implanon are virtually identical. The main difference between the two is that Nexplanon is radiopaque, meaning it can be seen on x-ray, ultrasound, CT scan, or MRI to determine if placement is correct. It is also easier to insert than Implanon (Mansour, 2010; Rowlands et al., 2010). The manufacturer anticipates phasing out Implanon over the next few years.

The cost of the subdermal implant and insertion ranges from $400 to $800. Removal ranges from $75 to $150. It is estimated that there were close to 500,000 American women using subdermal implants for contraception in 2012 ("Contraceptive Use in the United States," 2016; see Table 13.2).

How They Work

A subdermal contraceptive implant is inserted during the first 5 days of a woman's menstrual cycle (to ensure she is not pregnant). The implant time-releases progestin, and like other hormonal methods, it works by suppressing ovulation, thickening cervical mucus, and changing the endometrial lining. Subdermal implants can be left in place for up to 4 years, and women may have a rapid return to fertility after use. Once removed, ovulation usually returns anywhere from 1 to 6 weeks later.

Effectiveness

Effectiveness rates for subdermal implants are approximately 99%. Like other hormonal methods, effectiveness rates may be lower in women who are significantly overweight.

Advantages

Subdermal implants are a highly effective, long-lasting, easily reversible contraceptive method with a rapid onset of protection (Hatcher et al., 2011). They can decrease menstrual flow, cramping, and risk for endometrial cancer, and they can be used by women who are unable to take estrogen. In addition, they can be left in place for up to 4 years and can be removed any time.

Disadvantages

Subdermal implants require a prescription and medical office visit, which may be expensive depending on where it is done. They do not offer any protection from STIs. Possible side effects include irregular or heavy bleeding, especially within the first 6 to 12 months of usage. Other possible side effects include headaches, dizziness, nausea, weight gain, development of ovarian cysts, decreases in sexual desire, vaginal dryness, arm pain, and bleeding from the injection site (Hatcher et al., 2011). Removal may be difficult and generally takes longer than insertion. Researchers are working on a system that involves self-dissolving cylinders so that removal is unnecessary.

Cross-Cultural

Subdermal implants have low usage rates around the world and are more commonly used in less-developed regions (see Figure 13.7). They are approved in more than 60 countries and have been used by more than 11 million women worldwide (Hatcher et al.,

---

minipills
A type of contraceptive pill that contains only synthetic progesterone and no estrogen.

subdermal contraceptive implant
Contraceptive implant that time-releases a constant dose of progestin to inhibit ovulation.

Norplant
A contraceptive implant that consisted of six progestin capsules, which were implanted into the upper arm. Norplant is not currently available in the United States.

2011; Meirik et al., 2003). Prior to U.S. FDA approval, subdermal implants had been used throughout Europe, Latin America, Australia, and Asia.

Hormonal Injectables

The most commonly used hormonal injectable is depo-medroxy-progesterone acetate (DMPA, or **Depo-Provera**; DEP-poe PRO-vair-uh), which was approved by the FDA for contraceptive use in 1992. Depo-Provera is injected once every 3 months, and each injection costs anywhere from $35 to $70 (an initial examination/visit may cost anywhere from $35 to $250, although subsequent visits will be less). It is estimated that there were close to 1.7 million American women using hormonal injectables for contraception in 2012 ("Contraceptive Use in the United States," 2016; see Table 13.2).

How It Works

Depo-Provera is a progestin injected into the muscle of a woman's arm or buttock. It begins working within 24 hours. Like other hormonal methods, it works by suppressing ovulation, thickening cervical mucus, and changing the endometrial lining.

Effectiveness

Effectiveness rates for Depo-Provera range from 97% to 99.7%.

Advantages

Depo-Provera is highly effective, does not interfere with spontaneity, and reduces menstrual flow, cramping, and premenstrual syndrome. It does not contain estrogen, lasts for 3 months, is only moderately expensive, and is reversible (Hatcher et al., 2011). In addition, users need only four shots per year.

Disadvantages

Women who use Depo-Provera must schedule office visits every 3 months for their injections, and they experience a range of possible side effects, including irregular bleeding and spotting, fatigue, dizzy spells, weakness, headaches or migraines, weight gain (it is estimated that a woman will gain an average of 5.4 pounds in the first year of Depo-Provera use), and an increased risk of osteoporosis (Green, 2013; Hatcher et al., 2011). However, studies have found that bone loss is reversible after a woman stops using Depo-Provera (Kaunitz et al., 2008; Pitts & Emans, 2008). In addition, it may take a couple months to restore fertility after the last injection (Hatcher et al., 2011; Kaunitz, 2002).

Cross-Cultural Use

Injectable contraception also has low usage rates around the world and is more commonly used in less-developed regions (see Figure 13.7). This is mainly due to the long-term effectiveness rates of injectibles. They are common in Southeast Asia, along with East and South Africa ("Trends in Contraceptive Use Worldwide," 2015). They are also widely used in some of the poorest countries in Latin America and the Caribbean. Depo-Provera has been approved for use in more than 80 countries, including Botswana, Denmark, Finland, Great Britain, France, Sweden, Mexico, Norway, Germany, New Zealand, South Africa, and Belgium (Francoeur & Noonan, 2004; Hatcher et al., 2004). In addition, another combination injectable, Lunelle, is popular cross-culturally but is not available within the United States.

Review Questions

1 Explain how minipills differ from combined hormone oral contraceptives.

2 Explain how minipills, subdermal implants, and hormonal injectables work to prevent pregnancy.

3 Identify the advantages and disadvantages of each of the progestin-only hormone methods.

4 What do we know about the cross-cultural usage of progestin-only hormone methods?

Chemical Methods for Women

Spermicides come in a variety of forms, including creams, suppositories, gels, foams, foaming tablets, capsules, and films. Nonoxynol-9 is a spermicide that has been used for many years. It is available over-the-counter in many forms (creams, gels, suppositories, film, and condoms with spermicide) and can be used alone or in conjunction with another contraceptive method. However, as you saw from the nearby "Sex in Real Life" feature, there has been some controversy surrounding the use of nonoxynol-9. Today in the United States, the cost for most spermicides ranges from $5 to $10. They are generally less expensive in clinics.

How They Work

Spermicides contain two components: One is an inert base such as jelly, cream, foam, or film that holds the spermicide close to the cervix; the second is the spermicide itself. Foam, jelly, cream, and film are usually inserted into the vagina with either an applicator

Depo-Provera
Depo-medroxyprogesterone, an injectable contraceptive that prevents ovulation and thickens cervical mucus.

or a finger. **Vaginal contraceptive film** contains nonoxynol-9 and comes in a variety of package sizes. The film is wrapped around the index finger and inserted into the vagina.

Some spermicides are applied using suppositories, which are inserted in the vagina 10 to 30 minutes before intercourse to allow time for the outer covering to melt. It is important to read manufacturer's directions for spermicide use carefully. Douching and tampon use should be avoided for 6 to 8 hours after the use of spermicides because they interfere with effectiveness rates.

Effectiveness

Effectiveness rates for spermicides range from 71% to 82%. However, effectiveness depends on the type of spermicide and how consistently it is used. Overall, foam is more effective than jelly, cream, film, or suppositories.

Advantages

Spermicides do not require a prescription and can be easily purchased in drug stores, they can be discreetly carried in a pocket or purse, do not interfere with a woman's hormones, can be inserted during foreplay, provide lubrication during intercourse, have minimal adverse effects, and can be used by a woman who is breast-feeding.

Disadvantages

Spermicides must be used each time a couple engages in vaginal intercourse, which may be expensive depending on frequency of intercourse. In addition, there is an increase in postcoital drip, and

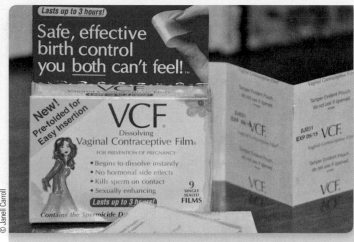

Vaginal contraceptive film is a paper-thin translucent film that dissolves in the vagina and releases spermicide.

some couples may be allergic or have adverse reactions. Spermicides often have an unpleasant taste, and they may cause vaginal irritations or an increase in urinary tract infections (Hatcher et al., 2011).

Cross-Cultural Use

Spermicides are widely used in some countries, including Argentina, Australia, Colombia, Costa Rica, Cuba, and many European and Scandinavian countries (Francoeur & Noonan, 2004). However, in many other countries they are not widely used, most probably because of the relatively high cost and/or required genital touching.

Review Questions

1 Identify the various forms of spermicidal contraception.

2 What are some of the risks and controversies surrounding the use of nonoxynol-9 spermicide?

3 Explain how spermicides work and discuss effectiveness rates.

4 Identify the advantages and disadvantages of spermicidal contraceptive use.

Intrauterine Methods for Women

An intrauterine device (IUD) is a small device made of flexible plastic that is placed in the uterus to prevent pregnancy (Figure 13.12). The Dalkon Shield was a popular IUD up until 1975, when the A. H. Robins Company recommended removal in all users after complaints of severe pain, bleeding, and pelvic inflammatory disease, which led to sterility in some cases. The problems with the Dalkon Shield involved the multifilament string that allowed bacteria to enter into the uterus through the cervix. As of 2017, there were five types of IUDs available in the United States: ParaGard, Liletta, Mirena, Skyla (also called Jaydess),

and Kyleena. Although the ParaGard IUD contains copper, unlike the other four, it does not contain hormones. While the ParaGuard IUD was FDA-approved in the mid-1980s, it wasn't until 2000 that the Mirena IUD was approved. Both of these IUDs were marketed to women who had already had children. The Skyla IUD was FDA-approved in 2013, while the Liletta and Kyleena IUD were FDA-approved in 2015 and 2016, respectively. The Skyla, Liletta, and Kyleena IUDs were marketed to all women, including those who had not had children.

The cost for an IUD, a medical examination, insertion, and follow-up visits can range from $500 to $1,000. It is estimated that there were close to 4 million American women using IUDs for

vaginal contraceptive film
Spermicidal contraceptive film that is placed in the vagina.

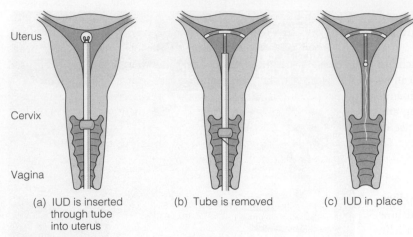

Uterus

Cervix

Vagina

(a) IUD is inserted
through tube
into uterus

(b) Tube is removed

(c) IUD in place

FIGURE **13.12** Insertion of an intrauterine device.

contraception in 2012 ("Contraceptive Use in the United States," 2016; see Table 13.2). Increases in use are due to many factors, including higher safety standards, more physicians and health care providers being trained in insertion and removal techniques, immigration from areas where IUDs are popular (e.g., Mexico), increased advertising, and positive word of mouth from other users (Hubacher et al., 2010). In addition, while the Paraguard and Mirena IUDs were mainly marketed to women who had already had children, many of the newer IUDs are being marketed to women who have not had children, increasing IUD use in younger women.

How They Work

The ParaGard IUD is placed in the uterus and causes an increase in copper ions and enzymes, which impairs sperm function and prevents fertilization (Hatcher et al., 2011). It can be left in place for up to 10 years. The other types of IUDs contain progestin, which is time-released into the uterus, causing an increased thickness in the cervical mucus, inhibiting sperm survival, and suppressing the buildup of the endometrium (Hatcher et al., 2011). The Mirena and Liletta IUDs contain the highest levels of progestin (52 mg), while the Kyleena and Skyla IUDs have lower levels of progestin (19.5 mg and 13.5 mg, respectively). The main differences in the levels of hormones in these IUDs is in how much they alter menstrual flow. The Mirena and Liletta IUDs are more likely to inhibit

all menstrual flow, while users of the Kyleena and Skyla IUDs may experience light periods. Studies have found that after one year of IUD use, 20% of Mirena users, 12% of Kyleena users, and 6% of Skyla users stopped having monthly periods (Mejia et al., 2016). Whether or not a woman will have periods while using an IUD also has to do with how heavy her periods were prior to using the IUD. Women who had moderate periods prior to using an IUD are more likely than women who had heavy periods to stop having periods. Black women and those who had been pregnant before are less likely to stop bleeding while using IUDs (Mejia et al., 2016). This may be due to the increased risk of uterine fibroids in Black women (see Chapter 5).

The Mirena and Kyleena IUDs can be left in for up to 5 years, while the Liletta and Skyla IUDs can be left in for up to 3 years (although one study found the Liletta IUD may last up to 5 years; Creinin et al., 2016). The string of an IUD hangs down from the cervix, and a woman can check the string to make sure the device is still properly in place.

Effectiveness

Effectiveness rates for IUDs range from 99.2% to 99.9%.

Advantages

IUDs are one of the least expensive method of contraception (for women) over time, they do not interfere with spontaneity, can be used during breast-feeding, and have long-lasting contraceptive effects. In addition, hormonal IUDs reduce or eliminate menstrual flow and cramping. They can also be used as emergency contraception (we discuss emergency contraception later in this chapter). Once an IUD is removed, fertility is quickly restored.

Disadvantages

IUDs require moderately painful insertion and removal procedures, may cause irregular bleeding patterns and spotting at the beginning of use (and heavier periods if using the ParaGard IUD), and offer no protection from STIs. Although the IUD has a small

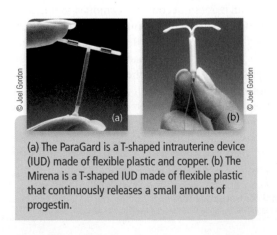

(a) The ParaGard is a T-shaped intrauterine device (IUD) made of flexible plastic and copper. (b) The Mirena is a T-shaped IUD made of flexible plastic that continuously releases a small amount of progestin.

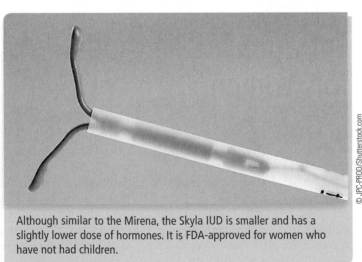

Although similar to the Mirena, the Skyla IUD is smaller and has a slightly lower dose of hormones. It is FDA-approved for women who have not had children.

risk for uterine perforation, this risk is lower in the newer types of IUDs, since they are smaller. It is possible that the string of the IUD may be felt by a sexual partner.

Cross-Cultural Use

Worldwide, 14% of reproductive-age women use intrauterine contraception, although there is much variability among usage rates. While in some countries usage rates are <2%, in other countries it is much higher (Buhling et al., 2014; see Figure 13.7). Various factors influence usage rates including governmental policies, geographic differences, and educational levels.

GyneFix, an IUD containing a flexible row of copper beads instead of a rigid plastic frame like other IUDs, has been used for many years in countries such as England, Asia, Canada, Latin America, and Africa (Wildemeersch & Andrade, 2010). The Gyne-Fix is similar to the Paraguard IUD, in that it releases copper ions and does not contain progestin. However, unlike any of the other IUDs we have discussed, the GyneFix is anchored to the upper portion of the uterus and hangs down.

Review Questions

1 What is an intrauterine device, and how does it work to prevent pregnancy?

2 How effective are IUDs, and what factors are important in determining effectiveness rates?

3 Identify some of the advantages and disadvantages of IUD use.

4 Are IUDs popular outside the United States? Explain.

Natural Methods

Natural methods of contraception do not alter any physiological function. They include natural family planning and **fertility awareness**, withdrawal, and abstinence.

Fertility Awareness–Based Methods

Fertility awareness–based methods involve identifying a woman's fertile period and either abstaining from vaginal intercourse or using another contraceptive method during this time. With the **rhythm method**, a couple simply keeps track of a woman's cycle; other, more intensive methods involve charting and recording physical fertility signs (such as monitoring daily **basal body temperature [BBT]** and checking cervical mucus; Hatcher et al., 2011). Typically, these intensive methods are referred to as **natural family planning**, or the **symptothermal method**. It is estimated that there were 509,000 American women using fertility awareness–based methods for contraception in 2012 ("Contraceptive Use in the United States," 2016; see Table 13.2).

How They Work

With the symptothermal method, a woman takes her BBT every morning before she gets out of bed and records it on a BBT chart. Changes in hormonal levels cause body temperature to increase 0.4° to 0.8°F (0.2°–0.4°C) immediately before ovulation, and it remains elevated until menstruation begins. A woman using this method monitors her cervical mucus, which becomes thin and stretchy during ovulation to help transport sperm. At other times of the month, cervical mucus is thicker.

After 6 months of consistent charting, a woman will be able to estimate the approximate time of ovulation, and she can then either abstain from vaginal intercourse or use contraception during her high-risk times (usually this period is between 1 and 2 weeks).

Effectiveness

Effectiveness rates for fertility awareness–based methods range from 88% to 97%. However, effectiveness rates depend on the accuracy of identifying a fertile period and a couple's ability to avoid intercourse (or use another contraceptive method) during this time.

Advantages

Fertility awareness–based methods are an acceptable form of contraception for those who cannot use another method for religious reasons. These methods can involve the male partner, help teach

fertility awareness
Basal body temperature charting used in conjunction with another method of contraception.

fertility awareness–based methods
Contraceptive or family planning method that involves identifying a fertile period in a woman's cycle.

rhythm method
A contraceptive method that involves calculating the period of ovulation and avoiding sexual intercourse around this time.

basal body temperature (BBT)
The body's resting temperature used to calculate ovulation in the symptothermal method of contraception.

natural family planning
A contraceptive method that involves calculating ovulation and avoiding sexual intercourse during ovulation and at other unsafe times.

symptothermal method
A contraceptive method that involves monitoring both cervical mucus and basal body temperature to determine ovulation.

Cyclebeads can be used with fertility awareness–based methods to help determine fertile days. A ring is moved over a series of color-coded beads that represent low- and high-fertility days.

couples about the menstrual cycle, may encourage couples to communicate more about contraception, are inexpensive, and have no medical side effects. These methods can also be helpful when a woman is ready to get pregnant because she may be familiar with the signs of ovulation. Couples who use these methods often use a variety of sexual expressions when they avoid intercourse during the fertile period.

Disadvantages

Fertility awareness–based methods restrict spontaneity and provide no protection from STIs. In addition, they take time and commitment to learn, and require several cycles of records before they can be used reliably. The majority of failures with this method are due to couples engaging in intercourse too close to ovulation. A woman may ovulate earlier or later than usual because of diet, stress, or alcohol use. These methods are often best suited for those needing to space pregnancies, rather than for those who want to avoid pregnancy.

Cross-Cultural Use

Fertility awareness–based contraceptive methods are popular around the world. Mostly this is because they are inexpensive and do not require much assistance from health care providers. These methods are commonly used in parts of Asia, Europe, Latin American countries, and the Caribbean (see Figure 13.7). They are often the only form of acceptable contraception in predominantly Catholic countries such as Ireland, Brazil, and the Philippines. In the Philippines, natural family planning and the rhythm method are thought to improve a couple's relationship because they need to work together to use the method (remember our earlier discussion about pressure from the Church against using modern methods of contraception in the Philippines; Leyson, 2004). Like other contraceptive methods, societal issues and marketing may also affect the use of these methods. For example, cultural resistance to condom use has increased the popularity of these fertility

awareness–based methods in Kenya, where they are the most commonly used contraceptive method (Brockman, 2004). Today, many women's groups from the United States travel to developing countries to teach fertility awareness–based methods. Studies have found that teaching women about fertility awareness–based contraceptive methods can significantly increase usage rates (Rossier et al., 2014).

Withdrawal

Withdrawal, or **coitus interruptus**, involves withdrawing the penis from the vagina before ejaculation. It's estimated that 5% of U.S. women use withdrawal as their contraceptive method. Many couples report using it because of convenience and dissatisfaction with other methods (Whittaker et al., 2010). When women in the National Survey of Family Growth (see Chapter 2) were asked about using withdrawal, 31% reported they had used it at some point as a contraceptive method (Dude et al., 2013). However, many female users expressed anxiety about using it because it relies on the male to pull out in time. Overall, withdrawal users are more likely to have used emergency contraception (we will discuss emergency contraception later in this chapter; Dude et al., 2013). It is estimated that there were close to 2 million American women using withdrawal for contraception in 2012 ("Contraceptive Use in the United States," 2016; see Table 13.2).

How It Works

Withdrawal does not require any advance preparation. A couple engages in vaginal intercourse and before ejaculation, the male withdraws his penis away from the vaginal opening of the woman. The ejaculate does not enter the vagina.

Effectiveness

Effectiveness rates for withdrawal range from 73% to 96%.

Advantages

Withdrawal is an acceptable method of contraception for those who cannot use another method for religious reasons. It is free, does not require any devices or chemicals, and is better than using no method at all (Hatcher et al., 2011).

Disadvantages

Withdrawal provides no protection from STIs, can be difficult and stressful to use, and may contribute to ejaculatory problems. Many men experience a mild to extreme "clouding of consciousness" just before orgasm when physical movements become involuntary (Hatcher et al., 2011). This method also requires trust from the female partner.

Cross-Cultural Use

Withdrawal is a popular contraceptive method throughout the world. It is widely practiced in Southern Europe and selected

> **coitus interruptus**
> A contraceptive method that involves withdrawal of the penis from the vagina before ejaculation.

countries in Western Asia (Ford & Holder, 2016; "Trends in Contraceptive Use Worldwide," 2015). Overall, it is a popular method for couples with limited contraceptive choices or for those who are reluctant to use modern contraceptive methods. In some countries, such as Iran, a lack of education and misconceptions about withdrawal have led to low usage rates (Rahnama et al., 2010). Many Iranians believe that withdrawal does not work and will lead to multiple health problems, which it does not.

Abstinence

Abstinence (or not engaging in vaginal intercourse at all) is the only 100% effective contraceptive method (Hatcher et al., 2011). It has probably been the most important factor in controlling fertility throughout history. Abstinence may be primary (never having engaged in vaginal intercourse) or secondary (not currently engaging in vaginal intercourse). Couples may choose abstinence to prevent pregnancy, to protect against STIs, or for many other reasons.

Review Questions

1 Differentiate between the various types of fertility awareness–based methods. What factors influence the effectiveness rates of these methods?

2 Explain how changes in cervical mucus and body temperature provide information about ovulation.

3 Explain the use and effectiveness of withdrawal as a contraceptive method.

4 Identify the advantages and disadvantages of natural contraceptive methods.

5 Explain the cross-cultural use of natural contraceptive methods.

Permanent Contraceptive Methods

Male and female **sterilization** methods are the most commonly used contraceptive methods in the world. In 2012, there were approximately 10 million women and 3 million men using these methods in the United States (Guttmacher Institute, 2016; see Table 13.2).

The primary difference between sterilization and other methods of contraception is that sterilization is typically considered irreversible. Although some people have been able to have their sterilizations reversed, this can be expensive and time-consuming (George et al., 2013). The majority of people who request sterilization reversals do so because they have remarried and desire children with their new partners. Reversal difficulties have led some couples to seek out IVF to achieve pregnancies (Hirshfeld-Cytron & Winter, 2013).

Female Sterilization

In a female sterilization, or **tubal sterilization**, a health care provider may close or block both Fallopian tubes so that the ovum and sperm cannot meet. Blocking the tubes can be done with **cauterization**; a ring, band, or clamp (which pinches the tube together); or **ligation** or nonsurgical procedures that involve placing inserts

to block the Fallopian tubes (see Figure 13.13). In the United States, female sterilization procedures are generally done with the use of a laparoscope through a small incision either under the navel or lower in the abdomen. After the procedure, a woman continues to ovulate, but the ovum does not enter the uterus. The costs for female sterilization vary but generally range from $2,000 to $5,000.

Less invasive alternatives to tubal sterilization include Essure, a permanently implanted sterilization method for women that was approved by the FDA in 2002. Essure is a tiny, spring-like device that is threaded into the Fallopian tubes. Within 3 months, the body's own tissue grows around the device, blocking fertilization. A woman using this method must undergo testing to make sure that the Fallopian tubes are fully blocked. Essure is considered an irreversible method of female sterilization, although there have been women who have tried to have the procedure reversed (Albright et al., 2013; Hatcher et al., 2011). In 2015, after a growing number

sterilization	cauterization
Surgical contraceptive method that causes permanent infertility.	A sterilization procedure that involves burning or searing the Fallopian tubes or vas deferens for permanent sterilization.
tubal sterilization	
A surgical procedure in which the Fallopian tubes are cut, tied, or cauterized for permanent contraception.	**ligation**
	A sterilization procedure that involves the tying or binding of the Fallopian tubes or vas deferens.

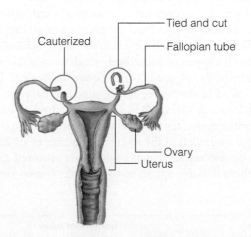

FIGURE **13.13** In a tubal sterilization, the Fallopian tubes are clipped, cut, or cauterized.

of complaints including pain, abnormal bleeding, perforation of the uterus and/or Fallopian tubes, and allergic reactions, the FDA developed an advisory committee to monitor the benefits and risks of Essure ("FDA Activities," 2015). It's possible that this method will be discontinued by the FDA.

Female sterilization is most common among Black and Hispanic women ages 35 or older (Daniels et al., 2013). Although it is much more common among married women, single women also use this method (Eeckhaut, 2015). Overall, the majority of women who choose permanent sterilization are content with their decision to do so (although the risk for regret is highest in women who undergo these procedures before age 30; Gizzo et al., 2014; McMartin, 2013). There are no hormonal changes, and ovaries continue to work and produce estrogen. Women maintain their levels of sexual interest and desire after permanent sterilization and report more positive than negative sexual side effects.

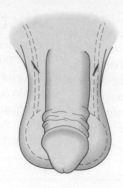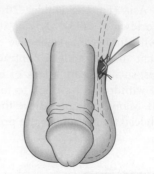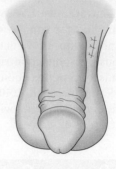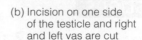

(a) Possible incision sites　　(b) Incision on one side of the testicle and right and left vas are cut　　(c) Incision closed

FIGURE **13.14** In a vasectomy, the vas deferens are clipped, cut, or cauterized.

Male Sterilization

Male sterilization, or **vasectomy**, blocks the flow of sperm through the vas deferens (see Chapter 6). Typically, this procedure is simpler, less expensive, and has lower rates of complications than female sterilization (Shih et al., 2011). Even so, vasectomies are performed at less than half the rate of female sterilizations (see Table 13.2). Unlike users of female sterilization, most men using this contraceptive method are married (Eeckhaut, 2015). Vasectomy rates are lowest among Black and Latino populations, which have the highest rates of female sterilization (Hubert et al., 2016; Rayala & Viera, 2013).

After a vasectomy, the testes continue to produce viable sperm cells, but with nowhere to go, they die and are absorbed by the body. Semen normally contains approximately 98% fluid and 2% sperm, and after a vasectomy, the man still ejaculates semen, but the semen contains no sperm (there is no overall change in volume or texture of the semen after a vasectomy). All other functions, such as the manufacturing of testosterone, erections, and urination, are unaffected by a vasectomy procedure.

The surgery for a vasectomy is performed as **outpatient surgery** with local anesthesia. After local anesthesia, a small incision about one fourth to one half inch long is made in the scrotum, and the vas deferens is clipped or cauterized, which usually takes approximately 20 minutes (Figure 13.14). A newer "no-scalpel" technique has been found to shorten operative time and decrease pain and swelling (Rayala & Viera, 2013). Men are advised to use another form of contraception for 12 weeks after a vasectomy to ensure that there are no sperm left in the ejaculate (Hatcher et al., 2011). Typically, one or two repeat semen analyses are required to evaluate whether there is viable sperm in the sample. Semen samples can be collected during masturbation or through the use of a special condom during vaginal intercourse. In 2008, the FDA approved a postvasectomy home sperm test called SpermCheck, which allows a man to test his semen sample at home rather than returning to a medical facility (Coppola et al., 2010).

After a vasectomy, a man may experience swelling, bleeding, bruising, or pain, but generally these subside within 2 weeks. Like tubal sterilization, vasectomy is considered irreversible. Vasectomy reversals have been done and are more likely to be successful if they are done within 15 years after the procedure (Rayala & Viera, 2013). The cost for the procedure varies widely, depending on where it is done. Overall, the cost for a vasectomy ranges from $300 to $1,000, making it one of the least expensive contraceptive methods over time.

Effectiveness

Effectiveness for both male and female sterilization procedures ranges from 99% to 99.9%. Tubal sterilizations are effective immediately, whereas vasectomies require semen analysis for 12 weeks after the procedure to ensure no viable sperm remains.

Advantages

Sterilization is a highly effective permanent method of contraception. It offers a quick recovery, few long-term adverse effects, and once completed does not interfere with spontaneity (Rayala & Viera, 2013; Shih et al., 2011).

Disadvantages

Sterilization requires medical intervention and/or surgery, can be expensive, provides no protection from STIs, and is considered irreversible.

Cross-Cultural Use

Female sterilization is the most widely used contraceptive method in the world (Hatcher et al., 2011; "Trends in Contraceptive Use Worldwide," 2015). While it is more common in some parts of the world, such as Asia and North America, it is less common

vasectomy	outpatient surgery
A surgical procedure in which each vas deferens is cut, tied, or cauterized for permanent contraception.	Surgery performed in the hospital or doctor's office, after which a patient is allowed to return home.

in others, such as Africa and Europe (see Figure 13.7). In many countries, female sterilization is the primary contraceptive method among low-income women (Brault et al., 2016; Dhungana et al., 2016). Female sterilization is more common than male,

even though these procedures are often expensive and have more potential risks. As we have discussed, access to and promotion of a certain method, along with cultural acceptance, also contribute to its popularity.

Review Questions

1 Identify the two main differences between sterilization and other contraceptive methods.

2 Explain some of the procedures used for female sterilization.

3 Explain some of the procedures used for male sterilization.

4 What are the advantages and disadvantages of sterilization as a contraceptive method?

5 Is sterilization a popular contraceptive method outside the United States? Explain.

Emergency Contraception

Many couples use ineffective methods in an attempt to avoid pregnancy, and some experience unintended pregnancies. **Emergency contraception** (**EC**; also referred to as "morning after" contraception, or emergency contraceptive pills) can prevent pregnancy when taken shortly after unprotected vaginal intercourse. EC is designed to be used in cases in which no contraception was used, contraception was used improperly (such as missed or delayed oral contraceptive pills, hormonal injections, replacement vaginal rings or patches), a male condom slipped or broke, a female condom or barrier device was improperly inserted or dislodged during intercourse, an IUD was expelled, or a sexual assault occurred (Hatcher et al., 2011).

There are some misconceptions about emergency contraception. Although it is referred to as the "morning after pill," this is

misleading because it can be used up to 5 days after unprotected intercourse and not just the morning after. In addition, it is important to point out that emergency contraception does *not* cause an abortion. Emergency contraception is contraception in that it works to *prevent* pregnancy (we will talk more about abortion later in this chapter).

The majority of emergency contraceptive pills are progestin-only. The first emergency contraceptive, Plan B, was approved by the FDA in 1999. It was a two-pill progestin-only method that works by inhibiting ovulation, thickening cervical mucus, and reducing endometrial buildup. In 2013, the FDA approved Plan B One-Step for over-the-counter sale. Today there are several different brands of emergency contraception, such as Take Action, Next Choice One-Dose, My Way, and various generics. All of these methods of emergency contraception are available without a prescription (or age restrictions) and should be taken within 3 days (72 hours) after vaginal intercourse (although they can be taken up to 5 days after intercourse, they are significantly less effective on days 4 and 5).

In 2010, the FDA approved ella, containing ulipristal acetate, which can prevent pregnancy up to 5 days (120 hours) after unprotected intercourse. Not only does ella have a longer window in which it can be used (5 days versus 3 days), it is also more effective in women with a higher body mass index (while Plan B is less effective in women with a BMI over 25, ella is effective for women with a BMI up to 35; Fok, 2016; Rovner, 2013). However, unlike other emergency contraception, ella requires a prescription. The cost of emergency contraception pills varies widely depending on where it is purchased, but typically it ranges from $35 to $60.

Other options for emergency contraception include the use of ordinary combination oral contraceptives or the insertion of a copper-releasing IUD (Hatcher et al., 2011). Oral contraceptives work by inhibiting or delaying ovulation, making the endometrium

Several generic forms of progestin-only emergency contraception are available without age restrictions in the family planning aisle of your pharmacy or drug store.

Martin Shields/Science Source

emergency contraception (EC)
Contraception that is designed to prevent pregnancy after unprotected vaginal intercourse.

less hospitable for implantation of an embryo, thickening the cervical mucus, altering the transportability of the Fallopian tubes, and inhibiting fertilization. The IUD insertion method is used much less frequently than other methods of emergency contraception. Adverse effects for emergency insertion of a copper-releasing IUD include abdominal discomfort and vaginal bleeding or spotting.

Using ordinary oral contraceptives as emergency contraception can lead to nausea, vomiting, cramping, breast tenderness, headaches, abdominal pain, fatigue, and dizziness (Hatcher et al., 2011). The incidence of nausea and vomiting is significantly higher in women who use ordinary oral contraceptive pills as emergency contraception (compared to women who use emergency contraceptive pills), since ordinary oral contraceptive pills contain estrogen.

It is estimated that close to 6 million sexually active women had ever used emergency contraception in the United States as of 2013 (Daniels et al., 2013b). This was significantly more than the estimated 4.2% of sexually active women who had used EC as of 2002. More than half of the women who used EC reported having used it because of method failures or unprotected sex. Most of the women (59%) used it only once, although 24% reported using it twice, and 17% reported using it three times or more (Daniels et al., 2013b). The typical user of emergency contraception is single, educated, and between the ages of 15 and 29 (see Figure 13.15).

Outside the United States, many women have never heard of emergency contraception, even though as of 2013 it was available in 71 countries (14 of those countries require a prescription, while 57 do not; Westley et al., 2014). Large majorities of women in low-income countries are unaware of emergency contraception—for example, 85% of women living in Africa have never heard of emergency contraception (Westley et al., 2013). In addition, in many countries, providers don't talk about emergency contraception because of negative attitudes about providing it to their patients. Women who have heard of emergency contraception often are unclear about how it works or when it should be taken. Overall, knowledge levels and use of emergency contraception are highest in Latin America, followed by Europe, West Asia, and Africa (Westley et al., 2013). In almost every country, wealthier, more-educated women know the most about emergency contraception.

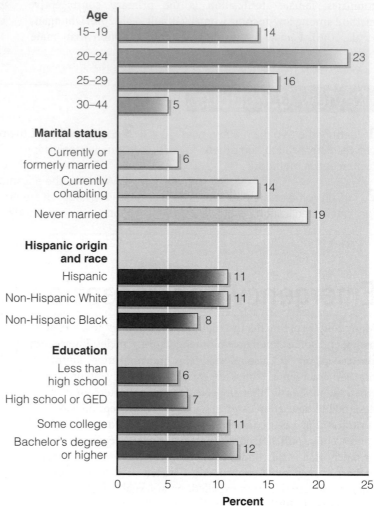

Use of Emergency Contraception

FIGURE **13.15** Percentage of sexually experienced women aged 15–44 who have ever used emergency contraception by marital status, Hispanic origin, and education, United States, 2006–2010.

SOURCE: "Contraceptive Use in the U.S.," 2016; Guttmacher Institute.

Emergency contraception is not an option in some Catholic countries, such as Costa Rica, Honduras, and the Philippines, where strong opposition has made it unavailable (Westley et al., 2013). Various organizations are working to raise overall awareness about emergency contraception and increase availability in all the world's countries.

Review Questions

1 Identify the various types of emergency contraception available today.

2 Identify some of the reasons why a woman might use emergency contraception, and explain how it works.

3 How soon does a woman need to take emergency contraception to have it be effective?

4 Identify some of the adverse effects of emergency contraception.

5 Who is the typical user of emergency contraception in the United States?

6 What do we know about the global use of emergency contraception?

Contraception in the Future

Although many pregnancies occur because couples didn't use contraception, it is estimated that half of all unintended pregnancies occur because of contraceptive failures (Hatcher et al., 2011). Researchers and scientists today continue to look for effective contraceptive methods that are easy to use and have few or no side effects. A consistent concern has been finding a method that can offer high effectiveness rates along with STI protection.

What's Ahead for Men?

Historically, contraception has been considered a female's responsibility, and that may be why the condom and vasectomy are the only contraceptive methods available to men. Many feminists claim that the lack of research into male contraceptive methods has to do with the fact that contraception research is done primarily by men. As a result, women are responsible for using contraception and must live with the potential adverse effects. Others claim that there are few male methods because it is easier to block the one ovum women produce each month than the millions of sperm in each ejaculation. Other arguments cite the fact that chemical contraception may decrease testosterone production, reduce the male sex drive, and harm future sperm production. Many men express a willingness to share the burden of contraception (Kanakis & Goulis, 2015). An international study of 4,000 people found that if a male oral contraceptive pill were available, more than 65% of men said they'd take it, and 75% of women said they'd trust their partners to take it (Glasier et al., 2000; Martin et al., 2000).

As of 2017, research into male contraception continues to explore chemical and hormonal contraception, reversible vasectomies, vas deferens implants and plugs, herbal contraceptives, and vaccines. Two of the most promising vas-based methods involve injectable implants known as RISUG (India) and Vasalgel (United States). RISUG (which is an acronym for *reversible inhibition of sperm under guidance*) is a polymer gel that is injected into the vas deferens to block the passage of sperm (Kanakis & Goulis, 2015; Lohiya et al., 2010). Vasalgel, which is being developed in the United States, is another type of polymer gel that is injected into the vas deferens. These gel implants do not require surgery and are reversible, unlike vasectomies. When a man wants to restore his fertility, the implants are flushed out of the vas deferens. Human trials have already begun on RISUG, but since the research is being done in India it may be a while before this method is available in the United States. On the other hand, since the research on Vasalgel is being done in the United States and researchers are following FDA protocol, it is possible that Vasalgel will be available here within the next few years. Other vas-based methods involve using high-intensity ultrasound to close the vas and block sperm, although these methods have shown less promise (Acker et al., 2003).

Scientists are also exploring the possibility of a male contraceptive pill using hormones that would inhibit sperm production. One pill that is getting a lot of attention is what's known as the "clean sheets" pill for men, which enables a man to have an orgasm without ejaculation (Dawar, 2006; Hisasue et al., 2006). Men have expressed interest in learning more about this method (Clinkenbeard, 2012). Studies are also exploring whether male hormones could be delivered via patches, gels, injections, or implants to suppress spermatogenesis (Behre et al., 2016). Although these methods have been successful in suppressing sperm production, they also have resulted in multiple adverse side effects, such as depression and other mood disorders, muscle pain, and acne.

Scientists also continue working on contraceptive vaccines (called **immunocontraceptives**) that would suppress testicular function, causing infertility until pregnancy is desired (Li et al., 2012; Tamburrino et al., 2014; Zheng et al., 2013). Antisperm contraceptive vaccines and genetically produced human antibodies inhibit sperm functions. Other studies explore the use of herbal extracts, such as Gendarussa, an herbal extract from Indonesia, as well as anticancer drugs, such as Lonidamine, for their ability to reduce sperm production (Maranghi et al., 2005). Studies have also been evaluating the use of ultrasound as a male contraceptive. Short-term use of ultrasound, directed at the testicles, has been found to decrease sperm production, although further studies are needed to ensure that the effects are reversible and there are no long-term side effects from using it as a contraceptive method (Tsuruta et al., 2012).

Although there continues to be ongoing research into new contraceptive options for men, it is possible that it will be several years before any new options are available.

What's Ahead for Women?

Women report that they want contraceptives that are simpler to use, have fewer adverse effects, and offer additional noncontraceptive benefits, such as STI protection, clearer skin, or less weight gain (Hatcher et al., 2011). Research is ongoing in an attempt to find a contraceptive method that addresses all these concerns.

Research continues to explore immunocontraceptives for women that would inhibit the function of human chorionic gonadotropin (see Chapter 12) and interrupt a woman's ability to become pregnant (Talwar et al., 2009). Other researchers are looking at vaccines that target sex hormones or gamete production (An et al., 2009; Naz, 2005; Wang et al., 2009a,b). Unfortunately, vaccines often negatively affect other functions and do not offer adequate effectiveness yet. New implants, injections, and permanent sterilization procedures are also being evaluated. Other research is evaluating longer-acting versions of existing methods, such as the contraceptive patch and hormonal ring. Finally, natural methods of contraception are also being studied. The FDA has approved a fertility computer for use at home, along with ovulation urine test strips. Although these devices are not approved for use as contraceptive devices, research is ongoing to explore these options. Although we still have a long way to go in making better methods available for controlling whether pregnancy occurs, many improvements are in the works and may be available in the near future.

Financial factors, political pressure, and legal concerns hold back most of the contraceptive research today. Private funding is often difficult because such large amounts are necessary for most research. Unfortunately, the threat of lawsuits has effectively scared most big pharmaceutical companies away from contraceptive research.

---

immunocontraceptives
Contraception that uses the body's immune response to prevent pregnancy by suppressing testicular or ovarian functions.

Review Questions

1 What do couples look for in new contraceptive methods?

2 Describe why there have been fewer contraceptive options for men and what the future holds for new male contraception.

3 Describe what the future holds for new female contraceptive methods.

Abortion

Because family planning involves controlling conception and birth, there are two main methods to achieve these goals—contraception and abortion (Leonard, 2006). At the beginning of this chapter we pointed out that the typical American woman spends at least 30 years trying *not* to get pregnant. Although the majority of women have used contraception, we know that many methods are difficult to use consistently and/or effectively, and no method is 100% effective. Unintended pregnancies do occur when a woman is using effective contraception, even though they are much more likely to occur when a woman uses no contraception. In fact, 52% of unintended pregnancies occur in the 16% of the women who use no contraception (Finer & Zolna, 2013). The rate of unintended pregnancy in the United States is significantly higher than rates in many other developed countries (Singh et al., 2010).

As we discussed earlier in this chapter, certain groups of women have higher rates of unintended pregnancies, including those who are young, unmarried, or poor. For women with stable relationships or the resources to raise a child, or both, an unintended pregnancy might not present much of a hardship. However, for many women, an unintended pregnancy is a stressful event that can potentially lead to serious consequences.

In this section, we discuss the abortion debate, historical perspectives, legal versus illegal abortions, statistics, abortion procedures, reactions to abortion, and cross-cultural research on abortion.

The Abortion Debate

Today, abortion is an issue that leads many people to question the role that the government should play in their lives. Disagreements about this issue have been very emotional and, at times, even violent. In 2009, Dr. George Tiller, one of only a few doctors in the country who provided abortions late in a pregnancy, was murdered in Wichita, Kansas. He had several death threats before his murder and was even shot in both arms in 1993 in an attempt to get him to stop performing abortions (Stumpe & Davey, 2009).

Although some people are unsure about how they feel about abortion or feel somewhat in the middle, the majority of us fall on one side or the other of the abortion debate.

pro-life supporter	pro-choice supporter
Individual who believes that abortion should be illegal or strictly regulated by the government.	Individual who believes that the abortion decision should be left up to the woman and not regulated by the government.

Pro-life supporters believe that human life begins at conception, and thus an embryo, at any stage of development, is a person. Although some pro-life supporters believe that aborting a fetus is murder and that the government should make all abortions illegal, others believe that abortion should be available only for specific cases (such as rape or danger to a mother's life).

On the other side of the issue, **pro-choice supporters** believe that a woman should have control over her fertility. Many people who are pro-choice believe there are a number of situations in which a woman may view abortion as a necessary option. Because not everyone agrees that life begins at conception, pro-choice supporters believe that it is a woman's choice whether to have an abortion, and they strongly believe that the government should not interfere with her decision.

The abortion debate often polarizes people into pro-life and pro-choice camps. However, both sides of the abortion debate came together recently to celebrate a report that showed that the United States has had the lowest abortion rates since abortion was legalized in 1973. Pro-life groups suggested the decreased abortion rates were a result of more women carrying unintended pregnancies to term, while pro-rights groups claimed greater contraceptive access was responsible for the decreased rates. In the United States, 6 in 10 adults (59%) believe that abortion should be legal in all or most cases, while 37% believe that it should be illegal all or most of the time (Lipka & Gramlich, 2017).

ON YOUR MIND

In the future, is abortion going to be illegal?

The current makeup of the U.S. Supreme Court makes it possible that *Roe v. Wade* could be overturned, giving full regulation of abortion back to the states. If *Roe v. Wade* were overturned, several states would likely ban abortion, including Louisiana, Mississippi, North Dakota, and South Dakota, whereas others would likely protect a woman's right to choose. Still other states would either retain their pre–*Roe v. Wade* abortion bans or restrict the right to legal abortion in the absence of *Roe v. Wade*.

Historical Perspectives

Abortion has been practiced in many societies throughout history; in fact, there are few large-scale societies in which it has not been practiced. Aristotle argued that abortion was necessary as a backup to contraception. He believed that a fetus was not alive until certain organs had been formed; for males, this occurred 40 days after conception, and for females, 90 days. In early Roman society, abortions were also allowed, but husbands had the power to determine whether their wives would undergo abortion.

Throughout most of Western history, religion determined general attitudes toward abortion, and both Judaism and Christianity have generally condemned abortion and punished those who used it. Still, throughout recorded history, abortions were performed. Many women died or were severely injured by illegal surgical abortions performed by semiskilled practitioners. Although it was little discussed publicly, abortion was apparently quite common; the Michigan Board of Health estimated in 1878 that one third of all pregnancies in that state ended in abortion (D'Emilio & Freedman, 1988).

In 1965, all 50 states banned abortion, although there were exceptions that varied by state (for instance, to save the mother's life, or in cases of rape or incest or fetal deformity). Those who could not have a legal abortion had the baby or underwent an illegal abortion (others may have used self-induced abortion methods, such as inserting sticks in the vagina, applying pressure to the abdomen, or drinking bleach). Illegal abortions, known as **back-alley abortions**, were very dangerous because they were often performed under unsanitary conditions and resulted in multiple complications, sometimes ending in death (recall my chapter-opening Notebook feature about a woman who underwent an illegal abortion). In 1967, abortion laws in England were liberalized, and many American women traveled to England for an abortion. By 1970, "package deals" appeared in the popular media advertising roundtrip airfare, airport transfers, passport assistance, lodging, meals, and the procedure itself (Gold, 2003).

In 1973, the Supreme Court ruled in the *Roe v. Wade* decision that a woman's right to an abortion is constitutionally protected, but not absolute (Boonstra et al., 2006). After the point of fetal viability (when a fetus can live on its own outside of the womb), a state could restrict or prohibit abortion unless it was necessary to protect the life and health of the woman. Since the Supreme Court handed down its decision in *Roe v. Wade* in 1973, individual states have regulated and limited whether, and under what circumstances, a woman can obtain an abortion. Following are some of the provisions of some of these state laws as of 2017:

- *Physician and hospital requirements:* Some states require abortions to be performed by licensed physicians, whereas others require procedures to be done in hospitals.

- *Public funding restrictions:* Limit the use of state funds for women who cannot afford abortion. South Dakota limits funding to cases of life endangerment only, which is against federal requirements.

- *State-mandated counseling:* Require women who choose abortion to undergo counseling that informs her of certain risks, including the development of breast cancer (5 states), the ability of the fetus to feel pain (12 states), and long-term mental health consequences (8 states).

- *Waiting periods:* Require women who want to have an abortion wait a specified period (usually 24 hours) between when she receives counseling and when the procedure is done. In Missouri, Oklahoma, South Dakota, and Utah, there is a 72-hour (3-day) waiting period, the longest in the nation.

- *Parental involvement:* **Parental notification** and **parental consent** regulations require minors to involve their parents

and get their consent before undergoing an abortion. Thirty-seven states require some type of parental involvement in a minor's decision to have an abortion.

- *Refusal:* Many states allow individual health care providers and/or institutions to refuse to provide abortion.

It is likely that these types of restrictions will continue to increase over the next few years, even though they can interfere with a woman's access to abortion. In fact, women who live in states that require counseling prior to an abortion are less likely to obtain an early abortion procedure (Jones & Jerman, 2017a).

There has been growing concern about the legality of safe abortion since the 2016 presidential election. President Donald Trump has expressed a commitment to overturning *Roe v. Wade* and eliminating the constitutional guarantee of the right to an abortion. Ultimately this will be the decision of the Supreme Court, so it will depend on the makeup of the justices on the bench. In the meantime, however, President Trump and his administration could do several things to erode a woman's access to abortion, including defunding Planned Parenthood and making the Hyde Amendment, which bans federal funding for many abortions, a permanent law rather than a one-year provisional law that is extended each year.

If the Supreme Court were to overturn *Roe v. Wade*, the decision on whether or not elective abortion would be legal would be left up to each individual state. Studies have found that if this were to happen, many of the central and southern states would outright ban abortion. In fact, four states—Louisiana, Mississippi, and North and South Dakota—already have laws in place that would make abortion illegal if *Roe v. Wade* is overturned (Marty, 2017). It is possible that only a handful of states would allow abortion if *Roe v. Wade* were overturned, including New York, California, parts of Illinois, and New Mexico.

Legal Versus Illegal Abortions

Although legalization of abortion in the United States gave women the right to choose abortion, it also led to the development of safer abortion procedures. As a result, fewer women were hospitalized for abortion-related complications and fewer died. Abortion-related deaths dropped significantly after *Roe v. Wade* was passed in 1973.

Many experts believe that making abortion illegal does not affect the underlying cause for abortion—unintended pregnancies (Boonstra et al., 2006). Legal or illegal, unintended pregnancies still occur and women will seek out options.

Abortion Statistics

The abortion rate hit a historic low in 2014 and has continued to decline since that time (Jones & Jerman, 2014). In 2014, the abortion rate was 14.6 abortions per 1,000 women, which was the

---

back-alley abortion
Illegal abortion, which was all that was available before the legalization of abortion in the 1970s.

parental notification
Abortion legislation that requires the

notification of the parents of a minor before an abortion procedure.

parental consent
Abortion legislation that requires the consent of the parents of a minor before an abortion procedure.

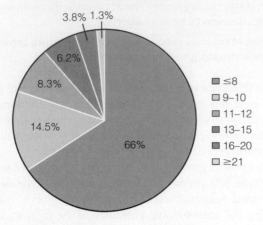

When do Women have Abortions?*

3.8% 1.3%
6.2%
8.3%
14.5%
66%

- ≤8
- 9–10
- 11–12
- 13–15
- 16–20
- ≥21

*In weeks from the last menstrual period.

FIGURE **13.16 Abortion and Length of Pregnancy in the U.S., 2017**
Two-Thirds of abortions in the United States occur at 8 weeks of pregnancy or earlier; 89% occur in the first 12 weeks of pregnancy.

SOURCE: *"Induced Abortion in the U.S." 2017; Guttmacher Institute.*

lowest rate ever recorded in the United States. Slightly fewer than 1 million abortions were performed in the United States in 2014, which was 12% less than the number performed in 2011 (Jones & Jerman, 2017). Even so, it is estimated that close to half of all pregnancies in the United States are unintended and that 42% of these pregnancies end in abortion (Finer & Zolna, 2016).

The majority of abortions occur early in pregnancy (see Figure 13.16), which may be the result of improved surgical procedures and/or the development of the "abortion pill." In 2014, 69% of all early abortions were done in a clinic, while 31% were done using the "abortion pill" (Jones & Jerman, 2017). Let's now explore the typical profile of a woman in the United States who has an abortion.

Who Has Abortions in the United States?

The majority of women who have abortions are young. In 2014, 60% were in their 20s and 25% were in their 30s (Jerman et al., 2016). They are also more likely to be unmarried, poor or low-income, and have had at least one previous birth (Jerman et al., 2016). Higher abortion rates are directly related to rates of unintended pregnancy, which is typically a result of the lack of access to high-quality contraception, as well as a lack of consistency in using certain methods. While close to 40% of women having abortions in 2014 reported no religious affiliation, 24% identified as Catholic, 17% as mainline Protestant, 13% as evangelical Protestant, and the rest reported some other religious affiliation (Jerman et al., 2016). There were no ethnic/racial differences in the number of women having abortions: 39% were White, 28% were Black, 25% were Hispanic, 6% were Asian or Pacific Islander, and 3% were of some other ethnicity/race (Jerman et al., 2016).

Why Do Women Have Abortions?

Women choose abortion for many different reasons—an inability to care for a child, financial reasons, partner or relationship issues, as well as work, school, or family issues. One study found that most common reasons given for having an abortion included the belief that a baby would interfere with work, school, or other children, a lack of financial resources, and concern and/or responsibilities for others (Finer et al., 2005). There is no simple answer to the question of why a woman decides to have an abortion.

The majority of women—regardless of age, marital status, income, ethnicity, education, or number of children—cite a concern for others as a main factor in their decision to have an abortion (Boonstra et al., 2006). Many women consult with others when they are deciding what to do about an unintended pregnancy. In fact, 60% report talking to someone, most often their partner, when they make their decision (Finer et al., 2006).

Abortion Procedures

Since 1973, abortion has been one of the most common surgical procedures in the United States, and many abortion procedures are performed in specialized abortion clinics. However, after *Roe v. Wade,* the majority of abortions were performed in hospitals. The move away from hospitals and into clinics reduced the cost of an abortion. In 2000, the availability of medication abortions, or the "abortion pill," in the United States enabled women to terminate their pregnancies in the privacy of their own homes.

Today, a woman can choose between a surgical ("in-clinic") or medication ("abortion pill") procedure (see Table 13.5 for more information about early abortion options). The most important

Table 13.5 Early Abortion Options

In-Clinic Abortion	The Abortion Pill
Highly effective	Highly effective
Often must wait until at least 6 weeks pregnant (up to 16 weeks LMP)	Can be used as soon as find out pregnant (up to 9 weeks LMP)
Relatively brief procedure	Procedure can take up to several days or more to complete
Involves invasive procedure	No invasive procedure (unless incomplete)
Allows local or general anesthesia	No anesthesia
Usually requires only one clinic visit	Involves at least two clinic visits
Bleeding is typically lighter after procedure; can last from a few days or more	Bleeding is typically heavier after procedure and can last a few days to 2 weeks
Moderate cramping during or after procedure	Strong cramping often occurs
Occurs in medical setting	Can occur in privacy of own home

factor in determining which procedure a woman should choose is the duration of a woman's pregnancy. An in-clinic abortion can be used up to 16 weeks after the first day of a woman's last menstrual period (LMP), whereas the abortion pill can only be used up to 70 days from LMP (before 10 weeks).

In-Clinic Abortion Procedures

A **first-trimester surgical abortion** (also called **vacuum aspiration**) can be performed up to 16 weeks after a woman's last period. It is simpler and safer than abortions performed after this time. The procedure can be done in a private clinic, physician's office, or hospital. The availability of these procedures depends on the laws in each state. For example, while some states ban abortion procedures after 6 weeks (North Dakota), others ban them at 12 weeks (Arkansas), 20 weeks (Arizona and North Carolina), or have no restrictions (such as New Hampshire, Oregon, Vermont, and West Virginia).

In a first-trimester in-clinic abortion procedure, a woman is often offered some type of sedative. She lies on an examining table with her feet in stirrups, and a speculum is placed in her vagina to view the cervix. Local anesthesia is injected into the cervix, which numbs it slightly. **Dilation rods** are used to open the cervix and usually cause mild cramping of the uterus. After dilation, a **cannula** is inserted into the cervix and is attached to a **vacuum aspirator**, which empties the contents of the uterus. A first-trimester procedure usually takes between 4 and 6 minutes.

Second-trimester in-clinic abortions are those performed later than 16 weeks after a woman's last period. These procedures are only available in states that allow this procedure and can be done in a private clinic, physician's office, or hospital. A woman may undergo a second-trimester procedure for several reasons, such as medical complications, fetal deformities that were not revealed earlier, divorce or marital problems, miscalculation of date of last menstrual period, financial or geographic problems (such as not living near a clinic that offers the procedure), or a denial of the pregnancy until the second trimester.

A **dilation and evacuation (D&E)** is often used in second-trimester procedures. The procedure is similar to a vacuum aspiration, but dilation may be done differently. Because the fetal tissue is larger, the cervix must be dilated more than it is in a first-trimester procedure. Dilators such as **laminaria** (lam-in-AIR-ree-uh) may be inserted into the cervix 12 to 24 hours before the procedure to help begin the dilation process. These dilators absorb fluid and slowly dilate the cervix. When a woman returns to the clinic or hospital, she will be given pain medication and numbing medication will be injected into the cervix. The dilators are removed, and the uterus is then emptied with suction and various instruments. A D&E usually takes about 15 to 20 minutes. Second-trimester abortion procedures are more difficult to find, have higher risks, and are more expensive than first-trimester procedures (Janiak et al., 2014).

After an in-clinic abortion procedure, most women experience bleeding and cramping. Over-the-counter pain relievers, such as ibuprofen, can reduce the pain and cramping. Although the heaviest bleeding might last only a few days, spotting can last for up to 6 weeks. Because these are medical procedures, potential risks are associated with these procedures, and these risks increase the longer a woman has been pregnant. Possible risks include an allergic reaction to medications, excessive bleeding, infection, injury to the cervix, uterine perforation, and/or an incomplete abortion. Health care providers advise women who are considering abortion to have an earlier procedure because the risks are lower in first-trimester procedures.

Most clinics and medical offices require a woman to stay a few hours after the procedure so that she can be monitored. If a woman is Rh-negative, she will be given RhoGAM after these procedures (see Chapter 12). Once home, she is advised to rest, not to lift heavy objects, to avoid vaginal intercourse, and not to use tampons for at least 1 week; all of these activities may increase the risk for infection. Typically, a woman's period will return within 4 to 8 weeks. Most clinics advise a follow-up visit 2 to 4 weeks after the procedure.

Medication Abortion

A medication abortion involves the use of an "abortion pill" to end an early pregnancy. This pill is actually a drug known as **mifepristone** (MYFE-priss-tone). Mifepristone was first approved for use in pregnancy termination in France in 1988, during which time it was referred to as RU-486. It was given FDA approval for use in the United States in 2000. In a medication abortion, mifepristone is used in conjunction with a second pill containing **misoprostol**. As we pointed out earlier, medication abortions accounted for 31% of abortion procedures in 2014, up from 24% in 2011 (Jones & Jerman, 2017).

Many clinics require a physical examination, blood work, and an ultrasound to determine the length of the pregnancy before prescribing the abortion pill. During this visit, medication abortion is explained and a woman is given antibiotics to reduce the possibility of infection. The actual medication abortion involves three steps. The first step involves taking the abortion pill, mifepristone. A woman will usually begin bleeding within 4 to 5 hours after taking this pill. Mifepristone works by blocking the hormone progesterone, which is responsible for maintaining the buildup of the endometrium (see Chapter 5). Without progesterone, the endometrial lining will break down and a pregnancy can no longer continue.

---

first-trimester surgical abortion
Termination of pregnancy within the first 16 weeks of pregnancy.

vacuum aspiration
The termination of a pregnancy by using suction to empty the contents of the uterus.

dilation rods
A series of graduated metal rods that are used to dilate the cervical opening during an abortion procedure.

cannula
A tube, used in an abortion procedure, through which the uterine contents are emptied.

vacuum aspirator
A vacuum pump that is used during abortion procedures.

second-trimester surgical abortion
Termination of pregnancy between the 16th and 21st weeks of pregnancy.

dilation and evacuation (D&E)
A second-trimester abortion procedure that involves cervical dilation and vacuum aspiration of the uterus.

laminaria
Seaweed used in second-trimester abortion procedures to dilate the cervix. Used dried, it can swell three to five times its original diameter.

mifepristone
Drug used in medication abortion procedures; it blocks the development of progesterone, which causes a breakdown in the uterine lining.

misoprostol
A synthetic prostaglandin drug used for early abortion.

The second step involves taking another medication, misoprostol. This is usually taken within 3 days of the abortion pill. Misoprostol is a **prostaglandin**, and it causes the uterus to contract and expel the uterine contents. Many women experience heavy bleeding, cramping, nausea, diarrhea, abdominal pain, dizziness, or a minor fever and chills. This process may take 4 to 5 hours or more, and during this time a woman will experience an abortion. The bleeding will continue for up to 4 weeks after the medications are taken, and women can use pads or tampons during this time.

ON YOUR MIND
How much does an abortion cost?

Abortions are available at many Planned Parenthood health clinics and the offices of various health care providers. The cost for a first-trimester in-clinic abortion ranges from $350 to $950. These fees usually include an examination, laboratory tests, medications, the procedure, and a follow-up examination. Second-trimester procedures are more expensive, and it may be difficult to find a clinic that offers these procedures today. The costs of abortion procedures vary depending on how long a woman has been pregnant and where she goes for the procedure. Generally, hospitals cost more than clinics. The cost for the "abortion pill" ranges from $350 to $650, and costs may be more or less depending on what additional tests, visits, or examinations may or may not be needed.

The third, and final, step involves a follow-up visit to the health care provider, usually within two weeks, to make sure that the abortion is complete. A blood test, ultrasound, or both may be performed. Women who have a medication abortion must be prepared to have an in-clinic abortion if they experience an incomplete abortion. Because the drugs for medication abortion are known to cause birth defects, in the event the abortion is incomplete, women are advised to not continue a pregnancy after using these drugs.

Medication abortion is a safe and effective procedure, and research indicates that it may be safer than in-clinic abortion procedures (Gatter et al., 2015; Singh et al., 2008). Some women choose medication abortion over in-clinic abortion because it feels more "natural," offers privacy, can be done earlier, does not use anesthesia, and provides more control (see Table 13.5). However, medication abortions often cause heavier bleeding and cramping than in-clinic abortions, and some women worry about being away from a medical facility (Lie et al., 2008). Finally, the length of time to expulsion (days compared with minutes) often makes medication abortion less appealing than an in-clinic abortion.

Reactions to Abortion

Although the decision to have an abortion is a difficult one, the physiological and psychological effects vary from person to person, and they depend on many factors. Here we'll explore the reactions of women, men, and teens.

Women's Reactions

The majority of evidence from research studies has found that legal abortion is safe and has few long-term physiological, psychological, or fertility-related problems later in life (Boonstra et al., 2006; Munk-Olsen et al., 2011; Warren et al., 2010). Although we know less about reactions to medication abortion, preliminary research has found that women are pleased with this type of procedure because it allows them more control and privacy (Cameron et al., 2010).

As we have discussed, physiological symptoms after an abortion often depend on the type of abortion procedure. Common physiological symptoms include cramping, bleeding with possible clots, and nausea. These symptoms may persist for several days, but if any of these are severe, a health care provider should be seen for an evaluation. Severe complications are much more frequent in second-trimester surgical procedures, as we discussed earlier. They include hemorrhaging, **cervical laceration**, **uterine perforation**, and infection. Of these complications, uterine perforation is the most serious, although the risk for occurrence is small. Earlier, we mentioned a state provision that involved informing women about the risks for breast cancer and impaired future fertility after an abortion. Reviews of scientific literature have found that women who have an abortion do not have an increased risk for breast cancer or long-term risks to future fertility (Guo et al., 2015).

Although women experience a range of emotions after an abortion, the most prominent response is often relief (Fergusson et al., 2009). Even though relief may be the immediate feeling, there are other categories of psychological reactions to abortion. Positive emotions include relief and happiness; socially based emotions include shame, guilt, and fear of disapproval; and internally based emotions include regret, anxiety, depression, doubt, and anger, which are based on the woman's feelings about the pregnancy (Bellieni & Buonocore, 2013). A woman may cycle through each of these reactions—feeling relief one minute, depression or guilt the next. Other possible negative psychological symptoms include self-reproach, increased sadness, and a sense of loss.

ON YOUR MIND
If you had an abortion, could it make you infertile later on?

Women who undergo an abortion can become pregnant and give birth later on in their life without complications (Bord et al., 2014; Costescu et al., 2016; Hatcher et al., 2007; Woolner et al., 2014). However, there are rare cases of unexpected complications of abortion that can lead to infertility, such as uterine perforation or severe infection. Because medication abortion procedures are nonsurgical, they have less risk for uterine perforation or infection.

prostaglandin
Compounds that can cause changes in the smooth muscle cells, leading to strong cramping.

cervical laceration
Cuts or tears on the cervix.

uterine perforation
Tearing a hole in the uterus.

Certain conditions may put a woman more at risk for development of severe psychological symptoms. These include being young, being persuaded to have an abortion when a woman doesn't want one, having a difficult time making the decision to have an abortion, blaming the pregnancy on another person or on oneself, having a strong religious and moral background, having an abortion for medical or genetic reasons, having a history of psychiatric problems before the abortion, not having family or partner support, and/or having a late abortion procedure (Major et al., 2000, 2008; Ralph et al., 2014; Rue et al., 2004). One study found that when women shared their abortion experiences with others, the reactions to their disclosures fell into three categories, including negative, supportive, or sympathetic (Cowan, 2017). While the majority of disclosures received either supportive or sympathetic reactions, over one third of reactions were negative, which researchers believed could have a negative impact on a person's well-being (Cowan, 2017).

In most cases, although discovering an unintended pregnancy and deciding to terminate the pregnancy are stressful decisions, in the majority of cases, the emotional aftermath does not appear to be severe (Fergusson et al., 2008; Major et al., 2000, 2008; Munk-Olsen et al., 2011; Warren et al., 2010). Still, it is very beneficial for a woman (and her partner) who is contemplating an abortion to discuss this with a counselor or health care provider.

Men's Reactions

A woman's choice to have an abortion forces many couples to reevaluate their relationship and ask themselves some difficult questions. Do they both feel the same about each other? Where is the relationship going? Keeping the lines of communication open during this time is very important. The male partner's involvement makes the abortion experience less traumatic for the woman; in fact, women whose partners support them and help them through the procedure show more positive responses after the abortion (Jones et al., 2011). Women who have no support from their partners or who make the decision themselves often experience greater emotional distress. In some cases, women have been found to conceal abortion decisions from their partners (Coker, 2007; Woo et al., 2005).

Although we know that an unintended pregnancy is difficult for many women, we often fail to acknowledge that men can also have a difficult time and may experience sadness, a sense of loss, and fear for their partner's well-being (Holmes, 2004). What makes it even more difficult for most men is that they often do not discuss the pregnancy with anyone other than their partner (Naziri, 2007).

Finally, unintended pregnancy is associated with higher levels of violence in intimate relationships. Research has found that some men try to control their partner's abortion-related decisions (Chibber et al., 2014). These behaviors are part of a larger pattern of behaviors involving forced sex, condom refusal, and contraceptive control (we will discuss this more in Chapter 17). Abusive men have been found to be more involved in unintended pregnancies ending in abortion than their nonabusive counterparts, especially in cases where there are repeat abortions (Silverman et al., 2010). This is an area of research that will continue to be explored in the future.

Teens and Abortion

As we have been discussing, the majority of women who have abortions in the United States are young. However, like the overall levels of abortion, the proportion of abortions done on adolescents declined significantly from 2008 to 2014 (Jerman et al., 2016). Overall, 12% of women who had abortions in 2014 were adolescents—8% were 18–19 years old, 3% were 15–17 years old, and 0.2% were younger than 15. Teenagers may be more vulnerable to postabortion anxiety, depression, sleep problems, and substance use/abuse, mostly because of developmental limitations and a lack of emotional support from those around them (Coleman, 2006; Ely et al., 2010). As we discussed earlier, women who have no support often experience increased emotional distress after an abortion.

Earlier we discussed the laws and regulations that individual states impose on access to abortion. Many of these are designed to control teenagers' access to abortion. The majority of states require parental involvement in a teen's decision to have an abortion. These restrictions often cause adolescents to delay abortion procedures. In fact, they are less likely than older women to have early abortion procedures (Jones & Jerman, 2016). Some states offer a medical emergency exception or a **judicial bypass option**, in which a minor can obtain consent from a judge rather than from her parents. Laws and regulations that restrict a teenager's access to abortion disproportionately affect ethnic and racial minority teens, leading to higher rates of unintended births (Coles et al., 2010).

Cross-Cultural Aspects of Abortion

Abortion laws vary dramatically around the world—it is legal and available in some countries, legal under certain circumstances in others, and completely illegal in others. Like in the United States, the availability of abortion is often dependent on many factors, including political views, religion, and economic issues. It's estimated that 96% of all countries allow abortion to save a woman's life, whereas six countries do not allow abortion under any circumstances (including Chile, the Dominican Republic, El Salvador, Nicaragua, Malta, as well as the Vatican City; Theodorou & Sandstrom, 2015). In most of Europe, with the exception of Malta and the Vatican, abortion is legal. France, Germany, Greece, and Russia all allow abortion for any reason. Ironically, countries with liberal abortion laws have been found to have lower rates of abortion. For example, in the Netherlands, abortion is legal, free, and widely available, yet abortion rates are among the world's lowest (and the rate of abortion in the Netherlands is significantly lower than in the United States; Boonstra et al., 2006). The Netherlands also has comprehensive sexuality education programs and liberal access to contraception, both of which contribute to low abortion rates (see Chapter 8 for more information about comprehensive sexuality education). Some countries in Europe, including Ireland, permit abortion only if a woman's life is at risk and impose up to 14 years' imprisonment on women who have illegal abortions.

> **judicial bypass option**
> Abortion legislation that allows for a judge to bypass parental consent or notification for a minor to acquire an abortion.

In Latin American countries, including Chile, the Dominican Republic, El Salvador, and Nicaragua, most people believe that abortion should be illegal in most or all cases ("Religion in Latin America," 2014). The only exception to this is in Uruguay, which has some of the most liberal abortion laws in Latin America. Throughout the Middle East and in sub-Saharan Africa abortion is legal to save a mother's life in most countries, but only Cape Verde and South Africa allow abortion for any reason (Theodorou & Sandstrom, 2015). Finally, in the Asian-Pacific region, some countries allow abortions for any reason, including Australia, China, and Turkey.

Although many countries have relied on support from the United States to help fund women's reproductive health care, in 2017, President Trump reinstated the Mexico City Policy, known as the "global gag rule," which bars U.S. governmental funding to international organizations that perform or promote abortion. There was controversy about this decision, and opponents believed it could contribute to 6.5 million unintended pregnancies and 2.1 million unsafe abortions throughout the world (Mackintosh, 2017).

Worldwide, approximately 56 million abortions occur each year ("Induced Abortion Worldwide," 2016). While the global rate of abortion is 35 per 1,000 women of childbearing age, the highest rates of abortion are in the Caribbean (65 per 1,000 women), followed by South America (47 per 1,000 women: "Induced Abortion Worldwide," 2016). To help put these numbers in perspective, recall that the abortion rate in the United States was 14.6 per 1,000 women in 2014.

The largest declines in abortion rates were in Eastern Europe (from 88 in 1990–1994 to 42 in 2010–2014); even so, there are significant differences in the abortion rates in Eastern and Western Europe (42 to 18; "Induced Abortion Worldwide," 2016). This was probably due to less use of effective contraceptive methods. Abortion rates have remained fairly stable in countries such as Africa, Latin America, and Asia. Most women who have abortions in other countries do so because they didn't have access to effective contraception. Similar to the United States, abortion rates are higher among unmarried women.

Researchers and experts are working to help legalize abortion around the world to help reduce the incidence of illegal abortions and postabortion complications. However, this is only the first step to ensuring that women have adequate access to abortion services. In some countries where abortion is legal, safe services are unavailable to many women because of prohibitive prices or certain restrictions, such as the necessity of getting the consent of multiple physicians (as is the case in Zambia, where abortion has been legal since 1994; Cohen, 2009).

Abortion remains a controversial procedure in the United States, as well as in the rest of the world. In the United States, both sides of the issue battle from what they believe are basic principles: one side from a fetus's right to be born and the other from a woman's right to control her own body. The pendulum of this debate continues to swing back and forth. Current politics may influence whether *Roe v. Wade* is one day overturned. Although new developments such as medication abortion may take the fight out of the abortion clinics and into women's homes, the only real certainty about the future of abortion is that it will remain one of the most controversial areas of American public life.

Review Questions

1 Trace the status of abortion throughout history and differentiate between legal and illegal abortion.

2 Differentiate between first- and second-trimester surgical abortion procedures.

3 Differentiate between in-clinic abortion and the abortion pill, and explain how a woman might decide which procedure would be best for her.

4 Identify some physiological and psychological reactions to abortion, and discuss the research on men and abortion.

5 Discuss the laws that have been imposed in an attempt to decrease abortion in adolescent populations.

6 Describe what we know about abortion outside the United States.

Chapter Review

Summary Points

1 Contraception is not a modern invention. The ancient Greeks and Egyptians used a variety of techniques to try to control their fertility. Several groups began to explore controlling fertility in the early 1800s, and Margaret Sanger was one of the first people to advocate the importance contraception.

2 Contraception use is more common in developed countries, and throughout the world it has always been affected by social and economic issues, knowledge levels, religion, and gender roles. The Catholic Church's position on contraception was formally presented in 1968 with the publication of the *Humanae Vitae*, the document that prohibits Catholics from using artificial contraception. Even though the Catholic Church prohibits contraceptive use, many residents of predominately Catholic countries support the use of contraception.

3 The FDA has approved several methods of contraception, but no method is best for everyone. The FDA is responsible for approving all prescription medicine in the United States. A pharmaceutical company must submit proof that the drug is safe for human use. It is estimated that it takes 10 to 14 years to develop a new contraceptive method.

4 Issues that must be considered when choosing a contraceptive method include personal health, number of sexual partners, frequency of vaginal intercourse, risk for acquiring a sexually transmitted infection, responsibility of partners, method cost, and method advantages and disadvantages.

5 Barrier methods of contraception work by preventing the sperm from entering the uterus. Barrier methods include male and female condoms, cervical barriers, and the contraceptive sponge. Male condoms can be made of latex, polyurethane, or lambskin. There are many types of male condoms on the market, including lubricated, non-lubricated, colored, glow-in-the-dark, flavored, and studded or textured.

6 Cervical barriers include diaphragms and the FemCap cervical cap, which work by blocking the entrance to the uterus and deactivating sperm through the use of spermicides. The diaphragm is one of the oldest contraceptive methods, and it was the most frequently prescribed contraceptive method in the United States in 1930. While the diaphragm is made of either latex or silicone, the FemCap is made of silicone. Cervical barriers are one of the least common methods of contraception in the United States today.

7 The contraceptive sponge is a barrier method that contains spermicide and is made of polyurethane. It is available over the counter. Although they are fairly popular in European countries, they are not widely used in other parts of the world.

8 Combined hormone methods use a blend of hormones to suppress ovulation and thicken the cervical mucus to prevent sperm from joining the ovum. Combined hormone methods include oral contraceptives, hormonal injections, rings, and patches. Combination oral contraceptives contain synthetic estrogen and a type of progestin. The increase in estrogen and progesterone prevents the pituitary gland from

sending hormones to cause the ovaries to begin maturation of an ovum. Most combination oral contraceptives come in 28- or 21-day packs and have been designed to mimic an average menstrual cycle.

9 Combination oral contraceptives can either be monophasic, biphasic, or triphasic, and breakthrough bleeding is more common in pills that have fluctuating hormone levels. Extended-cycle oral contraceptives, which use a continuous 84-day active pill with a 7-day placebo pill, became available in 2003.

10 There has been an ongoing debate about whether oral contraceptives increase the risk of various cancers, including ovarian, endometrial, cervical, and breast cancers. The results of research studies can be inconsistent, confusing, and not always clear-cut. The risk of developing cancer is highest in women who took oral contraceptives before 1975, because hormonal levels were much higher than the oral contraceptives available today. Overall, oral contraceptive use decreases the risks of ovarian and endometrial cancers, but it may increase the risks of cervical and breast cancers. The risks are lower with low-dose estrogen pills, and oftentimes the risk goes back to normal after discontinuing the pill. It is important for women to talk to their health care providers about these risks.

11 Other combination hormonal contraceptive options include NuvaRing, a small plastic ring inserted in the vagina that releases a constant dose of estrogen and progestin and is changed once a month; and the Ortho Evra patch, which sticks to the skin and time-releases synthetic estrogen and progestin into the bloodstream. These work by inhibiting ovulation, increasing cervical mucus, and/or rendering the uterus inhospitable to implantation.

12 Progestin-based methods include minipills, implants, and injectables. Mini-pills are similar to combination oral contraceptives, except they do not contain any estrogen and have lower levels of progestin. They must be taken every day with no hormone-free days. They are less popular than combined-hormonal oral contraceptives.

13 Implanon and Nexplanon are subdermal contraceptive implants, which are surgically inserted under the skin and time-release progestin. They have low usage rates around the world and are more commonly used in less-developed regions. The most commonly used hormonal injectable is Depo-Provera, which is injected into a woman's arm or buttock once every

3 months. Like other hormonal methods, it works by suppressing ovulation, thickening cervical mucus, and changing the endometrial lining.

14 Chemical methods of contraception include spermicides such as creams, jellies, foams, suppositories, and films. Spermicides work by reducing the survival of sperm in the vagina. Since they require genital touching, they are not widely used in most countries.

15 Intrauterine devices are placed in the uterus and inhibit ovulation, thereby causing an increase in cervical mucus and endometrial buildup. There are five types of IUDs available today: the ParaGard, Liletta, Mirena, Skyla, and Kyleena IUDs. While the ParaGard IUD contains copper, unlike the other four, it does not contain hormones. While the ParaGard and Mirena IUDs have been mostly marketed to women who already have children, the Liletta, Skyla, and Kyleena IUDs have been marketed to all women, including those who have not had children.

16 The ParaGard IUD has no hormones and can be left in place for up to 10 years. The Mirena and Liletta IUDs have the highest levels of progestin, while the Kyleena and Skyla have lower levels. Progestin levels help regulate menstrual bleeding. The Mirena and Kyleena IUDs can be left in place for up to 5 years, while the Skyla and Liletta IUDs can be left in place for 3 years.

17 Fertility awareness–based methods identify a woman's fertile period so she can abstain from vaginal intercourse or use another method of contraception. A more intensive method involves charting and recording physical fertility signs, such as monitoring daily body temperature.

18 Withdrawal, or coitus interruptus, is a method of contraception in which the man withdraws his penis from the vagina before ejaculation. This method can be used in conjunction with other contraceptive methods.

19 Tubal sterilization is the most widely used method of contraception in the world. In this procedure, a health care provider may sever or block both Fallopian tubes so that the ovum and sperm cannot meet. A vasectomy blocks the flow of sperm through the vas deferens, and although the testes will continue to produce viable sperm cells, the cells die and are reabsorbed by the body.

20 The majority of emergency contraceptive pills are progestin-only and prevent pregnancy when taken after unprotected vaginal intercourse. Today there are several different brands of emergency contraception, such as Take Action, Next Choice One-Dose, My Way, and various generics. All of these methods of emergency contraception should be taken within 3 days (72 hours). They are available without a prescription to teens 17 and older. Teens under the age of 16 need a prescription to get emergency contraception. Ella, a nonhormonal form of emergency contraception, is the newest form of emergency contraception. It can prevent pregnancy up to 5 days after unprotected intercourse. In addition, it is more effective in women with a higher body mass index.

21 Contraception has long been thought to be a female's responsibility, and that may be why the condom and vasectomy are the only contraceptive methods available to men. Many feminists claim the lack of male methods is because most of those doing the contraceptive research are men, whereas others claim that most methods are for women because it is easier to interfere with one ovum a month than thousands of sperm a day.

22 Many new contraceptive methods are on the horizon, and many will be easier to use, longer acting, and have higher effectiveness rates. As of 2017, research into male contraception continues to explore chemical and hormonal contraception, reversible vasectomies, vas deferens implants and plugs, herbal contraceptives, and vaccines. Two of the most promising vas-based methods involve injectable implants known as RISUG (India) and VasalGel (United States).

23 There are two methods of controlling conception: contraception and abortion. Although the majority of sexually active women use contraception, many methods are difficult to use effectively and/or consistently, and no method is 100% effective. In the United States, disagreements about abortion have been emotional and, at times, violent. Whereas some are pro-life supporters, others are pro-choice supporters.

24 Abortion has been practiced in many societies throughout history; in fact, there are

few large-scale societies where it has not been practiced. Before abortion was legalized, illegal abortions were common. Throughout most of Western history, religion determined general attitudes toward abortion.

25 In 1973, the court case *Roe v. Wade* gave women a constitutionally protected right to have an abortion in the early stages of pregnancy. In the first trimester of pregnancy, a woman has a right to choose abortion without the state interfering. In the second trimester, a state can regulate abortion to protect a woman's health. Since 1973, individual states have regulated and limited whether, and when, a woman can obtain an abortion. Provisions include physician and hospital requirements, gestational limits, public funding restrictions, state-mandated counseling, waiting periods, and parental involvement.

26 Legalization of abortion in the United States gave women the right to choose abortion but also increased the safety of abortion. Experts believe the legality of abortion does not affect the incidence of unintended pregnancy, the real underlying cause of abortion. The abortion rate hit a historic low in 2014 and has continued to decline since that time.

27 The typical woman who has an abortion in the United States is most likely to be in her 20s, poor or low-income, and unmarried. Although women choose abortion for many different reasons, some of the most common include an inability to care for a child, financial reasons, partner or relationship issues, or work, school, or family commitments.

28 Today a woman can choose between an in-clinic, surgical abortion and the abortion pill. The most important factor in determining which procedure a woman should have is the duration of her pregnancy and the side effects of each procedure.

29 The decision to have an abortion is a difficult one, and physiological and psychological effects vary from person to person and depend on many factors. The most

prominent reaction after an abortion is relief. Men may also experience difficulties, but the male partner's involvement makes the abortion experience less traumatic for the woman.

30 Intimate partner violence is higher in couples with unintended pregnancies. There are men who try to control their partner's abortion-related decisions. Abusive men are more involved in pregnancies ending in abortion, especially in cases where there are repeat abortions.

31 Teens may be more vulnerable to postabortion anxiety, depression, sleep problems, and substance use and abuse, especially if there is a lack of emotional support from those around them. Many state laws have been enacted to limit teenagers' access to abortion.

32 Abortion laws vary dramatically around the world—it is legal and available in some countries, legal under certain circumstances in others, and completely illegal in others. Like in the United States, the availability of abortion is often dependent on many factors, including political views, religion, and economic issues.

33 Worldwide, 56 million abortions occur each year. Countries that have liberal abortion laws have been found to have lower rates of abortion. Although many countries have relied on support from the United States to help fund women's reproductive health care, in 2017, President Trump reinstated the "global gag rule," which bars U.S. governmental funding to international organizations that perform or promote abortion.

34 Abortion remains a controversial procedure in the United States as well as in the rest of the world. In the United States, both sides of the issue battle from what they believe are basic principles: one side from a fetus's right to be born and the other from a woman's right to control her own body. The only real certainty about the future of abortion is that it will remain one of the most controversial areas of American public life.

Critical Thinking Questions

1 If you found out tomorrow that you (or your partner) were 6 weeks pregnant, what would your options be? Where would you go for help, and who would you talk to? What would your biggest concerns be?

2 Suppose a good friend of yours, Sylvia, tells you that she is 10 weeks pregnant, and she and

her boyfriend have decided that they will have an abortion. She knows that you are taking a human sexuality course and asks you about their options. What can you tell her?

3 What method of contraception do you think would work best for you at this time in your life? In 5 years? In 10 years? Why?

4 Do you think women who use herbal contraceptives should be taught about newer, more modern methods of contraception? What if the methods they are using are working for them?

Websites

Planned Parenthood Federation of America   Planned Parenthood Federation of America is the world's largest voluntary reproductive health care organization providing reproductive health care, sex education, and information. This website offers information on contraception, emergency contraception, STIs, safer sex, pregnancy, abortion, and other health-related concerns.

Guttmacher Institute   The Guttmacher Institute is a nonprofit organization that focuses on sexual and reproductive health research, policy analysis, and public education. The institute's mission is to protect the reproductive choices of all people in the United States and throughout the world.

National Abortion Federation   The National Abortion Federation (NAF) is the professional association of abortion providers in the United States and Canada. NAF members provide the broadest spectrum of abortion expertise in North America.

National Abortion Rights Action League   National Abortion Rights Action League (NARAL) is a pro-choice league that strives to help find workable answers to ultimately reduce the need for abortions. NARAL believes that ignoring limited access to contraception, reproductive health care, and sex education while taking away a woman's right to choose will only result in more unintended pregnancies and more abortions.

Male Contraception Information Project   The Male Contraception Information Project is a nonprofit organization that works to raise public awareness of promising male contraceptives and also provides resources and support for increased and expedited governmental research on male contraceptive methods.

14 Challenges to Sexual Functioning

From Dr. Carroll's Notebook...

Dr. Woet Gianotten, cofounder of the International Society in Sexuality and Cancer, is an expert in oncosexology, an area of medicine that focuses on the sexual and relationship needs of patients with cancer. As a physician and sexologist, he has spent many years exploring how disease, physical impairments, and medical interventions affect sexual functioning. Intrigued by the benefits of a satisfying sexual relationship, he began asking, "How can a good sex life affect physical health?" He strongly believes that an active and satisfying sex life can improve one's health and quality of life.

Petra Laribert

Dr. Gianotten's work with cancer patients has reaffirmed his belief in the importance of regular sexual expression. A regular and satisfying sex life can help people feel loved, secure, and alive. Unfortunately, many patients and physicians don't talk about sex. Dr. Gianotten explained that even though cancer patients are worried about sexual functioning, many are too embarrassed to talk with their physicians about their concerns. Many physicians are also uncomfortable and don't bring it up. Dr. Gianotten finds it interesting that while physicians are often uncomfortable talking about sex, sex therapists are often uncomfortable talking about cancer. His work has shown him that even in the end stages of people's lives, many still want sex. One woman told him that she had more sex during the last days of her husband's life than they had in the prior months just because they were afraid that each day would be his last. Another 65-year-old woman he worked with had been prescribed medications to alleviate the depression she experienced after the death of her husband. Sometime later when she entered into a new relationship she found the medication made it difficult for her to reach orgasm. When she shared her concerns with her physician, he questioned whether an orgasm was really that important to her. She responded, "If I can't get an orgasm, please give me pills to die!" Our thought-provoking conversation really made me think more about the benefits of a healthy and satisfying sex life.

Janell Carroll

S exual health is important to our overall health and quality of life. Although many might believe that satisfactory sexual functioning comes naturally, we know that many people experience challenges to their sexual functioning. In this chapter, we explore how physiological and psychological issues, together with chronic illnesses and disabilities, can create problems in sexual functioning, and we explore current treatments for these problems.

Challenges to Sexual Functioning

As we begin our exploration of challenges to sexual functioning, it is important to point out that sexual problems are quite common. Many of us experience times when we do not feel sufficiently aroused, have a lower level of enthusiasm, or have trouble relaxing during sex. In fact, the majority of couples report periodic problems with sexual functioning (Frank et al., 1978). Most of the time these problems do not interfere with overall sexual functioning and they go away on their own. However, for some people, the problems continue and may even get worse over time.

Defining a sexual problem can be difficult. If a person can't reach orgasm or can't get an erection one night, would you say this constitutes a sexual problem? To help clarify definitions, some sex therapists in the United States use the American Psychiatric Association's *Diagnostic and Statistical Manual of Mental Disorders* (*DSM*), which is a classification and diagnostic tool that includes criteria for sexual dysfunctions (terminology can be confusing, but to clarify, we will use the terms *dysfunction* and *disorder* interchangeably). The *DSM* is occasionally updated and continues to evolve and reflect the prevailing thinking and understanding about sexual dysfunction (remember that homosexuality was removed from the *DSM* in 1973; see Chapter 11). The *DSM* is currently in the fifth edition (referred to as the *DSM-5*). It has three chapters related to sexual disorders: sexual dysfunction, gender dysphoria, and paraphilic disorders (we will explore paraphilic disorders more in Chapter 16). The *DSM-5* includes three types of female sexual dysfunction and four types of male sexual dysfunction. We will explore all of these in this chapter.

One major concern with past editions of the *DSM* was its overreliance on Masters and Johnson's and Kaplan's linear models of sexual response in the classification of sexual dysfunctions (see Chapter 10). Diagnoses were often dependent on where in the sexual response cycle the symptoms occurred. However, recent research has raised important questions about the usefulness of applying these models of sexual functioning, especially

Although our sexual response changes as we age, many older couples still enjoy an active, satisfying sex life.

REAL RESEARCH Many people who experience sexual problems do not talk about their concerns with their health care providers, mostly because they feel embarrassed and/or lack the communication skills to do so (KINGSBERG & KNUDSON, 2011).

in women (Basson, 2000a,b; Basson et al., 2004; Janssen et al., 2008; Sungur & Gündüz, 2014; Tiefer, 2002, 2004, 2006). Like most revisions to the *DSM*, there were controversies and disagreements about the changes and updates (Campell et al., 2015; Duschinsky & Chachamu, 2013; Sarin et al., 2013; Welch et al., 2013).

It is also important to point out that not everyone who experiences sexual problems is distressed by them. Those who are might seek out sex therapy, and if they do, this typically begins with a medical evaluation to explore any physiological issues that might be contributing to the problem. This is not always an easy task because psychological and physiological factors can overlap (McCabe & Connaughton, 2014). Let's take a look at some of these factors.

Psychological Challenges to Sexual Functioning

A variety of psychological factors can challenge sexual functioning, including unconscious fears, ongoing stress, anxiety, depression, guilt, anger, fear of intimacy, dependency, abandonment, and concern over loss of control. Anxiety plays an important role in developing and maintaining sexual dysfunctions (Figure 14.1). **Performance fears**, distractions, shifts in attention, or preoccupation during sexual arousal may interfere with the ability to respond sexually (Bancroft et al., 2005; Kaplan, 1974; Masters &

performance fears
The fear of not being able to perform during sexual behavior.

Masters and Johnson's sexual response cycle (see Chapter 10) and the *Diagnostic and Statistical Manual of Mental Disorders* medical classifications have long been used as the foundation for treating sexual dysfunctions. However, critics have challenged how these models apply to female sexuality and contend that they are incomplete by not encompassing psychosocial dimensions of sexual expression (see Figure 10.9). In 2000, Leonore Tiefer, a leading sex therapist and feminist sexologist, and a group of colleagues proposed the New View of Women's Sexual Problems that included a revision in the classification system for female sexual dysfunction (Kaschak & Tiefer, 2001).

According to Tiefer and colleagues, most sexual problems occur when there is emotional, physical, or relational dissatisfaction with some aspect of a sexual experience (Tiefer, 2001). The New View of Women's Sexual Problems includes four categories that account for most of the limitations in women's sexual functioning:

I. Sexual problems caused by sociocultural, political, economic factors: Some contributing factors may include ignorance and anxiety because of lack of sex education, lack of access to reproductive health services, or other social constraints and pressures; perceived inability to meet cultural norms for ideal sexuality; and conflict between the sexual norms of culture of origin and another culture.

II. Sexual problems relating to partner and relationship factors: May include inhibition, avoidance, or distress arising from betrayal, dislike, or fear of partner; partner's abuse or unequal power; partner's negative patterns of communication; or discrepancies in desire for various sexual activities.

III. Sexual problems caused by psychological factors: These factors include sexual aversion, mistrust, or inhibition of sexual pleasure because of past experiences of physical, sexual, or emotional abuse; depression and anxiety; or general personality problems.

IV. Sexual problems caused by medical factors: Such problems can arise from a wide variety of factors, including numerous local or systemic medical conditions affecting neurological, neurovascular, circulatory, endocrine, or other systems of the body; pregnancy, sexually transmitted diseases, or other sex-related conditions; and adverse effects of many drugs, medications, or medical treatments.

New View proponents believe that an overmedicalization of female sexuality has resulted in an obsessive focus on the physical (genital) aspect of sexuality, leaving psychological and social aspects trivialized or ignored (Tiefer, 1996, 2002). The medical approaches to women's sexual problems have evolved into an increasing emphasis on pills, creams, gels, and other pharmaceutical agents, to the dismay of those who believe sexual behavior is multidimensional, complex, and context dependent (see websites listed at the end of the chapter for more information on the New View Campaign).

Johnson, 1970). When anxiety levels are high, physiological arousal may be impossible. A lack of privacy or feeling rushed can also contribute to sexual dysfunctions.

Throughout this textbook we have discussed various components of healthy and successful relationships, including trust, respect, and the ability to communicate one's needs. Because sexual dysfunctions often occur within the context of intimate relationships, many issues can affect sexual functioning. Feeling unappreciated, anger, insecurity, resentment, conflict, or a lack of trust can lead to problems with sexual functioning. In addition, worrying about whether a partner is being faithful can cause stress and anxiety, increasing the chances of a sexual dysfunction developing. Overall, relationship issues are more strongly related to the development of female sexual dysfunctions (McCabe & Connaughton, 2014).

Physiological Challenges to Sexual Functioning

Healthy sexuality depends on a fine interplay of vascular, hormonal, and neurological functioning. However, a variety of physiological factors, including injuries, disabilities, illnesses, and diseases, can interfere with these functions (Shivananda & Rao, 2016). Treatments for various diseases, such as chemotherapy and radiation, can also contribute to problems with sexual functioning (Frechette et al., 2013).

We also know that prescription drugs, such as **psychotropic medications** and contraceptive pills, as well as nonprescription

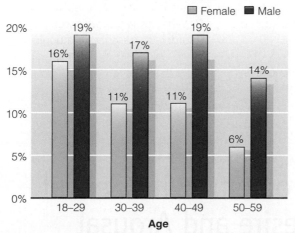

Anxiety About Sexual Performance

FIGURE **14.1** Data from the National Health and Social Life Survey found gender and age differences in self-reported anxiousness about performance during sex.

SOURCE: Laumann et al., 1999.

---

psychotropic medications
Medications prescribed for psychological disorders, such as depression.

drugs, such as alcohol, marijuana, and cocaine, can affect certain aspects of sexual functioning (see Chapter 13 for more information about contraceptive use). Finally, the common physical changes of aging can also affect sexual functioning (see Table 10.2).

Evaluating Challenges to Sexual Functioning

It's important for a sex therapist to understand how a person experiences a sexual problem. For example, have the symptoms always occurred or did they recently develop? A **lifelong sexual dysfunction** is one that has always existed, whereas an **acquired sexual dysfunction** is one that develops after a period of adequate functioning.

Therapists also need to know the context of the problem: Do the symptoms occur only at certain times or in every sexual situation? A **situational sexual dysfunction** is a problem that occurs during certain sexual activities or with certain partners (for instance, a man who can get an erection with his girlfriend but not his wife, or a woman who can have orgasms during masturbation but not during oral sex). A **generalized sexual dysfunction** is a problem that occurs in every situation, during every type of sexual activity, and with every sexual partner. It is important to clarify these differences, for they may affect treatment strategies. For instance, lifelong dysfunctions tend to have more biological or physiological causes, whereas acquired dysfunctions tend to have more psychological causes.

In addition to this information, therapists gather information about contributing psychological and relationship factors. The *DSM-5* includes a group of criteria to explore these issues, including the following:

1. Partner factors (e.g., sexual or health problems in partner)

2. Relationship factors (e.g., different levels of sexual interest or poor communication)

3. Individual vulnerability factors (e.g., body image issues or a history of sexual or emotional abuse), including depression, anxiety, or increased stress (e.g., loss of job, bereavement)

4. Cultural or religious factors

5. Medical factors (e.g., diagnosis or treatment issues)

It's important for therapists to evaluate each of these factors to gain a better understanding of exactly what could be contributing to any sexual disorder.

Sexual Disorders in Transgender People

Although sexual problems can present in similar ways in transgender people, oftentimes medical interventions can contribute to specific sexual disorders (Wylie et al., 2016). Although there are limited studies on sexual disorders in transgender people, it's important for us to consider the available research. Hormonal replacements and genital surgery can affect sexual desire and functioning. After gender affirmation surgery (see Chapter 4), transgender women are more likely than transgender men to experience problems with sexual desire. One study found that 62% of transgender women experienced a decrease in sexual desire after medical transition; 73% reported a lack of responsive sexual desire; and many reported significant distress about these changes (Wierckx et al., 2014). Transgender men, on the other hand, were more likely to experience increases in sexual desire after medical transition. The only exceptions to this were transgender men who underwent and were dissatisfied with their surgery. Dissatisfaction with surgery was more likely to contribute to problems with sexual desire after gender affirmation interventions. This is an area of research that will continue to grow in the future.

Let's now turn our attention to specific problems with sexual desire, arousal, orgasm, and pain during sexual behavior.

Review Questions

1 Identify and describe some of the psychological factors that have been found to interfere with sexual functioning.

2 Identify and describe some of the physiological factors that have been found to interfere with sexual functioning.

3 Explain how sexual dysfunctions are evaluated and how this might affect treatment strategies.

4 What do we know about sexual disorders in transgender people?

---

lifelong sexual dysfunction
A sexual dysfunction that has always existed.

acquired sexual dysfunction
A sexual dysfunction that occurs after a period of normal sexual functioning.

situational sexual dysfunction
A sexual dysfunction that occurs only in specific situations.

generalized sexual dysfunction
A sexual dysfunction that occurs in every sexual situation.

responsive sexual desire
Sexual desire that builds when a person engages in sexual activity.

Problems with Sexual Desire and Arousal

For many people, sexual desire leads them to seek out and initiate sexual activity. For others, sexual desire builds when they engage in sexual activity (referred to as **responsive sexual desire**). Problems with sexual desire and arousal in the *DSM-5* include **sexual interest/arousal disorder** in women and male **hypoactive sexual desire disorder (HSDD)** and **erectile disorder (ED)**. Although the diagnosis of "hypoactive sexual desire disorder" is not listed in the *DSM-5* for women, sometimes it is still used to describe low sexual desire in women.

Problems with sexual desire and arousal are characterized by a deficient or absent interest or arousal for sexual activity, which can lead to both psychological (e.g., a lack of desire) and physiological (e.g., arousal problems such as a lack of lubrication or erection) symptoms. To meet the criteria for an interest/arousal disorder, a person needs to have experienced symptoms 75% to 100% of the time for at least 6 months (American Psychiatric Association, 2013; see Figure 14.2 for more information on the lack of interest in sex). Decreased sexual desire and interest is common in people as they age (Birnbaum et al., 2016; Reis & Abdo, 2014) and some turn to **aphrodisiacs** for help (see the accompanying "Sex in Real Life" feature).

People with desire and arousal disorders experience a lack of sexual fantasies, reduced or absent initiation of sexual activity, and decreased self-stimulation. There has been considerable controversy associated with this diagnosis, primarily because it pathologizes **asexuality**, or the lack of a sexual drive or interest. Although there has been some ambiguity about what asexuality involves, many experts today believe it involves a lack of sexual attraction, rather than a lack of sexual desire (Chasin, 2011). In addition, this lack of sexual attraction typically does not create significant distress for asexuals.

Desire and arousal disorders are considered problematic only when they are persistent and cause significant distress. Sometimes it's not one partner's level of desire that is the problem but the **discrepancy in desire** between the partners. Many couples experience differences in their levels of desire—one partner may desire sex more often than the other. For example, if Lisa wants to have sex once a week but her partner wants sex every day, which partner do you think would be most likely to be diagnosed with a sexual disorder? If you guessed Lisa, you're right. Often the partner with a lower level of desire will show up at a therapist's office and not the partner with higher desire (Rosen & Leiblum, 1987). But if Lisa had a partner with a similar level of desire, there wouldn't be a sexual problem. Below we'll explore desire and arousal disorders, along with available treatments.

Problems with Sexual Desire in Women

Although the prior version of the *DSM* had two separate diagnoses for desire and arousal disorders in women, these were combined into one category of sexual interest/arousal in the *DSM-5*. This was mainly because many experts had found that desire and arousal problems were highly interrelated in women (Sarin et al., 2016). Criteria for sexual interest/arousal disorder involve absent or decreased sexual interest and erotic thoughts or fantasies, as well as decreased or absent initiation of sexual activity or responsiveness to a partner's attempts to initiate; sexual excitement and pleasure; response to sexual cues; and/or physical sensations during sexual activity (e.g., vasocongestion and vaginal lubrication).

Female desire/arousal disorders are one of the most prevalent types of female sexual dysfunctions (McCabe & Goldhammer, 2013; Parish & Hahn, 2016). In fact, a nationally representative sample of U.S. women found that 27% of premenopausal women and 52% of naturally menopausal women experienced such

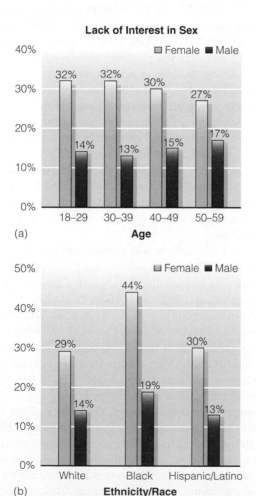

(a) Age

(b) Ethnicity/Race

FIGURE **14.2** Data from the National Health and Social Life Survey found gender differences in levels of self-reported lack of interest in sex in (a) various age and (b) ethnic/racial groups.
SOURCE: Laumann et al., 1999.

sexual interest/arousal disorder
A category of sexual dysfunctions that involves a lack of sexual interest and/or arousal in women.

hypoactive sexual desire disorder (HSDD)
A sexual dysfunction that involves diminished or absent sexual interest or desire in men.

erectile disorder (ED)
A sexual dysfunction that involves a diminished or absent ability to attain or maintain an adequate erection.

aphrodisiac
A substance that increases, or is believed to increase, a person's sexual desire.

asexuality
A condition in which a person does not experience sexual attraction to others. Unlike celibacy or abstinence, which are chosen, asexuality is an intrinsic part of who a person is.

discrepancy in desire
Differences in levels of sexual desire in a couple.

problems (West et al., 2008). Other studies have found rates between 7% and 15% in adult women (Rosen et al., 2012). Many of the inconsistencies in rates of desire disorders in women often have to do with how the problem is defined and measured. It's also important to keep in mind that due to embarrassment issues, less than half of women with sexual problems seek help or initiate discussions with their health care providers (Parish & Hahn, 2016).

There are many things that can affect a woman's sexual interest/arousal, including partner and relationship factors, such as a lack of attraction to one's partner, partner illness or health problems, marital or relationship conflicts, and differences in sexual interest. Individual issues, such as depression, anxiety, stress, a negative body image, negative messages about sex while growing up, eating disorders, fear of intimacy or pregnancy, or a concern over loss of control can also contribute (Rellini & Meston, 2011; Thomas & Thurston, 2016). A history of sexual or emotional abuse can also be contributing factors (Kelley & Gidycz, 2016; Meston & Lorenz, 2013).

A variety of physiological factors, including chronic illness, hormonal problems, medication side effects, chronic use of alcohol, and treatment for various illnesses may also contribute to decreased sexual desire and arousal (Basson et al., 2010; Ho et al., 2011; Ochsenkühn et al., 2011; Smith, 2010). Let's look at the various treatment options for desire disorders in women.

Treating Sexual Desire and Arousal Disorders in Women

Many therapists consider desire and arousal disorders in women to be some of the most complicated sexual problems to treat. In the United States, treatment of most sexual disorders begins with a medical history and workup to identify any physiological causes. A psychological evaluation will explore partner, relationship, individual, religious, and cultural issues, as well as any past sexual trauma or abuse that may interfere with sexual desire or interest. After identifying potential causes, the next step is to determine a plan of treatment. Such treatment may be **multimodal**, involving more than one type of therapy.

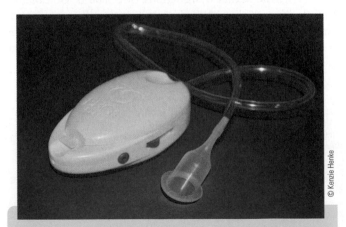

The EROS-CTD is a handheld device that increases blood flow to the clitoris. The plastic cup is placed directly over the clitoris during use and a gentle suction causes genital vasocongestion.

A variety of different treatment options are available. Cognitive–behavioral therapy, a form of psychotherapy that emphasizes the importance of how a person thinks and the effect these thoughts have on a person's feelings and behaviors, has offered promising results. These types of therapy are brief, highly instructional, and structured. Homework assignments are often assigned to help identify sexual motivations.

Another treatment option involves the EROS clitoral therapy device, which was approved by the FDA in 2000 as a prescription device for female sexual desire disorders (see nearby photo; Wilson et al., 2001). The small, battery-powered device creates a gentle suction on the clitoris and genital area, which increases blood flow and leads to clitoral engorgement. Clitoral engorgement triggers responses in the vaginal nerves, which increases sexual stimulation and sensations, leading to vaginal lubrication. Studies have found that the EROS device can help increase vaginal lubrication and vasocongestion (Billups et al., 2001).

Since the release of Viagra for men in 1998, there has been a rush of research trying to find the magic pill for women. Although some studies have evaluated the use of Viagra in women, overall, it has been found to provide little benefit in the treatment of female sexual desire and arousal disorders (Alexander et al., 2011; Basson et al., 2002). In 2015, the FDA approved the first medication to treat interest/arousal disorders in premenopausal women, Addyi (Flibanserin; Holt & Tingen, 2016; Puppo & Puppo, 2016). Although this medication was originally developed as an antidepressant, it was found to increase neurotransmitters associated with sexual excitement (Jayne et al., 2012; Simon et al., 2014). However, the FDA had rejected the medication twice before it was approved because of safety and efficacy issues. Studies have found that Addyi is modestly effective and reasonably safe (Aftab et al., 2017). However, experts point out that it should be discontinued if there is no improvement in sexual desire after taking the medication for 8 weeks (Joffe et al., 2016). Controversy about the FDA approval of Addyi, whether female sexual desire can be fixed with a pill, and concerns about side effects continue (Chańska & Grunt-Mejer, 2016; Katz, 2016).

In the mid-2000s, there was growing interest in a nasal spray inhaler dubbed PT-141 (bremelanotide) for treatment of female sexual arousal and desire disorders, which showed some promise in increasing sexual interest and behaviors in women by stimulating the central nervous system (Clayton et al., 2016; Safarinejad, 2008). However, because of safety concerns revolving around the nasal spray application of the medication, the FDA discontinued clinical trials in 2008. Other studies have been exploring the use of testosterone and dehydroepiandrosterone (DHEA) to treat sexual desire and arousal disorders in women. While DHEA has yielded some promising outcomes, the results of the studies of testosterone have been contradictory (Achilli et al., 2017; Bloch et al., 2013; Reis & Abdo, 2014). Even so, research continues to explore a variety of pharmacological treatments for women, medications that act on the central nervous system, and alternative methods of testosterone administration (Fabre et al., 2011; Gelman & Atrio,

multimodal
Using a variety of techniques.

Sex in Real Life   What Is an Aphrodisiac?

Throughout history, people from primitive—and not so primitive—cultures have searched for the ultimate aphrodisiac to enhance sexual interest and performance. Oysters, for example, have been reported to increase sexual desire, although this has never been proven. The idea that oysters are an aphrodisiac may have originated from their resemblance to male testicles, or even to female ovaries. Ancient people believed that food with the shape or qualities of the genitals possessed aphrodisiac qualities; seeds of all kinds were associated with fertility and desire.

In various cultures, carrots, cucumbers, chili peppers, rhino horns, and various seafood, as well as eggs and poppy seeds, were thought to increase sexual desire. The market for so-called aphrodisiacs in some countries has added to the decline of some endangered species, such as the rhinoceros, valued for its horn.

In Bangkok, Thailand, a vendor is pushing cobra blood to increase sexual drive. Customers choose their own snake; then the snake is split open with a razor blade. An incision is made in the major artery of the snake, and all the blood is drained into a wineglass. The blood is then mixed with warm whiskey and a dash of honey. Users believe it is an aphrodisiac.

There are no proven aphrodisiacs, but it is possible that if a person thinks something will increase their sexual desire, it just might do so (Shamloul, 2010). Simply believing something will increase desire may cause it to work. Overall, to increase sexual desire, rely on regular exercise, a healthy diet, candlelight, the use of scents, romantic music, and whatever else enhances your personal sexual arousal. Following are some of the most popular substances that have been thought to increase sexual desire.

Alcohol: Although some people believe that alcohol increases their sexual desire, in actuality, it merely decreases anxiety and inhibitions, and then only in low doses. In large amounts, alcohol can impair sexual functioning.

Amyl nitrate: Amyl nitrate (also called "snappers" or "poppers") is inhaled from capsules that are "popped" open for quick use. Amyl nitrate causes a rapid dilation of arteries that supply the heart and other organs with blood, including the brain, causing euphoria or giddiness. It is also thought to relax the involuntary smooth muscles, such as the throat and anus, and increase orgasmic sensations. Adverse effects include severe dizziness, migraine headaches, sweating, and fainting.

Bufo toad: Various toads, including the Bufo toad, secrete toxins from their skin in an effort to protect themselves from predators. Some believe these toxins have aphrodisiac qualities, although studies have found they can cause heart attacks and death (West & Krychman, 2015).

Cocaine: Thought to increase frequency of sexual behavior, sexual desire, and orgasmic sensations. In actuality, cocaine may reduce inhibitions, possibly leading to risky sexual behaviors. Long-term use can result in depression, addiction, and increased anxiety.

Ginseng: An herb that has been thought to increase sexual desire. Preliminary research has found it may have some positive aphrodisiac properties, but more research is needed to confirm (Shamloul, 2010).

Marijuana: Many states have legalized reactional use of marijuana, and users believe it enhances sexual desire, sexual stamina, and orgasmic intensity, while reducing inhibitions and improving mood. While research does support the relaxing effects of marijuana (Ramikie et al., 2014), there are no proven studies documenting improved sexual functioning.

Methamphetamine: Methamphetamine (also known as "crystal meth" or "ice") is a stimulant that is used recreationally as a potent aphrodisiac. It often has long-lasting euphoric effects that increase sexual desire, allowing users to engage in prolonged sexual activity (Hittner, 2016). Methamphetamine can be smoked, injected, snorted, swallowed, or inserted into the anus or urethra. It is a highly addictive drug that can lead to various adverse side effects, including convulsions, heart palpitations, tremors, profuse sweating, hallucinations, paranoia, extreme aggression, dry mouth ("meth mouth"), acne, facial sores, and even death. Over time, the use of methamphetamine destroys dopamine receptors in the brain, making it impossible to feel pleasure.

Spanish fly: Consists of ground-up beetle wings (cantharides) from Europe and causes inflammation of the urinary tract and dilation of the blood vessels. Although some people find the burning sensation arousing, Spanish fly may cause death from its toxic side effects. Studies have found the risks associated with Spanish fly use outweigh any potential benefits (West & Krychman, 2015).

Yohimbine: From the African yohimbe tree. Preliminary research has found it may have some mild aphrodisiac properties, but this does not support its widespread use (Shamloul, 2010). Side effects include elevated blood pressure, increased heart rate, and anxiety (West & Krychman, 2015).

2017; Min, 2014). **Vasoactive agents** are also being explored, including Vasomax, or phentolamine. These agents have been found to increase physiological sexual arousal by stimulating vaginal lubrication (Min, 2014; Sun et al., 2014).

---

vasoactive agent
Medication that causes dilation of the blood vessels.

IN OUR WORLD

Sex therapy in the United States has been criticized for its adherence to Western sexual attitudes and values, with an almost total ignorance of cultural differences in sexual problems and therapy. Our view of sex tends to emphasize that activity is pleasurable (or at least natural), both partners are equally involved, couples need and want to be educated about sex, and communication is important to have good sexual relationships (Lavee, 1991; So & Cheung, 2005). It is important to recognize, however, that these ideas might not be shared outside the United States or within different ethnic groups; therefore, Masters and Johnson's classic therapy model is much less acceptable to these groups. Sexual goals are different among cultural groups with an egalitarian ideology than among those without (Lau et al., 2005). An egalitarian ideology views mutual sexual pleasure and communication as important, whereas nonegalitarian ideologies view heterosexual intercourse as the goal and men's sexual pleasure as more important than women's (Reiss, 1986). Double standards of sexual pleasure are common, for example, in many Portuguese, Mexican, Puerto Rican, and Latino groups. Some Asian groups also often have strong cultural prohibitions about discussing sexuality. Relying on U.S. values such as open communication, mutual satisfaction, and accommodation to a partner's sexuality may not be appropriate in working with people from these cultures.

In cultures where low female desire is not seen as a problem, sexual interest/arousal disorder wouldn't be viewed as a sexual problem; it would be an acceptable part of female sexuality. In some Muslim groups, for example, the only problems that exist are those that interfere with men's sexual behavior (Lavee, 1991).

Approaches to sexual problems also differ outside the United States. For example, in Cuernavaca, Mexico, many working-class men who experience ED reject the use of erectile medications, believing that "mature" sexuality involves a focus on family and home instead of sexual functioning (Wentzell, 2013). Some cultures believe in supernatural causes of sexual disorders (such as the man being cursed by a powerful woman or being given the evil eye; So & Cheung, 2005). Malay and Chinese men who experience erectile disorders tend to blame their wives for the problem, whereas Indian men attribute their problem to fate (Low et al., 2002). However, Asian culture has also produced the Tantric ceremonial sexual ritual, which might be viewed as therapy for sexual disorders.

Tantric sex involves five exercises (Voigt, 1991). First, a couple begins by developing a private ritual to prepare them to share sexual expression: the lighting of candles; using perfume, lotions, music, a special bed or room; certain lighting patterns; massage; reciting poetry together; or meditating. Then they synchronize their breathing by lying together and "getting in touch" with each other. Direct eye contact is sustained throughout the ritual. (Couples often say that they feel uncomfortable using eye contact, but with practice it becomes very powerful.)

Next, "motionless intercourse" begins, in which the couple remains motionless at the peak of the sensual experience. For many couples, this may be during the time of initial penetration. Initially, this motionlessness may last only a few minutes, building up to increasingly longer periods. The final aspect of the Tantric ritual is to expand the sexual exchange without orgasm, resulting in an intensification of the sexual–spiritual energy (this is similar to Masters and Johnson's technique of delaying orgasm to enjoy the physical sensations of touching and caressing).

A variety of herbal products are available for female sexual desire and arousal disorders, including Lyriana, a nonprescription daily supplement, and Zestra, a botanical massage oil formulated to increase female arousal and pleasure. Studies have found that Zestra can increase sexual desire, arousal, and sexual satisfaction, although there are side effects associated with these products (Ferguson et al., 2003, 2010). Alura, an amino acid–based cream that contains menthol, has also been used for problems with sexual desire in women. The makers of Alura claim that when it is applied to the clitoris, blood flow increases through dilation of clitoral blood vessels. Studies are also testing other agents to increase female sexual arousal, including the aphrodisiac **yohimbine** (yo-HIM-bean). Yohimbine is a substance produced in the bark of the African yohimbe tree, which has been found to improve sexual functioning. Although these products do not require FDA approval, more research is needed to assess their possible adverse effects, including dizziness, irritation, and/or increased blood pressure. Despite a great deal of research, few of these hormonal and vasoactive agents have withstood scientific scrutiny (Perelman, 2007). In addition, safety issues have not been addressed for many of these products, adding to concerns of potential harm that these products may produce.

Finally, other recommendations for inclusion in the *DSM-5* that were not included in the final version were **hypersexual disorder** and **persistent sexual arousal syndrome**. Hypersexual disorder involves recurrent and intense sexual fantasies, sexual urges, and sexual behavior, which causes significant distress and can impair social, occupational, or other areas of functioning (Montgomery-Graham, 2016). Persistent sexual arousal syndrome involves an excessive and unremitting level of sexual arousal. Genital arousal can last for hours or days despite a lack of sexual desire or stimulation and can be distressing and worrisome to women, although many may be reluctant to discuss it with health care providers (Jackowich et al., 2016; Levin & Wylie, 2010). There was controversy over the fact that these diagnoses were not included

---

yohimbine
Produced from the bark of the African yohimbe tree; often used as an aphrodisiac.

hypersexual disorder
Recurrent and intense sexual fantasies, sexual urges, and sexual behavior.

persistent sexual arousal syndrome
An excessive and unremitting level of sexual arousal. May also be referred to as persistent genital arousal disorder.

in the *DSM-5* (Katehakis, 2012; Reid, 2015). While some believed that they were both "sex negative" diagnoses that shouldn't be listed in the *DSM*, others believed that omitting them could affect how therapists work with sexually compulsive patients. In addition, treatment for these problems could be inaccessible since it would not be covered by insurance (typically treatment for disorders listed in the *DSM* is covered by many insurance plans). More research is needed to shed light on these disorders.

Problems with Sexual Desire and Arousal in Men

The problems with sexual desire and arousal in men include hypoactive sexual desire disorder (HSDD) and erectile disorder (ED). While HSDD is characterized by a deficient or absent desire for sexual activity in men, ED refers to the inability to obtain or maintain an erection sufficient for sexual penetration. ED can occur with or without HSDD. Although there has not been a great deal of research on HSDD in men, studies have found that low sexual desire can be distressing to many men (Derogatis et al., 2012). As with desire/arousal disorders in women, a diagnosis requires that a man experiences desire/arousal symptoms 75% to 100% of the time for at least 6 months (American Psychiatric Association, 2013).

Although low sexual desire is more common in women than in men, studies have found that approximately 20% of men are affected by HSDD (Rubio-Aurioles & Bivalacqua, 2013). Since many people believe that sexual interest and desire are integral parts of masculinity, a loss of sexual desire in men can trigger many negative emotions. In addition, partners of men with HSDD may be distressed by the lack of physical affection and touch.

Erectile disorder, an arousal disorder, involves persistent or recurrent inability to attain, or maintain, an erection adequate for sexual activity. Erectile disorder is one of the most common sexual problems in men, and the incidence increases with age (see Figure 14.3). Whereas 12% of men younger than 59 experience ED, 22% of men aged 60 to 69, and 30% of men older than 69

experience ED (Bacon et al., 2003; Costabile et al., 2008; Liu et al., 2010; Lue, 2000). Erectile disorder can be lifelong or, more commonly, acquired. It can also be generalized (occurring in every sexual situation) or situational (occurring only in certain types of sexual situations).

Normal erectile functioning involves neurological, endocrine, vascular, and muscular factors. Many physiological factors can affect erectile functioning including hormones, vascular or neurological problems, chronic illnesses, alcoholism, obesity, smoking, injuries, as well as prescription and nonprescription medication use.

In addition to physical factors, erectile functioning can be affected by depression, anxiety, stress, body image issues, performance anxiety, fear of failure, and a history of sexual/emotional abuse. Anxiety has been found to have a cyclical effect on erectile functioning: If a man experiences a problem getting an erection one night, the next time he engages in sexual behavior he remembers the failure and becomes anxious. This anxiety, in turn, interferes with his ability to have an erection. These problems can occur even when a person reports adequate focus, intensity, and duration of sexual stimulation. Partner and relationship factors such as sexual problems in a partner, different levels of sexual interest, and poor communication can also contribute to erectile problems, as can cultural and religious issues.

Overall, EDs in younger men (20–35 years old) are more likely to be psychologically based, whereas EDs in older men (60 and older) are more likely to be due to physical factors (Lue, 2000). In many cases, it's a combination of both.

ON YOUR MIND

Is erectile disorder hereditary?

No, erectile disorder itself is not hereditary. However, certain diseases, such as diabetes, may be inherited and can lead to an erectile disorder or other sexual disorders. It is important to catch these diseases early so that medical intervention can decrease any possible sexual adverse effects.

REAL RESEARCH The regular use of pornography, along with masturbation, has been found to contribute to decreased sexual desire for partnered sex in men (CARVALHEIRA ET AL., 2015; we will discuss the use of pornography in Chapter 18).

To help clarify the causes of erectile disorder, health care providers and sex therapists may use tests such as the **nocturnal penile tumescence test**. Since men normally experience two or three erections a night during stages of rapid eye movement (REM) sleep, if these erections do not occur this could indicate a physiological problem. Alternatively, if erections do occur during

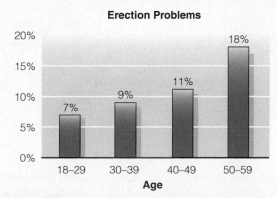

FIGURE **14.3** Data from the National Health and Social Life Survey found that the prevalence of erection problems in men increases with age.
SOURCE: Laumann et al., 1999.

nocturnal penile tumescence test
A study performed to evaluate erections during sleep that helps clarify the causes of erectile disorder.

the night but not during sexual activity, this may indicate psychological causes (Elhanbly et al., 2009). The nocturnal penile tumescence test requires a man to spend the night in a sleep laboratory, but newer devices, such as a RigiScan or stamp tests, allow men to monitor sleep erections in the privacy of their own homes.

Treating Sexual Desire Disorders in Men

Of all the sexual dysfunctions, there are more treatment options for male erectile disorder than for any other disorder. A tremendous amount of research has been dedicated to finding causes and treatment options for ED. Depending on the cause, treatment for ED includes psychological treatment, pharmacological treatment (drugs), hormonal and intracavernous injections, vascular surgery, vacuum constriction devices, and prosthesis implantation. Let's explore each of these treatment options.

REAL RESEARCH Sexual functioning may be affected by a partner's sexual disorder, leading to the development of other sexual problems. In fact, it is common for sexual disorders to coexist in couples even though there may only be awareness or focus just on one partner's sexual problem (WEEKS ET AL., 2016).

The primary psychological treatments for ED include **systematic desensitization** and sex therapy that includes education, **sensate focus**, and communication training (Heiman, 2002). These treatments can help reduce feelings of anxiety and can evaluate issues that are interfering with erectile response. Relationship therapy can also help explore issues in a relationship that might contribute to ED, such as unresolved anger, bitterness, or guilt.

Pharmacological action, including erectile medications, can treat erectile disorder. The first oral medication for ED, Viagra, was approved by the FDA in 1998, and since then, four other medications have received FDA approval to treat erectile disorder: Cialis, Levitra, Staxyn, and Stendra. In 2016, the FDA approved the first generic version of Viagra (Brennan, 2016). These medications can be used in a variety of ED cases—those that are **psychogenic** (sike-oh-JEN-nick), illness related, or have physical causes. These medications are often considered the first line of treatment for ED (Eardley, 2010; Palit & Eardley, 2010).

All of these drugs produce muscle relaxation in the penis, dilation of the arteries supplying the penis, and an inflow of blood, which can lead to penile erection. They do not increase a man's sexual desire and will not produce an erection without adequate sexual stimulation. Typically, they must be taken 30 to 60 minutes before sexual activity. Improvements in erections can last up to 4 hours, although Cialis can aid in erections for up to 36 hours (Japsen, 2003; Morales et al., 2011).

Erectile medications have several potential adverse effects, including headaches, a flushing in the cheeks and neck, nasal congestion, and indigestion. Less common adverse effects include an increased risk for vision problems, including changes in color vision and possible total vision loss, and ringing in the ears or total hearing loss (Martins et al., 2015; Mukherjee & Shivakumar, 2007; Sajjad & Weng, 2016). Critics of pharmacological treatment for ED point out that drug use focuses solely on an erection and fails to take into account the multidimensional nature of male sexuality (B. W. McCarthy & Fucito, 2005).

Earlier we discussed the use of yohimbine in the treatment of sexual desire disorders in women. Yohimbine has also been found to improve erections and can be successfully used with various erectile medications (Tanweer et al., 2010; Zhang et al., 2010). It works by stimulating the parasympathetic nervous system, which is linked to erectile functioning. Adverse effects include dizziness, nervousness, irritability, and an increased heart rate and blood pressure. In addition, nitroglycerin and nitrates have been used to treat ED (Wimalawansa, 2008).

Hormonal treatments are also used to improve erectile functioning in men who have hormonal irregularities (Lue, 2000). A man with low testosterone levels can be prescribed testosterone therapy through injections, patches, gels, creams, or oral delivery. An FDA-approved testosterone patch is applied directly to the scrotum, whereas gels and creams can be applied to other parts of the body such as the arms or stomach. AndroGel, a clear, colorless, odorless gel, was approved by the FDA in 2000 for the treatment of low testosterone (Morley & Perry, 2000). It is applied daily and is absorbed into the skin. Another FDA-approved testosterone method, Striant, is a tablet that adheres to the roof of the mouth and time-releases testosterone into the body. Adverse effects are rare but include headaches, acne, depression, gynecomastia, and hypertension. More serious risks include strokes, heart attacks, and death. In fact, in 2016, the FDA announced that all manufacturers of testosterone must include a label that warns users about the dangers associated

systematic desensitization
A treatment method for sexual disorders that involves neutralizing the anxiety-producing aspects of sexual situations and behavior by a process of gradual exposure.

sensate focus
A series of touching experiences that are assigned to couples in sex therapy

to teach nonverbal communication and reduce anxiety.

psychogenic
Relating to psychological causes.

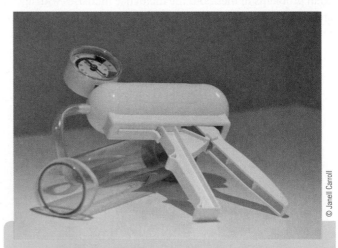

Vacuum constriction devices, such as the ErecAid, are often used in the treatment of erectile disorder. A man places his penis in the cylinder and vacuum suction increases blood flow to the penis, creating an erection.

© Janell Carroll

with the use of testosterone ("FDA Drug Safety Communication," 2016). Even though research has not been able to show a consistent and beneficial role of testosterone in increasing sexual functioning in men, these medications are commonly used to treat erectile disorder (Allan et al., 2008; Isidori et al., 2005). Interestingly, the majority of men who experience low sexual desire have normal levels of testosterone (Wespes & Schulman, 2002).

Another FDA-approved treatment for erectile disorder involves **intracavernous** (in-truh-CAV-er-nuss) **injections** (Alexandre et al., 2007; Lue, 2000). Men self-inject these preparations directly into the corpora cavernosa (see Chapter 6) while the penis is gently stretched out. The medication causes the blood vessels to relax, increasing blood flow to the penis. Erections typically occur within 20 minutes and can last for an hour and a half. Side effects include priapism, pain, bleeding, or bruising (Alexandre et al., 2007; Israilov et al., 2002).

Surgical intervention has increased as a treatment for ED. In some cases, physicians perform **revascularization** to improve erectile functioning; in other cases, **prosthesis** (pross-THEE-sis) **implantation** may be recommended. Today there are two main types of implants: **semirigid rods**, which provide a permanent state of erection but can be bent up and down; and inflatable devices that become firm when the man pumps them up (Simmons & Montague, 2008). Penetrative sexual behaviors may safely be engaged in 4 to 8 weeks after surgery. After prosthesis implantation, a man is still able to orgasm, ejaculate, and impregnate.

Sexual satisfaction after a prosthesis implantation has been found to be related to several factors, such as a man's relationship with his partner and feelings about his own masculinity (Vakalopoulos et al., 2013). While many couples report increased sexual satisfaction after surgery, between 10% and 20% of patients remain dissatisfied, dysfunctional, or sexually inactive (Minervini et al., 2006). If a man has psychological factors that contribute to his

ON YOUR MIND

A couple of guys I know have some Viagra, and they have been trying to get me to take it. Is it safe to use this drug if you don't have ED?

Although recreational use of Viagra and other erectile drugs is not uncommon, it does not always live up to expectations. Men who use these drugs are often disappointed because it doesn't always lead to longer and firmer erections, and it can often contribute to physical adverse effects, such as harmful changes in blood pressure (Crosby & Diclemente, 2004; Eloi-Stiven et al., 2007; Fisher et al., 2006; Musacchio et al., 2006). Men who use these drugs recreationally are more likely to engage in unsafe sex compared with those not using these drugs, which puts them at greater risk for sexually transmitted infections (Harte & Meston, 2011). They also may become dependent on the medications for erections (Harte & Meston, 2011). Finally, it's also important to point out that Internet sites that claim to sell authentic Viagra often ship counterfeit medications instead (Campbell et al., 2012).

erectile difficulties, these issues are likely to resurface after a prosthesis is implanted.

Vacuum constriction devices, which use suction to induce erections, have become more popular over the last few years, in part because they are less invasive and safer than injections. One such device, the ErecAid System, involves putting the flaccid penis into a vacuum cylinder and pumping it to draw blood into the corpora cavernosa (similar to the one Austin Powers was caught with in the movie *Austin Powers: International Man of Mystery*). A constriction ring is rolled onto the base of the penis after it is removed from the vacuum device to keep the blood in the penis. This ring is left on the penis until the erection is no longer desired. Negative side effects include possible bruising and, in rare cases, testicular entrapment in the vacuum chamber (Lue, 2000). Overall, these devices can be expensive, bulky, and noisy, and they reduce spontaneity, which some couples find unappealing.

REAL RESEARCH Injuries to the male genitalia, including the penis, scrotum, testes, and/or urethra, from underground explosive devices are common among U.S. service members who were deployed to Iraq and Afghanistan (Janak et al., 2017). These genital injuries often contribute to sexual dysfunctions, although sexual problems may not be addressed during medical care.

© Kenzie Henke

Semirigid prostheses are surgically implanted in the penis and can enable a man with erectile disorder to have an erection suitable for penetrative sexual behavior.

intracavernous injection
A treatment method for erectile disorder in which vasodilating drugs are injected into the penis for the purpose of creating an erection.

revascularization
A procedure used in the treatment of vascular erectile disorder in which the vascular system is rerouted to ensure better blood flow to the penis.

prosthesis implantation
A treatment method for erectile disorder in which a prosthesis is surgically implanted into the penis.

semirigid rod
A flexible rod that is implanted into the penis during prosthetic surgery.

vacuum constriction device
Treatment device for erectile disorder used to pull blood into the penis.

Review Questions

1 Identify and explain the problems with sexual desire in people.

2 Define sexual interest/arousal disorder in women. What are the criteria for this sexual dysfunction?

3 Identify possible treatment strategies for desire disorders in women.

4 Define HSDD in men. What are the criteria for this sexual dysfunction?

5 Define ED. What are the criteria for this sexual dysfunction?

6 Identify and explain tests used to diagnose male ED and the possible treatment options.

Problems with Orgasm

Every individual reaches orgasm differently and has different wants and needs to build sexual excitement. Some people need very little stimulation, while others need a great deal of stimulation. Some people never reach orgasm. The *DSM-5* includes one orgasm disorder in women, female **orgasmic disorder**, and two in men, **early ejaculation** and **delayed ejaculation**. Let's explore these disorders.

Problems with Orgasm in Women

Historically, a woman who had problems with orgasm was referred to as "frigid," which implied a lack of emotional warmth. The *DSM-5* defines female orgasmic disorder as a marked delay in, marked infrequency of, or absence of orgasm. Orgasmic disorders are a common complaint among women, and studies have found that approximately one quarter of women report problems reaching orgasm (Ishak et al., 2010; Laumann et al., 1994; Meston et al., 2004). However, it's important to point out that many women are not able to reach orgasm during penetration since it typically does not provide enough clitoral stimulation. You can see why clear definitions are important. A woman who cannot reach orgasm during penetration because of inadequate stimulation probably wouldn't be classified as having a sexual dysfunction. Lifelong orgasmic disorder describes a condition in which a woman has never had an orgasm, while acquired orgasmic disorder is a condition in which a woman was able to have orgasms previously but then develops problems reaching orgasm. Situational orgasmic disorder refers to a condition in which a woman can have orgasms only with one type of stimulation, while a global orgasmic disorder encompasses all types of stimulation. Studies have found that problems with

orgasm may be related to educational levels. Those with higher levels of education report lower levels of orgasmic problems (Figure 14.4).

Women with orgasmic disorders, compared with orgasmic women, often report less relationship satisfaction and lower levels of emotional closeness (González et al., 2006). They also have more difficulties in asking their partners for direct clitoral stimulation, discussing how slow or fast they want to go, or how hard or soft stimulation should be. Some women worry about what their partners might think if they make sexual suggestions or feel uncomfortable receiving stimulation (such as cunnilingus or manual stimulation) without stimulating their partners at the same time. Distracting thoughts, such as "his hand must be falling asleep" or "she can't be enjoying this," can increase existing anxiety and interfere with orgasm (Birnbaum et al., 2001; Kelly et al., 1990).

REAL RESEARCH A nationally representative study of U.S. women found that although 40% of women reported experiencing low sexual desire, decreased sexual arousal, and/or problems reaching orgasm, only 12% indicated these issues were a source of personal distress (SHIFREN ET AL., 2008).

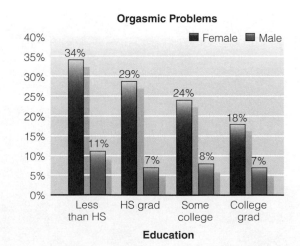

Orgasmic Problems

■ Female ■ Male

FIGURE **14.4** Data from the National Health and Social Life Survey found that although women report more orgasmic problems than men overall, higher levels of education are negatively associated with orgasmic problems in both men and women.

SOURCE: Laumann et al., 1999.

---

orgasmic disorder
A delay or absence of orgasm after a normal phase of sexual excitement.

early ejaculation
Pattern of ejaculating with minimal sexual stimulation before, on, or shortly after penetration and before the person

wishes it (also referred to as premature ejaculation).

delayed ejaculation
An orgasm disorder characterized by a delay, an infrequency, or the absence of ejaculation.

Physical factors can also contribute to female orgasmic disorder. Severe chronic illness and disorders such as diabetes, neurological problems, hormonal deficiencies, and alcoholism can all interfere with orgasmic response. Certain prescription drugs can also impair this response. For example, some women who take certain psychotropic drugs, including many types of antidepressants, experience delayed or absent orgasms (Labbate, 2008).

Treating Problems with Orgasm in Women

Today, the majority of treatment programs for orgasmic disorder involve a combination of different treatment approaches, such as homework assignments, sex education, communication skills training, cognitive restructuring, desensitization, and other techniques. The most effective treatment for female orgasmic disorder was developed by LoPiccolo and Lobitz (1972) and involves teaching a woman to masturbate to orgasm.

On a psychological level, masturbation also helps increase the pleasurable anticipation of sex. Education, self-exploration, communication training, and body awareness are also included in masturbation training for orgasmic problems. Masturbation exercises begin with a woman examining her body and vulva with mirrors. Then she is instructed to find which areas of her body feel the most pleasurable when touched and to stroke them. If this does not result in orgasm, a vibrator is used. As a woman progresses through these stages, she may involve her sexual partner so that the partner is able to learn which areas are more sensitive than others.

Although masturbation training is the most effective treatment for female orgasmic disorder, some therapists do not incorporate it into their treatment for a variety of reasons (including patient or therapist discomfort). Interestingly, improving orgasmic responses does not always increase sexual satisfaction. Heterosexual women may report increased satisfaction with vaginal intercourse over masturbation because it provides more intimacy and closeness (Jayne, 1981), even though masturbation may be a better means of reaching orgasm (Dodson, 1993).

Two additional treatments involve systematic desensitization and **bibliotherapy**. Both of these have been found to be helpful in cases in which there is a great deal of sexual anxiety. In systematic desensitization, events that cause anxiety are recalled into imagination; then a relaxation technique is used to decrease the anxiety. With enough repetition and practice, eventually the anxiety- producing events lose the ability to create anxiety. Both masturbation training and systematic desensitization have been found to be effective; however, masturbation training has higher effectiveness rates (Heiman & Meston, 1997).

Bibliotherapy, which uses written works as therapy, has also been found to be helpful for not only orgasmic disorders but other disorders as well. It can help a person regain some control and understand the problems they are experiencing. Although the results

may be short-lived, bibliotherapy has been found to improve sexual functioning (van Lankveld et al., 2001).

Problems with Orgasm in Men

Although ejaculation and orgasm are controlled by separate physiological processes (see Chapter 6), these have been merged into one category of orgasm problems in the *DSM* since they typically occur at the same time. Problems with orgasm in men typically involve ejaculation issues, including early or delayed ejaculation. The ejaculatory process is controlled by various endocrine factors, including testosterone, oxytocin, prolactin, and thyroid hormones (Corona et al., 2011). In the following subsections, we discuss these problems with orgasm.

ON YOUR MIND

I seem to have problems achieving orgasm with my partner, yet I am able to with the help of a vibrator. Are there different levels of orgasm? Sometimes it is so deep and complete and emotional; other times it is very satisfying but not to the tips of my toes! Is this normal? I would love to be able to achieve the same satisfaction with my partner as I can by myself or with a vibrator.

Different levels of sexual satisfaction result from orgasms. Orgasms differ based on stress, emotions, thoughts, physical health, menstrual cycles, sexual position, and method of stimulation. However, Masters and Johnson did find that masturbation usually evoked more powerful orgasms than penetration. To experience these orgasms with your partner, you might try masturbating together or using a vibrator with your partner.

Over the years, there have been issues about what to call early ejaculation in men. Some argue it should be called *premature* ejaculation, while others believe it should be called *rapid* ejaculation. Since premature and rapid both have negative connotations, the *DSM-5* recommended changing the term to *early ejaculation*, and we will use this term here. One of the most difficult issues about early ejaculation is how to define it. What does early mean? There weren't enough penile thrusts before orgasm? Not enough time elapsed between penetration and orgasm? A man reached orgasm before his partner did? All of these definitions are problematic because they involve individual differences in sexual functioning. Although the time it takes to ejaculate may vary based on a man's age, sexual experience, health, and stress level, early ejaculation refers to a persistent or recurrent pattern of ejaculation occurring during partnered sexual activity within approximately 1 minute of beginning of sexual activity and before a man wishes it. This last part of the definition is important because if a man believes it's a problem for him, therapists should consider it a problem. Like other sexual dysfunctions, to meet the criteria for early ejaculation, a man needs to have experienced symptoms 75% to 100% of the time for at least 6 months (American Psychiatric Association, 2013).

bibliotherapy
Using books and educational material for the treatment of sexual dysfunctions or other problems.

Early ejaculation is a common sexual disorder, and it can affect men of all ages (Figure 14.5; Linton & Wylie, 2010; Rowland et al., 2010; Serefoglu et al., 2011; Vardi et al., 2008). In the United States, estimates are that close to 30% of men report experiencing early ejaculation in the previous year (Laumann et al., 1994). Early ejaculation can lead to decreases in sexual satisfaction and quality of life for both men and their partners.

Historically, early ejaculation had been considered a psychological disorder (Benson et al., 2009). Psychological factors that can contribute include stress, anxiety, unresolved conflict, guilt, shame, and performance pressures (i.e., wanting to satisfy a partner). Some evolutionary theorists claim that early ejaculation may provide a biological advantage in that a man who ejaculates quickly would be more likely to impregnate a partner than a man who requires prolonged stimulation. Masters and Johnson (1970) originally proposed that early ejaculation develops when a man's early sexual experiences are rushed because of the fear of being caught or discovered. These fears, they believed, could condition a man to ejaculate rapidly. Others have pointed out that early ejaculation occurs in men who are unable to accurately judge their own levels of sexual arousal, which would enable them to use self-control and avoid rapid ejaculation (Kaplan, 1974).

The *DSM-5* included additional criteria about individual and relationship factors that may interfere with ejaculation. Studies have found low levels of relationship satisfaction are related to more severe levels of early ejaculation (McCabe & Connaughton, 2014). In addition, early ejaculation has been found to contribute to higher levels of partner frustration, anger, and disappointment (Revicki et al., 2008). All of these are important to consider in the diagnosis of early ejaculation.

Physiological factors may also contribute to early ejaculation. Research has found that some men might have "hyperexcitability" or an "oversensitivity" of their penis, which prevents them from delaying orgasm. Nerves in the lumbar spine are related to ejaculation, and research continues to explore medications to decrease the increased sensitivity (Benson et al., 2009). Other physiological factors that may contribute to early ejaculation include hormones, infections, as well as prescription and nonprescription drug use. Interestingly, there is also evidence that early ejaculation may have

a genetic component, wherein a male has a higher chance of experiencing it if his father did (Jern et al., 2009).

Another orgasmic disorder in men involves the opposite of early ejaculation—delayed ejaculation. Delayed ejaculation is defined as a delayed, infrequent, or absent ejaculation that has occurred 75% to 100% of the time for at least 6 months. Delayed ejaculation is one of the least understood, least common, and least studied of the sexual dysfunctions (Althof, 2012). It's estimated that less than 3% of men experience it (Perelman & Rowland, 2006). However, those who do experience it often have significant distress and relationship problems related to the problem. Studies have found that many men with delayed ejaculation have a history of high masturbatory activity, lower levels of sexual satisfaction, and higher levels of anxiety and depression (Abdel-Hamid & Saleh, 2011). Many men with delayed ejaculation problems often are pressured to "fake orgasm" with their partners to avoid partner conflict (Althof, 2012).

Delayed ejaculation can be the result of both psychological and physiological factors. Psychological factors include stress, a lack of attraction to one's partner, a strict religious background, atypical masturbation patterns, or past traumatic events such as sexual abuse. Physiological factors include the use of certain drugs and various illnesses, nerve damage, and spinal cord injury (SCI).

Although not specifically listed in the *DSM-5*, another relatively uncommon ejaculatory disorder involves **retrograde ejaculation**, in which the ejaculate empties into the bladder instead of being ejaculated outside the body through the urethra. A man with retrograde ejaculation typically experiences orgasm with little or no ejaculation (also called a "dry orgasm"; Ohl et al., 2008; Rowland et al., 2010). Some experts refer to this condition as **anejaculation**. Although this condition is not harmful, it can be frustrating for a man and can cause infertility issues in couples who are trying to get pregnant (Aust & Lewis-Jones, 2004; Zhao et al., 2004).

Treating Problems with Orgasm in Men

Treatment for orgasmic disorders in men often depends on the duration, context, and causes of the ejaculatory problem. Lifelong and generalized ejaculatory problems are often treated with medications or topical anesthetics, whereas acquired or situational cases might be treated with behavioral therapy, with or without medications (Althof, 2014; DeCarufel, 2017; Waldinger, 2014).

A variety of psychological, topical, and oral therapies have been used to treat early ejaculation, with varying levels of success. A common treatment has been the use of selective serotonin reuptake inhibitors (SSRIs), because a common side effect of these drugs is delayed ejaculation (Bai et al., 2015; Hisasue, 2016; McMahon, 2016). However, these medications need to be taken daily and oftentimes need a couple of months to work. Alternative treatments, including acupuncture and Chinese herbal medicines, have also shown some success in decreasing early ejaculation (Cooper et al., 2017). Although research continues to explore a variety of other drugs for the treatment of early ejaculation, one

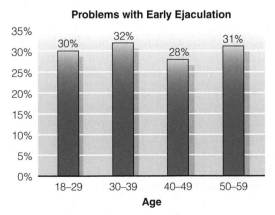

Problems with Early Ejaculation

FIGURE **14.5** Data from the National Health and Social Life Survey found that although early ejaculation is often associated with younger males, it can occur at any age.

SOURCE: Laumann et al., 1999.

retrograde ejaculation	anejaculation
A condition in which the male ejaculate is released into the bladder instead of being ejaculated outside the body through the urethra.	A sexual dysfunction that involves an absence of ejaculation.

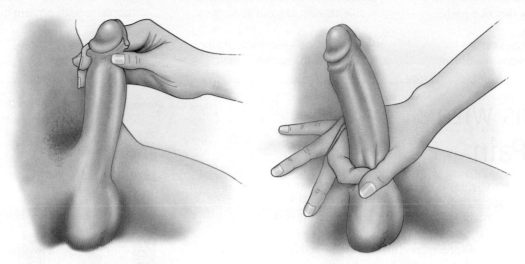

FIGURE **14.6** The squeeze technique is often recommended in the treatment of early ejaculation. Pressure is applied either at the top or to the base of the penis for several seconds until the urge to ejaculate subsides.

promising drug, Dapoxetine, has undergone several large Phase III trials. Originally approved as an antidepressant, Dapoxetine has been found to improve sexual functioning in men with early ejaculation (Corona et al., 2011; Lee et al., 2013; Simsek et al., 2014).

Treatment for early ejaculation may also include the use of behavioral techniques known as the **squeeze** or **stop–start techniques**. Both involve stimulating the penis to the point just before ejaculation. With the squeeze technique, sexual stimulation or masturbation is engaged in until just short of orgasm; then stimulation is stopped. The man or his partner puts a thumb on the frenulum and the first and second fingers on the dorsal side of the penis (Figure 14.6). Pressure is applied for 3 to 4 seconds, until the urge to ejaculate subsides. With the stop–start technique, stimulation is simply stopped until the ejaculatory urge subsides. Stimulation is then repeated up until that point, and this process is repeated over and over. Using these methods, a man can usually gain some control over his erection within 2 to 10 weeks and can have excellent control within several months. Suggested effectiveness rates have been as high as 98%, although it is unclear how this effectiveness is being measured (Masters & Johnson, 1970). In addition, many studies fail to mention whether the treatment permanently solves the problem or if periodic repetition of the techniques is necessary.

Treating Delayed Ejaculation

Treatments for delayed ejaculation include both psychological and physical interventions. Psychological treatments may include homework activities in which a man uses situations in which he is able to achieve ejaculation to help him during situations in which he is not able to ejaculate. For example, if a man can ejaculate during masturbation while fantasizing about being watched during sexual activity, he is told to use this fantasy while he is with his partner. Gradually, the man is asked to incorporate his partner into the sexual fantasy and to masturbate while with the partner.

It can be challenging to treat delayed ejaculation caused by psychological factors. One 43-year-old man shared with me his lifelong problem in reaching orgasm with his partner. He had been sexually abused as a child for many years by an uncle who was a few years older than he. During this abuse, the uncle tried to make him reach orgasm. However, as a boy, he had learned to withhold the orgasmic response. Later on in life, this pattern continued even though he was not consciously trying to do so.

Physical treatments for delayed ejaculation can include changing prescription medications, discontinuing the use of nonprescription drugs or alcohol, or sex therapy. In addition, various drug therapies have been used as treatment, including testosterone, yohimbine, and oxytocin (Abdel-Hamid et al., 2016). A novel treatment uses penile vibratory stimulation, which involves increasing penile sensations during sexual activity with a small vibrator, although more research is needed. A variety of medications, including Bupropion, are being evaluated for the treatment of delayed ejaculation (Abdel-Hamid et al., 2016; Sadowski et al., 2016). Delayed ejaculation can be difficult to treat, and no evidence-based treatments have been proved to eliminate this disorder (Nelson et al., 2007; Richardson et al., 2006).

REAL RESEARCH Sexual problems are common in people who experience posttraumatic stress disorder, which can affect overall sexual activity, desire, arousal, orgasm, and satisfaction (YEHUDA ET AL., 2015).

squeeze technique
A technique in which the ejaculatory reflex is reconditioned using a firm grasp on the penis.

stop–start technique
A technique in which the ejaculatory reflex is reconditioned using intermittent pressure on the glans of the penis.

Review Questions

1 Identify the various problems with orgasm and briefly describe each.

2 Identify the various causes for problems with orgasm in women.

3 Identify the various treatments for problems with orgasm in women.

4 Identify the various causes for problems with orgasm in men.

5 Identify the various treatments for problems with orgasm in men.

Problems with Sexual Pain

Pain during sexual activity, especially penetration, is common. However, the pain is often temporary or occurs only once in a while. Sexual pain disorders typically cause ongoing pain that leads to significant distress. While the prior version of the *DSM* had two categories of pain disorders, **vaginismus** (vadg-ih-NISS-muss) and **dyspareunia** (diss-par-ROON-ee-uh), the revised *DSM-5* collapsed these into one diagnosis called **genito-pelvic pain and penetration disorder**. This was done mainly because vaginismus and dyspareunia often co-occurred and were difficult to distinguish. While the *DSM* does not formally recognize sexual pain in men, there is evidence that some men experience pelvic pain associated with sexual behavior (Davis et al., 2009). Experts suspect male pelvic pain is caused by prostatitis (a swelling of the prostate gland). Much more research is needed in this area.

Problems with Sexual Pain in Women

Women with genito-pelvic pain and penetration disorder often experience one of the following symptoms: an inability to engage in vaginal penetration; significant vaginal or pelvic pain during vaginal penetration; marked fear or anxiety about vaginal/pelvic pain or vaginal penetration; and marked tensing of the pelvic floor muscles during vaginal penetration. To

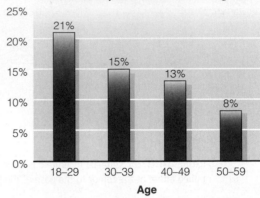

Women's Experience of Pain During Sex

FIGURE **14.7** Data from the National Health and Social Life Survey found that younger women self-report more pain during sex than older women, although older women are less likely to be sexually active than younger women.
SOURCE: Laumann et al., 1999.

meet the criteria for a genito-pelvic pain and penetration disorder, a woman needs to have experienced symptoms 75% to 100% of the time for at least 6 months (American Psychiatric Association, 2013).

The **pubococcygeus** (pub-oh-cock-SIGH-gee-us) **muscle** surrounds the entrance to the vagina and controls the vaginal opening. Involuntary spasms of this muscle can make penetration painful and virtually impossible (Lahaie et al., 2010; Ozdemir et al., 2008; Rosenbaum, 2011). Many women tolerate the sexual pain to meet their partner's needs or expectations. These conditions may be situation-specific, meaning that a woman may be able to allow penetration under certain circumstances but not in others (e.g., during a pelvic examination but not during sex; LoPiccolo & Stock, 1986). It is estimated that between 4% and 42% of women have experienced involuntary spasms of the vaginal muscles (Hope et al., 2010), whereas approximately 15% of heterosexual women report experiencing pain during penetration (Ben-Aroya & Edwards, 2015; Laumann et al., 1999; see Figure 14.7).

ON YOUR MIND

Why do women fake orgasms rather than honestly telling their partners what they are doing wrong?

Faking orgasms often occurs as a result of a sexual problem. A person who experiences problems with orgasm or delayed ejaculation may think that faking an orgasm is the best way to end the sexual activity or to please the partner. However, such deceptions are not healthy in a committed relationship, and partners are generally advised to discuss any sexual problems they have instead of covering them up. Some people may have difficulties communicating sexual needs and desires. So instead of talking to their partners about what sexually excites them, they hope that their partners just know what to do. However, what feels best to one person may not feel good to another, and what feels good may change over time. Many variables can also interfere with sexual pleasure, such as stress, fatigue, anxiety, or depression. It is important that couples communicate their desires so that their sex life is satisfying for both of them.

vaginismus
Involuntary spasms of the muscles around the vagina in response to attempts at penetration.

dyspareunia
Genital pain associated with sexual behavior.

genito-pelvic pain and penetration disorder
A category of sexual dysfunctions that involve persistent or recurrent difficulties with penetrative sex, pelvic pain, and/or fear or anxiety about pelvic pain, which causes significant distress.

pubococcygeus muscle
A muscle that surrounds and supports the vagina.

Sexual pain can occur before, during, or after sexual behavior and may range from slight pain to severe. When severe, it can make sexual behavior and penetration difficult, if not impossible. One woman had been in a relationship with her partner for more than 3 years, but they had never been able to engage in penile–vaginal intercourse because she felt as if her vagina "was closed up" (Author's files). Penetration of her vagina with her partner's fingers was possible and enjoyable, but once penile penetration was attempted, her vagina was impenetrable. She also had a history of past sexual abuse that was contributing to her sexual pain.

Unfortunately, few well-controlled studies exist on causes of sexual pain. However, we know that a number of factors may contribute to sexual pain and fear of penetration, from physical problems to allergies or infections. Vulvodynia and **vulvar vestibulitis** (vess-tib-u-LITE-is) **syndrome**, a type of vulvodynia, are considered common causes of sexual pain today (Domenici et al., 2016; Goldstein et al., 2016; Pacik & Geletta, 2017; see Chapter 5 for more information about vulvodynia).

Individual vulnerability issues, such as past sexual abuse, depression, anxiety, and stress, can also contribute. Sexual pain and fear of penetration is more common in women who have experienced sexual violence, and these problems often occur together with other sexual dysfunctions, such as desire or arousal problems (Neilson et al., 2016; Staples et al., 2016). In addition, religious and cultural issues can also contribute. Women with conservative values and relatively strict sex-related moral standards have been found to be at greater risk for sexual pain disorders (Borg et al., 2011).

Treating Problems with Sexual Pain

Although many women who experience sexual pain and fear of penetration do not seek treatment, medical evaluations and counseling can help isolate possible causes and solutions. It is important to consult with a health care provider. A physical examination can check for physiological problems that may be contributing to

these disorders. It is also helpful for couples to become educated about these disorders to reduce their anxiety or tension. If a history of sexual abuse exists, it is important to work through the trauma before beginning treatment specifically aimed at reducing the pain or fear associated with sexual behavior.

Although there is no "gold standard" treatment method for sexual pain in women, treatments can include medication, surgery, physical therapy, psychological therapy, and combined treatment methods (Al-Abbadey et al., 2016). Antidepressants have shown some promise in the treatment of vulvodynia and sexual pain disorders (Leo & Dewani, 2013). Cognitive–behavioral therapy has been found to reduce pain and increase comfort with penetration. After undergoing cognitive–behavioral therapy, 81% of women experiencing sexual pain reported they were able to engage in penetrative sex and had experienced increases in self-esteem and self-worth as a sexual partner (Engman et al., 2010).

Other treatment options include biofeedback, surgery, and the use of Botox to reduce vaginal and pelvic pain (Morrissey et al., 2015; Pacik & Geletta, 2017). Some health care providers teach women experiencing pain and penetration disorders to use **dilators**, which can help to open and relax the vaginal muscles. If this is successful, penetration can be attempted. In some cases, however, it may be necessary to use a dilator on a regular basis just before penetration. It is estimated that between 75% and 100% of women who use this technique are able to experience penetrative sex by the end of treatment (Heiman, 2002). Health care providers generally begin treatment with less invasive options and then move on to more invasive options if necessary (Goldstein et al., 2016).

Recent studies have begun to explore the impact of sexual pain on intimate relationships and have revealed that couples experiencing sexual pain had lower levels of sexual satisfaction, along with poorer sexual communication and erectile functioning (Smith & Pukall, 2014). More research is needed to understand the impact of sexual pain on intimate relationships.

Review Questions

1 Identify and differentiate among the various sexual pain disorders.

2 Explain how genito-pelvic pain and penetration disorders are treated.

Illness, Disability, and Sexual Functioning

We all need love, and we all need touching and contact with others. Yet, somehow we have grown to think that sexuality is the privilege of the healthy. Health care providers often rely on the International Classification of Diseases (ICD), an official system of identifying various illnesses. Several of these illnesses and their treatments can interfere with a person's sexual desire, physiological functioning, or both. Sexual functioning involves a complex physiological process, which can be impaired by pain, immobility, changes in bodily functions, or medications. Often problems

involve psychological issues as well. Sudden illness causes shock, anger, resentment, anxiety, and depression, all of which can adversely affect sexual desire and functioning. Many illnesses cause disfiguration and force a person to deal with radical changes in body image; after removal of a limb, breast, testicle, or the need to wear an external bag to collect bodily waste, many people wonder: How could anyone possibly find me sexually attractive?

---

vulvar vestibulitis syndrome
Syndrome that causes pain and burning in the vaginal vestibule and often occurs during penetration, tampon insertion, gynecological examinations, bicycle riding, and wearing tight pants.

dilators
A graduated series of metal rods used in the treatment of vaginismus.

Serious illness often puts strains on loving relationships. A partner may be forced to become nurse, cook, maid, and caretaker as well as lover. The caretaker of an ill person may worry that the sick partner is too weak or fragile for sex or be too concerned with their illness to want sexual contact. Still, many couples do enjoy loving, full relationships despite a serious illness. Recall my chapter-opening Notebook feature about Dr. Woet Gianotten, who affirmed that many terminally ill people desire sexual intimacy. Maintaining a healthy and satisfying sex life can increase personal happiness and satisfaction for those who are chronically ill or suffering from a variety of medical conditions.

As Dr. Gianotten explained, the real questions that sick people and their partners have about their sexuality are too often ignored by medical professionals. They may be questions of mechanics: "What positions can I get into now that I have lost a leg?"; questions of function: "Will my genitals still work now that I have a spinal cord injury?"; or questions of attractiveness: "Will my husband still want me now that I have lost a breast?" In the Netherlands, regular sexual expression is so important that if a handicapped man or woman is unable to find a sexual partner, the government may cover the expense of providing one. Let's review a sample of physical and mental challenges that confront people, and also some of the sexual questions and problems that can arise.

Cardiovascular Illnesses

Heart disease, including **hypertension**, **angina**, and **myocardial infarction**, is the number one cause of death in the United States. A person with heart disease—even a person who has had a heart transplant—can return to a normal sex life shortly after recovery. Most cardiologists allow sexual behavior as soon as the patient feels up to it, although they usually recommend that heart transplant patients wait from 4 to 8 weeks to give the incision time to heal. However, researchers have found that the frequency of sexual behavior after myocardial infarctions does decrease. In fact, only 1 in 4 couples returns to their previous levels of sexual behavior (Ben-Zion & Shiber, 2006). Why does this occur?

One reason is fear. Many patients (or their partners) fear that their damaged (or new) heart is not up to the strain of sexual behavior or orgasm (Bispo et al., 2013; Masoomi et al., 2010). This fear can be triggered by the fact that, when people become sexually excited, their heartbeat and respiration increases, and

they may break out into a sweat (these are also signs of a heart attack). Some people with heart disease actually do experience some angina during sexual activity. Although not usually serious, these incidents may be frightening. Although sexual activity can trigger a myocardial infarction, this risk is extremely low (Baylin et al., 2007; Muller et al., 1996). In fact, except for patients with very serious heart conditions, sex puts no more strain on the heart than walking up a flight or two of stairs.

Some problems also involve physical factors. Because penile erection is a vascular process, involving the flow of blood into the penis, it is not surprising that ED is a common problem in male patients with cardiovascular problems (Hebert et al., 2008). Some heart medications also can dampen desire or cause erectile problems, or, less often, women may experience a decrease in lubrication. Sometimes adjusting medications can help couples who are experiencing such problems.

After a heart attack or other heart problems, it is not uncommon to have feelings of depression, inadequacy (especially among men), or loss of attractiveness (especially among women; Duarte Freitas et al., 2011; Eyada & Atwa, 2007). In addition, in older patients, a partner often assumes the responsibility of enforcing the doctor's orders: "Watch what you eat!" "Don't drink alcohol!" "Don't put so much salt on that!" "Get some exercise!" This is hardly a role that leads to sexual desire. Any combination of these factors may lead one or both partners to avoid sex.

Strokes, also called cerebrovascular accidents, happen when blood is cut off from part of the brain, usually because a small blood vessel bursts. Although every stroke is different depending on what areas of the brain are damaged, some common results are **hemiplegia** (he-mi-PLEE-jee-uh), **aphasia** (uh-FAY-zhee-uh), and other cognitive, perceptual, and memory problems. As with other types of brain injury (such as those caused by automobile accidents), damage to the brain can affect sexuality in a number of ways.

In most cases of stroke, sexual functioning itself is not damaged, and many stroke victims do go on to resume sexual activity. After a stroke, the problems that confront a couple with normal functioning are similar to those with cardiovascular disease: fear of causing another stroke, worries about sexual attractiveness, and the stresses and anxieties of having to cope with a major illness. However, a stroke can also cause physiological changes that affect sexuality. Some men may experience priapism after a stroke, because the nerves controlling the erectile tissue on one side of the penis are affected. Hemiplegia can result in spasticity (jerking motions) and reduced sensation on one side of the body. Paralysis can also contribute to a feeling of awkwardness or unattractiveness. In addition, aphasia can affect a person's ability to communicate or understand sexual cues.

Some stroke victims also go through periods of **disinhibition**, in which they exhibit behavior that, before the stroke, they would have been able to suppress. Often this includes hypersexuality, in which the patient may make lewd comments, masturbate in public, disrobe publicly, or make inappropriate sexual advances (Larkin, 1992). Others may experience **hyposexuality**, in which they show decreased sexual desire, or they may experience ED. Sexual intervention programs have been designed for use in rehabilitation hospitals, and they can be of great help in teaching couples how to deal with the difficulties of adjusting to life after a stroke.

---

hypertension
Abnormally high blood pressure.

angina
Chest pains that accompany heart disease.

myocardial infarction
A cutoff of blood to the heart muscle, causing damage to the heart; also referred to as a heart attack.

stroke
Occurs when blood is cut off from part of the brain, usually because a small blood vessel bursts.

hemiplegia
Paralysis of one side of the body.

aphasia
Defects in the ability to express and/or understand speech, signs, or written communication, caused by damage to the speech centers of the brain.

disinhibition
The loss of normal control over behaviors such as expressing sexuality or taking one's clothes off in public.

hyposexuality
Abnormal suppression of sexual desire and behavior; the term usually refers to behavior caused by some disturbance of the brain.

Cancer

We discussed cancers of the female and male reproductive organs in Chapters 5 and 6. Cancer can involve almost any organ of the body and has a reputation of being invariably fatal. In fact, cure rates have increased dramatically, and some cancers are now more than 90% curable. Still, cancer can kill, and a diagnosis of cancer is usually accompanied by shock, numbness, and gripping fear. As in other illnesses, partners may need to become caretakers, and roles can change. Cancer treatments are likely to disrupt a patients' sexual functioning, and these disruptions may be temporary or long lasting (Bedell et al., 2017; Benedict et al., 2016; Tucker et al., 2016).

For example, surgery is required for a number of cancers of the digestive system, and it can lead to **ostomies** (OST-stome-mees). People with cancer of the colon often need to have part or all of the large intestine removed; the rectum may be removed as well. A surgical opening, called a **stoma** (STOW-mah), is made in the abdomen to allow waste products to exit the body. This is collected in a bag, which, for many patients, must be worn at all times (others can take it off periodically). Ostomy bags are visually unpleasant and may emit an odor, and the adjustment to their presence can be difficult for some couples. Having a new opening in the body to eliminate bodily wastes is itself a hard thing to accept for many people, but most eventually adjust to it and, barring other problems related to their disease, go on to live healthy and sexually active lives.

Cancer can affect sexual functioning in other ways as well. Physical scars, the loss of limbs or body parts, changes in skin texture when radiation therapy is used, the loss of hair, nausea, bloating, weight gain or loss, and acne are just some of the ways that cancer and its treatment can affect the body and one's body image. In addition, the psychological trauma and the fear of death can lead to depression, which can inhibit sexual relations. Perhaps the most drastic situations, however, occur when cancer affects the sexual organs themselves.

Breast Cancer

In American society, breasts are a focal part of female sexual attractiveness, and women often invest much of their feminine self-image in their breasts. For many years, a diagnosis of breast cancer usually meant that a woman lost that breast; **mastectomy** was the preferred treatment. **Simple mastectomies** meant that the breast tissue alone was removed, whereas radical mastectomies involved the removal of the breast together with other tissues and lymph nodes. As we discussed in Chapter 5, the numbers of mastectomies have decreased today, and many women are opting for lumpectomies. These are often coupled with chemotherapy, radiation therapy, or both.

Some women undergo breast reconstruction after a mastectomy (Juhl et al., 2017). However, reports of risk associated with implants have led to growing concerns about reconstructive surgeries (Hersher, 2017). An increasing number of breast cancer patients decide to "go flat" or opt out of reconstructive surgery after mastectomies (Brown & McElroy, 2017; Rabin, 2016).

Breast cancer and cancer treatments can negatively affect several physiological, psychological, and interpersonal aspects of sexual functioning and satisfaction (Advani et al., 2017; DeMorais et al., 2016; Kamen et al., 2017; Rottmann et al., 2017). Chemotherapy and endocrine treatments have been found to create abrupt menopause in young women, leading to vaginal dryness, pain, discomfort, and significantly reduced levels of sexual desire (Falk & Bober, 2016; Farthmann et al., 2016). Mastectomies have also been found to have a negative impact on women's sexuality and body images (Hart et al., 2015). A woman who loses a breast may worry that her partner will no longer find her attractive or desirable.

One study found that although 80% of women reported a satisfying sex life before breast cancer, 70% reported sexual problems after their treatment for breast cancer (Panjari et al., 2011). Sexual problems included decreased arousal and desire, problems with body image, as well as an increase in menopausal symptoms (i.e., hot flashes and night sweats). Educating women about these changes and providing them with information on how to cope with them can improve sexual functioning (Carter et al., 2011). Lesbian and bisexual breast cancer survivors may experience higher rates of psychological distress after a breast cancer diagnosis than heterosexual women because of the added stressors of being sexual minorities (Kamen et al., 2017). More research is needed in this area.

WENN Ltd Alamy

Angelina Jolie was found to carry a genetic mutation which predisposes her to breast cancer (see Chapter 5 for more information about genetic risks for breast cancer). She decided to undergo a preventative double mastectomy in 2013 to reduce her chances of breast cancer. Jolie's risk of developing breast cancer prior to the surgery was 87%, but this risk dropped to below 5% after the surgery. There have been many discussions about preventative surgery and genetic testing for breast and ovarian cancers that continue to be debated today.

ostomies
Operations to remove part of the small or large intestine or the bladder, resulting in the need to create an artificial opening in the body for the elimination of bodily wastes.

stoma
Surgical opening made in the abdomen to allow waste products to exit the body.

mastectomy
Surgical removal of a breast.

simple mastectomy
Surgical removal of the breast tissue.

Pelvic Cancer and Hysterectomies

Cancer can also strike a woman's vagina, uterus, cervix, or ovaries. Although women with vaginal and cervical cancers often experience more sexual problems than women without these cancers, rates of sexual activity and partnering are similar (Lindau et al., 2007). Negative changes in sexual functioning have been found in some studies but not in others (Donovan et al., 2007; Dunn, 2015; Greenwald & McCorkle, 2008; Stabile et al., 2015). Common sexual issues include insufficient vaginal lubrication, shortened vaginas, reduced vaginal elasticity, and sexual pain. Overall, a woman's feelings about her cancer treatment and her social support network are both important in sexual recovery from these treatments. As we mentioned earlier, educating women about the possible sexual effects of cancer can help improve sexual functioning.

Cancer of the reproductive organs may result in a hysterectomy. In a total hysterectomy, the uterus and cervix are removed; in a radical hysterectomy, the ovaries are also removed (**oophorectomy**; oh-uh-for-RECT-toe-mee), together with the Fallopian tubes and surrounding tissue. Hysterectomies are also performed for conditions other than cancer, such as fibroids, endometriosis, and uterine prolapse. In fact, the Centers for Disease Control and Prevention report that hysterectomy is the second most frequently performed surgical procedure on women in the United States.

A hysterectomy may or may not affect sexual functioning, but many health care providers neglect to discuss the sexual implications of hysterectomy (Jongpipan & Charoenkwan, 2007). If the ovaries are removed with the uterus, a woman will experience hormonal imbalances that can lead to reduced vaginal lubrication, hot flashes, night sweats, insomnia, mood swings, and other bodily changes. In Chapter 10, we discussed myotonia and the importance of the uterine muscles during sexual response. When the uterus is removed, some women may experience fewer uterine contractions during orgasm. Whether removal of the uterus decreases physical sexual response is controversial, with some studies claiming that it does and others claiming it does not (Goktas et al., 2015; Thakar, 2015; Xiao et al., 2016). Women with a history of depression or sexual problems are often at increased risk for development of more of these symptoms after a hysterectomy (Shifren & Avis, 2007).

Prostate Cancer

As we discussed in Chapter 6, prostate cancer is one of the most common cancers in men older than 50. When men are diagnosed with prostate cancer, many worry about sexual functioning after treatment (O'Shaughnessy et al., 2013). In the past, when a man experienced an enlarged prostate or was diagnosed with prostate cancer, a **prostatectomy** (pross-tuh-TECK-toe-mee) may have been performed, sometimes along with a **cystectomy**. These procedures often involved cutting the nerves necessary for erection, resulting in ED. A possible adverse effect of prostatectomy may be **incontinence**, sometimes necessitating an **indwelling catheter**. Many couples fear that this means the end of their sex life because removing and reinserting the catheter can lead to infection. For men who experience ED from the surgery, penile prostheses or intracavernous injections are possible.

As in all surgeries of this kind, the man must also cope with the fear of disease, concern about his masculinity and body image, concern about the reactions of his sexual partner, and the new sensations or sexual functioning that can accompany prostate surgery. Overall, many men do experience declines in sexual functioning after prostate cancer treatment (Hamilton et al., 2015; Schantz-Laursen, 2017; Wittmann et al., 2011). Many gay and bisexual men with prostate cancer report negative experiences with health care providers who assume they are heterosexual, making discussions about sexual functioning after prostate cancer difficult (Kelly et al., 2017; Rose et al., 2017).

Although improved prostate cancer screening has led to higher survival rates, the development of androgen deprivation therapy to decrease the development of prostate cancer has been found to contribute to sexual problems (Elliott et al., 2010; Hamilton et al., 2015; Wassersug, 2016). Because men begin this therapy earlier, many experience decreases in sexual performance and satisfaction.

Testicular and Penile Cancers

Cancer of the penis or scrotum is rare, and cancer of the testes is only slightly more common. Still, the sexual problems that result from these diseases are similar to those from prostate cancer. Testicular cancer is most common in men who are in their most productive years. Research has found that although sexual issues, including ejaculatory problems, are common after treatment for testicular cancer, there is considerable improvement 1 year after diagnosis.

In Chapter 6, we discussed testicular cancer, and although the surgical removal of a testicle (orchiectomy) because of cancer usually does not affect the ability to reproduce (sperm can be banked, and the remaining testicle may produce enough sperm and adequate testosterone), some men do experience psychological difficulties. This is mainly because of feelings that they have lost part of their manhood or fears about the appearance of their scrotum. The appearance of the scrotum can be helped by inserting a testicular prosthesis that takes the place of the missing testicle. In some rare cases, cancer of the penis may necessitate a partial or total penectomy (pee-NECK-toe-mee). In a total penectomy, the man's urethra is redirected downward to a new opening that is created between the scrotum and anus. Even with a penectomy, some men can have orgasms by stimulating the tissue that is left where the penis was, and the ejaculate leaves the body through the urethra (Schover & Jensen, 1988).

It is well documented that sexual problems can occur as a result of any type of cancer or cancer treatment. However, in some cases, the problems may only be a temporary result of the stress associated with the situation.

---

oophorectomy
Surgical removal of the ovaries.

prostatectomy
The surgical removal of the prostate gland.

cystectomy
Surgical removal of the bladder.

incontinence
Lack of normal voluntary control of urinary functions.

indwelling catheter
A permanent catheter, inserted in the bladder, to allow the removal of urine in those who are unable to urinate or are incontinent.

Diabetes

Diabetes is caused by the inability of the pancreas to produce insulin, which is used to process blood sugar into energy, or by the inability of the body to use the insulin produced. Diabetes may affect children (Type I diabetes), who must then depend on insulin injections for the rest of their lives, or it may appear later (Type II diabetes) and may then be controlled through diet or oral medication. Diabetes is a serious condition that can ultimately lead to blindness, renal failure, and other problems.

People with diabetes often experience multiple and complex sexual difficulties. While the most common difficulties in men include decreased sexual desire, ejaculatory problems, and/or erectile dysfunction, common difficulties in women include decreased sexual desire and painful intercourse (Kizilay et al., 2017). Erectile dysfunction may be one of the first signs of diabetes in men. A large number of men in the later stages of diabetes have penile prostheses implanted.

Differentiating between how much of a person's sexual difficulty is due to underlying physiological problems and how much is due to psychological issues is often difficult. Depression, fear of ED, lack of sexual response, anxiety about the future, and the life changes that diabetes can bring can all dampen sexual desire. Sex therapy is often an important part of diabetes treatment.

Multiple Sclerosis

Multiple sclerosis (MS) involves a breakdown of the myelin sheath that protects all nerve fibers, and it can be manifested in a variety of symptoms, such as dizziness, weakness, blurred or double vision, muscle spasms, spasticity, and loss of control of limbs and muscles. Symptoms can come and go without warning, but MS is progressive and may worsen over time. MS often strikes people between the ages of 20 and 50, at a time when they are establishing sexual relationships and families.

Sexual dysfunctions are common in people with MS, although they are often underdiagnosed (Lew-Starowicz & Gianotten, 2015). Difficulties with erection are the most common problem in men with MS, while decreased sexual interest and desire are most common in women with MS (Francomano et al., 2017; Gumus et al., 2014; Lew-Starowicz & Rola, 2013; Marck et al., 2016; Winder et al., 2016). People with MS may become hypersensitive to touch, experiencing even light caresses as painful or unpleasant. Fatigue, muscle spasms, and loss of bladder and bowel function can also inhibit sexual contact. Overall, sexual problems have been found to negatively affect the quality of life in people with MS (Lew-Starowicz & Gianotten, 2015). Since fatigue often makes sexual problems worse in the late afternoon and early evening, therapists may recommend sexual activity earlier in the day (Marck et al., 2016). Sex therapy and counseling can also help a person overcome some of these difficulties.

Cerebral Palsy

Cerebral palsy (CP) is caused by damage to the motor control centers of the developing brain during pregnancy, delivery, or in early childhood. This damage permanently affects body movement and muscle coordination. Classic symptoms include decreased muscle mass, spasms or other involuntary movements, unsteady gait, and balance problems. However, the symptoms of CP vary from person to person. A person with mild CP may experience slight clumsiness, while a person with severe CP may experience a complete inability for coordinated movement.

Many people with CP feel embarrassed and shameful about their bodies, making it difficult for them to see themselves as sexual beings. This may lead to a total avoidance of sexual interactions. One Dutch study that explored the sexuality of 20- to 24-year-old adults with CP found that 20% of the participants had never engaged in partnered sex (Wiegerink et al., 2011). Although many people with CP experience sexual desire and sexual interest, the disorder may limit their ability to engage in certain sexual positions or activities (Wiwanitkit, 2008). Since many are dependent on their parents or caregivers for their daily activities, they might also find it difficult to establish intimate relationships. Many experts in this field believe that medical providers should talk about sexuality with their CP patients. Studies have found that people with CP who have high sexual self-esteem are more likely to be involved in romantic relationships (Wiegerink et al., 2012). Unfortunately, very few people with CP are ever asked about sexual concerns during their medical visits.

Alcoholism

Alcohol dependence and alcohol abuse can both contribute to sexual problems. Alcohol is a general nervous system depressant that has both long- and short-term effects on sexual functioning. It can impair spinal reflexes and decrease serum testosterone levels, which can lead to ED. **Hyperestrogenemia** (high-per-ess-troh-jen-EE-mee-uh) can result from the liver damage caused by alcoholism, which, combined with lower testosterone levels, may cause gynecomastia (which we discussed in Chapter 6), testicular atrophy, sterility, ED, and desire problems. In women, liver disease can lead to decreased or absent menstrual flow, ovarian atrophy, loss of vaginal membranes, infertility, and miscarriages. Alcohol can affect almost every bodily system; after a while, the damage it causes, including the damage to sexual functioning, can be irreversible, even if the person stops drinking alcohol.

Alcoholism also has a dramatic impact on relationships. It often coexists with anger, resentment, depression, and other familial and relationship problems. Some people become abusive when drunk, whereas others may withdraw and become noncommunicative. Problem drinking may lead a person into a spiral of guilt, lowered self-esteem, and even thoughts of suicide. Recovery is a long, often difficult process, and one's body and sexuality need time to recover from periods of abuse.

Spinal Cord Injuries (SCIs)

The spinal cord brings impulses from the brain to the various parts of the body; damage to the cord can cut off those impulses in any areas served by nerves below the damaged section. SCIs can sig-

---

hyperestrogenemia
Having an excessive amount of estrogen in the blood.

nificantly affect sexual health and functioning (Alexander et al., 2009; Borisoff et al., 2010; Cardoso et al., 2009). However, to assess potential problems, a physician must know exactly where on the spine the injury occurred and how extensively the cord has been damaged. Although some return of sensation and movement can be achieved in many injuries, most people are left with permanent disabilities. In more extreme cases, SCI can result in total or partial **paraplegia** (pah-ruh-PLEE-jee-uh) or total or partial **quadriplegia** (kwa-druh-PLEE-jee-uh). In these cases, the person is rendered extremely dependent on his or her partner or caretaker.

Men are four times more likely than women to experience SCI, and if the injury is above a certain vertebra, a man may still be able to have an erection through the body's reflex mechanism. However, it may be difficult to maintain an erection because there are reduced skin sensations in the penis. Injuries to the lower part of the spine are more likely to result in erectile difficulties in men, but they are also more likely to preserve some sensation in the genitals. Men without disabilities maintain erections, in part, through psychic arousal, such as sexual thoughts, feelings, and fantasies; however, with SCI, psychic arousal cannot provide continuing stimulation. Most men with SCIs who are capable of having erections are not able to climax or ejaculate, which involves a more complex mechanism than an erection (Benevento & Sipski, 2002). A number of men report experiencing orgasm without ejaculation (Sipski et al., 2006).

Women with SCI can lose sensation in the genitals, and with it the ability to lubricate during sexual activity, making penetrative sex difficult (Cramp et al., 2015; Lombardi et al., 2009, 2010). However, many people with SCIs maintain orgasmic ability (Alexander & Rosen, 2008; Kreuter et al., 2011). "Phantom orgasm," a psychic sensation of having an orgasm without the corresponding physical reactions, is also common. Skin sensation in the areas unaffected by the injury can become greater, and new erogenous zones can appear (Brown et al., 2005; Ferreiro-Velasco et al., 2005).

Many people enjoy a variety of sexual activities after SCI, including kissing, hugging, and touching. A healthy sex life after SCI is possible if a person can learn to overcome the physical and psychological obstacles of their injuries (Kreuter et al., 2008). Unfortunately, many people with spinal cord injuries do not receive adequate information about how to participate in sexual activity after their injury (Eglseder & Demchick, 2017). Sexual problems develop over time as the full impact of their situation takes effect. Although men with SCI can resume sexual activity within a year of their injury, their frequency of sexual activity often decreases after the injury.

Rehabilitation from SCI can be a long, difficult process. Still, with a caring partner, meaningful sexual contact can be achieved.

---

paraplegia	**neuroleptics**
Paralysis of the legs and lower part of the body, affecting both sensation and motor response.	A class of antipsychotic drugs.
	major depression
quadriplegia	A persistent, chronic state in which the person feels they have no worth, cannot function normally, and entertains thoughts of or attempts suicide.
Paralysis of all four limbs.	
schizophrenia	**affective disorders**
Any of a group of mental disorders that affect the individual's ability to think, behave, or perceive things normally.	A class of mental disorders that affect mood.

Men incapable of having an erection can still use their mouths and sometimes their hands. If penetrative sex is desired, couples can use "stuffing" techniques, in which the flaccid penis is pushed into the vagina or anus. Possible treatment methods include prosthesis implantation, vacuum erection devices, and the injection of vasoactive drugs. Prosthesis implantation in men with SCIs has shown high satisfaction and low complication rates (Kim et al., 2008). Research has found that various erectile drugs can significantly improve erections in men with SCI (Garcia-Perdomo et al., 2016).

Mental Illness

People with psychological disorders have sexual fantasies, needs, and feelings, and they have the same right to a fulfilling sexual expression as others do. However, historically they have either been treated as asexual or their sexuality has been viewed as illegitimate, warped, or needing external control (Apfel & Handel, 1993).

People with **schizophrenia**, for example, can be among the most impaired and difficult psychiatric patients. **Neuroleptics**, antipsychotic drugs such as Thorazine and Haldol, can cause increased or decreased desire for sex; painful enlargement of the breasts, reproductive organs, or testicles; difficulty in achieving or maintaining an erection; delayed or retrograde ejaculation; and changes, including pain, in orgasm.

Outside of the effects of neuroleptics, people with schizophrenia have been found to grapple with the same sexual questions and problems as other people. The same is true of people with **major depression** and other **affective disorders**. They may experience hyposexuality when depressed or hypersexuality in periods of mania. Both can also occur as a result of antidepressant medications. Otherwise, their sexual problems do not differ significantly from those of people without major psychiatric problems (Schover & Jensen, 1988).

Sexual issues among those with intellectual disabilities are often neglected in psychiatric training, and health care providers who treat these patients have often spent more time trying to control and limit patients' sexual behavior than they have in treating sexual problems. For years, those with intellectual disabilities have been kept from learning about sexuality and having sexual relationships. It's as if an otherwise healthy adult is supposed to display no sexual interest or activity at all. Educators have designed special sexuality education programs for the intellectually and developmentally disabled to make sure that they express their sexuality in a socially approved manner (Young et al., 2012). However, to deny people with psychiatric problems or disabilities the pleasure of a sexual life is unnecessary.

Many people with intellectual disabilities (and physical disabilities) must spend long periods of their lives—sometimes their entire lives—in institutions, which makes developing a sex life difficult. Institutions differ greatly in the amount of sexual contact they allow; some allow none whatsoever, whereas others allow mutually consenting sexual contact, with the staff carefully overseeing the patients' contraceptive and hygienic needs (Young et al., 2012). For many people suffering from severe mental illnesses, intimate relationships are positively associated with recovery, even though this is often neglected by health care professionals (Boucher et al., 2016).

Another aspect of institutional life involves the sexual exploitation of patients with mental illness or intellectual disabilities. This is well known but seldom discussed by those who work in such institutions. About half of all women in psychiatric hospitals report having been abused as children or adolescents, and many are then abused in a hospital or other institutional setting. Children who grow up with developmental disabilities are between 4 and 10 times more likely to be abused than children without those difficulties (Baladerian, 1991). Therefore, it is difficult to separate the sexual problems of mental illness, developmental disability, and psychiatric illness from histories of sexual abuse (Apfel & Handel, 1993; Monat-Haller, 1992). We will discuss sexual abuse in Chapter 17.

Other Conditions

Many other conditions, such as chronic pain from illnesses such as arthritis, migraine headaches, and back pain, can make sexual behavior difficult or impossible at times. Respiratory illnesses, such as **chronic obstructive pulmonary disease (COPD)** and asthma, can also have a significant negative effect on sexual functioning. Not only do these diseases make physical exertion difficult, but they can also impair perceptual and motor skills. Millions of people who have COPD learn to take medicine before sexual activity and slow down their pace of sexual activity; their partners learn to use positions that allow the person with COPD to breathe comfortably.

Review Questions

1 Explain how physical illness and its treatment can interfere with sexual desire, physiological functioning, or both.

2 Explain why it is important for health care workers to ask patients about their sex lives.

3 Explain how cardiovascular illnesses can affect sexual functioning.

4 Explain how various cancers can affect sexual functioning.

5 Explain how diabetes, MS, alcoholism, SCIs, and mental illness can affect sexual functioning.

Getting Help

People who are ill have the same sexual needs and desires as everyone else. In the past, these needs have too often been neglected not because the individuals themselves were not interested in sexuality, but because health care providers and other health care professionals were uncomfortable learning about their sexual needs and discussing them with their patients. Fortunately, this has been changing, and now sexuality counseling is a normal part of the recuperation from many diseases and injuries in many hospitals. It is important for all of us to learn that those with illnesses are just like everybody else and simply desire to be treated as such.

Regardless of your health status, if you are experiencing problems with sexual functioning, it is important to seek help as soon as possible. Often, when the problems are ignored, they lead to bigger problems down the road. If you are in college and have a student counseling center available to you, this may be a good place to start looking for help. Request a counselor who has received training in sexuality or ask to be referred to one who has.

Today, many therapists receive specific training in sexuality. One of the best training organizations in the United States is the American Association of Sexuality Educators, Counselors, and Therapists (AASECT; see Chapter 2). This organization offers certification programs in human sexuality for counselors, educators, and therapists and can also provide information on those who are certified as therapists or counselors.

Review Questions

1 Explain how the sexual needs of people with various illnesses have been neglected over the years.

2 Explain why sexuality counseling is an important part of the recovery process.

3 Why might it be beneficial to seek help and not ignore a sexual problem?

---

chronic obstructive pulmonary disease (COPD)
A disease of the lung that affects breathing.

Chapter Review

1 Sexual health is important to our overall health and quality of life. Healthy sexuality depends on good mental and physical functioning. Sexual problems are common and may occur when we don't feel sufficiently aroused, have a lower level of enthusiasm, or have trouble relaxing during sex. The majority of couples report periodic sexual problems, but most of the time these problems do not interfere with overall sexual functioning and they go away on their own.

2 Defining a sexual problem can be difficult. To help clarify definitions, some sex therapists in the United States use the *Diagnostic and Statistical Manual of Mental Disorders (DSM)*, which is a classification and diagnostic tool. This manual is occasionally updated, and it continues to evolve and reflect the prevailing thinking and understanding about sexual disorders. The *DSM* is currently in the 5th edition (referred to as the *DSM-5*). Many of the changes in the *DSM* were aimed at simplification and clarification.

3 Psychological factors that can challenge sexual functioning include unconscious fears, stress, anxiety, depression, guilt, anger, fear of intimacy, dependency, abandonment, concern over loss of control, and performance fears. In addition, relationship issues can contribute to sexual problems, such as feeling unappreciated, anger, insecurity, resentment, conflict, or a lack of trust.

4 Physiological factors that can challenge sexual functioning include various injuries, disabilities, illnesses, diseases, medications, street drugs, and aging. Treatments for various diseases, such as chemotherapy and radiation, can also contribute to sexual problems.

5 Sexual problems can be lifelong or acquired, and situational or generalized. Having this information can help with diagnosis. Research has found that lifelong problems have more biological or physiological causes, whereas acquired problems tend to have more psychological causes.

6 The *DSM-5* lists a group of criteria to help evaluate psychological and relationship factors. These include sexual or health problems in partners, relationship factors, individual vulnerability factors, cultural or religious factors, and any medical factors. It's important for therapists to evaluate each of these factors to gain a better understanding of exactly what could be contributing to any sexual problems.

7 The *DSM-5* identifies sexual dysfunctions related to sexual desire, arousal, orgasm, and pain during sexual behavior and includes three types of female sexual dysfunction and four types of male sexual dysfunction. These include sexual interest/arousal disorder in women, male hypoactive sexual desire disorder, erectile disorder, female orgasmic disorder, early ejaculation, delayed ejaculation, and sexual pain disorders.

8 For many people, sexual desire leads them to seek out and initiate sexual activity. For others, sexual desire builds when they engage in sexual activity (responsive sexual desire). Problems with sexual desire include sexual interest/arousal disorder in women and HSDD and ED in men. These disorders are characterized by a deficient or absent desire for sexual activity, which can lead to both psychological and physiological symptoms. People with desire disorders experience a lack of sexual fantasies, reduced or absent initiation of sexual activity, and decreased self-stimulation. To meet the criteria for a desire/arousal disorder, a person needs to have experienced symptoms 75% to 100% of the time for at least 6 months.

9 Female desire/arousal disorders are one of the most prevalent types of female sexual dysfunctions. Many issues can affect a woman's sexual desire, including a lack of attraction to one's partner, partner illness or health problems, marital or relationship conflicts, and differences in sexual interest. Individual issues, such as depression, anxiety, stress, a negative body image, eating disorders, fear of intimacy or pregnancy, a concern over loss of control, or a history of sexual or emotional abuse, can also contribute. Physiological factors, including chronic illness, hormonal problems, medication side effects, chronic use of alcohol, and treatment for various illnesses, may also contribute to decreased sexual desire and arousal.

10 Many therapists consider problems with sexual desire and arousal to be one of the most complicated sexual problems to treat. A variety of different treatment options are available. Cognitive–behavioral therapy, a form of psychotherapy that emphasizes the importance of how a person thinks and the effect these thoughts have on a person's feelings and behaviors, has offered promising results. Pharmacological and herbal treatments have also been used. The FDA approved the first medication to treat interest/arousal disorders in premenopausal women in 2015.

11 Erectile disorder involves persistent or recurrent inability to attain, or maintain, an erection adequate for sexual activity. Erectile disorder is one of the most common sexual problems in men and the incidence increases with age. EDs in younger men are more likely to be psychologically based, whereas EDs in older men are more likely to be due to physical factors. There are more treatment options for male ED than for any other sexual disorder.

12 Treatment options include psychological treatment (including systematic desensitization and sex therapy); psychopharmacological, hormonal, and intracavernous injections; vascular surgery; vacuum constriction devices; and prosthesis implantation. The treatment of ED has changed considerably since erectile drugs became available.

13 The *DSM-5* includes one orgasm disorder in women, female orgasmic disorder, and two in men, early ejaculation and delayed ejaculation. Female orgasmic disorder involves a marked delay in, marked infrequency of, or absence of orgasm. This is a common complaint among women. Women with orgasmic disorders often report less relationship satisfaction and lower levels of emotional closeness. They also have more communication difficulties in asking their partners for what they need. Physical factors can also contribute to female orgasmic disorder, including chronic illness and disorders such as diabetes, neurological problems, hormonal deficiencies, and alcoholism. Certain prescription drugs can interfere with orgasmic response.

14 The majority of treatment programs for female orgasmic disorder involve a combination of different treatment approaches, such as homework assignments, sex education, communication skills training, cognitive restructuring, desensitization, and other techniques.

15 The ejaculatory process is controlled by various endocrine factors, including testosterone, oxytocin, prolactin, and thyroid hormones. There is a wide spectrum of ejaculatory disorders, ranging from early ejaculation to a delay or absence of ejaculation. Early ejaculation refers to a condition in which a man reaches orgasm just before, or immediately following, penetration. Early ejaculation is a common sexual problem affecting men.

16 Delayed ejaculation involves a delayed, infrequent, or absent ejaculation that has occurred for 6 months or more and occurs on most occasions of sexual activity. Delayed ejaculation is one of the least understood, least common, and least studied sexual dysfunctions. Men who experience it often have significant distress and relationship problems related to the problem. Studies have found that many men with delayed ejaculation have a history of high masturbatory activity, lower levels of sexual satisfaction, and higher levels of anxiety and depression.

17 Another ejaculatory disorder is retrograde ejaculation, in which the ejaculate empties into the bladder instead of being ejaculated outside the body through the urethra. A man with retrograde ejaculation typically experiences orgasm with little or no ejaculation. Treatment for ejaculatory disorders often depends on the duration, context, and causes of the disorder. Lifelong ejaculatory problems are often treated with medications or topical anesthetics, whereas other cases might be treated with behavioral therapy, with or without medications.

18 Temporary pain during sexual activity, especially penetrative sex, is common. Sexual pain disorders typically cause ongoing pain that leads to significant distress. While the *DSM-4* included vaginismus and dyspareunia as pain disorders, the *DSM-5* collapsed these into one diagnosis, genito-pelvic pain and penetration disorder. Mainly this was because vaginismus and dyspareunia often co-occurred and were difficult to distinguish.

19 Although there is no gold standard treatment method for sexual pain in women, treatments can include medication, surgery, physical therapy, psychological therapy, and combined treatment methods. Cognitive–behavioral therapy has been found to reduce pain and increase comfort with penetration. After treatment, many women report being able to engage in penetrative sex, as well as increases in self-esteem and self-worth. Other treatment options include biofeedback, surgery, and the use of Botox to reduce vaginal and pelvic pain. Health care providers generally begin treatment with less invasive options and then move on to more invasive options if necessary.

20 Physical illness and its treatment can interfere with a person's sexual desire, physiological functioning, or both. Cardiovascular problems, including hypertension, myocardial infarctions, strokes, and cancer, can all affect sexual functioning. There can be physical problems that interfere with physiological functioning, or there can be psychological problems or fear of sexual activity that can interfere with sexual functioning.

21 Breast cancer and cancer treatments can negatively affect several physiological, psychological, and interpersonal aspects of sexual functioning and satisfaction. Lesbian and bisexual breast cancer survivors may experience higher rates of psychological distress post breast cancer

diagnosis than heterosexual women because of the added stressors of being a sexual minority. Some women undergo breast reconstruction after a mastectomy; however, an increasing number of women today decide to "go flat," or opt out of reconstructive surgery, after mastectomies.

22 Almost all men will experience a normal enlargement of the prostate gland if they live long enough. When men are diagnosed with prostate cancer, many worry about sexual functioning after treatment. Many gay and bisexual men with prostate cancer report negative experiences with health care providers who assume they are heterosexual, making discussions about sexual functioning after prostate cancer difficult.

23 Illnesses such as heart disease, cancer, diabetes, multiple sclerosis, cerebral palsy, alcoholism, spinal cord injuries, mental illness, respiratory illnesses, and asthma can also negatively affect sexual functioning or present specific challenges. People who are ill have the same sexual needs and desires that able-bodied, healthy people do.

24 People who are experiencing sexual problems, illness, or disease should seek treatment as soon as possible to avoid the development of further problems. When problems are ignored, they tend to lead to bigger problems down the road.

Critical Thinking Questions

1 Suppose that one night you discover that you are having trouble reaching orgasm with your partner. What do you do about it? When it happens several times, what do you do? Who would you feel comfortable talking to about this problem?

2 If you were suddenly disabled or developed a chronic illness, would you lose your desire to love and be loved, to touch and be touched, to be regarded by another as sexy and desirable?

3 Do you think insurance plans should cover treatment for sexual dysfunction? Why or why not?

4 Do you think that drug companies could convince us that a sexual problem exists when there is none? Should researchers be doing more work to uncover the causes of female sexual problems, even if the pharmaceutical companies are paying for this research? Why or why not?

5 How do you think the *DSM* helps and doesn't help in the diagnosis and evaluation of sexual problems? Explain.

Websites

International Society for the Study of Women's Sexual Health (ISSWSH) The ISSWSH is a multidisciplinary, academic, and scientific organization that works to provide opportunities for communication among scholars, researchers, and practitioners about women's sexual functioning, as well as to provide the public with accurate information about women's sexual health.

Disability Resources This website offers information on sexuality for people with disabilities and for parents of children with disabilities. General disability information can be found, as well as disability-specific information.

New View Campaign Formed in 2000, this campaign challenges the medicalization of sex by the pharmaceutical companies. The website contains information, contacts, and media interviews.

Female Sexual Dysfunction ALERT (FSD-ALERT) This website, founded by Leonore Tiefer, a sex therapist and activist whose research we discussed in this chapter, challenges the myths promoted by the pharmaceutical industry and calls for research on the many causes of women's sexual problems. A variety of links to sexual health organizations are available.

The Sexual Health Network The Sexual Health Network is dedicated to providing easy access to sexuality information, education, mutual support, counseling, therapy, health care, products, and other resources for people with disabilities, illness, or natural changes throughout the life cycle and those who love them or care for them.

15 | Sexually Transmitted Infections

*T*hroughout this chapter we'll discuss sexually transmitted infections (STIs) and behaviors that can put a person at risk for acquiring an STI. Being able to talk with your partner about any infections or sexual experiences that might put you at risk is an important aspect of avoiding STIs. However, these are not easy issues to talk about. One of my students, Jessica, came to me to talk about her recent STI infection. Jessica and her boyfriend, Ryan, had an "on and off" relationship throughout their junior year of college. Like many couples, they didn't have great communication skills. When they left school for the summer they both had different ideas about the status of their relationship. Jessica thought they would be monogamous over the summer, but Ryan thought they were free to explore sex outside of their relationship. When they returned to school in the fall they resumed their sexual relationship. However, a few weeks into the semester Jessica began experiencing a variety of symptoms. A visit to the health center on campus confirmed her worst fears: She had been infected with herpes.

Jessica told me she remembered the phone call in which she got the news. She had been in class and ran back to her room after the call and locked herself in the bathroom. Ryan admitted to a hookup over the summer and told her he became infected with herpes during the hookup. It took weeks for Jessica to land back on her feet again—she closed herself off and couldn't talk with friends or family about her feelings. She ended up taking a semester leave from school to work things out. Although Jessica is still healing and taking care of herself today, she wants other college students to understand the importance of sexual communication. She has had two sexual partners in her life. Her story was heartbreaking and illustrates the importance of communication and safe sex.

Janell Carroll

Lisa Belval

In the United States, more than 20 million cases of sexually transmitted infections (STIs) are reported each year, and almost half of these are in young people ages 15 to 24 (Centers for Disease Control and Prevention [CDC], 2016). However, because many STIs are either unreported or undiagnosed, the actual number of STIs is much higher. We live in a society that is often reluctant to openly discuss issues related to sexuality and, as a result, communication about infections is difficult for many of us. STIs often create fear and judgment, and because of this, many college students are apprehensive about getting tested for STIs even when they are worried they might have one. Some students say they would feel "embarrassed" to get tested and would just "rather not know" if they were infected (Barth et al., 2002). Many people are unaware of the risk and consequences of many of the STIs, and it is clear that these infections are a global public health challenge today.

Sexually Transmitted Infections

Although the CDC collects and analyzes data on many STIs in the United States, only cases of chlamydia, chancroid, gonorrhea, hepatitis, syphilis, and HIV have mandatory reporting rules. This means that health care providers in the United States are required to report any of these STI cases to their local and/or state departments of public health, who in turn release them to the CDC. This enables the CDC to monitor, analyze, and interpret trends in an effort to reduce the occurrence of these STIs. While gonorrhea rates were at historic lows a few years ago and syphilis was close to being completely eliminated, the CDC has noted increasing rates of these two STIs since then. This is especially troubling because we are close to running out of treatment options for gonorrhea (Barton et al., 2016).

REAL RESEARCH Adolescents who hold negative attitudes about sexually transmitted infections are less likely to get tested for them (CUNNINGHAM ET AL., 2009).

STIs can be caused by parasitic, bacterial, or viral infections. The causal agents are important in treating STIs, which we will discuss in this chapter. The most effective way to avoid STI transmission is to abstain from oral, vaginal, and anal sex or to be in a long-term, mutually monogamous relationship with someone who is free from STIs.

contagion
Disease transmission by direct or indirect contact.

punishment concept
The idea that people who had become infected with certain diseases, especially sexually transmitted infections, did something wrong and are being punished.

asymptomatic
Without recognizable symptoms.

Attitudes About Sexually Transmitted Infections

The sudden appearance of a new disease has always elicited fear about the nature of its **contagion**. Cultural fears about disease and sexuality in the early 20th century gave way to many theories about casual transmission (Brandt, 1985). At the turn of the 20th century, physicians believed that STIs could be transmitted on pens, pencils, toothbrushes, towels, and bedding. In fact, during World War I, the U.S. Navy removed doorknobs from its battleships, claiming that they were responsible for spreading sexual infections (Brandt, 1985).

STIs have historically been viewed as symbols of corrupt sexuality (Allen, 2000). When compared with other illnesses, such as cancer or diabetes, attitudes about STIs have been considerably more negative, and many people believe that people so afflicted "got what they deserved." This has been referred to as the **punishment concept** of disease. It was generally believed that to acquire an STI, one must break the silent moral code of sexual responsibility. Those who become infected therefore have done something bad, for which they are being punished.

Kopelman (1988) suggested that this conceptualization has endured because it serves as a defense mechanism. By believing that a person's behavior is responsible for acquiring an STI, we think we are safe by not engaging in that behavior. For example, if we believe that herpes happens only to people who have more than 10 sexual partners, we may feel safe if we have fewer partners. Whether we are safe, of course, depends on whether our beliefs about the causes of transmission are true. Negative beliefs and stigma about STIs persist. One study found that many people who are diagnosed with STIs experience "self-stigmatization," which is an acceptance of the negative aspects of stigma (feeling inadequate and ashamed; Fortenberry, 2002). These negative feelings can also interfere with the act of getting tested at all.

High-Risk Groups and Sexually Transmitted Infections

Since 1946, the CDC has been monitoring public health issues, including sexually transmitted infections, with an eye on gaps and vulnerabilities in certain U.S. residents (Frieden, 2011). Large discrepancies have been found in STI prevalence, with higher rates in young people, certain racial/ethnic groups and minority populations, and men who have sex with men (MSM). Young adults are disproportionately affected by STIs, and the incidence of these infections continues to grow in this population, primarily because many engage in high-risk sexual behaviors, such as multiple partners or inconsistent condom use, or both. Studies have found that 1 in 4 sexually active adolescent females are infected with an STI (CDC, 2014b; Forhan et al., 2009; Satterwhite et al., 2013; see the accompanying "Sex in Real Life" feature for more information).

Overall, women are at greater risk for long-term complications from STIs because vaginal tissue is much more fragile than penile skin. Heterosexual and bisexual women have another additional risk because semen often remains in the female reproductive tract if a condom isn't used (Bolton et al., 2008; CDC, 2007). Women are also more likely than men to be **asymptomatic** and not know they are infected. Some infections,

Sex in Real Life   Safe Sex in College

The following story was written by a college student who had just completed her freshman year:

Sex in college was nothing like I expected. I was disappointed not only by the thin dorm walls and rickety twin beds but by the lack of safe sex. While my college promoted condoms, I was surprised they weren't used as often as they should be. No one ever thought of using them during oral. In fact, hook-up driven college students were more likely to talk about whether they preferred "spitting" or "swallowing" than what they used to protect themselves. Many students exposed themselves and their partners to a wide range of STIs. When it came to cunnilingus, most students had never even heard of a dental dam. Regardless of whether it's through an introduction at a party or a match on Tinder, one-night stands are common, which means that many students have multiple partners in a short amount of time. In addition, many hook-up decisions are influenced by alcohol, which can make negotiating safe sex difficult. A hook-up culture that focuses solely on pleasure without considering safety and communication is a tough one to live in.

This student's story is thought-provoking and brings up many good points. What can you do to decrease your risk for acquiring a sexually transmitted infection (STI)? Make sure you know your partner's STI history, maintain a monogamous sexual relationship, and use condoms and barriers for all sexual activities. It is also important to understand that certain sexual behaviors—called *high-risk* sexual behaviors—increase your risk for acquiring an STI. As the student mentioned, alcohol use can increase your risk of STIs because people are often more likely to engage in high-risk sexual behaviors when they have been drinking.

Following are some of these high-risk behaviors:

- Engaging in unprotected vaginal or anal intercourse without the use of a male or female condom unless this occurs in a long-term, single-partner, monogamous relationship in which both partners have been tested for STIs

- Engaging in oral sex with a partner without using a condom or dental dam (see nearby photo) unless this occurs in a long-term, single-partner, monogamous relationship in which both partners have been tested for STIs

- Engaging in vaginal or anal intercourse before age 18

- Having multiple sex partners

- Engaging in vaginal or anal intercourse with a partner who has multiple sex partners

- Engaging in oral sex with a partner who has multiple sex partners

- Engaging in any sexual behaviors with a partner who has ever injected drugs

- Engaging in sex work or sexual activity with a partner who has ever engaged in sex work

- Engaging in sexual activity with a partner who has a history of STIs

- Engaging in sexual activity with a partner with an unknown STI history

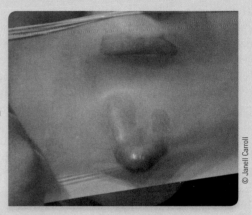

A dental dam is a thin sheet of latex that is used for STI protection during cunnilingus and anilingus.

© Janell Carroll

---

such as herpes and HIV, also have properties of **latency**. A person can have the virus that causes the infection but not have symptoms, and tests may even show up negative. As a result, the person may be unaware that they are infecting others. This is why it's always important to inform all sexual partners if you are diagnosed with an STI.

Surveillance data have found higher rates of reported STIs among certain racial/ethnic groups in the United States. Overall, Blacks have higher rates of many STIs than any other racial/ethnic group in the United States. National STI surveillance data have found that Blacks had the highest rates of chlamydia, gonorrhea, syphilis, and HIV cases in 2015 (Barton et al., 2016). This may be partially because Blacks are more likely to be treated in public clinics, which are more likely to report STIs (Arrington-Sanders et al., 2007). Even so, this cannot explain all of the racial/ethnic differences in STI rates. Other factors, such as access to health care, the ability to seek help, poverty, and sexual practices, are also responsible for some of the rate disparities.

Over the past several decades, the rates of STIs in MSM have been increasing. Researchers believe this is due to several factors, including increased Internet access to sexual partners, a decreased

fear of acquiring HIV, increased use of alcohol and other drugs, a lack of knowledge about STIs, and an increase in high-risk sexual behaviors, including oral sex and a lack of condom use in this population (Brooks et al., 2008; Eaton et al., 2015; Mackesy-Amiti et al., 2008; Ogilvie et al., 2008). Overall, MSM engage in more sexual risk-taking compared to heterosexual men and women (Workowski & Berman, 2010).

---

latency
A period in which a person is infected with a sexually transmitted infection but does not test positive for it.

While some might believe that women who have sex with women (WSW) are at low, or no, risk for STIs, WSW can, in fact, acquire STIs, along with vaginal infections (Workowski & Berman, 2010). WSW often have fewer sexual partners and engage in less penetrative sex than heterosexual women, which can reduce their overall risk for STIs, but transmission can occur with skin-to-skin contact, oral sex, and vaginal or anal sex using hands, fingers, or sex toys, especially when toys are shared (VanderLaan & Vasey, 2008). Bisexual women have a significantly higher rate of STIs than lesbians (Koh et al., 2005; Morrow & Allsworth, 2000; Tao, 2008). It's important for lesbian and bisexual women to obtain yearly pelvic examinations to reduce their risk for adverse complications of STIs (Reiter & McRee, 2014; Tjepkema, 2008).

Sexually Transmitted Infections in Transgender Persons

Transgender individuals may have sex with women, men, or both and consider themselves to be heterosexual, lesbian, gay, or bisexual (see Chapters 4 and 11 for more information). However, like cisgender people, transgender individuals who engage in high-risk sexual behaviors are at increased risk of developing STIs. Less access to adequate STI information may contribute to this increased risk among transgender individuals (Toibaro et al., 2009).

One study found that nearly half of transgender individuals had been diagnosed with an STI at some point in their lifetimes (24% HPV, 11% chlamydia, 11% HSV, 9% bacterial vaginosis (BV), 7% gonorrhea, and 7% trichomoniasis; Reisner et al., 2014; Sevelius, 2009). While some studies have found no differences in rates of HIV among transgender men and transgender women in the United States, others have found higher rates of HIV among transgender women, especially among those who are Black (Herbst et al., 2008; Stephens et al., 2011). Transgender men may have a lower prevalence of HIV than transgender women due to the fact that they engage in less risky sexual behaviors (Reisner et al., 2010; Sevelius, 2009). It's important to understand that engaging in high-risk sexual behaviors increases the risk of STIs (see the nearby Sex in Real Life).

Sexually Transmitted Infections and Pelvic Inflammatory Disease

Pelvic inflammatory disease (PID) is an infection of the female genital tract, including the endometrium, Fallopian tubes, and the lining of the pelvic area. Two of the most common causes of PID are chlamydia and gonorrhea (Kreisel et al., 2017). Although the exact rates of PID are unknown, the CDC estimates that 750,000 women experience acute cases of PID each year (with a total of 2.5 million women in the United States with a reported lifetime history of PID).

Symptoms of PID vary from none to severe. The most common symptom is lower abdominal pain. Severe symptoms may include acute pelvic pain, fever, painful urination, and abnormal vaginal bleeding or discharge. There are a variety of treatment

approaches to PID, and treatment is usually dependent on how progressed the infection is. For women with mildly to moderately severe PID, antibiotics are typically used. Women with acute cases may be required to undergo injections or intravenous treatments. Sexual partners should be treated if they have had sexual contact with the woman during the 60 days before the onset of her symptoms. Long-term complications of PID include ectopic and tubal pregnancies, chronic pelvic pain, and infertility (see Chapter 12 for more information on the role that PID plays in infertility).

Contraception, Pregnancy, and Sexually Transmitted Infections

We discussed in Chapter 13 how contraceptive methods offer varying levels of protection from STIs. The U.S. Food and Drug Administration (FDA) approved labeling contraceptives for STI protection in 1993. Barrier methods, such as condoms, diaphragms, or contraceptive sponges, can decrease the risk for acquiring an STI. Overall, male condoms are the most effective contraceptive method for reducing STI risk. They also offer protection from pelvic inflammatory disease in women (Workowski & Bolan, 2015). When heterosexual couples who are serodiscordant for HIV (one is HIV positive but the other is not) consistently use male condoms, they are 80% less likely to become infected with HIV compared to similar couples who do not use male condoms (Weller & Davis, 2002). The degree of protection from male condoms, however, depends on proper use. STI infections acquired while using male condoms are usually due to inconsistent or incorrect use. Female condoms also offer some STI protection, although not as much as male condoms.

ON YOUR MIND

Can sexually transmitted infections (STIs) be transmitted through oral sex?

It's often difficult to study the exact risk for acquiring an STI from oral sex, because many couples engage in other sexual behaviors, such as vaginal or anal intercourse. But studies have shown that oral sex can transmit STIs, such as herpes, syphilis, gonorrhea, HPV, HIV, and hepatitis A (CDC, 2010c). Although the risks for acquiring an STI from oral sex may be slightly smaller than the risk during other sexual behaviors, there is still a risk, especially if fluids are swallowed. To decrease your risk for acquiring an STI from oral sex, condoms or dental dams should always be used.

Other barrier methods, such as diaphragms, offer some protection against cervical STI infections but they cannot be relied on for protection from all STIs (Workowski & Bolan, 2015). Nonoxynol-9 (N-9) spermicide can cause vaginal and anal irritation with frequent use, which may lead to increased genital ulceration and a higher risk for STI infection (Workowski & Bolan, 2015).

The role of hormonal contraceptives in preventing STIs is complicated. The increased hormones change the cervical mucus and the lining of the uterus, which can help prevent any infectious substance from moving up into the genital tract. In addition, the reduced buildup of the endometrium decreases the possibility of an infectious substance growing (because there is less nutritive material for bacteria to survive; Workowski & Bolan, 2015). However, hormonal contraceptives may also cause the cervix to be more susceptible to infections because of changes in the vaginal discharge. Experts recommend that women using hormonal contraceptives also use condoms to prevent STIs.

When a woman does become pregnant, untreated sexually transmitted infections can adversely affect her pregnancy. Many of the STIs can cause miscarriage, stillbirth, early onset of labor, premature rupture of the amniotic sac, low birth weight, early infant pneumonia, infant eye infections, and/or fetal death (Dong et al., 2016; Gomez et al., 2013; Gupta & Bowman, 2012; Workowski & Bolan, 2015). The CDC recommends that all pregnant women be screened for chlamydia, gonorrhea, syphilis, hepatitis B and C, and HIV at their first prenatal visit, and they may require additional testing again during the third trimester. Women who do not know their partner's STI history should always use latex condoms during pregnancy.

Some STIs can be treated during pregnancy with antibiotics, and if treatment is begun immediately, there is less chance the newborn will become infected. It's estimated that untreated early syphilis will infect a fetus 80% of the time, and in 40% of these cases, the fetus will die (Barton et al., 2016). Other STIs may be treated with antiviral medications (Bardeguez et al., 2008; Kriebs, 2008). If there are active vaginal lesions or sores from an STI at the time of delivery, a health care provider may recommend a cesarean section.

Like many STIs, HIV can be passed from a mother to her child during pregnancy and/or labor and delivery. Risks are reduced when HIV is detected before pregnancy or early in the pregnancy, pregnant women receive HIV medications during pregnancy, and when a woman has a cesarean delivery (see Chapter 12). In addition, to reduce the risk of infection in babies born to HIV-infected mothers, HIV medications are given to newborns for 4 to 6 weeks after delivery. Unlike women infected with other STIs, HIV-positive mothers are advised not to breast-feed their newborns ("Preventing Mother-to-Child Transmission of HIV," 2016). In the following section, we will explore several categories of STIs, including ectoparasitic, bacterial, and viral, and then examine cross-cultural aspects of STIs.

Review Questions

1 Define the punishment concept of disease, and explain how the punishment concept might make people neglect protecting themselves from STIs.

2 Identify specific populations that are at higher risk for STIs, and explain the reasons they are high risk.

3 Define the "asymptomatic" and "latent" aspects of STIs, and explain how these may affect an individual.

4 Define pelvic inflammatory disease (PID) and identify causes, symptoms, and long-term risks.

5 Discuss the role of contraception in lessening STI risk.

6 Explain how untreated STIs can affect pregnancy, labor, and the fetus.

Ectoparasitic Infections: Pubic Lice and Scabies

Ectoparasitic infections are those that are caused by parasites that live on the skin's surface. The two ectoparasitic infections that are sexually transmitted are pubic lice and scabies.

Pubic Lice

Pubic lice (or "crabs") are a parasitic STI; the lice are very small, wingless insects that can attach themselves to pubic hair with their claws. They feed off the tiny blood vessels just beneath the skin and are often difficult to detect on light-skinned people. They may also attach themselves to other hairy parts of the body, although they tend to prefer pubic hair. When not attached to the human body, pubic lice cannot survive more than 24 hours. However, they reproduce rapidly, and the female cements her eggs to the sides of pubic hair. The eggs hatch in 7 to 9 days, and the newly hatched nits (baby pubic lice) reproduce within 17 days.

Incidence

Pubic lice are common and regularly seen by health clinics and various health care providers. Although there are no mandated reporting laws, pubic lice affect millions of people worldwide.

Symptoms

The most common symptom is a mild to unbearable itching, which often increases during the evening hours. This itching is thought to be a result of an allergic reaction to the saliva that the lice secrete during their feeding. The itching usually forces a person to seek treatment, although some people detect the lice visually first. People who are not allergic to this saliva may not experience any itching.

Diagnosis

A pubic lice infection is diagnosed by finding the parasites or eggs in the pubic hair. Although they can typically be seen with the naked eye, a magnifying lens may also be used.

> **pubic lice**
> A parasitic sexually transmitted infection that infests the pubic hair and can be transmitted through sexual contact; also called crabs.

Treatment

It is necessary to kill both the parasites and their eggs to treat pubic lice. In addition, the eggs must be destroyed on sheets and clothing. Over-the-counter creams or shampoos can be used to treat pubic lice. If necessary, prescription creams and shampoos can be prescribed if the over-the-counter methods do not work. Sheets and any articles of clothing that have been worn 2 to 3 days prior to treatment should be machine washed and dried. Hot water and dryer cycles should be used. Items that cannot be washed can be dry-cleaned or stored in a sealed plastic bag for 2 weeks. As with the other STIs, it is important to inform all sexual partners within the previous month that they are at risk for pubic lice.

Pubic lice attach to pubic hair and feed off the tiny blood vessels beneath the skin.

E. Gray/Science Source

Scabies

Scabies is an ectoparasitic infection of the skin with the mite *Sarcoptes scabiei*. It is spread during skin-to-skin contact, during both sexual and nonsexual contact. The mites can live for up to 48 hours on bed sheets and clothing and are impossible to see with the naked eye.

Incidence

Infection with scabies occurs worldwide and among all races, ethnic groups, and social classes. Like pubic lice, there are no mandated reporting laws, but scabies affects millions of people worldwide.

Symptoms

Usually the first symptoms include a rash and intense itching. The first time a person is infected, the symptoms may take between 4 and 6 weeks to develop. If a person has been infected with scabies before, the symptoms usually develop more quickly.

Diagnosis

A diagnosis can usually be made on examination of the skin rash. A skin scraping can be done to confirm the diagnosis. A delay in diagnosis can lead to a rapid spread of scabies, so immediate diagnosis and treatment are necessary (Tjioe & Vissers, 2008).

Treatment

Prescription creams are available to treat scabies. All bed sheets, clothing, and towels must be washed in hot water, and all sexual partners should be treated. Usually itching continues for 2 to 3 weeks after infection, even after treatment.

> ## ON YOUR MIND
>
> *Can crabs be spread through casual contact, such as sleeping on the same sheets or sharing clothes? What if someone with crabs sat on my couch and I sat down right after them?*
>
> If you slept in the bed of a person who was infected with pubic lice or wore the same clothes without washing them, there is a chance that you could become infected. Although they are usually spread through sexual contact, it is possible to acquire them if you share a bed or towels, linens, articles of clothing, combs and brushes, or toilet seats with a person who is infected.

Review Questions

1 Identify the two ectoparasitic STIs and describe how common they are.

2 Identify the most common symptoms associated with ectoparasitic STIs, and explain what a person should do if they experience any of these symptoms.

3 Identify the treatment for ectoparasitic STIs.

Bacterial Infections: Gonorrhea, Syphilis, Chlamydia, and More

Bacterial infections include gonorrhea, syphilis, chlamydia, chancroid, and a variety of vaginal infections. In this section, we explore the incidence, symptoms, diagnosis, and treatment for these bacterial infections.

Gonorrhea

Gonorrhea (the "clap" or "drip") is caused by the bacterium *Neisseria gonorrhoeae*, which can survive only in the mucous membranes of the body. These areas, such as the cervix, urethra, mouth, throat,

scabies
A parasitic sexually transmitted infection that affects the skin and is spread during skin-to-skin contact, during both sexual and nonsexual contact.

gonorrhea
A bacterial sexually transmitted infection that causes a puslike discharge and frequent urination in men; many women are asymptomatic.

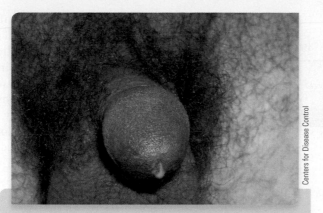

The majority of men infected with gonorrhea experience symptoms and will seek out treatment. However, this may not happen until they have already infected others.

Table 15.1 Prevalence of Sexually Transmitted Infections in the United States

Human Papillomavirus (HPV)	14,000,000/year
Chlamydia*	1,526,658/year
Gonorrhea*	395,216/year
HIV*	40,000/year
Syphilis*	23,872/year
Congenital Syphilis*	458/year
Hepatitis A*	1,200/year
Hepatitis B*	2,800/year
Hepatitis C*	2,200/year
Chancroid*	11/year
Herpes Simplex Virus I** (HSV-1)	6 million women; 5 million men with more than 178 million women and 142 million men infected
Herpes Simplex Virus II** (HSV-2)	500,000/year with more than 50 million people infected
Trichomoniasis	3.7 million infected in the United States; yearly prevalence unknown

There are more than 20 million new STIs in the United States each year and more than half of these are among young people (Barton et al., 2016). Above are the yearly rates for STIs, which have been collected through notifiable infection reporting, projects that monitor STI prevalence, and other national surveys. Keep in mind, however, that actual rates may be much higher since many STIs are asymptomatic and people do not get tested.
*nationally reportable infections
**data from 2012; Looker et al., 2015, 2015a

SOURCES: Barton et al., 2016; Bowen et al., 2015; "Genital HPV Infection," 2017; Looker et al., 2015; Looker et al., 2015a; "Surveillance for Viral Hepatitis," 2016.

rectum, and even the eyes, provide moisture and warmth that help the bacterium survive. *N. gonorrhoeae* is actually fragile and can be destroyed by exposure to light, air, soap, water, or a change in temperature, and so it is nearly impossible to transmit gonorrhea nonsexually. The only exception to this is the transmission of gonorrhea from a mother to her baby as the baby passes through the vagina during delivery. Transmission of gonorrhea occurs when mucous membranes come into contact with each other; this can occur during vaginal intercourse, oral sex, vulva-to-vulva sex, and anal sex. The CDC recommends that all sexually active women who are at higher risk of infection (e.g., have new sex partners, multiple sex partners, a sex partner with multiple partners, or a sex partner infected with an STI) be tested every year for gonorrhea (Barton et al., 2016).

Incidence

Gonorrhea is a nationally reportable infection, and data reveal it is a prevalent STI in the United States today. Although national rates of gonorrhea reached an all-time low in 2009, they have increased almost every year since then. In 2015, there were close to 400,000 cases of gonorrhea reported in the United States (Barton et al., 2016; see Table 15.1). Four main factors are related to gonorrhea prevalence in the United States: age, gender, race/ethnicity, and geographical area. In 2015, the highest rates were among 20- to 24-year-olds, although overall rates were higher among males (Barton et al., 2016; see Figure 15.1). From 2011 to 2015, gonorrhea rates increased 44% among males and decreased 0.7% among females (Barton et al., 2016). Researchers believe this may be due to increases in testing among men and/or increased numbers of men having sex with men.

Research has also found differences in gonorrhea rates among certain racial and/or ethnic groups. For example, in 2015, gonorrhea rates were close to 10 times higher in Blacks than Whites and almost 2 times higher in Hispanics than Whites (Barton et al., 2016; see Figure 15.2). Geographically, gonorrhea rates were highest in the South (followed by the West, Midwest, and Northeast).

Symptoms

Most men who are infected with gonorrhea experience symptoms alerting them of the infection, although they can infect others before the onset of symptoms (Workowski & Berman, 2010). Symptoms include a urethral discharge, painful urination, and/or an increase in the frequency and urgency of urination, as well as **epididymitis** (epp-pih-did-ee-MITE-us). Symptoms usually

epididymitis
An inflammation of the epididymis in men, usually resulting from sexually transmitted infections.

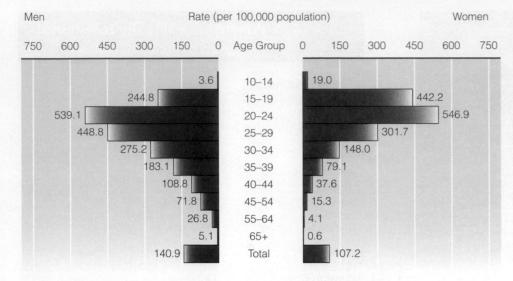

FIGURE **15.1** Gonorrhea Rates by Age Group and Sex: United States, 2015

SOURCE: Centers for Disease Control and Prevention, 2016; Barton et al., 2016.

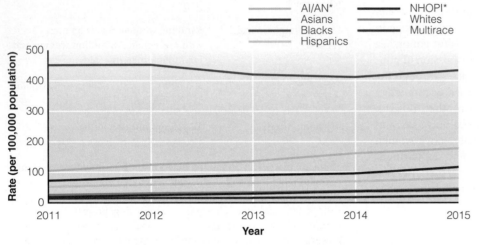

*AI/AN = American Indians/Alaska Natives; NHOPI = Native Hawaiians/Other Pacific Islanders.
NOTE: Includes 45 states reporting race/ethnicity data in Office of Management and Budget compliant formats during 2011–2015.

FIGURE **15.2** Gonorrhea Rates by Race/Ethnicity: United States, 2011–2015

SOURCE: Centers for Disease Control and Prevention, 2016; Barton et al., 2016.

appear between 2 and 6 days after infection.

Unlike men, the majority of women do not experience symptoms until complications develop, such as pelvic inflammatory disease (PID). As we discussed, gonorrhea is a major cause of PID in women. If symptoms do develop, they typically begin within 3 to 5 days and include an increase in urinary frequency, abnormal uterine bleeding, and bleeding after vaginal penetration, which results from an irritation of the cervix. The cervical discharge can irritate the vaginal

gonococcus bacterium
The bacterium that causes gonorrhea (*Neisseria gonorrhoeae*).

lining, causing pain and discomfort. Urination can be difficult and painful.

Rectal gonorrhea, which can be transmitted to individuals during anal intercourse, may cause bloody stools and a puslike discharge. If left untreated, gonorrhea can move throughout the body and settle in various areas, including the joints, causing swelling, pain, and pus-filled infections.

Diagnosis

Testing for gonorrhea can be done with a urine test that detects the bacteria, or through a sample of the discharge from the cervix, urethra, or another infected area with a cotton swab. The discharge is incubated to allow the bacteria to multiply. It is then put on a slide and examined under a microscope for the presence of the **gonococcus bacterium**. Several at-home STI kits are now available that provide gonorrhea testing (see the website section at the end of this chapter).

Treatment

The recommended treatment for gonorrhea infection is antibiotics, but the bacteria responsible for gonorrhea has developed resistance to almost every antibiotic that has been used for treatment. Today the CDC recommends the use of dual therapy, with two antibiotics, to treat gonorrhea (Barton et al., 2016). All sexual partners should also be tested for gonorrhea, regardless of whether they are experiencing symptoms. If a sexual partner is unlikely to seek treatment, some health care providers will provide patients with antibiotics or a prescription for them. Typically, becoming infected again after treatment is most likely caused by the failure of sex partners to get tested or receive treatment.

ON YOUR MIND

Which sexually transmitted infections (STIs) do gynecologists check for during a regular examination?

During a woman's yearly visit, health care providers perform a Pap test, which is designed to evaluate the cervical cells. Close to half of women believe that a Pap test can identify STIs (HAWKINS ET AL., 2011). This is not necessarily true. Although it is possible that some STIs, such as HPV and herpes, may show up during Pap testing, many will not. If you think that you may have been exposed to any STIs, it is important for you to ask your health care provider to perform specific tests to screen for these. Specific tests can be run for BV, chlamydia, gonorrhea, hepatitis, HIV, HPV, HSV, syphilis, and trichomoniasis.

Syphilis

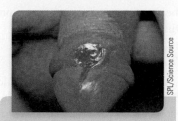

The chancre, which appears on the underside of the penis in this photo, is the classic painless ulcer of syphilis.

Syphilis is caused by an infection with the bacterium *Treponema pallidum*. The bacteria enter the body through small tears in the skin and live in the mucous membranes. Syphilis is transmitted during sexual contact, and it usually first infects the cervix, penis, anus, lips, or other area of the body. **Congenital syphilis** may also be transmitted through the placenta during the first or second trimester of pregnancy. While the CDC does not recommend annual testing for those who have a low risk of infection, it does recommend yearly testing for MSM and testing every 3 to 6 months for men at high risk (Barton et al., 2016).

after infection (typically this happens within 2 to 6 weeks after infection). During this stage, there may be one or more small, red-brown sores, called *chancres*, that appear on the vulva, penis, vagina, cervix, anus, mouth, or lips. The **chancre** (SHANK-ker), which is a round sore with a hard, raised edge and a sunken center, is usually painless and does not itch. If left untreated, the chancre will heal in 3 to 8 weeks. However, during this time, the person can still transmit the infection to other sexual partners.

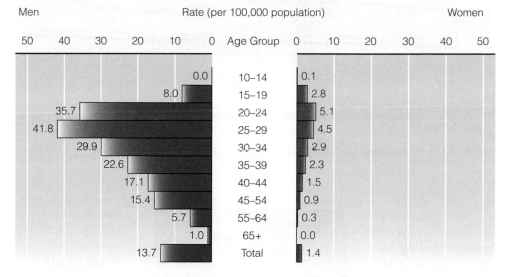

FIGURE **15.3** **Primary and Secondary Syphilis Rates by Age Group and Sex: United States, 2015**

SOURCE: Centers for Disease Control and Prevention, 2016; Barton et al., 2016.

Incidence

Like gonorrhea, syphilis is a nationally reportable infection. Data reveal that the syphilis rate in 2000 was the lowest it had ever been since reporting began in 1941. At that time the surgeon general announced a plan to eliminate syphilis from the United States. Unfortunately, syphilis rates have been increasing since then. In 2015, there were close to 24,000 reported cases of syphilis, which was the highest rate since 1994 (Barton et al., 2016). Experts believe this was due to increases in rates of MSM. Rates of congenital syphilis have also been increasing, and in 2015 there were close to 500 reported cases (Barton et al., 2016).

Like gonorrhea rates, four main factors are related to syphilis prevalence in the United States: age, gender, race/ethnicity, and geographical area. In 2015, syphilis rates were highest among males who were 25 to 29 years old (see Figures 15.3, 15.4, and 15.7). In fact, men accounted for over 90% of all syphilis cases in 2015. The majority of these infections (60%) were acquired in MSM (Barton et al., 2016).

Racial/ethnic differences in syphilis rates have been decreasing: While rates were 24 times higher in Blacks than Whites in 1999, by 2015, they were only 5 times higher (this disparity was higher among Black women than Black men; see Figure 15.5; Barton et al., 2016). Syphilis rates are highest in the West (followed by the South, Northeast, and Midwest).

Symptoms

Infection with syphilis is divided into three stages. The first stage, primary or early syphilis, occurs anywhere from 10 to 90 days

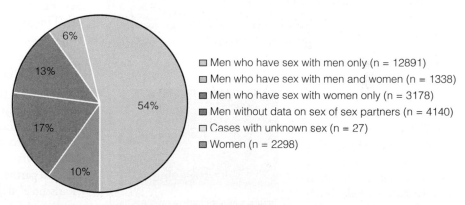

FIGURE **15.4** **Primary and Secondary Syphilis Distribution of Cases by Sex and Sexual Behavior, United States, 2015**

As in previous years, men accounted for a large majority (90%) of syphilis cases in 2015.

SOURCE: Centers for Disease Control and Prevention, 2016; Barton et al., 2016.

---

syphilis
A bacterial sexually transmitted infection that is divided into primary, secondary, and tertiary stages.

congenital syphilis
A syphilis infection acquired by an infant from the mother during pregnancy.

chancre
A small, red-brown sore that results from syphilis infection; the sore is actually the site at which the bacteria entered the body.

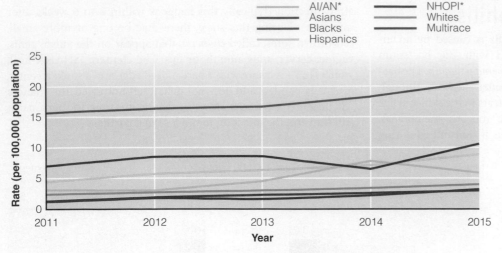

Legend:
- AI/AN*
- Asians
- Blacks
- Hispanics
- NHOPI*
- Whites
- Multirace

*AI/AN = American Indians/Alaska Natives; NHOPI = Native Hawaiians/Other Pacific Islanders.
NOTE: Includes 45 states reporting race/ethnicity data in Office of Management and Budget compliant formats during 2011–2015.

FIGURE **15.5** Primary and Secondary Syphilis Rates by Race/Ethnicity, United States, 2011–2015

SOURCE: Centers for Disease Control and Prevention, 2016; Barton et al., 2016.

After the chancre disappears, the infected person enters the second stage, secondary syphilis, which begins anywhere from 3 to 6 weeks after the chancre has healed. During this stage, the syphilis invades the central nervous system. The infected person develops reddish patches on the skin that look like a rash or hives. If the rash develops on the scalp, hair loss can also occur. The lymph glands in the groin, armpit, neck, or other areas enlarge and become tender. Additional symptoms at this stage include headaches, fevers, anorexia, flulike symptoms, and fatigue.

In the third and final stage of the infection, tertiary or late syphilis, the infection goes into remission. The rash, fever, and other symptoms go away, and the person usually feels fine. However, an infected individual is still able to transmit the infection for about 1 year. After this time they are no longer infectious. Left untreated, however, syphilis can spread to the brain and nervous system and cause neurological problems, including numbness,

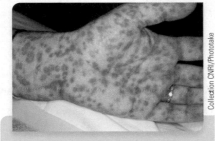

A secondary syphilis infection produces rashes on the palms or soles, as well as a generalized body rash.

Collection CNRI/Phototake

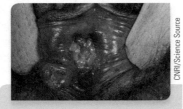

Typical syphilis chancre on the inside of a woman's labia minora.

CNRI/Science Source

chlamydia
A bacterial sexually transmitted infection; although often asymptomatic, it is thought to be one of the most damaging of all the STIs.

headaches, paralysis, changes in vision, dementia, and possibly death.

Diagnosis

Anyone who develops a chancre should immediately go to a health care provider to be tested for the presence of the syphilis-causing bacteria. Several at-home STI kits are now available that provide syphilis testing (see the website section at the end of this chapter). A diagnosis can be made by culturing and evaluating the lesion or through a blood test. Blood tests check for the presence of antibodies, which develop after a person is infected with the bacteria. However, during late syphilis, blood tests may appear negative or weakly positive even if the infection exists (Singh et al., 2008). All sexual partners should also be tested for syphilis, regardless of whether they are experiencing symptoms. If a person thinks that they may have been exposed to syphilis but test negative, they should consult with a health care provider immediately.

Treatment

In its early stages, syphilis is relatively easy to treat. Treatment typically involves a single injection of an antibiotic for persons who have been infected less than a year. Additional doses may be required if a person has been infected longer than a year (Workowski & Berman, 2010). Treatment can cure syphilis in the early stages, but it might not undo any damages already caused by the bacteria (such as any neurological damage).

Chlamydia

Chlamydia is the common name for infections caused by the bacterium *Chlamydia trachomatis*. Chlamydia can be transmitted during various sexual behaviors that include genital contact, such as vaginal intercourse, oral sex, and/or anal sex, and it can infect the penis, cervix, vagina, anus, urethra, eye, or throat. Oral sex with an infected partner can lead to pharyngeal (throat) chlamydia infection (Karlsson et al., 2011). The CDC recommends that all sexually active women who have a high risk of infection (e.g., have new sex partners, multiple sex partners, a sex partner with multiple partners, or a sex partner infected with an STI) be tested every year for chlamydia (Barton et al., 2016). While the CDC has not recommended routine screening for sexually active young men, it does recommend yearly testing for MSM and testing every 3 to 6 months for men at high risk.

Incidence

Chlamydia is a nationally reportable infection, and data reveal it is one of the most prevalent of all STIs in the United States today (Barton et al., 2016). Rates have been increasing since the late 1980s when the first screening programs were established. In 2015, there were more than 1.5 million cases of chlamydia in the United States

(Barton et al., 2016). Greater numbers may be because of more active screening for chlamydia, but experts believe they represent a true increase in the infection. Like other STIs, there are age, gender, race/ethnicity, and geographical differences in the prevalence of chlamydia.

Chlamydia rates are highest among adolescents and young adults ages 15 to 24 years (see Figures 15.6 and 15.7). Although rates among women were double those in men in 2015, experts believe this may be a result of more women being screened for infections. Rates of chlamydia in men increased 20% during 2011–2015, compared to a 0.3% increase among women during this period (Barton et al., 2016). However, lower overall rates among men indicates that many of the sex partners of infected women are not being diagnosed or treated.

Research has also found differences in certain racial/ethnic groups. In 2015, the chlamydia rate in Black women was close to 6 times the rate among White women, while the rate among Hispanic women was 2 times the rate among White women (Barton et al., 2016). Among Black men the chlamydia rate was close to 7 times the rate among White men. Geographical differences were also found, with rates of chlamydia highest in the South (followed by the Midwest, West, and the Northeast).

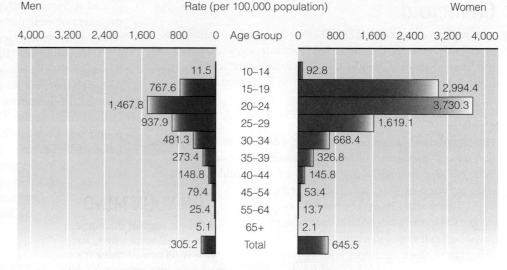

FIGURE **15.6** Chlamydia Rates by Age Group and Sex, United States, 2015

SOURCE: Centers for Disease Control and Prevention, 2016; Barton et al., 2016.

FIGURE **15.7** Gonorrhea and Chlamydia Rates by Age, United States, 2012

SOURCE: Centers for Disease Control and Prevention, 2016.

Symptoms

Chlamydia has been called a "silent disease" because there are often no symptoms. While some men may experience symptoms, the majority of women do not. Those who do have symptoms usually develop them within 1 to 3 weeks after becoming infected. If there are symptoms, a woman might experience burning during urination, pain during penetration, and pain in the lower abdomen. In most women, the cervix is the site of infection with chlamydia, so cervical bleeding or spotting may occur. Men may experience a penile discharge, burning sensations during urination, burning and itching around the opening of the urethra, and a pain or swelling in the testicles. The bacterium that causes chlamydia can also cause epididymitis and **nongonococcal urethritis** in men. With or without symptoms, chlamydia is contagious, which explains why rates are increasing.

As we discussed, chlamydial infections in women are a major cause of pelvic inflammatory disease (PID). Risk of PID is also increased when a woman with a chlamydia infection undergoes a surgical abortion or vaginal birth (Boeke et al., 2005).

Diagnosis

Chlamydia can be diagnosed through urine testing, but it can also be diagnosed from cultures of the vagina, cervix, urethra, rectum, or mouth. People who have engaged in oral or anal sex with infected partners should also undergo oral and rectal testing (Mangin et al., 2012; Papp et al., 2014). Like many of the other STIs, at-home kits are now available that provide multiple-site testing for chlamydia (see the website section at the end of this chapter).

Treatment

Chlamydia can easily be treated with antibiotics. All sexual partners should also be tested, even if they are not experiencing symptoms. As we discussed earlier, some health care providers may provide antibiotics for partners who are unwilling to get treated (Schembri & Schober, 2011). Rapid reinfection is usually due to the failure of sex partners to get tested or receive treatment. Patients are advised to abstain from penetrative sexual behaviors for 7 days after beginning antibiotic treatment, and they should be retested within 3 months of treatment.

---

nongonococcal urethritis
Urethral infection in men that is usually caused by an infection with chlamydia.

Sexually Transmitted Infections **409**

Chancroid

Although a **chancroid** (SHANK-kroyd) may look similar to a syphilis chancre, the difference lies in its soft edges compared with the hard edges of a syphilis sore. Chancroids are sexually transmitted through the *Haemophilus ducreyi* bacterium.

Incidence

Chancroid is a nationally reportable infection, and data reveal that it has decreased steadily in the United States since 1987. Whereas approximately 5,000 cases of chancroid were reported in 1987, only 11 were reported in 2015 (Barton et al., 2016). The majority of cases diagnosed in the United States involve a person who has traveled to a country where the infection is more common, such as countries in Africa, Asia, and the Caribbean.

Symptoms

People infected with chancroid experience development of a small lesion or several lesions at the point of entry. Four to 7 days after infection, a small lump appears and ruptures within 2 or 3 days, forming a shallow ulcer. These ulcers are painful, with ragged edges, and may persist for weeks and even months (Lewis, 2000). The infection may spread to the lymph nodes of the groin, which can cause swelling and pain.

Diagnosis

Diagnosis can be difficult, mainly because of problems culturing *H. ducreyi*, the responsible bacteria. A fluid sample from the ulcers is collected to examine for the presence of the bacteria. Difficulties with diagnosis may be responsible for the underdiagnosis of chancroid.

Treatment

Chancroids are treated with antibiotics. Ulcers typically improve between 3 and 7 days after treatment is begun. All recent sexual contacts should be told to seek testing and treatment.

Vaginal Infections

Vaginal infections are characterized by a discharge, itching, and/or odor. In Chapter 5, we discussed bacterial vaginosis (BV) and candidiasis. Although these infections can be transmitted sexually, they can also be acquired through nonsexual means. Having multiple sex partners can change the balance of bacteria in the vagina, which in turn can increase a woman's risk of acquiring BV. A BV infection can also increase a woman's risk for developing an STI. As we discussed in Chapter 5, a woman who experiences multiple vaginal infections should ask her partner to get evaluated and

treated. Although bacteria for BV can be found in the male urethra, treatment of male partners has not been found to decrease recurrences of BV in their female partners (Workowski & Bolan, 2015).

Trichomoniasis (trick-oh-mun-NYE-iss-sis; also called trich) is a vaginal infection caused by *Trichomonas vaginalis* bacteria. Although there are no national reporting requirements for trichomoniasis, studies have found that it is one of the most prevalent STIs in the United States. It's estimated that approximately 3.7 million people are infected with trichomoniasis (Workowski & Bolan, 2015). Rates are highest in non-Hispanic Black women (13% compared to 2% in White women). Women can get trichomoniasis from an infected man or woman, whereas a man usually contracts it only from an infected woman. This is because the bacteria is acquired through heterosexual or lesbian sexual behavior and is rarely transmitted through gay male sexual behavior. Symptoms usually appear anywhere from 3 to 28 days after infection.

> **ON YOUR MIND**
>
> *I have a vaginal discharge that is yellowish white, but there is no odor. I think it's a yeast infection because it's kind of itchy. Should I use an over-the-counter cream?*

Remember that having a discharge doesn't mean that you definitely have a vaginal infection. Normal vaginal discharge can range from white to slightly yellow, and it varies throughout the menstrual cycle. A yeast infection often causes vaginal itching and burning, pain during sex and urination, and a thick, white discharge. Keep in mind, however, that research has found only one in four women who seek treatment for a yeast infection actually has one (HOFFSTETTER ET AL., 2008). Vaginal itching can also be caused by inflammation, dry skin, STIs, and bacterial vaginosis (BV). Like a yeast infection, BV can sometimes be triggered by the use of antibiotics or the use of feminine hygiene products. However, over-the-counter medications for yeast infections, which fight fungus, are ineffective against BV.

Although some women are asymptomatic or have minimal symptoms of bacterial vaginal infections (Workowski & Berman, 2010), if there are symptoms, the most common is an increase in vaginal discharge. The discharge may be yellowish or green-yellow, frothy, and foul smelling; it may cause a burning or itching sensation in the vagina. Men can also be asymptomatic although if there are symptoms, these include a slight increase in burning on the tip of the penis, mild discharge, or slight burning after urination or ejaculation. Like many of the other STIs, at-home kits

REAL RESEARCH A group of teenage inventors have developed "fluorescing" condoms that light up when exposed to STIs (TARANTOLA, 2015). A layer of molecules in the condoms will cause a chemical reaction when exposed to STIs, turning them green when exposed to chlamydia, blue for syphilis, yellow for herpes, and purple for HPV. It's unclear whether this invention will become an actual product.

---

chancroid
A bacterial sexually transmitted infection characterized by small bumps that eventually rupture and form painful ulcers.

trichomoniasis
A vaginal infection that may result in discomfort, discharge, and inflammation.

are now available that provide testing for trichomoniasis (see the website section at the end of this chapter).

Both BV and trichomoniasis are easily treated with medications, such as Metronidazole (Flagyl) or Clindamycin. Metronidazole can cause adverse effects such as nausea, headaches, loss of appetite, diarrhea, cramping, and a metallic taste in the mouth.

Alcohol should also be avoided for 24 hours after this medication, since it can increase adverse side effects. Women who are infected with trichomoniasis should recommend all sex partners be treated. While it may not be necessary to treat male sexual partners of women infected with BV, all female partners should be treated.

Review Questions

1 Identify the bacterial STIs, and describe those that are most common today.

2 Explain how age, gender, race, ethnicity, geographic area, and sexual orientation have been found to affect incidence rates.

3 Explain the asymptomatic nature of the bacterial STIs and identify possible symptoms.

4 Identify the common treatments for bacterial STIs.

5 Discuss common vaginal infections and explain how they may be sexually transmitted.

Viral Infections: Herpes, Human Papillomavirus, and Hepatitis

STIs can also be caused by viruses. Once a virus invades a body cell, it is able to reproduce itself, so most of the time people will have the virus for the rest of their lives. Viruses can live in the body, and although people may not experience symptoms, they still have the virus. We now discuss herpes, HPV, and viral hepatitis; later in this chapter we will explore HIV and AIDS.

Herpes

Herpes simplex 1 (HSV-1) and **herpes simplex 2 (HSV-2)** are members of the **herpes** virus family. The CDC believe that most HSV-1 infections are typically acquired during childhood, while most HSV-2 infections are transmitted during penetrative sexual behavior (Barton et al., 2016). Although HSV-1 prefers the mouth or lips, it can also be transmitted to the genitals. HSV-2 prefers the genitals but can also be transmitted to the mouth or lips. When the virus infects a nonpreferred site (i.e., HSV-1 infects the genitals or HSV-2 infects the mouth or lips), symptoms are often less severe. Overall, recurrences and outbreaks are less frequent with an HSV-1, compared to an HSV-2, infection.

HSV is highly contagious and the virus may be released between outbreaks from the infected skin (often referred to as **viral shedding**). Because of this, it is possible to transmit the virus even when the infected partner does not have any active symptoms (Mertz, 2008; Schiffer et al., 2014). Viral shedding is more

common in genital HSV-2 infection than genital HSV-1 infection, especially during the first year after infection (Schiffer et al., 2014; Workowski & Berman, 2010). Infected people can also **autoinoculate** themselves by touching a cold sore or blister and then rubbing another part of their body.

Incidence

The herpes simplex virus is not a nationally reportable infection in the United States, but studies have found that infections are very common. In fact, 62% of people have been infected with HSV-1 by adolescence, and 85% have been infected by the age of 60. It's estimated that as many as 25% of women and 12.5% of men are currently infected with HSV-2, although only about 20% of these are aware of the infection (Horn et al., 2015). This is mainly because some people might not have symptoms, or have mild or unrecognized infections (Workowski & Berman, 2010). The majority of people who become infected with HSV-2 are infected by someone who doesn't even know they have it.

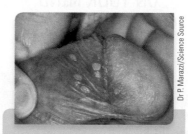

This is a typical patch of HSV-2 blisters on the penis.

Dr. P. Marazzi/Science Source

---

herpes simplex 1 (HSV-1)
A viral infection that is usually transmitted through kissing or sharing eating or drinking utensils and can cause cold sores or blisters on the face and mouth.

herpes simplex 2 (HSV-2)
A viral infection that is often sexually transmitted and is responsible for genital ulcerations and blisters.

herpes
A highly contagious viral infection that causes eruptions of the skin or mucous membranes.

viral shedding
The release of viral infections between outbreaks from infected skin.

autoinoculate
To cause a secondary infection in the body from an already existing infection.

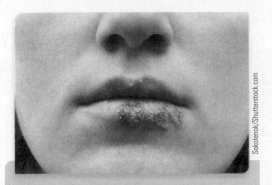

This is a typical patch of HSV-1 blisters, which often appear on the lips or mouth.

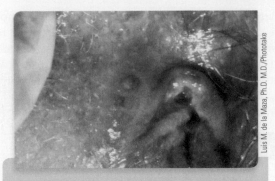

HSV-2 infection in women can cause blisters on the vulva, vagina, or any place the virus entered the body.

esteem, and depression. All of these reactions may also trigger an outbreak (Chida & Mao, 2009; Horn et al., 2015). Persons with supportive partners and social relationships tend to do better psychologically. In addition, those who receive psychological support services may experience a greater reduction in recurrent episodes of herpes (Horn et al., 2015).

Symptoms

Many people infected with HSV do not develop symptoms. If blisters do develop, they usually appear within 2 to 12 days after infection. At the onset, there is usually a tingling or burning feeling in the affected area, which can grow into an itching and a red, swollen appearance of the genitals (this period is often referred to as the **prodromal phase**). The amount of pain they cause can range from mild to severe, and depending on the amount of pain, urination may be difficult. Small blisters may appear externally on the vagina or penis. The blisters, which are usually red and sometimes have a grayish center, will eventually burst and ooze a yellowish discharge. As they begin to heal, a scab will form over them. Generally, the first episode of blisters is the most painful, and symptoms become less severe in subsequent outbreaks (Workowski & Berman, 2010). Other possible symptoms of HSV include a fever, headaches, pain, itching, vaginal or urethral discharge, and general fatigue. These symptoms peak within 4 days of the appearance of the blisters.

The frequency and severity of recurrent episodes of HSV depend on several things, including the amount of infectious agent (how much of the virus was contained in the original infecting fluids), the type of HSV, location of the infection, and the timing of treatment (Mark et al., 2008). Men and women who experience symptoms during their first outbreak of genital HSV-2 infection will most likely experience recurrent episodes of blisters, but those infected with genital HSV-1 infections may not have recurrences (Workowski & Berman, 2010). Certain triggers may increase the likelihood of an HSV outbreak, including exposure to sunlight (natural or tanning beds), lip trauma or chapping, sickness, menstruation, fatigue, and persistent anxiety and stress (Cohen et al., 1999). After several years, a person may no longer experience outbreaks, although they may still be contagious and able to infect others.

Psychological reactions to HSV outbreaks can include anxiety, guilt, anger, frustration, helplessness, a decrease in self-

Diagnosis

During the first several weeks after infection, antibodies to HSV develop and will remain in the body indefinitely. The presence of blisters caused by the herpes virus may be enough to diagnose HSV, but virologic and serologic (blood) tests are also used. Virologic tests involve taking a fluid sample from a lesion and monitoring it for the development of the virus (usually the virus will reproduce within 1 to 10 days). These tests are highly accurate if done within the first 3 days of the appearance of lesions. Serologic tests can also be used to identify antibodies and distinguish between HSV-1 and HSV-2. These tests are highly accurate when done 12 to 16 weeks after exposure to the virus. It's important for a health care provider to determine whether a person is infected with HSV-1 or HSV-2, since this can influence treatment recommendations. No test for the detection of HSV is 100% accurate because tests depend on the amount of infectious agent and the stage of the infection. False-negative results can occur when tests are performed too early. Like for many of the other STIs, at-home kits are now available that provide testing for HSV-2 (see the website section at the end of this chapter).

ON YOUR MIND

Because herpes is not curable, can people still transmit it when they are in their "downtime" between flare-ups?

Although rates of viral shedding have been found to decrease over time after the initial infection, it is possible to transmit the virus in the absence of active cold sores or lesions (HORN ET AL., 2015). Overall, viral shedding is more common in genital HSV-2 infections than genital HSV-1 infections, especially during the first year after infection. Health care providers recommend that people who have been infected with HSV use condoms to decrease the risk for infecting their partners.

Treatment

The standard treatment for HSV infection today are oral antiviral drugs, which are typically started during the first outbreak and continued for 7 to 10 days. These drugs shorten the duration of an outbreak and can prevent complications (such as itching

prodromal phase
The tingling or burning feeling that precedes the development of herpes blisters.

or scarring). Since people with HSV infection may experience recurrent episodes of blisters, medications can be used as needed to shorten the duration of outbreaks. Medications can also be taken during the prodromal phase before the appearance of blisters. Alternatively, daily **suppressive therapy** can be used to reduce recurrences. Suppressive therapy has also been found to decrease the risk of viral shedding and infections in sexual partners (Mujugira et al., 2013; Schiffer et al., 2014). Although topical medications were used in the past to manage HSV symptoms, they are no longer recommended since they have been shown to have little benefit.

Natural remedies for herpes outbreaks include applying an ice pack to the affected area during the prodromal phase and applying cooling or drying agents such as witch hazel. Increasing intake of foods rich in certain amino acids, such as L-lysine, which includes fish or yogurt, and decreasing the intake of sugar and nuts (which are high in another amino acid, arginine) may also help reduce recurrences (Griffith et al., 1987; Vukovic, 1992). Lysine can also be purchased from the vitamin section of any drugstore. Herbal treatments have also been used, including lemon balm (to dry cold sores), aloe (to decrease healing time of blisters), and peppermint oil (to inhibit the virus from replicating). However, the use of herbs can trigger outbreaks in some people, so it is recommended that they be used under medical supervision.

Support groups, relaxation training, hypnosis, yoga, and individual therapy have also been found to reduce the stress associated with HSV infections. As we discussed, reducing stress can also reduce the frequency and severity of outbreaks. Researchers have been working on the development of a vaccine to prevent HSV for decades; although progress has been made, as of 2017 there was no vaccine available. Clinical trials continue to evaluate several proposed vaccines. Some of the vaccines prompt the immune system to develop antibodies to the virus, while others try to find ways to destroy already infected cells in the body (Cooney, 2013; Kempner, 2013). If successful, an HSV vaccine could be used like the HPV vaccine and administered before a person becomes sexually active.

Human Papillomavirus

There are more than 100 different types of human papillomavirus (HPV), and more than 40 of them can be spread through various sexual behaviors, including vaginal and anal intercourse, oral sex, and vulva-to-vulva contact. There are two types of "low-risk" HPV that can cause **genital warts** (condyloma acuminata, venereal warts) and may also cause respiratory papillomatosis (warts in the respiratory tract). Seven additional "high-risk" HPV types can cause cervical, anal, oropharyngeal (throat), vaginal, penile, and other cancers (Alemany et al., 2014; Joura et al., 2015).

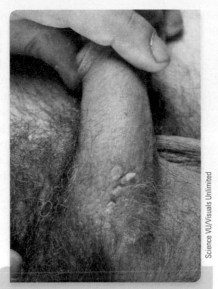
Science VU/Visuals Unlimited

Genital warts, caused by HPV, are usually skin-colored and may have a bumpy appearance on the penis.

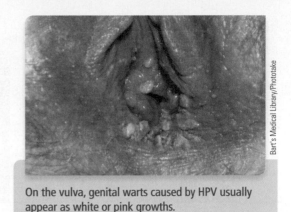
Bart's Medical Library/Phototake

On the vulva, genital warts caused by HPV usually appear as white or pink growths.

While virtually 100% of cervical cancer is caused by HPV, 95% of anal cancer, 70% of oropharyngeal cancer, 65% of vaginal cancer, and 35% of penile cancers are also caused by HPV (Chaturvedi et al., 2011; Gillison et al., 2008; Joura et al., 2015; Winer et al., 2006). Regular Pap tests for women enable health care providers to monitor precancerous changes in the cervical cells (often referred to as **cervical dysplasia**). Identifying problems early can significantly reduce the risk of the infection developing into cancer.

MSM are disproportionately affected by HPV-related cancers. In fact, rates of anal cancer in MSM are over 15 times higher than in heterosexual men (Lawton et al., 2013). HPV can also be spread during female-to-female sex, and it's important for lesbian and bisexual women to get regular Pap testing (Reiter & McRee, 2014). HPV is highly contagious, and sexual partners often are both infected, although it's impossible to determine who was infected first. Since there can be a long period of latency, being infected with HPV does not necessarily mean that a partner was unfaithful (Workowski & Bolan, 2015).

REAL RESEARCH Home HPV testing kits may be a useful method for screening lesbian and bisexual women who are risk for STIs (REITER & MCREE, 2014). Many young lesbian and bisexual women do not have routine Pap tests and are not aware of their HPV status.

Incidence

Although human papillomavirus is not a nationally reportable infection, studies have found that it is very common in the United States. In fact, HPV is so common that experts believe most sexually active people will get it at some point in their lifetimes (Workowski & Bolan, 2015). It's estimated that more than

suppressive therapy
Long-term use of antiviral medications to reduce the frequency of genital herpes recurrences.

genital warts
Wartlike growths on the genitals; also called venereal warts, condylomata, or papilloma.

cervical dysplasia
Disordered growth of cells in the cervix, typically diagnosed with Pap testing.

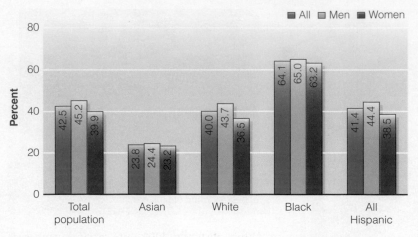

FIGURE **15.8** Prevalence of any Genital HPV among Adults aged 18-59, by Race/Ethnicity and Sex, United States, 2013–2014

SOURCE: National Health and Nutrition Examination Survey; McQuillan et al., 2017.

79 million Americans are infected with genital HPV and another 14 million become newly infected each year ("Genital HPV Infection," 2017). There are racial/ethnicity differences in the prevalence of HPV, with the highest rates among non-Hispanic Black adults and lowest among Asian adults (see Figure 15.8).

Symptoms

Symptoms for HPV are dependent on the type of HPV infection. As we discussed, certain types of HPV cause genital warts and/or growths in the throat, nose, and mouth. Warts are usually flesh colored, with a bumpy surface. Genital warts can develop in women on the vagina, vulva, introitus, or cervix, and in men on the penile shaft or under the foreskin in an uncircumcised penis (Workowski & Berman, 2010). Warts can also appear on the anus in both men and women. Warts are generally asymptomatic, and unless they are large, many people do not notice them and unknowingly infect their sexual partners. If warts grow in the throat, they can potentially block the airway, causing breathing difficulties and/or a hoarse voice.

Infection with high-risk types of HPV often have no symptoms, with the exception of oropharyngeal cancer. If a person does have symptoms, they can include persistent sore throat, hoarseness, pain when swallowing, earaches, and enlarged lymph nodes. It's estimated that 9,000 people are diagnosed with oropharyngeal cancer from HPV in the United States every year. It is four times more common in men than in women ("HPV and Oropharyngeal Cancer," 2017). Using condoms and dental dams during oral sex can lower a person's risk of acquiring oral HPV (see the "Sex in Real Life" feature earlier in this chapter).

Diagnosis

Several tests have been approved by the FDA to detect HPV infection in women and are often used during Pap testing. These tests are recommended by the CDC for women ages 20 to 26. Health care providers recommend that women who have more than one sexual partner should ask their medical provider for an HPV test. If genital warts are suspected, a health care provider can soak the infected area with acetic acid (white vinegar), which turns the warts white and makes them easier to see under magnification. An examination of the cervix under magnification (called *colposcopy*) can also be used. Currently there is no HPV test recommended for men, although some experts recommend that MSM undergo yearly anal cancer screening, since there is an increased risk of anal cancer in these groups. Like many of the other STIs, at-home kits are now available that provide testing for HPV (see the website section at the end of this chapter).

Treatment

While close to 90% of low-risk HPV infections are asymptomatic and resolve spontaneously within two years without treatment (Barton et al., 2016; Corneanu et al., 2011), it's important to seek treatment if a person notices the development of genital warts because they can quickly grow and multiply. Genital warts can be treated in several ways, and no treatment method is superior to another or best for all patients with HPV. Important factors for a health care provider to consider when deciding treatment options include the number and size of the warts, patient preference, treatment costs, convenience, and adverse effects.

Treatment alternatives include chemical topical solutions (to destroy external warts), cryotherapy (freezing the warts with liquid nitrogen), electrosurgical interventions (removal of warts using a mild electrical current, often referred to as a LEEP, or "loop electrosurgical excision procedure"), or laser surgery (high-intensity lasers to destroy the warts). Women with high-risk types of HPV may be encouraged to have pelvic examinations and Pap tests more frequently.

ON YOUR MIND

Could I get human papillomavirus (HPV) from the HPV vaccine? Can I get the vaccine if I've already had sex?

Unlike most vaccines, the HPV vaccines do not contain live viruses and are not infectious (MEITES ET AL., 2016). The vaccines contain inactivated virus-like particles from the HPV, which stimulate a person's body to produce antibodies against HPV (SCHLEGEL, 2007). Current recommendations are for women and men to have the vaccine before age 26, and ideally before becoming sexually active. However, if you are already sexually active but have not been exposed to HPV types 6, 11, 16, and 18, the vaccine will protect you from the types you have not already been exposed to. It is important to discuss these issues with your health care provider, but keep in mind that providers' opinions and attitudes about the vaccine influence whether they offer or promote the vaccine (ISHIBASHI ET AL., 2008).

Although there have been two HPV vaccines available in the United States—Gardasil and Cervarix—both of these were phased out in 2017. The newest HPV vaccine, Gardasil-9, is currently the only available HPV vaccine (Meites et al., 2016). It offers protection from nine types of HPV and can be given to both males and females. Ideally, the HPV vaccine should be given between the ages of 9 and 14, before an individual is sexually active. Done early, HPV vaccines are given as a two-dose injection (the second dose should be given 6 months after the first dose; see Figure 15.9 for more information on the HPV vaccine).

Teens and young adults who have not been vaccinated can have the HPV vaccine between the ages of 15 and 26. Later vaccines may require a three-dose injection (with the second dose 1 to 2 months after the first, and the third dose 6 months after the second). There is some evidence that the vaccine can protect sexually active individuals from HPV types they have not been exposed to and may offer some protection from types they have already been exposed to.

Vaccine side effects may include arm soreness, possible joint and muscle pain, fatigue, and general weakness (Garnock-Jones & Giuliano, 2011). Some women have reported feeling light-headed after the injection, and health care providers recommend waiting 15 minutes after the vaccine is given before leaving a health care provider's office (National Cancer Institute, 2009).

Because the vaccines are relatively new, the actual duration of immunity is unknown. Research continues to evaluate immunity duration, but it appears the vaccines are effective for at least 10 years in women who were not infected with HPV at the time of vaccination ("HPV Vaccine Information, 2017"). However, women who have had the HPV vaccine will still need to have regular Pap tests, since a small percentage of cervical cancers are caused by types other than those covered by the vaccine (Workowski & Bolan, 2015). Although HPV vaccines were developed to prevent cervical and other cancers, there have not been studies to determine if these vaccines offer protection from oral HPV and oropharyngeal cancers. However, experts are hopeful that they do offer protection from oral HPV.

Viral Hepatitis

Viral hepatitis is an infection that causes an inflammation of the liver. The three main types of viral hepatitis include hepatitis A virus (HAV), hepatitis B virus (HBV), and hepatitis C virus (HCV). Viral hepatitis is the leading cause of liver cancer in the United States. While HAV is transmitted through fecal–oral contact and is often spread by food handlers, it can also be spread through anal–oral contact. HBV is predominantly spread during high-risk sexual behaviors (see earlier "Sex in Real Life" feature), while HCV can be spread through sexual behavior but is mostly caused by illegal intravenous drug use or unscreened blood transfusions.

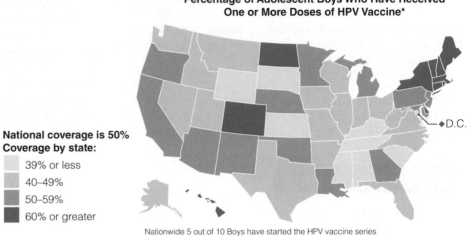

Percentage of Adolescent Girls Who Have Received One or More Doses of HPV Vaccine*

National coverage is 63%
Coverage by state:
- 59% or less
- 60–64%
- 65–69%
- 70% or greater

Nationwide 6 out of 10 Girls have started the HPV vaccine series

Percentage of Adolescent Boys Who Have Received One or More Doses of HPV Vaccine*

National coverage is 50%
Coverage by state:
- 39% or less
- 40–49%
- 50–59%
- 60% or greater

Nationwide 5 out of 10 Boys have started the HPV vaccine series

*Estimated coverage with ≥1 dose of human papillomavirus (HPV) vaccine among adolescents aged 13–17 years.

FIGURE **15.9** (a) Percentage of Adolescent Girls Who Have Received One or More Doses of the HPV Vaccine. (b) Percentage of Adolescent Boys Who Have Received One or More Doses of the HPV Vaccine

SOURCE: National Cancer Institute; Centers for Disease Control, 2016.

Incidence

Although viral hepatitis is a nationally reportable infection, it is typically underreported. In 2014, there were approximately 1,200 reported new cases of HAV in the United States, which was 30% less than in 2013 ("Surveillance for Viral Hepatitis," 2016). However, experts point out that because of underreporting and the exclusion of asymptomatic infections, the number of new cases of HAV in the United States was probably closer to 2,500 in 2014. There were 2,800 reported new cases of HBV in the United States in 2014, which was slightly up from 2011. But, again, because of underreporting and the exclusion of asymptomatic infections, experts believe the number of new cases of HBV in the United States was probably closer to 19,000. Finally, there were 2,200 reported

> **viral hepatitis**
> A viral infection; three main types of viral hepatitis include hepatitis A, B, and C.

new cases of HCV in the United States in 2014, which was one of the highest reported rates ever. Taking into consideration under-reporting, experts believe that the actual number of new cases of HCV in the United States was probably closer to 30,500 in 2014 ("Surveillance for Viral Hepatitis," 2016).

Symptoms

HAV, HBV, and HCV are all infections caused by different viruses, and they affect the liver in different ways. HAV often occurs as an acute infection that doesn't become chronic, and some people get better without treatment. Symptoms of HAV usually occur within 4 weeks and include fatigue, abdominal pain, loss of appetite, and diarrhea. HBV and HCV can also begin as acute infections, although they can also become chronic and lead to long-term liver problems. Symptoms of HBV usually occur anywhere from 6 weeks to 6 months after infection, although infection with HBV is usually asymptomatic. Possible symptoms may include nausea, vomiting, jaundice, headaches, fever, a darkening of the urine, moderate liver enlargement, and fatigue. Finally, most people infected with HCV are asymptomatic or have a mild illness, which develops within 8 to 9 weeks.

Diagnosis

Blood tests are used to identify viral hepatitis infections. Like for many of the other STIs, at-home kits are now available that provide testing for HCV (see the website section at the end of this chapter).

Treatment

Antiviral therapies are available for the treatment and management of hepatitis. These therapies have been designed to reduce **viral load** by interfering with the life cycle of the virus and also causing the body to generate an immune response against the virus (Guha et al., 2003). Health care providers generally recommend bed rest and adequate fluid intake so that a person does not experience dehydration. Usually after a few weeks, an infected person feels better, although this can take longer in persons with severe and chronic infections.

Vaccines are available for the prevention of both HAV and HBV, and persons at high risk for contracting either of these should have the vaccine. Young children are often routinely vaccinated against both HAV and HBV (Workowski & Bolan, 2015). High-risk individuals include health care workers who may be exposed to blood products, intravenous drug users and their sex partners, people with multiple sexual partners, people with chronic liver disease, MSM, people traveling to countries with high rates of hepatitis, and housemates of anyone with hepatitis (Workowski & Bolan, 2015). Although there is no vaccine currently available for HCV, research into the development of a vaccine is ongoing.

Review Questions

1 Identify the viral STIs, and describe those that are most common today.

2 Differentiate between "high-risk" and "low-risk" HPV, and explain long-term consequences of these risk types. What types of cancer has HPV been associated with?

3 Explain how the HPV vaccines work. What are current recommendations for their use?

4 Differentiate between HAV, HBV, and HCV. What hepatitis vaccines are available, and what are the current recommendations for their use?

The Human Immunodeficiency Virus and the Acquired Immune Deficiency Syndrome

Although the **human immunodeficiency virus (HIV)** is a viral infection, several factors set it apart from other STIs and also shed some light on why the **acquired immune deficiency syndrome (AIDS)** debate became so politically charged. HIV/AIDS appeared in the early 1980s, a time when modern medicine was believed to be well on its way to reducing epidemic disease (Altman, 1986). In addition, AIDS was first identified among gay and bisexual men and intravenous drug users. Because of this early identification, the disease was linked with "socially marginal" groups in the population (Altman, 1986; Kain, 1987). The media gave particular

viral load
The measure of the severity of a viral infection calculated by estimating the amount of virus in body fluid.

human immunodeficiency virus (HIV)
The retrovirus responsible for the development of AIDS; can be transmitted during vaginal or anal intercourse.

acquired immune deficiency syndrome (AIDS)
A condition of increased susceptibility to opportunistic diseases; results from an infection with HIV, which destroys the body's immune system.

attention to the lifestyle of "victims" and implied that social deviance has a price (similar to the punishment concept we discussed earlier in this chapter). We will talk more about public attitudes about AIDS later in this chapter.

AIDS is caused by a viral infection with HIV, a virus primarily transmitted through body fluids, including semen, vaginal fluid, breast milk, and blood. During vaginal or anal intercourse, this virus can enter the body through the vagina, penis, or rectum. Intravenous drug users can also transmit the virus by sharing needles. Oral sex may also transmit the virus, although the research has shown that the risk for HIV transmission from unprotected oral sex is lower than that of unprotected vaginal or anal sex (Baggaley et al., 2008). Kissing has been found to be low risk for transmitting HIV, especially when there are no cuts in the mouth or on the lips.

Like the herpes virus, HIV never goes away; it remains in the body for the rest of a person's life. However, unlike the herpes virus, an untreated HIV infection is often fatal. After a person is infected, the virus may remain dormant and cause no symptoms. This is why many people who are infected with HIV may not be aware of the infection. However, they can transmit the virus to other people immediately after infection. No one knows exactly why some people acquire the virus from one sexual encounter, whereas others may not be infected even after repeated exposures. We do know that a person who has an STI is at greater risk for acquiring HIV (Workowski & Bolan, 2015).

HIV attacks the **T lymphocytes** (tee-LIM-foe-sites; **T helper cells**) in the blood, which are responsible for a healthy immune system. Since HIV cannot reproduce on its own, it injects its infectious RNA into the fluid of the T helper cell. The RNA contains an enzyme known as **reverse transcriptase** (trans-SCRIPT-ace), which allows HIV to take control of the cell's DNA. Eventually, the new DNA destroys the cells and releases new cells infected with HIV into the blood, causing the immune system to be less effective in its ability to fight infections. When the immune system becomes compromised, a variety of **opportunistic diseases** can infect people with HIV. Without treatment, many opportunistic diseases can be fatal.

Perinatal HIV infections can occur at any time during a woman's pregnancy, labor, delivery, and/or breastfeeding. Today, HIV tests are routinely offered to pregnant women, and if a test is positive, medications can be used to reduce viral load and decrease the chances of maternal-fetal transmission (see the section on Treatment). A planned cesarean section can also be done to reduce the risk for transmission to the infant during delivery.

It is unknown exactly where HIV came from, although scientists have many theories. None of these theories has been proven,

however. In the early 1980s, a number of gay men, mostly in Los Angeles and New York City, began coming down with rare forms of pneumonia and skin cancer. At first, the disease was called GRID, for "gay-related immunodeficiency syndrome." Three hypotheses were offered: that there was a new infectious agent causing the disease, that the immune system was being suppressed by a drug that the infected persons were using, and that perhaps a sexual lubricant was involved. Many medical experts believed that this infectious agent would quickly be isolated and wiped out.

Incidence

As mentioned earlier in this chapter, HIV is a nationally reportable infection in the United States. To help encourage testing, some states use confidential codes to keep HIV-positive people anonymous. These statistics help to track the spread of the virus. The Centers for Disease Control estimates that more than 1.2 million people are living with HIV in the United States and that 1 in 8 are unaware of the infection ("HIV in the U.S.," 2016). In 2015, close to 40,000 people were diagnosed with HIV, which was 19% lower than 2005.

Like other STIs, there are age, gender, race/ethnicity, and geographical differences in the prevalence of HIV. In 2015, HIV rates were highest for those ages 20 to 29 (37%), followed by those ages 30 to 39 (24%) and 40 to 49 (17%). Rates were also highest among males, Blacks, and Hispanics (see Figure 15.10), along with gay and bisexual men (Weinert et al., 2016; see Figure 15.11 for information about transmission categories). Geographically, HIV rates were highest in the South and lowest in the Midwest (see Figure 15.12).

Although there is limited information on HIV among transgender adults and adolescents in the United States, it's estimated that from 2009 to 2014 approximately 2,400 transgender individuals were diagnosed with HIV (Clark et al., 2016). Rates were highest among transgender women (84%; see Figure 15.13).

The annual number of maternal-infant HIV infections has decreased by more than 90% since 1990 ("HIV Among Pregnant Women," 2017). While there were 216 infections in infants born to HIV-infected mothers in 2001, by 2013 this number had dropped to 69 (Taylor et al., 2017). These decreases were mostly due to improvements in obstetric care and treatments. HIV-infected mothers who take HIV medications throughout pregnancy, labor, and delivery and also have their newborns take HIV medications for 4 to 6 weeks after birth have a less that 1% chance of infecting their baby with HIV (we will discuss treatments more later in this chapter).

T lymphocyte (T helper cell) Type of white blood cell that helps to destroy harmful bacteria in the body.	**opportunistic disease** Disease that occurs when the immune system is weakened.
reverse transcriptase A chemical that is contained in the RNA of HIV; it helps to change the virus's DNA.	**perinatal HIV infections** HIV transmission from mother to child during pregnancy, labor and delivery, or breast-feeding.

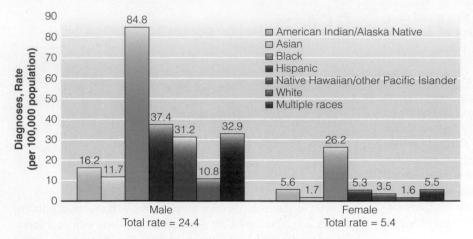

NOTE: Data include persons with a diagnosis of HIV infection regardless of stage of disease at diagnosis. Data for the year 2015 are preliminary and based on 6 months reporting delay.

FIGURE **15.10** Rates of Diagnoses of HIV Infection among Adults and Adolescents by Sex and Race-Ethnicity, United States, 2015

SOURCE: Centers for Disease Control, 2016.

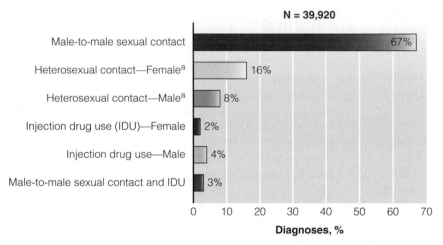

NOTE: Data include persons with a diagnosis of HIV infection regardless of stage of disease at diagnosis. Data for the year 2015 are preliminary and based on 6 months reporting delay. Data have been statistically adjusted to account for missing transmission category. "Other" transmission category not displayed as it comprises less than 1% of cases.
[a]Heterosexual contact with a person known to have, or to be at high risk for, HIV infection.

FIGURE **15.11** Diagnoses of HIV Infection Among Adults and Adolescents, by Transmission Category, United States, 2015

SOURCE: Centers for Disease Control, 2016.

Knowledge and Attitudes About AIDS

Knowledge levels about HIV/AIDS among U.S. college students are generally high, although knowledge levels do not consistently correlate with behavior changes or the practice of safer sex (Bruce & Walker, 2001; Shapiro et al., 1999). High-risk behaviors in college students, including multiple sexual partners, inconsistent condom use, high rates of sexual activity, and the use of alcohol during sexual activity, increase risks for all STIs, including HIV.

We've discussed the negative attitudes that many people have toward those infected with STIs, and this includes HIV/AIDS. Many people are afraid and uncomfortable around someone infected with HIV and have many mistaken beliefs about how it is transmitted.

Symptoms

As we discussed earlier, HIV infection results in a gradual deterioration of the immune system through the destruction of T helper cells. For those who are not being treated, this decline takes an average of 3 years in those who are emotionally depressed, and more than 5 years in those who are nondepressed (B. Bower, 1992). The average person who is HIV-positive and is not on any type of treatment will experience development of AIDS within 8 to 10 years.

HIV advances in stages, gradually overwhelming the immune system. The stages include acute HIV infection, latency, and AIDS. The first stage of the acute HIV infection usually begins within 2 to 4 weeks after HIV infection. Many people experience flu-like symptoms, including fever, sore throat, rash, muscle and joint pain, headaches, **oral candidiasis**, diarrhea, night sweats, and fatigue (Friedman-Kien & Farthing, 1990). During this time, the virus is multiplying and slowly destroying the T helper cells. After a period of time, an infected person will move into the second stage of latency, when they seem to recover and feel better. Symptoms may either be very mild or nonexistent. However, the virus is still reproducing, and infected persons can still infect others.

In the third stage of the HIV infection, the deterioration of the immune system makes it easier for opportunistic diseases to develop (i.e., those that can make people sick when their immune systems are compromised). Common opportunistic diseases include *Pneumocystis carinii* **pneumonia, toxoplasmosis, cryptococcosis, cytomegalovirus**, tuberculosis, and **Kaposi's sarcoma (KS)**. Lesions from KS frequently occur around the

oral candidiasis
An infection in the mouth caused by the excess growth of a fungus that naturally occurs in the body.

***Pneumocystis carinii* pneumonia (PCP)**
A rare type of pneumonia; an opportunistic disease that often occurs in people with AIDS.

toxoplasmosis
A parasite that can cause headache, sore throat, seizures, altered mental status, or coma.

cryptococcosis
An acute or chronic infection that can lead to pulmonary or central nervous system infection.

cytomegalovirus
A virus that can lead to diarrhea, weight loss, headache, fever, confusion, or blurred vision.

Kaposi's sarcoma (KS)
A rare form of cancer that often occurs in untreated men with AIDS.

ankle or foot, or they may be on the tip of the nose, face, mouth, penis, eyelids, ears, chest, or back. Other STIs may appear or progress quickly, such as genital warts or syphilis, which may be resistant to treatment. In general, the incidences of opportunistic illnesses are similar in men and women with a few exceptions. In women, cervical cancer may develop as an AIDS-defining condition (Hader et al., 2001).

A person who develops one or more opportunistic diseases may be considered to have progressed to AIDs, but blood tests can also be done. Viral load and **CD4 cell count** tests can determine how much HIV is in a person's system and also estimate the T helper cell count (which can show how well a person's immune system is controlling the virus). In a healthy person, T helper cell counts are usually between 500 to 1,600 cells per cubic millimeter of blood. However, since HIV slowly destroys the immune system, the level of T helper cells falls drastically. Once these levels fall below 200 cells per cubic millimeter of blood, a person is considered to have progressed to AIDs. How fast the disease progresses can depend on several factors, including how fast a person received treatment, age, stress, diet, infections with other viruses, and a person's genetic background.

Diagnosis

There are several ways to test for HIV, including blood tests to detect the virus, oral/blood tests to detect antibodies to the virus, and combination tests to detect both the virus and antibodies (also called antibody/antigen tests). A nucleic acid test is a blood test that can detect the presence of HIV in

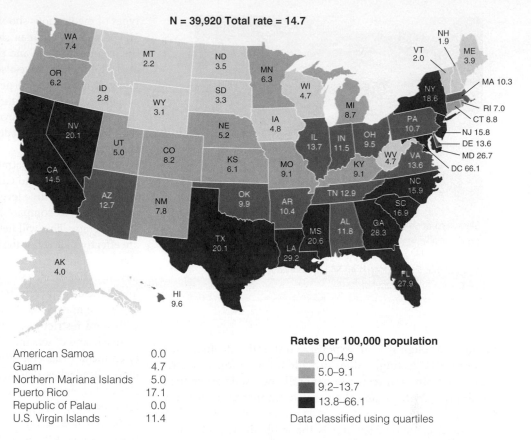

N = 39,920 Total rate = 14.7

American Samoa	0.0
Guam	4.7
Northern Mariana Islands	5.0
Puerto Rico	17.1
Republic of Palau	0.0
U.S. Virgin Islands	11.4

Rates per 100,000 population
- 0.0–4.9
- 5.0–9.1
- 9.2–13.7
- 13.8–66.1

Data classified using quartiles

NOTE: Data include persons with a diagnosis of HIV infection regardless of stage of disease at diagnosis. Data for the year 2015 are preliminary and based on 6 months reporting delay.

FIGURE **15.12** **Rates of Diagnoses of HIV Infection among Adults and Adolescents, United States, 2015**

SOURCE: Centers for Disease Control, 2016.

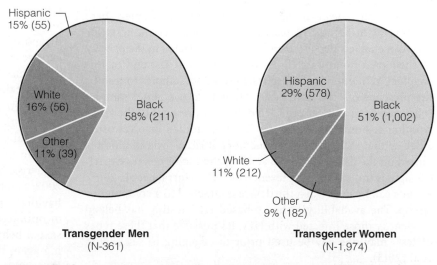

Transgender Men
(N-361)

Transgender Women
(N-1,974)

FIGURE **15.13** **HIV Diagnoses Among Transgender People by Race/Ethnicity, United States, 2009–2014**

SOURCE: Clark et al., 2016.

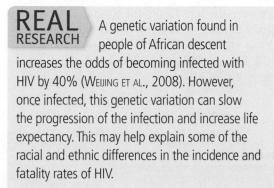

REAL RESEARCH A genetic variation found in people of African descent increases the odds of becoming infected with HIV by 40% (WEIJING ET AL., 2008). However, once infected, this genetic variation can slow the progression of the infection and increase life expectancy. This may help explain some of the racial and ethnic differences in the incidence and fatality rates of HIV.

CD4 cell count
Test that measure the number of T helper white blood cells, which will show how well a person's immune system is controlling HIV.

Several companies offer at-home STI testing with lab-certified results available within a few days. Physician consults for positive results, along with prescription treatment, may also be available. Costs range from $80 for individual tests, to $400 for a full STI panel of tests.

the blood. Although it is an expensive test and not often used for routine HIV testing, it does provide information about viral load. Combination tests can generally be used earlier than an antibody-only tests, and they are commonly used in many labs today.

The most common HIV test is the antibody screening test, which can be done on oral or blood fluids, either in a lab or as a rapid test. This test can determine the presence or absence of antibodies that develop when a person is infected with HIV. If there are none, the test results are negative, indicating that the person is probably not infected with HIV. It takes some time for the body to develop antibodies; thus, there is a period in which a person is infected with HIV but the test will not reveal it.

As we have been discussing throughout this chapter, there are several in-home STI tests available today. Home-tests for HIV can enable a person to check their HIV status in the privacy of their own home (see the website section at the end of this chapter). While some of these tests use saliva samples to test for the presence of HIV antibodies, other tests use blood samples (obtained from a finger prick) to detect the presence of the virus. Another at-home blood test that is being studied involves using a device that looks like a USB memory stick. A drop of blood is placed on the device and a pH sensing conductor creates electrical signals indicating the presence of HIV (Gurrala et al., 2016). Results can be read when the device is attached to a computer or laptop. The availability of home-based HIV testing has helped to identify those infected with HIV. It's possible that these types of tests may one day be used prior to engaging in sex (Eaton et al., 2015).

Treatment

Since 1995, there has been a tremendous decrease in HIV- and AIDS-related deaths, primarily because of the development of **antiretroviral therapy (ART)**. ART is the combination of three or more HIV drugs, often referred to as "drug cocktails." These types of medications should be started as soon as possible after an HIV diagnosis and can slow the progression of HIV, strengthen the immune system, and prevent opportunistic infections (Lifson et al., 2017). They have also significantly increased the life expectancy of children with perinatal HIV (Fowler et al., 2016). ART can also reduce the chances of infecting others. By mid-2016, more than 18 million people around the world were using ART, but less than half those who needed it had access to it (World Health Organization, 2016).

Before starting treatment for HIV infection, a person should be given viral load and CD4 cell count tests. Results of these tests will establish baseline levels to give a health care provider a starting measure to compare to later tests after a person has started drug therapy. This will help in determining if drug combinations are effective. How fast the viral load decreases depends on several factors, including baseline CD4 cell counts, whether the person has any AIDS-related illnesses, and how closely the person has followed the drug therapy protocol.

In the mid-1990s, ART involved taking 20 to 30 or more pills with food restrictions (some drugs must be taken on an empty stomach, and others must be taken just after eating). This therapy often includes adverse effects such as fatigue, nausea, fever, nightmares, headaches, diarrhea, changes in a person's fat distribution, elevated cholesterol levels, the development of diabetes, decreased bone density, liver problems, and skin rashes. Newer drug regimens have used fewer pills with fewer side effects; research continues to explore single-tablet antiretroviral regimens (Cohen et al., 2011; DeJesus et al., 2009).

Once a person begins ART, it is important that the dosages are taken exactly the way they were prescribed. Missing a dose or taking it late could give the virus an opportunity to multiply and/or cause the virus to become resistant to the medications. Individuals who begin drug therapy will most probably continue it for their entire life.

Many health care providers believe that people who have been diagnosed with HIV should be given psychological counseling to explore coping strategies, gain information on the virus, promote a healthier lifestyle, and reduce the risk for transmission to others. Without this intervention, it is possible that people who are diagnosed with HIV will be more likely to become anxious, depressed, and/or suicidal (Brandt et al., 2017).

Finally, it is also important to point out that the advent of ART in the late 1990s brought with it a substantial increase in high-risk behavior among HIV-positive gay men (Katz et al., 2002; Stephenson et al., 2003; Wolitski et al., 2001). These behavioral changes were thought to be due to increased feelings of optimism and reduced levels of HIV. Since mid-2005, risky sexual behaviors in HIV-positive gay men have been increasing again (Hart & Elford, 2010; Kembabazi et al., 2013; Mor & Dan, 2012).

> **antiretroviral therapy (ART)**
> A combination of antiretroviral drugs for the treatment of HIV.

The most frequently diagnosed STIs among women who have been sexually assaulted include trichomoniasis, BV, gonorrhea, and chlamydia (Workowski & Bolan, 2015). Tests for chlamydia and gonorrhea should be performed at the sites of penetration (vagina, mouth, anus), and urine or vaginal specimens should be taken to test for vaginal infections. Blood tests for HIV, hepatitis B, and syphilis tests should also be performed (Workowski & Bolan, 2015). In addition to emergency contraception (see Chapter 13), sexual assault survivors should be given treatment for chlamydia, gonorrhea, and trichomoniasis prophylactically. The HPV and hepatitis B vaccines should be given to survivors who have not had these vaccines prior to the sexual assault (and follow-up doses for the HPV vaccines should be 1 to 2 and 6 months after the initial HPV vaccine, and 1 to 2 and 4 to 6 months after the initial hepatitis B vaccine; Workowski & Bolan, 2015). An HIV test may be recommended on an individual basis.

Since some testing might not reveal infections at the time of the sexual assault, survivors are encouraged to have follow-up examinations for possible repeat testing, to check for new STIs, review test results, update vaccination protocols, and receive counseling and treatment for any infections (Workowski & Bolan, 2015). Tests for syphilis and HIV can be repeated at 6 weeks and 3 months post sexual assault.

Studies have found that the risk of an HIV infection during a one-time sexual assault are fairly low during forced oral or vaginal intercourse and slightly higher during forced anal intercourse (Workowski & Bolan, 2015). Bleeding during oral, vaginal, or anal penetration increases the risk of infection. As we've discussed in this chapter, risk of STI infection depends on exposure to infected ejaculate, viral load in the ejaculate, and the presence of other STIs in the assailant or survivor. If the assailant was known to be HIV-positive or if there are characteristics that make a survivor more likely to be at risk for HIV infection (e.g., genital lesions), health care providers may recommend prophylactic HIV treatment within 72 hours of the assault (Workowski & Bolan, 2015).

Although in some cases, the presence of STIs in children may be related to infections acquired during birth, most of the time they are strongly associated with sexual abuse (Workowski & Bolan, 2015). Children who have been sexually abused may be at a higher risk for STIs since there are typically multiple episodes of abuse. Since children who are sexually abused are often at increased risk of engaging in unsafe sexual behaviors earlier than those who have not been sexually abused, experts recommend they be given the HPV vaccine if they are > or = 9 years old (Workowski & Bolan, 2015). We will discuss sexual assault and abuse more in Chapter 17.

Prevention

Some people who are at high risk for acquiring HIV may take daily antiretroviral medications (called pre-exposure prophylaxis) to decrease their chances of infection. Antiretroviral medications help prevent HIV from spreading throughout a person's body. Higher doses of these medications may be used in emergency situations if a person was potentially exposed to HIV (called post-exposure prophylaxis). This would include situations in which a person was sharing needles, sexually assaulted, or exposed to HIV from a partner. To be effective, the medications must be started within 72 hours after exposure.

To prevent the further spread of HIV, people's behavior must change. Many programs have been started to achieve this goal, including educational programs, advertising, and mailings. Public service announcements about HIV/AIDS have increased on radio stations, and many television programs have agreed to address HIV/AIDS in upcoming episodes. A variety of television shows have also included the topic of HIV/AIDS in their programming. Many schools today are also including HIV education in their classes. These programs provide students with information about HIV, risky sexual behaviors, and prevention strategies. Different educational programs emphasize different messages.

As with other STIs, after a diagnosis of HIV has been made, it is important to inform all past sexual contacts to prevent the spread of the disease. Because the virus can remain in the body for several years before the onset of symptoms, some people may not know that they have the virus and are capable of infecting others.

It seems reasonable that before we can determine what will reduce high-risk behaviors that contribute to increases in HIV and AIDS, we need to know the behaviors that people are engaging in. However, data on sexual practices are lacking in the United States. As discussed in Chapter 2, many of our assumptions about current sexual behaviors are based on the Kinsey studies from the 1940s and 1950s. Little is known about current rates of high-risk behaviors, such as anal intercourse, extramarital or teenage sexuality, and homosexuality. The recent National Survey of Sexual Health and Behavior helped shed some light on these behaviors, and two ongoing surveys, the Behavioral Risk Factor Surveillance Survey (BRFSS) and the Youth Risk Behavior Surveillance Survey (YRBSS), continue to collect and monitor information about risk behaviors at the state level (see Chapters 2 and 8 for more information about these studies).

Researchers continue to explore the development of AIDS vaccines. However, HIV is one of the most difficult viruses to eradicate, because it has developed ways of dodging the immune system and becoming resistant to specific treatments. In the United States, the majority of AIDS vaccine research is funded through the National Institutes of Health. The Global HIV Vaccine Enterprise, an alliance of independent organizations around the world, has organized to accelerate HIV vaccine research and development. The development of a vaccine is a long process. In fact, the polio vaccine took 47 years to produce, and it is anticipated that the HIV vaccine may take just as long (Markel, 2005).

Global Aspects of HIV/AIDS

By the end of 2015, there were approximately 37 million people living with HIV worldwide (UNAIDS, 2016). However, this represented a 35% decrease in new HIV infections in adults and adolescents since 2000, along with a 58% decrease in new HIV infections among children. Children are grossly affected by the AIDS epidemic worldwide. Throughout the epidemic, more than 17 million children have lost one or both parents to AIDS, and the majority of these children live in sub-Saharan Africa (see accompanying "Sexual Diversity in Our World" feature). In South Africa, the show *Sesame Street* added an HIV-positive Muppet character, Kami. Kami is a 5-year-old orphan whose parents died of AIDS. Kami's character was designed to help children in South Africa understand AIDS and teach them that it's all right to play with HIV-positive children. The United Nations is committed to ending the global AIDS epidemic by 2030 (UNAIDS, 2016b).

In this section, we explore HIV in Asia and the Pacific, Eastern Europe and Central Asia, Western and Central Europe and North America, Eastern and Southern Africa, Latin America and the Caribbean, the Middle East and Northern Africa, and Western and Central Africa.

Asia and the Pacific

There were 5.1 million people living with HIV in Asia and the Pacific in 2015, and 300,000 adults and adolescents, along with 19,000 children were newly infected with HIV that year (UNAIDS, 2016a). The main modes of HIV transmission in Asia and the Pacific region are from clients of sex workers and their partners, MSM, injecting drug use, and sex workers (see Figure 15.14 for more information about HIV transmission rates). Increasing rates of HIV have also been found among transgender individuals in this region. A large proportion of HIV infections occur in married women whose husbands frequent sex workers or inject drugs.

Antiretroviral therapy is available in this region, although it's estimated that 59% of HIV-infected people do not have access to it. Even so, AIDS-related deaths decreased by 24% between 2010 and 2015 in Asia and the Pacific region.

Eastern Europe and Central Asia

There were 1.5 million people living with HIV in Eastern Europe and Central Asia in 2015, and an estimated 190,000 adults and adolescents became newly infected with HIV that year (UNAIDS, 2016a). This is one of the only regions in the world where HIV infections continue to climb. Between 2010 and 2015, there was a 57% increase in annual new HIV infections (UNAIDS, 2016). However, rates of childhood infections decreased, and there were fewer than 1,000 new HIV infections in children. The main modes of HIV transmission in Eastern Europe and Central Asia are injecting drug use, clients of sex workers and their partners, MSM, and sex workers. Antiretroviral therapy is available in this region, although it's estimated that 79% of HIV-infected people do not have access to it. As a result, between 2010 and 2015, AIDS-related deaths increased by 22% in Eastern Europe and Central Asia.

Western and Central Europe and North America

There were 2.4 million people living with HIV in Western and Central Europe and North America in 2015, and an estimated 91,000 adults and adolescents became newly infected with HIV that year (UNAIDS, 2016a). While more than half of new HIV infections were in the United States, another 25% were in France, Germany, Italy, Spain, Turkey, and the United Kingdom. The main modes of HIV transmission in this region are MSM, clients of sex workers and their partners, and injecting drug use.

Antiretroviral therapy is available in this region, and approximately half of HIV-infected people in this region are using it. The World Health Organization aims to increase the use of ART in this region to 90% by 2030. In fact, Sweden met this goal in September 2016 (Gisslén et al., 2016). Pre-exposure prophylaxis (PrEP) is also available in some countries in this region, including the United States, Canada, and France. All of this has contributed to a 24% decrease in AIDS-related deaths between 2010 and 2015.

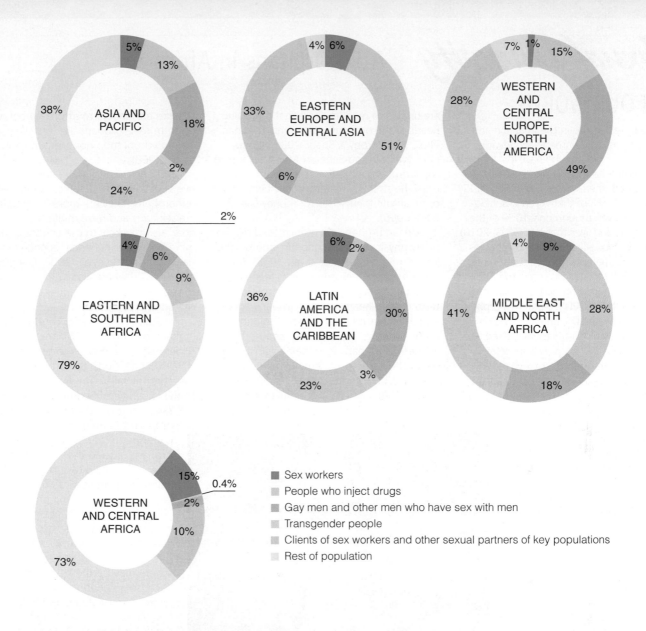

Methodological note: Estimated numbers of new HIV infections by key population were compiled from country Spectrum files submitted in 2015 to UNAIDS (2014 data), available modes-of-transmission studies and additional sources of data drawn from GARPR reports. Where data were lacking, regional medians were calculated from available data and applied to countries' populations.

FIGURE **15.14** Distribution of new HIV infections among Population groups by Region, 2014

SOURCE: UNAIDS, 2016b.

Eastern and Southern Africa

Eastern and Southern Africa has been one of the hardest hit regions by HIV, with almost half the global total of new HIV infections. An estimated 19 million people were living with HIV in 2015, and close to 1 million adults and adolescents and 56,000 children were newly infected with HIV that year (UNAIDS, 2016a). The highest rates of HIV are in South Africa (with 40% of the new infections), along with Ethiopia, Kenya, Uganda,

and Zimbabwe. Women account for more than half of the adults living with HIV in this region, and in 2015 there were roughly 4,500 new HIV infections in young women every week (UNAIDS, 2016a).

The main modes of HIV transmission are from clients of sex workers and their partners, MSM, injection drug use, and sex workers. Sexual violence among sex workers and young girls forced into marriage have also contributed to increased rates of HIV. Antiretroviral therapy is available in this region, although it's estimated that 46% of HIV-infected people do not have access to it. Voluntary medical male circumcision in this region has also been found to reduce the risk of HIV transmission (WHO/UNAIDS, 2011). AIDS-related deaths decreased by 38% between 2010 and 2015 in Eastern and Southern Africa.

Sexual Diversity AIDS Orphans in Africa

IN OUR WORLD

Despite all the declines in HIV infection and increased access to treatments worldwide, the number of children who have lost their parents to AIDS has not declined (UNAIDS, 2010). In 2009, there were 16.6 million AIDS orphans, and 90 % of them lived in sub-Saharan Africa (even though only 10 % of the world's population lives there; UNAIDS, 2010). Although we typically think of an orphan as a child without parents, the word is used a bit differently by those involved in the AIDS epidemic. A maternal orphan is a child who has lost a mother to AIDS, a paternal orphan has lost a father to AIDS, and a double orphan has lost both parents to AIDS (Fredriksson et al., 2008). AIDS orphans are often young—15 % are newborn to 4 years old, 35 % are 5 to 9 years old, and 50 % are 10 to 14 years old (Monasch & Boerma, 2004).

At the beginning of the AIDS epidemic in the 1980s, orphanages were set up in many African communities to help care for the many children whose parents had died. However, the number of orphans quickly surpassed the amount of space available in the orphanages. Extended family members care for over 90% of orphans in sub-Saharan Africa (Heymann et al., 2007). In fact, more than one third of working adults in sub-Saharan Africa care for orphans in their households, but the majority of these families live in poverty and

are unable to meet the essential caregiving needs of the orphans in their care (Kidman et al., 2007; Roby & Shaw, 2006). Ongoing poverty in sub-Saharan Africa has forced some orphans either into the labor market or to the streets where they may beg, steal, or prostitute themselves for money (Amanpour, 2006).

African orphans are at increased risk for many physical, socioeconomic, and psychological problems (Sherr et al., 2008). Many experience anxiety, depression, fear, anger, and guilt, which can contribute to long-term mental health issues. Orphans are also at increased risk for social isolation, abuse, neglect, malnutrition, and homelessness, and many lose their opportunities for health care, future employment, and adequate education (Li et al., 2008; Rivers et al., 2008). In fact, because many extended

Friedrich Stark/Alamy Stock Photo

families are unable to afford school and uniform fees, orphans are less likely to attend school than nonorphans (Kürzinger et al., 2008).

Orphans are also at greater risk for negative sexual health outcomes compared with nonorphans. They are more likely to initiate sex early and have multiple sex partners, are less likely to use condoms, and more likely to experience teenage pregnancy (Birdthistle et al., 2008; Gregson et al., 2005). They are also at greater risk for forced sex and have a higher prevalence of HIV and herpes infections.

As the HIV/AIDS rates continue to climb in many countries around the globe, it is imperative to find ways to both reduce HIV/AIDS infections and increase access to antiretroviral treatment. In addition to this, however, finding care and assistance for orphans also remains a priority. Local and global communities continue to reach out to help AIDS orphans around the globe, ensuring adequate access to services and providing support services for caregivers and families. Some groups provide psychological support, food, and/or clothing and offer resources to keep orphans in school. Many believe that finding ways to keep orphans in school may be the key to this crisis, because an adequate education can increase self-esteem and help ensure financial independence in the future (Fredriksson et al., 2008).

Latin America and the Caribbean

There were 2 million people living with HIV in Latin America and the Caribbean, and an estimated 100,000 adults and adolescents and 2,100 children were newly infected with HIV in 2015 (UNAIDS, 2016a). The main modes of HIV transmission are MSM, clients of sex workers and their partners, and sex workers. Increasing rates of HIV have also been found among transgender people in this region. In fact, HIV prevalence among transwomen has been found to be 49 times higher than the general population (UNAIDS, 2014).

Antiretroviral therapy is available in Latin America and the Caribbean, although it's estimated that 45% of HIV-infected people do not have access to it. Between 2010 and 2015, AIDS-related deaths decreased by 18% in this region.

Middle East and Northern Africa

The Middle East and Northern Africa have one of the lowest HIV prevalence rates in the world with an estimated 230,000 people living with HIV in 2015, and an estimated 21,000 adults and adolescents, along with 2,100 children were newly infected with HIV that year (UNAIDS, 2016a).

The main modes of HIV transmission in the Middle East and Northern Africa are transgender transmission, injecting drug use, MSM, and sex workers and their partners/clients. Antiretroviral therapy is available in this region, although it's estimated that 83% of people do not have access to it. This region has one of the lowest rates of ART use in the world (UNAIDS, 2014). Although programs have been established to decrease HIV infections in those who inject drugs, MSM, and pregnant mothers infected with HIV, AIDS-related deaths increased by 22% in the Middle East and Northern Africa from 2010 to 2015.

In South Africa, an HIV-positive Muppet, orphaned by AIDS, was added to the cast of *Sesame Street*. Her name is Kami, which is derived from the Tswana word for "acceptance."

Western and Central Africa

There were 6.5 million people were living with HIV in Western and Central Africa in 2015, and women accounted for over half of the total number of people living with HIV in this region (UNAIDS,

2016a). Close to 410,000 adults and adolescents and 66,000 children became newly infected with HIV in 2015 (UNAIDS, 2016a). Infections among children have decreased 31% since 2010. The main modes of HIV transmission in Western and Central Africa are clients of sex workers and their partners, MSM, sex workers, and injecting drug use. Barriers to decreasing HIV include limited information on how to prevent HIV/AIDS, high levels of HIV-related stigma and discrimination, and forced child marriage. It's estimated that 42% of girls in West and Central Africa were married by the time they were 18 years old (UNAIDS, 2015).

Antiretroviral therapy is available in Western and Central Africa, although it's estimated that 72% of HIV-infected people do not have access to it. Although pre-exposure prophylaxis (PrEP) is not currently available in this region, there are ongoing trials evaluating the effectiveness of these treatments. Between 2010 and 2015, AIDS-related deaths decreased by 10% in this region.

In summary, recent research suggests that counseling and educational interventions are being increasingly recognized as important aspects of care for people with HIV and their families in developing countries. In addition, home-based health care is being established to remove some of the burden from the hospitals, increase quality health care, and reduce costs.

Review Questions

1 Explain the global impact of the AIDS epidemic on children.

2 Identify the main mode of HIV transmission in Asia and the Pacific. What do you think could be done to decrease HIV infections in this particular area?

3 Identify the main mode of HIV transmission in Eastern Europe and Central Asia. What do you think could be done to decrease HIV infections in this particular area?

4 Identify the main mode of HIV transmission in Western and Central Europe and North America. What do you think could be done to decrease HIV infections in this particular area?

5 Identify the main mode of HIV transmission in Eastern and Southern Africa. What do you think could be done to decrease HIV infections in this particular area?

6 Identify the main mode of HIV transmission in Latin America and the Caribbean. What do you think could be done to decrease HIV infections in this particular area?

7 Identify the main mode of HIV transmission in Western and Central Africa. What do you think could be done to decrease HIV infections in this particular area?

Preventing Sexually Transmitted Infections and AIDS

You might be feeling pretty overwhelmed with all this new information about STIs. It is important not to lose sight of the fact that there is much that you can do to avoid becoming infected with a sexually transmitted infection. If you are sexually active, one of the most important things you can do is to get

yourself tested. When you get into a sexual relationship, make sure your partner is also tested. Today's experts recommend full testing for STIs for sexually active people, including HIV testing.

You can also make sure that you carefully choose your sexual partners and use barrier methods such as condoms and dental dams to reduce your chances of acquiring an STI. Unless you are in a monogamous relationship, it is important to avoid high-risk sexual behaviors (see the "Sex in Real Life" feature, "Safe Sex in College," earlier in the chapter). In addition, it is also important to be sure you are knowledgeable about STIs. Knowledge and education are powerful tools in decreasing the frequency of STIs.

Early Detection

If you already have an STI, early detection and management of the infection are important and can help lessen the possibility of infecting others. Be sure to notify your sexual partners as soon as a positive diagnosis is made to help reduce the chances that someone else will become infected. As discussed earlier in this chapter, many college students are apprehensive about getting tested for STIs, especially when they think they might be positive. It is important to be proactive in these matters and seek testing and treatment if you think you may have become infected. Many of the bacterial STIs can be treated with antibiotics. However, delaying treatment may result in more long-term consequences to your health, such as pelvic inflammatory disease or infertility (for you or your partner).

Talking About Sexually Transmitted Infections

Talking about STIs is not always easy to do, and although people might not always respond positively to such a discussion, it is important. Honesty, trust, and communication are key elements to any successful relationship. To begin a conversation about STIs, choose a time when you can be alone and uninterrupted. Sometimes it's a little easier to start by bringing up the importance of honesty in relationships. You could talk about what you've learned in this class and how it's made you think about your current and future health. Talk about any infections and past behaviors that may have put you or your partner at risk. Suggest STI testing and the importance of monogamy in your relationship.

Overall, as we discussed at the beginning of this chapter, it is important that we continue to try to break the silence about STIs and work to reduce the negative beliefs and stigma associated with them. Only then can we help encourage responsibility and safe behaviors.

Review Questions

1 Identify some strategies that a person can use to decrease the possibility of acquiring an STI.

2 If you have already been infected with an STI, what can you do to help manage the infection?

3 Explain how communication can be an important tool in decreasing STIs.

Chapter Review

Summary Points

1 Sexually transmitted infections (STIs) can be caused by ectoparasitic, bacterial, or viral infections. The causal agents are important in treating STIs. The most effective way to avoid STI transmission is to abstain from oral, vaginal, and anal sex or to be in a long-term, mutually monogamous relationship with someone who is free from STIs.

2 STIs have historically been viewed as symbols of corrupt sexuality, which is why there has been a "punishment concept" of disease. College students are at an increased risk for acquiring STIs because they engage in many behaviors that put them at greater risk, such as having multiple partners and engaging in unprotected sexual behaviors.

3 Large discrepancies have been found in STI prevalence, with higher rates in young people, certain racial/ethnic groups and minority populations, and MSM. Young adults are disproportionately affected by STIs, and the incidence of these infections continues to grow in this population, primarily because many engage in high-risk sexual behaviors, such as multiple partners, inconsistent condom use, or both.

4 Transgender persons who engage in high-risk sexual behaviors are at increased risk of developing STIs. Transgender men have been found to have lower rates of HIV than transgender women.

5 Untreated STIs contribute to the development of pelvic inflammatory disease (PID). Two of the most common causes of PID are chlamydia and gonorrhea. The most common symptom is lower abdominal pain. Severe symptoms may include acute pelvic pain, fever, painful urination, and abnormal vaginal bleeding or discharge. Long-term complications of PID include ectopic and tubal pregnancies, chronic pelvic pain, and infertility.

6 Contraceptive methods offer varying levels of protection from STIs. In 1993, the FDA approved labeling contraceptives for STI protection. Overall, condoms are the most effective contraceptive method for reducing STI risk. STIs acquired while using male condoms are usually due to inconsistent or incorrect use.

7 The role of hormonal contraceptives in preventing STIs is complicated. Increased hormones can change cervical mucus and the endometrium, which can prevent STIs. However, they may make the cervix more susceptible.

8 Untreated STIs can adversely affect a woman's pregnancy. Many of the STIs can cause miscarriage, stillbirth, early onset of labor, premature rupture of the amniotic sac, and fetal or uterine infection. The CDC recommends that all pregnant women be screened for chlamydia, gonorrhea, syphilis, hepatitis B and C, and HIV at their first prenatal visit, and they may require additional testing again during the third trimester. Some STIs can be treated during pregnancy with antibiotics, and early treatment may reduce newborn infections.

9 Ectoparasitic infections are those that are caused by parasites that live on the skin's surface and include pubic lice and scabies. First symptoms include a rash and intense itching. Treatment is with topical creams to kill the parasites and their larvae.

10 Bacterial STIs include gonorrhea, syphilis, chlamydia, and a variety of vaginal infections. Untreated, many of these can lead to pelvic inflammatory disease. Gonorrhea is a nationally reportable infection, and four main factors are related to gonorrhea prevalence in the United States: age, gender, race/ethnicity, and geographical area. Gonorrhea rates are highest in adolescents and young adults. Gonorrhea rates have increased in men and decreased in women. Researchers believe this may be due to increases in testing in men as well as increases in MSM.

11 The majority of women who are infected with gonorrhea are asymptomatic, whereas men are symptomatic. Testing for gonorrhea involves collecting a sample of the discharge from the cervix, urethra, or another infected area with a cotton swab. Home testing kits are also available. Gonorrhea can be treated effectively with antibiotics. Antibiotics are usually administered orally, but in severe cases, intramuscular injections may be necessary.

12 Syphilis is a nationally reportable infection. Although rates in 2000 were the lowest since reporting started in 1941, they have been increasing every year since then. Four main factors are related to syphilis prevalence in the United States: age, gender, race/ethnicity, and geographical area. Syphilis usually infects the cervix, penis, anus, or lips first. It can also infect a baby during birth. Infection with syphilis is divided into three stages: primary or

early syphilis, secondary syphilis, and tertiary or late syphilis. A diagnosis can be made by culturing and evaluating the lesion or through a blood test. Home testing kits are also available. Antibiotics are the treatment of choice today.

13 Chlamydia is a nationally reportable infection, and data reveal it is one of the most prevalent STIs in the United States today. Rates have been increasing, but increased numbers may be due to more active screening for chlamydia. Like other STIs, there are age, gender, race/ethnicity, and geographical differences in the prevalence of chlamydia. It is often called the "silent disease" because the majority of people with a chlamydia infection are asymptomatic. Chlamydia infections are a major cause of pelvic inflammatory disease. It can be diagnosed through urine testing, but it can also be diagnosed from cultures of the vagina, cervix, urethra, rectum, or mouth. Home testing kits are also available. Antibiotics are the treatment of choice today for chlamydia.

14 Chancroid is relatively rare in the United States. Once infected, people often experience development of small lesions where the infection entered the body. The infection may spread to the lymph nodes of the groin, which can cause swelling and pain. Chancroids are treated with antibiotics.

15 Vaginal infections are characterized by a discharge, itching, and/or odor. Although these infections can be sexually transmitted, they can also be acquired through nonsexual means. Having multiple sex partners can change the balance of bacteria in the vagina, which in turn can increase a woman's risk of acquiring bacterial vaginosis. A woman who experiences multiple vaginal infections should ask her partner to get evaluated and treated. Trichomoniasis is a prevalent STI. The most common symptoms include an increase in vaginal discharge and odor. Home testing kits for trichomoniasis are available.

16 Viral infections include herpes simplex virus, human papillomavirus, viral hepatitis, and HIV. Herpes is not a nationally reportable infection, but studies have found that it is very common. It is caused by either HSV-1 or HSV-2; however, once a person is infected, the symptoms can overlap. Although HSV-1 prefers the mouth or lips and HSV-2 prefers the genitals, they can infect either area. When the virus infects a nonpreferred site, symptoms are often less severe. Overall, recurrences and outbreaks are less frequent with an HSV-1, compared to an HSV-2, infection.

17 The presence of blisters caused by the herpes virus may be enough to diagnose the disease, but virologic and serologic (blood) tests are also used. Home testing kits are also available for HSV-2. Oral antiviral drugs can be used to shorten the duration of an HSV outbreak and can prevent complications. Daily suppressive therapy can be used to reduce recurrences and decrease viral shedding.

18 HPV is not a nationally reportable infection, although studies have found that it is very common. There are more than 40 types of HPV that can infect the genitals, anus, mouth, and throat during sexual behaviors. The majority of HPV infections are asymptomatic and go away without treatment. Low-risk HPV can cause genital warts and may also cause respiratory papillomatosis. High-risk HPV can cause cervical, anal, throat, vaginal, penile, and other cancers. HPV has been found to cause virtually 100% of cervical, 95% of anal, 70% of throat, 65% of vaginal, and 35% of penile cancers. MSM are disproportionately affected by HPV-related cancers.

19 Several tests have been approved by the FDA to detect HPV infection in women and are often used during Pap testing. There is no HPV test recommended for men, although the CDC recommends that MSM undergo yearly anal cancer screenings. Home testing kits for HPV are available. Close to 90% of low-risk HPV infections are asymptomatic and resolve spontaneously within two years without treatment.

20 Viral hepatitis is a nationally reportable infection that is typically underreported. An infection with viral hepatitis can lead to impaired liver function. There are three types of viral hepatitis: hepatitis A (HAV), hepatitis B (HBV), and hepatitis C (HCV). HAV infection is usually symptomatic, whereas infection with HBV and HCV is asymptomatic. Blood tests are used to identify viral hepatitis infections. Home testing kits for HCV are available. Vaccines are available for the prevention of both HAV and HBV, and research on a vaccine for HCV is in progress. Antiviral therapies are available for the treatment and management of hepatitis.

21 The human immunodeficiency virus is a nationally reportable infection that is primarily transmitted through body fluids, including semen, vaginal fluid, and blood. HIV attacks the T helper cells in the blood, changing the DNA in these cells. HIV antibodies can be detected in the bloodstream anywhere from 2 weeks to 6 months after infection. The attack on the T helper cells causes the immune system to be less effective in its ability to fight disease, and so many infected people develop opportunistic diseases.

22 Like other STIs, there are age, gender, race/ethnicity, and geographical differences in the prevalence of HIV. HIV rates were highest in those ages 20 to 29, followed by those ages 30 to 39. Rates were also highest among males, Blacks and Hispanics, and gay and bisexual men. In addition, HIV rates have increased among transgender adults and adolescents in the United States.

23 Perinatal HIV infections have declined in the United States mainly due to improvements in obstetric care and treatments. HIV-infected mothers who take HIV medications throughout pregnancy, labor, and delivery and also have their newborns take HIV medications after birth reduce their risks of infecting their babies.

24 The stages of HIV infection include acute HIV infection, latency, and AIDS. The first stage of the acute HIV infection usually begins within 2 to 4 weeks after HIV infection. Many people experience flu-like symptoms, including fever, sore throat, rash, muscle and joint pain, headaches, diarrhea, night sweats, and fatigue. During this time, the virus is multiplying and slowly destroying the T helper cells. In the second stage a person usually feels better and may not have symptoms. However, the virus is still reproducing, and infected persons can still infect others.

25 In the third stage of the HIV infection, the deterioration of the immune system makes it easier for opportunistic diseases to develop. Common opportunistic diseases include *Pneumocystis carinii* pneumonia, toxoplasmosis, cryptococcosis, cytomegalovirus, tuberculosis, and Kaposi's sarcoma.

26 Tests for HIV can look for either the virus itself or for antibodies that the body has developed to fight HIV. At-home HIV tests use either oral or blood samples, and positive results should be followed up by laboratory testing. A new test that looks like a USB flash drive is being tested for use.

27 Since 1995, there has been a tremendous decrease in HIV- and AIDS-related deaths, primarily because of the development of antiretroviral therapy (ART). This therapy has

also significantly increased the life expectancy of children infected with HIV at birth. ART should be started as soon as possible after an HIV diagnosis and can slow the progression of HIV, strengthen the immune system, prevent opportunistic infections, increase the life expectancy of children with perinatal HIV, and reduce the chances of infecting others.

28 Pre-exposure prophylaxis involves giving high-risk individuals daily antiretroviral medications to decrease their chances of HIV infection. Post-exposure prophylaxis can be used in emergency situations (such as needle sharing or sexual assault) and involve higher doses of these medications. To be effective, the medications must be started within 72 hours after exposure

29 Prevention and educational programs have begun to help reduce the spread of HIV. Educational programs, advertising, mailings, public service announcements, and television shows all have helped to increase knowledge levels about HIV/AIDS. Researchers continue to explore the development of AIDS vaccines. However, HIV is one of the most difficult viruses to eradicate because it has developed ways of dodging the immune system and becoming immune to specific treatments.

30 There has been a significant decrease in new HIV infections in adults, adolescents, and children. We explored HIV in Asia and the Pacific, Eastern Europe and Central Asia, Western and Central Europe and North America, Eastern and Southern Africa, Latin America and the Caribbean, the Middle East and Northern Africa, and Western and Central Africa.

31 In Asia and the Pacific, the main modes of transmission were clients of sex workers and their partners, MSM, injecting drug use, and sex workers. Increasing rates of HIV have also been found among transgender people in this region. It's estimated that 59% of HIV-infected people do not have access to ART in this region. AIDS-related deaths have been decreasing since 2010.

32 In Eastern Europe and Central Asia, the main modes of transmission were MSM, clients of sex workers and their partners, and injecting drug use. It's estimated that half of HIV-infected people do not have access to ART

in this region. AIDS-related deaths have been decreasing since 2010.

33 In Western and Central Europe and North America, the main modes of transmission were injecting drug use, clients of sex workers and their partners, MSM, and sex workers. It's estimated that half of HIV-infected people do not have access to ART in this region. Pre-exposure prophylaxis is available in the United States, Canada, and France. AIDS-related deaths have been decreasing in this region since 2010.

34 Eastern and Southern Africa is one of the hardest hit regions by HIV. The main modes of transmission were from clients of sex workers and their partners, MSM, injection drug use, and sex workers. Sexual violence among sex workers and young girls forced into marriage have also contributed to increased rates of HIV. It's estimated that nearly half of HIV-infected people do not have access to ART in this region. However, AIDS-related deaths have been decreasing in this region since 2010.

35 In Latin America and the Caribbean the main modes of transmission were MSM, clients of sex workers and their partners, and sex workers. Increasing rates of HIV have been found among transgender people in this region, with significantly higher rates among transwomen. It's estimated that nearly half of HIV-infected people do not have access to ART in this region. However, AIDS-related deaths have been decreasing in this region since 2010.

36 The Middle East and Northern Africa has one of the lowest HIV prevalence rates in the world. The main modes of transmission were transgender transmission, injecting drug use, MSM, and sex workers and their partners/clients. It's estimated that 83% of HIV-infected people do not have access to ART in this region. AIDS-related deaths have been increasing in this region since 2010.

37 There are ways to protect yourself from becoming infected with an STI. If you do become infected, early treatment can reduce long-term consequences. Although it's not always easy to talk to a sexual partner about STIs, it's important to do so. We need to continue to break the silence about STIs and work to reduce the negative beliefs and stigma associated with these infections.

Critical Thinking Questions

1 How will reading this chapter affect your own sexual practices? What material has had the biggest impact on you? Why?

2 Suppose that your best friend has never heard of chlamydia. What can you tell your friend about the symptoms, long-term risks, diagnosis, and treatment of chlamydia? Should your friend be worried?

3 Suppose that one late night when you are talking to a group of friends, the topic of STIs comes up. In your argument to encourage your friends to use condoms, what can you say about the asymptomatic nature of STIs? The properties of latency? How women are more at risk? How do you think your friends will respond?

4 Do you think the United States should provide medication to HIV-infected people in developing countries who cannot afford it? Or should the United States provide sexuality education or HIV/AIDS prevention to those who are not infected? How do you think the money be best spent? Why?

5 Have you ever dated someone with an STI? If so, when did you find out about it?

How did you feel? Did it affect your sex life? How so?

6 The HPV vaccines offer some protections from genital warts, as well as a variety of cancers. Have you had the vaccine? Why or why not? If you have children, would you get them vaccinated? Would you vaccinate both your sons and daughters? Why or why not?

7 If you needed to get tested for STIs, how would you go about this? Where would you go? Would you consider at-home testing? Why or why not?

Websites

American Sexual Health Association The American Sexual Health Association provides information on sexually transmitted infections (STIs). The website contains support, referrals, resources, and in-depth information about STIs.

Centers for Disease Control and Prevention (CDC) The CDC's division of STI prevention provides information about STIs, including surveillance reports and disease facts. The CDC's division of HIV/AIDS prevention provides information about HIV and AIDS, including surveillance reports and facts about the infection.

Herpes.org Herpes.org is an online resource for people with herpes and the human papillomavirus. The website provides information about the infections, what nonprescription and prescription treatments work, and where to find medical help and medication.

Joint United Nations Program on HIV and AIDS (UNAIDS) UNAIDS provides monitoring and evaluation of AIDS research and also provides access to various links and information about AIDS. Information on AIDS scenarios for the future, antiretroviral therapy, and HIV/AIDS in children and orphans is available.

LesbianSTDs This website provides information and resources regarding sexual health and STIs in women who have sex with women.

myLABbox A relatively new online service that offers home STI testing for chlamydia (genital, throat, rectal), gonorrhea (genital, throat, rectal), hepatitis C, herpes simplex 2, HIV, syphilis, trichomoniasis, and HPV. Individual tests, as well as complete STI testing panels are available. Reasonably priced with free shipping and fast results.

16 | Varieties of Sexual Expression

Meeting Kiki helped me more fully understand sexual variations and the "kink" culture. Kiki is a 25-year-old queer, femme-identified woman who works as a professional dominatrix and submissive. For the last 8 years, she has actively been involved in the sexual kink culture, which can range from playful to intense and may include spanking, power play, bondage, dominance and submission, and/or sadomasochism. Today she lives with her primary partner in a nonmonogamous relationship. She explained how various sensations during sexual behavior can heighten sexual arousal. Having a clothespin on your nipple can create an unbearable amount of physical pain, but then hot wax dripping on your thigh requires your attention to another powerful sensation. Kiki loves these sensations, and if she is tied up or blindfolded during these experiences, there is an additional sense of arousal.

Kiki told me about a recent "scene" she had been in that revolved around a simulated gang-rape encounter. There were four men and another woman, all of whom were good friends of hers. She was comfortable with all of them and knew they all cared very much about her. They acted out a two-hour scene in a hotel room. Throughout the scene, Kiki was degraded and humiliated, and at one point she was thrown out into the hallway naked. She was also held underwater in a bathtub repeatedly. She told me that although the experience was intense and difficult, it was also exhilarating. All the people involved in the scene knew what her boundaries were and how far they could take things. They had prearranged "safe words" to use if she had wanted to stop. "Red" meant to stop everything, "yellow" meant things were getting close to her boundaries, and "green" meant it was all a go.

Kiki realizes that not all people can understand why she does what she does. She knows her sexual interests probably seem "quirky" to many people. But she also believes that exploring these sexual interests in a healthy and thoughtful way doesn't make her crazy. She lives for seeking out new and different experiences and feels this is just another part of her exploration.

Listening to Kiki articulate her motivations helped me contemplate the diversity of sexual expression. How do people decide what sexual behaviors are acceptable for themselves and for others?

Janell Carroll

© Nicholas Tsacoyeanes

Human sexuality can be expressed in many ways. We tend to celebrate individual and cultural differences in most aspects of human life—in what people eat, how they dress, or how they dance, for example. Yet, we have been less tolerant of sexual diversity, and we have historically considered such behavior "deviant" or "perverted" (Laws & O'Donohue, 2008). More modern views of sexuality, however, do not categorize people as "deviant" versus "normal." For example, the sexual world is not really split into those who become sexually excited from looking at others naked or having sex and those who do not; most people get aroused to some degree from visual sexual stimuli. Some people get more aroused than others, and at the upper limits are those who can get aroused only when watching sexual scenes; such people have taken a normal behavior to an extreme. In this chapter, we explore variations of sexual behavior, including differences in sexual desire and the **paraphilias**.

What Is "Typical" Sexual Expression?

Some medical and sexuality texts still categorize certain kinds of behavior as sexual deviance. Many undergraduate texts discuss these behaviors in chapters that include words such as *abnormal*, *unusual*, or *atypical* in their titles. Yet how exactly do we decide whether a behavior is "normal"? What is "typical" sexual activity? Where do we draw the line? Do we call it "atypical" if 5% of sexually active people do it? Ten percent? Twenty-five percent?

Sexual behaviors increase and decrease in popularity; oral sex, for example, was once considered a perversion, but now it is a commonly reported sexual behavior. Perhaps, then, we should consider as "deviant" only behaviors that may be harmful in some way. Masturbation was once believed to

A strong and varied fantasy life is the sign of healthy sexuality, and acting out fantasies in a safe sexual situation can add excitement to one's sex life. Problems may arise when the fantasy or desire becomes so prominent or preoccupying that you are unable to function sexually in its absence; sexual play is taken to the point of physical or psychological injury; you feel extreme levels of guilt about the desire; or your compulsion to perform a certain type of sexual behavior interferes with everyday life, disrupts your personal relationships, or risks getting you in trouble with the law. Under any of these circumstances, it is advisable to see a qualified sex therapist or counselor.

ON YOUR MIND

If I fantasize about watching other people having sex or if I get turned on by being spanked, does that mean I have a paraphilia?

paraphilia
Clinical term used to describe types of sexual expressions that are seen as unusual and potentially problematic. A person who engages in paraphilias is often referred to as a paraphiliac.

lead to hairy palms, acne, and stunted growth; now it is considered a normal, healthy part of sexual expression. If many of these desires exist to some degree in all of us, then any such desire itself is not atypical, just the degree of the desire.

REAL RESEARCH Although the earliest treatments for paraphilias involved surgical castration, in the 1940s, a shift in treatment led to the popularity of hormonal treatments and soon thereafter to psychotherapy (GORDON, 2008).

Social value judgments, not science, primarily determine which sexual behaviors are considered "normal" by a society. For example, in 1906, Krafft-Ebing defined sexual deviance as "every expression of (the sexual instinct) that does not correspond with the purpose of nature—i.e., propagation" (Brown, 1983, p. 227). Certainly, most people would not go so far today. Freud himself stated that the criterion of normalcy was love and that defenses against "perversion" were the bedrock of civilization because perversion trivializes or degrades love (Cooper, 1991). Note that Freud's objections to perversion were not medical, as they were to most other mental disturbances, but moral.

Even "modern" definitions can contain hidden value judgments: "The sexually variant individual typically exhibits sexual arousal or responses to inappropriate people (e.g., minors), objects (e.g., leather, rubber, garments), or activities (e.g., exposure in public, coercion, violence)" (Gudjonsson, 1986, p. 192). "Appropriate" or "inappropriate" people, objects, or activities of sexual attention differ in different times, in different cultures, and for different people.

Despite these objections, certain groups of behaviors are considered the most common deviations from conventional heterosexual or homosexual behaviors.

Popular culture also influences our attitudes about what is acceptable sexual behavior. For example, in 2011 the widespread popularity of the erotic fiction series *Fifty Shades of Grey* by E. L. James brought many sexual practices, including bondage, discipline, and domination, into mainstream consciousness and everyday conversations. The trilogy was among the top-selling books of all time with a total worldwide sale of 100 million copies (Russon, 2014). *Fifty Shades of Grey* appealed to people of all ages and brought sexual kink into people's minds and homes.

Society may view sexual behavior as either solely the business of the individual in the privacy of the bedroom (e.g., sexual excitement from pain or certain clothing), as a sign that the person is mentally ill (e.g., having sex with animals), or as dangerous and illegal (e.g., sex with underage children). The U.S. Department of Justice coordinates the National Sex Offender Registry, which enables individuals to search for the identity and location of known sex offenders (see the accompanying "Sex in Real Life" feature). In this chapter, we explore variations in sexual behaviors, theories of why people are attracted to unusual sexual objects, and how therapists have tried to help those who are troubled by their sexual desires.

Sex in Real Life Megan's Law

In 1994, 7-year-old Megan Kanka was lured into her neighbor's home in Hamilton Township, New Jersey, by the promise of a puppy. There she was raped, strangled, and suffocated by a two-time convicted sexual offender. Shortly thereafter, the governor of New Jersey, Christine Todd Whitman, signed the toughest sex offender registration act in the country, known as "Megan's Law." In 1996, Megan's Law became federal law and mandated that every community have access to information about the presence of convicted sex offenders in their neighborhoods. Two years earlier, in 1994, a federal statute known as the Jacob Wetterling Crimes against Children and Sexually Violent Offender Registration Program was passed, which also requires all states to create registration programs for convicted sex offenders (Trivits & Reppucci, 2002).

Today, all 50 states require that convicted sex offenders register on their release from prison into the community and require the listing (with the offenders' names, addresses, photographs, crimes, and sometimes physical descriptions) to be made available to the public. Although all require sex offenders to register, the statutes vary in what information is made available and for how long (Trivits & Reppucci, 2002). Many convicted sex offenders have protested the law, claiming that it violates their constitutional rights; however, the government has decided that the safety of children is a higher priority than the privacy of convicted sex offenders. Critics argue that the public shaming that results from these listings can impair the offender's ability to be rehabilitated (Hamilton, 2017). In addition, some argue that having such lists creates instant mailing lists for those who wish to connect with other offenders (Sommerfeld, 1999).

If a sex offender moves to a new state, they must provide written notice of the relocation to local police within a few days. States have various rules about this. For example, if an offender moves to Maine, they have only 24 hours to notify police of their relocation (Shim, 2014). In Kansas, they must register every three days to police if they are homeless. Other states have added regulations to their sex offender registry laws. For example, in 2005, certain towns in New York, Florida, and New Jersey banned convicted child molesters from being within 2,500 feet of any school, day-care center, playground, or park (Koch, 2005). Other states use electronic monitoring in addition to their online registries. For example, Florida, Alabama, New Jersey, Missouri, Ohio, and Oklahoma all passed laws requiring electronic monitoring (ankle bands that monitor the offender's whereabouts).

In 2006, a federal statute was signed into law called the Adam Walsh Act. This law classified sexual offender registries into three tiers, depending on the severity of the offense. Offenders on the top tier must update their whereabouts every 3 months for life, whereas those on the middle tier must update their whereabouts every 6 months for 25 years. Those on the bottom tier include minors and those younger than 14, who must update their whereabouts every year for 15 years. In 2014, the U.S. House of Representatives voted to pass the International Megan's Law to Prevent Demand for Child Sex Trafficking, which would require foreign governments to be informed when an American who is registered as a sex offender is traveling there (McGrath, 2014).

Unfortunately, the registries may have given many parents and caregivers a false sense of security. Sex offender registries contain only those offenders who have been convicted of sexual offenses and not all who commit such crimes. Nonetheless, many of these new laws and tracking devices may help to discourage sexual offenders from engaging in these behaviors.

A sexual offender registry.

Review Questions

1 Explain how medical and sexuality texts categorize sexual behaviors and how this might affect popular opinions.

2 Explain how a sexual behavior can increase or decrease in frequency and how this affects society's definition of normal.

3 How do social value judgments determine which sexual behaviors are viewed as normal?

4 How did the trilogy Fifty Shades of Grey influence people's attitudes about sexual behavior?

Paraphilias

The word *paraphilia* (pear-uh-FILL-ee-uh) is derived from the Greek "para" (besides) and "philia" (love or attraction). In other words, paraphilias are sexual behaviors that involve a craving for an erotic object that is unusual or different. In Chapter 14, we introduced the *Diagnostic and Statistical Manual of Mental Disorders* (*DSM*) and talked about how it was used to diagnose sexual dysfunction. The *DSM-5* also contains information on paraphilic disorders, or atypical sexual behaviors that either cause mental distress to a person or could potentially harm others. To be diagnosed with a paraphilic disorder, the *DSM-5* requires a person to feel personal distress for at least 6 months about their sexual interest, or to have a sexual desire or behavior that involves distress, injury, or death of another person, or a desire for sexual behavior that involves unwilling people or those who are not able to consent ("Paraphilic Disorders," 2013). The *DSM-5* includes eight conditions: fetishistic, transvestic, sexual sadistic, sexual masochistic, exhibitionistic, voyeuristic, frotteuristic, and pedophilic disorders. We will discuss all of these in the upcoming sections.

Paraphilic disorders are recurrent and intense. The behavior causes significant distress and interferes with a person's ability to work, interact with friends, and other important areas of one's life. For some people with paraphilic disorder, the fantasy or presence of the object of their desire is necessary for arousal and orgasm; in others, the desire occurs periodically or exists separately from their other sexual relationships.

Most people with atypical sexual interests do not have a paraphilic disorder. Recall Kiki from my chapter-opening Notebook feature, who views her behaviors as an exciting aspect of her sexuality. Others might be distressed and uncomfortable with their sexual interests or behaviors and seek out help. Experts point out that the discomfort that a person feels should come from within and should not be the result of society's disapproval of the behavior. Keep in mind that paraphilias are not considered paraphilic disorders unless they cause significant distress to an individual or harm to others.

Individuals who engage in paraphiliac behaviors are a heterogeneous group with no true factors that set them apart from nonparaphiliacs, with the exception of gender—the majority of those with paraphilias are men. Other than this, people with paraphilias come from every socioeconomic bracket, every ethnic and racial group, and from every sexual orientation (Seligman & Hardenburg, 2000).

Although there are no classic profiles that fit all paraphilias, certain factors appear to be related to the development of a paraphilia. Research has found that those with some of the more serious paraphilias have experienced significant family problems during childhood that contribute to poor social skills and distorted views of sexual intimacy (Seligman & Hardenburg, 2000). The intensity of these behaviors varies; someone with a mild case might use certain sexual fantasies during masturbation, whereas someone with a severe case may engage in unwanted sexual behavior with a child.

fetishist
A person who engages in a fetishistic behavior.

Some of the extreme cases of paraphilias are similar to many impulse-control disorders, such as substance abuse, gambling, and eating disorders (Goodman, 1993). Some people may feel conflicted about their behavior and develop tension and a preoccupation with certain behaviors. They may have repeatedly tried to suppress their sexual desires but have not been able to do so (Seligman & Hardenburg, 2000).

Many people find lingerie exciting, enjoy watching sexual scenes, or enjoy being lightly scratched during sex. However, in an extreme case, the lingerie itself becomes the object of sexual attention, not a means of enhancing the sexuality of the partner. For this reason, some have suggested that the defining characteristic of paraphilia is that it replaces a whole with a part, that it allows people to distance themselves from complex human sexual contact and replace it with the undemanding sexuality of an inanimate object, scene, or single action (Kaplan, 1991).

Motivations for paraphilic behaviors vary. Some people with paraphilias claim that their behaviors provide meaning to their lives and give them a sense of self, whereas others say the behaviors relieve their depression and loneliness or help them express rage (Goodman, 1993; S. B. Levine et al., 1990). Some violent or criminal paraphiliacs have little ability to feel empathy for their victims and may convince themselves that their victims enjoy the experiences, even though the victims do not consent to them (Seligman & Hardenburg, 2000).

Research on paraphilias has been drawn mostly from clinical and incarcerated samples, which are almost certainly not representative of the population as a whole. The number of people who live comfortably with sexual behaviors that are outside the realm of what is considered "typical" is hard to determine because many might not be comfortable disclosing their sexual behaviors, even on confidential questionnaires.

Throughout history, people with paraphilias have been portrayed as sick and/or perverted. There is thus an attempt to draw a clear line between those who engage in such behaviors and "normal" people; yet the line is rarely that clear. Certainly there are paraphilic behaviors that can be dangerous or can threaten others. Men who expose themselves to young girls, people who violate corpses, strangers who rub against people on buses, or adults who seduce underage children must not be allowed to continue their behavior. There can even be legal problems with the paraphilias that are not in themselves dangerous; some **fetishists** resort to stealing the object of interest to them, and occasionally a voyeur will break into people's homes. A number of therapies have been developed to help these people, but as you will see, it is difficult to change a person's arousal patterns.

Many others live comfortably with their paraphilias. A man who has a fetish for lingerie, for example, may find a partner who enjoys wearing it for him. As discussed in my chapter-opening Notebook feature, Kiki is engaging in consensual sexual behavior and has no desire to change her behavior. Why should she want to put it to an end just because some other people might find it distasteful or weird? In what sense is such a person sick?

For this reason, paraphilias and paraphilic disorders have become controversial. Some theorists suggest that the term describes a society's value judgments about sexuality and not a psychiatric or

IN OUR WORLD

Although there has not been much research documenting the incidence, expression, and treatment of paraphilias outside the United States, there have been limited studies. The majority of information available concerns pedophilia and transvestic disorder. A limited amount of research exists on other paraphilias, such as sadomasochism. Here we explore what we do know about paraphilias in a variety of countries.

Brazil

Brazil is a conservative and religious country and, as such, there is not a great deal of acceptance for paraphilic behaviors. Although there are no legal restrictions against transvestic disorders, researchers estimate that there are few who engage in this practice (de Freitas, 2004). We do know that throughout history, zoophilia has been found to occur in Brazil, and it has been found to be more common in both men and those living in rural areas (de Freitas, 2004).

China

China has very strict policies against behaviors it deems inappropriate, and paraphilias certainly fall into this category. Sex offenders in China are often charged with "hooliganism,"

which is a term that includes a wide range of uncivil and sexually unrestrained behavior (Ruan & Lau, 2004). China has very severe penalties for those who engage in such behaviors, and harsh punishments are common. For example, one review reported that the Chinese government enforced the death penalty for certain sexual crimes, including forced sex and pedophilia (Ruan & Lau, 2004).

Czech Republic

Paraphiliacs in the Czech Republic have many more opportunities for communication and contact with other paraphiliacs than they did when they were under communist control (Zverina, 2004). This would include clubs, magazines, newspapers, and the Internet. Sadomasochism and fetishes are the most common paraphilias in the Czech Republic (Zverina, 2004). Sexual offenders who are charged with crimes are referred for counseling and treatments, which are covered under national health insurance plans.

Denmark

Denmark and many of the Scandinavian countries have much more liberal attitudes about sexuality, so they are less likely to sweep behaviors under the carpet if they

don't agree with them. Paraphilias are viewed as criminal behaviors, and those found engaging in such behaviors are appropriately charged. Denmark also has high reporting and treatment rates for paraphilias (Graugaard et al., 2004). In reaction to increased rates of child sexual abuse, Denmark opened a center for the treatment of sexually abused children at the University Hospital in Copenhagen in 2000, and today many groups actively educate professionals and the lay public about incest and child sexual abuse (Graugaard et al., 2004).

Japan

Sadism and masochism are well known in Japanese art and literature (Hatano & Shimazaki, 2004). Thousands of sadomasochism magazines are sold each month, and many nightclubs cater to the sadomasochism subculture. Like China, Japan has strict laws and punishments for people who engage in child sexual abuse. In 1999, Japan enacted a Child Prostitution and Child Pornography Prohibition law that prohibits sexual activity with minors and enforces strict punishments for those charged with these behaviors (Hatano & Shimazaki, 2004).

SOURCE: Francoeur & Noonan (2004).

---

clinical category (Silverstein, 1984). Robert J. Stoller, a well-known psychoanalytic theorist, objected to the idea of trying to create psychological explanations that group people by their sexual habits (Stoller, 1996).

Theories About Paraphilias

Many researchers have theorized as to why and how paraphilias develop, but little consensus has been reached. Paraphilias are undoubtedly complex behavior patterns, which may have biological, psychological, or social origins—or aspects of all three.

Biological Theories

Biological researchers have found that a number of conditions can initiate paraphilic behavior, such as illnesses, disturbances of brain structure and brain chemistry, and higher levels of certain hormones, such as testosterone (Giotakos et al., 2005;

Rahman & Symeonides, 2008; Sartorius et al., 2008). However, this does not mean that everyone with a paraphilia has one of these conditions. At most, these conditions are factors that may lead some people to be more likely to develop a paraphilia, but they do not explain the majority of such behaviors.

ON YOUR MIND

Why are paraphilias more common in men?

No one really knows, although theories abound. Some researchers suggest that perhaps paraphilias are developed visually, and males tend, for some biological reason, to be more sexually aroused by visual stimuli than females. Maybe cultural variables give men more sexual latitude in expressing what excites them. It could also have something to do with the way we look at it; women may express their paraphilias in different, less obvious ways than men. There could also be power differentials that contribute to higher rates in men.

Psychoanalytic Theory

Psychoanalytic thought suggests that paraphilias can be traced back to the difficult time the infant has in negotiating their way through the Oedipal crisis and castration anxiety. This can explain why paraphilias are more common among men because both boys and girls identify strongly with their mothers, but girls can continue that identification, whereas boys must, painfully, separate from their mothers to establish a male identity.

Louise Kaplan, a psychoanalyst, suggests that every paraphilia involves issues of masculinity or femininity; as she writes, "Every male perversion entails a masquerade or impersonation of masculinity and every female perversion entails a masquerade or impersonation of femininity" (1991, p. 249). For example, a man who exposes himself in public may be coping with castration anxiety by evoking a reaction to his penis from women. The exhibitionist in this view is "masquerading" as a man to cover up feelings of nonmasculinity; he is saying, in effect, "Let me prove that I am a man by showing that I possess the instrument of masculinity." He even needs to demonstrate that his penis can inspire fear, which may be why exhibitionists disproportionately choose young girls, who are more likely to display a fear reaction (Kline, 1987). This confirms to the exhibitionist the power of his masculinity.

In contrast, voyeurs, who are excited by looking at others nude or having sex, may be fixated on the experience that aroused their castration anxieties as children—the sight of genitals and sexuality (Kline, 1987). Looking allows the person to gain power over the fearful and hidden world of sexuality while safe from the possibility of contact. The visual component of castration anxiety occurs when the boy sees the power and size of the father's genitals and the lack of a penis on his mother or sisters. The act of looking initiates castration anxiety, and in the voyeur, the looking has never ceased. Yet looking itself cannot really relieve the anxiety permanently, and so the voyeur is compelled to peep again and again.

Developmental Theories

Freud suggested that children are polymorphously perverse; that is, at birth we have a general erotic potential that can be attached to almost anything. We learn from an early age which sexual objects society deems appropriate for us to desire, but society's messages can get off track. For example, advertising tries to "sexualize" its products—we have all seen shoe commercials, for example, that emphasize the long, sexy legs of the model while focusing on the shoes she wears. Some boys may end up focusing on those shoes as objects of sexual fantasy, which can develop into a fetish.

A theory that builds on similar ideas is John Money's (1984, 1986, 1990) **lovemaps**. Money suggests that the auditory, tactile, and (especially) visual stimuli we experience during childhood sex play form a template in our brain that defines our ideal lover and ideal sexual situation. If our childhood sex play remains undisturbed, development goes on toward heterosexual desires. If, however, the child is punished for normal sexual curiosity or if there are traumas during this stage, such as sexual abuse, the development of the lovemap can be disrupted in one of three ways.

In **hypophilia** (high-po-FILL-ee-uh), negative stimuli prevent the development of certain aspects of sexuality, and the genitals may be impaired from full functioning. Overall, females are more likely to experience hypophilia than men, resulting in an inability to orgasm, vaginal pain, or lubrication problems later in life. A lovemap can also be disrupted to cause a condition called **hyperphilia** (high-per-FILL-ee-uh), in which a person defies the negative sexual stimulus and becomes overly sexually active, even becoming compulsively sexual. Finally, a lovemap can be disrupted when there is a substitution of new elements into the lovemap, and a paraphilia can develop. Because normal sexual curiosity has been discouraged or made painful, the child redirects erotic energy toward other objects that are not forbidden, such as shoes, rubber, or just looking; in other cases, the child turns their erotic energy inward and becomes excited by pain or humiliation.

Once this lovemap is set, it becomes stable, which explains why changing it is so difficult. For example, Money (1984) suggests that sexual arousal to objects may arise when a parent makes a child feel shame about interest in an object. For example, a boy may be caught with his mother's panties in the normal course of curiosity about the woman's body, but when he is severely chastised, the panties become forbidden, dirty, and promising of sexual secrets, and he may begin to seek them out.

Another theory about how these fixations occur is the idea of **courtship disorders** (Freund & Blanchard, 1986; Freund et al., 1983, 1984). Organizing paraphilias into "courtship" stages suggests that the paraphiliac's behavior becomes fixed at a preliminary stage of mating that would normally lead to vaginal intercourse. Thus, a person becomes fixated on a particular person, object, or activity and does not progress to typical mating behaviors.

Behavioral Theories

Behaviorists suggest that paraphilias develop because some behavior becomes associated with sexual pleasure through **conditioning** (Wilson, 1987). For example, imagine that a boy gets a spanking. While receiving it, the boy has an erection, either by coincidence or because he finds the stimulus of the spanking pleasurable (it becomes a reinforcement). Later, remembering the spanking, he becomes excited and masturbates. As he repeats his masturbatory fantasy, a process called *conditioning* occurs, whereby sexual excitement becomes so associated with the idea of the spanking that he has trouble becoming excited in its absence.

---

lovemap
Term coined by John Money to refer to the template of an ideal lover and sexual situation we develop as we grow up.

hypophilia
Lack of full functioning of the sexual organs because of missing stages of childhood development.

hyperphilia
Compulsive sexuality caused by over-compensating for negative reactions to childhood sexuality.

courtship disorder
Theory that asserts that paraphilias develop from abnormalities in the normal courtship process, which involves looking for sexual partners, interacting with partners, touching or embracing them, and sexual intercourse.

conditioning
In behaviorism, a type of associative learning in which a person associates a particular behavior with a positive response.

You can imagine how similar situations could lead to other types of fetishes: A boy lies naked on a fur coat, or takes a "pony" ride on his aunt's leg while she's wearing her black leather boots, or puts on his sister's panties, or spies on a female houseguest through the bathroom keyhole. All of these behaviors become positively reinforced, and thus are more likely to be repeated.

Sociological Theories

Another way of looking at the causes of paraphilias is to examine the ways society encourages certain behaviors. Feminists, for example, argue that in societies that treat women as sexual objects, it can be a natural development to replace the woman with another, inanimate sexual object. When men and their sexual organs are glorified, some men may need to reinforce their masculinity by exposing themselves and evoking fear.

American society is ruled by images, saturated with television, movies, commercials, advertisements, and magazines; most of these images have highly charged sexual imagery (Collins, 2005). The result, some argue, is a world where the image takes the place of the reality, where it becomes common to substitute fantasies for reality. Surrounded by media, the society experiences things vicariously, through reading about it or seeing it rather than actually doing it. In such a climate, representations of eroticism may be easily substituted for sex itself, and so paraphilias become common.

Review Questions

1 Define *paraphilia* and explain the essential features of paraphilic disorder as determined by the *DSM-5*.

2 Identify and explain some of the motivations for paraphilias.

3 Differentiate between consensual and nonconsensual paraphilias.

4 Compare and contrast how the biological and psychoanalytic theories explain paraphilias, and provide an example.

5 Compare and contrast how the developmental and sociological theories explain paraphilias, and provide an example.

Types of Paraphilic Disorders

Paraphilic disorders have been grouped into a number of major categories by researchers and clinicians. We review in this section some of the more common types of paraphilic disorders that are included in the *DSM-5*, as well as some of the more obscure and less common paraphilias.

Fetishistic Disorder

A **fetishistic** (FEH-tish-is-tic) **disorder** involves a recurrent and intense sexual arousal manifested in fantasies, urges, or behaviors that involve the use of nonliving objects (such as shoes, boots, panties, or bras; or a fabric, such as leather, silk, fur, or rubber), or focus on nongenital body parts (such as feet or hair). These behaviors are recurrent and intense and have occurred for at least 6 months, causing significant social and/or occupational distress. As is the case with most paraphilias, the majority of fetishists are male (Darcangelo, 2008).

Many people enjoy using lingerie or other fabrics as part of their sexual behavior without becoming dependent on them for arousal. The fetishist, in contrast, needs the presence or the fantasy of the object to achieve arousal and sometimes cannot achieve orgasm in its absence. Some fetishists integrate the object of their desire into their sexual life with a partner; for others it remains a secret fetish, with hidden collections of shoes, or panties, or photographs of a body part, over which they masturbate in secret, ever fearful of discovery.

REAL RESEARCH People who are knowledgeable about sadomasochistic behavior or who know someone who has engaged in it have more positive attitudes about sadomasochism than those with less knowledge or acquaintances (YOST, 2010).

Different cultures hold up different body parts, objects, colors, or smells as symbols of attraction and sexuality for mating (see Chapter 7 for more information about attraction in different cultures). Fetishism involves a person becoming sexually attracted to a symbol itself instead of what it represents. Put another way, for the fetishist, the object—unlike the living, breathing person—is itself erotic, rather than the person, which also eliminates having to deal with another person's feelings, wants, and needs. It can be a refuge from the complexity of interpersonal sexual relations. In that sense, all the paraphilias we discuss can be seen as a type of fetishism; pain and humiliation, or women's clothes, or looking at people having sex can each be a substitute for interpersonal sexuality.

---

fetishistic disorder
A recurrent and intense sexual arousal manifested in fantasies, urges, or behaviors involving the use of nonliving objects or nongenital body parts.

A person with a foot fetish often has an inability to experience sexual arousal or orgasm without contact or a sexual fantasy about feet.

Transvestic Disorder

In Chapter 4, we discussed the transgender community that includes a variety of gender-diverse individuals. This is different from a **transvestic** (trans-VESS-tick) **disorder**, which involves wearing clothes of the other gender, intense sexual arousal from the cross-dressing, and distress about this behavior. These behaviors are recurrent and intense and have occurred for at least 6 months, causing significant social and/or occupational distress. This has been a controversial diagnosis, with many arguing that it pathologizes gender variance and implies that all cross-dressing is the result of a mental disorder (Kamens, 2011; Winters, 2009, 2010). As we discussed in Chapter 4, gender expression that differs from social expectations of sex assigned at birth should not be viewed as a mental health problem.

The goal of therapy for transvestic disorder is to cope with anxieties and guilt and the way a person relates interpersonally and sexually with their partner and family (Newring et al., 2008). Transvestite support groups have been organized in cities all over the country and may offer a good support system for those with transvestic disorder (Newring et al., 2008).

Sexual Sadism and Sexual Masochism Disorders

Sexual sadism disorder refers to an intense sexual arousal from the physical or psychological suffering of another person, which can be manifested by fantasies or behaviors. Sadistic behaviors may include restraint, blindfolding, strangulation, spanking, whipping, pinching, beating, burning, and electrical shocks. The term **sadism** is derived from a man named Donatien Alphonse François de Sade (1740–1814), known as the Marquis de Sade. De Sade was sent to prison for kidnapping and terrorizing a beggar girl and then later for tricking some prostitutes into eating "Spanish fly," supposedly an aphrodisiac, but which caused such burning and

blistering that one threw herself out a window. While in prison, de Sade wrote novels describing such tortures as being bound hand and foot, suspended between trees, set upon by dogs, almost being eviscerated (cut open), and so on. De Sade believed that the highest form of sexual activity for women was pain, not pleasure, because pleasure could be too easily faked. De Sade spent much of his life in prison (Bullough, 1976).

Sexual masochism disorder (MASS-oh-kiz-um) refers to an intense sexual arousal from the act of being humiliated, beaten, bound, or suffering in other ways. **Masochism** was named after another novelist, Leopold Baron Von Sacher-Masoch (1836–1895), who believed that women were created to subdue men's "animal passions" (Bullough, 1976). The *DSM-5* diagnosis for sexual sadism and sexual masochism disorders requires ongoing recurrent and intense sexually sadistic or masochistic fantasies or behaviors, which have caused significant social and/or occupational distress for at least 6 months. Many people, like Kiki, who engage in BDSM behaviors find enjoyment in these behaviors and are not distressed by them. Unless their behaviors caused distress, injury, or death to someone or their behavior involved partners who were unwilling or unable to consent, they would not be diagnosed with sadism or masochism disorders.

Sadism and masochism both associate sexuality and pain, and most people who practice one are also involved with the other. Therefore, the phenomenon as a whole is often referred to as **sadomasochism** (say-doe-MASS-oh-kiz-um), or S&M. The acronym *BDSM*—bondage, discipline, sadism, and masochism—is commonly used today because it illustrates the diverse range of possible experiences. BDSM refers to an eroticized exchange of power and the application or receipt of painful and/or intense sensations that may include physical restriction (e.g., bondage, handcuffs), administration of pain (e.g., spanking, clothespins), and/or humiliation (e.g., verbal or physical; Ambler et al., 2017; Turley & Butt, 2015). Some individuals may participate in only one behavior or activity, whereas others may engage in a variety of practices (Kleinplatz & Moser, 2006; Wiseman, 2000).

Because BDSM encompasses a wide variety of behaviors, the number of people who engage in it depends on how one defines it. Kinsey and his colleagues (1953) found that 3% to 12% of women and 10% to 20% of men reported getting sexually aroused to S&M narratives. However, researchers believe that sexual fantasies involving BDSM are much more prevalent. One study found that 23% of people have occasional sexual fantasies involving BDSM (Arndt et al., 1985).

transvestic disorder
A paraphilia that involves recurrent and intense sexual arousal from fantasies or behaviors involving cross-dressing, which often causes significant distress.

sexual sadism disorder
A paraphilia that involves a recurrent and intense sexual arousal from fantasies or behaviors involving the physical or psychological suffering of another person.

sadism
Deriving sexual pleasure from administering or watching pain and humiliation.

sexual masochism disorder
A paraphilia that involves recurrent and intense sexual arousal from fantasies or behaviors involving the act of being humiliated, beaten, bound, or suffering in other ways.

masochism
Deriving sexual pleasure from receiving pain or being humiliated.

sadomasochism
Broad term that refers to the receiving of sexual pleasure from acts involving the infliction or receiving of pain and humiliation.

Freud and his followers made sadomasochism central to their theories about adult sexuality. Freud believed that to some degree we all feel ambivalent about the ones we love and even, at times, feel the desire to hurt them. However, we also feel guilty about it, especially in early childhood, and the guilt we feel is satisfied by turning that hurt on ourselves. Later psychoanalytic theorists believed that the goal of masochism was not pain or punishment itself, but rather relinquishing the self to someone else to avoid responsibility or anxiety for sexual desires.

Sexual responses to pain exist, to some degree, in many sexual relationships. Kinsey and his colleagues (1953), for example, found that about 50% of the people in his sample experienced erotic response to sexual biting, and 24% of men and 12% of women had some erotic response to sadomasochistic stories. Another study found that 25% of people reported occasionally engaging in sadomasochistic behavior (Rubin, 1990). For example, some couples use bondage as a variation in their sexual lives without any other sadomasochistic elements (Comfort, 1987).

In most S&M encounters, one partner plays the **dominant** role ("master" or "top") and the other the **submissive** ("slave" or "bottom"). Female dominants are often referred to as Mistress, and male dominants are referred to as Master or Lord. Bondage and restraint are the most common expressions of these behaviors, although it is power, rather than pain, that is the most important aspect (Cross & Matheson, 2006; Seligman & Hardenburg, 2000).

A variety of techniques are commonly used to physically dominate the submissive partner. Tying up the submissive partner or using restraints to render them helpless is often referred to as B&D (for bondage and discipline). B&D may be accompanied by **flagellation**, **caning**, **birching**, or other painful or shocking stimuli on the skin such as the use of hot wax, ice, or biting. Psychological techniques can include sensory deprivation (through

A dominatrix is paid by submissive clients to engage in bondage and discipline fantasy play.

the use of face masks, blindfolds, earplugs), humiliation (being subject to verbal abuse or being made to engage in embarrassing behaviors such as boot-licking, **scatophagia** [scat-oh-FAJ-ee-uh], **urolagnia** [yur-oh-LOG-nee-uh], or acting like a dog), forced cross-dressing, or **infantilism** (American Psychiatric Association, 2000; Moser, 1988). This is accompanied by verbal descriptions of what is to come and why the person deserves it, increasing in intensity over time to eventual sexual climax. Note that the pain is used as part of a technique to enhance sexual arousal—the pain itself is not exciting. Many people involved in BDSM report increased sexual arousal and decreased psychological stress and negative affect when engaging in these behaviors (Ambler et al., 2017).

People can participate in BDSM to different degrees. For some couples, BDSM is an occasional diversion in their sexual behavior. Others, like Kiki, pursue it outside of a committed relationship; for example, most big cities have active kink subcultures that offer a variety of sadomasochistic services, including **dominatrixes** and submissives.

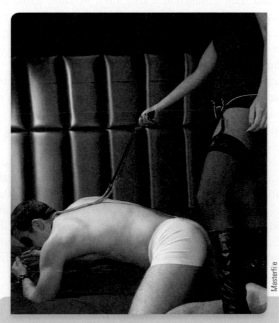

Sadomasochists often use props, such as leather clothes, studs, chains, and nipple clamps.

dominant
Describes the active role in sadomasochistic sexuality.

submissive
Describes the passive role in sadomasochistic activity.

flagellation
Striking a partner, usually by whipping.

caning
Beating someone with a rigid cane.

birching
Whipping someone using the stripped branch of a tree.

scatophagia
A paraphilic behavior that involves recurrent and intense sexual arousal from fantasies or behaviors involving feces.

urolagnia
A paraphilic behavior that involves recurrent and intense sexual arousal from fantasies or behaviors involving urine.

infantilism
A paraphilic behavior that involves recurrent and intense sexual arousal from fantasies or behaviors involving being treated like a baby (such as dressing in diapers).

dominatrix
A woman who takes the dominant role in bondage and discipline behaviors with male or female submissives.

A sadomasochistic (or "kink") subculture exists for those who have adopted BDSM as a lifestyle. A variety of organizations cater to consensual BDSM (such as the Eulenspiegel Society or the Society of Janus), and partners can meet at conferences and learn more in various BDSM newsletters and magazines. Specialty shops cater to BDSM advocates, selling restraints, whips, leather clothing, and other items. The sadomasochistic encounter, or "scene," is really a kind of drama or performance, which is enhanced by both sides knowing their roles and dressing the part. The encounter is carefully planned, and the dominant partner is usually very careful not to actually hurt the submissive partner while "torturing" them. As Kiki explained to me, a "safe word" is usually agreed on so that the submissive partner can signal if they are in real distress. The *Master's and Mistress' Handbook,* a guide to S&M encounters, offers a set of rules on how to torture one's partner without causing harm:

> Remember that a slave may suddenly start to cough or feel faint. If masked and gagged, choking or lack of oxygen may result in serious consequences within seconds.... Never leave a bound and gagged slave alone in a room.... It is essential that gags, nostril tubes, enema pipes, rods and other insertions should be scrupulously clean and dipped into mild antiseptic before use.... Never use cheap or coarse rope. This has no "give" and can quickly cause skin-sores. (Quoted in Gosselin, 1987, pp. 238–239)

Sadomasochistic subcultures exist among heterosexual and LGBT adults. In heterosexual BDSM, power relations between the sexes may be overturned, with the female being the dominant partner and the male submissive. The sadomasochistic "scene" is used to explore the nature of social relations by using sex as a means to explore power. Gay men who engage in BDSM have been found to prefer the use of leather, dildos, and wrestling, whereas heterosexual men tend to prefer humiliation, masks, gags, and straitjackets (Nordling et al., 2006). BDSM participants derive sexual excitement from playing with power relations, from either being able to dominate another completely or to give in completely to another's will.

The BDSM subculture takes symbols of authority and dominance from the general culture, such as whips, uniforms, and handcuffs, and uses them in a safe erotic drama in which scripted roles take the place of "real self." It even mocks these symbols of authority by using them for erotic pleasure. Well-known social psychologist R. F. Baumeister (1988) suggests that sadomasochism is a reaction to modern society itself. Noting that sexual masochism proliferated when Western culture became highly individualistic, Baumeister suggests that it relieves the submissive partner of a sense of responsibility for the self by placing one's behavior completely under someone else's control.

Exhibitionistic and Voyeuristic Disorders

Visual stimuli are basic aspects of sexuality; most sexually active people enjoy looking at the nude bodies of their partners, and such things as lingerie and the act of undressing one's partner can enhance the sexual nature of the human form. The enormous industry of adult magazines, books, and online websites, the almost obligatory nude scene in modern movies, the embarrassment most people feel when seen naked inappropriately, and even the common night-time dream of being caught naked in public all show the fundamental psychological power of visual sexual stimuli.

For some people, looking at nudity or sexual acts, or being seen naked or engaging in sex, become the paramount activities of sexuality. The person who becomes sexually aroused primarily from displaying their genitals, nudity, or sexuality to strangers is an **exhibitionist**; the person whose primary mode of sexual stimulation is to watch others naked or engaging in sex is called a **voyeur**. Langevin and Lang (1987) reviewed a number of studies that show that there is a close connection between exhibitionism and voyeurism; most exhibitionists engaged in voyeuristic habits before beginning to expose themselves.

Exhibitionistic Disorder

Exhibitionistic disorder involves recurrent and intense arousal from exposing one's genitals to an unsuspecting stranger. These behaviors cause significant social and/or occupational distress and have occurred for more than 6 months. As such, this behavior is nonconsensual. The exhibitionist (or "flasher"), who is usually male, achieves sexual gratification from exposing his genitals in public or to unsuspecting people, who are usually female (Murphy & Page, 2008). What excites the exhibitionist is not usually the nudity itself but the lack of consent of the victim as expressed in her shocked or fearful reaction. True exhibitionists would not get the same sexual charge being naked on a nude beach, for example, where everyone is naked.

Exhibitionists usually have erections while exposing themselves, and they masturbate either then or later, while thinking about the reactions of their victims. Usually exhibitionism begins in the teen years and decreases as a man ages; however, it may worsen in times of stress or disappointment (Murphy & Page, 2008; Seligman & Hardenburg, 2000).

Exhibitionism is legally classified as "indecent exposure," and it is one of the most common sexual offenses (along with voyeurism and pedophilia). However, it is important to keep in mind that exhibitionists have a witness to their crimes and because of this, there is a higher likelihood of being caught.

Research has failed to confirm any personality characteristics that might be common to exhibitionists except that the behavior is compulsive and difficult to stop (Rabinowitz et al., 2002). Many exhibitionists are shy and withdrawn but have normal dating and sexual histories. They are married or in committed partnerships and have normal sexual relations with their spouses or partners and have been found to have low levels of

exhibitionist	voyeur
A person who experiences recurrent and intense arousal from exposing their genitals to an unsuspecting stranger.	A person who experiences a recurrent and intense arousal from observing unsuspecting persons undressing or engaging in sex acts.

Although female exhibitionism is rare, it is interesting how much more acceptable it is for a woman to expose her body in U.S. society. Rihanna wore a see-through sparkly gown at a recent award ceremony and various media sources called her a fashion icon.

psychopathology (Hopkins et al., 2016). Although we don't know exactly how many exhibitionists there are, we do know that many women are "flashed"—in fact, 40% to 60% of female college students report having been flashed at some point (Murphy & Page, 2008).

Exhibitionism in women is rare, although cases of it are reported in the literature (Grob, 1985; Rhoads & Boekelheide, 1985). Female exhibitionists may seek approval to feel feminine and appreciated, and seeing men admire her naked body reinforces her sense of sexual value and femininity. Perhaps, then, exhibitionism in women just takes a different form than in men (see the nearby Real Research). Women have more legitimate ways to expose their bodies than men do, and women exposing breast cleavage is acceptable by today's fashion standards. In fact, many female celebrities have been known to flash various parts of their bodies for attention. For example, Rihanna appeared at a red-carpet event in a transparent fishnet dress that exposed her entire body. Would you consider her an exhibitionist?

REAL RESEARCH Taking a self-portrait of oneself, or a "selfie," is positively associated with social exhibitionism (SOROKOWSKA ET AL., 2016). One study found that students posted an average of 3 selfies of themselves, 1.4 selfies with their romantic partners, and 2.2 group selfies to Facebook each month (with women posting more than men).

Voyeuristic Disorder

Voyeuristic disorder involves individuals whose main means of sexual gratification is watching unsuspecting persons undressing, naked, or engaging in sexual activity. Some would argue that we are a voyeuristic society; our major media—newspapers, television, movies, advertisements—are full of sexual images that are intended to interest and arouse us. Magazines and movies featuring nude women or couples are popular. Even television shows display far more nudity and sexuality than would have been allowed just a few years ago. In modern society, it seems, we have all become casual voyeurs to some degree.

Those with voyeuristic disorder, however, are those for whom watching others naked or viewing erotica is a compulsion. These behaviors are recurrent and intense and have occurred for at least 6 months, causing significant social and/or occupational distress. Voyeurs are often called "Peeping Toms," a revealing term because implicit in it are two important aspects of voyeurism. First, a "peeper" is one who looks without the knowledge or consent of the person being viewed, and true voyeurs are excited by the illicit aspect of their peeping. Second, voyeurs are usually male. Although it is becoming more acceptable for women in society to watch porn or to go to see male strippers, clinically speaking, there are few "Peeping Janes" (Lavin, 2008).

The typical voyeur is a heterosexual male who begins his voyeuristic behaviors before age 15 (Lavin, 2008; Seligman & Hardenburg, 2000). **Primary voyeurism** is rare. More often, voyeurism is mixed in with a host of other paraphiliac behaviors (Langevin & Lang, 1987; Lavin, 2008). Still, voyeurs are generally harmless and are satisfied just with peeping, although they certainly can scare an unsuspecting person who sees a strange man peering in the window.

Many voyeurs satisfy some of their urges by watching pornography. For most voyeurs, however, this is ultimately unsatisfying, because part of the excitement is the knowledge that the victims do not know or approve of the fact that the voyeur sees them. Like exhibitionists, voyeurs tend to be immature, sexually frustrated, poor at developing relationships, and chronic masturbators (Lavin, 2008).

Over the last few years there has been an increase in "video voyeurism," in which a person uses cameras, cell phones, or other surveillance equipment to record nonconsenting persons undressing or having sex (Nolan & Maguire, 2016; Stuyvesant et al., 2014). In 2010, a Colgate University student secretly recorded having sex with his girlfriend in his bedroom (Citron, 2014). After they broke up, he threatened to post the video online but he was convicted under "Stephanie's Law," New York's unlawful surveillance statute. This statute makes it illegal to use a device to secretly record a person undressing or having sex (it was named after a woman whose landlord installed a camera in her smoke detector to secretly watch her). The student was given 4 years of jail time and was labelled a sexual offender. There have been a variety of new legislation in response to video voyeurism. Newly developed laws

primary voyeurism
Voyeurism as the main and exclusive paraphilia.

Sexual Diversity — Dutch Pedophilia Party?

IN OUR WORLD

In 2006, a new Dutch political party, known as the *Party for Neighbourly Love, Freedom, and Diversity* (*PNVD* or *Partij voor Naasten-liefde*), was founded in the Netherlands by three known pedophiles, Ad van den Berg, Martin Uittenbogaard, and Nobert de Jonge. The party became known as the "pedophil-ia" party in the media, since the two major issues on their platform involved lowering the age of consent and legalizing child pornography in the Netherlands. The main rationale for the development of the party was to give a voice to pedophiles, many of whom felt they had been ignored and silenced over the years. Creating a political party gave them an opportunity to have their voices heard. Although many Dutch citizens believed that the PNVD was a one-issue party, the group's founders argued that they had several additional proposed provisions, including the following:

- Allowing the private possession of child pornography.

- Everybody will have the freedom to ap-pear naked in public.

- People, aged 16 and older, can appear in pornographic productions.

- Pornography can be broadcast during the daytime hours.

- Allowing sexual contact for young people from the age of 12 on.

- Legalizing soft drugs (for those ages 12 and older) and hard drugs (for those 16 and over).

- Legalizing smoking, gambling, and alco-hol consumption from the age of 12 on.

- Allowing sexual contact in public nature reserves (intervention only when the nuisance becomes too great).

- Punishing the circumcision of boys and girls under the age of 16.

- Legalizing prostitution for those over the age of 16.

- Providing sexual education beginning in nursery school.

As you can imagine, the PNVD created a sig-nificant amount of controversy in Holland. To become a legally recognized party they needed at least 60,000 signatures. However, few people were willing to support the PNVD. In 2010, the party disbanded due to a lack of public support.

During a recent visit to the Netherlands, I had the opportunity to meet with two of the party's founders, Ad van den Berg and Martin Uittenbogaard. I really wanted to un-derstand more about them and their ideas for creating such a group. Martin Uittenbo-gaard told me that it has been difficult be-ing so open and public about his interests in pedophilia. He has experienced multiple death threats, and several of his windows have been broken with rocks. But the main reason he believes that society is against pedophilia is because it is "taboo." Martin explained that young children experience sexual interest and several do engage in sexual relationships with other young chil-dren. The problem, he believes, is that the government wants to control *who* people have sex with. That is why he thinks certain sexual behaviors, such as homosexuality or pornography, were il-legal—so the govern-ment could control it.

Ad van den Berg agreed with Martin and said that it was difficult to explain why he was attract-ed to young boys. He remembers the

Petra Lambert

attractions started when he was young but he didn't act on them until he was about 32 years old. He has never been attracted to girls, women, or adult men—only young boys. He was 65 years old when I spoke with him and he told me about several pla-tonic and sexual relationships he had with young boys. The youngest was 10 years old, but most are 11 to 13 years old. When I asked him what they talked about he told me they mostly talk about the boy's day and he helps them with homework. Most of the boys are not interested in his life or work, but they do like the attention he gives them. He doesn't see himself as a predator or a "hunter." When a boy tells him he doesn't want to be touched, he claims to respect this. Some boys just like to be with him, while others are looking simply for sex with-out a relationship.

One 11-year-old boy came to his house one day after a soccer game and asked him why he didn't have a wife. Ad explained that he didn't like women and that he liked boys instead. He explained that being honest about his feelings didn't scare the boy off. They trusted each other. One day the boy came over and told him that he was going to show himself to Ad. He un-dressed himself and walked around naked in the house. Ad stresses that he didn't ask the boy to do this—he did it on his own free will.

Both men told me if there is a power is-sue involved, it is the minor child who has all the power. If a boy goes to the police and tells them they were touched by an adult, the adult can be arrested. But the main point that both Martin and Ad wanted oth-ers to understand is that their love for boys is real and they feel they should be allowed to have loving relationships with them.

You might be wondering how a party with such a controversial platform could even exist. Their beliefs are disturbing to most of us, and many would argue that known pedophiles who are openly advo-cating child pornography and sexual con-tact with children belong in prison. What do you think? Does everyone have the right to express themselves, or does the safety of children preclude this right?

also make other practices, including "upskirting" or "downblousing," in which devices are used to look up women's skirts or down their blouses, illegal (Nolan & Maguire, 2016). Research in this area is sure to continue as technology continues to evolve.

Although it technically refers to a single couple engaging in sexual intercourse in front of others, **troilism** (TROY-ill-iz-um) has come to mean any sex sessions involving multiple partners. Troilism is not new; in 1631, Mervyn Touchet, the Second Earl of Castlehaven, was executed in England for ordering his servants to have sex with his wife while he watched. The fact that they were servants and thus beneath his station was as damaging to him as the actual act (Bullough, 1976).

Troilism may involve aspects of voyeurism, exhibitionism, and, sometimes, latent homosexual desires; an observer who gets excited, for example, by watching his partner give oral sex to another man may be subconsciously putting himself in his partner's place. Some troilists install ceiling mirrors, video cameras, and other means to capture the sexual act for viewing later on. Others engage in sharing a sexual partner with a third party while they look on, or they engage in swinging (see Chapter 9). Many couples experiment with group sex, but to the troilist, engaging in or fantasizing about such sexual activity is the primary means of sexual arousal.

Frotteuristic Disorder

Frotteurism (frah-TOUR-iz-um) involves a man rubbing his genitals against a person's (usually a woman) thighs or buttocks in a crowded place (such as a subway) where he can claim it was an accident and get away quickly. In some cases, he may fondle a woman's breasts with his hand while he is rubbing up against her. This is similar to **toucheurism**, which is the compulsive desire to touch strangers with one's hands for sexual arousal. This desire, usually in men, finds expression on buses, trains, in shopping malls, while waiting in line, at crowded concerts, anyplace where bodies are pressed together. There have also been cases of frotteurism or toucheurism among doctors or dentists who rub against or touch their patients. Frotteurism, however, does not usually appear in isolation but as one of a number of paraphilias in an individual (Langevin & Lang, 1987).

Like other paraphilic disorders, to be diagnosed with frotteuristic disorder a person must experience recurrent and intense behaviors that have occurred for at least 6 months, causing significant social and/or occupational distress.

Pedophilic Disorder

Throughout history, **pedophilia** (pee-doh-FILL-ee-uh) has been called many things, including child-love, cross-generational sex, man–child (or adult–child) interaction, boy-love, pederasty, and Greek love (Bullough, 1990). The variety of terms shows how differently adult–child sexual interactions have been viewed in different periods of history. In Chapter 17, we discuss child sexual abuse and incest, whereas in this chapter we concentrate our attention on pedophilia.

Pedophilic disorder involves recurrent and intense sexual arousal from prepubescent or pubescent children, which causes distress or impairment in important areas of functioning for at least 6 months. Pedophilia is one of the most common paraphilias and is most likely to be seen in treatment because of its harmful and illegal nature (O'Grady, 2001).

Pedophiles are often 18 years or older and at least 5 years older than their victims (American Psychiatric Association, 2010). However, even though many people consider sexual contact between adults and children to be one of the most objectionable of crimes today, in many periods of history and in different cultures today, various types of child–adult sexual contact have been seen as acceptable (see Chapter 1 for more information about Greek pederasty, or Chapter 11 for more information on the Sambian culture). Even so, pedophilia is illegal in every country in the world.

What exactly constitutes such contact in a society may be unclear. For example, as recently as the 1980s, a girl in the state of New Mexico could get married at age 13. If a 30-year-old man marries a 13-year-old girl and has legal, consensual marital intercourse with her, is it pedophilia? What if they have consensual sex but are not married? Why should a piece of paper—a marriage certificate—make a difference in our definition?

Throughout most of history, a girl was considered ready for marriage and an adult sexual relationship as soon as she "came of age," that is, at menarche. It was common for much older men to be betrothed to very young women, and such marriages were seen as proper. For example, Saint Augustine decided to get married to try to curb his sexual promiscuity, and so he was betrothed to a prepubertal girl. Although intercourse was not permitted until she reached puberty, such early marriages were apparently common (Bullough, 1990). In England in the 18th to 19th centuries, 12 years was considered the age of consent. In the 18th century as well, adult–child sex (especially same-sex pairings) was accepted in China, Japan, parts of Africa, Turkey, Arabia, Egypt, and the Islamic areas of India (Ames & Houston, 1990).

To some degree or another, then, what legally constitutes pedophilia is a matter of the laws in different societies. Yet, clinically speaking, pedophilia refers to sexual activity with a prepubescent child (under age 14). Many times these behaviors are also referred to as child sexual abuse. In fact, it has been shown that heterosexual males in almost all cultures are attracted to younger females, and homosexual males are attracted to younger (or younger appearing) males (O'Grady, 2001; see the nearby "Sexual Diversity in Our World" feature).

Pedophiles often report an attraction to children of a particular age range, most often 8- to 10-year-olds in those attracted to girls, and slightly older in those attracted to boys (attraction to prepubescent girls is more common; Murray, 2000). Some

troilism
Any sex sessions involving multiple partners, typically witnessed by others.

frotteurism
A paraphilic behavior that involves recurrent and intense sexual arousal from fantasies or behaviors that involve touching and/or rubbing the genitals against a nonconsenting person in a crowded place.

toucheurism
A paraphilic behavior that involves recurrent and intense sexual arousal

from fantasies or behaviors involving compulsively touching strangers.

pedophilia
A paraphilia that involves recurrent and intense sexual arousal from prepubescent or pubescent children, which usually causes distress or impairment in important areas of functioning. People who engage in this behavior are called pedophiles, or sexual offenders.

pedophiles are unable to function sexually with an adult, whereas others also maintain adult sexual relationships (Seligman & Hardenburg, 2000). Many pedophiles believe that pedophilia will become more socially acceptable over time, much like homosexuality did (O'Grady, 2001).

Pedophilic behavior is often obsessive. Pedophiles are usually obsessed with their fantasies, and they tend to dominate their lives. They are also predators—they know which child they like, and they work hard to get the trust and support from the parents or caretakers first. Pedophiles are good at winning the trust of parents. In fact, parents often trust the pedophile so much that they often take the pedophile's word over their own child's (O'Grady, 2001).

Some pedophiles threaten their victims and tell them they must keep their sexual activity secret. One therapist tells of a patient who had been repeatedly threatened by her assailant:

As a young teen, she and a friend were raped repeatedly by a friend of their parents. It went on for years. He would rape the girls in front of each other and threatened the lives of both of them if they told. They didn't. They were both afraid of him and convinced they wouldn't be believed anyway, given his high standing in the community and his friendship with their parents. There is a song she still hates, she tells me, because he used to sing it as he undressed them. (Salter, 2003, p. 13)

In the United States, an adult who has sexual contact with a boy or girl younger than the age of consent (see Table 17.1 for more information about the age of consent) to whom they are not married is guilty of child sexual abuse. A child sexual abuser may or may not be a pedophile; a person may sexually abuse a child because an adult is not available, because children are easier to seduce than adults, out of anger, or because of other sexual, psychological, or familial problems.

Toys that sexualize girls, such as Bratz dolls, can encourage girls to think about and treat their bodies as sexual objects.

Girls are twice as likely as boys to be victims of pedophilic behavior. In one study, 44% of pedophiles chose only girls, 33% chose only boys, and 23% abused both boys and girls (Murray, 2000). Boys are less likely to reject sexual advances and to report their sexual advances to authorities than girls (Brongersma, 1990). This may be the reason that violence is less common in sexual contact between men and boys than between men and girls.

Some pedophiles only look at children and never touch, whereas others engage in a variety of sexual acts with their victims, with the most common behavior being fondling and exhibitionism, rather than penetration. As we discussed earlier, some pedophiles often have a lack of empathy and believe that their behavior does not cause any negative psychological or physical consequences for their victims (Miranda & Fiorello, 2002).

REAL RESEARCH Sex offender registries have been hotly debated, with one side arguing they offer valuable information to the public while the other side argues they are expensive and ineffective (BIERIE, 2016). Evidence has shown that those on the sex offender registry are more likely to commit a sex offense than the general public and that the registries have decreased sex offenses.

Unfortunately, some pedophiles, realizing the chance of the child reporting the act, kill their victims. After one such murder of a young New Jersey girl named Megan Kanka in July 1994, her parents spearheaded "Megan's Law," which was signed into state law in October 1994. This law made it mandatory for authorities in New Jersey to tell parents when a convicted child molester moved into the neighborhood and increased penalties for child molesters. In 1996, Megan's Law became federal law (see the "Sex in Real Life" feature earlier in the chapter, "Megan's Law," for more information).

Female pedophiles also exist, although they often abuse children in concert with another person, usually their male partner. They may act to please their adult sexual partners rather than to satisfy their own pedophilic desires. Although less common, female pedophiles have been found to have a higher incidence of psychiatric disorders than male pedophiles (Chow & Choy, 2002).

A number of small organizations in Western countries, usually made up of pedophiles, argue that man–boy love should be legalized, usually under the pretense of guarding "the sexual rights of children and adolescents" (Okami, 1990). In America, the North American Man–Boy Love Association (NAMBLA) supports the abolition of age-of-consent laws. NAMBLA believes that there is a difference between those who simply want to use children for sexual release and those who develop long-lasting, often exclusive, and even loving relationships with a single boy. Suppe (1984) agrees that pederasty among postpubescent boys need not necessarily be harmful (which is not to deny that it often may be). In contrast, those who work with sexually abused children vehemently deny the claim, pointing to children whose lives were ruined by sex with adults.

Several factors may go into pedophilic behavior. Pedophiles have been described as having had arrested psychological development, which makes them childlike with childish emotional needs. They may also have low self-esteem and poor social relations with adults, may be trying to overcome their own humiliations and pains from their childhood, or may exaggerate the social male role of dominance and power over a weaker sexual partner. Conditions such as alcoholism may lessen the barriers to having sex with children. Other studies have found that pedophiles have brain abnormalities that contribute to their sexual behaviors (Eastvold et al., 2011; Poeppl et al., 2015). When asked why they engaged in sex with children, the most common response was because the children didn't fight it, followed by a lack of sexual outlets with adults, intoxication, and victim initiation of sexual behavior (Pollock & Hashmall, 1991).

Over the years, research has found that being a victim of sexual abuse in childhood is one of the most frequently reported risk factors for becoming a pedophile (Kärgel et al., 2015; Tenbergen et al., 2015). It is estimated that 35% of pedophiles were sexually abused as children (Keegan, 2001). Studies have also found that the choice of gender and age of victims often reflects the pattern of past sexual abuse in the pedophile's life (Pollock & Hashmall, 1991).

Pedophiles have high rates of **recidivism** (re-SID-iv-iz-um) and for some unknown reason, these rates are higher in homosexual men (Murray, 2000). The recidivism rate is the main impetus for legislation such as Megan's Law (Alexander, 1999).

The Internet has been a two-edged sword when it comes to pedophilia. On one hand, it has helped pedophiles find each other and talk about their behaviors. This can validate their behaviors because they are no longer feeling isolated, as though they are the only person who engages in child sex behaviors. Pedophiles are also able to gather information and

ON YOUR MIND

What should I do if I receive an obscene telephone call?

You should react calmly and not exhibit the reactions of shock, fright, or disgust that the caller finds exciting. Without getting upset, simply hang up the phone. An immediate ring again is probably a callback; ignore it, or pick up the phone and hang up quickly without listening. Sometimes a gentle suggestion that the person needs psychological help disrupts the caller's fantasy. Persistent callers can be discouraged by suggesting that you have contacted the police. If you do get more than one call, block the number and notify the telephone company.

can actually share images with each other. On the other hand, the Internet has also become a powerful tool to combat pedophilia, both in the online reporting of sex offenders and the ability of law officials to go undercover and seek out pedophiles online (Trivits & Reppucci, 2002; see the nearby Real Research feature).

Other Paraphilias and Sexual Variations

People can be sexually attracted to almost anything. An article in the *Journal of Forensic Sciences* tells of a man who was erotically attracted to his tractor; he wrote poetry to it, he had a pet name for it, and his body was found after he was asphyxiated by suspend-

REAL RESEARCH Federal investigators have found that many pedophiles are using powerful encryption tools in social media and other programs to illegally share child pornography online (VEDANTAM, 2011). Because law enforcement officers are prohibited from providing images of child porn, would-be members to these sites are required to share photos and videos of children being sexually abused to gain access to the sites.

ing himself by the ankles from the tractor's shovel to masturbate (O'Halloran & Dietz, 1993). However, a number of other paraphilias are relatively more common, and we now review a sample of them. Although these paraphilias are not listed as specific disorders in the *DSM-5*, they fall under a category of "Other Specified Paraphilic Disorders."

Obscene Telephone Callers

Scatolophilia (scat-oh-low-FILL-ee-uh), or obscene telephone calling, is when a person, almost always male, calls women and becomes excited as the victims react to his obscene suggestions. Most scatolophiliacs masturbate either during the call or afterward. Like exhibitionism, scatolophilia is nonconsensual, and the scatolophiliac becomes excited by the victim's reactions of fear, disgust, or outrage.

Most scatolophiliacs have problems in their relationships and suffer from feelings of isolation and inadequacy. For many, scatolophilia is the only way they can express themselves sexually (Holmes, 1991). Scatolophiliacs often have coexisting paraphilias, such as exhibitionism or voyeurism (Price et al., 2002).

Koichi Kamoshida/Getty Images

Problems with groping and frotteurism on public transportation have led to the establishment of women-only passenger cars in places such as Tokyo, Japan, and Seoul, South Korea.

recidivism	**scatolophilia**
Tendency to repeat crimes, such as sexual offenses.	Sexual arousal from making obscene telephone calls.

The obscene telephone caller may boast of sexual acts he will perform on the victim, may describe his masturbation in detail, may threaten the victim, or may try to entice the victim to reveal aspects of her sexual life or even perform sexual acts such as masturbating while he listens on the phone. Some callers are very persuasive; many have great success in talking women into performing sexual acts while posing as product representatives recalling certain products, as the police, or even as people conducting a sexual survey. (Note: No reputable sexuality researchers conduct surveys over the phone. If you receive such a call, do not answer any sexually explicit questions.) Others threaten harm to the victim or her family if she does not do what he asks (obscene callers often know the victim's address, if only from the phone book). Some will get a woman's phone number while observing her writing a check at a place like the supermarket and then will frighten her more because he knows her address, appearance, and even some of her food preferences (Matek, 1988).

Zoophilia

Zoophilia (zoo-uh-FILL-ee-uh; also referred to as bestiality), or sexual contact with animals, is rare, although Kinsey and his colleagues (1948, 1953) found that 1 out of 13 men engages in this behavior. Contact between people and animals has been both practiced and condemned since earliest times.

Studies of people who engage in sex with animals have found that a male dog is the most popular animal sex partner (Miletski, 2002). Sexual behaviors included masturbating the animal, submitting to anal sex performed by the animal, or active or passive oral sex with the animal.

Necrophilia

Tales of **necrophilia** (neck-row-FILL-ee-uh), or having sex with corpses, have been found even in ancient civilizations. The Egyptians prohibited embalmers from taking immediate delivery of corpses of the wives of important men for fear that the embalmers would violate them (Rosman & Resnick, 1989). More recently, the legends of the vampires imply necrophilia in the highly sexual approaches of the "undead." The stories of Sleeping Beauty, Snow White, and Romeo and Juliet all convey a sense of the restorative powers of loving the dead and thereby bringing the corpse back to life.

Rosman and Resnick (1989) suggest that necrophiliacs desire a partner who is unresisting and unrejecting; to find one, many seek out professions that put them in contact with corpses. They identify three types of genuine necrophilia: necrophiliac fantasy, in which a person has persistent fantasies about sex with dead bodies without actually engaging in such behavior; "regular" necrophilia, which involves the use of already-dead bodies for sexual pleasure; and necrophiliac homicide, in which the person commits murder to obtain a corpse for sexual pleasure. However, necrophilia is extremely rare and accounts for only a tiny fraction of murders (Milner et al., 2008).

An infamous case of necrophiliac homicide was that of serial killer Jeffrey Dahmer. Dahmer admitted to killing 17 men and having sex with their corpses; he also mutilated their bodies, tried to create a "shrine" out of their organs that he thought would give him "special powers," and ate their flesh. In keeping with Rosman and Resnick's claim that necrophiliacs desire a partner who is unresisting and unrejecting, Dahmer bored holes into his victims' skulls while they were alive and poured in acid or boiling water, trying to create "zombies" who would fulfill his every desire.

On the other hand, Dahmer also had sex with his victims while they were alive; perhaps he was an **erotophonophiliac**, which is someone who gets sexual excitement from the act of murder itself. Dahmer admitted his deeds but claimed he was insane. A jury found him sane and guilty, and he was sentenced to life in prison with no chance of parole; he was killed by another inmate in 1994.

Sexual Addictions

Although there is a great range in frequency of sexual contact in the general population (see Chapter 10), some argue that certain people cross over the line from a vigorous sex life to an obsessed sex life. Sexuality, like drugs, alcohol, gambling, and all other behaviors that bring a sense of excitement and pleasure, should involve some degree of moderation. Yet for some people, the need for repeated sexual encounters, which often end up being fleeting and unfulfilling, becomes almost a compulsion (Kraus et al., 2016; Wéry et al., 2016). An addiction involves an uncontrollable craving and compulsive need for a specific object. A typical sexual addict is a married man whose obsession with masturbation increases to an obsession with pornography, cybersex, visits to sex workers, or multiple sexual affairs (Keane, 2004).

In the past, derogatory terms, mostly for women, were used to describe these people; an example is **nymphomaniac**. Terms for men were more flattering and included **Don Juanism**, **satyriasis**, or in other cases "studs." Perhaps nowhere else is the double standard between the sexes so blatant—women who enjoy frequent sexual encounters are considered "whores" or "sluts," whereas men who enjoy similar levels of sexual activity have been admired. However, on some college campuses across the United States, men who engage in sex with many partners are often referred to as "players" or "horn dogs" (Author's files).

Sexual addiction, or hypersexual disorder, involves recurrent and intense sexual fantasies, sexual urges, and sexual behavior, and excessive time spent on these behaviors and an inability to control these fantasies (American Psychiatric Association, 2010). Sexual addiction was first written about by Patrick Carnes (2001) in his book *Out of the Shadows: Understanding Sexual Addiction.* Carnes wrote about the parallels between sexual addiction and

---

zoophilia
A paraphilic behavior that involves recurrent and intense sexual arousal from fantasies or behaviors involving sexual contact with animals (also referred to as bestiality).

necrophilia
A paraphilic behavior that involves recurrent and intense sexual arousal from fantasies or behaviors involving sexual contact with dead bodies.

erotophonophiliac
A paraphilia that involves recurrent and intense sexual arousal from real or imagined acts of committing murder.

nymphomaniac
A pejorative term used to describe women who engage in frequent or promiscuous sex.

Don Juanism, or satyriasis
Terms used to describe men who engage in frequent or promiscuous sex.

Sex in Real Life   Internet Sexual Addiction

For some people, obsessions develop for online sexual behavior, such as cybersex, pornography, or telephone sex. It's not hard to understand how an addiction might develop when we learn that hundreds of new sex-related sites are added to the Internet every day.

A person who has an Internet sexual addiction routinely spends significant amounts of time on pornographic websites and chat rooms with the intent of getting sex; feels preoccupied with using the Internet to find online sexual partners; discusses personal sexual fantasies not typically expressed offline; masturbates while engaging in online chats; obsesses about the next opportunity to engage in online sex; moves from cybersex to phone sex or face-to-face meetings; hides online chat sessions from others; obsessively seeks out Internet pornography sites; feels guilty; and has decreasing interest in real-life sexual partners (Beveridge, 2015; Grove

et al., 2011). People with low self-esteem, a distorted body image, an untreated sexual dysfunction, or a prior diagnosed sexual addiction are at greater risk for development of an Internet sexual addiction, and those who seek out Internet pornography have been found to have higher levels of loneliness compared with those who do not (Paul, 2009; Paul & Shim, 2008; Yoder et al., 2005; Young et al., 2000).

Many people with paraphilias turn to the Internet as a "safe" outlet for their sexual fantasies and urges. Psychotherapy and support groups often offer the most help for those with Internet sexual

addictions. More research is needed into this new and growing problem. Research has shown that there is a small minority of people who experience significant disturbances caused by their online sexual activity (Griffiths, 2001).

PornAtWork/Alamy Stock Photo

compulsive gambling, both of which involve an obsessive and compulsive addiction.

Cases of sexual addiction in the media involving celebrities such as Kanye West, Charlie Sheen, Tiger Woods, and Arnold Schwarzenegger prompted experts to include hypersexual disorder in the DSM-5.

© Everett Collection/Shutterstock.com

According to Carnes, sexual addicts go through four cycles repeatedly: a preoccupation with thoughts of sex, ritualization of preparation for sex (such as primping oneself and going to bars), compulsive sexual behavior over which addicts feel they have no control, and despair afterward as the realization hits that they have again repeated the destructive sequence of events.

Although hypersexual disorder is not a paraphilia, it is seen as a compulsive sexual behavior. It typically interferes with a person's daily functioning and may include compulsive masturbation or an obsession with pornography, whereas for others it may progress to multiple sex partners or exhibitionistic behaviors. Hypersexual disorder can lead to emotional suffering and problems in one's occupational functioning and marital and family relationships (Miles et al., 2016).

Although there are no definite numbers, the Society for the Advancement of Sexual Health estimates that 3% to 5% of Americans have a sexual addiction, with men outnumbering women five to one (Beck, 2008; Society for the Advancement of Sexual Health, 2008). However, these numbers are based only on those who seek treatment, so actual numbers are probably much higher. The availability of online pornography and sexual chat rooms has increased the number of cases of sexual addiction (Landau, 2008).

Typically, treatment for sexual addiction involves individual or group therapy as part of a 12-step recovery process (similar to the Alcoholics Anonymous program), originated by Carnes (2001). Medications may also be used, especially if a person also has bipolar disorder or depression, each of which is commonly associated with compulsive sexual behavior.

Many have criticized the idea of hypersexuality, however. They argue that terms such as "sexual addiction" are really disguised social judgments. Before the sexual freedom of the 1960s, those who engaged in promiscuous sex were often considered physically, mentally, or morally sick. Some scholars suggest that there has been an attempt to return to a pathological model of sexuality using the concept of addiction (Irvine, 1990). Although this is a growing area of research, limited research is available on hypersexuality. A number of self-help groups have been organized, including Sexaholics Anonymous, Sex Addicts Anonymous, Sex and Love Addicts Anonymous, and Co-Dependents of Sexual Addicts.

Review Questions

1 Define fetish and identify the key features of this paraphilia. What are the most common fetish items? Differentiate a fetish from fetishistic and transvestic disorder.

2 Define sadism and masochism and identify the key features of these paraphilias. Differentiate these from sexual sadism and sexual masochism disorders.

3 Define exhibitionistic and voyeuristic disorders. Identify the key features of these disorders.

4 Define frotteuristic disorder and identify the key features of this disorder.

5 Define pedophilic disorder and identify the key features of this disorder.

6 Identify some of the other less common paraphilias and identify the key features of each.

7 Explain how sexuality can be viewed as a behavior that brings excitement and pleasure, similar to gambling, drugs, and alcohol.

8 What is sexual addiction, or hypersexual disorder, and how is it manifested in people? Explain any gender differences in the perceptions of hypersexual disorder.

9 Explain the issues contributing to the debate about whether sexual addiction exists.

Assessing and Treating Paraphilic Disorders and Sexual Variations

Although the majority of those with paraphilias and sexual variations do not seek treatment and are content with balancing the pleasure and guilt of their behaviors, others find their behaviors to be an unwanted disruption to their lives. Their sexual desires may get in the way of forming relationships, may get them into legal trouble, or may become such a preoccupation that they dominate their lives. For these people, a number of therapeutic solutions have been tried, with varying success.

Assessment

It is difficult to assess and measure sexual variations. Part of the problem is that many people tend to feel uncomfortable talking about their sexual practices, especially if they are socially stigmatized. In addition, sexual behaviors often occur in private and may involve the use of sexual fantasy, which is nearly impossible to measure (Laws & O'Donahue, 2008). There are also ethical issues that make assessment difficult.

Although some people with paraphilias are referred to clinicians by law enforcement, for others, assessment is often done through self-report, through behavioral observation, or by physiological tests or personality inventories (Laws & O'Donahue, 2008; Seligman & Hardenburg, 2000). Self-reports may not be reliable, however; individuals under court order to receive treatment for pedophilia may be highly motivated to report that the behavior has ceased. Also, people are not necessarily the best judge of their own desires and behavior; some may truly believe they have overcome their sexual desires when, in fact, they have not. The second technique, behavioral observation, is limited by the fact that it cannot assess fantasies and desires; also, most people can suppress these behaviors for periods of time.

Physiological tests may be a bit more reliable. The most reliable technique for men is probably **penile plethysmography**, which is often used with male sex offenders. For example, a pedophile can be shown films of nude children and the plethysmograph can record his penile blood volume. If he becomes excited at the pictures, then he is probably still having pedophilic desires and fantasies. A similar test is also available to test the sexual response of female offenders. However, both of these physiological tests have been found to be of limited use in this population because there are no outward signs of arousal (Laws & O'Donahue, 2008; Seligman & Hardenburg, 2000).

Personality inventories, such as the **Minnesota Multiphasic Personality Inventory (MMPI)**, can help establish personality patterns and determine whether there are additional psychological

---

penile plethysmography
A test performed by measuring the amount of blood that enters the penis in response to a stimulus, which can indicate how arousing the stimulus is for the male.

Minnesota Multiphasic Personality Inventory (MMPI)
Psychological test used to assess general personality characteristics.

disorders (Seligman & Hardenburg, 2000). Other psychological inventories for depression and anxiety are often also used. In the future, the development of methodologies to assess these behaviors will be a priority in this field.

Treatment Options

For the most part, treatment for paraphilic disorders today is multifaceted and may include group, individual, and family therapy; medication; education; and self-help groups (Laws & O'Donahue, 2008; Seligman & Hardenburg, 2000; see Table 16.1). Overall, treatment is aimed at the reduction or elimination of the paraphilic symptoms, relapse prevention, and increasing victim empathy (d'Amora & Hobson, 2003).

Whatever the technique, the most important goal of therapy must be to change a person's behavior. If behavior can be changed, even if fantasies and inner emotional life are not altered, then at least the individuals will not be harming others or themselves. That is why behavioral techniques have been the most commonly used and most successful of the paraphilic disorder treatments.

Therapy to resolve earlier childhood trauma or experiences that help maintain the paraphilic behaviors is also helpful (Kaplan et al., 1994). This therapy can help increase self-esteem and social skills, which are often lacking in people with paraphilic disorders. Positive behaviors can be encouraged by teaching them how to improve their social skills, allowing them to meet more people as potential sexual partners. Counseling, modeling (taking after a positive role model), or feedback to change emotions and thoughts can be used to change a person's attitudes toward the sexual object. In empathy training, which is useful when there is a victim, individuals are taught to increase their compassion by putting themselves in the same situation as the victim. Incarcerated sex offenders may be exposed to relapse prevention therapies, which focus on

ON YOUR MIND

I think about sex a lot—it seems like it is almost all the time. I also like to have sex as often as I can. Do I have a sexual addiction?

Probably not. Thinking about sex is a universal human pastime, especially when a person is younger and just beginning to mature as a sexual being. Sexual addiction becomes a problem when people find their sexual behavior becoming dangerous or uncomfortable. People who find that they cannot stop themselves from engaging in behaviors that put them at physical risk, that they find immoral, that make them feel extremely guilty, or that intrude on their ability to do other things in their life should probably seek counseling—but that is true whether or not the behavior is sexual.

controlling the cycle of troubling emotions, distorted thinking, and fantasies that accompany their activities (Goleman, 1992). These techniques can be used in either group psychotherapy or individual counseling sessions. Group therapy has been found to be an important tool in reducing isolation, improving social skills, and reducing shame and secrecy (Seligman & Hardenburg, 2000).

Yet most find their desires difficult to suppress, and for them aversion therapy is one of the most common treatment strategies (Laws & O'Donahue, 2008; Seligman & Hardenburg, 2000). In aversion therapy, the undesirable behavior is linked with an unpleasant stimulus. For example, the person might be shown pictures of nude boys or asked to fantasize about exposing himself to a girl while an unpleasant odor, a drug that causes nausea, or an electric shock is administered. This technique has had some success, although its effectiveness decreases over time. In **shame aversion**, the unpleasant stimulus is shame; for example, an exhibitionist may be asked to expose himself in front of an audience.

Although removing the behavior itself may protect any victims, the person who still fantasizes about the behavior or has the same underlying attitude that led to it (such as fear of women) may not really be that much better off. The psychological underpinnings of the paraphilic disorder also must be changed. In systematic desensitization, the person is taught to relax and is then taken through more and more anxiety-provoking or arousing situations until eventually the person learns to relax during even the most extreme situations.

A number of therapies incorporate masturbation to try to reprogram a person's fantasies. In **orgasmic reconditioning**, the paraphiliac masturbates; just as they feel orgasm is inevitable, they switch to a more socially desirable fantasy, hoping thereby to increasingly associate orgasm and, later, erection with the desirable stimulus. Similarly, in **satiation therapy**, the person masturbates to a conventional fantasy and then right away masturbates again to the undesirable fantasy (Marshall, 1979). The decreased sex drive and low responsiveness of the second attempt makes the experience less exciting than usual, and eventually the behavior may lose its desirability.

In addition to these behavioral therapies, pharmacotherapy (drug therapy) has become more popular (Chopin-Marcé, 2001). The research shows that certain drugs can lead to a significant decrease in deviant sexual fantasies, urges, and behaviors (Keegan, 2001). Testosterone-suppressing drugs (antiandrogen) can produce castration levels of testosterone for up to 5 years (Reilly et al., 2000). Antidepressants have also been found to be helpful. In fact, many therapists believe that the compulsive nature of many paraphilias is related to a psychological condition known as **obsessive–compulsive disorder (OCD)**. Because of these similarities, treatment options

shame aversion
A type of aversion therapy in which the behavior that one wishes to extinguish is linked with strong feelings of shame.

orgasmic reconditioning
A sex therapy technique in which a person switches fantasies just at the moment of masturbatory orgasm to try to condition themselves to become excited by more conventional fantasies.

satiation therapy
A therapy to lessen excitement to an undesired stimulus by masturbating to a

desired stimulus and then immediately masturbating again, when desire is lessened, to an undesired stimulus.

obsessive–compulsive disorder (OCD)
A psychological disorder in which a person experiences recurrent and persistent thoughts, impulses, or images that are intrusive and inappropriate, and that cause marked anxiety and repetitive behaviors.

Table 16.1 Paraphilic Disorder Treatment Options

Treatment for paraphilic disorder may often involve several approaches. Overall, the goal of treatment is to reduce or eliminate the paraphilic behaviors, reduce or eliminate the chances of relapse, and increase personal feelings of self-esteem, as well as victim empathy. Although many sexual offenders are mandated by courts to go to therapy, those who seek out therapy on their own have been found to be more motivated and successful in their treatment. Although many convicted sex offenders will reduce their paraphilic behavior after treatment, some may not. Those who are engaging in high levels of paraphilic behavior and/or those with multiple psychological disorders are often less successful in therapy. Following are the various treatment options for paraphilias.

Type of Therapy	Therapeutic Methods
Individual	One-on-one therapy with a psychologist or counselor; work on improving self-esteem and social skills. Often uses modeling, empathy, and social-skills training, controlling the cycle of troubling emotions, distorted thinking, and fantasies that accompany their activities.
Group	A form of psychotherapy in which a therapist works with multiple paraphiliacs with similar conditions. The interactions between the members of the group are analyzed and considered to be therapeutic.
Family	Treatment of more than one member of a family in the same session. Family relationships and processes are explored and evaluated for their potential role in the paraphiliac's behavior.
Cognitive–behavioral	Combination of cognitive and behavior therapy. Works to help weaken the connections between certain situations and emotional/physical reactions to them (including depression, self-defeating, or self-damaging behaviors), whereas also examining how certain thinking patterns help contribute to behavior. Emphasizes relaxation and improving emotional health.
Systematic desensitization	A technique used in behavior therapy to treat behavioral problems involving anxiety. Clients are exposed to threatening situations under relaxed conditions until the anxiety reaction is extinguished.
Aversion	A behavior-modification technique that uses unpleasant stimuli in a controlled fashion to change behavior in a therapeutic way. An example would be a pedophile who is given an electric shock or a nausea drug while looking at naked pictures of children.
Shame aversion	A behavior-modification technique that uses shame as the unpleasant stimuli to change behavior in a therapeutic way. An example would be an exhibitionist who is asked to expose themself in front of an audience.
Orgasmic reconditioning	A behavioral technique that involves reprogramming a person's fantasies. An example would be to have a paraphiliac masturbate, and when orgasm is inevitable, they would switch their fantasy to a more socially desirable one, hoping thereby to increasingly associate orgasm and, later, erection with the desirable stimulus.
Satiation	A behavioral technique in which a person masturbates to a conventional fantasy and then immediately masturbates again to an undesirable fantasy. The decreased sex drive and low responsiveness of the second attempt makes the experience less exciting than usual, and eventually the behavior may lose its desirability.
Pharmacotherapy	Medications may be used to improve symptoms, delay the progression, or reduce the urge to act on paraphilic behaviors. A variety of medications have been used, including antidepressants and testosterone-suppressing drugs.
Surgical	Procedures such as castration are used to stop the paraphilic behavior.
Chemotherapy	Using medication to either decrease sexual drive or to treat psychological pathologies that are believed to underlie the paraphilic behavior.

for sexual paraphilias have begun to evaluate the use of selective serotonin reuptake inhibitors (SSRIs; these antidepressant drugs have been successful in the treatment of OCD; Abouesh & Clayton, 1999; Baez-Sierra et al., 2016). SSRIs have been found to reduce deviant sexual fantasies, urges, and behaviors.

Surgery has also been used in the treatment of paraphilic disorders. However, castration may not be the answer to the violent or pedophilic offender; some use foreign objects on their victims, and so the inability to achieve erection is not necessarily an impediment to their activity. Others cite the fact that although castration may cause a decrease in testosterone, it does not always result in a decrease in sex drive (Santen, 1995). To the degree that such crimes are crimes of aggression, rather than of sex, castration may not address the underlying cause.

Ultimately, there is no certain way to change a person's sexual desires. For many people with paraphilic disorder whose desires are socially or legally unacceptable, life is a struggle to keep their sexuality tightly controlled. As we mentioned earlier, recidivism rates for those with paraphilic disorders are generally high, so long-term treatment is often necessary. Those who do best are motivated and committed to treatment (as opposed to being mandated by the court to appear in therapy), seek treatment early, and have normal adult sexual outlets (Seligman & Hardenburg, 2000). Those with less treatment success often have multiple psychological disorders, low empathy levels, and a high frequency of paraphilic behavior (Kaplan et al., 1994).

Overall, this is an area of research that is also in need of further study. Unfortunately, few studies have shown promising treatment results for paraphilic disorders. In fact, current research does not support the fact that treatments lead to long-term behavioral changes (Laws & O'Donahue, 2008). Treatment modalities for paraphilic disorders will be another priority research area in the future.

Review Questions

1 Explain some of the reasons a paraphiliac may, or may not, seek out therapy.

2 How are paraphilias assessed? Are self-reports reliable? Why or why not?

3 Identify the various treatment options for paraphilic disorder.

4 Explain how aversion therapy has been used for the treatment of paraphilic disorder.

5 What is often the main goal of therapy for a paraphiliac?

Variations or Deviations

What criteria should we use to decide whether a sexual behavior is "normal"? The number of people who engage in it? What a particular religion says about it? Popular opinion? Should we leave it up to the courts or psychiatrists? Stoller (1991) suggests that we are all perverse to some degree. Why should some people be singled out as being too perverse, especially if they do no harm to anyone else?

Perhaps the need we feel to brand some sexual behaviors as perverse is summed up by S. B. Levine and colleagues (1990, p. 92): "Paraphiliac images often involve arousal without the pretense of caring or human attachment." We tend to be uncomfortable with sex for its own sake, separate from ideas of love, intimacy, or human attachment, which is one reason that masturbation was seen as evil or sick for so many years (Laws & O'Donohue, 2008).

Paraphilias are often still labeled "perversions" by law and often carry legal penalties. Because even consensual adult sexual behavior, such as anal intercourse, is illegal in some states, it is not surprising that paraphilias are as well. Yet these laws also contain contradictions; for example, why is it illegal for men to expose themselves, yet women are not arrested for wearing revealing clothing? We must be careful in deciding that some sexual behaviors are natural and others are unnatural, or some normal and others abnormal. Those that we call paraphilias may simply be part of human sexual diversity, unproblematic unless they cause distress, injury, or involve an unconsenting or underage partner.

Review Questions

1 Identify some of the ways that people may determine whether a sexual behavior is "normal."

2 Explain how there are contradictions in laws regulating sexual behaviors.

3 How might paraphilias be viewed as normal variations of human sexual behavior?

Chapter Review

Summary Points

1 People celebrate individual differences for most aspects of human life, with the exception of sexual diversity. Sexual behavior can be viewed as a continuum, but social value judgments, rather than science, determine which sexual behaviors are considered acceptable in society. Attitudes about which behaviors are acceptable vary over time, and there are cultural variations.

2 The word *paraphilia* is derived from the Greek "para" (besides) and "philia" (love or attraction). Paraphilic disorders are recurrent, intense sexually arousing fantasies, sexual urges, or behaviors that involve a craving for an erotic object for 6 months or more and that involve a nonhuman object, the suffering or humiliation of oneself or one's partner, or children or other nonconsenting persons. This behavior causes significant distress and interferes with a person's ability to work, interact with friends, and other important areas.

3 The *DSM-5* includes eight paraphilic conditions: fetishistic, transvestic, sexual sadistic, sexual masochistic, exhibitionistic, voyeuristic, frotteuristic, and pedophiliac disorders.

4 Most people with atypical sexual interests do not have a paraphilia. Others might be distressed and uncomfortable with their sexual interests or behaviors and seek out help. In a move to depathologize unusual sexual behaviors, experts point out that the discomfort that a person feels should come from within and should not be the result of society's disapproval of the behavior.

5 People with paraphilias come from every socioeconomic bracket, every ethnic and racial group, and every sexual orientation. The factors that have been found to be related to the development of a paraphilia include a person's sex, growing up in a dysfunctional family or experiencing family problems during childhood, and past sexual abuse.

6 Several theories attempt to explain the development of paraphilias. The biological theories claim physical factors are responsible for the development of paraphilic behavior. Psychoanalytic theorists suggest that the causes can be traced back to problems during the Oedipal crisis and with castration anxiety. Developmental theories claim that individuals form a template in their brain that defines their ideal lover and sexual situation, and this can be disrupted in several ways.

7 Paraphilias may also be caused by courtship disorders in which the behavior becomes fixed at a preliminary stage of mating that would normally lead to sexual intercourse. Behaviorists suggest that paraphilias develop because a behavior becomes associated with sexual pleasure through conditioning. Sociologists look at the ways in which society shapes and encourages certain behaviors.

8 A fetishistic disorder involves an inanimate object or a body part that becomes the primary or exclusive focus of sexual arousal and orgasm in an individual. A transvestic disorder involves recurrent and intense sexual arousal from cross-dressing. Fetishistic disorder is a controversial diagnosis with many arguing that it pathologizes gender variance.

9 Sexual sadistic disorder involves the intentional infliction of physical or psychological pain on another person to achieve sexual excitement. Sexual masochistic disorder involves deriving sexual pleasure through one's own physical pain or psychological humiliation. The *DSM-5* diagnosis requires ongoing recurrent and intense sexually sadistic or masochistic fantasies or behaviors, which have caused significant social and/or occupational distress for at least 6 months. However, many people who engage in BDSM behaviors find enjoyment in these behaviors and are not distressed by them.

10 Exhibitionistic disorder is the most common of all reported sexual offenses, and it involves a person becoming sexually aroused primarily from displaying their genitals. Voyeuristic disorder involves watching unsuspecting persons undressing, naked, or engaging in sexual activity. These behaviors cause significant social and/or occupational distress and have occurred for more than 6 months. There has been an increase in "video voyeurism," in which people use cameras, cell phones, or other surveillance equipment to record nonconsenting persons undressing or having sex.

11 Frotteuristic disorder typically involves a man rubbing his genitals against a person's thighs or buttocks in a crowded place where he can claim it was an accident and get away quickly. Like other paraphilias, to be diagnosed with frotteuristic disorder a person must experience recurrent and intense behaviors that have occurred for at least 6 months, causing significant social and/or occupational distress.

12 Pedophilic disorder involves recurrent and intense sexual arousal from prepubescent or pubescent children, which usually causes distress or impairment in important areas of functioning. Pedophiles most often report an attraction to children of a particular age range. Many choose children because they are available and vulnerable; some pedophiles are unable to function sexually with an adult. The Internet has been both helpful and detrimental in the elimination of pedophilia: pedophiles use it to find each other and talk about their behaviors, yet it has also helped to identify pedophiles.

13 People can be sexually attracted to almost anything. Other paraphilias include scatolophilia (obscene telephone calling), zoophilia (sexual contact with animals), and necrophilia (sexual contact with dead bodies).

14 Although there is a great range in frequency of sexual contact in the general population, some argue that certain people cross over the line from a vigorous sex life to an obsessed sex life. Sexuality, like drugs, alcohol, gambling, and all other behaviors that bring a sense of excitement and pleasure, should involve some degree of moderation. Yet for some people, the need for repeated sexual encounters, which often end up being fleeting and unfulfilling, becomes almost a compulsion; this is often referred to as a sexual addiction or hypersexuality. Many have criticized this concept and argue that terms such as these are really disguised social judgments.

15 Treatment for paraphilic disorder first involves an assessment. This can be done through self-report, behavioral observation, physiological tests, or personality inventories. Overall, the most important goal of therapy must be to change a person's behavior. Treatments for paraphilic disorder may include group, individual, and family therapy; medication; education; and self-help groups. Behavioral methods are most common; techniques include aversion therapy, shame aversion, systematic desensitization, orgasmic reconditioning, and satiation therapy. Pharmacological and surgical interventions, such as testosterone-suppressing drugs, antidepressants, and chemotherapy, are also used.

16 It is difficult to determine how to decide whether a sexual behavior is normal or abnormal. Much of society feels uncomfortable with the idea of sex for its own sake, separate from love, intimacy, and human attachment.

Critical Thinking Questions

1 How do you decide whether a sexual behavior is "normal"? What is your definition of "typical" sexual activity, and where do you draw the line for yourself?

2 Do you think people should be allowed to engage in any sexual behaviors they choose, as long as they don't hurt anyone? Explain.

3 If the majority of people feel that Kiki's behavior (described in my chapter-opening Notebook feature) is distasteful, perverted, or abnormal, should we as a society make her stop doing it? Do you think she is sick? Why or why not?

4 Which theory do you think best explains why a paraphilia might develop? What aspects of this theory make the most sense to you? Why?

5 Suppose that tonight when you are walking by yourself, you are approached by a middle-aged man who flashes you and begins stroking his erect penis. What do you do? Whom do you tell?

6 Do you think a pedophile's address and photograph should be made public in a sex offender registry so that neighbors can be aware of their crimes against young children? How long should this information be listed? For 1 year? 5 years? 10 years? The rest of the person's life? Explain.

Websites

Community-Academic Consortium for Research on Alternative Sexualities (CARAS) CARAS is dedicated to the support and promotion of excellence in the study of alternative sexualities and the dissemination of research results to the alternative sexuality communities, the public, and the research community.

Sexaholics Anonymous (SA) SA is a fellowship of individuals who share their experience, strength, and hope with each other so they may overcome their sexual addiction and help others recover from sexual addiction or dependency.

Silent Lambs Silent Lambs is a website dedicated to reducing the ability of churches to adopt a "code of silence" when it comes to child sexual abuse that occurs within the church. This website has a variety of links and helpful information; a variety of videos and transcripts are available from recent clergy sexual abuse cases.

National Sex Offender Public Registry The National Sex Offender Public Registry, coordinated by the Department of Justice, is a cooperative effort between the state agencies hosting public sexual offender registries and the federal government. This website's search tool has a number of search options that allow a user to submit a single national query to obtain information about sex offenders.

17 | Power and Coercion

I worked as a rape crisis counselor for many years, and while I found it enormously rewarding, it was also one of the hardest jobs I've ever had. The self-blame that many women experienced after a rape was one of the most difficult aspects of this work. We live in a blame-the-victim society that seems to take sexual violence seriously only when a person is overcome by a stranger in a dark alley. But we all know that a rapist can also be our friend, date, or classmate. Each of us makes hundreds of decisions every day, and while many of these are good decisions (such as driving the speed limit or wearing a seat belt), some may be neutral decisions. Going to a particular party, having one too many drinks, or walking home alone may not be good decisions, but a person doesn't deserve to be punished for such decisions. When something bad happens to us as a result of that decision, we often second-guess ourselves, wondering: Why did I go to that party? Why did I get drunk? Although second-guessing is normal, many people fail to realize that rape often involves one person disrespecting another person. All of these thoughts were running through my head when I met Meg last fall. Although she had agreed to talk to me about her recent experience with sexual violence, I knew it was going to be difficult for her to share her story with me.

Meg had gone out to a party one night—everyone knew each other and they drove out to the woods for a bonfire. They drank during the drive and although Meg was usually the designated driver when she was out with partying friends, this time she decided to kick back and have a good time. Everyone was drinking, laughing, and dancing. At one point, Meg realized she'd had too much to drink and she needed to lie down. One of the couples at the party had brought a tent and told her she could use it. She didn't remember getting into the tent, but she woke up with a man forcing himself on her. Meg blamed herself for years and wished she hadn't had so much to drink. She wondered what she did to lead the guy on even though she knew she wasn't responsible. Meg's story was difficult for me to hear, but it helped motivate me to continue to work toward changing our culture's blame-the-victim mentality.

Janell Carroll

© Matthew Sorenson

455

Power is an aspect of all sexual relationships. Sexual relationships are healthy when power is shared and when the relationship empowers the partners. In sexuality, however, as everywhere in human life, power can also be used to degrade and oppress. For example, the act of seduction is usually an interaction between each partner's power, which is partly what makes dating and sexual anticipation so exciting. However, coercive sexuality involves the clash of personal power, with one partner overpowering the other.

Sexual violence is an all-encompassing term that includes sexual acts that are committed against someone without their consent. The National Intimate Partner and Sexual Violence Survey (NISVS) collects data on five types of sexual violence, including **rape, sexual coercion, unwanted sexual contact, forced penetration**, and **non-contact unwanted sexual behavior** (Smith et al., 2017). There have been several incidents involving sexual violence in the news recently, including the sexual assault of an unconscious woman by a Stanford University student, livestreamed gang rapes on Facebook Live, and sexual harassment charges and firings at several large corporations. This chapter begins with discussions of sexual violence and then goes on to explore other ways that power can be misused in relationships.

ON YOUR MIND

Why do people rape?

There are several theories as to why rape exists in our society. Feminists argue that the nature of the relationships between the sexes fosters rape. Others argue that it exists because of the rapist's psychopathology. Still others claim it is because of how women dress, act, or behave. Today, most theorists agree that rape is a crime of power in which sex is used as a weapon.

Sexual Violence: Definitions, Incidence, Perpetrators, and Theories

Rape (also referred to as **sexual assault**) is defined by the NISVS as completed or attempted unwanted vaginal, oral, or anal penetration through the use of physical force (by being held down), threats of violence, or when a victim is under the influence of alcohol or drugs. This would also include situations in which a person is passed out and unable to consent and can include penetration by a penis, fingers, or an object.

The line that separates rape from other categories of sexual activity can be blurry because of the fine distinctions between forced and consensual sex, as well as societal patterns of female passivity and male aggression (LaFree, 1982). For instance, societal and cultural rules often dictate that men, not women, should initiate sexual activity. Defining rape and sexual assault is also complicated by the fact that sometimes unwanted sex can be consensual. Studies have found that a significant percentage of college students claim they have engaged in sexual activity in dating relationships when they didn't want to (Brousseau et al., 2011; O'Sullivan & Allgeier, 1998).

The second type of sexual violence outlined by the NISVS is *sexual coercion*, which involves being pressured to engage in sexual activity when a person doesn't want to. It can include using threats to get sex or continuous requests to have sex until a person finally relents and gives in. The third type of sexual violence, *unwanted sexual contact,* includes unwanted sexual behaviors that do not involve penetration, such as kissing, touching, fondling, or groping. Touching may be through clothing or directly and may include the genitals, buttocks, groin, breast, or legs.

The fourth type of sexual violence, *forced penetration*, involves forcing a person (with physical force, threats of violence, or while they are under the influence of alcohol or drugs) to vaginally, orally, or anally penetrate another person. Finally, *non-contact unwanted sexual behavior* includes unwanted exposure to sexual situations including pornography, verbal or behavioral **sexual harassment**, or the creation of a sexually hostile climate. Although the legal definitions of sexual violence, rape, and sexual assault are often determined by individual states, we will refer to these various types of sexual violence throughout this chapter.

Debate is ongoing about the appropriate term for a person who has experienced sexual violence. Although the word *victim* emphasizes the person's lack of responsibility for the incident, it may also imply they were a passive recipient of the attack. The term *victim* can also become a permanent label. Some prefer the term *survivor*, which implies

sexual violence
A sexual act committed against someone without their consent.

rape
Completed or attempted unwanted vaginal, oral, or anal penetration through the use of physical force, threats of violence, or when a victim is under the influence of alcohol or drugs.

sexual coercion
A form of sexual violence that involves being pressured to engage in sexual activity when a person doesn't want to.

unwanted sexual contact
A form of sexual violence that includes unwanted sexual behaviors that do not involve penetration, such as kissing, touching, fondling, or groping.

forced penetration
A form of sexual violence that includes forcing a person to penetrate someone else

using physical force, threats of violence, or while they are under the influence of alcohol or drugs.

non-contact unwanted sexual behavior
A form of sexual violence that includes unwanted exposure to sexual situations including pornography, verbal or behavioral sexual harassment, or the creation of a sexually hostile climate.

sexual assault
Any type of sexual contact or behavior that occurs without the explicit consent of the recipient.

sexual harassment
Unwanted sexual attention from someone in school or the workplace; also includes unwelcome sexual jokes, glances, or comments, or the use of status or power to coerce or attempt to coerce a person into having sex.

REAL RESEARCH Many college-age women say they experience "rape anxiety," or fears and anxieties related to the danger of rape, when they are walking alone at night (KARUTURI, 2017).

	Lifetime		
	Weighted %	**95% CI**	**Estimated Number of Victims***
Contact sexual violence[1]	36.3	(35.3, 37.2)	43,758,000
Rape/sexual assault	19.1	(18.3, 19.9)	22,992,000
Completed or attempted forced penetration	14.4	(13.7, 15.1)	17,412,000
Completed alcohol/drug-facilitated penetration	9.0	(8.4, 9.6)	10,883,000
Made to penetrate	0.5	(0.4, 0.6)	592,000
Sexual coercion	13.2	(12.5, 13.9)	15,954,000
Unwanted sexual contact	27.5	(26.7, 28.4)	33,237,000
Non-contact unwanted sexual experiences	32.1	(31.1, 33.0)	38,707,000

Abbreviation: CI = confidence interval.
[1]Contact sexual violence includes rape, being made to penetrate someone else, sexual coercion, and/or unwanted sexual contact.
*Rounded to the nearest thousand.

FIGURE **17.1** Lifetime Prevalence of Sexual Violence in U.S. Women, 2010–2012.

SOURCE: National Intimate Partner and Sexual Violence Survey; Smith et al., 2017.

that the person had within themselves the strength to overcome and to survive the experience. However, for clarity, in this chapter we use the term *victim* to refer to a person who has survived sexual violence.

Sexual Violence Statistics

It's estimated that more than 1 in 3 women and 1 in 6 men in the United States have experienced some form of sexual violence in their lifetime (see Figures 17.1 and 17.2; Smith et al., 2017). The National Intimate Partner and Sexual Violence Survey found that the majority of sexual violence is perpetrated by someone known to the victim. Studies have found that sexual violence can happen to anyone; 75% of bisexual women, 46% of lesbians, and 43% of heterosexual women, along with 48% of bisexual men, 40% of gay men, and 21% of heterosexual men have experienced sexual violence in their lifetime (Walters et al., 2013). Below are some current statistics about lifetime sexual violence:

- One in 5 women (19% or an estimated 23 million) and 1.5% of men (an estimated 1.7 million) have experienced an attempted or completed rape (Smith et al., 2017).

	Lifetime		
	Weighted %	**95% CL**	**Estimated Number of Victims***
Contact sexual violence[1]	17.1	(16.3, 17.9)	19,522,000
Rape/sexual assault	1.5	(1.3, 1.7)	1,692,000
Completed or attempted forced penetration	1.0	(0.8, 1.2)	1,114,000
Completed alcohol/drug-facilitated penetration	0.8	(0.6, 1.0)	935,000
Made to penetrate	5.9	(5.4, 6.5)	6,764,000
Made to penetrate - completed or attempted forced	2.0	(1.7, 2.3)	2,283,000
Made to penetrate - completed alcohol/drug-facilitated	4.8	(4.3, 5.3)	5,441,000
Sexual coercion	5.8	(5.3, 6.3)	6,626,000
Unwanted sexual contact	11.0	(10.3, 11.7)	12,521,000
Non-contact unwanted sexual experiences	13.2	(12.5, 14.0)	15,097,000

Abbreviation: CI = confidence interval.
[1]Contact sexual violence includes rape, being made to penetrate someone else, sexual coercion, and/or unwanted sexual contact.
*Rounded to the nearest thousand.

FIGURE **17.2** Lifetime Prevalence of Sexual Violence in U.S. Men, 2010–2012.

SOURCE: National Intimate Partner and Sexual Violence Survey; Smith et al., 2017.

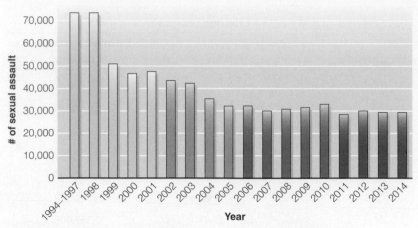

FIGURE **17.3** **Rates of Sexual Violence, United States, 1994–2014**
Rates of sexual violence have fallen by more than half since 1994.

SOURCE: The Rape, Abuse & Incest National Network (RAINN). Retrieved online from https://www.rainn.org/statistics/scope-problem

- There were 431,840 reported rapes in the United States in 2015 (Truman & Morgan, 2016).

- Thirteen percent of women and 6% of men reported experiencing sexual coercion (Basile et al., 2014).

- More than 27% of women and 11% of men report experiencing unwanted sexual contact (Basile et al., 2014).

- Nearly 1 in 3 women and 1 in 8 men reported non-contact unwanted sexual experiences (Basile et al., 2014).

- One in 17 men (6% or an estimated 7 million men) reported being forced to penetrate someone else (Basile et al., 2014).

- More than 32% of women and 13% of men report having some type of non-contact unwanted sexual experience (Basile et al., 2014). (See Figures 17.3, 17.4,17.5 and Table 17.1 for more detail.)

Keep in mind, however, that sexual violence includes some of the most underreported crimes in the United States, so it is difficult to assess the actual number of victims. We know that close to half of victims don't report sexual violence. Like Meg in my chapter-opening Notebook feature, some victims do not report it because they feel shameful, guilty, embarrassed, or humiliated and don't want people to know. Since many also know their perpetrators, they also blame themselves for being with them, which makes them less comfortable reporting their attacks. Many also worry that their reports will not be taken seriously, their confidentiality will not be maintained, or the perpetrator will retaliate (Sable et al., 2006).

Characteristics of Perpetrators of Sexual Violence

Perpetrators of sexual violence are primarily male, single, and between the ages of 15 and 30 (Amir, 1971; Russell, 1984). They have been found to have high levels of impulsivity and aggression, sexist views about women, and high levels of rape myth acceptance (Beech et al., 2006; Langevin et al., 2007; Masser et al., 2006). Men who commit sexual violence often have histories of personal violence, such as child physical or sexual abuse, dating violence, or **intimate partner violence** (**IPV**; we will discuss IPV further later in this chapter; Cavanaugh et al., 2011; Davis et al., 2012). In addition, sexual violence has been found to be related to the use of pornography (Bouffard, 2010; Hald et al., 2010; Malamuth et al., 2000). Even so, despite the assumption that men who commit sexual violence are psychologically disturbed individuals, research does not support the assumption that they are very different from men who don't commit such acts (Oliver et al., 2007; Voller & Long, 2010).

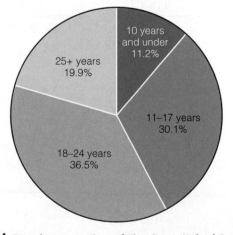

FIGURE **17.4** **Female Age at Time of First Rape, United States, 2010–2012**
Nearly 1 in 3 female victims of rape experienced it for the first time between the ages of 11–17 years of age.

SOURCE: National Intimate Partner and Sexual Violence Survey; Smith et al., 2017. Retrieved from https://www.cdc.gov/violenceprevention/pdf/NISVS -StateReportBook.pdf

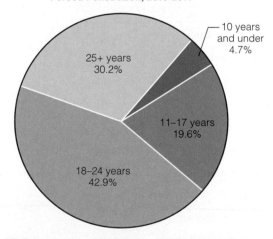

FIGURE **17.5** **Male Age at Time Forced to Penetrate, United States, 2010–2012**
Close to one-quarter (24.3%) of males who were forced to penetrate someone experienced their first victimization prior to the age of 18.

SOURCE: National Intimate Partner and Sexual Violence Survey; Smith et al., 2017. Retrieved from https://www.cdc.gov/violenceprevention/pdf/NISVS -StateReportBook.pdf

Studies have found that men who commit sexual violence often do so more than once (Swartout et al., 2015). In fact, research has found that the majority of sexual violence is perpetrated by serial offenders who have an average of six victims (Lisak & Miller, 2002). Thus, a relatively small number of men are responsible for a large amount of sexual violence, which explains the disparities between the number of men who say they do it and the number of women who say they have experienced it (Lisak & Miller, 2002).

The idea of using sexual coercion and forcing a person to engage in sex is not unusual. In a classic study about the potential to rape, 356 college-age heterosexual men were asked, "If you could be assured that no one would know and that you could in no way be punished for forcing a woman to do something she really didn't want to do (rape), how likely, if at all, would you be to commit such acts?" Sixty percent indicated that under the right circumstances, there was some likelihood that they would use force, rape, or both (Briere & Malamuth, 1983, p. 318). However, this study is very dated, so it is difficult to know whether the results would be different today. Other studies have found anywhere from 10% to 30% of men admit they might force sex under certain conditions (Lev-Wiesel, 2004; Lisak & Miller, 2002). One study found that 58% of college men reported they had forced sex when a woman was unable to consent or didn't make her consent clear (Parkhill & Abbey, 2008).

Sexual violence can be perpetrated by or against members of any sex. Studies have found that 17% of the perpetrators of campus sexual assaults on male victims were female, while 1% of the perpetrators on female victims were female (Budd et al., 2017). We will talk more about female perpetrators of sexual assault later in this chapter.

REAL RESEARCH One study found that 45% of females and 30% of males who were in a relationship reported being forced into sexual activity by their partner when they didn't want it (Brousseau et al., 2011). Such sexual coercion can lead to depression, anxiety, low self-esteem, and a negative view of one's sexual self.

intimate partner violence (IPV) A pattern of coercive behavior designed to exert power and control over a person in an intimate relationship through the use of intimidation, threats, or harmful or harassing behavior.

Table 17.1 Age of Consent

Many countries, and states within the United States, have legal ages of consent. The age of consent is how old a person must be to be considered capable of legally giving informed consent to engage in sexual acts with another person. It is considered a crime for a person to engage in sexual behavior with someone younger than the age of consent. Around the world, the age of consent varies from 12 to 20 years old and in some countries where there is no legal age of consent, all sexual relations are forbidden outside of marriage. In the United States, the legal age of consent varies from 16 to 18 years old.

Country	Age	Country	Age
Afghanistan	MUST BE MARRIED	Laos	15
Angola, Africa	12	Libya	MUST BE MARRIED
Argentina	18	Malaysia	16
Australia	16	Mexico	17
Bahrain, Asia	21	Netherlands	16
Bolivia	14	Nicaragua	18
Brazil	14	Norway	16
Burundi, Africa	18	Pakistan	MUST BE MARRIED
Chile	18	Peru	14
China	14	Poland	15
Cuba	16	Qatar	MUST BE MARRIED
Dominican Republic	18	Russia	16
Germany	14	Saudi Arabia	MUST BE MARRIED
Greece	15	Singapore	16
Iceland	15	South Korea	20
Iran	MUST BE MARRIED	Spain	16
Iraq	18	Sweden	15
Ireland	17	United Arab Emirates	MUST BE MARRIED
Italy	14	United States	16–18
Kenya	18	Vietnam	18
Kuwait	MUST BE MARRIED	Yemen	MUST BE MARRIED
Laos	15		

SOURCE: Age of Consent, https://www.ageofconsent.net/what-is-age-of-consent

The term *date-rape drug* is slang for any drug that may be used during a sexual assault. This would include Rohypnol (also called *roofies, Forget Pill,* or *Mind Eraser*), gamma-hydroxy-butyric acid (GHB; also called *Liquid Ecstasy, Georgia Home Boy,* or *Easy Lay*), and ketamine (also called *Special K, Kit Kat,* or *Cat Valium*). Today, experts refer to rapes using these drugs as "drug-facilitated sexual assault." The effects of these drugs are similar to those of Valium, but they are much more powerful. The drugs go to work quickly, and the time they last varies. If a person has been drinking alcohol when the drugs were ingested, the drug effects will last longer. Adverse effects of these drugs may include drowsiness, memory problems, lower blood pressure, sleepiness, problems talking, dizziness, and impaired motor functions. With higher doses, convulsions, vomiting, loss of consciousness, and coma or death can occur.

Rohypnol is illegal in the United States but is legal in several countries and has been smuggled into the United States. Rohypnol comes in tablet form and is typically placed in a drink, where it quickly dissolves. Once dissolved, the tablets are undetectable—there is no taste or color change to the liquid. Ketamine is a white powder that easily dissolves in a drink, whereas GHB can come in tablet, liquid, or powder form. Ketamine and GHB are both legal and used for different medical purposes. The effects of these drugs usually begin within 30 minutes, peak within 2 hours, and can last a total of 8 hours. An individual may feel nauseous, hot or cold, and dizzy within 10 minutes after ingesting these drugs.

You can protect yourself from drug-facilitated sexual assault by never accepting drinks from other people, opening your drinks yourself, and never leaving your drink unattended. If you think you have been drugged, it is important to go to a police station or hospital as soon as possible because a urine test can check for the presence of the drugs. These drugs can leave your body within 12 to 72 hours, so it is important to get a urine test as soon as possible.

Although it is important to be aware of these drugs, many experts argue that focusing on these drugs in sexual crimes often turns our attention away from other drugs, such as alcohol and/or street drugs, that are often associated with sexual violence (Németh et al., 2010).

A variety of devices have been invented to detect the presence of date-rape drugs, including coasters, dip-sticks, and color-changing drinkware.

Stephen Coburn/Shutterstock.com

Theories about Sexual Violence

What drives someone to be sexually violent? To understand this we turn to the most prominent theories of why rape occurs, including rapist psychopathology, victim precipitation, and feminist, sociological, and evolutionary theories.

Rapist Psychopathology: A Disease Model

Modern ideas about why rape occurs evolved first from psychiatric theories, which suggested that men rape because of mental illness, uncontrollable sexual urges, or alcohol intoxication. This theory of **rapist psychopathology** suggests that it is either disease or intoxication that forces men to rape, and that if they did not have these problems, they would not rape.

According to this theory, the rape rate can be reduced by finding these sick individuals and rehabilitating them. The theory makes people feel safer because it suggests that only sick individuals rape, not "normal" people. However, research consistently fails to identify any significant distinguishing characteristics of rapists (Fernandez & Marshall, 2003). Perhaps it is easier to see rapists as somehow sick than realize that the potential to rape exists in many of us.

Theories of rapist psychopathology were very common until the 1950s, when feminist researchers began to refocus attention on rape's effect on the victim rather than on the offender. However, there are still those who accept psychopathological theories today. In fact, college students often report that this theory helps to explain stranger rape but does not help us to understand date or acquaintance rape (Cowan, 2000).

ON YOUR MIND

My ex-boyfriend forced me to have sex with him. Since I have had sex with him in the past, does that mean this is not rape?

It does not matter if you have had a sexual relationship with someone in the past—if it is nonconsensual, it is rape. Rape can, and does, occur between an offender and victim who have a preexisting relationship (often referred to as "date rape" or "acquaintance rape"), and even between spouses and partners.

rapist psychopathology
A theory of rape that identifies psychological issues in a rapist that contribute to rape behavior.

victim precipitation theory
A theory of rape that identifies victim characteristics or behaviors that contribute to rape.

feminist theory
A theory that contends that rape is a tool used in society to keep women in their place.

sociological theory
A theory that identifies power differentials in society as contributing to rape.

Victim Precipitation Theory: Blaming the Victim

In my chapter-opening Notebook feature, I discussed how many people might believe that a woman does something to put herself at risk for sexual violence. The **victim precipitation theory** explores the ways victims make themselves vulnerable, such as how they dress or act or where they walk (Wakelin, 2003). By focusing on the victim and ignoring the motivations of the perpetrator, many have labeled this a blame-the-victim theory.

The victim precipitation theory shifts the responsibility from the person who knowingly attacked the innocent victim (Sawyer et al., 2002): "She shouldn't have been drinking if she didn't want to have fun," "She should have stayed with her friends," or "Her outfit was begging for attention!" Women who wear revealing clothing and drink alcohol are perceived as having greater sexual intent and therefore are viewed as more responsible for a sexual assault than women who wear neutral attire and do not drink alcohol (Maurer & Robinson, 2008).

The victim precipitation theory also serves to distance people from the reality of sexual violence and lulls them into the false assumption that it could not happen to them or someone close to them because they would not act like "those other women." If we believe bad things happen to people who take risks, then we believe we are safe if we do not take those risks.

In Susan Brownmiller's (1975) classic work on gender and rape, she argues that rape forces a woman to stay in at night, to monitor her behavior, and to look to men for protection. This attitude also contributes to a rape victim's guilt because she then wonders, "If I hadn't worn what I did, walked where I walked, or acted as I did, maybe I wouldn't have been raped." Overall, men perceive rape victims more negatively than women do (Hockett et al., 2016).

Feminist Theory: Keeping Women in Their Place

Feminist theorists contend that rape and the threat of rape are tools used in our society to keep women in their place. This fear keeps women in traditional sex roles, which are subordinate to men's. Feminist theorists believe that the social, economic, and political separation of the genders has encouraged sexual violence, which is viewed as an act of domination of men over women. Sex-role stereotyping—which reinforces the idea that men are supposed to be strong, aggressive, and assertive, whereas women are expected to be slim, submissive, and passive—encourages sexual violence in our culture (Murnen et al., 2002).

Sociological Theory: Balance of Power

Sociological theory and feminist theory have much in common; in fact, many feminist theorists are sociologists. Sociologists believe that rape is an expression of power differentials in society (Martin, 2003). When men feel disempowered by society, by changing sex roles, or by their jobs, overpowering women with the symbol of their masculinity (a penis) reinforces, for a moment, men's control over the world.

Sociologists explore the ways people guard their interests in society. For example, the wealthy class in a society may fear the poorer classes, who are larger in number and envy the possessions of the upper class. Because women have been viewed as "possessions" of men throughout most of Western history, fear of the lower classes often manifested itself in a belief that lower-class males were "after our wives and daughters." During the slavery period in the United States, for example, it was widely believed that, if given the chance, Black males would rape White women. Yet the truth was just the opposite: The rape of White women by Black males was relatively rare, whereas many White slave masters routinely raped their Black slaves. Once again, this supports the idea that rape is a reflection of power issues rather than just sexual issues.

Evolutionary Theory: Product of Evolution

Finally, a controversial theory on the origins of rape came out of evolutionary theory. Randy Thornhill and Craig Palmer, authors of *A Natural History of Rape: Biological Bases of Sexual Coercion*, proposed that rape was rooted in human evolution (Thornhill & Palmer, 2000). According to evolutionary theory, men and women have developed differing reproductive strategies, wherein men desire frequent mating to spread their seed, and women are designed to protect their eggs and be more selective in choosing mates (see Chapter 2 for more information about evolutionary theory). Rape has developed as a consequence of these differences in reproductive strategies. The majority of perpetrators are male, Thornhill and Palmer assert, because men are designed to impregnate and spread their seed.

As we pointed out, this theory is controversial, and many feminists and sociologists alike do not support these ideas (Brownmiller, 2000; Roughgarden, 2004). However, controversial or not, it is an interesting argument for us to consider when discussing theories on the development of sexual violence.

Review Questions

1 Explain why there is no single definition of sexual violence.

2 Describe the problems that have been encountered in attempting to identify the actual incidence of sexual violence.

3 Identify what researchers have found about the characteristics of perpetrators of sexual violence.

4 Explain the disparities between the number of women who say they experienced sexual violence and the number of men who say they have perpetrated it.

5 Identify and differentiate between the five theories of rape.

Attitudes about Sexual Violence and Cultural Variations

Studies have found gender and racial/ethnic variations in attitudes about sexual violence. In addition, cultural issues can affect how a society defines sexual violence and the attitudes toward it. We discuss these issues in the following sections.

Gender Differences in Attitudes about Sexual Violence

Researchers have used many techniques to measure attitudes about sexual violence, such as questionnaires, written vignettes, mock trials, videotaped scenarios, still photography, and newspaper reports. Overall, men are less empathetic and sensitive than women toward victims of sexual violence, believe more rape myths, and tend to blame victims more than women (Carroll et al., 2016; Hockett et al., 2016; Pistorio, 2016; see Table 17.2).

However, some hope exists about changing these attitudes. Men who take sexual violence education workshops or college courses on violence against women have less rape myth acceptance than men who do not take such workshops or courses (Currier &

Carlson, 2009; Foubert & Cremedy, 2007). Rape prevention programs for male college students have also been related to both attitudinal and behavioral changes (Foubert et al., 2010a, 2010b). In addition, men who were involved in these programs also reported less likelihood to commit sexual violence when they or a potential partner was under the influence of alcohol.

A number of studies have found that having male friends who support violence against women is a risk factor for committing sexual violence (Tharp et al., 2013). When a man brags to his friends about having sex with a woman who was drunk the night before, the responses of his friends will shape how he feels about the event. Do they high-five him? Do they sit by quietly and say nothing? Or do they speak up and tell him he was wrong? Overall, men are less likely than women to intervene or say something when they notice sexual violence occurring (Amar et al., 2014; Hoxmeier et al., 2015). Mentors in Violence Prevention (MVP), a program that has been used on college campuses to decrease sexual violence, matches male juniors and seniors with groups of incoming male students and facilitates discussions about sexual violence and alcohol use (Katz, 2014). By discussing these issues and educating males about violence against women, experts are hopeful that rates of sexual violence will decrease on college campuses (Starecheski, 2014).

Ethnic Differences in Attitudes about Sexual Violence

Although the majority of the research has examined gender differences in attitudes about sexual violence, there is research on racial/ethnic attitudinal differences. Overall, racial/ethnic minorities have been found to have more traditional attitudes toward women, which have been found to affect attitudes about sexual violence. For example, among college students, non-Hispanic Whites are more sympathetic than Blacks to women who have been victims of sexual violence (Nagel et al., 2005). However, Blacks are more sympathetic than Hispanic college students (Littleton et al., 2007; Yamawaki & Tschanz, 2005). Asian American students have the least sympathy for women who have been victims of sexual violence and are more likely to hold victims responsible for the assaults (Devdas & Rubin, 2007; Lee et al., 2005; Yamawaki & Tschanz, 2005).

Researchers suggest that these differences are due to variations in cultural gender roles and conservative attitudes about sexuality. It is important to keep in mind that within these ethnic groups, there are also gender differences in attitudes about sexual violence, with women more supportive of victims than men.

Sexual Violence in Different Cultures

Sexual violence is defined differently around the world, so the incidence of sexual violence varies depending on a culture's definition. One culture might accept sexual behavior that is considered sexually violent in another culture. For example, sexual violence has been

---

Table 17.2 Rape Myths

Martha Burt (1980) defined rape myths as prejudicial and stereotyped beliefs about rape, rape victims, and rapists. Rape myths enable people to distance themselves from the possibility of being raped and can also lead people to justify rape by rationalizing what happened and who might be at fault. Although there are many rape myths, the ones listed here are among the most common.

- Only "bad" women get raped.
- Women make false reports of rape.
- Women fantasize about rape.
- Men can't be raped.
- You can tell a rapist by the way he looks.
- No one can be raped against their will.
- A man can't rape his wife.
- Rape only happens to young, attractive women.
- Most rapists rape only once.
- False reporting of rape is common.

Sexual Diversity
Sexual Entitlement and the Rape of Women and Children in South Africa

IN OUR WORLD

South Africa has one of the highest reported rape rates in the world. In fact, a female born in South Africa has a greater chance of being raped in her lifetime than of learning to read (Dempster, 2002). High rape rates are primarily due to a wide variety of social and cultural issues, including economic issues, gender inequality, the sexual entitlement of men, and an acceptance of violence against women (Jewkes et al., 2009a, 2009b). Poverty and economic issues often force large families to sleep in the same bedroom, which exposes young children to sex at an early age (Phillips, 2001). South African men are raised with a strong sense of male sexual entitlement. This shouldn't be surprising, especially when you consider that South Africa's president, Jacob Zuma, was tried for rape in 2006, but later acknowledged engaging in unprotected sex with the HIV-positive daughter of a family friend (McDougall, 2010). Throughout the trial, Zuma's supporters burned photographs of the woman who accused him.

Rapex, an antirape condom worn by women, was unveiled in South Africa in 2005. The South African inventor, shown here, explains that during rape, metal barbs in the condom will hook into penile skin and immediately disable an assailant, allowing the woman to get away. The assailant must seek medical attention to get the barbs surgically removed, enabling the police to identify them.

Overall, a female born in South Africa has a 50% chance of being raped in her lifetime (Shields, 2010). Many of these rapes involve gang rapes or involve multiple acts of penetration (Vetten et al., 2008). Gang rapes are often viewed as a part of the culture and may be considered a form of male bonding. In addition to high rape rates, South Africa also has the largest number of people living with HIV. In fact, a woman who is raped by a man older than 25 years has a 25% chance of her rapist being HIV-positive (Jewkes et al., 2009b). Women who are raped in South Africa often do not report the rape and instead live in social isolation and fear. Those who do report the rape often face retribution and threats of murder.

A study by the Medical Research Council of South Africa found that 1 in 4 men had raped a woman or a girl in their lifetime, and nearly half of these men said they raped more than once (Jewkes et al., 2009a). Several factors were associated with the likelihood of having committed rape, including age, levels of education, and early childhood experiences. Men who raped were more likely to be between the ages of 20 and 40 years and have higher levels of education than those who did not rape. They were also more likely to have experienced teasing, harassment, or bullying in childhood, and engage in various risky sexual behaviors, including multiple sex partners, sex with a sex worker, and a lack of condom use.

South Africa also has the highest rates of child rape in the world. It is estimated that a child is raped every 26 seconds (Jewkes et al., 2009a; McDougall, 2010). Studies have found that approximately 40% of girls and boys report being sexually abused at some point in their childhood (for comparison, sexual abuse rates in U.S. children are 28% and 17% in girls and boys, respectively; Lichtenberg, 2011). Children are often raped first by relatives in South Africa. One father, who had been raping his 11-year-old daughter for a year, said, "My child cannot sleep with other men until I have slept with her first" (Shields, 2010). Even Oprah Winfrey was forced to take notice of these events when several girls at her exclusive school for underprivileged girls outside of Johannesburg were victims of sexual violence (Lichtenberg, 2011). For many years, a persistent myth existed that having sex with a

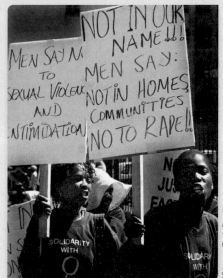

virgin can cure AIDS (Phillips, 2001). As a result, babies, some as young as 8 months old, were being gang-raped by HIV-positive men. The rape of infants poses many challenges, including the inability of the child to identify the rapist and a lack of DNA evidence because highly absorbent, disposable diapers often make it impossible to retrieve evidence (McDougall, 2010). Overall, the conviction rate of child and baby rapists in South Africa is extremely low—studies have found only about 7% of rapists are ever found guilty (Ghanotakis, 2008).

Finally, another troubling practice in South Africa is that of *corrective rape*, in which a lesbian woman is raped to "cure" her of her sexual orientation (Kelly, 2009). Homophobia is rampant in South Africa, and this became painfully clear when Eudy Simelane, a star of South Africa's national female soccer team who was living openly as a lesbian, was gang-raped and brutally beaten and stabbed in 2008 (Bearak, 2009). A South African gay rights organization found that 86% of Black lesbians say they live in fear of sexual violence (Kelly, 2009).

Efforts to reduce the rape rates include educational campaigns, improved legislation, and increasing the prosecution of rapists and the penalties for rape. Educational interventions are now available to empower children and other adults and help them to understand sexual violence. It is hoped that all of these efforts will eventually decrease the skyrocketing rape rates in South Africa.

accepted as a punishment in some cultures throughout history. Among the Cheyenne Indians, a husband who suspected his wife of infidelity could put her "out to field," where other men were encouraged to rape her (Hoebel, 1954). In the Marshall Islands of the Pacific Ocean, women were seen as the property of the males, and any male could force sexual intercourse on them (Sanday, 1981). In Kenya, the Gusii people view intercourse as an act in which males overpower their female partners and cause them considerable pain. In fact, if the female has difficulty walking the next morning, the man is seen as a "real man" and will boast of his ability to make his partner cry (Bart & O'Brien, 1985). In 2002, an 11-year-old Pakistani boy was found guilty of walking unchaperoned with a girl from a different tribe. His punishment involved the gang-raping of his 18-year-old sister, which was done to shame his family. The gang rape took place in a mud hut while hundreds of people stood by and laughed and cheered (Tanveer, 2002).

Sexual violence has also been used for initiation purposes. In East Africa, the Kikuyu previously had an initiation ritual in which a young boy was expected to rape to prove his manhood (Broude & Greene, 1976). Until he did this, he could not engage in sexual intercourse or marry a woman. In Australia, among the Arunta, rape serves as an initiation rite for girls. After the ceremonial rape, she is given to her husband, and no one else has access to her.

REAL RESEARCH Nonconsensual condom removal during sexual penetration, a practice referred to as "stealthing," can transform consensual sex into nonconsensual sex (Bonos, 2017; Brodsky, 2017). Although experts consider this practice to be an act of sexual violence, there are currently no laws against it.

Many cultural beliefs and societal issues are responsible for the high rates of sexual violence in South Africa, including the fact that South African women have a difficult time saying no to sex; many men believe they are entitled to sex and believe that women enjoy being raped (Meier, 2002). In 2005, an anti-rape female condom was unveiled in South Africa. This device was controversial, with some believing that it put the responsibility for the problem on the shoulders of South African women, and others believing that the device was a valuable tool in decreasing the climbing rates of sexual violence in South Africa (Dixon, 2005; see the accompanying "Sexual Diversity in Our World" feature for more information about sexual violence in South Africa).

Research by Sanday (1981) indicates that the primary cultural factors that affect the incidence of sexual violence in a society include relations between the sexes, the status of women, and male attitudes in the society. Not surprisingly, societies that socialize men to be aggressive, dominating, and to use force to get what they want have higher incidences of sexual violence.

Review Questions

1 Discuss the research on gender differences in attitudes about sexual violence.

2 Explain the impact of educational programs on attitudes and behaviors about sexual violence.

3 Discuss the research on ethnicity differences in attitudes about sexual violence.

4 Explain how sexual violence is defined differently around the world and how rates vary depending on a culture's definition.

Sexual Violence on College Campuses

Sexual violence is common on college campuses. In fact, female college students are more likely to experience sexual violence compared to women in any other age group (and women in the same age group who are not attending college; Breiding et al., 2014). Studies have found that first-year women are particularly at risk for sexual violence during the first couple of months of college, which has led some experts to refer to this period as the "red zone" (Megan, 2014). More than half of college sexual assaults occur from August to November (Kimble et al., 2007). Vulnerability is increased because many students are living away from home for the first time and often don't have an established support system.

College men are also victims of sexual violence, although less often than women (we will discuss male victims more later in this chapter).

In Chapter 7, we discussed stalking in intimate relationships. Stalking is another form of sexual violence and includes unwanted phone calls, texts, voicemails, messages through social media, e-mails, perpetrator showing up or approaching them at certain locations, such as home, school, or work; and being watched, followed, or spied on. The Centers for Disease Control found that approximately 1 in 6 women and 1 in 19 men in the United States have experienced stalking at some point in their lifetime (Smith et al., 2017). The perpetrators are often current or former intimate partners, and they typically make threats of physical harm. Although stalking is often one of the least discussed behaviors on college campuses, the highest rates occur in 18- to 24-year-olds (Gray, 2012).

Sexual Violence Legislation on Campus

In 1990, Congress passed the Student Right to Know and Campus Security Act, which resulted from the rape and murder of Jeanne Clery at Lehigh University in 1986. After Jeanne's murder, her parents found out that 38 violent crimes had occurred on the Lehigh campus in the 3 years before her murder. Working with other parents and groups, they fought for Congress to pass a law requiring colleges and universities to make information about sexual violence public. In 1992, the Campus Sexual Assault Victims' Bill of Rights was added, which required colleges and universities to develop prevention policies and provide victims with certain protections and rights after sexual assault, including the ability to change classes or dormitories if necessary.

Student-led protests demanding better treatment for victims of sexual violence, along with new rules set forth by the U.S. government, have led to changes on many college and university campuses designed to increase education and decrease sexual violence statistics (Shapiro, 2014). The Campus Sexual Violence Elimination Act (Campus Save Act) requires schools to educate students, faculty, and staff on the prevention of sexual violence. Required programs include information on consent, alcohol use, dating violence, and sexual assault. All U.S. colleges and universities were required to comply with the Campus Save Act by the end of 2014.

The momentum began to build after several events related to sexual violence occurred at various prestigious universities. In 2014, the Obama administration began a national sexual assault awareness campaign on college campuses. Schools that failed to protect their students from sexual assault and rape were in violation of Title IX of the 1972 Education Amendments; Title IX requires all universities receiving federal funds to provide equal access to education for all students, regardless of gender. Because many students believe that Title IX funding only has to do with equality in college athletics, another campaign entitled *Know Your IX* was launched aimed at educating students about Title IX and empowering them to stop sexual violence on college campuses. The White House Task Force to Protect Students from Sexual Assault was established to help students and schools more effectively prevent sexual violence on their campuses. The task force launched a website, NotAlone.gov, a centralized site to collect data on sexual assault and rape on college campuses ("Not Alone," 2014). The task force has also set up multiple requirements for colleges and universities to improve educational efforts (for example, all schools must designate at least one employee to coordinate the school's Title IX responsibilities and students are required to have access to this person).

ON YOUR MIND

What if you are drunk and she is, too, and when you wake up in the morning, she says you raped her?

Claims of rape must be taken seriously. If you have been drinking, it's best to delay sexual activity until you're absolutely sure your partner can give their consent. Legally, someone who is incapacitated by alcohol or drugs cannot give consent to engage in sexual activity. Even if they beg you to have sex and tell you they want it, this does not constitute consent. While this might not sound fair, it is very important to be clear about the role that alcohol may play in sexual consent.

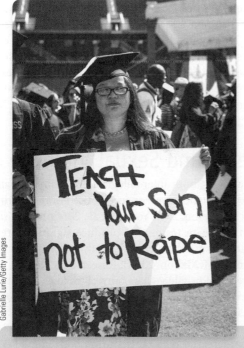

Gabrielle Lurie/Getty Images

A controversial ruling on a rape case at Stanford University in 2014, in which a student who sexually assaulted a classmate was allowed to remain on campus and graduate, prompted a national debate about how rape on college campuses should be handled.

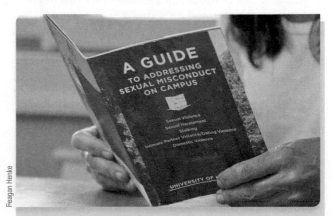

Feagan Henke

Know Your IX is a campaign that aims to educate all college students about their rights under Title IX. This can help students who have been sexually assaulted advocate for themselves during their schools' proceedings and, if necessary, file a complaint against their colleges with the U.S. Department of Education's Office for Civil Rights.

Alcohol and Sexual Violence

Alcohol use is also a pervasive problem on college campuses and is one of the strongest predictors of sexual violence (Fantasia et al., 2015; Lawyer et al., 2010; Mouilso et al., 2012). One study found that 80% of female students who were drinking alcohol experienced verbal or physical coercion by their male partner when they were too intoxicated to resist (Downing-Matibag & Geising, 2009). Another found that more than half of female students said they would not have had sex with a person they had been with if they had not been drinking (Labrie et al., 2014).

Although there have been few studies on ethnic/racial differences in alcohol-related sexual violence, one study found these types of sexual violence were more common among White college students than among Black college students (Abbey et al., 1996). This may have to do with the fact that White college students have been found to use alcohol more than Black college students (Chartier & Caetano, 2010).

Alcohol reduces inhibitions, which increases the chances of engaging in risky sexual behaviors (Aicken et al., 2011; Bersamin et al., 2011; Klein et al., 2007; see Chapter 15 for a discussion of high-risk sexual behaviors). However, alcohol use on college campuses, as it relates to sexual violence, is viewed very differently for men and women. A man who is drunk and is accused of sexual violence is seen as less responsible because he was drinking ("Lighten up; he didn't even know what he was doing."), whereas a woman who has been drinking is seen as more responsible for her behavior ("Can you believe her? She's acting like a slut!"; Parks & Scheidt, 2000; Peralta, 2008; Richardson & Campbell, 1982; Scully & Marolla, 1983). One female college student who had been drinking when a sexual assault occurred said, "Alcohol put me in the mood for petting, kissing, holding and hugging, and he may have interpreted that as going further with sexual activity" (Harrington & Leitenberg, 1994). A male college student who had been drinking during a sexual assault said, "Alcohol loosened us up and the situation occurred by accident. If no alcohol was consumed, I would never have crossed that line" (Abbey, 2002, p. 118). Alcohol seems to "sexualize" the environment for men—cues that might be taken as neutral if the men were not drunk (such as a certain woman talking to them or dancing with them) may be seen as an indication of sexual interest (Abbey et al., 2005; Montemurro & McClure, 2005; Peralta, 2008).

Fraternities and Sexual Violence

Initially, Greek organizations were established to help students join together to participate in social issues that they felt were largely ignored by their respective universities (Bryan, 1987). Today, however, many fraternities and sororities operate primarily for socializing. Although sexual violence does occur in residence halls and off-campus apartments, there are several ways in which fraternities create a riper environment for sexual violence.

> **rape crisis centers**
> Organizations that offer support services to victims of sexual violence, their families, and friends. Many offer information, referrals, support groups, counseling, educational programs, and workshops.

Alcohol use is a pervasive problem on college campuses and is one of the strongest predictors of sexual violence.

Many fraternities revolve around an ethic of masculinity. Values that the members see as important include competition, dominance, willingness to drink alcohol, and sexual prowess. There is considerable pressure to be sexually successful, and the members gain respect from other members through sex (Flanagan, 2011; Kingree & Thompson, 2013). The emphasis on masculinity, secrecy, and the protection of the group often provides a fertile environment for sexual violence (Adams-Curtis & Forbes, 2004). Greek men have been found to have higher levels of rape myth acceptance than non-Greek men (Canan et al., 2016; see Table 17.2).

Many fraternities today sponsor sexual violence prevention programs and invite guest speakers from **rape crisis centers** to discuss sexual violence. As we discussed earlier, studies have found that these programs contribute to positive attitudinal and behavioral changes (Cook, 2012; Foubert et al., 2010a, 2010b; Moynihan & Banyard, 2008).

Athletes and Sexual Violence

Student athletes, both intercollegiate and recreational, have been found to have higher levels of acceptance of rape-myths than non-athletes (McMahon, 2015; Young et al., 2016). In addition, athletes who participate on teams that produce significant revenue have higher rates of sexual violence than athletes on teams that produce less revenue (McMahon, 2004). Researchers suggest that perhaps it is the sense of privilege that contributes to a view of the world in which sexual violence is legitimized. Playing sports may also help connect aggression and sexuality.

One study found that Division I college football games significantly increased rape rapes during both home (41% increase) and away games (15% increase; Lindo et al., 2016). This may be due to increased partying and "hypermasculinity," which promotes the idea that violence and aggression are "manly" (Muehlenhard & Cook, 1988). Other studies have also found that drinking increases during sporting events; in fact, it's estimated that 20–30% of college students drink more when their teams win (Lindo et al., 2012).

The need to be aggressive and tough while playing sports can create problems off the field (Boeringer, 1999; Brown et al., 2002). Many male athletes may also have a distorted view of women, which often revolves around views expressed in the locker room. Locker room talk often includes derogatory language about women (including the use of words such as *sluts* or *bitches* to describe them), whereas those athletes who are not playing well are referred to as *girls* (McMahon, 2004; Murnen & Kohlman, 2007).

Like male athletes, female athletes are more likely to blame the victim for a rape than female nonathletes, and believe that some women who are raped put themselves in a bad situation (McMahon, 2004, 2015). They also are less likely to believe they could be at risk for sexual violence. When asked about the potential for a female athlete to experiencing sexual violence, one woman said:

I think it would be a shock to a female athlete—because, we feel that we're so tough. . . . I always am kidding around that like, I could sit on a guy and knock the wind out of him and the idea of a guy taking advantage of me seems. . . well, that could never happen. . . . I work out all the time, I'm so strong. . . . I'm not some little girl. I'm tough. (McMahon, 2004, p. 16)

REAL RESEARCH Research has found that many sexual assault victims report experiencing a kind of temporary paralysis called "tonic immobility," making them unable to yell or fight back during an assault (MÖLLER ET AL., 2017).

Review Questions

1 Explain what we know about sexual violence on campus.

2 Explain the role that alcohol plays in sexual violence on college campuses.

3 Explain the research on fraternity membership and sexual violence on college campuses.

4 Explain the research on athletes, athletics, and sexual violence on college campuses.

Effects of Sexual Violence

Sexual violence is emotionally, physically, and psychologically destructive for the victim. Some deny that it occurred at all, to avoid the pain of dealing with it. Others express self-blame, disbelief, anger, vulnerability, and increased feelings of dependency. As time goes by, the healing process begins, and feelings may shift to self-pity, sadness, and guilt. Anxiety attacks, nightmares, and fear slowly begin to decrease, although the incident is never forgotten. Some victims never return to prior functioning levels and must create an entirely new view of themselves. Researchers Burgess and Holmstrom (1979) coined the term **rape trauma syndrome (RTS)**, which describes the effects of rape (although the researchers developed this model specifically to apply to victims of rape, we believe that it can apply to victims of other forms of sexual violence as well).

Rape Trauma Syndrome

The rape trauma syndrome (RTS) is a two-stage stress response pattern characterized by physical, psychological, behavioral, sexual problems, or a combination of these, and it occurs after forced, nonconsenting sexual activity. Although the *Diagnostic and Statistical Manual of Mental Disorders* does not recognize RTS, symptoms are similar to posttraumatic stress disorder (PTSD), which occurs after a traumatic event. Research has found that a significant number of rape survivors develop PTSD within 2 weeks after the rape (Littleton & Henderson, 2009; Taft et al., 2009; Zinzow et al., 2012).

Although not all victims respond to rape in the same manner, what follows is a description of what typically occurs. During the first stage of RTS, the **acute phase**, most victims fear being alone, with strangers, or even in their bedroom or their car if that is where the sexual violence took place. Other emotional reactions include anger (at the perpetrator, the sexual assault, health care workers, family, oneself, court), anxiety, depression, confusion, shock, disbelief, incoherence, guilt, humiliation, shame, and self-blame (Frazier, 2000). A victim may also experience wide mood fluctuations. Difficulties with sleeping, including recurrent nightmares, are common. This phase begins immediately after the assault, may last from days to weeks, and involves several stress-related symptoms.

The majority of victims eventually talk to someone about the sexual assault (Fisher et al., 2003). Most of the time a victim will talk to friends or family members rather than to the police. Younger victims are more likely to tell someone than are older victims, perhaps because older victims blame themselves more for the sexual assault and may fear that others also will blame them. One study found that 50% of the women who experienced a sexual assault waited years before telling anyone (Monroe et al., 2005). Overall, women who speak out about their sexual assault and experience negative reactions often stop talking about it (Ahrens, 2006). Negative reactions lead to increased self-blame and uncertainty about whether the experience qualified as a sexual assault, and they increase the likelihood of PTSD (Ullman et al., 2007).

rape trauma syndrome (RTS)	acute phase
A two-stage stress response pattern that occurs after a rape or sexual assault.	First stage of the rape trauma syndrome, in which a victim often feels shock, fear, anger, or other related feelings.

Emotional reactions also vary depending on whether the victims knew their perpetrators. Women who report being sexually assaulted by strangers experience more anxiety, fear, and startle responses, whereas those who were sexually assaulted by acquaintances usually report more depression and guilt and decreased self-confidence (Sorenson & Brown, 1990). The majority of women who are sexually assaulted know their perpetrators and may have initially trusted them and agreed to be with them. After the sexual assault, they may second-guess themselves, wondering how they could have had such bad judgment or why they didn't see it coming. Many also feel a sense of betrayal. Women who feel guilty or responsible for a sexual assault have lower levels of psychological well-being than women who do not feel responsible or guilty (Glenn & Byers, 2009).

Depression often follows a sexual assault, and some victims report still feeling depressed 8 to 12 months after the incident. Women who have a history of prior psychological problems, prior victimization, and/or a tendency to self-blame have a greater risk for depression (Zinzow et al., 2012). Substance abuse may also occur, and studies have found that women involved in alcohol-related sexual assault have a higher prevalence of substance abuse after the incident compared to women who weren't using alcohol (Rhew et al., 2017).

Physical symptoms after a rape or sexual assault can include general body soreness, bruises, nausea, throat soreness and difficulties swallowing (if there was oral sex), genital itching or burning, and rectal bleeding or pain (if there was anal sex). In women, the emotional stress of the sexual assault may also cause menstrual irregularities. However, some of these symptoms (nausea and menstrual irregularities) are also signs of pregnancy, which is why a pregnancy test is of utmost importance after a victim has been sexually assaulted. Research has found there is a greater incidence of pregnancy in women who have been sexually assaulted than in women who engage in consensual unprotected vaginal intercourse (Gottschall & Gottschall, 2003). However, it is also true that women in prime fertile ages are overrepresented in sexual assault statistics.

Long-term reorganization, stage two of RTS, involves restoring order in the victim's lifestyle and reestablishing control. Many victims report that changing some aspect of their lives, such as changing addresses, roommates, universities, or even cell phone numbers, helped them to gain control. Symptoms from both stages can persist for 1 to 2 years after the sexual assault (Nadelson et al., 1982), although Burgess and Holmstrom (1979) found that 74% of rape victims recovered within 5 years. Recovery is affected by the amount and quality of care that the victim received after the sexual assault. Positive crisis intervention and the support of others decrease the symptoms of the trauma.

In the past, many researchers have argued that sexual assault is a violent crime, not a sexual one. "Desexualizing" rape, or taking the sexual aspect out of it, has de-emphasized post-assault sexual concerns (Wakelin, 2003). Sexual assault is indeed both a violent and a sexual crime, and the majority of victims report experiencing sexual problems post-assault, even though these problems may not be lifelong (Burgess & Holmstrom, 1979; Perilloux et al., 2012).

Changes in sexual behaviors and sexual difficulties can persist for a considerable period after the sexual assault (Postma et al., 2013). It can take weeks, months, or even years to work through sexual difficulties such as fear of sex, desire and arousal disorders, and specific problems with sexual behaviors including penetrative sex, genital fondling, and oral sex. Avoiding sexual interactions is also common after a sexual assault. One 20-year-old woman who had been sexually assaulted when she was 13 years old said: "[I] never wanted to have sex again. I wanted to prove that I really didn't want sex. I wanted to prove this to myself and to everyone else that I knew about the situation. I wanted to prove that I wasn't a slut" (Perilloux et al., 2012, p. 1103). Other women may become hypersexual post-assault. One study found alcohol consumption after a sexual assault increased the likelihood of engaging in risky sexual behaviors with multiple partners (Deliramich & Gray, 2008; Rhew et al., 2017).

Counseling can be helpful for women suffering from post-assault sexual difficulties. It is not uncommon for a woman to seek help for a sexual problem, such as a lack of orgasm, and during the course of therapy reveal an experience with sexual violence that she had never discussed. See Figure 17.6 for statistics on other health conditions that may be associated with sexual assault.

ON YOUR MIND

Do women who are sexually assaulted eventually have a normal sex life?

Although it may take months or even years, most sexual assault victims report that their sex lives get back to what is normal for them (Perilloux et al., 2012). Common problems include fear of sex and arousal problems. Studies have found that lesbian women may have more difficulties with sexual problems post-rape (Long et al., 2007). Overall, it's not uncommon for women to avoid sexual interactions for a period of time after a sexual assault. Counseling, a supportive partner, and emotional support are extremely helpful.

Silent Rape Reaction

Some victims never discuss their rape with anyone and carry the burden of the assault alone. Burgess and Holmstrom (1974) call this the **silent rape reaction**, and in many ways, it is similar to RTS. Feelings of fear, anger, and depression and physiological symptoms still exist; however, they remain locked inside. In fact, those who take longer to confide in someone usually suffer a longer recovery period (Cohen & Roth, 1987).

The silent rape reaction occurs because some victims deny and repress the incident until a time when they feel stronger emotionally. This may be months or even years later. A student of mine, who had been sexually assaulted 3 years earlier, was taking a course in psychology and noticed with frustration that as she read each chapter of the textbook, she would become extremely anxious

---

long-term reorganization
The second stage of the rape trauma syndrome, which involves a restoration of order in the victim's lifestyle and reestablishment of control.

silent rape reaction
A type of rape trauma syndrome in which a victim does not talk to anyone after the rape or sexual assault.

It is common to experience emotions such as sadness, confusion, anger, guilt, and/or humiliation after experiencing sexual violence. Taking to a counselor can be very helpful in working through these feelings.

Health Condition	Weighted %	
	History	No History
Asthma	22.1*	14.7
Irritable Bowel Syndrome	11.4*	6.2
Diabetes	11.2	10.7
High Blood Pressure	28.3	29.3
Frequent Headaches	27.4*	15.6
Chronic Pain	28.0*	15.7
Difficulty Sleeping	37.5*	19.7
Activity Limitations	33.6*	19.1
Poor Physical Health	6.2*	3.0
Poor Mental Health	3.6*	1.1

*Chi-square test of independence statistically significant; p-value < .05.

FIGURE **17.6 Prevalence of Physical/Mental Conditions Among Women with and without a History of Sexual Violence, United States, 2010–2012** The proportion of women reporting physical and mental conditions was significantly higher among those with a history of sexual violence compared to those without a history of such violence.

SOURCE: National Intimate Partner and Sexual Violence Survey; Smith et al., 2017. Retrieved from https://www.cdc.gov/violenceprevention/pdf/NISVS -StateReportBook.pdf

when she saw the word *therapist.* When she explored why this produced anxiety, she realized that she could read the word only as *the rapist,* and it terrified her. Perhaps her subconscious was letting her know that she was finally ready to work through the repressed experience. Slowly the memories of the assault came back, as did all of the emotional pain. After 2 months in counseling, she had worked through the memories sufficiently to feel that she was on her way to resolving her feelings about the sexual assault.

Sexual Violence, Partners and Other Special Populations

Although we have learned from the research that certain groups are at greater risk for sexual violence, we also know that some special populations are also at risk, including spouses, lesbians, bisexuals, transgender individuals, older women, women with disabilities, and sex workers.

Marital Sexual Violence

Marital sexual violence involves nonconsensual sexual behavior between married partners (this is also referred to as intimate partner violence, which we will discuss later in this chapter). For many years the legal definition of rape and sexual assault was "forced sexual intercourse by a male with a female not his wife," which indicated that the law didn't apply to married couples. Although marital sexual violence was ignored by the law for many years, since 1993 it has been a crime in all 50 states. However, the laws have continued to evolve, and each state determines how these cases will be handled (Jackson, 2015).

Although their symptoms are similar to those who are victims of nonmarital sexual assault, many of these women report feeling extremely betrayed and may lose the ability to trust others, especially men. In addition, there is often little social support for wives who are sexually assaulted, and those who stay with their husbands often endure repeated attacks (Bergen & Bukovec, 2006). Unfortunately, marital sexual assault may be one of the least discussed and reported types of sexual violence.

Lesbians and Bisexuals

Stereotypical beliefs about sexual violence continue to exist in American culture, leading many to assume that the typical victims are heterosexual women (Miller, 2015). However, sexual violence is a common experience in both lesbian and bisexual women (Balsam et al., 2005). As we discussed earlier, studies have found that the prevalence of sexual violence among lesbians and bisexual women is often higher than the prevalence in heterosexual women (Langenderfer-Magruder et al., 2016; Ollen et al., 2017; Rhew et al., 2017; Walters et al., 2013).

Like heterosexual women lesbian and bisexual women often experience RTS after a rape or sexual assault, although there may be more intense emotional repercussions compared with heterosexual women (Campbell, 2008; Long et al., 2007). Lesbians may also experience difficulties in assimilating the experience of sexual violence into their own self-image. They may be "feminist-identified" in most areas of their lives, and the assault may force them to reexamine the patriarchal society and their feelings about men. Some lesbians may have never experienced penetration by a man and may be unaccustomed to dealing with the fear of pregnancy, let alone the extreme feelings of being violated and abused. Lesbians can also be sexually assaulted by women, although more research is needed in this area.

Transgender Populations

As we pointed out earlier, the prevalence of sexual violence among sexual minorities is often higher than the prevalence among heterosexuals (Langenderfer-Magruder et al., 2016). Transgender, queer, and gender nonconforming college students also have high rates of sexual violence (Cantor et al., 2015; see Chapter 4 for more information on transgender populations). Many transgender persons are targeted because of their transgender status (Lev & Lev, 1999). However, they often do not feel welcome at rape crisis centers, which may be unprepared to work with transgender clients who have experienced sexual assault or sexual violence. Overall, transgender persons consistently have lower levels of rape myth acceptance than other sexual minorities (Schulze & Koon-Magnin, 2017). This will be an important area of research in the future.

Older Women

Many people believe that sexual violence happens only to younger women. It is difficult to think about our mothers or grandmothers being sexually assaulted. The stereotype that only young, heterosexual, attractive women are assaulted prevents our thinking about the risk for sexual assault for other groups, including older women. Although it is true that younger women are more at risk for sexual violence, older women are also at risk (Ball, 2005; Burgess & Morgenbesser, 2005; Jeary, 2005). Older women are likely to be even more traumatized by sexual assault than younger women because many have very conservative attitudes about sexuality, may have undergone menopausal changes (lack of lubrication and/or thinning of the vaginal walls) that can increase the severity of physical

Older women are also victims of sexual violence and may experience increased trauma because of declining physical health and more conservative attitudes about sexuality.

injury, and have less social support after a sexual assault, which reinforces and intensifies their sense of vulnerability (Burgess & Morgenbesser, 2005).

Women with Disabilities

The National Intimate Partner and Sexual Violence Survey found that persons with disabilities, regardless of their age, race, ethnicity, sexual orientation, or socioeconomic class, are at an increased risk for sexual violence (Basile et al., 2016). Although both women and men with disabilities are at increased risk for sexual coercion and noncontact unwanted sexual experiences, women with disabilities are also at an increased risk for rape (Basile et al., 2016). They may be more vulnerable because of their diminished ability to fight back. In addition, women with disabilities may have a more difficult time reading the preliminary cues that would alert them to danger. The impact of a sexual assault may be intense for these people because of a lack of knowledge about sexuality, loss of a sense of trust in others, and the lack of knowledgeable staff who can effectively work with them. In many cases, persons with severe mental disabilities who have been sexually assaulted may not realize that their rights have been violated and, therefore, may not report the crime. Because of these factors, the intensity and length of time of RTS is usually prolonged. Educational interventions, together with solid support networks, have been found to help those with disabilities cope with sexual violence (Basile et al., 2016; Foster & Sandel, 2010).

Sex Workers

Due to the nature of their work, sex workers are especially vulnerable to sexual violence (Lea et al., 2016). Because a sex worker's job is to provide sex in exchange for payment, the question of consent is often difficult to judge. Sexual assaults are also common from a sex worker's pimp. In fact, one study found that sex workers reported being sexually assaulted an average of 16 times and beaten 58 times each year by their pimps (Chesler, 1993). Also, because of the general disapproval of sex work, a sex worker who reports a rape or sexual assault is often treated with disdain. People tend not to believe that she was assaulted or may think that she is angry because she was not paid. Many sex workers who are sexually assaulted begin to question their involvement in sex work. College students are more likely to blame sex workers for a rape or sexual assault and have less empathy toward them compared to non-sex work victims (Sprankle et al., 2017). Believing and trusting all women's reports of sexual assault and performing a comprehensive medical checkup are imperative.

Secondary Victims of Sexual Violence

Sexual violence is traumatic for the victim but also for partners, family members, and friends. When a person is sexually assaulted, their partner, friends, and family members often feel anger, frustration, and intense feelings of revenge. In addition, some partners experience a sense of loss, guilt, and self-blame. PTSD is also common in partners, friends, and family members after a loved one has been a victim of sexual violence (Christiansen et al., 2012).

The development of PTSD is more likely when a friend or family member feels guilty about not being able to prevent the assault or has little social support.

Emotional reactions to a partner's sexual assault may affect people's feelings about their partner and can negatively affect their relationship. Partners may lose trust in their significant others and worry that they might have expressed sexual interest in the perpetrator. Overall, after a rape or sexual assault, negative judgments and reactions by a victim's partner are common (A. Brown & Testa, 2008). These reactions further isolate the victim and reinforce feelings of guilt. Although some relationships dissolve due to the stress of the sexual assault, studies have found some friends and partners report their relationships became closer and more intimate following the assault (Ahrens & Campbell, 2000).

All in all, sexual violence places a great deal of stress on relationships. Many people avoid dealing with the assault entirely, believing that talking about it would be too stressful. Many partners feel uncomfortable sharing their feelings about a sexual assault because they worry about burdening the victim. However, open communication is extremely beneficial and should be encouraged. Even though dealing with sexual violence can be traumatic, women who have stable and supportive partners, friends, and family members recover from sexual violence more quickly than those who do not have such support.

Review Questions

1 Define and describe the rape trauma syndrome.

2 Identify the stages of the rape trauma syndrome and explain what typically happens during these stages.

3 Define and describe the silent rape reaction and discuss the long-term effects.

4 Describe the effects of sexual violence in special populations, including married partners, lesbians, bisexuals, transgender individuals, older women, women with disabilities, and sex workers.

5 Describe the typical reactions of people whose partners have been raped or sexually assaulted.

When Men Are Victims of Sexual Violence

There are many myths about the sexual assault of men, such as "Real men can't be sexually assaulted," "Male sexual assault is about homosexuality," and "A man can't be sexually assaulted by a woman" (O'Brien et al., 2015; Turchik & Edwards, 2012). The prevalence of these myths contributes to victim-blaming and underreporting. Earlier we pointed out that approximately 1.5% of men have experienced an attempted or completed rape at some point in their lifetime, and many men have reported experiencing other types of sexual violence (Basile et al., 2014; Smith et al., 2017).

The majority of men who experience sexual violence are under the age of 18 the first time they experience it (Masho & Anderson, 2009). Male victims of sexual violence are more likely to be Black (Scarce, 1997). However, the higher frequency of rape in Black men may be because much of the research on male rape has been done in Black communities.

Although the long-term effects of sexual assault are common in men and can include depression, anger, anxiety, self-blame, and increased vulnerability, few men ever seek out medical care or counseling (Masho & Anderson, 2009; Walker et al., 2005). Sexual dysfunction is common after a sexual assault and can continue for years after the assault (Walker et al., 2005). Some male sexual assault victims may increase their post-assault sexual activity to reaffirm their manhood. (See Figure 17.7 for statistics on health conditions.)

As we discussed earlier, the National Intimate Partner and Sexual Violence Survey found that persons with disabilities are at an increased risk for sexual violence (Basile et al., 2016). While men with disabilities are at an increased risk for sexual coercion and noncontact unwanted sexual experiences, they are also at an increased risk of forced penetration. Unfortunately, male mental health professionals have been found to be less supportive of bisexual and gay male victims of sexual violence and attribute more pleasure to the victim's assault than to assaults in other groups (Miller, 2015).

© luxorphoto/Shutterstock.com

Although long-term effects of sexual violence are common in men, including depression, anger, anxiety, and self-blame, few men ever seek out medical care or counseling.

Sexual Assault of Men by Women

Students often dismiss the idea that a man could be sexually assaulted by a woman because they believe men are always willing to have sex and because a man must be sexually aroused to have an erection. Both of these misconceptions make male sexual assault more humiliating for men. Since male erectile response is involuntary, a man can have an erection when he is not aroused (see the nearby "On Your Mind").

Females can commit sexual assault on males (Russell et al., 2017). As we discussed earlier, studies have found that 17% of the perpetrators offending male victims are female (Budd et al., 2017). Female perpetrators have been found to engage in a wide range of sexually aggressive behaviors, including forced sex and the use of verbal coercion (Anderson & Savage, 2005). The majority of male sexual assaults by women use psychological or pressured contact, such as verbal persuasion or emotional manipulation, rather than physical force. Men who are sexually assaulted by women often experience significant shame and rarely seek treatment (O'Brien et al., 2015).

Sexual Assault of Men by Men

The majority of men who are sexually assaulted report having male perpetrators (Smith et al., 2017). Although there is a myth that only gay men are sexually assaulted (O'Brien et al., 2015), all

	Weighted %	
Health Condition	History	No History
Asthma	16.1*	11.9
Irritable Bowel Syndrome	4.3*	3.0
Diabetes	9.3	10.1
High Blood Pressure	29.4	29.4
Frequent Headaches	15.3*	7.7
Chronic Pain	23.0*	12.6
Difficulty Sleeping	33.5*	17.9
Activity Limitations	29.1*	18.1
Poor Physical Health	4.9*	2.8
Poor Mental Health	2.9*	1.4

*Chi-square test of independence statistically significant; p-value < .05.

FIGURE **17.7** **Prevalence of Physical/Mental Conditions Among Men with and without a History of Sexual Violence, United States, 2010–2012** The proportion of men reporting physical and mental conditions was significantly higher among those with a history of sexual violence compared to those without a history of such violence.

SOURCE: National Intimate Partner and Sexual Violence Survey; Smith et al., 2017. Retrieved from https://www.cdc.gov/violenceprevention/pdf/NISVS -StateReportBook.pdf

men are at risk for sexual violence. While studies have found that gay men are more likely to experience sexual coercion and rape (Anderson et al., 2017), another study found that close to 40% of male victims of sexual violence were heterosexual (Larsen & Hilden, 2016).

As in the case of female sexual assault, male sexual assault is an expression of power, a show of strength and masculinity that uses sex as a weapon. The most common emotional reactions to the sexual assault of men by men include shame, embarrassment, self-blame, hostility, and depression (Tewksbury, 2007). Like women, men who have been sexually assaulted may go through RTS. Many heterosexual victims question their sexual orientation and feel that the assault makes them less of a "real man." Men who are sexually assaulted by men are also much less likely to report their assaults to the police than female victims. Fearing others will think they are gay is a barrier to reporting for some men (Larsen & Hilden, 2016; Sable et al., 2006).

ON YOUR MIND

Technically, can a man really be raped?

Some people think that it is impossible for a woman to rape a man because he might not get an erection. Even though men are anxious, embarrassed, or terrorized during a rape, they are able to have erections. Having an erection while being raped may be confusing and humiliating, just as an orgasm is for females. In fact, for some, it may be the most distressing aspect of the assault (Sarrel & Masters, 1982). Women who rape men can also use dildos, hands, or other objects to penetrate the anus. In addition, men can be orally or anally raped by men and forced to penetrate others.

Unlike female victims of sexual assault, male victims are more likely to be assaulted by a stranger, have more than one perpetrator, and are more likely to have been under the influence of alcohol or drugs (Larsen & Hilden, 2016). The most common type of activity in the sexual assault of men by men is anal penetration followed by oral penetration (Groth & Burgess, 1980; Scarce, 1997).

Prison Sexual Assault

The Prison Rape Elimination Act, a federal law that reduces tolerance for prison sexual assault, became effective in 2003. It mandated the collection of national data on the incidence of prison rape and provides funding for research and program development. This law has helped reduce prison sexual assault, support those who have been sexually assaulted in prison, and also provides yearly data on prison sexual assault. Even so, the largest number of male rapes occurs in prison or jail settings (Turchik & Edwards, 2012). From 2011 to 2012, 3% to 4% of inmates in U.S. jails and prisons were sexually victimized (Beck et al., 2013). However, since this study was based on inmate reports, the actual numbers are probably much higher. Rates were higher among female inmates; among Whites than Blacks; and among inmates with higher educations than those who had not completed high school. Studies have found that approximately 18% of prison inmates report sexual threats from other prisoners (Hensley et al., 2005). Many Americans hold indifferent attitudes toward prison rape and believe that prisoners "get what they deserve" in prison (Turchik & Edwards, 2012).

Men in prison learn stereotypic avoidance techniques that women may use in society—physical modesty, no eye contact, no accepting of gifts, and tempering of friendliness (Bart & O'Brien, 1985). Prison sexual assault has been found to be an act of asserting one's own masculinity in an environment that rewards dominance and power (Peeples & Scacco, 1982). Sex, violence, and conquest are the only avenues open to men in the restrictive confines of prison. To sexually assault another man is seen as the "ultimate humiliation" because it forces the victim to assume a feminine role. The victim becomes the "property" of his perpetrator, who will, in turn, provide protection in return for sex. However, the perpetrator often will "sell" sexual favors from his man to other inmates in exchange for cigarettes or money.

Women who are in U.S. prisons are often victims of sexual violence, including harassment, fondling, sexual coercion, and sexual assault, with the majority of this abuse being perpetuated by prison staff (Struckman-Johnson & Struckman-Johnson, 2002). Female inmates also experience sexual pressure in their interactions with other female inmates (Alarid, 2000). The majority of women who are sexually assaulted in prison never report the crime for fear of retaliation.

Like sexual assault in other populations, inmates who have been sexually assaulted also experience RTS. Because these inmates must continue to interact with their perpetrators, long-term reorganization may take longer to work through. In addition, oftentimes there are no sexual assault services for those in prison and little sympathy from prison employees. Prison sexual assault has also contributed to the increased prevalence of HIV and other sexually transmitted infections in U.S. prisons (Pinkerton et al., 2007). Rectal and vaginal trauma is common during prison sexual assault, which increases the risk for sexually transmitted infections and HIV (Dumond & Dumond, 2002).

Review Questions

1 How has the myth that a man could never be sexually assaulted by a woman made male sexual assault more humiliating for male victims?

2 Explain how female perpetrators use verbal persuasion or emotional manipulation more often than physical force.

3 Explain how male sexual assault of men has been viewed as an expression of power.

4 What does the research tell us about sexual violence in prison?

Coping with Sexual Violence, Reporting Sexual Violence, and Treating Perpetrators

As discussed earlier in the chapter, the majority of victims of sexual violence do not report the assaults to the police. We now explore coping with sexual violence, reporting statistics and reasons for nonreporting, and the process of telling the police, pressing charges, and going to court. We also examine treating the perpetrators of sexual violence.

Coping with Sexual Violence

Sexual assault is the only violent crime in which the victim is expected to fight back. If a person does not struggle, people question whether they wanted to have sex. Only with visible proof of a struggle (bruises and cuts) does society seem to have sympathy.

Some victims of sexual assault have said that at the time of the assault, they felt frozen with fear, that it was impossible to move because they just could not believe what was happening to them. One victim explains:

> Did you ever see a rabbit stuck in the glare of your headlights when you were going down a road at night? Transfixed—like it knew it was going to get it—that's what happened. (Brownmiller, 1975, p. 358)

After a sexual assault, it's important for a victim to write out as much as they remember in as much detail as possible. When did the sexual assault occur? Where was the victim? What time was it? Who was with the victim? What was the perpetrator wearing? What happened? Was alcohol involved? Was anyone else present? Victims should keep this for their own records, for if they decide to press charges, it will be helpful.

Immediately after a sexual assault a person should get help—call a friend, family member, campus police, or a crisis hotline (see the websites listed at the end of this chapter for the RAINN online crisis center). They should not shower, clean up, or brush their teeth before going for medical help, in case they decide to have a sexual assault evidence collection (also called a "rape kit") done. This kit collects the perpetrator's DNA and keeps the evidence safe in case a victim decides to report the sexual assault at a later time. These kits can be done for any type of sexual assault and can be done up to 3–4 days after the assault. Health care providers can screen for STIs and provide emergency contraception if necessary.

Reporting Sexual Violence

While there is no legal obligation to report sexual violence, many victims claim that reporting it helped them regain a sense of control. Women who report their sexual assault to the police have been subsequently found to have a better adjustment and fewer emotional symptoms than those who do not report it (Sable et al., 2006). The likelihood of reporting is increased if the perpetrator was a stranger, if there was violence, or if a weapon was involved. Female victims of female perpetrators are less likely than those of male perpetrators to report incidents of sexual violence mainly because female-female sexual assault is often not taken as seriously as male-female sexual assault (Beck, 2016).

Barriers to reporting sexual violence may be increased for sexual minorities who often worry about further marginalization (Ollen et al., 2017). Heteronormative ideas about sex may create difficulties navigating services for help. One student said:

> [The] "face" most people think of when they think "relationship abuse" is the heteronormative....a man abusing a woman. So any variant of that, even a heterosexual couple, a woman abusing a man, is not brought up nearly enough. LGBT people are questioning: "Is this really abuse? Is this in my head?" (Ollen et al., 2017).

Telling the Police

On college campuses, campus police are often notified about sexual violence before the local police. Campus police may be able to take disciplinary action, such as fines or dismissal if the assailant is a student, but they are not able to press formal charges. Pressing charges with the local police may be important for two reasons. First, it alerts the police to a crime, and thus may prevent others from being victimized. Second, if the victim decides to take legal action, they will need to have a formal report from the local police (not the campus police).

Although police officers have become more sensitive to the plight of victims of sexual violence in the past few years, some victims still report negative experiences. Police must interrogate

Project Unbreakable, an online photography project, works to increase awareness of the issues surrounding sexual violence and encourages the act of healing through art. The project features survivors holding handwritten posters with their assailants' most memorable phrases. Many survivors find these phrases swirl around their heads post-assault, causing increased emotional pain and suffering. Being able to publically share them can help some survivors begin to heal. For more information, go to http://projectunbreakable.tumblr.com.

Courtesy Project Unbreakable

each case completely, which can be very difficult for a victim who has just been through a traumatic experience. Still, many report that taking such legal action lets them feel back in control and doing something about their situation.

Many victims of sexual violence are unsure about whether or not they might want to pursue prosecution. They might want to talk with partners, family members, and/or friends before making a decision. If a person is thinking they might want to pursue prosecution, it's important to make a police report and get a physical examination immediately.

Pressing Charges

The decision to press official charges is a difficult one that takes much consideration. It has often been said that victims of sexual violence go through a second assault because they can be put on trial more than the accused perpetrator. Court proceedings take up a great deal of time and energy, and they create considerable anxiety.

Victims of sexual violence report that they pressed charges because they were angry, to protect others, or they wanted justice to be served. Reasons for refusing to press charges include being afraid of revenge, wanting to just forget, feeling sorry for the perpetrator, or feeling as though it would not matter anyway because nothing would be done. Victims of sexual violence can also file a civil lawsuit and sue the perpetrator for monetary damages. See Table 17.3 for more information about what to do if someone is a victim of sexual violence.

A variety of devices have been invented to detect the presence of date-rape drugs, including coasters, dip-sticks, and color-changing drinkware.

AP Images/Eric Risberg

Treating Perpetrators of Sexual Violence

Can people who commit sexual violence be treated so they lose their desire to be sexually violent? Because the majority of perpetrators of sexual violence are male, this section concentrates on treating male perpetrators. Many therapies have been tried,

Table 17.3	What to Do If You Are Sexually Assaulted
1	Know that it was not your fault. When a person is sexually assaulted, they often spends a long time trying to figure out exactly what they did to put themselves at risk. Women are more likely to do this because they have always been told to "be careful," "watch how you dress," or "don't drink too much." In reality, a rape might happen anywhere and at any time. No one asks to be raped.
2	Talk to a counselor. Some people like to talk to a rape crisis counselor before going to the hospital or police. This is very helpful because counselors are knowledgeable about sexual assault and the aftermath of symptoms. Many hospitals have on-site counselors. Talking to a counselor also helps give a person back their sense of control (see the list of websites at the end of this chapter).
3	Go to a hospital for a medical examination. An immediate medical evaluation is imperative. If there is a nurse or health care provider on campus, you can see either of them, but it is better to go to a local emergency department to have a thorough physical examination. A rape kit, which allows for an anonymous collection of evidence during the medical evaluation, should also be done. The results of this kit will only be released if a person decides to press charges. Medical evaluations are important to administer emergency contraception if necessary; check for sexually transmitted infections that may have been transmitted during the sexual assault; and check for the presence of date-rape drugs (if a person thinks they may have been drugged, they should try not to urinate before getting tested).
4	As we discussed in Chapter 15, prophylactic treatment for chlamydia, gonorrhea, and trichomoniasis, along with blood tests for HIV, hepatitis B, and syphilis, should be given after a sexual assault. The HPV and hepatitis B vaccines should be given to victims who have not had these vaccines prior to the sexual assault. If necessary, health care providers may recommend prophylactic HIV treatment within 72 hours of the assault.
5	Do not throw away any evidence of the sexual assault. Do not shower before you go to the hospital. If you decide to change your clothes, do not wash or destroy what you were wearing. If anything was damaged in the assault, such as glasses, clothing, or book bags, keep these, too. Put everything in a plastic bag and store it in a safe place. It is necessary to preserve the evidence of the sexual assault, which will be very important if a person decides to press charges at some point.
6	Decide whether to file a police report and/or press charges. A person can file either a formal or informal report. This is something that you will need to sort through and decide. Talking to a counselor and getting more information about possible options are very important (see websites at the end of this chapter for more information).

including psychotherapy, behavioral treatment, support groups, shock treatment, and the use of Depo-Provera, a drug that can diminish a man's sex drive. The idea behind Depo-Provera is that if the sex drive is reduced, so, too, is the likelihood of sexual violence. However, these treatments have yielded inconclusive results. Many feminists argue that because aggression, not sexual desire, causes sexual violence, eliminating sexual desire will not decrease the incidence of sexual violence. For many men in treatment, the most important first step is to accept responsibility for their actions.

Many programs have been developed to decrease rape myths and increase knowledge levels. As we have discussed, all-male programs have been found to reduce significantly the belief in rape myths. However, although attitudes about sexual violence appear to change after these programs, research has yet to show that this results in changes in sexual violence (Foubert & Cremedy, 2007). Treatments for repeat offenders has not been found to be overwhelmingly successful (Lalumière et al., 2005a).

Review Questions

1 What gender differences have been found in the reporting of sexual violence?

2 Explain how a victim-precipitated view of sexual violence might affect police attitudes.

3 Identify some of the reasons a victim might press (and not press) charges after experiencing sexual violence.

4 Explain the process of telling the police, pressing charges, and going to court. What are some of the problems

victims of sexual violence might experience along the way?

5 Identify some of the therapies that have been used in the treatment of perpetrators of sexual violence.

Sexual Abuse of Children

So far we have been talking about forced sexual relations between adults. But what happens when the coercive behavior involves children? **Child sexual abuse** is defined as sexual behavior that occurs between an adult and a minor. One important characteristic of child sexual abuse is the dominant, powerful position of the adult or older teen that allows them to force a child into sexual activity. The sexual activity can include genital/breast fondling, making a child fondle an adult, masturbation, voyeurism (looking at a child's naked body), exhibitionism (making a child look at an adult's naked body), digital penetration with fingers or sex toys, or oral, vaginal, or anal intercourse (Finkelhor et al., 2008). In addition, child sexual abuse can include making a child view pornography or participate in pornography, and/or child sexual exploitation (Putnam, 2003).

As straightforward as this seems, the definition of child sexual abuse can become fuzzy. For instance, do you consider sexual play between a 13-year-old brother and his 7-year-old sister sexual abuse? How about an adult male who persuades a 14-year-old girl to touch his genitals? Or a mother who caresses her young son's genitals? How about a 14-year-old boy who willingly has sex with a 25-year-old woman? How would you define the sexual abuse of children? Personal definitions of sexual abuse affect how we perceive those who participate in this behavior (Finkelhor, 1984).

Many researchers differentiate between child sexual abuse or molestation, which usually involves nonrelatives; pedophilia, which

involves a compulsive desire to engage in sex with a particular age of child; and **incest**, which is sexual contact between a child or adolescent who is related to the abuser. There are several types of incest, including father–daughter, father–son, brother–sister, grandfather–grandchild, mother–daughter, and mother–son. Incest can also occur between stepparents and stepchildren or aunts and uncles and their nieces and nephews. Sexual behavior between a child and someone who is responsible for the child's care (such as a babysitter) may also be considered incest, although definitions for incest vary from state to state.

Because most children look to their parents for nurturing and protection, incest involving a parent, guardian, or someone else the child trusts can be extremely traumatic. The incestuous parent exploits this trust to fulfill sexual or power needs of his or her own. The particularly vulnerable position of children in relation to their parents has been recognized in every culture. The **incest taboo**—the absolute prohibition of sex between family members—is universal (Herman, 1981).

Sociologists suggest that social restrictions against incest may have originally formed to reduce role conflicts (Henslin, 2005). Parents who have sexual relationships with their child will have one role (i.e., parent) that conflicts with another, which can interfere with responsibilities. We must also understand, however, that definitions of incest vary cross-culturally. The Burundi, a tribal group in tropical Africa, believe that a mother causes her son's erectile dysfunction by allowing the umbilical cord to touch his penis during birth (Henslin, 2005). To rectify this situation, the mother must engage in sexual intercourse with her son. Although this practice may sound bizarre to us, the culture of the Burundi supports this practice and does not view it as incestuous.

Although there are various types of incest, father–daughter and sibling incest are two of the most common types of incest in the United States (Caffaro & Conn-Caffaro, 2005; Thompson, 2009). Many siblings play sex games with each other while growing up, and the line between harmless sex play and incest can be difficult to ascertain. Sex play often involves siblings who are no more

---

child sexual abuse
Sexual contact with a minor by an adult.

incest
Sexual contact between persons who are related or have a caregiving relationship.

incest taboo
The absolute prohibition of sex between family members.

than 5 years apart, is nonabusive, is mutually desired, and often involves experimentation (Kluft, 2010). Sibling incest, in contrast, often involves siblings with a large age difference, repeated sexual contact, and motivations other than curiosity (Kluft, 2010; Rudd & Herzberger, 1999; Thompson, 2009).

Although by far the majority of incest offenders are male, some women do sexually abuse children. Mother–son incest is more likely to be subtle, including behaviors that may be difficult to distinguish from normal mothering behaviors (including genital touching; Kelly et al., 2002). Men who have been sexually abused by their mothers often experience more trauma symptoms than do other sexually abused men.

Incidence of Child Sexual Abuse

Accurate statistics on the prevalence of child sexual abuse are difficult to come by for many reasons: Some victims are uncertain about the precise definition of sexual abuse, might be unwilling to report, or are uncomfortable about sex and sexuality in general (Ephross, 2005; Finkelhor, 1984). Overall, studies have found that

- approximately 9.2% of children are sexually abused;
- 1 in 5 girls and 1 in 20 boys are victims of child sexual abuse; and
- as adults, 20% of females and 5–10% of males recall being sexually abused as children.

However, the overall reported incidence of child sex abuse has been increasing. Perhaps the increases are a reflection of the changing sexual climate (in which there is less tolerance for such behavior), rather than an actual increase in the number of sexual assaults on children. Women's groups often teach that child sexual abuse is due to the patriarchal social structure and must be treated through victim protection. The child protection movement views the problem as one that develops out of a dysfunctional family and is treated through family therapy.

Some argue that children can't be trusted when making a claim of sexual abuse. Would a child ever "make up" such a story? Research has shown that false reports of child sexual abuse occur in less than 10% of reported cases (Besharov, 1988). This is important because a child's report of sexual abuse remains the single most important factor in diagnosing abuse (Heger et al., 2002).

Victims of Child Sexual Abuse

Although research is limited because of sampling and responding rates, it's estimated that children are the most vulnerable for child sexual abuse between the ages of 7–13 years old ("Child Sexual Abuse Statistics," 2012). Studies have found that 12% of women were 10 or younger when they were first sexually abused, and 30% of women were between the ages of 11 and 17 years old (Black et al., 2011). Nearly 30% of men were 10 or younger when they were first sexually abused.

Boys are more likely to be sexually abused by strangers (40% of boys, 21% of girls), whereas girls are more likely to be sexually abused by family members (29% of girls, 11% of boys; Finkelhor

et al., 1990). Finkelhor (1984) proposes three reasons why the reported rates of male sexual abuse may be lower than those for females: boys often feel they should be more self-reliant and should be able to handle the abuse; the stigma of homosexuality; and the fear of a loss of freedoms.

Reactions to sexual abuse vary. Many victims are scared to reveal the abuse because of shame, fear of retaliation, belief that they themselves are to blame, or fear that they will not be believed. Some incest victims try to get help only if they fear that a younger sibling is threatened. When they do get help, younger victims are more likely to go to a relative for help, whereas older victims may run away or enter into early marriages to escape the abuse (Herman, 1981). Victims of sexual abuse with a biological father often delay reporting the longest, whereas those who have been victims of stepfathers or live-in partners have been found to be more likely to tell someone (Faller, 1989).

How Children Are Affected

Child sexual abuse can have long-lasting effects that may lead to other psychological problems (Gray, 2017; Hall & Hall, 2011). Keep in mind that what follows is a discussion of what is typically experienced by a victim of childhood sexual abuse or incest. As we have discussed before, it is impossible to predict what a child's experience will be; the reaction of each child is different. A few factors make the abuse more traumatic, including the intensity of the sexual contact and how the sexual abuse is handled in the family. If a family handles the sexual abuse in a caring and sensitive manner, the effects on the child are often reduced.

Psychological and Emotional Reactions

Sexual abuse can be devastating for a child and often causes feelings of betrayal, powerlessness, fear, anger, self-blame, low self-esteem, and problems with intimacy and relationships later in life (Martens, 2007; Thompson, 2009; Valente, 2005). Overall, incest behaviors are the most traumatic when they occur over a long period, the offender is a person who is trusted, penetration occurs, and there is aggression. Children who hide their sexual abuse often experience shame and guilt, and they fear the loss of affection from family and friends (Seymour et al., 2000). They also feel frustrated about not being able to stop the abuse.

Regardless of whether they tell someone about their sexual abuse, many victims experience psychological symptoms such as depression, increased anxiety, nervousness, emotional problems, and personality and intimacy disorders. Similar to reactions of rape victims, PTSD and depression are common symptoms and may occur more often in victims who are abused repeatedly (Jonas et al., 2011; Thompson, 2009). Guilt is usually severe, and many children blame themselves for the sexual abuse. While female victims of child sexual abuse are more likely to experience depressive symptoms and suicidality, male victims are more likely to abuse substances after sexual abuse (Gray, 2017).

Victims may also try to cut themselves off from a painful or unbearable memory, which can lead to what psychiatrists refer to as a **dissociative disorder**. In its extreme form, dissociative disorder may result in a **dissociative identity disorder**, in which a person maintains two or more distinct personalities. Although it has long been a controversial issue in psychology, there is research to support the claim that some abuse victims are unable to remember past abuse (Malmo & Laidlaw, 2010). Some experts claim that although the memories are classified as bad, disgusting, and confusing, many times they are not "traumatic." Because of this, the memories are simply forgotten and not repressed (McNally et al., 2004, 2005). This issue continues to be controversial, even though many victims of sexual abuse often report an inability to remember details or the entirety of the abuse.

Women who were sexually abused as children have higher rates of personality disorders and PTSD than those who experienced sexual abuse later in life (Jonas et al., 2011; McLean & Gallop, 2003). Earlier in this chapter, we discussed the increased risk for engaging in risky sexual behaviors post-sexual assault. Both antisocial and high-risk sexual behaviors are also related to a history of child sexual abuse (Deliramich & Gray, 2008; Wells et al., 2016). The most devastating emotional effects occur when the sexual abuse is done by someone the victim trusts. In a study of the effects of sexual abuse by relatives, friends, or strangers, it was found that the stronger the emotional bond and trust between the victim and the assailant, the more distress the victim experienced (Feinauer, 1989).

Long-Term Effects

It is not uncommon for children who are sexually abused to display what Finkelhor and Browne (1985) refer to as **traumatic sexualization**. Children may begin to exhibit compulsive sex play or masturbation and show an inappropriate amount of sexual knowledge. When they enter adolescence, they may begin to show indiscriminate and compulsive sexual behavior, which may lead to sexually abusing others in adulthood (Rudd & Herzberger, 1999; Valente, 2005). These children have learned that it is through their sexuality that they get attention from adults.

Children who were sexually abused often experience sexual problems in adulthood. The developmentally inappropriate sexual behaviors that they learned as children can contribute to a variety of sexual dysfunctions later in life (Najman et al., 2005; Stephenson et al., 2014). Research has found that a large proportion of patients who seek sex therapy have histories of incest, rape, and other forms of sexual abuse (Maltz, 2002).

There is also a connection between the development of eating disorders and child sexual abuse (Berger, 2015; Caslini et al., 2016; Madowitz et al., 2015). Many people who have been sexually abused turn to food to decrease stress and tension. They may try to "de-sexualize" themselves by gaining or losing too much weight (Cohen, 2016). Gay and bisexual men who experience childhood sexual abuse are significantly more likely to have an eating disorder than men without a history of sexual abuse (Feldman & Meyer, 2007). Individuals who can discuss the sexual abuse are often able to make significant changes in their eating patterns.

Problems with drug and alcohol addiction are also more common in adults with a history of child sexual abuse. In fact, high rates of alcohol and drug use have been found even as early as age 10 (Valente, 2005). Finkelhor and Browne (1985) hypothesize that because of the stigma that surrounds the early sexual abuse, the children believe they are "bad," and the thought of "badness" is incorporated into their self-concept. As a result, they often gravitate toward behaviors that society sees as deviant.

It is not unusual for adults who had been abused as children to confront their offenders later in life, especially among those who have undergone some form of counseling or psychotherapy to work through their own feelings about the experience. They may feel a strong need to deal with the experience and often get help to work through it. The accompanying "Sex in Real Life" feature is a letter written by an 18-year-old woman who had been sexually abused by her father throughout her childhood. This letter was the first time that she had confronted him.

Characteristics of Child Sexual Abusers

Research on child sexual abusers has found several factors that distinguish abusers from those who do not abuse children. Sexual abusers are more likely to be male, older, have poor social skills, low IQs, unhappy family histories, low self-esteem, and less happiness in their lives than nonabusers (Finkelhor et al., 1990; Hunter et al., 2003; National Sexual Violence Resource Center, 2011). Most of the time they are acquainted with the child they sexually abuse and in 34% of cases they are family members.

Several motivations have been identified for engaging in child sexual abuse (Kluft, 2010). An abuser with an affection motivation views the behaviors as a part of family closeness with an emphasis on the "special" relationship between the victim and abuser. An erotic-based motivation usually involves sexual contact between several family members and is motivated by an eroticization of family roles. Aggression-based and rage-based motivations revolve around the abuser's sexualized anger and frustration, which is often taken out on a victim. Rage-based motivations also involve an overly hostile and sadistic abuser.

Denying responsibility for the offense and claiming they were in a trancelike state is also common. The majority of offenders are also good at manipulation, which they develop to prevent discovery by others. One man told his 13-year-old victim, "I'm sorry this had to happen to you, but you're just too beautiful," demonstrating the typical abuser's trait of blaming the victim for the abuse (Vanderbilt, 1992, p. 66).

The Development of a Sexual Abuser

Three prominent theories—learning, gender, and biological—propose factors that make abuse more likely. Proponents of learning theories believe that what children learn from their environment or

---

dissociative disorder
Psychological disorder involving a disturbance of memory, identity, and consciousness, usually resulting from a traumatic experience.

dissociative identity disorder
A disruption of identity characterized by two or more distinct personality states.

traumatic sexualization
A common result of sexual abuse in which a child displays compulsive sex play or masturbation and shows an inappropriate amount of sexual knowledge.

The following letter was written by an 18-year-old college student to her father. She had just begun to recall past sexual abuse by her father and was in counseling working on her memories. She decided to confront her father with this letter.

Dad: I can't hide it any longer! I remember everything about when I was a little girl. For years I acted as if nothing ever happened; it was always there deep inside but I was somehow able to lock it away for many years. But Daddy, something has pried that lock open, and it will never be able to be locked away again. I remember being scared or sick and crawling into bed with my parents only to have my father's hands touch my chest and rear. I remember going on a Sunday afternoon to my father's office, innocently wanting to spend time with him, only to play with some machine that vibrated.

I remember sitting on my father's lap while he was on the phone. I had a halter top on at the time. I remember wondering what he was doing when he untied it then turned me around to face him so he could touch my stomach and chest. I remember many hugs, even as a teenager, in which my father's hand was on my rear. I remember those words, "I like what is underneath better," when I asked my father if he liked my new outfit. But Daddy, more than anything, I remember one night when mom wasn't home. I was scared so I crawled into bed with my father who I thought was there to protect me. I remember his hands caressing my still undeveloped breast. I remember his hand first rubbing the top of my underwear then the same hand working its way down my underwear. I remember thinking that it tickled, but yet it scared me.

Others had never tickled me like this. I felt frozen until I felt something inside me. It hurt, and I was scared. I said stop and started shaking. I remember jumping out of bed and running to my room where I cried myself to sleep. I also remember those words I heard a few days later, "I was just trying to love you. I didn't mean to hurt you. No one needs to know about this. People would misunderstand what happened."

You don't have to deal with the memories of what this has done to my life, my relationships with men, my many sleepless nights, my days of depression, my feelings of filth being relieved through making myself throw up and the times of using—abusing—alcohol in order to escape. You haven't even had to see the pain and confusion in my life because of this. I have two feelings, pain and numbness. You took my childhood away from me by making me lock my childhood away in the dark corners of my mind. Now that child is trying to escape, and I don't know how to deal with her.

I felt it was only fair that you know that it is no longer a secret. I have protected you long enough. Now it is time to protect myself from all of the memories. Daddy, I must tell you, even after all that has happened, for some reason I'm not sure of, I still feel love for you—that is, if I even know what love is.

SOURCE: Author's files.

those around them contributes to their behavior later in life. Many child sex abusers were themselves sexually abused as children (Levenson & Grady, 2016). Many reported an early initiation into sexual behavior that taught them about sex at a young age. Many learned that such behavior was how adults show love and affection to children.

Proponents of gender theories identify gender as an important aspect in the development of an abuser—sexual abusers are overwhelmingly male (Finkelhor et al., 1990; Seto, 2008). Males are not often taught how to express affection without sexuality, which leads to needing sex to confirm their masculinity, being more focused on the sexual aspect of relationships, and being socialized to be attracted to mates who are smaller. Keep in mind that the incidence of female offenders may be lower because of lower reporting rates for boys or because society is more accepting of intimate female interactions with children (Groth, 1978; McLeod, 2015). It's estimated that women are the abusers in about 14% of cases among boys and 6% of among girls (Statistics on Perpetrators, 2012). Like male offenders, many female offenders were sexually abused as children (Levenson et al., 2015).

Proponents of biological theories suggest that physiology contributes to the development of sexual abusers. One study found that male offenders had normal levels of the male sex hormone testosterone but increased levels of other hormones (Lang et al., 1990). There have also been reports of neurological differences between incest offenders and non–sex criminal offenders that are thought to contribute to violence (Langevin et al., 1988).

Treating Child Sexual Abuse

We know that sexual abuse can have many short- and long-term consequences—for victims and abusers. As a result, it is important to help victims of child sexual abuse to heal and help abusers learn ways to eliminate their abusive behaviors.

Helping the Victims Heal

Currently, the most effective treatments for victims of child sexual abuse include a combination of cognitive and behavioral psychotherapies, which teach victims how to understand and handle the trauma of their assaults more effectively. Many victims of sexual abuse also have difficulties developing and maintaining intimate relationships. Being involved in a relationship that is high in emotional intimacy and low in expectations for sex is beneficial (Maltz, 1990). Learning that they have the ability to say no to sex is very important and usually develops when they establish relationships based first on friendship, rather than sex. Many times the partners of victims of sexual abuse are confused; they do not fully understand the effects of abuse in the lives of their partners, and so they may also benefit from counseling (Cohen, 1988).

Treating the Abusers

In Chapter 16, we discussed treatment for pedophilia. The treatment of child sexual abusers is similar in that the primary goal

REAL RESEARCH Victims of childhood sexual, physical, and emotional abuse lose at least 2 years of life expectancy, compared with persons who did not experience childhood maltreatment (Corso et al., 2008). This typically occurs because of the increased risk for obesity, depression, and heart disease, in addition to the development of unhealthy behaviors such as substance abuse or sexual promiscuity.

is to decrease the level of sexual arousal to inappropriate sexual objects—in this case, children. This is done through behavioral treatment, psychotherapy, or drugs. Other goals of therapy include teaching sexual abusers to interact and relate better with adults, assertiveness skills training, empathy and respect for others, increasing sexual education, and evaluating and reducing any sexual difficulties that they might be experiencing with their sexual partners (Abel et al., 1980). Because recidivism is high in these abusers, it is also important to find ways to reduce the incidence of engaging in these behaviors (Firestone et al., 2005).

Preventing Child Sexual Abuse

How can we prevent child sexual abuse? Increasing the availability of sexuality education has been cited as one way to decrease the incidence of child sexual abuse. Children from traditional, authoritarian families who have no sexuality education are at greater risk for sexual abuse. Education about sexual abuse—teaching that it does not happen to all children—may help children to understand that it is wrong. Telling children where to go and whom to talk to is also important. One program that has been explored is the Just Say No campaign, which teaches young children how to say no to inappropriate sexual advances by adults. This program has received much attention. How effective is such a strategy? Even if we can teach children to say no to strangers, can we also teach them to say no to their fathers or sexually abusive relatives? These are a few questions that future research will need to address.

Another important factor in prevention is adequate funding and staffing of child welfare agencies. Social workers may be among the first to become aware of potentially dangerous situations. Health care providers and educators must also be adequately trained to identify the signs of abuse.

Review Questions

1 Define child sexual abuse and discuss its incidence.

2 Discuss victims' psychological and emotional reactions to child sexual abuse.

3 Explain what the research tells us about sexual abusers and the development of such behavior.

4 Describe the most effective treatments for victims and perpetrators of childhood sexual abuse.

5 Identify some ways in which society can help prevent childhood sexual abuse.

Intimate Partner Violence

Intimate partner violence (IPV) includes physical and sexual violence, stalking, psychological aggression (e.g., name calling/insulting), and/or control of reproductive or sexual health (e.g., refusing to use condoms; Smith et al., 2017). Although **intimate partner sexual violence (IPSV)** is a significant aspect of IPV, it has often been overlooked in the research on sexual violence (Bagwell-Gray et al., 2015).

In the United States, 1 in 3 people reported experiencing IPV during their lifetime, with higher rates among multiracial Americans and lower rates among Asian or Pacific Islanders (Smith et al., 2017). In Chapter 16, we discussed the popularity of the erotic fiction series *Fifty Shades of Grey*. This best-selling novel depicted a romantic relationship between a millionaire and a college student that many believe was characterized by IPV, including emotional abuse, stalking, intimidation, isolation, and sexual violence (Bonomi et al., 2013). The perpetuation of sexual violence in popular culture continues to promote dangerous violence standards in intimate relationships.

Although IPV is common in adolescent and college-age populations, it can happen to people at any age (Bonomi et al., 2007; Forke et al., 2008). It is often related to stress. Studies have found that risk factors include early parenthood, problem drinking in the abuser, severe poverty, and unemployment ("National Institute of Justice," 2007). Earlier in this chapter we discussed how rape rates increase on college campuses during home football games, and the incidence of IPV has also been found to increase during certain sporting events. Unexpected losses in NFL football games have been found to be related to a 10% increase in rates of IPV (Card & Dahl, 2011).

Finally, some people are killed by their violent partners (known as intimate partner homicide [IPH])—76% of IPH victims were women, whereas 24% were men (Fox & Zawitz, 2004). Studies on men who commit IPH have found that 42% have past criminal charges, 15% have a psychiatric history, and 18% have both (Eke et al., 2011).

Defining Intimate Partner Violence

IPV is coercive behavior that uses threats, harassment, or intimidation. It can involve physical (shoving, hitting, hair pulling), emotional (extreme jealousy, intimidation, humiliation), or sexual (forced sex, physically painful sexual behaviors) abuse. Some offenders even are violent toward pets, especially pets that are close to the victim. Generally there is a pattern of abuse rather than a single isolated incident.

---

intimate partner sexual violence (IPSV)
Intimate partner violence that involves sexual aspects and can include sexual coercion, sexual abuse, and/or forced sexual activity.

Intimate Partner Violence in Lesbian Relationships

Although we don't often hear much about it, IPV occurs at about the same rate in lesbian relationships as it does in heterosexual relationships (Eaton et al., 2008; Hewlett, 2008). Many women in same-sex relationships do not feel comfortable discussing the violence with others and worry about being outed by their partner (Brown, 2008). Following is one woman's story about the violence in her relationship.

I met my girlfriend at a party that a friend hosted. She was intelligent, beautiful, and had a wonderful sense of humor. Our relationship developed rapidly and the closeness we shared was something I had never experienced before. It is difficult to remember exactly when the abuse began because it was subtle. She criticized me because she didn't like my cooking, and she occasionally called me names when we argued. I didn't think much about it because she had recently lost custody of her daughter to her ex-husband because of her sexual orientation and was angry, irritable, and depressed. She often threatened suicide and attempted it during an argument that we had and then blamed me for calling 911 for help. Despite the stress she was experiencing, she was very supportive of me when my family "disowned" me after I came out to them. When I bought my first car, she insisted I put it in her name. Although we had periods of profound happiness, our arguments increased in frequency as did her drinking and drug use. I kept telling myself that things would get better but they never did. She continually accused me of being unfaithful (I wasn't) and even once raped me after claiming I had flirted with a supermarket cashier. The first time she hit me I grabbed her wrist and twisted her arm to keep from being hit again. My response frightened me so much I suggested we see a couple's counselor, and she agreed.

Couple counseling was not helpful, and although things felt worse, our therapist said that was normal so we persevered. I began scrutinizing my own behavior believing that if I could only do things better or differently, our life together would improve. It wasn't until she pulled a knife on me that I realized that it wasn't going to change for the better . . . it was only going to get worse. I called a crisis line and the counselor suggested that what I was experiencing was domestic violence. That had actually never occurred to me because we were both women. Leaving her was the hardest thing I have ever done.

It's still difficult to think of my situation as domestic violence but with the help of my counselor and support group, I am learning that women can be violent to other women, that anger, stress, depression, alcohol, and drugs do not cause violence, that violence is a choice the abuser makes, and finally, that I am not to blame.

SOURCE: National Coalition of Anti-Violence Programs (1998).

Many women in abusive relationships claim their relationship started off well and that they believed the first incidence of violence was a one-time occurrence that would not happen again. They often excuse their partner's behavior and accept their partner's apologies. In time, the abuser convinces his partner that it is really her fault that he became violent and that if she changes, it won't happen again. Most women in this situation begin to believe that the problems are indeed their fault, so they stay in the abusive relationship. Many actually believe that it is safer in the relationship than outside of it. Things that may make it more difficult for some women to leave include issues such as finances, low self-esteem, fear, or isolation.

Intimate partner violence also occurs among college students. One 21-year-old college student told me:

No one could understand why I wanted my relationship with Billy to work. After all, no relationship is perfect. He didn't mean to slam me that hard. Why would he want to leave bruises on me? Look at him. He's a big guy. Anyone can tell he might have trouble seeing his own strength. He means well. He gives the best hugs, like a big sweet bear. He always says he's sorry. He loves me and tells me this in letters all the time. He thinks I'm sweet, pretty, and kind. Maybe my friends are just jealous. After all, he is a really good-looking guy. I know a lot of girls who want him. He tells me girls throw themselves at him every day. Why would he lie? (Author's files)

Although we know less about IPV in same-sex relationships, a survey by National Violence Against Women found that 22% of men and 35% of women reported experiencing physical abuse from a same-sex partner they were living with (Tjaden & Thoennes, 2000).

Another study found that 1 in 3 men in same-sex relationships have been abused (Houston & McKirnan, 2008). Other groups, including transgender individuals, may experience even higher levels of IPV. In one survey, transgender respondents reported lifetime physical abuse rates by a partner of 37% (Landers & Gilsanz, 2009). Although many aspects of IPV in LGBTQ relationships are similar to IPV in heterosexual couples, there are some things that are unique to LGBTQ individuals. They may have fewer social supports, less availability of medical and psychological services, and may have a fear of being "outed" when seeking help (Ard & Makadon, 2011; St. Pierre & Senn, 2010).

© Joel Gordon

Although less is known about the prevalence and experience of intimate partner violence in lesbian relationships, it is known that IPV in lesbian relationships looks similar to IPV in heterosexual relationships.

Reactions to Intimate Partner Violence

Victims of IPV experience both physical and psychological symptoms, and the symptoms depend on both the frequency and the severity of the violence (Beeble et al., 2011; Campbell et al., 2002). Common psychological symptoms, similar to those experienced by victims of other coercive sexual behaviors, include depression, antisocial behavior, increased anxiety, low self-esteem, a fear of intimacy, substance abuse, suicidality, and the development of PTSD (Stewart et al., 2016). Physical symptoms may include headaches, back pain, broken bones, gynecological disorders, and stomach problems. Children who witness IPV are also negatively affected both short- and long-term (Stewart et al., 2016).

Preventing Intimate Partner Violence

Earlier in this chapter, we discussed the fact that violence tends to repeat itself in people's lives—victims of violence often experience it more than once, known as *poly-victimization* (Cavanaugh et al., 2011). IPV victims often have a history of violence in their families, child sexual abuse, and/or teen dating violence (Leonard, 2005; Lipsky et al., 2005). In fact, people who are victims of child sexual abuse or teen dating violence are significantly more likely to perpetrate or become victims of IPV as adults than those who were not victims of child sexual abuse (Gómez, 2011).

Educational programs can help educate the public about IPV, and prevention programs can be designed to reach out to those who have been victimized to help them learn ways to reduce violent tendencies. Safe housing for victims of IPV can also reduce the likelihood of future abuse. Today, there are thousands of battered-women's shelters across the United States. These shelters provide women with several important things, including information and a safe haven. Often these centers have 24-hour hotlines that can help women who are struggling with issues related to domestic violence (see the websites listed at the end of this chapter for other hotline options). Increasing the availability of safe houses and counseling and education is imperative. In addition, increasing the availability of services for lesbian, gay, bisexual, transgender, elderly, and disabled people will help ensure that help is available for all who may need it.

Review Questions

1 Define intimate partner violence (IPV) and give one example.

2 Identify some common psychological and physiological symptoms of IPV.

3 How is IPV in same-sex relationships similar to and different from heterosexual relationships?

4 Explain how IPV relates to sexual and physical abuse.

Sexual Harassment

Although we have mentioned sexual harassment earlier in this chapter, it is a broad term that includes anything from unwanted sexual advances, telling sexual jokes, an "accidental" brush on a person's body, or making offensive comments about a person's sex. It can also include unwanted online sexual attention. Because of the wide variety of actions that fall under this definition, many people are confused about what exactly constitutes sexual harassment.

In the United States, the courts recognize two types of sexual harassment, including **quid pro quo harassment** and **hostile environment harassment**. Quid pro quo (meaning "this for that") harassment occurs when a person is required to engage in some type of sexual conduct in exchange for a certain grade, employment, or other benefit. For example, a teacher or employer might offer someone a better grade or opportunity for engaging in sexual behavior. Another type of sexual harassment involves being subjected to unwelcome repeated sexual comments or visually offensive material that creates a hostile work environment and interferes with work or school. For example, a student or employee might repeatedly tell sexual jokes or send them electronically.

It may seem that sexual harassment is not as troubling as other forms of sexual violence, but the effects of harassment on the victim can be traumatic and often cause long-term difficulties. Fitzgerald and Ormerod (1991) claim, "There are many similarities between sexual harassment and other forms of sexual victimization, not only in the secrecy that surrounds them but also in the [myth] that supports them" (p. 2). Severe or chronic sexual harassment can cause psychological side effects similar to rape and sexual assault, and in extreme cases, it has been known to contribute to suicide.

In 2016, a sexual harassment scandal began to surface at the Fox Network when more than 20 women came forward to file a lawsuit accusing Fox's CEO, Roger Ailes, of long-term sexual harassment (Pallotta, 2017). Several women accused Ailes of propositioning them for sex and not hiring or even firing them when they refused. One accuser claimed Ailes had pressured her for sex in exchange for a job, saying, "You know if you want to play with the big boys, you have to lay with the big boys" (Redden, 2016). Although Ailes categorically denied all the accusations of sexual harassment, he was forced to resign in 2016. Another Fox News icon, Bill O'Reilly, was also forced out for sexual harassment in 2017. All of these events have helped to bring more attention to sexual harassment in the workplace.

---

quid pro quo harassment
A type of sexual harassment that involves submission to a particular type of conduct, either explicitly or implicitly, to get education or employment.

hostile environment harassment
A type of sexual harassment that occurs when an individual is subjected to unwelcome repeated sexual comments, innuendoes, or visually offensive material or touching that interferes with school or work.

Sexual harassment is still an all-too frequent reality in the workplace today. In 2017, a sexual harassment scandal at the Fox News Channel involved several high-profile men, including top-rated television personality, Bill O'Reilly, and CEO Roger Ailes. Both were fired from the network and although Ailes died a few months later, O'Reilly continues to deny any wrongdoing.

Slaven Vlasic/Getty Images

REAL RESEARCH Sexual victimization, including sexual assault and child sexual abuse, is a risk factor for poorer college academic performance (BAKER et al., 2016). It was found to predict students' GPA in their final semester better than any established academic predictor and was the only factor related to transferring or quitting college.

REAL RESEARCH A longitudinal study found that aggression and suicide attempts during male adolescence were related to poor intimate partner relationships and an increased likelihood of partner violence in young adulthood (KERR & CAPALDI, 2011).

Incidence and Reporting of Sexual Harassment

Sexually harassing behaviors are common on many college campuses. It's estimated that 66% of college students experience some form of sexual harassment, yet less than 10% report these incidences (Lundy-Wagner & Winkel-Wagner, 2013). Federal law prohibits the sexual harassment of college students, and victims of sexual harassment can sue their schools for damages for sexual harassment.

Studies have found that the majority of people never tell anyone about being sexually harassed. According to a 2016 Equal Employment Opportunity Commission (EEOC) Task Force Report, 70% of people who experienced sexual harassment never talked to their supervisors or bosses about the harassment (Feldblum & Lipnic, 2016). In addition, less than 13% file a formal

complaint about the sexual harassment. Some do verbally confront their offenders or leave their jobs to get away from it. Assertiveness is the most effective strategy, either by telling someone about it or confronting the offender. Many fear, however, that confronting a boss or teacher who is harassing them could jeopardize their jobs or their grades. If you are being sexually harassed by someone in a university setting, the best advice is to talk to a counselor or your advisor about it. Remember that you are protected by federal law (recall the earlier discussion about Title IX).

Preventing Sexual Harassment

The first step in reducing the incidence of sexual harassment is to acknowledge the problem. Too many people deny its existence. Because sexual harassers usually have more power, it is difficult for victims to come forward to disclose their victimization. University officials and administrators need to work together to provide educational opportunities and assistance for all students, staff, and employees. Establishing policies for dealing with these problems is necessary. Workplaces also need to design and implement strong policies against sexual harassment.

Education, especially about the role of women, is imperative. Studies have shown that sexual harassment education and training can reduce these behaviors (Diehl et al., 2014). As our society continues to grow and the workplace changes, we need to educate people about how to understand these changes. Throughout history, when women have broken out of their traditional roles, there have always been difficulties.

Throughout this chapter we have explored how power can be used to degrade and oppress. Sexual violence, rape, sexual assault, the sexual abuse of children, IPV, and sexual harassment are problems in our society today. The first step in reducing these crimes is to acknowledge the problems and not hide them. Education, especially about the sexuality, sexual consent, and the role of women, is necessary; without it, these crimes will undoubtedly continue to escalate.

Review Questions

1 Define sexual harassment and differentiate between the various types of sexual harassment.

2 Explain how sexual harassment can affect a person's employment.

3 Identify some strategies for dealing with, and preventing, sexual harassment.

Chapter Review

1 Power is an aspect of all sexual relationships. Sexual relationships are healthy when power is shared and when the relationship empowers the partners. In sexuality, however, as everywhere in human life, power can also be used to degrade and oppress. Sexual violence is an all-encompassing term that includes sexual acts that are committed against someone without their consent.

2 The National Intimate Partner and Sexual Violence Survey collects data on five types of sexual violence, including rape, sexual coercion, unwanted sexual contact, forced penetration, and non-contact unwanted sexual behavior.

3 Rape (also referred to as sexual assault) is defined by the NISVS as completed or attempted unwanted vaginal, oral, or anal penetration through the use of physical force (by being held down), threats of violence, or when a victim is under the influence of alcohol or drugs. This would also include situations in which a person is passed out and unable to consent and can include penetration by a penis, fingers, or an object.

4 The second type of sexual violence is sexual coercion, which involves being pressured to engage in sexual activity when a person doesn't want to. It can include using threats to get sex or continuous requests to have sex until a person finally relents and gives in. The third type of sexual violence, unwanted sexual contact, includes unwanted sexual behaviors that do not involve penetration, such as kissing, touching, fondling, or groping. Touching may be through clothing or directly, and may include the genitals, buttocks, groin, breast, or legs.

5 The fourth type of sexual violence involves forcing a person (with physical force, threats of violence, or while they are under the influence of alcohol or drugs) to vaginally, orally, or anally penetrate another person. The last type is non-contact unwanted sexual behavior and includes unwanted exposure to sexual situations including pornography, verbal or behavioral sexual harassment, or the creation of a sexually hostile climate. The exact definitions of sexual violence, rape, and sexual assault are often determined by individual states.

6 It's estimated that more than 1 in 3 women and 1 in 6 men in the United States have experienced some form of sexual violence in their lifetime. However, sexual violence includes some of the most underreported crimes in the United States, so it is difficult to assess the actual number of victims. We know that close to half of all victims don't report sexual violence.

7 Perpetrators of sexual violence are primarily male and single. They have high levels of impulsivity and aggression, sexist views about women, and high levels of rape myth acceptance. Men who commit sexual violence often have histories of personal violence, such as child physical abuse, child sexual abuse, dating violence, or intimate partner violence.

8 Four theories that explain why rape occurs are the rapist psychopathology, victim precipitation, feminist, and sociological theories. The rapist psychopathology theory suggests that either disease or intoxication forces men to rape. Victim precipitation theory shifts the responsibility from the person who knowingly attacked to the innocent victim. Feminists believe that rape and the threat of rape are tools used in our society to keep women in their place. The social, economic, and political separation of the sexes has also encouraged rape, which is viewed as an act of domination of men over women. Finally, sociologists believe that rape is an expression of power differentials in society. When men feel disempowered by society, by changing sex roles, or by their jobs, overpowering women with the symbol of their masculinity (a penis) reinforces, for a moment, men's control over the world.

9 There are gender differences in attitudes toward rape. Men have been found to be less empathetic and sensitive toward rape victims than women, believe more rape myths, and blame victims more than women. Men who take sexual violence education workshops or college courses on violence against women have less rape myth acceptance than men who do not take such workshops or courses. Having male friends who support violence against women is a risk factor for committing sexual violence.

10 Racial/ethnic minorities have been found to have more traditional attitudes toward women, which has been found to

affect rape attitudes. Non-Hispanic Whites are more sympathetic than Blacks to women who have been raped, whereas Blacks are more sympathetic than Hispanic college students. Asian American students have the least sympathy for women who have been raped and are more likely to hold a rape victim responsible for the rape.

11 Sexual violence is defined differently around the world, so the incidence of sexual violence varies depending on a culture's definition. The primary cultural factors that affect the incidence of sexual violence in a society include relations between the sexes, the status of women, and male attitudes in the society. Not surprisingly, societies that socialize men to be aggressive, dominating, and to use force to get what they want have higher incidences of sexual violence.

12 Female college students are more likely to experience sexual violence compared to women in any other age group and women in the same age group who are not attending college. Studies have found that first-year women are particularly at risk for sexual violence during the first couple of months of college, called the "red zone."

13 Stalking is another form of sexual violence and includes unwanted phone calls, texts, voicemails, messages through social media, e-mails, perpetrator showing up or approaching them at certain locations, such as home, school, or work; and being watched, followed, or spied on.

14 After the rape and murder of a Lehigh college student, congress passed the Student Right to Know and Campus Security Act which requires universities to make information about sexual violence public. The Campus Sexual Assault Victims' Bill of Rights was also passed, requiring universities to develop prevention policies and provide victims with protections and rights. Finally, the Campus Sexual Violence Elimination Act (Campus Save Act) requires schools to educate students, faculty, and staff on the prevention of rape, dating violence, sexual assault, and stalking.

15 The momentum began to build after several events related to sexual assault occurred at various prestigious universities. Schools that failed to protect their students from sexual assault and rape were in violation of Title IX of the 1972 Education Amendments; Title IX requires all universities receiving federal funds to provide equal access to education for all students, regardless of gender.

16 Sexual assault and alcohol abuse are pervasive problems on college campuses. Numerous studies have found links between sexual assaults and alcohol use. Alcohol use is one of the strongest predictors of rape on college campuses. Although there have been few studies on ethnic/racial differences in alcohol-related sexual assaults, one study found these types of sexual assaults are more common among White college students than among Black college students.

17 Alcohol use on college campuses, as it relates to rape, is viewed very differently for men and women. College students view victims who were drinking as more responsible for the assaults, but view perpetrators who were drinking as less responsible.

18 Fraternities tend to tolerate and may actually encourage the sexual coercion of women, because they tend to host large parties with lots of alcohol and little university supervision. Greek men have been found to have higher levels of rape myth acceptance than non-Greek men. The ethic of masculinity also helps foster an environment that may increase the risk for rape.

19 Student athletes, both intercollegiate and recreational, have been found to have higher levels of acceptance of rape myths than nonathletes. Many athletes have been found to view the world in a way that helps to legitimize rape, and many feel a sense of privilege. Female athletes have been found to be more likely than nonathletes to believe in the blame-the-victim theory of rape and believe that some women put themselves in a bad situation.

20 Rape trauma syndrome (RTS) is a two-stage stress response pattern characterized by physical, psychological, behavioral, or sexual problems (or a combination of these). Two stages, the acute and long-term reorganization, detail the symptoms that many women feel after a rape. Rape may cause sexual difficulties that can persist for a considerable period after the rape. Some victims have a silent rape reaction because they never report or talk about their rape.

21 The effects of rape are similar in special populations, including rape between marital partners and rape of lesbians, bisexuals, transgender, older women, women with disabilities, and sex workers. Partners of women who have been raped also experience emotional symptoms. Overall, rape places a great deal of stress on a relationship.

22 Men can be raped by women and also by other men. The majority of male rapes by women use psychological or pressured contact, such as verbal persuasion or emotional manipulation, rather than physical force. The true incidence is unknown because the rape of men by men is infrequently reported to the police. Male rape is an expression of power, a show of strength and masculinity that uses sex as a weapon. Rape also occurs in prison.

23 Rapists are primarily from younger age groups and tend to reduce their rape behavior as they get older. They have also been found to have experienced overwhelmingly negative early interpersonal experiences, most of which were with their fathers; have sexist views about women; accept myths about rape; have low self-esteem; and be politically conservative.

24 Different therapies for rapists include shock treatment, psychotherapy, behavioral treatment, support groups, and the use of medications. Many programs have been developed to decrease myths about rape and increase knowledge levels. All-male programs have been found to reduce significantly the belief in rape myths.

25 The likelihood that a rape will be reported increases if the assailant was a stranger, if there was violence, or if a weapon was involved. Women who report their rapes to the police have been found to have a better adjustment and fewer emotional symptoms than those who do not report. Some victims refuse to press charges because they are afraid of revenge, want to forget the event, feel sorry for the rapist, or feel as though it would not matter anyway because nothing will be done.

26 Child sexual abuse refers to sexual contact between a child or adolescent who is related to the abuser. One important characteristic of child sexual abuse is the dominant, powerful position of the adult or older teen that allows them to force a child into sexual activity. The sexual activity can include genital/breast fondling, making a child fondle an adult, masturbation, voyeurism, exhibitionism, digital penetration with fingers or sex toys, or oral, vaginal, or anal intercourse. It can also include making a child view pornography or participate in pornography, and/or child sexual exploitation.

27 Accurate statistics on the prevalence of child sexual abuse are difficult to come by because some victims are uncertain about the definition of sexual abuse, unwilling to report, or uncomfortable about sex and sexuality in general. Many victims are scared to reveal the abuse. Victims of incest with a biological father delay reporting the longest, whereas those who have been victims of stepfathers or live-in partners tell more readily.

28 Children who hide their sexual abuse often experience shame and guilt and fear the loss of affection from family and friends. They also have low self-esteem and feel frustrated about not being able to stop the abuse. Regardless of whether they tell someone about their sexual abuse, many victims experience psychological symptoms such as depression, increased anxiety, nervousness, emotional problems, low self-esteem, and personality and intimacy disorders.

29 While female victims of child sexual abuse are more likely to experience depressive symptoms and suicidality, male victims are more likely to abuse substances after sexual abuse. The most devastating emotional effects occur when the sexual abuser is someone the victim trusts.

30 Research comparing child sexual abusers with nonabusers has shown that molesters tend to have poorer social skills, lower IQs, unhappy family histories, lower self-esteem, and less happiness in their lives. Three prominent theories that propose factors that make abuse more likely are learning, gender, and biological theories.

31 Currently, the most effective treatments for victims of sexual abuse include a combination of cognitive and behavioral psychotherapies. Many victims of sexual abuse also have difficulties developing and maintaining intimate relationships. Goals for therapy of child sex abusers include decreasing sexual arousal to inappropriate sexual objects, teaching them to interact and relate better with adults, assertiveness skills training, empathy and respect for others, increasing sexual education, and evaluating and reducing any sexual difficulties that they might be experiencing with their sexual partners.

32 Increasing the availability of sex education can also help decrease child sexual abuse. Adequate funding and staffing of child welfare agencies may also be helpful.

33 Intimate partner violence includes physical and sexual violence, stalking, psychological aggression, and/or control of reproductive or sexual health. Intimate partner sexual violence is a significant aspect of IPV but it has often been overlooked in the research on sexual violence. Although IPV is common in adolescent and college-age populations, it can happen to people at any age.

34 In the United States, 1 in 3 people reported experiencing IPV during their lifetime, with higher rates among multiracial Americans and lower rates among Asian or Pacific Islanders. Studies have found that risk factors for IPV include early parenthood, problem drinking in the abuser, severe poverty, and unemployment. Sexual harassment includes jokes, unwanted sexual advances, a friendly pat, an "accidental" brush on a person's body, or an arm around a person. Severe or chronic sexual harassment can cause psychological side effects similar to those experienced by rape and sexual assault victims, and in extreme cases, it has been known to contribute to suicide. It may seem that sexual harassment is not as troubling as other forms of sexual violence, but the effects of harassment on the victim can be traumatic and often cause long-term difficulties.

35 Studies have found that the majority of people never tell anyone about being sexually harassed. The first step in reducing the incidence of sexual harassment is to acknowledge the problem. Too many people deny its existence. Because sexual harassers usually have more power, it is difficult for victims to come forward to disclose their victimization.

Critical Thinking Questions

1 Why do you think a woman who was sexually assaulted after she had too much to drink is often blamed more for the assault than a woman who was sexually assaulted in the street by an unknown assailant? Explain.

2 Many professional athletes have been charged with sexual assault or intimate partner violence—for example, Mike Tyson, Kobe Bryant, and Ray Rice. Do you think professional athletes make poor decisions with women who are drawn to them? Do you think a woman would say they were raped without just cause? Why or why not?

3 Do you consider sexual intercourse between a 17-year-old male and his 14-year-old girlfriend sexual abuse? How would you define the sexual abuse of children?

4 In a handful of divorce cases, one spouse accuses the other of child sexual abuse. Do you think that these accusations originate from a vengeful ex-spouse wanting custody, or do you think it might be easier to discuss the sexual abuse once the "bonds of secrecy" have been broken, as they typically are during divorce?

Websites

Adult Survivors of Child Abuse (ASCA)   Designed specifically for adult survivors of physical, sexual, and emotional child abuse or neglect, ASCA offers an effective support program. This website's mission is to reach out to as many survivors of child abuse as possible, and it offers information on individual and group support groups.

Rape, Abuse & Incest National Network (RAINN)   RAINN is the nation's largest anti–sexual assault organization. It operates the National Sexual Assault Hotline at 1-800-656-HOPE and carries out programs to prevent sexual assault, help victims, and ensure that rapists are brought to justice. The website includes statistics, counseling resources, prevention tips, news, and more.

National Violence Against Women Prevention Research Center   National Violence Against Women Prevention Research Center provides information on current topics related to violence against women and its prevention. The website contains statistics and information on many topics, including evaluations of college sexual assault programs across the nation.

Know Your IX   A campaign aimed to empower students to stop sexual violence on college campuses. Provides information about Title IX violations, dealing with and combating sexual assault, harassment, and abuse on college and university campuses.

Not Alone: Together Against Sexual Assault   Information for students, schools, and anyone interested in finding resources on how to respond to and prevent sexual assault on college and university campuses. Information on students' rights, resources, filing complaints, crisis intervention, and school-level enforcement activities are available.

Men Can Stop Rape (MCSR)   MCSR is a nonprofit organization that works to increase men's involvement and efforts to reduce male violence. MCSR empowers male youths and the institutions that serve them to work as allies with women in preventing rape and other forms of men's violence. MCSR uses education and community groups to build men's capacity to be strong without being violent.

Clery Center for Security on Campus   The Clery Center for Security on Campus is a nonprofit organization that works to make campuses safe for college and university students. It was cofounded in 1987 by Connie and Howard Clery, following the murder of their daughter at Lehigh University. Security on Campus educates students and parents about crime on campus and assists victims in understanding laws pertaining to these crimes.

Male Survivor   Male Survivor works to help people better understand and treat adult male survivors of childhood sexual abuse. Information about male sexual abuse and a variety of helpful links are available.

Northwest Network of Bi, Trans, Lesbian, and Gay Survivors of Abuse   The Northwest Network provides support and advocacy for bisexual, transsexual, lesbian, and gay survivors of abuse. Information about sexual abuse and a variety of helpful links are available.

National Coalition Against Domestic Violence (NCADV)   The NCADV works to eliminate domestic violence, empower battered women and children, promote direct service programs, educate the public, and promote partnerships with corporations to fund programs to eliminate domestic violence. Website provides information, statistics, resources, volunteer opportunities, and helpful links.

18 Sexual Images and Selling Sex

© 2012 Cengage Learning

Like many of you, I love reality television shows. I'm curious about the people who are in them and the reasons why the shows are so popular. The shows are often completely unrealistic, using sensationalism to attract viewers and advertisers. One show you might remember, Jersey Shore, followed a group of housemates at the New Jersey shore. The show was called a "cultural phenomenon," generating record ratings for MTV and earning the title as the "most watched television series EVER" (Gorman, 2011). Not surprisingly, many college students spent hours watching Jersey Shore and analyzing its content. Two students of mine, Alex and Raelynn, talked to me about how Jersey Shore affect people's attitudes about gender, sexuality, and relationships. Although they were appalled by how the female characters behaved like stereotypical "bimbos," they loved watching the show. What I couldn't figure out was why so many women loved the show when the female characters were portrayed so negatively?

Male college students also watched Jersey Shore and told me they looked up to the men on the show and found themselves treating the women in their lives in similar ways. Raelynn remembered one male friend who brought a girl home and then decided that the girl wasn't attractive enough to stay; he asked her to leave and went out and found someone else to bring home. Reality shows like Jersey Shore often affect people's views about gender, sexuality, and relationships. The popularity of such reality shows definitely makes us wonder about the future of American television and how it will continue to shape our views.

Janell Carroll

Our lives today are full of visual media: magazines, television, websites, and product packaging. Even food products are adorned with pictures of people and scenes. Advertisements stare at us, between articles in magazines and newspapers, plastered on billboards, walls, buses, taxis, and from the sidebars of social media. Moving images on television, in the movies, on computers and smartphones surround us almost everywhere we go, and we will depend on them even more as technology continues to develop. We live in a visual culture with images we simply cannot escape.

We begin this chapter with a brief history of erotic representations. Next, we examine how erotic representations are presented to us every day in books, television, advertising, and other media. Only then do we turn to the graphic sexual images of pornography. We also explore how sex itself is sold today, from lap dances in strip clubs to sex work. Along the way, ask yourself the following questions: What influence do sexual representations and selling sex have on us? What are they trying to show us about ourselves? How do they subtly affect the way we think about gender and sexuality?

Early erotic art was often public art. The city of Pompeii included large, erect phalluses on street corners, and erotic frescoes adorned many people's homes.

Erotic Representations in History

Human beings have been making representations of themselves and the world around them since ancient times. Many of the earliest cave drawings and animal bone sculptures have been representations of the human form, usually scantily dressed or naked. Often, the poses or implications of the art seem explicitly erotic. Yet it is hard to know to what degree these images were considered erotic by preliterate people, for early erotic art was also sacred art; the purpose was to represent those things most important to early people—the search for food and the need to reproduce (Lucie-Smith, 1991). However, by the dawn of the great ancient civilizations such as Egypt, people were drawing erotic images on walls or pieces of papyrus just for the sake of eroticism (Manniche, 1987). Since that time, human beings have been fascinated with representations of the human form naked or engaged in sexually explicit behavior; in turn, many governments have been equally intent on limiting or eradicating those images.

Erotic representations have appeared in most societies throughout history, and they have been greeted with different degrees of tolerance. Ancient cultures often created public erotic tributes to the gods, including temples dedicated to phallic worship. India's sacred writings are full of sexual accounts, and some of the most explicit public sculptures in the world adorn its temples. Greece is famous for the erotic art that decorated objects such as bowls and urns. When archaeologists in the 18th and 19th centuries uncovered the Roman city of Pompeii, buried in a volcanic blast in 79 A.D., they were startled and troubled to find that this jewel of the Roman Empire, which they had so admired, was full of brothels, had carved phalluses protruding at every street corner, and had private homes full of erotic **frescoes** (FRESS-cohs; Kendrick, 1987). Authorities hid these findings for years by keeping the erotic objects in locked museum rooms and publishing pictures of the city in which the phalluses were made to taper off like candles.

Not all sexual representations are explicit, and many of our greatest artists and writers included sexual components in their creations. The plays of Shakespeare, although hardly shocking by today's standards, do contain references to sexuality and sexual intercourse. The art of Michelangelo and Leonardo da Vinci also included graphic nudity without being titillating. Still, in their day, these pictures caused controversy; in the 16th century, for example, priests painted loincloths over nude pictures of Jesus and the angels. What people in one society or one period in history see as obscene, another group—or the same group later—can view as great art.

Development of Pornography

Most sexual representations created throughout history had a specific purpose, whether it was to worship the gods, to adorn pottery, or, later, to criticize the government or religion. Very little erotic art seems to have been created simply for the purpose of arousing the viewer, as much of modern erotic art is. So most of history's erotic art cannot be considered "pornographic" in the modern sense (Hunt, 1993).

Pornography, which tends to portray sexuality for its own sake, did not emerge as a distinct, separate category until the middle of the 18th century in the United States. For most of history, sexuality itself was so imbedded in religious, moral, and legal contexts that it was not thought of as a separate sphere of life (Kendrick, 1987). Explicit words and pictures (together with other

fresco	pornography
A type of painting done on wet plaster so that the plaster dries with the colors incorporated into it.	Any sexually oriented material that is created simply for the purpose of arousing the viewer.

forms of writing, such as political writings) were controlled in the name of religion or in the name of politics, not in the name of public **decency** (Hunt, 1993). For example, **obscenity** was illegal among the Puritans (punishable originally by death and later by boring through the tongue with a hot iron) because it was an offense against God. That may explain why before the 19th century, **hard-core** sexual representations were rare.

Another strong influence on the development of pornography in the United States was the development of the printing press and the mass availability of the printed word (sexually explicit books were printed within 50 years of the invention of movable type in the Western world). For most of history, written or printed work was available only to a small elite because only they could afford it and, more importantly, only they could read.

The most famous pornographic work of the 18th century was John Cleland's *Memoirs of a Woman of Pleasure* (better known as *Fanny Hill*), first published in 1748. Cleland's work was solely aimed at sexually arousing the reader. Before Cleland, most sexually explicit books were about prostitutes because these women did "unspeakable" things (that could be described in graphic detail) and because they could end up arrested, diseased, and alone, thereby reinforcing society's condemnation of their actions. In fact, the word *pornography* literally means "writing about harlots."

Cases such as *Fanny Hill* teach us that to really understand the meaning of "pornography," we must understand the desire of the U.S. government and other groups to control it and suppress it.

In other words, the story of pornography is not just about publishing erotic material but also about the struggle between those who try to create it and those who try to stop them. Both sides must be included in any discussion of pornography; without those who try to suppress it, pornography just becomes erotic art. In fact, the term **erotica**, often used to refer to sexual representations that are not pornographic, really just means pornography that a particular person finds acceptable. One person's pornography can be another person's erotica. As we shall see in this chapter, the modern arguments about pornography are some of the most divisive in the country, pitting feminists against feminists, allying some of the most radical feminist scholars with fundamentalist preachers of the religious right, and pitting liberals against liberals and conservatives against conservatives in arguments over the limits of free speech.

But sexually explicit representations are not the only sexual images in U.S. society. Sexuality is present in almost all of our **media**, from the model sensuously sipping a bottle of beer to the offhand sexual innuendos that are a constant part of television sitcoms. In fact, the U.S. entertainment media seems to be almost obsessed by sexual imagery; Michel Foucault (1998), French philosopher and historian of sexuality, has called it a modern compulsion to speak incessantly about sex. Before we discuss the sexually explicit representations of "pornography" with the heated arguments they often inspire, let us turn to the erotic images that present themselves to us in the popular media every day.

Review Questions

1 Explain how erotic representations have appeared throughout history.

2 Differentiate among pornography, obscenity, and erotica.

3 Describe the development of pornography.

Sexuality in the Media and the Arts

Since the early 1990s, representations in the U.S. **mass media** have become more explicitly erotic. Many of the images we see today are explicitly or subtly sexual. Barely clothed females and shirtless, athletic males are so common in our ads that we scarcely notice them anymore. Some even feature full nudity (in fact, some clothing companies, such as Abercrombie & Fitch, are notorious for using naked models or models with very little clothing—which appears rather odd when you remember they're trying to sell clothes!). Many of today's movies, even some directed at children, have sexual scenes that would not have been permitted in movie theaters even 20 years ago. The humor in television shows has become more and more sexual, and nudity has begun to appear on primetime networks. In addition, graphic depictions of sexuality, which until recently could be found only in adult bookstores and theaters, can now be easily accessed via the Internet.

We like to believe that we are so used to the media that we are immune to its influences. Does sex (or violence) on television, for example, really influence how sexual (or violent) our society becomes? Do the constant sexual stereotypes paraded before us in advertisements really help shape our attitudes toward gender relations? Does constant exposure to sexual images erode family life, encourage casual sex, and lead to violence against women, as some conservative and feminist groups claim? Also, if we find out that

decency
Conformity to recognized standards of propriety, good taste, and modesty—as defined by a particular group (standards of decency differ among groups).

obscenity
A legal term for materials that are considered offensive to standards of sexual decency in a society.

hard core
Describes explicit, genitally oriented sexual depictions, more explicit than soft

core, which displays sexual activity often without portrayals of genital penetration.

erotica
Sexually oriented media that are considered by a viewer or society as within the acceptable bounds of decency.

media
All forms of public communication.

mass media
Media intended for a large, public audience.

sex and violence in the media do have an effect on how we behave, what should we do about it?

Erotic Literature

Although the portrayal of sexuality is as old as art itself, pornography and censorship are more modern concepts, products of the mass production of erotic art in society. Throughout Western history, reactionary forces (usually the clergy) often censored nudity in public art, especially when it featured religious figures. For example, on the walls of Michelangelo's Sistine Chapel, clerics painted over the genitals of nudes with loincloths and wisps of fabric. Still, because there was no way to mass-produce these kinds of art, the Church's reactions varied on a case-by-case basis.

Pornography in the modern sense began to appear when printing became sophisticated enough to allow large runs of popular books, beginning in the 16th century. Intellectuals and clergy were often against this mass production of books. They worried that if everybody had books and could learn about things for themselves, why would anyone need teachers, scholars, or theologians? Religious and secular intellectuals quickly issued dire warnings about the corrupting effects of allowing people direct access to knowledge and established censorship mechanisms. By the 17th century, the Church was pressuring civic governments to allow them to inspect bookstores, and soon forbidden books, including erotica, were being removed; such books then became rarer and more valuable, and a clandestine business arose in selling them. It was this struggle between the illicit market in sexual art and literature and the forces of censorship that started what might be called a pornographic subculture—one that still thrives today.

Today, erotic literature of almost any kind is readily available in the United States. The sexual scenes described in the average romance novel today would have branded it as pornographic only a few decades ago. In Chapter 16, we discussed the enormous popularity of the erotic fiction series that begins with *Fifty Shades of Grey* and how the series brought many sexual practices into mainstream consciousness and everyday conversations. One would think that such books would be the main targets of people trying to censor sexually explicit materials. Yet, most censorship battles over sexually explicit material involve images rather than the written word.

Although the early court cases that established the U.S. legal opinion toward pornography in the United States were often about books (especially about sending them through the mail), modern debates about pornography tend to focus more on explicit pictures and movies. Still, it was the erotic novel that first established pornographic production as a business in the Western world and provoked a response from religious and governmental authorities.

Television and Film

Television has a strong influence on the modern American outlook toward life. Whether it's network television, Netflix, or HBO, the world we see on TV is only a small slice of the real world. For example, although literally hundreds of acts of sexual intercourse

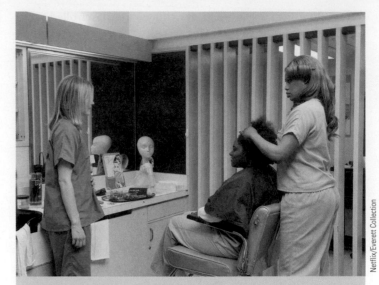

Television shows, such as *Orange Is the New Black,* boldly explore themes related to sexual orientation and gender identity, with strong lesbian, bisexual, and transgender characters. In 2014, Laverne Cox, who plays Sophia Burset, (the hairdresser in this photo) became the first openly transgender person to be nominated for an Emmy.

are portrayed or suggested on shows and movies every day, we rarely see a couple discuss or use contraception, discuss the morality of their actions, contract a sexually transmitted infection (STI), experience a sexual dysfunction, or regret the act afterward. Many couples end up in bed shortly after initial physical attraction and take no time to build an emotional relationship before having sex. Values and morals about sexuality seem nonexistent in many shows.

Relatively new shows such as *Game of Thrones, Orange Is the New Black, Shameless,* and *Girls* are graphically explicit in their treatment of sex. Full frontal nudity is not uncommon in many of these shows, and various sexual issues, such as masturbation and oral sex, are commonly explored in story lines. When talking about the amount of sex allowed on television, Doug Herzog, president of MTV Networks Entertainment Group, said, "The line moves every day, so you got to move with it" (quoted in Strauss, 2010).

Television magazine shows that imitate news reports but concentrate on two or three stories (for example, *Dateline* or *20/20*) often search for stories with lurid content, and if there is a sexual scandal or a sexual assault accusation in the news, they are sure to feature it. Even the "hard" news shows, such as the networks' evening news reports, have turned a corner in their willingness to use graphic descriptions of sexual events. News shows, after all, also need ratings to survive, and one way to interest audiences is to report legitimate news stories that have a sexual content in a graphic and provocative way. These news reports deliver the sexually explicit information with the implicit message that they disapprove of it; but they still deliver it.

A 2005 study of sexual content on American television analyzed more than 1,000 hours of programming, including all genres of television shows. Researchers found that 70% of the shows studied

Sexual Diversity

Spuiten en Slikken—Sex and Drugs on Television

IN OUR WORLD

The first chapter of this textbook opened with a cross-cultural exploration of sexuality in three countries: Japan, the Netherlands, and the United States. Each of these countries has rules about how much sex is tolerated on television. In a conservative country, such as Japan, there is less tolerance, whereas in more liberal countries, such as the Netherlands, there is more tolerance. On a recent trip to the Netherlands, I had the opportunity to attend the taping of a popular Dutch television show *Spuiten en Slikken*. The title of the show is a play on words that can mean either "Shoot Up and Swallow" or "Ejaculate and Swallow," referencing sex and drugs. *Spuiten en Slikken* explores sex and drugs in a very open and matter-of-fact

© Janell Carroll

fashion and is aimed at 13- to 19-year-olds. The weekly show has between 500,000 and 750,000 viewers each week, representing about 4% of the Netherlands population (for comparison, MTV's hit show *Jersey Shore* averaged about 3 million viewers, which is roughly 1% of the U.S. population; Henke, 2011).

Hosts of the show experiment with sex and drugs in every show, while young audience members watch and learn what can happen. Typical sex-related story lines for the show involve oral and anal sex, partner swapping, pornography, and semen tasting, whereas typical drug-related story lines include exploring the effects of psychedelic mushrooms, hash, or marijuana. On one show, the host smoked pot to show audience members the effect of marijuana use on memory (they forgot most of their lines).

To come up with show topics, a group of researchers keeps tabs on sexual and drug trends in the young adult population. Noticing that many teens had been experimenting with recording their sexual interactions on their smartphones, producers decided to explore these practices in more depth. The show explored the reasons why teens might decide to do this and

the consequences of doing so. Hosts discussed the negative possibilities of doing so (i.e., it could get into the wrong hands) as well as the suggestions for doing it right (i.e., getting the lighting right).

I had the opportunity to talk with Pim Castelijn, the director of programming for the station that broadcasts the show in the Netherlands. I told him that critics might think the show "glorified" sex and drugs. Did he think it made kids want to experiment with things they showcased? He told me that teens already know that sex and drugs *are* glorious, and that's what draws them toward experimentation. He wondered why so many Americans are afraid to talk to teens about how good sex is. He believes that ignoring the positives only makes teens distrustful. *Spuiten en Slikken* attempts to highlight both the positives and negatives associated with various sexual behaviors (and drug use) and doesn't automatically claim that all sex and drugs are bad. It presents a balanced approach in hope that kids who watch will be able to make up their own minds.

Probably the most interesting thing I learned about the show that day was that the station it airs on, BNN, is a public television station, funded with taxpayer money. Do you think a show like this would air in the United States? Why or why not?

SOURCES: P. Castelijn, personal communication, September 26, 2008; A. Gnocchi, personal communication, September 26, 2008.

included some sexual content, averaging five sexual scenes per hour (Kunkel et al., 2005). These numbers were up from 1998, when 56% of shows included sexual content, and 3.2 sexual scenes occurred every hour. During primetime programming, sexual content increased and averaged close to six sexual scenes per hour. Only 11% of primetime network shows made references to sexual risks or responsibilities, and this percentage has remained virtually the same since 1998.

The AIDS epidemic was a key factor in opening up the way in which news organizations spoke about sexuality (for example, the word *condom* would never have appeared on a major news network before the outbreak of AIDS). Another landmark came in 1998 when news broke of a sex scandal between then-president Bill Clinton and Monica Lewinsky. The Clinton–Lewinsky story was one of the biggest of the decade and was covered by most evening news shows in explicit detail. This story broke precedent and allowed the networks to use language and sexual

references that would have been unthinkable just a few years earlier.

Television, Film, and Minority Sexuality

As sexually explicit as the U.S. visual media has become, it has generally had a poor track record in its portrayals of certain sexual behaviors, such as same-sex behavior and sexuality among certain minorities, such as the elderly, the disabled, and racial and ethnic minorities. Today, thanks to popular shows such as *Orange Is the New Black*, *Modern Family*, and *Shameless*, LGBTQ people become more mainstream on television.

One place where minorities, especially female minorities, have had a high representation has been in reality television. However, reality shows such as *Real Housewives of Atlanta*, *Love and Hip Hop*, and *She's in Charge* often portray Black women as bossy, manipulative, and stubborn. Although many White women are portrayed in equally negative ways in reality shows (take *Jersey Shore,* for example), the difference lies in the fact that White women have a less stereotyped presence on many major television networks. Although television shows starring Black women have been few and far between, this has slowly been changing. In fact, *Scandal* was the first television show in 30 years that starred a Black woman (McDaniel & Good, 2016).

Television, Film, and Gender

American television offers its viewers sexual information both explicitly (through such things as news, documentaries, and public service announcements) and implicitly (through the ways it portrays sexuality or gender relations in its programming; Gunter & McAleer, 1990; Peter & Valkenburg, 2007). One implicit message of American television programming, almost since its inception, has been that men are in positions of leadership (whether they are chief legal counsel or the head of the family), whereas women, even if they are high ranking, are often sexualized. Even today, the stereotyping of women is often extreme in television commercials, which is considered in the "Advertising" section later in this chapter. Although the types of portrayals of women's roles are changing and improving on television today, men still outnumber women in major roles, and the traditional role of woman as sex object still predominates on television.

Many gender stereotypes persist on American television. As we have discussed, this is especially true in popular reality television shows. For example, in one show, *Keeping Up with the Kardashians,* women are portrayed as self-centered and preoccupied with their looks and wealth. A national sex-tape scandal involving Kim Kardashian was the impetus for the start of the show, which documents the everyday actions of the Kardashian family. The goal was to show how one wealthy family functions (or doesn't) day to day. The underlying message seems to be that women can use their looks and fame to get ahead. As Kim Kardashian said in the first episode of the show, "There's a lot of baggage that comes with us. But it's like Louis Vuitton baggage—you always want it" (McClain, 2013). Another popular reality show, *The Bachelor,* portrays women as catty, backstabbing, and preoccupied with the goal of finding Prince Charming. The women are typically stereotypically beautiful, thin, and personable. Stereotyping is common in reality shows and is often used to engage viewers. Since ratings are the most important aspect of these shows, the storylines and outcomes are often not based on truth or reality.

Gender roles in other television shows are changing. Men are now being shown as single or stay-at-home dads, and there is a tendency to mock the old "macho man" stereotypes on shows such as *The Family Guy.* Shows like *How to Get Away with Murder* feature women in leading roles and have helped establish the new television woman: forceful, working outside the home, and

dealing with the real-life problems of balancing social life, personal issues, and work. These women are smart, motivated, and self-confident. Gender stereotypes have also been changing with the increasing popularity of reality television shows such as *Survivor, The Biggest Loser, Naked and Afraid,* and *Top Chef.* Shows like these not only portray women as strong and independent but also often portray men as sensitive and emotional.

Television and Children

American teenagers watch more than 4 hours of television each day (Rideout et al., 2010). The proliferation of new technologies on which to watch television, such as smartphones, iPads, laptops, and tablets, has significantly increased the overall amount of time that teens spend watching television shows. Like adults, the majority of teens record and watch their shows later and/or watch them on devices other than the television.

Television viewing also begins early in the United States: 2- to 5-year-olds spend almost 28 hours a week watching television and teenagers about 22 hours. In 1961, the average age to begin watching television was 3 years old, but by 2007, it was 9 months old (Zimmerman et al., 2007). The biggest leap in hours spent watching television occurs from 11 to 14 years old when children watch an average of 5 hours of television and movie content—either live or recorded—each day (Rideout et al., 2010). When these numbers are evaluated by racial/ethnic groups, Black and Hispanic youths have been found to watch nearly 6 hours of television per day, compared with a little more than 3 hours per day for Whites.

Researchers have begun to ask serious questions about the impact of extensive television watching, especially because television is so inundated with sexuality and gender stereotypes. For example, children are concerned with gender roles, and they often see the world in terms of "boy" behavior and "girl" behavior. As discussed in Chapter 4, children are often pressured into behaving in gender-appropriate ways, and they quickly begin to tease other children who do not follow these stereotypes. Still, research shows that when children are exposed to books or films that portray nonstereotyped gender behaviors, the children's gender stereotypes are reduced (Abad & Pruden, 2013).

Historically, many children's shows have lacked positive female role models and offered stereotyped portrayals of men and women. For example, although *Sesame Street* has had a human cast of mixed ethnicities and genders, and even a number of female Muppets, its most notable Muppet figures (from Kermit to Bert and Ernie to Big Bird to the Count) have all been male. It was only with the introduction of Zoe in 1993 that a female Muppet managed to gain a high profile. Many other popular children's shows contain male characters as leads, including *Arthur, SpongeBob SquarePants,* and *Phineas and Ferb.*

Television executives argue that boys will not watch cartoons with a female lead, but girls will watch cartoons with a male lead, and so it makes economic sense to produce cartoons featuring males. The result is that it is hard for young girls to find good gender role models in cartoons. It is understandable that researchers

Sex in Real Life — Generation M

The face of media is quickly changing all around us. Today we can hear music from devices smaller than our finger and access the Internet through our smartphones. Many cars and vans have optional built-in television monitors on seat backs and smartphones download e-mails and can record digital images and video. Today's adolescents spend a significant amount of time each day using electronic media, including television, movies, Internet, video, smartphones, GameCubes, and PlayStations (not including the time they spend using computers for school work or the time spent texting and talking on a smartphone; Rideout et al., 2010). When you add in the fact that they are often multitasking and using more than one medium at a time, the overall time spent with electronic media is more than 11 hours each day.

In 2010, the Henry J. Kaiser Family Foundation released "Generation M: Media in the Lives of 8–18-Year-Olds," the results of a study that included responses to anonymous questionnaires from more than 2,000 8- to 18-year-olds. Whereas 39% of teens had their own cell phone in 2005, by 2010, 66% had cell phones (Rideout et al., 2010). Following are other interesting findings from this important study. On average, adolescents between the ages of 8 and 18 were found to:

- Watch 4 hours 29 minutes of television each day
- Listen to 2 hours 31 minutes of music each day
- Spend 1 hour 29 minutes using the computer for recreational use per day
- Play video games for 1 hour 13 minutes per day
- Read recreational material for 38 minutes a day

© Reagan Herke

In the average home in America, 84% have Internet access (59% have high-speed Internet), 84% have cable or satellite (47% of these also get premium cable channels, such as HBO), and 52% have TiVo or other DVRs. What is interesting, however, is the number of adolescents who have access to this material in their bedrooms.

Forty-five percent of 8- to 18-year-olds report there are no rules about television watching (Rideout et al., 2010). The study also found that in the average adolescent bedroom:

- 71% have a television
- 49% have cable television
- 50% have a video game console
- 36% have a computer

Gender differences were found: Boys were twice as likely as girls to play video games, but girls spent more time listening to music than boys. As for the overall types of music listened, rap and hip-hop were the clear favorites (60% of Whites, 70% of Hispanics, and 81% of Blacks reported this genre of music as their favorite; Rideout et al., 2005). Ethnic differences revealed that Black youths spent more time watching television than Hispanic or White Americans.

Adolescents' increased access to the Internet gives them much greater access to information. Many adolescents report that their parents are unaware of what they see online (Cameron et al., 2005). Because research has shown that the exposure to sexuality in the media has been found to be related to adolescent sexual behavior, the content of these media is worth exploring. This generation of adolescents is certainly a media generation, but now the question for researchers is this: What long-term impact will this have on adolescents?

SOURCE: Rideout et al. (2005, 2010).

---

have found that more television viewing is correlated with greater gender stereotyping in certain groups of children (Myers, 2012; Schiau et al., 2013). However, the situation has slowly improved, with cartoons such as *Odd Squad* and *Peg + Cat* that have strong leading female characters.

One might also wonder what effect television has on the developing sexuality of children and adolescents. Sex is a common theme on many television programs today. How does this affect the sexual behavior of teens? Research has shown that increasing sexual content on television is related to early sexual initiation in adolescents (Collins et al., 2004). Teens who watch a lot of television are likely to believe their peers are sexually active (Eggermont, 2005).

Movement Against the Sexualization of the Visual Media

The irony is that American networks have turned to sex to increase their ratings, yet the constant presence of sexual themes on television is beginning to turn viewers away. The majority of Americans want stronger regulation of sexual content and profanity (Kunkel et al., 2005).

Portrayal of sexuality in movies has also long been a source of controversy. There was no control over motion picture content until the 1930s, when the industry began policing itself with the Motion Picture Code. However, the rating system has not stopped the filmmakers from trying to be as sexually explicit as they can within the rating categories. Hollywood seems to try to push the limits of the R rating as far as possible, and a number of directors have had to cut sexually explicit scenes out of their movies. In fact, some movies are made in two or three versions; the least sexually explicit version is for release in the United States, a more explicit copy is released in Europe (where standards are looser), and a third, even more explicit version is released on DVD.

A backlash does seem to be developing, and Hollywood has been reducing the sexual explicitness of its general release movies. Michael Medved (1992), a noted movie critic, argued in his book *Hollywood vs. America* that the movie and television industries are out of touch; too dedicated to violence, profanity, and sex; and do not really understand what consumers want to see on television and in the movies. He claimed that G- and PG-rated movies actually make more money than R-rated movies.

However, some of the shows boycotted by groups, such as the American Family Association, get high ratings for the very reasons that they are boycotted—they are willing to deal with complex issues such as abortion and homosexuality in a frank and honest (if sometimes sensationalistic) manner. It will be interesting to see whether advertisers are scared away by these groups or continue to sponsor provocative and controversial programs.

After a controversial season full of negative reviews for the scandalous nature of the show, Gossip Girl launched a highly successful ad campaign that used negative quotes from several watchdog organizations to promote the show. Ad campaigns included the acronyms "OMFG" and "WTF." Producers claimed that "WTF" simply referred to "Watch This Fall."

ON YOUR MIND

Most kids today know all about sex at an early age. So why are people so uptight about showing nudity on television? What do they think it will do to their kids?

Even in a society like ours, which has begun to discuss sex more openly, sexuality is still a difficult subject for children to understand. Many parents believe that it is their job to introduce the topic to their children, to explain it to them, and to teach their children whatever values the parents believe are appropriate. This may be undermined when children see fairly uncensored sexuality on television, which is usually shown without any discussion of values and without any way to address the children's questions about what they are seeing. The accompanying "Sex in Real Life" feature, "Generation M," discusses research on the media consumption habits of children and teenagers.

Advertising

Advertising is a modern medium, and its influence pervades modern life. There is practically no area free from its effects, from social media to consumer products and even to nature itself—billboards obscure our views from highways, and planes drag advertising banners at our beaches. People proudly wear advertisements for fashion designers on their shirts, sneakers, or hats, not realizing that they are paying money to help the company advertise.

According to estimates, children watch more than 40,000 commercials on television every year (Bakir & Palan, 2010). Studies have shown that advertising has a profound effect on the way children think about the world (forming a mind-set of

"products I want to have," for example), and it influences the way they begin to form their ideas of sexuality and gender roles (Gunter & McAleer, 1990; Lynch, 2012).

Advertising and Gender Role Portrayals

In his groundbreaking book *Gender Advertisements*, Erving Goffman (1976) used hundreds of pictures from print advertising to show how men and women are positioned or displayed to evoke sexual tension, power relations, or seduction. Advertisements, Goffman suggested, do not show actual portrayals of men and women but present clear-cut snapshots of the way we think they behave. Advertisements try to capture ideals of each sex: Men are shown as more confident and authoritative, whereas women are more childlike and deferential (Belknap & Leonard, 1991). Since Goffman's book was published, advertisements have become more blatantly sexual, and analyzing the gender role and sexual content of advertisements has become a favorite pastime of those who study the media.

Although studies indicate that advertising is becoming less sexist today, gender differences still exist (Eisend, 2010). An examination of gender-role portrayals in television advertising from seven countries, including Brazil, Canada, China, Germany, South Korea, Thailand, and the United States, found that females were still portrayed in stereotypical ways (Paek et al., 2011).

As you flip through popular magazines today, it's obvious that advertising companies are trying to put more women into ads in positions of authority and dominance. Men are also being shown in less stereotypic roles, such as cuddling babies or cooking. However, the naked body is still a primary means of selling products, and even if gender roles are becoming more egalitarian, portrayals of sexuality are still blatant.

Calvin Klein often challenges the limits in advertising campaigns by featuring graphic nudity and sexual themes. This controversial 50-foot billboard in a New York City neighborhood featured a scantily-clothed man and woman.

AP Images

A J. Crew ad in 2011 created controversy by showing a woman painting her son's toenails pink.

Advertising and Portrayals of Sexuality

The purpose of advertising is threefold—to get your attention, to get you physiologically excited, and to associate that excitement with the product being advertised. The excitement can be intellectual, emotional, physical (sports, for example), or visual (fast-moving action, wild colors). But when you think of "getting excited," what immediately comes to mind? Well, that is what comes to the mind of advertising executives also, and so ads often use sexual images or suggestions to provoke, to entice—in short, to seduce.

Sexuality (especially female sexuality) has been used to sell products for decades. In an analysis comparing magazine advertisements in 1964 with advertisements in 1984, Soley and Kurzbard (1986) found that although the percentage of advertisements portraying sexuality did not change, sexual illustrations had become more overt and visually explicit by 1984. By the late 1990s, a variety of advertisers, including Calvin Klein and Abercrombie & Fitch, were challenging the limits with advertising campaigns that featured graphic nudity or strong sexual implications. Although Abercrombie & Fitch was forced to withdraw many of its catalogs because of public outcry, today clothing manufacturers and perfume companies constantly try to out-eroticize each other.

Not all portrayals of sexuality are this blatant, however. Some are suggestive, such as sprays of soda foam near the face of an ecstatic looking woman, models posing with food or appliances placed in obviously phallic positions, models posed in sexual positions even if clothed, or ads that show women and, less often, men whose faces are contorted in what looks like sexual pleasure.

Some authors even claim that advertisements have tried to use **subliminal** sexuality—pictures of phalluses or breasts or the word *sex* worked into advertisements so they cannot be seen without extreme scrutiny (Levine, 1991). Whether these strategies work is a matter of much debate, but Calvin Klein's ads were so provocative that news reports about them appeared in newspapers and on television news shows—and that is just what advertisers want most for their ads and the products they represent, for people to talk and think about them.

Advertisements have the power to both shape and reflect culture. Many advertisers attempt to push mainstream themes but find themselves mired in controversy. Yet, as we said, controversy can bring more attention to issues. Two examples can illustrate this. In 2011, J. Crew released an ad featuring J. Crew's president painting her son's toenails pink (see accompanying photo). Critics argued that painting a boy's toenails would increase the chances of the boy being gay or transgender (James, 2011). More recently, Dove released an ad about celebrating motherhood. The ad featured a variety of women talking about motherhood and included a transgender woman holding a baby. Critics argued that the "cross-dressing man" cannot call herself a mother ("Dove Ad Features," 2017). Although critics were vocal about both of these

subliminal
Existing or functioning below the threshold of consciousness, such as images or words, often sexual, that are not immediately apparent to the viewer of an advertisement, intended to excite the subconscious mind and improve the viewer's reaction to the ad.

advertisements and debate was strong, in the end, the ads did exactly what they were supposed to do—create a buzz, drawing more attention to the products.

Electronic Technologies and the Internet

The growth of new technologies has tremendously increased the amount of time that children and adults spend with various forms of electronic media (see the nearby "Sex in Real Life" feature). It is estimated that the average teen spends more than 11 hours a day with various electronic media (Roman, 2015). For context, the American Academy of Pediatrics recommends no more than two hours of electronic media per day for teenagers and young adults (Strasburger & Hogan, 2013).

We are currently living in a high-tech world that exposes children to new technologies in many areas of their lives. Their classrooms are even high-tech these days with smartboards and Internet accessibility. The benefit of incorporating technology into schools includes increased diversity,

student interaction, and access to new knowledge (DeLoatch, 2015). But today's adolescents are spending more time than ever in front of screens, which may also have negative effects. For example, studies have found that technology can change the way that children think and focus, affecting areas such as attention, information overload, decision-making, learning, and memory (Taylor, 2012). An overuse of technology may also make it more difficult for adolescents to read emotions and have empathy for others. One study by UCLA researchers found that sixth graders who went five days without electronic devices were better able to read human emotions compared to sixth graders who were allowed to use their electronic devices (Uhls et al., 2014).

The power of the Internet has been discussed throughout this text, but it is mentioned here once again because the Internet allows for completely unregulated interaction among millions of children and adults. The Internet has generated whole new forms of communications, and as new forms of media are developed, sex and gender issues are arising there, too. Sexuality manifests itself online today in a variety of ways, including pornography sites, explicit videos and photos, image sharing, forums/subreddits, Tumblr, merchandising, and streaming and **camming** (web-

ON YOUR MIND

I've heard that people who are looking for child pornography often use the Internet. What kind of images do they look for? How often do they get caught?

Although the distribution of child pornography is illegal and banned by federal law in all 50 states, the crimes still occur. In 2006, Project Safe Childhood, a nationwide program designed to protect children from online exploitation and abuse, was implemented through the U.S. Department of Justice. This program increased the number of international, federal, state, and local investigations involving child sexual exploitation, leading to increased federal prosecutions. From 2007 to 2012, close to 12,000 defendants were convicted in federal courts for offenses related to the sexual exploitation of children ("Project Safe Childhood," 2012). In addition, Project Safe Childhood has helped identify more than 3,500 children who have participated in child pornography. In 2017, Project Safe Childhood helped identify a Cleveland man who was sentenced to 26 years in prison for running an online group that shared images of toddlers being sexually assaulted and tortured (Tobin, 2017). Those typically arrested for such crimes have access to minor children, either by living with them, through a job, or in organized youth activities. The offenders are typically White (91%), older than 25 (86%), and unmarried (Wolak et al., 2005). When law officials reviewed the child pornography that offenders had in their possession, they found 83% had images of 6- to 12-year-olds and 19% had images of children younger than 3. These images contained children involved in a range of sexual behaviors including oral sex, genital touching, and penetration (Wolak et al., 2005).

Google Glass, a type of wearable technology, enables users to access e-mail, texts, and the Internet via voice and physical commands. An app called "Sex with Glass" allows users to record themselves having sex from their partner's perspective.

Sergio Azenha/Alamy Stock Photo

camming
A slang term for webcamming, which involves using a webcam to feed or stream images or video through a computer or computer network.

wearable computers
Miniature electronic devices worn by a user to enable constant interaction between the computer and user.

camming) sites. Even spam e-mail is often sex-related (how many spam e-mails have you received alerting you to "sexy singles in your area!" or "enlarge your penis in under a week!"?). We will discuss pornography later in this chapter.

The development of **wearable computers** takes technology to a whole new place and embeds technology in watches, glasses, shirts, or any other wearable item. These technologies allow users constant access to their devices. The sales of wearable computers has exploded from $1.8 million in 2013 to an estimated $325 million in 2016 (Statista, 2017). It is expected to reach $929 million by 2021. One product that foreshadowed the power of wearable technology, Google Glass, provides smartphone-like technology in a hands-free format. Using an optical head-mounted display connected to Wifi, users can perform a variety of functions, such as browsing the Internet, getting directions, taking photographs, recording video, sending text messages, and more, while doing other activities. Google Glass apps allow users to record a variety of events, including sexual interactions (Bradley, 2014; Pocklington, 2014; Thomas, 2014). The app "Sex with Glass" enables people to watch themselves having sex through their partner's eyes. Users put on their glasses and to begin recording a sexual interaction they say "Okay Glass, it's time." To stop the recording they simply say, "Okay, Glass, pull out." They may even be able to access sexual tips by saying "Okay, Glass, give me ideas" if they need to spice things up a bit. After recording, users can connect their phones to the app to replay the footage (Pocklington, 2014).

redsnapper/Alamy Stock Photo

Although camming was once thought of as a small niche in the adult entertainment industry, it has become very popular over the last few years. Cam models broadcast themselves live from the privacy of their own homes and can interact with the people watching them.

Review Questions

1 Identify the early reactionary forces that began a censorship of erotic literature.

2 Explain how television uses sex to attract viewers and increase ratings.

3 In what ways do television and movies influence our perceptions of gender?

4 Identify and explain how television has been found to socialize children from a young age.

5 Explain how gender roles have been portrayed in various types of advertising.

6 Explain how advances in technology can provide people with greater access to sexual content and may affect our sexual interactions.

Pornography: Graphic Images and Obscenity

Pornography has always aroused passions, but the debate over pornography is particularly active today because pornography is so widely available. Today pornography can be easily viewed online or purchased in stores. Yet conflicts have arisen between free-speech advocates, antiporn (and anti-antiporn) feminists, religious groups, presidential commissions, the American Civil Liberties Union, and a powerful pornography industry.

Defining Obscenity

This section begins by reviewing the disputes over the legal and governmental definitions of pornography as they have been argued in presidential commissions and in the highest courts in the country. Then we look at how those same debates are discussed among the scholars and activists who try to influence the country's policies toward pornography. We also examine the basic claim of modern opponents of pornography: that pornography is harmful in its effects on individuals and society as a whole. Finally, we examine the public's attitudes toward pornography.

Sex in Real Life   My Short-Lived Porn Career

A few years ago, one of my students came to me to discuss an issue that came up in her relationship with her boyfriend. He had gone to Los Angeles to star in some adult films and she was distressed. How would this affect their relationship? The two of them came to talk with me and he shared the story of his short-lived porn career. Unfortunately, in the end he lost his girlfriend, who was really unhappy about his decision to participate in the films. What would you have done in this situation? Would you support a partner who wanted to star in a porn film? Why or why not?

It's not like I've always wanted to be a porn star. Of course I've wondered what the lifestyle would be like, and how I would perform if I were one. One night I found out that a famous porn star, Ginger Lynn, was dancing at a local strip club. We went to see her, and after her dance she offered to sign autographs. She also mentioned that she was sponsoring a competition to earn a chance to star in an adult porno film with her. I was intrigued and decided to approach her to ask her about it. After speaking with her for a while about the opportunity she took some information from me and told me that she would call me.

After a battery of tests to check for STIs, I flew out west to make my porn debut a few months later. I was given $700 to pay for travel expenses and my "services." My head was spinning on the plane because I was consumed by anticipation, excitement, nervousness, and fear. I was mostly worried about my relationship with my girlfriend. I knew that she was having a hard time understanding why I wanted to do this. To be honest, I wasn't even sure why I wanted to do it. I guess I looked at it as the opportunity of a lifetime. But I still questioned it. Was I trying to prove something?

It is hard to explain the feelings I had when I first arrived to the set where the filming would take place. There were many people walking around freely observing the sex scenes. The people there were all very courteous and professional. Each of us was taken aside and asked about what types of scenes and sex acts we were willing to participate in. The producers stressed that we should not participate in anything we were uncomfortable with.

George Steinmetz/Getty Images

The days on the set were long. There were about two dozen males and females participating, and each of us had to do a minimum of three scenes. Each scene lasted about an hour. The male performers were encouraged to take a Viagra pill for insurance after consulting the onsite doctor. On this first day I participated in two scenes. The first involved an oral sex competition with seven girls and seven guys. The guys serviced the girls first while the girls were blindfolded. We had to kneel and perform cunnilingus on each girl for three minutes. By a show of fingers in the air the girls were asked to "score" the guys on a scale of 1 to 10. There was a cash prize for the guy with the highest score.

The second scene was much like the first only it involved the guys seated on the couches and the girls on their knees. I was blindfolded and each of the seven girls came around and gave me oral sex for three minutes each. When each of the girls had given action to each of us, we removed our blindfolds to watch the grand finale—our ejaculations. During all the scenes the cameramen moved around freely filming video and taking still photos.

My third scene was filmed on the final day of shooting. I was to be dominated by two women. We participated in a kinky threesome the likes of which I have never known. The women performed oral sex on each other and on me. We switched positions repeatedly, and there was much groping and licking. The scene lasted for about an hour, but the time seemed to go by very quickly. At one point I was lying down and one girl was sitting on my face while the other was sucking my cock.

The experience was very interesting. Although I was glad to have the experience I did not find that it was an appealing career for me to pursue, and I have been troubled by the potential aftermath of my participation. I realize that I might lose my relationship with my girlfriend. I wonder if she'll decide to let me go because she is so unhappy that I even wanted to do it in the first place.

SOURCE: Author's files.

Court Decisions

The First Amendment to the Constitution of the United States, enacted in 1791, includes the words "Congress shall make no law . . . abridging the freedom of speech, or of the press." Ever since, the court system has struggled with the meaning of those words, for it is obvious that they cannot be taken literally; we do not have the right to make false claims about other people, lie in court under oath, or in the most famous example, yell "fire" (falsely) in a crowded theater, even though that limits our freedom of speech.

Court cases in the United States have established the following three-part definition of obscenity that has determined how courts define pornography. For something to be obscene, it must (a) appeal to the **prurient** (PRURE-ee-ent) interest; (b) offend contemporary community standards; and (c) lack serious literary, artistic, political, or scientific value.

> **prurient**
> Characterized by lascivious thoughts; used as criterion for deciding what is pornographic.

However, these criteria are not without critics. Important questions remain about topics such as the definitions of community standards and prurient interest, and who gets to decide. Some argue that the criteria of prurience, offensiveness, and community standards turn moral fears into legal "harms," which are more imaginary than real, and so we end up with arbitrary discussions of what is "prurient" and which speech has "value" (Hunter et al., 1993). In contrast, antiporn feminists argue that pornography laws were made to reflect a male preoccupation with "purity" of thought and insult to moral sensibilities, and to ignore the true harms of pornography: the exploitation of women.

> **REAL RESEARCH** Male college students watch more Internet pornography and report using it at an earlier age than female college students (HARPER & HODGINS, 2016). High levels of Internet porn use have been found to be related to decreased psychosocial functioning, along with problems with alcohol, marijuana, gambling, and video game use.

Presidential Commissions

A presidential commission is a special task force developed by the president of the United States that performs an investigation or research on a specific topic. Although presidential commissions date back to George Washington, they became more popular in the 20th century (Rosenbaum, 2005). There have been more than 100 presidential commissions that have examined issues such as bioethics, chemical warfare, terrorist attacks, and oil spills. These commissions issued detailed reports and recommended changes in public policy. Even though presidential commissions often do not lead to an adoption of new policies, they do help educate Americans about important issues. Now we'll explore two of the commissions on pornography.

1970 COMMISSION ON OBSCENITY AND PORNOGRAPHY
In 1967, President Lyndon Johnson set up a commission to study the impact of pornography on American society. The commission was headed by a behavioral scientist who brought on other social scientists, and although the commission also included experts in law, religion, broadcasting, and publishing, its findings were based on empirical research, and much of its $2 million budget was used to fund more scientific studies (Einsiedel, 1989). The commission (which used the terms *erotica* or *explicit sexual material* rather than *pornography*) studied four areas: pornography's effects, traffic and distribution of pornography, legal issues, and positive approaches to cope with pornography (Berger et al., 1991).

The 1970 commission operated without the benefit of the enormous research on pornography that has appeared since that time, and so it has been criticized for such things as not distinguishing between different kinds of erotica (for example, violent versus nonviolent); for including homosexuals, exhibitionists, and rapists all under the same category of "sex offenders"; and for relying on poor empirical studies. Still, although calling for more research and better designed and funded studies in the future, the commission did perform the most comprehensive study of the evidence

up until that time, and concluded that no reliable evidence was found to support the idea that exposure to explicit sexual materials is related to the development of delinquent or criminal sexual behavior among youths or adults, so adults should be able to decide for themselves what they will or will not read (Einsiedel, 1989).

In other words, the commission recommended that the state stop worrying so much about pornography, which the commission saw as a relatively insignificant threat to society. The U.S. Senate was not happy with the commission's conclusions and condemned its members.

1986 ATTORNEY GENERAL'S COMMISSION ON PORNOGRAPHY (THE "MEESE COMMISSION")
In 1985, President Ronald Reagan appointed Attorney General Edwin Meese to head a new commission that he expected to overturn the 1970 commission's findings. In fact, the official charter of the Meese Commission was to find "more effective ways in which the spread of pornography could be contained" (Berger et al., 1991, p. 25); thus, it already assumed that pornography was dangerous or undesirable and needed containment. Whereas the 1970 commission focused on social science, the Meese Commission listened to experts and laypeople through public hearings around the country, most of whom supported restricting or eliminating sexually graphic materials. Virtually every claim made by antipornography activists was cited in the report as fact with little or no supporting evidence, and those who did not support the commission's positions were treated rudely or with hostility (Berger et al., 1991).

The Meese Commission divided pornography into several categories: violent pornography, "degrading" pornography (e.g., anal sex, group sex, homosexual depictions), and nonviolent/nondegrading pornography. The commission used a selection of scientific studies to claim that the first two categories are damaging and may be considered a type of social violence, and that they hurt women most of all. Overall, the Meese Commission came to the opposite conclusions of the 1970 commission and made a number of recommendations:

- Antipornography laws were sufficient as they were written, but law enforcement efforts should be increased at all levels.

- Convicted pornographers should forfeit their profits and be liable to have property used in production or distribution of pornography confiscated, and repeat offenses against the obscenity laws should be considered felonies.

- Religious and civic groups should picket and protest institutions that peddle offensive materials.

- Congress should ban obscene cable television, telephone sex lines, and child pornography in any form.

Reaction to the Meese Commission was immediate and strong. Many of the leading sexuality researchers cited by the commission in support of its conclusions condemned the report and accused the commission of intentional misinterpretation of their scientific evidence. The Moral Majority, the religious right, and conservative supporters hailed the findings as long overdue. Women's groups were split on how to react to the report. On the one hand, the report used feminist language and adopted the position that pornography damages women. Antiporn feminists saw in Meese a possible ally to get pornography banned or at least restricted, and thus supported the Meese Commission's conclusions, if not its spirit. Other women's groups, however, were very wary of the commission's antigay postures and conservative bent, and they worried that the report would be used to justify wholesale censorship.

The Pornography Debates

The religious conservative opposition to pornography is based on a belief that people have an inherent human desire to sin, and that pornography reinforces that tendency and so undermines the family, traditional authority, and the moral fabric of society (Berger et al., 1991). Unless strong social standards are kept, people will indulge themselves in individual fulfillment and pleasure, promoting material rather than spiritual or moral values (Downs, 1989). Users of pornography become desensitized to shocking sexual behaviors, and pornography teaches them to see sex as simple physical pleasure rather than a part of a loving, committed relationship. This leads to increased teen pregnancy rates, degradation of females, and sexual assault; in this, at least, the religious conservative antipornography school agrees with the antiporn feminists.

Nowhere has the issue of pornography been as divisive as among feminist scholars, splitting them into two general schools. The antipornography feminists see pornography as an assault on women that silences them, renders them powerless, reinforces male dominance, and indirectly encourages sexual and physical abuse against women. The other side, which includes groups such as the Feminist Anticensorship Taskforce (FACT), argues that censorship of sexual materials will eventually (if not immediately) be used to censor such things as feminist writing and gay erotica, and would therefore endanger women's rights and freedoms of expression (Cowan, 1992). Some who argue against the antipornography feminists call themselves the "anti-antiporn" contingent, but for simplicity's sake, we refer to them simply as the "anticensorship" group.

ON YOUR MIND

I've watched pornography, and I'm just curious about condom use. Are there any rules about using condoms on the sets of pornographic movies?

Although many adult film actors are not legally required to use condoms during filming, some production companies require them. Producers who don't mandate the use of condoms argue that viewers don't want to watch safe sex in porn and that scenes with condoms take too long to shoot (Liu, 2004; Madigan, 2004). Actors are required to undergo monthly testing for STIs, but as you learned from Chapter 15, many infections may not show up in testing until many weeks after a person becomes infected. As we have discussed, some states, including California, have passed legislation that requires condom use during filming.

Antipornography Arguments

One of the scholars who has written most forcefully and articulately against pornography is Catherine MacKinnon (1985, 1987, 1993). MacKinnon argues that pornography cannot be understood separately from the long history of male domination of women, and that it is, in fact, an integral part and a reinforcing element of women's second-class status. According to MacKinnon, pornography is less about sex than power. She argues that pornography is a discriminatory social practice that institutionalizes the inferiority and subordination of one group by another, the way segregation institutionalized the subordination of Blacks by Whites.

MacKinnon suggests that defending pornography on First Amendment terms as protected free speech is to misunderstand the influence of pornography on the everyday lives of women in society. She suggests thinking of pornography itself as a violation of a woman's right not to be discriminated against, guaranteed by the Fourteenth Amendment. Imagine, she suggests, if the thousands of movies and books produced each year by the pornographic industry were not showing women, but rather Jews, Blacks, the handicapped, or some other minority splayed naked, often chained or tied up, urinated and defecated on, with foreign objects inserted into their orifices, while at the same time physical and sexual assaults against that group were epidemic in society (as they are against women). Would people still appeal to the First Amendment to prevent some kind of action?

Other feminists take this argument a step further and claim that male sexuality is by its nature subordinating; Andrea Dworkin (1981, 1987), for example, is uncompromising about men and their sexuality. Dworkin, like MacKinnon, sees pornography as a central aspect of male power, which she sees as a long-term strategy to elevate men to a superior position in society by forcing even strong women to feign weakness and dependency. Even sexuality reflects male power: Dworkin sees every act of intercourse as an assault, because men are the penetrators and women are penetrated.

Because pornography is harmful in and of itself, such authors claim it should be controlled or banned. Although they have not had much success passing such laws in the United States, their strong arguments have set the agenda for the public debate over pornography.

Anticensorship Arguments

A number of critics have responded to the arguments put forth by people like MacKinnon and Dworkin (Kaminer, 1992; Posner, 1993; Wolf, 1991). First, many argue that a restriction against pornography cannot be separated from a restriction against writing or pictures that show other oppressed minorities in subordinate positions. Once we start restricting all portrayals of minorities being subordinated, we are becoming a society ruled by censorship. Many Hollywood movies, television shows, and even women's romance novels portray women as subordinate or secondary to men. Are all of those to be censored, too? MacKinnon seems to make little distinction between *Playboy* and movies that portray violent rape. Are all sexual portrayals of the female body or of intercourse harmful to women?

Also, what about lesbian pornography, in which the models and the intended audience are female, and men almost wholly excluded? Many of these portrayals are explicitly geared toward resisting society's established sexual hierarchies (Henderson, 1991). Should they also be censored? Once sexually explicit portrayals are suppressed, anticensorship advocates argue, so are the portrayals that try to challenge sexual stereotypes.

A more complicated issue is the antiporn group's claim that pornography harms women. One response is to suggest that such an argument once again casts men in a more powerful position than women and, by denying women's power, supports the very hierarchy it seeks to dismantle. But the question of whether it can be demonstrated that pornography actually harms women is a difficult one.

Studies on the Harmful Effects of Pornography

Both sides of the pornography debate have produced reams of studies that support their side; the Meese Commission and antiporn feminists such as MacKinnon and Dworkin have produced papers showing that pornography is tied to rape, assault, and negative attitudes toward women, and others have produced studies showing that pornography has no effects or is secondary to more powerful forces (Fisher & Barak, 1991). More recent experts argue that pornography is linked to failed relationships and negative attitudes about women (Paul, 2005). Who is right?

Society-Wide Studies

In 1969, J. Edgar Hoover, director of the FBI, submitted evidence to the Presidential Commission on Obscenity and Pornography claiming that police observation had led him to believe the following:

A disproportionate number of sex offenders were found to have large quantities of pornographic materials in their residences . . . more, in the opinion of witnesses, than one would expect to find in the residences of a random sample of non-offenders of the same sex, age, and socioeconomic status, or in the residences of a random sample of offenders whose offenses were not sex offenses. (Quoted in Hunter et al., 1993, p. 226)

Correlations like these have been used since the early 19th century to justify attitudes toward pornography (Hunter et al., 1993). Such claims are easily criticized on scientific grounds because a "witness's opinion" cannot be relied on (and there has never been a study that has reliably determined the amount of pornography in the "average" nonoffender or non–sex offender's home). Better evidence is suggested in the state-by-state studies (Baron & Straus, 1987; Scott & Schwalm, 1988). Both groups of researchers found a direct nationwide correlation between rape and sexually explicit magazines: Rape rates are highest in those places with the highest circulation of sex magazines.

However, Denmark, which decriminalized pornography in the 1960s, and Japan, where pornography is sold freely and tends to be dominated by rape and bondage scenes, have low rates of reported rape, relative to the United States (Davies, 1997; Posner, 1993). In a study of four countries over 20 years, Kutchinsky (1991) could find no increase in rape relative to other crimes in any of the countries, even as the availability of pornography increased dramatically. Baron (1990), the same researcher who found that rape rates correlated with explicit magazines, did a further study, which showed that gender equality was higher in states with higher circulation rates of sexually explicit magazines. This may be because those states are generally more liberal. Women in societies that forbid or repress pornography (such as Islamic societies) tend to be more oppressed than those in societies in which it is freely available. All in all, the effects of pornography on a society's violence toward women are far from clear.

Individual Studies

Several laboratory studies have sought to determine the reactions of men exposed to different types of pornography. In most cases, men are shown pornography and then a test is done to determine whether their attitudes toward women, sex crimes, and the like are altered. Although little evidence indicates that nonviolent, sexually explicit films provoke antifemale reactions in men, many studies have shown that violent or degrading pornography does influence attitudes (Davies, 1997; Malamuth et al., 2012). Viewing sexual violence and degradation increases fantasies of sexual assault, the belief that some women secretly desire to be sexually assaulted, acceptance of violence against women, insensitivity to sexual assault victims, desire for sex without emotional involvement, the treatment of women as sex objects, and desire to see more violent pornography (Coyne, 2016; Fisher & Barak, 1991; Gervais & Eagan, 2017).

However, these studies take place under artificial conditions (Would these men have chosen to see such movies if not in a study?), and feelings of sexual aggression in a laboratory may not mirror a person's activities in the real world. It is also unclear how long such feelings last and whether they really influence behavior (Kutchinsky, 1991). Other studies show that men's aggression tends to increase after seeing any violent movie, even if it is not sexual, and so the explicit sexuality of the movies may not be the important

Ian Dagnall/Alamy Stock Photo

Pornhub, founded in 2007, is the single largest pornographic website on the Internet. In 2015, the company announced plans to shoot the first porn video in space, titled *Sexplorations*.

factor (Arriaga et al., 2015; Linz & Donnerstein, 1992). A study on the self-perceived effects of pornography use in Danish men and women 18 to 30 years old found few negative effects (Hald & Malamuth, 2008). In fact, participants reported that the use of pornography had an overall positive effect on various aspects of their lives.

Are We Missing the Point?

Lahey (1991) argues that the attempt to determine the effects of viewing pornography misses the point because, once again, the focus is on men and their reactions. Is it not enough that women feel belittled, humiliated, and degraded? The voice of women is silent in pornography studies. The questions focus on whether pornography induces sexual violence in men. Pornography, Lahey (after MacKinnon and Dworkin) argues, harms women by teaching falsehoods about them (that they enjoy painful sex, are not as worthy as men, secretly desire sex even when they refuse it, and do not know what they really like); it harms women's self-esteem; and it harms women by reproducing itself in men's behavior toward women.

Certainly, there is an argument to be made that certain kinds of sexually explicit materials contribute little to society and cause much pain directly and indirectly to women. Many who defend sexually explicit materials that show consensual sex abhor the violent and degrading pornography that is the particular target of feminist ire. Whether the way to respond to such materials is through new laws (which may do little to stop its production; for example, child pornography, which is illegal, flourishes in the United States; Wolak et al., 2005) or through listening to the voices of women, who are its victims, is an open question.

> **REAL RESEARCH** Heterosexual men who watch pornographic videos containing images of naked men with a woman have been found to have higher quality sperm than heterosexual men who watch similar videos containing only women (KILGALLON & SIMMONS, 2005). Researchers suggest this is due to a perceived sperm competition, wherein a heterosexual male produces higher quality sperm when there is a threat of a female choosing another male.

The Adult Entertainment Industry

The global adult entertainment industry is one of the largest and most profitable industries in the world. It includes pornographic products such as magazines, comics, movies, pay-per-view, and online porn. To give you a better idea of the profits involved, consider this: the adult film industry makes more than $13 billion in profits each year, while mainstream Hollywood movies make around $9 billion in profits each year (Alessi, 2014). Many of the online buying features available through the Internet and smartphones today (such as real-time credit card processing) were developed by the pornography industry (Griffiths, 2003). The accessibility, anonymity, and ease of use have all contributed to the growing popularity of the Internet. It's estimated that up to 87% of young adult men and 37% of young adult women report regular use of pornography (Wright et al., 2013). The move from magazine

Virtual reality headsets have changed how people can use pornography. They can give users an opportunity to become participants in porn, rather than just observers.

porn to Internet porn has been found to potentially be associated with more explicit and violent content (Wood et al., 2017).

There has been a vocal debate about mandatory condom use in adult films. Measure B, known as the County of Los Angeles Safer Sex in the Adult Film Industry Act, imposed the use of condoms during all vaginal and anal sex scenes in pornographic productions. The overwhelming majority of U.S. porn films are made in California. Supporters believed that Measure B would stop the spread of disease, protect industry workers, and save tax dollars. However, those who opposed the legislation claimed it was a waste of taxpayer money and would drive the porn industry out of California (which is has—a growing number of pornographic films are shot in Las Vegas, which does not require condom use). In 2014, the California Assembly passed a bill to require condom use in pornographic films shot in the state (Greenblatt, 2014). Many in the adult film industry opposed the bill, believing that voluntary safeguards such as routine testing for sexually transmitted infections were enough to protect adults who star in pornographic films.

While some experts believe that pornography is related to greater sexual knowledge and openness to new sexual experiences (Grov et al., 2011; Weinberg et al., 2010), other studies have found that it can have negative effects (Armstrong, 2017; Nelson et al., 2016; Wood et al., 2017). Men who regularly use pornography are less likely to be sexually satisfied with their real-life partner sex (Sun et al., 2014; see Chapter 14). A number of studies have found that pornography can contribute to mental health issues and cause relationship difficulties (Lambert et al., 2012; Ley et al., 2014; Short et al., 2012; see Chapter 16 for more information about Internet sexual addictions). Although porn addiction is not a clinically diagnosed condition, there are a significant number of men who admit

> **virtual reality pornography**
> Online pornography that enables users to become an active part of virtual sexual experiences using headsets to view 360-degree content.

they were addicted to pornography (mostly online). Today many websites cater to men who want to stop watching porn and/or those who have successfully given it up (such as the "Pornfree" subreddit).

Finally, **virtual reality (VR) pornography**, which enables users to become an active part of virtual sexual experiences using headsets to view 360-degree content, has also gained in popularity. There was a 250% increase in the availability of VR pornography in 2016 alone (Weston, 2017). VR porn raises many issues involving sexual consent, cheating, and the exploitation of women. Certainly, the development of new technologies will present challenges to those who want to regulate or control the public's access to sexually explicit materials. Over the next few years it will be interesting to see what happens to the adult entertainment industry.

Public Attitudes About Pornography

It is not only scholars and activists who disagree about pornography; the general public seems profoundly ambivalent about it as well. The majority want to ban violent pornography and feel that such pornography can lead to a loss of respect for women and increases in sexual violence.

Pornography is a difficult and controversial problem in American society. By arguing that sex is the only part of human life that should not be portrayed in our art and media, the core conflict over sexuality is revealed: People seem to believe that although sexuality is a central part of human life, it should still be treated differently than other human actions, as a category unto itself.

Review Questions

1 Explain how courts define *pornography* and *obscenity*.

2 Discuss and differentiate between the two commissions on pornography, and explain the findings of each.

3 Differentiate between the antipornography and anticensorship arguments.

4 Describe the studies that have been done on the harmful effects of pornography.

5 Discuss the adult entertainment industry.

6 Discuss public attitudes about pornography.

Sex Work: Trading Sex for Money

Thus far we have explored how sexual images have been used to sell everything from jeans to perfume and how sex has been used in television, movies, and films to increase viewership and ratings. We also looked at pornography's history, its presence on the Internet, and the public's response to it. Now we turn our attention to those who work in the sex industry, such as sex workers and those who work in the porn industry (in the accompanying "Sex in Real Life" feature, one college student talks about his experiences being a "porn star"). One of the oldest forms of sex work is prostitution (also referred to as "hooking," with prostitutes being referred to as "hookers"), which we focus on in this section.

Defining sex work and prostitution is not easy. The U.S. legal code is ambiguous about what constitutes sex work; for instance, some state penal codes define it as the act of hiring out one's body for sexual intercourse, whereas other states define it as sexual intercourse in exchange for money or as any sexual behavior that is sold for profit. This text defines sex work as the exchange of money or goods for sexual services. This can include a wide range of sexual behaviors from erotic interactions without physical contact to high-risk sexual behaviors (Harcourt & Donovan, 2005).

Researchers have found the study of sex work a challenge, because the exact size of the population is unknown, making a representative sample difficult to come by (Shaver, 2005). Also, because sex work is illegal in the United States, except for certain counties

Yaacov Dagan/Alamy Stock Photo

People get involved in the pornographic industry for a variety of different reasons. While some claim they chose to get involved for financial or personal reasons, others report being pressured or forced to participate.

in Nevada, many sex workers are hidden, so their behaviors cannot be measured. It is estimated that there are as many as 2 million sex workers in the United States today, some full time and some part time. Overall, there are more female sex workers working with male clients than all other forms combined (Goode, 1994; Perkins & Bennett, 1985). Although the use of sex workers is significantly underreported, studies have found that 2% to 3% of adult male residents of large metropolitan areas in the United States have patronized local sex workers (Brewer et al., 2008).

Sociological Aspects of Sex Work

Society has created social institutions such as marriage and the family in part to regulate sexual behavior. However, it is also true that, throughout history, people have had sexual relations outside these institutions. Sex work has existed, in one form or another, as long as marriage has, which has led some to argue that it provides a needed sexual release. Whether a society should recognize this by allowing legal, regulated sex work, however, raises a number of controversial social, political, economic, and religious questions.

Some sociologists suggest that sex work developed out of the patriarchal nature of most societies. In a society in which men are valued over women and men hold the reins of economic and political power, some women exploit the only asset that cannot be taken away from them—their sexuality. Other sociologists used to claim that women actually benefited from sex work because, from a purely economic point of view, they get paid for giving something away that is free to them. Kingsley Davis, one of the most famous sociologists of the 20th century, wrote:

> The woman may suffer no loss at all, yet receive a generous reward, resembling the artist who, paid for his work, loves it so well that he would paint anyway. Purely from the angle of economic return, the hard question is not why so many women become prostitutes, but why so few of them do. (Quoted in Benjamin, 1961, p. 876)

Types of Sex Workers

Sex work is mostly a gendered phenomenon, with women doing most of the selling and men doing most of the buying (Oselin, 2010). By far, the main motivation for becoming a sex worker is economic (Harcourt & Donovan, 2005). In this section, we discuss female, male, and adolescent sex workers.

Female Sex Workers

Female sex workers (FSWs) in the United States are young. The average age of entry into sex work is 14 years old (Dittmann, 2005). One study found that 75% of FSWs were younger than 25 and single (Medrano et al., 2003; Potterat et al., 1990).

Typically, FSWs live in an apartment or home with several other sex workers and one pimp. This is known as a **pseudofamily**. The pseudofamily operates much like a family does; there are rules

and responsibilities for all family members (Romenesko & Miller, 1989). The pimp is responsible for protecting the FSWs, whereas the women are responsible for bringing home the money. Other household responsibilities are also agreed on. When the female ages or the pimp tires of her, she may be traded like a slave or simply disowned.

Psychological problems are common in female sex workers and more common in older FSWs compared to younger (deSchampheleire, 1990). Dangers associated with a life of sex work, including stressful family situations and mistreatment by clients or pimps, often lead to drugs or alcohol, although many enter sex work to enable them to make enough money to support their pre-existing addictions. Many women who become sex workers have drug addictions and use the sex work as a way to help pay for their drugs (Potterat et al., 1998).

Entry into sex work is often a gradual process. At first, the activity may bother FSWs, but as time goes by, they become accustomed to the life and begin to see themselves and the profession differently (Goode, 1994). A regular customer visits the FSW at least once a week, and some have sexual encounters two or three times each week or spend several hours at a hotel (or one of their homes) together. Many FSWs want to escape from sex work (Farley et al., 2003).

ON YOUR MIND

Do sex workers enjoy having sex?

Having sex with whom? The majority of sex workers have sexual lives outside of their professional lives. As for sex with clients, although some sex workers report that they enjoy both sexual intercourse and oral sex, the majority do not. Some do experience orgasms in their interactions with clients, but again, the majority do not. In fact, in Masters and Johnson's early research on sexual functioning, they included sex workers (see Chapter 2) but found that the pelvic congestion in sex workers, which resulted from having sex without orgasms, made them poor subjects for their studies.

PREDISPOSING FACTORS FOR ENGAGING IN FEMALE SEX WORK
Some common threads run through the lives of many FSWs. The most common factor, according to researchers, is an economically deprived upbringing (Goode, 1994). However, because high-class sex workers, who often come from wealthy backgrounds, are less likely to be caught and arrested, research studies may concentrate too much on poorer women.

Early sexual contact with multiple partners has also been found to be related to female sex work. FSWs are also more often victims of sexual abuse, initiate sexual activity at a younger age, and experience a higher frequency of sexual assault. Intrafamilial violence and past physical and sexual abuse are also common (Mitchell et al., 2010; Murphy, 2010). Overall, Black women who

pseudofamily
A type of family that develops when sex workers and pimps live together; rules, household responsibilities, and work activities are agreed on by all members of the family.

have a history of emotional or physical abuse have been found to be more likely to engage in sex work than White or Hispanic women with similar abuse (Medrano et al., 2003).

Keep in mind that although these factors contribute to a predisposition to sex work, they do not cause a woman to become a sex worker. For example, it is known that many FSWs have had no early sex education either in school or from their family; however, this does not mean that the lack of sex education caused them to become FSWs. Many different roads lead to a life of sex work.

TYPES OF FEMALE SEX WORKERS Female sex workers can solicit their services in the street, clubs, brothels, as **call girls** or **courtesans**, or out of an **escort agency** (Harcourt & Donovan, 2005; Perkins & Bennett, 1985). These types of FSWs differ with respect to the work setting, prices charged, and safety from violence and arrest.

The most widespread type of FSWs is streetwalkers (Harcourt & Donovan, 2005). To attract customers, they dress in tight clothes and high heels and may work on street corners or in transportation stops (Riccio, 1992). This type of sex work is considered the most dangerous type because streetwalkers are often victims of violence, sexual assault, and robbery (Dalla, 2002; Romero-Daza et al., 2003).

Streetwalkers generally approach customers and ask them questions, such as "Looking for some action?" or "Do you need a date?" If the client is interested, the sex worker will suggest a price, and they will go to a place where the service can be provided (an alley, car, or cheap hotel room). In places where there is a lack of privacy, streetwalkers often provide oral sex or "hand relief" (Harcourt & Donovan, 2005). Other sex workers actively seek out clients via CB radio while driving on the highway, stopping at truck or rest stops to service the clients (Harcourt & Donovan, 2005; Luxenburg & Klein, 1984).

Indoor sex work offers more protection from violence and less police arrests. It includes club or bar sex workers, who solicit clients and perform services on site or at an agreed-on location (Harcourt & Donovan, 2005). **Brothel** sex work is another type of indoor sex work. Brothels vary with respect to their size and design, but they are typically found in places where there is an active sex industry, and they are regulated by the state (Harcourt & Donovan, 2005). In the United States, Nevada is the only state with counties in which brothels are legal, and sex workers carry identification cards and are routinely examined for STIs. When a customer walks into a brothel in Nevada, they may be given a "menu" of choices. From this menu they pick an appetizer (such as a hot bath or a pornographic video) and a main course (such as the specific sexual position). Then the customer can choose a person from a **lineup**, and the couple goes into a private room. The typical rate is $2 per minute, with more exotic services being more expensive. Usually conventional sexual intercourse costs $30 to $40, and oral sex may cost $50 or more.

Probably the most covert form of sex work is done through escort agencies (Harcourt & Donovan, 2005). High-class call girls and courtesans can be reached by phone and services are performed in a client's home or hotel room. In 2008, New York governor Eliot Spitzer was found to have had multiple liaisons with a variety of sex workers at the Emperor's Club V.I.P. The Emperor's

Xaveria Hollander, one of New York's leading madams for many years, opened the Vertical Whorehouse in 1969 but was arrested for prostitution and thrown out of the country a few years later. Today, she operates Xaverla's Happy House, a bed and breakfast, out of her home in Amsterdam, where I met with her and talked about her life in sex work.

Club operated out of New York, Washington, Miami, Paris, and London and offered sex workers for anywhere from $1,000 to $5,500 per hour.

Finally, another type of FSW includes **bondage and discipline (B&D) sex workers** who provide B&D services, using such things as leather, whips, and chains. Women who specialize in B&D will advertise with pseudonyms such as Madam Pain or Mistress Domination (Perkins & Bennett, 1985). B&D sex workers may have dungeons, complete with whips, racks, and leg irons, and wear black leather, studded belts, and masks. L

Male Sex Workers

Male sex workers (MSWs) may service both men and women. MSWs who service men are referred to as **hustlers** or "boys." Many MSWs who have sex with men may identify as heterosexual. Approximately 50% of MSWs are homosexual, 25% are bisexual, and 25% are heterosexual (Pleak & Meyer-Bahlburg, 1990). In many beach resorts around the globe, male "beachboys" or **gigolos** (JIG-uh-lows) are available to wealthier women for both social and

call girl
A higher class female sex worker who is often contacted by telephone and may either work by the hour or the evening or for longer periods.

courtesan
A sex worker who often interacts with men of rank or wealth.

escort agency
An agency set up to arrange escorts for unaccompanied males; sexual services are often involved.

brothel
A house of sex workers.

lineup
The lining up of sex workers in a brothel so that when clients enter a brothel, they can choose the worker they want.

bondage and discipline (B&D) sex worker
A sex worker who is paid to engage in bondage and discipline fantasy play with clients.

hustler
A male sex worker who provides sexual services to men.

gigolo
A man who is hired to have a sexual relationship with a woman and receives financial support from her.

Investigators believe that Eliot Spitzer spent up to $80,000 for sex workers over a period of several years. One woman he hired was Ashley Dupré, a $1,000-an-hour call girl working with the Emperor's Club V.I.P.

sexual needs (Harcourt & Donovan, 2005). Like women, men tend to enter into the life of sex work early, usually by the age of 16 (with a range from 12 to 19; Cates & Markley, 1992). The majority of MSWs are between the ages of 16 and 29 and are White (West, 1993). Like the pimp for FSWs, many MSWs also have mentors, or "sugar daddies."

When MSWs are asked what types of sexual behavior they engage in with their clients, 99% say that they perform fellatio, either alone or in combination with other activities; 80% say that they engage in anal sex, and 63% participate in anal rimming (anal oral sex; Morse et al., 1992).

PREDISPOSING FACTORS FOR ENGAGING IN MALE SEX WORK Like females, males engage in sex work mainly for economic reasons (Kaye, 2007). They typically view their work as a valid source of income (Bimbi, 2007). Several factors predispose a man to become a sex worker, including early childhood sexual experience (such as coerced sexual behavior) combined with a homosexual orientation (Earls & David, 1989). MSWs often experience their first sexual experience at a young age (approximately 12 years old) and have older partners. They often have fewer career aspirations than those not in the sex worker industry and are more likely to view themselves as addicted to either drugs or alcohol (Cates & Markley, 1992).

Like female streetwalkers, male streetwalkers have more psychopathologies than non–sex workers, which may have to do with their dangerous and chaotic environments (Simon et al., 1992). They are more suspicious, mistrustful, hopeless, lonely, and often lack meaningful interpersonal relationships (Leichtentritt & Arad, 2005). These feelings may develop out of the distrust that many

have for their clients; clients may refuse to pay for services, hurt them, or force them to do things that they do not want to do. In fact, more than half of MSWs report a fear of violence while they are hustling (Scott, 2005). Although many would like to stop prostituting, they feel that they would not be able to find other employment (Simon et al., 1992).

TYPES OF MALE SEX WORKERS   Male sex workers, like female sex workers, may engage in street hustling, bar hustling, and escort sex work. The differences between these types of sex workers are in income potential and personal safety.

Male street and bar hustlers solicit clients on the street or in parks that are known for the availability of the sexual trade. The majority of male sex workers begin with street hustling, especially if they are too young to get into bars. MSWs, like FSWs, ask their clients if they are "looking for some action."

Because of increasing fear and danger on the streets, many street hustlers eventually move into bars. One MSW explains:

> You got a lot of different kinds of assholes out there. When someone pulls up and says "get in," you get in. And you can look at their eyes, and they can be throwing fire out of their eyes, and have a knife under the seat. You're just in a bad situation. I avoid it by not hustling in the street. I hustle in the bars now. (Luckenbill, 1984, p. 288)

MSWs also report that bar hustling enables them to make more money than street hustling because they get to set their own prices. The average price for a bar trick ranges from $50 to $75. A natural progression after bar hustling is working as an escort, which involves finding someone who arranges clients but also takes a share of the profits. Each date that is arranged for an escort can bring from $150 to $200, and the sex worker usually keeps 60% for themselves. However, escort services are not always well-run or honest operations, and problems with escort operators may force a MSW to return to bar hustling. Compared with other types of MSWs, however, escorts are least likely to be arrested.

Adolescent Sex Workers

What is known about adolescent sex workers is disheartening. For adolescents who run away from home, sex work offers a way to earn money and to establish their autonomy. Many of these adolescents have been sexually abused and have psychological problems (Thompson, 2005; Walker, 2002). Adolescent sex work can have long-term psychological and sociological effects on the adolescents and their families (Landau, 1987).

Many teenagers run away from home each year in the United States, and more than 85% of those who do eventually become involved in sex work (Hammer et al., 2002; Landau, 1987). Others engage in sex work while living at home. Stories about adolescent sex workers are often tragic, like the following from Lynn, a 13-year-old sex worker:

> It was freezing cold that Friday afternoon as I stood on the street corner looking for buyers. The harsh wind made the temperature feel as though it was below zero, and I had been outdoors for almost two and a half hours already. I was wearing a

short fake fur jacket, a brown suede miniskirt and spike heels. Only a pair of very sheer hose covered my legs, and I shook as I smiled and tried to flag down passing cars with male drivers.

Finally, a middle-aged man in an expensive red sports car pulled up to the curb. He lowered the car window and beckoned me over to him with his finger. I braced myself to start my act. Trying as hard as I could to grin and liven up my walk, I went over to his car, rested my chest on the open window ledge and said, "Hi ya, Handsome." He answered, "Hello, Little Miss Moffet. How'd you like Handsome to warm you up on a cold day like this?" I wished that I could have told him that I wouldn't like it at all. That even the thought of it made me sick to my stomach. I hid my feelings and tried to look enthusiastic. So with the broadest smile I could manage, I answered, "There's nothing I'd like better than to be with you, Sir." I started to get into his car, but he stopped me, saying, "Not so fast, Honey, how much is this going to cost me?" I hesitated for a moment. I really wanted twenty dollars, but it had been a slow day and I had a strong feeling that this guy wasn't going to spring for it, so I replied, "Fifteen dollars, and the price of the hotel room."

We had sex in the same run-down dirty hotel that I always take my tricks to. It doesn't cost much, and usually that's all that really matters to them. Being with that guy was horrible, just like it always turns out to be. That old overweight man sweated all over me and made me call him Daddy the whole time. He kept calling me Marcy, and later he explained that Marcy was his youngest daughter. Once he finished with me, the guy seemed in a big hurry to leave. He dressed quickly, and just as he was about to rush out the door, I yelled out, "But what about my money?" He pulled a ten-dollar bill out of his back pocket and laid it on the dresser, saying only, "Sorry, kid, this is all I've got on me right now."

At that moment I wished that I could have killed him, but I knew that there was nothing I could do. The middle-class man in the expensive red sports car had cheated his 13-year-old hooker. That meant that I had to go back out on the street and brave the cold again in order to find another taker. (Landau, 1987, pp. 25–26)

Pimps look for scared adolescent runaways on the street or at train and bus stations, luring them with promises of friendship and potential love relationships. A pimp will approach a runaway in a very caring and friendly way, offering to buy her a meal or give her a place to stay. At first, he makes no sexual demands whatsoever. He buys her clothes and meals and does whatever it takes to make her feel indebted to him. To him, all of his purchases are a debt she will one day repay. As soon as the relationship becomes sexual and the girl has professed her love for the pimp, he begins asking her to "prove" her love by selling her body. The girl may agree to do so only once, not realizing the destructive cycle she is beginning. This cycle is based on breaking down her self-esteem and increasing her feelings of helplessness. Male adolescents may enter into the life of sex work in similar ways. Some may choose a life of sex work to meet their survival needs or to support a drug habit.

Outside the United States, adolescent sex work is prevalent in many countries, such as Brazil and Thailand. Female adolescents in Brazil are drawn to sex work primarily for economic reasons (Penna-Firme et al., 1991; sex trafficking is discussed later in this chapter). In Thailand, some parents sell their daughter's virginity for money or act as their managers and arrange jobs for them.

Other Players in the Business

Sex workers are not the only people involved in the business. Other players include pimps and clients.

Pimps

Pimps play an important role in sex work, although not all sex workers have pimps. In exchange for money, a pimp offers a sex worker protection from both clients and the police. Many pimps take all of a female sex worker's earnings and manage the money, providing her with clothes, jewels, food, and sometimes a place to live. Many pimps feel powerful within their peer group and enjoy the fact that their job is not particularly stressful for them. Pimps often require that their FSWs make a certain amount of money (Dalla, 2002). A pimp recruits FSWs and will often manage a group of sex workers, known as his "stable" (Ward et al., 1994). He is typically sexually involved with many of them.

Clients

Clients of sex workers are often referred to as **johns** or **tricks** (Brooks-Gordon & Geisthorpe, 2003). The term *trick* has also been used to describe the behavior requested by the client. This term originated from the idea that the client was being "tricked" out of something, mainly his money (Goode, 1994).

What motivates people to use sex workers? Sigmund Freud believed that some men preferred sex with workers because they were incapable of sexual arousal without feeling that their partner was inferior or a "bad" woman. Carl Jung went a step further and claimed that sex work was tied to various unconscious **archetypes**, such as the "Great Mother." This archetype includes feelings of hatred and sexuality, which are connected to mother figures. This, in turn, leads men to have impersonal sex with partners whom they do not love or to whom they have no attraction.

There is much confusion about clients and the reasons they visit sex workers (Brooks-Gordon & Geisthorpe, 2003). What is known is that the majority of clients of sex workers are male, and they visit sex workers for a variety of reasons: for guaranteed sex, to eliminate the risk for rejection, for greater control in sexual encounters, for companionship, to have undivided attention, a lack of sexual outlets, physical or mental handicaps, for adventure or curiosity, or to relieve loneliness (Jordan, 1997; McKeganey & Bernard, 1996; Monto, 2000, 2001). Married men may seek out sex workers when their wives will not perform certain sexual behaviors, when they feel guilty about asking their wives to engage

pimp	**trick**
A slang term that refers to the male in charge of organizing clients for a female sex worker.	A slang term that refers to the sexual services of a sex worker; also may refer to a john.
john	**archetypes**
A slang term that refers to a sex worker's client.	Ancient images that Carl Jung believed we are born with and influenced by.

in an activity, or when they feel the behaviors are too deviant to discuss with their wives (Jordan, 1997). A nonscientific study done in 2008 interviewed men who had paid for sex and found that the majority of men felt highly conflicted about their behavior (Heinzmann, 2008). Eighty-three percent of men said they kept returning to sex workers because it was an "addiction," and 40% said they were drunk when they went. One client felt it was all about business: "Prostitutes are a product, like cereal. You go to the grocery, pick the brand you want and pay for it. It's business" (Heinzmann, 2008).

When men who were arrested for soliciting sex workers were asked which sexual behaviors they engaged in, 81% had received fellatio, 55% had engaged in sexual intercourse, whereas others engaged in a little of both or manual masturbation (i.e., hand jobs; Monto, 2001). Sadomasochistic behavior, with the woman as dominant and the man submissive, is the most common form of "kinky" sexual behavior requested from sex workers (Goode, 1994). Other commonly requested behaviors include clients dressing as women, masturbating in front of nude clients, and rubber fetishes. One FSW recalled a job in which she was paid $300 to dress up in a long gown and urinate in a cup while her client masturbated, and another was asked to have sex with a client in his daughter's bed (Dalla, 2002).

Clients may also seek out sex workers because they are afraid of emotional commitments and want to keep things uninvolved (which is what Eliot Spitzer, the governor of New York, said about his liaisons with call girls); to build up their egos (many FSWs fake orgasm and act very sexually satisfied); because they are starved for affection and intimacy; or because they travel a great deal or work in heavily male-populated areas (such as in the armed services) and desire sexual activity.

Kinsey found that clients of sex workers are predominantly White, middle-class, unmarried men who are between the ages of 30 and 60 (Kinsey et al., 1948). More recent research supports Kinsey's findings—the majority of men who visit sex workers are middle-aged and unmarried (or unhappily married; Monto & McRee, 2005). They also tend to be regular or repeat clients: Almost 100% go monthly or more frequently, and 50% of these go weekly or more frequently (Freund et al., 1991). "Regulars" often pay more than new customers and are a consistent source of income (Dalla, 2002).

The majority of clients are not concerned with the police because law enforcement is usually directed at the sex workers rather than clients. However, some authorities have gone so far as videotaping license plates and enrolling clients in "john school" to stop their behaviors (Fisher et al., 2002).

REAL RESEARCH The National Health and Social Life Survey found a substantial discrepancy between men's and women's interest in fellatio. Although 45% of men reported receiving fellatio as very appealing, only 17% of women found giving it appealing (Monto, 2001). Not surprisingly, fellatio is the most requested sexual behavior from sex workers (Monto, 2001).

The Government's Role in Sex Work

Sex work is illegal in every state in the United States, except, as noted earlier, for certain counties in Nevada. However, even though it is illegal, it still exists in almost every large U.S. city. In general, the government could address the issue of sex work in two ways. It could remain a criminal offense, or it could be legalized and regulated. If sex work were legalized, it would be subject to government regulation over such things as licensing, location, health standards, and advertising.

The biggest roadblock to legalized sex work in the United States is that it is viewed as an immoral behavior by the majority of people (Rio, 1991). Laws that favor legal sex work would, in effect, be condoning the behavior. Overall, however, the strongest objections to legalized sex work are reactions to streetwalking. Today the majority of Americans believe that the potential benefits of legalized sex work should be evaluated.

Those who feel that sex work should be legalized believe that this would result in lower levels of STIs (because sex workers could be routinely checked for STIs) and less disorderly conduct. Another argument in favor of legalization is that if sex work were legal, the government would be able to collect taxes on the money earned by both sex workers and their pimps. Assuming a 25% tax rate, this gross income would produce more than $20 billion each year in previously uncollected taxes.

In parts of Nevada where sex work is legal, the overwhelming majority of people report that they favor legalized sex work. Ordinances in Nevada vary by county, with each county responsible for deciding whether sex work is legal throughout the county, only in certain districts, or not at all. For instance, there are no legal brothels in Reno or Las Vegas, perhaps because these cities enjoy large conventions and because many men attend these conventions without their partners. City officials felt that if a convention was held in a town with legalized sex work, many partners might not want the men to attend; thus, there would be a decrease in the number of convention participants. Even so, there are several brothels near Reno and Las Vegas, and also several that are close to state borders. Usually, these are the largest of all the Nevada brothels. Brothels are locally owned small businesses that cater to both local and tourist customers. Although sex work in Nevada is not a criminal offense, there are laws against enticing people into sex work, such as pimping or advertising for sex workers (Reynolds, 1986).

Crackdowns on sex work in other areas of the United States (where it is not legal) often result in driving it further underground. This is exactly what happened in New York City in the 1980s. After law officials closed down several brothels in Manhattan, many of them moved to Queens. Some of the sex workers began operating out of "massage parlors" or private homes, which were supported through drug money.

Many groups in the United States and abroad are working for the legalization of prostitution. In San Francisco in 1973, an organization called COYOTE ("Call Off Your Old Tired Ethics") was formed by an ex–sex worker named Margo St. James to change the public's views of sex work. COYOTE's mission was to repeal all laws against sex work, to reshape sex work into a credible occupation, and to protect the rights of sex workers. Members argued that contrary to popular belief, not all sex work is forced—some women voluntarily choose to become sex workers, and it should be respected as a career choice.

Delores French, a sex worker, author, president of the Florida COYOTE group, and president of HIRE ("Hooking Is Real Employment"), argued:

> A woman has the right to sell sexual services just as much as she has the right to sell her brains to a law firm when she works as a lawyer, or to sell her creative work to a museum when she works as an artist, or to sell her image to a photographer when she works as a model, or to sell her body when she works as a ballerina. Since most people can have sex without going to jail, there is no reason except old fashioned prudery to make sex for money illegal. (Quoted in Jenness, 1990, p. 405)

Sex Work and Sexually Transmitted Infections

Most U.S. sex workers are knowledgeable about STIs. They try to minimize their risks by using condoms, rejecting clients with obvious STIs, and routinely taking antibiotics. However, although female sex workers often do feel they are at risk for infection with STIs with clients, they usually do not feel this way with their longterm partners (Dorfman et al., 1992). Condoms are used less frequently with their own sexual partners than with clients. Among male sex workers who have sex with men, receptive anal intercourse without a condom is the most common mode of HIV transmission (Elifson et al., 1993), whereas among FSWs, intravenous drug use is the most common mode of HIV transmission.

Many opponents of legalized sex work claim that legalization would lead to increases in the transmission of various STIs. However, STI transmission and sex work have been found to have less of a relationship than you might think. Rates of STIs in Europe were found to decrease when sex work was legalized and to increase when it was illegal (Rio, 1991). This is probably because legalization can impose restrictions on the actual practice and require medical evaluations. Many sex workers take antibiotics sporadically to reduce the risk for STIs; however, this practice has led some strains of STIs to become resistant to various antibiotics. Also, as we discussed in Chapter 15, viral STIs, such as HIV and herpes, are not cured by antibiotics.

Quitting Sex Work

Sex work is considered by many to be a deviant, and often low-status, line of work. People in this industry are often labeled and stigmatized for working in an area that violates societal norms (Ebaugh, 1988; Oselin, 2010). Their job creates a role for them in society, which influences their view of the world and the behaviors they engage in. Because many sex workers see themselves as deviant, this makes it especially difficult to leave. In addition, few have support systems that could help them get out.

Women who do leave often have many reasons for doing so. One common reason involves religion and wanting to reestablish a religious lifestyle. One FSW who left the industry said:

> When I was working on the streets, I kept praying to God: This is not me. Why do I keep doing this? Why can't I stop? God help me stop. . . He was always there knocking I just had to open up the door to allow him to come in and help me stop. (Oselin, 2010, p. 532)

Other women leave because of fear and the experience of seeing all the violence on the streets. One FSW who left for this reason said:

> I thought I was going to die in the life because I didn't see any way out no matter how much I wanted it to end. Things were getting worse on the streets day by day. I've seen about five prostitutes I knew end up dead in garbage cans. (Oselin, 2010, p. 533)

Other women cite personal and family relationships, exhaustion, sobriety, and feeling too old to continue as reasons for quitting (Oselin, 2010). Research has found that between 60% and 75% of FSWs were sexually assaulted, whereas 70% to 95% were physically assaulted (U.S. Department of State, 2005). These experiences along with jail time, multiple pregnancies, and STIs can also be turning points for quitting the industry.

Another key factor in leaving sex work is finding an agency that offers assistance, such as a prostitution-helping organization (PHO; Oselin, 2010). These organizations provide information, assistance, and shelter for women who want to leave sex work. Sometimes their first interaction with a PHO is through a mobile outreach unit that appears in their neighborhood (Oselin, 2010). Other women find out about PHOs from counselors, jail personnel, friends, or advertising. One woman who found a PHO said:

> I couldn't do it alone. I tried before but it didn't work. I started to get back on drugs. And the only thing I knew was to go and get money from men [through sex] and once I started doing that I started using drugs too. The program offered me a different way out. I knew they helped you get an education, a job, and maintain sobriety. (Oselin, 2010, p. 544)

REAL RESEARCH More than 1 in 12 U.S. men report exchanging drugs, money, or a place to stay for sex with a female in the last year (DECKER et al., 2008).

Sex Work Around the World

During World War II, it is estimated that 200,000 women from Japan, Korea, China, the Philippines, Indonesia, Taiwan, and the Netherlands were taken by the Imperial Japanese Army from their hometowns and put in brothels for Japanese soldiers (Kakuchi, 2005).

In 1993, Japan finally admitted to having forced women to prostitute themselves as **comfort girls**, and in the early 2000s, these women demanded compensation for the suffering they were forced to endure. In 2005, the Women's Active Museum on War and Peace in Tokyo was opened to honor the women who worked as sex slaves during World War II.

A group named GABRIELA (General Assembly Binding Women for Reforms, Integrity, Equality, Leadership, and Action) has formed in the Philippines in an attempt to fight sex work, sexual harassment, rape, and battering of women. More than 100 women's organizations belong to GABRIELA, which supports the economic, health, and working conditions of women. GABRIELA operates free clinics for sex workers and also provides seminars and activities to educate the community about sex work (West, 1989).

Sex work has long been a part of the cultural practices in Thailand. Many countries, including the United States, Japan, Taiwan, South Korea, Australia, and Europe, organize "sex tours" to Thailand. Sex workers are so prevalent in Thailand that Thai men view a trip to a sex worker almost in the same regard as going to the store for milk (Sexwork.com, 1999a). It has also been suggested that because many Thais are Buddhists, they believe in reincarnation and hope that they will not be a sex worker in their next life. This belief in reincarnation often reduces the fear of death (Kirsch, 1985; Limanonda et al., 1993; Sexwork.com, 1999b). Sex work is endorsed by both men and women in Thailand, mainly because of the prevailing belief that men have greater sex drives than women (Taywaditep et al., 2004). In fact, college students in Thailand often report that sex work protects "good women" from being raped.

It is estimated that there are between 500,000 and 700,000 FSWs and between 5,000 and 8,000 MSWs in Thailand—working "direct" (in brothels or massage parlors) or "indirect" (available for dates and also offering sex for their customers). Direct sex workers make between $2 and $20 for a service, whereas indirect sex workers make between $20 and several hundred dollars (Taywaditep, 2004). Sex workers in Thailand are required to participate in the governmental STI monitoring system, which has helped decrease STI prevalence. Thailand has instituted a "100% condom use" program targeted at the sex work industry (Sharma, 2001). As a result, condom use by sex workers and clients is high. One study found that 79% of men used condoms with sex workers (compared with 4% of men using them with regular partners; Ford & Chamrathrithirong, 2007).

In Amsterdam, Holland, De Wallen is the largest and best known red-light district. This area is crowded with sex shops, adult movie and live theater shows, and street and window prostitutes. They are called "window" prostitutes because they sit behind a window and sell their bodies. There are approximately 200 such windows in the red-light district, which is one of the biggest tourist attractions in Amsterdam. Travel services run tours through the red-light district, although these tourists do not generally hire the sex workers. Sex work in Amsterdam is loosely regulated by authorities. Sex workers pay taxes, get regular checkups, and

At a beach resort in Thailand, young prostitutes wait for a buyer.

Stephen Shaver/Getty Images

participate in government-sponsored health and insurance plans (McDowell, 1986).

In Cuba, MSWs and FSWs who solicit tourists are known as *jineteros* (Espín et al., 2004). *Jineteros* exchange sex for clothing or other luxuries brought over from other countries. In Havana, teenagers offer sex to older tourists in exchange for a six-pack of cola or a dance club's cover charges. FSWs in Cuba also ply the tourist trade.

Although sex work exists all over the world, it is dealt with differently in each culture. We have much to learn from the way that other cultures deal with sex work. There are many places throughout the world where young girls are forced into sexual slavery against their will, which is discussed next.

De Wallen, also known as Rosse Buurt or the Red Light District, is a designated area for legalized sex work in Amsterdam, Holland.

Stefano Paterna/Alamy Stock Photo

comfort girl
A woman in Japan or the Philippines during World War II who was forced into sex work by the government to provide sex for soldiers; also called a hospitality girl.

Sex Trafficking: Modern-Day Slavery

Sex trafficking is the most common form of modern-day slavery and is one of the fastest growing organized crimes (Schauer & Wheaton, 2006; Walker-Rodriguez & Hill, 2011). Victims tend to come from countries such as Asia, the former Soviet Union, Africa, Eastern Europe, and the United States, and are most commonly trafficked to Italy, the United States, Germany, and the Netherlands (Hodge, 2008). The United States is the second largest destination and market country in the world for women and children trafficked by the sex industry (Germany is number one; Schauer & Wheaton, 2006).

Some victims are recruited via false-front agencies (such as modeling or employment agencies that pose as legitimate organizations), or they are approached because they are already working in sex work in their native country and are promised more money in wealthier nations (Hodge, 2008). Because many cannot afford the trip, they agree to work off their debts once they arrive in their new location (referred to as "debt bondage"; Hodge, 2008). For many others, there is no choice involved in the process—they are sold by poor family members or kidnapped.

Statistics

It is estimated that between 600,000 and 800,000 people are trafficked across international borders every year—80% of whom are female and 50% children (Hodge, 2008). Although we tend to think of sex trafficking as only an international problem, it is estimated that between 100,000 to 300,000 children are trafficked in the United States each year (Carr, 2009; Siskin & Wyler, 2013).

Victims

Traffickers often use force, drugs, and financial methods to control their victims (Walker-Rodriguez & Hill, 2011). Gang rapes and other forms of violence are common to force the victims to stay. Continuous abuse makes victims more likely to comply with the demands of the traffickers. One victim, a teen runaway from

Baltimore, Maryland, was gang-raped by an acquaintance of the trafficker, who "rescued" her and demanded she repay him by working as his prostitute (Walker-Rodriguez & Hill, 2011). Many of the women and girls are frightened and afraid to speak out against the traffickers.

The physical and psychological costs to victims of sexual trafficking are high. Many are locked in homes or brothels for weeks or months and are beaten and raped. Physical symptoms often include broken bones, bruises, cuts, and vaginal bleeding (Raymond & Hughes, 2001), whereas emotional symptoms include depression, anxiety, and posttraumatic stress disorder (Hodge, 2008).

Following is one young woman's testimony before the U.S. Senate Foreign Relations Committee in 2000:

When I was 14, a man came to my parents' house in Veracruz, Mexico, and asked me if I was interested in making money in the United States. He said I could make many times as much money doing the same things that I was doing in Mexico. At the time, I was working in a hotel cleaning rooms and I also helped around my house by watching my brothers and sisters. He said I would be in good hands, and would meet many other Mexican girls who had taken advantage of this great opportunity. My parents didn't want me to go, but I persuaded them.

A week later, I was smuggled into the United States through Texas to Orlando, Florida. It was then the men told me that my employment would consist of having sex with men for money. I had never had sex before, and I had never imagined selling my body. And so my nightmare began. Because I was a virgin, the men decided to initiate me by raping me again and again, to teach me how to have sex. Over the next three months, I was taken to a different trailer every 15 days. Every night I had to sleep in the same bed in which I had been forced to service customers all day. I couldn't do anything to stop it. I wasn't allowed to go outside without a guard. Many of the bosses had guns. I was constantly afraid. One of the bosses carried me off to a hotel one night, where he raped me. I could do nothing to stop him.

Because I was so young, I was always in demand with the customers. It was awful. Although the men were supposed to wear condoms, some didn't, so eventually I became pregnant and was forced to have an abortion. They sent me back to the

brothel almost immediately. I cannot forget what has happened. I can't put it behind me. I find it nearly impossible to trust people. I still feel shame. I was a decent girl in Mexico. I used to go to church with my family. I only wish none of this had ever happened. (Polaris Project, 2005)

Looking Forward

In 2000, the U.S. Congress passed the Trafficking Victims Protection Act, which was the first federal law that specifically addressed trafficking. This law has been reauthorized multiple times and has helped protect victims of sexual trafficking by increasing awareness and enforcing laws against sexual trafficking. It has also helped to create a "T-visa," which allows international victims to stay in the United States to assist federal authorities in the prosecution of traffickers. Victims may be moved into the witness protection program and granted permanent residency after 3 years (Hodge, 2008). The law helped to increase awareness, monitor the situation, and improve prosecution. The Federal Bureau of Investigation with the U.S. Immigration and Customs Enforcement agencies and other local, state, and federal law enforcement agencies work together to help combat sex trafficking of both U.S. and international victims.

Throughout this chapter, we have explored erotic representations in books, television, advertising, other media, and how sex is used to sell products. We have also examined the sale of sex itself through sex work. There are many effects to living in a society so saturated with sexual representations, and these effects certainly help shape our opinions and thoughts about men, women, and sexuality today.

Review Questions

1 Define sex trafficking and identify countries that are often involved in such practices.

2 Provide one way in which people become victims of sex trafficking.

3 Explain the methods that traffickers use to control their victims.

4 What is the U.S. government doing to help protect victims of trafficking?

Chapter Review

Summary Points

1 Our lives today are full of visual media: magazines, television, websites, billboards, and product packaging. Even food products are adorned with pictures of people and scenes. Advertisements stare at us, between articles in magazines and newspapers, plastered on billboards, walls, buses, taxis, and from the sidebars of social media. Moving images on television, in the movies, and on computers or smartphones surround us almost everywhere we go. Erotic representations have existed in almost all societies at almost all times; they have also been the subject of censorship by religious or governmental powers.

2 Pornography emerged as a separate category of erotic art during the 18th century. The printing press made it more readily available. Erotic novels first established pornography production as a business in the Western world, and it provoked a response of censorship from church and governmental authorities.

3 Since the early 1990s, representations in the U.S. mass media have become more explicitly erotic. Many of the images we see today are explicitly or subtly sexual. Barely clothed females and shirtless, athletic males are so common in our ads that we scarcely notice them anymore. Television and, to a lesser extent, movies have become the primary media in the United States, and they contain enormous amounts of sexually suggestive material. Certain groups have begun to organize to change the content of television programming.

4 Advertising has commercialized sexuality and uses an enormous amount of sexual imagery to sell products. Advertisements are becoming more sexually explicit in the general media in the United States. The purpose of advertising is threefold—to get your attention, to get you physiologically excited, and to associate that excitement with the product being advertised. The excitement can be intellectual, emotional, physical (sports, for example), or visual (fast-moving action, wild colors). Sexuality, especially female sexuality, has been used to sell products for decades.

5 Many gender stereotypes persist on American television. This is especially true in popular reality television shows, such as *Keeping Up with the Kardashians* or *The Bachelor*. Women in these shows are often self-centered and preoccupied with their looks and wealth. Stereotyping is often used to engage viewers. Since ratings are the most important aspect of these shows, the storylines and outcomes are often not based on truth or reality.

6 American teenagers watch a lot of television per day and the proliferation of new technologies on which to watch television, such as smartphones, iPads, laptops, and tablets, has significantly increased the overall amount of time that teens spend watching television shows. Like adults, the majority of teens record and watch their shows later and/or watch them on devices other than the television.

7 Historically, many children's shows have lacked positive female role models and offered stereotyped portrayals of men and women. American networks have turned to sex to increase their ratings, yet the constant presence of sexual themes on television is beginning to turn viewers away. Many Americans want stronger regulation of sexual content and profanity.

8 Advertising is a modern medium, and its influence pervades everyday life. There is practically no area free from its effects, from social media to consumer products and even to nature itself. Although studies indicate that advertising is becoming less sexist today, gender differences still exist.

9 The growth of new technologies has tremendously increased the amount of time that children and adults spend with various forms of electronic media. The average teen spends more than 11 hours a day with various electronic media (and the American Academy of Pediatrics recommends no more than two hours of electronic media per day for teenagers and young adults). An overuse of technology may also make it more difficult for adolescents to read emotions and have empathy for others.

10 Sexuality manifests itself online today in a variety of ways, including pornography sites, explicit videos and photos, image sharing, forums/subreddits, Tumblr, merchandising, streaming and camming, sites. Even spam email is often sex-related.

11 Pornography is one of the most difficult issues in public life in America. Feminists, conservatives, and the religious right argue that pornography is destructive, violates the rights of women, corrupts children, and should be banned or severely restricted. Liberals and critics of banning pornography argue that creating a definition of pornography that protects art and literature is impossible, that people have the right to read whatever materials they want in their own homes, and that censorship is a slippery slope that leads to further censorship. The public is split between these positions.

12 Court cases in the United States have established a three-part definition of obscenity that has determined how courts define pornography. For something to be obscene, it must appeal to the prurient interest, offend contemporary community standards, and lack serious literary, artistic, political, or scientific value.

13 A presidential commission is a special task force developed by the president of the United States that performs an investigation or research on a specific topic. There have been more than 100 presidential commissions that have issued detailed reports and recommended

changes in public policy. Even though presidential commissions often do not lead to an adoption of new policies, they do help educate Americans about important issues.

14 Two presidential commissions on pornography were the 1970 Commission on Obscenity and Pornography set up by President Lyndon Johnson and the 1986 Meese Commission set up by President Ronald Reagan. While the first commission found that pornography posed a relatively insignificant threat to society, the second had opposite conclusions.

15 The religious conservative opposition to pornography is based on a belief that people have an inherent human desire to sin, and that pornography reinforces that tendency and so undermines the family, traditional authority, and the moral fabric of society. There are both antipornography and anticensorship arguments about pornography.

16 The global adult entertainment industry is one of the largest and most profitable industries in the world. It includes pornographic products such as magazines, comics, movies, pay-per-view, and online porn. The accessibility, anonymity, and ease of use have all contributed to the growing popularity of the Internet. While some experts believe that pornography is related to greater sexual knowledge and openness to new sexual experiences, other studies have found that it can have negative effects.

17 It is not only scholars and activists who disagree about pornography; the general public seems profoundly ambivalent about it as well. The majority want to ban violent pornography and feel that such pornography can lead to a loss of respect for women and increases in sexual violence.

18 Defining sex work is not easy. The U.S. legal code is ambiguous about what constitutes sex work; for instance, some state penal codes define it as the act of hiring out one's body for sexual intercourse, whereas other states define it as sexual intercourse in exchange for money or as any sexual behavior that is sold for profit.

19 Sex work involves the exchange of money or goods for sexual services. This can include a wide range of sexual behaviors, from erotic interactions without physical contact to high-risk sexual behaviors. Sex workers may be cisgender or transgender.

20 The sex industry includes sex workers, escorts, phone sex operators, strippers, and porn stars. One of the oldest forms of sex work

is prostitution. Sex work is mostly a gendered phenomenon, with women selling and men buying. By far, the main motivation for becoming a sex worker is economic.

21 Female sex workers (FSWs) often experience an economically deprived upbringing. However, because high-class sex workers, who often come from wealthy backgrounds, are less likely to be caught and arrested, research studies may concentrate too much on poorer women.

22 FSWs are also more often victims of sexual abuse, initiate sexual activity at a younger age, and experience a higher frequency of rape. Intrafamilial violence and past physical and sexual abuse are also common. FSWs can solicit their services in the street, clubs, brothels, on CB radios, as call girls or courtesans, or out of an escort agency. These types of FSWs differ with respect to the work setting, prices charged, and safety from violence and arrest. The most widespread type of FSW is streetwalkers.

23 Male sex workers (MSWs) engage in sex work mainly for economic reasons and view their work as a valid source of income. Many experienced early childhood sexual experience (such as coerced sexual behavior) combined with a homosexual orientation, first sexual experience at a young age (approximately 12 years old), and have older partners. They often have fewer career aspirations than those not in the sex worker industry and are more likely to view themselves as addicted to either drugs or alcohol. MSWs, like FSWs, may engage in street hustling, bar hustling, and escort sex work. The differences between these types of sex work are in income potential and personal safety.

24 Many teens run away from home each year in the United States, and more than 85% eventually become involved in sex work. Outside the United States, adolescent sex work is prevalent in many countries, such as Brazil and Thailand. Female adolescents in Brazil are drawn to sex work primarily for economic reasons.

25 Pimps play an important role in sex work. They offer protection, recruit other prostitutes, may manage a group of sex workers, and try to keep them hustling to make money. Successful pimps can make a great deal of money and often feel powerful in their role as a pimp.

26 Clients go to sex workers for a variety of reasons, including guaranteed sex, to eliminate the risk for rejection, for companionship, to have the undivided attention of the prostitute, because they have no other sexual outlets, for adventure or curiosity, or to relieve loneliness.

27 Many people believe that sex work should be legalized so that it can be subjected to government regulation and taxation. However, others think that it would be immoral to legalize sex work.

28 Different groups, such as COYOTE, have organized to change the public's views of sex work and to change the laws against it. These groups are also common outside the United States.

29 Sex workers are at high risk for acquiring STIs. Overall, they are knowledgeable about these risks and use condoms some of the time. STIs have been found to decrease when sex work is legalized.

30 FSWs cite personal and family relationships, exhaustion, sobriety, and feeling too old to continue as reasons for quitting sex work. Research has found that between 60% and 75% of FSWs were raped, whereas 70% to 95% were physically assaulted. These experiences, along with jail time, multiple pregnancies, and/or STIs, can also be turning points for quitting the industry.

31 Sex workers exist all over the world. "Comfort girls" were forced into sex work in Japan during World War II. "Hospitality girls" were used for the same purposes in the Philippines. Sex work has long been a part of the cultural practices in Thailand. Sex work is legal and supported by people in Thailand mainly because of the prevailing belief that men have greater sex drives than women. College students in Thailand often report that sex work protects "good women" from being raped. Sex workers in Thailand are required to be under a governmental STI monitoring system, which has helped decrease STI prevalence.

32 Sex trafficking is the most common form of modern-day slavery and is one of the fastest growing organized crimes. Victims tend to come from countries such as Asia, the former Soviet Union, Africa, Eastern Europe, and the United States, and are most commonly trafficked to Italy, the United States, Germany, and the Netherlands. The United States is the second largest destination and market country in the world for women and children trafficked by the sex industry.

33 Traffickers often use force, drugs, and financial methods to control their victims. Many of the victims are drugged and/or beaten and raped. Gang rapes and other forms of violence are common to force the victims to stay.

34 The Federal Bureau of Investigation with the U.S. Immigration and Customs Enforcement agencies and other local, state, and federal law enforcement agencies work together to help combat sex trafficking of both U.S. and international victims.

Critical Thinking Questions

1 When you read through one of your favorite magazines and see the various advertisements that use sex to sell their products, what effect do these ads have on you? Do you think there are any effects of living in a society so saturated with sexual images? Why or why not?

2 Do you think that sex or violence on television influences how promiscuous or violent our society becomes? Do the sexual stereotypes paraded before us in commercials and advertisements shape our attitudes toward gender relations? What do you think can be done about this?

3 What television shows did you watch as a child? What messages about gender, sexuality, and relationships did you learn from these shows? Would you let your own child watch these shows today? Why or why not?

4 Would you ever go to a strip club? If so, what would be your reasons for going? For not going? If you have been, what types of reactions did you have?

5 The United States is the second largest destination and market country in the world for women and children trafficked by the sex industry. If you were to design a strategy to reduce trafficking in the United States, what would you do?

Websites

Sex Workers Without Borders (SWWB) SWWB is a harm-reduction advocacy, education, direct services, and activist organization for individuals and issues involving the sex trade. Its website contains harm-reduction information and strategies offered by current or former sex workers.

Coalition Against Trafficking in Women (CATW) Founded in 1988, CATW was the first international, nongovernmental organization to focus on human sex trafficking, especially in women and children. CATW promotes women's human rights by working internationally to combat sexual exploitation in all its forms.

GABRIELA Network, USA (GABNet) The GABRIELA (General Assembly Binding Women for Reforms, Integrity, Equality, Leadership, and Action) Network is a U.S.-based multiracial, multiethnic women's solidarity organization that works on issues that affect women and children of the Philippines but have their roots in decisions made in the United States. The Purple Rose Campaign, spearheaded by GABRIELA, addresses the issue of sex trafficking of Filipino women and children.

Henry J. Kaiser Family Foundation The Kaiser Foundation conducts original survey research on a wide range of topics related to health policy and public health, as well as major social issues, including sexuality. The goal of Kaiser's surveys is to better understand the public's knowledge, attitudes, and behaviors.

Prostitution Research and Education Prostitution Research and Education, sponsored by the San Francisco Women's Centers, develops research and educational programs to document the experiences of people in sex work through research, public education, and arts projects. Links are provided to fact sheets about sex work, arguments for and against legalization, outreach programs for those who want to leave the business, information on female slavery outside the United States, and many other important topics.

Victims of Pornography Victims of Pornography is a website aimed to educate and create awareness that there are real victims of pornography. The site includes news; letters from people who have been involved with pornography; and links to advocacy and outreach groups.

APPENDIX

Human Sexuality Timelines

518

Human Sexuality: Past and Present

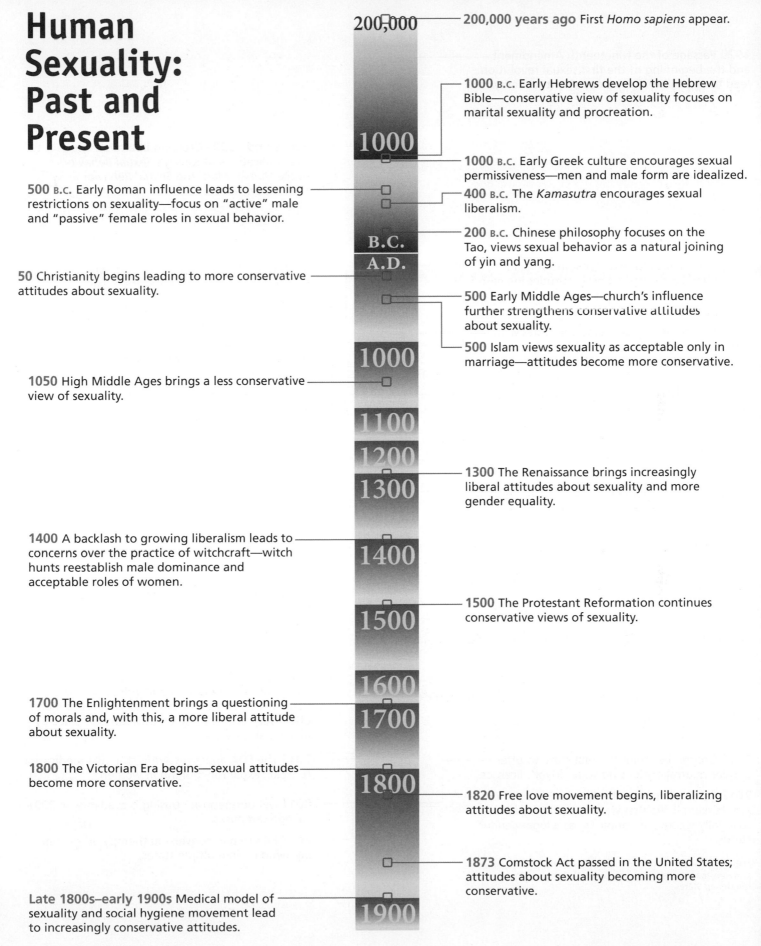

200,000 years ago First *Homo sapiens* appear.

200,000

1000 B.C. Early Hebrews develop the Hebrew Bible—conservative view of sexuality focuses on marital sexuality and procreation.

1000

1000 B.C. Early Greek culture encourages sexual permissiveness—men and male form are idealized.

500 B.C. Early Roman influence leads to lessening restrictions on sexuality—focus on "active" male and "passive" female roles in sexual behavior.

400 B.C. The *Kamasutra* encourages sexual liberalism.

200 B.C. Chinese philosophy focuses on the Tao, views sexual behavior as a natural joining of yin and yang.

B.C.
A.D.

50 Christianity begins leading to more conservative attitudes about sexuality.

500 Early Middle Ages—church's influence further strengthens conservative attitudes about sexuality.

500 Islam views sexuality as acceptable only in marriage—attitudes become more conservative.

1000

1050 High Middle Ages brings a less conservative view of sexuality.

1100

1200

1300 The Renaissance brings increasingly liberal attitudes about sexuality and more gender equality.

1300

1400 A backlash to growing liberalism leads to concerns over the practice of witchcraft—witch hunts reestablish male dominance and acceptable roles of women.

1400

1500 The Protestant Reformation continues conservative views of sexuality.

1500

1600

1700 The Enlightenment brings a questioning of morals and, with this, a more liberal attitude about sexuality.

1700

1800 The Victorian Era begins—sexual attitudes become more conservative.

1800

1820 Free love movement begins, liberalizing attitudes about sexuality.

1873 Comstock Act passed in the United States; attitudes about sexuality becoming more conservative.

Late 1800s–early 1900s Medical model of sexuality and social hygiene movement lead to increasingly conservative attitudes.

1900

1920 Passage of the Nineteenth Amendment and the beginning of the first sexual revolution lead to more liberal attitudes about sexuality.

1910

1920

1940s and 1950s Growing liberalism with the publications of Kinsey's *Sexual Behavior in the Human Male* and *Sexual Behavior in the Human Female*.

1930

1940

1950

Early 1960s Second sexual revolution leads to more liberal attitudes. Liberal attitudes increase when FDA approves first contraceptive pill.

1960

1965 U.S. Supreme Court strikes down Comstock laws, increasing liberal views of sexuality.

1969 Stonewall Riots and the beginning of the gay liberation movement.

1966 Liberal view of sexuality continues with the publication of Masters and Johnson's *Human Sexual Response*.

1970s Liberal attitudes continue; coeducational residence halls are offered on a handful of U.S. college campuses.

1973 *Roe v. Wade*, landmark decision by the U.S. Supreme Court, legalizes abortion.

1970

1973 Homosexuality is removed from the *DSM*.

1980

1990

1998 Viagra is approved by the FDA; liberal attitudes about sexuality continue.

2000

2004 Massachusetts legalizes same-sex marriage.*

2008 Gender-neutral housing available on several U.S. college campuses.

2010

2015 The U.S. Supreme Court rules that the Constitution allows for same-sex couples to marry, effectively overturning all restrictions in place by individual states.

2017 Oregon becomes the first state to offer gender-neutral options on state driver's licenses.

2015 The FDA approves *Addyi*, the first medication to treat sexual functioning in women.

2017 California passes the Gender Recognition Act, making it the first state in the United States to legally recognize nonbinary as a legal gender status.

2017 Gender-neutral housing is available on 200+ college campuses.

2017 Bills to ban conversion therapy on minors are pending in multiple states.

*Liberal attitudes continued to prevail with the passage of same-sex marriage and bans on conversion therapy in the United States.

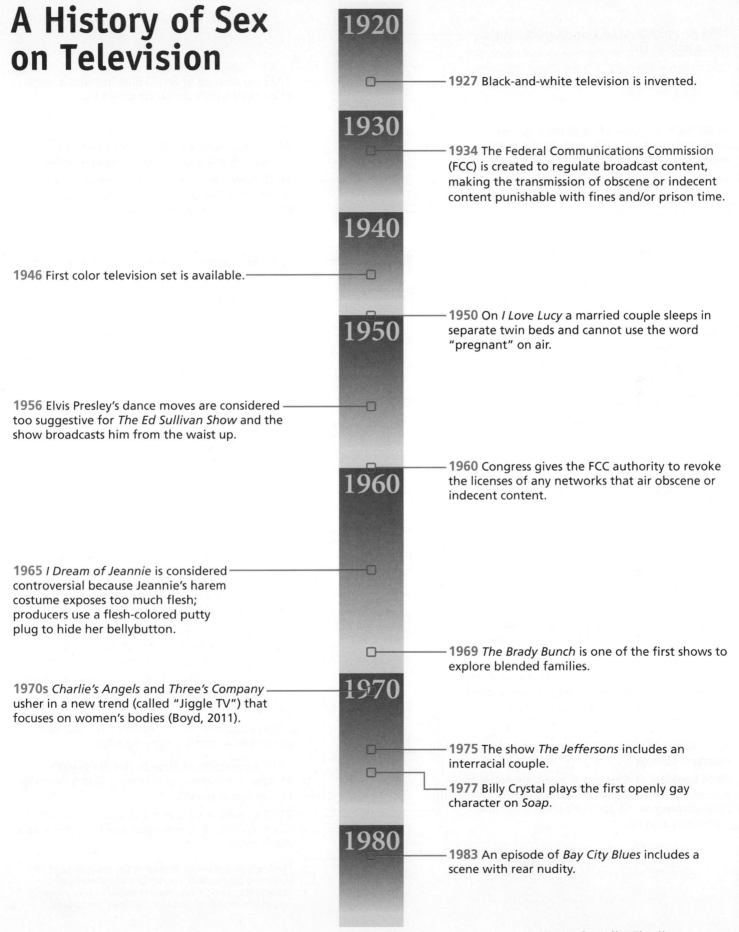

A History of Sex on Television

1920

1927 Black-and-white television is invented.

1930

1934 The Federal Communications Commission (FCC) is created to regulate broadcast content, making the transmission of obscene or indecent content punishable with fines and/or prison time.

1940

1946 First color television set is available.

1950 On *I Love Lucy* a married couple sleeps in separate twin beds and cannot use the word "pregnant" on air.

1950

1956 Elvis Presley's dance moves are considered too suggestive for *The Ed Sullivan Show* and the show broadcasts him from the waist up.

1960 Congress gives the FCC authority to revoke the licenses of any networks that air obscene or indecent content.

1960

1965 *I Dream of Jeannie* is considered controversial because Jeannie's harem costume exposes too much flesh; producers use a flesh-colored putty plug to hide her bellybutton.

1969 *The Brady Bunch* is one of the first shows to explore blended families.

1970s *Charlie's Angels* and *Three's Company* usher in a new trend (called "Jiggle TV") that focuses on women's bodies (Boyd, 2011).

1970

1975 The show *The Jeffersons* includes an interracial couple.

1977 Billy Crystal plays the first openly gay character on *Soap*.

1980

1983 An episode of *Bay City Blues* includes a scene with rear nudity.

A History of Sex on Television

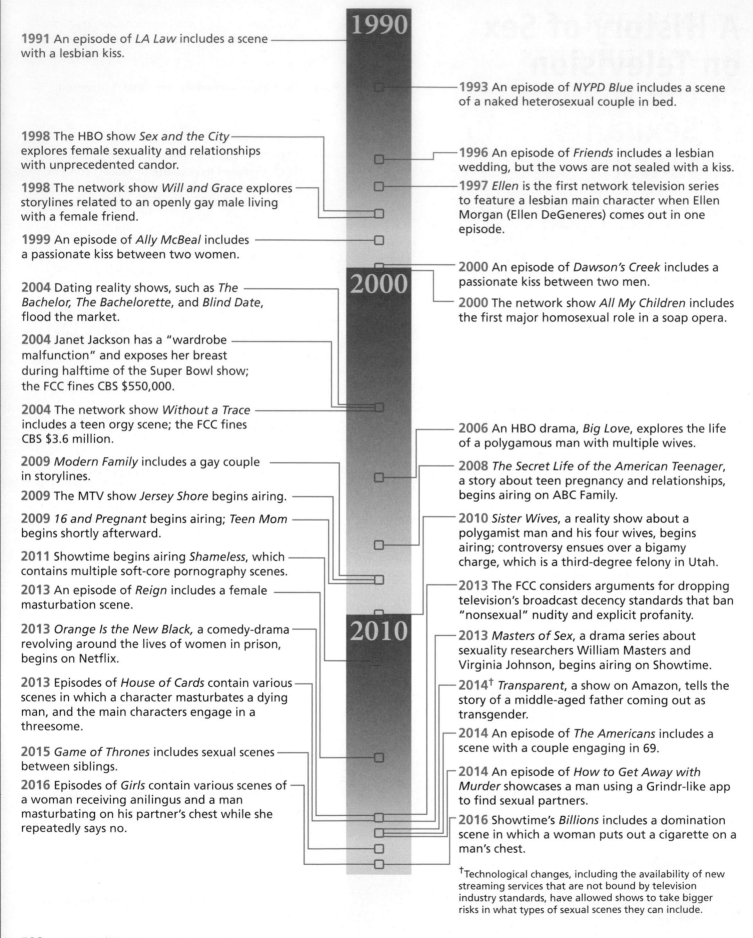

1990

1991 An episode of *LA Law* includes a scene with a lesbian kiss.

1993 An episode of *NYPD Blue* includes a scene of a naked heterosexual couple in bed.

1998 The HBO show *Sex and the City* explores female sexuality and relationships with unprecedented candor.

1996 An episode of *Friends* includes a lesbian wedding, but the vows are not sealed with a kiss.

1998 The network show *Will and Grace* explores storylines related to an openly gay male living with a female friend.

1997 *Ellen* is the first network television series to feature a lesbian main character when Ellen Morgan (Ellen DeGeneres) comes out in one episode.

1999 An episode of *Ally McBeal* includes a passionate kiss between two women.

2000

2000 An episode of *Dawson's Creek* includes a passionate kiss between two men.

2004 Dating reality shows, such as *The Bachelor*, *The Bachelorette*, and *Blind Date*, flood the market.

2000 The network show *All My Children* includes the first major homosexual role in a soap opera.

2004 Janet Jackson has a "wardrobe malfunction" and exposes her breast during halftime of the Super Bowl show; the FCC fines CBS $550,000.

2004 The network show *Without a Trace* includes a teen orgy scene; the FCC fines CBS $3.6 million.

2006 An HBO drama, *Big Love*, explores the life of a polygamous man with multiple wives.

2009 *Modern Family* includes a gay couple in storylines.

2008 *The Secret Life of the American Teenager*, a story about teen pregnancy and relationships, begins airing on ABC Family.

2009 The MTV show *Jersey Shore* begins airing.

2009 *16 and Pregnant* begins airing; *Teen Mom* begins shortly afterward.

2010 *Sister Wives*, a reality show about a polygamist man and his four wives, begins airing; controversy ensues over a bigamy charge, which is a third-degree felony in Utah.

2011 Showtime begins airing *Shameless*, which contains multiple soft-core pornography scenes.

2013 An episode of *Reign* includes a female masturbation scene.

2013 The FCC considers arguments for dropping television's broadcast decency standards that ban "nonsexual" nudity and explicit profanity.

2010

2013 *Orange Is the New Black,* a comedy-drama revolving around the lives of women in prison, begins on Netflix.

2013 *Masters of Sex*, a drama series about sexuality researchers William Masters and Virginia Johnson, begins airing on Showtime.

2013 Episodes of *House of Cards* contain various scenes in which a character masturbates a dying man, and the main characters engage in a threesome.

2014† *Transparent*, a show on Amazon, tells the story of a middle-aged father coming out as transgender.

2014 An episode of *The Americans* includes a scene with a couple engaging in 69.

2015 *Game of Thrones* includes sexual scenes between siblings.

2014 An episode of *How to Get Away with Murder* showcases a man using a Grindr-like app to find sexual partners.

2016 Episodes of *Girls* contain various scenes of a woman receiving anilingus and a man masturbating on his partner's chest while she repeatedly says no.

2016 Showtime's *Billions* includes a domination scene in which a woman puts out a cigarette on a man's chest.

†Technological changes, including the availability of new streaming services that are not bound by television industry standards, have allowed shows to take bigger risks in what types of sexual scenes they can include.

Important Developments in the History of Sexuality Research

1840

1843 Russian physician Heinrich Kaan publishes *Psychopathia Sexualis*.

1850

1860

1870

1880

1886 Richard von Krafft-Ebing, a German psychiatrist, expands and refines Kaan's earlier work in *Psychopathia Sexualis*.

1890

1892 American physician Clelia Mosher begins a survey among educated middle-class women concerning sexual attitudes and experiences.

1896 English private scholar Havelock Ellis begins *Studies in the Psychology of Sex*.

1897 Berlin physician Magnus Hirschfeld founds the **Scientific Humanitarian Committee**, the world's first "gay rights" organization.

1897 Berlin physician Albert Moll publishes *Investigations Concerning the Libido Sexualis*.

1899 Magnus Hirschfeld begins editing of the *Yearbook for Sexual Intermediate Stages* for the Scientific Humanitarian Committee.

1900

1903–4 Magnus Hirschfeld begins his statistical surveys on homosexuality but they are quickly terminated by legal action.

1905 Sigmund Freud publishes *Three Essays on the Theory of Sex*.

1907 Berlin dermatologist Iwan Bloch coins the term *Sexualwissenschaft* (sexology) and publishes *The Sexual Life of Our Time*.

1908 Magnus Hirschfeld publishes the first issue of *The Journal for Sexology*.

1909 Albert Moll publishes *The Sexual Life of the Child*, challenging Freud's psychoanalytic theory.

1911 Albert Moll publishes *The Handbook of Sexual Sciences*.

1910

1914 Iwan Bloch publishes the *Journal of Sexology*.

1913 Magnus Hirschfeld, Iwan Bloch, and others found the **Society of Sexology** in Berlin.

1913 Albert Moll founds the **International Society for Sex Research** in Berlin.

1914 Magnus Hirschfeld publishes *Homosexuality in Men and Women*.

1919 Magnus Hirschfeld opens the **Institute for Sexology** in Berlin.

1926 Moll organizes **International Congress of Sex Research** in Berlin.

1920

1930

1933 Nazis close the **Institute for Sexology** and destroy the data.

1938 Alfred Kinsey begins his studies of human sexual behavior in the United States.

1940

1947 Alfred Kinsey founds the **Institute for Sex Research** at Indiana University.

1948 Alfred Kinsey and colleagues publish *Sexual Behavior in the Human Male*.

1949 Simone de Beauvoir publishes *The Second Sex*.

1951 Clellan S. Ford and Frank A. Beach publish *Patterns of Sexual Behavior.*

1953 Alfred Kinsey and his colleagues publish *Sexual Behavior in the Human Female.*

1964 An American physician, Mary Calderone, founds the **Sexuality Information and Education Council of the United States** (SIECUS).

1966 William Masters and Virginia Johnson publish *Human Sexual Response.*

1970 William Masters and Virginia Johnson publish *Human Sexual Inadequacy.*

1971 American psychiatrist Richard Green founds the **International Academy of Sex Research**; organization publishes *Archives of Sexual Behavior.*

1973 Data collection begins in the United States for the *National Survey of Family Growth.*

1974 Hans Lehfeldt organizes the first **World Congress of Sexology.**

1974 The first issue of *Journal of Homosexuality* is published.

1981 Alan Bell and Martin Weinberg publish *Sexual Preferences.*

1986 The **American Board of Sexology** organizes in Washington, D.C.

1990 The **Asian Federation for Sexology** is founded in Hong Kong.

1991 Data collection begins in the United States for the *Youth Risk Behavior Survey.*

1992 Data collection begins in the United States for the *National Health and Social Life Survey.*

2000 Data collection begins in the United States for the *National College Health Assessment.*

2002 Pfizer Pharmaceuticals publishes the *Global Study of Sexual Attitudes and Behaviors.*

2002 The *National Survey of Family Growth* begins including males in data collection.

2007 The Durex Corporation publishes the *Durex Sexual Wellbeing Global Survey.*

2010 The *National Survey of Sexual Health and Behavior* is published.

2016 The World Health Organization and UNAIDS publish the *Global AIDS Update* as well as global studies on adolescent contraceptive use and violence against women.

1950

1960

1970

1980

1990

2000

2010

1954 William Masters and Virginia Johnson begin researching sexuality in the United States.

1957 American gynecologist Hans Lehfeldt founds the **Society for the Scientific Study of Sexuality** (SSSS).

1965 SSSS publishes the first issue of the *Journal of Sex Research.*

1967 The **American Association of Sex Educators, Counselors and Therapists** (AASECT) is founded.

1970 Morton Hunt begins a large-scale sexuality study and eventually publishes *Sexual Behavior in the 1970s.*

1974 The first World Health Organization (WHO) is convened in Geneva. The following year, it publishes *Education and Treatment in Human Sexuality: The Training of Health Professionals.*

1976 The **Institute for Advanced Study of Sexuality** is founded in San Francisco.

1978 Alan Bell and Martin Weinberg publish *Homosexualities.*

1978 The **World Association for Sexology** is founded in Rome.

1988 The *German Journal of Sex Research* is first published.

1989 The **European Federation of Sexology** is founded in Geneva.

1994 The Robert Koch Institute opens the **Archive for Sexology** in Berlin.

1994 Researchers from the National Opinion Research Center publish the *National Health and Social Life Study.*

1994 Data collection begins in the United States for the *National Longitudinal Study of Adolescent Health.*

2013 The World Health Organization publishes global study on the prevalence of violence against women.

2013 The United Nations Children's Fund publishes global study on children and AIDS.

2013 The Joint United Nations Programme on HIV/AIDS (UNAIDS) publishes global AIDS study.

Same-Sex Relationships Around the Globe

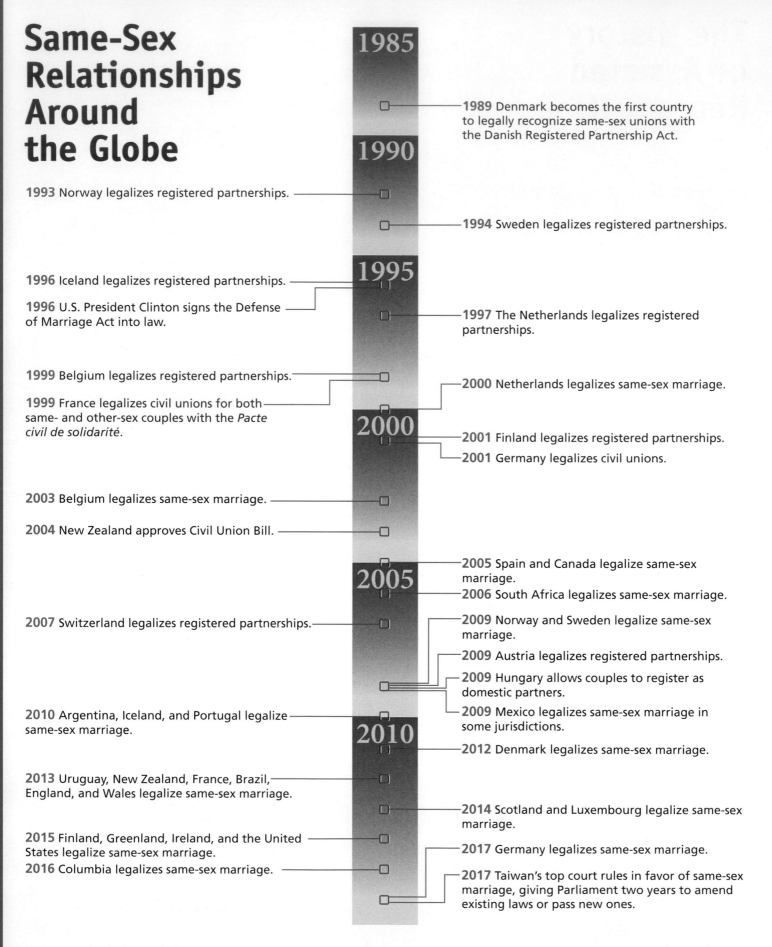

1985

1989 Denmark becomes the first country to legally recognize same-sex unions with the Danish Registered Partnership Act.

1990

1993 Norway legalizes registered partnerships.

1994 Sweden legalizes registered partnerships.

1995

1996 Iceland legalizes registered partnerships.

1996 U.S. President Clinton signs the Defense of Marriage Act into law.

1997 The Netherlands legalizes registered partnerships.

1999 Belgium legalizes registered partnerships.

1999 France legalizes civil unions for both same- and other-sex couples with the *Pacte civil de solidarité*.

2000 Netherlands legalizes same-sex marriage.

2000

2001 Finland legalizes registered partnerships.

2001 Germany legalizes civil unions.

2003 Belgium legalizes same-sex marriage.

2004 New Zealand approves Civil Union Bill.

2005 Spain and Canada legalize same-sex marriage.

2005

2006 South Africa legalizes same-sex marriage.

2007 Switzerland legalizes registered partnerships.

2009 Norway and Sweden legalize same-sex marriage.

2009 Austria legalizes registered partnerships.

2009 Hungary allows couples to register as domestic partners.

2009 Mexico legalizes same-sex marriage in some jurisdictions.

2010 Argentina, Iceland, and Portugal legalize same-sex marriage.

2010

2012 Denmark legalizes same-sex marriage.

2013 Uruguay, New Zealand, France, Brazil, England, and Wales legalize same-sex marriage.

2014 Scotland and Luxembourg legalize same-sex marriage.

2015 Finland, Greenland, Ireland, and the United States legalize same-sex marriage.

2017 Germany legalizes same-sex marriage.

2016 Columbia legalizes same-sex marriage.

2017 Taiwan's top court rules in favor of same-sex marriage, giving Parliament two years to amend existing laws or pass new ones.

The History of Assisted Reproduction

1600

1677 Human sperm is discovered by Dutch scientist.

1700

1800

1827 Human ovum is discovered by Russian scientist.

1843 Scientists discover that human conception occurs when sperm enters the ovum, which reveals that contributions from both male and female create life.

1900

1910

1928 First pregnancy test is developed by German gynecologists.

1920

1934 Progesterone is discovered by German scientist who goes on to win the Nobel Prize in chemistry.

1930

1937 *New England Journal of Medicine* discusses the concept of in vitro fertilization (IVF) techniques.

1945 *British Medical Journal* discusses artificial insemination using donor sperm.

1940

1953 First cryopreservation of human sperm.

1950s First ultrasounds developed for use during pregnancy.

1950

1960

1978 Louise Brown, the first baby conceived via IVF, is born in England.

1970

1973 IVF is first attempted in the United States. First IVF pregnancy is reported in Australia but does not produce a child.

1979 Two babies conceived by IVF are born in France and Germany.

1980

1981 First IVF baby is born in the United States.

1983 Sperm Bank of California opens.

1983 First cryopreservation of human embryo.

1984 First baby developed from a frozen embryo is born in Australia.

1983 First baby conceived with donor ova is born in Australia.

1987 Embryo transfer procedure is patented.

1988 Custody battle over "Baby M" results in custody given to the genetic father and his wife with visitation rights to the surrogate.

1990

1991 A 42-year-old woman becomes a surrogate mother for her daughter after becoming pregnant with the daughter's embryo.

1994 First baby born in France conceived through ICSI.

1992 Intracytoplasmic sperm injection (ICSI) for male infertility is introduced.

1996 Policy is drawn up by the American Society for Reproductive Medicine on what to do with abandoned embryos.

1996 First baby born in the United States conceived with intracellular sperm injection (ICSI).

1998 First embryonic stem cells isolated.

1999 First cryopreservation of human ova.

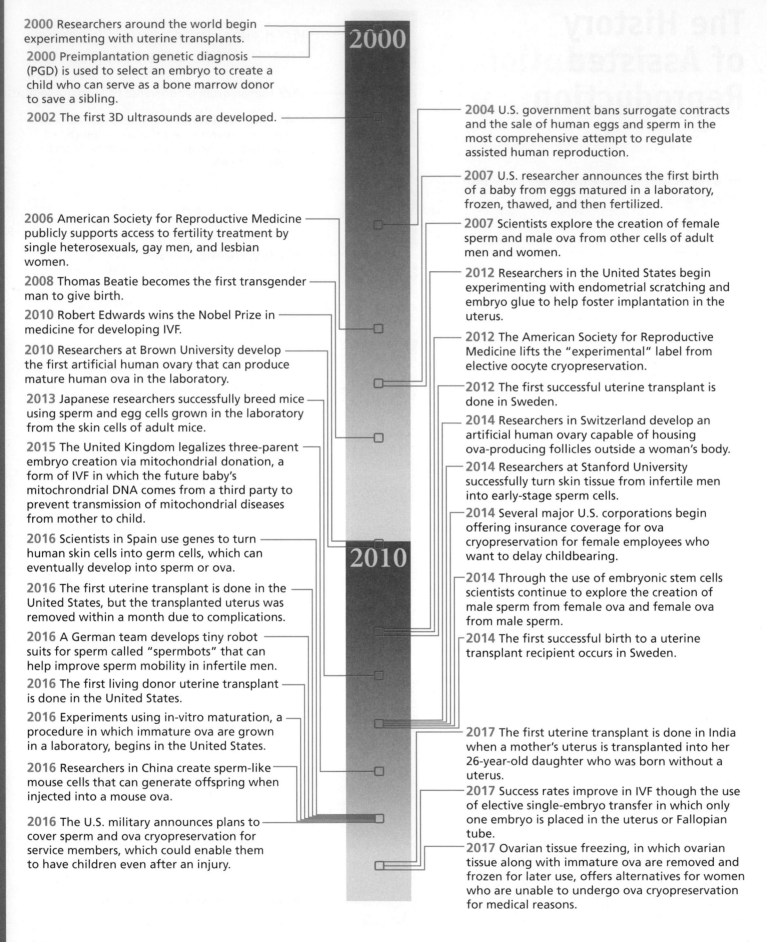

2000 Researchers around the world begin experimenting with uterine transplants.

2000 Preimplantation genetic diagnosis (PGD) is used to select an embryo to create a child who can serve as a bone marrow donor to save a sibling.

2002 The first 3D ultrasounds are developed.

2006 American Society for Reproductive Medicine publicly supports access to fertility treatment by single heterosexuals, gay men, and lesbian women.

2008 Thomas Beatie becomes the first transgender man to give birth.

2010 Robert Edwards wins the Nobel Prize in medicine for developing IVF.

2010 Researchers at Brown University develop the first artificial human ovary that can produce mature human ova in the laboratory.

2013 Japanese researchers successfully breed mice using sperm and egg cells grown in the laboratory from the skin cells of adult mice.

2015 The United Kingdom legalizes three-parent embryo creation via mitochondrial donation, a form of IVF in which the future baby's mitochondrial DNA comes from a third party to prevent transmission of mitochondrial diseases from mother to child.

2016 Scientists in Spain use genes to turn human skin cells into germ cells, which can eventually develop into sperm or ova.

2016 The first uterine transplant is done in the United States, but the transplanted uterus was removed within a month due to complications.

2016 A German team develops tiny robot suits for sperm called "spermbots" that can help improve sperm mobility in infertile men.

2016 The first living donor uterine transplant is done in the United States.

2016 Experiments using in-vitro maturation, a procedure in which immature ova are grown in a laboratory, begins in the United States.

2016 Researchers in China create sperm-like mouse cells that can generate offspring when injected into a mouse ova.

2016 The U.S. military announces plans to cover sperm and ova cryopreservation for service members, which could enable them to have children even after an injury.

2000

2010

2004 U.S. government bans surrogate contracts and the sale of human eggs and sperm in the most comprehensive attempt to regulate assisted human reproduction.

2007 U.S. researcher announces the first birth of a baby from eggs matured in a laboratory, frozen, thawed, and then fertilized.

2007 Scientists explore the creation of female sperm and male ova from other cells of adult men and women.

2012 Researchers in the United States begin experimenting with endometrial scratching and embryo glue to help foster implantation in the uterus.

2012 The American Society for Reproductive Medicine lifts the "experimental" label from elective oocyte cryopreservation.

2012 The first successful uterine transplant is done in Sweden.

2014 Researchers in Switzerland develop an artificial human ovary capable of housing ova-producing follicles outside a woman's body.

2014 Researchers at Stanford University successfully turn skin tissue from infertile men into early-stage sperm cells.

2014 Several major U.S. corporations begin offering insurance coverage for ova cryopreservation for female employees who want to delay childbearing.

2014 Through the use of embryonic stem cells scientists continue to explore the creation of male sperm from female ova and female ova from male sperm.

2014 The first successful birth to a uterine transplant recipient occurs in Sweden.

2017 The first uterine transplant is done in India when a mother's uterus is transplanted into her 26-year-old daughter who was born without a uterus.

2017 Success rates improve in IVF though the use of elective single-embryo transfer in which only one embryo is placed in the uterus or Fallopian tube.

2017 Ovarian tissue freezing, in which ovarian tissue along with immature ova are removed and frozen for later use, offers alternatives for women who are unable to undergo ova cryopreservation for medical reasons.

The History of Contraception

1872 Anthony Comstock creates the New York Society for the Suppression of Vice and proposes the Comstock Act.

1914 Margaret Sanger publishes *The Woman Rebel*, a monthly newsletter promoting contraception. She is indicted and flees to England to escape arrest.

1915 Supporters of Sanger form the first U.S. contraceptive organization, the National Birth Control League.

1916 Sanger opens the first U.S. contraceptive clinic.

1936 Federal appeals court finds (*United States v. One Package*) that the federal government cannot interfere with medical doctors providing contraception to their patients.

1936 The American Medical Association officially recognizes contraception as an integral part of medicine and education.

1965 U.S. Supreme Court strikes down Comstock Act.

1965 The Supreme Court strikes down *Griswold v. Connecticut*.

1970 President Nixon signs into law Title X of the Public Health Service Act.

1970 Congress increases Title X's mandate to provide sexuality education programs and contraceptive services to teens at risk for pregnancy.

1973 *Roe v. Wade* legalizes abortion in the United States.

‡This timeline does not include the development of the majority of oral contraceptive pills that followed the first pill in 1960. Since that time, a variety of different contraceptive pills have been introduced with major improvements, including lower estrogen doses.

1830
1840
1850
1860
1870
1880
1890
1900
1910
1920
1930
1940
1950
1960
1970

1839 Charles Goodyear vulcanizes rubber and begins manufacturing rubber condoms.

1873 Congress passes the Comstock Act.

1882 A German physician, Wilhelm Mensinga, invents the diaphragm.

1906 The U.S. Food and Drug Administration (FDA) is founded.

1921 Sanger founds the American Birth Control League.

1925 First diaphragms (originally called womb veils) available in the United States.

1932 U.S. Postal Service confiscates a package that Margaret Sanger orders from Japan containing diaphragms. Sanger files a lawsuit against the federal government.

1938 Judge lifts the federal obscenity ban on contraception, but contraception remains illegal in most U.S. states.

1942 The American Birth Control League becomes the Planned Parenthood Federation of America, creating a national network of contraceptive clinics.

1960 The first oral contraceptive pill, Enovid, is approved by the FDA.‡

1968 Pope Paul VI publishes *Humanae Vitae*, which states that the Catholic Church opposes all forms of contraception, except the rhythm method.

1968 The Lippes Loop and Cooper 7 IUDs are approved by the FDA.

1971 The Dalkon Shield IUD is approved by the FDA.

1972 The Supreme Court (*Baird v. Eisenstadt*) legalizes contraception for everyone, regardless of marital status.

1975 The FDA advises A. H. Robins to withdraw the Dalkon Shield from the market.

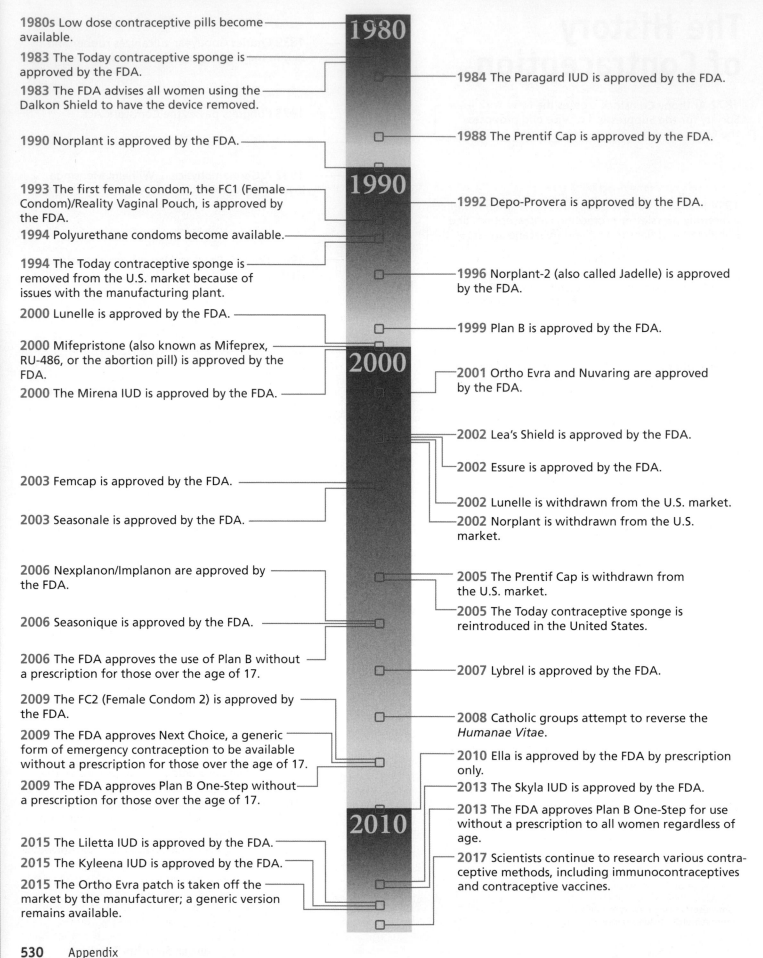

1980s Low dose contraceptive pills become available.

1983 The Today contraceptive sponge is approved by the FDA.

1983 The FDA advises all women using the Dalkon Shield to have the device removed.

1990 Norplant is approved by the FDA.

1993 The first female condom, the FC1 (Female Condom)/Reality Vaginal Pouch, is approved by the FDA.

1994 Polyurethane condoms become available.

1994 The Today contraceptive sponge is removed from the U.S. market because of issues with the manufacturing plant.

2000 Lunelle is approved by the FDA.

2000 Mifepristone (also known as Mifeprex, RU-486, or the abortion pill) is approved by the FDA.

2000 The Mirena IUD is approved by the FDA.

2003 Femcap is approved by the FDA.

2003 Seasonale is approved by the FDA.

2006 Nexplanon/Implanon are approved by the FDA.

2006 Seasonique is approved by the FDA.

2006 The FDA approves the use of Plan B without a prescription for those over the age of 17.

2009 The FC2 (Female Condom 2) is approved by the FDA.

2009 The FDA approves Next Choice, a generic form of emergency contraception to be available without a prescription for those over the age of 17.

2009 The FDA approves Plan B One-Step without a prescription for those over the age of 17.

2015 The Liletta IUD is approved by the FDA.

2015 The Kyleena IUD is approved by the FDA.

2015 The Ortho Evra patch is taken off the market by the manufacturer; a generic version remains available.

1980

1990

2000

2010

1984 The Paragard IUD is approved by the FDA.

1988 The Prentif Cap is approved by the FDA.

1992 Depo-Provera is approved by the FDA.

1996 Norplant-2 (also called Jadelle) is approved by the FDA.

1999 Plan B is approved by the FDA.

2001 Ortho Evra and Nuvaring are approved by the FDA.

2002 Lea's Shield is approved by the FDA.

2002 Essure is approved by the FDA.

2002 Lunelle is withdrawn from the U.S. market.

2002 Norplant is withdrawn from the U.S. market.

2005 The Prentif Cap is withdrawn from the U.S. market.

2005 The Today contraceptive sponge is reintroduced in the United States.

2007 Lybrel is approved by the FDA.

2008 Catholic groups attempt to reverse the *Humanae Vitae*.

2010 Ella is approved by the FDA by prescription only.

2013 The Skyla IUD is approved by the FDA.

2013 The FDA approves Plan B One-Step for use without a prescription to all women regardless of age.

2017 Scientists continue to research various contraceptive methods, including immunocontraceptives and contraceptive vaccines.

References

Aaronson, I., & Aaronson, A. (2010). How should we classify intersex disorders? *Journal of Pediatric Urology*, *6*(5), 443–446.

Abad, C., & Pruden, S. (2013). Do storybooks really break children's gender stereotypes? *Frontiers in Psychology*, *4*, 986.

Abbate, D., Campisi, S., Marzola, E., Rocca, G., Peris, C., Campagnoli, C., Peloso, A., et al. (2012). Amenorrhea in eating disorders: Poor stability of symptom after a one-year treatment. *Eating and Weight Disorders*, *17*(2), 78–85.

Abbey, A. (2002). Alcohol-related sexual assault: A common problem among college students. *Journal of Studies on Alcohol*, (Suppl. 14), 118–128.

Abbey, A., Roxx, L., McDuffie, D., & McAuslan, P. (1996). Alcohol and dating risk factors for sexual assault among college women. *Psychology of Women Quarterly*, *20*(1), 147–169.

Abbey, A., Zawacki, T., & Buck, P. O. (2005). The effects of past sexual assault perpetration and alcohol consumption on men's reactions to women's mixed signals. *Journal of Social & Clinical Psychology*, *24*(2), 129–155.

Abboud, L. N., & Liamputtong, P. (2003). Pregnancy loss: What it means to women who miscarry and their partners. *Social Work in Health Care*, *36*(3), 37–62.

Abdel-Hamid, I., Elsaied, M., & Mostafa, T. (2016). The drug treatment of delayed ejaculation. *Translational Andrology and Urology*, *5*(4), 576–591.

Abdel-Hamid, I. A., & Saleh, E. S. (2011). Primary lifelong delayed ejaculation: Characteristics and response to bupropion. *Journal of Sexual Medicine*, *8*(6), 1772–1779.

Abel, G., Becker, J., & Skinner, L. (1980). Aggressive behavior and sex. *Psychiatric Clinics of North America*, *3*, 133–135.

Abel, I. (2013, January 12). Did porn warp me forever? *Salon*. Retrieved August 13, 2013, from http://www.salon.com/2013/01/13/did_porn_warp_me_forever.

Abma, J. C., Martinez, G. M., & Copen, C. E. (2010). Teenagers in the United States: Sexual activity, contraceptive use, and childbearing, National Survey of Family Growth 2006–2008. National Center for Health Statistics. *Vital Health Statistics*, *23*(30), 1–47.

"Abortion Policy in the Absence of *Roe*." (2014, May 1). State policies in brief. Guttmacher Institute. Retrieved May 26, 2014, from http://www.guttmacher.org/statecenter/spibs/spib_APAR.pdf.

Abouesh, A., & Clayton, A. (1999). Compulsive voyeurism and exhibitionism: A clinical response to paroxetine. *Archives of Sexual Behavior*, *28*(1), 23–30.

AbouZeid, A. A., Mousa, M. H., Soliman, H. A., Hamza, A. F., & Hay, S. A. (2011). Intra-abdominal testis: Histological alterations and significance of biopsy. *Journal of Urology*, *185*(1), 269–274.

Abraham, L., Morn, M., & Vollman, A. (2010). Women on the web: How women are shaping the Internet. ComScore, Inc. Retrieved January 30, 2014, from http://uxscientist.com/public/docs/uxsci_5.pdf.

Abramson, A. (2003). *The history of television: 1942–2000*. Jefferson, NC: McFarland Publishers.

Achilli, C., Pundir, J., Ramanathan, P., Sabatini, L., Hamoda, H., Panay, N. (2017). Efficacy and safety of transdermal testosterone in postmenopausal women with hypoactive sexual desire disorder: a systematic review and meta-analysis. *Fertility and Sterility*, *107*(2), 475–482.

Acker, D., Kavoussi, L., Pant, B., Lopath, P., & Ebbin, E. (2003). Occlusion of tubular anatomical structures by energy application. *U.S. Patent No. 6,599,256*. Washington, DC: U.S. Patent and Trademark Office.

Adam, B. D. (1987). *The rise of a gay and lesbian movement*. Boston: Twayne.

Adams, H. E., Wright, L. W., Jr., & Lohr, B. A. (1996). Is homophobia associated with homosexual arousal? *Journal of Abnormal Psychology*, *105*, 440–445.

Adams, J., & Light, R. (2015). Scientific consensus, the law, and same sex parenting outcomes. *Social Science Research*, *53*, 300–310.

Adams, R. (2015). 21 men reveal how porn shaped their views of sex. *Huffington Post*. Retrieved January 11, 2017, from http://www.huffingtonpost.com/entry/21-men-reveal-how-porn-shaped-their-views-of-sex_us_55d3459ae4b055a6dab16ef0.

Adams-Curtis, L. E., & Forbes, G. B. (2004). College women's experiences of sexual coercion: A review of cultural, perpetrator, victim, and situational variables. *Trauma, Violence & Abuse*, *5*(2), 91–122.

ADD Health. (2002). Add Health and Add Health 2000: A national longitudinal study of adolescent health. Retrieved June 14, 2002, from http://www.cpc.unc.edu/addhealth.

Adler, R. B., Rosenfeld, L. B., & Proctor, R. F. (2007). *Interplay: The process of interpersonal communication* (10th ed.). New York: Oxford University Press.

Adotas. (2016, April 28). OpenMarket survey/infographic reveal millennials prefer texting but marketers miss the boat. *Adotas Newsletter*. Retrieved January 11, 2017, from http://www.openmarket.com/news/millennials-prefer-texting-versus-talking/.

Advani, P., Brewster, A., Baum, G., & Scholver, L. (2017). A pilot randomized trial to prevent sexual dysfunction in postmenopausal breast cancer survivors starting adjuvant aromatase inhibitor therapy. *Journal of Cancer Survivorship: Research and Practice*. Retrieved April 15, 2017, from https://www.ncbi.nlm.nih.gov/pubmed/28229275.

Afifi, T., McManus, T., Steuber, K., & Coho, A. (2009). Verbal avoidance and dissatisfaction in intimate conflict situations. *Human Communication Research*, *35*(3), 357.

Aftab, A., Chen, C., & McBrid, J. (2017). Flibanserin and its discontents. *Archives of Women's Mental Health*, *20*(2), 243–247.

Agarwal, A., Deepinder, F., Sharma, R. K., Ranga, G., & Li, J. (2008). Effect of cell phone usage on semen analysis in men attending infertility clinic: An observational study. *Fertility and Sterility*, *89*, 124–128.

Agarwal, A., Singh, A., Hamada, A., & Kesari, K. (2011). Cell phones and male infertility. *International Brazilian Journal of Urology*, *37*(4), 432–454.

Agénor, M., Bailey, Z., Krieger, N., Austin, S., & Gottlieb, B. (2015). Exploring the cervical cancer screening experiences of Black lesbian, bisexual, and queer women: The role of patient-provider communication. *Women & Health*, *55*(6), 717–736.

Agnihotri, S. (2016, March 20). India finally has a gay marriage bureau. *India Today*. Retrieved March 15, 2017, from http://indiatoday.intoday.in/story/india-homosexuality-gay-marriage-bureau/1/624683.html.

Ahern, N., & Bramlett, T. (2016). An update on teen pregnancy. *Journal of Psychosocial*

Nursing and Mental Health Services, 54(2), 25–28.

Ahmadi, A. (2013, June 13). Ethical issues in hymenoplasty: Views from Tehran's physicians. *Journal of Medical Ethics.* Retrieved February 19, 2014, from http://www.ncbi.nlm.nih.gov/pubmed/23764547.

Ahmadi, A. (2016). Recreating virginity in Iran: Hymenoplasty as a form of resistance. *Medical Anthropology Quarterly, 30*(2), 222–237.

Ahmed, J. (1986). Polygyny and fertility differentials among the Yoruba of western Nigeria. *Journal of Biosocial Sciences, 18,* 63–73.

Ahmetoglu, G., Swami, V., & Chamorro-Premuzic, T. (2010). The relationship between dimensions of love, personality, and relationship length. *Archives of Sexual Behavior, 39*(5), 1181–1190.

Ahrens, C. E. (2006). Being silenced: The impact of negative social reactions on the disclosure of rape. *American Journal of Community Psychology, 38,* 263–274.

Ahrens, C., & Campbell, R. (2000). Assisting rape victims as they recover from rape. *Journal of Interpersonal Violence, 15*(9), 959–986.

Ahrold, T., Farmer, M., Trapnell, P., & Meston, C. (2011). The relationship among sexual attitudes, sexual fantasy, and religiosity. *Archives of Sexual Behavior, 40*(3), 619–630.

Aicken, C., Nardone, A., & Mercer, C. (2011). Alcohol misuse, sexual risk behavior, and adverse sexual health outcomes. *Journal of Public Health, 33*(2), 262–271.

Ainsworth, M. D. S., Blehar, M. C., Waters, E., & Wall, S. (1978). *Patterns of attachment: A psychological study of the strange situation.* Hillsdale, NJ: Erlbaum.

Akbag, M., & Imamoglu, S. (2010). The prediction of gender and attachment styles on shame, guilt, and loneliness. *Educational Sciences: Theory and Practice, 10*(2), 669–682.

Akers, A. Y., Gold, M. A., Bost, J. E., Adimora, A. A., Orr, D. P., & Fortenberry, J. D. (2011). Variation in sexual behaviors in a cohort of adolescent females: The role of personal, perceived peer, and perceived family attitudes. *Journal of Adolescent Health, 48*(1), 87–93.

Ako, T., Takao, H., Yoshiharo, M., Osamu, I., & Yutaka, U. (2001). Beginnings of sexual reassignment surgery in Japan. *International Journal of Transgenderism.* Retrieved June 1, 2003, from http://www.symposion.com/ijt/ijtvo05no01_02.htm.

Al-Abbadey, M., Liossi, C., Curran, N., Schoth, D., & Graham, C. (2016). Treatment of female sexual pain disorders: A systematic review. *Journal of Sex & Marital Therapy, 42*(2), 99–142.

Alan Guttmacher Institute. (2014, June 1). Sex and HIV education. *State Policies in Brief.* Retrieved April 9, 2014, from https://www.guttmacher.org/statecenter/spibs/spib_SE.pdf.

Alan Guttmacher Institute. (2017). State laws and policies: Sex and HIV education. Retrieved February 11, 2017, from https://www.guttmacher.org/search/site/sex%20education.

Alanko, K., Santtila, P., Harlaar, N., Witting, K., Varjonen, M., Jern, P., Johansson, A., von der Pahlen, B., & Sandnabba, N. K. (2010). Common genetic effects of gender atypical behavior in childhood and sexual orientation in adulthood: A study of Finnish twins. *Archives of Sexual Behavior, 39*(1), 81–92.

Alarid, L. F. (2000). Sexual assault and coercion among incarcerated women prisoners: Excerpts from prison letters. *The Prison Journal, 80*(4), 391–406.

Alarie, M., & Gaudet, S. (2013). "I don't know if she is bisexual or if she just wants to get attention": Analyzing the various mechanisms through which emerging adults invisibilize bisexuality. *Journal of Bisexuality, 13*(2), 191–214.

Albers, K. (2007). Comprehensive care in the prevention of ectopic pregnancy and associated negative outcomes. *Midwifery Today with International Midwife,* (84), 26–27, 67.

Albert, A., & Porter, J. R. (1988). Children's gender-role stereotypes: A sociological investigation of psychological models. *Sociological Forum, 3,* 184–210.

Albert, B. (2009). With one voice: A 2009 survey of adults and teens on parental influence, abstinence, contraception, and the increase in the teen birth rate. National Campaign to Prevent Teen Pregnancy. Retrieved January 24, 2011, from http://www.thenationalcampaign.org/resources/pdf/pubs/WOV_Lite_2009.pdf.

Albert, R. T., Elwell, S. L., & Idelson, S. (2001). *Lesbian rabbis: The first generation.* Piscataway, NJ: Rutgers University Press.

Albright, C., Frishman, G., & Bhagavath, B. (2013). Surgical aspects of removal of Essure microinsert. *Contraception, 88*(3), 334–336.

Aleccia, J. (2013, April 4). 'The new normal': Cohabitation on the rise, study finds. *NBC News.* Retrieved August 23, 2017, from https://www.nbcnews.com/health/new-normal-cohabitation-rise-study-finds-1C9208429.

Alemany, L., de Sanjosé, S., Tous, S., Quint, W., Vallejos, C., Shin, H., Bravo, L., Alonso, P., Lima, M., et al. (2014). Time trends of human papillomavirus types in invasive cervical cancer, from 1940 to 2007. *International Journal of Cancer, 135*(1), 88–95.

Alexa. (2014). *Top sites: The top 500 sites on the web.* Alexa Internet. Retrieved February 10, 2014, from http://www.alexa.com/topsites.

Alexander, M. A. (1999). Sexual offender treatment efficacy revisited. *Sexual Abuse: A Journal of Research and Treatment, 11,* 101–116.

Alexander, M. S., Brackett, N. L., Bodner, D., Elliott, S., Jackson, A., Sonksen, J.; National Institute on Disability and Rehabilitation Research. (2009). Measurement of sexual functioning after spinal cord injury: Preferred instruments. *Journal of Spinal Cord Medicine, 32*(3), 226–236.

Alexander, M., & Rosen, R. (2008). Spinal cord injuries and orgasm: A review. *Journal of Sex and Marital Therapy, 24,* 308–324.

Alexander, M. S., Rosen, R. C., Steinberg, S., Symonds, T., Haughie, S., & Hultling, C. (2011). Sildenafil in women with sexual arousal disorder following spinal cord injury. *Spinal Cord, 49*(2), 273–279.

Alexandre, B., Lemaire, A., Desvaux, P., & Amar, E. (2007). Intracavernous injections of prostaglandin E1 for erectile dysfunction: Patient satisfaction and quality of sex life on long-term treatment. *Journal of Sexual Medicine, 4,* 426–431.

Alkatout, K., Honemeyer, U., Strauss, A., Tinelli, A., Malvasi, A., Jonat, W., Mettler, L., & Schollmeyer, T. (2013). Clinical diagnosis and treatment of ectopic pregnancy. *Obstetrical & Gynecological Survey, 68*(8), 571–581.

Alkhuja, S., Mnekel, R., Patel, B., & Ibrahimbacha, A. (2001). Stidor and difficult airway in an AIDS patient. *AIDS Patient Care and Sexually Transmitted Diseases, 15*(6), 293–295.

Allan, C., Forbes, E., Strauss, B., & McLachlan, R. (2008). Testosterone therapy increases sexual desire in ageing men with low-normal testosterone levels and symptoms of androgen deficiency. *International Journal of Impotence Research, 20,* 396–401.

Allaway, H., Southmayd, E., & DeSouza, M. (2016). The physiology of functional hypothalamic amenorrhea associated with energy deficiency in exercising women and in women with anorexia nervosa. *Hormone Molecular Biology and Clinical Investigation, 25*(2), 91–119.

Allen, C., Bowdin, S., Harrison, R., Sutcliffe, A., Brueton, L., Kirby, G., et al. (2008, June 3). Pregnancy and perinatal outcomes after assisted reproduction: A comparative study. *Irish Journal of Medical Science, 177*(3), 233–241.

Allen, E., & Atkins, D. (2012). The association of divorce and extramarital sex in a representative U.S. sample. *Journal of Family Issues, 33*(11), 1477–1493.

Allen, K., & Goldberg, A. (2009). Sexual activity during menstruation: A qualitative study. *Journal of Sex Research, 46*(6), 535–545.

Allen, M., Emmers-Sommer, T. M., & Crowill, T. L. (2002). Couples negotiating safer sex behaviors: A meta-analysis of the impact of conversation and gender. In M. Allen & R. Preiss (Eds.), *Interpersonal communication research.* Mahwah, NJ: Erlbaum.

Allen, N., Beral, V., Casabonne, E., et al. (2009). Moderate alcohol intake and cancer incidence in women. *Journal of the National Cancer Institute, 101*(5), 296–305.

Allen, P. L. (2000). *The wages of sin: Sex and disease, past and present.* Chicago: University of Chicago Press.

Allison, R., & Risman, B. (2014). "It goes hand in hand with the parties": Race, class, and residence in college student negotiations of hooking up. *Sociological Perspectives, 57*(1), 102–123.

Allyn, D. (1996). Private acts—public policy: Alfred Kinsey, the American Law Institute and the privatization of American sexual morality. *Journal of American Studies, 30,* 405–428.

Allyn, D. (2000). *Make love not war: The sexual revolution: An unfettered history.* Boston: Little, Brown.

Aloni, M., & Bernieri, F. J. (2004). Is love blind? The effects of experience and infatuation on the perception of love. *Journal of Nonverbal Behavior, 28*(4), 287–295.

Alonso-Zaldivar, R., & Neuman, J. (2005, November 11). FDA suggests warning for condoms. *Los Angeles Times,* p. A-15.

Al-Shawaf, T., Zosmer, A., Dirnfeld, M., & Grudzinskas, G. (2005). Safety of drugs used in assisted reproduction techniques. *Drug Safety, 28*(6), 513–528.

Althaus, F. (1997). Most Japanese students do not have intercourse until after adolescence. *Family Planning Perspectives, 29*(3), 145–147.

Althof, S. (2012). Psychological interventions for delayed ejaculation/orgasm. *International Journal of Impotence Research, 24*(4), 131–136.

Althof, S. (2014). Treatment of premature ejaculation: Psychotherapy, pharmacotherapy, and combined therapy. In Y. Binik & K. Hall (Eds.), *Principles and practice of sex therapy* (5th ed., pp. 112–137). New York: Guilford Press.

Altman, C. (2000). Gay and lesbian seniors: Unique challenges of coming out in later life. *SIECUS Report, 4,* 14.

Altman, D. (1986). *AIDS in the mind of America.* New York: Anchor Press, Doubleday.

"AMA Calls for Modernizing Birth Certificate Policies." (2014, June 9). American Medical Association News Room. Retrieved June 16, 2014, from http://www.ama-assn.org/ama /pub/news/news/2014/2014-06-09 -modernizing-birth-certificate-policies .page.

Amador, J., Charles, T., Tait, J., & Helm, H. (2005). Sex and generational differences in desired characteristics in mate selection. *Psychological Reports, 96*(1), 19–25.

Amanpour, C. (2006). World fails to save Africa's AIDS orphans: Africa's HIV-infected children also ignored. *CNN Online.* Retrieved November 3, 2008, from http://www.cnn.com /2006/WORLD/africa/07/17/amanpour .africa.btsc/index.html.

Amar, A., Sutherland, M., & Laughon, K. (2014). Gender differences in attitudes and beliefs associated with bystander behavior and sexual assault. *Journal of Forensic Nursing, 10*(2), 84–91.

Amato, P., & DeBoer, D. (2001). The transmission of marital instability across generations: Relationship skills or commitment to marriage? *Journal of Marriage and the Family, 63,* 1038–1051.

Amato, P. R., & Hohmann-Marriott, B. (2007). A comparison of high- and low-distress marriages that end in divorce. *Journal of Marriage and Family, 69,* 621–639.

Ambady, N., Koo, J., Lee, F., & Rosenthal, R. (1996). More than words: Linguistic and nonlinguistic politeness in two cultures. *Journal of Personality and Social Psychology, 70,* 996–1011.

Ambler, J., Lee, E., Klement, K., Loewald, T., Comber, E., Hanson, S., Cutler, B., Cutler, N., & Sagarin, B. (2017). Consensual BDSM facilitates role-specific altered states of consciousness: A preliminary study. *Psychology of Consciousness: Theory, Research, and Practice, 4*(1), 75–91.

American Academy of Pediatrics. (2012). *Circumcision policy statement.* Retrieved March 2, 2014, from http://pediatrics .aappublications.org/content/early/2012 /08/22/peds.2012-1989.full.pdf+html.

American Academy of Pediatrics. (2012). Section of breastfeeding. Policy statement: Breastfeeding and the use of human milk. *Pediatrics, 129*: e827–41.

American Academy of Pediatrics. (2013). Promoting the well-being of children whose parents are gay or lesbian. *Pediatrics, 131*(4), 827–830.

American Cancer Society. (2007a). *How to perform a breast self exam.* Retrieved March 22, 2008, from http://www.cancer.org /docroot/CRI/content/CRI_2_6x_How_to _perform_a_breast_self_exam_5.asp.

American Cancer Society. (2010). *Cancer: Facts and figures, 2010.* Atlanta, GA: American Cancer Society. Retrieved January 5, 2011, from http://www.cancer.org/acs/groups /content/@epidemiologysurveilance /documents/document/acspc-026238.pdf.

American Cancer Society. (2011). *Breast cancer in men.* Retrieved April 19, 2011, from http:// www.cancer.org/acs/groups/cid/documents /webcontent/003091-pdf.pdf.

American Cancer Society. (2014a). *Breast cancer facts & figures 2013–2014.* Atlanta, GA: American Cancer Society. Retrieved February 21, 2014, from http://www.cancer .org/acs/groups/content/@research /documents/document/acspc-040951.pdf.

American Cancer Society. (2014b). *Key statistics about endometrial cancer.* American Cancer Society. Retrieved February 23, 2014, from http://www.cancer.org/cancer /endometrialcancer/detailedguide /endometrial-uterine-cancer-key-statistics.

American Cancer Society. (2014c). *Key statistics about cervical cancer.* American Cancer Society. Retrieved June 24, 2014, from http:// www.cancer.org/cancer/cervicalcancer /detailedguide/cervical-cancer-key -statistics.

American Cancer Society. (2014d). *Breast awareness and self-exam.* Retrieved June 24, 2014, from http://www.cancer.org/cancer /breastcancer/moreinformation /breastcancerearlydetection/breast-cancer -early-detection-acs-recs-bse?docSelected =breast-cancer-early-detection-acs-recs -clinical-breast-exam.

American Cancer Society. (2014e). *Prostate cancer.* Retrieved June 24, 2014, from http:// www.cancer.org/cancer/prostatecancer.

American Cancer Society. (2017a). Breast cancer at a glance. Retrieved January 20, 2017, from https://cancerstatisticscenter.cancer.org /#/cancer-site/Breast.

American Cancer Society. (2017b). Cervical cancer at a glance. Retrieved January 20, 2017, from https://cancerstatisticscenter.cancer .org/#/cancer-site/Cervix.

American Cancer Society. (2017c). Uterine corpus cancer at a glance. Retrieved January 20, 2017, from https://cancerstatisticscenter.cancer.org /#/cancer-site/Uterine%20corpus.

American Cancer Society. (2017d). Ovarian cancer at a glance. Retrieved January 20, 2017, from https://cancerstatisticscenter.cancer .org/#/cancer-site/Ovary.

American Cancer Society. (2017e). What are the key statistics about breast cancer in men? Retrieved January 25, 2017, from https:// www.cancer.org/cancer/breast-cancer-in -men/about/key-statistics.html.

American Cancer Society. (2017f). What are the key statistics about penile cancer? Retrieved January 25, 2017, from https://www.cancer .org/cancer/penile-cancer/about/key -statistics.html.

American Cancer Society. (2017g). What are the key statistics about testicular cancer? Retrieved January 25, 2017, from https:// www.cancer.org/cancer/testicular-cancer /about/key-statistics.html.

American Cancer Society. (2017h). What are the key statistics for prostate cancer? Retrieved January 25, 2017, from https://www.cancer .org/cancer/prostate-cancer/about/key -statistics.html.

American College Health Association. (2009). American College Health Association National College Health Assessment Spring

2008 reference group data report. *Journal of American College Health, 57*(5), 477–488.

American College Health Association. (2013). Reference Group Executive Summary. Retrieved November 22, 2013, from http://www.acha-ncha.org/docs/ACHA-NCHA-II_ReferenceGroup_ExecutiveSummary_Spring2013.pdf.

American College Health Association. (2016). National College Health Assessment II: Reference Group Executive Summary, Spring, 2016. Hanover, MD. Retrieved January 29, 2017, from http://www.acha-ncha.org/docs/ACHA-NCHA-II_ReferenceGroup_Executive Summary_Spring2016.pdf.

American College of Obstetricians and Gynecologists. (2007). Screening for fetal chromosomal abnormalities. Washington, DC: American College of Obstetricians and Gynecologists (ACOG); 2007 Jan. 11. (*ACOG Practice Bulletin; No. 77*).

American Psychiatric Association. (1998). *Media information: Position statement on hate crimes*. Retrieved October 4, 2008, from http://www.apa.org/releases/hate.html.

American Psychiatric Association. (2000). *Diagnostic and statistical manual of mental disorders* (4th ed., Text. Rev.). Washington, DC: Author.

American Psychiatric Association. (2010). About the DSM. Retrieved June 18, 2011, from http://www.dsm5.org/about/Pages/Default.aspx.

American Psychiatric Association. (2013). *Diagnostic and statistical manual of mental disorders* (5th ed.). Washington, DC: Author.

American Society of Plastic Surgeons. (2013). *2012 Plastic surgery statistics report*. Retrieved February 19, 2014, from http://www.plasticsurgery.org/Documents/news-resources/statistics/2012-Plastic-Surgery-Statistics/plastic-surgery-trends-quick-facts.pdf.

Ames, M. A., & Houston, D. A. (1990). Legal, social, and biological definitions of pedophilia. *Archives of Sexual Behavior, 19*, 333–342.

Amir, M. (1971). *Patterns in forcible rape*. Chicago: University of Chicago Press.

Amis, D. (2007). Care practice #1: Labor begins on its own. *Journal of Perinatal Education, 16*, 16–20.

An, G., Huang, T. H., Wang, D. G., Xie, Q. D., Ma, L., & Chen, D. Y. (2009). In vitro and in vivo studies evaluating recombinant plasmid pCXN2-mIzumo as a potential immunocontraceptive antigen. *American Journal of Reproductive Immunology, 61*(3), 227–235.

Anderson, M. (2016, January 29). More Americans using smartphones for getting directions, streaming TV. FACTANK, Pew Research Center. Retrieved January 11, 2017, from http://www.pewresearch.org/fact-tank/2016/01/29/us-smartphone-use/.

Anderson, P. B., & Savage, J. S. (2005). Social, legal, and institutional context of heterosexual aggression by college women. *Trauma, Violence, & Abuse, 6*(2), 130–140.

Anderson, R., Wandrey, R., Klossner, S., Cahill, S., & Delahanty, D. (2017). Sexual minority status and interpersonal victimization in college men. *Psychology of Sexual Orientation and Gender Diversity, 4*(1), 130–136.

Anderton, D., & Emigh, R. (1989). Polygynous fertility: Sexual competition vs. progeny. *American Journal of Sociology, 94*(4), 832–855.

Andre, A. (2006). The study of sex. Retrieved January 2, 2008, from http://www.alternet.org/story/33347/.

Andrisani, A., Sabbadin, C., Minardi, S., Favaro, A., Donà, G., Bordin, L., Ambrosini, G., & Armanini, D. (2016). Persistent amenorrhea and decreased DHEAS to cortisol ratio after recovery from anorexia nervosa. *Gynecological Endocrinology*, 1–4.

Angier, N. (1999). *Woman: An intimate geography*. New York: Anchor Books.

Anorlu, R. (2008). Cervical cancer: The sub-Saharan African perspective. *Reproductive Health Matters, 16*(32), 41–49.

Antheunis, M., Valkenburg, P. M., & Peter, J. (2007). Computer-mediated communication and interpersonal attraction: An experimental test of two explanatory hypotheses. *CyberPsychology & Behavior, 10*, 831–836.

Apfel, R. J., & Handel, M. H. (1993). *Madness and loss of motherhood*. Washington, DC: American Psychiatric Press.

Aran, I. (2016, February 18). Wait, why does the Catholic Church oppose birth control again? *Fusion*. Retrieved April 5, 2017, from http://fusion.net/wait-why-does-the-catholic-church-oppose-birth-control-1793854826.

Ard, K., Makadon, H. (2011). Addressing intimate partner violence in lesbian, gay, bisexual, and transgender patients. *Journal of General Internal Medicine, 26*(8), 930–933.

Arena, J. M., & Wallace, M. (2008). Issues regarding sexuality. In E. Capezuti, D. Zwicker, M. Mezey, T. Fuller, D. Gray-Miceli, & M. Kluger (Eds.), *Evidence-based geriatric nursing protocols for best practice* (3rd ed., pp. 629–647). New York: Springer Publishing Company.

Aries, E. (1996). *Men and women in interaction: Reconsidering the differences*. New York: Oxford University Press.

Aries, P. (1962). *Centuries of childhood: A social history of family life*. New York: Vintage Books.

Armour, B. S., Wolf, L., Mitra, M., Brieding, M. (2008). Differences in intimate partner violence among women with and without a disability. American Public Health Association's 136th Annual Meeting, San Diego, CA. October 27. Retrieved November 14, 2008, from http://apha.confex.com/apha/136am/webprogram/Paper182004.html.

Arndt, W., Foehl, J., & Good, F. (1985). Specific sexual fantasy themes: A multidimensional study. *Journal of Personality and Social Psychology, 48*(2), 472–480.

Aron, A., Fisher, H., Mashek, D, Strong, G., Li, H., & Brown, L. (2005). Reward, motivation and emotion systems associated with early-stage intense romantic love. *Journal of Neurophysiology, 94*(1), 327–337.

Arrington-Sanders, R., Dyson, J., & Ellen, J. (2007). STDs in adolescents. In J. Klausner & E. Hook (Eds.), *Current diagnosis and treatment of STDs* (pp. 160–166). New York: McGraw-Hill.

Arroba, A. (2004). Costa Rica. In R. T. Francoeur & R. J. Noonan (Eds.), *The Continuum international encyclopedia of sexuality* (pp. 227–240). New York/London: Continuum International.

Arsenault, C. (2011, October 30). Millions of aborted girls imbalance India. *Aljazeera*. Retrieved July 30, 2014, from http://www.aljazeera.com/indepth/features/2011/10/201110415385524923.html.

Asadi, K., Oloomi, M., Mahdavid, M., Habibi, M., & Bouzari, S. (2013). Vaccination with recombinant FimH fused with flagellin enhances cellular and humoral immunity against urinary tract infection in mice. *Vaccine, 3*(8), 1210–1216.

Ashley, R., Barthold, J., & Kolon, T. (2010). Cryptorchidism: Pathogenesis, diagnosis, treatment and prognosis. *Urologic Clinics of North America, 37*(2), 183–193.

"Attorney General Eric Holder Announces Revisions to the Uniform Crime Report's Definition of Rape." (2012, January 6). U.S. Department of Justice Office of Public Affairs. Retrieved June 16, 2014, from http://www.justice.gov/opa/pr/2012/January/12-ag-018.html.

Aubrey, J., Behm-Morawitz, E., & Kim, K. (2014). Understanding the effects of MTV's *16 and Pregnant* on adolescent girls' beliefs, attitudes, and behavioral intentions toward teen pregnancy. *Journal of Health Communication*. Retrieved April 1, 2014, from http://www.ncbi.nlm.nih.gov/pubmed/24628488.

Auchus, R., & Arlt, W. (2013). Approach to the patient: The adult with congenital adrenal hyperplasia. *The Journal of Clinical Endocrinology and Metabolism, 98*(7), 2645–2655.

Audebert, A., Lecointre, L., Afors, K., Koch, A. Wattiez, A., & Akladios, C. (2015). Adolescent endometriosis: Report of a series of 55 cases with a focus on clinical presentation and long-term issues. *Journal of Minimally Invasive Gynecology, 22*(5), 834–840.

Aust, T. R., & Lewis-Jones, D. I. (2004). Retrograde ejaculation and male infertility. *Hospital Medicine, 65*(6), 361–364.

Auster, C. J., & Leone, J. M. (2001). Late adolescents' perspectives on marital rape. *Adolescence, 36*, 141–152.

Auster, C. J., & Ohm, S. C. (2000). Masculinity and femininity in contemporary American Society. *Sex Roles, 43*(7–8), 499–528.

Avegant. (2014). Glyph: A mobile personal theater with built-in premium audio. Retrieved June 17, 2014, from http://www .avegant.com.

Avendaño, C., Mata, A., Sanchez, C., & Doncel, G. (2012). Use of laptop computers connected to internet through wi-fi decreases human sperm motility and increases sperm DNA fragmentation. *Fertility and Sterility, 97*(1), 39–45.

Aversa, T., Messina, M., Mazzanti, L., Salerno, M., Mussa, A., Faienza, M., Scarano, E., DeLuca, F., & Wasniewska, M. (2015). The association with Turner syndrome significantly affects the course of Hashimoto's thyroiditis in children. *Endocrine, 50*(3), 777–782.

Aviram, I. (2005). Online infidelity: Aspects of dyadic satisfaction, self-disclosure, and narcissism. Retrieved May 9, 2005, from http://jcmc.indiana.edu/vol10/issue3/aviram .html.

Awwad, J., Nassar, A., Usta, I., Shaya, M., Younes, Z., & Ghazeeri, G. (2013). Attitudes of Lebanese university students towards surgical hymen reconstruction. *Archives of Sexual Behavior, 42*(8), 1627–1635.

Ayala, M. (2009). Brain serotonin, psychoactive drugs, and effects on reproduction. *Central Nervous System Agents in Medical Chemistry, 9*(4), 258–276.

Baams, L., Grossman, A., & Russel, S. (2015). Minority stress and mechanisms of risk for depression and suicidal ideation among lesbian, gay, and bisexual youth. *Developmental Psychology, 51*(5), 688–696.

Babin, E. A. (2013). An examination of predictors of nonverbal and verbal communication of pleasure during sex and sexual satisfaction. *Journal of Social and Personal Relationships, 30*(3), 270–292.

Bachai, S. (2014, March 20). Time management isn't for men: 70% would give up friendships for more time in the day. *Medical Daily*. Retrieved May 2, 2014, from http://www .medicaldaily.com/time-management -isntmen-70-would-give-friendships-more -time-day-271750.

Bacon, C. G., Mittleman, M. A., Kawachi, I., et al. (2003). Sexual function in men older than 50 years of age: Results from the health professionals follow-up study. *Annals of Internal Medicine, 139*, 161–168.

Badawy Z. S., Chohan K. R., Whyte D. A., Penefsky H. S., Brown O. M., & Souid A. K. (2008). Cannabinoids inhibit the respiration of human sperm. Fertility and Sterility. Retrieved October 13, 2008, from http://www .fertstert.org/article/S0015–0282(08)00750 –4/abstract.

Badgett, M., Lau, H., Sears, B., & Ho, D. (2007). *Bias in the workplace: Consistent evidence of sexual orientation and gender identity discrimination*. The Williams Institute. Retrieved May 15, 2014, from http:// williamsinstitute.law.ucla.edu/wp-content /uploads/Badgett-Sears-Lau-Ho-Bias-in-the -Workplace-Jun-2007.pdf.

Baer, D. (2015, July 1). Japan's huge sex problem is setting up a 'demographic time bomb' for the country. *Business Insider*. Retrieved August 23, 2017, from http://www .businessinsider.com/half-of-japanese -people-arent-having-sex-2015-7.

Baez-Sierra, D., Balgobin, C., & Wise, T. (2016). Treatment of paraphilic disorders. In R. Balon (Ed.), *Practical guide to paraphilia and paraphilic disorders* (pp. 430–462). Cham, Switzerland: Springer International.

Bagemihl, B. (1999). *Biological exuberance: Animal homosexuality and natural diversity*. New York: St. Martin's Press.

Baggaley, R., White, R., & Boily, M. C. (2008). Systematic review of orogenital HIV-1 transmission probabilities. *International Journal of Epidemiology, 37*(6), 1255–1265.

Bagley, D. (2005). Personal communication.

Bagwell-Gray, M., Messing, J., & Baldwin-White, A. (2015). Intimate partner sexual violence: A review of terms, definitions, and prevalence. *Trauma, Violence & Abuse, 16*(3), 316–335.

Bai, Y., Pu, C., Han, P., Li, J., Yuan, H., Tang, Y., Wang, X., & Wei, Q. (2015). Selective serotonin reuptake inhibitors plus phosphodiesterase-5 inhibitors for premature ejaculation: A systematic review and meta-analysis. *Urology, 86*(4), 758–764.

Bailey, A., & Hurd, P. (2005). Finger length ratio correlates with physical aggression in men but not in women. *Biological Psychology, 68*(3), 215–222.

Bailey, B. P., Gurak, L. J., & Konstan, J. A. (2003). Trust in cyberspace. In J. Ratner (Ed.), *Human factors and Web development* (2nd ed., pp. 311–321). Mahwah, NJ: Erlbaum.

Bailey, J. M., & Pillard, R. C. (1995). Genetics of human sexual orientation. *Annual Review of Sex Research, 6*, 126–150.

Bailey, R., Egesah, O., & Rosenberg, S. (2008). Male circumcision for HIV prevention: A prospective study of complications in clinical and traditional settings in Bungoma, Kenya.

Bulletin of the World Health Organization, 86, 669–677.

Baiocco, R., Fontanesi, L., Santamaria, F., Loverno, S., Marasco, B., Baumgartner, E., Willoughby, B., & Laghi, F. (2014, March 27). Negative parental responses to coming out and family functioning in a sample of lesbian and gay young adults. *Journal of Child and Family Studies*. Retrieved May 12, 2014, from http://link.springer.com/article/10.1007% 2Fs10826-014-9954-z#page-1.

Baird, D., Dunson, D., Hill, M., Cousins, D., & Schectman, J. (2003). High cumulative incidence of uterine leiomyoma in black and white women. *American Journal of Obstetrics and Gynecology, 188*(1), 100–107.

Baker, M., Frazier, P., Greer, C., Paulsen, J., Howard, K., Meredith, L., Anders, S., & Shallcross, S. (2016). Sexual victimization history predicts academic performance in college women. *Journal of Counseling Psychology, 63*(6), 685–692.

Bakir, A., & Palan, K. (2010). How are children's attitudes toward ads and brands affected by gender-related content in advertising? *Journal of Advertising, 39*(1), 35–48.

Baladerian, N. J. (1991). Sexual abuse of people with developmental disabilities. *Sexuality and Disability, 9*, 323–335.

Ball, H. (2005). Sexual offending on elderly women: A review. *Journal of Forensic Psychiatry & Psychology, 16*(1), 127–138.

Balon, R. (2008). The DSM criteria of sexual dysfunction: Need for a change. *Journal of Sex and Marital Therapy, 34*(3), 186–197.

Balsam, K. F., Beauchaine, T., Rothblum, E., & Solomon, S. (2008). Three-year follow-up of same-sex couples who had civil unions in Vermont, same-sex couples not in civil unions, and heterosexual married couples. *Developmental Psychology, 44*, 101–116.

Balsam, K., Molina, Y., Beadnell, B., Simoni, J., & Walters, K. (2011). Measuring multiple minority stress: The LGBT people of color microaggressions scale. *Cultural Diversity and Ethnic Minority Psychology, 17*(2), 163–174.

Balsam, K., Rothblum, E., & Beauchaine, T. (2005). Victimization over the life span: A comparison of lesbian, gay, bisexual and heterosexual siblings. *Journal of Counseling and Clinical Psychology, 73*, 477–487.

Bancroft, J. (2004). Alfred C. Kinsey and the politics of sex research. *Annual Review of Sex Research, 15*, 1–39.

Bancroft, J., & Vukadinovic, Z. (2004). Sexual addiction, sexual compulsivity, or what? Toward a theoretical model. *Journal of Sex Research, 41*(3), 225–234.

Bancroft, J., Graham, C., Janssen, R., & Sanders, S. (2009). The dual control model: Current status and future directions. *Journal of Sex Research, 46*(2–3), 121–142.

Bancroft, J., Herbenick, D., Barnes, T., Hallam-Jones, R., Wylie, K., & Janssen, E. (2005). The relevance of the dual control model to male sexual dysfunction: The Kinsey Institute/BASRT collaborative project. *Sexual & Relationship Therapy, 20*(1), 13–30.

Bandura, A. (1969). *Principles of behavior modification*. Austin, TX: Holt, Rinehart & Winston.

Banyard, V., Moynihan, M., Walsh, W., Cohn, E., & Ward, S. (2010). Friends of survivors: The community impact of unwanted sexual experiences. *Journal of Interpersonal Violence, 25*(2), 242–256.

Bao, A., & Swaab, D. (2010). Sex differences in the brain, behavior, and neuropsychiatric disorders. *Neuroscientist, 16*(5), 550–565.

Barbach, L. (1982). *For each other: Sharing sexual intimacy*. New York: Penguin Group.

Barber, N. (2008). Explaining cross-national differences in polygyny intensity. *Cross-Cultural Research, 42*, 103.

Bardeguez, A., Lindsey, J., Shannon, M., Tuomala, R., Cohn, S., Smith, E., et al. (2008). Adherence to antiretrovirals among US women during and after pregnancy. *Journal of Acquired Immune Deficiency Syndrome, 48*, 408–417.

Barford, V. (2008, February, 25). Iran's 'diagnosed transsexuals.' *BBC News*. Retrieved December 20, 2010, from http://news.bbc.co.uk/2/hi/7259057.stm.

Barker, D. J. (1997). Maternal nutrition, fetal nutrition, and disease in later life. *Nutrition, 13*(9), 807–813.

Barnes, D., & Meyer, I. (2012). Religious affiliation, internalized homophobia, and mental health in lesbians, gay men, and bisexuals. *American Journal of Orthopsychiatry, 82*(4), 505–515.

Baron, L. (1990). Pornography and gender equality: An empirical analysis. *The Journal of Sex Research, 27*, 363–380.

Baron, L., & Straus, M. A. (1987). Four theories of rape: A macrosociological analysis. *Social Problems, 34*, 467–489.

Baron, N. (2008). *Always on: Language in an online and mobile world*. New York, NY: Oxford University Press.

Baron, N. S. (2004). See you online: Gender issues in college student use of instant messaging. *Journal of Language & Social Psychology, 23*(4), 397–423.

Baron, N., & Ling, R. (2007). Emerging patterns of American mobile phone use: Electronically-mediated communication in transition. In G. Goggin & L. Hjorth (Eds.), *Mobile Media 2007: Proceedings of an International Conference on Social and Cultural Aspects of Mobile Phones, Media and Wireless Technologies,* June 2–4. University of Sydney, Sydney, Australia.

Barral, M., de Oliveira, G., Lobato, R., Mendoza-Sassi, R., Martinez, A., & Gonçalves, C. (2014). Risk factors of HIV-1 vertical transmission and the influence of antiretroviral therapy in pregnancy outcome. *Revista Do Instituto De Medicina Topical De São Paulo, 56*(2), 133–138.

Baron-Cohen, S., Lombardo, M., Augeung, B., Ashwin, E., Chakrabarti, B., & Knickmeyer, R. (2011). Why are autism spectrum conditions more prevalent in males? *PLoS Biology, 9*(6). Retrieved from http://www.plosbiology.org/article/info%3Adoi%2F10.1371%2Fjournal.pbio.1001081.

Barratt, C., Mansell, S., Beaton, C., Tardif, S., & Oxenham, S. (2011). Diagnostic tools in male infertility—The question of sperm dysfunction. *Asian Journal of Andrology, 13*(1), 53–58.

Barros, A., & Sampaio, M. (2012). Gynecomastia: Physiopathology, evaluation and treatment. *São Paulo Medical Journal, 130*(3), 187–197.

Barrow, R., Newman, L., & Douglas, J. (2008). Taking positive steps to address STD disparities for African-American communities. *Sexually Transmitted Diseases, 35*(12), S1–S3.

Bart, P. B., & O'Brien, P. H. (1985). *Stopping rape: Successful survival strategies*. New York: Pergamon Press.

Barth, K. R., Cook, R. L., Downs, J. S., Switzer, G. E., & Fischoff, B. (2002). Social stigma and negative consequences: Factors that influence college students' decision to seek testing for STIs. *Journal of American College Health, 50*(4), 153–160.

Bartholomew, K., & Horowitz, L. (1991). Attachment styles among young adults: A test of a four-category model. *Journal of Personality and Social Psychology, 61*, 226–244.

Barton, J., Braxton, J., Davis, D., DeVoux, A., Flagg, E., Grier, L., Harvey, A., Kidd, S., Kirkcaldy, R., Kreisel, K., et al. (2016) Sexually transmitted disease surveillance, 2015. U.S. Centers for Disease Control and Prevention, Department of Health and Human Services, Atlanta, GA. Retrieved April 26, 2017, from https://www.cdc.gov/std/stats15/std-surveillance-2015-print.pdf.

Bar-Yosef, Y., Greenstein, A., Beri, A., Lidawi, G., Matzkin, H., & Chen, J. (2007). Doral vein injuries observed during penile exploration for suspected penile fracture. *Journal of Sexual Medicine, 4*, 1142–1146.

Basaran, H., Akgü., S., Kanbur, N., Gümrük, F., Cetin, M., & Derman, O. (2013). Dysfunctional uterine bleeding in adolescent girls and evaluation of their response to treatment. *Turkish Journal of Pediatrics, 55*(2), 186–189.

Basaria, S., Coviello, A., Travison, T., Storer, T., Farwell, W., Jette, A. M., et al. (2010). Adverse events associated with testosterone administration. *New England Journal of Medicine, 363*, 109–122.

Basile, K., Breiding, M., & Smith, S. (2017). Disability and risk of recent sexual violence in the United States. *American Journal of Public Health, 106*(5), 928–933.

Basile, K., Smith, S., Breiding, M., Black, M., & Mahendra, R. (2014). Sexual violence surveillance: Uniform definitions and recommended data elements. Centers for Disease Control and Prevention, Atlanta, GA.

Basile, K., Smith, S., Fowler, D., Walters, M., Hamburger, M. (2016). Sexual violence victimization and associations with health in a community sample of African American women. *Journal of Aggression, Maltreatment & Trauma, 25*(3). Retrieved August 23, 2017, from http://www.tandfonline.com/doi/abs/10.1080/10926771.2015.1079283.

Basow, S., & Minieri, A. (2011). "You owe me": Effects of date cost, who pays, participant gender, and rape myth beliefs on perceptions of rape. *Journal of Interpersonal Violence, 26*(3), 479–497.

Basson, R. (2000a). The female sexual response: A different model. *Journal of Sex and Marital Therapy, 26*, 51–65.

Basson, R. (2000b). The female sexual response revisited. *Journal of Obstetrics and Gynaecology of Canada, 22*, 383–387.

Basson, R. (2001). Using a different model for female sexual response to address women's problematic low sexual desire. *Journal of Sex and Marital Therapy, 27*, 395–403.

Basson, R. (2005). Women's sexual dysfunction: Revised and expanded definitions. *Canadian Medical Association Journal, 172*(10), 1327–1333.

Basson, R., Leiblum, S., Brotto, L., Derogatis, L., Fourcroy, J., Fugl-Meyer, K., Graziottin, A., Heiman, J., Laan, E., Meston, C., Schover, L., Van Lankveld, J., & Schultz, W. (2004). Revised definitions of women's sexual dysfunction. *Journal of Sexual Medicine, 1*(1), 40–48.

Basson, R., McInnes, R., Smith, M., Hodgson, G., & Koppiker, N. (2002). Efficacy and safety of sildenafil citrate in women with sexual dysfunction associated with female sexual arousal disorder. *Journal of Women's Health and Gender-Based Medicine, 11*(4), 367–377.

Basson, R., Rees, P., Wang, R., Montejo, A. L., & Incrocci, L. (2010). Sexual function in chronic illness. *Journal of Sexual Medicine, 7*(1 Pt 2), 374–388.

Bassuk, S., & Manson, J. (2015). Oral contraceptives and menopausal hormone therapy: Relative and attributable risks of cardiovascular disease, cancer, and other health outcomes. *Annals of Epidemiology, 25*(3), 193–200.

Batabyal, A. A. (2001). On the likelihood of finding the right partner in an arranged marriage. *Journal of Socio-Economics*, *30*(3), 273–281.

Bauer, G. R., & Welles, S. L. (2001). Beyond assumptions of negligible risk: STDs and women who have sex with women. *American Journal of Public Health*, *91*(8), 1282–1287.

Bauermeister, J. A., Johns, M. M., Sandfort, T. G., Eisenberg, A., Grossman, A. H., & D'Augelli, A. R. (2010). Relationship trajectories and psychological well-being among sexual minority youth. *Journal of Youth and Adolescence*, *39*(10), 1148–1163.

Baumeister, L. M., Flores, E., & Marin, B. V. (1995). Sex information given to Latina adolescents by parents. *Health Education Research*, *10*(2), 233–239.

Baumeister, R. F. (1988). Masochism as escape from self. *Journal of Sex Research*, 25, 28–59.

Baxter, J., & Hewitt, B. (2010). Pathways into marriage: Cohabitation and the domestic division of labor. *Journal of Family Issues*, *31*(11), 1507–1529.

Bayer, R. (1981). *Homosexuality and American psychiatry: The politics of diagnosis*. New York: Basic Books.

Baylin, A., Hernandez-Diaz, S., Siles, X., Kabagambe, E., & Campos, H. (2007). Triggers of nonfatal myocardial infarction in Costa Rica: Heavy physical exertion, sexual activity, and infection. *Annals of Epidemiology*, *17*, 112–118.

Bazarova, N., & Yuan, Y. (2013). Expertise recognition and influence in intercultural groups: Differences between face-to-face and computer-mediated communication. *Journal of Computer-Mediated Communication*, *18*(4), 437–453.

Bazi, T. (2016). Female genital mulilation: The role of medical professional orgasnizations. *International Urogynecology Journal*. Retrieved January 21, 2017, from http://link.springer.com/article/10.1007/s00192-016-3202-6.

Beaber, E., Buist, D., Barlow, W., Malone, K., Reed, S., & Li, C. (2014). Recent oral contraceptive use by formulation and breast cancer risk among women 20 to 49 years of age. *Cancer Research*, *74*(15), 2028–2035.

Beaber, E., Buist, D., Barlow, W., Malone, K., Reed, S., & Li, C. (2014a). Recent oral contraceptive use by formulation and breast cancer risk among women 20 to 49 years of age. *Cancer Research*, *74*(15), 4078–4089.

Beaber, E., Malone, K., Tang, M., Barlow, W., Porter, P., Daling, J., & Li, C. (2014). Oral contraceptives and breast cancer risk overall and by molecular subtype among young women. *Cancer Epidemiology, Biomarkers & Prevention*, *23*(5), 755–764.

Beacher, F., Minati, L., Baron-Cohen, S., Lombardo, M., Lai, Gray, M., Harrison, N., & Critchley, H. (2012). Autism attenuates sex differences in brain structure: A combined voxel-based morphometry and diffusion tensor imaging study. *American Journal of Neuroradiology*, *33*(1), 83–89.

Beals, K. P., & Peplau, L. A. (2005). Identity support, identity devaluation, and well-being among lesbians. *Psychology of Women Quarterly*, *29*(2), 140–148.

Bearak, B. (2009, September 22). Mixed verdict in S. African lesbian's murder trial. *New York Times*. Retrieved April 20, 2011, from http://www.nytimes.com/2009/09/23/world/africa/23safrica.html.

Bearman, P., & Bruckner, H. (2001). Promising the future: Virginity pledges and first intercourse. *American Journal of Sociology*, *106*(4), 859–912.

Beaton, A. A., & Mellor, G. (2007). Direction of hair whorl and handedness. *Laterality*, *12*, 295–301.

Beck, A., Berzofsky, M., Caspar, R., & Krebs, C. (2013). Sexual victimization in prisons and jails reported by inmates. U.S. Department of Justice, Bureau of Justice Statistics. Retrieved June 17, 2014, from http://www.bjs.gov/content/pub/pdf/svpjri1112.pdf.

Beck, K. (2016, March 30). When your rapist is a woman. *Marie Claire*. Retrieved from http://www.marieclaire.com/culture/a19495/women-raped-by-women/.

Beck, M. (2008, September 30). Is sex addiction a sickness, or excuse to behave badly? *Wall Street Journal*, (Eastern edition). New York, p. B.9.

Becker, J. V., et al. (1986). Level of postassault sexual functioning in rape and incest victims. *Archives of Sexual Behavior*, *15*, 37–50.

Becker, M., Weinberger, T., Chandy, A., & Schmukler, S. (2016). Depression during pregnancy and postpartum. *Current Psychiatry Reports*, *18*(3), 32.

Beckett, M. K., Elliott, M. N., Martino, S., Kanouse, D. E., Corona, R., Klein, D. J., & Schuster, M. A. (2010). Timing of parent and child communication about sexuality relative to children's sexual behaviors. *Pediatrics*, *125*(1), 34–42.

Beckmann, M., Dittrick, R., Findeklee, S., & Lotz, L. (2016). Surgical aspects of ovarian tissue removal and ovarian tissue transplantation for fertility preservation. *Geburtshilfe and Frauenheilkunde*, *76*(10), 1057–1064.

Bedell, S., Manders, D., Kehoe, S., Lea, J., Miller, D., Richardson, D., & Carlson, M. (2017). The opinions and practices of providers toward the sexual issues of cervical cancer patients undergoing treatment. *Gynecologic Oncology*, *144*(3), 586–591.

Beeble, M., Sullivan, C., & Bybee, D. (2011). The impact of neighborhood factors on the well-being of survivors of intimate partner violence over time. *American Journal of Community Psychology*, *47*(3–4), 287–306.

Beech, A., Ward, T., & Fisher, D. (2006). The identification of sexual and violent motivations in men who assault women: Implication for treatment. *Journal of Interpersonal Violence*, *21*, 1635.

Begley, S. (2007, May 7). Just say no—to bad science. *Newsweek*, p. 57.

Begley, S. (2010, July 2). The anti-lesbian drug. *Newsweek*. Retrieved November 16, 2010, from http://www.newsweek.com/2010/07/02/the-anti-lesbian-drug.html.

Behre, H., Zitzmann, M., Anderson, R., Handelsman, D., Lestari, S., McLachlan, R., Meriggiola, M., Misro, M., et al. (2016). Efficacy and safety of an injectable combination hormonal contraceptive for men. *The Journal of Clinical Endocrinology and Metabolism*, *101*(12), 4779–4788.

Belkin, L. (2011, February 11). The IRS, breast pumps and other updates. *New York Times*. Retrieved May 30, 2011, from http://parenting.blogs.nytimes.com/2011/02/11/the-irs-breast-pumps-and-other-updates/.

Belknap, P., & Leonard II, W. M. (1991). A conceptual replication and extension of Erving Goffman's study of gender advertisements. *Sex Roles*, *25*, 103–118.

Bell, A. P., Weinberg, M. S., & Hammersmith, S. K. (1981). *Sexual preference: Its development in men and women*. Bloomington: Indiana University Press.

Bellieni, C., & Buonocore, G. (2013). Abortion and subsequent mental health: Review of the literature. *Psychiatry and Clinical Neurosciences*, *67*(5), 301–310.

Bellino, S., Renocchio, M., Zizzo, M., Rocca, G., Bogetti, P., & Bogetto, F. (2010). Quality of life of patients who undergo breast reconstruction after mastectomy: Effects of personality characteristics. *Plastic Reconstructive Surgery*, *127*(1), 10–17.

Bellot, G. (2016, November 1). On being queer in the Caribbean. *New York Times*. Retrieved January 18, 2017, from https://www.nytimes.com/2015/11/01/opinion/sunday/on-being-queer-in-the-caribbean.html.

Belsky, J., Houts, R., & Fearon, R. (2010). Infant attachment security and the timing of puberty: Testing an evolutionary hypothesis. *Psychological Science*, *21*(9), 1195–1201.

Bem, D. J. (2000). Exotic becomes erotic: Interpreting the biological correlates of sexual orientation. *Archives of Sexual Behavior*, *29*(6), 531–548.

Bem, S. L. (1974). The measurement of psychological androgyny. *Journal of Consulting and Clinical Psychology*, *42*, 155–162.

Bem, S. L. (1977). On the utility of alternative procedures for assessing psychological androgyny. *Journal of Consulting and Clinical Psychology, 45*, 196–205.

Bem, S. L. (1981). Gender schema theory: A cognitive account of sex-typing. *Psychological Review, 88*, 354 364.

Ben-Aroya, Z., & Edwards, L. (2015). Vulvodynia. *Seminars in Cutaneous Medicine and Surgery, 34*(4), 192–198.

Benedict, C., Philip, E., Baser, R., Carter, J., Schuler, T., Jandorf, L., DuHamel, K., & Nelson, C. (2016). Body image and sexual function in women after treatment for anal and rectal cancer. *Psycho-Oncology, 25*(3), 316–323.

Benevento, B. T., & Sipski, M. L. (2002). Neurogenic bladder, neurogenic bowel, and sexual dysfunction in people with spinal cord injury. *Physical Therapy, 82*(6), 601–612.

Benjamin, H. (1961). *Encyclopedia of sexual behavior*. New York: Hawthorn Books.

Bennett, J. (2009). Only you. And you. And you. *Newsweek*. Retrieved July 3, 2011, from http:// www.newsweek.com/2009/07/28/only-you -and-you-and-you.html.

Bennett, J. (2016, January 31). She? Ze? They? (Hmm?) What's in a gender pronoun? *New York Times*. Retrieved January 18, 2017, from https://www.nytimes.com/2016/01/31 /fashion/pronoun-confusion-sexual-fluidity .html.

Benokraitis, N. V. (1993). *Marriages and families*. Englewood Cliffs, NJ: Prentice Hall.

Bensley, L., Eenwyk, J., & Simmons, K. (2000). Self-reported childhood sexual and physical abuse and adult HIV-risk behaviors and heavy drinking. *American Journal of Preventive Medicine, 18*(2), 151–158.

Benson, A., Ost, L., Noble, M., & Laakin, M. (2009). Premature ejaculation. *Emedicine*. Retrieved March 25, 2010, from http:// emedicine.medscape.com/article/435884 -overview.

Benson, L., McGinn, M., & Christensen, A. (2012). Common principles of couple therapy. *Behavior Therapy, 43*(1), 25–35.

Benton, T. (2008). Depression and HIV/AIDS. *Current Psychiatry Reports, 10*, 280–285.

Ben-Zeev, A., Scharnetzki, L., Chan, L., & Dennehy, T. (2012). Hypermasculinity in the media: When men "walk into the fog" to avoid affective communication. *Psychology of Popular Media Culture, 1*(1), 53–61.

Ben-Zion, I., & Shiber, A. (2006). Heart to heart: Rehabilitation of sexuality in cardiac patients. *Harefuah, 145*, 350–351.

Benzer, A. (2009, October 16). How to be a multiorgasmic man. *Huffington Post*. Retrieved April 20, 2014, from http://www .huffingtonpost.com/dr-alex-benzer/how-to -be-a-multiorgasmic_b_319087.html.

Berenbaum, S., & Beltz, A. (2011). Sexual differentiation of human behavior: Effects of prenatal and pubertal organizational hormones. *Frontiers in Neuroendocrinology, 32*(2), 183–200.

Berenbaum, S., Korman Bryk, K., & Beltz, A. (2012). Early androgen effects on spatial and mechanical abilities: Evidence from congenital adrenal hyperplasia. *Behavioral Neuroscience, 126*(1), 86–96.

Berenbaum, S. A., & Snyder, E. (1995). Early hormonal influences on childhood sex-typed activity and playmate preferences. *Developmental Psychology, 31*(1), 31–43.

Bergen, K., Kirby, E., & McBride, C. (2007). "How do you get two houses cleaned?": Accomplishing family caregiving in commuter marriages. *Journal of Family Communication, 7*(4), 287–307.

Bergen, R., & Bukovec, P. (2006). Men and intimate partner rape: Characteristics of men who sexually abuse their partner. *Journal of Interpersonal Violence, 21*, 1375.

Berger, R. J., Searles, P., & Cottle, C. E. (1991). *Feminism and pornography*. New York: Praeger.

Berger, V. (2015). Clinician confidence in treating eating disorders manifesting in survivors of child sexual abuse. *Dissertation Abstracts International: Section B: The Sciences and Engineering, 76*(2-B), 978-1-321-27073-0.

Bergman, K., Rubio, R., Green, R., & Padron, E. (2010). Gay men who become fathers via surrogacy: The transition to parenthood. *Journal of GLBT Family Studies, 6*, 111–141.

Bergmann, M. S. (1987). *The anatomy of living*. New York: Fawcett Columbine.

Bergstrand, C., & Williams, B. (2000, October 10). Today's alternative marriage styles: The case of swingers. *Electronic Journal of Human Sexuality, 3*. Retrieved September 14, 2008, from http://www.ejhs.org/volume3/swing /body.htm.

Berkey, B. R., Perelman-Hall, T., & Kurdek, L. A. (1990). The multidimensional scale of sexuality. *Journal of Homosexuality, 19*, 67–87.

Berkowitz, D., & Marsiglio, W. (2007). Gay men: Negotiating procreative, father, and family identities. *Journal of Marriage and Family, 69*, 366–382.

Bernstein, E. (2010, October 19). I'm very, very, very sorry—really? *Wall Street Journal*, D1.

Bersamin, M. M., Paschall, M. J., Saltz, R. F., & Zamboanga, B. L. (2011). Young adults and casual sex: The relevance of college drinking settings. *Journal of Sex Research, 20*, 1–8.

Bertone-Johnson, E., Hankinson, S., Johnson, S., & Manson, J. (2008). Cigarette smoking and the development of premenstrual syndrome. *American Journal of Epidemiology, 168*(8), 938–945.

Besharov, D. (1988). *Protecting children from abuse and neglect: Policy and practices*. Springfield, IL: Charles C. Thomas.

Beshay, S., Rivera, G., Balthasar, J., & Florea, N. (2015). Efficacy and clinical value of commonly compounded hormone replacement therapy: A literature review. *International Journal of Pharmaceutical Compounding, 19*(1), 6–12.

Bestic, L. (2005). When a patch works. Retrieved August 30, 2005, from http:// www.timesonline.co.uk/article/0,,8124 –1716899,00.html

Bethlehem, J. (2010). Selection bias in web surveys. *International Statistical Review, 78*(2), 161–188.

Beveridge, J. (2015). A tangled web: Internet pornography, sexual addiction, and the erosion of attachment. In L. Cundy (Ed.), *Love in the age of the Internet: Attachment in the digital era* (pp. 31–52). London: Karnac.

Bezemer, D., de Wolf, F., Boerlijst, M. C., van Sighem, A., Hollingsworth, T. D., Prins, M., Geskus, R. B., Gras, L., Coutinho, R. A., & Fraser, C. (2008). A resurgent HIV-1 epidemic among men who have sex with men in the era of potent antiretroviral therapy. *AIDS, 22*(9), 1071–1077.

Bhide, A., Nama, V., Patel, S., & Kalu, E. (2010). Microbiology of cysts/abscesses of Bartholin's gland: Review of empirical antibiotic therapy against microbial culture. *Journal of Obstetrics and Gynecology, 30*(7), 701–703.

Bialik, C. (2007). Sorry you have gone over your limit of network friends. *Wall Street Journal*. Retrieved February 10, 2008, from http:// online.wsj.com/article/SB119518271549595364 .html?mod=googlenews_wsj.

Bialik, C. (2010, October 9). Research into human sexuality leaves a lot to be desired. *Wall Street Journal*, p. A2.

Bianchi., D., Parker, R., Wentworth, J., Madankumar, R., Saffer, C., Das, A., Craig, J., Chudova, D., et al. (2014). DNA sequencing versus standard prenatal aneuploidy screening. *New England Journal of Medicine, 370*, 799–808.

Bianco, S. (2012). A potential mechanism for the sexual dimorphism in the onset of puberty and incidence of idiopathic central precocious puberty in children. *Frontiers in Endocrinology, 3*, 149.

Biblarz, T., & Savci, E. (2010). Lesbian, gay, bisexual, and transgender families. *Journal of Marriage and Family, 72*, 480–497.

Bick, R. L., Maden, J., Heller, K. B., & Toofanian, A. (1998). Recurrent miscarriage: Causes, evaluation, and treatment. *Medscape Women's Health, 3*(3), 2.

Bieber, I., et al. (1962). *Homosexuality: A psychoanalytic study*. New York: Basic Books.

Biello, D. (2007, December 5). What is the best age difference for husband and wife? *Scientific American*. Retrieved May 11, 2011,

from http://www.scientificamerican.com
/article.cfm?id5what-is-the-best-age
-difference-for-husband-and-wife.

Bigelow, B. J. (1977). Children's friendship expectations: A cognitive developmental study. *Child Development, 48,* 246–253.

Biglia, N., Moggio, G., Peano, E., Sgandurra, P., Ponzone, R., Nappi, R. E., & Sismondi, P. (2010). Effects of surgical and adjuvant therapies for breast cancer on sexuality, cognitive functions, and body weight. *Journal of Sexual Medicine, 7*(5), 1891–1900.

Bilardi, J., Walker, S., Temple-Smith, M., McNair, R., Mooney-Somers, J., Bellhouse, C., Fairley, C., Chen, M., & Bradshaw, C. (2013). The burden of bacterial vaginosis: Women's experience of the physical, emotional, sexual and social impact of living with recurrent bacterial vaginosis. *PLOS ONE, 8*(9), 1–13.

Billups, K., Berman, L., Berman, J., Metz, M., Glennon, M., & Goldstein, I. (2001). A new non-pharmacological vacuum therapy for female sexual dysfunction. *Journal of Sex and Marital Therapy, 27*(5), 435–441.

Bimbi, D. S. (2007). Male prostitution: Pathology, paradigms and progress in research. *Journal of Homosexuality, 53*(1–2), 7–35.

Bingham, J. (2014, January 27). Working mothers plagued with guilt—as men secretly pine to be stay-at-home fathers. *The Telegraph.* Retrieved February 14, 2014, from http://www.telegraph.co.uk/women/mother -tongue/10597883/Working-mothers -plagued-with-guilt-as-men-secretly-pine -to-be-stay-at-home-fathers.html.

Binik, Y., Brotto, L., Graham, C., & Segraves, R. (2010). Response of the DSM-V sexual dysfunctions subworkgroup to commentaries published in the JSM. *Journal of Sexual Medicine, 7*(7), 2382–2387.

Bird, M. H. (2006). Sexual addiction and marriage and family therapy: Facilitating individual and relationship healing through couple therapy. *Journal of Marital and Family Therapy, 32*(3), 297–310.

Birdthistle, I., Floyd, S., Machingura, A., Mudziwapasi, N., Gregson, S., Glynn, J. R. (2008). From affected to infected? Orphanhood and HIV risk among female adolescents in urban Zimbabwe. *Epidemiology and Social AIDS, 22*(6), 759–766.

Birnbaum, G., Glaubman, H., & Mikulincer, M. (2001). Women's experience of heterosexual intercourse. *Journal of Sex Research, 38*(3), 191–194.

Birnbaum, G., Reis, H., Mizrahi, M., Kanat-Maymon, Y., Sass, O., & Granovski-Milner, C. (2016). Intimately connected: The importance of partner responsiveness for experiencing sexual desire. *Journal of Personality and Social Psychology, 111*(4), 530–546.

Biro, F., Galvez, M., Greenspan, L., Succop, P., Vangeepuram, N., Pinney, S., Teitelbaum, S., Windham, G., Kushi, L., & Wolff, M. (2010). Pubertal assessment method and baseline characteristics in a mixed longitudinal study of girls. *Pediatrics, 6*(11), 595.

Biro, F., Greenspan, L., Galvez, M., Pinney, S., Teitelbaum, S., Windham, G., Deardorff, J., Herrick, R., Succop, P., Hiatt, R., Kushi, L., & Wolff, M. (2013). Onset of breast development in a longitudinal cohort. *Pediatrics, 132*(6), 1019–1027.

Bish, C. L., Chu, S. Y., Shapiro-Mendoza, C., Sharma, A., & Blanck, H. (May 1, 2008). Trying to lose or maintain weight during pregnancy—United States, 2003. *Maternal and Child Health Journal.* Retrieved October 14, 2008, from http://www.springerlink.com /content/n76tk678r07j87v1/?p=13a0415474414 3e6be60537c74733c0d&pi=1.

Bispo, G., De Lima Lopes, J., & De Barros, A. (2013). Cardiovascular changes resulting from sexual activity and sexual dysfunction after myocardial infarction. *Journal of Clinical Nursing, 22*(23–24), 3522–3531.

Bisson, M., & Levine, T. (2009). Negotiating a friends with benefits relationship. *Archives of Sexual Behavior, 38*(1), 66–73.

Biswas, S. (2005, May 17). Fear and loathing in gay India. *BBC News.* Retrieved September 15, 2008, from http://news.bbc.co.uk/2/hi/south _asia/4304081.stm.

Bittles, A. H., Mason, W. M., & Greene, J. (1991). Reproductive behavior and health in consanguineous marriages. *Science, 252*(5007), 789–794.

Bivona, J., & Critelli, J. (2009). The nature of women's rape fantasies: An analysis of prevalence, frequency, and contents. *Journal of Sex Research, 46*(1), 33–45.

Bivona, J., Critelli, J., Clark, M. (2012). Women's rape fantasies: An empirical evaluation of the major explanations. *Archives of Sexual Behavior, 41*(5), 1107–1119.

Bjornelv, S., Nordahl, H. M., & Holmen, T. L. (2011). Psychological factors and weight problems in adolescents. The role of eating problems, emotional problems, and personality traits: The Young-HUNT Study. *Social Psychiatry and Psychiatry Epidemiology, 46*(5), 353–362.

Black, K., & Gold, D. (2008). Gender differences and socioeconomic status biases in judgments about blame in date rape scenarios. *Violence and Victims, 23*(1), 115–128.

Black, M., Basile, K., Breiding, M., Smith, S., Walters, M., Merrick, M., Chen, J., & Stevens, M. (2011). The National Intimate Partner and Sexual Violence Survey (NISVS): 2010 Summary Report. Atlanta, GA. Retrieved from https://www.cdc.gov/violenceprevention/pdf /nisvs_report2010-a.pdf.

Black, M., Shetty, A., & Bhattacharya, S. (2008). Obstetric outcomes subsequent to intrauterine death in the first pregnancy. *British Journal of Gynecology, 115,* 269–274.

Blackwood, E. (1984). Sexuality and gender in Native American tribes: The case of cross-gender females. In A. C. Herrmann & A. J. Stewart (Eds.), *Theorizing feminism: Parallel trends in the humanities and social sciences* (pp. 301–315). Boulder, CO: Westview Press.

Blair, A. (2000). Individuation, love styles and health-related quality of life among college students. *Dissertation Abstracts International,* University of Florida, #0-599-91381-9.

Blake, L., Carone, N., Raffanello, E., Slutsky, J., Ehrhardt, A., & Golombok, S. (2017). Gay fathers' motivations for and feelings about surrogacy as a path to parenthood. *Human Reproduction, 32*(4), 860–867.

Blake, S. M., Ledsky, R., Lehman, T., Goodenow, C., Sawyer, R., & Hack, T. (2001). Preventing sexual risk behaviors among gay, lesbian, and bisexual adolescents: The benefits of gay-sensitive HIV instruction in schools. *American Journal of Public Health, 91,* 940–946.

Blanchard, M. A., & Semoncho, J. E. (2006). Anthony Comstock and his adversaries: The mixed legacy of the battle for free speech. *Communication and Public Policy, 11,* 317–366.

Blanchard, R. (1997). Birth order and sibling sex ratio in homosexual versus heterosexual males and females. *Annual Review of Sex Research, 8,* 27–67.

Blanchard, R. (2004). Quantitative and theoretical analyses of the relation between older brothers and homosexuality in men. *Journal of Theoretical Biology, 230*(2), 173–187.

Blanchard, R. (2008). Review and theory of handedness, birth order, and homosexuality in men. *Laterality, 13,* 51–70.

Blanchard, R., Cantor, J. M., Bogaert, A., Breedlove, S., & Ellis, L. (2006). Interaction of fraternal birth order and handedness in the development of male homosexuality. *Hormones & Behavior, 49,* 405–414.

Bleakley, A., Hennessey, M., & Fishbein, M. (2006). Public opinion on sex education in U.S. schools. *Archives of Pediatrics and Adolescent Medicine, 160,* 1151–1156.

Blecher, S. R., & Erickson, R. P. (2007). Genetics of sexual development: A new paradigm. *American Journal of Medical Genetics, 143,* 3054–3068.

Bleecker, E., & Murnen, S. (2005). Fraternity membership, the display of degrading sexual images of women, and rape myth acceptance. *Sex Roles, 53,* 487–493.

Bloch, M., Meiboom, H., Zaig, I., Schreiber, S., & Abramov, L. (2013). The use of dehydroepiandrosterone in the treatment of hypoactive sexual desire disorder. *Euopean Neuropsychopharmacology, 23*(8), 910–918.

Block, J. D. (1999). *Sex over 50*. Paramus, NJ: Reward Books.

Bloom, B., Cohen, R., & Freeman, G. (2012). *Summary health statistics for US children: National Health Interview Survey*. National Center for Health Statistics, Vital Health Statistics, Series 10 (No. 254). Retrieved February 14, 2014, from http://www.cdc.gov/nchs/data/series/sr_10/sr10_254.pdf.

Blosnich, J., Nasuti, L., Mays, V., & Cochran, S. (2016). Suicidality and sexual orientation: Characteristics of symptom severity, disclosure, and timing across the life course. *American Journal of Orthopsychiatry, 86*(1), 69–78.

Blumstein, P., & Schwartz, P. (1983). *American couples*. New York: William Morrow.

Bocklandt, S., & Vilain, E. (2007). Sex differences in brain and behavior: Hormones versus genes. *Advances in Genetics, 59*, 245–266.

Bodenmann, G., Meuwly, N., Bradbury, T., Gmelch, S., & Ledermann, T. (2010). Stress, anger, and verbal aggression in intimate relationships: Moderating effects of individual and dyadic coping. *Journal of Social and Personal Relationships, 27*(3), 408–424.

Boehmer, U. (2002). Twenty years of public health research: Inclusion of lesbian, gay, bisexual and transgender populations. *American Journal of Public Health, 92*(7), 1125–1131.

Boehmer, U., Bowen, D., & Bauer, G. (2007). Overweight and obesity in sexual–minority women: Evidence from population-based data. *American Journal of Public Health, 97*(6), 1134–1140.

Boeke, A. J., van Bergen, J. E., Morre, S. A., & van Everdingen, J. J. (2005). The risk of pelvic inflammatory disease associated with urogenital infection with chlamydia trachomatis: Literature review. *Ned Tijdschr Geneeskd, 149*(16), 878–884.

Boeringer, S. (1999). Associations of rape-supportive attitudes with fraternal and athletic participation. *Violence Against Women, 5*(1), 81–90.

Bogaert, A. (1996). Volunteer bias in human sexuality research: Evidence for both sexuality and personality differences in males. *Archives of Sexual Behavior, 25*(2), 125–140.

Bogaert, A. (2010). Physical development and sexual orientation in men and women: An analysis of NATSAL-2000. *Archives of Sexual Behavior, 39*(1), 110–116.

Bogaert, A. F. (2005). Gender role/identity and sibling sex ratio in homosexual men. *Journal of Sex and Marital Therapy, 31*, 217–227.

Bogaert, A. F., & Skorska, M. (2011). Sexual orientation, fraternal birth order, and the maternal immune hypothesis: A review. *Frontiers in Neuroendocrinology, 32*(2), 247–254.

Bogaert, A., Visser, B., & Pozzebon, J. (2015). Gender differences in object of desire self-consciousness sexual fantasies. *Archives of Sexual Behavior, 44*(8), 2299–2310.

Bogaerts, S., Vanheule, S., Leeuw, F., & Desmet, M. (2006). Recalled parental bonding and personality disorders in a sample of exhibitionists: A comparative study. *Journal of Forensic Psychiatry & Psychology, 17*(4), 636–646.

Bogle, K. (2008). *Hooking Up: Sex, Dating, and Relationships on Campus*. NYU Press, New York, NY.

Bohm-Starke, N. (2010). Medical and physical predictors of localized provoked vulvodynia. *Acta Obstetrics and Gynecology Scandinavia, 89*(12), 1504–1510.

Bolso, A. (2005). Orgasm and lesbian sexuality. *Sex Education, 5*(1), 29–48.

Bolton, M., van der Straten, A., & Cohen, C. (2008). Probiotics: Potential to prevent HIV and sexually transmitted infections in women. *Sexually Transmitted Diseases, 35*(3), 214–225.

Bonetti, A., Tirelli, F., Catapano, A., Dazzi, D., Dei Cas, A., Solito, F., et al. (2007). Side effects of anabolic androgenic steroids abuse. *International Journal of Sports Medicine, 29*(8), 679–687.

Bongaarts, J., & Blanc, A. (2015). Estimating the current mean age of mothers at the birth of their first child from household surveys. *Population Health Metrics, 13*(25). Retrieved March 29, 2017, from https://www.ncbi.nlm.nih.gov/pmc/articles/PMC4570715/.

Bonomi, A., Altenburger, L., & Walton, N. (2013). "Double crap!" abuse and harmed identity in Fifty Shades of Grey. *Journal of Women's Health, 22*(9), 733–744.

Bonomi, A., Anderson, M., Reid, R., Carrell, D., Fishman, P., Rivara, F., & Thompson, R. (2007). Intimate partner violence in older women. *The Gerontologist, 47*, 34–41.

Bonos, L. (2017, May 5). "I'm not sure this is rape, but…" What a law student found when she asked women about "stealthing." *Washington Post*. Retrieved from https://www.washingtonpost.com/news/soloish/wp/2017/05/05/im-not-sure-this-is-rape-but-what-a-law-student-found-when-she-asked-women-about-stealthing/?tid=ss_mail&utm_term=.ef97e01a9203.

Boomer, D. S. (1963). Speech disturbances and body movement in interviews. *Journal of Nervous and Mental Disease, 136*, 263–266.

Boon, S., & Alderson, K. (2009). A phenomenological study of women in same-sex relationships who were previously married to men. *Canadian Journal of Human Sexuality, 18*(4), 149–169.

Boonstra, H. (2005, May). Condoms, contraceptives and nonoxynol-9: Complex issues obscured by ideology. *The Guttmacher Report on Public Policy, 8*(2), pp. 4–7.

Boonstra, H., Gold, R., Richard, C., & Finer, L. (2006). *Abortion in women's lives*. New York: Guttmacher Institute. Retrieved June 4, 2011, from http://www.guttmacher.org/pubs/2006/05/04/AiWL.pdf.

Booth, R. (2014, June 29). Facebook reveals news feed experiment to control emotions. *The Guardian*. Retrieved January 9, 2017, from http://www.theguardian.com/technology/2014/jun/29/facebook-users-emotions-news-feeds.

Bord, I., Gdalevich, M., Nahum, R. Meltcer, S., Anteby, E., & Orvieto, R. (2014). Misoprostol treatment for early pregnancy failure does not impair future fertility. *Gynecological Endocrinology, 30*(4), 316–319.

Borg, C., de Jong, P. J., & Weijmar Schultz, W. (2011). Vaginismus and dyspareunia: Relationship with general and sex-related moral standards. *Journal of Sexual Medicine, 8*(1), 223–231.

Borini, A., Cattoli, M., Bulletti, C., & Coticchio, G. (2008). Clinical efficiency of oocyte and embryo cryopreservation. *Annals of the New York Academy of Sciences, 1127*, 49–58.

Borisoff, J., Elliott, S., Hocaloski, S., & Birch, G. (2010). The development of a sensory substitution system for the sexual rehabilitation of men with chronic spinal cord injury. *Journal of Sexual Medicine, 7*(11), 3647–3658.

Bornstein, D. (Ed.). (1979). *The feminist controversy of the Renaissance*. Delmar, NY: Scholars' Facsimiles & Reprints.

Boroughs, D. S. (2004). Female sexual abusers of children. *Children & Youth Services Review, 26*(5), 481–487.

Borrell, L., Rodriguez-Alvarez, E., Savitz, D., & Baquero, M. (2016). Parental race-ethnicity and adverse birth outcomes in New York City: 2000–2010. *American Journal of Public Health, 106*(8), 1491–1497.

Bos, H., & Gartrell, N. (2010). Adolescents of the USA National Longitudinal Lesbian Family Study: Can family characteristics counteract the negative effects of stigmatization? *Family Process, 49*(4), 559–572.

Bos, H., Knox, J., Van Rijn-van Gelderen, L., & Gartrell, N. (2016). Same-sex and different-sex parent households and child health outcomes: Findings from the National Survey of Children's Health. *Journal of Developmental and Behavioral Pediatrics, 37*(3), 179–187.

Bosch, F., Broker, T., Forman, D., Moscicki, A., Gillison, M., Doorbar, J., Stern, P., et al. (2013). Comprehensive control of human papillomavirus infections and related disease. *Vaccine, 31*(6), G1–31.

Bosello, R., Favaro, A., Zanetti, T., Soave, M., Vidotto, G., Huon, G., & Santanastaso, P. (2010). Tattoos and piercings in adolescents: Family conflicts and temperament. *Rivesta di Psichiatria, 45*(2), 102–106.

Bosse, J., & Chiodo, L. (2016). It is complicated: Gender and sexual orientation identity in LGBTQ youth. *Journal of Clinical Nursing, 25*(23–24), 3665–3675.

Bostwick, W., Boyd, C., Hughes, T., & McCabe, S. (2010). Dimensions of sexual orientation and the prevalence of mood and anxiety disorders in the U.S. *American Journal of Public Health, 100*(3), 468–475.

Boswell, J. (1980). *Christianity, social tolerance, and homosexuality: Gay people in western Europe from the beginning of the Christian era to the fourteenth century.* Chicago: The University of Chicago Press.

Boucher, M., Groleau, D., & Whitley, R. (2016). Recovery and severe mental illness: The role of romantic relationships, intimacy, and sexuality. *Psychiatric Rehabilitation Journal, 39*(2), 180–182.

Bouchlariotou, S., Tsikouras, P., Dimitraki, M., Athanasiadis, A., Papoulidis, I., Maroulis, G., Liberis, A., & Liberis, V. (2011). Turner's syndrome and pregnancy: Has the 45,X/47,XXX mosaicism a different prognosis? *Journal of Maternal and Fetal Neonatal Medicine, 24*(5), 668–672.

Bouffard, L. (2010). Exploring the utility of entitlement in understanding sexual aggression. *Journal of Criminal Justice, 38*(5), 870–879.

Boukhris, T., Sheehy, O., Mottron, L., & Bérard, A. (2016). Antidepressant use during pregnancy and the risk of autism spectrum disorder in children. *JAMA Pediatrics, 170*(2), 117–124.

Boushey, H., & O'Leary, A. (2010, March 8). How working women are reshaping America's families and economy and what it means for policymakers. Center for American Progress. Retrieved December 20, 2010, from http://www.americanprogress.org /issues/2010/03/our_working_nation.html /print.html.

Bowen, V., Su, J., Torrone, E., Kidd, S., & Weinstock, H. (2015). Increase in incidence of congenital syphilis—United States, 2012–2014. *MMWR, 64*(44), 1241–1245.

Bower, B. (1992). Depression, early death noted in HIV cases. *Science News, 142*, 53.

Bowlby, J. (1969). *Attachment and loss: Attachment.* New York: Basic Books.

Boxer, D. (1996). Ethnographic interviewing as a research tool in speech act analysis: The case of complaints. In S. M. Gass and J. Neu (Eds.), *Speech Acts Across Cultures* (pp. 217–239). New York: de Gruyter.

Boyd, H. (2011, July). Sex and television: How America went from 'I Love Lucy' to 'Playboy Club.' *Deseret News.* Retrieved May 26, 2014, from http://www.deseretnews.com/article /700167256/Sex-and-Television-How -America-went-from-I-Love-Lucy-to -Playboy-Club.html?pg=all.

Boyd, L. (2000). Morning sickness shields fetus from bugs and chemicals. *RN, 63*(8), 18–20.

Boyle, S., & Omoto, A. (2014). Lesbian community oughts and ideals: Normative fit, depression, and anxiety among young sexual minority women. *Psychology of Women Quarterly, 38*(1), 33–45.

Bradley, C. (2014, February 14). A bit too up close and personal? Google Glass wearers capture the 'marry me' moment. *Mirror Online.* Retrieved June 17, 2014, from http://www.mirror.co.uk/news/world-news/bit-up -close-personal-google-3145998.

Bradshaw, C., Kahn, A., & Saville, B. (2010). To hook up or date: Which gender benefits? *Sex Roles, 62*(9–10), 661–669.

Braithwaite, S., Doxey, R., Dowdle, K., & Fincham, F. (2016). The unique influences of parental divorce and parental conflict on emerging adults in romantic relationships. *Journal of Adult Development, 23*(4), 214–225.

Brandberg, Y., Sandelin, K., Erikson, S., Jurell, G., Liljegren, A., Lindblom, A., et al. (2008). Psychological reactions, quality of life, and body image after bilateral prophylactic mastectomy in women at high risk for breast cancer: A prospective 1-year follow-up study. *Journal of Clinical Oncology, 26*, 3943–3949.

Brandt, A. M. (1985). *No magic bullet: A social history of venereal disease in the United States.* New York: Oxford University Press.

Brandt, C., Zvolensky, M., Woods, S., Gonzalez, A., Safren, S., & O'Cleirigh, C. (2017). Symptoms and disorders among adults living with HIV and AIDS: A critical and integrative synthesis of the empirical literature. *Clinical Psychology Review, 51*, 164–184.

Brasky, T., Li, Y., Jaworowicz, D., Potischman, N., Ambrosone, C., Hutson, A., Nie, J., Shields, P., Trevisan, M., Rudra, C., Edge, S., & Freudenheim, J. (2013). Pregnancy-related characteristics and breast cancer risk. *Cancer Causes & Control, 24*(9), 1675–1685.

Bratter, J. L., & King, R. B. (2008). "But will it last?": Marital instability among interracial and same-race couples. *Family Relations, 57*, 160–172.

Brault, M., Schensul, S., Singh, R., Verman, R., & Jadhav, K. (2016). Multilevel perspectives on female sterilization in low-income communities in Mumbai, India. *Qualitative Health Research, 26*(11), 1550–1160.

Braüner, C., Overvad, K., Tjønneland, A., & Attermann, J. (2013). Induced abortion and breast cancer among parous women: A Danish cohort study. *Acta Obstetricia Et Gynecologica Scandinavia, 92*(6), 700–705.

Breastfeeding Report Card. (2016). Breastfeeding report card, Progressing toward national breastfeeding goals, United States, 2016. National Center for Chronic Disease Prevention and Health Promotion, Division of Nutrition, Physical Activity, and Obesity. Retrieved April 2, 2017, from https:// www.cdc.gov/breastfeeding/pdf/2016 breastfeedingreportcard.pdf.

"Breastfeeding State Laws." (2016). National Conference of State Legislatures. Retrieved April 2, 2017, from http://www.ncsl.org /research/health/breastfeeding-state-laws.aspx.

Brecher, E. M., & Brecher, J. (1986). Extracting valuable sexological findings from severely flawed and biased population samples. *Journal of Sex Research, 22*, 6–20.

Breedlove, S. (2017). Prenatal influences on human sexual orientation: Expectations versus data. *Archives of Sexual Behavior.* Retrieved March 19, 2017, from https://www .ncbi.nlm.nih.gov/pubmed/28176027.

Breiding, M., Smith, S., Basile, K., Walters, M., Chen, J., & Merrick, M. (2014). Prevalence and characteristics of sexual violence, stalking, and intimate partner violence victimization—National Intimate Partner and Sexual Violence Survey, United States, 2011. *Morbidity and Mortality Weekly Report, 63*(8), 1–18.

Brennan, A., Ayers, S., Ahmed, H., & Marshall-Lucette, S. (2007). A critical review of the Couvade syndrome: The pregnant male. *Journal of Reproductive and Infant Psychology, 25*(3), 173–189.

Brennan, B. P., Kanayama, G., Hudson, J. I., & Pope, H. G., Jr. (2011). Human growth hormone abuse in male weightlifters. *American Journal of Addiction, 20*(1), 9–13.

Brennan, Z. (2016, March 10). Teva wins FDA approval for first Viagra generic, will not launch until 2017. Regulatory Affairs Professionals Society. Retrieved April 15, 2017, from http://www.raps.org/Regulatory-Focus /News/2016/03/10/24515/Teva-Wins-FDA -Approval-for-First-Viagra-Generic-Will -Not-Launch-Until-2017/.

Brenner, M. (2014, January). Danger in the ring. *Vanity Fair.* Retrieved May 24, 2014, from http://www.vanityfair.com/politics/2014/01 /nuvaring-lethal-contraceptive-trial.

Breuss, C. E., & Greenberg, S. (1981). *Sex education: Theory and practice.* Belmont, CA: Wadsworth.

Brewer, D., Roberts, J., Muth, S., & Potterat, J. (2008). Prevalence of male clients of street prostitute women in the United States. *Human Organization, 67*, 346–357.

Brewer, G., & Hamilton, V. (2014). Female mate retention, sexual orientation, and gender identity. *Evolutionary Behavioral Sciences, 8*(1), 12–19.

Brewis, A., & Meyer, M. (2005). Marital coitus across the life course. *Journal of Biosocial Sciences*, 37, 499–518.

Brewster, K. L., & Tillman, K. H. (2008). Who's doing it? Patterns and predictors of youths' oral sexual experiences. *Journal of Adolescent Health*, 42, 73–80.

Brewster, P., Mullin, C., Dobrin, R., & Steeves, J. (2010). Sex differences in face processing are mediated by handedness and sexual orientation. *Laterality*, 9, 1–13.

Briere, J., & Elliott, D. (2003). Prevalence and psychological sequelae of self-reported childhood physical and sexual abuse in general population. *Child Abuse and Neglect*, 27(10), 1205–1222.

Briere, J., & Malamuth, N. (1983). Self-reported likelihood of sexually aggressive behavior: Attitudinal versus sexual explanations. *Journal of Research in Personality*, 17, 315–323.

Brinig, M. F., & Allen, D. A. (2000). "These boots are made for walking": Why most divorce filers are women. *American Law and Economics Review*, 2, 126–169.

Brink, S. (2015, August 26). Selecting boys over girls is a trend in more and more countries. NPR Goats and Soda: Stories of Life in a Changing World. Retrieved March 29, 2017, from http://www.npr.org/sections/goatsandsoda/2015/08/26/434616512/selecting-boys-over-girls-is-a-trend-in-more-and-more-countries.

Brinkman, S., Johnson, S., Codde, J., Hart, M., Straton, J., Mittinty, M., & Silburn, S. (2016). Efficacy of infant simulator programmes to prevent teenage pregnancy: A school-based cluster randomized controlled trail in Western Australia. *The Lancet*, 388(10057), 2264–2271.

Brinton, L. (2011). Breast cancer risk among patients with Klinefelter syndrome. *Acta Paediatrica*, 100(6), 814–818.

Brinton, L., Westhoof, C., Scoccia, B., Lamb, E., Trabert, B., Niwa, S., & Moghissi, K. (2013). Fertility drugs and endometrial cancer risk: Results from an extended follow-up of a large infertility cohort. *Human Reproduction*, 28(1), 2813–2821.

Brinton, R., Yao, J., Yin, F., Mack, W., & Cadenas, E. (2015). Perimenopause as a neurological transition state. *Nature Reviews Endocrinology*, 11(7), 393–405.

Brizendine, L. (2006). *The female brain*. New York, NY: Broadway Publishing.

Brizendine, L., & Allen, B. J. (2010). Are gender differences in communication biologically determined? In B. Slife (Ed.), *Taking sides: Clashing views on psychological issues* (16th ed., pp. 71–88). New York: McGraw-Hill.

Brockman, N. (2004). Kenya. In R. T. Francoeur & R. J. Noonan (Eds.), *The Continuum international encyclopedia of sexuality* (pp. 679–691). New York/London: Continuum International.

Broderick, G. (2012). Priapism and sickle-cell anemia: Diagnosis and nonsurgical therapy. *Journal of Sexual Medicine*, 9(1), 88–103.

Brodsky, A. (2017). "Rape-adjacent": Imagining legal responses to nonconsensual condom removal. *Columbia Journal of Gender and Law*, 32(2), 183–210.

Brogan, S., Fiore, A., & Wrench, J. (2009). Understanding the psychometric properties of the sexual communication style scale. *Human Communication*, 12(4), 421–445.

Brongersma, E. (1990). Boy-lovers and their influence on boys: Distorted research and anecdotal observations. *Journal of Homosexuality*, 20, 145–173.

Brooks-Gordon, B., & Geisthorpe, L. (2003). What men say when apprehended for kerb crawling: A model of prostitutes' clients' talk. *Psychology, Crime and Law*, 9(2), 145–171.

Brooks, K., Gruenwald, T., Karlamanga, A., Hu, P., Koretz, B., & Seeman, T. (2014). Social relationships and allostatic load in the MIDUS study. *Health Psychology*, 33(11), 1373–1381.

Brooks, R., Lee, S., Newman, P., & Leibowitz, A. (2008). Sexual risk behavior has decreased among men who have sex with men in Los Angeles but remains greater than that among heterosexual men and women. *AIDS Education and Prevention*, 20, 312–324.

Brooks-Gunn, J., & Furstenberg, F. F. (1989). Adolescent sexual behavior. *American Psychologist*, 44, 249–257.

Brooks-Gunn, J., & Furstenberg, F. F. (1990). Coming of age in the era of AIDS: Puberty, sexuality, and contraception. *Milbank Quarterly*, 68, 59–84.

Broude, G. J., & Greene, S. J. (1976). Cross-cultural codes on twenty sexual attitudes and practices. *Ethnology*, 15, 409–428.

Brousseau, M., Bergeron, S., & Hebert, M. (2011). Sexual coercion victimization and perpetration in heterosexual couples: A dyadic investigation. *Archives of Sexual Behavior*, 40(2), 363–372.

Brown, A., & Testa, M. (2008). Social influences on judgments of rape victims: The role of the negative and positive social reactions of others. *Sex Roles*, 58, 490–501.

Brown, B. B., Dolcini, M. M., & Leventhal, A. (1997). Transformations in peer relationships at adolescence: Implications for health related behavior. In J. Schulenberg, J. L. Maggs, & K. Hurrelmann (Eds.), *Health risks and developmental transitions during adolescence* (pp. 161–189). Cambridge, U.K.: Cambridge University Press.

Brown, C. (2008). Gender-role implications on same-sex intimate partner abuse. *Journal of Family Violence*, 23, 457–463.

Brown, C. (2017). The many ways society makes a man. *National Geographic*. Retrieved August 23, 2017, from http://www.nationalgeographic.com/magazine/2017/01/how-rites-of-passage-shape-masculinity-gender/.

Brown, D. J., Hill, S. T., & Baker, H. W. (2005). Male fertility and sexual function after spinal cord injury. *Progress in Brain Research*, 152, 427–439.

Brown, E. (2001). *Patterns of infidelity and their treatment* (2nd ed.). Philadelphia, PA: Brunner/Routledge.

Brown, J. C. (1983). Paraphilias: Sadomasochism, fetishism, transvestism and transsexuality. *British Journal of Psychiatry*, 143, 227–231.

Brown, J., & Trevethan, R. (2010). Shame, internalized homophobia, identity formation, attachment style, and the connection to relationship status in gay men. *American Journal of Men's Health*, 4(3), 267–276.

Brown, J., Pan, A., & Hart, R. J. (2010). Gonadotrophin-releasing hormone analogues for pain associated with endometriosis. *Cochrane Database of Systematic Reviews*, 12, CD008475.

Brown, M., McElroy, J. (2017). Sexual and gender minority breast cancer patients choosing bilateral mastectomy without reconstruction: "I now have a body that fits me" *Women & Health*. Retrieved August 23, 2017, from http://www.tandfonline.com/doi/abs/10.1080/03630242.2017.1310169.

Brown, S. L., Lee, G. R., & Bulanda, J. R. (2006). Cohabitation among older adults: A national portrait. *Journals of Gerontology Series B: Psychological Sciences and Social Science*, 61, S71–S79.

Brown, S., Morrison, L., Calibuso, M., & Christiansen, T. (2008). The menstrual cycle and sexual behavior: Relationship to eating, exercise, sleep and health patterns. *Women Health*, 48(4), 429–444.

Brown, T. J., Sumner, K. E., & Nocera, R. (2002). Understanding sexual aggression against women: An examination of the role of men's athletic participation and related variables. *Journal of Interpersonal Violence*, 17(9), 937–952.

Brown-James, A. (2017). Exploring the associations between Black women's rape fantasy and power. Dissertation Abstracts International: Section B: The Sciences and Engineering, 77(7-B), #970-1339491462.

Brownmiller, S. (1975). *Against our will: Men, women, and rape*. New York: Simon & Schuster.

Brownmiller, S. (2000). Rape on the brain: A review of Randy Thornhill and Craig Palmer. Retrieved December 5, 2005, from http://www.susanbrownmiller.com/html/review-thornhill.html.

Brubaker, L., Handa, V., Bradley, C., Connolly, A., Moalli, P., Brown, M., & Weber, A. (2008). Sexual function 6 months after first delivery. *Obstetrics and Gynecology*, 111, 1040–1044.

Bruce, K., & Walker, L. (2001). College students' attitudes about AIDS: 1986 to 2000. *AIDS Education and Prevention, 13*(5), 428–437.

Brucker, C., Karck, U., & Merkle, E. (2008). Cycle control, tolerability, efficacy and acceptability of the vaginal contraceptive ring, NuvaRing: Results of clinical experience in Germany. *European Journal of Contraceptive Reproductive Health Care, 13*, 31–38.

Brückner, H., & Bearman, P. (2005). After the promise: The STD consequences of adolescent virginity pledges. *Journal of Adolescent Health, 36*(4), 271–278.

Brumbaugh, C., & Fraley, C. (2010). Adult attachment and dating strategies: How do insecure people attract dates? *Personal Relationships, 17*(4), 599–614.

Brumberg, J. J. (1997). *The body project: An intimate history of American girls.* New York: Vintage Books.

Brummelte, S., & Galea, L. (2016). Postpartum depression: Etiology, treatment and consequences for maternal care. *Hormones and Behavior, 77*, 153–166.

Bruni, V., Pontello, V., Luisi, S., & Petraglia, F. (2008). An open-label multicentre trial to evaluate the vaginal bleeding pattern of the combined contraceptive vaginal ring NuvaRing. *European Journal of Obstetrics and Gynecological Reproductive Biology, 139*, 65–71.

Brunner Huber, L. R., & Ersek, J. L. (2011). Perceptions of contraceptive responsibility among female college students: An exploratory study. *Annals of Epidemiology, 21*(3), 197–203.

Brunner-Huber, L., & Toth, J. (2007). Obesity and oral contraceptive failure: Findings from the 2002 National Survey of Family Growth. *American Journal of Epidemiology, 166*, 1306–1311.

Bryan, W. A. (1987). Contemporary fraternity and sorority issues. *New Directions for Student Services, 40*, 37–56.

Bryant, C. (2010). Understanding the intersection of race and marriage: Does one model fit all? *Psychological Science Agenda.* Retrieved May 11, 2011, from http://www.apa.org/science/about/psa/2010/10/race-marriage.aspx.

Bryant, D., Hoeft, F., Lai, S., Lackey, J., Roeltgen, D., Ross, J., & Reiss, A. (2012). Sex chromosomes and the brain: A study of neuroanatomy in WYY syndrome. *Developmental Medicine and Child Neurology, 54*(12), 1149–1156.

Buckett, W., Chian, R., Holzer, H., Dean, N., Usher, R., & Tan, S. (2007). Obstetric outcomes and congenital abnormalities after in vitro maturation, IVF, and ICSI. *Obstetrics and Gynecology, 110*, 885–891.

Buckner, M. M., Ledbetter, A. M., & Bridge, M. C. (2013). Raised to dissent: Family-of-origin communication patterns as predictors of organizational dissent. *Journal of Family Communication, 13*(4), 263–279.

Buckwalter-Poza, R. (2014, May 5). The frozen children: The rise and complications of embryo adoption in the U.S. *Pacific Standard.* Retrieved May 21, 2014, from http://www.psmag.com/navigation/politics-and-law/frozen-children-rise-complications-embryo-adoption-u-s-80754.

Budd, K., Rocque, M., & Bierie, D. (2017). Deconstructing incidents of campus sexual assault: Comparing male and female victimizations. *Sexual Abuse: A Journal of Research and Treatment.* Retrieved from https://www.ncbi.nlm.nih.gov/pubmed/28471287.

Buffardi, A. L., Thomas, K. K., Holmes, K. K., & Manhart, L. E. (2008). Moving upstream: Ecosocial and psychosocial correlates of sexually transmitted infections among young adults in the United States. *American Journal of Public Health, 98*, 1128–1137.

Bugg, C., & Taira, T. (2016). Pelvic inflammatory disease: Diagnosis and treatment in the emergency department. *Emergency Medicine Practice, 18*(12), 1–24.

Buhling, K., Zite, N., Lotke, P., & Black, K. (2014). Worldwide use of intrauterine contraception: A review. *Contraception, 89*(3), 162–173.

Bui, N. (2017). Exploring similarity characteristics, identification, and parasocial interactions in choice of celebrities. *Psychology of Popular Media Culture, 6*(1), 12–31.

Bull, S. S., & Melian, L. M. (1998). Contraception and culture: The use of Yuyos in Paraguay. *Health Care for Women International, 19*(1), 49–66.

Bullivant, S., Sellergren, S., Stern, K., Spencer, N., Jacob, S., Mennella, J., & McClintock, M. (2004). Women's sexual experience during the menstrual cycle: Identification of the sexual phase by noninvasive measurement of luteinizing hormone. *Journal of Sex Research, 41*(1), 82–93.

Bullough, V. (1994). *Science in the bedroom: The history of sex research.* New York: Basic Books.

Bullough, V. L. (1973). *The subordinate sex: A history of attitudes toward women.* Urbana: University of Illinois Press.

Bullough, V. L. (1976). *Sexual variance in society and history.* New York: Wiley.

Bullough, V. L. (1979). *Homosexuality: A history.* New York: New American Library.

Bullough, V. L. (1990). History in adult human sexual behavior with children and adolescents in Western societies. In J. Feierman (Ed.), *Pedophilia biosocial dimensions* (pp. 69–90). New York: Springer-Verlag.

Bullough, V. L. (1998). Alfred Kinsey and the Kinsey Report: Historical overview and lasting contributions. *Journal of Sex Research, 35*(2), 127–131.

Bumpass, L., & Lu, H.-H. (2000). Trends in cohabitation and implications for children's family contexts in the U.S. *Population Studies, 54*, 29–41.

Burbidge, M., & Walters, J. (1981). *Breaking the silence: Gay teenagers speak for themselves.* London, U.K.: Joint Council for Gay Teenagers.

Burch, B. (1998). Lesbian sexuality. *Psychoanalytic Review, 85*(3), 349–372.

Burdette, A. M., Ellison, C. G., Sherkat, D. E., & Gore, K. A. (2007). Are there religious variations in marital infidelity? *Journal of Family Issues, 28*, 1553.

Burgess, A. W., & Holmstrom, L. L. (1979). *Rape: Crisis and recovery.* Bowie, MD: Robert J. Brady.

Burgess, A. W., & Morgenbesser, L. I. (2005). Sexual violence and seniors. *Brief Treatment & Crisis Intervention, 5*(2), 193–202.

Burke, D. (2008, July 26). Birth control ban marks 40 years. *The Ledger.* Retrieved October 28, 2008, from http://www.theledger.com/article/20080726/NEWS/807260367/1326&title=Birth_Control_Ban_Marks_40_Years.

Burke, D., & Cohen, E. (2016, February 18). Pope suggest contraceptives could be used to slow spread of Zika. CNN. Retrieved April 3, 2017, from http://www.cnn.com/2016/02/18/health/zika-pope-francis-contraceptives/.

Burkeman, O., & Younge, G. (2005). Being Brenda. Retrieved February 24, 2005, from http://www.godspy.com/life/Being-Brenda.cfm.

Burkman, R. T. (2002). The transdermal contraceptive patch: A new approach to hormonal contraception. *International Journal of Fertility and Women's Medicine, 47*(2), 69–76.

Burkman, R., Schlesselman, J. J., & Zieman, M. (2004). Safety concerns and health benefits associated with oral contraception. *American Journal of Obstetrics and Gynecology, 190*(Suppl. 4), S5–S22.

Burleson, B. R. (2003). The experience and effects of emotional support: What the study of cultural and gender differences can tell us about close relationships, emotion and interpersonal communication. *Personal Relationships, 10*(1), 1–23.

Burleson, B. R., Kunkel, A. W., Samter, W., & Werking, K. (1996). Men's and women's evaluations of communication skills in personal relationships: When sex differences make a difference—and when they don't. *Journal of Social and Personal Relationships, 13*, 201–224.

Burnett, A. (2016). Penile preserving and reconstructive surgery in the management of penile cancer. *Nature Reviews: Urology, 13*(5), 249–257.

Burns, M., Costello, J., Ryan-Woolley, B., & Davidson, S. (2007). Assessing the impact of late treatment effects in cervical cancer: An exploratory study of women's sexuality. *European Journal of Cancer Care, 16*, 364–372.

Burris, H., Collins, J., & Wright, R. (2011). Racial/ethnic disparities in preterm birth: Clues from environmental exposures. *Current Opinions in Pediatrics, 23*, 227–232.

Burt, M. (1980). Cultural myths and support for rape. *Journal of Personality and Social Psychology, 38*, 217–230.

Busby, D., Carroll, J., & Willoughby, B. (2010). Compatibility or restraint? The effects of sexual timing on marriage relationships. *Journal of Family Psychology, 24*(6), 766–774.

Buss, D. (1989). Sex differences in human mate preferences: Evolutionary hypotheses tested in 37 cultures. *Behavioral and Brain Sciences, 12*, 1–49.

Buss, D. (2000). *The dangerous passion: Why jealousy is as necessary as love and sex.* New York, NY: The Free Press.

Buss, D. M. (1994). *The evolution of desire: Strategies of human mating.* New York: Basic Books.

Buss, D. M. (2003). The dangerous passion: Why jealousy is as necessary as love and sex. *Archives of Sexual Behavior, 32*(1), 79–80.

Buss, D. M., Shackelford, T. K., Kirkpatrick, L., & Larsen, R. J. (2001). A half century of mate preferences: The cultural evolution of values. *Journal of Marriage & the Family, 63*(2), 491–503.

Busse, P., Fishbein, M., Bleakley, A., & Hennessy, M. (2010). The role of communication with friends in sexual initiation. *Communication Research, 37*(2), 239–255.

Butrick, C. W. (2009). Pelvic floor hypertonic disorders: Identification and management. *Obstetrics and Gynecology Clinics of North America, 36*(3), 707–722.

Buttke, D., Sircar, K., & Martin, C. (2012). Exposures to endocrine-disrupting chemicals and age of menarche in adolescent girls in NHANES (2003–2008). *Environmental Health Perspectives, 120*(11), 1613–1618.

Byers, E., Henderson, J., & Hobson, K. (2009). University students' definitions of sexual abstinence and having sex. *Archives of Sexual Behavior, 38*(5), 665–674.

Byers, E., O'Sullivan, L., & Brotto, L. (2016). Time out from sex or romance: Sexually experienced adolescents' decisions to purposefully avoid sexual activity or romantic relationships. *Journal of Youth and Adolescence, 45*, 831–845.

Byne, W. (2016). Regulations restrict practice of conversion therapy. *LGBT Health, 3*(2), 97–99.

Byrne, D., & Murnen, S. K. (1988). Maintaining loving relationships. In R. Sternberg & M. L. Barnes (Eds.), *Psychology of love* (pp. 293–310). New Haven, CT: Yale University Press.

Cabral, P., Wallander, J., Song, A., Elliott, M., Tortolero, S., Reisner, S., & Schuster, M. (2017). Generational status and social factors predicting initiation of partnered sexual activity among Latino/a youth. *Health Psychology, 36*(2), 169–178.

Caetano, R., Clark, C., & Tam, T. (1998). Alcohol consumption among racial/ethnic minorities: Theory and research. *Alcohol Health and Research World, 22*(4), 233–241.

Caffaro, J., & Conn-Caffaro, A. (2005). Treating sibling abuse families. *Aggression and Violent Behavior, 10*(5), 604–623.

Cahill, S., South, K., & Spade, J. (2000). *Outing age: Public policy issues affecting gay, lesbian, bisexual and transgender elders.* Washington, DC: National Gay and Lesbian Task Force.

Cai, D., Wilson, S. R., & Drake, L. E. (2000). Culture in the context of intercultural negotiation: Individualism-collectivism and paths to integrative agreements. *Human Communication Research, 26*(4), 591–617.

Calderone, M. (1983). On the possible prevention of sexual problems in adolescence. *Hospital and Community Psychiatry, 34*, 528–530.

Callahan, M. M. (2002). Safety and tolerance studies of potential microbicides following multiple penile applications. Annual Conference on Microbicides, May 12–15, 2002, Antwerp, Belgium.

Calzavara, L. M., Burchell, A. N., Lebovic, G., Myers, T., Remis, R. S., Raboud, J., Corey, P., Swantee, C., & Hart, T. A. (2011). The impact of stressful life events on unprotected anal intercourse among gay and bisexual men. *AIDS Behavior.* Retrieved February 20, 2011, from http://www.ncbi.nlm.nih.gov/pubmed/21274612.

Calzo, J., Roberts, A., Corliss, H., Blood, E., Kroshus, E., & Austin, S. (2014). Physical activity disparities in heterosexual and sexual minority youth ages 12–22 years old: Roles of childhood gender nonconformity and athletic self-esteem. *Annals of Behavioral Medicine: A Publication of the Society of Behavioral Medicine, 47*(1), 17–27.

Cameron, D., & Berkowitz, B. (2016, June 14). The state of gay rights around the world. *The Washington Post.* Retrieved March 15, 2017, from https://www.washingtonpost.com/graphics/world/gay-rights/.

Cameron, K. A., Salazar, L. F., Bernhardt, J. M., Burgess-Whitman, N., Wingood, G. M., & DiClemente, R. J. (2005). Adolescents' experience with sex on the web: Results from online focus groups. *Journal of Adolescence, 28*(4), 535–540.

Cameron, P. (2006). Children of homosexuals and transsexuals more apt to be homosexual. *Journal of Biosocial Science, 38*(3), 413–418.

Cameron, S., Glasier, A., Dewart, H., & Johnstone, A. (2010). Women's experiences of the final stage of early medical abortion at home: Results of a pilot survey. *Journal of Family Planning and Reproductive Health Care, 36*(4), 213–216.

Cammaert, L. (1985). How widespread is sexual harassment on campus? Special issue: Women in groups and aggression against women. *International Journal of Women's Studies, 8*, 388–397.

Cammu, H., Dony, N., Martens, G., & Colman, R. (2014). Common determinants of breech presentation at birth in singletons: A population-based study. *European Journal of Obstetrics, Gynecology, and Reproductive Biology, 177*, 106–109.

Campbell, J. C., Webster, D., Koziol-McLain, J., Block, C., Campbell, D., Curry, M. A., et al. (2002). Intimate partner violence and physical health consequences. *Archives of Internal Medicine, 162*(10), 1157–1163.

Campbell, L., Simpson, J., Boldry, J., & Rubin, H., (2010). Trust, variability in relationship evaluations, and relationship processes. *Journal of Personality and Social Psychology, 99*(1), 14–21.

Campbell, M., Artz, L., & Stein, D. (2015). Sexual disorders in *DSM-5* and *ICD-11*: A conceptual framework. *Current Opinion in Psychiatry, 28*(6), 435–439.

Campbell, N., Clark, J., Stecher, V., & Goldstein, I. (2012). Internet-ordered Viagra is rarely genuine. *Journal of Sexual Medicine, 9*(11), 2943–2951.

Campbell, P. P. (2008). Sexual violence in the lives of lesbian rape survivors. St. Louis: Saint Louis University, AAT #3324148.

Camperio-Ciani, A., Corna, F., & Capiluppi, C. (2004). Evidence for maternally inherited factors favouring male homosexuality and promoting female fecundity. *Proceedings: Biological Sciences, 271*(1554), 2217–2221.

Campione-Barr, N., Lindell, A., Short, S., Greer, K., & Drotar, S. (2015). First- and second-born adolescent's decision-making autonomy throughout adolescence. *Journal of Adolescence, 45*, 250–262.

Campos, B., Graesch, A., Repetti, R., Bradbury, T., & Ochs, E. (2009). Opportunity for interaction? A naturalistic observation study of dual-earner families after work and school. *Journal of Family Psychology, 23*(6), 798–807.

Canan, S., Jozkowski, K., & Crawford, B. (2016). Sexual assault supportive attitudes: Rape myth acceptance and token resistance in Greek and non-Greek college students from two university samples in the United States. *Journal of Impersonal Violence.* Retrieved from https://www.ncbi.nlm.nih.gov/pubmed/26944340.

Cantor, D., Fisher, B., Chibnall, S., Townsend, R., Lee, H., Bruce, C., & Thomas, G. (2015). Report on the AAU Campus Climate Survey on Sexual Assault and Sexual Misconduct. Westat, Rockville, MD. Retrieved from https://www.aau.edu/sites/default/files/%40%20Files/Climate%20Survey/AAU_Campus_Climate_Survey_12_14_15.pdf.

Cao, H., Fang, X., Fine, M., Ju, X., Lan, J., & Liu, X. (2015). Beyond the average marital communication: Latent profiles of the observed interactions among Chinese newlywed couples. *Journal of Family Psychology, 29*(6), 850–682.

Card, D., Dahl, G. (2011). Family violence and football: The effect of unexpected emotional cues on violent behavior. *The Quarterly Journal of Economics, 126*(1), 103.

Cardoso, F. L., Savall, A. C., & Mendes, A. K. (2009). Self-awareness of the male sexual response after spinal cord injury. *International Journal of Rehabilitation Research, 32*(4), 294–300.

Cardwell, M., & Center, P. (2012). Pregnancy sickness: A biopsychological perspective. *Obstetrical & Gynecological Survey, 67*(1), 645–652.

Carey, B. (2005). Straight, gay or lying? Bisexuality revisited. Retrieved July 5, 2005, from http://www.thetaskforce.org/downloads /07052005NYTBisexuality.pdf.

Carlson, D. (2012). Deviations from desired age at marriage: Mental health differences across marital status. *Journal of Marriage and Family, 74*(4), 743–758.

Carnes, P. (2001). *Out of the shadows: Understanding sexual addiction.* Center City, MN: Hazelden Information Education.

Carpentier, M. Y., & Fortenberry, J. D. (2010). Romantic and sexual relationships, body image, and fertility in adolescent and young adult testicular cancer survivors: A review of the literature. *Journal of Adolescent Health, 47*(2), 115–125.

Carpinello, O., Jacob, M., Nulsen, J., & Benadiva, C. (2016). Utilization of fertility treatment and reproductive choices by lesbians couples. *Fertility and Sterility, 106*(7), 1709–1713.

Carr, B. (2009, November 25). Sex trafficking: An American problem too. CNN Online. Retrieved May 7, 2011, from http://articles .cnn.com/2009–11–25/opinion/carr.human .trafficking_1_trafficking-victims-protection -act-tvpa-lena?_s5PM:OPINION.

Carrell, D. T., Wilcox, A. L., Lowry, L., Peterson, C. M., Jones, K. P., Erickson, L., et al. (2003). Elevated sperm chromosome aneuploidy and apoptosis in patients with unexplained recurrent pregnancy loss. *Obstetrics and Gynecology, 101*(6), 1229–1235.

Carrier, J. M. (1989). Gay liberation and coming out in Mexico. *Journal of Homosexuality, 17,* 225–252.

Carroll, A. (2016). State-sponsored homophobia: A world survey of sexual orientation laws: Criminalization, protection and recognition. 11th edition. Retrieved March 15, 2017, from http://ilga.org/downloads/02_ILGA_State _Sponsored_Homophobia_2016_ENG _WEB_150516.pdf.

Carroll, J. (2007). *Most Americans approve of interracial marriages.* Retrieved April 12, 2014, from http://libill.hartford.edu:2372/ehost /pdfviewer/pdfviewer?vid=5&sid=ea4b35e1 -726e-430c-876a-15d0963d9262%40sessionm gr111&hid=102.

Carroll, J. (2009). *The day Aunt Flo comes to visit.* Avon, CT: Best Day Media.

Carroll, J., Padilla-Walker, L., Nelson, L., Olsen, C., Barry, C., & Madsen, S. (2008). Generation XXX. *Journal of Adolescent Research, 23*(1), 6–30.

Carroll, J., Volk, K., & Hyde, J. (1985). Differences between males and females in motives for engaging in sexual intercourse. *Archives of Sexual Behavior, 14*(2), 131–139.

Carroll, M., Rosenstein, J., Foubert, J., Clark, M., & Korenman, L. (2016). Rape myth acceptance: A comparison of military service academy and civilian fraternity and sorority students. *Military Psychology, 28*(5), 306–317.

Carter, F., Carter, J., Luty, S., Jordan, J., McIntosh, V., Bartram, A., et al. (2007). What is worse for your sex life: Starving, being depressed, or a new baby? *International Journal of Eating Disorders, 40,* 664–667.

Carter, J. S., Corra, M., & Carter, S. K. (2009). The interaction of race and gender: Changing gender-role attitudes, 1974–2006. *Social Science Quarterly, 90*(1), 196–212.

Carter, J., Duncan, S., Stoilova, M., & Phillips, M. (2016). Sex, love and security: Accounts of distance and commitment in living apart together relationships. *Sociology, 50*(3), 576–593.

Carter, J., Goldfrank, D., & Schover, L. (2011). Simple strategies for vaginal health promotion in cancer survivors. *Journal of Sexual Medicine, 8*(2), 549–559.

Caruso, S., Agnello, C., Malandrino, C., LoPresti, L., Cicero, C., & Cianci, S. (2014). Do hormones influence women's sex? Sexual activity over the menstrual cycle. *Journal of Sexual Medicine, 11*(1), 211–221.

Caruso, S., Agnello, C., Malandrino, C., Presti, L., Cicero, C., & Cianci, S. (2014). Do hormones influence women's sex? Sexual activity over the menstrual cycle. *Journal of Sexual Medicine, 11*(1), 211–221.

Caruso, S., Iraci Sareri, M., Agnello, C., Romano, M., Lo Presti, L., Malandrino, C., & Cianci, A. (2011). Conventional vs. extended-cycle oral contraceptives on the quality of sexual life: Comparison between two regimens containing 3 mg drospirenone and 20 mg ethinyl estradiol. *Journal of Sexual Medicine, 8*(5), 1478–1485.

Carvalheira, A., Traeen, B., & Stulhofer, A. (2015). Masturbation and pornography use among coupled heterosexual men with decreased sexual desire: How many roles of masturbation? *Journal of Sex and Marital Therapy, 41*(6), 626–635.

Caslini, M., Bartoli, F., Crocamo, C., Dakanalis, A., Clerici, M., & Carrà, G. (2016). Disentangling the association between child abuse and eating disorders: A systematic review and meta-analysis. *Psychosomatic Medicine, 78*(1), 79–90.

Caspi, A., Williams, B., Kim-Cohen, J., Craig, I., Milne, B., Poulton, R., et al. (2007). Moderation of breastfeeding effects on the IQ by genetic variation in fatty acid metabolism. *Proceedings of the National Academy of Sciences of the United States of America, 104,* 18860–18865.

Cass, V. C. (1979). Homosexual identity formation: A theoretical model. *Journal of Homosexuality, 4,* 219–235.

Cass, V. C. (1984). Homosexual identity formation: Testing a theoretical model. *The Journal of Sex Research, 20,* 143–167.

Casteels, K., Wouters, C., VanGeet, C., & Devlieger, H. (2004). Video reveals self-stimulation in infancy. *Acta Paediatrics, 93*(6), 844–846.

Catania, J. A., Binson, D., Van Der Straten, A., & Stone, V. (1995). Methodological research on sexual behavior in the AIDS era. *Annual Review of Sex Research, 6,* 77–125.

Catania, J. A., Coates, T. J., Kegeles, S. M., et al. (1989). Implications of the AIDS risk-reduction model for the gay community: The importance of perceived sexual enjoyment and help-seeking behaviors. In V. M. Mays, G. W. Albee, & S. F. Schneider (Eds.), *Primary prevention of AIDS: Psychological approaches* (pp. 242–261). Newbury Park, CA: Sage.

Catania, J. A., McDermott, L. J., & Pollack, L. M. (1986). Questionnaire response bias and face-to-face interview sample bias in sexuality research. *Journal of Sex Research, 22,* 52–72.

Catarino, R., Petignat, P., Dongui, G., & Vassilakow, P. (2015). Cervical cancer screening in developing countries at a crossroad: Emerging technologies and policy choices. *World Journal of Clinical Oncology, 6*(6), 281–290.

Cates, J. A., & Markley, J. (1992). Demographic, clinical, and personality variables associated with male prostitution by choice. *Adolescence, 27,* 695–706.

Caughey, A., Hopkins, L., & Norton, M. (2006). Chorionic villus sampling compared with amniocentesis and the difference in the rate of pregnancy loss. *Obstetrics and Gynecology, 108,* 612–616.

Cavanaugh, C., Messing, J., Petras, H., Fowler, B., LaFlair, L., Kub, J., Agnew, J., Fitzgerald, S., Bolyard, R., & Campbell, J. (2011). Patterns of violence against women: A latent class analysis. *Psychological Trauma: Theory, Research, Practice, and Policy.* Retrieved August 26, 2011, from http://psycnet.apa.org /index.cfm?fa=buy.optionToBuy&id=2011 -07605-001.

Cecchetti, J. A. (2007). Women's attachment representations of their fathers and the experience of passionate love in adulthood. *Dissertation Abstracts International: Section B: The Sciences and Engineering, 68*, 3389.

Cederroth, C. R., Auger, J., Zimmermann, C., Eustache, F., & Nef, S. (2010). Soy, phytoestrogens and male reproductive function: A review. *International Journal of Andrology, 33*(2), 304–316.

Centers for Disease Control. (2016, November 10). Reproductive health: Preterm birth. Retrieved March 31, 2017, from https://www.cdc.gov /reproductivehealth/maternalinfanthealth /pretermbirth.htm.

Centers for Disease Control. (2016). Reported STDS in the United States, 2015: National data for chlamydia, gonorrhea, and syphilis. Retrieved April 26, 2017, from https://www .cdc.gov/nchhstp/newsroom/docs/factsheets /std-trends-508.pdf.

Centers for Disease Control and Prevention Fact Sheet. (2012). *New HIV infections in the United States*. Retrieved June 9, 2014, from http://www.cdc.gov/nchhstp/newsroom /docs/2012/HIV-Infections-2007-2010.pdf.

Centers for Disease Control and Prevention, Division of STD Prevention. (2007). *Sexually transmitted disease surveillance, 2006*. Retrieved September 17, 2008, from http:// www.cdc.gov/STD/stats/toc2006.htm.

Centers for Disease Control and Prevention. (2007a). *2005 assisted reproductive technology success rates: National summary and fertility clinic reports*. Atlanta, GA: Author.

Centers for Disease Control and Prevention. (2008). Male circumcision and risk for HIV transmission and other health conditions: Implications for the United States. Department of Health and Human Services. Retrieved December 18, 2008, from http://www.cdc.gov /hiv/resources/factsheets/circumcision.htm.

Centers for Disease Control and Prevention. (2010a). Youth Risk Behavior Surveillance— United States, 2009. *Morbidity and Mortality Weekly Report Surveillance Summaries, 59*(5), 1–142.

Centers for Disease Control and Prevention. (2010b). 2008 assisted reproductive technology success rates: National summary and fertility clinic reports. Atlanta, GA: U.S. Department of Health and Human Services. Retrieved March 1, 2011, from http://www .cdc.gov/art/ART2008/PDF/ART_2008 _Full.pdf.

Centers for Disease Control and Prevention. (2010c). Sexually transmitted diseases treatment guidelines, 2010. *Morbidity and Mortality Weekly Report, 59*(No. RR-12).

Centers for Disease Control and Prevention. (2011a). 2011 State and Local Youth Risk Behavior Survey. Retrieved November 22, 2013, from http://www.cdc.gov/healthyyouth /yrbs/pdf/questionnaire/2011_hs _questionnaire.pdf.

Centers for Disease Control and Prevention. (2011b). Sexual identity, sex of sexual contacts, and health-risk behaviors among students in grades 9–12—Youth risk behavior surveillance, selected sites, U.S., 2001–2009. *Morbidity and Mortality Weekly Report, 60*. Retrieved April 1, 2014, from http://www.cdc .gov/mmwr/pdf/ss/ss60e0606.pdf.

Centers for Disease Control and Prevention. (2011c). *2011 Assisted reproductive technology: Fertility clinic success rates report*. National Center for Chronic Disease Prevention and Health Promotion, Division of Reproductive Health. Retrieved May 21, 2014, from http:// www.cdc.gov/art/ART2011/PDFs/01_ART _2011_Clinic_Report-FM.pdf.

Centers for Disease Control and Prevention. (2011d). *Understanding intimate partner violence fact sheet*. CDC Violence Prevention. Retrieved April 29, 2011, from http://www .cdc.gov/violenceprevention/pdf/IPV _factsheet-a.pdf.

Centers for Disease Control and Prevention. (2012). *National ART success rates*. National Summary Data. Retrieved July 31, 2014, from http://nccd.cdc.gov/DRH_ART/Apps /NationalSummaryReport.aspx.

Centers for Disease Control and Prevention. (2013a). *Ovarian cancer statistics*. Retrieved February 23, 2014, from http://www.cdc.gov /cancer/ovarian/statistics.

Centers for Disease Control and Prevention. (2013b). *Key statistics from the National Survey of Family Growth*. Retrieved March 28, 2014, from http://www.cdc.gov/nchs/nsfg /key_statistics/s.htm#sexualactivity.

Centers for Disease Control and Prevention. (2013c). *Genital herpes CDC fact sheet*. Retrieved June 6, 2014, from http://www.cdc .gov/std/herpes/stdfact-herpes.htm.

Centers for Disease Control and Prevention. (2013d). *Surveillance for viral hepatitis— United States, 2011*. Division of Viral Hepatitis and National Center for HIV/AIDS, Viral Hepatitis, STD, and TB Prevention. Retrieved June 6, 2014, from http://www.cdc.gov /hepatitis/Statistics/2011Surveillance/index .htm.

Centers for Disease Control and Prevention. (2013e). *HIV surveillance report*. National Center for HIV/AIDS, Viral Hepatitis, STD, and TB Prevention. Retrieved June 6, 2014, from http://www.cdc.gov/hiv/pdf/statistics_2011 _HIV_Surveillance_Report_vol_23.pdf.

Centers for Disease Control and Prevention. (2014). Genital HPV infection—CDC fact sheet. Atlanta, GA.

Centers for Disease Control and Prevention. (2014a). Reported STDs in the United States. Retrieved June 9, 2014, from http://www .cdc.gov/nchhstp/newsroom/docs/STD -Trends-508.pdf.

Centers for Disease Control and Prevention. (2014b, January). *Sexually transmitted disease surveillance 2012*. U.S. Department of Health and Human Services. Retrieved June 5, 2014, from http://www.cdc.gov/sTD/stats12 /Surv2012.pdf.

Centers for Disease Control and Prevention. (2014c). *HIV among pregnant women, infants, and children*. Retrieved June 6, 2014, from http://www.cdc.gov/hiv/risk/gender /pregnantwomen/facts.

Centers for Disease Control and Prevention. (2016). CDC fact sheet: Information for teens and young adults: Staying healthy and preventing STDs. Retrieved February 11, 2017, from https://www.cdc.gov/std/life-stages -populations/stdfact-teens.htm.

Centers for Disease Control and Prevention. (2016a). HIV infection risk, prevention, and testing behaviors among men who have sex with men—National HIV behavioral surveillance, 20 U.S. cities, 2014. HIV Surveillance Special Report. Retrieved February 11, 2017, from https://www.cdc.gov/hiv/pdf/library/reports /surveillance/cdc-hiv-hssr-nhbs-msm-2014.pdf.

Centers for Disease Control and Prevention. (2017). Youth Risk Behavior Surveillance System (YRBSS) Questionnaires. Retrieved January 7, 2017, from https://www.cdc.gov /healthyyouth/data/yrbs/questionnaires.ht.

Chabarria, K., Racusin, D., Antony, K., Kahr, M., Suter, M., Mastrobattista, J., & Aagaard, K. (2016). Marijuana use and its effects in pregnancy. *American Journal of Obstetrics and Gynecology, 215*(4), 506,(e1–7).

Chagas, B., Gurgel, A., Da Cruz, H., Amaral, C., Cardoso, M., Silva, N., Da Silva, L., De Albuquerque, E., Muniz, M., & De Freitas, A. (2013). An interleukin-10 gene polymorphism associated with the development of cervical lesions in women infected with human papillomavirus and using oral contraceptives. *Infection, Genetics and Evolution: Journal of Molecular Epidemiology and Evolutionary Genetics in Infectious Diseases, 19*(1), 32–37.

Chakraborty, A., McManus, S., Brugha, T. S., Bebbington, P., & King, M. (2011). Mental health of the non-heterosexual population of England. *British Journal of Psychiatry, 198*, 143–148.

Chalabi, M. (2014, June 5). The 100 most-used emojis. *FiveThirtyEight*. Retrieved January 11, 2017, from https://fivethirtyeight.com /datalab/the-100-most-used-emojis/.

Chaladze, G. (2016). Heterosexual male carriers could explain persistence of homosexuality in men: Individual-based simulations of an X-linked inheritance model. *Archives of Sexual Behavior, 45*(7), 1705–1711.

Chalett, J. M., & Nerenberg, L. T. (2000). "Blue balls": A diagnostic consideration in testiculoscrotal pain in young adults: A case report and discussion. *Pediatrics, 106*, 843.

Chan, C. S. (1989). Issues of identity development among Asian-American lesbians and gay men. *Journal of Counseling and Development, 68*, 16–20.

Chan, J., Olivier, B., deJong, R., Snoeren, E., Kooijman, E., vanHasselt, F., et al. (2008). Translational research into sexual disorders: Pharmacology and genomics. *European Journal of Pharmacology, 585*, 426–435.

Chancer, L. S. (2006). *Sadomasochism in everyday life: The dynamics of power and powerlessness.* New Brunswick, NJ: Rutgers University Press.

Chandra, A., Copen, C., & Mosher, W. (2013). Sexual behavior, sexual attraction, and sexual identity in the U.S.: Data from the 2006–2010 National Survey of Family Growth. In A. K. Baumle (Ed.), *International Handbooks of Population, International Handbook of the Demography of Sexuality* (Vol. VI, pp. 45–66). Dordrecht, Netherlands: Springer Science and Business Media.

Chandra, A., Copen, C., & Stephen, E. (2014). Infertility service use in the United States: Data from the National Survey of Family Growth, 1982–2010. National Health Statistics Reports, Number 73. Retrieved March 29, 2017, from https://www.cdc.gov/nchs/data/nhsr/nhsr073.pdf#x2013;2010%20.

Chandra, A., Copen, C., & Stephen, H. (2013). *Infertility and impaired fecundity in the U.S., 1982–2010: Data from the National Survey of Family Growth* (No. 67). Retrieved May 21, 2014, from http://www.cdc.gov/nchs/data/nhsr/nhsr067.pdf.

Chandra, A., Mosher, W. D., Copen, C., & Sionean, C. (2011). Sexual behavior, sexual attraction, and sexual identity in the United States: Data from the 2006–2008 National Survey of Family Growth [National health statistics reports; no 36]. Hyattsville, MD: National Center for Health Statistics.

Chang, S., Chen, K., Lin, H., Chao, Y., & Lai, Y. (2011). Comparison of the effects of episiotomy and no episiotomy on pain, urinary incontinence, and sexual function 3 months postpartum: A prospective follow-up study. *International Journal of Nursing Studies, 48*(4), 409–418.

Chańska, W., & Grunt-Mejer, K. (2016). The unethical use of ethical rhetoric: The case of flibanserin and pharmacologisation of female sexual desire. *Journal of Medical Ethics, 42*(11). Retrieved April 14, 2017, from http://jme.bmj.com/content/42/11/701.

Chaplin, S. (2007). *Japanese love hotels: A cultural history.* London: Routledge.

Chaplin, T., & Aldao, A. (2013). Gender differences in emotion expression in children: A meta-analytic review. *Psychological Bulletin, 139*(4), 735–765.

Chartier, K., & Caetano, R. (2010). Ethnicity and health disparities in alcohol research. *Alcohol Research & Health, 33*(1–2), 152–160.

Chasin, C. (2011). Theoretical issues in the study of asexuality. *Archives of Sexual Behavior, 40*(1), 713–723.

Chaturvedi, A., Engels, E., Pfeiffer, R., Hernandez, B., Xiao, W., Kim, E., Jiang, B., Goodman, M., Sibug-Saber, M., Cozen, W., Liu, L., Lynch, C., Wentzensen, N. et al. (2011). Human papillomavirus and rising oropharyngeal cancer incidence in the United States. *Journal of Clinical Oncology: Official Journal of the American Society of Clinical Oncology, 29*(32), 4294–4301.

Chaudhury, R. R. (1985). Plant contraceptives translating folklore into scientific application. In D. B. Jelliffe & E. F. Jelliffe (Eds.), *Advances in international maternal and child health* (pp. 107–114). Oxford, U.K.: Claredon Press.

Chavarro, J. E., Toth, T. L., Sadio, S. M., & Hauser, R. (2008). Soy food and isoflavone intake in relation to semen quality parameters among men from an infertility clinic. *Human Reproduction, 23*(11), 2584–2590.

Chavarro, J. E., Willett, W. C., & Skerrett, P. J. (2007). *The fertility diet.* New York: McGraw Hill.

Chavez-Macgregor, M., Clarke, C., Lichtensztajn, D., Hortobagyi, G., & Giordano, S. (2013). Male breast cancer according to tumor subtype and race. *Cancer, 119*(9), 1611–1617.

Chcasty, M., Clare, A. W., & Collins, C. (2002). Child sexual abuse: A predictor of persistent depression in adult rape and sexual assault victims. *Journal of Mental Health, 11*(1), 79–84.

Check, J. H. (2010). The future trends of induction of ovulation. *Minerva Endocrinology, 35*(4), 227–246.

Chelimo, C., Wouldes, T., Cameron, L., & Elwood, J. (2013). Risk factors for and prevention of HPV, genital warts, and cervical cancer. *Journal of Infection, 66*(3), 207–213.

Chcmaly, S. (2013, September 15). The real boy crisis: 5 ways America tells boys not to be "girly." *Salon.* Retrieved February 14, 2014, from http://www.salon.com/2013/09/25/5_ways_america_tells_boys_not_to_be_girly.

Chemes, H., & Rawe, V. (2010). The making of abnormal spermatozoa: Cellular and molecular mechanisms. *Cell Tissue Research, 341*(3), 349–357.

Chen, C., Chou, Y., Wu, Y., Lin, C., Lin, S., & Lee, C. (2013). Phthalates may promote female puberty by increasing kisspeptin activity. *Human Reproduction, 28*(10), 2765–2773.

Chen, J., & Danish, S. (2010). Acculturation, distress disclosure, and emotional self-disclosure within Asian populations. *Asian American Journal of Psychology, 1*(3), 200–211.

Chen, J., & Shiu, C. (2016). Sexual orientation and sleep in the U.S.: A national profile. *American Journal of Preventive Medicine, 52*(4), 433–442.

Chen, M., Vu, B., Axelrad, M., Dietrich, J., Gargollo, P., Gunn, S., Macias, C., McCullough, L., Roth, D., Sutton, V., & Karaviti, L. (2015). Androgen insensitivity syndrome: Management considerations from infancy to adulthood. *Pediatric Endocrinology Reviews, 12*(4), 373–387.

Chen, P., Fullilove, R., & Jacobson, K. (2015). Community violence exposure and sexual behaviors in a nationally representative sample of young adults: The effects of race/ethnicity and gender. *Journal of Social Service Research, 41*(3), 295–306.

Chen, S. (2010, May 3). Serious legal hurdles for gay divorce. CNN. Retrieved January 31, 2011, from http://articles.cnn.com/2010-05-03/living/texas.gay.divorce_1_gay-marriage-gay-divorce-same-sex-divorce?_s5PM:LIVING.

Chen, W., Rosner, B., Hankinson, S., Colditz, G., & Willett, W. (2011). Moderate alcohol consumption during adult life, drinking patterns, and breast cancer risk. *Journal of the American Medical Association, 306*(17), 1884–1890.

Chen, X., Liu, X., Zhang, L., Li, S., Shi, Y., & Tong, X. (2013). Poorer survival of male breast cancer compared with female breast cancer patients may be due to biological differences. *Japanese Journal of Clinical Oncology, 43*(10), 954–963.

Chen, Y., Zhang, L., & Hao, Q. (2013). Candidate microRNA biomarkers in human epithelial ovarian cancer. *Cancer Cell International, 13*, 86–94.

Chen, Z., & Shi, Y. (2010). Polycystic ovary syndrome. *Front Medicine China, 4*(3), 280–284.

Cheng, D., Kettinger, L., Uduhiri, K., & Hurt, L. (2011). Alcohol consumption during pregnancy: Prevalence and provider assessment. *Obstetrics and Gynecology, 117*(2 Pt 1), 212–217.

Cheng, W., Ickes, W., & Kenworthy, J. (2013). The phenomenon of hate crimes in the U.S. *Journal of Applied Social Psychology, 43*(4), 761–794.

Cheng, W., & Warren, M. (2001). She knows more about Hong Kong than you do isn't it: Tags in Hong Kong conversational English. *Journal of Pragmatics, 33*, 1419–1439.

Cheng, Y., & Chien, A. (2017, January 18). On taking gay rights from Taipei to Beijing: Don't call it a "movement." *New York Times.* Retrieved March 15, 2017, from https://www.nytimes.com/2017/01/18/world/asia/china-taiwan-same-sex-gay.html?rref=collection%2Ftimestopic%2FSame-Sex%20Marriage%2C%20Civil%20Unions%2C%20and%20Domestic%20Partnerships&action=click&contentCollection=timestopics&region=stream&module=stream_unit&version=latest&contentPlacement=10&pgtype=collection.

Chesler, P. (1993, October). Sexual violence against women and a woman's right to self-defense: The case of Aileen Carol Wuornos. *Criminal Practice Law Report, 1*(9). Retrieved May 1, 2011, from http://www.phyllis-chesler.com/114/sexual-violence-against-women-self-defense-wuornos.

Chi, X., Van de Bongardt, D., & Hawk, S. (2015). Intrapersonal and interpersonal sexual behaviors of Chinese university students: Gender differences in prevalence and correlates. *Journal of Sex Research, 52*(5), 532–542.

Chia, M., & Abrams, D. (1997). *The multiorgasmic man: Sexual secrets every man should know.* San Francisco: HarperCollins.

Chibber, K., Biggs, M., Roberts, S., & Foster, D. (2014). The role of intimate partners in women's reasons for seeking abortion. *Women's Health Issues, 24*(1), 131–138.

Chida, Y., & Mao, X. (2009). Does psychosocial stress predict symptomatic herpes simplex virus recurrence? A meta-analytic investigation on prospective studies. *Brain, Behavior, and Immunity, 23*(7), 917–925.

"Child Sexual Abuse Statistics." (2012). The National Center for Victims of Crime. Retrieved from https://victimsofcrime.org/media/reporting-on-child-sexual-abuse/child-sexual-abuse-statistics.

Chinese Ministry of Industry and Information Technology (CMIIT). (2011). *2010 National Information Industry Report.* Retrieved February 2, 2014, from http://www.miit.gov.cn/n11293472/n11293832/n11294132/n12858447/13578942.html.

Chlebowski, R., Anderson, G., & Gass, M., et al. (2010). Estrogen plus progestin and breast cancer incidence and mortality in postmenopausal women. *Journal of the American Medical Association, 304*(15), 1684–1692.

Chmielewski, D. C., & Hoffman, C. (2006). Porn industry again at the tech forefront. *Los Angeles Times,* p. A1. Retrieved November 15, 2008, from http://articles.latimes.com/2006/apr/19/business/fi-porn19.

Choi, N. (2004). Sex role group differences in specific, academic, and general self-efficacy. *Journal of Psychology: Interdisciplinary & Applied, 138*(2), 149–159.

Choi, S., & Meyer, I. (2016). *LGBT aging: A review of research findings, needs, and policy implications.* Los Angeles: Williams Institute.

Chopin-Marcé, M. J. (2001). Exhibitionism and psychotherapy: A case study. *International Journal of Offender Therapy & Comparative Criminology, 45*(5), 626–633.

Chow, E. W., & Choy, A. L. (2002). Clinical characteristics and treatment response to SSRI in a female pedophile. *Archives of Sexual Behavior, 31*(2), 211–215.

Chrisler, J., Gorman, J., Manion, J., Murgo, M., Barney, A., Adams-Clark, A., Newton, J., &

McGrath, M. (2016). Queer periods: Attitudes toward and experiences with menstruation in the masculine of centre and transgender community. *Culture, Health & Sexuality, 18*(11), 1238–1250.

Chrisler, J., Marván, M., Gorman, J., & Rossini, M. (2015). Body appreciation and attitudes toward menstruation. *Body Image, 12,* 78–81.

Christiansen, D., Bak, R., & Elklit, A. (2012). Secondary victims of rape. *Violence and Victims, 27*(2), 246–262.

Christiansen, O. B. (1996). A fresh look at the causes and treatments of recurrent miscarriage, especially its immunological aspects. *Human Reproduction Update, 2*(4), 271–293.

Christiansen, S., Axelstad, M., Boberg, J., Vinggaard, A., Pedersen, G., Hass, U. (2013). Low-dose effects of bisphenol A on early sexual development in male and female rates. *Reproduction, 147*(4), 477–487.

Chumlea, W. C., Schubert, C. M., Roche, A. F., Kulin, H. E., Lee, P. A., Himes, J. H., & Sun, S. S. (2003). Age at menarche and racial comparisons in U.S. girls. *Pediatrics, 111,* 110–113.

Churches, O., Nicholls, M., Thiessen, M., Kohler, M., & Keage, H. (2014). Emoticons in mind: An event-related potential study. *Journal of Neuroscience, 9*(2), 196–202.

Cianciotto, J., & Cahill, S. (2006). *Youth in the crosshairs: The third wave of the ex-gay movement.* National Gay and Lesbian Task Force Policy Institute. Retrieved October 2, 2008, from http://www.thetaskforce.org/downloads/reports/reports/YouthInTheCrosshairs.pdf.

Cibula, D., Gompel, A., Mueck, A. O., La Vecchia, C., Hannaford, P. C., Skouby, S. O., Zikan, M., & Dusek, L. (2010). Hormonal contraception and risk of cancer. *Human Reproduction Update, 16*(6), 631–650.

Ciebiera, M., Wodarczyk, M., Stabuszewska-Jóźwiak, A., Nowicka, G., & Jakiel, G. (2016). Influence of vitamin D and transforming growth factor serum concentrations, obesity, and family history on the risk for uterine fibroids. *Fertility and Sterility, 106*(7), 1787–1792.

Citron, D. (2014, May 15). Nonconsensual taping of sex partners is a crime. *Forbes.* Retrieved May 1, 2017, from https://www.forbes.com/sites/daniellecitron/2014/05/15/nonconsensual-taping-of-sex-partners-is-a-crime/#97fab086ce08.

Clapp, I., & Lopez, B. (2007). Size at birth, obesity and blood pressure at age five. *Metabolic Syndrome and Related Disorders, 5,* 116–126.

Clapp, J. F. (1996). Morphometric and neurodevelopmental outcome at age five years of the offspring of women who continued to exercise regularly throughout pregnancy. *Journal of Pediatrics, 129*(6), 856–863.

Clark, H., Babu, A., Wiewel, E., Opoku, J., & Crepaz, N. (2016). Diagnosed HIV infection

in transgender adults and adolescents: Results from the National HIV Surveillance System, 2009–2014. *AIDS Behavior.* Retrieved April 26, 2017, from https://www.ncbi.nlm.nih.gov/pubmed/28035497.

Clark, M. S., & Reis, H. T. (1988). Interpersonal processes in close relationships. *Annual Review of Psychology, 39,* 609–672.

Clark, P. M., Atton, C., Law, C. M., Shiell, A., Godfrey, K., & Barker, D. J. (1998). Weight gain in pregnancy, triceps skinfold thickness, and blood pressure in offspring. *Obstetrics and Gynecology, 91*(1), 103–107.

Clarke, A. K., & Miller, S. J. (2001). The debate regarding continuous use of oral contraceptives. *Annals of Pharmacotherapy, 35,* 1480–1484.

Clarke, L., & Korotchenko, A. (2010). Shades of grey: To dye or not to dye one's hair in later life. *Ageing and Society, 30*(6), 1011–1026.

Claxton, A., & Perry-Jenkins, M. (2008). No fun anymore: Leisure and marital quality across the transition to parenthood. *Journal of Marriage and Family, 70,* 28–44.

Clay, K. (2014, June 18). Microsoft enters wearable sector with phone charging pants. *Forbes.* Retrieved June 17, 2014, from http://www.forbes.com/sites/kellyclay/2014/06/18/microsoft-enters-wearables-sector-with-phone-charging-pants.

Clayton, A., Althof, S., Kingsberg, S., DeRogatis, L., Kroll, R., Goldstein, I., Kaminetsky, J., Spana, C., Lucas, J., Jordan, R., & Portman, D. (2016). Bremelanotide for female sexual dysfunctions in premenopausal women: A randomized, placebo-controlled dose-finding trial. *Women's Health, 12*(3), 325–337.

Clift, E. (2012, February 2). Could DSM-5 be harmful to your mental health? *Women's Media Center.* Retrieved May 31, 2014, from http://www.womensmediacenter.com/feature/entry/could-dsm-5-be-harmful-to-your-mental-health.

Clinkenbeard, J. (2012, March 29). Could this male contraceptive pill make a vas deferens in the fight against HIV? *Techcitement.* Retrieved May 26, 2014, from http://techcitement.com/culture/could-this-male-contraceptive-pill-make-a-vas-deferens-in-the-fight-against-hiv/#.U4Olt8a9ypU.

Clinton, C., & Gillespie, M. (1997). *Sex and race in the early South.* Oxford, England: Oxford University Press.

Clipson, T., Wilson, S., & DuFrene, D. (2012). The social networking arena: Battle of the sexes. *Business Communication Quarterly, 75*(1), 64–67.

Coan, J. (2014, February). *Marriage as a moderator of threat-related hypothalamic regulation in straight- and same-sex couples.* Paper presented at 15th Annual Society of Personality and Social Psychology Conference, Austin, TX.

Coast, E. (2007). Wasting semen: Context and condom use among the Maasai. *Culture, Health and Sexuality, 9*, 387–401.

Coccia, M., & Rizzello, F. (2008). Ovarian reserve. Assessment of human reproductive function. *Annals of the New York Academy of Science, 1127*, 27–30.

Cochran, B. M., Ginzler, J., & Cauce, A. (2002). Challenges faced by homeless sexual minorities: Comparison of gay, lesbian, bisexual, and transgendered homeless sexual minorities with their heterosexual counterparts. *Journal of Public Health, 92*, 773–777.

Cohen, C., Elion, R., Ruane, P., Shamblaw, D., DeJesus, E., Rashbaum, B., Chuck, S., Yale, K., Liu, H., Warren, D., Ramanathan, S., & Kearney, B. (2011). Randomized, phase 2 evaluation of two single-tablet regimenselvitegravir/cobicistat/emtricitabine/tenofovir disoproxil fumarate versus efavirenz/emtricitabine/tenofovir disoproxil fumarate for the initial treatment of HIV infection. *AIDS, 25*(6), F7–12.

Cohen, F., Kemeny, M., Kearney, K., Zegans, L., Neuhaus, J., & Conant, M. (1999). Persistent stress as a predictor of genital herpes recurrence. *Archives of Internal Medicine, 159*, 2430–2436.

Cohen, J., & Byers, E. (2013). Beyond lesbian bed death: Enhancing our understanding of the sexuality of sexual-minority women in relationships. *Journal of Sex Research, 51*(8), 893–903.

Cohen, J., Byers, E., & Walsh, L. (2008). Factors influencing the sexual relationships of lesbians and gay men. *International Journal of Sexual Health, 20*(3), 162–176.

Cohen, J. K., Miller, R. J., Ahmed, S., Lotz, M. J., & Baust, J. (2008c). Ten-year biochemical disease control for patients with prostate cancer treated with cryosurgery as primary therapy. *Urology, 71*, 515–518.

Cohen, K. M., & Savin-Williams, R. C. (1996). Developmental perspectives on coming out to self and others. In R. C. Savin-Williams & K. M. Cohen (Eds.), *The lives of lesbians, gays, and bisexuals: Children to adults* (pp. 113–151). Fort Worth, TX: Harcourt Brace.

Cohen, L. (1988). Providing treatment and support for partners of sexual-assault survivors. *Psychotherapy, 25*, 94–98.

Cohen, L., & Roth, S. (1987). The psychological aftermath of rape: Long-term effects and individual differences in recovery. *Journal of Social and Clinical Psychology, 5*, 525–534.

Cohen, M. (2016). Sexual abuse and eating disorders. Eating Disorder & Referral Information Center. Retrieved online from https://www.edreferral.com/blog/sexual-abuse-and-eating-disorders-by-mary-anne-cohen-csw-director-aaa-the-new-york-center-for-eating-disorders-206.

Cohen, S. A. (2009). Facts and consequences: Legality, incidence and safety of abortion worldwide. *Guttmacher Policy Review, 12*(4). Retrived June 4, 2010, from http://www.guttmacher.org/pubs/gpr/12/4/gpr120402.html.

Cohen-Bendahan, C., van de Beek, C., & Berenbaum, S. (2005). Prenatal sex hormone effects on child and adult sex-typed behavior: Methods and findings. *Neuroscience & Biobehavioral Reviews, 29*(2), 353–384.

Cohen-Kettenis, P. T., & Pfäfflin, F. (2010). The DSM diagnostic criteria for gender identity disorder in adolescents and adults. *Archives of Sexual Behavior, 39*(2), 499–513.

Cohn, D. (2009). The states of marriage and divorce. Pew Research Council, October 15, Retrieved July 4, 2011, from http://pewresearch.org/pubs/1380/marriage-and-divorce-by-state.

Cohn, D. (2012, February 16). Intermarried couples: Trends and characteristics. Pew Research Center, Social & Demographic Trends. Retrieved March 6, 2017, from http://www.pewsocialtrends.org/2012/02/16/intermarried-couples-trends-and-characteristics/.

Coker, A. L. (2007). Does physical intimate partner violence affect sexual health? A systematic review. *Trauma Violence Abuse, 8*, 149–177.

Colapinto, J. (2001). *As nature made him: The boy who was raised as a girl*. New York: HarperCollins.

Colby, S., Ortman, J. (2015). Projections of the size and composition of the U.S. population: 2014 to 2060. *Current Population Reports*. Retrieved August 23, 2017, from https://www.census.gov/content/dam/Census/library/publications/2015/demo/p25-1143.pdf.

Coleman, E. (1982). Developmental stages of the coming-out process. *American Behavioral Scientist, 25*, 469–482.

Coleman, M., Ganong, L., & Fine, M. (2000). Reinvestigating remarriage: Another decade of progress. *Journal of Marriage and Family, 62*(4), 1288–1308.

Coleman, P. (2002). *How to say it for couples*. New York: Prentice Hall Press.

Coleman, P. K. (2006). Resolution of unwanted pregnancy during adolescence through abortion versus childbirth: Individual and family predictors and psychological consequences. *Journal of Youth and Adolescence, 35*, 903–911.

Coles, M., Makino, K., Stanwood, N., Dozier, A., & Klein, J. (2010). How are restrictive abortion statutes associated with unintended teen birth? *Journal of Adolescent Health, 47*(2), 160–167.

Colley, A., Todd, Z., White, A., & Turner-Moore, T. (2010). Communication using camera phones among young men and women: Who sends what to whom? *Sex Roles, 63*(5/6), 348–360.

Collier, J. F., & Rosaldo, M. Z. (1981). Politics and gender in simple societies. In S. Ortner & H. Whitehead (Eds.), *Sexual meanings* (pp. 275–329). Cambridge, U.K.: Cambridge University Press.

Collier, K., Bos, H., Merry, M., & Sandfort, T. (2013). Gender, ethnicity, religiosity, and same-sex sexual attraction and the acceptance of same-sex sexuality and gender non-conformity. *Sex Roles, 68*(11–12), 724–737.

Collins, P. H. (1998). The tie that binds: Race, gender and U.S. violence. *Ethnic and Racial Studies, 21*(5), 917–939.

Collins, P. H. (2000). It's all in the family. *Women and Language, 23*(2), 65–69.

Collins, R. (2005). Sex on television and its impact on American youth: Background and results from the RAND television and adolescent sexuality study. *Child & Adolescent Psychiatric Clinics of North America, 14*(3), 371–385.

Collins, R. L., Ellickson, P. L., & Klein, D. J. (2007). Research report: The role of substance use in young adult divorce. *Addiction, 102*, 786.

Collins, R. L., Elliott, M. N., Berry, S. H., Kanouse, D. E., Kunkel, D., Hunter, S. B., & Miu, A. (2004). Watching sex on television predicts adolescent initiation of sexual behavior. *Pediatrics, 114*(3), 280–289.

Collisson, B., Howell, J., Rusbasan, D., & Rosenfeld, E. (2016). Date someone your own size: Prejudice and discrimination toward mixed-weight relationships. *Journal of Social and Personal Relationships*, 1–31. Retrieved March 7, 2017, from http://journals.sagepub.com/doi/abs/10.1177/0265407516644067.

Cólon-López, V., Fernàndez-Espada, N., Vélez, C., Gonzalez, V., Dias-Toro, E., et al. (2016). Communication and sex and HPV among Puerto Rican mothers and daughters. *Ethnicity & Health*, 1–13. Retrieved February 11, 2017, from http://www.tandfonline.com/doi/abs/10.1080/13557858.2016.1246938?journalCode=ceth20.

Colón-López, V., Fernández-Espada, N., Vélez, C., Gonzalez, E., Diaz-Toro, E., Calo, W. (2017). Communication about sex and HPV among Puerto Rican mothers and daughters, *Ethnicity & Health, 22*(4), 348–360.

Comfort, A. (1987). Deviation and variation. In G. D. Wilson (Ed.), *Variant sexuality: Research and theory* (pp. 1–20). Baltimore: Johns Hopkins University Press.

Comfort, A., & Rubenstein, J. (1992). The new joy of sex: A gourmet guide to lovemaking in the nineties. New York: Simon & Schuster.

Compton, J. (2016, September 7). For some same-sex couples, divorce is legal nightmare. NBC News. Retrieved March 6, 2016, from http://www.nbcnews.com/feature/nbc-out/some-same-sex-couples-divorce-legal-nightmare-n643891.

Condon, P. (2010, July 8). Presbyterian church's general assembly oks gay clergy. *Huffington Post*. Retrieved February 20, 2011, from http://www.huffingtonpost.com/2010/07/08/presbyterian-gay-clergy_n_640189.html.

Conley, T., Moors, A., Matsick, J., & Ziegler, A. (2013). The fewer the merrier?: Assessing stigma surrounding consensually non-monogamous romantic relationships. *Analyses of Social Issues and Public Policy*, 13, 1–30.

Conron, K. J., Mimiaga, M. J., & Landers, S. J. (2010). A population-based study of sexual orientation identity and gender differences in adult health. *American Journal of Public Health*, 100(10), 1953–1960.

"Contraceptive Use in the United States." (2016). Fact Sheet, Alan Guttmacher Institute. Retrieved April 5, 2017, from https://www.guttmacher.org/fact-sheet/contraceptive-use-united-states.

Conway, A. M. (2005). Girls, aggression, and emotional regulation. *American Journal of Orthopsychiatry*, 75(2), 334–339.

Conway, G., Band, M., Doyle, J., & Davies, M. (2010). How do you monitor the patient with Turner's syndrome in adulthood? *Clinical Endocrinology*, 73(6), 696–699.

Cook, R., & Dickens, B. (2009). Hymen reconstruction: Ethical and legal issues. *International Journal of Gynecology and Obstetrics*, 107(3), 266–269.

Cook, S. (2012). How to progress from a rape-supportive culture. *Women in Higher Education*, 21(7), 16.

Cooks, S., & Calebs, B. (2016). The integrated attachment and sexual minority stress model: Understanding the role of adult attachment in the health and well-being of sexual minority men. *Behavioral Medicine*, 42(3), 164–173.

Cooney, E. (2013, November). Targeting HSV: NIH launches trial of genital herpes vaccine. *Harvard Medical School*. Retrieved June 6, 2014, from http://hms.harvard.edu/news/targeting-hsv-11-8-13.

Cooper, A. M. (1991). The unconscious core of perversion. In G. I. Fogel & W. A. Myers (Eds.), *Perversions and near-perversions in clinical practice: New psychoanalytic perspectives* (pp. 17–35). New Haven: Yale University Press.

Cooper, K., Martyn-St James, M., Kaltenthaler, E., Dickinson, K., Cantrell, A., Ren, S., Wylie, K., Frodsham, L., & Hood, C. (2017). Complementary and alternative medicine for management of premature ejaculation: A systematic review. *Sexual Medicine*, 5(1), e1–e18.

Coordt, A. K. (2005). Young adults of childhood divorce: Intimate relationships prior to marriage. *Dissertation Abstracts International, Section A: Humanities and Social Sciences*, 66, 500.

Copeland, K., Brown, J., Creasman, J., Van Den Eeden, S., Subak, L., Thom, D., Ferrara, A., & Huang, A. (2012). Diabetes mellitus and sexual function in middle-aged and older women. *Obstetrics and Gynecology*, 120 (2 Pt. 1), 331–340.

Copen, C., Chandra, A., & Febo-Vazquez, M. (2016). Sexual behavior, sexual attraction, and sexual orientation among adults aged 18–44 in the United States: Data from the 2011–2013 National Survey of Family Growth. National Health Statistics Reports, #88. Retrieved March 24, 2017, from https://www.cdc.gov/nchs/data/nhsr/nhsr088.pdf.

Copen, C., Chandra, A., & Martinez, G. (2012a). Prevalence and timing of oral sex with opposite-sex partners among females and males aged 15–24 years: U.S., 2007–2010. *National Health Statistics Reports*, 56. Retrieved March 27, 2014, from http://www.cdc.gov/nchs/data/nhsr/nhsr056.pdf.

Copen, C., Chandra, A., & Martinez, G. (2012b). Prevalence and timing of oral sex with opposite-sex partners among females and males aged 15–24 Years: United States, 2007–2010 (National Health Statistics Reports, No. 56). Washington, DC: Centers for Disease Control and Prevention.

Copen, C., Daniels, K., & Mosher, W. (2013). *First premarital cohabitation in the United States: 2006–2010 National Survey of Family Growth* (National Health Statistics Report No. 64). Hyattsville, MD: National Center for Health Statistics.

Copen, C., Daniels, K., Vespa, J., & Mosher, W. (2012). *First marriages in the United States: Data from the 2006–2010 National Survey of Family Growth* (National Health Statistics Report No. 49). Hyattsville, MD: National Center for Health Statistics.

Coppola, M. A., Klotz, K. L., Kim, K. A., Cho, H. Y., Kang, J., Shetty, J., Howards, S. S., Flickinger, C. J., & Herr, J. C. (2010). SpermCheck Fertility, an immunodiagnostic home test that detects normozoospermia and severe oligozoospermia. *Human Reproduction*, 25(4), 853–861.

Corey, L., & Handsfield, H. (2000). Genital herpes and public health. *Journal of the American Medical Association*, 283, 791–794.

Corneanu, L. M., Stănculescu, D., & Corneanu, C. (2011). HPV and cervical squamous intraepithelial lesions: Clinicopathological study. *Romanian Journal of Morphology and Embryology*, 52(1), 89–94.

Cornelius, T., Shorey, R., & Beebe, S. (2010). Self-reported communication variables and dating violence: Using Gottman's marital communication conceptualization. *Journal of Family Violence*, 25(4), 439.

Corona, G., Jannini, E. A., Lotti, F., Boddi, V., De Vita, G., Forti, G., Lenzi, A., Mannucci, E., & Maggi, M. (2011). Premature and delayed ejaculation: Two ends of a single continuum influenced by hormonal milieu. *International Journal of Andrology*, 34(1), 41–48.

Corso, P., Edwards, V., Fang, X., & Mercy, J. (2008). Health-related quality of life among adults who experience maltreatment during childhood. *American Journal of Public Health*, 98, 1094–1100.

Corte, C., Matthews, A., Stein, K., & Lee, C. (2016). Early drinking onset moderates the effect of sexual minority stress on drinking identity and alcohol use in sexual and gender minority women. *Psychology of Sexual Orientation and Gender Diversity*, 3(4), 480–488.

Corty, E. W., Guardiani, J. M. (2008) Canadian and American sex therapists' perceptions of normal and abnormal ejaculatory latencies: How long should intercourse last. *Journal of Sexual Medicine 5*, 1251–1256.

Costa-Martins, J., Pereira, M., Martins, H., Moura-Ramos, M., Coelho, R., & Tavares, J. (2014). The influence of women's attachment style on the chronobiology of labour pain, analgesic consumption and pharmacological effect. *Chronobiology International*, 31(6), 787–796.

Costabile, R., Mammen, T., & Hwang, K. (2008). An overview and expert opinion on the use of alprostadil in the treatment of sexual dysfunction. *Expert Opinions in Pharmacotherapy*, 9, 1421–1429.

Costescu, D., Guilbert, E., Bernardin, J., Black, A., Dunn, S., Fitzsimmons, B., Norman, W., et al. (2016). Medical abortion. *Journal of Obstetrics and Gynaecology Canada*, 38(4), 366–389.

Coulson, N. J. (1979). Regulation of sexual behavior under traditional Islamic law. In Al-Sayyid-Marsot & A. Lutfi (Eds.), *Society and the sexes in medieval Islam* (pp. 63–68). Malibu, CA: Undena Publications.

Coulter, R., Birkett, M., Corliss, H., Hatzenbuehler, M., Mustanski, B., & Stall, R. (2016). Associations between LGBTQ-affirmative school climate and adolescent drinking behaviors. *Drug and Alcohol Dependence*, 161(1), 340–347.

Courtenay, W. H. (2000). Behavioral factors associated with disease, injury, and death among men: Evidence and implications for prevention. *The Journal of Men's Studies*, 9(1), 81–142.

Courvant, D., & Cook-Daniels, L. (1998). Transgender and intersex survivors of domestic violence: Defining terms, barriers and responsibilities. In *National Coalition Against Domestic Violence Conference*

Manual, Denver, CO. Retrieved June 17, 2014, from http://www.survivorproject.org /defbarresp.html.

Cowan, G. (1992). Feminist attitudes toward pornography control. *Psychology of Women Quarterly*, 165–177.

Cowan, G. (2000). Beliefs about the causes of four types of rape. *Sex Roles*, *42*(9–10), 807–823.

Cowan, S. (2017). Enacted abortion stigma in the United States. *Social Science & Medicine*, *177*, 259–268.

Cox, N., Vanden Berghe, W., Dewaele, A., & Vincke, J. (2010). Acculturation strategies and mental health in gay, lesbian, and bisexual youth. *Journal of Youth and Adolescence*, *39*(10), 1199–1210.

Cox, S., Pazol, K., Warner, L., Romero, L., Spitz, A., Gavin, L., & Barfield, W. (2014). Vital Signs: Births to teens aged 15–17 years— United States, 1991–2012. *Morbidity and Mortality Weekly Report*, *63*(14), 312–318.

Coyne, S., Stockdale, L., Busby, D., Iverson, B., & Grant, D. (2011). "I luv u ☺": A descriptive study of the media use of individuals in romantic relationships. *Family Relations*, *60*(2), 150–162.

Craig, S., Austin, A., & Alessi, E. (2013). Gay affirmative cognitive behavioral therapy for sexual minority youth: A clinical adaptation. *Clinical Social Work Journal*, *41*(3), 258–266.

Cramer, R., Golom, F., LoPresto, C., & Kirkley, S. (2008). Weighing the evidence: Empirical assessment and ethical implications of conversion therapy. *Ethics & Behavior*, *18*, 93–114.

Cramer, R., Kehn, A., Pennington, C., Wechsler, H., Clark, J., & Nagle, J. (2013). An examination of sexual orientation and transgender-based hate crimes in the post-Matthew Shepard era. *Psychology, Public Policy, and Law*, *19*(3), 355–368.

Cramp, J., Courtois, F., & Ditor, D. (2015). Sexuality for women with spinal cord injury. *Journal of Sex and Marital Therapy*, *41*(3), 238–253.

Cranney, S. (2015). Internet pornography use and sexual body image in a Dutch sample. *International Journal of Sexual Health*, *27*(3), 316–323.

Crary, D. (2010, October 4). Indiana University survey on sex in U.S., biggest since 1994. *Courier-Journal.com*. Retrieved October 9, 2010, from http://www.courier-journal .com/article/20101004/FEATURES03 /310040046/1010/Indiana1University1 survey1on1sex1in1US11biggest1since11994.

Cravens, J., Whiting, J. (2016). Fooling around on Facebook: The perceptions of infidelity behavior on social networking sites. *Journal of Couple and Relationship Therapy*, *15*(3), 213–231.

Cravens, J., Leckie, K., & Whiting, J. (2013). Facebook infidelity: When poking becomes problematic. *Contemporary Family Therapy: An International Journal 35*(1), 74–90.

Crawford, J., Boulet, M., & Drea, C. (2011). Smelling wrong: Hormonal contraception in lemurs alters critical female odour cues. *Proceedings of the Royal Society B*, *278*, 122–130.

Crawford, J. T., Leynes, P. A., Mayhorn, C. B., & Bink, M. L. (2004). Champagne, beer, or coffee? A corpus of gender-related and neutral words. *Behavior Research Methods, Instruments & Computers*, *36*(3), 444–459.

Crawford, M. (2006). *Transformations: Women, gender & psychology*. New York: McGraw-Hill.

Creinin, M., Jansen, R., Starr, R., Gobburu, J., Gopalakrishnan, M., & Olariu, A. (2016). Levonorgestrel release rates over 5 years with the Liletta 520mg intrauterine system. *Contraception*, *94*(4), 353–356.

Cremer, M., Phan-Weston, S., & Jacobs, A. (2010). Recent innovations in oral contraception. *Seminars in Reproductive Medicine*, *28*(2), 140–146.

Critelli, J., & Bivona, J. (2008). Women's erotic rape fantasies: An evaluation of theory and research. *Journal of Sex Research*, *45*(1), 57–70.

Critelli, J. W., Myers, E. J., & Loos, V. E. (1986). The components of love: Romantic attraction and sex role orientation. *Journal of Personality*, *54*(2), 354–370.

Crivelli, C., Jarillo, S., Russell, J., & Fernández-Dols, J. (2016). Reading emotions from faces in two indigenous societies. *Journal of Experimental Psychology*, *145*(7), 830–843.

Croft, M. L., Morgan, V., Read, A. W., & Jablensky, A. S. (2010). Recorded pregnancy histories of the mothers of singletons and the mothers of twins. *Twin Research and Human Genetics*, *13*(6), 595–603.

Crosby, A., Han, B., Ortega, L., Parks, S., & Gfroerer, J. (2011). Suicidal thoughts and behaviors among adults aged.18 years— United States, 2008–2009. *Morbidity and Mortality Weekly Report*, *60*(SS13), 1–22.

Crosby, R., & Diclemente, R. (2004). Use of recreational Viagra among men having sex with men. *Sexually Transmitted Infections*, *80*, 466–468.

Crosby, R., Diclemente, R., Wingood, G., Salazar, L., Lang, D., Rose, E., et al. (2008a). Co-occurrence of intoxication during sex and sexually transmitted infections among young African American women: Does partner intoxication matter? *Sexual Health*, *5*, 285–289.

Cross, P., & Matheson, K. (2006). Understanding sadomasochism: An empirical examination of four perspectives. *Journal of Homosexuality*, *50*, 133–166.

Crossland, K. (2014). Shotgun cohabitation. *World Magazine*. Retrieved April 12, 2014, from http://www.worldmag.com/2014/01 /shotgun_cohabitation.

Crow, S., Agras, W., Crosby, R., Halmi, K., & Mitchell, J. (2008). Eating disorder symptoms in pregnancy: A prospective study. *International Journal of Eating Disorders*, *41*, 277–279.

Crowley, I. P., & Kesner, K. M. (1990). Ritual circumcision (umkhwetha) amongst the Xhosa of the Ciskei. *British Journal of Urology*, *66*(3), 318–321.

Croydon, H. (2014, April 24). Screw the fairy tale, it's time to rethink monogamy. *New Statesman*. Retrieved July 7, 2014, from http://www.newstatesman.com/lifestyle /2014/04/screw-fairy-tale-it-s-time-rethink -monogamy.

Cruz, D., Lume, C., Silva, J., Nunes, A., Castro, I., Silva, R., Silva, V., Ferreira, R., & Fardilha, M. (2015). Oxidative stress markers: Can they be used to evaluate human sperm quality? *Turkish Journal of Urology*, *41*(4), 198–207.

Cruz, J. M. (2003). "Why doesn't he just leave?": Gay male domestic violence and the reasons victims stay. *Journal of Men's Studies*, *11*, 309.

Cunningham, G. (2013). Andropause or male menopause? Rationale for testosterone replacement therapy in older men with low testosterone levels. *Endocrine Practice*, *19*(5), 847–852.

Cunningham, G. R., & Toma, S. M. (2011). Why is androgen replacement in males controversial? *Journal of Clinical Endocrinological Metabolism*, *96*(1), 38–52.

Cunningham, S. D., Kerrigan, D. L., Jennings, J. M., & Ellen, J. M. (2009). Relationships between perceived STD-related stigma, STD-related shame and STD screening among a household sample of adolescents. *Perspectives on Sexual and Reproductive Health*, *41*(4), 225–230.

Currier, D., & Carlson, J. (2009). Creating attitudinal change through teaching: How a course on "women and violence" changes students' attitudes about violence against women. *Journal of Interpersonal Violence*, *24*(10), 1735–1754.

Cusitar, L. (1994). *Strengthening the link: Stopping the violence*. Toronto: Disabled Women's Network.

Czaja, S., Sabbag, S., Lee, C., Schulz, R., Lang, S., Vlahovic, T., Jaret, A., & Thurston, C. (2015). Concerns about aging and caregiving among middle-aged and older lesbian and gay adults. *Aging and Mental Health*, *20*(11) 1107–1118.

D'Aloisio, A., Baird, D., DeRoo, L., & Sandler, D. (2010). Association of intrauterine and early-life exposures with diagnosis of uterine leiomyomata by 35 years of age in the sister study. *Environmental Health Perspectives*, *118*(3), 375–381.

d'Amora, D., & Hobson, B. (2003). Sexual offender treatment. Retrieved March 31, 2003, from http://www.smith-lawfirm.com/Connsacs_offender_treatment.htm.

D'Augelli, A. R. (2005). Stress and adaptation among families of lesbian, gay, and bisexual youth: Research challenges. *Journal of GLBT Family Studies, 1*, 115–135.

D'Augelli, A. R., Grossman, A. H., Hershberger, S., & O'Connell, T. (2001). Aspects of mental health among older lesbian, gay, and bisexual adults. *Aging and Mental Health, 5*, 149–158.

D'Augelli, A. R., Grossman, A. H., & Starks, M. (2006). Childhood gender atypicality, victimization, and PTSD among lesbian, gay, and bisexual youth. *Journal of Interpersonal Violence, 21*, 1462–1482.

D'Augelli, A., Grossman, A., Starks, M., & Sinclair, K. (2010). Factors associated with parents' knowledge of gay, lesbian, and bisexual youths' sexual orientation. *Journal of GLBT Family Studies, 6*(2), 178–198.

D'Cruz, H., & Stagnitti, K. (2010). When parents love and don't love their children: Some children's stories. *Child & Family Social Work, 15*(2), 216.

D'Emilio, J. (1998). *Sexual politics, sexual communities*. Chicago: University of Chicago Press.

D'Emilio, J., & Freedman, E. (1988). *Intimate Matters: A History of Sexuality in America*. Chicago, IL: University of Chicago Press.

D'Onofrio, B., Rickert, M., Frans, E., Kuja-Halkola, R., Almqvist, C., Sjölander, A., Larsson, H., & Lichtenstein, P. (2014). Paternal age at childbearing and offspring psychiatric and academic morbidity. *Journal of the American Medical Association, 71*(4), 432–438.

D'Souza, G., Cullen, K., Bowie, J., Thorpe, R., & Fakhry, C. (2014). Differences in oral sexual behaviors by gender, age, and race explain observed differences in prevalence of oral human papillomavirus infection. *PLOS ONE, 9*(1) 1–12.

Daan, N., Koster, M., de Wilde, M., Dalmeijer, G., Evelein, A., Fauser, B., & de Jager, W. (2016). Biomarker profiles in women with PCOS and PCOS offspring: A pilot study. *PLOS ONE, 11*(11). Retrieved January 20, 2017, from https://www.ncbi.nlm.nih.gov/pmc/articles/PMC5091782/.

Dade, L. R., & Sloan, L. R. (2000). An investigation of sex-role stereotypes in African Americans. *Journal of Black Studies, 30*(5), 676.

Dake, J. A., Price, J. H., Ward, B. L., & Welch, P. J. (2011). Midwestern rural adolescents' oral sex experience. *Journal of School Health, 81*(3), 159–165.

Daley, E., Perrin, K., Vamos, C., Hernandez, N., Anstey, E., Baker, E., Kolar, S., & Ebbert, J. (2013). Confusion about pap smears: Lack of knowledge among high-risk women. *Journal of Women's Health, 22*(1), 67–74.

Dalla, R. L. (2002). Night moves: A qualitative investigation of street-level sex work. *Psychology of Women Quarterly, 26*(1), 63–74.

Daltveit, A., Tollances, M., Pihlstrom, H., & Irgens, L. (2008). Cesarean delivery and subsequent pregnancies. *Obstetrics and Gynecology, 111*, 1327–1334.

Danby, C., & Margesson, L. (2010). Approach to the diagnosis and treatment of vulvar pain. *Dermatology Therapy, 23*(5), 485–504.

Dancey, C. P. (1990). Sexual orientation in women: An investigation of hormonal and personality variables. *Biological Psychology, 30*, 251–264.

Daniels M. C., & Adair, L. S. (2005). Breast-feeding influences cognitive development in Filipino children. *Journal of Nutrition, 135*(11), 2589–2595.

Daniels, K., Daugherty, J., Jones, J., Mosher, W. (2015). Current contraceptive use and variation by selected characteristics among women aged 15–44: United States, 2011–2013. National Health Statistics Reports, No. 86.

Daniels, K., Jones, J., & Abma, J. (2013a). Use of emergency contraception among women aged 15–44: United States, 2006–2010, NCHS Data Brief, No. 112.

Daniels, K., Jones, J., & Abma, J. (2013b). Use of emergency contraception among women aged 15–44: U.S., 2006–2010. NCHS Data Brief (No. 112). Retrieved May 26, 2014, from http://www.cdc.gov/nchs/data/databriefs/db112.pdf.

Daniels, K., Mosher, W., & Jones, J. (2013). Contraceptive methods women have ever used: United States, 1982–2010, National Health Statistics Reports, No. 62.

Daniels, K., Mosher, W., & Jones, J. (2013a). Contraceptive methods women have ever used: U.S., 1982–2010. National Health Statistics Reports (No. 62). Retrieved May 24, 2014, from http://www.cdc.gov/nchs/data/nhsr/nhsr062.pdf.

Daniels, K., Mosher, W. (2014). Contraceptive methods women have ever used: United States, 1982–2010. *National Health Statistics Report, 62*, 1–15.

Daniluk, J., & Browne, N. (2008). Traditional religious doctrine and women's sexuality reconciling the contradictions. *Women and Therapy, 31*(1), 129–142.

Danno, K., Colas, A., Terxan, L., & Bordet, M. (2013). Homeopathic treatment of premenstrual syndrome: A case series. *Journal of the Faculty of Homeopathy, 102*(1), 59–65.

Dante, G., & Facchinetti, F. (2011). Herbal treatments for alleviating premenstrual symptoms: A systematic review. *Journal of Psychosomatic Obstetrics and Gynecology, 32*(1), 42–51.

Daragahi, B., & Dubin, A. (2001). Can prenups be romantic? *Money, 30*(2), 30–38.

Darcangelo, S. (2008). Fetishism: Psychopathology and theory. In D. Laws & W. O'Donohue (Eds.), *Sexual deviance: Theory, assessment and treatment* (2nd ed., pp. 108–118). New York: Guilford Press.

Darwiche, J., Favez, N., Maillard, F., Germond, M., Guex, P., Despland, J., & Roten, Y. (2013). Couples' resolution of an infertility diagnosis before undergoing IVF. *Swiss Journal of Psychology, 72*(2), 91–102.

Das, A. (2007). Masturbation in the U.S. *Journal of Sex and Marital Therapy, 33*(4), 301–317.

Das, A., Parish, W., & Laumann, E. (2009). Masturbation in urban China. *Archives of Sexual Behavior, 38*(1), 108–120.

Das, M. (2010). Gender role portrayals in Indian television ads. *Sex Roles, 64*, 208–222.

Dattijo, L. M., Nyango, D. D., & Osagie, O. E. (2010). Awareness, perception and practice of female genital mutilation among expectant mothers in Jos University Teaching Hospital Jos, north-central Nigeria. *Nigerian Journal of Medicine, 19*(3), 311–315.

Davé, S., Petersen, I., Sherr, L., & Nazareth, I. (2010). Incidence of maternal and paternal depression in primary care. *Archives of Pediatric Adolescent Medicine, 164*(11), 1038–1044.

Davidson, J. (2002). Working with polyamorous clients in the clinical setting. *Electronic Journal of Human Sexuality, 5*. Retrieved September 13, 2008, from http://www.ejhs.org/volume5/polyoutline.html.

Davidson, J., Moore, N., Earle, J., & Davis, R. (2008). Sexual attitudes and behavior at four universities: Do region, race, and/or religion matter? *Adolescence, 433*(170), 189–220.

Davies, J., Knight, E., Savage, A., Brown, J., & Malone, P. (2011). Evaluation of terminology used to describe disorders of sex development. *Journal of Pediatric Urology, 7*(4), 412–415.

Davies, K. A. (1997). Voluntary exposure to pornography and men's attitudes toward feminism and rape. *Journal of Sex Research, 34*(2), 131–138.

Davies, M., Boulle, A., Fakir, T., Nuttall, J., & Eley B. (2008). Adherence to antiretroviral therapy in young children in Cape Town, South Africa, measured by medication return and caregiver self-report: A prospective cohort study. *BMC Pediatrics, 4*(8), 34.

Davies, M., Rogers, P., & Whitelegg, L. (2009). Effects of victim gender, victim sexual orientation, victim response and respondent gender on judgments of blame in a hypothetical adolescent rape. *Legal and Criminological Psychology, 14*(2), 331–338.

Davis, K., Schraufnagel, T., Jacques-Tiura, A., Norris, J., George, W., & Kiekel, P. (2012). Childhood sexual abuse and acute alcohol effects on men's sexual aggression intentions. *Psychology of Violence, 2*(2), 179–193.

Davis, K. E., & Latty-Mann, H. (1987). Love styles and relationship quality: A contribution to validation. *Journal of Social & Personal Relationships, 4*(4), 409–428.

Davis, K. E., & Todd, M. J. (1982). Friendship and love relationships. *Advances in Descriptive Psychology, 2,* 79–122.

Davis, M. G., Reape, K. Z., & Hait, H. (2010a). A look at the long-term safety of an extended-regimen OC. *Journal of Family Practitioner, 59*(5), E3.

Davis, S., & Braunstein, G. (2012). Efficacy and safety of testosterone in the management of hypoactive sexual desire disorder in postmenopausal women. *Journal of Sexual Medicine, 9*(4), 1134–1148.

Davis, S., & Jane, F. (2011). Sex and perimenopause. *Australia Family Physician, 40*(5), 274–278.

Davis, S., Binik, Y., & Carrier, S. (2009). Sexual dysfunction and pelvic pain in men: A male sexual pain disorder? *Journal of Sex & Marital Therapy, 35,* 182–205.

Davis, S. C., Meneses, K., & Hilfinger Messias, D. K. (2010b). Exploring sexuality & quality of life in women after breast cancer surgery. *Nurse Practitioner, 35*(9), 25–31.

Dawar, A. (2006, November 28). British scientists invent male pill. *Telegraph.* Retrieved October 28, 2008, from http://www.telegraph.co.uk/news/migrationtemp/1535304/British-scientists-invent-male-pill.html.

Day, R. D., & Padilla-Walker, L. M. (2009). Mother and father connectedness and involvement during early adolescence. *Journal of Family Psychology, 23*(6), 900–904.

De Carufel, F. (2017). *Premature ejaculation: Theory, evaluation and therapeutic treatment.* New York: Routledge/Taylor & Francis Group, New York, NY.

de Freitas, S. (2004). Brazil. In R. T. Francoeur & R. J. Noonan (Eds.), *The Continuum complete international encyclopedia of sexuality* (pp. 98–113). New York/London: Continuum International.

De Munck, V., & Korotayev, A. (2007). Wife-husband intimacy and female status in cross-cultural perspective. *Cross-Cultural Research, 14*(4), 307–335.

de Vries, B. (2009). Brain sexuality and aging: A late blooming relationship. *Sexuality Research & Social Policy, 6*(4), 1–4.

DeBellis, M. D., Keshavan, M. S., Beers, S. R., Hall, J., Frustaci, K., Masalehdan, A., et al. (2001). Sex differences in brain maturation during childhood and adolescence. *Cerebral Cortex, 11*(6), 552–557.

Decker, M., Raj, A., Gupta, J., & Silverman, J. (2008). Sex purchasing and associations with HIV/STI among a clinic-based sample of U.S. men. *Journal of Acquired Immune Deficiency Syndrome, 48*(3), 355–359.

DeCuypere, G., T'Sjoen, G., Beerten, R., Selvaggi, G., Sutter, P., Hoebeke, P., et al. (2005). Sexual and physical health after sex reassignment surgery. *Archives of Sexual Behavior, 34,* 679–690.

Deepinder, R., Makker, K., & Agarwal, A. (2007). Cell phones and male infertility: Dissecting the relationship. *Reproductive BioMedicine Online, 15*(3), 266–270.

Defendi, G. L. (2016). Klinefelter syndrome. Medscape. Retrieved January 17, 2017, from http://emedicine.medscape.com/article/945649-overview#a6.

Degges-White, S., & Marszalek, J. (2008). An exploration of long-term, same-sex relationships: Benchmarks, perceptions, and challenges. *Journal of Lesbian, Gay, Bisexual, and Transgendered Issues in Counseling, 1,* 99–119.

DeJesus, E., Young, B., Morales-Ramirez, J., Sloan, L., Ward, D., Flaherty, J., Ebrahimi, R., Maa, J., Reilly, K., Ecker, J., McColl, D., Seekins, D., & Farajallah, A. (2009). Simplification of antiretroviral therapy to a single-tablet regimen consisting of efavirenz, emtricitabine, and tenofovir disoproxil fumarate verusss unmodified antirretroviarl therapy in virologiclaly suppressed HIV-1-infected patients. *Journal of Acquired Immune Deficiency Syndrome, 51*(2), 163–174.

DeJonge, A., Teunissen, D., van Diem, M., Scheepers, P., & Lagro-Janssen, A. (2008). Woman's positions during the second stage of labour: Views of primary care midwives. *Journal of Advanced Nursing, 63,* 347–356.

DeLamater, J. (1987). A sociological approach. In J. H. Geer & W. T. O'Donohue (Eds.), *Theories of human sexuality* (pp. 237–253). New York: Plenum Press.

DeLange, J. (1995). Gender and communication in social work education: A cross-cultural perspective. *Journal of Social Work Education, 31*(1), 75–82.

Delgado, M., Ettekal, A., Simpkins, S., & Schaefer, D. (2016). How do my friends matter? Examining Latino adolescents' friendships, school belonging, and academic achievement. *Journal of Youth and Adolescence, 45*(6), 1110–1125.

Deligeoroglou, E., & Karountzos, V. (2016). Dysfunctional uterine bleeding as an early sign of polycystic ovary syndrome during adolescence: An update. *Minerva Ginecologica.* Retrieved January 20, 2017, from https://www.ncbi.nlm.nih.gov/pubmed/27787478.

Deligeoroglou, E., Karountzos, V. & Creatsas, G. (2013). Abnormal uterine bleeding and dysfunctional uterine bleeding in pediatric and adolescent gynecology. *Gynecological Endocrinology, 29*(1)74–78

Deliramich, A., & Gray, M. (2008). Changes in women's sexual behavior following sexual assault. *Behavior Modification, 32*(5), 611–621.

Delmonico, D. L., & Griffin, E. J. (2008). Cybersex and the e-teen: What marriage and family therapists should know. *Journal of Marital and Family Therapy, 34*(4), 431–444.

Demerath, E., Liu, C., Franceschini, N., Chen, G., Palmer, J., Smith, E., Chen, C., Ambrosone, C., et al. (2013). Genome-wide association study of age at menarche in African-American women. *Human Molecular Genetics, 22*(16), 3329–3346.

Demissie, Z., Brener, N., McManus, T., Shanklin, S., Hawkins, J., & Kann, L. (2015). School health profiles 2014: Characteristics of health programs among secondary schools. U.S. Department of Health and Human Services, Centers for Disease Control and Prevention. Retrieved February 11, 2017, from https://www.cdc.gov/healthyyouth/data/profiles/pdf/2014/2014_profiles_report.pdf.

DeMorais, F., Freitas-Junior, R., Rahal, R., & Gonzaga, C. (2016). Sociodemographic and clinical factors affecting body image, sexual function and sexual satisfaction in women with breast cancer. *Journal of Clinical Nursing, 25*(11–12), 1557–1565.

Dempster, C. (2002). Silent war on South African women. Retrieved April 10, 2003, from www.new.bbc.co.uk/hi/english/world/africa/newsid_190900011909220.stm.

Denizet-Lewis, B. (2009, September 23). Coming out in middle school. *New York Times.* Retrieved February 20, 2011, from http://www.nytimes.com/2009/09/27/magazine/27out-t.html?pagewanted54&_r51.

Derogatis, L., Rosen, R., Goldstein, I., Werneburg, B., Kempthorne-Rawson, J., & Sand, M. (2012). Characterization of hypoactive sexual desire disorder in men. *Journal of Sexual Medicine, 9*(3), 812–820.

DeRoo, C., Tilleman, K., T'Sjoen, G., & DeSutter, P. (2016). Fertility options in transgender people. *International Review of Psychiatry, 2*(1), 112–119.

de-Schampheleire, D. (1990). MMPI characteristics of professional prostitutes: A crosscultural replication. *Journal of Personality Assessment, 54,* 343–350.

Desilver, D. (2013, June 26). How many same-sex marriages in the US.? At least 71,165, probably more. *Pew Research Center Fact Tank.* Retrieved April 20, 2014, from http://www.pewresearch.org/fact-tank/2013/06/26/how-many-same-sex-marriages-in-the-u-s-at-least-71165-probably-more.

Desruelles, F., Cunningham, S., & Dubois, D. (2013). Pubic hair removal: A risk factor for 'minor' STI such as molluscum contagiosum? *Sexually Transmitted Infections, 89*(3), 216.

Devdas, N., & Rubin, L. (2007). Rape myth acceptance among first-and second-generation south Asian American women. *Sex Roles, 56*, 701–705.

deVisser, R., & McDonald, D. (2007). Swings and roundabouts: Management of jealousy in heterosexual "swinging" couples. *British Journal of Social Psychology, 46*, 459–476.

Devlin, S., Diehr, P., Andersen, R., Goff, B., Tyree, P., & Lafferty, W. (2010). Identification of ovarian cancer symptoms in health insurance claims data. *Journal of Women's Health, 19*(3), 381–389.

Dhejne, C., Lichtenstein, P., Boman, M., Johansson, A., Långström, N., & Landén, M. (2011). Long-term follow-up of transsexual persons undergoing sex reassignment surgery: Cohort study in Sweden. *PLOS ONE, 6*(2). Retrieved February 14, 2014, from http://www.plosone.org/article/info%3Adoi%2F10.1371%2Fjournal.pone.0016885.

Dhungana, A., Nanthamongkolchai, S., & Pitkultang, S. (2016). Factors related to intention to undergo female sterilization among married women in rural Kathmandu, Nepal. *Nepal Journal of Epidemiology, 6*(1), 539–547.

Diamanti-Kandarakis, E. (2007). Role of obesity and adiposity in polycystic ovary syndrome. *International Journal of Obesity, 31*, s8–s13.

Diamond, L., & Fagundes, C. (2010). Psychobiological research on attachment. *Personal Relationships, 27*(2), 218.

Diamond, L., Earle, D., Heiman, J., Rosen, R., Perelman, M., & Harning, R. (2006). An effect on the subjective sexual response in premenopausal women with sexual arousal disorder by bremelanotide (PT-141), a melanocortin receptor agonist. *Journal of Sexual Medicine, 3*, 628–638.

Diamond, L. M. (2000). Sexual identity, attractions, and behavior among young sexual minority women over a 2-year period. *Developmental Psychology, 36*(2), 241–250.

Diamond, L. M. (2005). A new view of lesbian subtypes: Stable versus fluid identity trajectories over an 8-year period. *Psychology of Women Quarterly, 29*(2), 119–128.

Diamond, M. (1993). Homosexuality and bisexuality in different populations. *Archives of Sexual Behavior, 22*, 291–310.

Diamond, M., & Diamond, G. H. (1986). Adolescent sexuality: Biosocial aspects and intervention. In P. Allen-Meares & D. A. Shore (Eds.), *Adolescent sexualities: Overviews and principles of intervention* (pp. 3–13). New York: Haworth Press.

Diamond, M., & Sigmundson, H. K. (1997). Sex reassignment at birth: Long-term review and clinical implications. *Archives of Pediatric Medicine, 151*, 290–297.

Dickenson, J., & Huebner, D. (2016). The relationship between sexual activity and depressive symptoms in lesbian, gay, and bisexual youth: Effects of gender and family support. *Archives of Sexual Behavior, 45*(3), 671–681.

Dickey, L., Singh, A., Chang, S., Rehrig, M. (2016). *Advocacy and social justice: The next generation of counseling and psychological practice with transgender and gender-nonconforming clients.* In A. Singh & Dickey, L. (Eds.), Affirmative Counseling and Psychological Practice with Transgender and Gender Nonconforming Clients. American Psychological Association. Retrieved August 23, 2017, from http://www.apa.org/pubs/books/4317425.aspx?tab=1.

Dickson, G. (2012). Gynecomastia. *American Family Physician, 85*(7), 716–722.

Diehl, C., Glaser, T., & Bohner, G. (2014). Face the consequences: Learning about victim's suffering reduces sexual harassment myth acceptance and men's likelihood to sexually harass. *Aggressive Behavior, 40*(6), 489–503.

Diergaarde, B., & Kurta, M. (2014). Use of fertility drugs and risk of ovarian cancer. *Current Opinion in Obstetrics & Gynecology, 26*(3), 125–129.

Dietz, H. P. (2006). Pelvic floor trauma following vaginal delivery. *Current Opinions in Obstetrics and Gynecology, 18*, 528–537.

Dijkstra, P., Barelds, D., & Groothof, H. (2013). Jealousy in response to online and offline infidelity: The role of sex and sexual orientation. *Scandinavian Journal of Psychology, 54*(4), 328–336.

Dillow, M., Dunleavy, K., & Weber, K. (2009). The impact of relational characteristics and reasons for topic avoidance on relational closeness. *Communication Quarterly, 57*(2), 205.

Dimah, K., & Dimah, A. (2004). Intimate relationships and sexual attitudes of older African American men and women. *The Gerontologist, 44*, 612–613.

diMauro, D. (1995). *Sexuality research in the United States: An assessment of the social and behavioral sciences.* New York: Social Science Research Council.

Dimmick, J., Feaster, J., & Hoplamazian, G. (2011). News in the interstices: The niches of mobile media in space and time. *New Media & Society, 13*(1), 23–39.

DiNapoli, L., & Capel, B. (2008). SRY and the standoff in sex determination. *Molecular Endocrinology, 22*, 1–9.

Dindia, K. & Canary, D. J. (2006). (Eds.), *Sex differences and similarities in communication* (2nd. ed.). Mahwah, NJ: Erlbaum.

Dinger, J., Minh, T. D., Buttmann, N., & Bardenheuer, K. (2011). Effectiveness of oral contraceptive pills in a large U.S. cohort comparing progestogen and regimen. *Obstetrics and Gynecology, 117*(1), 33–40.

Dinh, M., Fahrbach, K., & Hope, T. (2011). The role of the foreskin in male circumcision: An evidence-based review. *American Journal of Reproductive Immunology, 65*(3), 279–283.

Dion, K., & Dion, K. (2010). Individualistic and collectivistic perspectives on gender and the cultural context of love and intimacy. *Journal of Social Issues, 49*(3), 53–69.

Dirkes, J., Hughes, T., Ramirez-Valles, J., Johnson, T., & Bostwick, W. (2016). Sexual identity development: Relationship with lifetime suicidal ideation in sexual minority women. *Journal of Clinical Nursing, 25*(23–24), 3545–3556.

Dittmann, M. (2005). Getting prostitutes off the streets. *Monitor on Psychology, 35*(9), 71.

DiVirqilio, A. (2013, December 1). Money in pornography: One of the most misunderstood industries. *The Richest.* Retrieved August 27, 2014, from http://www.therichest.com/expensive-lifestyle/money/money-in-pornography-one-of-the-most-misunderstood-industries.

Dixit, A. K., & Pindyck, R. S. (1994). *Investment under uncertainty.* Princeton, NJ: Princeton University Press.

Dixon, R. (2005). Controversy in South Africa over device to snare rapists. Retrieved October 19, 2005, from http://www.smh.com.au/news/world/controversy-in-south-africa-over-device-to-snare-rapists/2005/09/01/1125302683893.html.

Djordjevic, M., Bizic, M., Stanojevic, D., Bumbasievic, M., Kojovic, V., Majstorovic, M., Acimovic, M., Pandey, S., & Perovic, S. (2009). Urethral lengthening in metoidioplasty by combined buccal mucosa graft and labia minora flap. *Urology, 74*(2), 349–353.

Dodd, S. M. (2010). Ambivalent social support and psychneuroimmunologic relationships among women undergoing surgery for suspected endometrial cancer. University of Florida, AAT #34366330.

Dodge, B., Reece, M., Herbenick, D., Schick, V., Sanders, S. A., & Fortenberry, J. D. (2010). Sexual health among U.S. black and Hispanic men and women: A nationally representative study. *Journal of Sexual Medicine, 7*(Suppl. 5), 330–345.

Dodson, B. (1993). *Sex for one: The joy of selfloving.* New York: Crown.

Dolan, B. (2012). Duofertility wireless sensor receives FDA clearance. *Mobi Health News.* Retrieved May 26, 2014, from http://mobihealthnews.com/16028/duofertility-wireless-sensor-receives-fda-clearance.

Dolnick, S. (2007, December 31). India leads way in making commercial surrogacy a viable industry. *Hartford Courant*, p. A3.

Domenici, L., Perniola, G., Giorgini, M., Lecce, F., Bracchi, C., Musella, A., Marchetti, C., DiDonatro, V., Tomao, F., Palaia, I., Ciolli, P., Recine, N., Muzii, L., & Benedetti, P. (2016). Vulvodynia: Current opinion and treatment strategies. *Minerva Ginecologica, 68*(6), 727–732.

Domonoske, C. (2017, January 12). In majority Catholic Philippines, Duterte orders better access to birth control. National Public Radio. Retrieved April 3, 2017, from http://www.npr.org/sections/thetwo-way/2017/01/12/509462732/in-majority-catholic-philippines-duterte-orders-better-access-to-birth-control.

Dong, D., Binongo, J., & Kancherla, V. (2016). Maternal chlamydia infection during pregnancy and risk of cyanotic congenital heart defects in the offspring. *Maternal and Children Health Journal, 20*, 66–76.

Dong, Q., Deng, S., Wang, R., & Yuan, J. (2011). In vitro and in vivo animal models in priapism research. *Journal of Sexual Medicine, 8*(2), 347–359.

Donnan, H. (1988). *Marriage among Muslims: Preference and choice in Northern Pakistan.* New York: E. J. Brill.

Donnelly, D. A., & Burgess, E. O. (2008). The decision to remain in an involuntarily celibate relationship. *Journal of Marriage and Family, 70*, 519–536.

Donnez, J., Donnez, O., & Domans, M. (2016). Safety of treatment of uterine fibroids with the selective progesterone receptor modulator, ulipristal acetate. *Expert Opinion on Drug Safety, 15*(12), 1679–1686.

Donovan, K., Taliaferro, L., Alvarez, E., Jacobsen, P., Roetzheim, R., & Wenham, R. (2007). Sexual health in women treated for cervical cancer: Characteristics and correlates. *Gynecological Oncology, 104*, 428–434.

Doorduin, T., & Van Burlo, W. (2014). Trans people's experience of sexuality in the Netherlands: A pilot study. *Journal of Homosexuality, 61*(5), 654–672.

Dorfman, L. E., Derish, P. A., & Cohen, J. B. (1992). Hey girlfriend: An evaluation of AIDS prevention among women in the sex industry. *Health Education Quarterly, 19*, 25–40.

Dorgan, M. (2001, June 13). New divorce laws in China give rise to spying. *Hartford Courant,* A13.

Dorner, G., Schenk, B., Schmiedel, B., & Ahrens, L. (1983). Stressful events in perinatal life of bi- and homosexual men. *Experimental and Clinical Endocrinology, 81*(1), 83–87.

Dorr, C. (2001). Listening to men's stories: Overcoming obstacles to intimacy from childhood. *Families in Society, 82*, 509–515.

Doty, N. D., Willoughby, B. L., Lindahl, K. M., & Malik, N. M. (2010). Sexuality related social support among lesbian, gay, and bisexual youth. *Journal of Youth and Adolescence, 39*(10), 1134–1147.

Dougherty, C. (2010, September 29). New vow: I don't take thee. *Wall Street Journal.* Retrieved October 5, 2010, from http://online.wsj.com/article/SB10001424052748703882404575519871444705214.html.

Douglas, J., & Olshaker, M. (1998). *Obsession.* Sydney: Pocket Books.

Douglas, M., & Swenerton, J. (2002). Epidural anesthesia in three parturients with lumbar tattoos: A review of possible implications. *Canadian Journal of Anesthesia, 49*, 1057–1060.

Downing-Matibag, T., & Geisinger, B. (2009). Hooking up and sexual risk taking among college students: A health belief model perspective. *Qualitative Health Research, 19*(9), 1196–1209.

Downs, D. A. (1989). *The new politics of pornography.* Chicago: The University of Chicago Press.

Doyle, D. (2005). Ritual male circumcision: A brief history. *Journal of the Royal College of Physicians, 35*, 279–285. Retrieved April 8, 2008, from http://www.rcpe.ac.uk/publications/articles/journal_35_3/doyle_circumcision.pdf.

Drabble, L., Trocki, K., Hughes, T., Korcha, R., & Lown, A. (2013). Sexual orientation differences in the relationship between victimization and hazardous drinking among women in the National Alcohol Survey. *Psychology of Addictive Behaviors, 27*(3), 639–648.

Dreger, A., Feder, E., & Tamar-Mattis, A. (2010, June 29). Preventing homosexuality (and uppity women) in the womb? The Hastings Center. Retrieved November 13, 2010, from http://www.thehastingscenter.org/Bioethicsforum/Post.aspx?id54754.

Dreger, A., Feder, E., & Tamar-Mattis, A. (2012). Prenatal dexamethasone for congenital adrenal hyperplasia: An ethics canary in the modern medical mine. *Journal of Bioethical Inquiry, 9*(3), 277–294.

Dresner, E., & Herring, S. (2010). Functions of the nonverbal in CMC: Emoticons and illocutionary force. *Communication Theory, 20*(3), 249.

Drew, P. E. (2004). Iran. In The International Encyclopedia of Sexuality. In R. T. Francoeur & R. J. Noonan (Eds.), *The Continuum international encyclopedia of sexuality* (pp. 554–568). New York/London: Continuum International.

Driemeyer, W., Janssen, E., Wiltfang, J., & Elmerstig, E. (2016). Masturbation experiences of Swedish senior high school students: Gender differences and similarities. *Journal of Sex Research,* 1–11. Retrieved February 11, 2017, from http://www.tandfonline.com/doi/abs/10.1080/00224499.2016.1167814.

Droupy, S. (2010). [Sexual dysfunctions after prostate cancer radiation therapy]. *Cancer Radiotherapy, 14*(6–7), 504–509.

Drucker, D. (2012). Marking sexuality from 0–6: The Kinsey scale in online culture. *Sexuality & Culture, 16*, 241–262.

Drury, S., Scaramella, L., & Zeanah, C. (2016). The neurobiological impact of postpartum maternal depression: Prevention and intervention approaches. *Child and Adolescent Psychiatric Clinics of North America, 25*(2), 179–200.

Drydakis, N. (2014). Sexual orientation and labor market outcomes. IZA World of Labor, Retrieved March 19, 2017, from https://wol.iza.org/articles/sexual-orientation-and-labor-market-outcomes/long.

Duarte Freitas, P., Haida, A., Bousquet, M., Richard, L., Mauriège, P., & Guiraud T. (2011). Short-term impact of a 4-week intensive cardiac rehabilitation program on quality of life and anxiety-depression. *Annals of Physical and Rehabilitation Medicine, 54*(3), 132–143.

Dubuc, S., & Coleman, D. (2007). An increase in the sex ratio of births to India-born mothers in England and Wales: Evidence for sex-selective abortion. *Population and Development Review, 33*, 383–400.

Dude, A., Neustadt, A., Martins, S., & Gilliam, M. (2013). Use of withdrawal and unintended pregnancy among females 15–24 years of age. *Obstetrics and Gynecology, 122*(3), 595–600.

Duffin, T. (2016). The lowdown on the down low: Why some bisexually active men choose to self-identify as straight. *Journal of Bisexuality, 4*, 484–506.

Duffy, J., Warren, K., & Walsh, M. (2001). Classroom interactions: Gender of teacher, gender of student and classroom subject. *Sex Roles, 45*(9–10), 579–593.

Duijts, L., Jaddoe, V., Hofman, A., & Moll, H. (2010). Prolonged and exclusive breastfeeding reduces the risk of infectious diseases in infancy. *Pediatrics, 126*, e18–e25.

Dumond, R., & Dumond, D. (2002). The treatment of sexual assault victims. In C. Hensley (Ed.), *Prison sex: Practice and policy* (pp. 67–87). Boulder, CO: Lynne Reinner.

Dun, E., & Nezhat, C. (2012). Tubal factor infertility: Diagnosis and management in the era of assisted reproductive technology. *Obstetrics and Gynecology Clinics of North America, 39*(4), 551–566.

Dunbar, R. (1998). *Grooming, gossip, and the evolution of language.* Boston: Harvard University Press.

Dunham, C., Myers, F., McDougall, A., & Barnden, N. (1992). *Mamatoto: A celebration of birth.* New York: Penguin Group.

Dunn, J., Zhang, Q., Weeks, M., Li, J., Liao, S., & Li, F. (2016). Indigenous HIV prevention beliefs and practices among low-earning Chinese sex workers as context for introducing female condoms and other novel prevention options. *Qualitative Health Research.* Retrieved April 5, 2017, from https://www.ncbi.nlm.nih.gov/pubmed/27811288.

Dunn, M. W. (2015). Bladder cancer: A focus on sexuality. *Clinical Journal of Oncology Nursing, 19*(1), 68–73.

Dunne, E. (2007). *Genital warts.* U.S. Centers for Disease Control, Division of STD Prevention. Retrieved September 17, 2008, from http://www.cdc.gov/vaccines/recs/acip/downloads/mtg-slides-oct07/23HPV.pdf.

Dupre, M. E., & Meadows, S. O. (2007). Disaggregating the effects of marital trajectories on health. *Journal of Family Issues, 28,* 623–652.

Durex Network. (2008). The face of global sex 2008: The path to sexual confidence. Retrieved October 13, 2010, from http://www.durexnetwork.org/SiteCollectionDocuments/Research%20-%20Face%20of%20Global%20Sex%202008.pdf.

Durex.com. (2007). *Sexual wellbeing global study 2007–2008.* Retrieved January 20, 2008, from http://durex.com/cm/sexual_wellbeing_globeflash.asp.

Durham, L., Beltman, L., Davis, P., Ferguson, L., Hacker, M., Hooker, D., Larison, K., Pribyl, J., et al. (2008). Standardizing criteria for scheduling elective labor inductions. *Journal of Maternal Child Nursing, 33*(3), 159–165.

Durham, L., Veltman, L., Davis, P., Ferguson, L., Hacker, M., Hooker, D., et al. (2008). Standardizing criteria for scheduling elective labor inductions. *American Journal of Maternal Child Nursing, 33,* 159–165.

Durso, L., & Gates, G. (2012). *Serving our youth: Findings from a national survey of service providers working with LGBT youth who are homeless or at risk of becoming homeless.* Los Angeles, CA: The Williams Institute with True Colors Fund and the Palette Fund.

Durwood, L., McLaughlin, K., & Olson, K. (2017). Mental health and self-worth in socially transitioned transgender youth. *Journal of the American Academy of Child & Adolescent Psychiatry, 56*(2), 116–123.

Duschinsky, R., & Chachamu, N. (2013). Sexual dysfunction and paraphilias in the DSM-5: Pathology, heterogeneity, and gender. *Feminism & Psychology, 23*(1), 49–55.

Dush, C., & Amato, P. R. (2005). Consequences of relationship status and quality for subjective well-being. *Journal of Social and Personal Relationships, 22,* 607.

Dworkin, A. (1981). *Pornography: Men possessing women.* New York: Putnam.

Dworkin, A. (1987). *Intercourse.* New York: The Free Press.

Eaker, E. D., Sullivan, L. M., Kelly-Hayes, M., D'Agostino, R. B., Sr., & Benjamin, E. J. (2007). Marital status, marital strain and the risk of coronary heart disease or total mortality: The Framingham Offspring Study. *Psychosomatic Medicine, 69,* 509–513.

Eardley, I. (2010). Oral therapy for erectile dysfunction. *Archives of Españoles Urology, 63*(8), 703–714.

Earls, C. M., & David, H. (1989). A psychosocial study of male prostitution. *Archives of Sexual Behavior, 18,* 401–419.

Earnshaw, V., Pitipitan, E., & Chaudoir, S. (2011). Intended responses to rape as functions of attitudes, attributions of fault, and emotions. *Sex Roles, 64*(5–6), 382–393.

Easton, J. A., Confer, J. C., Goetz, C. D., & Buss, D. M. (2010). Reproduction expediting: Sexual motivations, fantasies, and the ticking biological clock. *Personality and Individual Differences, 49,* 516–520.

Eastvold, A., Suchy, Y., & Strassberg, D. (2011). Executive function profiles of pedophilic and nonpedophilic child molesters. *Journal of the International Neuropsychological Society, 17*(2), 295–308.

Eaton, A., & Rios, D. (2017). Social challenges faced by queer Latino college men: Navigating negative responses to coming out in a double minority sample of emerging adults. *Cultural Diversity and Ethnic Minority Psychology.* Retrieved March 24, 2017, from https://www.ncbi.nlm.nih.gov/pubmed/28252982.

Eaton, A., Rose, S., Interligi, C., Fernandez, K., & McHugh, M. (2016). Gender and ethnicity in dating, hanging out, and hooking up: Sexual scripts among Hispanic and White young adults. *Journal of Sex Research, 53*(7), 788–804.

Eaton, D., Kann, L., Kinchen, S., Shanklin, S., Flint, K., Hawkins, J., Harris, W., Lowry, R., McManus, T., Chyen, D., Whittle, L., Lim, C., Wechsler, H. (2012). Youth Risk Behavior Surveillance—United States, 2011. *Morbidity and Mortality Weekly Report, 61*(SS04), 1–162.

Eaton, D. K., Kann, L., Kinchen, S., Ross, J., Hawkins, J., Harris, W., et al. (2006, June 9). Youth risk behavior surveillance—United States, 2005. Surveillance Summaries. *Morbidity and Mortality Weekly Report, 55*(no. SS-5). Hyattsville, MD: U.S. Department of Health and Human Services, Centers for Disease Control. Retrieved September 2, 2008, from http://www.cdc.gov/mmwr/PDF/SS/SS5505.pdf.

Eaton, L., Driffin, D., Smith, H., White, D., & Cherry, C. (2015). Black men who have sex with men, sexual risk taking, and willingness to use rapid home HIV tests. *Prevention Science, 16*(2), 321–329.

Eaton, L., Kaufman, M., Fuhrel, A., Cain, D., Cherry, C., Pope, H., & Kalichman, S. (2008). Examining factors co-existing with interpersonal violence in lesbian relationships. *Journal of Family Violence, 23,* 697–706.

Ebaugh, H. (1988). *Becoming an ex: The process of role exit.* Chicago: University of Chicago Press.

Eckstein, D., & Goldman, A. (2001). The couples' gender-based communication questionnaire. *Family Journal of Counseling and Therapy for Couples and Families, 9*(1), 62–74.

Edelman, B. (2009). Red light states: Who buys online adult entertainment? *Journal of Economic Perspectives, 23*(1), 209–220.

Edwards, R. (1998). The effects of gender, gender role, and values. *Journal of Language and Social Psychology, 17*(1), 52–72.

Edwards, R., & Hamilton, M. A. (2004). You need to understand my gender role: An empirical test of Tannen's model of gender and communication. *Sex Roles, 50*(7–8), 491–504.

Eeckhaut, M. (2015). Marital status and female and male contraceptive sterilization in the United States. *Fertility and Sterility, 103*(6), 1509–1515.

Eggermont, S. (2005). Young adolescents' perceptions of peer sexual behaviours: The role of television viewing. *Child: Care, Health and Development, 31*(4), 459–468.

Eglseder, K., & Demchick, B. (2017). Sexuality and spinal cord injury. *OTJR: Occupation, Participation & Health.* Retrieved April 15, 2017, from https://www.ncbi.nlm.nih.gov/pubmed/28355966.

Ehmann, R., Boedeker, E., Friedrich, U., Sagert, J., Dippon, J., Friedel, G., & Walles, T. (2012). Canine scent detection in the diagnosis of lung cancer: Revisiting a puzzling phenomenon. *The European Respiratory Journal, 39*(3), 669–676.

Ehrenreich, S. E., & Underwood, M. K. (2016). Adolescents' internalizing symptoms as predictors of the content of their Facebook communication and responses received from peers. *Translational Issues in Psychological Science, 2*(3), 227–237.

Ehrich, K., Williams, C., Farsides, B., Sandall, J., & Scott, R. (2007). Choosing embryos: Ethical complexity and relational autonomy in staff accounts of PGD. *Sociology of Health and Illness, 29,* 1091–1106.

Ehsani-Ardakani, M., Fallahian, M., Rostami, K., Rostami-Nejad, M., Lotfi, S., Mohaghegh-Shalmani, H., Dabiri, R., Norouzinia, M., Azizpour-Shoobi, F., & Zali, M. (2014). Celiac disease and dysfunctional uterine bleeding: The efficiency of gluten free diet. *Bratislava Medical Journal, 115*(1), 19–21.

Einsiedel, E. (1989). Social science and public policy: Looking at the 1986 commission on pornography. In S. Gubar & J. Hoff (Eds.), *For adult users only* (pp. 87–107). Bloomington: Indiana University Press.

Eisenberg, M. (2001). Differences in sexual risk behaviors between college students with same-sex and opposite-sex experience. *Archives of Sexual Behavior, 30*(6), 575–589.

Eisenberg, M., Wall, M., & Neumark-Sztainer, D. (2012). Muscle-enhancing behaviors about adolescent girls and boys. *Pediatrics, 130*(6), 1019–1026.

Eisend, M. (2010). A meta-analysis of gender roles in advertising. *Journal of the Academy of Marketing Science, 38*(4), 418–440.

Eisenman, R., & Dantzker, M. (2006). Gender and ethnic differences in sexual attitudes at a Hispanic-Serving University. *Journal of General Psychology, 133*(2), 153–163.

Eke, A., Hilton, N., Harris, G., Rice, M., & Houghton, R. (2011). Intimate partner homicide: Risk assessment and prospects for prediction. *Journal of Family Violence, 26*(3), 211–216.

Ekman, P., & Friesen, W. (1969). The repertoire of nonverbal behavior: Categories, origins, usage and coding. *Semiotica, 1,* 49–98.

El Scheich, T., Weber, A., Klee, D., Schweiger, D., Mayatepek, E., & Karenfort, M. (2013). Adolescent ischemic stroke associated with anabolic steroid and cannabis abuse. *Journal of Pediatric Endocrinology & Metabolism 26*(1–2), 161–165.

Eldar-Avidan, D., Haj-Yahia, M., & Greenbaum, C. (2009). Divorce is a part of my life. Resilience, survival, and vulnerability. Young adults' perception of the implications of parental divorce. *Journal of Marital and Family Therapy, 35*(1), 30–47.

Elford, J. (2006). Changing patterns of sexual behaviour in the era of highly active antiretroviral therapy. *Current Opinions in Infectious Disease, 19*(1), 26–32.

Elford, J., Bolding, G., Maguire, M., & Sherr, L. (2000). Combination therapies for HIV and sexual risk behavior among gay men. *Journal of Acquired Immune Deficiency Syndrome, 23,* 266–271.

Elhanbly, S., Elkholy, A., Elbayomy, Y., Elsaid, M., & Abdel-gaber, S. (2009). Nocturnal penile erections: The diagnostic value of tumescence and rigidity activity units. *International Journal of Impotence Research, 21*(6), 376–381.

El-Helaly, M., Awadalla, N., Mansour, M., & El-Biomy, Y. (2010). Workplace exposures and male infertility: A case-control study. *International Journal of Occupational Medicine and Environmental Medicine, 23*(4), 331–338.

Elias, M. (2007, February 11). Gay teens coming out earlier to peers and family. *USA Today.* Retrieved October 2, 2008, from http://www.usatoday.com/news/nation/2007-02-07-gay-teens-cover_x.htm.

Eliason, M. J. (1997). The prevalence and nature of biphobia in heterosexual undergraduate students. *Archives of Sexual Behavior, 26*(3), 317–326.

Eliassen, A., Hankinson, S., Rosner, B., Holmes, M., & Willett, W. (2010). Physical activity and risk of breast cancer among postmenopausal women. *Archives of Internal Medicine, 170*(19), 1758–1764.

Elifson, K. W., Boles, J., Posey, E., Sweat, M., et al. (1993). Male transvestite prostitutes and HIV risk. *American Journal of Public Health, 83,* 260–261.

Eliot, L. (2009). *Pink brains, blue brains: How small differences grow into troublesome gaps—and what we can do about it.* Orlando, FL: Houghton Mifflin Harcourt.

Elischberger, H., Glazier, J., Hill, E., & Verduzco-Baker, L. (2016). "Boys don't cry"—or do they? Adult attitudes toward and beliefs about transgender youth. *Sex Roles, 75*(5), 197–214.

Elliott, S., Latini, D., Walker, L., Wassersug, R., & Robinson, J. (2010). Androgen deprivation therapy for prostate cancer: Recommendations to improve patient and partner quality of life. *Journal of Sexual Medicine, 7*(9), 2996–3010.

Elliott, S., & Umberson, D. (2008). The performance of desire: Gender and sexual negotiation in long-term marriages. *Journal of Marriage and Family, 70,* 392–407.

Ellis, B. (2013). The hypothalamic-pituitary-gonadal axis: A switch-controlled, condition-sensitive system in the regulation of life history strategies. *Hormones and Behavior, 64*(2), 215–225.

Ellis, B. J., & Essex, M. J. (2007). Family environments, adrenarche, and sexual maturation: A longitudinal test of a life history model. *Child Development, 78,* 1799–1817.

Ellis, B., Shirtcliff, E., Boyce, W., Deardorff, J., & Essex, M. (2011). Quality of early family relationships and the timing and tempo of puberty: Effects depend on biological sensitivity to context. *Development and Psychopathology, 23*(1), 85–99.

Ellis, D. G., & McCallister, L. (1980). Relational control sequences in sex-typed and androgynous groups. *Western Journal of Speech Communication, 44,* 35–49.

Ellis, H. (1910). *Studies in the psychology of sex* (Vols. I-VI). Philadelphia: F. A. Davis.

Ellis, L. (1988). Sexual orientation of human offspring may be altered by severe maternal stress during pregnancy. *Journal of Sex Research, 25*(1), 152–157.

Ellis, L., Burke, D., & Ames, M. (1987). Sexual orientation as a continuous variable: A comparison between the sexes. *Archives of Sexual Behavior, 16,* 523–529.

Ellison, C. R. (2000). *Women's sexualities.* Oakland, CA: New Harbinger.

Ellison, C. R. (2006). *Women's sexualities: Generations of women share intimate secrets of sexual self-acceptance.* Oakland, CA: New Harbinger Publications.

Ellison, N., Steinfield, C., & Lampe, C. (2007). The benefits of Facebook "friends": Social capital and college students' use of online social network sites. *Journal of Computer-Mediated Communication, 12*(4), 1143–1168.

Elmslie, B., & Tebaldi, E. (2007). Sexual orientation and labor market discrimination. *Journal of Labor Research, 28*(3), 436–453.

Eloi-Stiven, M., Channaveeraiah, N., Christos, P., Finkel, M., & Reddy, R. (2007). Does marijuana use play a role in the recreational use of sildenafil? *Journal of Family Practitioner, 56,* E1–E4.

Ely, G., Flaherty, C., & Cuddeback, G. (2010). The relationship between depression and other psychosocial problems in a sample of adolescent pregnancy termination patients. *Child and Adolescent Social Work Journal, 27*(4), 269–282.

Emhardt, E., Siegel, J., & Hoffman, L. (2016). Anatomic variation and orgasm: Could variations in anatomy explain differences in orgasmic success? *Clinical Anatomy, 29*(5), 665–672.

Emilee, G., Ussher, J. M., & Perz, J. (2010). Sexuality after breast cancer: A review. *Maturitas, 66*(4), 397–407.

Emmers-Sommer, T., Farrell, J., Gentry, A., Stevens, S., Eckstein, J., Battocletti, J., & Gardener, C. (2010). First date sexual expectations: The effects of who asked, who paid, date location, and gender. *Communication Studies, 61*(3), 339–355.

Emons, G., Fleckenstein, G., Hinney, B., Huschmand, A., & Heyl, W. (2000). Hormonal interactions in endometrial cancer. *Endocrine-Related Cancer, 7,* 227–242.

Engel, J. W., & Saracino, M. (1986). Love preferences and ideals: A comparison of homosexual, bisexual, and heterosexual groups. *Contemporary Family Therapy: An International Journal, 8*(3), 241–250.

Englund-Ögge, L., Brantsaeter, A., Haugen, M., Sengpiel, V., Khatibi, A., Myhre, R., Myking, S., et al. (2012). Association between intake of artificially sweetened and sugar-sweetened beverages and preterm delivery: A large prospective cohort study. *American Journal of Clinical Nutrition, 96*(3), 552–559.

Engman, M., Wijma, K., & Wijma, B. (2010). Long-term coital behaviour in women treated with cognitive behaviour therapy for superficial coital pain and vaginismus. *Cognitive and Behavioral Therapy, 39*(3), 193–202.

Ensign, J., Scherman, A., & Clark, J. (1998). The relationship of family structure and conflict to levels of intimacy and parental attachment in college students. *Adolescence, 33*(131), 575–582.

Ephross, P. H. (2005). Group work with sexual offenders. In G. L. Greif (Ed.), *Group work with populations at risk* (pp. 253–266). New York: Oxford University Press.

Epperson, C. (2013). Premenstrual dysphoric disorder and the brain. *American Journal of Psychiatry, 170*(3), 248–252.

Epperson, C., Steiner, M., Hartlage, S., Eriksson, E., Schmidt, P., Jones, I., & Yonders, K. (2012). Premenstrual dysphoric disorder: Evidence for a new category for DSM-5. *American Journal of Psychiatry, 169*(5), 465–475.

Epps, J., & Kendall, P. C. (1995). Hostile attributional bias in adults. *Cognitive Therapy and Research, 19*, 159–178.

Epstein, C. F. (1986). Symbolic segregation: Similarities and differences in the language and non-verbal communication of women and men. *Sociological Forum, 1*, 27–49.

Epstein, C. F. (1988). *Deceptive distinctions: Sex, gender, and the social order*. New Haven, CT: Yale University Press.

Epstein, H., & Morris, M. (2011). Concurrent partnerships and HIV: An inconvenient truth. *Journal of the International AIDS Society, 14*, 13.

Epstein, M., & Ward, L. M. (2008). "Always use protection": Communication boys receive about sex from parents, peers, and the media. *Journal of Youth and Adolescence, 37*, 113–127.

Epstein, R., McKinney, P., Fox, S., & Garcia, C. (2012). Support for a fluid-continuum model of sexual orientation: A large-scale Internet study. *Journal of Homosexuality, 59*(10), 1356–1381.

Epstein, Z. (2013, June 26). *Why low-end phones are so important: Mobile user base grows to 1.17 billion in China*. BRG Media. Retrieved February 3, 2014, from http://bgr.com/2013/06/26/china-mobile-phone-user-base-may-2013.

Ericksen, J. A. (1999). *Kiss and tell: Surveying sex in the twentieth century*. Cambridge, MA: Harvard University Press.

Erogul, O., Oztas, E., Yildirim, I., Kir, T., Aydur, E., Komesli, G., et al. (2006). Effects of electromagnetic radiation from a cellular phone on human sperm motility: An in vitro study. *Archives of Medical Research, 37*, 840–843.

Ersoy, B., Balkan, C., Gunay, T., & Egemen, A. (2005). The factors affecting the relation between the menarcheal age of mother and daughter. *Child: Care, Health & Development, 31*(3), 303–308.

Escoffier, J. (2003). *Sexual revolution*. New York: Thunder's Mouth Press.

Eshbaugh, E. M., & Gute, G. (2008). Hookups and sexual regret among college women. *Journal of Social Psychology, 148*, 77–89.

Eskenazi, B., Wyrobek, A. J., Sloter, E., Kidd, S. A., Moore, L., Young, S., & Moore, D. (2003). The association of age and semen quality in healthy men. *Human Reproduction, 18*, 447–454.

Espelage, D. L., Aragon, S. R., Birkett, M., & Koenig, B. W. (2008). Homophobic teasing, psychological outcomes, and sexual orientation among high school students: What influence do parents and schools have? *School Psychology Review, 37*, 202–216.

Espín, M. C., Llorca, M. D. C., Simons, B. C., Borrego, N. G., Cueto, G. M., Guerra, E. A., Rodríguez, B. T., et al. (2004). Cuba. In R. T. Francoeur & R. J. Noonan (Eds.), *The Continuum complete international encyclopedia of sexuality* (pp. 259–279). New York/London: Continuum International.

Esposito, K., Maiorino, M. I., Bellastella, G., Giugliano, F., Romano, M., & Giugliano, D. (2010). Determinants of female sexual dysfunction in type 2 diabetes. *International Journal of Impotence Research, 22*(3), 179–184.

Essén, B., Blomkvist, A., Helström, L., & Johnsdotter, S. (2010). The experience and responses of Swedish health professionals to patients requesting virginity restoration. *Reproductive Health Matters, 18*(35), 38–46.

Estacion, A., & Cherlin, A. (2010). Gender distrust and intimate unions among low-income Hispanic and African American women. *Journal of Family Issues, 31*(4), 475.

Estephan, A., & Sinert, R. (2010, February 1). *Dysfunctional uterine bleeding*. Retrieved December 26, 2010, from http://emedicine.medscape.com/article/795587-overview.

Etengoff, C., & Daiute, C. (2014). Family members' uses of religion in post-coming-out conflicts with their gay relative. *Psychology of Religion and Spirituality, 6*(1), 33–43.

Ethics Committee Report. (2006). *Access to fertility treatment by gays, lesbians, and unmarried persons*. Ethics Committee of the American Society for Reproductive Medicine. Retrieved from http://www.asrm.org/Media/Ethics/fertility_gaylesunmarried.pdf.

Euling, S., Selevan, S., Pescovitz, O., & Skakkebaek, N. (2008). Role of environmental factors in the timing of puberty. *Pediatrics, 121*(Suppl. 3), 167–171.

Evans, A., Scally, A., Wellard, S., & Wilson, J. (2007). Prevalence of bacterial vaginosis in lesbians and heterosexual women in a community setting. *Sexually Transmitted Infections, 83*, 424–425.

Evans, N. (2016, September 27). Equality Florida gives out $9.5M raised after Pulse. WFSU Public Media. Retrieved March 24, 2017, from http://news.wfsu.org/post/equality-florida-gives-out-95m-raised-after-pulse.

Eyada, M., & Atwa, M. (2007). Sexual function in female patients with unstable angina or non-ST-elevation myocardial infarction. *Journal of Sexual Medicine, 4*(5), 1373–1380.

Eyler, A., Pang, S., & Clark, A. (2014). LGBT assisted reproduction: Current practice and future possibilities. *LGBT Health, 1*(3), 151–156.

Fabes, R., Martin, C., & Hanish, L. (2003). Young children's play qualities in same-, other-, and mixed-sex peer groups. *Child Development, 74*(3), 921–932.

Fabre, L. F., Brown, C. S., Smith, L. C., & Derogatis, L. R. (2011). Gepirone-ER treatment of hypoactive sexual desire disorder (HSDD) associated with depression in women. *Journal of Sexual Medicine, 8*(5), 1411–1419.

Faculty of Sexual and Reproductive Healthcare. (2011). Drug interactions with hormonal contraception. *Faculty of Sexual and Reproductive Healthcare Clinical Guidance*. Retrieved May 26, 2014, from http://www.fsrh.org/pdfs/CEUguidancedruginteractionshormonal.pdf.

Faderman, L. (1981). *Surpassing the love of men: Romantic friendship and love between women from the Renaissance to the present*. New York: William Morrow.

Fahs, B. (2011). Sex during menstruation: Race, sexual identity, and women's accounts of pleasure and disgust. *Feminism and Psychology, 21*(2), 155–178.

Fahs, B. (2016). Methodological mishaps and slippery subjects: Stories of first sex, oral sex, and sexual trauma in qualitative sex research. *Qualitative Psychology, 3*(2), 209–225.

Falagas, M., Betsi, G., & Athanasiou, S. (2006). Probiotics for prevention of recurrent vulvovaginal candidiasis: A review. *Journal of Antimicrobial Chemotherapy, 58*(2), 266–272.

Falk, S., & Bober, S. (2016). Vaginal health during breast cancer treatment. *Current Oncology Reports, 18*(5), 32.

Faller, K. C. (1989). The role relationship between victim and perpetrator as a predictor of characteristics of intrafamilial sexual abuse. *Child and Adolescent Social Work Journal, 6*, 217–229.

Faludi, S. (1991). *Backlash: The undeclared war against American women*. New York: Crown.

Fantasia, H., Fontenot, H., Sutherland, M., & Lee-St. John, T. (2015). Forced sex and sexual consent among college women. *Journal of Forensic Nursing, 11*(4), 223–231.

Farah, M. (1984). *Marriage and sexuality in Islam*. Salt Lake City: University of Utah Press.

Farley, M., & Barkan, H. (1998). Prostitution, violence, and post-traumatic stress disorder. *Women and Health, 27*(3), 37–49.

Farley, M., Cotton, A., Lynne, J., et al. (2003). Prostitution and trafficking in nine countries: An update on violence and posttraumatic stress disorder. In M. Farley (Ed.), *Prostitution, trafficking and traumatic stress* (pp. 33–74). Binghamton, NY: Haworth Press.

Farr, R., Forssell, S., & Patterson, C. (2010). Parenting and child development in adoptive families: Does parental sexual orientation matter? *Applied Developmental Science, 14*(3), 164–178.

Farthmann, J., Hanjalic-Beck, A., Veit, J., Rautenberg, B., Stickeler, E., Erbes, T., Földi, M.,

& Hasenburg, A. (2016). The impact of chemotherapy for breast cancer on sexual function and health-related quality of life. *Supportive Care in Cancer, 24*(6), 2603–2609.

Fathalia, M. (2013). Incessant ovulation and ovarian cancer: A hypothesis re-visited. *Facts, Views & Vision in Obgyn, 5*(4), 292–297.

Faulkner, A. H., & Cranston, K. (1998). Correlates of same-sex sexual behavior in a random sample of Massachusetts high school students. *American Journal of Public Health, 88*(2), 262–266.

Faulkner, S., & Lannutti, P. (2010). Examining the content and outcomes of young adults' satisfying and unsatisfying conversations about sex. *Qualitative Health Research, 20*(3), 375–385.

Faupel-Badger, J., Arcaro, K., Balkam, J., et al. (2013). Postpartum remodeling, lactation, and breast cancer risk. *Journal of the National Cancer Institute, 105*(3), 166–174.

Fawzy, F., Hussein, A., Eid, M., El Kashash, A., & Salem, H. (2015). Cryptorchidism and fertility. Clinical Medicine insights. *Reproductive Health, 9*, 39–43.

Fay, R. E., Turner, C. F., Klassen, A. D., & Gagnon, J. H. (1989). Prevalence and patterns of same-gender sexual contact among men. *Science, 243*, 338–348.

"FDA Activities." (2015). September 2015 advisory committee to discuss Essure safety and effectiveness. Retrieved April 8, 2017, from https://www.fda.gov/MedicalDevices /ProductsandMedicalProcedures /ImplantsandProsthetics/EssurePermanent BirthControl/ucm452254.htm

"FDA drug safety communication." (2016). FDA cautions about using testosterone products for low testosterone due to aging; requires labeling change to inform of possible increased risk of heart attack and stroke with use. U.S. Food & Drug Administration. Retrieved April 15, 2017, from https://www .fda.gov/Drugs/DrugSafety/ucm436259.htm.

Federal Bureau of Investigation. (2013). Frequently asked questions about the change in the UCR definition of rape. Retrieved August 25, 2014, from http://www.fbi.gov /about-us/cjis/ucr/recent-program-updates /new-rape-definition-frequently-asked -questions.

Federal Bureau of Investigation. (2013). Hate crimes statistics. Washington, DC: U.S. Department of Justice. Retrieved May 15, 2014, from http://www.fbi.gov/about-us/cjis /ucr/hate-crime/2012.

Federation of Feminist Women's Health Centers. (1991). *A new view of a woman's body: An illustrated guide.* Los Angeles: The Feminist Press.

Feeney, J. A., & Noller, P. (1990). Attachment style as a predictor of adult romantic relationships. *Journal of Personality & Social Psychology, 58*(2), 281–291.

Feijoo, A. (2008). Adolescent sexual health in Europe and the U.S.—Why the difference? *Advocates for Youth.* Retrieved May 10, 2011, from http://www.circumcisionandhiv.com /files/fsest.pdf.

Feiler, B. (2010, August 27). The joys of vicarious divorce. *New York Times.* Retrieved September 16, 2010, from http://community .nytimes.com/comments/www.nytimes .com/2010/08/29/fashion/29FamilyMatters .html.

Feinauer, L. (1988). Relationship of long term effects of childhood sexual abuse to identity of the offender: Family, friend, or stranger. *Women and Therapy, 7*, 89–107.

Feinauer, L. (1989). Comparison of long-term effects of child abuse by type of abuse and by relationship of the offender to the victim. *American Journal of Family Therapy, 17*, 46–48.

Feinberg, M., Willer, R., Stellar, J., & Keltner, D. (2012). The virtues of gossip: Reputational information sharing as prosocial behavior. *Journal of Personality and Social Psychology, 102*(5), 1015–1030.

Feldblum, C., & Lipnic, V. (2016). Select Task Force on the Study of Harassment in the Workplace. U.S. Equal Employment Opportunity Commission. Retrieved from https://www.eeoc.gov/eeoc/task_force /harassment/report.cfm.

Feldman, M., & Meyer. I. (2007). Childhood abuse and eating disorders in gay and bisexual men. *International Journal of Eating Disorders, 40*(5), 418–423.

Ferdenzi, C., Schaal, B., & Roberts, S. C. (2009). Human axillary odor: Are there side-related perceptual differences? *Chemical Senses, 34*(7), 565–571.

Ferguson, C. J., Brown, J. M., & Torres, A. V. (2016). Education or indoctrination? The accuracy of introductory psychology textbooks in covering controversial topics and urban legends about psychology. *Current Psychology.* Retrieved January 11, 2017, from http://link.springer.com/article/10.1007 /s12144-016-9539-7.

Ferguson, D. M., Hosmane, B., & Heiman, J. R. (2010). Randomized, placebo-controlled, double-blind, parallel design trial of the efficacy and safety of Zestra in women with mixed desire/interest/arousal/orgasm disorders. *Journal of Sex and Marital Therapy, 36*(1), 66–86.

Ferguson, D. M., Steidle, C. P., Singh, G. S., Alexander, J. S., Weihmiller, M. K., & Crosby, M. G. (2003). Randomized placebo-controlled, double blind, crossover design trial of the efficacy and safety of Zestra for women with and without female sexual arousal disorder. *Journal of Sex and Marital Therapy, 29*(Suppl. 1), 33–44.

Ferguson, R. B. (2004). The associations among members' perceptions of intragroup relationship conflict, leader-member exchange quality, and leader gossiping behavior. *Dissertation Abstracts International, 64*(10-A), (#0419–4209).

Fergusson, D. M., Horwood, L. J., & Boden, J. M. (2009). Reactions to abortion and subsequent mental health. *British Journal of Psychiatry, 195*(5), 420–426.

Fergusson, D., Horwood, L., & Boden, J. (2008). Abortion and mental health disorders: Evidence from a 30-year longitudinal study. *British Journal of Psychiatry, 193*, 444–451.

Fernandes, H. B., Kennair, L., Hutz, C. S., Natividade, J. C., & Kruger, D. J. (2016). Are negative postcoital emotions a product of evolutionary adaption? Multinational relationships with sexual strategies, reputation, and mate quality. *Evolutionary Behavioral Sciences, 10*(4), 219–244.

Fernández, I. (2005). Go, Diego go. *Hispanic, 18, 20,* 68.

Fernandez, Y. M., & Marshall, W. L. (2003). Victim empathy, social self-esteem, and psychopathology in rapists. *Sexual Abuse: Journal of Research and Treatment, 15*(1), 11–26.

Ferree, M. M., & Hess, B. B. (1985). *Controversy and coalition: The new feminist movement.* Boston: Twayne.

Ferreira-Poblete, A. (1997). The probability of conception on different days of the cycle with respect to ovulation: An overview. *Advances in Contraception, 13*(2–3), 83–95.

Ferreiro-Velasco, M. E., Barca-Buyo, A., de la Barrera, S. S., Montoto-Marques, A., Vazquez, X. M., & Rodriguez-Sotillo, A. (2005). Sexual issues in a sample of women with spinal cord injury. *Spinal Cord, 43*(1), 51–55.

Fetters, A. (2015, June 1). The tampon: A history. *The Atlantic.* Retrieved January 20, 2017, from https://www.theatlantic.com/health/archive /2015/06/history-of-the-tampon/394334/.

Field, T., Diego, M., Pelaez, M., Deeds, O., & Delgado, J. (2010). Breakup distress and loss of intimacy in university students. *Psychology, 1*(3), 173–177.

Fielder, R., & Carey, M. (2009). Predictors and consequences of sexual hookups among college students: A short-term prospective study. *Archives of Sexual Behavior, 39*(5), 1105–1119.

Fielder, R., & Carey, M. (2010). Predictors and consequences of sexual "hookups" among college students: A short-term prospective study. *Archives of Sexual Behavior, 39*(5), 1105–1119.

Fieldman, J. P., & Crespi, T. D. (2002). Child sexual abuse: Offenders, disclosure and school-based initiatives. *Adolescence, 37*(145), 151–160.

Fields, E., DeWitt, P., Fisher, C., & Rabinovitch, R. (2013). Management of male breast cancer in the U.S.: A surveillance, epidemiology and end results analysis. *International Journal of Radiation Oncology, Biology, Physics, 87*(4), 747–752.

File, T. (2013). *Computer and Internet use in the United States: Population characteristics.* U.S. Department of Commerce, Economics and Statistics Administration, U.S. Census Bureau. Retrieved January 7, 2014, from http://www.census.gov/prod/2013pubs/p20-569.pdf.

Fincham, F., & Beach, S. (2010). Marriage in the new millennium: A decade of review. *Journal of Marriage and Family, 72*(3), 630–650.

Finer, L., & Hussain, R. (2013). Unintended pregnancy and unsafe abortion in the Philippines: Context and consequences. Alan Guttmacher Institute. Retrieved April 3, 2017, from https://www.guttmacher.org/report/unintended-pregnancy-and-unsafe-abortion-philippines-context-and-consequences.

Finer, L., & Philbin, J. (2013). Sexual initiation, contraceptive use, and pregnancy among young adolescents. *Pediatrics, 131*(5), 886–891.

Finer, L., & Philbin, J. (2014). Trends in ages at key reproductive transition in the United States, 1951–2010. *Women's Health Issues, 24*(3), e271–e279.

Finer, L., & Philbin, J. (2014). Trends in ages at key reproductive transitions in the U.S., 1951–2010. *Women's Health Issues.* Retrieved May 26, 2014, from http://www.guttmacher.org/pubs/journals/j.whi.2014.02.002.pdf.

Finer, L., & Zolna, M. (2013). Shifts in intended and unintended pregnancies in the U.S., 2001–2008. *American Journal of Public Health, 104*(S1), S44–S48.

Finer, L., & Zolna, M. (2016). Declines in unintended pregnancy in the United States, 2008–2011. *New England Journal of Medicine, 374*, 843–852. Retrieved April 9, 2017, from http://www.nejm.org/doi/full/10.1056/NEJMsa1506575#t=article.

Finer, L., Frohwirth, L., Dauphinee, L., Singh, S., & Moore, A. (2005). Reasons U.S. women have abortions: Quantitative and qualitative perspectives. *Perspectives on Sexual and Reproductive Health, 37*(3), 110–118.

Finer, L., Frohwirth, L., Dauphinee, L., Singh, S., & Moore, A. (2006). Timing of steps and reasons for delays in obtaining abortions in the United States. *Contraception, 74*(4), 334–344.

Finer, L. B., & Henshaw, S. K. (2006). Disparities in rates of unintended pregnancy in the United States, 1994 and 2001. *Perspectives on Sexual and Reproductive Health, 38*, 90–96.

Fingerhut, H. (2016). Support steady for same-sex marriage and acceptance of homosexuality. Pew Research Center. Fact Tank. Retrieved March 19, 2017, from http://www.pewresearch.org/fact-tank/2016/05/12/support-steady-for-same-sex-marriage-and-acceptance-of-homosexuality/.

Fink, H. A., MacDonald, R., Rutks, I. R., & Nelson, D. B. (2002). Sildenafil for male erectile dysfunction: A systematic review and meta-analysis. *Archives of Internal Medicine, 162*(12), 1349–1360.

Finkelhor, D. (1980). Sex among siblings: A survey on prevalence, variety, and effects. *Archives of Sexual Behavior, 9*, 171–194.

Finkelhor, D. (1984). *Child sexual abuse: New theory and research.* New York: The Free Press.

Finkelhor, D., & Browne, A. (1985). The traumatic impact of child sexual abuse. *American Journal of Ortho-Psychiatry, 55*, 530–541.

Finkelhor, D., Hammer, H., & Sedlak, A. (2008). Sexually Assaulted Children: National Estimates and Characteristics. National Incidence Studies of Missing, Abducted, Runaway, and Thrownaway Children. Retrieved from https://www.ncjrs.gov/pdffiles1/ojjdp/214383.pdf.

Finkelhor, D., Hotaling, G., Lewis, I. A., & Smith, C. (1990). Sexual abuse in a national survey of adult men and women: Prevalence, characteristics, and risk factors. *Child Abuse and Neglect, 14*, 19–28.

Fiot, E., Zenaty, D., Boizeau, P., Haigneré, J., Dos Santos, S., & Léger, J. (2016). X-chromosome gene dosage as a determinant of impaired pre and postnatal growth and adult height in Turner syndrome. *European Journal of Endocinology, 174*(3), 281–288.

Firestone, P., Nunes, K. L., Moulden, H., Broom, I., & Bradford, J. M. (2005). Hostility and recidivism in sexual offenders. *Archives of Sexual Behavior, 34*(3), 277–283.

Firger, J. (2015, December 11). U.S. schools still lack sufficient sex education programs. *Newsweek.* Retrieved February 11, 2017, from http://www.newsweek.com/us-schools-still-lack-sufficient-sex-education-programs-404328.

Firmin, M., & Firebaugh, S. (2008). Historical analysis of college campus interracial dating. *College Student Journal, 42*(3), 782–788.

Fischer, G. J. (1987). Hispanic and majority student attitudes toward forcible date rape as a function of differences in attitudes toward women. *Sex Roles, 17*(1–2), 93–101.

Fisher, B. S., Daigle, L. E., Cullen, F. T., & Turner, M. G. (2003). Reporting sexual victimization to the police and others: Results from a national-level study of college women. *Criminal Justice & Behavior, 30*(1), 6–38.

Fisher, B., Cullen, F., & Turner, M. (2000). The sexual victimization of college women. Bureau of Justice Statistics. Retrieved from https://www.ncjrs.gov/pdffiles1/nij/182369.pdf.

Fisher, B., Wortley, S., Webster, C., & Kirst, M. (2002). The socio-legal dynamics and implications of "diversion": The case study of the Toronto "John School" diversion programme for prostitution offenders. *Criminal Justice: International Journal of Policy and Practice, 2*(34), 385–410.

Fisher, D., Malow, R., Rosenberg, R., Reynolds, G., Farrell, N., & Jaffe, A. (2006). Recreational Viagra use and sexual risk among drug abusing men. *American Journal of Infectious Disease, 2*, 107–114.

Fisher, H. (2004). *Why we love: The nature and chemistry of romantic love.* New York: Henry Holt.

Fisher, H., Brown, L., Aron, A., Strong, G., & Mashek, D. (2010). Reward, addiction, and emotion regulation systems associated with rejection in love. *Journal of Neurophysiology, 104*(1), 51–60.

Fisher, W. A., & Barak, A. (1991). Pornography, erotica, and behavior: More questions than answers. *International Journal of Law and Psychiatry, 14*, 65–83.

Fitzgerald, L. F., & Ormerod, A. J. (1991). Perceptions of sexual harassment: The influence of gender and academic context. *Psychology of Women Quarterly, 15*, 281–294.

Flaherty, A., Kim, T., Giuliano, A., Magliocco, A., Hakky, T., Pagliaro, L., & Spiess, P. (2014). Implications for human papillomavirus in penile cancer. *Urologic Oncology, 32*(1), 53.

Flanagan, C. (2011, April 23). Shutter fraternities for young women's good. *Wall Street Journal.* Retrieved April 24, 2011, from http://online.wsj.com/article/SB10001424052748704658704576275152354071470.html?mod5WSJ_WSJ_News_BlogsModule.

Flanders, E., Gibson, M., Goldberg, A., & Ross, L. (2016). Postpartum depression among visible and invisible sexual minority women: A pilot study. *Archives of Women's' Mental Health, 19*(2), 299–305.

Fleischmann, A. A., Spitzberg, B. H., Andersen, P. A., Roesch, S. C., & Metts, S. (2005). Tickling the monster: Jealousy induction in relationships. *Journal of Social and Personal Relationships, 22*(1), 49–73.

Floyd, K. (2014). Empathetic listening as an expression of interpersonal affection. *The International Journal of Listening, 28*(1), 1–12.

Fok, W. (2016). Update on emergency contraception. *Current Opinion in Obstetrics & Gynecology, 28*(6), 522–529.

Foldes, P., & Buisson, O. (2009). The clitoral complex: A dynamic sonographic study. *Journal of Sexual Medicine, 6*(5), 1223–1231.

Folsom, L., & Fuqua, J. (2015). Reproductive issues in women with Turner syndrome. *Endocrinology and Metabolism Clinics of North America, 44*(4), 723–737.

Food and Drug Administration, Office of Women's Health. (2006, June). *Human papillomavirus.* Retrieved September 16,

2008, from http://www.fda.gov/WOMENS/getthefacts/hpv.html.

Food and Drug Administration. (2007a, December 18). *FDA mandates new warning for nonoxynol 9 OTC contraceptive products*. Retrieved October 28, 2008, from http://www.fda.gov/bbs/topics/NEWS/2007/NEW01758.html.

Food and Drug Administration. (2007b). Over-the-counter vaginal contraceptive and spermicide drug products containing nonoxynol 9; required labeling. Final rule. *Federal Register, 72*, 71769–71785.

Food and Drug Administration. (2008, January 18). *FDA approves update to label on birth control patch*. Retrieved October 28, 2008, from http://www.fda.gov/bbs/topics/NEWS/2008/NEW01781.html.

Food and Drug Administration (FDA). (2013). FDA approves first drug treatment for Peyronie's disease. U.S. Department of Health and Human Services. Retrieved March 2, 2014, from http://www.fda.gov/newsevents/newsroom/pressannouncements/ucm377849.htm.

Foote, W. E., & Goodman-Delahunty, J. (2005). Harassers, harassment contexts, same-sex harassment, workplace romance, and harassment theories. In W. E. Foote & J. Goodman-Delahunty (Eds.), *Evaluating sexual harassment: Psychological, social, and legal considerations in forensic examinations* (pp. 27–45). Washington, DC: American Psychological Association.

Ford, C. L., Whetten, K. D., Kaufman, J. S., & Thrasher, A. D. (2007). Black sexuality, social construction, and research targeting 'The down low' ('The DL'). *Annals of Epidemiology, 17*(3), 209–216.

Ford, K., & Chamrathrithirong, A. (2007). Sexual partners and condom use of migrant workers in Thailand. *AIDS Behavior, 11*, 905–914.

Ford, L., & Holder, J. (2016, March 8). Contraception and family planning around the world. *The Guardian*. Retrieved April 5, 2017, from https://www.theguardian.com/global-development/datablog/2016/mar/08/contraception-and-family-planning-around-the-world-interactive.

Forhan, S. (2008, March). *Prevalence of STIs and bacterial vaginosis among female adolescents in the U.S.: Data from the National Health and Nutritional Examination Survey 2003–2004*. Presented at the 2008 National STD Prevention Conference, Chicago, IL. Retrieved May 29, 2008, from http://www.cdc.gov/STDConference/2008/media/summaries-11march2008.htm#tues1.

Forhan, S., Gottlieb, S., Sternberg, M., Xu, F., Datta, S., McQuillan, G., Berman, S., & Markowitz, L. (2009). Prevalence of sexually transmitted infections among female

adolescents aged 14 to 19 in the United States. *Pediatrics, 124*(6), 1505–1512.

Forke, C., Myers, R., Catallozzi, M., & Schwarz, D. (2008). Relationship violence among female and male college undergraduate students. *Archives of Pediatric Adolescent Medicine, 162*, 634–641.

Forrester-Knauss, C., Stutz, E., Weiss, C., & Tschudin, S. (2011). The interrelation between PMS and major depression. *BMC Public Health, 11*, 795–806.

Forry, N. D., Leslie, L. A., & Letiecq, B. L. (2007). Marital quality in interracial relationships. *Journal of Family Issues, 28*, 1538.

Forste, R., & Fox, K. (2012). Household labor, gender roles, and family satisfaction: A cross-national comparison. *Journal of Comparative Family Studies, 43*(5), 613.

Forstein, M. (1988). Homophobia: An overview. *Psychiatric Annals, 18*, 33–36.

Fortenberry, J., Schick, V., Herbenick, D., Sanders, S., Dodge, B., & Reece, M. (2010). Sexual behaviors and condom use at least vaginal intercourse: A national sample of adolescents age 14 to 17 years. *Journal of Sexual Medicine, 7*(Suppl. 5), 305–314.

Fortenberry, J. D. (2002). Unveiling the hidden epidemic of STDs. *Journal of the American Medical Association, 287*(6), 768–769.

Forti, G., Corona, G., Vignozzi, L., Krausz, C., & Maggi, M. (2010). Klinefelter's syndrome: A clinical and therapeutical update. *Sex Development, 4*(4–5), 249–258.

Foster, K., & Sandel, M. (2010). Abuse of women with disabilities: Toward an empowerment perspective. *Sexuality and Disability, 28*(3), 177–187.

Foster-Gimbel, O., & Engeln, R. (2016). Fat chance! Experiences and expectations of antifat bias in the gay male community. *Psychology of Sexual Orientation and Gender Diversity, 3*(1), 63–70.

Foubert, J., & Cremedy, B. (2007). Reactions of men of color to a commonly used rape prevention program. *Sex Roles, 57*, 137–144.

Foubert, J., Godin, E., & Tatum, J. (2010a). In their own words: Sophomore college men describe attitude and behavior changes resulting from a rape prevention program 2 years after their participation. *Journal of Interpersonal Violence, 25*(12), 2237–2257.

Foubert, J., Tatum, J., & Godin, E. (2010b). First-year male students' perceptions of a rape prevention program 7 months after their participation: Attitude and behavior changes. *Journal of College Student Development, 51*(6), 707–715.

Foubert, J. D. (2000). The longitudinal effects of a rape: Prevention program on fraternity men's attitudes. *Journal of American College Health, 48*(4), 158–163.

Foubert, J. D., & McEwen, M. K. (1998). An all-male rape prevention peer education

program: Decreasing fraternity men's behavioral intent to rape. *Journal of College Student Development, 39*, 548–556.

Foucault, M. (1998). *The history of sexuality, Vol. 1: An introduction*. London: Penguin Books.

Foundation for AIDS Research. (2013). *The regional picture: Sub-Saharan Africa*. Retrieved June 10, 2014, from http://www.amfar.org/about-hiv-and-aids/facts-and-stats/statistics—worldwide.

Fowers, B. J. (1998). Psychology and the good marriage. *American Behavioral Scientist, 41*(4), 516.

Fowler, M., Qin, M., Fiscus, S., Currier, J., Flynn, P., Chipato, T., McIntrye, J., et al. (2016). Benefits and risks of antiretroviral therapy for perinatal HIV infection. *New England Journal of Medicine, 375*(18), 1726–1737.

Fowler, M. G., Gable, A. R., Lampe, M. A., Etima, M., & Owor, M. (2010). Perinatal HIV and its prevention: Progress toward an HIV-free generation. *Clinical Perinatology, 37*(4), 699–719.

Fox, J. A., & Zawitz, M. W. (2004). Homicide trends in the United States. Retrieved October 23, 2005, from www.ojp.usdoj.gov/bjs/homicide/homtrnd.htm.

Fox, M., & Thomson, M. (2010). HIV/AIDS and circumcision: Lost in translation. *Journal of Medical Ethics, 36*(12), 798–801.

Foxman, B., & Buxton, M. (2013). Alternative approaches to conventional treatment of acute uncomplicated urinary tract infection in women. *Current Infectious Disease Reports, 15*(2), 124–129.

Frackiewicz, E. J. (2000). Endometriosis: An overview of the disease and its treatment. *Journal of the American Pharmaceutical Association, 40*(5), 645–657.

Fraley, R. (2002). Attachment stability from infancy to adulthood: Meta-analysis and dynamic modeling of developmental mechanisms. *Personality and Social Psychology Review, 6*(2), 123–151.

France-Presse, A. (2010, September 28). Bishops to support protests against birth control. ABS/CBN News. Retrieved March 2, 2011, from http://www.abs-cbnnews.com/nation/09/28/10/bishops-support-protests-against-birth-control.

Franceschi, S. (2005). The IARC commitment to cancer prevention: The example of papillomavirus and cervical cancer. *Recent Results in Cancer Research, 166*, 277–297.

Francis, A. (2008). Family and sexual orientation: The family-demographic correlates of homosexuality in men and women. *Journal of Sex Research, 45*(4), 371–377.

Francoeur, R. T., & Noonan, R. J. (Eds.). (2004). *The Continuum International encyclopedia of sexuality*. New York/London: Continuum International.

Francomano, D., Ilacqua, A., Cortese, A., Tartaglia, G., Lenzi, A., Inghilleri, M., & Aversa, A. (2017). Effects of daily tadalafil on lower urinary tract symptoms in young men with multiple sclerosis and erectile dysfunction: A pilot study. *Journal of Endocrinological Investigation, 40*(3), 275–279.

Franiuk, R., Seefelt, J., & Vandello, J. (2008). Prevalence of rape myths in headlines and their effects on attitudes toward rape. *Sex Roles, 58,* 790–802.

Frank, E., Anderson, C., & Rubinstein, D. N. (1978). Frequency of sexual dysfunction in normal couples. *New England Journal of Medicine, 299,* 111–115.

Frankel, L. (2002). "I've never thought about it": Contradictions and taboos surrounding American males' experiences of first ejaculation (semenarche). *Journal of Men's Studies, 11*(1), 37–54.

Frappier, J., Toupin, I., Levy, J., Aubertin-Leheudre, M., & Karelis, A. (2013). Energy expenditure during sexual activity in young healthy couples. *PLoS One, 8*(10), e79342. Retrieved March 13, 2010, from https://www.ncbi.nlm.nih.gov/pmc/articles/PMC3812004/.

Frazier, P. A. (2000). The role of attributions and perceived control in recovery from rape. *Journal of Personal and Interpersonal Loss, 5*(2/3), 203–225.

Frechette, D., Paquet, L., Verma, S., Clemons, M., Wheatley-Price, P., Gertler, S., Song, X., Graham, N., & Dent, S. (2013). The impact of endocrine therapy on sexual dysfunction in postmenopausal women with early stage breast cancer. *Breast Cancer Research and Treatment, 141*(1), 111–117.

Frederick, D., Lever, J., Gillespie, B., & Garcia, J. (2017). What keeps passion alive? Sexual satisfaction is associated with sexual communication, mood setting, sexual variety, oral sex, orgasm, and sex frequency in a national U.S. study. *Journal of Sex Research, 54*(2), 186–201.

Frederick, D., Peplau, A., & Lever, J. (2008). The Barbie mystique: Satisfaction with breast size and shape across the lifespan. *International Journal of Sexual Health, 20*(3), 200–211.

Fredricksen-Goldsen, K., Kim, H. (2017). The science of conducting research with LGBT older adults – An introduction to aging with pride: National Health, Aging, and sexuality/Gender Study (NHAS). *The Gerontologist, 57*(S1), 1–14.

Fredriksen-Goldsen, K., Kim, H. J., Barkan, S., Muraco, A., & Hoy-Ellis, C. (2013). Health disparities among lesbian, gay, and bisexual older adults: Results from a population-based study. *American Journal of Public Health, 103*(10), 1802–1809.

Fredriksen-Goldsen, K., Kim, H., Emlet, C., Muraco, A., Erosheva, E., Hoy-Ellis, C.,

Goldsen, J., & Petry, H. (2011). The aging and health report: Disparities and resilience among lesbian, gay, bisexual, and transgender older adults. Institute for Multigenerational Health, Seattle, WA.

Fredriksson, J., Kanabus, A., Pennington, J., & Pembrey, G. (2008). AIDS orphans. Avert International AIDS Charity. Retrieved November 3, 2008, from http://www.avert.org/aidsorphans.htm.

Freedman, D., Khan, L., Serdula, M., Dietz, W., Srinivasan, S. R., & Berenson, G. S. (2002). Relation of age at menarche to race, time period, and anthropometric dimensions: The Bogalusa Heart Study. *Pediatrics, 110*(4), E43.

Freedman, D. H. (2010, November). Lies, damned lies, and medical science. *The Atlantic.* Retrieved January 2, 2011, from http://www.theatlantic.com/magazine/archive/2010/11/lies-damned-lies-and-medical-science/8269/.

Freeman, M. P. (2014). ADHD and pregnancy. *American Journal of Psychiatry, 171*(7), 723–728.

Freeman, N. (2007). Preschoolers' perceptions of gender appropriate toys and their parents' beliefs about genderized behaviors: Miscommunication, mixed messages, or hidden truths? *Early Childhood Education Journal, 34*(5), 357–366.

Freeman, S. B. (2008). Continuous oral contraception. Strategies for managing breakthrough bleeding. *Advance for Nurse Practitioners 16*(8), 36–38.

Fretts, R. C., Boyd, M. E., Usher, R. H., & Usher, H. A. (1992). The changing pattern of fetal death, 1961–1988. *Obstetrics and Gynecology, 79*(1), 35–39.

Freud, S. (1953). Three essays on the theory of sexuality. In J. Strachey (Ed. & Trans.), The standard edition of the complete psychological works of Sigmund Freud (Vol. 7, pp. 130–243). London: Hogarth Press. (Original work published 1905.)

Freund, K., & Blanchard, R. (1986). The concept of courtship disorder. *Journal of Sex and Marital Therapy, 12,* 79–92.

Freund, K., Scher, H., & Hucker, S. (1983). The courtship disorders. *Archives of Sexual Behavior, 12,* 369–379.

Freund, K., Scher, H., & Hucker, S. (1984). The courtship disorders: A further investigation. *Archives of Sexual Behavior, 13,* 133–139.

Freund, M., Lee, N., & Leonard, T. (1991). Sexual behavior of clients with street prostitutes in Camden, New Jersey. *Journal of Sex Research, 28,* 579–591.

Freund, M., Leonard, T. L., & Lee, N. (1989). Sexual behavior of resident street prostitutes with their clients in Camden, New Jersey. *Journal of Sex Research, 26,* 460–478.

Frick, K. D., Clark, M. A., Steinwachs, D. M., Langenberg, P., Stovall, D., Munro, M. G., &

Dickersin, K.; STOP-DUB Research Group. (2009). Financial and quality-of-life burden of dysfunctional uterine bleeding among women agreeing to obtain surgical treatment. *Women's Health Issues, 19*(1), 70–78.

Friday, L. (2013, August 13). University approves gender neutral housing. *BU Today.* Retrieved February 13, 2014, from http://www.bu.edu/today/2013/university-approves-gender-neutral-housing.

Friebe, A., & Arck, P. (2008). Causes for spontaneous abortion: What the bugs 'gut' to do with it? *International Journal of Biochemistry and Cell Biology, 40*(11), 2348–2352.

Frieden, T. R. (2011). CDC health disparities and inequalities report—United States, 2011. *Morbidity and Mortality Weekly Report, 60*(Suppl.), 1–2.

Friedenreich, C., & Cust, A. (2008). Physical activity and breast cancer risk. *British Journal of Sports Medicine, 42*(8), 636–647.

Friedler, S., Glasser, S., Azani, L., Freedman, L., Raziel, A., Strassburger, D., Ron-El, R., & Lerner-Geva, L. (2011). The effect of medical clowning on pregnancy rates after in vitro fertilization and embryo transfer. *Fertility and Sterility, 95*(6), 2127–2130.

Friedman, C. (2007). First comes love, then comes marriage, then comes baby carriage: Perspectives on gay parenting and reproductive technology. *Journal of Infant, Child, and Adolescent Psychotherapy, 6,* 111–123.

Friedman, S., Loue, S., Heaphy, E., & Mendez, N. (2011). Intimate partner violence victimization and perpetration by Puerto Rican women with severe mental illnesses. *Community Mental Health Journal, 47*(2), 156–163.

Friedman-Kien, A. E., & Farthing, C. (1990). Human immunodeficiency virus infection: A survey with special emphasis on mucocutaneous manifestations. *Seminars in Dermatology, 9,* 167–177.

Friedrich, W., Fisher, J., Broughton, D., Houston, M., & Shafran, C. (1998). Normative sexual behavior in children: A contemporary sample. *Pediatrics, 101*(4), 456–464.

Friedrich, W. N. (1998). Behavioral manifestations of child sexual abuse. *Child Abuse and Neglect, 22*(6), 523–531.

Friedrich, W. N., Grambsch, P., Broughton, D., Kuiper, J., & Beilke, R. L. (1991). Normative sexual behavior in children. *Pediatrics, 88,* 456–464.

Fritz, G. S., Stoll, K., & Wagner, N. N. (1981). A comparison of males and females who were sexually molested as children. *Journal of Sex & Marital Therapy, 7*(1), 54–59.

Froehner, M., Koch, R., Litz, R., Oehlschlaeger, S., Hakenberg, O., Wirth, M. (2005). Feasibility and limitations of comorbidity measurement in patients undergoing radical prostatectomy, *European Urology, 47*(2), 190–195.

Froehner, M., Koch, R., Wirth, M., Adam, M., Schlomm, T., Huland, H., & Graefen, M. (2014). Does increasing life expectancy affect competing mortality after radical prostatectomy? *Urologic Oncology, 32*(4), 413–418.

Frohlich, P. F., & Meston, C. M. (2000). Evidence that serotonin affects female sexual functioning via peripheral mechanisms. *Physiology and Behavior, 71*(3–4), 383–393.

Frost, J. J., Darroch, J. E., & Remez, L. (2008). Improving contraception use in the United States. *In Brief, 1.* New York: Alan Guttmacher Institute.

Frost, J. J., & Driscoll, A. K. (2006). *Sexual and reproductive health of U.S. Latinas: A literature review.* New York: Alan Guttmacher Institute. Retrieved May 27, 2008, from http://www .guttmacher.org/pubs/2006/02/07/or19.pdf.

Frostino, A. (2007). Guilt and jealousy associated with sexual fantasies among heterosexual married individuals. Widener University. *Dissertation Abstracts International: Section B: The Sciences and Engineering, 68*(3-B), 1924.

Fruth, A. (2007). Dating and adolescents' psychological well-being. *Dissertation Abstracts International Section A: Humanities and Social Sciences, 68*(1-A), 360.

Fryar, C. D., Hirsch, R., Porter, K. S., Kottiri, B., Brody, D., & Louis, T. (2007, June 28). Drug use and sexual behaviors reported by adults: United States, 1999–2002. Advance Data from Vital and Health Statistics, Centers for Disease Control, 384. Retrieved October 3, 2008, from http://www.cdc.gov/nchs/data /ad/ad384.pdf.

Fu, Y. (2010). Interracial marriage formation: Entry into first union and transition from cohabitation to marriage. University of North Carolina at Chapel Hill, AAT #1483777.

Fuller-Fricke., R. L. (2007). Interaction of relationship satisfaction, depressive symptoms, and self-esteem in college-aged women. *Fuller Theological Seminary, Dissertation Abstracts,* UMI #3267404.

Gaetz, S. (2004). Safe streets for whom? Homeless youth, social exclusion, and criminal victimization. *Canadian Journal of Criminology and Criminal Justice, 46,* 423–456.

Gaffield, M. E., Culwell, K. R., & Ravi, A. (2009). Oral contraceptives and family history of breast cancer. *Contraception, 80*(4), 372–380.

Gähler, M., Hong, Y., & Bernhardt, E. (2009). Parental divorce and union disruption among young adults in Sweden. *Journal of Family Issues, 30*(5), 688–713.

Gaither, G. A. (2000). The reliability and validity of three new measures of male sexual preferences (Doctoral dissertation, University of North Dakota). *Dissertation Abstracts International, 61,* 4981.

Gaither, G. A., Sellbom, M., & Meier, B. P. (2003). The effect of stimulus content on volunteering for sexual interest research among college students. *Journal of Sex Research, 40*(3), 240–249.

Gajilan, A. C. (2007, April 23). Thumbing your way to arthritis [Web log post]. Retrieved February 10, 2014, from http://www.cnn.com /HEALTH/blogs/paging.dr.gupta/2007/04 /thumbing-your-way-to-arthritis.html.

Galis, F., Broek, C., Van Dongen, S., & Wijnaendts, L. (2010). Sexual dimorphism in the prenatal digit ratio (2D:4D). *Archives of Sexual Behavior, 39,* 57–62.

Gallagher, J. (2001). Normal, China—The Chinese Psychiatric Association decides that being gay is no longer a disease. *The Advocate,* p. 22.

Gallagher, M., & Baker, J. K. (2004, May 4). Same-sex unions and divorce risk: Data from Sweden. *iMAPP Policy Brief.* Retrieved September 14, 2008, from http://www .marriagedebate.com/pdf/SSdivorcerisk.pdf.

Gallo, R. V. (2000). Is there a homosexual brain? *Gay and Lesbian Review, 7*(1), 12–16.

Gallup, G., & Frederick, D. (2010). The science of sex appeal: An evolutionary perspective. *Review of General Psychology, 14*(3), 240–250.

Galupo, M. P. (2006). Sexism, heterosexism, and biphobia: The framing of bisexual women's friendships. *Journal of Bisexuality, 6,* 35–45.

Gamel, C., Hengeveld, M., Davis, B. (2000). Informational needs about the effects of gynaecological cancer on sexuality: A review of the literature. *Journal of Clinical Nursing, 9*(5), 678–688.

Gan, C., Zou, Y., Wu, S., Li, Y., & Liu, Q. (2008). The influence of medical abortion compared with surgical abortion on subsequent pregnancy outcome. *International Journal of Gynecology and Obstetrics, 101,* 231–238.

Garbin, C., Deacon, J., Rowan, M., Hartmann, P., & Geddes, D. (2009). Association of nipple piercing with abnormal milk production and breastfeeding. *Journal of the American Medical Association, 301*(24), 2550–2551.

Garcia, J., & Rieber, C. (2008). Hook-up behavior: A biopsychosocial perspective. *Journal of Social, Evolutionary, and Cultural Psychology, 2,* 198–208.

Garcia, J., Rieber, C., Massey, S., & Merriwether, A. (2012). Sexual hookup culture: A review. *Review of General Psychology, 16*(2), 161–176.

Garcia-Falgueras, A., & Swaab, D. F. (2010). Sexual hormones and the brain: An essential alliance for sexual identity and sexual orientation. *Endocrine Development, 17,* 22–35.

Garcia-Perdomo, H., Echeverria-Garcia, F., & Tobias, A. (2016). Effectiveness of phosphodiesterase 5 inhibitors in the treatment of erectile dysfunction in patients with spinal cord trauma: Systematic review and meta-analysis. *Urologia Internationalis, 98*(2), 198–204.

Gard, C. (2000). What is he/she saying? *Current Health, 26*(8), 18–20.

Gardiner, P., Stargrove, M., & Low, D. (2011). Concomitant use of prescription medications and dietary supplements in menopausal women: An approach to provider preparedness. *Maturitas, 68*(3), 251–255.

Gardner, A. (2004). *Excess weight can compromise birth control pills.* Sexual Health Network. Retrieved October 1, 2008, from http://sexualhealth.e-healthsource. com/?p=news1&id=523135.

Gareis, E., Merkin, R., & Goldman, J. (2011). Intercultural friendship: Linking communication variables and friendship success. *Journal of Intercultural Communication Research, 40*(2), 153–171.

Garneau, C., Olmstead, S., Pasley, K., & Fincham, F. (2013). The role of family structure and attachment in college student hookups. *Archives of Sexual Behavior, 42*(8), 1473–1486.

Garnock-Jones, K. P., & Giuliano, A. R. (2011) Quadrivalent human papillomavirus (HPV) types 6, 11, 16, 18 vaccine: For the prevention of genital warts in males. *Drugs, 71*(5), 591–602.

Gartrell, N., & Bos, H. (2010). The US national longitudinal lesbian family study: Psychological adjustment of the 17-year-old adolescents. Retrieved June 7, 2010, from http://pediatrics.aappublications.org/cgi /content/abstract/peds.2009–3153v1.

Gartrell, N., & Bos, H. (2010). U.S. national longitudinal lesbian family study: Psychological adjustment of 17-year-old adolescents. *Pediatrics, 126*(1), 28–36.

Garver-Apgar, C. E., Gangestad, S. W., Thornhill, R., Miller, R. D., & Olp, J. J. (2006). Major histocompatibility complex alleles, sexual responsivity, and unfaithfulness in romantic couples. *Psychological Science, 17,* 830–835.

Gaskin, I. (2012). Has pseudocyesis become an outmoded diagnosis? *Birth: Issues in Perinatal Care, 39*(1), 77–79.

Gates, G. (2011). *How many people are lesbian, gay, bisexual and transgender?* UCLA-Williams Institute, Los Angeles, CA.

Gates, G. (2011). How many people are lesbian, gay, bisexual, and transgender? Williams Institute. Retrieved March 24, 2017, from https://williamsinstitute.law.ucla.edu /research/census-lgbt-demographics-studies /how-many-people-are-lesbian-gay-bisexual -and-transgender/.

Gates, G. (2013). *LGBT parenting in the United States.* The Williams Institute, Los Angeles, CA.

Gates, G. (2017, January 11). In US, more adults identifying as LGBT. Gallup Poll. Retrieved online from http://www.gallup.com /poll/201731/lgbt-identification-rises.aspx.

Gates, G., & Newport, F. (2015). An estimated 780,000 Americans in same-sex marriages. Gallup Social Issues. Retrieved March 7, 2017, from http://www.gallup.com/poll/182837/estimated-780-000-americans-sex-marriages.aspx.

Gates, G., & Renna, C. (2010). 2010 census analysis of same-sex couples: 1 in 7 not identified. Williams Institute. Retrieved May 11, 2011, from http://www3.law.ucla.edu/williamsinstitute/pdf/2010CensusAnalysis_PR_Sept7.pdf.

Gates, G., Badgett, L., Macomber, J. E., & Chambers, K. (2007, March 27). Adoption and foster care by lesbian and gay parents in the United States. Urban Institute. Retrieved October 2, 2008, from http://www.urban.org/url.cfm?ID=411437.

Gates, G., Badgett, L., Macomber, J., & Chambers, K. (2007). Adoption and foster care by lesbian and gay parents in the U.S. Washington, DC: Urban Institute Press.

Gates, G. J. (2008). Same-sex couples: U.S. census and the American Community Survey. Retrieved January 31, 2011, from http://www2.law.ucla.edu/williamsinstitute/pdf/CensusPresentation_LGBT.pdf.

Gates, G. J., & Sonenstein, F. L. (2000). Heterosexual genital sexual activity among adolescent males: 1988–1995. *Family Planning Perspectives*, 32(6), 295–304.

Gato, J., & Fontaine, A. (2013). Anticipation of the sexual and gender development of children adopted by same-sex couples. *International Journal of Psychology*, 48(3), 244–253.

Gatter, M., Cleland, K., & Nucatola, D. (2015). Efficacy and safety of medical abortion using mifepristone and buccal misoprostol through 63 days. *Contraception*, 91(4), 269–273.

Gauthreaux, C., Negron, J., Castellanos, D., Ward-Peterson, M., Castro, G., Rodriguez de la Vega, P., & Acuña, J. (2017). The association between pregnancy intendedness and experiencing symptoms of postpartum depression among new mothers in the United States, 2009 to 2011: A secondary analysis of PRAMS data. *Medicine*, 96(6), e5851.

Gavard, J., & Artal, R. (2008). Effect of exercise on pregnancy outcome. *Clinical Obstetrics and Gynecology*, 51, 467–480.

Gebhard, P., & Johnson, A. (1979). *The Kinsey data: Marginal tabulations of the 1938–1963 interviews conducted by the Institute for Sex Research*. Philadelphia: W. B. Saunders.

Geer, J. H., & O'Donohue, W. T. (1987). A sociological approach. In J. H. Geer & W. T. O'Donohue (Eds.), *Theories of human sexuality* (pp. 237–253). New York: Plenum Press.

Geiger, A. (2016). Sharing chores a key to good marriage, say majority of married adults. *FactTank*, Pew Research Center. Retrieved August 23, 2017, from http://www.pewresearch.org/fact-tank/2016/11/30/sharing-chores-a-key-to-good-marriage-say-majority-of-married-adults/.

Gelbard, M. (1988). Dystrophic penile classification in Peyronie's disease. *Journal of Urology*, 139, 738–740.

Gelez, H., Clement, P., Compagnie, S., Gorny, D., Laurin, M., Allers, K., Sommer, B., & Giuliano, F. (2013). Brain neuronal activation induced by flibanserin treatment in female rats. *Psychopharmacology*, 230(4), 639–652.

Gelman, F., & Atrio, J. (2017). Flibanserin for hypoactive sexual desire disorder: Place in therapy. *Therapeutic Advances in Chronic Disease*. Retrieved April 14, 2017, from http://journals.sagepub.com/doi/full/10.1177/2040622316679933.

Gemelli, R. J. (1996). *Normal child and adolescent development*. Arlington, VA: American Psychiatric Press.

"Genital HPV Infection." (2017). Fact Sheet. Centers for Disease Control and Prevention. Retrieved April 24, 2017, from https://www.cdc.gov/std/hpv/stdfact-hpv.htm.

Gentile, S. (2015). Prenatal antidepressant exposure and the risk of autism spectrum disorders in children. Are we looking at the fall of gods? *Journal of Affective Disorders*, 182, 132–137.

Gentzler, A., Kerns, K., & Keener, E. (2010). Emotional reactions and regulatory responses to negative and positive events: Associations with attachment and gender. *Motivation and Emotion*, 34(1), 78.

George, K., Kamth, M., & Tharyan, P. (2013, February 28). Minimally invasive versus open surgery for reversal of tubal sterilization. *Cochrane Database of Systematic Reviews*. Retrieved May 26, 2014, from http://www.ncbi.nlm.nih.gov/pubmed/23450598.

Geraghty, P. (2010). Beyond birth control. The health benefits of hormonal contraception. *Advanced Nurse Practitioner*, 17(2), 47–48, 50, 52.

Getahun, D., Ananth, C. V., Selvam, N., & Demissie, K. (2005). Adverse perinatal outcomes among interracial couples in the United States. *Obstetrics and Gynecology*, 106(1), 81–88.

Ghanem, H., Glina, S., Assalian, P., & Buvat, J. (2013). Position paper: Management of men complaining of a small penis despite an actually normal size. *Journal of Sexual Medicine*, 10(1), 294–303.

Ghanotakis, E. (2008, January 10). South Africa: An everyday crime. *Frontline Rough Cut*. Retrieved April 30, 2011, from http://www.pbs.org/frontlineworld/rough/2008/01/south_africa_ev.html.

Ghaziani, A. (2005). Breakthrough: The 1979 national march. Gay & Lesbian Review Worldwide, 12(2), 31–33.

Ghidini, A., & Bocchi, C. (2007). Direct fetal blood sampling: Cordocentesis. In J. T. Queenan, C. Y. Spong, & C. J. Lockwood (Eds.), *Management of high-risk pregnancy: An evidence-based approach*. Hoboken, NJ: Wiley Blackwell.

Ghosh, G., Grewal, J., Männistö, T., Mendola, P., Chen Z., Xie, Y., & Laughon, S. (2014). Racial/ethnic differences in pregnancy-related hypertensive disease in nulliparous women. *Ethnicity & Disease*, 24(3), 283–289.

Ghosh, M. K. (2005). Breech presentation: Evolution of management. *Journal of Reproductive Medicine*, 50(2), 108–116.

Giaccardi, S., Ward, L., Seabrook, R., Manago, A., & Lippman, J. (2016). Media and modern manhood: Testing associations between media consumption and young men's acceptance of traditional gender ideologies. *Sex Roles*, 75(3), 151–163.

Giahi, L., Mohammadmoradi, S., Javidan, A., Sadeghi, M. (2016). Nutritional modifications in male infertility: A systematic review covering 2 decades. *Nutrition Reviews*, 74(2), 118–130.

Gibbs, J. L., Ellison, N. B., & Heino, R. D. (2006). Self-presentation in online personals: The role of anticipated future interaction, self-disclosure, and perceived success in Internet dating. *Communication Research*, 33(2), 152–177.

Gibbs, N. (2010, April 22). The pill at 50: Sex, freedom and paradox. *Time Magazine*. Retrieved September 6, 2010, from http://www.time.com/time/health/article/0,8599,1983712,00.html.

Gibson, B. (2010). Care of the child with the desire to change genders—female to male transition. *Pediatric Nursing*, 36(2), 112–119.

Gierisch, J., Coeytaux, R., Urrutia, R., Havrilesky, L., Moorman, P., Lowery, W., Dinan, M., et al. (2013). Oral contraceptive use and risk of breast, cervical, colorectal, and endometrial cancers: A systematic review. *Cancer Epidemiology, Biomarkers & Prevention*, 22(11), 1931–1943.

Gil, E., & Johnson, T. (1993). *Sexualized children: Assessment and treatment of sexualized children and children who molest*. Rockville, MD: Launch Press.

Gill, S. (2009). Honour killings and the quest for justice in black and minority ethnic communities and in the UK. United Nations Division for the Advancement of Women, Expert Group Meeting on good practices in legislation to address harmful practices against women. Retrieved March 30, 2011, from http://www.un.org/womenwatch/daw/egm/vaw_legislation_2009/Expert%20Paper%20EGMGPLHP%20_Aisha%20Gill%20revised_.pdf.

Gilleard, C., & Higgs, P. (2000). *Cultures of ageing: Self, citizen and the body*. Upper Saddle River, NJ: Prentice Hall Publishers.

Gillison, M., Chaturvedi, A., Lowy, D. (2008). HPV prophylactic vaccines and the potential prevention of noncervical cancers in both men and women. *Cancer, 113*(10 suppl.), 3036–3046.

Gilmore, A. K., Schacht, R. L., George, W. H., Otto, J. M., Davis, K. C., Heiman, J. R., Norris, J., & Kajumulo, K. F. (2010). Assessing women's sexual arousal in the context of sexual assault history and acute alcohol intoxication. *Journal of Sexual Medicine, 7*(6), 2112–2119.

Gilmore, D. D. (1990). *Manhood in the making: Cultural concepts of masculinity.* New Haven, CT: Yale University Press.

Giltay, J. C., & Maiburg, M. C. (2010). Klinefelter syndrome: Clinical and molecular aspects. *Expert Review of Molecular Diagnostics, 10*(6), 765–776.

Ginsberg, T. B., Pomerantz, S. C., & Kramer-Feeley, V. (2005). Sexuality in older adults: Behaviours and preferences. *Age and Ageing, 34*, 475–480.

Ginty, M. M. (2005). New pills launch debate over menstruation. Retrieved March 19, 2005, from http://www.womensenews.org/article .cfm/dyn/aid/1879/context/archive.

Giordano, L. (2015). Do you know what's in your tampons and pads? Congress is considering letting us know. *The Huffington Post.* Retrieved January 20, 2017, from http:// www.huffingtonpost.com/lorraine-giordano /do-you-know-whats-in-your_1_b_6550408 .html.

Giotakos, O., Markianos, M., & Vaidakis, N. (2005). Aggression, impulsivity, and plasma sex hormone levels in a group of rapists, in relation to their history of childhood attention-deficit/hyperactivity disorder symptoms. *Journal of Forensic Psychiatry & Psychology, 16*(2), 423–433.

Giraldi, A., & Kristensen, E. (2010). Sexual dysfunction in women with diabetes mellitus. *Journal of Sex Research, 47*(2), 199–211.

Girard, L., Doyle, O., & Tremblay, R. (2017). Breastfeeding, cognitive and noncognitive development in early childhood: A population study. *Pediatrics, 139*(4). Retrieved April 2, 2017, from http://pediatrics .aappublications.org/content/pediatrics /early/2017/03/23/peds.2016-1848.full.pdf.

Girsh, E., Katz, N., Genkin, L., Girtler, O., Bocker, J., Bezdin, S., & Barr, I. (2008). Male age influences oocyte-donor program results. *Journal of Assisted Reproductive Genetics, 25*(4), 137–143.

Girshick, L. B. (1999). *No safe haven: Stories of women in prison.* Lebanon, NH: University Press of New England.

Gisslén, M., Svedhem, V., Lindborg, L., Flamholc, L., Norrgren, H., Wendahl, S., Axwlsson, M., & Sönnerborg, A. (2016). Sweden, the first country to achieve the Joint United Nations Programme on HIV/AIDS (UNAIDS)/World Health Organization (WHO) 90-90-90 continuum of HIV care targets. *HIV Medicine, 18*(4), 305–307.

Gizzo, S., Bertocco., A., Saccardi, C., DiGangi, S., Litta, P., D'antona, D., & Nardelli, G. (2014, March 28). Female sterilization: Update on clinical efficacy, side effects and contraindications. *Minimally Invasive Therapy & Allied Technologies.* Retrieved May 26, 2014, from http://www.ncbi.nlm.nih .gov/pubmed/24678788.

Glasier, A., Anakwe, R., Everington, D., Martin, C., Van Der Spuy, Z., Cheng, L., Ho., P., & Anderson, R. (2000). Would women trust their partners to use a male pill? *Human Reproduction, 15*(3), 646–649.

Glass, J., Simon, R., & Andersson, M. (2016). Parenthood and happiness: Effects of work-family reconciliation policies in 22 OECD countries. *American Journal of Sociology, 122*(3), 886–929.

Glasser, M., Kolvin, I., Campbell, D., Glasser, A., Leitch, I., & Farrelly, S. (2001). Cycle of child sexual abuse: Links between being a victim and becoming a perpetrator. *British Journal of Psychiatry, 179*, 482–494.

Gleicher, N., Weghofer, A., & Barad, D. (2008). Preimplantation genetic screening: "Established" and ready for prime time? *Fertility and Sterility, 89*, 780–788.

Glenn, C. L., Spieldenner, A. R. (2013). An intersectional analysis of television narrative of African American women with African American men on "the Down Low," *Sexuality & Culture, 17*(3), 401–416.

Glenn, N., & Marquardt, E. (2001). Hooking up, hanging out and hoping for Mr. Right: College women on mating and dating today. Retrieved October 19, 2005, from http://www.americanvalues.org/Hooking _Up.pdf.

Glenn, S., & Byers, E. (2009). The roles of situational factors, attributions, and guilt in the well-being of women who have experienced sexual coercion. *Canadian Journal of Human Sexuality, 18*(4), 201–220.

Glenwright, M., & Pexman, P. M. (2010). Development of children's ability to distinguish sarcasm and verbal irony. *Journal of Child Language, 37*(2), 429–451.

Glynn, S. (2016, December 19). Breadwinning mothers are increasingly the U.S. norm. *Center for American Progress.* Retrieved August 23, 2017, from https://www.americanprogress .org/issues/women/reports/2016/12/19/295203 /breadwinning-mothers-are-increasingly-the -u-s-norm/.

Godeau, E., Gabhainn, S., Vignes, C., Ross, J., Boyce, W., & Todd, J. (2008). Contraceptive use by 15-year-old students at their last sexual intercourse. *Archives of Pediatric and Adolescent Medicine, 162*(1), 66–73.

Godfrey, K., Robinson, S., Barker, D. J., Osmond, C., & Cox, V. (1996). Maternal nutrition in early and late pregnancy in relation to placental and fetal growth. *British Medical Journal, 312*(7028), 410–414.

Goffman, E. (1976). *Gender advertisements.* New York: Harper Colophon Books.

Goktas, S., Gun, I., Yildiz, T., Sakar, M., & Caglayan, S. (2015). The effect of total hysterectomy on sexual function and depression. *Pakistan Journal of Medical Sciences, 31*(3), 700–705.

Gokyildiz, S., & Beji, N. K. (2005). The effects of pregnancy on sexual life. *Journal of Sex and Marital Therapy, 31*(3), 201–215.

Gold, E., Bair, Y., Block, G., Greendale, G., Harlow, S., Johnson, S., Kravitz, H., Rasor, M., Siddiqui, A., Sternfeld, B., Utts, J., & Zhang, G. (2007). Diet and lifestyle factors associated with PMS in a racially diverse community sample. *Journal of Women's Health, 16*(6), 934.

Gold, J. C. (2004). Kiss of the yogini: "Tantric sex" in its South Asian contexts. *Journal of Religion, 84*(2), 334–336.

Gold, R. (2009). All that's old is new again: The long campaign to persuade women to forego abortion. *Guttmacher Policy Review, 12*(2). Retrieved March 17, 2011, from http://www .guttmacher.org/pubs/gpr/12/2/gpr120219 .html.

Gold, R. B. (2003, March). Lessons from before Roe: Will past be prologue? Retrieved September 3, 2005, from http://www.agi -usa.org/pubs/ib_5-03.html.

Gold, S. (2015). Why thousands of women are having their breast implant removed. *Health.* Retrieved January 20, 2017, from http://www .health.com/health/article/0,,20959083,00.html.

Goldbach, J., & Gibbs, J. (2015). Strategies employed by sexual minority adolescents to cope with minority stress. *Psychology of Sexual Orientation and Gender Diversity, 2*(3), 297–306.

Goldberg, A., Smith, J., & Kashy, D. (2010). Preadoptive factors predicting lesbian, gay, and heterosexual couples' relationship quality across the transition to adoptive parenthood. *Journal of Family Psychology, 24*(3), 221–232.

Golden, G. H. (2001). Dyadic-dystonic compelling eroticism: Can these relationships be saved? *Journal of Sex Education & Therapy, 26*(1), 50.

Golden, R., Furman, W., & Collibee, C. (2016). The risks and rewards of sexual debut. *Developmental Psychology, 52*(11), 1913–1925.

Goldenberg, T. (2016). "Struggling to be the alpha": Sources of tension and intimate partner violence in same-sex relationships between men. *Culture, Health & Sexuality, 18*(8), 875–889.

Goldman, A. (2016, July 16). FBI has found no evidence that Orlando shooter targeted Pulse because it was gay club. *Washington Post.*

Retrieved March 24, 2017, from https://www.washingtonpost.com/world/national-security/no-evidence-so-far-to-suggest-orlando-shooter-targeted-club-because-it-was-gay/2016/07/14/a7528674-4907-11e6-acbc-4d4870a079da_story.html?utm_term=.770896af7bc0.

Goldman, R. (1999). The psychological impact of circumcision. *British Journal of Urology International, 83*, 93–102.

Goldman-Mellor, S., Brydon, L., & Steptoe, A. (2010). Psychological distress and circulating inflammatory markers in healthy young adults. *Psychological Medicine, 40*, 2079–2087.

Goldstein, A. T., & Burrows, L. (2008). Vulvodynia. *Journal of Sexual Medicine, 5*, 5–15.

Goldstein, A., Pukall, C., Brown, C., Bergeron, S., Stein, A., & Kellogg-Spadt, S. (2016). Vulvodynia: Assessment and treatment. *Journal of Sexual Medicine, 13*(4), 572–590.

Goleman, D. (1992, April 14). Therapies offer hope for sexual offenders. *The New York Times*, pp. C1, C11.

Gollapalli, V., Liao, J., Dudakovic, A., Sugg, S., Scott-Conner, C., & Weigel, R. (2010). Risk factors for development and recurrence of primary breast abscesses. *Journal of the American College of Surgeons, 211*(1), 41–48.

Golombok, S., Mellish, L., Jennings, S., Casey, P., Tasker, F., & Lamb, M. (2014). Adoptive gay father families: Parent-child relationships and children's psychological adjustment. *Child Development, 85*(2), 456–468.

Gómez, A. (2011). Testing the cycle of violence hypothesis: Child abuse and adolescent dating violence as predictors of intimate partner violence in young adulthood. *Youth and Society, 43*(1), 171–192.

Gomez, G., Kamb, M., Newman, L., Mark, J., Broutet, N., & Hawkes, S. (2013). Untreated maternal syphilis and adverse outcomes of pregnancy: A systematic review and meta-analysis. *Bulletin of the World Health Organization, 91*(3), 217–226.

Gonzaga, G., Haselton, M., Smurda, J., Davies, M., & Poore, J. (2008). Love, desire, and the suppression of thoughts of romantic alternatives. *Evolution and Human Behavior, 29*, 119–126.

Gonzalez, J., Connell, N., Businelle, M., & Jennings, W., & Chartier, K. (2014). Characteristics of adults involved in alcohol-related intimate partner violence: Results from a nationally representative sample. *BMC Public Health, 14*, 466. Retrieved August 27, 2014, from http://www.biomedcentral.com/1471-2458/14/466.

González, M., Viáfara, G., Caba, F., Molina, T., & Ortiz, C. (2006). Libido and orgasm in middle-aged women. *Maturitas, 53*, 1–10.

González, R., & Ludwikowski, B. (2016). Should CAH in females be classified as DSD? *Frontiers in Pediatrics, 13*(4). Retrieved January 17, 2017, from http://journal.frontiersin.org/article/10.3389/fped.2016.00048/full.

Goode, E. (1994). *Deviant behavior*. Englewood Cliffs, NJ: Prentice Hall.

Goodman, A. (1993). Diagnosis and treatment of sexual addiction. *Journal of Sex and Marital Therapy, 19*(3), 225–251.

Goodman, M. P. (2009). Female cosmetic genital surgery. *Obstetrics and Gynecology, 113*(1), 154–159.

Goodman, M. P., Placik, O., Benson, R., Miklos, J., Moore, R., Jason, R., Matlock, D., Simopoulos, A., Stern, B., Stanton, R., et al. (2010). A large multicenter outcome study of female genital plastic surgery. *Journal of Sexual Medicine, 7*(4 Pt 1), 1565–1577.

Goodwin, J. (2007, June). Kill yourself or your family will kill you. *Marie Claire*, 155–157.

Goodwin, P. Y., Mosher, W. D., & Chandra, A. (2010). Marriage and cohabitation in the United States: A statistical portrait based on Cycle 6 (2002) of the National Survey of Family Growth. National Center for Health Statistics. DHHS Publication No. 2010–1980. *Vital Health Statistics, 23*(28), 1–45.

Goodwin, P., Mosher, W., & Chandra, A. (2010). Marriage and cohabitation in the United States: A statistical portrait based on Cycle 6 (2002) of the National Survey of Family Growth. *National Center for Health Statistics, Vital Health Statistics, 23*(28).

Gooren, L. (2006). The biology of human psychosexual differentiation. *Hormones & Behavior, 50*, 589–601.

Goossens, G., Kadji, C., & Delvenne, V. (2015). Teenage pregnancy: A psychopathological risk for mothers and babies. *Psychiatria Danubina, 27*(Suppl. 1), s499–s503.

Gordon, A. M., & Chen, S. (2016). Do you get where I'm coming from?: Perceived understanding buffers against the negative impact of conflict on relationship satisfaction. *Journal of Personality and Social Psychology, 110*(2), 239–260.

Gordon, B. N., & Schroeder, C. S. (1995). *Sexuality: A developmental approach to problems*. Chapel Hill, NC: Clinical Child Psychology Library.

Gordon, H. (2008). The treatment of paraphilias: A historical perspective. *Criminal Behaviour and Mental Health, 18*, 79–87.

Gordon, K., Baucom, D., Snyder, D. (2005). Treating couples recovering from infidelity: An integrative approach. *JCLP/In Session, 61*(11), 1393–1405.

Gordon, L. (2010, March 15). Mixed-gender dorm rooms are gaining acceptance. *Los Angeles Times*. Retrieved November 6, 2010, from http://articles.latimes.com/2010/mar/15/local/la-me-dorm-gender15-2010mar15.

Gordon, S. (1986). What kids need to know. *Psychology Today, 20*, 22–26.

Gorman, B. (January 7, 2011). "'Jersey Shore' Season Premiere Draws 8.45 Million Viewers; 4.2 Adults 18–49 Rating." TVbytheNumbers.com. Retrieved January 7, 2011, from http://tvbythenumbers.zap2it.com/2011/01/07/jersey-shore-season-premiere-draws-8-4-million-sets-mtv-all-time-series-high/77688.

Gosselin, C. C. (1987). The sadomasochistic contract. In G. D. Wilson (Ed.), *Variant sexuality: Research and theory* (pp. 229–257). Baltimore: Johns Hopkins University Press.

Gottfried, J. S., Vaala, S. E., Bleakley, A., Hennessy, M., Jordan, A. (2013). Does the effect of exposure to TV sex on adolescent sexual behavior vary by genre? *Communication Research, 40*(1), 73–95.

Gottman, J. M. (1994). *Why marriages succeed or fail*. New York: Simon & Schuster.

Gottman, J. M. (1999). *The seven principles for making marriage work*. New York: Random House.

Gottman, J., & Silver, N. (2000). *The seven principles for making marriage work*. New York: Crown.

Gottman, J., Levenson, R., Gross, J., Frederickson, B., McCoy, K., Rosenthal, L., Ruef, A., & Yoshimoto, D. (2003). Correlates of gay and lesbian couples' relationship satisfaction and relationship dissolution. *Journal of Homosexuality, 45*(1), 23–43.

Gottman, J., Levenson, R., Swanson, C., Swanson, K., Tyson, R., & Yoshimoto, D. (2003). Observing gay, lesbian and heterosexual couples' relationships: Mathematical modeling of conflict interaction. *Journal of Homosexuality, 45*, 65–91.

Gottschall, J. A., & Gottschall, T. A. (2003). Are per-incident rape-pregnancy rates higher than per-incident consensual pregnancy rates? *Human Nature, 14*(1), 1–20.

Gould, S. J. (1981). *The mismeasure of man*. New York: Norton.

Gourley, C. (2007). *Flappers and the new American woman: Perceptions of women from 1918 through the 1920s*. Breckenridge, CO: Twenty-First Century Books.

Graham, J., & Barnow, Z. (2013). Stress and social support in gay, lesbian, and heterosexual couples: Direct effects and buffering models. *Journal of Family Psychology, 27*(4), 569–578.

Graugaard, C., Eplov, L. F., Giraldi, A., Mohl, B., Owens, A., Risor, H., & Winter, G. (2004). Denmark. In R. T. Francoeur & R. J. Noonan (Eds.), *The Continuum complete international encyclopedia of sexuality* (pp. 329–344). New York/London: Continuum International.

Gray, R. (2012). Stalking stats. Retrieved June 16, 2014, from http://www.campussafety magazine.com/article/Stalking-Stats.

Gray, S. (2017). Gender and racial/ethnic differences in the effects of child sexual abuse. *Dissertation Abstracts International: Section B: The Sciences and Engineering, 77*(10-B), #978-1339729213.

Green, E. R. (2017, May 18). Personal communication.

Green, E. R., & Maurer, L. (2015). *The teaching transgender toolkit: A facilitator's guide to increasing knowledge, decreasing prejudice, & building skills* (2nd ed.). Ithaca, NY: Planned Parenthood of the Southern Finger Lakes.

Green, R. (1987). *The "sissy boy syndrome" and the development of homosexuality.* New Haven, CT: Yale University Press.

Green, R. (1988). The immutability of (homo)-sexual orientation: Behavioral science implications for a constitutional (legal) analysis. *The Journal of Psychiatry and the Law, 16,* 537–575.

Green, R. J. (2008a). Gay and lesbian couples: Developing resilience in response to social injustice. In M. McGoldrick & K. Hardy (Eds.), *Revisioning family therapy: Race, culture, and gender in clinical practice* (2nd ed.). New York: Guilford Press.

Green, R. J. (2008b, January 11). *What straights can learn from gays about relationships and parenting.* San Francisco: Rockway Institute. Retrieved December 19, 2008, from http://www.newswise.com/articles/view/536799/.

Green, R. J., & Mitchell, V. (2002). Gay and lesbian couples in therapy: Homophobia, relational ambiguity, and social support. In A. S. Gurman & N. S. Jacobson (Eds.), *Clinical handbook of couple therapy* (3rd ed., pp. 546–568). New York: Guilford Press.

Green, R. J., Bettinger, M., & Zacks, E. (1996). Are lesbian couples fused and gay male couples disengaged? Questioning gender straightjackets. In J. Laird & R. J. Green (Eds.), *Lesbians and gays in couples and families: A handbook for therapists* (pp. 185–230). New York: Jossey-Bass.

Green, S., Haber, E., McCabe, R., & Soares, C. (2013). Cognitive-behavioral group treatment for menopausal symptoms. *Archives of Women's Mental Health, 16*(4), 325–332.

Green, W. (2013). The FDA, contraceptive marketing approval and products liability litigation: Depo-Provera and the risk of osteoporosis. *Food and Drug Law Journal, 68*(2), 115–135.

Greenberg, M., Cheng, Y., Hopkins, L., Stotland, N., Bryant, A., & Caughey, A. (2006). Are there ethnic differences in the length of labor? *American Journal of Obstetrics and Gynecology, 195,* 743–748.

Greenberg, M., Cheng, Y., Sullivan, M., Norton, L., & Caughey, A. (2007). Does length of labor vary by maternal age? *American Journal of Obstetrics and Gynecology, 197,* 428.

Greenblatt, A. (2014, May 27). California lawmakers vote to require condom use in porn films. National Public Radio. Retrieved June 17, 2014, from http://www.npr.org/blogs/thetwo-way/2014/05/27/316471404/california-lawmakers-vote-to-require-condom-use-in-porn-films.

Greenwald, E., & Leitenberg, H. (1989). Longterm effects of sexual experiences with siblings and nonsiblings during childhood. *Archives of Sexual Behavior, 18,* 289–400.

Greenwald, H., & McCorkle, R. (2008). Sexuality and sexual function in long-term survivors of cervical cancer. *Journal of Women's Health, 17,* 955–963.

Greer, J. B., Modugno, F., Allen, G. O., & Ness, R. B. (2005). Androgenic progestins in oral contraceptives and the risk of epithelial ovarian cancer. *Obstetrics and Gynecology, 105,* 731–740.

Gregson, S., Nyamukapa, C., Garnett, G., Wambe, M., Lewis, J., Mason, P., Chandiwana, S., & Anderson, R. (2005). HIV infection and reproductive health in teenage women orphaned and made vulnerable by AIDS in Zimbabwe. *AIDS Care, 17*(7), 785–794.

Greif, J., Pezzi, C., Klimberg, V., Bailey, L., & Zuraek, M. (2012). Gender differences in breast cancer. *Annals of Surgical Oncology, 19*(10), 3199–3204.

Grello, C., Welsh, D., & Harper, M. (2006). No strings attached: The nature of casual sex in college students. *Journal of Sex Research, 43*(3), 255–267.

Griffen, G. M. (1995). *Penis size and enlargement: Fact, fallacies and proven methods.* Lindenhurst, IL: Hourglass Books.

Griffin, J., Umstattd, M., & Usdan, S. (2010). Alcohol use and high-risk sexual behavior among collegiate women: A review of research on alcohol myopia theory. *Journal of American College Health, 58*(6), 523–533.

Griffin, S. A. (2006). A qualitative inquiry into how romantic love has been portrayed by contemporary media and researchers. *Dissertation Abstracts International Section A: Humanities and Social Sciences, 67,* 2272.

Griffith, R. S., Walsh, D. E., Myrmel, K. H., Thompson, R. W., & Behforooz, A. (1987). Success of L-lysine therapy in frequently recurrent herpes simplex infection. Treatment and prophylaxis. *Dermatologica, 175*(4), 183–190.

Griffiths, M. (2001). Sex on the Internet: Observations and implications for Internet sex addiction. *Journal of Sex Research, 38*(4), 333–343.

Griffiths, M. (2003). Internet abuse in the workplace and concern for employers and employment counselors. *Journal of Employment Counseling, 40*(2), 87–97.

Griffiths, M. D. (2000). Excessive Internet use: Implications for sexual behavior. *Cyberpsychology and Behavior, 3,* 537–552.

Griffitt, W., & Veitch, R. (1971). Hot and crowded: Influences of population density and temperature on interpersonal affective behavior. *Journal of Personality and Social Psychology, 17,* 92–98.

Griggs, B. (2014, February 13). Facebook goes beyond 'male' and 'female' with new gender options. *CNN TECH.* Retrieved February 17, 2014, from http://www.cnn.com/2014/02/13/tech/social-media/facebook-gender-custom.

Grimbizis, G. F., & Tarlatzis, B. C. (2010). The use of hormonal contraception and its protective role against endometrial and ovarian cancer. *Best Practice & Research: Clinical Obstetrics & Gynaecology, 24*(1), 29–38.

Grimbos T., Dawood K., Burriss R. P., Zucker K. J., & Puts D. A. (2010). Sexual orientation and the second to fourth finger length ratio: A meta-analysis in men and women. *Behavioral Neuroscience, 124*(2), 278–287.

Grindley, L. (2014). Italy: Town must recognize gay marriage performed in the U.S. *Advocate.* Retrieved April 12, 2014, from http://www.advocate.com/world/2014/04/10/italy-town-must-recognize-gay-marriage-performed-us.

Grob, C. S. (1985). Single case study: Female exhibitionism. *Journal of Nervous and Mental Disease, 173,* 253–256.

Groer, M. W. (2005). Differences between exclusive breastfeeders, formula-feeders, and controls: A study of stress, mood, and endocrine variables. *Biological Research for Nursing, 7*(2), 106–117.

Groom, K., McCowan, L., Mackay, L., Lee, A., Said, J., Kane, S., Walker, S., vanMens, T., Hannan, N., et al. (2017). Enoxaparin for the prevention of preeclampsia and intrauterine growth restriction in women with a history: A randomized trial. *American Journal of Obstetrics and Gynecology, 216*(2), 1–296.

Gross, J. (2007, October 9). Aging and gay, and facing prejudice in twilight. *New York Times.* Retrieved September 3, 2008, from http://www.nytimes.com/2007/10/09/us/09aged.html.

Grosskurth, P. (1980). *Havelock Ellis: A biography.* New York: Alfred A. Knopf.

Grossman, J., Charmaraman, L., & Erkut, S. (2016). Do as I say, not as I did: How parents talk with early adolescents about sex. *Journal of Family Issues, 37*(2), 177–197.

Groth, A. N. (1978). Patterns of sexual assault against children and adolescents. In A. W. Burgess, A. N. Groth, L. L. Holmstrom, & S. M. Sgroi (Eds.), *Sexual assault of children and adolescents.* Toronto: Lexington Books.

Groth, N., & Burgess, A. (1980). Male rape: Offenders and victims. *American Journal of Psychiatry, 137,* 806–810.

Grove, C., Gillespie, B., Royce, T., & Lever, J. (2011). Perceived consequences of casual online sexual activities on heterosexual relationships: A US online survey. *Archives of Sexual Behavior, 40*(2), 429–439.

Groysman, V. (2010). Vulvodynia: New concepts and review of the literature. *Dermatology Clinics, 28*(4), 681–696.

Gruber, A. J., & Pope, H. G. (2000). Psychiatric and medical effects of anabolic-androgenic steroid use in women. *Psychotherapy and Psychosomatics, 69*(1), 19–26.

Gruenbaum, E. (2006). Sexuality issues in the movement to abolish female genital cutting in Sudan. *Medical Anthropology Quarterly, 20*, 121.

Grunbaum, J. A., Kann, L., Kinchen, S. A., Williams, B., Ross, J. G., Lowry, R., & Kolbe, L. (2002). Youth risk behavior surveillance: United States, 2001. *Morbidity and Mortality Weekly Report, 51*(no. SS-4).

Grünebaum, A., McCullough, L., Arabin, B., Dudenhausen, J., Orosz, B., & Chervenak, F. (2016). Underlying causes of neonatal deaths in term singleton pregnancies: Home births versus hospital births in the United States. *Journal of Perinatal Medicine*. Retrieved March 31, 2017, from https://www.ncbi.nlm.nih.gov/pubmed/27754969.

Grynberg, M., Bidet, M., Benard, J., Poulain, M., Sonigo, C., et al. (2016). Fertility preservation in Turner syndrome. *Fertility and Sterility, 105*(1), 13–19.

Guadagno, R., & Sagarin, B. (2010). Sex differences in jealousy: An evolutionary perspective on online infidelity. *Journal of Applied Social Psychology, 40*(10), 2636–2655.

Gudjonsson, G. H. (1986). Sexual variations: Assessment and treatment in clinical practice. *Sexual and Marital Therapy, 1*, 191–214.

Gudykunst, W., Ting-Toomey, S., & Nishida, T. (1996). *Communication in personal relationships across cultures*. Thousand Oaks, CA: Sage Publications.

Guerrera, M., Volpe, S., & Mao, J. (2009). Therapeutic uses of magnesium. *American Family Physician, 80*(2), 157–162.

Guerrero, L. K., & Afifi, W. (1999). Toward a goal-oriented approach for understanding communicative responses to jealousy. *Western Journal of Communication, 63*(2), 216–248.

Guerrero, L., & Bachman, G. (2010). Forgiveness and forgiving communication in dating relationships: An expectancy-investment explanation. *Journal of Social and Personal Relationships, 27*(6), 801.

Guffey, M. E. (1999). *Business communication: Process & product* (3rd ed.). Belmont, CA: Wadsworth.

Guftason, P., & Fransson, U. (2015). Age differences between spouses: Sociodemographic variation and selection. *Marriage & Family Review, 51*(7), 610–632.

Guha, C., Shah, S. J., Ghosh, S. S., Lee, S. W., Roy-Chowdhury, N., & Roy-Chowdhury, J. (2003). Molecular therapies for viral hepatitis. *BioDrugs, 17*(2), 81–91.

Gumus, H., Akpinar, Z., & Yilmaz, H. (2014). Effects of multiple sclerosis on female sexuality. *Journal of Sexual Medicine, 11*(2), 481–486.

Gundersen, B. H., Melas, P. S., & Skar, J. E. (1981). Sexual behavior of preschool children: Teachers' observations. In L. L. Constantine & F. M. Martinson (Eds.), *Children and sex: New findings, new perspectives* (pp. 45–61). Boston: Little, Brown.

Gundersen, T., Jøgensen, N., Andersson, A., Bang, A., Nordkap, L., Skakkebaek, N., Priskorn, L., Juul, A., & Jensen, T. (2015). Association between use of marijuana and male reproductive hormones and semen quality: A study among 1,215 health young men. *American Journal of Epidemiology, 182*(6), 473–481.

Gunter, B., & McAleer, J. L. (1990). *Children and television: The one-eyed monster?* London: Routledge, Chapman, Hall.

Gunter, J. (2007). Vulvodynia: New thoughts on a devastating condition. *Obstetrics and Gynecological Survey, 62*, 812–819.

Guo, J., Huang, Y., Yang, L., Xie, Z., Song, S., Yin, J., Kuang, L., & Qin, W. (2015). Association between abortion and breast cancer: An updated systematic review and meta-analysis based on prospective studies. *Cancer Causes and Control, 26*(6), 811–819.

Guo, Z., Si, T., Yang, X., & Xu, Y. (2015). Oncological outcomes of cryosurgery as primary treatment in T3 prostate cancer. *BJU International, 116*(1), 79–84.

Gupta, J. K., & Nikodem, V. C. (2000). Woman's position during second stage of labour. *Cochrane Database of Systematic Reviews, 2*, CD002006.

Gupta, N., & Bowman, C. (2012). Managing sexually transmitted infections in pregnant women. *Women's Health, 8*(3), 313–321.

Gurrala, Z., Lang, L., Shepherd, D., Davidson, E., Harrison, M., McClure, S., Kaye, C., Toumazou, G., & Cooke, S. (2016). Novel pH sensing semiconductor for point-of-care detection of HIV-1 viremia. *Scientific Reports, 6*. Retrieved April 28, 2017, from https://www.nature.com/articles/srep36000.

Guth, M. (2015). Compounded testosterone troches to optimize health and the testosterone controversy. *International Journal of Pharmaceutical Compounding, 19*(3), 195–203.

Gutierrez-Morfin, N. (2016, September 16). "Gender-fluid" among recent additions to Oxford English dictionary. NBC News. Retrieved January 17, 2017, from http://www.nbcnews.com/feature/nbc-out/gender-fluid-among-recent-additions-oxford-english-dictionary-n649571.

Guttmacher Institute. (2013). *Contraceptive use in the U.S.* Retrieved May 24, 2014, from http://www.guttmacher.org/pubs/fb_contr_use.html.

Guzzo, K. (2009). Marital intentions and the stability of first cohabitations. *Journal of Family Issues, 30*(2), 179–205.

Haas, S., & Whitton, S. (2015). The significance of living together and importance of marriage in same-sex couples. *Journal of Homosexuality, 9*, 1241–1263.

Hader, S. L., Smith, D. K., Moore, J. S., & Holmberg, S. D. (2001). HIV infection in women in the U.S.: Status at the millennium. *Journal of the American Medical Association, 285*(9), 1186–1192.

Haeberle, E. J. (1982). The Jewish contribution to the development of sexology. *Journal of Sex Research, 18*, 305–323.

Hafner, L. (2015). Pathogenesis of Fallopian tube damage caused by chlamydia trachomatis infections. *Contraception, 92*(2), 108–115.

Hagen, J. (2013, October 16). Gender-neutral housing sparks campus debates. *Rolling Stone*. Retrieved February 13, 2014, from http://www.rollingstone.com/politics/news/gender-neutral-housing-sparks-campus-debates-20131016.

Hahm, H., Lee, J., Zerden, L., & Ozonoff, A. (2008). Longitudinal effects of perceived maternal approval on sexual behaviors of Asian and Pacific Islander (API) young adults. *Journal of Youth and Adolescence, 37*, 74–85.

Haines, E., Deaux, K., & Lofaro, N. (2016). The times they are a-changing … or are they not? A comparison of gender stereotypes, 1983–2914. *Psychology of Women Quarterly, 40*(3), 1–11.

Hald, G. M., & Malamuth, N. M. (2008). Self-perceived effects of pornography consumption. *Archives of Sexual Behavior, 37*(4), 614–626.

Hald, G., Malamuth, N., & Yuen, C. (2010). Pornography and attitudes supporting violence against women: Revisiting the relationship in nonexperimental studies. *Aggressive Behavior, 36*(1), 14–20.

Halim, M., Ruble, D., Tamis-LeMonda, C., Zosuls, K., Lurye, L., & Greulich, F. (2013). Pink frilly dresses and the avoidance of all things "girly": Children's appearance rigidity and cognitive theories of gender development. *Developmental Psychology*. Retrieved February 14, 2014, from http://www.csulb.edu/~mhalim/pub/Halim%20Ruble%20Tamis-LeMonda%20PFD%20DP%20(in%20press).pdf.

Hall, E. T. (1976). *Beyond culture*. New York: Doubleday.

Hall, E. T. (1990). *Understanding cultural differences, Germans, French and Americans*. Yarmouth, ME: Intercultural Press.

Hall, J., Baym, N. (2011). Calling and texting (too much): Mobile maintenance expectations, (over) dependence, entrapment, and friendship satisfaction. *New Media and Society*, *14*(2), 316–331.

Hall, M., & Hall, J. (2011). The long-term effects of childhood sexual abuse: Counseling implications. Retrieved from https://www.counseling.org/docs/disaster-and-trauma_sexual-abuse/long-term-effects-of-childhood-sexual-abuse.pdf.

Hall, P., & Schaeff, C. (2008). Sexual orientation and fluctuating symmetry in men and women. *Archives of Sexual Behavior*, *37*(1), 158–165.

Halldorsson, T. I., Strøm, M., Petersen, S. B., & Olsen, S. F. (2010). Intake of artificially sweetened soft drinks and risk of preterm delivery: A prospective cohort study in 59,334 Danish pregnant women. *American Journal of Clinical Nutrition*, *92*(3), 626–633.

Halpern-Felsher, B., Kropp, R., Boyer, C., Tschann, J., & Ellen, J. (2004). Adolescents' self-efficacy to communicate about sex: Its role in condom attitudes, commitment, and use. *Adolescence*, *39*(155), 443–457.

Halpern, C., Joyner, K., Udry, R., & Suchindran, C. (2000). Smart teens don't have sex (or kiss much either). *Journal of Adolescent Health*, *26*(3), 213–222.

Halsall, P. (1996). *Thomas Aquinas: Summa theologiae*. Retrieved April 10, 2008, from http://www.fordham.edu/halsall/source/aquinas1.html.

Hamachek, D. E. (1982). *Encounters with others: Interpersonal relationships and you.* New York: Holt, Rinehart & Winston.

Hambaugh, J. (2012). *Gossipmongers: Interest in gossip as a function of gender and mode of transmission.* Dissertation Abstracts International Section B: The Sciences and Engineering, 73(3-B), ISBN 978-1-267-05531-6.

Hamberg, K. (2000). Gender in the brain: A critical scrutiny of the biological gender differences. *Lakartidningen*, *97*, 5130–5132.

Hamburg, B. A. (1986). Subsets of adolescent mothers: Developmental, biomedical, and psychosocial issues. In J. B. Lancaster & B. A. Hamburg (Eds.), *School-age pregnancy and parenthood: Biosocial dimensions* (pp. 115–145). New York: Aldine DeGruyter.

Hamer, D. H., et al. (1993). A linkage between DNA markers on the X chromosome and male sexual orientation. *Science*, *261*, 321–327.

Hamilton, B., Martin, J., & Osterman, M. (2016). Births: Preliminary data for 2015. *National Vital Statistics Report, 65*(3).

Hamilton, B., Martin, J., & Osterman, M. (2016). Births: Preliminary data for 2015. *National Vital Statistics Reports, 65*(3). Retrieved February 11, 2017, from https://www.cdc.gov/nchs/data/nvsr/nvsr65/nvsr65_03.pdf.

Hamilton, B., Martin, J., Osterman, M., Curtin, S., & Mathews, T. (2015). Births: Final data for 2014. *National Vital Statistics Reports*, *64*(12). Retrieved March 6, 2017, from https://www.cdc.gov/nchs/data/nvsr/nvsr64/nvsr64_12.pdf.

Hamilton, B., Martin, J., & Ventura, S. (2013). Births: Preliminary data for 2012. *National Vital Statistics Reports*, *62*(3), National Center for Health Statistics, Hyattsville, MD. Retrieved August 19, 2014, from http://www.cdc.gov/nchs/data/nvsr/nvsr62/nvsr62_03.pdf.

Hamilton, E. (2017). Identity concerns among sexual offenders: The narrative call. *Practice Innovations, 2*(1), 13–20.

Hamilton, K., Chambers, S., Legg, M., Oliffe, J., & Cormie, P. (2015). Sexuality and exercise in men undergoing androgen deprivation therapy for prostate cancer. *Supportive Care in Cancer, 23*(1), 133–142.

Hamilton, L., & Armstrong, E. (2009). Gendered sexuality in young adulthood: Double binds and flawed options. *Gender and Society*, *23*(5), 589–616.

Hamilton, T. (2002). *Skin flutes and velvet gloves.* New York: St. Martin's Press.

Hammer, H., Finkelhor, D., & Sedlak, A. (2002). Runaway/thrownaway children: National estimates and characteristics. National incidence studies of missing, abducted, runaway, and thrownaway children. Retrieved June 28, 2011, from http://www.ncjrs.gov/html/ojjdp/nismart/04/.

Handler, A., Davis, F., Ferre, C., & Yeko, T. (1989). The relationship of smoking and ectopic pregnancy. *American Journal of Public Health*, *79*, 1239–1242.

Handwerk, B. (2005, February 25). 4-D ultrasound gives video view of fetuses in the womb. *National Geographic News*. Retrieved October 14, 2008, from http://news.nationalgeographic.com/news/pf/80752382.html.

Haney-Caron, E., & Heilbrun, K. (2014). Lesbian and gay parents and determination of child custody: The changing legal landscape and implications for policy and practice. *Psychology of Sexual Orientation and Gender Diversity, 1*(1), 19–29.

Hankins, G. (1995). *Operative obstetrics.* Appleton and Lange, Stamford, CT.

Hannaford, P. C., Iversen, L., Macfarlane, T. V., Elliott, A. M., Angus, V., & Lee, A. J. (2010). Mortality among contraceptive pill users: Cohort evidence from Royal College of General Practitioners' Oral Contraception Study. *British Medical Journal*, *340*, c927.

Hans, J., Gillen, M., & Akande, K. (2010). Sex redefined: The reclassification of oral-genital contact. *Perspectives on Sexual and Reproductive Health*, *42*(2). Retrieved February 6, 2011, from http://www.guttmacher.org/pubs/psrh/full/4207410.pdf.

Hansen, B. (1989). American physicians' earliest writings about homosexuals, 1880–1900. *Milbank Quarterly*, *67*(Suppl. 1), 92–108.

Harcourt, C., & Donovan, B. (2005). The many faces of sex work. *Sexually Transmitted Diseases*, *81*, 201–206.

Harden, K., Mendle, J., & Kretsch, N. (2012). Environmental and genetic pathways between early pubertal timing and dieting in adolescence: Distinguishing between objective and subjective timing. *Psychological Medicine*, *42*, 183–193.

Hardt, J., Sidor, A., Nickel, R., Kappis, B., Petrak, P., & Egle, U. T. (2008). Childhood adversities and suicide attempts: A retrospective study. *Journal of Family Violence*, *23*, 713–719.

Hardy, S., & Raffaelli, M. (2003). Adolescent religiosity and sexuality: An investigation of reciprocal influences. *Journal of Adolescence*, *26*(6), 731–739.

Harkinson, J. (2016). "Game-changing" study links cellphone radiation to cancer. *Mother Jones*. Retrieved January 29, 2017, from http://www.motherjones.com/environment/2016/05/federal-study-links-cell-phone-radiation-cancer.

Harlow, B., Kunitz, C., Nguyen, R., Rydell, S., Turner, R., & MAcLehose, R. (2014). Prevalence of symptoms consistent with a diagnosis of vulvodynia: Population-based estimated from 2 geographic regions. *American Journal of Obstetrics and Gynecology*, *210*(1), 40, c1–8.

Harlow, H. F. (1959). Love in infant monkeys. *Scientific American*, *200*, 68–70.

Harmon, A. (2007, September 16). Cancer free at 33, but weighing a mastectomy. *New York Times*. Retrieved March 20, 2008, from http://www.nytimes.com/2007/09/16/health/16gene.html.

Harney, A. (2013, September 23). Wealthy Chinese seek U.S. surrogates for second child, green card. *Medscape*. Retrieved May 21, 2014, from http://www.medscape.com/viewarticle/811488?nlid=34463_2043&src=wnl_edit_medn_obgy&uac=149266AJ&spon=16.

Harrington, N., & Leitenberg, H. (1994). Relationship between alcohol consumption and victim behaviors immediately preceding sexual aggression by an acquaintance. *Violence and Victims*, *9*(4), 315–324.

Harris, L. (2012). Personality characteristics and attitudes towards infidelity in gay and lesbian individuals (Doctoral dissertation, Adelphi University). Available from UMI Dissertations Publishing (No. 3531144; ISBN 9781267721167).

Harris, L., & Josephs, L. (2010). *Personality characteristics and attitudes towards infidelity* in gay and lesbian individuals. Poster session presented at the Annual Conference of the New York State Psychological Association, Rochester, New York.

Harris, T. (2013). Female genital mutilation: A literature review. *Nursing Standard, 28*(1), 41–47.

Harrison, F. (2005). Iran's sex-change operations. *BBC News.* Retrieved May 25, 2008, from http://news.bbc.co.uk/2/hi/programmes/newsnight/4115535.stm.

Hart, A., Pinell-White, X., Egro, F., & Losken, A. (2015). The psychosexual impact of partial and total breast reconstruction: A prospective one-year longitudinal study. *Annals of Plastic Surgery, 75*(3), 281–286.

Hart, C. W. M., & Pilling, A. R. (1960). *The Tiwi of North Australia.* New York: Holt, Rinehart & Winston.

Hart, G. J., & Elford, J. (2010). Sexual risk behaviour of men who have sex with men: Emerging patterns and new challenges. *Current Opinions in Infectious Disease, 23*(1), 39–44.

Harte, C., & Meston, C. (2011). Recreational use of erectile dysfunction medications in undergraduate men in the U.S. *Archives of Sexual Behavior, 40*(3), 597–606.

Harvey, M., Bird, S., & Branch, M. (2004). A new look at an old method: The diaphragm. *Perspectives on Sexual and Reproductive Health, 35*(6), 270–273.

Harville, E., Taylor, C., Tesfai, H., Xiong, X., & Buekens, P. (2011). Experience of hurricane Katrina and reported intimate partner violence. *Journal of Interpersonal Violence, 26*(4), 833–845.

Haselton, M. G., Mortezaie, M., Pillsworth, E. G., Bleske-Recheck, A. E., & Frederick, D. A. (2007). Ovulation and human female ornamentation: Near ovulation, women dress to impress. *Hormones and Behavior, 51*, 40–45.

Hatano, Y., & Shimazaki, T. (2004). Japan. In R. T. Francoeur & R. J. Noonan (Eds.), *The Continuum International encyclopedia of sexuality* (pp. 636–678). New York/London: Continuum International.

Hatcher, R. (2004). Depo-Provera injections, implants, and progestin-only pills (minipills). In R. A. Hatcher et al. (Eds.), *Contraceptive technology* (18th Rev. ed., pp. 461–494). New York: Ardent Media.

Hatcher, R. A., Trussell, J., Nelson, A., Cates, W., Kowal, D., & Policar M. (2011). *Contraceptive technology* (20th ed.). New York: Ardent Media.

Hatcher, R. A., Trussell, J., Nelson, A., Cates, W., Steward, F., & Kowal, D. (2007). *Contraceptive technology* (19th ed.). New York: Ardent Media.

Hatemi, P., Crabtree, C., & McDermott, R. (2017). The relationship between sexual preferences and political orientations. Do positions in the bedroom affect positions in the ballot box? *Personality and Individual Differences, 105*(15), 318–325.

Hatfield, E. (1988). Passionate and companionate love. In R. J. Sternberg & R. J. Barnes (Eds.), *Psychology of love* (pp. 191–217). New Haven, CT: Yale University Press.

Hatfield, E., & Sprecher, S. (1986). Measuring passionate love in intimate relationships. *Journal of Adolescence, 9*(4), 383–410.

Hatfield, E., Mo, Y., & Rapson, R. (2015). Love, sex, and marriage across cultures. In L. A. Jensen (Ed.), *Oxford Handbook of Human Development and Culture* (pp. 570–585). New York: Oxford University Press.

Hatzenbuehler, M., Bellatorre, A., Lee, Y., Finch, B. Muennig, P., & Fiscella, K. (2014). Structural stigma and all-cause mortality in sexual minority populations. *Social Science & Medicine, 103*(33), 33–41.

Havrilesky, L., Gierisch, J., Moorman, P., Coeytaux, R., Peragallo-Urrutia, R., Lowery, W., Dinan, M., McBroom, A., Wing, L., et al. (2013). *Oral contraceptive use for the primary prevention of ovarian cancer.* Evidence Report/Technology Assessment No. 212 (AHRQ Publication No. 13-E002-EF). Rockville, MD: Agency for Healthcare Research and Quality.

Hawkins, N. A., Cooper, C. P., Saraiya, M., Gelb, C. A., & Polonec, L. (2011). Why the Pap test? Awareness and use of the Pap test among women in the United States. *Journal of Women's Health, 20*, 511–515.

Hawley, A., Mahoney, A., Pargament, K., & Gordon, A. (2015). Sexuality and spirituality as predictors of distress over a romantic breakup: Mediated and moderated pathways. *Spirituality in Clinical Practice, 2*(2), 145–159.

Haworth, A. (2013, October). Why have young people in Japan stopped having sex? The Guardian. Retrieved July 7, 2014, from http://www.theguardian.com/world/2013/oct/20/young-people-japan-stopped-having-sex.

Hayashi, A. (2004, August 20). Japanese women shun the use of the pill. *CBS News.* Retrieved October 28, 2008, from http://www.cbsnews.com/stories/2004/08/20/health/main637523.shtml.

Hayashi, Y., & Kohri, K. (2013). Circumcision related to urinary tract infections, sexually transmitted infections, HIV, and penile and cervical cancer. *International Journal of Urology, 20*(8), 769–775.

Hazelwood, R., & Burgess, A. (1987). *Practical aspects of rape investigation: A multidisciplinary approach.* New York: Elsevier.

Hazen, C., & Shaver, P. (1987a). Romantic love conceptualized as an attachment process. *Journal of Personality and Social Psychology, 52*(3), 511–524.

Hazen, C., & Shaver, P. (1987b). Attachment as an organization framework for research on close relationships. *Psychological Inquiry, 5*(1), 1–22.

Hebert, K., Lopez, B., Castellanos, J., Palacio, A., Tamariz, L., & Arcement, L. (2008). The prevalence of erectile dysfunction in heart failure patients by race and ethnicity. *International Journal of Impotence Research, 20*(5), 507–511.

Hebert, L., Lilleston, P., Jennings, J., & Sherman, S. (2015). Individual, partner, and partnership level correlates of anal sex among youth in Baltimore City. *Archives of Sexual Behavior, 44*(3), 619–629.

Heck, N., Flentje, A., & Cochran, B. (2013). Offsetting risks: High school gay-straight alliances and lesbian, bisexual, and transgender youth. *Psychology of Sexual Orientation and Gender Diversity, 1*(S), 81–90.

Heczko, P., Tomusiak, A., Adamski, P., Jakimiuk, A., Stafański, G., et al. (2015). Supplementation of standard antibiotic therapy with oral probiotics for bacterial vaginosis and aerobic vaginitis. *BMC Women's Health, 15*, 115.

Hefner, V. (2016). Tuning into fantasy: Motivations to view wedding television and associated romantic beliefs. *Psychology of Popular Media Culture, 5*(4), 307–323.

Heger, A., Ticson, L., Velasquez, O., & Bernier, R. (2002). Children referred for possible sexual abuse: Medical findings in 2384 children. *Child Abuse & Neglect, 26*(6–7), 645–659.

Hegna, K., & Rossow, I. (2007). What's love got to do with it? Substance use and social integration for young people categorized by same-sex experience and attractions. *Journal of Drug Issues, 37*, 229–256.

Heidari-Vala, H., Ebrahimi, H., Sadeghi, M., Akhondi, M., Ghaffari, N., & Heidari, M. (2013). Evaluation of an aqueous-ethanolic extract from rosmarinus officinalis for its activity on the hormonal and cellular function of testes in adult male rats. *Iranian Journal of Pharmaceutical Research, 12*(2), 445–451.

Heidari, M., Nejadi, J., Ghate, A., Delfan, B., & Iran-Pour, E. (2010). Evaluation of intralesional inject of verapamil in treatment of Peyronie's disease. *Journal of the Pakistan Urological Association, 60*(4), 291–293.

Heiman, J. (2002). Sexual dysfunction: Overview of prevalence, etiological factors, and treatments. *Journal of Sex Research, 39*(1), 73–79.

Heiman, J., & Meston, M. (1997). Empirically validated treatment for sexual dysfunction. *Annual Review of Sex Research, 8*, 148–194.

Heinzmann, D. (2008, May 6). Some men say using prostitutes is an addiction: 200 take part in a study about motivation. *Chicago Tribune.* Retrieved October 7, 2008, from http://libill.hartford.edu:2083/pqdweb?index=7&did=1473639221&SrchMode=1&sid=4&Fmt=3&VInst=PROD&VType=PQD&RQT=309&VName=PQD&TS=1223437846&clientId=3309.

Hellerstein, E., Olafson, L., Parker, H., & Offen, K. M. (1981). *Victorian women: A documentary account of women's lives in nineteenth-century England, France, and the United States.* Stanford, CA: Stanford University Press.

Hellmann, P., Christiansen, P., Johannes, T., Main, K., Duno, M., & Juul, A. (2012). Male patients with partial androgen insensitivity syndrome: A longitudinal follow-up of growth, reproductive hormones and the development of gynaecomastia. *Archives of Disease in Childhood, 97*(5), 403–409.

Helmore, K. (2010, July 1). Empowering women to protect themselves: Promoting the female condom in Zimbabwe. United Nations Population Fund. Retrieved March 15, 2011, from http://www.unfpa.org/public/News/pid/3913.

Hembree, W. C., Cohen-Kettenis, P., Delemare-van de Waal, H. A., et al. (2009). Endocrine treatment of transsexual persons: An Endocrine Society clinical practice guideline. *Journal of Clinical Endocrinology and Metabolism, 94*(9), 3132–3154.

Hemphill, E. (1991). *Brother to brother: New writings by black gay men.* Boston: Alyson.

Hemstrom, O. (1996). Is marriage dissolution linked to differences in mortality risks for men and women? *Journal of Marriage and the Family, 58,* 366–378.

Henderson, A., Lehavot, K., & Simoni, J. (2009). Ecological models of sexual satisfaction among lesbian/bisexual and heterosexual women. *Archives of Sexual Behavior, 38*(1), 50–66.

Henderson, H. (2009). Why lesbians should be encouraged to have regular cervical screening. *Journal of Family Planning and Reproductive Health Care, 35*(1), 49–52.

Henderson, L. (1991). Lesbian pornography: Cultural transgression and sexual demystification. *Women and Language, 14,* 3–12.

Henderson, S., Taylor, R., & Thompson, R. (2002). In touch: Young people, communication, and technologies. *Information, Communication, and Society, 5*(4), 494–512.

Hendrick, C., & Hendrick, S. S. (1989). Research on love: Does it measure up? *Journal of Personality & Social Psychology, 56*(5), 784–794.

Hendrick, C., & Hendrick, S. S. (2000). *Close relationships: A sourcebook.* Thousand Oaks, CA: Sage.

Henke, G. (2010, November 7). Personal communication.

Henke, G. (2011, May 11). Personal communication.

Henline, B., Lamke, L., & Howard, M. (2007). Exploring perceptions of online infidelity. *Personal Relationships, 14,* 113–238.

Hensel, D. J., Fortenberry, J. D., Harezlak, J., Anderson, J. G., & Orr, D. P. (2004). A daily diary analysis of vaginal bleeding and coitus among adolescent women. *Journal of Adolescent Health, 34*(5), 392–394.

Hensley, C., Koscheski, M., & Tewksbury, R. (2005). Examining the characteristics of male sexual assault targets in a Southern maximum-security prison. *Journal of Interpersonal Violence, 20*(6), 667–679.

Hensley, L. G. (2002). Treatment of survivors of rape: Issues and interventions. *Journal of Mental Health Counseling, 24*(4), 331–348.

Henslin, J. M. (2005). The sociology of human sexuality. In J. M. Henslin, *Sociology: A down-to-earth approach.* Online chapter retrieved November 30, 2005, from http://www.ablongman.com/html/henslintour/henslinchapter/ahead3.html.

Herbenick, C., Reece, M., Sanders, S., Dodge, B., Ghassemi, A., & Fortenberry, J. (2009). Prevalence and characteristics of vibrator use by women in the US.: Results from a nationally representative study. *Journal of Sexual Medicine, 6,* 1857–1866.

Herbenick, D. (2008, July 7). Can having sex help to alleviate menstrual cramps? *Kinsey Confidential.* Retrieved April 20, 2014, from http://kinseyconfidential.org/sex-alleviate-menstrual-cramps.

Herbenick, D., Reece, M., Schick, V., Sanders, S., Dodge, B., & Fortenberry, D. (2010a). Sexual behavior in the United States: Results from a National Probability Sample of men and women ages 14–94. *Journal of Sexual Medicine, 7*(Suppl. 5), 255–265.

Herbruck, L. F. (2008). The impact of childbirth on the pelvic floor. *Urological Nursing, 28,* 173–184.

Herbst, J., Jacobs, E., Finlayson, T., McKleroy, V., Neumann, M., & Crepaz, N. (2008). Estimating HIV prevalence and risk behaviors of transgender persons in the U.S.: A systematic review. *AIDS Behavior, 12,* 1–17.

Herbstrith, J., Tobin, R., Hesson-McInnis, M., & Schneider, W. (2013). Preservice teacher attitudes toward gay and lesbian parents. *School Psychology Quarterly, 28*(3), 183–194.

Herdt, G. (1981). *Guardians of the flutes: Idioms of masculinity.* New York: McGraw-Hill.

Herdt, G. (1988). Cross-cultural forms of homosexuality and the concept "gay." *Psychiatric Annals, 18,* 37–39.

Herdt, G. (1989). Introduction: Gay and lesbian youth, emergent identities, and cultural scenes at home and abroad. In G. Herdt (Ed.), *Gay and lesbian youth* (pp. 1–42). New York: Harrington Park Press.

Herdt, G., & Stoller, R. (1990). *Intimate communications: Erotics and the study of culture.* New York: Columbia University Press.

Herek, G. (1993). Documenting prejudice against lesbians and gay men on campus: The Yale sexual orientation survey. *Journal of Homosexuality, 25*(4), 15–30.

Herek, G. (2002). Heterosexuals' attitudes toward bisexual men and women in the United States. *Journal of Sex Research, 39*(4), 264–274.

Herek, G. (2006). Legal recognition of same-sex relationship in the United States: A social science perspective. *American Psychologist, 61,* 606–621.

Herek, G. M. (1984). Beyond "homophobia": A social psychological perspective on attitudes toward lesbians and gay men. In J. P. DeCecco (Ed.), *Homophobia: An overview* (pp. 1–21). New York: The Haworth Press.

Herek, G., Cogan, J. C., & Gillis, J. (2002). Victim experiences in hate crimes based on sexual orientation. *Journal of Social Issues, 58*(2), 319–339.

Herlihy, A., & McLachlan, R. (2015). Screening for Klinefelter syndrome. *Current Opinion in Endocrinology, Diabetes, and Obesity, 22*(3), 224–229.

Herman, J. L. (1981). *Father-daughter incest.* Cambridge, MA: Harvard University Press.

Herman, J., & Schatzow, E. (1987). Recovery and verification of memories of childhood sexual trauma. *Psychoanalytic Psychology, 4,* 1–14.

Hernàndez, A. (2013, July 7). Panamanians prefer texting to talking. *La Prensa.* Retrieved February 3, 2014, from http://www.prensa.com/impreso/panorama/panamenos-prefieren-enviar-mensajes-texto-que-hablar/190021.

Hernandez, B., Goodman, M., Unger, E., Steinau, M., Powers, A., Lynch, C., et al. (2014). Human papillomavirus genotype prevalence in invasive penile cancers from registry-based U.S. population. *Frontiers in Oncology, 4*(9), 9.

Heron, J., McGuinness, M., Blackmore, E., Craddock, N., & Jones, I. (2008). Early postpartum symptoms in puerperal psychosis. *British Journal of Obstetrics and Gynecology, 115,* 348–353.

Herrick, A. L., Matthews, A. K., & Garofalo, R. (2010). Health risk behaviors in an urban sample of young women who have sex with women. *Journal of Lesbian Studies, 14*(1), 80–92.

Hersher, R. (2017, March 22). Breast implants linked to rate blood cancer in small proportion of women. National Public Radio. Retrieved May 22, 2017, from http://www.npr.org/sections/health-shots/2017/03/22/521081964/breast-implants-linked-to-rare-blood-cancer-in-small-proportion-of-women.

Herting, M., & Sowell, E. (2017). Puberty and structural brain development in humans. *Frontiers in Neuroendocrinology, 44*, 122–137.

Hertlein, K., & Piercy, F. (2012). Essential elements of Internet infidelity treatment. *Journal of Marital and Family Therapy, 38*(Suppl. 1), 257–270.

Herz, R. (2007). *The scent of desire: Discovering our enigmatic sense of smell.* New York: William Morrow Publishers.

Hetherington, E. (2003). Intimate pathways: Changing patterns in close personal relationships across time. *Family Relations, 52*, 318–331.

Hewlett, M. (2008, September 17). Getting help is hard for gay domestic violence victims. *McClatchy—Tribune Business News.* Retrieved October 5, 2008, from http://libill .hartford.edu:2083/pqdweb?index=2&did =1556431461&SrchMode=1&sid=1&Fmt=3& VInst=PROD&VType=PQD&RQT=309& VName=PQD&TS=1223252228&clientId=3309.

Heymann, J., Earle, A., Rajaraman, D., Miller, C., & Bogen, K. (2007). Extended family caring for children orphaned by AIDS: Balancing essential work and caregiving in a high HIV prevalence nation. *AIDS Care, 19*(3), 337–345.

Hicks, C. W., & Rome, E. S. (2010). Menstrual manipulation: Options for suppressing the cycle. *Cleveland Clinic Journal of Medicine, 77*(7), 445–453.

Hicks, T., & Leitenberg, H. (2001). Sexual fantasies about one's partner versus someone else: Gender differences in incidence and frequency. *Journal of Sex Research, 38*, 43–50.

Hickson, F. C. I., Davies, P. M., & Hunt, A. J. (1994). Gay men as victims of nonconsensual sex. *Archives of Sexual Behavior, 23*(3), 281–294.

Hiew, D., Halford, W., & Van De Vijver, F. (2016). Communication and relationship satisfaction in Chinese, Western, and Intercultural Chinese-Western couples. *Journal of Family Psychology, 30*(2), 193–202.

Hiew, D., Halford, W., Van de Vijver, F., & Liu, S. (2015). The Chinese-Western intercultural couple standards scale. *Psychological Assessment, 27*(3), 816–826.

Hill, B., Janssen, E., Kvam, P., Amick, E., & Sanders, S. (2014). The effect of condoms on penile vibrotactile sensitivity thresholds in young, heterosexual men. *Journal of Sexual Medicine, 11*(1), 102–106.

Hill, B., Sanders, S., & Reinisch, J. (2016). Variability in sex attitudes and sexual histories across age groups of bisexual women and men in the United States. *Journal of Bisexuality, 16*(1), 20–40.

Hill, B. F., & Jones, J. S. (1993). Venous air embolism following orogenital sex during pregnancy. *American Journal of Emergency Medicine, 11*, 155–157.

Hill, C., & Silva, E. (2005). *Drawing the line: Sexual harassment on campus.* Washington, DC: AAUW Educational Foundation.

Hill, S. (2007). Overestimation bias in mate competition. *Evolution and Human Behavior, 28*(2), 118–123.

Hill, S. A. (2002). Teaching and doing gender in African American families. *Sex Roles, 47*, 493–506.

Hillebrand, R. (2008). The Oneida community. Retrieved April 10, 2008, from http://www .nyhistory.com/central/oneida.htm.

Hinchley, G. (2007). Is infant male circumcision an abuse of the rights of the child? Yes. *British Medical Journal, 8, 335*(7631), 1180.

Hines, M., Brook, C., & Conway, G. (2004). Androgen and psychosexual development: Core gender identity, sexual orientation and recalled childhood gender role behavior in women and men with CAH. *Journal of Sex Research, 41*(1), 75–81.

Hinshelwood, M. (2002). Early and forced marriage: The most widespread form of sexual exploitation of girls? Retrieved August 27, 2003, from http://www.kit.nl/ils /exchange_content/html/forced_marriage _-_sexual_healt.asp.

Hipwell, A., Stepp, S., Chung, T., Durand, V., & Keenan, K. (2012). Growth in alcohol use as a developmental predictor of adolescent girls' sexual risk-taking. *Prevention Science, 13*(2), 118–128.

Hirayama, H., & Hirayama, K. (1986). The sexuality of Japanese Americans. Special issue: Human sexuality, ethnoculture, and social work. *Journal of Social Work and Human Sexuality, 4*(3), 81–98.

Hirshfeld-Cytron, J., & Winter, J. (2013). Laparoscopic tubal reanastomosis versus in vitro fertilization: Cost-based decision analysis. *American Journal of Obstetrics and Gynecology, 209*(1), 56–62.

Hirshkowitz, M., & Schmidt, M. H. (2005). Sleep-related erections: Clinical perspectives and neural mechanisms. *Sleep Medicine Reviews, 9*(4), 311–329.

Hirvikoski, T., Nordenström, A., Wedell, A., Ritzén, M., & Lajic, S. (2012). Prenatal dexamethasone treatment of children at risk for congenital adrenal hyperplasia: The Swedish experience and standpoint. *Journal of Clinical Endocrinology and Metabolism, 97*(6), 1881–1883.

Hisasue, S. (2016). The drug treatment of premature ejaculation. *Translational Andrology and Urology, 5*(4), 482–486.

Hisasue, S., Furuya, R., Itoh, N., Kobayashi, K., Furuya, S., & Tsukamoto, T. (2006). Ejaculatory disorder caused by alpha-1 adrenoceptor antagonists is not retrograde ejaculation but a loss of seminal emission. *International Journal of Urology, 13*(10), 1311–1316.

Hitsch, G., Hortacsu, A., & Ariely, D. (2010). What makes you click? Mate preferences in online dating. *Quantitative Marketing and Economics, 8*(4), 393.

Hitti, M. (2008, January 18). *FDA strengthens warning on blood clot risk for users of Ortho Evra birth control skin patch.* WebMD. Retrieved October 28, 2008, from http:// www.webmd.com/sex/birth-control /news/20080118/birth-control-patch -stronger-warning.

Hittner, J. (2016). Meta-analysis of the association between methamphetamine use and high-risk sexual behavior among heterosexuals. *Psychology of Addictive Behaviors, 30*(2), 147–157.

HIV among pregnant women, infants, and children. (2017). Fact sheet. Retrieved April 29, 2017, from https://www.cdc.gov/hiv/group /gender/pregnantwomen/index.html.

HIV among transgender people. (2017, April 21). Centers for Disease Control and Prevention. Retrieved April 26, 2017, from https://www .cdc.gov/hiv/group/gender/transgender /index.html.

HIV in the U.S. (2016). HIV in the U.S.: At a glance. Centers for Disease Control and Prevention. Retrieved April 26, 2017, from https://www.cdc.gov/hiv/statistics/overview /ataglance.html.

Ho, S., Cheong, A., Adgent, M., Veevers, J., Suen, A., Tam, N., Leung, Y., Jefferson, W., & Williams, C. (2016). Environmental factors, epigenetics, and developmental origin of reproductive disorders. *Reproductive Toxicology, 16*, 30268-4. Retrieved January 29, 2017, from https://www.ncbi.nlm.nih.gov /pubmed/27421580.

Ho, V. P., Lee, Y., Stein, S. L., & Temple, L. K. (2011). Sexual function after treatment for rectal cancer: A review. *Diseases of the Colon and Rectum, 54*(1), 113–125.

Hobbs, K., Symonds, T., Abraham, L., May, K., & Morris, M. (2008). Sexual dysfunction in partners of men with premature ejaculation. *International Journal of Impotence Research, 20*(5), 512–517.

Hobern, K. (2014). Religion in sexual health: A staff perspective. *Journal of Religion and Health, 53*(2), 461–468.

Hoburg, R., Konik, J., Williams, M., & Crawford, M. (2004). Bisexuality among self-identified heterosexual college students. *Journal of Bisexuality, 4*, 25–36.

Hockett, J., Smith, S., Klausing, C., & Saucier, D. (2016). Rape myth consistency and gender differences in perceiving rape victims: A meta-analysis. *Violence Against Women, 22*(2), 139–167.

Hodes-Wertz, B., Druckenmiller, S., Smith, M., & Noyes, N. (2013). What do reproductive-age women who undergo oocyte cryopreservation think about the process as a means to preserve fertility? *Fertility and Sterility, 100*(5), 1343–1349.

Hodge, D. R. (2008). Sexual trafficking in the U.S.: A domestic problem with transnational dimensions. *Social Work, 53*(2), 143–152.

Hoebel, E. A. (1954). *The law of primitive man.* Cambridge, MA: Harvard University Press.

Hoff, C., Beougher, S., Chakravarty, D., Darbes, L., & Neilands, T. (2010). Relationship characteristics and motivations behind agreements among gay male couples: Differences by agreement type and couple serostatus. *AIDS Care, 22*(7), 827–835.

Hoffman, M. C. (2008, July 23). Philippines in struggle against abortionist population control initiative. *LifeSite News.com.* Retrieved October 28, 2008, from http://www.lifesitenews.com/ldn/2008/jul/08072201.html.

Hoffstetter, S., Barr, S., LeFevre, C., Leong, F., & Leet, T. (2008). Self reported yeast symptoms compared with clinical wet mount analysis and vaginal yeast culture in a specialty clinic setting. *Journal of Reproductive Medicine, 53,* 402–406.

Hofman, B. (2005). "What is next?": Gay male students' significant experiences after coming-out while in college. *Dissertation Abstracts International Section A: Humanities & Social Sciences, 65*(8-A), #0419–4209.

Hogan, H. (2005). Title IX requires colleges & universities to eliminate the hostile environment caused by campus sexual assault. Retrieved October 25, 2005, from http://www.securityoncampus.org/victims/titleixsummary.html.

Holland, J., Ramasanoglu, C., & Sharpe, S. (2004). *The male in the head: Young people, heterosexuality and power.* London: Tufnell Press.

Hollander, D. (2001). Users give new synthetic and latex condoms similar ratings on most features. *Family Planning Perspectives, 33*(1), 45–48.

Holmberg, D., & Blair, K. (2009). Sexual desire, communication, satisfaction, and preferences of men and women in same-sex versus mixed-sex relationships. *Journal of Sex Research, 46*(1), 57–66.

Holmes, J. G., & Rempel, J. K. (1989). Trust in close relationships. In C. Hendrick (Ed.), *Close relationships* (Vol. 10, pp. 187–219). Newbury Park, CA: Sage.

Holmes, M. C. (2004). Reconsidering a "woman's issue:" Psychotherapy and one man's postabortion experiences. *American Journal of Psychotherapy, 58*(1), 103–115.

Holmes, R. (1991). *Sex crimes.* Newbury Park, CA: Sage.

Holmstrom, A. J. (2009). Sex and gender similarities and differences in communication values in same-sex and cross-sex friendships. *Communication Quarterly, 57*(2), 224–238.

Holt, H., & Tingen, J. (2016). Flibanserin (Addyi) for hypoactive sexual desire disorder in premenopausal women. *American Family Physician, 93*(10), 826–828.

Holway, G. (2015). Vaginal and oral sex initiation timing: A focus on gender and race/ethnicity. *International Journal of Sexual Health, 27*(3), 351–367.

Hook, E. B. (1981). Rate of chromosome abnormalities at different maternal ages. *Obstetrics and Gynecology, 58*(3), 282–285.

Hooker, E. (1957). The adjustment of the male overt homosexual. *Journal of Projective Techniques, 21,* 18–31.

Hooton, T. M. (2003). The current management strategies for community-acquired urinary tract infection. *Infectious Disease Clinics of North America, 17*(2), 303–332.

Hoover, K., Tao, G., & Kent, C. (2010). Trends in the diagnosis and treatment of ectopic pregnancy in the United States. *Obstetrics and Gynecology, 115*(3), 495–502.

Hope, M. E., Farmer, L., McAllister, K. F., & Cumming, G. P. (2010). Vaginismus in peri- and postmenopausal women: A pragmatic approach for general practitioners and gynaecologists. *Menopause International, 16*(2), 68–73.

Hopkins, T., Green, B., Carnes, P., & Campling, S. (2016). Varieties of intrusion: Exhibitionism and voyeurism. *Sexual Addiction & Compulsivity, 23*(1), 4033.

Horan, S. M. (2016). Further understanding sexual communication: Honesty, deception, safety, and risk. *Journal of Social and Personal Relationships, 33*(4), 449–468.

Horn, E., Turkheimer, E., & Strachan, E. (2015). Psychological distress, emotional stability, and emotion regulation moderate dynamics of herpes simplex virus type 2 recurrence. *Annals of Behavioral Medicine, 49*(2), 187–198.

Horn, M., & Geraci, S. (2013). Polycystic ovary syndrome in adolescents. *Southern Medical Journal, 106*(10), 570–576.

Horowitz, S. M., Weis, D. I., & Laflin, M. T. (2001). Differences between sexual orientation behavior groups and social background, quality of life, and health behaviors. *Journal of Sex Research, 38*(3), 205–219.

Horta, B., Loret de Mola, C., & Victoria, C. (2015). Breastfeeding and intelligence: A systematic review and meta-analysis. *Acta Paediatrica, 104*(467), 14–19.

Houser, M. L., Fleuriet, C., & Estrada, D. (2012). The cyber factor: An analysis of relational maintenance through the use of computer-mediated communication. *Communication Research Reports, 29*(1), 34–43.

Houston, E., & McKirnan, D. (2008). Intimate partner abuse among gay and bisexual men: Risk correlates and health outcomes. *Journal of Urban Health, 84,* 681–690.

Howard, L. M., Hoffbrand, S., Henshaw, C., Boath, L., & Bradley, E. (2005). Antidepressant prevention of postnatal depression. *The Cochrane Database of Systematic Reviews, 2,* art. no. CD004363.

Howe, N., Rinaldi, C., & Recchia, H. (2010). Patterns in mother-child internal state discourse across four contexts. *Merrill-Palmer Quarterly, 56*(1), 1–20.

Howell, E. A., Mora, P. A., Horowitz, C. R., & Leventhal, H. (2005). Racial and ethnic differences in factors associated with early postpartum depressive symptoms. *Obstetrics & Gynecology, 105*(6), 1442–1450.

Howlader N., Noone, A., Krapcho, M., Garshell, J., Neyman, N., Altekruse, S., Kosary, C., Yu, M., Ruhl, J., Tatalovich, Z., Cho, H., Mariotto, A., Lewis, D., Chen, H., Feuer, E., & Cronin, K. (2013). *SEER cancer statistics review, 1975–2010.* Bethesda, MD: National Cancer Institute. Retrieved from http://seer.cancer.gov/csr/1975_2010.

Howlett, K., Koetters, T., Edrington, J., West, C., Paul, S., Lee, K., Aouizerat, B. E., Wara, W., Swift, P., & Miaskowski, C. (2010). Changes in sexual function on mood and quality of life in patients undergoing radiation therapy for prostate cancer. *Oncology Nursing Forum 37*(1), E58–E66.

Hoxmeier, J., Flay, B., & Acock, A. (2015). When will students intervene? Differences in students' intent to intervene in a spectrum of sexual assault situations. *Violence and Gender, 2*(3), 179–184.

HPV and Oropharyngeal Cancer. (2017, January 3). Centers for Disease Control and Prevention Fact Sheet. Retrieved April 24, 2017, from https://www.cdc.gov/std/hpv/stdfact-hpvandoropharyngealcancer.htm.

HPV Vaccine Coverage. (2016). Infographic, Centers for Disease Control and Prevention. Retrieved April 26, 2017, from https://www.cdc.gov/hpv/infographics/vacc-coverage.html.

Hsi, R., Hotaling, J., Hartzier, A., Hold, S., & Walsh, T. (2013). Validity and reliability of a smartphone application for the assessment of penile deformity in Peyronie's disease. *Journal of Sexual Medicine, 10*(7), 1867–1873.

Hu, S., Wei, N., Wang, Q., Yan, L., Wei, E., Zhang, M., Hu, J., Huang, M., Zhou, W., & Xu, Y. (2008). Patterns of brain activation during visually evoked sexual arousal differ between homosexual and heterosexual men. *American Journal of Neuroradiology, 29,* 1890–1896.

Huang, C. Y., Yao, C. J., Wang, C., Jiang, J. K., & Chen, G. (2010). Changes of semen quality in Chinese fertile men from 1985 to 2008. *National Journal of Andrology, 16*(8), 684–688.

Huang, J. (2007). Hormones and female sexuality. In M. Tepper & A. F. Owens (Eds.), *Sexual Health, Vol 2: Physical Foundations* (pp. 43–78). Westport, CT: Praeger.

Huang, Y., Zhang, Z., Tashkin, D., Feng, B., Straif, K., & Hashibe, M. (2015). An epidemiologic review of marijuana and cancer: An update. *Cancer Epidemiology, Biomarkers & Prevention*, 24(1), 15–31.

Huang, Z., Gao, Y., Wen, W., Li, H., Zheng, W., Shu, X., & Beeghly-Fadiel, A. (2015). Contraceptive methods and ovarian cancer risk among Chinese women: A report from the Shanghai women's health study. *International Journal of Cancer*, 137(3), 607–614.

Hubacher, D., Finerb, L., & Espeyc, E. (2010). Renewed interest in intrauterine contraception in the United States: Evidence and explanation. *Contraception*, 83(4), 291–294.

Hubayter, Z., & Simon, J. (2008). Testosterone therapy for sexual dysfunction in postmenopausal women. *Climacteric*, 11, 181–191.

Hubert, C., White, K., Hopkins, K., Grossman, D., & Potter, J. (2016). Perceived interest in vasectomy among Latina women and their partners in a community with limited access to female sterilization. *Journal of Health Care for the Poor and Underserved*, 27(2), 762–777.

Huebner, D., Mandic, C., Mackaronis, J., Beougher, S., & Hoff, C. (2012). The impact of parenting on gay male couples' relationships, sexuality, and HIV risk. *Couple and Family Psychology: Research and Practice*, 1(2), 106–119.

Huff-Hannon, J. (2011). A campaign goes viral to stop 'corrective rape,' used to 'cure' south African women of homosexuality. Retrieved February 20, 2011, from http://www.alternet .org/rights/149491/a_campaign_goes_viral _to_stop_%2527corrective_rape%252C%2527 _used_to_%2527cure%2527_south_african _women_of_homosexuality/.

Huffstutter, P. J. (2004). Smallest surviving preemie will go home soon. Retrieved December 23, 2004, from http://www.latimes .come/news/nationworld/nation/la-na -baby22dec,0,3320847,print.story.

Hughes, J. R. (2006). A general review of recent reports on homosexuality and lesbianism. *Sexuality and Disability*, 24, 195–205.

Hull, S., Hennessy, M., Bleakley, A., Fishbein, M., & Jordan, A. (2010). Identifying the causal pathways from religiosity to delayed adolescent sexual behavior. *Journal of Sex Research*, 19, 1–11.

Human Rights Campaign. (2010). Surrogacy laws and legal considerations. Retrieved February 24, 2011, from http://www.hrc.org /issues/parenting/surrogacy/2485.htm.

Human Rights Campaign. (2017). Gender-neutral housing. Retrieved January 16, 2017, from http://www.hrc.org/resources/gender -neutral-housing.

Hunt, L. (1993). Introduction: Obscenity and the origins of modernity, 1500–1800. In L.

Hunt (Ed.), *The invention of pornography* (pp. 9–45). New York: Zone Books.

Hunt, L., Eastwick, P., & Finkel, E. (2015). Leveling the playing field: Longer acquaintance predicts reduced assortative mating on attractiveness. *Psychological Science*, 26(7), 1046–1053.

Hunt, M. (1974). *Sexual behavior in the 1970's*. New York: Dell.

Hunter, D., Colditz, G., Hankinson, S., Malspeis, S., Spiegelman, D., Chen, W., Stampfer, M., & Willett, W. (2010). Oral contraceptive use and breast cancer: A prospective study of young women. *Cancer Epidemiology, Biomarkers & Prevention*, 19(10), 2496–2502.

Hunter, I., Saunders, D., & Williamson, D. (1993). *On pornography: Literature, sexuality and obscenity law*. New York: St. Martin's Press.

Hunter, J. A., Figueredo, A. J., Malamuth, N. M., & Becker, J. V. (2003). Juvenile sex offenders: Toward the development of a typology. *Sexual Abuse: Journal of Research & Treatment*, 15(1), 27–48.

Hunter, L. (2014). Vaginal breech birth: Can we move beyond the term breech trial? *Journal of Midwifery & Women's Health*, 59(3), 320–327.

Huober-Zeeb, C., Lawrenz, B., Popovici, R. M., Strowitzki, T., Germeyer, A., Stute, P., & von Wolff, M. (2011). Improving fertility preservation in cancer: Ovarian tissue cryobanking followed by ovarian stimulation can be efficiently combined. *Fertility and Sterility*, 95(1), 342–344.

Hussain, A., Nicholls, J., & El-Hasani, S. (2010). Technical tips following more than 2000 transabdominal preperitoneal (TAPP) repair of the groin hernia. *Surgical Laparoscopy, Endoscopy, and Percutaneous Techniques*, 20(6), 384–388.

Hutcheon, J. A., Lisonkova, S., & Joseph, K. S. (2011). Epidemiology of pre-eclampsia and the other hypertensive disorders of pregnancy. *Best Practice and Research in Clinical Obstetrics and Gynecology*, 25(4), 391–403.

Hutter, M. (1981). *The changing family: Comparative perspective*. New York: Wiley.

Huyghe, E., Delannes, M., Wagner, F., Delaunay, B., Nohra, J., Thoulouzan, M., Shut-Yee, J. Y., Plante, P., Soulie, M., Thonneau, P., & Bachaud, J. M. (2009). Ejaculatory function after permanent 125I prostate brachytherapy for localized prostate cancer. *International Journal of Radiation Oncology*, 74(1), 126–132.

Hwang, E., Lichtensztajn, D., Gomez, S., Fowble, B., & Clarke, C. (2013). Survival after lumpectomy and mastectomy for early stage invasive breast cancer. *Cancer*, 119(7), 1402–1411.

Hyde, J. (2014). Gender similarities and differences. *Annual Review of Psychology*, 65, 373–398.

Hyde, J. (2014). The gender similarities hypothesis. *American Psychologist*, 60(6), 581–592.

Hyde, J., & Mertz, J. (2008). Gender, culture, and mathematics. *Proceedings of the National Academy of Science*, 106(22), 8801–8807.

Iatrakis, G., Iavazzo, C., Zervoudis, S., Koumousidis, A., Sofoudis, C., Kalampokas, T., & Salakos, N. (2011). The role of oral contraception use in the occurrence of breast cancer. A retrospective study of 405 patients. *Clinical and Experimental Obstetrics & Gynecology*, 38(3), 225–227.

Iavazzo, C., Sardi, T., & Gkegkes, I. (2013). Female genital mutilation and infections: A systematic review of the clinical evidence. *Archives of Gynecology and Obstetrics*, 287(6), 1137–1149.

Iemmola, F., & Camperio Ciani, A. (2009). New evidence of genetic factors influencing sexual orientation in men: Female fecundity increase in the maternal line. *Archives of Sexual Behavior*, 38(3), 393–399.

Ignatius, E., & Kokkonen, M. (2007). Factors contributing to verbal self-disclosure. *Nordic Psychology*, 59(4), 362–391.

Igras, S., Macieira, M., Murphy, E., & Lundgren, R. (2014). Investing in very young adolescents' sexual and reproductive health. *Global Public Health*, 9(5), 555–569.

Ilic, M., Vlajinac, H., Marinkovic, J., & Sipetic-Grujicic, S. (2013). Abortion and breast cancer: Case-control study. *Tumori*, 99(4), 452–457.

Impett, E. A., Beals, K. P., & Peplau, L. A. (2001). Testing the investment model of relationship commitment and stability in a longitudinal study of married couples. *Current Psychology*, 20(4), 312–327.

"Induced Abortion Worldwide." (2016). Global incidence and trends. Guttmacher Institute. Retrieved April 12, 2017, from https://www .guttmacher.org/fact-sheet/induced-abortion -worldwide.

Ingalhalikar, M., Smith, A., Parker, D., Satterthwaite, T., Elliott, M., Ruparel, K., Hakonarson, H., Gur, R., Gur, R., & Verma, R. (2013). Sex differences in the structural connectome of the human brain. *Proceedings of the National Academy of Science of the United States of America*. Retrieved February 14, 2014, from http://www.pnas .org/content/early/2013/11/27/1316909110.

International Gay and Lesbian Human Rights Commission. (2010). Middle East and North America. Retrieved August 26, 2011, from http://www.iglhrc.org/cgi-bin/iowa/region /10.html.

Intersexual Society of North America. (2014). *What does ISNA recommend for children with intersex?* Retrieved February 17, 2014, from http://www.isna.org/faq/patient-centered.

Ioverno, S., Belser, A., Baiocco, R., Grossman, A., & Russell, S. (2016). The protective role of gay-straight alliances for lesbian, gay, bisexual, and questioning students: A prospective analysis. *Psychology of Sexual Orientation and Gender Diversity, 3*(4), 397–406.

Irvine, J. (1990). *Disorders of desire, sex, and gender in modern American sexology*. Philadelphia: Temple University Press.

Irving, C., Basu, A., Richmond, S., Burn, J., & Wren, C. (2008, July 2). Twenty-year trends in prevalence of survival of Down syndrome. *European Journal of Human Genetics*. Retrieved October 14, 2008, from http://www.nature.com/ejhg/journal/vaop/ncurrent/abs/ejhg2008122a.html.

Irwig, M. S., & Kolukula, S. (2011). Persistent sexual side effects of finasteride for male pattern hair loss. *Journal of Sexual Medicine, 8*(6), 1747–1753.

Isaacs, A. M. (2013). *Let's talk about sex. How family communication patterns and family sexual communication impact adolescents' and emerging adults' sexual outcomes*. Dissertation Abstracts International Section A: Humanities and Social Sciences, *74*(2-A), ISBN 978-1-267-66723-6.

Isaiah Green, A. (2007). Queer theory and sociology: Locating the subject and the self in sexuality studies. *Sociological Theory, 25*, 26–45.

Ishak, W. W., Berman, D. S., & Peters, A. (2008). Male anorgasmia treated with oxytocin. *Journal of Sexual Medicine, 5*, 1022–1024.

Ishak, W., & Tobia, G. (2013). DSM-5 changes in diagnostic criteria of sexual dysfunction. *Reproductive System & Sexual Disorders, 2*(2). Retrieved August 13, 2014, from http://omicsonline.org/dsm-5-changes-in-diagnostic-criteria-of-sexual-dysfunctions-2161-038X.1000122.pdf.

Ishak, W., Bokarius, A., Jeffrey, J., Davis, M., & Bakhta, Y. (2010). Disorders of orgasm in women: A literature review of etiology and current treatments. *Journal of Sexual Medicine, 7*(10), 3254–3268.

Ishibashi, K. L., Koopmans, J., Curlin, F. A., Alexander, K., & Ross, L. (2008). Paediatricians' attitudes and practices towards HPV vaccination. *Acta Paediatrician, 97*(11), 1550–1556.

Isidori, A., Giannetta, E., Gianfrilli, D., Greco, E., Bonifacio, V., Aversa, A., et al. (2005). Effects of testosterone on sexual function in men: Results of a meta-analysis. *Clinical Endocrinology, 63*, 381–394.

Israilov, S., Niv, E., Livne, P. M., Shmeuli, J., Engelstein, D., Segenreich, E., & Baniel, J. (2002). Intracavernous injections for erectile dysfunction in patients with cardiovascular diseases and failure or contraindications for sildenafil citrate. *International Journal of Impotence Research, 14*(1), 38–43.

Iversen, L., Sivasubramaniam, S., Lee, A., Fielding, S., & Hannaford, P. (2017). Lifetime cancer risk and combined oral contraceptives: The Royal College of General Practitioners' oral contraception study. *American Journal of Obstetrics and Gynecology*. Retrieved April 5, 2017, from https://www.ncbi.nlm.nih.gov/pubmed/28188769.

Iverson, J. S. (1991). A debate on the American home: The antipolygamy controversy, 1880–1890. *Journal of the History of Sexuality, 1*, 585–602.

Jackman, L. P., Williamson, D. A., Netemeyer, R. G., & Anderson, D. A. (1995). Do weight-preoccupied women misinterpret ambiguous stimuli related to body size? *Cognitive Therapy and Research, 19*, 341–355.

Jackowich, R., Pink, L., Gordon, A., & Pukall, C. (2016). Persistent genital arousal disorder. A review of its conceptualizations, potential origins, impact, and treatment. *Sexual Medicine Reviews, 4*(4), 329–342.

Jackson, A. (2015). State contexts and the criminalization of marital rape across the United States. *Social Science Research, 51*, 290–306. Retrieved from https://www.ncbi.nlm.nih.gov/pubmed/25769868.

Jackson, B. (1998). *Splendid slippers: A thousand years of an erotic tradition*. Berkeley, CA: Ten Speed Press.

Jackson, H., Raj, H., Raj, R., & Mobley, S. (2007) *Myths, misperceptions and fears: Addressing condom use barriers*. International Planned Parenthood Federation. Retrieved May 24, 2014, from http://www.unfpa.org/webdav/site/global/shared/documents/publications/2007/myths_condoms.pdf.

Jackson, J., Miller, R., Oka, M., & Henry, R. (2014). Gender differences in marital satisfaction: A meta-analysis. *Journal of Marriage and Family, 76*(1), 105–129.

Jackson, M. (1984). Sex research and the construction of sexuality: A tool of male supremacy? *Women's Studies International Forum, 7*, 43–51.

Jackson, S. (2007). 'She might not have the right tools... and he does': Children's sense-making of gender, work and abilities in early school readers. *Gender and Education, 19*(1), 61–77.

Jacob, H., Kreifelts, B., Bruck, C., Nizielski, S., Schutz, A., & Wildgruber, D. (2013). Nonverbal signals speak up: Association between perceptual nonverbal dominance and emotional intelligence. *Cognitive and Emotion, 27*(5), 783–799.

Jacobs, S. E., Thomas, W., & Lang, S. (1997). *Two-spirit people: Native American gender identity, sexuality, and spirituality*. Chicago: University of Illinois Press.

Jacobson, J., Likis, F., & Murphy, P. (2012). Extended and continuous combined contraceptive regimens for menstrual suppression. *Journal of Midwifery and Women's Health, 57*(6), 585–592.

Jacquet, S. E., & Surra, C. A. (2001). Parental divorce and premarital couples: Commitment and other relationship characteristics. *Journal of Marriage and Family, 63*(3), 627–639.

Jain, J. K., Minoo, P., Nucatola, D. L., & Felix, J. C. (2005). The effect of nonoxynol-9 on human endometrium. *Contraception, 71*(2), 137–142.

Jamanadas, K. (2008). Sati was started for preserving caste. Retrieved April 8, 2008, from http://www.ambedkar.org/research/Sati_Was_Started_For_Preserving_Caste.htm.

James, S. D. (2011, April 13). J Crew ad with boy's pink toenails creates stir. *ABC News*. Retrieved May 5, 2011, from http://abcnews.go.com/Health/crew-ad-boy-painting-toenails-pink-stirs-transgender/story?id513358903.

Janak, J., Orman, J., Soderdahl, D., & Hudak, S. (2017). Epidemiology of genitourinary injuries among male U.S. service members deployed to Iraq and Afghanistan: Early findings from the Trauma Outcomes and Urogenital Health (TOUGH) Project. *Journal of Urology, 197*(2), 414–419.

Jang, S., Kim, D., & Choi, M. (2014). Effects and treatment methods of acupuncture and herbal medicine for PMS/PMDD: Systematic Review. *BMC Complementary and Alternative Medicine, 14*(1), 11.

Janiak, E., Kawachi, I., Goldberg, A., & Gottlieb, B. (2014). Abortion barriers and perceptions of gestational age among women seeking abortion care in the latter half of the second trimester. *Contraception, 89*(4), 322–327.

Janssen, E., McBride, K., Yarber, W., Hill, B., & Butler, S. (2008). Factors that influence sexual arousal in men: A focus group study. *Archives of Sexual Behavior, 37*(2) 252–265.

Janus, S. S., & Janus, C. L. (1993). *The Janus report on sexual behavior*. New York: Wiley.

Japsen, B. (2003). Viagra faces 1st rivals by year's end. Retrieved July 18, 2003, from http://www.webprowire.com/summaries/5357111.html.

Jaworski, A., & Coupland, J. (2005). Othering in gossip: "You go out you have a laugh and you can pull yeah okay but like ...." *Language and Society, 34*, 667–695.

Jayne, C. (1981). A two-dimensional model of female sexual response. *Journal of Sex and Marital Therapy, 7*, 3–30.

Jayne, C., Simon, J., Taylor, L., Kimura, T., & Lesko, L (2012). Open-label extension study of Flibanserin in women with hypoactive sexual desire disorder. *Journal of Sexual Medicine, 9*(12), 3180–3188.

Jeary, K. (2005). Sexual abuse and sexual offending against elderly people: A focus on perpetrators and victims. *Journal of Forensic Psychiatry & Psychology, 16*(2), 328–343.

Jellesma, F., & Vingerhoets, A. (2012). Crying in middle childhood: A report on gender differences. *Sex Roles, 67*(7–8), 412–421.

Jelovsek, J. E., Walters, M. D., & Barber, M. D. (2008). Psychosocial impact of chronic vulvovaginal conditions. *Journal of Reproductive Medicine, 53*, 75–82.

Jenkins, D., & Johnston, L. (2004). Unethical treatment of gay and lesbian people with conversion therapy. *Families in Society, 85*(4), 557–561.

Jenkins, S. (2009). Marital splits and income changes over the longer term. In M. Brynin & J. Ermisch (Eds.), *Changing relationships*. London: Routledge.

Jenkins, W. (2010). Can anyone tell me why I'm gay? What research suggests regarding the origins of sexual orientation. *North American Journal of Psychology, 12*(2), 279–296.

Jenness, V. (1990). From sex as sin to sex as work: COYOTE and the reorganization of prostitution as a social problem. *Social Problems, 37*, 403–420.

Jerman, J., Jones, R., & Onda, T. (2016). Characteristics of U.S. abortion patients in 2014 and changes since 2008. Guttmacher Institute. Retrieved April 9, 2017, from https://www.guttmacher.org/report/characteristics-us-abortion-patients-2014.

Jern, P., Santtila, P., Johansson, A., Varjonen, M., Witting, K., von der Pahlen, B., & Sandnabba, N. K. (2009). Evidence for a genetic etiology to ejaculatory dysfunction. *International Journal of Impotence Research, 21*(1), 62–67.

Jetter, A. (1991). Faye's crusade. *Vogue, 147*–151, 202–204.

Jewkes, R., Abrahams, N., Mathews, S., Seedat, M., Niekerk, A., Suffla, S., & Ratele, K. (2009a). Preventing rape and violence in South Africa: Call for leadership in a new agenda for action. MRC Policy Brief. Retrieved April 30, 2011, from http://www.mrc.ac.za/gender/prev_rapedd041209.pdf.

Jewkes, R., Sikweyiya, Y., Morrell, R., & Dunkle, K. (2009b). Understanding men's health and use of violence: Interface of rape and HIV in South Africa. Medical Research Council of South Africa. Retrieved April 30, 2011, from http://gender.care2share.wikispaces.net/file/view/MRCISA1men1and1rape1ex1summary1june2009.pdf.

Jha, A. (2010, October 4). British IVF pioneer Robert Edwards wins Nobel prize for medicine. Retrieved March 1, 2011, from http://www.guardian.co.uk/science/2010/oct/04/ivf-pioneer-robert-edwards-nobel-prize-medicine.

Jha, P., Kumar, R., Vasa, P., Dhingra, N., Thiruchelvam, D., & Moineddin, R. (2006). Low male-to-female sex ratio of children born in India: National survey of 1.1 million households. *The Lancet, 367*, 211–218.

Jha, R. K., Jha, P. K., & Guha, S. K. (2009). Smart RISUG: A potential new contraceptive and its magnetic field-mediated sperm interaction. *International Journal of Nanomedicine, 4*, 55–64.

Jiang, L., & Hancock, J. (2013). Absence makes the communication grow fonder: Geographic separation, interpersonal media, and intimacy in dating relationships. *Journal of Communication, 63*(3), 556–577.

Jick, S., & Hernandez, R. (2011). Risk of non-fatal venous thromboembolism in women using oral contraceptives containing drospirenone compared with contraceptives containing levonorgestrel. *British Medical Journal*. Retrieved June 5, 2011, from http://www.bmj.com/content/342/bmj.d2151.full.

Jin, F., Tao, M., Teng, Y., Shao, H., Li, C., & Mills, E. (20156). Knowledge and attitude towards menopause and hormone replacement therapy in Chinese women. *Gynecologic and Obstetric Investigation, 79*(1), 40–45.

Joel, D. (2012). Genetic-gonadal-genitals sex and the misconception of brain and gender, or why 3G-males and 3G-females have intersex brain and intersex gender. *Biology of Sex Differences, 3*(1), 27.

Joffe, H., Chang, C., Sewell, C., Easley, O., Nguyen, C., Dunn, S., Lehrfeld, K., Lee, L., Kim, M., Slagle, A., & Beitz, J. (2016). FDA approval of flibanserin—Treating hypoactive sexual desire disorder. *New England Journal of Medicine, 374*(2), 101–104.

Johannsen, T., Ripa, C., Carlsen, E., Starup, J., Nielsen, O., Schwartrz, M., Drzewiecki, K., Mortensen, E., & Main, K. (2010). Long-term gynecological outcomes in women with congenital adrenal hyperplasia due to 21-hydroxylase deficiency. *International Journal of Pediatric Endocrinology*. Retrieved November 13, 2010, from http://www.ncbi.nlm.nih.gov/pmc/articles/PMC2963122/.

Johansson, A., Sundbom, E., Hojerback, T., & Bodlund, O. (2010). A five-year follow-up study of Swedish adults with gender identity disorder. *Archives of Sexual Behavior, 39*(6), 1429–1437.

John, E. M., Miron, A., Gong, G., Phipps, A. I., Felberg, A., Li, R. P., et al. (2007). Prevalence of pathogenic BRCA1 mutation carriers in 5 U.S. racial/ethnic groups. *Journal of the American Medical Association, 298*, 2910–2911.

Johns, M., Zimmerman, M., Harper, G., & Bauermeister, J. (2017). Resilient minds and bodies: Size discrimination, body image, and mental health among sexual minority women. *Psychology of Sexual Orientation and Gender Diversity, 4*(1), 34–42.

Johnson, A. J. (2009). A functional approach to interpersonal argument: Differences between public-issue and personal-issue arguments. *Communication Reports, 22*(1), 13.

Johnson, A. M. (2001). Popular belief in gender-based communication differences and relationship success. *Dissertation Abstracts*, University of Massachusetts, Amherst, #0-599-95739-5.

Johnson, A. M., Mercer, C. H., Erens, B., Copas, A. J., McManus, S., Wellings, K., Fenton, K. A., Korovessis, C., Macdowall, W., Nanchahal, K., Purdon, S., & Field, J. (2001). Sexual behaviour in Britain: Partnerships, practices, and HIV-risk behaviours. *Lancet, 358*, 1835–1842.

Johnson, H., Ollus, N., & Nevala, S. (2008). *Violence against women: An international perspective*. New York: Springer Science and Business.

Johnson, J. (2001). *Male multiple orgasm: Step by step* (4th ed.). Jack Johnson Seminars.

Johnson, J., & Alford, R. (1987). The adolescent quest for intimacy: Implications for the therapeutic alliance. *Journal of Social Work and Human Sexuality* (Special issue: Intimate Relationships), 5, 55–66.

Johnson, K., Gill, S., Reichman, V., Tassinary, L. (2007). Swagger, sway, and sexuality: Judging sexual orientation from body motion and morphology. *Journal of Personality and Social Psychology, 93*(3), 321–334.

Johnson, K. C., & Daviss, B. A. (2005). Outcomes of planned home births with certified professional midwives: Large prospective study in North America. *British Medical Journal, 330*(7505), 1416–1420.

Johnson, N. (2010, September 11). For-profit hospitals leading in cesareans. *Daily News Los Angeles*. Retrieved September 13, 2010, from http://www.dailynews.com/news/ci_16051899.

Johnson, R., & Murad, H. (2009). Gynecomastia: Pathophysiology, evaluation, and management. *Mayo Clinic Proceedings, 84*(11), 1010–1015.

Johnson, S. E. (1996). *Lesbian sex: An oral history*. Tallahassee, FL: Naiad Press.

Johnson, T. (2007). *Understanding children's sexual behaviors: What's natural and healthy*. San Diego, CA: Institute on Violence, Abuse and Trauma.

Jonas, S., Bebbington, P., McManus, S., Meltzer, H., Jenkins, R., Kuipers, E., Cooper, C., King, M., & Brugha, T. (2011). Sexual abuse and psychiatric disorder in England: Results from the 2007 adult psychiatric morbidity survey. *Psychological Medicine, 41*(4), 709–720.

Jones, J. (2013, May 13). Same-sex marriage support solidifies above 50% in U.S. *Gallup Politics*. Retrieved April 15, 2014, from http://www.gallup.com/poll/162398/sex-marriage-support-solidifies-above.aspx.

Jones, J., & Jerman, J. (2014). Abortion incidence and service availability in the U.S., 2011.

Perspectives on Sexual and Reproductive Health, 46(1). Retrieved May 26, 2014, from http://www.guttmacher.org/pubs/journals/psrh.46e0414.pdf.

Jones, J., Mosher, W., & Daniels, K. (2012a). Current contraceptive use in the U.S., 2006–2010, and changes in patterns of use since 1995. National Health Statistics Report (No. 60). Retrieved May 26, 2014, from http://www.cdc.gov/nchs/data/nhsr/nhsr060.pdf.

Jones, J. H. (1997). *Alfred C. Kinsey: A public/private life*. New York: W. W. Norton.

Jones, R. (1984). *Human reproduction and sexual behavior*. Englewood Cliffs, NJ: Prentice Hall.

Jones, R., & Jerman, J. (2017). Abortion incidence and service availability in the United States. *Perspectives on Sexual and Reproductive Health, 49*(1), 17–27.

Jones, R., & Jerman, J. (2017a). Characteristics and circumstances of U.S. women who obtain very early and second-trimester abortions. *PLOS One*. Retrieved April 9, 2017, from http://journals.plos.org/plosone/article?id=10.1371/journal.pone.0169969.

Jones, R., & Kooistra, K. (2011). Abortion incidence and access to services in the U.S., 2008. *Perspectives in Sex and Reproductive Health, 43*(1), 41–50.

Jones, R., Darroch, J., & Singh, S. (2005). Religious differentials in the sexual and reproductive behaviors of young women in the United States. *Journal of Adolescent Health, 36*(4), 279–288.

Jones, R., Finer, L., & Singh, S. (2010, May). Characteristics of U.S. abortion patients, 2008. New York: Alan Guttmacher Institute. Retrieved June 5, 2011, from http://www.guttmacher.org/pubs/US-Abortion-Patients.pdf.

Jones, R., Frohwirth, L., & Moore, A. (2012). More than poverty: Disruptive events among women having abortions in the USA. *Journal of Family Planning and Reproductive Health Care, 39*(1), 36–43.

Jones, R. K., Moore, A. M., & Frohwirth, L. F. (2011). Perceptions of male knowledge and support among U.S. women obtaining abortions. *Women's Health Issues, 21*(2), 117–123.

Jongpipan, J., & Charoenkwan, K. (2007). Sexual function after radical hysterectomy for early-stage cervical cancer. *Journal of Sexual Medicine, 4*, 1659–1665.

Jordan, J. (1997). User buys: Why men buy sex. *Australian and New Zealand Journal of Criminology, 30*, 55–71.

Jordan, S., Morris, J., Davies, G., Tucker, D., Thayer, D., Leteijn, J., Morgan, M., et al. (2016). Selective serotonin reuptake inhibitor antidepressants in pregnancy and congenital anomalies: Analysis of linked database in Wales, Norway and Funen, Denmark. *PLOS One, 11*(12). Retrieved April 2, 2017, from http://journals.plos.org/plosone/article?id=10.1371/journal.pone.0165122.

Jorgensen, C. (1967). *Christine Jorgenson: Personal biography*. New York: Erickson.

Jose, A., O'Leary, D., & Moyer, A. (2010). Does premarital cohabitation predict subsequent marital stability and marital quality? A meta-analysis. *Journal of Marriage and Family, 72*(1), 105–116.

Joung, I. M., Stronks, K., & van de Mheen, H. (1995). Health behaviours explain part of the differences in self-reported health associated with partner/marital status in the Netherlands. *Journal of Epidemiology and Community Health, 49*(5), 482–488.

Joura, E., Giuliano, A., Iversen, O., Bouchard, C., Mao, C., Mehlsen, J., Moreira, E., Ngan, Y., Petersen, L., Lazcano-Ponce, E., et al. (2015). A 9-valent HPV vaccine against infection and intraepithelial neoplasia in women. *New England Journal of Medicine, 372*(8), 711–723.

Juhl, A., Christensen, S., Zachariae, R., & Damsgaard, T. (2017). Unilateral breast reconstruction after mastectomy—Patient satisfaction, aesthetic outcome and quality of life. *Acta Oncologica, 56*(2), 225–231.

Julien, D., Chartrand, E., Simard, M., Bouthillier, D., & Bégin, J. (2003). Conflict, social support, and relationship quality: An observational study of heterosexual, gay male, and lesbian couples' communication. *Journal of Family Psychology, 17*(3), 419–428.

Junco, R., Merson, D., Salter, D. (2010). The effect of gender, ethnicity, and income on college students' use of communication technologies. *CyberPsychology, Behavior, and Social Networking, 13*(6), 619–627.

Juntti, S. A., Tollkuhn, J., Wu, M. V., Fraser, E., Soderborg, T., Tan, S., Honda, S., Harada, N., & Shah, N. M. (2010). The androgen receptor governs the execution, but not the programming, of male sexual and territorial behavior. *Neuron, 66*(2), 167–169.

Juraska, J., & Willing, J. (2017). Pubertal onset as a critical transition for neural development and cognition. *Brain Research, 1654*(Part B), 87–94.

Juster, R., Almeida, D., Cardoso, C., Raymond, C., Johnson, P., Pfaus, J., Mendrek, A., Duchesne, A., Pruessner, J., & Lupien, S. (2016). Gonads and strife: Sex hormones vary according to sexual orientation for women and stress indices for both sexes. *Psychoneuroendocrinology, 72*, 119–130.

Justman, J., Goldberg, A., Reed, J., Bock, N., Njeuhmeli, E., & Goldzier, T. (2013). Adult male circumcision: Reflections on successes and challenges. *Journal of Acquired Immune Deficiency Syndromes, 63*(2), 140–143.

Kaats, G. R., & Davis, K. E. (1971). Effects of volunteer biases in studies of sexual behavior and attitudes. *Journal of Sex Research, 7*, 26–34.

Kaestle, C., & Allen, K. (2011). The role of masturbation in healthy sexual development: Perceptions of young adults. *Archives of Sexual Behavior, 40*(5), 983–994. Retrieved February 4, 2011, from http://www.springerlink.com/content/a61r62w728335l00/.

Kaestle, C., & Halpern, C. (2007). What's love got to do with it? Sexual behaviors of opposite sex couples through emerging adulthood. *Perspectives on Sexual and Reproductive Health, 39*(3), 134–140.

Kagan, J. (1996). Three pleasing ideas. *American Psychologist, 51*(9), 901–908.

Kahn, Y. (1989–90). Judaism and homosexuality: The traditionalist/progressive debate. *Journal of Homosexuality, 18*, 47–82.

Kahr, B. (2008). *Who's been sleeping in your head: The secret world of sexual fantasies*. New York: Basic Books.

Kain, E. L. (1987). A note on the integration of AIDS into the Sociology of Human Sexuality. *Teaching Sociology, 15*, 320–323.

Kakuchi, S. (2005). New museum documents lives of Japan's "comfort women." Retrieved November 6, 2005, from http://www.womensenews.org/article.cfm?aid=2509.

Kalb, A., Kalb, A., Cardoso, T., Fernandes, C., Corcini, C., Varela, J., & Martinez, P. (2015). Maternal transfer of bisphenol A during nursing causes sperm impairment in male offspring. *Archives of Environmental Contamination and Toxicology, 70*(4), 793–801.

Kalra, S., Ratcliffe, S., & Dokras, A. (2013). Is the fertile window extended in women with polycystic ovary syndrome? *Fertility and Sterility, 100*(1), 208–213.

Kalyani, R., Basavaraj, P. B., & Kumar, M. L. (2007). Factors influencing quality of semen: A two year prospective study. *Indian Journal of Pathology and Microbiology, 50*, 890–895.

Kamali, H. (2010, December 20). Personal communication.

Kamen, C., Jabson, J., Mustian, K., & Boehmer, U. (2017). Minority stress, psychosocial resources, and psychological distress among sexual minority breast cancer survivors. *Health Psychology*. Retrieved April 15, 2017, from https://www.ncbi.nlm.nih.gov/pubmed/28165265.

Kamens, S. (2011). On the proposed sexual and gender identity diagnoses for *DSM-5*: History and controversies. *The Humanistic Psychologist, 39*(1), 37–59.

Kaminer, W. (1992, November). Feminists against the first amendment. *Atlantic Monthly*, pp. 111–117.

Kanakis, G., & Goulis, D. (2015). Male contraception: A clinically-oriented review. *Hormones, 14*(4), 598–614.

Kanayama, G., Hudson, J. I., & Pope, H. G., Jr. (2010). Illicit anabolic-androgenic steroid use. *Hormones and Behavior, 58*(1), 111–121.

Kandaraki, E., Chatzigeorgiou, A., Livadas, S., Palioura, E., Economou, F., Koutsilieris, M., Palimeri, S., Panidis, D., & Diamanti-Kandarakis, E. (2011). Endocrine disruptors and polycystic ovary syndrome: Elevated serum levels of bisphenol A in women with PCOS. *Journal of Clinical Endocrinology and Metabolism, 96*(3), E480–E484.

Kann, L., Kinchen, S., Shanklin, S., Flint, K., Hawkins, M., Harris, W., Lowry, R., et al. (2014). Youth risk behavior surveillance—United States, 2013. *Morbidity and Mortality Weekly Report, 63*(ss04), 1–168.

Kann, L., McManus, T., Harris, W., Shanklin, S., Flint, K., Hawkins, J., Queen, B., Lowry, R., Olsen, E., et al. (2016). Youth risk behavior surveillance—United States, 2015. *Morbidity and Mortality Weekly Report, Surveillance Summary, 65*(6). Retrieved February 11, 2017, from https://www.cdc.gov/healthyyouth/data/yrbs/pdf/2015/ss6506_updated.pdf.

Kann, L., McManus, T., Harris, W., Shanklin, S., Flint, K., Hawkins, J., Queen, B., Lowry, R., O'Malley, E., et al. (2016). Youth Risk Behavior Surveillance—United States, 2015. *Morbidity and Mortality Weekly Report*, Centers for Disease Cotnrol and Prevention, 65(6). Retrieved January 9, 2017, from https://www.cdc.gov/healthyyouth/data/yrbs/pdf/2015/ss6506_updated.pdf.

Kann, L., Olsen, E., McManus, T., Harris, W., Shanklin, S., Flint, K., et al. (2016). Sexual identity, sex of sexual contacts, and health-related behaviors among students in grades 9-12—United States and selected sites, 2015. *Morbidity and Mortality Weekly Report, 65*(9), 1–202.

Kantor, L. (1992). Scared chaste? Fear based educational curricula. *SIECUS Reports, 21*, 1–15.

Kantor, M. (2015). Why a gay person can't be made un-gay: The truth about reparative therapies. Santa Barbara, CA: Praeger Publishers.

Kaplan, G. (1977). Circumcision: An overview. *Current Problems in Pediatrics, 1*, 1–33.

Kaplan, H., Kohl, R., Pomeroy, W., Offit, A., & Hogan, B. (1974). Group treatment of premature ejaculation. *Archives of Sexual Behavior, 3*(5), 443–452.

Kaplan, H., Sadock, B., & Grebb, J. (1994). *Synopsis of psychiatry* (7th ed.). Baltimore, MD: Williams and Wilkins.

Kaplan, H. S. (1974). *The new sex therapy*. New York: Bruner/Mazel.

Kaplan, L. J. (1991). Women masquerading as women. In G. I. Fogel & W. A. Meyers (Eds.), *Perversions and near-perversions in clinical practice: New psychoanalytic perspectives* (pp. 127–152). New Haven, CT: Yale University Press.

Kappas, A., & Krämer, N. (2011). *Face-to-face communication over the Internet: Emotions in a web of culture, language and technology*. New York, NY: Cambridge University Press.

Kapsimalakou, S., Grande-Nagel, I., Simon, M., Fischer, D., Thill, M., & Stökelhuber, B. (2010). Breast abscess following nipple piercing: A case report and review of the literature. *Archives of Gynecology and Obstetrics, 282*(6), 623–626.

Karabay, C., Kocabay, G., Oduncu, V., Kalayci, A., Guler, A., Karagöz, A., Candan, O., Basaran, O., Zehir, R., Izgi, A., Esen, A., & Kirma, C. (2013). Drospirenone-containing oral contraceptives and risk of adverse outcomes after myocardial infarction. *Catheterization and Cardiovascular Interventions, 82*(3), 387–383.

Karacan, M., Alwaeely, F., Erkan, S., Çebi, Z., Berberoglugil, M., Batukan, M., Ulug, M., Arvas, A., & Camlibel, T. (2013). Outcome of intracytoplasmic sperm injection cycles with fresh testicular spermatozoa obtained on the day of or the day before oocyte collection and with cryopreserved testicular sperm in patients with azoospermia. *Fertility and Sterility, 100*(4), 975–980.

Kärgel, C., Massau, C., Walter, M., Kruger, T., & Schiffer, B. (2015). Diminished functional connectivity on the road to child sexual abuse in pedophilia. *Journal of Sexual Medicine, 12*(3), 783–795.

Kårhus, L., Egerup, P., Skovlund, C., & Lidegaard, O. (2014). Impact of ectopic pregnancy for reproductive prognosis in next generation. *Acta Obstetrics and Gynecology Scandinavia, 93*(4), 416–419.

Karlsson, A., Sterlund, A., & Forss, N. (2011). Pharyngeal chlamydia trachomatis is not uncommon any more. *Scandinavian Journal of Infectious Disease, 43*, 344–348.

Karniol, R. (2001). Adolescent females' idolization of male media stars as a transition into sexuality. *Sex Roles, 44*(1–2), 61–77.

Karuturi, R. (2017, May 4). Rape anxiety. Stanford Daily. Retrieved from http://www.stanforddaily.com/2017/05/04/rape-anxiety/.

Kaschak, E., & Tiefer, L. (2001). *A new view of women's sexual problems*. Binghamton, NY: Haworth Press.

Kaslow, F. (2000). *Handbook of couple and family forensics: A sourcebook for mental health and legal professionals*. Hoboken, NJ: John Wiley & Sons Inc.

Katehakis, A. (2012). Sex addiction beyond the *DSM-V. Psychology Today*. Retrieved April 15, 2017, from https://www.psychologytoday.com/blog/sex-lies-trauma/201212/sex-addiction-beyond-the-dsm-v.

Kato, T. (2016). Effects of partner forgiveness on romantic break-ups in dating relationships: A longitudinal study. *Personality and Individual Differences, 95*, 185–189.

Katz-Wise, S., Budge, S., Orovecz, J., Nguyen, B., & Nava-Coulter, B. (2017). Imagining the future: Perspectives among youth and caregivers in the trans Youth Family Study. *Journal of Counseling Psychology, 64*(1), 26–40.

Katz, A. (2016). The circle of female sexual desire—Have we come a long way? *Nursing for Women's Health, 20*(3), 235–238.

Katz, J. (2014). Mentors in violence prevention: Gender violence prevention education & training. Retrieved August 24, 2014, from http://www.jacksonkatz.com/mvp.html.

Katz, M. H., Schwarcz, S. K., Kellogg, T. A., Klausner, J. D., Dilley, J. W., Gibson, S., et al. (2002). Impact of highly active antiretroviral treatment on HIV seroincidence among men who have sex with men. *American Journal of Public Health, 92*(3), 388–395.

Kaufman, B. S., Kaminsky, S. J., Rackow, E. C., & Weil, M. H. (1987). Adult respiratory distress syndrome following orogenital sex during pregnancy. *Critical Care Medicine, 15*, 703–704.

Kaufman, M., Smelyanskaya, M., VanLith, L., Mallalieu, E., Waxman, A., Hatzhold, K., Marcell, A., Kasedde, S., et al. (2016). Adolescent sexual and reproductive health services and implications for the provision of voluntary medical male circumcision. *PLOS One, 11*(3), e0149892.

Kaunitz, A. (2002). Current concepts regarding use of DMPA. *Journal of Reproductive Medicine, 47*(9 Suppl.), 785–789.

Kaunitz, A. M., Arias, R., & McClung, M. (2008). Bone density recovery after depot medroxyprogesterone acetate injectable contraception use. *Contraception, 77*, 67–76.

Kaushic, C., Roth, K. L., Anipindi, V., & Xiu, F. (2011). Increased prevalence of sexually transmitted viral infections in women: The role of female sex hormones in regulating susceptibility and immune responses. *Journal of Reproductive Immunology, 88*(2), 204–209.

Kawwass, J., Monsour, M., & Crawford, S. (2013). Trends and outcomes for donor oocyte cycles in the United States, 2000–2010. *JAMA, 310*(22), 2426–2434.

Kaye, K. (2007). Sex and the unspoken in male street prostitution. *Journal of Homosexuality, 53*, 37–73.

Kayongo-Male, D., & Onyango, P. (1984). *The sociology of the African family*. London: Longman.

Kazmierczak, M., Kielbratowska, B., & Pastwa-Wojciechowska, B. (2013). Couvade syndrome among Polish expectant fathers. *Medical Science Monitor: International Medical Journal of Experimental and Clinical Research, 19*, 132–138.

Keane, H. (2004). Disorders of desire: Addiction and problems of intimacy. *Journal of Medical Humanities, 25*(3), 189–197.

Keasler, M. (2006). *Love hotels*. San Francisco: Chronicle Books.

Keegan, J. (2001). The neurobiology, neuropharmacology and pharmacological treatment of the paraphilias and compulsive sexual behavior. *Canadian Journal of Psychiatry, 46*(1), 26–33.

Keijsers, L., & Poulin, F. (2013). Developmental changes in parent-child communication throughout adolescence. *Developmental Psychology, 49*(12), 2301–2308.

Keller, J. C. (2005). Straight talk about the gay gene. *Science & Spirit, 16*, 21.

Keller, M. (2013). Social media and interpersonal communication. *Social Work Today, 13*(3), 10.

Kelley, E., & Gidycz, C. (2016). Mediators of the relationship between sexual assault and sexual functioning difficulties among college women. *Psychology of Violence*. Retrieved April 14, 2017, from http://psycnet.apa.org /psycinfo/2016-43611-001/.

Kellogg, N. (2009). Clinical report: The evaluation of sexual behaviors in children. *Pediatrics, 124*(3), 992–998.

Kelly, A. (2009, March 12). Raped and killed for being a lesbian: South Africa ignores 'corrective' attacks. *The Guardian*. Retrieved April 30, 2011, from http://www.guardian .co.uk/world/2009/mar/12/eudy-simelane -corrective-rape-south-africa.

Kelly, D., Sakellariou, D., Fry, S., & Vougioukalou, S. (2017). Heteronormativity and prostate cancer: A discursive paper. *Journal of Clinical Nursing*. Retrieved April 15, 2017, from http://onlinelibrary.wiley.com /doi/10.1111/jocn.13844/abstract.

Kelly, J. M. (2005). *Zest for life: Lesbians' experiences of menopause*. North Melbourne, Australia: Spinifex Press.

Kelly, L., Keaten, J., Becker, B., Cole, J., Littleford, L., & Rothe, B. (2012). "It's the American lifestyle!": An investigation of text messaging by college students. *Qualitative Research Reports in Communication, 13*(1), 1–9.

Kelly, M. P., Strassberg, D. S., & Kircher, J. R. (1990). Attitudinal and experiential correlates of anorgasmia. *Archives of Sexual Behavior, 19*, 165–177.

Kelly, R. J., Wood, J., Gonzalez, L., MacDonald, V., & Waterman, J. (2002). Effects of mother-son incest and positive perceptions of sexual abuse experiences on the psychosocial adjustment of clinic-referred men. *Child Abuse and Neglect, 26*(4), 425–441.

Kelly-Vance, L., Anthis, K. S., & Needelman, H. (2004). Assisted reproduction versus spontaneous conception: A comparison of the developmental outcomes in twins. *Journal of Genetic Psychology, 165*(2), 157–168.

Kelsey, J., Gammon, M., & John, E. (1993). Reproductive factors and breast cancer. *Epidemiology Review, 15*(1), 36–47.

Kembabazi, A., Bajunirwe, F., Hunt, P., Martin, J., Muzoora, C., Haberer, J., Bangsberg, D., & Siedner, M. (2013). Disinhibition in risky sexual behavior in men, but not women, during four years of antiretroviral therapy in rural, Southwestern Uganda. *PLoS One, 8*(7). Retrieved April 29, 2017, from https://www .ncbi.nlm.nih.gov/pmc/articles/PMC3716596/.

Kempner, M. (2013, November). Progress seen in efforts to create herpes vaccine. *RH Reality Check*. Retrieved June 6, 2014, from http://rhrealitycheck.org/article/2013/11/12 /progress-seen-in-efforts-to-create-herpes -vaccine.

Kendrick, W. M. (1987). *The secret museum: Pornography in modern culture*. New York: Viking.

Kennedy, H. (2002). Research and commentaries on Richard von Krafft-Ebing and Karl Heinrich Ulrichs. *Journal of Homosexuality, 42*(1), 165–178.

Kenner, W., & Nicolson, S. (2015). Psychosomatic disorders of gravida status: False and denied pregnancies. *Psychosomatics: Journal of Consultation and Liaison Psychiatry, 56*(2), 119–128.

Kerckhoff, A. (1964). Patterns of homogamy and the field of eligibles. *Social Forces, 42*(3), 289–297.

Kerr, D., & Capaldi, D. (2011). Young men's intimate partner violence and relationship functioning: Long-term outcomes associated with suicide attempt and aggression in adolescence. *Psychological Medicine, 41*(4), 759–769.

Kerr, D., Santurri, L., & Peters, P. (2013). A comparison of lesbian, bisexuals, and heterosexual college undergraduate women on selected mental health issues. *Journal of American College Health, 61*(4), 185–194.

Kerrigan, D., Mobley, S., Rutenberg, N., Fisher, A., & Weiss, E. (2000). The female condom: Dynamics of use in urban Zimbabwe. New York: The Population Council. Retrieved July 24, 2008, from http://www .popcouncil.org/pdfs/horizons/fcz.pdf.

Kerrigan, D., Mobley, S., Rutenberg, N., Fisher, A., & Weiss, E. (2004). *The female condom: Dynamics of use in urban Zimbabwe*. New York, NY: Population Council.

Kershaw, S. (2009, October 15). Rethinking the older woman-young man relationship. *New York Times*. Retrieved October 15, 2009, from http://www.nytimes.com/2009/10/15 /fashion/15women.html.

Kertzner, R. M., Meyer, I. H., Frost, D. M., & Stirratt, M. J. (2009). Social and psychological well-being in lesbians, gay men, and bisexuals: The effects of race, gender, age, and sexual identity. *American Journal of Orthopsychiatry, 79*(4), 500–510.

Kessous, R., Aricha-Tamir, B., Sheizaf, B., Steiner, N., Moran-Gilad, J., & Weintraub, A. (2013). Clinical and microbiological characteristics of Bartholin gland abscesses. *Obstetrics and Gynecology, 122*(4), 794–799.

Keuroghlian, A., Shtasel, D., & Bassuk, E. (2014). Out on the street: A public health and policy agenda for lesbian, gay, bisexual, and transgender youth who are homeless. *American Journal of Orthopsychiatry, 84*(1), 66–72.

Keyes, H. (2016, August 25). Contraception in Japan. Savvy Tokyo. Retrieved April 3, 2017, from https://savvytokyo.com/contraception -in-japan/.

Khadivzadeh, T., & Parsai, S. (2005). Effect of exclusive breastfeeding and complementary feeding on infant growth and morbidity. *Eastern Mediterranean Health Journal, 10*(3), 289–294.

Khosropour, C. M., Johnson, B. A., Ricca, A. V., Sullivan, P. S. (2013). Enhancing retention of an Internet-based cohort study of men who have sex with men via text messaging: Randomized controlled study. *Journal of Medical Internet Research, 15*(8). Retrieved January 4, 2014, from http://www.ncbi.nlm .nih.gov/pubmed/23981905.

Kidd, S., & Workowski, K. (2015). Management of gonorrhea in adolescents and adults in the United States. *Clinical Infectious Diseases, 61*(Suppl. 8), S785–801.

Kidman, R., Petrow, S., & Heymann, S. (2007). Africa's orphan crisis: Two community-based models of care. *AIDS Care, 19*(3), 326–329.

Kiernan, C. (2014). A tattoo that completes a new breast. *New York Times*. Retrieved July 17, 2014, from http://well.blogs.nytimes .com/2014/06/02/a-tattoo-that-completes-a -new-breast/?_php=true&_type=blogs&_r=0.

Kilchevsky, A., Vardi, Y., Lowenstein, L., & Gruenwald, I. (2012). Is the female G-spot truly a distinct anatomic entity? *Journal of Sexual Medicine, 9*(3), 719–726.

Kilgallon, S., & Simmons, L. (2005). Image content influences men's semen quality. *Biology Letters, 1*(3), 253–255.

Killick, S., Leary, C., Trussell, J., & Guthrie, K. (2010). Sperm content of pre-ejaculatory fluid. *Human Fertility, 14*(1), 48–52.

Killick, S., Leary, C., Trussell, J., & Guthrie, K. (2011). Sperm content of pre-ejaculatory fluid. *Human Fertility, 14*(1), 48–52.

Kim, D., Byun, I., Lee, W., Rah, D., Kim, J., & Lee, D. (2016). Surgical management of gynecomastia: Subcutaneous mastectomy and liposuction. *Aesthetic Plastic Surgery, 40*(6), 877–884.

Kim, J., & Hatfield, E. (2004). Love types and subjective well-being: A cross-cultural study. *Social Behavior and Personality, 32*, 173–182.

Kim, Y. (2013, November 26). A closer look at the explosion of cell phone subscribers in North Korea. *38 North*. Retrieved February 3, 2014, from http://38north.org/2013/11 /ykim112613.

Kim, Y., Yang, S., Lee, J., Jung, T., & Shim, H. (2008). Usefulness of a malleable penile prosthesis in patients with a spinal cord injury. *International Journal of Urology, 15*(10), 919–923.

Kimble, M., Neacsiu, A., Flack, W., & Horner, J. (2008). Risk of unwanted sex for college women: Evidence for a red zone. *Journal of American College Health, 57*(3), 331–338.

Kimbrough, A., Guadagno, R., Muscanell, N., & Dill, J. (2013). Gender differences in mediated communication: Women connect more than do men. *Computers in Human Behavior, 29*(3), 896–900.

Kimmel, M. S., & Plante, R. F. (2007). Sexualities. *Contexts, 6*, 63–65.

King, M., & Ussher, J. (2012). It's not all bad: Women's construction and lived experience of positive premenstrual change. *Feminism Psychology, 23*(3), 399–417.

King, M., Semlyen, J., Tai, S., Killaspy, H., Osborn, D., Popelyuk, D., & Nazareth, I. (2008). A systematic review of mental disorder, suicide, and deliberate self harm in lesbian, gay and bisexual people. *BMC Psychiatry, 8*, 70. Retrieved January 24, 2011, from http://www.biomedcentral.com/1471-244X/8/70.

King, P., & Boyatzis, C. (2004). Exploring adolescent spiritual and religious development: Current and future theoretical and empirical perspectives. *Applied Developmental Science, 8*, 2–6.

Kingree, J., & Thompson, M. (2013). Fraternity membership and sexual aggression: An examination of mediators of the association. *Journal of American College Health, 61*(4), 213–221.

Kingsberg, S. A., & Knudson, G. (2011). Female sexual disorders: Assessment, diagnosis, and treatment. *Urological Clinics of North America, 34*(4), 497–506.

Kingsberg, S., Derogatis, L., Edelson, J., Jordan, R., & Krychman, M. (2014). Distress reduction in female sexual dysfunctions: A dose-ranging study of subcutaneous bremelanotide. *Obstetrics and Gynecology, 123*(Suppl. 1), 29–30.

Kinnunen, L. H., Moltz, H., Metz, J., & Cooper, M. (2004). Differential brain activation in exclusively homosexual and heterosexual men produced by the selective serotonin reuptake inhibitor, fluoxetine. *Brain Research, 1024*(1–2), 251–254.

Kinsey, A. C., Pomeroy, W., Martin, C. E., & Gebhard, P. (1953). *Sexual behavior in the human female*. Philadelphia: Saunders.

Kinsey, A., Pomeroy, W. B., & Martin, C. E. (1948). *Sexual behavior in the human male*. Philadelphia: Saunders.

Kirby, D. (1992). Sexuality education: It can reduce unprotected intercourse. *SIECUS Report, 21*, 19–25.

Kirby, D. (2001, May). Emerging answers: Research findings on programs to reduce teen pregnancy. National Campaign to Prevent Teen Pregnancy.

Kirby, D. (2007). Emerging answers: 2007. Research findings on programs to reduce teen pregnancy and sexually transmitted diseases. Washington, DC: National Campaign to Prevent Teen and Unplanned Pregnancy. Retrieved May 29, 2008, from http://www.thenationalcampaign.org/EA2007/EA2007_full.pdf.

Kirsch, A. T. (1985). Text and context: Buddhist sex roles/culture of gender revisited. *American Ethnologist, 12*(2), 302–320.

Kirshenbaum, S. (2011). *The science of kissing: What our lips are telling us*. New York, NY: Grand Central Publishing.

Kitazawa, K. (1994). Sexuality issues in Japan. *SIECUS Report*, 7–11.

Kito, M. (2005). Self-disclosure in romantic relationships and friendships among American and Japanese college students. *Journal of Social Psychology, 145*, 127–140.

Kizilay, F., Gali, H., & Serefoglu, E. (2017). Diabetes and sexuality. *Sexual Medicine Reviews, 5*(1), 45–51.

Klausen, P. (2007). *Trends in birth defect research*. Hauppauge, NY: Nova Science Publishers.

Klausner, J. (2013). The sound of silence: Missing the opportunity to save lives at birth. *Bulletin of the World Health Organization, 91*, 158–158a.

Klawitter, M. (2014). Meta-analysis of the effects of sexual orientation on earnings. *Industrial Relations, 54*(1), 4–32.

Kleese, C. (2011). Notions of love in polyamory. Elements in a discourse on multiple loving. *Laboratorium*. Retrieved October 7, 2014, from http://www.soclabo.org/index.php/laboratorium/article/view/250/588.

Klein, C., & Gorzalka, B. (2009). Sexual functioning in transsexuals following hormone therapy and genital surgery: A review. *Journal of Sexual Medicine, 6*(11), 2922–2932.

Klein, F. (1978). *The bisexual option: A concept of one-hundred percent intimacy*. New York: Arbor House.

Klein, F. (1990). The need to view sexual orientation as a multivariable dynamic process: A theoretical perspective. In D. P. McWhirter, S. A. Sanders, & J. M. Reinisch (Eds.), *Homosexuality/heterosexuality: Concepts of sexual orientation* (pp. 277–282). New York: Oxford University Press.

Klein, F. (1993). *The bisexual option* (2nd ed.). Philadelphia: Haworth Press.

Klein, F., Sepekoff, B., & Wolf, T. (1985). Sexual orientation: A multi-variable dynamic process. *Journal of Homosexuality, 11*(1–2), 35–49.

Klein, W., Geaghan, T., & MacDonald, T. (2007). Unplanned sexual activity as a consequence of alcohol use: A prospective study of risk perceptions and alcohol use among college freshman. *Journal of American College Health, 56*(3), 317–323.

Kleinplatz, P., & Moser, C. (2006). *Sadomasochism: Powerful pleasures*, Routledge, NY: Haworth Press.

Klimkiewicz, J. (2008, April 24). Outsourcing labor. *Hartford Courant*, pp. D1–D4.

Kline, P. (1987). Sexual deviation: Psychoanalytic research and theory. In G. D. Wilson (Ed.), *Variant sexuality: Research and theory* (pp. 150–175). Baltimore: Johns Hopkins University Press.

Klonoff-Cohen, H., Natarajan, L., & Chen, R. (2006). A prospective study of the effects of female and male marijuana use on in vitro fertilization (IVF) and gamete intrafallopian transfer (GIFT) outcomes. *American Journal of Obstetrics and Gynecology, 194*(2), 369–376.

Klotz, L., & Emberton, M. (2012). Management of low risk prostate cancer: Active surveillance and focal therapy. *Current Opinion in Urology, 24*(3), 270–279.

Kluft, R. (2010). Ramifications of incest. *Psychiatric Times, 27*(12), 48–56.

Kluger, J. (2008, January 17). The science of romance: Why we love. *Time Magazine*. Retrieved August 17, 2008, from http://www.time.com/time/magazine/article/0,9171,1704672-2,00.html.

Kluger, N. (2010). Body art and pregnancy. *European Journal of Obstetrics and Gynecological Reproductive Biology, 153*(1), 3–7.

Knapp, M. L., & Hall, J. A. (2005). *Nonverbal communication in human interaction* (6th ed.). Belmont, CA: Wadsworth.

Knibbs, K. (2013, May 22). KTHXBA!! How internet-speak is changing the way we talk IRL (in real life). *Digital Trends*. Retrieved November 10, 2013, from http://www.digitaltrends.com/social-media/how-the-internet-is-changing-the-way-we-talk.

Knight, S. J., & Latini, D. M. (2009). Sexual side effects and prostate cancer treatment decisions: Patient information needs and preferences. *Cancer Journal, 15*(1), 41–44.

Knoester, M., Helmerhorst, F., Vandenbroucke, J., van der Westerlaken, L., Walther, F., Veen, S., et al. (2008). Perinatal outcome, health growth, and medical care utilization of 5- to 8-year old intracytoplasmic sperm injection singletons. *Fertility and Sterility, 89*, 1133–1146.

Knöfler, T., & Imhof, M. (2007). Does sexual orientation have an impact on nonverbal behavior in interpersonal communication? *Journal of Nonverbal Behavior, 31*(3), 189–204.

Knox, D., Breed, R., & Zusman, M. (2007). College men and jealousy. *College Student Journal, 41*, 435–444.

Knox, D., Zusman, M. E., & Mabon, L. (1999). Jealousy in college student relationships. *College Student Journal, 33*(3), 328–329.

Knox, D., Zusman, M., & McNeely, A. (2008). University student beliefs about sex: Men vs. women. *College Student Journal, 42*, 181–186.

Ko, D. (2001). *In every step a lotus: Shoes for bound feet*. Berkeley: University of California Press.

Ko, D. (2007). *Cinderella's sisters: A revisionist history of footbinding*. Berkeley: University of California Press.

Ko, J., Rockhill, K., Tong, V., Morrow, B., & Farr, S. (2017). Trends in postpartum depressive symptoms—27 states, 2004, 2008, and 2012. *Morbidity and Mortality Weekly Report, 66*, 153–158.

Koch, W. (2005). Despite high-profile cases, sex-offense crimes decline. Retrieved October 9, 2005, from http://www.usatoday.com/news/nation/2005-08-24-sex-crimes-cover_x.htm?POE=NEWISVA.

Koci, A., & Strickland, O. (2007). Relationship of adolescent physical and sexual abuse to perimenstrual symptoms in adulthood. *Issues in Mental Health Nursing, 28*, 75–87.

Koerner, A., & Fitzpatrick, M. (1997). Family type and conflict: The impact of conversation orientation and conformity orientation on conflict in the family. *Communication Studies, 48*, 59–75.

Koh, A. S., Gomez, C. A., Shade, S., & Rowley, E. (2005). Sexual risk factors among self-identified lesbians, bisexual women, and heterosexual women accessing primary care settings. *Sexually Transmitted Diseases, 32*(9), 563–569.

Kohl, J. V., & Francoeur, R. (2002). *The scent of eros: Mysteries of odor in human sexuality*. Lincoln, NE: iUniverse, Author's Choice Press.

Kohler, P. K., Manhart, L. E., & Lafferty, W. E. (2008). Abstinence-only and comprehensive sex education and the initiation of sexual activity and teen pregnancy. *Journal of Adolescent Health, 42*, 344–351.

Kohn, C., Hasty, S., & Henderson, C. W. (2002, September 3). Study confirms infection from receptive oral sex occurs rarely. *AIDS Weekly*, 20–22.

Kolata, G. (2007, August 12). The myth, the math, the sex. *New York Times*. Retrieved October 14, 2010, from http://www.nytimes.com/2007/08/12/weekinreview/12kolata.html.

Komarowska, M., Hermanowicz, A., & Debek, W. (2015). Putting the pieces together: Cryptorchidism—do we know everything? *Journal of Pediatric Endocrinology & Metabolism, 28*(11–12), 1247–1256.

Kon, I. S. (2004). Russia. In R. T. Francoeur & R. J. Noonan (Eds.), *The Continuum International encyclopedia of sexuality* (pp. 888–908). New York/London: Continuum International.

Kong, S., & Bernstein, K. (2009). Childhood trauma as a predictor of eating psychopathology and its mediating variables in patients with eating disorders. *Journal of Clinical Nursing, 18*(13), 1897–1907.

Kontula, O., & Haavio-Mannila, E. (2004). Finland. In R. T. Francoeur & R. J. Noonan (Eds.), *The Continuum International encyclopedia of sexuality* (pp. 381–411). New York/London: Continuum International.

Koon-Magnin, S., & Ruback, R. (2012). Young adults' perceptions of non-forcible sexual activity: The effects of participant gender, respondent gender, and sexual act. *Sex Roles, 67*(11–12), 646–658.

Kopelman, L. (1988). The punishment concept of disease. In C. Pierce & D. Vandeveer (Eds.), *AIDS, ethics, and public policy*. Belmont, CA: Wadsworth.

Kopelman, L. (2014). Make her a virgin again: When medical disputes about minors are cultural clashes. *Journal of Medical Philosophy, 39*(1), 8–25.

Koropeckyj-Cox, T., Romano, V., & Moras, A. (2007). Through the lenses of gender, race, and class. Students' perceptions of childless/childfree individuals and couples. *Sex Roles, 56*, 415–428.

Kosciw, J., Diaz, E., & Greytak, E. (2008). *The 2007 national school climate survey: The experiences of lesbian, gay, bisexual and transgender youth in our nation's schools*. New York, NY: Gay, Lesbian and Straight Education Network.

Kosfeld, M., Heinrichs, M., Zak, P. J., Fischbacher, U., & Fehr, E. (2005). Oxytocin increases trust in humans. *Nature, 435*, 676–676.

Koskimäki, J., Shiri, R., Tammela, T., Häkkinen, J., Hakama, M., & Auvinen, A. (2008). Regular intercourse protects against erectile dysfunction: Tampere aging male urologic study. *American Journal of Medicine, 121*, 592–596.

Koster, W., Bruinderink, M., & Janssens, W. (2015). Empowering women or pleasing men? Analyzing male views on female condom use in Zimbabwe, Nigeria and Cameroon. *International Perspectives on Sexual and Reproductive Health, 41*(3), 126–135.

Kotchick, B. A., Dorsey, S., & Miller, K. S. (1999). Adolescent sexual risk-taking behavior in single-parent ethnic minority families. *Journal of Family Psychology, 13*(1), 93–102.

Kotlyar, I., & Ariely, D. (2013). The effect of nonverbal cues on relationship formation. *Computers in Human Behavior, 29*(3), 544–551.

Kovac, J., Scovell, J., Ramasamy, R., Rajanahally, S., Coward, R., Smith, R., & Lipshultz, L. (2015). Men regret anabolic steroid use due to a lack of comprehension regarding the consequences on future fertility. *Andrologia, 47*(8), 872–878.

Kramer, A., Guillory, J., Hancock, J. (2014). Experimental evidence of massive-scale emotional contagion through social networks. *Proceedings of the National Academy of Sciences of the United States of America, 111*(24), 8788–8790.

Kraus, S., Voon, V., & Potenza, M. (2016). Should compulsive sexual behavior be considered an addiction? *Addiction, 111*(12), 2097–2106.

Krebs, C. P., Lindquist, C. H., Warner, T. D., Fisher, B. S., & Martin, S. L. (2007). *The Campus Sexual Assault (CSA) Study*. Washington, DC: National Institute of Justice, U.S. Department of Justice.

Krebs, C., Lindquist, C., Warner, T., Fisher, B., & Martin, S. (2009). College women's experiences with physically forced, alcohol- or other drug-enabled, and drug-facilitated sexual assault before and since entering college. *Journal of American College Health, 57*(6), 639–649.

Kreider, R. M. (2005). Number, timing and duration of marriages and divorces: 2001. *Current Population Reports* (P70–97). Washington, DC: U.S. Census Bureau.

Kreisel, K., Torrone, E., Bernstein, K., Hong, J., & Gorwitz, R. (2017). Prevalence of pelvic inflammatory disease in sexually experienced women of reproductive age-U.S., 2013–2014. *MMWR, 66*(3), 80–83.

Kreuter, M., Siosteen, A., & Biering-Sorensen, F. (2008). Sexuality and sexual life in women with spinal cord injury: A controlled study. *Journal of Rehabilitative Medicine, 40*, 61–69.

Kreuter, M., Taft, C., Siösteen, A., & Biering-Sørensen, F. (2011). Women's sexual functioning and sex life after spinal cord injury. *Spinal Cord, 49*(1), 154–160.

Kriebs, J. (2008). Understanding herpes simplex virus: Transmission, diagnosis, and considerations in pregnancy management. *Journal of Midwifery Women's Health, 53*, 202–208.

Krishnan, A., & Muthusami, S. (2017). Hormonal alterations in PCOS and its influence on bone metabolism. *Journal of Endocrinology, 232*(2), 99–113.

Krishnan, S., & Kiley, J. (2010). The lowest-dose, extended-cycle combined oral contraceptive pill with continuous ethinyl estradiol in the U.S. *International Journal of Women's Health, 2*, 235–239.

Kristof, N. D. (1996, February 11). Who needs love! In Japan, many couples don't. *New York Times*, p. A1.

Kroll R., Reape, K., & Margolis, M. (2010). The efficacy and safety of a low-dose, 91-day, extended-regimen oral contraceptive with continuous ethinyl estradiol. *Contraception, 81*(1), 41–48.

Krone, N., Hanley, N. A., & Arlt, W. (2007). Age-specific changes in sex steroid biosynthesis and sex development. *Best Practice & Research: Clinical Endocrinology Metabolism, 21*, 393–401.

Krüger, T., Schiffer, B., Eikermann, M., Haake, P., Gizewski, E., & Schedlowsk, M. (2006). Serial neurochemical measurement of cerebrospinal fluid during the human sexual response cycle. *European Journal of Neuroscience, 24*, 3445–3452.

Kuczkowski, K. M. (2006). Labor analgesia for the parturient with lumbar tattoos: What does an obstetrician need to know? *Archives of Gynecology and Obstetrics, 274*, 310–312.

Kuefler, M. (2006). *The Boswell thesis: Essays on Christianity, social tolerance, and homosexuality.* Chicago: University of Chicago Press.

Kuhle, B., Melzer, D., Cooper, C., Merkle, A., Pepe, N., Ribanovic, A., Verdesco, A., Wettstein, T. (2015). The 'birds and the bees' differ for boys and girls: Sex differences in the nature of sex talks. *Evolutionary Behavioral Sciences, 9*(2), 107–115.

Kühn, S., & Gallinat, J. (2014). Brain structure and functional connectivity associated with pornography consumption: The brain on porn. *Journal of the American Medical Association, 71*(7), 827–834.

Kuliev, A., & Verlinsky, Y. (2008). Impact of preimplantation genetic diagnosis for chromosomal disorders on reproductive outcome. *Reproductive Biomedical Online, 16*, 9–10.

Kulkarni, A., Jamieson, D., Jones, H., Kissin, D., Gallo, M., Macaluso, M., & Adashi, E. (2013). Fertility treatments and multiple births in the United States. *The New England Journal of Medicine, 369*(23), 2218–2225.

Kumar, S., Roy, S., Chaudhury, K., Sen, P., & Guha, S. K. (2008). Study of the micro-structural properties of RISUG—a newly developed male contraceptive. *Journal of Biomedical Materials Research, 86*(1), 154–161.

Kunkel, A. W., & Burleson, B. R. (1998). Social support and the emotional lives of men and women: An assessment of the different cultures perspective. In D. Canary & K. Dindia (Eds.), *Sex differences and similarities in communication: Critical essays and empirical investigations of sex and gender in interaction* (pp. 101–125). Mahwah, NJ: Lawrence Erlbaum Associates.

Kunkel, D., Eyal, K., Finnerty, K., Biely, E., & Donnerstein, E. (2005). Sex on TV4. Retrieved November 9, 2005, from http://www.kff.org/entmedia/upload/Sex-on-TV-4-Full-Report.pdf.

Kuperberg, A., Padgett, J. (2016). The role of culture in explaining college students' selection into hookups, dates, and long-term romantic relationships. *Journal of Social and Personal Relationships, 33*(8). Retrieved August 23, 2017, from http://journals.sagepub.com/doi/abs/10.1177/0265407515616876?journalCode=spra.

Kurdek, L. A. (2006). Differences between partners from heterosexual, gay, and lesbian cohabiting couples. *Journal of Marriage and Family, 68*, 509–528.

Kurdek, L. A. (2008). Change in relationship quality for partners from lesbian, gay male, and heterosexual couples. *Journal of Family Psychology, 22*(5), 701–711.

Kurtzleben, D. (2013, March 1). Gay couples more educated, higher-income than heterosexual couples. *U.S. News and World Report.* Retrieved May 15, 2014, from http://www.usnews.com/news/articles/2013/03/01/gay-couples-more-educated-higher-income-than-heterosexual-couples.

Kürzinger, M., Pagnier, J., Kahn, J., Hampshire, R., Wakabi, T., & Dye, T. (2008). Education status among orphans and non-orphans in communities affected by AIDS in Tanzania and Burkina Faso. *AIDS Care, 20*(6), 726–732.

Kutchinsky, B. (1991). Pornography and rape: Theory and practice? *International Journal of Law and Psychiatry, 14*, 47–64.

Kuvalanka, K., Leslie, L., & Radina, R. (2014). Coping with sexual stigma: Emerging adults with lesbian parents reflect on the impact of heterosexism and homophobia during their adolescence. *Journal of Adolescent Research, 29*(2), 241–270.

Labbate, L. (2008). Psychotropics and sexual dysfunction: The evidence and treatments. *Advances in Psychosomatic Medicine, 29*, 107–130.

Labonte-Lemoyne, E., Curnier, D., & Ellemberg, D. (2017). Exercise during pregnancy enhances cerebral maturation in the newborn: A randomized controlled trial. *Journal of Clinical and Experimental Neuropsychology, 39*(4), 347–354.

Labrie, J., Hummer, J., Ghaidarov, T., Lac, A., & Kenney, S. (2014). Hooking up in the college context: The event-level effects of alcohol use and partner familiarity on hookup behaviors and contentment. *Journal of Sex Research, 51*(1), 62–72.

LaBrie, J., Hummer, J., Ghaidarov, T., Lac, A., & Kenney, S. (2014). Hooking up in the college context: The event-level effects of alcohol use and partner familiarity on hookup behaviors and contentment. *Journal of Sex Research, 51*(1), 62–73.

Lacerda, H. M., Richiardi, L., Pettersson, A., Corbin, M., Merletti, F., & Akre, O. (2010). Cancer risk in mothers of men operated for undescended testis. *PLoS One, 5*(12), e14285.

Lacey, R. S., Reifman, A., Scott, J. P., Harris, S. M., & Fitzpatrick, J. (2004). Sexual-moral attitudes, love styles, and mate selection. *The Journal of Sex Research, 41*(2), 121–129.

Ladizinski, B., Lee, K., Nutan, F., Higgins, H., & Federman, D. (2014). Gynecomastia: Etiologies, clinical presentations, diagnosis, and management. *Southern Medical Journal, 107*(1), 44–49.

LaFree, G. (1982). Male power and female victimization. *American Journal of Sociology, 88*, 311–328.

Lahaie, M. A., Boyer, S. C., Amsel, R., Khalifé, S., & Binik, Y. M. (2010). Vaginismus: A review of the literature on the classification/diagnosis, etiology and treatment. *Women's Health, 6*(5), 705–719.

Lahey, K. A. (1991). Pornography and harm—learning to listen to women. *International Journal of Law and Psychiatry, 14*, 117–131.

Lai, M., Bombardo, J., Suckling, A., Ruigrok, B., Chakrabarti, C., Ecker, S., Deoni, M., Craig, D., Murphy, E., Bullmore, M., & Baron-Cohen, S. (2013). Biological sex affects the neurobiology of autism. *Brain, 136*(9), 2799–2815.

Lakhey, M., Ghimire, R., Shrestha, R., & Bhatta, A. D. (2010). Correlation of serum free prostate-specific antigen level with histological findings in patients with prostatic disease. *Kathmandu University Medical Journal, 8*(30), 158–163.

Lakoff, R. (1975). *Language and woman's place.* New York: Harper.

Lalumière, M. L., Harris, G. T., Quinsey, V., & Rice, M. E. (2005a). Clinical assessment and treatment of rapists. In M. L. Lalumière & G. Harris (Eds.), *Causes of rape: Understanding individual differences in male propensity for sexual aggression* (pp. 161–181). Washington, DC: American Psychological Association.

Lalumière, M. L., Harris, G. T., Quinsey, V., & Rice, M. E. (2005b). Forced copulation in the animal kingdom. In M. L. Lalumière & G. Harris (Eds.), *Causes of rape: Understanding individual differences in male propensity for sexual aggression* (pp. 31–58). Washington, DC: American Psychological Association.

Lalumière, M. L., Harris, G. T., Quinsey, V., & Rice, M. E. (2005c). Sexual interest in rape. In M. L. Lalumière & G. Harris (Eds.), *Causes of rape: Understanding individual differences in male propensity for sexual aggression* (pp. 105–128). Washington, DC: American Psychological Association.

Lam, A. G., Russell, S. T., Tan, T. C., & Leong, S. J. (2008). Maternal predictors of noncoital sexual behavior: Examining a nationally representative sample of Asian and White American adolescents who have never had sex. *Journal of Youth and Adolescence, 37*, 62–74.

Lamb, J., Dawson, S., Gagan, M., & Peddie, D. (2013). Cigarette smoking and the frequency of colposcopy visits, treatments and re-referral. *Nursing Praxis in New Zealand, 29*(1), 24–33.

Lambda. (2001). State-by-state map of sodomy laws. Retrieved October 15, 2003, from http://lambdalegal.org/cgi_bin/pages/states/sodomy-map.

Lambe, M., Hsieh, C., Trichopoulos, D., Ekbom, A., Pavia, M., & Adami, H. (1994). Transient increase in the risk of breast cancer after giving birth. *New England Journal of Medicine*, *331*(1), 5–9.

Lambert, N., Negash, S., Stillman, T., Olmstead, S., & Fincham, F. (2012). A love that doesn't last: Pornography consumption and weakened commitment to one's romantic partner. *Journal of Social and Clinical Psychology*, *31*(4), 410–438.

Lamidi, E., & Payne, K. (2012). Marital status in the U.S., 2012. National Center for Family & Marriage Research Family Profiles (FP-14-07). Retrieved July 7, 2014, from http://www.bgsu.edu/content/dam/BGSU/college-of-arts-and-sciences/NCFMR/documents/FP/FP-14-07-marital-status.pdf.

Lampiao, F. (2009). Variation of semen parameters in healthy medical students due to exam stress. *Malawi Medical Journal*, *21*(4), 166–170.

Lancaster, J. B., & Hamburg, B. A. (Eds.), *School-Age Pregnancy and Parenthood: Biosocial Dimensions*. New York, NY: Aldine DeGruyter.

Landau, E. (1987). *On the streets: The lives of adolescent prostitutes*. New York: Julian Messner.

Landau, E. (2008, September 5). When sex becomes an addiction. CNN.com. Retrieved October 2, 2008, from http://www.cnn.com/2008/HEALTH/09/05/sex.addiction/.

Landers, S., & Gilsanz, P. (2009). The health of lesbian, gay, bisexual, and transgender (LGBT) persons in Massachusetts. Massachusetts Department of Public Health. Retrieved from http://www.masstpc.org/wp-content/uploads/2012/10/DPH-2009-lgbt-health-report.pdf.

Lang, P., Samaras, D., & Samaras, N. (2012). Testosterone replacement therapy in reversing "andropause": What is the proof-of-principle? *Rejuvenation Research*, *15*(5), 453–465.

Lang, R., Flor-Henry, P., & Frenzel, R. (1990). Sex hormone profiles in pedophilic and incestuous men. *Annals of Sex Research*, *3*, 59–74.

Langenderfer-Magruder, L., Walls, N., Kattari, S., Whitfield, D., & Ramos, D. (2016). Sexual victimization and subsequent police reporting by gender identity among lesbian, gay, bisexual, transgender, and queer adults. *Violence and Victims*, *31*(2), 320–331.

Langevin, R., & Lang, R. A. (1987). The courtship disorders. In G. D. Wilson (Ed.), *Variant sexuality: Research and theory* (pp. 202–228). Baltimore: Johns Hopkins University Press.

Langevin, R., Langevin, M., & Curnoe, S. (2007). Family size, birth order, and parental age among male paraphilics and sex offenders. *Archives of Sexual Behavior*, *36*, 599–609.

Langevin, R., Wortzman, G., Dickey, R., Wright, P., et al. (1988). Neuropsychological impairment in incest offenders. *Annals of Sex Research*, *1*, 401–415.

Langstrom, N., Grann, M., & Lindblad, F. (2000). A preliminary typology of young sex offenders. *Journal of Adolescence*, *23*, 319–329.

Lanigan, J. (2009). A sociotechnological model for family research and intervention: How information and communication technologies affect family life. *Marriage and Family Review*, *45*(6–8), 587–609.

Lanz, M., & Tagliabue, S. (2007). Do I really need someone in order to become an adult? Romantic relationships during emerging adulthood in Italy. *Journal of Adolescent Research*, *22*, 531–549.

Laqueur, T. W. (2003). *Solitary sex: A cultural history of masturbation*. Cambridge, MA: Zone Books.

Larkin, M. (1992). Reacting to patients with sexual problems. *Headlines*, *3*, 2, 3, 6, 8.

Larsen, M., & Hilden, M. (2016). Male victims of sexual assault: 10 years' experience from a Danish assault center. *Journal of Forensic and Legal Medicine*, *13*, 8–11.

Larson, C. M. (2015). Do hormonal contraceptives alter mate choice and relationship functioning in humans? *Dissertation Abstracts International: Section B: The Sciences and Engineering*, *75*(9-B), 978-1-303-95971-4.

Larsson, I., & Svedin, C. (2002). Sexual experiences in childhood: Young adults' recollections. *Archives of Sexual Behavior*, *31*(3), 263–273.

LaSala, M. (2004). Extradyadic sex and gay male couples: Comparing monogamous and nonmonogamous relationships. *Families in Society: The Journal of Contemporary Social Services*, *85*(3), 405–412.

LaSala, M. C. (2000). Lesbians, gay men and their parents: Family therapy for the coming out crisis. *Family Process*, *39*(2), 257–266.

LaSala, M. C. (2001). The importance of partners to lesbians' intergenerational relationships. *Social Work Research*, *25*(1), 27–36.

Lassche, H., & Martinez, I. (2010). *What do men and women require to gratify their desire? Gender differences in emotional and sexual intimacy* (Faculty of Social and Behavioural Theses, Universiteit Utrecht). Retrieved March 24, 2014, from http://dspace.library.uu.nl/handle/1874/45162.

Lassri, D., Luyten, P., Cohen, G., & Shahar, G. (2016). The effect of childhood emotional maltreatment on romantic relationships in young adulthood: A double mediation model involving self-criticism and attachment. *Psychological Trauma: Theory, Research, Practice, and Policy*, *8*(4), 504–511.

Lathi, R., Liebert, C., Brookfield, K., Taylor, J., Vom Saal, F., Fujimoto, V., & Baker, V. (2014). Conjugated bisphenol A (BPA) in maternal serum in relation to miscarriage risk. *Fertility and Sterility*, *102*(1), 123–128. Retrieved May 24, 2014, from http://www.fertstert.org/article/S0015-0282(14)00265-9/abstract.

Lau, J., Kim, J. H., & Tsui, H. Y. (2005). Prevalence of male and female sexual problems, perceptions related to sex and association with quality of life in a Chinese population. *International Journal of Impotence Research*, *17*(6), 494–505.

Laumann, E. O., Gagnon, J., Michael, R., & Michaels, S. (1994). *The social organization of sexuality: Sexual practices in the United States*. Chicago: University of Chicago Press.

Laumann, E. O., Paik, A., & Rosen, R. (1999). Sexual dysfunction in the United States. *Journal of the American Medical Association*, *281*, 537–544.

Laumann, E. O., Paik, A., Glasser, D. B., Kang, J., Wang, T., Levinson, B., et al. (2006). A cross-national study of subjective sexual well-being among older women and men: Findings from the Global Study of Sexual Attitudes and Behaviors. *Archives of Sexual Behavior*, *35*, 145–161.

Laumann, E., Nicolosi, A., Glasser, D., Paik, A., Gingell, C., Moreira, E., Wang, T., for the GSSAB Investigators' Group. (2005). Sexual problems among women and men aged 40–80-y: Prevalence and correlates identified in the Global Study of Sexual Attitudes and Behaviors. *International Journal of Impotence Research*, *17*, 39–57.

Laurence, J. (2006). Treating HIV infection with one pill per day. *AIDS Patient Care and STDs*, *20*, 601–603.

Lavee, Y. (1991). Western and non-Western human sexuality: Implications for clinical practice. *Journal of Sex and Marital Therapy*, *17*, 203–213.

Lavin, M. (2008). Voyeurism: Psychopathology and theory. In D. Laws & W. O'Donohue (Eds.), *Sexual deviance: Theory, assessment and treatment* (2nd ed., pp. 305–319). New York: Guilford Press.

Lavner, J., & Bradbury, T. (2012). Why do even satisfied newlyweds eventually go on to divorce? *Journal of Family Psychology*, *26*(1), 1–10.

Lavner, J., Waterman, J., & Peplau, L. (2014). Parent adjustment over time in gay, lesbian, and heterosexual parent families adopting from foster care. *American Journal of Orthopsychiatry*, *84*(1), 46–53.

Law Library of Congress. (2014). Laws on homosexuality in African nations. Global Legal Research Center. Retrieved March 19, 2017, from https://www.loc.gov/law/help/criminal-laws-on-homosexuality/homosexuality-laws-in-african-nations.pdf.

Lawrence, A. A. (2006). Patient-reported complications and functional outcomes of male and female sex reassignment surgery. *Archives of Sexual Behavior, 35*, 717–727.

Laws, D., & O'Donohue, W. (2008). *Sexual deviance: Theory, assessment, and treatment.* New York: Guilford Press.

Lawton, M., Nathan, M., & Asboe, D. (2013). HPV vaccination to prevent anal cancer in men who have sex with men. *Sexually Transmitted Infections, 89*(5), 342–343.

Lawyer, S., Resnick, H., Bakanic, V., Burkett, T., & Kilpatrick, D. (2010). Forcible, drug-facilitated, and incapacitated rape and sexual assault among undergraduate women. *Journal of American College Health, 58*(5), 453–461.

Layer, E., Beckham, S., Momburi, R., & Kennedy, C. (2013). Understanding the partial protection of male circumcision for HIV prevention among women in Iringa Region, Tanzania. *AIDS Care, 25*(8), 1045–1050.

Layton-Tholl, D. (1998). Extramarital affairs: The link between thought suppression and level of arousal. *Dissertation Abstracts*, Miami Institute of Psychology of the Caribbean Center for Advanced Studies, #AAT9930425.

Le Cornet, C., Lortet-Tieulent, J., Forman, D., Béranger, R., Flechon, A., Fervers, B., Schüz, J., & Bray, F. (2014). Testicular cancer incidence to rise by 25% by 2025 in Europe? *European Journal of Cancer, 50*(4), 831–839.

Lea, S., Callaghan, L., Grafton, I., Falcone, M., & Shaw, S. (2016). Attrition and rape case characteristics: A profile and comparison of female sex workers and non-sex-workers. *Journal of Interpersonal Violence, 31*(12), 2175–2195.

Leaper, C. (2000). The social construction and socialization of gender during development. In P. H. Miller & E. K. Scholnick (Eds.), *Toward a feminist developmental psychology* (pp. 127–152). New York: Routledge.

Leaper, C., & Robnett, R. D. (2011). Women are more likely than men to use tentative language, aren't they? A meta-analysis testing for gender differences and moderators, *Psychology of Women Quarterly, 35*(1), 129–142.

Leaver, R. B. (2016). Male infertility: An overview of causes and treatment options. *British Journal of Nursing, 25*(18), S35–S40.

Ledbetter, A. (2010). Communication patterns and communication competence as predictors of online communication attitude: Evaluating a dual pathway model. *Journal of Family Communication, 10*(2), 99–115.

Ledermann, T., Bodenmann, G., Rudaz, M., & Bradbury, T. (2010). Stress, communication, and martial quality in couples. *Family Relations, 59*(2), 195–207.

Lee, J. A. (1974). The styles of loving. *Psychology Today, 8*, 43–51.

Lee, J. A. (1988). Love-styles. In R. Sternberg & M. Barnes (Eds.), *The psychology of love*. New Haven, CT: Yale University Press.

Lee, J. A. (1998). Ideologies of lovestyle and sexstyle. In V. de Munck (Ed.), *Romantic love and sexual behavior* (pp. 33–76). Westport, CT: Praeger.

Lee, J., Pomeroy, E. C., Yoo, S., & Rheinboldt, K. (2005). Attitudes toward rape: A comparison between Asian and Caucasian college students. *Violence Against Women, 11*(2), 177–196.

Lee, L. (1984). Sequences in separation: A framework for investigating endings of the personal (romantic) relationship. *Journal of Social and Personal Relationships, 1*(1), 49–73.

Lee, P., & Houk, C. (2013). Cryptorchidism. *Current Opinion in Endocrinology, Diabetes, and Obesity, 20*(3), 210–216.

Lee, W., Lee, S., Cho, S., Lee, Y., Oh, C., Yoo, C., Cho, J., Lee, S., & Yang, D. (2013). Comparison between on-demand dosing of dapoxetine alone and dapoxetine plus mirodenafil in patients with lifelong premature ejaculation. *Journal of Sexual Medicine, 10*(11), 2832–2841.

Leeker, O., & Carlozzi, A. (2014). Effects of sex, sexual orientation, infidelity expectations, and love on distress related to emotional and sexual infidelity. *Journal of Marital and Family Therapy, 40*(1), 68–91.

Leemaqz, S., Dekker, G., McCowan, L., Kenny, L., Myers, J., Simpson, N., Poston, L., & Roberts, C. (2016). Maternal marijuana has independent effects on risk for spontaneous preterm birth but not other common late pregnancy complications. *Reproductive Toxicology, 62*, 77–86.

Lefkowitz, E., Vasilenko, S., & Leavitt, C. (2016). Oral vs. vaginal sex experiences and consequences among first-year college students. *Archives of Sexual Behavior, 45*(2), 329–337.

Lehmann, J., Nuevo-Chiquero, A., & Vidal-Fernandez, M. (2016). The early origins of birth order differences in children's outcomes and parental behavior. *Journal of Human Resources.* Retrieved February 13, 2017, from http://jhr.uwpress.org/content/early/2016/11/01/jhr.53.1.0816-8177.full.pdf+html

Leiblum, S. R., & Goldmeier, D. (2008). Persistent genital arousal disorder in women: Case reports of association with anti-depressant usage and withdrawal. *Journal of Sex and Marital Therapy, 34*(2), 150–159.

Leiblum, S. R., & Seehuus, M. (2009). FSFI scores of women with persistent genital arousal disorder compared with published scores of women with female sexual arousal disorder and healthy controls. *Journal of Sexual Medicine, 6*, 469–473.

Leiblum, S., Koochaki, P., Rodenberg, X., Barton, I., & Rosen, R. (2006). Hypoactive sexual desire disorder in postmenopausal women: US results from the women's international study of health and sexuality. *Menopause, 13*, 46–56.

Leibo, S. P. (2008). Cryopreservation of oocytes and embryos: Optimization by theoretical versus empirical analysis. *Theriogenology, 69*, 37–47.

Leichtentritt, R. D., & Arad, B. D. (2005). Young male street workers: Life histories and current experiences. *British Journal of Social Work, 35*(4), 483–509.

Leitenberg, H., & Henning, K. (1995). Sexual fantasy. *Psychological Bulletin, 117*(3), 469–496.

LeMoyne, E., Curnier, D., St-Jacques, S., & Ellemberg, D. (2012). The effects of exercise during pregnancy on the newborn's brain: Study protocol for a randomized controlled trial. *Cell & Bioscience, 13*. Retrieved May 24, 2014, from http://www.trialsjournal.com/content/13/1/68.

Lenhard, M., Nehring, S., Nagel, D., Mayr, D., Kirschenhofer, A., Hertlein, L., et al. (2009). Predictive value of CA 125 and CA 72-4 in ovarian borderline tumors. *Clinical Chemistry and Laboratory Medicine, 47*(5), 537–542.

Lenhart, A. (2010). *Cell phones and American adults*. Pew Internet & American Life Project. Pew Research Center. Retrieved February 1, 2014, from http://pewinternet.org/~/media//Files/Reports/2010/PIP_Adults_Cellphones_Report_2010.pdf.

Lenhart, A. (2015). Teens, social media & technology overview, 2015. *Pew Research Center Internet & Technology.* Retrieved August 23, 2017, from http://www.pewinternet.org/2015/04/09/teens-social-media-technology-2015/.

Leo, R., & Dewani, S. (2013). A systematic review of the utility of antidepressant pharmacotherapy in the treatment of vulvodynia pain. *Journal of Sexual Medicine, 10*(10), 2497–2505.

Leo, S., & Sia, A. (2008). Maintaining labour epidural analgesia: What is the best option? *Current Opinions in Anesthesiology, 21*, 263–269.

Leonard, A. S. (2006, September 25). Hong Kong appeals court strikes down differential age of consent law on "buggery." Leonard Link, New York Law School. Retrieved October 2, 2008, from http://newyorklawschool.typepad.com/leonardlink/2006/09/hong_kong_appea.html.

Leonard, K. E. (2005). Editorial: Alcohol and intimate partner violence: When can we say that heavy drinking is a contributing cause of violence? *Addiction, 100*(4), 422–425.

Leone, T., & Padmadas, S. (2007). The proliferation of a sterilization culture in women's lives: A comparison of Brazil and India. London School of Economics. *Genus, 63*(3/4), 77–97.

Leopold, T. (2016). Gender differences in the consequences of divorce: A multiple-outcome comparison of former spouses.

SOEP Papers on Multidisciplinary Panel Data Research: The German Socio-Economic Panel Study. Retrieved March 8, 2017, from https://www.diw.de/documents/publikationen/73/diw_01.c.534419.de/diw_sp0841.pdf.

Lepkowski, J. M., Mosher, W. D., Davis, K. E., Groves, R. M., & Van Hoewyk, J. (2010). The 2006–2010 National Survey of Family Growth: Sample design and analysis of a continuous survey. National Center for Health Statistics. *Vital Health Statistics, 2*(150), 1–36.

Lete, I., Cristóbal, I., Febrer, L., Crespo, C., Arbat, A., Hernández, F., Brosa, M. (2011). Economic evaluation of the levonorgestrel-releasing intrauterine system for the treatment of dysfunctional uterine bleeding in Spain. *European Journal of Obstetrics, Gynecology, and Reproductive Biology, 154*(1), 71–80.

Leushuis, E., Van der Steeg, J., Steures, P., Repping, S., Bossuyt, P., Mol, B., Hompes, P., & Van der Veen, F. (2014). Semen analysis and prediction of natural conception. *Human Reproduction, 29*(7), 1360–1367. Retrieved May 21, 2014, from http://humrep.oxfordjournals.org/content/early/2014/05/02/humrep.deu082.abstract.

Lev, A., & Lev, S. (1999). Sexual assault in the lesbian, gay, bisexual and transgender communities. In J. C. McClennen and J. Gunther (Eds.), *Same-sex partner abuse: A professional's guide to practice intervention,* (pp. 35–61). Lewiston, NY: Mellen Press.

LeVay, S. (1991). A difference in hypothalamic structure between heterosexual and homosexual men. *Science, 253,* 1034–1037.

Levenson, J., & Grady, M. (2016). The influence of childhood trauma on sexual violence and sexual deviance in adulthood. *Traumatology, 22*(2), 94–103.

Levenson, J., Willis, G., & Prescott, D. (2015). Adverse childhood experiences in the lives of female sex offenders. *Sexual Abuse: A Journal of Research and Treatment, 27*(3), 258–283.

Levin, R. J. (2007). Sexual activity, health and well-being—the beneficial roles of coitus and masturbation. *Sexual and Relationship Therapy, 22,* 135–148.

Levin, R., & Wylie, K. (2010). Persistent genital arousal disorder: A review of the literature and recommendations for management. *International Journal of STDs and AIDS, 21*(5), 379–380.

Levine, D. (2007). Ectopic pregnancy. *Radiology, 245,* 385–397.

Levine, J. (1991). Search and find. *Forbes, 148,* 134–135.

Levine, R., Sato, S., & Hashimoto, T. (1995). Love and marriage in eleven cultures. *Journal of Cross-Cultural Psychology, 26*(5), 554–571.

Levine, S. B., Risen, C. B., & Althof, S. E. (1990). Essay on the diagnosis and nature of paraphilia. *Journal of Sex and Marital Therapy, 16*(2), 89–102.

Lev-Wiesel, R. (2004). Male university students' attitudes toward rape and rapists. *Child & Adolescent Social Work Journal, 21,* 199.

Lew-Starowicz, M., & Gianotten, W. (2015). Sexual dysfunction in patients with multiple sclerosis. *Handbook of Clinical Neurology, 130,* 357–370.

Lew-Starowicz, M., & Rola, R. (2013). Prevalence of sexual dysfunctions among women with multiple sclerosis. *Sexuality and Disability, 31*(2), 141–153.

Lewes, K. (1988). *The psychoanalytic theory of male homosexuality.* New York: Meridian.

Lewin, R. (1988). New views emerge on hunters and gatherers. *Science, 240*(4856), 1146–1148.

Lewis, D. A. (2000). Chancroid: From clinical practice to basic science. *AIDS Patient Care and STDs, 14*(1), 19–36.

Lewis, M. (1997). *Altering fate: Why the past does not predict the future.* New York, NY: Guilford.

Lewis, M. (1999). On the development of personality. In L. A. Pervin & O. P. John (Eds.), *Handbook of personality: Theory and research* (2nd ed., pp. 327–346). New York, NY: Guilford.

Lewis, M., Atkins, D., Blayney, J., Dent, D., & Kaysen, D. (2013). What is hooking up? Examining definitions of hooking up in relation to behavior and normative perceptions. *Journal of Sex Research, 50*(8), 757–766.

Lewis, M., Granato, H., Blayney, J., Lostutter, T., & Kilmer, J. (2012). Predictors of hooking up sexual behaviors and emotional reactions among U.S. college students. *Archives of Sexual Behavior, 41*(5), 1219–1229.

Lewis, R. J., & Janda, L. H. (1988). The relationship between adult sexual adjustment and childhood experiences regarding exposure to nudity, sleeping in the parental bed, and parental attitudes toward sexuality. *Archives of Sexual Behavior, 17,* 349–362.

Lewis, R., & Ford-Robertson, J. (2010). Understanding the occurrence of interracial marriage in the United States through differential assimilation. *Journal of Black Studies, 41*(2), 405–420.

Lewis, R., & Marston, C. (2016). Oral sex, young people, and gendered narratives of reciprocity. *Journal of Sex Research, 53*(7), 776–787.

Ley, D. J. (2016, April 21). Political values and sex research. *Psychology Today.* Retrieved January 11, 2017, from https://www.psychologytoday.com/blog/women-who-stray/201604/political-values-and-sex-research.

Leyendecker, G., Kunz, G., Herbertz, M., Beil, D., Huppert, P., Mall, G., Kissler, S., Noe, M., & Wildt, L. (2004, December). Uterine peristaltic activity and the development of endometriosis. *Annals of the New York Academy of Sciences, 1034,* 338–355.

Leyson, J. F. (2004). Philippines. In R. T. Francoeur & R. J. Noonan (Eds.), *The Continuum International encyclopedia of sexuality* (pp. 825–845). New York/London: Continuum International.

Li, C. C., & Rew, L. (2010). A feminist perspective on sexuality and body image in females with colorectal cancer: An integrative review. *Journal of Wound Ostomy and Continence Nursing, 37*(5), 519–525.

Li, C. I., Malone, K. E., Daling, J. R., Potter, J. D., Bernstein, L., Marchbanks, P. A., et al. (2008). Timing of menarche and first full-term birth in relation to breast cancer risk. *Journal of Epidemiology, 167,* 230–239.

Li, D. K., Zhou, Z., Miao, M., He, Y., Wang, J., Ferber, J., Herrinton, L. J., Gao, E., & Yuan, W. (2011). Urine bisphenol-A (BPA) level in relation to semen quality. *Fertility and Sterility, 95*(2), 625–630, e1-e4.

Li, G., Pollitt, A., & Russell, S. (2016). Depression and sexual orientation during young adulthood: Diversity among sexual minority subgroups and the role of gender nonconformity. *Archives of Sexual Behavior, 45*(3), 697–711.

Li, H., Ding, X., Guo, C., Guan, H., & Xiong, C. (2012). Immunization of male mice with B-cell epitopes in transmembrane domains of CatSper1 inhibits fertility. *Fertility and Sterility, 97*(2), 445–452.

Li, Q., Davila, J., Bagchi, M., & Bagchi, I. (2016). Chronic exposure to bisphenol A impairs progesterone receptor-mediated signaling in the uterus during early pregnancy. *Receptors & Clinical Investigation, 3*(3). Retrieved March 30, 2017, from https://www.ncbi.nlm.nih.gov/pubmed/28239613.

Li, Y., Cohen, A. (2014). Religion, sexuality and family. In V. Saroglou (Ed.), *Religion, personality, and social behaviors* (pp. 213–229). New York: Psychology Press.

Liao, C., Wei, J., Li, Q., Li, L., Li, J., & Li, D. (2006). Efficacy and safety of cordocentesis for prenatal diagnosis. *International Journal of Gynecology and Obstetrics, 93,* 13–17.

Liao, L., Michala, L., & Creighton, S. (2010). Labial surgery for well women: A review of the literature. *British Journal of Obstetrics and Gynecology, 117*(1), 20–25.

Liben, L. S., & Bigler, R. S. (2002). The developmental course of gender differentiation. *Monographs of the Society of Research in Child Development, 67*(2), vii–147.

Lichtenberg, I. (2011, February 27). Child rape in South Africa persists unabated. *Monsters and Critics News.* Retrieved April 30, 2011, from http://www.monstersandcritics.com/news/africa/features/article_1622267.php/Child-rape-in-South-Africa-persists-unabated-Feature.

Liddicoat, A. (2009). Communication as culturally contexted practice. *Australian Journal of Linguistics, 29*(1), 115–133.

Lie, M. L., Robson, S. C., & May, C. R. (2008). Experiences of abortion: A narrative review of qualitative studies. *BMC Health Services Research, 8*, 150.

Lienemann, B., & Stopp, H. (2013). The association between media exposure of interracial relationships and attitudes toward interracial relationships. *Journal of Applied Social Psychology, 43*(Suppl. 2), 398–415.

Lifson, A., Grund, B., Gardner, E., Kaplan, R., Denning, E., Engen, N., Carey, C., Chen, F., Dao, S., Florence, E., Sanz, J., & Emery, S. (2017). Improved quality of life with immediate versus deferred initiation for antiretroviral therapy in early asymptomatic HIV infection. *AIDS, 31*(7), 953–963.

Light, A., Obedin-Maliver, J., Sevelius, J., & Kerns, J. (2014). Transgender men who experienced pregnancy after female-to-male gender transitioning. *Obstetrics and Gynecology, 124*(6) 1120–1127.

Lim, J. (2014, July 8). Popular testosterone therapy lacks evidence. *Live Science*. Retrieved July 8, 2014, from http://www.livescience.com/46703-popular-testosterone-therapy-lacks-evidence.html?cmpid=514645.

Lim, M. M., & Young, L. J. (2006). Neuropeptidergic regulation of affiliative behavior and social bonding in animals. *Hormones and Behavior, 50*, 506–517.

Limanonda, B., Chongvatana, N., Tirasawat, P., & Auwanit, W. (1993). *Summary report on the demographic and behavioral study of female commercial sex workers in Thailand*. Bangkok, Thailand: Institute of Population Studies.

Lindau, S., & Gavrilova, N. (2010). Sex, health, and years of sexually active life gained due to good health: Evidence from two US population based cross sectional surveys of ageing. *British Medical Journal, 340*, c810. Retrieved from http://www.bmj.com/content/340/bmj.c810.full.pdf.

Lindau, S., Gavrilova, N., & Anderson, D. (2007). Sexual morbidity in very long term survivors of vaginal and cervical cancer: A comparison to national norms. *Gynecologic Oncology, 106*(2), 413–418.

Lindau, S., Schumm, L., Laumann, E., Levinson, W., O'Muircheartaigh, C., & Waite, L. (2007). A study of sexuality and health among older adults in the United States. *The New England Journal of Medicine, 357*(8), 762–774.

Lindberg, L. D., Jones, R., & Santelli, J. S. (2008, July). Non-coital sexual activities among adolescents. *Journal of Adolescent Health*. Retrieved May 26, 2008, from http://www.guttmacher.org/pubs/JAH_Lindberg.pdf.

Lindberg, L., Maddow-Zimet, I., & Boonstra, H. (2016). Changes in adolescents' receipt of sex education, 2006–2013. *Journal of Adolescent Health, 58*(6), 621–627.

Lindh, I., Skjeldestad, F., Gemzell-Danielsson, K., Heikinheimo, O., Hognert, H., Milsom, I., & Lidegaard, Ø. (2016). Contraceptive use in the Nordic countries. *Acta Obstetricia et Gynecologica Scandinavica, 96*(1), 19–28.

Lindo, J., Siminski, P., & Swensen, I. (2016). College party culture and sexual assault. IZA Discussion Paper, #9700. Retrieved from http://ftp.iza.org/dp9700.pdf.

Lindo, J., Swensen, G., & Waddell, G. (2012). "Are big-time sports a threat to student achievement?" *American Economic Journal: Applied Economics, 4*(4), 254–274.

Ling, R., Baron, N., Lenhart, A., & Campbell, S. (2014). "Girls text really weird": Gender, testing and identity among teens. *Journal of Children and Media, 8*(4), 423–439.

Ling, R., Bertel, T., & Sundsoy, P. (2011). The socio-demographics of texting: An analysis of traffic data. *New Media & Society, 14*(2), 281–298.

Linton, K. D., & Wylie, K. R. (2010). Recent advances in the treatment of premature ejaculation. *Journal of Drug Design, Development and Therapy, 18*(4), 1–6.

Linz, D. (1989). Exposure to sexually explicit materials and attitudes toward rape: A comparison of study results. *The Journal of Sex Research, 26*, 50–84.

Linz, D., & Donnerstein, E. (1992, September 30). Research can help us explain violence and pornography. *The Chronicle of Higher Education*, B3–B4.

Lip, S., Murchison, L., Cullis, P., Govan, L., & Carachi, R. (2013). A meta-analysis of the risk of boys with isolated cryptorchidism developing testicular cancer in later life. *Archives of Disease in Childhood, 98*(1), 20–26.

Lipka, M., & Gramlich, J. (2017, January 26). Five facts about abortion. Pew Research Center. Retrieved April 12, 2017, from http://www.pewresearch.org/fact-tank/2017/01/26/5-facts-about-abortion/.

Lippa, R. A., & Tan, F. P. (2001). Does culture moderate the relationship between sexual orientation and gender-related personality trait? *Journal of Comparative Social Science, 35*(1), 65–87.

Lips, H. (2008). *Sex & gender: An introduction* (6th ed.). New York: McGraw-Hill.

Lips, N. (2016, July 15). Each country's most popular emoji revealed. *Refinery 29*. Retrieved January 11, 2017, from http://www.refinery29.uk/2016/07/116909/most-tweeted-emoji-by-country.

Lipsky, S., Caetano, R., Field, C. A., & Larkin, G. (2005). Psychosocial and substance-use risk factors for intimate partner violence. *Drug & Alcohol Dependence, 78*(1), 39–47.

Lipton, L. (2003). The erotic revolution. In J. Escoffier (Ed.), *Sexual revolution* (pp. 20–30). New York: Thunder's Mouth Press.

Lisak, D., & Miller, P. (2002). Repeat rape and multiple offending among undetected rapists. *Violence and Victims, 17*(1), 73–84.

Litosseliti, L. (2006). *Gender and language: Theory and practice*. London: Arnold.

Litt, D., Lewis, M., Blayney, J., & Kaysen, D. (2013). Protective behavioral strategies as a mediator of the generalized anxiety and alcohol use relationship among lesbian and bisexual women. *Journal of Studies on Alcohol and Drugs, 74*(1), 168–174.

Little, A. C., Burt, D. M., & Perrett, D. I. (2006). What is good is beautiful: Face preference reflects desired personality. *Personality and Individual Differences, 41*, 1107–1118.

Littleton, H., & Henderson, C. (2009). If she is not a victim, does that mean she was not traumatized? Evaluation of predictors of PTSD symptomatology among college rape victims. *Violence Against Women, 15*(2), 148–167.

Littleton, H., Breitkopf, C., & Berenson, A. (2007). Rape scripts of low-income European American and Latina women. *Sex Roles, 56*, 509–516.

Littleton, H., Grills-Taquechel, A., & Axsom, D. (2009a). Impaired and incapacitated rape victims: Assault characteristics and post-assault experiences. *Violence and Victims, 24*(4), 439–457.

Littleton, H., Tabernik, H., Canales, E., & Backstrom, T. (2009b). Risky situation or harmless fun? A qualitative examination of college women's bad hook-up and rape scripts. *Sex Roles, 60*(11–12), 793–805.

Liu, C. (2004). County health officials call for condoms in porn movies. *LA Times*. Retrieved November 15, 2008, from http://articles.latimes.com/2004/oct/08/local/me-porn8.

Liu, C., Xie, J., Wang, L., Zheng, Y., Ma, Z., Yang, H., Chen, X., Shi, G., Li, S., Zhao, J., et al. (2011). Immediate analgesia effect of single point acupuncture in primary dysmenorrhea: A randomized controlled trial. *Pain Medication, 12*(2), 300–307.

Liu, D. F., Jiang, H., Hong, K., Zhao, L. M., Tang, W. H., & Ma, L. L. (2010). Influence of erectile dysfunction course on its progress and efficacy of treatment with phosphodiesterase type 5 inhibitors. *Chinese Medical Journal, 123*(22), 3258–3261.

Liu, E., Nisenblat, V., Farquhar, C., Fraswer, I., Bossuyt, P., Johnson, N., & Hull, M. (2015). Urinary biomarkers for the non-invasive diagnosis of endometriosis. The Cochrane Database of Systematic Reviews. Retrieved January 20, 2017, from http://www.cochrane.org/CD012019/MENSTR_urinary-biomarkers-non-invasive-diagnosis-endometriosis.

Liu, H., Waite, L., Shen, S., & Wang, D. (2016). Is sex good for your health? A national study on partnered sexuality and cardiovascular risk among older men and women. *Journal of Health and Social Behavior, 57*(3), 276–296.

Livingston, G. (2014, November 14). The demographics of remarriage. Pew Research Center, Social & Demographic Trends. Retrieved March 6, 2017, from http://www .pewsocialtrends.org/2014/11/14/chapter-2 -the-demographics-of-remarriage/.

Livingston, G., & Caumont, A. (2017, February 13). 5 facts on love and marriage in America. Pew Research Center, Fact Tank. Retrieved March 6, 2017, from http://www.pewresearch .org/fact-tank/2017/02/13/5-facts-about-love -and-marriage/.

Livingston, G., & Cohn, D. (2010). The new demography of American motherhood. Pew Research Center. Retrieved July 2, 2011, from http://pewsocialtrends.org/files/2010/10/754 -new-demography-of-motherhood.pdf.

Lloyd, R., Files, J., & Mayer, A. (2012). Perimenopause: Counting sheep and still no sleep. *Journal of Women's Health, 21*(11), 1209–1210.

Lloyd, T., Hounsome, L., Mehay, A., Mee, S., Verne, J., & Cooper, A. (2015). Lifetime risk of being diagnosed with, or dying from, prostate cancer by major ethnic group in England 2008–2010. *BMC Medicine, 13*(1), 171.

Lobo, R., Pickar, J., Stevenson, J., Mack, W., & Hodis, H. (2016). Back to the future: Hormone replacement therapy as part of prevention strategy for women at the onset of menopause. *Atherosclerosis, 254*, 282–290.

Lock, J., & Steiner, H. (1999). Gay lesbian and bisexual youth risks for emotional, physical, and social problems: Results from a community-based survey. *Journal of American Academy of Child and Adolescent Psychiatry 38*(3), 297–305.

Locker, L., McIntosh, W., Hackney, A., Wilson, J., & Wiegand, K. (2010). The breakup of romantic relationships: Situational predictors of perception of recovery. *North American Journal of Psychology, 12*(3), 565–578.

Lohiya, N. K., Suthar, R., Khandelwal, A., Goyal, S., Ansari, A. S., & Manivannan, B. (2010). Sperm characteristics and teratology in rats following vas deferens occlusion with RISUG and its reversal. *International Journal of Andrology, 33*(1), e198-e206.

Lombardi, G., Del Popolo, G., Macchiarella, A., Mencarini, M., & Celso, M. (2010). Sexual rehabilitation in women with spinal cord injury: A critical review of the literature. *Spinal Cord, 48*(12), 842–849.

Lombardi, G., Macchiarella, A., Cecconi, F., & Del Popolo, G. (2009). Ten-year follow-up of sildenafil use in spinal cord-injured patients with erectile dysfunction. *Journal of Sexual Medicine, 6*(12), 3449–3457.

Lombardo, W., Cretser, G., & Roesch, S. (2001). For crying out loud—the differences persist into the '90s. *Sex Roles, 45*(7–8), 529–547.

Long, M., Faubion, S., MacLaughlin, K., Pruthi, S., & Casey, P. (2015). Contraception and hormonal management in the perimenopause. *Journal of Women's Health, 24*(1), 3–10.

Long, S., Ullman, S., Long, L., Mason, G., & Starzynski, L. (2007). Women's experiences of male-perpetrated sexual assault by sexual orientation. *Violence and Victims, 22*, 684–701.

Long, V. E. (2003). Contraceptive choices: New options in the U.S. market. *SIECUS Report, 31*(2), 13–18.

Longua, P. (2010). "I love you" (but I can't look you in the eyes): Explicit and implicit self-esteem predict verbal and nonverbal response to relationship threat. Chicago: Loyola University, AAT #3434370.

Lonsway, K., Cortina, L., & Magley, V. (2008). Sexual harassment mythology: Definition, conceptualization, and measurement. *Sex Roles, 58*, 599–616.

Looker, K., Magaret, A., May, M., Turner, K., Vickerman, P., Gottlieb, S., & Newman, L. (2015). Global and regional estimates of prevalent and incident herpes simplex virus type 1 infections in 2012. *PLoS One*. Retrieved April 30, 2017, from http://journals.plos .org/plosone/article?id=10.1371/journal .pone.0140765.

Looker, K., Magaret, A., May, M., Turner, K., Vickerman, P., Gottlieb, S., & Newman, L. (2015a). Global and regional estimates of prevalent and incident herpes simplex virus type 2 infections in 2012. *PLoS One*. Retrieved April 30, 2017, from http://journals .plos.org/plosone/article?id=10.1371/journal .pone.0114989.

Lopez, L., Grimes, D. A., Gallo, M., & Schulz, K. (2008). Skin patch and vaginal ring versus combined oral contraceptives for contraception. *Cochrane Database Systems Review, 23*, CD003552.

LoPiccolo, J., & Lobitz, W. C. (1972). The role of masturbation in the treatment of orgasmic dysfunction. *Archives of Sexual Behavior, 2*, 163–171.

LoPiccolo, J., & Stock, W. E. (1986). Treatment of sexual dysfunction. *Journal of Consulting and Clinical Psychology, 54*, 158–167.

Lorenz, K., & Ullman, S. (2016). Alcohol and sexual assault victimization: Research finding and future directions. *Aggression and Violent Behavior, 31*, 82–94.

LoRusso, G., Tomao, F., Spinelli, G., Prete, A., STati, V., Panici, P., Papa, A., & Tomao, S. (2015). Fertility drugs and breast cancer risk. *European Journal of Gynacological Oncology, 36*(2), 107–113.

Lott, A. J., & Lott, B. E. (1961). Group cohesiveness, communication level, and conformity. *Journal of Abnormal & Social Psychology, 62*, 408–412.

Loucks, A. B., & Nattiv, A. (2005). The female athlete triad. *Lancet, 366*, s49–s50.

Love, E., Bhattacharya, S., Smith, N., & Bhattacharya, S. (2010). Effect of interpregnancy interval on outcomes of pregnancy after miscarriage: Retrospective analysis of hospital episode statistics in Scotland. *British Medical Journal, 341*, c3967.

Lovejoy, F. H., & Estridge, D. (Eds.). (1987). *The new child health encyclopedia*. New York: Delacorte Press.

Lovejoy, M. C. (2015). Hooking up as an individualistic practice: A double-edged sword for college women. *Sexuality & Culture, 19*(3), 464–492.

Low, W. Y., Wong, Y. L., Zulkifli, S. W., & Tan, H. (2002). Malaysian cultural differences in knowledge, attitudes and practices related to erectile dysfunction. *International Journal of Impotence Research, 14*(6), 440–445.

Lu, W., Mueser, K., Rosenberg, S., & Jankowski, M. (2008). Correlates of adverse childhood experiences among adults with severe mood disorders. *Psychiatric Services, 59*, 1018–1026.

Luby, J., Belden, A., Whalen, D., Harms, M., & Barch, D. (2016). Breastfeeding and childhood IQ: The mediating role of gray matter volume. *Journal of the American Academy of Child and Adolescent Psychiatry, 55*(5), 367–375.

Luchies, L., Rusbult, C., Eastwick, P., Wieselquist, J., Kumashiro, M., Coolsen, M., & Finkel, E. (2013). Trust and biased memory of transgressions in romantic relationships. *Journal of Personality and Social Psychology, 104*(4), 673–694.

Luciano, E., & Orth, U. (2017). Transitions in romantic relationships and development of self-esteem. *Journal of Personality and Social Psychology, 112*(2), 307–328.

Lucie-Smith, E. (1991). *Sexuality in western art*. London: Thames & Hudson.

Luckenbill, D. F. (1984). Dynamics of the deviant scale. *Deviant Behavior, 5*, 337–353.

Ludermir, A., Lewis, G., Valongueiro, S., de Araujo, T., & Araya, R. (2010). Violence against women by their intimate partner during pregnancy and postnatal depression: A prospective cohort study. *Lancet, 376*(9744), 903–910.

Lue, T. (2000). Erectile dysfunction. *New England Journal of Medicine, 342*(24), 1802–1813.

Lundsberg, L., Pal, L., Gariety, A., Xu, X., Chu, M., & Illuzzi, J. (2014). Knowledge, attitudes, and practices regarding conception and fertility: A population-based survey among reproductive-age U.S. women. *Fertility and Sterility, 101*(3), 767–774.

Lundy-Wagner, V., & Winkel-Wagner, R. (2013). A harassing climate? Sexual harassment and campus racial climate research. *Journal of Diversity in Higher Education, 6*(1), 51–68.

Luo, S., & Tuney, S. (2015). Can texting be used to improve romantic relationships? The effects of sending positive text messages on relationship satisfaction. *Computers in Human Behavior, 49*, 670–678.

Luo, X., & Jiang, K. (2016). Relationship between jealousy and attachment in college students. *Chinese Mental Health Journal, 30*(3), 231–236.

Lurie, S., Kedar, D., Boaz, M., Golan, A., & Sadan, O. (2013). Need for episiotomy in a subsequent delivery following previous delivery with episiotomy. *Archives of Gynecology and Obstetrics, 287*(2), 201–204.

Lutfey, K. E., Link, C., Rosen, R., Wiegel, M., & McKinlay, J. (2008, January 11). Prevalence and correlates of sexual activity and function in women: Results from the Boston Area Community Health (BACH) survey. *Archives of Sexual Behavior.* Retrieved October 30, 2008, from http://www.springerlink.com /content/f47306253471w048/?p=efd510bd7d9 a43c29bd1f1b7ca8b33b3&pi=0.

Luxenburg, J., & Klein, L. (1984). CB radio prostitution: Technology and the displacement of deviance. In Chaneles. S (Ed.), *Gender issues, sex offences, and criminal justice: Current trends* (pp. 71–87). New York: The Haworth Press.

Lynch, M. (2012). Food messages in television programs for preschoolers: A call for research. *Canadian Journal of Communication, 37*(2), 345–353.

Lyons, H., Manning, W., Longmore, M., & Giordano, P. (2014). Young adult casual sexual behavior: Life-course-specific motivations and consequences. *Sociological Perspectives, 57*(1), 79–101.

Maas, C. P., ter Kuile, M. M., Laan, E., Tuynman, C. C., Weyenborg, P., Trimbos, J. B., & Kenter, G. G. (2004). Objective assessment of sexual arousal in women with a history of hysterectomy. *British Journal of Obstetrics and Gynaecology, 111*, 456–462.

Maas, J. (1998). *Power sleep.* New York: HarperCollins.

MacArthur, H., & Shields, S. (2015). There's no crying in baseball, or is there? Male athletes, tears, and masculinity in North America. *Emotional Review, 7*(1), 39–46.

MacArthur, T., Bachmann, G., & Ayers, C. (2016). Menopausal women requesting egg/embryo donation: Examining health screening guidelines for assisted reproductive technology. *Menopause, 23*(7), 799–802.

Maccio, E. M. (2010). Influence of family, religion, and social conformity on client participation in sexual reorientation therapy. *Journal of Homosexuality, 57*(3), 441–458.

Maccoby, E. E. (2002). Gender and group process: A developmental perspective. *Current Directions in Psychological Science, 11*(2), 54–58.

Maccoby, E. E., Jacklin, C. N. (1987). Gender segregation in childhood. In H. W. Reese (Ed.), *Advances in child development and behavior,* (Vol. *20,* pp. 239–287). San Diego, CA: Academic Press.

MacDonald, T., Noel-Weiss, J., West, D., Walks, M., Biener, M., Kibbe, A., Myler, E. (2016). Transmasculine individuals' experiences with lactation, chestfeeding, and gender identity: A qualitative study. *BMC Pregnancy & Childbirth,* 16(16). Retrieved May 9, 2017, from https://bmcpregnancychildbirth.biomedcentral .com/articles/10.1186/s12884-016-0907-y.

Macdorman, M. F., Declercq, E., & Menacker, F. (2011). Trends and characteristics of home births in the United States by race and ethnicity, 1990–2006. *Birth, 38*(1), 17–23.

MacDorman, M., & Gregory, E. (2015). Fetal and perinatal mortality: United States, 2013. *National Vital Statistics Reports, 64*(8).

Macdowall, W., Wellings, K., Stephenson, J., & Glasier, A. (2008). Summer nights: A review of the evidence of seasonal variations in sexual health indicators among young people. *Health Education, 108*, 40.

Mackay, J. (2000). *The Penguin atlas of human sexual behavior.* New York: Penguin.

Mackesy-Amiti, M., Fendrich, M., & Johnson, T. (2008). Substance-related problems and treatment among men who have sex with men in comparison to other men in Chicago. *Journal of Substance Abuse and Treatment.* Epub ahead of print. Retrieved September 19, 2008, from http://www.ncbi.nlm.nih.gov /pubmed/18715744.

MacKinnon, C. A. (1985, March 26). Pornography: Reality, not fantasy. *The Village Voice.*

MacKinnon, C. A. (1986). Pornography: Not a moral issue. (Special Issue: Women and the law.) *Women's Studies International Forum, 9,* 63–78.

MacKinnon, C. A. (1987). *Feminism unmodified: Discourses on life and law.* Cambridge, MA: Harvard University Press.

MacKinnon, C. A. (1993). *Only words.* Cambridge, MA: Harvard University Press.

Mackintosh, E. (2017). Abortion laws around the world: From bans to personal choice. CNN. Retrieved April 12, 2017, from http:// www.cnn.com/2017/01/25/health/abortion -laws-around-the-world/.

Macneil, S. (2004). It takes two: Modeling the role of sexual self-disclosure in sexual satisfaction. *Dissertation Abstracts International: Section B: The Sciences & Engineering, 65* (1-B), 481. (#0419–4217).

Macur, J. (2012, October 22). Lance Armstrong is stripped of his 7 Tour de France titles. *New York Times.* Retrieved January 27, 2017, from http://www.nytimes.com/2012/10/23/sports /cycling/armstrong-stripped-of-his-7-tour -de-france-titles.html.

Madan, R. A., & Gulley, J. L. (2010). The current and emerging role of immunotherapy in prostate cancer. *Clinical Genitourinary Cancer, 8*(1), 10–16.

Madigan, N. (2004). Man, 86, convicted under new law against Americans who go abroad to molest minors. Retrieved November 11, 2004, from http://travel2.nytimes.com/2004/11/20 /national/20predator.html?ex=1129003200& en=8275e98301fbe992&ei=5070&n=Top%2 fFeatures%2fTravel%2fDestinations%2fUnit ed%20States%2fRegions.

Madowitz, J., Matheson, B., & Liang, J. (2015). The relationship between eating disorders and sexual trauma. *Eating and Weight Disorders, 20*(3), 281–293.

Maestripieri, D., Henry, A., & Nickels, N. (2016). Explaining financial and prosocial biases in favor of attractive people: Interdisciplinary perspectives from economics, social psychology, and evolutionary psychology. *Behavioral and Brain Sciences,* 1–76.

Maestripieri, D., Klimczuk, A., Traficonte, D., & Wilson, M. (2014). Ethnicity-related variation in sexual promiscuity, relationship status, and testosterone levels in men. *Evolutionary Behavioral Sciences, 8*(2), 96–108.

Maguen, S, & Armistead, L. (2006). Abstinence among female adolescents: Do parents matter above and beyond the influence of peers? *American Journal of Orthopsychiatry, 76*(2), 260–264.

Mah, K., & Binik, Y. (2005). Are orgasms in the mind or the body? Psychosocial versus physiological correlates of orgasmic pleasure and satisfaction. *Journal of Sex & Marital Therapy, 31*(3), 187–200.

Mahabir, S., Spitz, M. R., Barrera, S. L., Dong, Y. Q., Eastham, C., & Forman, M. R. (2008). Dietary boron and hormone replacement therapy as risk factors for lung cancer in women. *American Journal of Epidemiology* (Epub). Retrieved March 18, 2008, from http://www.ncbi.nlm.nih.gov/sites/entrez.

MaHood, J., & Wenburg, A. R. (1980). *The Mosher survey.* New York: Arno.

Maines, R. (1999). *Hysteria, the vibrator, and women's sexual satisfaction.* Baltimore: The Johns Hopkins University Press.

Major, B., Appelbaum, M., Beckman, L., Dutton, M., Russo, N., & West, C. (2008). *Report of the APA Task Force on Mental Health and Abortion.* Retrieved May 26, 2014, from http://www.apa.org/pi/women/programs /abortion/mental-health.pdf.

Major, B., Cozzarelli, C., Cooper, L., Zubek, J., Richards, C., Wilhite, M., & Gramzow, R. (2000). Psychological responses of women after first-trimester abortion. *Archives of General Psychiatry, 57*(8), 777–784.

Makı, K., Kaspar, K., Khoo, C., Derrig, L., Schild, A., & Gupta, K. (2016). Consumption of a cranberry juice beverage lowered the number of clinical urinary tract infection episodes in women with a recent history of urinary tract infection. *The American Journal of Clinical Nutrition, 103*(6), 1434–1442.

Malacad, B., & Hess, G. (2010). Oral sex: Behaviors and feelings of Canadian young females and implications for sex education. *European Journal of Contraception and Reproductive Health Care, 15*(3), 177–185.

Malamuth, N., Addison, T., & Koss, M. (2000). Pornography and sexual aggression: Are there reliable effects and can we understand them? *Annual Review of Sex Research, 11*(1), 26–91.

Malamuth, N., Hald, G., & Koss, M. (2012). Pornography, individual differences in risk and men's acceptance of violence against women in a representative sample. *Sex Roles, 66*, 427–439.

Malik, M., Norian, J., McCarthy-Keith, D., Britten, J., & Catherino, W. (2010). Why leiomyomas are called fibroids: The central role of extracellular matrix in symptomatic women. *Seminars in Reproductive Medicine, 28*(3), 169–179.

Malmo, C., & Laidlaw, T. (2010). Symptoms of trauma and traumatic memory retrieval in adult survivors of childhood sexual abuse. *Journal of Trauma and Dissociation, 11*(1), 22–43.

Malone, P., & Steinbrecher, H. (2007). Medical aspects of male circumcision. *British Medical Journal, 335*(7631), 1206–1290.

Maltz, D. W., & Borker, R. A. (1982). A cultural approach to male-female communication. In J. J. Gumperz (Ed.), *Language and social identity* (pp. 196–216). New York. Cambridge University Press.

Maltz, W. (1990, December). Adult survivors of incest: How to help them overcome the trauma. *Medical Aspects of Human Sexuality*, 38–43.

Maltz, W. (2002). Treating the sexual intimacy concerns of sexual abuse survivors. *Sexual and Relationship Therapy, 17*(4), 321–327.

Maltz, W., & Boss, S. (2001). *Private thoughts: Exploring the power of women's sexual fantasies.* Novato, CA: New World Library.

Manago, A., Taylor, T., & Greenfield, P. (2012). Me and my 400 friends: The anatomy of college students' Facebook networks, their communication patterns, and well-being. *Developmental Psychology, 48*(2), 369–380.

Mandelbaum, J. (2010). What motivates female suicide bombers? Open Salon. Retrieved April 10, 2010, from http://open.salon.com/blog/judy_mandelbaum/2010/04/05/what_motivates_female_suicide_bombers.

Maness, D. L., Reddy, A., Harraway-Smith, C. L., Mitchell, G., & Givens, V. (2010). How best to manage dysfunctional uterine bleeding. *Journal of Family Practice, 59*(8), 449–458.

Manganiello, A., Hoga, L., Reberte, L., Miranda, C., & Rocha, C. (2011). Sexuality and quality of life of breast cancer patients post mastectomy. *European Journal of Oncology Nursing, 15*(2), 167–172.

Mangin, D., Murdoch, D., Wells, J., Coughlan, E., Bagshaw, S., Corwin, P., Chambers, S., & Toop, L. (2012). Chlamydia trachomatis testing sensitivity in midstream compared with first-void urine specimens. *Annals of Family Medicine, 10*(1), 50–53.

Manley, M., Diamond, L., & Van Anders, S. (2015). Polyamory, monoamory, and sexual fluidity: A longitudinal study of identity and sexual trajectories. *Psychology of Sexual Orientation and Gender Diversity, 2*(2), 168–180.

Mannheimer, S., Friedland, G., Matts, J., Child, C., & Chesney, M. (2002). The consistency of adherence to antiretroviral therapy predicts biologic outcome for HIV-infected persons in clinical trials. *Clinical Infectious Disease, 34*(8), 1115–1121.

Manniche, L. (1987). *Sexual life in ancient Egypt.* London: KPI Ltd.

Manning, W., Brown, S., & Stykes, J. (2016). Same-sex and different-sex cohabiting couple relationship stability. *Demography, 53*(4), 937–953.

Manning, W., Fettro, M., & Lamidi, E. (2014, May). Child well-being in same-sex parent families: Review of research prepared for American Sociological Association Amicus Brief. *Population Research and Policy Review, 33*(4), 485–502. Retrieved May 19, 2014, from http://link.springer.com/article/10.1007/s11113-014-9329-6#.

Mansour, D. (2010). Nexplanon: What Implanon did next. *Journal of Family Planning and Reproductive Health Care, 36*(4), 187–189.

Maranghi, F., Mantovani, A., Macrì, C., Romeo, A., Eleuteri, P., Leter, G., Rescia, M., Spanò, M., & Saso, L. (2005). Long-term effects of lonidamine on mouse testes. *Contraception, 72*(4), 268–272.

Marazziti, D., Falaschi, V., Lombardi, A., Mungai, F., & Dell'Osso, L. (2015). Stalking: A neurobiological perspective. *Rivista di Psichiatria, 50*(1), 12–18.

Marchbanks, P., Curtis, K., Mandel, M., Wilson, H., Jeng, G., Folger, S., McDonald, J., Daling, J., et al. (2012). Oral contraceptive formation and risk of breast cancer. *Contraception, 85*(4), 342–350.

Marck, C., Jelinek, P., Weiland, T., Hocking, J., DeLivera, A., Taylor, K., Neate, S., Pereira, N., & Jelinek, G. (2016). Sexual function in multiple sclerosis and associations with demographic, disease and lifestyle characteristics: An international cross-sectional study. *BMC Neurology, 16*(1), 210.

Margari, L., Lamanna, A., Craig, F., Simone, M., & Gentile, M. (2014). Autism spectrum disorders in XYY syndrome: Two new cases and systematic review of the literature. *European Journal of Pediatrics.* Retrieved February 14, 2014, from http://www.ncbi.nlm.nih.gov/pubmed/24464091.

Margolis, J. (2004). *O: The intimate history of the orgasm.* New York: Grove/Atlantic Press.

Margulies, S. (2003). The psychology of prenuptial agreements. *Journal of Psychiatry & Law, 31*(4), 415–432.

Margulis, L., & Sagan, D. (1991). *Mystery dance: On the evolution of human sexuality.* New York: Summit Books.

Marín, R., Christensen, A., & Atkins, D. (2014). Infidelity and behavioral couple therapy: Relationship outcomes over 5 years following therapy. *Couple and Family Psychology: Research and Practice, 3*(1), 1–12.

Marinakis, G., & Nikolaou, D. (2011). What is the role of assisted reproduction technology in the management of age-related infertility? *Human Fertility, 14*, 8–15.

Maritz, G. S. (2008). Nicotine and lung development. Birth Defects Research, Part C. 84, 45–53.

Marjoribanks, J., Brown, J., O'Brien, P., Wyatt, K. (2013). Selective serotonin reuptake inhibitors for premenstrual syndrome. *Cochrane Database of Systematic Reviews.* Retrieved February 21, 2014, from http://www.ncbi.nlm.nih.gov/pubmed/23744611.

Mark, K., Desai, A., & Terplan, M. (2016). Marijuana use and pregnancy: Prevalence, associated characteristics, and birth outcomes. *Archives of Women's Mental Health, 19*(1), 105–111.

Mark, K., Garcia, J., & Fisher, H. (2015). Perceived emotional and sexual satisfaction across sexual relationship contexts: Gender and sexual orientation differences and similarities. *The Canadian Journal of Human Sexuality, 24*(2), 120–130.

Mark, K., & Jozkowski, K. (2013). The mediating role of sexual and nonsexual communication between relationship and sexual satisfaction in a sample of college-age heterosexual couples. *Journal of Sex and Marital Therapy, 39*(5), 410–427.

Mark, K., Rosenkrantz, D., & Kerner, I. (2014). "Bi"ing into monogamy: Attitudes toward monogamy in a sample of bisexual-identified adults. *Psychology of Sexual Orientation and Gender Diversity, 1*(3), 263–269.

Mark, K., Wald, A., Mageret, A., Selke, S., Olin, I., Huang, M., & Corey, L. (2008). Rapidly cleared episodes of herpes simplex virus reactivation in immunocompetent adults. *Journal of Infectious Disease.* Epub ahead of print. Retrieved September 19, 2008, from http://www.ncbi.nlm.nih.gov/sites/entrez.

Markel, H. (2005). The search for effective HIV vaccines. *The New England Journal of Medicine, 353*(8), 753–757.

Marques, J., & Aires, S. (2016). Association of Turner syndrome and growth hormone deficiency: A review. *Pediatric Endocrinology Reviews, 13*(1), 455–457.

Marrazzo, J. (2004). Barriers to infectious disease care among lesbians. *Emerging Infectious Disease, 10*, 1974–1978.

Marrazzo, J., Cook, R., Wiesenfeld, H., Murray, P., Busse, B., Krohn, M., & Hillier, S. (2007). *Lactobacillus* capsule for the treatment of bacterial vaginosis. *Journal of Women's Health, 15*, 1053–1060.

Marrazzo, J., Thomas, K., Fiedler, T., Ringwood, K., & Fredricks, D. (2008). Relationship of specific vaginal bacteria and bacterial vaginosis treatment failure in women who have sex with women. *Annals of Internal Medicine, 149*, 20–28.

Marrazzo, M., Thomas, K., Fiedler, T., Ringwood, K., & Fredricks, D. (2010). Risks for acquisition of bacterial vaginosis among women who report sex with women: A cohort study. *PLoS One, 5*(6), e11139.

Marshal, M. P., Friedman, M. S., Stall, R., & Thompson, A. L. (2009). Individual trajectories of substance use in lesbian, gay and bisexual youth and heterosexual youth. *Addiction, 104*(6), 974–981.

Marshall, D. S. (1971). Sexual behavior on Mangaia. In D. S. Marshall & R. C. Suggs (Eds.), *Human sexual behavior*. New York: Basic Books.

Marshall, D. S., Suggs, R. C. (1971). *Human sexual behavior: Variations in the ethnographic spectrum*. New York, NY: Basic Books.

Marshall, W. L. (1979). Satiation therapy: A procedure for reducing deviant sexual arousal. *Journal of Applied Behavior Analysis, 12*(3), 377–389.

Martell, C., & Prince, S. (2005). Treating infidelity in same-sex couples. *Journal of Clinical Psychology, 61*(11), 1429–1438.

Martenies, S., & Perry, M. (2013). Environmental and occupational pesticide exposure and human sperm parameters: A systematic review. *Toxicology, 307*, 66–73.

Martens, W. (2007). Optimism therapy: An adapted psychotherapeutic strategy for adult female survivors of childhood sexual abuse. *Annals of the American Psychotherapy Association, 10*, 30–38.

Martin-Storey, A., & Crosnoe, R. (2014). Peer harassment and risky behavior among sexual minority girls and boys. *American Journal of Orthopsychiatry, 84*(1), 54–65.

Martin, C., Anderson, R., Cheng, L., Ho, P., Van der Spuy, Z., Smith, K., Glasier, A., Everington, D., & Baird, D. (2000). Potential impact of hormonal male contraception: Cross-cultural implications for development of novel preparations. *Human Reproduction, 15*(3), 637–645.

Martin, D., Martin, M., & Carvalho, K. (2008). Reading and learning-disabled children: Understanding the problem. *The Clearing House, 81*, 113–118.

Martin, H. P. (1991). The coming-out process for homosexuals. *Hospital and Community Psychiatry, 42*, 158–162.

Martin, J. A., Hamilton, B. E., Sutton, P. D., Ventura, S. J., Menacker, F., Kirmeyer, S., & Mathews, T. J. (2009). Births: Final data for 2006. *National Vital Statistics Reports, 57*(7), National Center for Health Statistics.

Martin, J. A., Hamilton, B. E., Sutton, P., Ventura, S., Menacker, F., Kirmeyer, S., & Munson, M. (2007, December 5). Births: Final data for 2005. *National Vital Statistics Report, 56*(6). Retrieved May 31, 2008, from http://www.cdc.gov/nchs/data/nvsr/nvsr56/nvsr56_06.pdf.

Martin, J., Hamilton, B., & Osterman, M. (2016). Births in the United States, 2015. National Vital Statistics Reports, 258, National Center for Health Statistics. Retrieved March 27, 2017, from https://www.cdc.gov/nchs/data/databriefs/db258.pdf.

Martin, J., Hamilton, B., Osterman, M., Curtin, S., & Mathews, T. (2013). Births: Final data for 2012. *National Vital Statistics Reports, 52*(9). Retrieved May 21, 2014, from http://www.cdc.gov/nchs/data/nvsr/nvsr62/nvsr62_09.pdf.

Martin, J., Hamilton, B., Venture, S., Osterman, M., Curtin, S., & Matthews, T. (2013). Births: Final data for 2012. *National Vital Statistics Report, 62*(9).

Martin, K., & Luke, K. (2010). Gender differences in the ABC's of the birds and bees: What mothers teach young children about sexuality and reproduction, *Sex Roles, 62*(3–4), 278–291.

Martin, T. A. (2003). Power and consent: Relation to self-reported sexual assault and acquaintance rape. *Dissertation Abstracts International: Section B: The Sciences & Engineering, 64*(3-B), #0419–4217.

Martin, W. E. (2001). A wink and a smile: How men and women respond to flirting. *Psychology Today, 34*(5), 26–27.

Martins, Kolomiets, B., Caplette, R., Sahel, J., Castelo-Branco, M., Ambrósio, A., Picaud, S. (2015). Sildenafil acutely decreases visual responses in ON and OFF retinal ganglion cells, *Investigative Ophthalmology & Visual Science, 56*(4), 2639–2648.

Martínez-Burgos, M., Herrero, L., Megías, D., Salvanes, R., Montoya, M. C., Cobo, A. C., & Garcia-Velasco, J. A. (2011). Vitrification versus slow freezing of oocytes: Effects on morphologic appearance, meiotic spindle configuration, and DNA damage. *Fertility and Sterility, 95*(1), 374–377.

Martinez, G., & Abma, J. (2015). Sexuality activity, contraceptive use, and childbearing of teenagers aged 15–19 in the United States, National Center for Health Statistics Data Brief, 209. Retrieved February 11, 2017, from https://www.cdc.gov/nchs/data/databriefs/db209.pdf.

Martinez, G., Abma, J., & Casey, C. (2010). Educating teenagers about sex in the United States (National Center for Health Statistics, *Data Brief No. 44*).

Martinez, G., Abma, J., & Copen, C. (2010). Educating teenagers about sex in the United States. *NCHS Data Brief, 44*, 1–8.

Martinez, G., Copen, C., & Abma, J. (2011). Teenagers in the United States: Sexual activity, contraceptive use, and childbearing, 2006–2010. *National Survey of Family Growth, Vital and Health Statistics, Series 23* (31). Retrieved April 14, 2014, from http://www.cdc.gov/nchs/data/series/sr_23/sr23_031.pdf.

Martinez, G. M., Chandra, A., Abma, J. C., Jones, J., & Mosher, W. D. (2006). Fertility, contraception, and fatherhood: Data on men and women from cycle 6 (2002) of the National Survey of Family Growth. *Vital Health Statistics, 23*(26). Hyattsville, MD: National Center for Health Statistics, Centers for Disease Control.

Martins, J., Kolomiets, B., Caplette, R., Sahel, J., Castelo-Branco, M., Ambrósio, A., & Picaud, S. (2015). Sildenafil acutely decreases visual responses in on and off retinal ganglion cells. *Investigative Ophthalmology & Visual Science, 56*(4), 2639–2648.

Martins, N., Malacane, M., Lewis, N., & Kraus, A. (2016). A content analysis of teen parenthood in "Teen Mom" reality programming. *Health Communication, 31*(12), 1548–1556.

Martinson, F. M. (1981). Eroticism in infancy and childhood. In L. L. Constantine & F. M. Martinson (Eds.), *Children and sex: New findings, new perspectives* (pp. 23–35). Boston: Little, Brown.

Marty, R. (2017, February 7). What will happen if *Roe v. Wade* is overturned? Retrieved April 12, 2017, from http://www.care2.com/causes/what-will-happen-if-roe-v-wade-is-overturned.html.

Marx, R., & Kettrey, H. (2016). Gay-straight alliances are associated with lower levels of school-based victimization of LGBTQ+ youth: A systematic review and meta-analysis. *Journal of Youth and Adolescence, 45*(7), 1269–1282.

Maseroli, E., Rastrelli, G., Corona, G., Boddi, V., Amato, A., Mannucci, E., Forti, G., & Maggi, M. (2014). Gynecomastia in subjects with sexual dysfunction. *Journal of Endocrinological Investigation, 37*(6), 525–532.

Masho, S., & Anderson, L. (2009). Sexual assault in men: A population-based study of Virginia. *Violence and Victims, 24*(1), 98–110.

Mason, M. A., Fine, M. A., & Carcochan, S. (2001). Family law in the new millennium: For whose families? *Journal of Family Issues, 22*(7), 859–882.

Mason, P. (2013). Intersex genital autonomy: A rights-based framework for medical interventions with intersex infants. In G. C. Denniston, F. Hodges, & M. Fayre Milos (Eds.), *Genital cutting: Protecting children from medical, cultural, and religious infringements* (pp. 149–184). New York, NY: Springer Science & Business Media.

Masoomi, M., Zare, J., Kahnooj, M., Mirzazadeh, A., & Sheikhvatan, M. (2010). Sex differences in potential daily triggers of the onset of acute myocardial infarction: A case-crossover analysis among an Iranian population. *Journal of Cardiovascular Medicine, 11*(10), 723–726.

Massa, G., Verlinde, F., DeSchepper, J., Thomas, M., Bourguignon, J. P, Craen, M., de Segher, F., Francois, I., Du Caju, M., Maes, M., & Heinrichs, C. (2005). Trends in age at diagnosis of Turner syndrome. *Archives of Disease in Childhood, 90*(3), 267–275.

Massart, F., & Saggese, G. (2010). Morphogenetic targets and genetics of undescended testis. *Sexual Development, 4*(6), 326–335.

Masser, B., Viki, T., & Power, C. (2006). Hostile sexism and rape proclivity amongst men. *Sex Roles, 54*, 565–574.

Mast, M. S., & Sczesny, S. (2010). Gender, power, and nonverbal behavior. In J. C. Chrisler & D. R. McCreary (Eds.), *Handbook of Gender Research in Psychology* (pp. 411–425). New York, NY: Springer.

Masters, W. H., & Johnson, V. E. (1966). *Human sexual response*. Boston: Little, Brown.

Masters, W. H., & Johnson, V. E. (1970). *Human sexual inadequacy*. Boston: Little, Brown.

Masters, W. H., & Johnson, V. E. (1979). *Homosexuality in perspective*. Boston: Little, Brown.

Masters, W. H., Johnson, V. E., & Kolodny, R. C. (1982). *Human sexuality*. Boston: Little, Brown.

Masterton, G. (1987). *How to drive your woman wild in bed*. New York: Penguin Books.

Masumori, N. (2012). Status of sex reassignment surgery for gender identity disorder in Japan. *International Journal of Urology, 19*(5), 402–414.

Matek, O. (1988). Obscene phone callers. (Special issue: The sexually unusual: Guide to understanding and helping.) *Journal of Social Work and Human Sexuality, 7*, 113–130.

Mathenjwa, T., & Maharaj, P. (2012). 'Female condoms give women greater control': A qualitative assessment of the experiences of commercial sex workers in Swaziland. *European Journal of Contraception and Reproductive Health Care, 17*(5), 383–392.

Mather, M., & Lavery, D. (2010). In U.S., proportion married at lowest recorded levels. Population Reference Bureau. Retrieved May 11, 2011, from http://www.prb.org /Articles/2010/usmarriagedecline.aspx.

Mathers, M., Degener, S., & Roth, S. (2011). Cryptorchidism and infertility from the perspective of interdisciplinary guidelines. *Urologe A, 50*(1), 20–25.

Mathes, E. W. (2005). Relationship between short-term sexual strategies and sexual jealousy. *Psychological Reports, 96*(1), 29–35.

Mathews, T., MacDorman, M., & Thoma, M. (2015). Infant mortality statistics from the 2014 period linked birth/infant death data sex. *National Vital Statistics Reports, 64*(9), 1–30.

Matsubara, H. (2001, June 20). Sex change no cure for torment. *Japan Times*.

Matsumoto, D. (1996). *Culture and psychology*. Pacific Grove, CA: Brooks/Cole.

Matthews, A., Dowswell, T., Haas, D. M., Doyle, M., & O'Mathúna, D. P. (2010). Interventions for nausea and vomiting in early pregnancy. *Cochrane Database Systems Review, 8*(9), CD007575.

Matthews, A. K., Tartaro, J., & Hughes, T. L. (2003). A comparative study of lesbian and heterosexual women in committed relationships. *Journal of Lesbian Studies, 7*, 101–114.

Matthews, T., & Hamilton, B. (2009, August). Delayed childbearing: More women are having their first child later in life. *NCHS Data Brief, 21*, 1–8.

Matthews, T., & Hamilton, B. (2014). *First births to older women continue to rise*. NCHS Data Brief (No. 152), U.S. Department of Health and Human Services. Retrieved May 21, 2014, from http://www.cdc.gov/nchs/data /databriefs/db152.pdf.

Matthews, T., MacDorman, M., Thoma, M. (2015). Infant mortality statistics from the 2013 period linked birth/infant death data set. *National Vital Statistics Reports, 64*(9), 1–30.

Maugh, T. H. (2006, July 14). Rates of prematurity, low birth weight highest ever. *Los Angeles Times*. Retrieved from http:// articles.latimes.com/2006/jul/14/science/sci -children14.

Maunder, R., & Hunter, J. (2008). Attachment relationships as determinants of physical health. *Journal of the American Academy of Psychoanalysis and Dynamic Psychiatry, 36*(1), 11–33.

Maurer, T., & Robinson, D. (2008). Effects of attire, alcohol, and gender on perceptions of date rape. *Sex Roles, 58*, 423–435.

Maynard, E., Carballo-Dieguez, A., Ventuneac, A., Exner, T., & Mayer, K. (2009). Women's experiences with anal sex: Motivations and implications for STD prevention. *Perspectives on Sexual and Reproductive Health, 41*(3), 142–149.

Mays, V. M., Yancy, A. K., Cochran, S. D., Weber, M., & Fielding, J. E. (2002). Heterogeneity of health disparities among African-American, Hispanic and Asian American women. *American Journal of Public Health, 92*(4), 632–640.

Mazman, S., & Usluel, Y. (2011). Gender differences in using social networks. *The Turkish Online Journal of Educational Technology, 10*(2), 133–139.

Mbah, A., Alio, A., Marty, P., Bruder, K., Wilson, R., & Salihu, H. (2011). Recurrent versus isolated pre-eclampsia and risk of feto-infant morbidity outcomes: Racial/ethnic disparity. *European Journal of Obstetrics and Gynecological and Reproductive Biology, 156*(1), 23–28.

Mbügua, K. (2006). Reasons to suggest that the endocrine research on sexual preference is a degenerating research program. *History & Philosophy of the Life Sciences, 28*, 337–358.

McAndrew, F. T., Bell, E. K., & Garcia, C. M. (2007). Who do we tell and whom do we tell on? Gossip as a strategy for status enhancement. *Journal of Applied Social Psychology, 37*, 1562–1577.

McBride, J. L. (2007). The family. *In The behavorial sciences and health care* (2nd ed., Section VI, #19), Ashland, OH: Hogrefe & Huber.

McCabe, M., & Connaughton, C. (2014). Psychosocial factors associated with male sexual difficulties. *Journal of Sex Research, 51*(1), 31–42.

McCabe, M., & Goldhammer, D. (2013). Prevalence of women's sexual desire problems: What criteria do we use? *Archives of Sexual Behavior, 42*(6), 1073–1078.

McCabe, M., & Wauchope, M. (2005). Behavioral characteristics of men accused of rape: Evidence for different types of rapists. *Archives of Sexual Behavior, 34*, 241–253.

McCabe, M. P. (2002). Relationship functioning among people with MS. *Journal of Sex Research, 39*(4), 302–309.

McCabe, S., Bostwick, W., Hughes, T., West, B., & Boyd, C. (2010). The relationships between discrimination and substance use disorders among lesbian, gay, and bisexual adults in the U.S. *American Journal of Public Health, 100*(10), 1946–1952.

McCall, L. (2005). The complexity of intersectionality. *Signs: Journal of Women in Culture and Society, 30*(3), 1771–1800.

McCarthy, B., & Casey, T. (2008). Love, sex, and crime: Adolescent romantic relationships and offending. *American Sociological Review, 73*(6), 944–969.

McCarthy, B. W., & Fucito, L. M. (2005). Integrating medication, realistic expectations, and therapeutic interventions in the treatment of male sexual dysfunction. *Journal of Sex and Marital Therapy, 31*(4), 319–328.

McCarthy, M. (2015). More U.S. men with low risk prostate cancer opt for watchful waiting. *British Medical Journal, 351,* h3777.

McCay, T., Misra, S., & Lindquist, C. (2017). Violence and LGBTQ+ communities: What do we know, and what do we need to know? *RTI International.* Retrieved March 24, 2017, from http://www.rti.org/sites/default/files/rti_violence_and_lgbtq_communities.pdf.

McClelland, S. (2011). Who is the "self" in self reports of sexual satisfaction? Research and policy implications. *Sexuality Research & Social Policy, 8*(4), 304–320.

McClintock, E. (2010). When does race matter? Race, sex, and dating at an elite university. *Journal of Marriage and Family, 72*(1), 45–73.

McClowry, S., Rodriguez, E., Tamis-LeMonda, C., Spellmann, M., Carlson, A., & Snow, D. (2013). Teacher/student interactions and classroom behavior: The role of student temperament and gender. *Journal of Research in Childhood Education, 27*(3), 283–301.

McConaghy, N., Hadzi-Pavlovic, D., Stevens, C., Manicavasagar, V., Buhrich, N., & Vollmer-Conna, U. (2006). Fraternal birth order and ratio of heterosexual/homosexual feelings in women and men. *Journal of Homosexuality, 51*(4), 161–174.

McConnell, E., Birkett, M., & Mustanski, B. (2016). Families matter: Social support and mental health trajectories among lesbian, gay, bisexual, and transgender youth. *Journal of Adolescent Health, 59*(6), 674–680.

McCoubrey, C. (2002, May 24). Alan P. Bell, 70, researcher of influences on homosexuality. *New York Times.* Retrieved October 12, 2010, from http://www.nytimes.com/2002/05/24/us/alan-p-bell-70-researcher-of-influences-on-homosexuality.html.

McCracken, P. (2006, August 20). Bullying women into suicide to restore honor. *San Francisco Chronicle.* Retrieved October 5, 2010, from http://www.sfgate.com/cgi-bin/article.cgi?file5/chronicle/archive/2006/08/20/INGD9KJ5U61.DTL.

McDaniel, B., Drouin, M., Cravens, J. (2017). Do you have anything to hide? Infidelity-related behaviors on social media sites and marital satisfaction. *Computers in Human Behavior, 66,* 88–95.

McDaniel, B. T., & Coyne, S. M. (2016). "Technoference": The interference of technology in couple relationships and implications for women's personal and relationship well-being. *Psychology of Popular Media Culture, 5*(1), 85–98.

McDermott, R., Schwartz, J., Lindley, L., & Proietti, J. (2014). Exploring men's homophobia: Associations with religious fundamentalism and gender role conflict domains. *Psychology of Men and Masculinity, 15*(2), 191–200.

McDonald, E., & Brown, S. (2013). Does method of birth make a difference to when women resume sex after childbirth? *International Journal of Obstetrics and Gynaecology, 120*(7), 823–830.

McDonald, J., & Rapkin, A. (2012). Multilevel local anesthetic nerve blockade for the treatment of generalized vulvodynia. *Journal of Sexual Medicine, 9*(11), 2919–2926.

McDougall, D. (2010, May 30). Cries from the beloved country. *The Sunday Times.* Retrieved April 30, 2011, from http://www.timesonline.co.uk/tol/news/world/africa/article7133312.ece.

McDowall, A., & Khan, S. (2004, November 25). The Ayatollan and the transsexual. *The Independent.* Retrieved December 20, 2010, from http://www.independent.co.uk/news/world/middle-east/the-ayatollah-and-the-transsexual-534482.html.

McDowell, B. (1986). The Dutch touch. *National Geographic, 170,* 501–525.

McElrath, K., Stana, A., Taylor, A., & Johnson-Arnold, L. (2017). Race/sex interactions and HIV testing among college students. *Journal of Racial and Ethnic Health Disparities, 4*(1), 112–121.

McEwen, G. N., Jr., & Renner, G. (2006). Validity of anogenital distance as a marker of in utero phthalate exposure. *Environmental Health Perspectives, 114*(1), A19–A20.

McFadden, D. (2011). Sexual orientation and the auditory system. *Front Neuroendocrinology.* Retrieved February 20, 2011, from http://www.ncbi.nlm.nih.gov/pubmed/21310172.

McFadden, D., Loehlin, J. C., Breedlove, S., Lippa, R. A., Manning, J. T., & Rahman, Q. (2005). A reanalysis of five studies on sexual orientation and the relative length of the 2nd and 4th fingers (the 2D:4D). *Archives of Sexual Behavior, 34,* 341–356.

McGlynn, K. A., Sakoda, L. C., Rubertone, M. V., Sesterhenn, I. A., Lyu, C., Graubard, B. I., & Erickson, R. L. (2007). Body size, dairy consumption, puberty, and risk of testicular germ cell tumors. *American Journal of Epidemiology, 165*(4), 355–363.

McGrath, B. (2014, May 20). International Megan's law passed by U.S. House of Representatives. *NJ.com.* Retrieved June 11, 2014, from http://www.nj.com/mercer/index.ssf/2014/05/international_megans_law_passed_by_us_house_of_representatives.html.

McGregor, S., Tachedjian, G., Haire, B., & Kaldor, J. (2013). The seventh (and last?) international microbicides conference: From discovery to delivery. *Sexual Health, 10*(3), 240–245.

McGuirk, E. M., & Pettijohn, T. F. (2008). Birth order and romantic relationship styles and attitudes in college students. *North American Journal of Psychology, 10,* 37–52.

McKeganey, N., & Bernard, M. (1996). *Sex work on the streets: Prostitutes and their clients.* Philadelphia: Open University Press.

McLaren, A. (1990). *A history of contraception.* Cambridge, MA: Basil Blackwell.

McLaughlin, K., Hatzenbuehler, M., Xuan, Z., & Conron, K. (2012). Disproportionate exposure to early-life adversity and sexual orientation disparities in psychiatric morbidity. *Child Abuse & Neglect, 36*(9), 645–655.

McLean, L. M., & Gallop, R. (2003). Implications of childhood sexual abuse for adult borderline personality disorder and complex post traumatic stress disorder. *American Journal of Psychiatry, 160*(2), 369–371.

McLeod, D. (2015). Female offenders in child sexual abuse cases: A national picture. *Journal of Child Sexual Abuse, 24*(1), 97–114.

McMahon, C. (2016). Emerging and investigational drugs for premature ejaculation. *Translational Andrology and Urology, 5*(4), 487–501.

McMahon, S. (2004). Student-athletes, rape-supportive culture, and social change. Retrieved October 16, 2005, from http://sexualassault.rutgers.edu/pdfs/student-athletes_rape-supportive_culture_and_social_change.pdf.

McMahon, S. (2015). Participation in high school sports and bystander intentions, efficacy to intervene, and rape myth beliefs. *Journal of Interpersonal Violence, 30*(17), 2980–2998.

McMartin, K. (2013). Hysteroscopic tubal sterilization: An evidence-based analysis. *Ontario Health Technology Assessment Series, 13*(21), 1–35.

McMillan, C., & Jenkins, A. (2016). "A magical little pill that will relieve you of your womanly issues": What young women say about menstrual suppression. *International Journal of Qualitative Studies on Health and Well-Being, 11,* 329–32.

McMullin, D., & White, J. (2006). Long-term effects of labeling a rape experience. *Psychology of Women Quarterly, 30*(1), 96–105.

McNally, R. J., Clancy, S. A., Barrett, H. M., & Parker, H. A. (2004). Inhibiting retrieval of trauma cues in adults reporting histories of childhood sexual abuse. *Cognition and Emotion, 18*(4), 479–493.

McNally, R. J., Clancy, S. A., Barrett, H. M., & Parker, H. A. (2005). Reality monitoring in adults reporting repressed, recovered, or continuous memories of childhood sexual abuse. *Journal of Abnormal Psychology, 114*(1), 147–152.

McNamara, M., Batur, P., & DeSapri, K. (2015). In the clinic: Perimenopause. *Annals of Internal Medicine, 162*(3), 1–15.

McNulty, J., Wenner, C., & Fisher, T. (2015). Longitudinal associations among relationship satisfaction, sexual satisfaction, and frequency of sex in early marriage. *Archives of Sexual Behavior, 45*(1), 85–97.

McPhillips, D. (2016). The 10 countries with the highest smartphone penetration. *US News.* Retrieved January 11, 2017, from http://www.usnews.com/news/best-countries/articles/2016-03-21/the-10-countries-with-the-highest-smartphone-penetration.

McQuillan, G., Kruszon-Moran, D., Markowitz, L., Unger, E., & Paulose-Ram, R (2017). Prevalence of HPV in adults aged 18-69: United States, 2011–2014. NCHS Data Brief, #280. Retrieved April 28, 2017, from https://www.cdc.gov/nchs/data/databriefs/db280.pdf.

Mead, M. (1935/1988/2001). *Sex and temperament in three primitive societies.* New York: William Morrow.

Medoff, M. (2012). Restrictive abortion laws, antiabortion attitudes and women's contraceptive use. *Social Science Research, 41*(1), 160–169.

Medrano, M. A., Hatch, J. P., & Zule, W. A. (2003). Childhood trauma and adult prostitution behavior in a multiethnic heterosexual drug-using population. *American Journal of Drug and Alcohol Abuse, 29*(20), 463–486.

Medved, M. (1992). *Hollywood vs. America: Popular culture and the war on traditional values.* New York: HarperCollins.

Megan, K. (2014, August 24). Starting college at high risk. *Hartford Courant.* A1, A12.

Mehl, M. R., Vazire, S., Ramirez-Esparza, N., Slatcher, R. B., & Pennebaker, J. W. (2007). Are women really more talkative than men? *Science, 317*, 82.

Mehrabian, A. (2009). *Nonverbal communication.* Piscataway, NJ: Transaction Publishers.

Mehta, C., & Strough, J. (2010). Gender segregation and gender-typing in adolescence. *Sex Roles, 64*(3–4), 251–263.

Meier, E. (2002). Child rape in South Africa. *Pediatric Nursing, 28*(5), 532–535.

Meirik, O., Fraser, I., & d'Arcangues, C. (2003). Implantable contraceptives for women. *Human Reproduction Update, 9*(1), 49–59.

Meites, E., Kempe, A., & Markowitz, L. (2016). Use of a 2-does schedule for human papillomavirus vaccination—Updated recommendations of the advisory committee on immunization practices. *MMWR, 65*(49), 1405–1408.

Mejia, M., McNicholas, C., Madden, T., & Peipert, J. (2016). Association of baseline bleeding pattern on amenorrhea with levonorgestrel intrauterine system use. *Contraception, 94*(5), 556–560.

Melisko, M. E., Goldman, M., & Rugo, H. S. (2010). Amelioration of sexual adverse effects in the early breast cancer patient. *Journal of Cancer Survivorship, 4*(3), 247–255.

Melwani, S. (2013). *A little bird told me so … : The emotional, attributional, relational and team-level outcomes of engaging in gossip.* Dissertation Abstracts International Section A: Humanities and Social Sciences, *73*(9-A), ISBN 978-1-267-35690-1.

Ménard, K. S., Nagayama Hall, G., Phung, A., Erian Ghebrial, M., & Martin, L. (2003). Gender differences in sexual harassment and coercion in college students. *Journal of Interpersonal Violence, 18*(10), 1222–1239.

Mendelsohn, G., Taylor, L., Fiore, A., & Cheshirt, C. (2014). Black/White dating online: Interracial courtship in the 21st century. *Psychology of Popular Media Culture, 3*(1), 2–18.

Mendoza, N., & Motos, M. (2013). Androgen insensitivity syndrome. *Gynecological Endocrinology, 29*(1), 1–5.

Menke, L., Sas, T., Keizer-Schrama, S., Zandwijken, G., Ridder, M., Odink, R., Jansen, M., et al. (2010). Efficacy and safety of oxandrolone in growth hormone-treated girls with Turner syndrome. *Journal of Clinical Endocrinology & Metabolism, 95*(3), 1151–1160.

Menon, R. (2008). Spontaneous preterm birth, a clinical dilemma: Etiologic, pathophysiologic and genetic heterogeneities and racial disparity. *Acta Obstetrica Gynecologic Scandinavica, 87*, 590–600.

Menon, S., Timms, P., Allan J., Alexander, K., Rombauts, L., Horner, P., Keltz, M., Hocking, J., & Huston, W. (2015). Human and pathogen factors associated with chlamydia trachomatis-related infertility in women. *Clinical Microbiology Reviews, 28*(4), 969–985.

Menzler, K., Belke, M., Wehrmann, E., Kradow, K., Lengler, U., Jansen, A., Hamer, H., Oertel, W., Rosenow, F., & Knake, S. (2011). Men and women are different: Diffusion tensor imaging reveals sexual dimorphism in the microstructure of the thalamus, corpus callosum and cingulum. *Neuroimage, 54*, 2557–2562.

Merki-Feld, G. S., & Hund, M. (2007). Clinical experience with NuvaRing in daily practice in Switzerland: Cycle control and acceptability among women of all reproductive ages. *European Journal of Contraceptive and Reproductive Health Care, 12*, 240–247.

Merki-Feld, G. S., Seeger, H., & Mueck, A. O. (2008). Comparison of the proliferative effects of ethinylestradiol on human breast cancer cells in an intermittent and a continuous dosing regime. *Hormone and Metabolic Research.* Retrieved March 18, 2008, from http://www.thieme-connect.com/ejournals/abstract/hmr/doi/10.1055/s-2007-1004540.

Mernitz, S., Dush, C. (2016). Emotional health across the transition to first and second unions among emerging adults. *Journal of Family Psychology, 30*(2), 233–244.

Mertz, G. (2008). Asymptomatic shedding of herpes simplex virus 1 and 2: Implications for prevention of transmission. *Journal of Infectious Diseases, 198*(8), 1098–1100.

Merzenich, H., Zeeb, H., & Blettner, M. (2010). Decreasing sperm quality: A global problem? *MBC Public Health, 10*, 24–29.

Meschke, L. L., Bartholomae, S., & Zentall, S. R. (2000). Adolescent sexuality and parent-adolescent processes: Promoting healthy teen choices. *Family Relations, 49*(2), 143–155.

Messenger, J. C. (1993). Sex and repression in an Irish folk community. In D. N. Suggs & A. W. Miracle (Eds.), *Culture and human diversity.* Pacific Grove, CA: Brooks/Cole.

Messina, M. (2010). Soybean isoflavone exposure does not have feminizing effects on men: A critical examination of the clinical evidence. *Fertility and Sterility, 93*(7), 2095–2104.

Meston, C. M., Hull, E., Levin, R., & Sipski, M. (2004). Disorders of orgasm in women. *Journal of Sexual Medicine, 1*, 66–68.

Meston, C. M., Trapnell, P. D., & Gorzalka, B. B. (1996). Ethnic and gender differences in sexuality: Variations in sexual behavior between Asian and non-Asian university students. *Archives of Sex Behavior, 25*(1), 33–71.

Meston, C. M., & Worcel, M. (2002). The effects of yohimbine plus L-arginine glutamate on sexual arousal in post menopausal women with sexual arousal disorders. *Archives of Sexual Behavior, 31*(4), 323–332.

Meston, C., & Buss, D. (2007). Why humans have sex. *Archives of Sexual Behavior, 36*(4), 477–507.

Meston, C., & Lorenz, T. (2013). Physiological stress responses predict sexual functioning and satisfaction differently in women who have and have not been sexually abused in childhood. *Psychological Trauma, 5*(4), 350–358.

Meston, C., Lorenz, T., & Stephenson, K. (2013). Effects of expressive writing on sexual dysfunction, depression, and PTSD in women with a history of childhood sexual abuse: Results from a randomized clinical trial. *Journal of Sexual Medicine, 10*(9), 2177–2189.

Metropolitan Community Churches. (2005). About us. Retrieved November 7, 2005, from http://www.mccchurch.org/AM/Text Template.cfm?Section=About_Us&Template=/CM/HTMLDisplay.cfm&ContentID=877.

Metz, T., & Stickrath, E. (2015). Marijuana use in pregnancy and lactation: A review of the evidence. *American Journal of Obstetrics and Gynecology, 213*(6), 761–778.

Meuleman, C., Vandenabeele, B., & Fieuws, S. (2009). High prevalence of endometriosis in infertile women with normal ovulation and normospermic partners. *Fertility and Sterility, 92*(1), 68–74.

Meyer-Bahlburg, H. F., Dolezal, C., Baker, S. W., & New, M. I. (2008). Sexual orientation in women with classical or non-classical CAH as a function of degree of prenatal androgen excess. *Archives of Sexual Behavior, 37*, 85–99.

Meyer-Bahlburg, H., Ehrhardt, A., Feldman, J., Rosen, L., Veridiano, N., & Zimmerman, I. (1985). Sexual activity level and sexual functioning in women prenatally exposed to diethylstilbestrol. *Psychosomatic Medicine, 47*(6), 497–511.

Mhloyi, M. M. (1990). Perceptions on communication and sexuality in marriage in Zimbabwe. *Women and Therapy, 10*(3), 61–73.

Mi, T., Abbasi, S., Zhang, H., Uray, K., Chunn, J., Wei, L., Molina, J., Weisbrodt, N., Kellems, R., Blackburn, M., & Xia, Y. (2008). Excess adenosine in murine penile erectile tissues contributes to priapism via A2B adenosine receptor signaling. *Journal of Clinical Investigation, 118*(4), 1491–1501.

Micali, S., Isgro, G., Bianchi, G., Miceli, N., Calapai, G., & Navarra, M. (2014). Cranberry and recurrent systitis: More than marketing? *Critical Reviews in Food Science and Nutrition, 54*(8), 1063–1075.

Michael, R. T., Gagnon, J. H., Laumann, E. O., & Kolata, G. (1994). *Sex in America.* Boston, MA: Little, Brown.

Mihalik, G. (1988). Sexuality and gender: An evolutionary perspective. *Psychiatric Annals, 18*, 40–42.

Miles, L., Cooper, R., Nugent, W., & Ellis, R. (2016). Sexual addiction: A literature review of treatment interventions. *Journal of Human Behavior in the Social Environment, 26*(1), 89–99.

Miletski, H. (2002). *Understanding bestiality and zoophilia.* Bethesda, MD: East-West.

Miller, A., Wall, C., Baines, C., Sun, P., To, T., & Narod, S. (2014). Twenty five year follow-up for breast cancer incidence and mortality of the Canadian National Breast Screening Study. *British Medical Journal, 348*(g366), 1–10.

Miller, G., Kors, S., & Macfie, J. (2017). No differences? Meta-analytic comparisons of psychological adjustment in children of gay fathers and heterosexual parents. *Psychology of Sexual Orientation and Gender Diversity, 4*(1), 14–22.

Miller, J. E. (2015). Mental health professionals' perceptions, attitudes, and beliefs about lesbian, gay, bisexual, and transgender rape victims. *Dissertation Abstracts International: Section B: The Sciences an Engineering, Vol 76*(3-B), #978-1-321-32218-7.

Miller, K., Gleaves, D., Hirsch, T., Green, B., Snow, A., & Corbett, C. (2000). Comparisons of body image dimensions by race/ethnicity and gender in a university population. *International Journal of Eating Disorders, 27*(3), 310–316.

Miller, Peter V. (1995). A review: They said it couldn't be done: The National Health and Social Life Survey. *The Public Opinion Quarterly, 59*(3), 404–419.

Miller, W., & Witchel, S. (2013). Prenatal treatment of congenital adrenal hyperplasia: Risks outweigh the benefits. *American Journal of Obstetrics and Gynecology, 208*(5), 354–359.

Miller-Ott, A., Kelly, L., & Ruran, R. (2012). The effects of cell phone usage rules on satisfaction in romantic relationships. *Communication Quarterly, 60*(1), 17–34.

Milner, J., Dopke, C., & Crouch, J. (2008). Paraphilia not otherwise specified. In D. Laws & W. O'Donohue (Eds.), *Sexual deviance: Theory, assessment and treatment* (2nd ed., pp. 384–418). New York: Guilford Press.

Milner, J., & Robertson, K. (1990). Comparison of physical child abusers, intrafamilial sexual child abusers, and child neglecters. *Journal of Interpersonal Violence, 5*, 37–48.

Min, K. S. (2014). AB52: What's new in treatment of female sexual dysfunction? *Translational Andrology and Urology, 3*(Suppl. 1). Retrieved April 15, 2017, from https://www.ncbi.nlm.nih.gov/pmc/articles/PMC4708387/.

Miner, M. H., Coleman, E., Center, B., Ross, M., & Simon Rosser, B. (2007). The compulsive sexual behavior inventory: Psychometric properties. *Archives of Sexual Behavior, 36*(4), 579–587.

Minervini, A., Ralph, D., & Pryor, J. (2006). Outcome of penile prosthesis implantation for treating erectile dysfunction: Experience with 504 procedures. *British Journal of Urology, 97*, 129–133.

Miranda, A., & Fiorello, K. (2002). The connection between social interest and the characteristics of sexual abuse perpetuated by male pedophiles. *Journal of Individual Psychology, 58*, 62–75.

Mirbagher-Ajorpaz, N., Adib-Hajbaghery, M., & Mosaebi, F. (2010). The effects of acupressure on primary dysmenorrheal: A randomized controlled trial. *Complementary Practices in Clinical Practices, 17*(1), 33–36.

Mishna, F., Newman, P., Daley, A., & Soloman, S. (2008, January 5). Bullying of lesbian and gay youth: A qualitative investigation. *British Journal of Social Work.* Retrieved October 2, 2008, from http://bjsw.oxfordjournals.org/cgi/content/abstract/bcm148.

Misra, G. (2009). Decriminalising homosexuality in India. *Reproductive Health Matters, 17*(34), 20–28.

Misri, S., Kostaras, X., Fox, D., & Kostaras, D. (2000). The impact of partner support in the treatment of postpartum depression. *Canadian Journal of Psychiatry, 45*(6), 554–559.

Mitchell, K., Finkelhor, D., & Wolak, J. (2003). The exposure of youth to unwanted sexual material on the Internet: A national survey of risk, impact, and prevention. *Youth and Society, 34*, 330–358.

Mitchell, K., Finkelhor, D., & Wolak, J. (2010). Conceptualizing juvenile prostitution as child maltreatment: Findings from the National Juvenile Prostitution Study. *Child Maltreatment, 15*(1), 18–36.

Mithun, M. (2012). Tags: Cross-linguistic diversity and commonality. *Journal of Pragmatics, 44*(15), 2165–2182.

Mittendorf, R., Williams, M. A., Berkey, C. S., & Cotter, P. F. (1990). The length of uncomplicated human gestation. *Obstetrics and Gynecology, 75*(6), 929–932.

Mize, T. D. (2016). Sexual orientation in the labor market. *American Sociological Review.* Retrieved March 18, 2017, from http://journals.sagepub.com/doi/abs/10.1177/0003122416674025.

Mock, S. E., & Cornelius, S. W. (2007). Profiles of interdependence: The retirement planning of married, cohabiting, and lesbian couples. *Sex Roles, 56*(11–12), 793–800.

Modan, B., Hartge, P., Hirsh-Yechezkel, G., Chetrit A., Lubin F., Beller U., et al. (2001). Parity, oral contraceptives, and the risk of ovarian cancer among carriers and noncarriers of a BRCA1 or BRCA2 mutation. *New England Journal of Medicine, 345*, 235–240.

Moegelin, L., Nilsson, B., & Helström, L. (2010). Reproductive health in lesbian and bisexual women in Sweden. *Acta Obstet Gynecol Scand, 89*(2), 205–209.

Moen, V., & Irestedt, L. (2008). Neurological complications following central neuraxial blockades in obstetrics. *Current Opinions in Anesthesiology, 21*, 275–280.

Mohamad, N., Soelaiman, I., & Chin, K. (2016). A concise review of testosterone and bone health. *Clinical Interventions in Aging, 11*, 1317–1324.

Moleiro, C., & Pinto, N. (2015). Sexual orientation and gender identity: Review of concepts, controversies and their relation to psychopathology classification systems. *Frontiers in Psychology, 6.* Retrieved May 1, 2017, from https://www.ncbi.nlm.nih.gov/pmc/articles/PMC4589638/.

Molina, B. (2014, June 16). Tech Five: Yahoo sinks, more clues on Apple's 'iWatch.' *USA Today.* Retrieved June 17, 2014, from http://www.usatoday.com/story/tech/2014/06/16/tech-stocks-apple/10570615.

Möller, A., Söndergaard, H., Helström, L. (2017). Tonic immobility during sexual assault—a common reaction predicting post-traumatic stress disorder and severe depression. *Acta Obstetricia et Gynecologica Scandinavica*. Retrieved August 8, 2017, from http://onlinelibrary.wiley.com/doi/10.1111/aogs.13174/full#.

Monasch, R., & Boerma, J. (2004). Orphanhood and childcare patterns in sub-Saharan Africa: An analysis of national survey from 40 countries. *AIDS*, *18*(Suppl. 2), S55-S65.

Monat-Haller, R. K. (1992). *Understanding and experiencing sexuality*. Baltimore: Brookes.

Money, J. (1955). Hermaphroditism, gender, and precocity in hyper-adrenocorticism: Psychologic findings. *Bulletin of the Johns Hopkins Hospital*, *96*, 253–254.

Money, J. (1975). Ablatio penis: Normal male infant sex-reassigned as a girl. *Archives of Sexual Behavior*, *4*(1), 65–71.

Money, J. (1984). Paraphilias: Phenomenology and classification. *American Journal of Psychotherapy*, *38*, 164–179.

Money, J. (1986). *Venuses penuses: Sexology, sexophy, and exigency theory*. Buffalo, NY: Prometheus Books.

Money, J. (1990). Pedophilia: A specific instance of new phylism theory as applied to paraphiliac lovemaps. In J. Feierman (Ed.), *Pedophilia: Biosocial dimensions* (pp. 445–463). New York: Springer-Verlag.

Monroe, L. M., Kinney, L., Weist, M., Dafeamekpor, D., Dantzler, J., & Reynolds, M. (2005). The experience of sexual assault: Findings from a statewide victim needs assessment. *Journal of Interpersonal Violence*, *20*(7), 767–776.

Montemurro, B., & McClure, B. (2005). Changing gender norms for alcohol consumption. *Sex Roles*, *52*, 279–288.

Montemurro, B., & Siefken, J. M. (2012). MILFS and matrons: Images and realities of mothers' sexuality. *Sexuality & Culture*, *16*(4), 366–388.

Montgomery-Graham, S. (2016). Conceptualization and assessment of hypersexual disorder: A systematic review of the literature. *Sexual Medicine Reviews*, *5*(2), 146–162.

Montirosso, R., Peverelli, M., Frigerio, E., Crespi, M., & Borgatti, R. (2010). The development of dynamic facial expression recognition at different intensities in 4- to 18-year-olds. *Social Development*, *19*(1), 71.

Monto, M. A. (2000). Why men seek out prostitutes. In R. Weitzer (Ed.), *Sex for sale: Prostitution, pornography, and the sex industry* (pp. 67–83). New York: Routledge.

Monto, M. A. (2001). Prostitution and fellatio. *Journal of Sex Research*, *38*(2), 140–146.

Monto, M. A., & McRee, N. (2005). A comparison of the male customers of female street prostitutes with national samples of men. *International Journal of Offender Therapy and Comparative Criminology*, *49*(5), 505–529.

Mookodi, G., Ntshebe, O., & Taylor, I. (2004). Botswana. In R. T. Francoeur & R. J. Noonan (Eds.), *The Continuum International encyclopedia of sexuality* (pp. 89–97). New York/London: Continuum International.

Mooney, P. (2016). Explant breast surgery: Why women are getting their breast implants removed. *Inquisitr*. Retrieved January 20, 2017, from http://www.inquisitr.com/2981002/explant-breast-surgery-why-women-are-getting-their-breast-implants-removed-graphic-photos/.

Moor, B., Crone, E., & der Molen, M. (2010). The heartbrake of social rejection: Heart rate deceleration in response to unexpected peer rejection. *Psychological Science*, *21*(9), 1326–1333.

Moore, E., Berkley-Patton, J., & Hawes, S. (2013). Religiosity, alcohol use, and sex behaviors among college student-athletes. *Journal of Religion and Health*, *52*(3), 930–940.

Moore, M. E. (2010). Communication involving long-term dating partners' sexual conversations: The connection between religious faith and sexual intimacy. *Dissertation Abstract International*, *48*/05. University of Arkansas, AAT #1484652.

Mor, Z., & Dan, M. (2012). The HIV epidemic among men who have sex with men—Behavior beats science. *EMBO Reports, 13*(11), 948–953.

Morales, A. M., Casillas, M., & Turbi, C. (2011). Patients' preference in the treatment of erectile dysfunction: A critical review of the literature. *International Journal of Impotence Research*, *23*(1), 1–8.

Morbidity and Mortality Weekly Report (MMWR). (2013, February 8). Progress in increasing breastfeeding and reducing racial/ethnic differences—U.S., 2000–2008 births. *Morbidity and Mortality Weekly Report*. Retrieved May 23, 2014, from http://www.cdc.gov/mmwr/preview/mmwrhtml/mm6205a1.htm?s_cid=mm6205a1_w.

Morbidity and Mortality Weekly Report (MMWR). (2014, January 3). Announcements: National birth defects prevention month and folic acid awareness week—January 2014. *Morbidity and Mortality Weekly Report*. Retrieved July 31, 2014, from http://www.cdc.gov/mmwr/preview/mmwrhtml/mm6251a6.htm.

Morcos, R., & Kizy, T. (2012). Gynecomastia: When is treatment indicated? *Journal of Family Practice*, *61*(12), 719–725.

Moreno-Garcia, M., Fernandez-Martinez, F. J., & Miranda, E. B. (2005). Chromosomal anomalies in patients with short stature. *Pediatric International*, *47*(5), 546–549.

Morgan, S. P., & Rindfuss, R. (1985). Marital disruption: Structural and temporal dimensions. *American Journal of Sociology*, *90*(5), 1055–1077.

Moriel D., & Schembri, M. (2014). Vaccination approaches for the prevention of urinary tract infection. *Current Pharmaceutical Biotechnology*, *14*(11), 967–974.

Morley, J., & Perry, H. (2000). Androgen deficiency in aging men. *Journal of Laboratory and Clinical Medicine*, *135*(5), 370–378.

Morran, C. (2014, February 7). Merck agrees to pay $100 million to settle NuvaRing lawsuits. *Consumerist*. Retrieved May 24, 2014, from http://consumerist.com/2014/02/07/merck-agrees-to-pay-100-million-to-settle-nuvaring-lawsuits.

Morris, B., & Wiswell, T. (2013). Circumcision and lifetime risk of urinary tract infection: A systematic review and meta-analysis. *Journal of Urology*, *189*(6), 2118–2124.

Morris, B., Wamai, R., Henebeng, E., Tobian, S., Klausner, J., Banerjee, J., & Hankins, C. (2016). Estimation of country-specific and global prevalence of male circumcision. *Population Health Metrics*, *14*(4). Retrieved January 29, 2017, from https://pophealthmetrics.biomedcentral.com/articles/10.1186/s12963-016-0073-5.

Morris, C. (2014, January 14). After rough 2013, porn studios look for a better year. CNBC. Retrieved June 17, 2014, from http://www.cnbc.com/id/101326937.

Morris, C., Reiber, C., & Roman, E. (2015). Quantitative sex differences in response to the dissolution of a romantic relationship. *Evolutionary Behavioral Sciences*, *9*(4), 270–282.

Morris, D. Z. (2017, January 1). New French law bars work email after hours. *Fortune*. Retrieved January 11, 2017, from http://fortune.com/2017/01/01/french-right-to-disconnect-law/.

Morris, R. J. (1990). Aikane: Accounts of Hawaiian same-sex relationships in the journals of Captain Cook's third voyage (1776–1780). *Journal of Homosexuality*, *19*, 21–54.

Morrison-Beedy, D., Carey, M. P., Cote-Arsenault, D., Seibold-Simpson, S., & Robinson, K. A. (2008). Understanding sexual abstinence in urban adolescent girls. *Journal of Obstetric, Gynecologic, and Neonatal Nursing*, *37*, 185.

Morrison, T. G. (2007). Children of homosexuals and transsexuals more apt to be homosexual: A reply to Cameron. *Journal of Biosocial Science*, *39*(1), 153–156.

Morrissey, D., El-Khawand, D., Ginzburg, N., Wehbe, S., O'Hare, P., Whitmore, K. (2015). Botulinum toxin A injections into pelvic floor muscles under electromyographic guidance for women with refractory high-tone pelvic floor dysfunction. *Female Pelvic Medicine & Reconstructive Surgery*, *21*(5), 277–282.

Morrow, K. M., & Allsworth, J. E. (2000). Sexual risk in lesbians and bisexual women. *Journal of Gay and Lesbian Medical Association*, 4(4), 159–165.

Morse, E. V., Simon, P. M., Balson, P. M., & Osofsky, H. J. (1992). Sexual behavior patterns of customers of male street prostitutes. *Archives of Sexual Behavior*, 21, 347–357.

Mortenson, S. T. (2002). Sex, communication, values, and cultural values. *Communication Reports*, 15(1), 57–71.

Mosconi, A. M., Roila, F., Gatta, G., & Theodore, C. (2005). Cancer of the penis. *Critical Reviews in Oncology/Hematology*, 53(2), 165–178.

Moser, C. (1988). Sadomasochism. Special issue: The sexually unusual: Guide to understanding and helping. *Journal of Social Work and Human Sexuality*, 7, 43–56.

Mosher, W. D., Martinez, G. M., Chandra, A., Abma, J. C., & Wilson, S. J. (2004). Use of contraception and use of family planning services in the United States: 1982–2002. *Advance Data from Vital and Health Statistics*, no. 350. Retrieved May 27, 2008, from http://www.cdc.gov/nchs/data/ad/ad350.pdf.

Moskowitz, C. (2008, May 16). Same sex couples common in the wild. *LiveScience*. Retrieved October 2, 2008, from http://www.livescience.com/animals/080516-gay-animals.html.

Mouilso, E., Fischer, S., & Calhoun, K. (2012). A prospective study of sexual assault and alcohol use among first-year college women. *Violence and Victims*, 27(1), 78–94.

"Mounting challenge to brain sex differences." (2017, January 17). Science Daily. Retrieved January 17, 2017, from https://www.sciencedaily.com/releases/2017/01/170117135943.htm.

Mouritsen, A., Aksglaede, L., Sorensen, K., Mogensen, S., Leffers, H., Main, K., Frederiksen, H., Andersson, A., Skakkebaek, N., & Juul, A. (2010). Hypothesis: Exposure to endocrine-disrupting chemicals may interfere with timing of puberty. *International Journal of Andrology*, 33(2), 346–359.

Moyer, V. (2012). Screening for cervical cancer: U.S. preventive services task force recommendation statement. *Annals of Internal Medicine*, 156(12), 880–891.

Moynihan, M., & Banyard, V. (2008). Community responsibility for preventing sexual violence: A pilot study with campus Greeks and intercollegiate athletes. *Journal of Prevention and Intervention in the Community*, 36(1–2), 23–38.

Mruk, D. D. (2008). New perspectives in non-hormonal male contraception. *Trends in Endocrinology and Metabolism*, 19(2), 57–64.

Mueck, A. O., & Seeger, H. (2008). The World Health Organization defines hormone replacement therapy as carcinogenic: Is this implausible? *Gynecological Endocrinology*, 24, 129–132.

Mueck, A. O., Seeger, H., & Rabe, T. (2010). Hormonal contraception and risk of endometrial cancer: A systematic review. *Endocrine Related Cancer*, 17(4), R263–R271.

Muehlenhard, C., & Shippee, S. (2010). Men's and women's reports of pretending orgasm. *Journal of Sex Research*, 47(6), 552–567.

Muehlenhard, C. L., & Cook, S. W. (1988). Men's self-reports of unwanted sexual activity. *Journal of Sex Research*, 24, 58–72.

Mueller, A., James, W., Abrutyn, S., & Levin, M. (2015). Suicide ideation and bullying among U.S. adolescents: Examining the intersections of sexual orientation, gender, and race/ethnicity. *American Journal of Public Health*, 105(5), 980–985.

Muir, J. G. (1993, March 31). Homosexuals and the 10% fallacy. *The Wall Street Journal*, p. A14.

Muise, A., Kim, J., McNulty, J., & Impett, E. (2016). The positive implications of sex for relationships. In C. K. H. Reis (Ed.), *Advances in Personal Relationships: Vol. 1, Positive Approaches to Optimal Relationship Development*. Cambridge, UK: Cambridge University Press.

Mujugira, A., Magaret, A., Celum, C., Baeten, J., Lingappa, J., Morrow, R., Fife, K., Delany-Moretiwe, S., de Bruyn, G., et al. (2013). Daily acyclovir to decrease herpes simplex virus type 2 transmission from HSV-2/HIV-1 co-infected persons: A randomized controlled trial. *Journal of Infectious Disease*, 208(9), 1366–1374.

Mukherjee, B., & Shivakumar, T. (2007). A case of sensorineural deafness following ingestion of sildenafil. *Journal of Laryngology and Otology*, 121, 395–397.

Mulick, P. S., & Wright, L. W. (2002). Examining the existence of biphobia in the heterosexual and homosexual populations. *Journal of Bisexuality*, 2, 45–65.

Muller, J. E., Mittleman, M. A., Maclure, M., Sherwood, J. B., & Toffer, G. H. (1996). Triggering myocardial infarction by sexual activity. *Journal of the American Medical Association*, 275(18), 1405–1409.

Mulligan, E., & Heath, M. (2007). Seeking open minded doctors. How women who identify as bisexual, queer or lesbian seek quality health care. *Australian Family Physician*, 36, 385–480.

Mulvaney, B. M. (1994). Gender differences in communication: An intercultural experience. Paper prepared by the Department of Communication, Florida Atlantic University.

Mumba, M. (2010). A phenomenological study of how college students communicate about anal sex and its implications for health. *Dissertation Abstracts*, Ohio University, AAT #3433979.

Munk-Olsen, T., Laursen, T. M., Pedersen, C. B., Lidegaard, Ø., & Mortensen, P. B. (2011). Induced first-trimester abortion and risk of mental disorder. *New England Journal of Medicine*, 364(4), 332–339.

Munsey, C. (2009, October). Insufficient evidence to support sexual orientation change efforts. *Monitor on Psychology*, 40(9), 29.

Munson, M. (1987). How do you do it? *On Our Backs*, 4(1).

Muratori, M., Marchiani, S., Tamburrino, L., Forti, G., Luconi, M., & Baldi, E. (2011). Markers of human sperm functions in the ICSI era. *Frontiers in Bioscience*, 1(16), 1344–1363.

Murina F., Bernorio R., & Palmiotto, R. (2008). The use of amielle vaginal trainers as adjuvant in the treatment of vestibulodynia: An observational multicentric study. *Medscape Journal of Medicine*, 10(1), 23.

Murina, F., Bianco, V., Radici, G., Felice, R., & Signaroldi, M. (2010). Electrodiagnostic functional sensory evaluation of patients with generalized vulvodynia: A pilot study. *Journal of Lower Genital Tract Diseases*, 14(3), 221–224.

Murnen, S. K., Wright, C., & Kaluzny, G. (2002). If boys will be boys then girls will be victims? A meta-analytic review of the research that relates masculine ideology to sexual aggression. *Sex Roles*, 46(11–12), 359–375.

Murnen, S., & Kohlman, M. (2007). Athletic participation, fraternity membership, and sexual aggression among college men: A meta-analysis review. *Sex Roles*, 57, 145–157.

Murphy, H. E. (2012). Improving the lives of students, gay and straight alike: Gay-straight alliances and the role of school psychologists. *Psychology in the Schools*, 49(9), 883–891.

Murphy, L. (2010). Understanding the social and economic contexts surrounding women engaged in street-level prostitution. *Issues in Mental Health Nursing*, 31(12), 775–784.

Murphy, L. R. (1990). Defining the crime against nature: Sodomy in the United States appeals courts, 1810–1940. *Journal of Homosexuality*, 19, 49–66.

Murphy, W., & Page, J. (2008). Exhibitionism: Psychopathology and theory. In D. Laws & W. O'Donohue (Eds.), *Sexual deviance: Theory, assessment and treatment* (2nd ed., pp. 61–75). New York: Guilford Press.

Murray, J. (2000). Psychological profile of pedophiles and child molesters. *Journal of Psychology*, 134(2), 211–224.

Murray, K. M., Ciarrocchi, J. W., & Murray-Swank, N. A. (2007). Spirituality, religiosity, shame, and guilt as predictors of sexual attitudes and experiences. *Journal of Psychology and Theology*, 35, 222–234.

Murray, S., & Dynes, W. (1999). Latin American gays: Snow Whites and snake charmers. *The Economist*, 353(8150), 82.

Murray, S., & Holmes, J. (2009). Motivating mutual responsiveness: The architecture of interdependent minds. *Psychological Review*, 116(4), 908–928.

Musacchio, N., Hartrich, M., & Garofalo, R. (2006). Erectile dysfunction and Viagra use: What's up with college males? *Journal of Adolescent Health, 39*, 452–454.

Musick, K., & Bumpass, L. (2012). Reexamining the case for marriage: Union formation and changes in well-being. *Journal of Marriage and Family, 74*, 1–18.

Mustanski, B. (2001). Getting wired: Exploiting the internet for the collection of valid sexuality data. *Journal of Sex Research, 38*(4), 292–302.

Mustanski, B., & Liu, R. (2013). A longitudinal study of predictors of suicide attempts among lesbian, gay, bisexual, and transgender youth. *Archives of Sexual Behavior, 42*(3), 437–448.

Musters, A. M., Taminiau-Bloem, E. F., van den Boogaard, E., van der Veen, F., & Goddijn, M. (2011). Supportive care for women with unexplained recurrent miscarriage: Patients' perspectives. *Human Reproduction, 26*, 873–877.

Mustich, E. (2013, July 16). 'The mask you live in': Jennifer Siebel Newsom documentary will examine masculinity. *Huffington Post.* Retrieved February 14, 2014, from http://www.huffingtonpost.com/2013/07/16/the-mask-you-live-in-jennifer-siebel-newsom-masculinity_n_3599812.html.

Myers, K. (2012). "Cowboy Up!": Non-hegemonic representations of masculinity in children's television programming. *Journal of Men's Studies, 20*(2), 125–143.

Nacci, P. L., & Kane, T. R. (1983). The incidence of sex and sexual aggression in federal prisons. *Federal Probation, 47*, 31–36.

Nadeem, M., & Roche, F. (2014). Bone mineral density in Turner's syndrome and the influence of pubertal development. *Acta Paediatrica, 103*(1), 38–42.

Nadelson, C. C., Notman, M. T., Zackson, H., & Gornick, J. (1982). A follow-up study of rape victims. *American Journal of Psychiatry, 139*, 1266–1270.

Nagai, A. (2013). Editorial comment to status of SRS for gender identity disorder in Japan. *International Journal of Urology, 19*(5), 415.

Nagel, B., Matsuo, H., McIntyre, K. P., & Morrison, N. (2005). Attitudes toward victims of rape: Effects of gender, race, religion, and social class. *Journal of Interpersonal Violence, 20*(6), 725–737.

Nagel, J. (2003). *Race, ethnicity and sexuality.* New York: Oxford University Press.

Nahshoni, K. (2010, July 28). US rabbis: Accept homosexuals. *Ynet news.* Retrieved February 19, 2011, from http://www.ynetnews.com/articles/0,7340,L-3926452,00.html.

Nahuis, M., Oosterhuis, G., Hompes, P., Van Wely, M., Mol, B., Van der Veen, F. (2013). The basic fertility workup in women with polycystic ovary syndrome. *Fertility and Sterility, 100*(1), 219–225.

Najman, J. M., Dunne, M. P., Purdie, D. M., Boyle, F. M., & Coxeter, P. D. (2005). Sexual abuse in childhood and sexual dysfunction in adulthood: An Australian population-based study. *Archives of Sexual Behavior, 34*(5), 517–526.

Nanda, S. (2001). *Gender diversity: Crosscultural variations.* Prospect Heights, IL: Waveland Press.

Napper, L., Montes, K., Kenney, S., LaBrie, J. (2016). Assessing the personal negative impacts of hooking up experienced by college students: Gender differences and mental health, *Journal of Sex Research, 53*(7), 766–775.

Naqaish, T., Rizvi, F., Khan, A., & Afzal, M. (2012). Patient satisfaction for levonorgestrel intrauterine system and norethisterone for treatment of dysfunctional uterine bleeding. *Journal of Ayub Medical College, 24*(1), 23–26.

Nass, C. (2012, May/June). The keyboard and the damage done. *Pacific Standard,* pp. 22–25.

National Campaign to Prevent Teen and Unplanned Pregnancy. (2013). *National and state data.* Retrieved April 3, 2014, from http://thenationalcampaign.org/data/landing.

National Cancer Institute. (2009). Human papillomavirus (HPV) vaccines. U.S. National Institutes of Health, National Cancer Institute. Retrieved April 1, 2010, from http://www.cancer.gov/cancertopics/factsheet/prevention/HPV-vaccine.

National Cancer Institute. (2014) NIH study confirms risk factors for male breast cancer. Press Release. Retrieved January 28, 2017, from https://www.cancer.gov/news-events/press-releases/2014/BreastCancerMalePoolingStudy.

National Center for Health Statistics. (2015). Sexual orientation and health among U.S. adults aged 18 and over: By sex and age group: United States, 2015. National Health Interview Survey. Retrieved March 15, 2017, from https://www.cdc.gov/nchs/data/nhis/sexual_orientation/asi_2015_stwebsite_tables.pdf.

National Conference of State Legislatures. (2014). Breastfeeding state laws. June 11. Retrieved July 31, 2014, from http://www.ncsl.org/research/health/breastfeeding-state-laws.aspx.

National Institute of Justice. (2007). Causes and consequences of intimate partner violence. Office of Justice Programs. Retrieved from https://www.nij.gov/topics/crime/intimate-partner-violence/pages/causes.aspx.

National Sexual Violence Resource Center. (2011). Child Sexual Abuse Prevention. Retrieved from http://www.nsvrc.org/sites/default/files/Publications_NSVRC_Overview_Child-sexual-abuse-prevention_0.pdf.

National Survey on Drug Use and Health. (2013). The NSDUH Report. Substance Abuse and Mental Health Services Administration. Retrieved March 31, 2017, from https://www.samhsa.gov/data/sites/default/files/spot123-pregnancy-alcohol-2013/spot123-pregnancy-alcohol-2013.pdf.

Natsuaki, M., Leve, L., & Mendle, J. (2011). Going through the rites of passage: Timing and transition of menarche, childhood sexual abuse, and anxiety symptoms in girls. *Journal of Youth and Adolescence, 40*(10), 1357–1370.

Nauru, T., Suleiman, M., Kiwi, A., Anther, M., Wear, S. Q., Irk, S., & Rive, J. (2008). Intracytoplasmic sperm injection outcome using ejaculated sperm and retrieved sperm in azoospermic men. *Urology, 5*, 106–110.

Naus, M. J., Philipp, L. M., Samsi, M. (2009). From paper to pixels: A comparison of paper and computer formats in psychological assessment. *Computers in Human Behavior, 25*(1), 1–7.

Navai, R. (2009, March 27). Women told: 'You have dishonoured your family, please kill yourself.' *The Independent.* Retrieved October 5, 2010, from http://www.independent.co.uk/news/world/europe/women-told-you-have-dishonoured-your-family-please-kill-yourself-1655373.html.

Naz, R. K. (2005). Contraceptive vaccines. *Drugs, 65*, 593–603.

Naziri, D. (2007). Man's involvement in the experience of abortion and the dynamics of the couple's relationship: A clinical study. *European Journal of Contraceptive and Reproductive Health Care, 12*, 168–174.

Neal, J., & Frick-Horbury, D. (2001). The effects of parenting styles and childhood attachment patterns on intimate relationships. *Journal of Instructional Psychology, 28*(3), 178–183.

Nebehay, S. (2004). Cervical cancer epidemic in poor countries. Retrieved December 12, 2004, from http://www.reuters.co.uk/printerFriendlyPopup.jhtml?type=healthNews&storyID=7114888.

Needham, B. L., & Austin, E. L. (2010). Sexual orientation, parental support, and health during the transition to young adulthood. *Journal of Youth and Adolescence, 39*(10), 1189–1198.

Neff, L., & Karney, B. (2005). To know you is to love you: The implications of global adoration and specific accuracy for marital relationships. *Journal of Personality & Social Psychology, 88*(3), 480–497.

Neilson, E., Norris, J., Bryan, A., & Stappenbeck, C. (2016). Sexual assault severity and depressive symptoms as longitudinal predictors of the quality of women's sexual experiences. *Journal of Sex and Marital Therapy,* 1–16. Retrieved April 15, 2017, from http://www.tandfonline.com/doi/abs/10.1080/0092623X.2016.1208127.

Neisen, J. H. (1990). Heterosexism: Redefining homophobia for the 1990s. *Journal of Gay and Lesbian Psychotherapy*, *1*, 21–35.

Nelson, A. (2015). Transdermal contraception methods: Today's patches and new options on the horizon. *Expert Opinions in Pharmacotherapy*, *16*(6), 863–873.

Nelson, C., Ahmed, A., Valenzuela, R., & Melhall, J. (2007). Assessment of penile vibratory stimulation as a management strategy in men with secondary retarded orgasm. *Urology*, *69*, 552–555.

Nelson, H., Zakher, B., Cantor, A. , Fu, R., Griffin, J., O'Meara, E., Buist, D., et al. (2012). Risk factors for breast cancer for women aged 40 to 49 years: A systematic review and meta-analysis. *Annals of Internal Medicine*, *156*(9), 635–648.

Nelson, J. (2013). An examination of sexual fantasy with specific emphasis on both fluid and constant variables: The effect of gender, sexual orientation, ethnicity, religion, and personality on sexual fantasy. *Dissertation Abstracts International: Section B: The Sciences and Engineering*, *73*(12-B)(E).

Nelson, R. (2005). Gottman's sound medical house model. Retrieved September 3, 2005, from http://www.psychpage.com/family /library/gottman.html.

Németh, Z., Kun, B., & Demetrovics, Z. (2010). The involvement of gamma-hydroxybutyrate in reported sexual assaults: A systematic review. *Journal of Psychopharmacology*, *24*(9), 1281–1287.

Neri, Q., Takeuchi, T., & Palermo, G. (2008). An update of assisted reproductive technologies results in the U.S. *Annals of the New York Academy of Sciences*, *1127*, 41–49.

Neruda, B. (2005). Development and current status of combined spinal epidural anaesthesia [article in German]. *Anasthesiol Intensivemed Nofallmed Schmerzther*, *40*(8), 459–468.

Ness, R. B., Dodge, R. C., Edwards, R. P., Baker, J. A., & Moysich, K. B. (2011). Contraception methods, beyond oral contraceptives and tubal ligation, and risk of ovarian cancer. *Annals of Epidemiology*, *21*(3), 188–196.

New, J. F. H. (1969). *The Renaissance and Reformation: A short history*. New York: Wiley.

Newbem, E., Anschuetz, G., Eberhart, M., Salmon, M., Brady, K., Reyes, A., Baker, J., Asbel, L., Johnson, C., & Schwarz, D. (2013). Adolescent sexually transmitted infections and risk for subsequent HIV. *American Journal of Public Health*, *103*(10), 1874–1861.

Newberger, D. (2000). Down syndrome: Prenatal risk assessment and diagnosis. *American Family Physician*, *62*(4), 825–832.

Newcomb, M. (2013). Moderating effect of age on the association between alcohol use and sexual risk in MSM: Evidence for elevated risk among younger MSM. *AIDS and Behavior*, *17*(5), 1746–1754.

Newcomb, M. E., & Mustanski, B. (2010). Internalized homophobia and internalizing mental health problems: A meta-analytic review. *Clinical Psychology Review*, *30*(8), 1019–1029.

Newell, M., Coovadia, H., Cortina-Borja, M., Rollins, N., Gaillard, P., & Dabis, F. (2004). Mortality of infected and uninfected infants born to HIV-infected mothers in Africa: A pooled analysis. *Lancet*, *364*(9441), 1236–1243.

Newfield, E., Hart, S., Dibble, S., & Kohler, L. (2006). Female-to-male transgender quality of life. *Quality of Life Research*, *15*, 1447–1457.

Newman, L., & Nyce, J. (Eds.). (1985). *Women's medicine: A cross-cultural study of indigenous fertility regulation*. New Brunswick, NJ: Rutgers University Press.

Newman, L., Kamb, M., Hawkes, S., Gomez, G., Say, L., Seuc, A., & Broutet, N. (2013). Global estimates of syphilis in pregnancy and associated adverse outcomes: Analysis of multinational antenatal surveillance data. *PLOS Medicine*, *10*(2). Retrieved June 6, 2014, from http://www.plosmedicine.org/article /info%3Adoi%2F10.1371%2Fjournal.pmed .1001396.

Newring, K., Wheeler, J., & Draper, C. (2008). Transvestic fetishism: Assessment and treatment. In D. Laws & W. O'Donohue (Eds.), *Sexual deviance: Theory, assessment and treatment* (2nd ed., pp. 285–304). New York: Guilford Press.

Ng, E., & Ma, J. L. (2004). Hong Kong. In R. T. Francoeur & R. J. Noonan (Eds.), *The Continuum International encyclopedia of sexuality* (pp. 489–502). New York/London: Continuum International.

Ngun, T., Guo, W., Ghahramani, N., Purkayastha, K., Conn, D., Sanchez, F., Bocklandt, S., Zhang, M., Ramirez, C., Pellegrini, M., & Vilain, E. (2015). A novel predictive model of sexual orientation using epigenetic markers. Presented at the American Society of Human Genetics Annual Meeting, October 6–10, 2015, Baltimore, MD. Concurrent Platform Session B. Retrieved March 24, 2017, from http:// www.ashg.org/2015meeting/pdf/program-at -a-glance-ASHG-2015.pdf.

Ngun, T. C., Ghahramani, N., Sanchez, F. J., Bocklandt, S., & Vilain, E. (2011). The genetics of sex differences in brain and behavior. *Frontiers in Neuroendocrinology*, *32*(2), 227–246.

Nicholas, D. R. (2000). Men, masculinity and cancer. *Journal of American College Health*, *49*(1), 27–33.

Nichols, M. (1990). Lesbian relationships: Implications for the study of sexuality and gender. In D. McWhiter, S. A. Sanders, & J. Reinish (Eds.), *Homosexuality/heterosexuality: Concepts of sexual orientation* (pp. 350–364). The Kinsey Institute Series. New York: Oxford University Press.

Nichols, M. (2004). Lesbian sexuality/female sexuality: Rethinking 'lesbian bed death'. *Sexual and Relationship Therapy*, *19*(4), 363–371.

Nicoll, L. M., & Skupski, D. W. (2008). Venous air embolism after using a birth-training device. *Obstetrics and Gynecology*, *111*, 489–491.

Nielsen Mobile Netview. (2016, December 28). Tops of 2016: Digital. Retrieved January 11, 2017, from http://www.nielsen.com/us/en /insights/news/2016/tops-of-2016-digital.html.

Nielsen Newswire. (2010). *U.S. teen mobile report: Calling yesterday, texting today, using apps tomorrow*. Retrieved February 1, 2014, from http://www.nielsen.com/us/en /newswire/2010/u-s-teen-mobile-report -calling-yesterday-texting-today-using-apps -tomorrow.html.

Nieman, L. K., Blocker, W., Nansel, T., Mahoney, S., Reynolds, J., Blithe, D., Wesley, R., & Armstrong, A. (2011). Efficacy and tolerability of CDB-2914 treatment for symptomatic uterine fibroids: A randomized, double-blind, placebo-controlled, phase IIb study. *Fertility and Sterility*, *95*(2), 767–772.e1–2.

Nieschlag, E., & Vorona, E. (2015). Mechanisms in endocrinology: Medical consequences of doping with anabolic androgenic steroids: Effects on reproductive functions. *European Journal of Endocrinology*, *173*(2), R47–58.

Nilsson, L. (1990). *A child is born*. New York: Delacorte Press, Bantam Books.

Njus, D., & Bane, C. (2009). Religious identification as a moderator of evolved sexual strategies of men and women. *Journal of Sex Research*, *46*(6), 546–557.

Nolan, T., & Maguire, M. (2016). Sex offenders and their treatment. In H. Fradella & J. Sumner (Eds.), *Sexuality, law, and (in)justice* (pp. 402–435). New York: Taylor & Francis.

Noller, P. (1993, March-June). Gender and emotional communication in marriage: Different cultures or differential social power? *Journal of Language & Social Psychology*, *12*(1–2), 132–152.

Nonnemaker, J., McNeely, C., & Blum, R. (2003). Public and private domains of religiosity and adolescent health risk behaviors: Evidence from the National Longitudinal Study of Adolescent Health. *Social Science & Medicine*, *57*(11), 2049–2054.

Noorimotlagh, Z., Haghighi, N., Ahmadimoghadam, M., & Rahim, F. (2016). An updated systematic review on the possible effect of nonylphenol on male fertility. *Environmental Science and Pollution Research International*. Retrieved January 29, 2017, from https://www.ncbi.nlm.nih.gov /pubmed/27826822.

Nordling, N., Sandnabba, N., Santilla, P., & Alison, L. (2006). Differences and similarities between gay and straight individuals involved in the SM subculture. *Journal of Homosexuality, 50*(2–3), 41–67.

Nordtveit, T., Melve, K., Albrechtsen, S., & Skjaerven, R. (2008). Maternal and paternal contribution to intergenerational recurrence of breech delivery: Population based cohort study. *British Medical Journal, 336*, 843–844.

Nelson, A. (2015). Transdermal contraception methods: Today's patches and new options on the horizon. *Expert Opinions in Pharmacotherapy, 16*(6), 863–873.

"Not Alone." (2014). The First Report of the White House Task Force to Protect Students from Sexual Assault. Retrieved June 16, 2014, from http://www.whitehouse.gov/sites /default/files/docs/report_0.pdf.

Notman, M. T. (2002). Changes in sexual orientation and object choice in midlife in women. *Psychoanalytic Inquiry, 22*, 182–195.

Nour, N. M. (2004). Female genital cutting: Clinical and cultural guidelines. *Obstetrical & Gynecological Survey, 59*(4), 272–279.

Nour, N. M. (2006). Health consequences of child marriage in Africa. *Emerging Infectious Diseases, 12*(11). Retrieved June 26, 2008, from http://www.cdc.gov/ncidod/EID /vol12no11/06–0510.htm.

Nuttall, F., Warrier, R., & Gannon, M. (2015). Gynecomastia and drugs: A critical evaluation of the literature. *European Journal of Clinical Pharmacology, 71*(5), 569–578.

O'Brien, C., Keith, J., & Shoemaker, L. (2015). Don't tell: Military culture and male rape. *Psychological Services, 12*(4), 357–365.

O'Connell, H. E., & DeLancey, D. O. (2005). Clitoral anatomy in nulliparous, healthy, premenopausal volunteers using enhanced magnetic resonance imaging. *Journal of Urology, 173*, 2060–2063.

O'Connell, M., & Feliz, S. (2011). *Same-sex couple household statistics from the 2010 census* (SEHSD Working Paper No. 2011–26). Washington, DC: U.S. Bureau of the Census.

O'Connor, M. (2008). Reconstructing the hymen: Mutilation or restoration? *Journal of Law, Medicine, and Ethics, 16*(1), 161–175.

O'Grady, R. (2001). Eradicating pedophilia toward the humanization of society. *Journal of International Affairs, 55*(1), 123–140.

O'Halloran, R. L., & Dietz, P. E. (1993). Autoerotic fatalities with power hydraulics. *Journal of Forensic Sciences, 38*, 359–364.

O'Leary, A., DiNenno, E., Honeycutt, A., Allaire, B., Neuwahl, S., Hicks, K., & Sansom, S. (2017). Contribution of anal sex to HIV prevalence among heterosexuals: A modeling analysis. *AIDS and Behavior*. Retrieved March 10, 2017, from https://www.ncbi.nlm .nih.gov/labs/articles/28058564/.

O'Neill, N., & O'Neill, G. (1972). *Open marriage: A new life style for couples.* New York: Evans.

O'Shaughnessy, P., Ireland, C., Pelentsov, L., Thomas, L., & Esterman, A. (2013). Impaired sexual function and prostate cancer: A mixed method investigation into the experiences of men and their partners. *Journal of Clinical Nursing, 22*(23–24), 3492–3502.

O'Sullivan, L., & Allgeier, E. (1998). Feigning sexual desire: Consenting to unwanted sexual activity in heterosexual dating relationships. *Journal of Sex Research, 35*, 234–243.

O'Sullivan, L. F., Udell, W., Montrose, V. A., Antoniello, P., & Hoffman, S. (2010). A cognitive analysis of college students' explanations for engaging in unprotected sexual intercourse. *Archives of Sexual Behavior, 39*(5), 1121–1131.

Oakes, M., Eyvazzadeh, A., Quint, E., & Smith, Y. (2008). Complete androgen insensitivity syndrome—a review. *Journal of Pediatric and Adolescent Gynecology, 21*, 305–310.

Occhipinti., A., Germano, A., & Maffei, M. (2016). Prevention of urinary tract infection with oximacro, a cranberry extract with a high content of A-type proanthocyanidins. *Urology Journal, 13*(2), 2640–2649.

Ochsenkühn, R., Hermelink, K., Clayton, A. H., von Schönfeldt, V., Gallwas, J., Ditsch, N., Rogenhofer, N., & Kahlert, S. (2011). Menopausal status in breast cancer patients with past chemotherapy determines long-term hypoactive sexual desire disorder. *Journal of Sexual Medicine, 8*(5), 1486–1494.

Odenweller, K. G., Rittenour, C. E., Myers, S. A., & Brann, M. (2013). Father-son communication patterns and gender ideologies: A modeling and compensation analysis. *Journal of Family Communication, 13*(4), 340–357.

Ofir, K., Kalter, A., Moran, O., Sivan, E., Schiff, E., & Simchen, M. (2013). Subsequent pregnancy after stillbirth: Obstetrical and medical risks. *Journal of Perinatal Medicine, 41*(5), 543–548.

Ofman, U. (2004). "... And how are things sexually?": Helping patients adjust to sexual changes before, during, and after cancer treatment. *Supportive Cancer Therapy, 1*, 243–247.

Ogilvie, G., Taylor, D., Trussler, T., Marchand, R., Gilbert, M., Moniruzzaman, A., & Rekart, M. (2008). Seeking sexual partners on the Internet: A marker for risky sexual behavior in men who have sex with men. *Canadian Journal of Public Health, 99*, 185–188.

Ogletree, S. M., & Ginsburg, H. J. (2000). Kept under the hood: Neglect of the clitoris in common vernacular. *Sex Roles, 43*(11–12), 917–927.

Olil, D. A., Quallich, S. A., Sønksen, J., Brackett, N. L., & Lynne, C. M. (2008). Anejaculation

and retrograde ejaculation. *Urology Clinics of North America, 35*(2), 211–220.

Ojanen, T., Sijtsema, J., Hawley, P., & Little, T. (2010). Intrinsic and extrinsic motivation in early adolescents' friendship development: Friendship selection, influence, and prospective friendship quality. *Journal of Adolescence, 33*(6), 837.

Okami, P. (1990). Sociopolitical biases in the contemporary scientific literature on adult human sexual behavior with children and adolescents. In J. Feierman (Ed.), *Pedophilia* (pp. 91–121). New York: Springer Verlag.

Okami, P., Olmstead, R., & Abramson, P. R. (1998). Early childhood exposure to parental nudity and scenes of parental sexuality ("primal scenes"): An 18-year longitudinal study of outcome. *Archives of Sexual Behavior, 27*(4), 361–384.

Okeowo, A. (2014, February 28). A rising tide of anti-gay sentiment in Africa. *The New Yorker*. Retrieved April 12, 2014, from http://www .newyorker.com/online/blogs/newsdesk /2014/02/a-rising-tide-of-anti-gay-sentiment -in-africa.html.

Okon, B. A., & Ansa, S. A. (2012). Language, culture and communication: The Ibibio worldview. *Studies in Literature and Language, 5*(3), 70–74.

Oliver, C., Beech, A., Fisher, D., & Beckett, R. (2007). A comparison of rapists and sexual murderers on demographic and selected psychometric measures. *International Journal of Offender Therapy and Comparative Criminology, 51*, 298.

Ollen, E., Ameral, V., Reed, K., & Hines, D. (2017). Sexual minority college students' Perceptions on dating violence and sexual assault. *Journal of Counseling Psychology, 64*(1), 112–119.

Olmstead, S., Pasley, K., & Fincham, F. (2013). Hooking up and penetrative hookups: Correlates that differentiate college men. *Archives of Sexual Behavior, 42*(4), 573–583.

Olson, K., Durwood, L., DeMeules, M., & McLaughlin, K. (2016). Mental health of transgender children who are supported in their identities. *Pediatrics, 137*(3). Retrieved February 11, 2017, from http://pediatrics .aappublications.org/content/early/2016/02/24 /peds.2015-3223.

Olson, K., Key, A., & Eaton, N. (2015). Gender cognition in transgender children. *Psychological Science, 26*(4), 467–474.

Olsson, S. E., & Möller, A. (2006). Regret after sex reassignment surgery in a male-to-female transsexual: A long-term follow up. *Archives of Sexual Behavior, 35*, 501–506.

Oner, B. (2001). Factors predicting future time orientation for romantic relationships with the opposite sex. *Journal of Psychology: Interdisciplinary & Applied, 135*(4), 430–438.

Operario, D., Soma, T., & Underhill, K. (2008). Sex work and HIV status among transgender women: Systematic review and meta-analysis. *Journal of Acquired Immune Deficiency Syndrome, 48*(1), 97–103.

Ornish, D. (1999). *Love and survival: The scientific basis for the healing power of intimacy*. New York: Harper Paperbacks.

Orosz, G., Szekeres, A., Kiss, Z., Farkas, P., & Roland-Lévy, C. (2015). Elevated romantic love and jealousy if relationship status is declared on Facebook. *Frontiers in Psychology, 6*, 214. Retrieved February 7, 2017, from https://www.ncbi.nlm.nih.gov/pmc/articles/PMC4341541/.

Ortigue, S., Bianchi-Demicheli, F., Patel, N., Frum, C., & Lewis, J. (2010). Neuroimaging of love: fMRI meta-analysis evidence toward new perspectives in sexual medicine. *Journal of Sexual Medicine, 7*(11), 3541–3552.

Ortiz, C. A., Freeman, J. L., Kuo, Y. F., & Goodwin, J. S. (2007). The influence of marital status on stage at diagnosis and survival of older persons with melanoma. *Journals of Gerontology, Series A: Biological Sciences and Medical Sciences, 62*, 892–898.

Osazuwa-Peters, N. (2013). Human papillomavirus (HPV), HPV-associated oropharyngeal cancer, and HPV vaccine in the United States—Do we need a broader vaccine policy? *Vaccine, 31*(47), 5500–5505.

Oselin, S. (2010). Weighing the consequences of a deviant career: Factors leading to an exit from prostitution. *Sociological Perspectives, 53*(4), 527–549.

Osterman, M., Martin, J. (2014). Recent declines in induction of labor by gestational age. NCHS Data Brief No. 155. Centers for Disease Control and Prevention, Atlanta GA. Retrieved August 25, 2014, from http://www.cdc.gov/nchs/data/databriefs/db155.htm.

Oswald, R., & Clausell, E. (2005). Same-sex relationships and their dissolution. In M. Fine & J. Harvey (Eds.), *Handbook of divorce and relationship dissolution* (pp. 499–513). New York: Routledge.

Othman, A., Edrees, G., El-Missiry, M., Ali, D., Aboel-Nour, M., & Dabdoub, B. (2016). Melatonin controlled apoptosis and protected the testes and sperm quality against bisphenol A-induced oxidative toxicity. *Toxicology and Industrial Health, 32*(9), 1537–1549.

Otis, M. D., & Skinner, W. F. (1996). The prevalence of victimization and its effects on mental well-being among lesbian and gay people. *Journal of Homosexuality, 30*, 93–121.

Ouellette, G., & Michaud, M. (2016). Generation text: Relations among undergraduates' use of text messaging, textese, and language and literacy skills. *Canadian Journal of Behavioural Science, 48*(3), 217–221.

Oultram, S. (2009). All hail the new flesh: Some thoughts on scarification, children and adults. *Journal of Medical Ethics, 35*(10), 607–610.

Owen, J., & Fincham, F. (2011). Young adults' emotional reactions after hooking up encounters. *Archives of Sexual Behavior, 40*(2), 321–341.

Owen, J., Fincham, F., & Moore, J. (2011). Short-term prospective study of hooking up among college students. *Archives of Sexual Behavior, 40*(2), 331–341.

Owen, J., Rhoades, G., Stanley, S., & Fincham, F. (2010). Hooking up among college students: Demographic and psychosocial correlates. *Archives of Sexual Behavior, 39*(3), 653–663.

Owen, R. (2009). Dapoxetine: A novel treatment for premature ejaculation. *Drugs Today, 45*(9), 669–678.

Owens, Z. (2017). Is it Facebook official? Coming out and passing strategies of young adult gay men on social media. *Journal of Homosexuality, 64*(4), 431–449.

Ozdemir, O., Simsek, F., Ozkardes, S., Incesu, C., & Karakoc, B. (2008). The unconsummated marriage: Its frequency and clinical characteristics in a sexual dysfunction clinic. *Journal of Sex and Marital Therapy, 34*, 268–279.

Pacey, A., Povey, A., Clyma, J., McNamee, R., Moore, H., Baillie, H, & Cherry, N. (2014). Modifiable and non-modifiable risk factors for poor sperm morphology. *Human Reproduction*. Retrieved June 24, 2014, from http://humrep.oxfordjournals.org/content/early/2014/06/03/humrep.deu116.abstract?sid=66725767-40f3-4c49-8240-591c88a5822b.

Pachankis, J. E., & Goldfried, M. R. (2004). Clinical issues in working with lesbian, gay, and bisexual clients. *Psychotherapy: Theory, Research, Practice, and Training, 41*(3), 227–246.

Pacik, P., & Geletta, S. (2017). Vaginismus treatment: Clinical trials follow up 241 patients. *Sexual Medicine*. Retrieved April 15, 2017, from https://www.ncbi.nlm.nih.gov/pubmed/28363809.

Pacik, P. T. (2009). Botox treatment for vaginismus. *Plastic and Reconstructive Surgery, 124*(6), 455e–456e.

Padgett, V. R., Brislin-Slutz, J. A., & Neal, J. A. (1989). Pornography, erotica, and attitudes toward women: The effects of repeated exposure. *The Journal of Sex Research, 26*, 479–491.

Paek, H., Nelson, M., & Vilela, A. (2011). Examination of gender-role portrayals in television advertising across seven countries. *Sex Roles, 64*(3–4), 192–207.

Paik, A. (2010). "Hookups," dating, and relationship quality: Does the type of sexual involvement matter? *Social Science Research, 39*(5), 739–753.

Paik, A., Sanchagrin, K., & Heimer, K. (2016). Broken promises: Abstinence pledging and

sexual and reproductive health. *Journal of Marriage and Family*. Retrieved February 13, 2017, from http://onlinelibrary.wiley.com/doi/10.1111/jomf.12279/abstract.

Palacios, S. (2011). Hypoactive sexual desire disorder and current pharmacotherapeutic options in women. *Women's Health, 7*(1), 95–107.

Palca, J. (1991). Fetal brain signals time for birth. *Science, 253*, 1360.

Palit, V., & Eardley, I. (2010). An update on new oral PDE5 inhibitors for the treatment of erectile dysfunction. *Nature Reviews Urology, 7*(11), 603–609.

Pallotta, F. (2017, April 20). Nine months of sex harassment scandals take down two Fox News icons. CNN Media. Retrieved from http://money.cnn.com/2017/04/20/media/fox-news-sex-harassment/.

Palombi, L., Nielsen-Saines, K., Giuliano, M., & Marazzi, M. (2011). Easier said than done: World Health Organization recommendations for prevention of mother-to-child transmission of HIV-areas of concern. *AIDS Research and Human Retroviruses, 27*(8), 807–808.

Pan, S., Leung, C., Shah, J., & Kilchevsky, A. (2015). Clinical anatomy of the G-spot. *Clinical Anatomy, 28*(3), 363–367.

Panay, N., & Fenton, A. (2015). Severe PMS/PMDD—Is it time for a new approach? *Climacteric, 18*(3), 331–332.

Pandey, S., & Bhattacharyta, S. (2010). Impact of obesity on gynecology. *Women's Health, 6*(1), 107–117.

Pang, R., Bello, M., Stone, M., Kirkpatrick, M., Huh, J., Monterosso, J., Hastelton, M., Fales, M., & Leventhal, A. (2016). Premenstrual symptoms and smoking-related expectancies. *Addictive Behaviors, 57*, 38–41.

Panjari, M., Bell, R., & Davis, S. (2011). Sexual function after breast cancer. *Journal of Sexual Medicine, 8*(1), 294–302.

Papp, J., Schachter, J., Gaydos, C., & Van Der Pol, B. (2014). Recommendations for the laboratory-based detection of chlamydia trachomatis and *Neisseria gonorrhoeae*—2014. Morbidity and Mortality Weekly Report, *63*(RR02), 1–19.

"Paraphilic Disorders." (2013). American Psychiatric Association. Retrieved June 11, 2014, from http://www.dsm5.org/Documents/Paraphilic%20Disorders%20Fact%20Sheet.pdf.

Pardue, A., & Arrigo, B. (2008). Power, anger, and sadistic rapists: Toward a differentiated model of offender personality. *International Journal of Offender Therapy and Comparative Criminology, 52*, 378–400.

Pardun, C. J., L'Engle, K. L., & Brown, J. D. (2005). Linking exposure to outcomes: Early adolescents' consumption of sexual content in six media. *Mass Communication & Society,* *8*(2), 75–91.

Parish, S., & Hahn, S. (2016). Hypoactive sexual desire disorder: A review of epidemiology, biopsychology, diagnosis, and treatment. *Sexual Medicine Reviews, 4*(2), 103–120.

Park, A. J., & Paraiso, M. F. (2009). Successful use of botulinum toxin type A in the treatment of refractory postoperative dyspareunia. *Obstetrics and Gynecology, 114*(2 Pt 2), 484–487.

Park, H., Mykhyalyshyn, I. (2016). LGBT people are more likely to be targets of hate crimes than any other minority group. *New York Times,* Retrieved August 23, 2017, from https://www.nytimes.com/interactive/2016/06/16/us/hate-crimes-against-lgbt.html?mcubz=0.

Parker, S. E., Mai, C. T., Canfield, M. A., Rickard, R., Wang, Y., Meyer, R. E., Anderson, P., Mason, C. A., Collins, J. S., Kirby, R. S., & Correa, A. (2010). Updated national birth prevalence estimates for selected birth defects in the United States, 2004–2006. National Birth Defects Prevention Network. *Birth Defects Research: Part A, Clinical and Molecular Teratology, 88*(12), 1008–1016.

Parker, S. K., & Griffin, M. A. (2002). What is so bad about a little name calling? *Journal of Occupational Health Psychology, 7*(3), 195–210.

Parker, S., Troisi, R., Wise, L., Palmer, J., Titus-Ernstoff, L., Strohsnitter, W., & Hatch, E. (2014). Menarche, menopause, years of menstruation, and the incidence of osteoporosis. *Journal of Clinical Endocrinology and Metabolism, 99*(2), 594–601.

Parker-Pope, T. (2010). *For better: The science of marriage.* Boston: Dutton.

Parkhill, M., & Abbey, A. (2008). Does alcohol contribute to the confluence model of sexual assault perpetration? *Journal of Social and Clinical Psychology, 27,* 529–554.

Parks, K. A., & Scheidt, D. M. (2000). Male bar drinkers' perspective on female bar drinkers. *Sex Roles, 43*(11/12), 927–935.

Parrott, D., & Peterson, J. (2008). What motivates hate crimes based on sexual orientation? Mediating effects of anger on antigay aggression. *Aggressive Behavior, 34,* 306–318.

Parry, B. L. (2008). Perimenopausal depression. *American Journal of Psychiatry, 165,* 23–27.

Parsonnet, J., Hansmann, M., Delaney, M., Modern, P., Dubois, A., Wieland-Alter, W., Wissemann, K., Wild, J., Jones, M., Seymour, J., & Onderdonk, A. (2005). Prevalence of toxic shock syndrome toxin 1-producing Staphylococcus aureus and the presence of antibodies to this superantigen in menstruating women. *Journal of Clinics in Microbiology, 43*(9), 4628–4634.

Parsons, J., Starks, T., Gamarel, K., & Grov, C. (2012). Non-monogamy and sexual relationship quality among same-sex male couples. *Journal of Family Psychology, 26*(5), 669–677.

Passel, J., Wang, W., & Taylor, P. (2010). Marrying out: One-in-seven new U.S. marriages is interracial or interethnic. Pew Research Center. Retrieved May 11, 2011, from http://pewresearch.org/pubs/1616/american-marriage-interracial-interethnic.

Pasterski, V. L., Brain, C., Geffner, M. E., Hindmarsh, P., Brook, C., & Hines, M. (2005). Prenatal hormones and postnatal socialization by parents as determinants of male-typical toy play in girls with congenital adrenal hyperplasia. *Child Development, 76*(1), 264–279.

Pasterski, V., Hindmarsh, P., Geffnew, M., Brook, C., Brain, C., & Hines, M. (2007). Increased aggression and activity level in 3- to 11-year old girls with congenital adrenal hyperplasia (CAH). *Hormones and Behavior, 52,* 368–374.

Pastor, Z. (2010). G spot—Myths and realities. *Czechoslovakian Gynecology, 75*(3), 211–217.

Pasupathy, D., & Smith, G. C. (2005). The analysis of factors predicting antepartum stillbirth. *Minerva Ginecology, 57*(4), 397–410.

Pathela, P., Hajat, A., Schillinger, J., Blank, S., Sell, R., & Mostashari, F. (2006). Discordance between sexual behavior and self-reported sexual identity: A population-based survey of New York City men. *Annals of Internal Medicine, 145*(6), 416–425.

Patrick, K. (2007). Is infant male circumcision an abuse of the rights of the child? No. *British Medical Journal, 335*(7631), 1181.

Pattatucci, A. M. (1998). Molecular investigations into complex behavior: Lessons from sexual orientation studies. *Human Biology, 70*(2), 367–387.

Patterson, C. (2005). *Lesbian & gay parenting.* Washington, DC: American Psychological Association, Public Interest Directorate. Retrieved May 15, 2014, from http://www.apa.org/pi/lgbt/resources/parenting.aspx.

Patterson, C. (2013). Children of lesbian and gay parents: Psychology, law, and policy. *Psychology of Sexual Orientation and Gender Diversity, 1*(S), 27–34.

Patton, G. C., & Viner, R. (2007). Pubertal transitions in health. *Lancet, 369,* 1130–1139.

Patzer, G. (2013, February). Physical attractiveness: Uncertainty of the presumptive causal direction. *Journal of Management and Marketing Research, 12*(12), 1–9.

Paul, B. (2009). Predicting Internet pornography use and arousal: The role of individual difference variables. *Journal of Sex Research, 46*(4), 344–357.

Paul, B., & Shim, J. (2008). Gender, sexual affect, and motivations for internet pornography use. *International Journal of Sexual Health, 20*(3), 187–199.

Paul, J. P. (1984). The bisexual identity: An idea without social recognition. *Journal of Homosexuality, 9,* 45–63.

Paul, P. (2005). *Pornified: How pornography is transforming our lives, our relationships and our families.* New York: Times Books.

Paul, P. (2010, July 30). The un-divorced. *New York Times.* Retrieved August 6, 2010, from http://www.nytimes.com/2010/08/01/fashion/01Undivorced.html.

Pauls, R. (2015). Anatomy of the clitoris and the female sexual response. *Clinical Anatomy, 28*(3), 376–384.

Payer, P. J. (1991). Sex and confession in the thirteenth century. In J. E. Salisbury (Ed.), *Sex in the Middle Ages.* New York: Garland.

Pazol, K., Creanga, A., Burley, K., Hayes, B., & Jamieson, D. (2013, November 29). Abortion surveillance—U.S., 2010. *Morbidity and Mortality Weekly Report (Surveillance Summaries), 62*(8), 1–44.

Pearce, A., Chuikova, T., Ramsey, A., & Galyautdinova, S. (2010). A positive psychology perspective on mate preferences in the U.S. and Russia. *Journal of Cross-Cultural Psychology, 41*(5–6), 742.

Pearson, C. (2015, January 15). The app that could be a 99 percent effective form of birth control. *The Huffington Post.* Retrieved April 9, 2017, from http://www.huffingtonpost.com/2015/01/15/contraceptive-app-natural-cycles_n_6472642.html.

Peck, S. (1978). *The road less traveled: A new psychology of love, traditional values and spiritual growth.* Oxford, England: Simon & Schuster.

Peddada, S., Laughlin, S., Miner, K., Guyon, J., Haneke, K., Vahdat, H., Semelka, R., Kowalik, A., Armao, D., Davis, B., & Baird, D. (2008). Growth of uterine leiomyomata among premenopausal black and white women. *Proceedings of the National Academy of Sciences of the U.S., 105*(50), 19887–19892.

Pedrera-Zamorano, J. D., Lavado-Garcia, J. M., Roncero-Martin, R., Calderon-Garcia, J. F., Rodriguez-Dominguez, T., & Canal-Macias, M. L. (2009). Effect of beer drinking on ultrasound bone mass in women. *Nutrition, 25*(10), 1057–1063.

Peele, S., & Brodsky, A. (1991). *Love and addiction.* Jersey City, NJ: Parkwest.

Peeples, E. H., & Scacco, A. M. (1982). The stress impact study technique: A method for evaluating the consequences of male-on-male sexual assault in jails, prisons, and other selected single-sex institutions. In A. M. Scacco (Ed.), *Male rape: A casebook of sexual aggressions* (pp. 241–278). New York: AMS Press.

Penke, L., & Asendorpf, J. B. (2008). Evidence for conditional sex differences in emotional but not in sexual jealousy at the automatic level of cognitive processing. *European Journal of Personality, 22,* 3–30.

Penna-Firme, T., Grinder, R. E., & Linhares-Barreto, M. S. (1991). Adolescent female prostitutes on the streets of Brazil: An exploratory investigation of ontological issues. *Journal of Adolescent Research, 6,* 493–504.

Peplau, L., Frederick, D., Yee, C., Maisel, N., Lever, J., Ghavami, N. (2009). Body image satisfaction in heterosexual, gay, and lesbian adults. *Archives of Sexual Behavior, 38,* 713–725.

Peplau, L. A., & Fingerhut, A. (2004). The paradox of the lesbian worker. *Journal of Social Issues, 60*(4), 719–736.

Peplau, L. A., Garnets, L. D., & Spalding, L. R. (1998). A critique of Bem's "Exotic becomes erotic" theory of sexual orientation. *Psychological Review, 105*(2), 387–394.

Perales, M., Calabria, I., Lopez, C., Franco, E., Coteron, J., & Barakat, R. (2016). Regular exercise throughout pregnancy is associated with a shorter first stage of labor. *American Journal of Health Promotion, 30*(3), 149–154.

Peralta, R. L. (2008). "Alcohol allows you to not be yourself": Toward a structured understanding of alcohol use and gender difference among gay, lesbian, and heterosexual youth. *Journal of Drug Issues, 38,* 373–400.

Perelman, M. (2007). Clinical application of CNS-acting agents in FSD. *Journal of Sexual Medicine, 4*(Suppl. 4), 280–290.

Perelman, M., & Rowland, D. (2006). Retarded ejaculation. *World Journal of Urology, 24,* 645–652.

Perilloux, C., & Buss, D. (2008). Breaking up romantic relationships: Costs experienced and coping strategies deployed. *Evolutionary Psychology, 6*(1), 164–181.

Perilloux, C., Duntley, J., & Buss, D. (2012). The costs of rape. *Archives of Sexual Behavior, 41*(5), 1099–1106.

Perkins, R., & Bennett, G. (1985). *Being a prostitute: Prostitute women and prostitute men.* Boston: Allen & Unwin.

Perlman, D. (2007). The best of times, the worst of times: The place of close relationships in psychology and our daily lives. *Canadian Psychology, 48,* 7–24.

Perovic, S. V., & Djinovic, R. P. (2010). Current surgical management of severe Peyronie's disease. *Archives of Españoles Urology, 63*(9), 755–770.

Perper, K., Peterson, K., & Manlove, J. (2010). *Diploma attainment among teen mothers.* Washington, DC: Child Trends. Retrieved April 14, 2014, from http://childtrends .org/wp-content/uploads/2010/01/child _trends-2010_01_22_FS_diplomaattainment .pdf.

Perper, T. (1985). *Sex signals: The biology of love.* Philadelphia, PA: ISI Press.

Perrigouard, C., Dreval, A., Cribier, B., & Lipsker, D. (2008). Vulvar vestibulitis syndrome: A clinicopathological study of 14 cases. *Annals of Dermatologie et de Venereologie, 135,* 367–372.

Perrow, C., & Guillén, M. F. (1990). *The AIDS disaster.* New Haven, CT: Yale University Press.

Perry, S. (2013). Religion and interracial romance: The effects of religious affiliation, public and devotional practices, and biblical literalism. *Social Science Quarterly, 94*(5), 1308–1327.

Peter, J., & Valkenburg, P. (2007). Adolescents' exposure to a sexualized media environment and their notions of women as sex objects. *Sex Roles, 56,* 381–395.

Peterman, T., O'Connor, K., Bradley, H., Torrone, E., & Bernstein, K. (2016). Gonorrhea control, United States, 1972–2015, a narrative review. *Sexually Transmitted Diseases, 43*(12), 725–730.

Peters, T., Schatzkin, A., Gierach, G., et al. (2009). Physical activity and postmenopausal breast cancer risk in the NIH-AARP diet and health study. *Cancer Epidemiology Biomarkers Prevention, 18*(1), 289–296.

Peterson, C., Johnstone, E., Hammound, A., Standord, J., Varner, M., Kennedy, A., Chen, Z., Sun, L., et al. (2013). Risk factors associated with endometriosis. *American Journal of Obstetrics and Gynecology, 208*(6), 452–462.

Pettigrew, J. (2009). Text messaging and connectedness within close interpersonal relationships. *Marriage and Family Review, 45*(6–8), 697–716.

Pew Research Center. (2010). The decline of marriage and rise of new families. Pew Research Center's Social and Demographic Trends Project. Retrieved May 12, 2011, from http://pewsocialtrends.org/files/2010/11/pew -social-trends-2010-families.pdf.

Pew Research Center. (2013). The world's Muslims: Religion, politics and society. Retrieved March 24, 2017, from http://www .pewforum.org/2013/04/30/the-worlds -muslims-religion-politics-society-morality/.

Pew Research Center. (2013a). *The global divide on homosexuality.* Washington, DC: Author. Retrieved May 6, 2014, from http://www .pewglobal.org/files/2013/06/Pew-Global -Attitudes-Homosexuality-Report-FINAL -JUNE-4-2013.pdf.

Pew Research Center. (2013b). *A survey of LGBT Americans: Attitudes, experiences and values in changing times.* Washington, DC: Author. Retrieved May 15, 2014, from http://www .pewsocialtrends.org/files/2013/06/SDT _LGBT-Americans_06-2013.pdf.

Pew Research Center. (2017, January 12). Mobile fact sheet. Retrieved January 11, 2017, from http://www.pewinternet.org/fact-sheet /mobile/.

Pfaus, J., Giuliano, F., & Gelez, H. (2007). Bremelanotide: An overview of preclinical CHS effects of female sexual function. *Journal of Sexual Medicine, 4*(Suppl. 4), 269–279.

Phillips, B. (2001, December 11). Baby rapes shock South Africa. *BBC News.* Retrieved April 30, 2011, from http://news.bbc.co.uk /2/hi/africa/1703595.stm.

Phipps, W., Saracino, M., Magaret, A., Selke, S., Remington, M., Huang, M. L., Warren, T., Casper, C., Corey, L., & Wald, A. (2011). Persistent genital herpes simplex virus-2 shedding years following the first clinical episode. *Journal of Infectious Disease, 203*(2), 180–187.

Piacentino, D., Kotzalidis, G., del Casale, A., Aromatario, M., Pomara, C., Girardi, P., & Sani, G. (2015). Anabolic-androgenic steroid use and psychopathology in athletes. A systematic review. *Current Neuropharmacology, 13*(1), 101–121.

Piaget, J. (1951). *Play, dreams, and imitation in children.* New York: Norton.

Pialoux, G., Vimont, S., Moulignier, A., Buteux, M., Abraham, B., & Bonnard, P. (2008). Effect of HIV infection on the course of syphilis. *AIDS Review, 10,* 85–92.

Piccinino, L. J., & Mosher, W. D. (1998). Trends in contraceptive method use in the United States: 1982–1994. *Family Planning Perspectives, 30,* 4–10.

Pickert, K. (2014, February 17). The abortion debate. *Time, 183*(6), 18.

Pilishvili, T., & Koyanongo, E. (2016). The representation of love among Brazilians, Russians and Central Africans: A comparative analysis. *Psychology in Russia: State of the Art, 9*(1), 84–97.

Pillard, R. C. (1991). Masculinity and femininity in homosexuality: "Inversion" revisited. In J. C. Gonsiorek & J. D. Weinrich (Eds.), *Homosexuality: Research implications for public policy* (pp. 32–43). Newbury Park, CA: Sage.

Pillard, R. C. (1998). Biologic theories of homosexuality. *Journal of Gay and Lesbian Psychotherapy, 2*(4), 75–76.

Pillard, R. C., & Bailey, J. M. (1998). Human sexual orientation has a heritable component. *Human Biology, 70*(2), 347–366.

Pilver, C., Kasi, S., Desai, R., & Levy, B. (2010). Health advantage for black women: Patterns in premenstrual dysphoric disorder. *Psychological Medicine,* 1–10.

Pilver, C., Kasl, S., Desai, R., Levy, B. (2011). Health advantage for black women: Patterns in pre-menstrual dysphoric disorder. *Psychological Medicine, 41*(8), 1741–1750.

Pines, A. (2011). Male menopause: Is it a real clinical syndrome? *Climacteric, 14*(1), 15–17.

Ping, W. (2002). *Aching for beauty: Footbinding in China.* New York: Random House.

Pinheiro, A. P., Raney, T. J., Thornton, L. M., Fichter, M. M., Berrettini, W. H., Goldman, D., Halmi, K. A., Kaplan, A. S., Strober, M., Treasure, J., Woodside, D. B., Kaye, W. H., & Bulik, C. M. (2010). Sexual functioning in women with eating disorders. *International Journal of Eating Disorders*, 43(2), 123–129.

Pinheiro, A. P., Thorton, L., & Plotonicov, K. (2007). Patterns of menstrual disturbance in eating disorders. *International Journal of Eating Disorders*, 40(5), 424.

Pinkerton, J., & Stovall, D. (2010). Reproductive aging, menopause, and health outcomes. *Annals of the New York Academy of Science*, 1204, 169–178.

Pinkerton, S., Galletly, C., & Seal, D. (2007). Model-based estimates of HIV acquisition due to prison rape. *The Prison Journal*, 87(3), 295–310.

Pino, N. W., & Meier, R. F. (1999). Gender differences in rape reporting. *Sex Roles*, 40(11–12), 979–990.

Pinquart, M., Stotzka, C., & Silberreisen, R., (2008). Personality and ambivalence in decisions about becoming parents. *Social Behavior and Personality*, 36, 87–96.

Piot, P. (2000). Global AIDS epidemic: Time to turn the tide. *Science*, 288(5474), 2176–2188.

Pisetsky, E. M., Chao, Y., Dierker, L. C., May, A. M., & Striegel-Moore, R. (2008). Disordered eating and substance use in high-school students: Results from the Youth Risk Behavior Surveillance System. *International Journal of Eating Disorders*, 41, 464.

Pistorio, J. M. (2016). Mental health professionals' attitudes toward rape survivors. *Dissertation Abstracts International: Section B: The Sciences and Engineering*, 77(1-B), 978-1339145778.

Pitkin, J. (2010). Cultural issues and the menopause. *Menopause International*, 16(4), 156–161.

Pitts, S., & Emans, S. (2008). Controversies in contraception. *Current Opinion in Pediatrics*, 20(4), 383–389.

Pivarnik, J. M. (1998). Potential effects of maternal physical activity on birth weight: Brief review. *Med Science Sports Exercise*, 30(3), 400–406.

Piwko, C., Koren, G., Babashov, V., Vicente, C., & Einarson, T. (2013). Economic burden of nausea and vomiting of pregnancy in the U.S.A. *Journal of Population Therapeutics and Clinical Pharmacology*, 20(2), 149–160.

Piyamongkol, W., Wanapirak, C., Sirchotiyakul, S., Srisupundit, K., & Tongsong, T. (2012). A comparison of cordocentesis outcomes between early and conventional procedures. *Journal of Maternal-Fetal and Neonatal Medicine*, 25(11), 2298–2301.

Planned Parenthood Federation of America. (2005). Abstinence-only "sex" education.

Retrieved May 30, 2005, from http://www.plannedparenthood.org/pp2/portal/medicalinfo/teensexualhealth/fact-abstinence-education.xml.

Plante, A. F., & Kamm, M. A. (2008). Life events in patients with vulvodynia. *British Journal of Obstetrics and Gynecology*, 115, 509–514.

Planty, M., Langton, L., Krebs, C., Berzofsky, M., & Smiley-McDonald, H. (2013). Female victims of sexual violence, 1994–2010. Bureau of Justice Statistics. Retrieved August 24, 2014, from http://www.bjs.gov/content/pub/pdf/fvsv9410.pdf.

Plaud, J. J., Gaither, G. A., Hegstand, H. J., Rowan, L., & Devitt, M. K. (1999). Volunteer bias in human psychophysiological sexual arousal research: To whom do our research results apply? *The Journal of Sex Research*, 36, 171–179.

Plaut, A., & Kohn-Speyer, A. C. (1947). The carcinogenic action of smegma. *Science*, 105, 392.

Pleak, R. R., & Meyer-Bahlburg, H. F. (1990). Sexual behavior and AIDS knowledge of young male prostitutes in Manhattan. *Journal of Sex Research*, 27, 557–587.

Plummer, K. (1991). Understanding childhood sexualities. *Journal of Homosexuality*, 20, 231–249.

Pocklington, R. (2014, Jan 21). New Google Glass app records you having sex through your partner's eyes. *Mirror Online*. Retrieved June 17, 2014, from http://www.mirror.co.uk/news/weird-news/sex-glass-new-google-glass-3047298.

Poeppl, T., Eickhoff, S., Fox, P., Laird, A., Rupprecht, R., Langguth, B., & Bzdok, D. (2015). Connectivity and functional profiling of abnormal brain structures in pedophilia. *Human Brain Mapping*, 36(6), 2374–2386.

Pogatchnik, S. (1995, November 26). Ireland legalized divorce. *Hartford Courant*, p. A1.

Polaris Project. (2005). Testimony of Rosa. Retrieved December 13, 2005, from http://www.humantrafficking.com/humantrafficking/features_ht3/Testimonies/testimonies_mainframe.htm.

Pollock, N. L., & Hashmall, J. M. (1991). The excuses of child molesters. *Behavioral Sciences and the Law*, 1, 53–59.

Polman, R., Kaiseler, M., & Borkoles, E. (2007). Effect of a single bout of exercise on the mood of pregnant women. *Journal of Sports Medicine and Physical Fitness*, 47, 102–111.

Pomeroy, W. B. (1972). *Dr. Kinsey and the Institute for Sex Research*. New Haven, CT: Yale University Press.

Ponseti, J., Bosinski, H., Wolff, S., Peller, M., Jansen, O., Mehdorn, H., Buchel, C., & Siebner, H. (2006). A functional endophenotype for sexual orientation in humans. *Neuroimage*, 33(3), 825–833.

Ponseti, J., Granert, O., Jansen, O., Wolff, S., Mehdorn, H., Bosinski, H., & Siebner, H. (2009). Assessment of sexual orientation using the hemodynamic brain response to visual sexual stimuli. *Journal of Sexual Medicine*, 6(6), 1628–1634.

Poortman, A., & Mills, M. (2012). Investments in marriage and cohabitation: The role of legal and interpersonal commitment. *Journal of Marriage and Family*, 74(2), 357–376.

Poosari, A., Promthet, S., Kamsa-Ard, S., Suwanrungruang, K., Longkul, J., & Wiangnon, S. (2014). Hormonal contraceptive use and breast cancer in Thai women. *Journal of Epidemiology*, 24(3), 216–220.

Pope, H., & Kanayama, G. (2012). Anabolic-androgenic steroids. In J. Verster, K. Brady, M. Galanter, & P. Conrod (Eds.), *Drug abuse and addiction in medical illness: Causes, consequences and treatment* (pp. 251–264). New York, NY: Springer Science and Business Media.

Popkin, S., Scott, M., & Galvez, M. (2016). Impossible choices: Teens and food insecurity in America. Urban Institute. Retrieved February 11, 2017, from http://www.urban.org/research/publication/impossible-choices-teens-and-food-insecurity-america.

Popova, S., Lange, S., Probst, C., Gmel, G., & Rehm, J. (2017). Estimation of national, regional, and global prevalence of alcohol use during pregnancy and fetal alcohol syndrome: A systematic review and meta-analysis. *The Lancet*, 5(3), e290–e299.

Popovic, M. (2005). Intimacy and its relevance in human functioning. *Sexual and Relationship Therapy*, 20(1), 31–49.

Porter, R. (1982). Mixed feelings: The Enlightenment and sexuality in eighteenth-century Britain. In P.-G. Goucé (Ed.), *Sexuality in eighteenth-century Britain* (pp. 1–27). Manchester, U.K.: Manchester University Press.

Portio Research. (2013). *Portio Research Mobile Factbook 2013*. Retrieved February 3, 2014, from http://www.portioresearch.com/media/3986/Portio%20Research%20Mobile%20Factbook%202013.pdf.

Portman, D., Edelson, J., Jordan, R., Clayton, A.,& Krychman, M. (2014). Bremelanotide for hypoactive sexual desire disorder. *Obstetrics and Gynecology*, 123(1), 31S.

Posey, C., Lowry, P., Roberts, T., & Ellis, T. (2010). Proposing the online community self-disclosure model: The case of working professionals in France and the UK who use online communities. *European Journal of Information Systems*, 19(2), 181–196.

Posner, R. A. (1993). Obsession. *The New Republic*, 209, 31–36.

Postma, R., Bicanic, I., Vaart, H., & Laan, E. (2013). Pelvic floor muscle problems mediate sexual problems in young adult rape victims. *Journal of Sexual Medicine*, 10(8), 1978–1987.

Pothen, S. (1989). Divorce in Hindu society. *Journal of Comparative Family Studies, 20*(3), 377–392.

Potterat, J. J., Rothenberg, R. B., Muth, S. Q., Darrow, W. W., & Phillips-Plummer, L. (1998). Pathways to prostitution: The chronology of sexual and drug abuse milestones. *Journal of Sex Research, 35*(4), 333–340.

Potterat, J. J., Woodhouse, D. E., Muth, J. B., & Muth, S. Q. (1990). Estimating the prevalence and career longevity of prostitute women. *Journal of Sex Research, 27*, 233–243.

Poulson, R. L., Eppler, M. A., Satterwhite, T. N., Wuensch, K. L., & Bass, L. A. (1998). Alcohol consumption, strength of religious beliefs, and risky sexual behavior in college students. *Journal of American College Health, 46*(5), 227–233.

Povey, A., & Stocks, S. (2010). Epidemiology and trends in male subfertility. *Human Fertility, 13*(4), 182–188.

Power, T., Langlois, N., & Byard, R. (2013). The forensic implications of Turner's syndrome. *Journal of Forensic Sciences.* Retrieved February 14, 2014, from http://www.ncbi.nlm.nih.gov/pubmed/24313855.

Pozniak, A. (2002). Pink versus blue: The things people do to choose the sex of their baby. Retrieved June 3, 2002, from http://abcnews.go.com/sections/living/DailyNews/choosingbabysex020603.html.

Practice Committee of the American Society for Reproductive Medicine. (2016). Fertility drugs and cancer: A guideline. *Fertility & Sterility, 106*(7), 1617–1626.

Predrag, S. (2005). LGBT news and views from around the world. *Lesbian News, 30*(9), 19–21.

Preiss, D., & Shahi, P. (2016, May 31). The dwindling options for surrogacy abroad. *The Atlantic.* Retrieved March 28, 2017, from https://www.theatlantic.com/health/archive/2016/05/dwindling-options-for-surrogacy-abroad/484688/.

Prejean, J., Song, R., Hernandez, A., Ziebell, R., Green, T., Walker, F., Lin, L., An, Q., Mermin, J., Lansky, A., et al. (2011). Estimated HIV incidence in the United States, 2006–2009. *PLOS ONE, 6*(8). Retrieved June 9, 2014, from http://www.plosone.org/article/info%3Adoi%2F10.1371%2Fjournal.pone.0017502.

Preventing Mother-to-Child Transmission of HIV. (2016). HIV Prevention, Department of Health and Human Services. Retrieved April 29, 2017, from https://aidsinfo.nih.gov/understanding-hiv-aids/fact-sheets/20/50/preventing-mother-to-child-transmission-of-hiv.

Previti, D., & Amato, P. (2004). Is infidelity a cause or a consequence of poor marital quality? *Journal of Social and Personal Relationships, 21*(2), 217–230.

Price, J. (2008). Parent-child quality time: Does birth order matter? *Journal of Human Resources, 43*, 240–265.

Price, M., Ades, A., Welton, N., Macleod, J., Turner, K., Simms, I., & Horner, P. (2012). How much tubal factor infertility is caused by chlamydia? Estimates based on serological evidence corrected for sensitivity and specificity. *Sexually Transmitted Diseases, 39*(8), 608–613.

Price, M., Kafka, M., Commons, M., Gutheil, T., & Simpson, W. (2002). Telephone scatologia: Comorbidity with other paraphilias and paraphilia-related disorders. *International Journal of Law & Psychiatry, 25*(1), 37–49.

Priddler, H. (2015). How well are lesbians treated in UK fertility clinics? *Human Fertility, 18*(3), 194–199.

Prinsen, T., & Punyanunt-Carter, N. (2009). The difference in nonverbal behaviors and how it changes in different stages of a relationship. *Texas Speech Communication Journal, 34*(1), 1–7.

Prior, V., & Glaser, D. (2006). *Understanding attachment and attachment disorders: Theory, evidence and practice.* London: Jessica Kingsley.

"Progress in increasing breastfeeding." (2013). Progress in increasing breastfeeding and reducing racial/ethnic differences—United States, 2000–2008 births. *Morbidity and Mortality Weekly Report, 62*(05), 77–80.

"Project Safe Childhood." (2012). Fact Sheet: Project Safe Childhood. U.S. Department of Justice. Retrieved August 27, 2014, from http://www.justice.gov/sites/default/files/psc/docs/psc-fact-sheet_2-21-12_.pdf.

"Protection of Life During Pregnancy Act 2013." (2013). *Irish Statute Book*, Number 35 of 2013. Retrieved August 1, 2014, from http://www.irishstatutebook.ie/pdf/2013/en.act.2013.0035.pdf.

Proto-Campise, L., Belknap, J., & Wooldredge, J. (1998). High school students' adherence to rape myths. *Violence Against Women, 4*, 308–328.

Proulx, N., Caron, S., & Logue, M. (2006). Older women/younger men: A look at the implications of age difference in marriage. *Journal of Couple & Relationship Therapy, 5*(4), 43–64.

Prüss-Ustün, A., Wold, J., Driscoll, T., Degenhardt, L., Neira, M., Calleja, J. (2013). HIV due to female sex work: Regional and global estimates. *PLoS One, 8*(5). Retrieved January 4, 2014, from http://www.plosone.org/article/info%3Adoi%2F10.1371%2Fjournal.pone.0063476.

Pryzgoda, J., & Chrisler, J. C. (2000). Definitions of gender and sex: The subtleties of meaning. *Sex Roles, 43*(7–8), 499–528.

Puckett, J., Ryan, D., Swann, G., Garofalo, R., & Mustanski, B. (2017). Internalized homophobia and perceived stigma: A validation study of stigma measures in a sample of young men who have sex with men. *Sexuality Research & Social Policy: A Journal of the NSRC, 14*(1), 1–16.

Puckett, J., Woodward, E., Mereish, E., & Pantalone, D. (2015). Parental rejection following sexual orientation disclosure: Impact on internalized homophobia, social support, and mental health. *LGBT Health, 2*(3), 265–269.

Puente, S., & Cohen, D. (2003). Jealousy and the meaning (or nonmeaning) of violence. *Personality and Social Psychology Bulletin, 29*(4), 449–460.

Puppo, G., & Puppo, V. (2016). U.S. food and drug administration approval of Addyi (flibanserin) for treatment of hypoactive sexual desire disorder. *European Urology, 69*(2), 379–380.

Puppo, V. (2012). Does the G-spot exist? A review of the current literature. *International Urogynecology Journal, 23*(12), 1665–1669.

Puppo, V., & Puppo, G. (2015). Anatomy of sex: Revision of the new anatomical terms used for the clitoris and the female orgasm by sexologists. *Clinical Anatomy, 28*(3), 293–304.

Putnam, F. (2003). Ten-year research update review: Child sexual abuse. *Journal of the American Academy of Child and Adolescent Psychiatry, 42*(3), 269–278.

Puttabyatappa, M., Cardoso, R., & Padmanabhan, V. (2016). Effect of maternal PCOS and PCOS-like phenotype on the offspring's health. *Molecular and Cellular Endocrinology, 435*, 329–39.

Putterman, A. (2014, July 16). Archies death: Comic book vendors like the take on serious issue. *Hartford Courant.* Retrieved July 16, 2014, from http://articles.courant.com/2014-07-16/news/hc-archie-dies-20140716_1_veronica-lodge-betty-cooper-archie-fans.

Pyne, J., Asch, S., Lincourt, K., Kilbourne, A., Bowman, C., Atkinson, H., & Gifford, A. (2008). Quality indicators for depression care in HIV patients. *AIDS Care, 20*, 1075–1083.

Qin, J., Sheng, X., Wu, D., Gao, S., You, Y., Yang, T., & Wang, H. (2017). Worldwide prevalence of adverse pregnancy outcomes among singleton pregnancies after in vitro fertilization/intracytoplasmic sperm injection: A systematic review and meta-analysis. *Archives of Gynecology and Obstetrics, 295*(2), 285–301.

Quadagno, D., Sly, D. F., & Harrison, D. F. (1998). Ethnic differences in sexual decisions and sexual behavior. *Archives of Sexual Behavior, 27*(1), 57–75.

Quinlan, C., McVeigh, K., Driver, C., Govind, P., & Karpari, A. (2015). Parental age and autism spectrum disorders among New York city children 0–36 months of age. *Maternal and Child Health Journal, 19*(8), 1783–1790.

Quinn, S., & Gedroyc, W. (2015). Thermal ablative treatment of uterine fibroids. *International Journal of Hyperthermia, 31*(3), 272–279.

Rabbee, Z., & Grogan, S. (2016). Young men's understandings of male breast cancer: "Pink ribbons" and "war wounds." *International Journal of Men's Health, 15*(3), 210–217.

Rabin, R. (2016, October 31). "Going flat" after breast cancer. *New York Times.* Retrieved May 22, 2017, from https://www.nytimes .com/2016/11/01/well/live/going-flat-after -breast-cancer.html.

Rabin, R. C. (2010a, October 9). Grown-up, but still irresponsible. *New York Times.* Retrieved October 10, 2010, from http://www.nytimes .com/2010/10/10/weekinreview/10rabin.html.

Rabin, R. C. (2010b, May 10). New spending for a wider range of sex education. *New York Times.* Retrieved January 24, 2011, from http://www.nytimes.com/2010/05/11/health /policy/11land.html.

Rabinovici, J., David, M., Fukunishi, H., Morita, Y., Gostout, B. S., & Stewart, E. A.; MRgFUS Study Group. (2010). Pregnancy outcome after magnetic resonance-guided focused ultrasound surgery (MRgFUS) for conservative treatment of uterine fibroids. *Fertility and Sterility, 93*(1), 199–209.

Rabinowitz Greenberg, S. R., Firestone, P., Bradford, J., & Greenberg, D. M. (2002). Prediction of recidivism in exhibitionists: Psychological, phallometric, and offense factors. *Sexual Abuse: Journal of Research & Treatment, 14*(4), 329–347.

Rabkin, J. (2008). HIV and depression: 2008 review and update. *Current HIV/AIDS Reports, 5,* 163–171.

Radestad, I., Olsson, A., Nissen, E., & Rubertsson, C. (2008). Tears in the vagina, perineum, spincter ani, and rectum and first sexual intercourse after childbirth: A nationwide follow up. *Birth, 35,* 98–106.

Rado, S. (1949, rev. 1955). An adaptational view of sexual behavior. *Psychoanalysis of behavior: Collected papers.* New York: Grune & Stratton.

Radosh, A., & Simkin, L. (2016). Acknowledging sexual bereavement: A path out of disenfranchised grief. *Reproductive Health Matters, 24*(48), 25–33.

Raffaelli, M., & Green, S. (2003). Parent-adolescent communication about sex; retrospective reports by Latino college students. *Journal of Marriage and the Family, 65,* 474–481.

Rahbar, N., Asgharzadeh, N., & Ghorbani, R. (2012). Effect of omega-3 fatty acids on intensity of primary dysmenorrhea. *International Journal of Gynecology and Obstetrics, 117*(1), 45–47.

Rahman, Q. (2005). Fluctuating asymmetry, second to fourth finger length ratios and human sexual orientation. *Psychoneuroendocrinology, 30*(4), 382–391.

Rahman, Q., & Koerting, J. (2008). Sexual orientation-related differences in allocentric spatial memory tasks. *Hippocampus, 18,* 55–63.

Rahman, Q., & Symeonides, D. (2008). Neurodevelopmental correlates of paraphilic sexual interests in men. *Archives of Sexual Behavior, 37,* 166–171.

Rahnama, P., Hidarnia, A., Amin Shokravi, F., Kazemnejad, A., Ghazanfari, Z., & Montazeri, A. (2010). Withdrawal users' experiences of and attitudes to contraceptive methods: A study from Eastern district of Tehran, Iran. *BMC Public Health, 10,* 779.

Rai, D., Lee, B., Dalman, C., Golding, J., Lewis, G., & Magnusson, C. (2013). Parental depression, maternal antidepressant use during pregnancy, and risk of autism spectrum disorders: Population based case control study. *British Medical Journal, 346.* Retrieved May 24, 2014, from http://www .bmj.com/content/346/bmj.f2059.

Raifman, J., Moscoe, E., Austin, B., & McConnell, M. (2017). Difference-in-differences analysis of the association between state same-sex marriage policies and adolescent suicide attempts. *JAMA Pediatrics.* Retrieved March 24, 2017, from https://www .ncbi.nlm.nih.gov/pubmed/28241285.

Rajaraman, P., Simpson, J., Neta, G., Berrington de Gonzalez, A., Ansell, P., Linet, M. S., Ron, E., & Roman, E. (2011). Early life exposure to diagnostic radiation and ultrasound scans and risk of childhood cancer: Case-control study. *British Medical Journal, 342,* d472.

Raley, R., Sweeney, M., & Wondra, D. (2015). The growing racial and ethnic divide in U.S. marriage patterns. *The Future of Children, 25*(2). Retrieved March 7, 2017, from http:// files.eric.ed.gov/fulltext/EJ1079383.pdf.

Ralph, L., Gould, H., Baker, A., & Foster, D. (2014). The role of parents and partners in minors' decisions to have an abortion and anticipated coping after abortion. *Journal of Adolescent Health, 54*(4), 428–434.

Ramikie, T., Nyilas, R., Bluett, R., Gamble-George, J., Hartley, N., Mackie, K., Watanabe, M., Katona, I., & Patel, S. (2014). Multiple mechanistically distinct modes of endocannabinoid mobilization at central amygdala glutamatergic synapses. Neuron. Retrieved April 16, 2017, from http://www .cell.com/neuron/abstract/S0896 -6273(14)00017-8.

Ramirez, E. (2016, November 17). The crazy reason nearly every phone in Japan is waterproof. *Mashable.* Retrieved January 11, 2017, from http://mashable.com/2016/11/17 /waterproof-phones-japan/#Ihu9twXA_OqV.

Rammouz, I., Tahiri, D., Aalouane, R., Kjiri, S., Belhous, A., Ktiouet, J., & Sekkat, F. (2008). Infanticide in the postpartum period: About a clinical case. *Encephale, 34,* 284–288.

Ramsey, F., Hill, M., & Kellam, C. (2010). Black lesbians matter: An examination of the unique experiences, perspectives, and priorities of the Black lesbian community. Retrieved February 20, 2011, from http:// zunainstitute.org/2010/research/blm /blacklesbiansmatter.pdf.

Rancour-Laferriere, D. (1985). *Signs of the flesh.* New York: Mouton de Gruyter.

Rand, M. R. (2009). Criminal victimization, 2008. National Crime Victimization Survey, Bureau of Justice Statistics. *Bureau of Justice Statistics Bulletin.* Retrieved April 13, 2011, from http://bjs.ojp.usdoj.gov/content/pub /pdf/cv08.pdf.

Randall, H., & Byers, E. (2003). What is sex? Students' definitions of having sex, sexual partner, and unfaithful sexual behavior. *Canadian Journal of Human Sexuality, 12*(2), 87–96.

Rankin, P. T. (1952). The measurement of the ability to understand spoken language. *Dissertation Abstracts.* University of Michigan, 1953–06117–001.

Rapkin, A., & Mikacich, J. (2013). Premenstrual dysphoric disorder and severe premenstrual syndrome in adolescents. *Pediatric Drugs, 15,* 191–202.

Rapkin, A., Berman, S., & London, E. (2014). The cerebellum and premenstrual dysphoric disorder. *AIMS Neuroscience, 1*(2), 120–141.

Rapkin, A., Berman, S., Mandelkern, M., Silverman, D., Morgan, M., & London, E. (2011). Neuroimaging evidence of cerebellar involvement in premenstrual dysphoric disorder. *Biological Psychiatry, 69*(4), 374–380.

Rapkin, A. J., & Winer, S. A. (2008). The pharmacologic management of premenstrual dysphoric disorder. *Expert Opinions in Pharmacotherapy, 9,* 429–445.

Rapkin, M. (2013, May 16). The gay retiree utopia. *Bloomberg Businessweek.* Retrieved May 19, 2014, from http://www.businessweek .com/articles/2013-05-16/the-gay-retiree -utopia.

Raskin, N. J., & Rogers, C. R. (1989). Person-centered therapy. In R. J. Corsini & D. Wedding (Eds.), *Current psychotherapies* (4th ed., pp. 155–196), Pacific Grove, CA: F. E. Peacock.

Rasmussen, P. R. (2005). The sadistic and masochistic prototypes. In P. R. Rasmussen (Ed.), *Personality-guided cognitive-behavioral therapy* (pp. 291–310). Washington, DC: American Psychological Association.

Rauer, A. J., & Volling, B. L. (2007). Differential parenting and sibling jealousy: Developmental correlates of young adults' romantic relationships. *Personal Relationships, 14,* 495–511.

Raval, A. P., Hirsch, N., Dave, K. R., Yavagal, D. R., Bramlett, H., & Saul, I. (2011). Nicotine and estrogen synergistically exacerbate cerebral ischemic injury. *Neuroscience*, *181*, 216–225.

Ravert, A. A., & Martin, J. (1997). Family stress, perception of pregnancy, and age of first menarche among pregnant adolescents. *Adolescence*, *32*(126), 261–269.

Ravn, P., Haugen, A., & Glintborg, D. (2013). Overweight in polycystic ovary syndrome. An update on evidence based advice on diet, exercise and metformin use for weight loss. *Minerva Endocrinologica*, *38*(1), 59–76.

Ray, N. (2006). Lesbian, gay, bisexual and transgendered youth: An epidemic of homelessness. National Gay and Lesbian Task Force Policy Institute. Retrieved February 17, 2011, from http://www.thetaskforce.org/downloads/reports/reports/HomelessYouth.pdf.

Raya, B., Bamberger, E., Kerem, N., Kessel, A., & Srugo, I. (2012). Beyond "safe sex"—can we fight adolescent pelvic inflammatory disease? *European Journal of Pediatrics*, *172*(5), 581–590.

Rayala, B., & Viera, A. (2013). Common questions about vasectomy. *American Family Physician*, *88*(11), 757–761.

Raymond, J. G., & Hughes, D. M. (2001). Sex trafficking of women in the United States. Retrieved November 16, 2008, from http://www.uri.edu/artsci/wms/hughes/sex_traff_us.pdf.

Read, C. M. (2010). New regimens with combined oral contraceptive pills—moving away from traditional 21/7 cycles. *European Journal of Contraceptive and Reproductive Health Care*, *15*(Suppl. 2), S32–S41.

Redden, M. (2016, July 21). Roger Ailes accused of harassment by at least 20 women, attorneys say. *The Guardian*. Retrieved from https://www.theguardian.com/media/2016/jul/21/roger-ailes-sexual-harassment-accusations-fox-news.

Redlick, M. (2016). The green-eyed monster: Mate value, relational uncertainty, and jealousy in romantic relationships. *Personal Relationships*, *23*(3), 505–516.

Redway, J., & Miville, M. (2013). Gender roles among African American women. In M. Miville (Ed.), *Multicultural gender roles: Applications for mental health and education* (pp. 65–95). Hoboken, NJ: John Wiley & Sons.

Reece, M., Herbenick, D., Sanders, S., Dodge, B., Ghassemi, A., & Fortenberry, J. (2009). Prevalence and characteristics of vibrator use by men in the US.: Results from a nationally representative study. *Journal of Sexual Medicine*, *6*, 1867–1874.

Reece, M., Herbenick, D., Sanders, S., Dodge, B., Ghassemi, A., & Fortenberry, J. (2010a). Prevalence and predictors of testicular self-exam among a nationally representative sample of men in the U.S. *International Journal of Sexual Health*, *22*(1), 1–4.

Reece, M., Herbenick, D., Schick, V., Sanders, S. A., Dodge, B., & Fortenberry, J. D. (2010b). Background and considerations on the National Survey of Sexual Health and Behavior (NSSHB). *Journal of Sexual Medicine*, *7*(Suppl. 5), 243–245.

Reece, M., Herbenick, D., Schick, V., Sanders, S., Dodge, B., & Fortenberry, D. (2010c). Condom use rates in a national probability sample of males and females ages 14–94 in the United States. *Journal of Sexual Medicine*, *7*(Suppl. 5), 266–276.

Reece, M., Herbenick, D., Schick, V., Sanders, S., Dodge, B., & Fortenberry, J. (2010d). Sexual behaviors, relationships, and perceived health among adult men in the United States: Results from a national probability sample. *Journal of Sexual Medicine*, *7*(Suppl. 5), 291–304.

Reese, J. B. (2011). Coping with sexual concerns after cancer. *Current Opinions in Oncology*, *23*(4), 313–321.

Reese, J. B., Keefe, F. J., Somers, T. J., & Abernethy, A. P. (2010e). Coping with sexual concerns after cancer: The use of flexible coping. *Support Care Cancer*, *18*(7), 785–800.

Regan, P. C. (2006). Love. In R. D. McAnulty & M. M. Burnette (Eds.), *Sex and sexuality: Sexual functions and dysfunctions* (pp. 87–113). Westport, CT: Praeger.

Regnerus, M. D., & Luchies, L. B. (2006). The parent-child relationship and opportunities for adolescents' first sex. *Journal of Family Issues*, *27*, 159–183.

Rehman, U., & Holtzworth-Munroe, A. (2007). A cross cultural examination of the relation of marital communication behavior and marital satisfaction. *Journal of Family Psychology*, *21*(4), 795–763.

Rehman, U., Janssen, E., Newhouse, S., Heiman, J., Holtzworth-Munroe, A., Fallis, E., & Rafaeli, E. (2011). Marital satisfaction and communication behaviors during sexual and nonsexual conflict discussions in newlywed couples. *Journal of Sex and Marital Therapy*, *37*(2), 94–103.

Reiber, C., & Garcia, J. (2010). Hooking up: Gender differences, evolution, and pluralistic ignorance. *Evolutionary Psychology*, *8*(3), 390–404.

Reid, J., Elliot, S., & Webber, G. (2011). Casual hookups to formal dates: Refining the boundaries of the sexual double standard. *Gender & Society*, *25*(5), 545–568.

Reid, R., Bonomi, A., Rivara, F., Anderson, M., Fishman, P., Carrell, D., & Thompson, R. (2008). Intimate partner violence among men: Prevalence, chronicity, and health effects. *American Journal of Preventive Medicine*, *34*, 478–485.

Reid, R. C. (2015). How should severity be determined for the *DSM-5* proposed classification of hypersexual disorder? *Journal of Behavioral Addictions*, *4*(4), 221–225.

Reig, A., Siles, G., & Solano, R. (2014). Attitudes towards female genital mutilation: An integrative review. *International Nursing Review*, *61*(1), 25–34.

Reilly, D. R., Delva, N. J., & Hudson, R. W. (2000). Protocols for the use of cyproterone, medroxyprogesterone, & leuprolide in the treatment of paraphilia. *Canadian Journal of Psychiatry*, *45*(6), 559–564.

Reilly, M. (2016, March 31). Same-sex couples can now adopt children in all 50 states. *Huffington Post*. Retrieved March 19, 2017, from http://www.huffingtonpost.com/entry/mississippi-same-sex-adoption_us_56fdb1a3e4b083f5c607567f.

Reips, U. D., & Bachtiger, M. T. (2000). Are all flies drosophilae? Participant selection bias in psychological research. Unpublished manuscript.

Reis, E. (2013). Intersex surgeries, circumcision, and the making of "normal." In G. C. Denniston, F. Hodges, & M. Fayre Milos (Eds.), *Genital cutting: Protecting children from medical, cultural, and religious infringements* (pp. 137–147). New York, NY: Springer Science & Business Media.

Reis, S., & Abdo, C. (2014). Benefits and risks of testosterone treatment for hypoactive sexual desire disorder in women. *Clinics*, *69*(4), 294–303.

Reisner, S., Perkovich, B., & Mimiaga, M. (2010). A mixed methods study of the sexual health needs of New England transmen who have sex with nontransgender men. *AIDS Patient Care STDS*, *24*(8), 501–513.

Reisner, S., Vetters, R., Leclerc, M., Zaslow, S., Wolfrum, S., Shumer, D., & Mimiaga, M. (2015). Mental heal of transgender youth in care at an adolescent urban community health center: A matched retrospective cohort study. *The Journal of Adolescent Health*, *56*, 274–279.

Reiss, I. L. (1982). Trouble in paradise: The current status of sexual science. *Journal of Sex Research*, *18*, 97–113.

Reiss, I. L. (1986). *Journey into sexuality: An exploratory voyage.* Englewood Cliffs, NJ: Prentice Hall.

Reiter, P., & McRee, A. (2014). Cervical cancer screening behaviors and acceptability of human papillomavirus self-testing among lesbian and bisexual women aged 21–26 years in the U.S.A. *Journal of Family Planning and Reproductive Health Care*, *41*(4), 259–264.

"Religion in Latin America." (2014). Pew Research Center. Retrieved April 12, 2017, from http://www.pewforum.org/2014/11/13/chapter-5-social-attitudes/#views-on-abortion.

Rellini, A. H., & Meston, C. M. (2011). Sexual self-schemas, sexual dysfunction, and the sexual responses of women with a history of childhood sexual abuse. *Archives of Sexual Behavior, 40*(2), 351–362.

Remez, L. (2000, November/December). Oral sex among adolescents: Is it sex or is it abstinence? *Family Planning Perspectives, 32*(6), 298–304.

Rempel, J. K., & Baumgartner, B. (2003). The relationship between attitudes towards menstruation and sexual attitudes, desires, and behavior in women. *Archives of Sexual Behavior, 32*(2), 155–163.

Remsberg, K. E., Demerath, E. W., Schubert, C. M., Chumlea, C., Sun, S. S., & Siervogel, R. M. (2005). Early menarche and the development of cardiovascular disease risk factors in adolescent girls: The Fels Longitudinal Study. *Journal of Clinical Endocrinology & Metabolism*, published online ahead of print. Retrieved March 22, 2005, from http://jcem.endojournals.org/cgi/content/abstract/jc.2004-1991v1.

Renaud, C. A., & Byers, E. S. (1999). Exploring the frequency, diversity, and content of university students' positive and negative sexual cognitions. *Canadian Journal of Human Sexuality, 8*(1), 17–30.

Rendas-Baum, R., Yang, M., Gricar, J., & Wallenstein, G. (2010). Cost-effectiveness analysis of treatments for premenstrual dysphoric disorder. *Applied Health Economics and Health Policy, 8*(2), 129–140.

Rensberger, B. (1994, July 25). Contraception the natural way: Herbs have played a role from ancient Greece to modern-day Appalachie. *Washington Post*, p. A3.

"Reporting Rape in 2013." (2014). Criminal Justice Information Services (CJIS) Division Uniform Crime Reporting (UCR) Program. Retrieved May 9, 2017, from https://ucr.fbi.gov/recent-program-updates/reporting-rape-in-2013-revised.

Resnick, H., Acierno, R., Kilpatrick, D. G., & Holmes, M. (2005). Description of an early intervention to prevent substance abuse and psychopathology in recent rape victims. *Behavior Modification, 29*(1), 156–188.

Resnick, M. D., Bearman, P. S., Blum, R. W., Bauman, K. E., Harris, K. M., Jones, J., et al. (1997). Protecting adolescents from harm: Findings from the National Longitudinal Study on Adolescent Health. *Journal of the American Medical Association, 278*(10), 823–832.

Rettenmaier, N., Rettenmaier, C., Wojciechowski, T., Abaid, L., Brown, J., Micha, J., & Goldstein, B. (2010). The utility and cost of routine follow-up procedures in the surveillance of ovarian and primary peritoneal carcinoma: A 16-year institutional review. *British Journal of Cancer, 103*(11), 1657–1662.

Revicki, D., Howard, K., Hanlon, J., Mannix, S., Greene, A., & Rothman, M. (2008). Characterizing the burden of premature ejaculation from a patient and partner perspective: A multicountry qualitative analysis. *Health and Quality of Life Outcomes, 6*, 33. Retrieved May 31, 2014, from http://www.ncbi.nlm.nih.gov/pmc/articles/PMC2390524.

Reynolds, G. (2013, November 20). Mother's exercise may boost baby's brain. *New York Times*. Retrieved May 24, 2014, from http://well.blogs.nytimes.com/2013/11/20/mothers-exercise-may-boost-babys-brain.

Reynolds, H. (1986). *The economics of prostitution*. Springfield, IL: Charles C. Thomas.

Reynolds, T., Vranken, G., Nueten, J. V., & Aldis, J. (2008). Down's syndrome screening: Population statistic dependency of screening performance. *Clinical Chemistry and Laboratory Medicine, 46*(5), 639–647.

Rhew, I., Stappenbeck, C., Bedard-Gilligan, M., Hughes, T., & Kaysen, D. (2017). Effects of sexual assault on alcohol use and consequences among young adult sexual minority women. *Journal of Consulting and Clinical Psychology, 85*(5), 424–433.

Rhoades, G., Stanley, S., Markman, H. (2009). Couples' reasons for cohabitation: Associations with individual well-being and relationship quality. *Journal of Family Issues, 30*(2), 233–258.

Rhoades, G. K., Stanley, S. M., & Markman, H. J. (2009). The pre-engagement cohabitation effect: A replication and extension of previous findings. *Journal of Family Psychology, 23*(1), 107–111.

Rhoads, J. M., & Boekelheide, P. D. (1985). Female genital exhibitionism. The Psychiatric Forum, Winter, 1–6.

Ricciardelli, R., Grills, S., & Craig, A. (2016). Constructions and negotiations of sexuality in Canadian federal men's prisons. *Journal of Homosexuality, 63*(12), 1660–1684.

Riccio, R. (1992). Street crime strategies: The changing schemata of streetwalkers. *Environment and Behavior, 24*, 555–570.

Rice, E., Barman-Adhikari, A., Rhoades, H., Winetrobe, H., Fulginti, A., Astor, R., Montoya, J., Plant, A., & Kordic, T. (2013). Homelessness experiences, sexual orientation, and sexual risk taking among high school students in Los Angeles. *Journal of Adolescent Health, 52*(6), 773–778.

Rice, M., Murphy, M., & Tworoger, S. (2012). Tubal libation, hysterectomy and ovarian cancer: A meta-analysis. *Journal of Ovarian Research, 5*(1), 13.

Rice, M., Murphy, M., Vitonis, A., Cramer, D., Titus, L., Twogoger, S., & Terry, K. (2013). Tubal ligation, hysterectomy and epithelial ovarian cancer in the New England Case-Control Study. *International Journal of Cancer, 133*(10), 2415–2421.

Rich, A. (1983). Compulsory heterosexuality and lesbian existence. In A. Snitow, C. Stinsell, & S. Thompson (Eds.), *Powers of desire: The politics of sexuality* (pp. 177–205). New York: Monthly Review Press.

Richards, M., Flanagan, M., Littman, A., Burke, A., & Callegari, L. (2016). Primary cesarean section and adverse delivery outcomes among women of very advanced maternal age. *Journal of Perinatology: Official Journal of the California Perinatal Association, 36*(4), 272–277.

Richardson, B. A. (2002). Nonoxynol-9 as a vaginal microbicide for prevention of sexually transmitted infections. *Journal of American Medication Association, 287*, 1171–1172.

Richardson, D., & Campbell, J. L. (1982). The effect of alcohol on attributions of blame for rape. *Personality and Social Psychology Bulletin, 8*, 468–476.

Richardson, D., Nalabanda, A., & Goldmeier, D. (2006). Retarded ejaculation: A review. *International Journal of STDs and AIDS, 17*, 143–150.

Richter, B., Lindahl, K., & Malik, N. (2017). Examining ethnic differences in parental rejection of LGB youth sexual identity. *Journal of Family Psychology, 31*(2), 244–249.

Richters, J., Hendry, O., & Kippax, S. (2003). When safe sex isn't safe. *Culture, Health & Sexuality, 5*(1), 37–52.

Rideout, V. J., Foehr, U. G., & Roberts, D. F. (2010). *Generation M2: Media in the lives of 8- to 18-year-olds*. Menlo Park, CA: Kaiser Family Foundation.

Rideout, V., Roberts, D. F., & Foehr, U. G. (2005). Generation M: Media in the lives of 8–18-year-olds. Retrieved November 7, 2005, from http://www.kff.org/entmedia/upload/Executive-Summary-Generation-M-Media-in-the-Lives-of-8-18-Year-olds.pdf.

Ridge, R. D., & Reber, J. S. (2002). "I think she's attracted to me": The effect of men's beliefs on women's behavior in a job interview scenario. *Basic and Applied Social Psychology, 24*(1), 1–14.

Rieger, G., Chivers, M. L., & Bailey, J. M. (2005). Sexual arousal patterns of gay men. *Psychological Science, 16*(8), 579–584.

Rieger, G., Savin-Williams, R., Chivers, M., & Bailey, J. (2016). Sexual arousal and masculinity-femininity of women. *Journal of Personality and Social Psychology, 111*(2), 265–283.

Riggle, E., Rostosky, S., & Horne, S. (2010). Psychological distress, well-being, and legal recognition in same-sex couple relationships. *Journal of Family Psychology, 24*(1), 82–86.

Riggs, J. M. (2005). Impressions of mothers and fathers on the periphery of child care. *Psychology of Women Quarterly*, *29*(1), 58.

Ringdahl, E., & Teague, L. (2006). Testicular torsion. *American Family Physician*, *74*(10), 1739–1743.

Rinker, D. (2016). Eat, drink, workout, and be merry: Emerging research on the association between alcohol use, eating, and physical activity. The 39th Annual Research Society on Alcoholism Meeting, New Orleans, Louisiana. June 25–29, 2016. Retrieved August 23, 2017, from http://www.rsoa.org/2016meet-1-RSA-PROGRAM-OUTLINE.pdf.

Rio, L. M. (1991). Psychological and sociological research and the decriminalization or legalization of prostitution. *Archives of Sexual Behavior*, *20*, 205–218.

Riordan, M., & Kreuz, R. (2010). Cues in computer-mediated communication: A corpus analysis. *Computers in Human Behavior*, *26*(6), 1806–1817.

Rischer, C. E., & Easton, T. (1992). *Focus on Human Biology*. New York: HarperCollins.

Riskind, R., & Patterson, C. (2010). Parenting intentions and desires among childless lesbian, gay, and heterosexual individuals. *Journal of Family Psychology*, *24*(1), 78–81.

Riskind, R., Patterson, C., & Nosek, B. (2013). Childless lesbian and gay adults' self-efficacy about achieving parenthood. *Couple and Family Psychology: Research and Practice*, *2*(3), 222–235.

Risman, B., & Schwartz, P. (1988). Sociological research on male and female homosexuality. *Annual Review of Sociology*, *14*, 125–147.

Rittenhouse, C. A. (1991). The emergence of premenstrual syndrome as a social problem. *Social Problems*, *38*(3), 412–425.

Rivers, J., Mason, J., Silvestre, E., Gillespie, S., Mahy, M., & Monasch, R. (2008). Impact of orphanhood on underweight prevalence in sub-Saharan Africa. *Food and Nutrition Bulletin*, *29*(1), 32–42.

Rizwan, S., Manning, J., & Brabin, B. J. (2007). Maternal smoking during pregnancy and possible effects of in utero testosterone: Evidence from the 2D:4D finger length ratio. *Early Human Development*, *83*, 87–90.

Rizzuto, I., Behrens, R., & Smith, L. (2013). Risk of ovarian cancer in women treated with ovarian stimulating drugs for infertility. *Cochrane Database of Systematic Reviews*, *138*. Retrieved May 21, 2014, from http://www.ncbi.nlm.nih.gov/pubmed/23943232.

Roan, S. (2010, August 15). Medical treatment carries possible side effect of limiting homosexuality. *Los Angeles Times*. Retrieved October 15, 2010, from http://articles.latimes.com/2010/aug/15/science/la-sci-adrenal-20100815.

Robb, A. (2014, July 7). How using emoji makes us less emotional. *New Republic*. Retrieved January 11, 2017, from https://newrepublic.com/article/118562/emoticons-effect-way-we-communicate-linguists-study-effects.

Roberts, A., Austin, S., Corliss, H., Vandermorris, A., & Koenen, K. (2010). Pervasive trauma exposure among US sexual orientation minority adults and risk of posttraumatic stress disorder. *American Journal of Public Health*, *100*(12), 2433–2441.

Roberts, B., & Reddy, V. (2008). Pride and prejudice: Public attitudes towards homosexuality. *HSRC Review*, *6*(4), 9–11.

Roberts, S. (2010, September 15). Study finds wider view of family. *New York Times*. Retrieved September 15, 2010, from http://query.nytimes.com/gst/fullpage.html?res5 9504E7DE163AF936A2575AC0A9669D8B63.

Roberts, S., & Roiser, J. P. (2010). In the nose of the beholder: Are olfactory influences on human mate choice driven by variation in immune system genes or sex hormone levels? *Experimental Biology and Medicine*, *235*(11), 1277–1281.

Roberts, S., Cobey, K., Klapilová, K., & Havlicek, J. (2013). An evolutionary approach offers a fresh perspective on the relationship between oral contraception and sexual desire. *Archives of Sexual Behavior*, *42*(8), 1369–1375.

Roberts, S., Gosling, L., Carter, V., & Petrie, M. (2008). MHC-correlated odour preferences in humans and the use of oral contraceptives. *Proceedings of the Royal Society B*, *275*(1652), 2715–2722.

Robin, G., Boitrelle, F., Marcelli, F., Colin, P., Leroy-Martin, B., Mitchell, V., Dewailly, D., & Rigot, J. M. (2010). Cryptorchidism: From physiopathology to infertility. *Gynecological Obstetrics and Fertility*, *38*(10), 588–599.

Robinson, P. (1993). *Freud and his critics*. Berkeley, CA: University of California Press.

Roby, J. L., & Shaw, S. A. (2006). The African orphan crisis and international adoption. *Social Work*, *51*(3), 199–210.

Rodriguez, I. (2004). Pheromone receptors in mammals. *Hormones & Behavior*, *46*(3), 219–230.

Rogers, P., D'Hooghe, T., Fazleabas, A., Giudice, L., Montgomery, G., Petraglia, F., & Taylore, R. (2013). Defining future directions for endometriosis research. *Reproductive Sciences*, *20*(5), 483–499.

Rogers, S. C. (1978). Woman's place: A critical review of anthropological theory. *Comparative Studies in Society and History*, *20*, 123–162.

Rogow, D., & Horowitz, S. (1995). Withdrawal: A review of the literature and an agenda for research. *Studies in Family Planning*, *26*(3), 140–153.

Rohde, P., Stice, E., & Marti, C. (2016). Development and predicative effects of eating disorder risk factors during adolescence: Implications for prevention efforts. *International Journal of Eating Disorders*, *48*(2), 187–198.

Rohmann, E., Führer, A., & Bierhoff, H. (2016). Relationship satisfaction across European cultures: The role of love styles. *Journal of Comparative Social Science*, *50*(2), 178–211.

Roisman, G., Clausell, Holland, A., Fortuna, K., & Elieff, C. (2008). Adult romantic relationships as contexts of human development: A multimethod comparison of same-sex couples with opposite-sex dating, engaged, and married dyads. *Developmental Psychology*, *44*(1), 91–101.

Romanowski, B. (2011). Long term protection against cervical infection with the human papillomavirus: Review of currently available vaccines. *Human Vaccines*, *7*(2), 161–169.

Rome, E. (1998). Anatomy and physiology of sexuality and reproduction. In The Boston Women's Health Collective (Eds.), *The new our bodies, ourselves* (pp. 241–258). Carmichael, CA: Touchstone Books.

Romenesko, K., & Miller, E. M. (1989). The second step in double jeopardy: Appropriating the labor of female street hustlers. (Special issue: Women and crime.) *Crime and Delinquency*, *35*, 109–135.

Romero-Daza, N., Weeks, M., & Singer, M. (2003). "Nobody gives a damn if I live or die": Violence, drugs, and street-level prostitution in inner-city Hartford, Connecticut. *Medical Anthropology*, *22*(3), 233–259.

Ronis, S., & O'Sullivan, L. (2011). A longitudinal analysis of predictions of male and female adolescents' transitions to intimate sexual behavior. *Journal of Adolescent Health*, *49*(3), 321–232.

Ropelato, J. (2008). Internet pornography statistics. *Top Ten Reviews*. Retrieved October 7, 2008, from http://internet-filter-review.toptenreviews.com/internet-pornography-statistics.html.

Rosario, M. (2015). Implications of childhood experiences for the health and adaptation of lesbian, gay, and bisexual individuals: Sensitivity to developmental process in future research. *Psychology of Sexual Orientation and Gender Diversity*, *2*(3), 214–224.

Rosario, M., Schrimshaw, E., & Hunter, J. (2004). Predictors of substance use over time among gay, lesbian, and bisexual youths. An examination of three hypotheses. *Addictive Behaviors*, *29*(8), 1623–1631.

Rosario, M., Schrimshaw, E., & Hunter, J. (2012). Risk factors for homelessness among lesbian, gay, and bisexual youths: A developmental milestone approach. *Children and Youth Services Review*, *34*(1), 186–193.

Rose, A., Smith, R., Glick, G., & Schwartz-Mette, R. (2016). Girls' and boys' problem talk: Implications for emotional closeness in friendships. *Developmental Psychology, 52*(4), 629–639.

Rose, D., Ussher, J., & Perz, J. (2017). Let's talk about gay sex: Gay and bisexual men's sexual communication with healthcare professionals after prostate cancer. *European Journal of Cancer Care, 26*(1). Retrieved April 15, 2017, from https://www.ncbi.nlm.nih.gov/labs /articles/26918877/.

Rose, J., Mackey-Kallis, S., Shyles, L., Barry, K., Biagini, D., Hart, C., & Jack, L. (2012). Face it: The impact of gender on social media images. *Communication Quarterly, 60*(5), 588–607.

Rosen, N., Sadikaj, G., Delisle, I., Bergeron, S., Glowacka, M., & Baxter, M. (2013). Impact of male partner responses on sexual function in women with vulvodynia and their partners. *Health Psychology*. Retrieved February 21, 2014, from http://www.ncbi.nlm.nih.gov /pubmed/24245835.

Rosen, R., Connor, M., Miyasato, G., Link, C., Shifren, J., Fisher, W., Derogatis, L., & Schobelock, M. (2012). Sexual desire problems in women seeking healthcare: A novel study design for ascertaining prevalence of hypoactive sexual desire disorder in clinic-based samples of U.S. women. *Journal of Women's Health, 21*(5), 505–515.

Rosen, R. C., & Leiblum, S. R. (1987). Current approaches to the evaluation of sexual desire disorders. *Journal of Sex Research, 23*, 141–162.

Rosenbaum, D. E. (2005, October 30). Commissions are fine, but rarely what changes the light bulb. Retrieved November 6, 2005, from http://www.nytimes.com/2005/10/30 /weekinreview/30rosenbaum.html?fta=y.

Rosenbaum, T. (2011). Addressing anxiety in vivo in physiotherapy treatment of women with severe vaginismus: A clinical approach. *Journal of Sex and Marital Therapy, 37*(2), 89–93.

Rosenblum, E. (2014, April 17). Later, baby: Will freezing your eggs free your career? *Bloomberg Businessweek*. Retrieved May 24, 2014, from http://www.businessweek.com /articles/2014-04-17/new-egg-freezing -technology-eases-womens-career-family -angst.

Rosenthal, R., & Rosnow, R. L. (1975). *The volunteer subject*. New York: Wiley.

Rosmalen-Noojjens, K., Vergeer, C., & Lagro-Janssen, A. (2008). Bed death and other lesbian sexual problems unraveled: A qualitative study of the sexual health of lesbian women involved in a relationship. *Women & Health, 48*(3), 339–362.

Rosman, J. P., & Resnick, P. J. (1989). Sexual attraction to corpses: A psychiatric review of necrophilia. *Bulletin of the American Academy of Psychiatry and the Law, 17*, 153–163.

Ross, C. A. (2009). Psychodynamics of eating disorder behavior in sexual abuse survivors. *American Journal of Psychotherapy, 63*(3), 211–227.

Ross, J., Tartaglia, N., Merry, D., Dalva, M., & Zinn, A. (2015). Behavioral phenotypes in males with XYY and possible role of increased NLFH4Y expression in autism features. *Genes, Brain, and Behavior, 14*(2), 137–144.

Ross, L. E. (2005). Perinatal mental health in lesbian mothers: A review of potential risk and protective factors. *Women Health, 41*(3), 113–128.

Ross, L. E., Steele, L., & Epstein, R. (2006a). Lesbian and bisexual women's recommendations for improving the provision of assisted reproductive technology services. *Fertility and Sterility, 86*, 735–738.

Ross, L. E., Steele, L. S., & Epstein, R. (2006b). Service use and gaps in services for lesbian and bisexual women during donor insemination, pregnancy, and the postpartum period. *Journal of Obstetrics and Gynecology Canada, 28*, 505–511.

Ross, L., Dobinson, C., & Eady, A. (2010). Perceived determinants of mental health for bisexual people: A qualitative examination. *American Journal of Public Health, 100*(3), 496–502.

Ross, L., O'Gorman, L., MacLeod, M., Bauer, G., MacKay, J., & Robinson, M. (2016). Bisexuality, poverty and mental health: A mixed methods analysis. *Social Science & Medicine, 156*, 64–72.

Ross, L. E., Steele, L., Goldfinger, C., & Strike, C. (2007). Perinatal depressive symptomatology among lesbian and bisexual women. *Archives of Women's Mental Health, 10*, 1434–1816.

Rossato M., Pagano C., & Vettor R. (2008). The cannabinoid system and male reproductive functions. *Journal of Neuroendocrinology, 20*(Suppl. 1), 90–93.

Rosser, B. R. (1999). Homophobia: Description, development and dynamic of gay bashing. *Journal of Sex Research, 36*(2), 211.

Rossi, A. S. (1978). The biosocial side of parenthood. *Human Nature, 1*, 72–79.

Rossi, N. E. (2010). "Coming out" stories of gay and lesbian young adults. *Journal of Homosexuality, 57*(9), 1174–1191.

Rossi, W. A. (1993). *The sex life of the foot and shoe*. Melbourne, FL: Krieger.

Rossier, C., Senderowicz, L., & Soura, A. (2014). Do natural methods count? Underreporting of natural contraception in urban Burkina Faso. *Studies in Family Planning, 45*(1), 171–182.

Roth, C., Satran, L., & Smith, S. (2015). Marijuana use in pregnancy. *Nursing for Women's Health, 19*(5), 431–437.

Rothblum, E., Balsam, K., & Solomon, S. (2008). Comparison of same-sex couples who were married in Massachusetts, had domestic partnerships in California, or had civil unions in Vermont. *Journal of Family Issues, 29*(1), 48–78.

Rothgerber, H., & Wolsiefer, K. (2014). A naturalistic study of stereotype threat in young female chess players. *Group Processes & Intergroup Relations, 17*(1), 79–90.

Rothman, S. M. (1978). *Woman's proper place*. New York: Basic Books.

Rottmann, N., Gilsa-Hansen, D., DePont, C., Hagedoorn, M., Frisch, M., Nicolaisen, A., Kroman, N., Flyer, H., & Johansen, C. (2017). Satisfaction with sex life in sexually active heterosexual couples deling with breast cancer: A nationwide longitudinal study. *Acta Oncologica, 56*(2), 212–219.

Roughgarden, J. (2004). A review of evolution, gender, and rape. *Ethology, 110*(1), 76.

Roumen, F., & Mishell, D. (2012). The contraceptive vaginal ring, NuvaRing, a decade after its introduction. *European Journal of Contraception & Reproductive Health Care, 17*(6), 415–427.

Rousseau, B. (2017, February 18). In Bali, babies are believed too holy to touch the earth. *New York Times*. Retrieved April 3, 2017, from https://www.nytimes.com/2017/02/18 /world/asia/bali-indonesia-babies -nyambutin.html?_r=0.

Rovner, J. (2013, November 26). Emergency contraceptive pill might be ineffective for obese. *NPR*. Retrieved May 26, 2014, from http://www.npr.org/blogs/health/2013/11/26 /247226093/emergency-contraceptive-pill -might-be-ineffective-for-obese.

Rowan, T., Gaither, T., Awad, M., Osterberg, E., Shindel, A., & Breyer, B. (2016). Pubic hair grooming prevalence and motivation among women in the U.S. *JAMA Dermatology, 152*(1), 1106–1113.

Rowland, D., McMahon, C. G., Abdo, C., Chen, J., Jannini, E., Waldinger, M. D., & Ahn, T. Y. (2010). Disorders of orgasm and ejaculation in men. *Journal of Sexual Medicine, 7*(4 Pt 2), 1668–1686.

Rowlands, S., Sujan, M. A., & Cooke, M. (2010). A risk management approach to the design of contraceptive implants. *Journal of Family Planning and Reproductive Health Care, 36*(4), 191–195.

Ruan, F., & Lau, M. P. (2004). China. In R. T. Francoeur & R. J. Noonan (Eds.), *The Continuum International encyclopedia of sexuality* (pp. 182–209). New York/London: Continuum International.

Ruan, F. F., & Tsai, Y. M. (1988). Male homosexuality in contemporary mainland China. *Archives of Sexual Behavior, 17*, 189–199.

Ruan, X., & Mueck, A. (2015). Oral contraception for women of middle age. *Maturitas, 82*(3), 266–270.

Rubin, L. (1990). *Erotic wars*. New York: Farrar, Straus, & Giroux.

Rubin, Z. (1970). Measurement of romantic love. *Journal of Personality & Social Psychology*, 16(2), 265–273.

Rubin, Z. (1973). *Liking and loving: An invitation to social psychology*. Oxford, England: Holt, Rinehart & Winston.

Rubio-Aurioles, E., & Bivalacqua, T. (2013). Standard operational procedures for low sexual desire in men. *Journal of Sexual Medicine*, 10(1), 94–107.

Ruble, D., & Brooks-Gunn, J. (1982). The experience of menarche. *Child Development*, 53(6), 1557–1566.

Rudd, J. M., & Herzberger, S. D. (1999). Brother-sister incest, father-daughter incest: A comparison of characteristics and consequences. *Child Abuse and Neglect*, 23(9), 915–928.

Rudolph, K., Caldwell, M. & Conley, C. (2005). Need for approval and children's well-being. *Child Development*, 76(2), 309–323.

Rudy, K. (2000). Queer theory and feminism. *Women's Studies*, 29(2), 195–217.

Rue, V. M., Coleman, P. K., Rue, J. J., & Reardon, D. C. (2004). Induced abortion and traumatic stress: A preliminary comparison of American and Russian women. *Medical Science Monitor*, 10(10), SR5–SR16.

Ruffman, T., Halberstadt, J., & Murray, J. (2009). Recognition of facial, auditory, and bodily emotions in older adults. *Journals of Gerontology*, 64B(6), 696.

Ruggles, S. (2009). Reconsidering the northwest European family system: Living arrangements of the aged in comparative historical perspective. *Population and Development Review*, 35(2), 249–273.

Rugh, A. B. (1984). *Family in contemporary Egypt*. Syracuse, NY: Syracuse University Press.

Ruhl, C. (2013). Update on chlamydia and gonorrhea screening during pregnancy. *Nursing for Women's Health*, 17(2), 143–146.

Ruigrok, A., Salimi-Khorshidi, G., Lai, M., Baron-Cohen, S., Lombardo, M., Tait, R., & Suckling, J. (2013). A meta-analysis of sex differences in human brain structure. *Neuroscience and Biobehavioral Reviews*. Retrieved February 14, 2014, from http://www.sciencedirect.com/science/article/pii/S0149763413003011.

Rupp, J. (2007). The photography of Joseph Rupp: Bound feet. Retrieved December 19, 2008, from http://www.josephrupp.com/.

Russell, D. E. H. (1984). *Sexual exploitation: Rape, child sexual abuse, and workplace harassment*. Beverly Hills, CA: Sage.

Russell, D. E. H., & Howell, N. (1983). The prevalence of rape in the United States revisited. *Signs: Journal of Women in Culture and Society*, 688–695.

Russell, T., Doan, C., & King, A. (2017). Sexually violent women: The PIC-5, everyday sadism, and adversarial sexual attitudes predict female sexual aggression and coercion against male victims. *Personality and Individual Differences*, 111, 242–249.

Russon, M. (2014, February 27). 50 Shades of Grey joins top 10 bestselling books: How many have you read? *International Business Times*. Retrieved June 11, 2014, from http://www.ibtimes.co.uk/50-shades-grey-joins-top-10-bestselling-books-how-many-have-you-read-1438234.

Rust, P. C. R. (2000). *Bisexuality in the U.S.* New York: Columbia University Press.

Rutkowska, A., & Rachoń, D. (2014). Bisphenol A (BPA) and its potential role in the pathogenesis of the polycystic ovary syndrome. *Gynecological Endocrinology*, 30(4), 260–265.

Ruuska, J., Kaltiala-Heino, R., Kiovisto, A., & Rantanen, P. (2003). Puberty, sexual development, and eating disorders in adolescent outpatients. *European Child and Adolescent Psychiatry*, 12(5), 214–220.

Ryan, C., & Futterman, D. (2001). Social and developmental challenges for lesbian, gay, bisexual youth. *SIECUS Report*, 29(4), 5–18.

Ryan, C., Huebner, D., Diaz, R. M., & Sanchez, J. (2009). Family rejection as a predictor of negative health outcomes in white and Latino lesbian, gay, and bisexual young adults. *Pediatrics*, 123(1), 346–352.

Ryan, C., Russell, S., Huebner, D., Diaz, R., & Sanchez, J. (2010). Family acceptance in adolescence and the health of LGBT young adults. *Journal of Child and Adolescent Psychiatric Nursing*, 23(4), 205–214.

Ryan, K. (2011). The relationship between rape myths and sexual scripts: The social construction of rape. *Sex Roles*, 65(11–12), 774–782.

Ryan, K., Cole, J., Saslow, K., Mitchell, B., McArdle, P., Sparks, M., Cheng, Y., & Kittner, S. (2014). Prevention opportunities for oral contraceptive-associated ischemic stroke. *Stroke: A Journal of Cerebral Circulation*, 45(3), 893–895.

Sabelli, H., Fink, P., Fawcett, J., & Tom, C. (1996). Sustained antidepressant effect of PEA replacement. *Journal of Neuropsychiatry and Clinical Neuroscience*, 8(2), 168–171.

Sable, M., Danis, F., Mauzy, D., & Gallagher, S. (2006). Barriers to reporting sexual assault for women and men: Perspectives of college students. *Journal of American College Health*, 55, 157–162.

Sabo, D. S., & Runfola, R. (1980). *Jock: Sports and male identity*. New York: Prentice Hall.

Sadovsky, R., Basson, R., Krychman, M., Morales, A., Schover, L., Wang, R., & Incrocci, L. (2010). Cancer and sexual problems. *Journal of Sexual Medicine*, 7(1 Pt 2), 349–373.

Sadowski, D., Butcher, M., & Köhler, T. (2016). A review of pathophysiology and management options for delayed ejaculation. *Sexual Medicine Reviews*, 4(2), 167–176.

Saewyc, E., Konishi, C., Rose, H., & Homma, Y. (2014). School-based strategies to reduce suicidal ideation, suicide attempts, and discrimination among sexual minority and heterosexual adolescents in western Canada. *International Journal of Child, Youth, & Family Studies*, 5(1), 89–112.

Saewyc, E. M., Bearinger, L. H., Heinz, P. A., Blum, R. W., & Resnick, M. (1998). Gender differences in health and risk behaviors among bisexual and homosexual adolescents. *Journal of Adolescent Health*, 23(2), 181–188.

Safarinejad, M. R. (2008). Evaluation of the safety and efficacy of bremelanotide, a melanocortin receptor agonist, in female subjects with arousal disorder: A double-blind placebo-controlled, fixed dose, randomized study. *Journal of Sexual Medicine*, 5, 887–897.

"Safer sex basics." (2005). Retrieved October 12, 2005, from http://sexuality.about.com/cs/safersex/a/safersexbasics.htm.

"Safer Sex." (2017). Safer sex ('Safe sex'). Planned Parenthood. Retrieved March 12, 2017, from https://www.plannedparenthood.org/learn/stds-hiv-safer-sex/safer-sex.

SAGE. (2010). Improving the lives of LGBT older adults. Retrieved May 15, 2014, from http://www.lgbtmap.org.

Saha, R., Pettersson, H., Svedberg, P., Olovsson, M., Bergqvist, A., Marions, L., Tornvall, P., & Kuja-Halkola, R. (2015). Heritality of endometriosis. *Fertility and Sterility*, 104(4), 947–952.

Sajjad, A., & Weng, C. (2016). Vision loss in a patient with primary pulmonary hypertension and long-term use of sildenafil. *Retinal Cases & Brief Reports*. Retrieved April 15, 2017, from https://www.ncbi.nlm.nih.gov/pubmed/27355186.

Sakorafas, G. H. (2005). The management of women at high risk for the development of breast cancer: Risk estimation and preventative strategies. *Cancer Treatment Reviews*, 29(2), 79–89.

Saleh, F. M., & Berlin, F. (2003). Sex hormones, neurotransmitters, and psychopharmacological treatments in men with paraphilic disorders. *Journal of Child Sexual Abuse*, 12, 233–253.

Salonia, A., Eardley, I., Giuliano, F., Hatzichristou, D., Moncada, I., Vardi, Y., Wespes, E., & Hatzimouratidis, K. (2014). European Association of Urology guidelines on priapism. *European Urology*, 65(2), 480–489.

Salter, D., McMillan, D., Richards, M., Talbot, T., Hodges, J., Bentovim, A., et al. (2003). Development of sexually abusive behavior in sexually victimized males. *Lancet*, 361(9356), 471–476.

Salzmann, Z. (2007). *Language, culture, and society* (4th ed.). Boulder, CO: Westview Press.

Samaras, N., Samaras, D., Lang, P., Forster, A., Pichard, C., Frangos, E., & Meyer, P. (2012). A view of geriatrics through hormones. *Maturitas*, 74(3), 213–219.

Sample, I. (2010). The price of love? Losing two of your closest friends. *Guardian*. Retrieved January 17, 2011, from http://www.guardian .co.uk/science/2010/sep/15/price-love-close -friends-relationship.

Samter, W., & Burleson, B. R. (2005). The role of communication in same-sex friendships: A comparison among African Americans, Asian Americans, and European Americans. *Communication Quarterly*, 53, 265–284.

Samuels, A. (2011, May 1). Reality TV trashes Black women. *Newsweek*. Retrieved May 5, 2011, from http://www.newsweek.com/2011 /05/01/reality-tv-trashes-black-women.html.

Sánchez, F., & Vilain, E. (2010). Genes and brain sex differences. *Progress in Brain Research*, 186, 65–76.

Sánchez, J. M., Milam, M. R., Tomlinson, T. M., & Beardslee, M. A. (2008). Cardiac troponin I elevation after orogenital sex during pregnancy. *Obstetrics and Gynecology*, 111, 487–489.

Sanday, P. R. (1981). The socio-cultural context of rape: A cross-cultural study. *Journal of Social Issues*, 37, 5–27.

Sanders, S. A., & Reinisch, J. M. (1999). Would you say you "had sex" if…? *Journal of the American Medical Association*, 281(3), 275–277.

Sandnabba, N. K., & Ahlberg, C. (1999). Parents' attitudes and expectations about children's cross-gender behavior. *Sex Roles*, 40(3–4), 249–263.

Sandowski, C. L. (1989). *Sexual concerns when illness or disability strikes*. Springfield, IL: Charles C. Thomas.

Sanghani, R. (2017). Meet the heterosexual couples campaigning to have civil partnerships. *The Telegraph*. Retrieved March 7, 2017, from http://www.telegraph .co.uk/women/life/meet-the-heterosexual -couples-campaigning-to-have-civil-partners/.

Sangkomkamhang, U., Lumbiganon, P., Laopaiboon, M., & Mol, B. (2013). Progestogens or progestogen-releasing intrauterine systems for uterine fibroids. *Cochrane Database of Systematic Reviews*. DOI: 10.1002/14651858.CD008994.pub2. Retrieved February 21, 2014, from http:// www.ncbi.nlm.nih.gov/pubmed/23450594.

Santelli, J., Robin, L., Brener, N., & Lowry, R. (2001). Timing of alcohol and other drug use and sexual risk behaviors among unmarried adolescents and young adults. *Family Planning Perspectives*, 33(5), 200–205.

Santen, R. J. (1995). The testis. In P. Felig, J. D. Baxter, & L. A. Frolman, (Eds.), *Endocrinology and metabolism* (3rd ed.). New York: McGraw-Hill.

Santos, P., Schinemann, J., Gabarcio, J., & da Graca, G. (2005). New evidence that the MHC influences odor perception in humans: A study with 58 Southern Brazilian students. *Hormones and Behavior*, 47(4), 384–388.

Sarin, S., Amsel, R., & Binik, Y. (2013). Disentangling desire and arousal: A classificatory conundrum. *Archives of Sexual Behavior*, 42(6), 1079–1100.

Sarin, S., Amsel, R., & Binik, Y. (2016). A streetcar name "Derousal"? A psychophysiological examination of the desire-arousal distinction in sexually functional and dysfunctional women. *Journal of Sex Research*, 53(6), 711–729.

Sarkisian, N., & Gerstel, N. (2008). Till marriage do us part: Adult children's relationships with their parents. *Journal of Marriage and Family*, 70, 360–377.

Sarno, E., Mohr, J., Jackson, S., & Fassinger, R. (2015). When identities collide: Conflicts in allegiances among LGB people of color. *Cultural Diversity and Ethnic Minority Psychology*, 21(4), 550–559.

Sarrel, P., & Masters, W. (1982). Sexual molestation of men by women. *Archives of Sexual Behavior*, 11, 117–131.

Sartorius, A., Ruf, M., Kief, C., & Demirakca, T. (2008). Abnormal amygdala activation profile in pedophilia. *European Archives of Psychiatry and Clinical Neuroscience*, 258, 271–279.

Saslow, B., Boetes, C., Burke, W., Harms, S., Leach, M., Lehman, C., et al. (2007). American Cancer Society guidelines for breast screening with MRI as an adjunct to mammography. *CA Cancer Journal for Clinicians*, 57, 75–89.

Sassler, S., Cunningham, A., & Lichter, D. (2009). Intergenerational patterns of union formation and relationship quality. *Journal of Family Issues*, 30(6), 757–786.

Sassler, S., Michelmore, K., & Holland, J. (2016). The progression of sexual relationships. *Journal of Marriage and Family*, 78(3), 587–597.

Sati, N. (1998). Equivocal lifestyles. The Living Channel. Retrieved July 7, 2003, from http:// www.glas.org/ahbab/Articles/arabia1.html.

Sato, R., & Iwasawa, M. (2006). Contraceptive use and induced abortion in Japan: How is it so unique among the developed countries? *Japanese Journal of Population*, 4(1), 34–54.

Sato, S. M., Schulz, K. M., Sisk, C. L., & Wood, R. I. (2008). Adolescents and androgens, receptors and rewards. *Hormones and Behavior* 53(5), 647–658.

Satterwhite, C., Torrone, E., Meites, E., Dunne, E., Mahajan, R., Ocfemia, M., Su, J., Xu, F., & Weinstock, H. (2013). Sexually transmitted infections among US women and men: Prevalence and incidence estimates, 2008. *Sexually Transmitted Diseases*, 40(3), 187–193.

Sauer, P., & Neubauer, D. (2014). Female genital mutilation: A hidden epidemic. *European Journal of Pediatrics*, 173(2), 237–238.

Saulny, S. (2010, January 30). Black? White? Asian? More young Americans choose all of the above. *New York Times*. Retrieved January 30, 2011, from http://www.nytimes .com/2011/01/30/us/30mixed.html?src5twrhp.

Sauter, D., Eisner, F., Ekman, P., & Scott, S. (2010). Cross-cultural recognition of basic emotions through nonverbal emotional vocalizations. *Proceedings of the National Academy of Sciences of the United States of America*, 107(6), 2408.

Savareux, L., Droupy, S.; les membres du comité d'andrologie de l'AFU. (2009). [Evaluation of sexual dysfunction in prostate cancer management]. *Progress in Urology*, 19(Suppl. 4), S189–S192.

Savaya, R., & Cohen, O. (2003). Divorce among Moslem Arabs living in Israel: Comparison for reasons before and after the actualization of the marriage. *Journal of Family Issues*, 24(3), 338–351.

Savic, I., Berglund, H., & Lindström, P. (2005). Brain response to putative pheromones in homosexual men. *Proceedings of the National Academy of Sciences*, 102, 7356–7361.

Savic, I., Garcia-Falgueras, A., & Swaab, D. (2010). Sexual differentiation of the human brain in relation to gender identity and sexual orientation. *Progress in Brain Research*, 186, 41–62.

Savic, I., & Lindström, P. (2008, June 16). PET and MRI show differences in cerebral asymmetry and functional connectivity between homo- and heterosexual subjects. *Proceedings of the National Academy of Sciences*. Retrieved October 3, 2008, from http://www.pnas.org /cgi/content/abstract/0801566105v1.

Savin-Williams, R. C. (2001). *"Mom, Dad. I'm gay." How families negotiate coming out*. Washington, DC: American Psychological Association.

Savin-Williams, R. C., & Diamond, L. M. (2000). Sexual identity trajectories among sexual minority youths: Gender comparisons. *Archives of Sexual Behavior*, 29, 607–627.

Savitz, L., & Rosen, L. (1988). The sexuality of prostitutes: Sexual enjoyment reported by "streetwalkers." *Journal of Sex Research*, 24, 200–208.

Sawyer, R. G., Thompson, E. E., & Chicorelli, A. M. (2002). Rape myth acceptance among intercollegiate student athletes. *American Journal of Health Studies*, 18(1), 19–25.

Scarce, M. (1997). *The hidden toll of stigma and shame*. New York: De Capo Press.

Schaan, V., & Vögele, C. (2016). Resilience and rejection sensitivity mediate long-term outcomes of parental divorce. *European Child & Adolescent Psychiatry*, 25(11), 1267–1269.

Schabrun, S., Van Den Hoom, W., Moorcroft, A., Greenland, C., & Hodges, P. (2014). Texting and walking: Strategies for postural control and implications for safety. *PLoS One, 9*(1). Retrieved February 3, 2014, from http://www.plosone.org/article/info%3Adoi%2F10.1371%2Fjournal.pone.0084312.

Schachter, S., & Singer, J. (1962). Cognitive, social, and physiological determinants of emotional state. *Psychological Review, 69*(5), 379–399.

Schachter, S., & Singer, J. (2001). Cognitive, social, and physiological determinants of emotional state. In W. Parrott (Ed.), *Emotions in social psychology: Essential readings* (pp. 76–93). New York: Psychology Press.

Schade, L., Sandberg, J., Bean, R., Busby, D., & Coyne, S. (2013). Using technology to connect in romantic relationships: Effects on attachment, relationship satisfaction, and stability in emerging adults. *Journal of Couple and Relationship Therapy, 12*(4), 314–338.

Schantz-Laursen, B. (2017). Sexuality in men after prostate cancer surgery: A qualitative interview study. *Scandinavian Journal of Caring Sciences, 31*(1), 120–127.

Schauer, E., & Wheaton, E. (2006). Sex trafficking into the U.S.: A literature review. *Criminal Justice Review*. Retrieved May 7, 2011, from http://www.worldwideopen.org/uploads/resources/files/631/TFGLO052_Lit_Review_Trafficking_into_the_US.pdf.

Schembri, G., & Schober, P. (2011). Risk factors for chlamydial infection in chlamydia contacts: A questionnaire-based study. *Journal of Family Planning and Reproductive Health Care, 37*(1), 10–16.

Schiau, S., Plitea, L., Fusita, A., Pjekny, S., & Iancu, L. (2013). How do cartoons teach children? A comparative analysis on preschoolers and schoolchildren. *Journal of Media Research, 3*(17), 37–49.

Schick, V., Herbenick, D., Reece, M., Sanders, S. A., Dodge, B., Middlestadt, S. E., & Fortenberry, J. D. (2010). Sexual behaviors, condom use, and sexual health of Americans over 50: Implications for sexual health promotion for older adults. *Journal of Sexual Medicine, 7*(Suppl. 5), 315–329.

Schierbeck, L., Rejnmark, L., Tofteng, C., Stilgren, L., Eiken, P., et al. (2012). Effect of hormone replacement therapy on cardiovascular events in recently postmenopausal women. *British Medical Journal, 345*. DOI: http://dx.doi.org/10.1136/bmj.e6409. Retrieved February 21, 2014, from http://www.bmj.com/content/345/bmj.e6409.

Schiffer, J., Mayer, B., Fong, Y., Swan, D., & Wald, A. (2014). Herpes simplex virus-2 transmission probability estimates based on quantity of viral shedding. *Journal of the Royal Society, Interface, 11*(95). Retrieved June 6, 2014, from http://rsif.royalsocietypublishing.org/content/11/95/20140160.abstract.

Schiffrin, H., Edelman, A., Falkenstern, M., & Stewart, C. (2010). The associations among computer-mediated communication, relationships, and well-being. *Cyberpsychology, Behavior, and Social Networking, 13*(3), 299–306.

Schildkraut, J. M., Calingaert, B., Marchbanks, P. A., Moorman, P. G., & Rodriguez, G. C. (2002). Impact of progestin and estrogen potency in oral contraceptives on ovarian cancer risk. *Journal of the National Cancer Institute, 94*, 32–38.

Schindler, A. E. (2010). Non-contraceptive benefits of hormonal contraceptives. *Minerva Ginecol, 62*(4), 319–329.

Schlegel, R. (2007, January 17). HPV vaccine. *Washington Post*. Retrieved September 16, 2008, from http://www.washingtonpost.com/wp-dyn/content/discussion/2007/01/16/DI2007011600929.html.

Schlichter, A. (2004). Queer at last? *GLW: A Journal of Lesbian and Gay Studies, 10*(4), 543–565.

Schliep, K., Mitchell, E., Mumford, S., Radin, R., Zarek, S., Sjaarda, & Schisterman, E. (2016). Trying to conceive after an early pregnancy loss: An assessment on how long couples should wait. *Obstetrics & Gynecology, 127*(2), 204–212.

Schmitt, D., & Fuller, R. (2015). On the varieties of sexual experience: Cross-cultural links between religiosity and human mating strategies. *Psychology of Religion and Spirituality, 7*(4), 314–326.

Schnarch, D. (1997). *Passionate marriage*. New York: Henry Holt.

Schneider, F., Habel, U., Kessler, C., Salloum, J. B., & Posse, S. (2000). Gender differences in regional cerebral activity during sadness. *Human Brain Mapping, 9*(4), 226–238.

Schneider, J. P. (2000). Effects of cybersex addiction on the family: Results of a survey. *Sexual Addiction & Compulsivity, 7*(1), 31–58.

Schneider, L., Mori, L., Lambert, P., & Wong, A. (2009). The role of gender and ethnicity in perceptions of rape and its aftereffects. *Sex Roles, 60*(5–6), 410–422.

Schneider, M. (1989). Sappho was a right-on adolescent: Growing up lesbian. *Journal of Homosexuality, 17*, 111–130.

Schoelwer, M., Donahue, K., Bryk, K., Didrick, P., Berenbaum, S., & Eugster, E. (2015). Psychological assessment of mothers and their daughters at the time of diagnosis of precocious puberty. *International Journal of Pediatric Endocrinology, 2015*(1), 5.

Schover, L., & Jensen, S. B. (1988). *Sexuality and chronic illness*. New York: Guilford Press.

Schrimshaw, E., Siegel, K., Downing, M., & Parsons, J. (2013). Disclosure and concealment of sexual orientation and the mental health of non-gay-identified, behaviorally bisexual men. *Journal of Consulting and Clinical Psychology, 81*(1), 141–153.

Schrodt, P. (2009). Family strength and satisfaction as functions of family communication environments. *Communication Quarterly, 57*(2), 171–186.

Schrodt, P., & Carr, K. (2012). Trait verbal aggressiveness as a function of family communication patterns. *Communication Research Reports, 29*(1), 54–63.

Schrodt, P., & Ledbetter, A. (2007). Communication processes that mediate family communication patterns and mental well-being: A means and covariance structures analysis of young adults from divorced and non-divorced families. *Human Communication Research, 33*, 330–356.

Schrodt, P., Ledbetter, A., Jembert, K., Larson, L., Brown, N., & Glonek, K. (2009). Family communication patterns as mediators of communication competence in the parent-child relationship. *Journal of Social and Personal Relationships, 26*(6–7), 853–874.

Schuberg, K. (2009, October 16). Despite widespread contraceptive use, 1/3 of pregnancies in France 'unplanned,' new study confirms. CBS News. Retrieved October 17, 2009, from http://www.cnsnews.com/node/55580.

Schubert, T. W. (2004). The power in your hand: Gender differences in bodily feedback from making a fist. *Personality and Social Psychology Bulletin, 30*(6), 757–769.

Schüklenk, U., Stein, E., Kerin, J., & Byne, W. (1997). The ethics of genetic research on sexual orientation. *Hastings Center Report, 27*(4), 6–13.

Schuler, P., Vinci, D., Isosaari, R., Philipp, S., Todorovich, J., Roy, J., & Evans, R. (2008). Body-shape perceptions and body mass index of older African American and European American Women. *Journal of Cross-Cultural Gerontology, 23*(3), 255–264.

Schüler, S., Ponnath, M., Engel, J., & Ortmann, O. (2013). Ovarian epithelial tumors and reproductive factors: A systematic review. *Archives of Gynecology and Obstetrics, 287*(6), 1187–1204.

Schultz, J. S. (2010, August 6). Divorce insurance (Yes, divorce insurance). *New York Times*. Retrieved October 12, 2010, from http://bucks.blogs.nytimes.com/2010/08/06/divorce-insurance-yes-divorce-insurance/.

Schulze, C., & Koon-Magnin, S. (2017). Gender, sexual orientation, and rape myth acceptance: Preliminary findings from a sample of primarily LGBQ-identified survey respondents. *Violence and Victims, 32*(1), 159–180.

Schumm, W. (2010). Children of homosexuals more apt to be homosexuals? A reply to Morrison and to Cameron based on an examination of the multiple sources of data. *Journal of Biosocial Science*, *42*(6), 721–743.

Schützwohl, A. (2008). The intentional object of romantic jealousy. *Evolution and Human Behavior*, *29*, 92–99.

Schuyler, A., Masvawure, T., Smit, J., Beksinska, M., Mabude, Z., Ngoloyi, C., & Mantell, J. (2016). Building young women's knowledge and skills in female condom use: Lessons learning from a South African intervention. *Health Education Research*, *31*(2), 260–272.

Schwartz, G., Kim, R., Kolundzija, A., Rieger, G., & Sanders, A. (2010). Biodemographic and physical correlates of sexual orientation in men. *Archives of Sexual Behavior*, *39*, 93–109.

Schwarz, S., & Hassebrauck, M. (2012). Sex and age differences in mate-selection preferences. *Human Nature*, *23*(4), 447–466.

Schweitzer, R., O'Brien, J., & Burri, A. (2015). Postcoital dysphoria: Prevalence and psychological correlates. *Sexual Medicine*, *3*(4), 235–243.

Scott, J. E., & Schwalm, L. A. (1988). Rape rates and the circulation rates of adult magazines. *Journal of Sex Research*, *24*, 241–250.

Scott, J. R. (2005). Episiotomy and vaginal trauma. *Obstetrics and Gynecology Clinics of North America*, *32*(2), 307–321.

Scott, S., Rhoades, G., Stanley, S., Allen, E., & Markman, H. (2013). Reasons for divorce and recollections of premarital intervention: Implications for improving relationship education. *Couple and Family Psychology: Research and Practice*, *2*(2), 131–145.

Scott-Sheldon, L., Carey, M., & Carey, K. (2010). Alcohol and risky sexual behavior among heavy drinking college students. *AIDS and Behavior*, *14*(4), 845–853.

Scully, D., & Marolla, J. (1983). *Incarcerated rapists: Exploring a sociological model*. Final Report for Department of Health and Human Services, NIMH.

Sedgh G., Finer, L., Bankole, A., Eilers, M., & Singh, S. (2015). Adolescent pregnancy, birth, and abortion rates across countries: Levels and recent trends. *Journal of Adolescent Health*, *56*(2), 223–230.

Sedgh, G., Hussain, R., Bankole, A., & Singh, S. (2007). Unmet need for contraception in developing countries: Levels and reasons for not using a method. Alan Guttmacher Institute, Occasional Report No. 37. Retrieved July 29, 2008, from http://www.guttmacher.org/pubs/2007/07/09/or37.pdf.

Sedgh, G., Singh, S., & Hussain, R. (2014). Intended and unintended pregnancies worldwide in 2012 and recent trends. *Studies in Family Planning*, *45*(3), 301–314.

Seeber, B., & Barnhart, K. (2006). Suspected ectopic pregnancy. *Obstetrics and Gynecology*, *107*(2 pt 1), 399–413.

Seelman, K., Adams, M., & Poteat, T. (2016). Interventions for healthy aging among mature Black lesbians: Recommendations gathered through community-based research. *Journal of Women & Aging*, 1–13.

Segal, C. (2016, June 11). Oregon court rules that "nonbinary" is a legal gender. PBS NewsHour. Retrieved January 19, 2017, from http://www.pbs.org/newshour/rundown/oregon-court-rules-that-nonbinary-is-a-legal-gender/.

Seidman, S. N., & Rieder, R. O. (1994). A review of sexual behavior in the U.S. *American Journal of Psychiatry*, *151*, 330–341.

Seiffge-Krenke, I., Shulman, S., & Klesinger, N. (2001). Adolescent precursors of romantic relationships in young adulthood. *Journal of Social & Personal Relationships*, *18*(3), 327–346.

Seiter, C. (2015, June 23). The psychology of emojis. *The Next Web*. Retrieved January 11, 2017, from http://thenextweb.com/insider/2015/06/23/the-psychology-of-emojis/.

Seki, K., Matsumoto, D., & Imahori, T. T. (2002). The conceptualization and expression of intimacy in Japan and the United States. *Journal of Cross Cultural Psychology*, *33*, 303–319.

Seligman, L., & Hardenburg, S. A. (2000). Assessment and treatment of paraphilias. *Journal of Counseling and Development*, *78*(1), 107–113.

Sell, R., Wells, J., & Wypij, D. (1995). The prevalence of homosexual behavior and attraction in the U.S., the U.K and France: Results of a national population-based sample. *Archives of Sexual Behavior*, *24*, 235–249.

Seltzer, L., Prososki, A., Ziegler, T., & Pollak, S. (2012). Instant messages vs speech: Hormones and why we still need to hear each other. *Evolution and Human Behavior*, *33*, 42–45.

Semlyen, J., King, M., Varney, J., & Hagger-Johnson, G. (2015). Sexual orientation and symptoms of common mental disorder or low wellbeing: Combined meta-analysis of 12 UK population health surveys. *BMC Psychiatry*, *16*, 67. Retrieved March 24, 2017, from https://bmcpsychiatry.biomedcentral.com/articles/10.1186/s12888-016-0767-z.

Sepede, G., Sarchione, F., Matarazzo, I., Di Giannantonio, M., & Salerno, R. (2016). Premenstrual dysphoric disorder without comorbid psychiatric conditions: A systematic review of therapeutic options. *Clinical Neuropharmacology*, *39*(5), 241–261.

Sepilian, V., & Wood, E. (2004). Ectopic pregnancy. Retrieved July 19, 2005, from http://www.emedicine.com/med/topic3212.htm.

Seppa, N. (2001). Study reveals male link to preeclampsia. *Science News*, *159*(12), 181–182.

Serefoglu, E. C., Yaman, O., Cayan, S., Asci, R., Orhan, I., Usta, M. F., Ekmekcioglu, O., Kendirci, M., Semerci, B., & Kadioglu, A. (2011). Prevalence of the complaint of ejaculating prematurely and the four premature ejaculation syndromes: Results from the Turkish Society of Andrology Sexual Health Survey. *Journal of Sexual Medicine*, *8*(2), 540–548.

Serjeant, G., & Hambleton, I. (2015). Priapism in homozygous sickle cell disease: A 40-year study of the natural history. *The West Indian Medical Journal*, *64*(3), 175–180.

Seshadri, K. (2016). The endocrinology of love. *Indian Journal of Endocrinology and Metabolism*, *20*(4), 558–563.

Seto, M. (2008). Pedophilia: Psychopathology and theory. In D. Laws & W. O'Donohue (Eds.), *Sexual deviance: Theory, assessment and treatment* (2nd ed., pp. 164–183). New York: Guilford Press.

Sevelius, J. (2009). "There's no pamphlet for the kind of sex I have": HIV-related risk factors and protective behaviors among transgender women who have sex with nontransgender men. *Journal of the Association of Nurses in AIDS Care*, *20*(5), 398–410.

Severson, N., Muñoz-Laboy, M., & Kaufman, R. (2014). 'At times, I feel like I'm sinning': The paradoxical role of non-lesbian, gay, bisexual and transgender-affirming religion in the lives of behaviorally-bisexual Latino men. *Culture, Health & Sexuality*, *16*(2), 136–148.

Seveso, M., Taverna, G., Giusti, G., Benetti, A., Maugeri, O., Piccinelli, A., & Graziotti, P. (2010). Corporoplasty by plication: Outpatient surgery for the correction of penile cancer. *Archives of Italian Urological Andrology*, *82*(3), 164–166.

Sexuality Information and Education Council of the United States. (2004). Guidelines for comprehensive sexuality education (3rd ed.). Retrieved September 22, 2005, from http://www.siecus.org/pubs/guidelines/guidelines.pdf.

Sexwork.com. (1999a). Thailand's long tradition of prostitution: Modern attitude shifts vs. huge economic benefits. Retrieved June 29, 2011, from http://www.sexwork.com/Thailand/traditions.html.

Sexwork.com. (1999b). The influence of Thai Buddhism on prostitution. Retrieved November 16, 2008, from http://www.sexwork.com/Thailand/buddhism.html.

Seymour, A., Murray, M., Sigmon, J., Hook, M., Edmunds, C., Gaboury, M., et al. (Eds.). (2000). Retrieved May 22, 2003, from http://www.ojp.usdoj.gov/ovc/assist/nvaa2000/academy/welcome.html.

Shackelford, T. K., & Goetz, A. T. (2007). Adaptation to sperm competition in humans. *Current Directions in Psychological Science*, *16*, 47–50.

Shackford, S. (2016, June 13). In America, Muslims are more likely to support gay marriage then evangelical Christians. *Reason: Free Minds and Free Markets*. Retrieved March 24, 2017, from http://reason.com/blog/2016/06/13/in-america-muslims-are-more-likely-to-su.

Shadiack, A., Sharma, S., Earle, D., Spana, C., & Hallam, T. (2007). Melanocortins in the treatment of male and female sexual dysfunction. *Current Topics in Medical Chemistry, 7*, 1137–1144.

Shafaat, A. (2004). Punishment for adultery in Islam: A detailed examination. Retrieved April 10, 2008, from http://www.islamicperspectives.com/Stoning4.htm.

Shamloul, R. (2005). Treatment of men complaining of short penis. *Urology, 65*(6), 1183–1185.

Shamloul, R. (2010). Natural aphrodisiacs. *Journal of Sexual Medicine, 7*(1 Pt 1), 39–49.

Shanmugalingam, T., Soultati, A., Chowdhury, S., Rudman, S., & Van Hemelrjck, M. (2013). Global incidence and outcome of testicular cancer. *Clinical Epidemiology, 5*, 417–427.

Shao, R., Wang, X., Wang, W., Stener-Victorin, E., Mallard, C., Brännström, M., & Billig, H. (2012). From mice to women and back again: Causalities and clues for chlamydia-induced tubal ectopic pregnancy. *Fertility and Sterility, 98*(5), 1175–1185.

Shapiro, J. (2014). Campus rape reports are up, and assaults aren't the only reason. National Public Radio News. Retrieved June 16, 2014, from http://www.npr.org/2014/04/30/308276181/campus-rape-reports-are-up-and-there-might-be-some-good-in-that.

Shapiro, J., Radecki, S., Charchian, A. S., & Josephson, V. (1999). Sexual behavior and AIDS-related knowledge among community college students in Orange County, California. *Journal of Community Health, 24*(1), 29–43.

Sharma, G. (2016, February 13). 10 amazing facts you probably don't know about mobile phones. *TechCrunch*. Retrieved January 11, 2017, from https://techcrunch.com/gallery/10-amazing-facts-you-probably-dont-know-about-mobile-phones/.

Sharma, O., & Haub, C. (2008). Sex ratio at birth begins to improve in India. Population Reference Bureau. Retrieved February 24, 2011, from http://www.prb.org/Articles/2008/indiasexratio.aspx.

Sharma, R. (2001). Condom use seems to be reducing number of new HIV/AIDS cases. *British Medical Journal, 323*(7310), 417–421.

Sharp, E., & Ispa, J. (2009). Inner-city single Black mothers' gender-related childrearing expectations and goals. *Sex Roles, 60*, 656–668.

Sharp, V., Kieran, K., & Arlen, A. (2013). Testicular torsion: Diagnosis, evaluation, and management. *American Family Physician, 88*(12), 835–840.

Sharpsteen, D. J., & Kirkpatrick, L. A. (1997). Romantic jealousy and adult romantic attachment. *Journal of Personality & Social Psychology, 72*(3), 627–640.

Shaver, F. M. (2005). Sex work research: Methodological and ethical challenges. *Journal of Interpersonal Violence, 20*(3), 296–319.

Shaver, P. R., Wu, S., & Schwartz, J. C. (1992). Cross-cultural similarities and differences in emotion and its representation: A prototype approach. In M. S. Clark (Ed.), *Emotion* (pp. 175–212). Newbury Park, CA: Sage.

Shaver, P., & Hazan, C. (1987). Being lonely, falling in love: Perspectives from attachment theory. *Journal of Social Behavior & Personality, 2*(2, Pt 2), 105–124.

Sheaffer, A. T., Lange, E., & Bondy, C. A. (2008). Sexual function in women with Turner syndrome. *Journal of Women's Health, 17*, 27–33.

Sheehan, P. (2007). Hyperemesis gravidarum—assessment and management. *Australian Family Physician, 36*, 698–701.

Sheldon, K. M. (2007). Gender differences in preferences for singles ads that proclaim extrinsic versus intrinsic values. *Sex Roles, 57*, 119–130.

Sheppard, C., & Wylie, K. R. (2001). An assessment of sexual difficulties in men after treatment for testicular cancer. *Sexual and Relationship Therapy, 16*(1), 47–58.

Sherfey, J. (1972). *The nature and evolution of female sexuality*. New York: Random House.

Shernoff, M. (2007). Male couples and monogamy: Clinical and cultural issues. In Paul R. Peluso (Ed.), *Infidelity: A Practitioner's Guide to Working with Couples in Crisis* (pp. 207–227). New York, NY: Routledge/Taylor & Francis Group.

Sherr, L., Varrall, R., Mueller, J., Richter, L., Wakhweya, A., Adato, M., Belsey, M., Chandan, U., Drimie, S., Haour-Knipe, V., Hosegood, M., Kimou, J., Madhavan, S., Mathambo, V., & Desmond, C. (2008). A systematic review on the meaning of the concept 'AIDS orphan': Confusion over definitions and implications for care. *AIDS Care, 20*(5), 527–536.

Shettles, L., & Rorvik, D. (1970). *Your baby's sex: Now you can choose*. New York: Dodd, Mead.

Sheynkin, Y., Jung, M., Yoo, P., Schulsinger, D., & Komaroff, E. (2005). Increase in scrotal temperature in laptop computer users. *Human Reproduction, 20*(2), 452–455.

Shibusawa, T. (2009). A commentary on "gender perspectives in cross-cultural couples." *Clinical Social Work Journal, 37*, 230–233.

Shields, R. (2010, May 16). South Africa's shame: The rise of child rape. *The Independent UK*. Retrieved April 20, 2011, from http://www.independent.co.uk/news/world/africa/south-africas-shame-the-rise-of-child-rape-1974578.html.

Shiffman, M., VanderLaan, D., Wood, H., Lumley, M., Lollis, S., & Zucker, K. (2016). Behavioral and emotional problems as a function of peer relationships in adolescents with gender dysphoria: A comparison with clinical and nonclinical controls. *Psychology of Sexual Orientation and Gender Diversity, 3*(1), 27–36.

Shifren, J. L., & Avis, N. E. (2007). Surgical menopause: Effects on psychological well-being and sexuality. *Menopause, 14*, 586–591.

Shifren, J. L., Monz, B. U., Russo, P., Segreti, A., & Johannes, C. (2008). Sexual problems and distress in United States women. *Obstetrics & Gynecology, 112*, 970–978.

Shih, G., Turok, D. K., & Parker, W. J. (2011). Vasectomy: The other (better) form of sterilization. *Contraception, 83*(4), 310–315.

Shilts, R. (2000). *And the band played on: Politics, people, and the AIDS epidemic*. New York: St. Martin's Press.

Shim, J. (2014, August 14). Listed for life. *Slate*. Retrieved May 1, 2017, from http://www.slate.com/articles/news_and_politics/jurisprudence/2014/08/sex_offender_registry_laws_by_state_mapped.html.

Shimanaka, K. (2008, August 8). Ominous rumblings on the love hotel front. *The Tokyo Reporter*. Retrieved August 23, 2008, http://www.tokyoreporter.com/2008/08/11/ominous-rumblings-on-the-love-hotel-front.

Shindel, A., Nelson, C., Naughton, C., & Mulhall, J. (2008). Premature ejaculation in infertile couples: Prevalence and correlates. *Journal of Sexual Medicine, 5*(2), 485–491.

Shivananda, M., & Rao, T. (2016). Sexual dysfunction in medical practice. *Current Opinions in Psychiatry, 29*(6), 331–335.

Shoard, C. (2013, June). Michael Douglas: Oral sex caused my cancer. *The Guardian*. Retrieved June 6, 2014, from http://www.theguardian.com/film/2013/jun/02/michael-douglas-oral-sex-cancer.

Shohel, M., Rahman, M., Zaman, A., Uddin, M., Al-Amin, M., & Reza, H. (2014). A systematic review of effectiveness and safety of different regimens of levonorgestrel oral tablets for emergency contraception. *BMC Women's Health, 14*(54), 1–10.

Shpigel, M., Belsky, Y., & Diamond, G. (2015). Clinical work with non-accepting parents of sexual minority children: Addressing causal and controllability attributions. *Professional Psychology: Research and Practice, 46*(1), 46–54.

Shrewsberry, A., Weiss, A., & Ritenour, C. W. (2010). Recent advances in the medical and surgical treatment of priapism. *Current Urological Reports, 11*(6), 405–413.

Shtarkshall, R. A., & Zemach, M. (2004). Israel. In R. T. Francoeur & R. J. Noonan (Eds.), *The Continuum International encyclopedia of sexuality* (pp. 581–619). New York/London: Continuum International.

Shteynshlyuger, A., & Freyle, J. (2011). Familial testicular torsion in three consecutive generations of first-degree relatives. *Journal of Pediatric Urology, 7*, 86–91.

Shteynshlyuger, A., & Yu, J. (2013). Familial testicular torsion: A meta analysis suggests inheritance. *Journal of Pediatric Urology, 9*(5), 683–690.

Shulman, J. L., & Horne, S. G. (2006). Guilty or not? A path model of women's sexual force fantasies. *Journal of Sex Research, 43*, 368–377.

Shulman, L. P. (2010). Gynecological management of premenstrual symptoms. *Current Pain and Headache Reports, 14*(5), 367–375.

Shulman, S., Davilla, J., & Shachar-Shapira, L. (2010). Assessing romantic competence among older adolescents. *Journal of Adolescence, 34*(3), 397–406.

Shutty, M. S., & Leadbetter, R. A. (1993). Case report: Recurrent pseudocyesis in a male patient with psychosis, intermittent hyponatremia, and polydipsia. *Psychosomatic Medicine, 55*, 146–148.

Siddiqui, S. (2013, December 18). Side effects may include death: The story of the biggest advance in birth control since the pill. *Huffington Post*. Retrieved May 24, 2014, from http://www.huffingtonpost.com/2013/12/18/nuvaring-blood-clots_n_4461429.html.

Sidhu, J. (2012, September 14). How to buy a daughter. *Slate*. Retrieved July 31, 2014, from http://www.slate.com/articles/health_and_science/medical_examiner/2012/09/sex_selection_in_babies_through_pgd_americans_are_paying_to_have_daughters_rather_than_sons_.html.

Siebenbruner, J. (2013). Are college students replacing dating and romantic relationships with hooking up? *Journal of College Student Development, 54*(4), 433–438.

SIECUS. (2016). 2016 Sex ed state legislative year-end report. Sexuality Information and Education Council of the United States. Retrieved February 12, 2017, from http://www.siecus.org/document/docWindow.cfm?fuseaction=document.viewDocument&documentid=655&documentFormatId=763.

Sieczkowski, C. (2012, April 11). Supermodels without Photoshop: Israel's 'Photoshop Law' puts focus on digitally altered images. *International Business Times*. Retrieved November 10, 2013, from http://www.ibtimes.com/supermodels-without-photoshop-israels-photoshop-law-puts-focus-digitally-altered-images-photos.

Sigal, J., Gibbs, M. S., Goodrich, C., Rashid, T., Anjum, A., Hsu, D., Perrino, C., Boratrav, H., Carson-Arenas, A., et al. (2005). Cross-cultural reactions to academic sexual harassment: Effects of individualist vs. collectivist culture and gender of participants. *Sex Roles, 52*(3–4), 201–215.

Sigamoney, V., & Epprecht, M. (2013). Meanings of homosexuality, same-sex sexuality, and Africanness in two South African townships: An evidence-based approach for rethinking same-sex prejudice. *African Studies Review, 56*(2), 83–107.

Siker, J. S. (1994). *Homosexuality in the Church: Both sides of the debate*. Louisville, KY: Westminster John Knox Press.

Silbert, M. (1998). Compounding factors in the rape of street prostitutes. In A. W. Burgess (Ed.), Rape and sexual assault II. London: Taylor & Francis.

Silva, C., Chu, C., Monahan, K., & Joiner, T. (2015). Suicide risk among sexual minority college students: A mediated moderation model of sex and perceived burdensomeness. *Psychology of Sexual Orientation and Gender Diversity, 2*(1), 22–33.

Silverman, B., & Gross, T. (1997). Use and effectiveness of condoms during anal intercourse. *Sexually Transmitted Diseases, 24*, 11–17.

Silverman, E. K. (2004). Anthropology and circumcision. *Annual Reviews in Anthropology, 33*(1), 419–445.

Silverman, J., Decker, M., McCauley, H., Gupta, J., Miller, E., Raj, A., & Goldberg, A. (2010). Male perpetration of intimate partner violence and involvement in abortions: An abortion-related conflict. *American Journal of Public Health, 1100*(8), 1415–1417.

Silverstein, B., Edwards, T., Gamma, A., Ajdacic-Gross, V., Rossler, W., & Angst, J. (2013). The role played by depression associated with somatic symptomatology in accounting for the gender difference in the prevalence of depression. *Social Psychiatry and Psychiatry Epidemiology, 48*(2), 257–263.

Silverstein, C. (1984). The ethical and moral implications of sexual classification: A commentary. *Journal of Homosexuality, 9*, 29–38.

Simmons, M., & Montague, D. (2008). Penile prosthesis implantation: Past, present and future. *International Journal of Impotence Research, 20*, 437–444.

Simon, J., Kingsberg, S., Shumel, B., Hanes, V., Garcia, M., & Sand, M. (2014). Efficacy and safety of flibanserin in postmenopausal women with hypoactive sexual desire disorder. *Menopause, 2*(6), 633–640.

Simon, L., & Daneback, K. (2013). Adolescents' use of the internet for sex education: A thematic and critical review of the literature. *International Journal of Sexual Health, 15*(4), 304–319.

Simon, P. M., Morse, E. V., Osofsky, H. J., & Balson, P. M. (1992). Psychological characteristics of a sample of male street prostitutes. *Archives of Sexual Behavior, 21*, 33–44.

Simon, S. (2015, October 20). American Cancer Society releases new breast cancer guideline.

Retrieved January 20, 2017, from http://www.cancer.org/latest-news/american-cancer-society-releases-new-breast-cancer-guidelines.html.

Simondsen, K., & Kolesar, J. (2013). New treatment options for castration-resistant prostate cancer. *American Journal of Health-System Pharmacy, 70*(10), 858–865.

Simons, M. (1996, January 26). African women in France battling polygamy. *New York Times*, p. A1.

Simons, R. L., & Whitbeck, L. B. (1991). Sexual abuse as a precursor to prostitution and victimization among adolescent and adult homeless women. *Journal of Family Issues, 12*, 361–379.

Simpson, J., Collins, W., Tran, S., & Haydon, K. (2007). Attachment and the experience and expression of emotions in romantic relationships: A developmental perspective. *Journal of Personality and Social Psychology, 92*(2), 355–367.

Simsek, A., Kirecci, S., Kucuktopcu, O., Ozgor, F., Akbulut, M., Sarilar, O., Oxkuvanci, U., & Gurbuz, Z. (2014). Comparison of paroxetine and dapoxetine, a novel selective serotonin reuptake inhibitor in the treatment of premature ejaculation. *Asian Journal of Andrology*. Retrieved June 1, 2014, from http://www.ncbi.nlm.nih.gov/pubmed/24830690.

Sinclair, H., & Frieze, I. (2015). Initial courtship behavior and stalking: How should we draw the line? In R. D. Maiuro (Ed.), *Perspectives on stalking: Victims, perpetrators, and cyberstalking* (pp. 55–73). New York: Spring Publishing.

Singh, A., Wong, T., & De, P. (2008). Characteristics of primary and late latent syphilis cases which were initially non-reactive with the rapid plasma regain as the screening test. *International Journal of STDs and AIDS, 19*, 464–468.

Singh, D., Vidaurri, M., Zambarano, R. J., & Dabbs, J. M. (1999). Lesbian erotic role identification: Behavioral, morphological, and hormonal correlates. *Journal of Personality and Social Psychology, 76*(6), 1035–1049.

Singh, S., & Darroch, J. (2012). *Adding it up: Costs and benefits of contraceptive services: Estimates for 2012*. Guttmacher Institute and United Nations Population Fund (UNFPA). Retrieved May 24, 2014, from http://www.guttmacher.org/pubs/AIU-2012-estimates.pdf.

Singh, S., Sedgh, G., & Hussain, R. (2010). Unintended pregnancy: Worldwide levels, trends and outcomes. *Studies in Family Planning, 41*(4), 241–250.

Sipski, M., Alexander, C., & Gomez-Marin, O. (2006). Effects of level and degree of spinal cord injury on male orgasm. *Spinal Cord, 44*, 798–804.

Skakkebaek, A., Wallentin, M., & Gravholt, C. (2015). Neuropsychology and socioeconomic aspects of Klinefelter syndrome: New developments. *Current Opinion in Endocrinology, Diabetes, and Obesity, 22*(3), 209–216.

Skakkebaek, N. (2016). A brief review of the link between environment and male reproductive health: Lessons from studies of testicular germ cell cancer. *Hormone Research in Paediatrics, 86,* 240–246.

Skakkebaek, N., Rajpert-DeMeyts, E., Buck, L., Toppari, J., Andersson, A., Eisenberg, M., Jensen, T., Jorgensen, N., Swan, S., Sapra, K., et al. (2016). Reproductive disorders and fertility trends: Influences of environment and genetic susceptibility. *Physiological Reviews, 96*(1), 55–97.

Skerrett, D. M., Kõlves, K., & DeLeo, D. (2016). Factors related to suicide in LGBT populations, *Crisis, 37*(5), 361–369.

Skinner, A., Hudac, C. (2016). "Yuck, you disgust me!" Affective bias against interracial couples. *Journal of Experimental Social Psychology, 68,* 68–77.

Skinner, B. F. (1953). *Science and human behavior.* New York: Macmillan.

Skoog, T., & Özdemir, S. (2016). Explaining why early-maturing girls are more exposed to sexual harassment in early adolescence. *The Journal of Early Adolescence, 36*(4), 490–509.

Skorska, M., & Bogaert, A. (2016). Pubertal stress and nutrition and their association with sexual orientation and height in the ADD health data. *Archives of Sexual Behavior, 46*(1), 217–236.

Skovlund, C., Mørch, L., & Kessing, L. (2016). Association of hormonal contraception with depression. *Journal of the American Medical Association, 73*(11), 1154–1162.

Slavney, P. R. (1990). *Perspectives on hysteria.* Baltimore, MD: Johns Hopkins University Press.

Slevin, K. F. (2010). "If I had lots of money...I'd have a body makeover": Managing the aging body. *Social Forces, 88*(3), 1003–1020.

Smith, B., Armelie, A., Boarts, J., Brazil, M., Delahanty, D. (2016). PTSD, depression, and substance use in relation to suicidality risk among traumatized minority lesbian, gay, and bisexual youth. *Archives of Suicide Research, 20*(1), 80–93.

Smith, C. J., McMahon, C., & Shabsigh, R. (2005). Peyronie's disease: The epidemiology, aetiology and clinical evaluation of deformity. *British Journal of Urology International, 95*(6), 729–732.

Smith, D. K., Taylor, A., Kilmarx, P. H., Sullivan, P., Warner, L., Kamb, M., Bock, N., Kohmescher, B., & Mastro, T. D. (2010). Male circumcision in the United States for the prevention of HIV infection and other adverse health outcomes: Report from a CDC consultation. *Public Health Report, 25*(Suppl. 1), 72–82.

Smith, J. L. (2016). Counseling for empowerment: Working with girls, parents, and women dealing with Turner's syndrome. *Social Work & Christianity, 42*(4), 488–496.

Smith, K. (2015). Paternal age bioethics. *Journal of Medical Ethics, 41*(9), 775–779.

Smith, K., & Pukall, C. (2014). Sexual function, relationship adjustment, and the relationship impact of pain in male partners of women with provoked vulvar pain. *Journal of Sexual Medicine, 11*(5), 1283–1293.

Smith, K. T. (1971). Homophobia: A tentative personality profile. *Psychological Reports, 29,* 1091–1094.

Smith, L. E. (2010). Sexual function of the gynecologic cancer survivor. *Oncology, 24*(10 Suppl.), 41–44.

Smith, M. (2013). Youth viewing sexually explicit material online: Addressing the elephant on the screen. *Sexuality Research & Social Policy, 10*(1), 62–75.

Smith, S. A., & Michel, Y. (2006). A pilot study on the effects of aquatic exercises on discomforts of pregnancy. *Journal of Obstetrics and Gynecological Neonatal Nursing, 35,* 315–323.

Smith, S., Chen, J., Basile, K., Gilbert, L., Merrick, M., Patel, N., Walling, M., & Jain, A. (2017). The national intimate partner and sexual violence survey (NISVS): 2010–2012 State Report, National Center for Injury Prevention and Control, Centers for Disease Control and Prevention. Atlanta, GA.

Snapp, S., Ryu, E., & Kerr, J. (2015). The upside to hooking up: College students' positive hookup experiences. *International Journal of Sexual Health, 27*(1), 43–56.

So, H. W., & Cheung, F. M. (2005). Review of Chinese sex attitudes & applicability of sex therapy for Chinese couples with sexual dysfunction. *Journal of Sex Research, 42*(2), 93–102.

Soares, C. (2010). Can depression be a menopause-associated risk? *BMC Medicine, 8,* 79.

Sobsey, D. (1994). *Violence and abuse in the lives of people with disabilities.* Baltimore, MD: Paul H. Brookes.

Society for the Advancement of Sexual Health. (2008). *Public service announcement: Sexual addiction.* Retrieved October 2, 2008, from http://www.sash.net/.

Sohrabi, N., Kashanian, M., Ghafoori, S., & Malakouti, S. (2013). Evaluation of the effect of omega-3 fatty acids in the treatment of premenstrual syndrome. *Complementary Therapies in Medicine, 21*(3), 141–146.

Soley, L., & Kurzbard, G. (1986). Sex in advertising: A comparison of 1964 and 1984 magazine advertisements. *Journal of Advertising, 15,* 46–54.

Solis, S. (2016, June 19). Voices: ISIL or not, Orlando shooting was hate crime against LGBT people. *USA Today.* Retrieved March 24, 2017, from http://www.usatoday.com/story/opinion/voices/2016/06/19/voices-orlando-shooting-hate-crime-lgbt/85940494/.

Soloman, S. E., Rothblum, D., & Balsam, K. F. (2005). Money, housework, sex, and conflict: Same-sex couples in civil unions, those not in civil unions, and heterosexual married siblings. *Sex Roles, 52,* 561–575.

Sommerfeld, J. (1999). Megan's Law expands to the Internet. Retrieved March 31, 2003, from http://www.msnbc.com/news/297969.asp?cp1=1.

Song, A., & Halpern-Felsher, B. (2011). Predictive relationship between adolescent oral and vaginal sex: Results from a prospective, longitudinal study. *Archives of Pediatrics and Adolescent Medicine, 165*(3), 243–249.

Sontag, S. (1979). The double-standard of aging. In J. H. Williams (Ed.), *Psychology of women: Selected readings* (pp. 462–478). New York: W. W. Norton Publishers.

Sorenson, S., & Brown, V. (1990). Interpersonal violence and crisis intervention on the college campus. *New Directions for Student Services, 49,* 57–66.

Sorokowska, A., Oleszkiewica, A., Frackowiak, T., Pisanski, K., Chmiel, A., & Sorokowski, P. (2016). Selfies and personality: Who posts self-portrait photographs? *Personality and Individual Differences, 90,* 119–123.

Sotirin, P. (2000). All they do is bitch, bitch, bitch: Political and interactional features of women's office talk. *Women and Language, 23*(2), 19.

Spack, N., Edwards-Leeper, L., Feldman, H., Leibowitz, S., Mandel, F., Diamond, D., & Vance, W. (2012). Children and adolescents with gender identity disorder referred to a pediatric medical center. *Pediatrics, 129*(3), 418–425.

Specht, I., Toft, G., Hougaard, K., Lindh, V., Jönsson, B., Heederik, D., Giwercman, A., & Bonde, J. (2014). Associations between serum phthalates and biomarkers of reproductive function in 589 adult men. *Environment International, 66,* 146–156.

Speck, N., Boechat, K., Santos, G., & Ribalta, J. (2016). Treatment of bartholin gland cyst with CO2laser. *Einstein, 14*(1), 25–29.

Spence, J. T. (1984). Gender identity and its implications for the concepts of masculinity and femininity. In T. B. Sonderegger (Ed.), *Psychology and gender* (pp. 59–95). Lincoln: University of Nebraska Press.

Spolan, S. (1991, March 22). Oh, by the way. *Philadelphia City Paper,* p. 7.

Sprankle, E., Bloomquist, K., Butcher, C., Gleason, N., & Schaefer, Z. (2017). The role of sex work stigma in victim blaming and empathy of sexual assault survivors. *Sexuality Research & Social Policy*. Retrieved from https://www.springerprofessional.de/en/the-role-of-sex-work-stigma-in-victim-blaming-and-empathy-of-sex/12176292.

Sprecher, S., & Hendrick, S. (2004). Self-disclosure in intimate relationships: Associations with individual and relationship characteristics over time. *Journal of Social and Clinical Psychology, 23*(6), 857–877.

Sprecher, S., & Regan, P. (1996). College virgins: How men and women perceive their sexual status. *Journal of Sex Research, 33*(1), 3–16.

Sprecher, S., & Toto-Morn, M. (2002). A study of men and women from different sides of earth to determine if men are from Mars and women are from Venus in their beliefs about love and romantic relationships. *Sex Roles, 46*(5–6), 131–147.

Sprecher, S., Cate, R., & Levin, L. (1998). Parental divorce and young adults' beliefs about love. *Journal of Divorce & Remarriage, 28*(3–4), 107–120.

Sprecher, S., Treger, S., Wondra, J., Hilaire, N., & Wallpe, K. (2013). Taking turns: Reciprocal self-disclosure promotes liking in initial interactions. *Journal of Experimental Social Psychology, 49*(5), 860–866.

Srinivasan, P., & Lee, G. R. (2004). The dowry system in Northern India: Woman's attitudes and social change. *Journal of Marriage and the Family, 66*(5), 1108–1118.

Srivastava, R., Thakar, R., & Sultan, A. (2008). Female sexual dysfunction in obstetrics and gynecology. *Obstetrics and Gynecology Survey, 63*, 527–537.

St Pierre, M., & Senn, C. (2010). External barriers to help-seeking encountered by Canadian gay and lesbian victims of intimate partner abuse: An application of the barriers model. *Violence and Victims, 25*(4), 536–551.

Stabile, C., Gunn, A., Sonoda, Y., & Carter, J. (2015). Emotional and sexual concerns in women undergoing pelvic surgery and associated treatment for gynecologic cancer. *Translational Andrology and Urology, 4*(2), 169–185.

Stacey, D. (2008). No more periods: The safety of continuous birth control. Retrieved March 18, 2008, from http://contraception.about.com/od/prescriptionoptions/p/MissingPeriods.htm.

Stacey, M. (2011). Distinctive characteristics of sexual orientation bias crimes. *Journal of Interpersonal Violence, 26*(15), 3013–3032.

Stafford, L., & Merolla, A. (2007). Idealization, reunions, and stability in long-distance dating relationships. *Journal of Social and Personal Relationships, 24*(1), 37–54.

Stanger, J. D., Vo, L., Yovich, J. L., & Almahbobi, G. (2010). Hypo-osmotic swelling test identifies individual spermatozoa with minimal DNA fragmentation. *Reproductive Biomedicine Online, 21*(4), 474–484.

Staples, J., Eakins, D., Neilson, E., George, W., Davis, K., & Norris, J. (2016). Sexual assault disclosure and sexual functioning. The role of trauma symptomatology. *Journal of Sexual Medicine, 13*(10), 1562–1569.

Starecheski, L. (2014, August 18). The power of the peer group in preventing campus rape. National Public Radio. Retrieved August 18, 2014, from http://www.npr.org/blogs/health/2014/08/18/339593542/the-power-of-the-peer-group-in-preventing-campus-rape.

Stark, R. (1996). *The rise of Christianity*. Princeton, NJ: Princeton University Press.

Starkman, N., & Rajani, N. (2002). The case for comprehensive sex education. *AIDS Patient Care and STDs, 16*(7), 313–318.

Starling, K. (1999). How to bring the romance back. *Ebony, 54*(4), 136–137.

"Statistics on Perpetrators." (2012). Statistics on Perpetrators of Child Sexual Abuse. The National Center for Victims of Crime. Retrieved from https://victimsofcrime.org/media/reporting-on-child-sexual-abuse/statistics-on-perpetrators-of-csa.

Steen, S., & Schwartz, P. (1995). Communication, gender, and power: Homosexual couples as a case study. In M. A. Fitzpatrick & A. L. Vangelisti (Eds.), *Explaining family interactions* (pp. 310–343). Thousand Oaks, CA: Sage.

Steensma, T., van der Ende, J., Verhulst, F., & Cohen-Kettenis, P. (2013). Gender variance in childhood and sexual orientation in adulthood: A prospective study. *Journal of Sexual Medicine, 10*(11), 2723–2733.

Steers, M., Quist, M., Bryan, J., Foster, D., Young, C., & Neighbors, C. (2016). I want you to like me: Extraversion, need for approval and time on Facebook as predictors of anxiety. *Translational Issues in Psychological Science, 2*(3), 283–293.

Steiger, H., Richardson, J., Schmitz, N., Israel, M., et al. (2010). Trait-defined eating disorder subtypes and history of childhood abuse. *International Journal of Eating Disorders, 43*(5), 428–432.

Stein, J. H., & Reiser, L. W. (1994). A study of white, middle-class adolescent boys' responses to 'semenarche'. *Journal of Youth and Adolescence, 23*(3), 373–384.

Steinauer, J., & Autry, A. (2007). Extended cycle combined hormonal contraception. *Obstetrics and Gynecological Clinics of North America, 34*(1), 43–55.

Steiner, A. Z., D'Aloisio, A. A., DeRoo, L. A., Sandler, D. P., & Baird, D. D. (2010). Association of intrauterine and early-life exposures with age at menopause in the Sister Study. *American Journal of Epidemiology, 172*(2), 140–148.

Stengers, J., & Van Neck, A. (2001). *Masturbation: The history of a great terror*. New York: Palgrave/St. Martins.

Stephens, S., Bernstein, K., & Philip, S. (2011). Male to female and female to male transgender persons have different sexual risk behaviors yet similar rates of STDs and HIV. *AIDS and Behavior, 15*(3), 683–686.

Stephenson, J. M., Imrie, J., Davis, M. M., Mercer, C., Black, S., et al. (2003). Is use of antiretroviral therapy among homosexual men associated with increased risk of transmission of HIV infection? *Sexually Transmitted Diseases, 79*(1), 7–10.

Stephenson, K., Ahrold, T., & Meston, C. (2011). The association between sexual motives and sexual satisfaction: Gender differences and categorical comparisons. *Archives of Sexual Behavior, 40*(3), 607–618.

Stephenson, K., Pulverman, C., & Meston, C. (2014). Assessing the association between childhood sexual abuse and adult sexual experiences in women with sexual difficulties. *Journal of Traumatic Stress, 27*, 274–282.

Stergiakouli, E., Thapar, A., & Davey-Smith, G. (2016). Association of acetaminophen use during pregnancy with behavioral problems in childhood: Evidence against confounding. *JAMA Pediatrics, 170*(1), 964–970.

Stern, B., Russell, C., & Russell, D. (2007). Hidden persuasions in soap operas: Damaged heroines and negative consumer effects. *International Journal of Advertising, 26*(1), 9–36.

Stern, C., West, T., Jost, J., & Rule, N. (2013). The politics of gaydar: Ideological differences in the use of gendered cues in categorizing sexual orientation. *Journal of Personality and Social Psychology, 104*(3), 520–541.

Sternberg, R. J. (1985): *Beyond IQ: A triarchic theory of human intelligence*. New York: Cambridge University Press.

Sternberg, R. J. (1987). Liking versus loving: A comparative evaluation of theories. *Psychological Bulletin, 102*(3), 331–345.

Sternberg, R. J. (1998). *Cupid's arrow: The course of love through time*. New Haven, CT: Yale University Press.

Sternberg, R. J. (1999). *Love is a story*. New York: Oxford University Press.

Sternberg, S. (2006). Once-a-day drug cocktail—in one pill—wins FDA approval. *USAToday*. Retrieved October 8, 2008, from http://www.usatoday.com/news/health/2006-07-12-hiv-pill_x.htm.

Stevens, A. (2014, April 12). Polyamory works for us. *Salon*. Retrieved April 20, 2014, from http://www.salon.com/2014/04/12/polyamory_works_for_us.

Stevenson, B., & Isen, A. (2010). Who's getting married? Education and marriage today and in the past. A briefing paper prepared for the Council on Contemporary Families, January 26, 2010. Retrieved January 29, 2011, from http://www.contemporaryfamilies.org/images/stories/homepage/orange_border/ccf012510.pdf.

Stevenson, B., & Wolfers, J. (2007). Marriage and divorce: Changes and their driving forces. *Journal of Economic Perspectives*, 21(2), 27–52.

Stewart, D., Vigod, S., & Riazantseva, E. (2016). New developments in intimate partner violence and management of its mental health sequelae. *Current Psychiatry Reports*, 18(1), 4.

Stewart, F., & Gabelnick, H. L. (2004). Contraceptive research and development. In R. A. Hatcher et al. (Eds.), *Contraceptive technology* (18th rev. ed., pp. 601–616). New York: Ardent Media.

Stewart, H. (2005). Senoritas and princesses: The quinceanera as a context for female development. *Dissertation Abstracts*, 65(7-A), 2770, #0419–4209.

Stewart, J. (1990). *The complete manual of sexual positions*. Chatsworth, CA: Media Press.

Stillwell, L. (2010). To date or not to date? Religious and racial dating choices among conservative Christians. Denton, TX: University of North Texas, AAT 3436546.

Stochholm, K., Juul, S., & Gravholt, C. (2013). Poor socio-economic status in 47, XXX—an unexpected effect of an extra X chromosome. *European Journal of Medical Genetics*, 56(6), 286–291.

Stokes, C., & Ellison, C. (2010). Religion and attitudes toward divorce laws among U.S. adults. *Journal of Family Issues*, 31(10), 1279–1304.

Stoller, R. J. (1991). The term perversion. In G. I. Fogel & W. A. Myers (Eds.), *Perversions and near-perversions in clinical practice: New psychoanalytic perspectives* (pp. 36–58). New Haven, CT: Yale University Press.

Stoller, R. J. (1996). The gender disorders. In I. Rosen (Ed.), *Sexual deviation* (3rd ed., pp. 111–133). London: Oxford University Press.

Stoller, R. J., & Herdt, G. H. (1985). Theories of origins of male homosexuality. *Archives of General Psychiatry*, 42, 399–404.

Storgaard, L., Bonde, J. P., Ernst, E., Spano, M., Andersen, C. Y., Frydenberg, M., & Olsen, J. (2003). Does smoking during pregnancy affect sons' sperm counts? *Epidemiology*, 14(3), 278–286.

Storm, L. (2011). Nurturing touch helps mothers with postpartum depression and their infants. Interview by Deb Discenza. *Neonatal Network*, 30(1), 71–72.

Storms, M. D. (1980). Theories of sexual orientation. *Journal of Personality and Social Psychology*, 38, 783–792.

Storms, M. D. (1981). A theory of erotic orientation development. *Psychological Review*, 88, 340–353.

Strand, L. B., Barnett, A. G., & Tong, S. (2011). The influence of season and ambient temperature on birth outcomes: A review of the epidemiological literature. *Environmental Research*, 111, 451–462.

Strandberg, K., Peterson, M., Schaefers, M., Case, L., Pack, M., Chase, D., & Schlievert, P. (2009). Reduction in staphylococcus aureus growth and exotoxin production and in vaginal interleukin 8 levels due to glycerol monolaurate in tampons. *Clinics in Infectious Diseases*, 49(11), 1718–1717.

Strandjord, S., & Rome, E. (2015). Monthly periods—Are they necessary? *Pediatric Annals*, 44(9), 231–236.

Strasburger, V. C., & The Council on Communications and Media. (2010). Sexuality, contraception, and the media. *Pediatrics*, 126, 576–582.

Stratton, K., & Culkin, D. (2016). A contemporary review of HPV and penile cancer. *Oncology*, 30(3), 245–249.

Strauss, G. (2010). Sex on TV: It's increasingly uncut and unavoidable. *USA Today*. Retrieved May 3, 2011, from http://www.usatoday.com/life/television/news/2010-01-20-sexcov20_CV_N.htm#.

Strickler, J. (2010, December 21). More couples saying 'I do' to prenups. *Chicago Tribune*. Retrieved May 11, 2011, from http://articles.chicagotribune.com/2010-12-21/travel/sc-fam-1221-prenup-20101221_1_prenups-moss-barnett-second-marriages.

Strommen, E. (1993). "You're a what?": Family member reactions to the disclosure of homosexuality. In L. D. Garnets and D. C. Kimmel (Eds.), *Psychological perspectives on lesbian and gay male experiences* (pp. 248–266). New York, NY: Columbia University Press.

Stromsvik, N., Raheim, M., Oyen, N., Engebretsen, L., & Gjengedal, E. (2010). Stigmatization and male identity: Norwegian males' experience after identification as BRCA1/2 mutation carriers. *Journal of Genetic Counseling*, 19(4), 360.

Struble, C. B., Lindley, L. L., Montgomery, K., Hardin, J., & Burcin, M. (2010). Overweight and obesity in lesbian and bisexual college women. *Journal of American College Health*, 59(1), 51–56.

Struckman-Johnson, C., & Struckman-Johnson, D. (1994). Men pressured and forced into sexual experience. *Archives of Sexual Behavior*, 23, 93–115.

Struckman-Johnson, C., & Struckman-Johnson, D. (2002). Sexual coercion reported by women in three midwestern prisons. *Journal of Sex Research*, 39(3), 217–227.

Strudwick, P. (2014, January 4). Crisis in South Africa: The shocking practice of "corrective rape"—aimed at "curing" lesbians. *The Independent*. Retrieved March 20, 2017, from http://www.independent.co.uk/news/world/africa/crisis-in-south-africa-the-shocking-practice-of-corrective-rape-aimed-at-curing-lesbians-9033224.html.

Strunz, S., Schermuck, C., Ballerstein, S., Ahlers, C., Dziobek, I., & Roepke, S. (2017). Romantic relationships and relationship satisfaction among adults with Asperger syndrome and high-functioning autism. *Journal of Clinical Psychology*, 73(1), 113–125.

Stuebe, A. M., Willett, W. C., Xue, F., & Michels, K. B. (2009). Lactation and incidence of premenopausal breast cancer. *Archives of Internal Medicine*, 169(15), 1364–1371.

Stumpe, J., & Davey, M. (2009, May 31). Abortion doctor shot to death in Kansas church. *New York Times*. Retrieved March 14, 2011, from http://www.nytimes.com/2009/06/01/us/01tiller.html.

Stuyvesant, R., Mercier, D., & Haidle, A. (2014). Voyeurism: A case study. In W. O'Donohue (Ed.), *Case studies in sexual deviance: Toward evidence-based practice* (pp. 117–148). New York: Routledge.

Su, J., Berman, S., Davis, D., Weinstock, H., & Kirkcaldy, R. (2010). Congenital syphilis, US, 2003–2008. Centers for Disease Control and Prevention. *MMWR Morbidity and Mortality Weekly Report*, 59, 413–417.

Subramaniam, A., Singh, R., Tilak, P., Devi, R., Kulandaivelu, M., & Kumarasamy, T. (2013). Androgen insensitivity syndrome: Ten years of our experience. *Frontiers in Bioscience*, 5(1), 779–784.

Sugimoto, C. R. (2013). Global gender disparities in science. *Nature*, 504(7479), 211–213.

Sugrue, D. P., & Whipple, B. (2001) The consensus-based classification of female sexual dysfunction: Barriers to universal acceptance. *Journal of Sex and Marital Therapy*, 27, 232.

Sukel, K. (2012). *Dirty minds: How our brains influence love, sex, and relationships*. New York, NY: Free Press Publishers.

Sulak, P. J., Scow, R. D., Preece, C., Riggs, M., & Kuehl, T. (2000). Withdrawal Symptoms in Oral Contraceptive Users. *Obstetrics & Gynecology*, 95, 261–266.

Sullivan, P. S., Drake, A. J., & Sanchez, T. H. (2007). Prevalence of treatment optimism-related risk behavior and associated factors among men who have sex with men in 11 states, 2000–2001. *AIDS Behavior*, 11(1), 123–129.

Sullivan, S., Sarrel, P., & Nelson, L. (2016). Hormone replacement therapy in young women with primary ovarian insufficiency and early menopause. *Fertility and Sterility*, 106(7), 1588–1599.

Sun, Z., Huang, J., Yang, D., Cao, X., & Zhou, W. (2014). Activation of B-adrenergic receptors during sexual arousal facilitates vaginal lubrication by regulating vaginal epithelial C1 secretion. *Journal of Sexual Medicine*. Retrieved June 2, 2014, from http://nlinelibrary.wiley.com/doi/10.1111/jsm.12583/abstract.

Sunderam, S., Kissin, D., Crawford, S., Anderson, J., Folger, S., Jamieson, D., & Barfield, W. (2013).

Assisted reproductive technology surveillance—U.S., 2010. *Morbidity and Mortality Weekly Report, 62*(SS09), 1–24.

Sunderam, S., Kissin, D., Crawford, S., Folger, S., Jamieson, D., Warner, L., & Barfield, W. (2015). Assisted reproductive technology surveillance—United States, 2012. *Morbidity and Mortality Weekly Report, 64* (SS06), 1–29.

Sungur, M., & Gündüz, A. (2014). A comparison of DSM-IV-TR and DSM-5 definitions for sexual dysfunctions: Critiques and challenges. *Journal of Sexual Medicine, 11*(2), 364–373.

Supornsilchai, V., Jantarat, C., Nosoognoen, W., Pornkunwilai, S., Wacharasindhu, S., & Soder, O. (2016). Increased levels of bisphenol A (BPA) in Thai girls with precocious puberty. *Journal of Pediatric Endocrinology and Metabolism, 29*(11), 1233–1239.

Suppe, F. (1984). Classifying sexual disorders: The diagnostic and statistical manual of the American Psychiatric Association. *Journal of Homosexuality, 9,* 9–28.

Surveillance for viral hepatitis. (2016). Statistics and Surveillance. Centers for Disease Control and Prevention. Retrieved April 24, 2017, from https://www.cdc.gov/hepatitis/statistics/2014surveillance/pdfs/2014hepsurveillancerpt_rev2016-09-26.pdf.

Suschinsky, K., Bossio, J., & Chivers, M. (2014). Women's genital sexual arousal to oral versus penetrative heterosexual sex varies with menstrual cycle phase at first exposure. *Hormones and Behavior, 65*(3), 319–327.

Sutphin, S. T. (2010). Social exchange theory and the division of household labor in same-sex couples. *Marriage and Family Review, 46*(3), 191–209.

Svoboda, E. (2006, December 5). All the signs of pregnancy except one: A baby. Retrieved from http://www.nytimes.com/2006/12/05/health/05pseud.html.

Svoboda, E. (2011). Breaking up is hard to do. *Psychology Today, 44*(1), 64.

Swaab, D. F. (2004). Sexual differentiation of the human brain: Relevance for gender identity, transsexualism and sexual orientation. *Gynecological Endocrinology, 19*(6), 201–312.

Swaab, D. F., & Hofman, M. A. (1990). An enlarged suprachiasmatic nucleus in homosexual men. *Brain Research, 537,* 141–148.

Swami, V., & Furnham, A. (2008). *The Psychology of Physical Attraction.* New York: Routledge/Taylor & Francis Group.

Swanson, J. M., Dibble, S., & Chapman, L. (1999). Effects of psychoeducational interventions on sexual health risks and psychosocial adaptation in young adults with genital herpes. *Journal of Advanced Nursing, 29*(4), 840–851.

Swartout, K., Koss, M., & White, J. (2015). Trajectory analysis of the campus serial rapist assumption. *JAMA Pediatrics, 169*(12), 1148–1154.

Swearingen, S., & Klausner, J. D. (2005). Sildenafil use, sexual risk behavior, and risk for sexually transmitted diseases, including HIV infection. *American Journal of Medicine, 118,* 571–577.

Sylva, D., Safron, A., Rosenthal, A., Reber, P., Parrish, T., & Bailey, J. (2013). Neural correlates of sexual arousal in heterosexual and homosexual women and men. *Hormones and Behavior, 121*(2), 673–684.

Szymanski, D. M., Chung, Y., & Balsam, K. (2001). Psychosocial correlates of internalized homophobia in lesbians. *Measurement and Evaluation in Counseling and Development, 34*(1), 27–39.

Taft, C., Resick, P., Watkins, L., & Panuzio, J. (2009). An investigation of posttraumatic stress disorder and depressive symptomatology among female victims of interpersonal trauma. *Journal of Family Violence, 24*(6), 407–416.

Tait, R. (2005, July 28). A fatwa for transsexuals. *Salon.* Retrieved December 14, 2010, from http://dir.salon.com/story/news/feature/2005/07/28/iran_transsexuals.

Talib, R., Ibrahim, M., & Cangüven, O. (2016). Nonsurgical treatment options in peyronie's disease: 2016 update. *Turkish Journal of Urology, 42*(4), 217–223.

Talley, A., Hughes, T., Aranda, F., Birkett, M., & Marshal, M. (2014). Exploring alcohol-use behaviors among heterosexual and sexual minority adolescents: Intersections with sex, age, and race/ethnicity. *Psychology of Addictive Behaviors, 25*(3), 530–541.

Talwar, G. P., Vyas, H. K., Purswani, S., & Gupta, J. C. (2009). Gonadotropin-releasing hormone/human chorionic gonadotropin beta based recombinant antibodies and vaccines. *Journal of Reproductive Immunology, 83*(1–2), 158–163.

Tamburrino, L., Marchiani, S., Minetti, F., Forti, G., Muratori, M., & Baldi, E. (2014). The catsper calcium channel in human sperm. *Human Reproduction, 29*(3), 418–428.

Tang, S., & Gui, G. (In press). A review of the oncologic and survival management of breast cancer in the augmented breast: Diagnostic, surgical, and surveillance challenges. *Annals of Surgical Oncology.*

Tannahill, R. (1980). *Sex in history.* New York: Stein & Day.

Tannen, D. (1990). *You just don't understand: Women and men in conversation.* New York: Ballantine Books.

Tannen, D., Kendall, S., & Gordon, C. (2007). *Family talk: Discourse and identity in four American families.* New York: Oxford University Press.

Tanveer, K. (2002, July 7). In Pakistan, gang rape as a tribal punishment. *The Hartford Courant,* A2.

Tanweer, M., Fatima, A., & Rahimnaijad, M. (2010). Yohimbine can be the new promising therapy for erectile dysfunction in type 2 diabetics. *Journal of the Pakistan Medical Association, 60*(11), 980.

Tao, G. (2008). Sexual orientation and related viral sexually transmitted disease rates among U.S. women aged 15–44 years. *American Journal of Public Health, 98,* 1007–1009.

Tao, P., & Brody, S. (2011). Sexual behavior predictors of satisfaction in a Chinese sample. *Journal of Sexual Medicine, 8*(2), 455–460.

Tarantola, A. (2015, June 24). Color-changing condoms could tell which VD you just got. Engadget. Retrieved April 28, 2017, from https://www.engadget.com/2015/06/24/color-changing-condoms/.

Tarin, J., Hermenegildo, C., García-Pérez, M., & Cano, A. (2013). Endocrinology and physiology of pseudocyesis. *Reproductive Biology and Endocrinology, 11*(39). Retrieved May 21, 2014, from http://www.rbej.com/content/11/1/39.

Tarkovsky, A. (2006). Sperm taste: 10 simple tips for better tasting semen. Ezine articles. Retrieved August 10, 2008, from http://ezinearticles.com/?Sperm-Taste—-10-Simple-Tips-For-Better-Tasting-Semen&id=164106.

Tay, J. I., Moore, J., & Walker, J. J. (2000). Ectopic pregnancy. *British Medical Journal, 320*(7239), 916–920.

Taylor, A., Nesheim, S., Zhang, X., Song, R., FitzHarris, L., Lampe, M., Weidle, P., & Sweeney, P. (2017). Estimated perinatal HIV infection among infants born in the United States, 2002–2013. *JAMA Pediatrics.* Retrieved April 29, 2017, from https://www.ncbi.nlm.nih.gov/pubmed/28319246.

Taylor, E., Banyard, V., Grych, J., & Hamby, S. (2016). Not all behind closed doors: Examining bystander involvement in intimate partner violence. *Journal of Interpersonal Violence.* Retrieved from http://journals.sagepub.com/doi/abs/10.1177/0886260516673629.

Taylor, H. E. (2000). Meeting the needs of lesbian and gay young adults. *The Clearing House, 73*(4), 221.

Taylor, J. (2007). Transgender identities and public policy in the U.S.: The relevance for public administration. *Administration & Society, 39*(7), 833–856.

Taywaditep, K. J., Coleman, E., & Dumronggittigule, P. (2004). Thailand. In R. T. Francoeur & R. J. Noonan (Eds.), *The Continuum complete international encyclopedia of sexuality* (pp. 1021–1053). New York/London: Continuum International.

Team, T. (2014, June 18). Is Google Glass the next big money maker? *Forbes.* Retrieved June 17, 2014, from http://www.forbes.com/sites/greatspeculations/2014/06/18/is-google-glass-the-next-big-money-maker.

Tebbe, E., & Moradi, B. (2016). Suicide risk in trans populations: An application of minority stress theory. *Journal of Counseling Psychology, 63*, 520–533.

Teitelman, A. (2004). Adolescent girls' perspectives of family interactions related to menarche and sexual health. *Qualitative Health Research, 14*(9), 1292–1308.

Teles, M., Bianco, S., Brito, V., Trarbach, E., Kuohung, W., Xu, S., Seminara, S., Mendonca, B., Kaiser, U., & Latronico, A. (2008). A GPR54-activiting mutation in a patient with central preconscious puberty. *New England Journal of Medicine, 358*, 709–715.

Telles, D. P., Souto, K., & Page-Shafer, K. (2006). Long-term female condom use among vulnerable populations in Brazil. *AIDS Behavior, 10*(Suppl. 4), 67–75.

Tenbergen, G., Wittfoth, M., Frieling, H., Ponseti, J., Walter, M., Beier, K., Schiffer, B., & Kruger, T. (2015). The neurobiology and psychology of pedophilia: Recent advances and challenges. *Frontiers in Human Neuroscience, 9*, 344. Retrieved May 1, 2017, from https://www.ncbi.nlm.nih.gov/pmc/articles/PMC4478390/.

Tenore, J. L. (2000). Ectopic pregnancy. *American Family Physician, 61*(4), 1080–1088.

Tepavcevic, D., Kostic, J., Basuroski, I., Stojsavljevic, N., Pekmezovic, T., & Drulovic, J. (2008). The impact of sexual dysfunction on the quality of life measured by MSQoL-54 in patients with multiple sclerosis. *Multiple Sclerosis, 14*(8), 1131–1136.

Terada, Y., Schatten, G., Hasegawa, H., & Yaegashi, N. (2010). Essential roles of the sperm centrosome in human fertilization: Developing the therapy for fertilization failure due to sperm centrosomal dysfunction. *Tohoku Journal of Experimental Medicine, 220*(4), 247–258.

Terasawa, E., Kurian, J., Keen, K., Shiel, N., Colman, R., & Capuano, S. (2012). Body weight impact on puberty: Effects of high-calorie diet on puberty onset in female rhesus monkeys. *Endocrinology, 153*(4), 1696–1705.

Terry, J. (1990). Lesbians under the medical gaze: Scientists search for remarkable differences. *The Journal of Sex Research, 27*, 317–339.

Teuscher, U., & Teuscher, C. (2006). Reconsidering the double standard of aging: Effects of gender and sexual orientation on facial attractiveness ratings. *Personality and Individual Differences, 42*(4), 631–639.

Tewksbury, R. (2007). Effects of sexual assaults on men: Physical, mental and sexual consequences. *International Journal of Men's Health, 6*, 22–36.

Thakar, R. (2015). Is the uterus a sexual organ? Sexual function following hysterectomy. *Sexual Medicine Reviews, 3*(4), 264–278.

Tharp, A., DeGue, S., Valle, L., Brookmeyer, K., Massetti, G., & Matjasko, J. (2013). A systematic qualitative review of risk and protective factors for sexual violence perpetration. *Trauma Violence and Abuse, 14*(2), 133–167.

Theodorou, A., & Sandstrom, A. (2015). How abortion is regulated around the world. Pew Research Center. Retrieved April 12, 2017, from http://www.pewresearch.org/fact-tank/2015/10/06/how-abortion-is-regulated-around-the-world/.

Thomas, E. (2014, January 21). Google Glass sex app lets you watch, record yourself in the act. *Huffington Post*. Retrieved June 17, 2014, from http://www.huffingtonpost.com/2014/01/21/google-glass-sex_n_4637741.html.

Thomas, H., & Thurston, R. (2016). A biopsychosocial approach to women's sexual function and dysfunction at midlife: A narrative review. *Maturitas, 87*, 49–60.

Thomas, H., Chang, C., Dillon, S., & Hess, R. (2014). Sexual activity in midlife women: Importance of sex matters. *JAMA Internal Medicine, 174*(4), 631–633.

Thomas, S. L., & Ellertson, C. (2000). Nuisance or natural and healthy: Should monthly menstruation be optional for women? *Lancet, 355*, 922–924.

Thomasset, C. (1992). The nature of woman. In C. Klapisch-Zuber (Ed.), *A history of women in the West, Volume II: Silences of the Middle Ages* (pp. 43–70). Cambridge, U.K.: Belknap Press.

Thompson, A. P. (1984). Emotional and sexual components of extramarital relations. *Journal of Marriage and the Family, 46*, 35–42.

Thompson, K. M. (2009). Sibling incest: A model for group practice with adult female victims of brother-sister incest. *Journal of Family Violence, 24*, 531–537.

Thompson, P. (2008). Desperate housewives? Communication difficulties and the dynamics of marital (un)happiness. *The Economic Journal, 118*(532), 1640–1669.

Thompson, S. J. (2005). Factors associated with trauma symptoms among runaway/homeless adolescents. *Stress, Trauma and Crisis: An International Journal, 8*(2–3), 143–156.

Thorbjarnardottir, T., Olafsdottir, E., Valdimarsdottir, U., Olafsson, O., & Tryggvadottir, L. (2014). Oral contraceptives, hormone replacement therapy and breast cancer risk. *Acta Oncologica, 53*(6), 752–758.

Thorne, N., & Amrein, H. (2003). Vomeronasal organ: Pheromone recognition with a twist. *Current Biology, 13*(6), R220–R222.

Thornhill, R., & Palmer, C. T. (2000). *A natural history of rape: Biological bases of sexual coercion*. Boston: MIT Press.

Thorpe, P., Gilboa, S., Hernandez-Diaz, S., Loind, J., Cragean, J., Briggs, G., Kweder, S., Friedman, J., Mitchell, A., & Honein, M. (2013). Medications in the first trimester of pregnancy: Most common exposures and critical gaps in understanding fetal risk. *Pharmacoepidemiology and Drug Safety, 22*(90), 1013–1018.

Thorsen, M. L. (2016). The adolescent family environment and cohabitation across the transition to adulthood. *Social Science Research*. In Press. Retrieved January 9, 2017, from http://www.sciencedirect.com/science/article/pii/S0049089X16300217.

Thorup, J., McLachlan, R., Cortes, D., Nation, T. R., Balic, A., Southwell, B. R., & Hutson, J. (2010). What is new in cryptorchidism and hypospadias—a critical review on the testicular dysgenesis hypothesis. *Pediatric Surgery, 45*(10), 2074–2086.

Tichelman, A., Kaufman, R., Edwards-Leeper, L., Mandel, F., Shumer, C., & Spack, D. (2015). Serving transgender youth: Challenges, dilemmas, and clinical examples. *Professional Psychology: Research and Practice, 46*(1), 37–45.

Tiefer, L. (1996). The medicalization of sexuality: Conceptual, normative and professional issues. *Annual Review of Sex Research, 7*, 252–282.

Tiefer, L. (2001). A new view of women's sexual problems: Why new? Why now? *Journal of Sex Research, 38*(2), 89–96.

Tiefer, L. (2002). Beyond the medical model of women's sexual problems: A campaign to resist the promotion of "female sexual dysfunction." *Sexual & Relationship Therapy, 17*(2), 127–135.

Tiefer, L. (2004). *Sex Is Not a Natural Act and Other Essays*. Boulder, CO: Westview Press.

Tiefer, L. (2006). Female sexual dysfunction: A case study of disease mongering and activist resistance. *PLoS Medicine, 3*(4). Retrieved June 19, 2008, from http://medicine.plosjournals.org/perlserv/?request=get-document&doi=10.1371/journal.pmed.0030178&ct=1.

Tiefer, L. (2012). Medicalizations and demedicalizations of sexuality therapies. *Journal of Sex Research, 49*(4), 311.

Timur, S., & Sahin, N. (2010). The prevalence of depression symptoms and influencing factors among perimenopausal and postmenopausal women. *Menopause, 17*(3), 545–551.

Ting-Toomey, S., Gao, G., & Trubisky, P. (1991). Culture, face maintenance, and styles of handling interpersonal conflicts: A study in five cultures. *International Journal of Conflict Management, 2*(4), 275–296.

Tishelman, A., Kaufman, R., Edwards-Leeper, L., Mandel, F., Shumer, D., Spack, N. (2015). Serving transgender youth: Challenges, dilemmas, and clinical examples. *Professional Psychology, Research and Practice, 46*(1), 37–45.

Tjaden, P., & Thoennes, N. (2000). Extent, nature, and consequences of intimate partner violence: Findings from the National Violence Against Women Survey. Washington, D.C.: U.S. Department of Justice, National Institute of Justice, Report #NCJ181867.

Tjaden, P., & Thoennes, N. (2000). *Extent, nature, and consequences of intimate partner violence: Findings from the National Violence Against Women Survey.* Washington, DC: National Institute of Justice and the Centers for Disease Control and Prevention.

Tjepkema, M. (2008). Health care use among gay, lesbian and bisexual Canadians. *Health Reports, 19,* 53–64.

Tjioe, M., & Vissers, W. (2008). Scabies outbreaks in nursing homes for the elderly: Recognition, treatment options, and control of reinfestation. *Drugs Aging, 25*(4), 299–306.

Toadvine, J. (2016). Out story too: Giving voice to lesbian couples' experience with infertility. *Dissertation Abstracts International Section A: Humanities and Social Science, 76*(12-A). #978-1321914474.

Tobian, A., Adamu, T., Reed, J., Kiggundu, V., Yazdi, Y., & Njeuhmeli, E. (2015). Voluntary medical male circumcision in resource-constrained setting. *Nature Reviews: Urology, 12*(12), 661–670.

Toibaro, J., Ebensrtejin, J., Parlante, A., Burgoa, P., Freyre, A., Romero, M., & Losso, M. (2009). Sexually transmitted infections among transgender individuals and other sexual identities. *Medicina, 69*(3), 327–330.

Tokushige, N., Markham, R., Crossett, B., Ah, S., Nelaturi, V., Khan, A., & Fraser, I. (2011). Discovery of a novel biomarker in the urine in women with endometriosis. *Fertility and Sterility, 95*(1), 46–49.

Toledo, M. (2009, January 30). First comes marriage, then comes love. *ABC News,* January 30. Retrieved April 20, 2014, from http://abcnews.go.com/2020/story?id=6762309.

Tom, S., Kuh, D., Guralnik, J., & Mishra, G. (2010). Self-reported sleep difficulty during the menopausal transition: Results from a prospective cohort study. *Menopause, 17*(6), 1128–1135.

Tomaso, B. (2008, July 25). After 40 years, birth control decree still divides American Catholics. *Dallas News.* Retrieved October 28, 2008, from http://religionblog.dallasnews.com/archives/2008/07/after-40-years-birth-control-d.html.

Tomassilli, J., Golub, S., Bimbi, D., & Parsons, J. (2009). Behind closed doors: An exploration of kinky sexual behaviors in urban lesbian and bisexual women. *Journal of Sex Research, 46*(5), 438–445.

Tomfohr, L., Pung, M., & Dimsdale, J. (2016). Mediators of the relationship between race and allostatic load in African and white Americans. *Health Psychology, 35*(4), 322–332.

Tommola, P., Unkila-Kallio, L., & Paavonen, J. (2010). Surgical treatment of vulvar vestibulitis: A review. *Acta Obstetrics and Gynecology Scandinavia, 89*(11), 1385–1395.

Tommola, P., Unkila-Kallio, L., & Paavonen, J. (2012). Long-term well-being after surgical or conservative treatment of severe vulvar vestibulitis. *Acta Obstetricia Et Gynecologica Scandinavica, 91*(9), 1086–1093.

Tong, V., Dietz, P., Morrow, B., D'Angelo, D., Farr, S., Rockhill, K., & England, L. (2013). Trends in smoking before, during, and after pregnancy—Pregnancy risk assessment monitoring system, U.S., 40 sites, 2000–2010. *Morbidity and Mortality Weekly Report, 62*(SS06), 1–19.

Toomey, R., & Russell, S. (2013). Gay-straight alliances, social justice involvement, and school victimization of lesbian, gay, bisexual, and queer youth: Implications for school well-being and plans to vote. *Youth and Society, 45*(4), 500–522.

Toporek, B. (2013). Steubenville athletes guilty in rape case. *Education Week, 32*(26), 4.

Topp, S. (2013). Against the quiet revolution: The rhetorical construction of intersex individuals as disordered. *Sexuality, 16*(1–2), 180–194.

Toppari, J., Virtanen, H. E., Main, K. M., & Skakkebaek, N. E. (2010). Cryptorchidism and hypospadias as a sign of testicular dysgenesis syndrome (TDS): Environmental connection. *Birth Defects Research, 88*(10), 910–919.

Torkelson, J. (2012). A queer vision of emerging adulthood: Seeing sexuality in the transition to adulthood. *Sexuality Research and Social Policy, 9*(2), 132–142.

Toro-Morn, M., & Sprecher, S. (2003). A cross-cultural comparison of mate preferences among university students: The United States vs. the People's Republic of China (PRC). *Journal of Comparative Family Studies, 34*(2), 151–170.

Toth, K., & Kemmelmeier, M. (2009). Divorce attitudes around the world: Distinguishing the impact of culture on evaluations and attitude structure. *Cross-Cultural Research: The Journal of Comparative Social Science, 43*(3), 280–297.

Towne, B., Czerwinski, S. A., Demerath, E. W., Blangero, J., Roche, A. F., & Siervogel, R. M. (2005). Heritability of age at menarche in girls from the Fels Longitudinal Study. *American Journal of Physical Anthropology,* published online ahead of print. Retrieved March 22, 2005, from http://www.ncbi.nlm.nih.gov/entrez/query.fcgi?cmd=Retrieve&db=pubmed&dopt=Abstract&list_uids=15779076.

Trabert, B., Sigurdson, A. J., Sweeney, A. M., Strom, S. S., & McGlynn, K. A. (2011). Marijuana use and testicular germ cell tumors. *Cancer, 117*(4), 848–853.

Treas, J., & Giesen, D. (2000). Sexual infidelity among married and cohabiting Americans. *Journal of Marriage and Family, 62*(1), 48–61.

Treat, T., Viken, R., Farris, C., & Smith, J. (2016). Enhancing the accuracy of men's perceptions of women's sexual interest in the laboratory. *Psychology of Violence, 6*(4), 562–572.

Tremble, B., Schneider, M., & Appathurai, C. (1989). Growing up gay or lebian in a multicultural context. In G. Herdt (Ed.), *Gay and lesbian youth* (pp. 253–267). New York: Harrington Park Press.

Trémollieres, F. (2013). Impact of oral contraceptive on bone metabolism. *Best Practice & Research, Clinical Endocrinology & Metabolism, 27*(1), 47–53.

"Trends in Abortion in the U.S.: 1973–2011." (2014, February). Guttmacher Institute. Retrieved May 26, 2014, from http://www.guttmacher.org/presentations/trends.pdf.

"Trends in Contraceptive Use Worldwide." (2015). United Nations, Department of Economic and Social Affairs, Population Division. Retrieved April 3, 2017, from http://www.un.org/en/development/desa/population/publications/pdf/family/trendsContraceptiveUse2015Report.pdf.

Trenholm, C., Devaney, B., Fortson, K., Quay, L., Wheeler, J., & Clark, M. (2007). Impact of four Title V, Section 510 Abstinence Education Programs. Princeton, NJ: Mathematic Policy Research. Retrieved from http://www.mathematica-mpr.com/publications/PDFs/impactabstinence.pdf.

Trivits, L. C., & Reppucci, N. D. (2002). Application of Megan's Law to juveniles. *American Psychologist, 57*(9), 690–704.

Troiden, R. R. (1989). The formation of homosexual identities. In G. Herdt (Ed.), *Gay and lesbian youth* (pp. 43–73). New York: Harrington Park Press.

Trost, J. E. (2004). Sweden. In R. T. Francoeur & R. J. Noonan (Eds.), *The Continuum International encyclopedia of sexuality* (pp. 984–994). New York/London: Continuum International.

Trotter, E. C., & Alderson, K. G. (2007). University students' definitions of having sex, sexual partner, and virginity loss: The influence of participant gender, sexual experience, and contextual factors. *Canadian Journal of Human Sexuality, 16,* 11–20.

Trudel, G., Villeneuve, L., Preville, M., Boyer, R., & Frechette, V. (2010). Dyadic adjustment, sexuality and psychological distress in older couples. *Sexual and Relationship Therapy, 25*(3), 306–315.

Truman, J., & Morgan, R. (2016). Criminal victimization, 2015. U.S. Department of Justice, Bureau of Justice Statistics. Retrieved May 9, 2017, from https://www.bjs.gov/content/pub/pdf/cv15.pdf.

Trumbach, R. (1990). Is there a modern sexual culture in the West, or, did England never change between 1500 and 1900? *Journal of the History of Sexuality, 1*, 206–309.

Tsai, S., Stafanick, M., & Stafford, R. (2011). Trends in menopausal hormone therapy use of US office-based physicians, 2000–2009. *Menopause, 18*(4), 385–392.

Tsui-Sui, A., Loveland-Cherry, C., & Guthrie, B. (2010). Maternal influences on Asian American-Pacific Islander adolescents' perceived maternal sexual expectations and their sexual initiation. *Journal of Family Issues, 31*(3), 381–406.

Tsuiji, K., Takeda, T., Li, B., Wakabayashi, A., Kondo, A., Kimura, T., & Yaegashi, N. (2011). Inhibitory effect of curcumin on uterine leiomyoma cell proliferation. *Gynecological Endocrinology, 27*(7), 512–517.

Tsunokai, G., Kposowa, A., & Adams, M. (2009). Racial preferences in internet dating: A comparison of four birth cohorts. *Western Journal of Black Studies, 33*(1), 1–16.

Tsuruta, J., Dayton, P., Gallippi, C., O'Rand, M., Streicker, M., Gessner, R., Gregory, T., Silva, E., Hamil, K., Moser, G., & Sokal, D. (2012). Therapeutic ultrasound as a potential male contraceptive. *Reproductive Biology and Endocrinology, 10*(7). Retrieved May 26, 2014, from http://www.ncbi.nlm.nih.gov/pubmed/22289508.

Tucker, S., Speer, S., & Peters, S. (2016). Development of an explanatory model of sexual intimacy following treatment for localized prostate cancer: A systematic review and meta-synthesis of qualitative evidence. *Social Science & Medicine, 163*, 80–83.

Tufekci, Z. (2010, May). Who acquires friends through social media and why? "Rich get richer" versus "seek and ye shall find." *Proceedings of the Fourth International AAAI Conference on Weblogs and Social Media.* Washington, DC.

Tufekci, Z. (2014). The social Internet: frustrating, enriching, but not lonely. *Public Culture, 26*(1), 13–23.

Tumlinson, K., Pence, B., Curtis, S., Marshall, S., & Speizer, I. (2015). Quality of care and contraceptive use in urban Kenya. *International Perspectives on Sexual and Reproductive Health, 41*(2), 69–79.

Turchik, J., & Edwards, K. (2012). Myths about male rape: A literature review. *Psychology of Men & Masculinity, 13*(2), 211–226.

Turley, E., & Butt, T. (2015). BDSM—Bondage and discipline; domination and submission; sadism and masochism. In C. Richards & M. Baker (Eds.), *The Palgrave handbook of the psychology of sexuality and gender* (pp. 24–41). New York: Palgrave Macmillan.

Turner, C. F., Ku, L., Rogers, S. M., Lindberg, L., Pleck, J., & Sonenstein, F. (1998). Adolescent sexual behavior, drug use, and violence: Increased reporting with computer survey technology. *Science, 280*, 867–873.

Turner, C. F., Villarroel, M., Chromy, J., Eggleston, E., & Rogers, S. (2005). Same-gender sex among U.S. adults. *Public Opinion Quarterly, 69*, 439–462.

Turner, W. (2000). *A genealogy of queer theory.* Philadelphia: Temple University Press.

Turner, Y., & Stayton, W. (2014). The twenty-first century challenges to sexuality and religion. *Journal of Religion and Health, 53*(2), 483–497.

Twiss, J., Wegner, J., Hunter, M., Kelsay, M., Rathe-Hart, M., & Salado, W. (2007). Perimenopause symptoms, quality of life, and health behaviors in users and nonusers of hormone therapy. *Journal of the American Academy of Nurse Practitioners, 19*, 602–613.

Tye, M. H. (2006). Social inequality and well-being: Race-related stress, gay-related stress, self-esteem, and life satisfaction among African American gay and bisexual men. *Dissertation Abstracts International: Section B, 67*(4-B), 0419–4217.

Tzeng, O. (1992). Cognitive/comparative judgment paradigm of love. In O. Tzeng (Ed.), *Theories of love development, maintenance, and dissolution: Octagonal cycle and differential perspectives,* pp. 133–149.

Tzortzis, V., Skriapas, K., Hadjigeorgiou, G., Mitsogiannis, I., Aggelakis, K., Gravas, S., et al. (2008). Sexual dysfunction in newly diagnosed multiple sclerosis women. *Multiple Sclerosis, 14*, 561–563.

U.S. Census Bureau. (2007, September 19). *Most people make only one trip down the aisle, but first marriages shorter, census bureau reports.* Retrieved September 20, 2007, from http://www.census.gov/Press-Release/www/releases/archives/marital_status_living_arrangements/010624.html.

U.S. Department of Justice, Bureau of Justice Statistics. (2006). Criminal victimization in the United States, 2005 statistical tables (U.S. Department of Justice Publication NCH 2152244, Table 2, Number of victimizations and victimization rates for persons age 12 and over, by type of crime and gender of victims). Washington, DC: Author.

U.S. Department of Justice, Office of Justice Programs. (2002). Rape and sexual assault: Reporting to police and medical attention, 1992–2000. Retrieved October 22, 2005, from http://www.ojp.usdoj.gov/bjs/pub/pdf/rsarp00.pdf.

U.S. Department of Justice, Office on Violence Against Women. (2008). Anonymous reporting and forensic examinations. Retrieved October 25, 2008, from http://www.ovw.usdoj.gov/docs/faq-arfe052308.pdf.

U.S. Department of State. (2005). Trafficking in persons report. Retrieved December 12, 2005, from http://www.state.gov/documents/organization/47255.pdf.

U.S. Food & Drug Association. (2015). Tampons and Asbestos, Dioxin, & Toxic Shock Syndrome. Medical Device Safety. Retrieved January 20, 2017, from http://www.fda.gov/MedicalDevices/Safety/AlertsandNotices/PatientAlerts/ucm070003.htm.

U.S. Preventive Services Task Force. (2016). Gynecological conditions: Periodic screening with the pelvic examination. Retrieved January 20, 2017, from https://www.uspreventiveservicestaskforce.org/Page/Document/draft-recommendation-statement157/gynecological-conditions-screening-with-the-pelvic-examination.

Uecker, J. (2012). Marriage and mental health among young adults. *Journal of Health and Social Behavior, 53*(1), 67–83.

Uecker, J., & Regnerus, M. (2010). BARE MARKET: Campus sex ratios, romantic relationships, and sexual behavior. *Sociological Quarterly, 51*(3), 408–435.

Ullman, S., Relyea, M., Peter-Hagene, L., & Vasquez, A. (2013). Trauma histories, substance use coping, PTSD, and problem substance use among sexual assault victims. *Addictive Behaviors, 38*(6), 2219–2223.

Ullman, S., Townsend, S., Filipas, H., & Starzynski, L. (2007). Structural models of the relations of assault severity, social support, avoidance coping, self-blame, and PTSD among sexual assault survivors. *Psychology of Women Quarterly, 31*, 23–37.

Umberson, D., Thomeer, M., Kroeger, R., Lodge, A., Xu, M. (2015). Challenges and opportunities for research on same-sex relationships. *Journal of Marriage and the Family, 77*(1), 96–111.

UNAIDS. (2005). AIDS Epidemic Update: December, 2005. Retrieved November 22, 2005, from http://www.unaids.org/epi2005/doc/report_pdf.html.

UNAIDS. (2008). 2008: Report on the global AIDS epidemic. UNAIDS Joint United Nations Programme on HIV/AIDS. Retrieved November 3, 2008, from http://www.unaids.org/en/KnowledgeCentre/HIVData/GlobalReport/2008/2008_Global_report.asp.

UNAIDS. (2010). *A global view of HIV infection.* Retrieved June 9, 2014, from http://www.unaids.org/documents/20101123_2010_HIV_Prevalence_Map_em.pdf.

UNAIDS. (2010). Global report on the AIDS epidemic. Joint United Nations Programme on HIV/AIDS. Retrieved April 1, 2011, from http://www.unaids.org/globalreport/documents/20101123_GlobalReport_full_en.pdf.

UNAIDS. (2014). The Gap Report. Retrieved April 30, 2017, from http://files.unaids.org

/en/media/unaids/contentassets/documents /unaidspublication/2014/UNAIDS_Gap _report_en.pdf.

UNAIDS. (2015). Ending child marriage in Africa: A brief by girls not brides. Retrieved April 30, 2017, from http://www.girlsnotbrides.org /wp-content/uploads/2015/02/Child-marriage -in-Africa-A-brief-by-Girls-Not-Brides.pdf.

UNAIDS. (2016, November). Fact Sheet: Global HIV statistics. Retrieved April 26, 2017, from http://www.unaids.org/sites/default/files /media_asset/UNAIDS_FactSheet_en.pdf.

UNAIDS. (2016). Global AIDS update 2016. Joint United Nations Programme on HIV/ AIDS, Switzerland. Retrieved January 9, 2017, from http://www.who.int/hiv/pub/arv /global-AIDS-update-2016_en.pdf?ua=1.

UNAIDS. (2016a). Fact Sheet: Global HIV statistics. Retrieved April 20, 2017, from http://www.unaids.org/sites/default/files /media_asset/UNAIDS_FactSheet_en.pdf.

UNAIDS. (2016b). Global AIDS Update. Retrieved April 29, 2017, from http://www .unaids.org/sites/default/files/media_asset /global-AIDS-update-2016_en.pdf.

UNICEF (2016). Female genital mutilation/ cutting: A global concern. New York. Retrieved January 20, 2017, from https:// www.unicef.org/media/files/FGMC_2016 _brochure_final_UNICEF_SPREAD.pdf.

Uniform Crime Reports. (2015). Hate crime statistics; victims. Retrieved March 24, 2017, from https://ucr.fbi.gov/hate-crime/2015 /topic-pages/victims_final.pdf.

United Nations Children's Fund (2013). Towards an AIDS-free generation—Children and AIDS: Sixth Stocktaking Report. New York, NY: UNICEF. Retrieved May 19, 2014, from http://www.unaids.org/en/media/unaids /contentassets/documents/unaidspublication /2013/20131129_stocktaking_report _children_aids_en.pdf.

United Nations Educational, Scientific, and Cultural Organization (UNESCO). (2008). Review of sex, relationships, and HIV education in the schools. UNESCO Global Advisory Group. Retrieved January 26, 2011, from http://unesdoc.unesco.org/images /0016/001629/162989e.pdf.

United Nations Educational, Scientific, and Cultural Organization (UNESCO). (2009). International technical guidance on sexuality education: An evidence-informed approach for schools, teachers, and health educators. Retrieved May 10, 2011, from http://unesdoc .unesco.org/images/0018/001832/183281e.pdf.

United Nations Population Fund. (2012). Marrying too young: End child marriage. Retrieved April 12, 2014, from https://www .unfpa.org/webdav/site/global/shared /documents/publications/2012/Marrying TooYoung.pdf.

United Nations Population Fund. (2017). News on Child Marriage. Retrieved March 8, 2017, from http://www.unfpa.org/child-marriage.

United Nations. (2013). World contraceptive patterns, 2013. Retrieved May 26, 2014, from http://www.un.org/en/development/desa /population/publications/pdf/family/world ContraceptivePatternsWallChart2013.pdf.

Untied, A., Orchowski, L., Mastroleo, N., & Gidycz, C. (2012). College students' social reactions to the victim in a hypothetical sexual assault scenario: The role of victim and perpetrator alcohol use. Violence and Victims, 27(6), 957–972.

Upchurch, D. M., Aneshensel, C. S., Mudgal, J., & McNeely, C. S. (2001). Sociocultural contexts of time to first sex among Hispanic adolescents. Journal of Marriage and Family, 63(4), 1138.

Upchurch, D. M., Levy-Storms, L., et al. (1998). Gender and ethnic differences in the timing of first sexual intercourse. Family Planning Perspectives, 30(3), 121–128.

Upson, K., Harmon, Q., & Baird, D. (2016). Soy-based infant formula feeding and ultrasound-detected uterine fibroids among young African-American women with no prior clinical diagnosis of fibroids. Environmental Health, 124(6), 769–775.

Urato, A. C., & Norwitz, E. R. (2011). A guide towards pre-pregnancy management of defective implantation and placentation. Best Practices and Research in Clinical Obstetrics and Gynecology, 25(3), 367–387.

Ussher, J., & Perz, J. (2008). Empathy, egalitarianism and emotion work in the relationship negotiation of PMS: The experience of women in lesbian relationships. Feminism and Psychology, 18(1), 87–111.

Vakalopoulos, I., Kampantais, S., Ioannidis, S., Laskaridis, L., Dimopoulos, P., Toutziaris, C., Koptsis, M., Henry, G., & Katsikas, V. (2013). High patient satisfaction after inflatable penile prostheses implantation correlates with female partner satisfaction. Journal of Sexual Medicine, 10(11), 2774–2781.

Valdiserri, R. O. (2002). HIV/AIDS stigma: An impediment to public health. American Journal of Public Health, 92(3), 341–343.

Valencia, M., Arias, M., González, J., Campos, E., Rodriguez, M., Alvarez, I., Vargas, M., Flores, J., Haro, S., Bonilla, M., Escuderto, R., & Campero, R. (2013). Safety of veralipride for the treatment of vasomotor symptoms of menopause. Menopause, 21(5), 484–492.

Valente, S. M. (2005). Sexual abuse of boys. Journal of Child and Adolescent Psychiatric Nursing, 18(1), 10–16.

Valentova, J., Kleisner, K., Havlicek, J., & Neustupa, J. (2014). Shape differences between the faces of homosexual and heterosexual men. Archives of Sexual Behavior, 43(2), 353–361.

Valenzuela, C. Y. (2008). Prenatal maternal mnemonic effects on the human neuro- psychic sex: A new proposition from fetus- maternal tolerance-rejection. La Revista Medica de Chile, 136(12), 1552–1558.

Valenzuela, C. Y. (2010). Sexual orientation, handedness, sex ratio and fetomaternal tolerance-rejection. Biological Research, 43(3), 347–356.

Valkenburg, P., & Peter, J. (2007). Online communication and adolescent well- being: Testing the stimulation versus the displacement hypothesis. Journal of Computer- Mediated Communication, 12(4), 1169–1182.

Van Berlo, W., & Ensink, B. (2000). Problems with sexuality after sexual assault. Annual Review of Sex Research, 11, 235–257.

Van de Ven, P., Campbell, D., & Kippax, S. (1997). Factors associated with unprotected anal intercourse in gay men's casual partnerships in Sydney, Australia. AIDS Care, 9(6), 637–649.

Van der Krogt, C. (2016). Homosexuality and Islam: What does the Qur'an actually say about gay people? Pink News. Retrieved March 24, 2017, from http://www.pinknews .co.uk/2016/06/23/homosexuality-and-islam -what-does-the-quran-actually-say-about -gay-people/.

Van Der Pol, C., Lacle, M., Witkamp, A., Kornegoor, R., Miao, H., Bouchardy, C., Borel, R., Van Der Wall, E., Verkooijen, H., & Van Diest, P. (2016). Prognostic models in male breast cancer. Breast Cancer Research and Treatment, 160(2), 339–346.

Van Gelderen, L., Bos, H., Gartrell, N., Hermanns, J., & Perrin, E. C. (2012). Quality of life of adolescents raised from birth by lesbian mothers: The US national longitudinal family study. Journal of Developmental and Behavioral Pediatrics, 33(1), 17–23.

van Lankveld, J., Everaerd, W., & Grotjohann, Y. (2001). Cognitive-behavioral bibliotherapy for sexual dysfunctions in heterosexual couples: A randomized waiting-list controlled clinical trial in the Netherlands. Journal of Sex Research, 38(1), 51–67.

Van Schalkwyk, J., Yudin, M., Yudin, M., Allen, V., Bouchard, C., Boucher, M., Boucoiran, I., et al. (2015). Vulvovaginitis: Screening for and management of trichomoniasis, vulvovaginal candidiasis, and bacterial vaginosis. Journal of Obstetrics and Gynaecology Canada, 37(3), 266–276.

van Teijlingen, E., Reid, J., Shucksmith, J., Harris, F., Philip, K., Imamura, M., Tucker, J., & Penney, G. (2007). Embarrassment as a key emotion in young people talking about sexual health. Sociological Research, 12(2). Retrieved April 15, 2011, from http://www .socresonline.org.uk/12/2/van_teijlingen.html.

Van Voorhis, B. J. (2006). Outcomes from assisted reproductive technology. *Obstetrics and Gynecology, 107*, 183–200.

Vance, S., Ehrensaft, D., & Rosenthal, S. (2014). Psychological and medical care of gender nonconforming youth. *Pediatrics, 134*(6), 1184–1192.

Vandenberg, L., Schaeberle, C., Rubin, B., Sonnenschein, C., Soto, A. (2013). The male mammary gland: A target for the xenoestrogen bisphenol A. *Reproductive Toxicology, 37*, 15–23.

Vanderbilt, H. (1992). Incest: A chilling report. *Lears*, (Feb.), 49–77.

VanderLaan, D., & Vasey, P. (2008). Mate retention behavior of men and women in heterosexual and homosexual relationships. *Archives of Sexual Behavior, 37*, 572–586.

Vanfossen, B. (1996). ITROWs women and expression conference. Institute for Teaching and Research on Women, Towson University, Towson, MD. Retrieved April 15, 2003, from http://www.towson.edu/itrow.

Vannier, S., & O'Sullivan, L. (2011). Communicating interest in sex: Verbal and nonverbal initiation of sexual activity in young adults' romantic dating relationships. *Archives of Sexual Behavior, 40*(5), 961–969.

Vannier, S., & O'Sullivan, L. (2016). Passion, connection, and destiny. *Journal of Social and Personal Relationships, 34*(2). Retrieved February 8, 2017, from http://journals.sagepub.com/doi/abs/10.1177/0265407516631156.

Vardi, Y., McMahon, C., Waldinger, M., Rubio-Aurioles, E., & Rabinowitz, D. (2008). Are premature ejaculation symptoms curable? *Journal of Sexual Medicine, 5*, 1546–1551.

Varner, J. (2013, March–May). MANopause (andropause). *The Alabama Nurse, 7*.

Varshini, J., Srinag, B., Kalthur, G., Krishnamurthy, H., Kumar, P., Rao, S., & Adiga, S. (2012). Poor sperm quality and advancing age are associated with increased sperm DNA damage in infertile men. *Andrologia, 44*, 642–649.

Vedantam, S. (2011, March 24). Pedophiles use online social networks to foil investigators. *The Washington Post*, p. A3.

Vendittelli, F., Riviere, O., Crenn-Hebert, C., Rozan, M., Maria, B., & Jacquetin, B. (2008). Is a breech presentation at term more frequent in women with a history of cesarean delivery? *American Journal of Obstetrics and Gynecology, 198*, 521.

Venkat, P., Masch, R., Ng, E., Cremer, M., Richman, S., & Arslan, A. (2008, May 23). Knowledge and beliefs about contraception in urban Latina women. *Journal of Community Health, 33*(5), 357–362.

Ventura, S. J., Abma, J. C., Mosher, W. D., & Henshaw, S. K. (2007). *Recent trends in teenage pregnancy in the United States, 1990–2002*. Hyattsville, MD: National Center for Health Statistics, Centers for Disease Control. Retrieved May 27, 2008, from http://www.cdc.gov/nchs/products/pubs/pubd/hestats/teenpreg1990–2002/teenpreg1990–2002.htm.

Vermeulen, J., Kornegoor, R., Wall, E., Groep, P., & Diest, P. (2013). Differential expression of growth factor receptors and membrane-bound tumor markers for imaging in male and female breast cancer. *PLOS ONE, 8*(1), 1–8.

Versfeld, N. J., & Dreschler, W. A. (2002). The relationship between the intelligibility of time-compressed speech and speech-in-noise in young and elderly listeners. *Journal of the Acoustical Society of America, 111*, 401–408.

Verweij, K., Shekar, S., Zietsch, B., Eaves, L., Bailey, J., Boomsma, D., & Martin, N. (2008). Genetic and environmental influences on individual differences in attitudes toward homosexuality: An Australian twin study. *Behavior Genetics, 38*, 257–265.

Vesperini, H. (2010, October 4). Rwanda working to curb population explosion. *Asia One News*. Retrieved October 5, 2010, from http://www.asiaone.com/News/AsiaOne%2BNews/World/Story/A1Story20101005–240682.html.

Vessey, M., Yeates, D., & Flynn, S. (2010). Factors affecting mortality in a large cohort study with special reference to oral contraceptive use. *Contraception, 82*(3), 221–229.

Vetten, L., Jewkes, R., Sigsworth, R., Christofides, N., Loots, L., & Dunseith, O. (2008). "Tracking justice: The attrition of rape cases through the criminal justice system in Gauteng." Johannesburg, South Africa: Tsh-waranang Legal Advocacy Centre, the South African Medical Research Council and the Centre for the Study of Violence and Reconciliation.

Vidaurri, M., Singh, D., Zambarano, R., & Dabbs, J. (1999). Lesbian erotic role identification: Behavioral, morphological, and hormonal correlates. *Journal of Personality and Social Psychology, 76*(6), 1035–1050.

Vierck, E., & Silverman, J. (2015). Brief report: Phenotypic differences and their relationship to paternal age and gender in autism spectrum disorder. *Journal of Autism and Developmental Disorders, 45*(6), 1915–1924.

Vigano, P., Parazzini, F., Somigliana, E., & Vercellini, P. (2004). Endometriosis: Epidemiology and aetiological factors. *Best Practice & Research Clinical Obstetrics & Gynaecology, 18*(2), 177–200.

Vignovic, J., & Thompson, L. (2010). Computer-mediated cross-cultural collaboration: Attributing communication errors to the person versus the situation. *Journal of Applied Psychology, 95*(2), 265–276.

Viloria, H. (2014, May 14). Op-ed: What's in a name: Intersex and identity. *The Advocate*. Retrieved January 18, 2017, from http://www.advocate.com/commentary/2014/05/14/op-ed-whats-name-intersex-and-identity.

Vincke, J., & van Heeringen, K. (2002). Confidant support and the mental well-being of lesbian and gay young adults: A longitudinal analysis. *Journal of Community and Applied Social Psychology, 12*, 181–193.

Virtanen, H., Sadov, S., & Toppari, J. (2012). Prenatal exposure to smoking and male reproductive health. *Current Opinion in Endocrinology, Diabetes, and Obesity, 19*(3), 228–232.

Voigt, H. (1991). Enriching the sexual experience of couples: The Asian traditions and sexual counseling. *Journal of Sex and Marital Therapy, 17*, 214–219.

Voisin, D., Chen, P., Fullilove, R., Jacobson, K. (2015). Community violence exposure and sexual behaviors in a nationally representative sample of young adults: The effects of race/ethnicity and gender. *Journal of Social Service Research, 41*(3). Retrieved August 23, 2017, from http://www.tandfonline.com/doi/abs/10.1080/01488376.2014.987941.

Voller, E., & Long, P. (2010). Sexual assault and rape perpetration by college men: The role of the big five personality traits. *Journal of Interpersonal Violence, 25*(3), 457–480.

Von Sydow, K. (2000). Sexuality of older women: The effect of menopause, other physical and social and partner-related factors. *Arztl Fortbild Qualitatssich, 94*(3), 223–229.

Vorsanova, S., Iurov, I., Kolotii, A., Beresheva, A., Demidova, I., Kurinnaia, O., Kravets, V., Monakhov, V., Solov'ev, I., & Iurov, I. (2010). Chromosomal mosaicism in spontaneous abortions: Analysis of 650 cases. *Genetika, 46*(10), 1356–1359.

Vostral, S. L. (2008). *Under wraps: A history of menstrual hygiene technology*. Lanham, MD: Lexington Books.

Vrabel, K., Hoffart, A., Ro, O., Martinsen, E., & Rosenvinge, J. (2010). Co-occurrence of avoidant personality disorder and child sexual abuse predicts poor outcome in long-standing eating disorder. *Journal of Abnormal Psychology, 119*(3), 623–629.

Vrangalova, Z. (2015). Hooking up and psychological well-being in college students: Short-term prospective links across different hookup definitions. *Journal of Sex Research, 52*(5), 485–498.

Vrbikova, J., Zamrazilova, H., Sedlackova, B., & Snajderova, M. (2011). Metabolic syndrome in adolescents with polycystic ovary syndrome. *Gynecological Endocrinology, 27*(1), 820–822.

Vrouenraets, L., Fredriks, A., Hannema, S., Cohen-Kettenis, P., & de Vries, M. (2016). Perceptions of sex, gender, and puberty suppression: A qualitative analysis of transgender youth. *Archives of Sexual Behavior, 45*(7), 1697–1703.

Vukovic, L. (1992, November-December). Cold sores and fever blisters. *Natural Health*, 119–120.

Waal, F. B. M. (1995). Bonobo sex and society. *Scientific American*, 82–88. Retrieved July 4, 2003, from http://songweaver.com/info/bonobos.html.

Wacker, J., Parish, S., & Macy, R. (2008). Sexual assault and women with cognitive disabilities: Codifying discrimination in the United States. *Journal of Disability Policy Studies*, 19, 86–95.

Waite, L., Joyner, K. (2001). Emotional satisfaction and physical pleasure in sexual unions: Time horizon, sexual behavior, and sexual exclusivity. *Journal of Marriage and Family*, 63(1), 247–264.

Waite, L., Luo, Y., & Lewin A. (2009). Marital happiness and marital stability: Consequences for psychological well-being. *Social Science Research*, 38(1), 201–212.

Wakefield, J. (2012). The DSM-5's proposed new categories of sexual disorder: The problem of false positives in sexual diagnosis. *Clinical Social Work Journal*, 40(2), 213–223.

Wakelin, A. (2003). Effects of victim gender and sexuality on attributions of blame to rape victims. *Sex Roles*, 49(9–10), 477–487.

Walch, K., Eder, R., Schindler, A., & Feichtinger, W. (2001). The effect of single-dose oxytocin application on time to ejaculation and seminal parameters in men. *Journal of Assisted Reproductive Genetics*, 18, 655–659.

Waldinger, M. (2005). Lifelong premature ejaculation: Definition, serotonergic neurotransmission and drug treatment. *World Journal of Urology*, 23, 102–108.

Waldinger, M. (2014). Pharmacotherapy for premature ejaculation. *Current Opinion in Psychiatry*, 27(6), 400–405.

Waldinger, M. D., & Schweitzer, D. H. (2009). Persistent genital arousal disorder in 18 Dutch women: Part II. A syndrome clustered with restless legs and overactive bladder. *Journal of Sexual Medicine*, 6(2), 482–497.

Waldinger, R., & Schulz, M. (2010). What's love got to do with it? Social functioning, perceived health, and daily happiness in married octogenarians. *Psychology and Aging*, 25(2), 422–431.

Waldman, K. (2013, November 1). RT if you're: (about someone dying. *Slate*. Retrieved November 10, 2013, from http://www.slate.com/blogs/xx_factor/2013/11/01/mourning_on_social_media_it_s_not_crass.html.

Walen, S. R., & Roth, D. (1987). A cognitive approach. In J. H. Geer & W. T. O'Donahue (Eds.), *Theories of human sexuality* (pp. 335–360). New York: Plenum Press.

Walker-Rodriguez, A., & Hill, R. (2011). Human sex trafficking. *FBI Law Enforcement Bulletin*, 80(3), 1–9.

Walker, J., & Milton, J. (2006). Teachers' and parents' roles in the sexuality education of primary school children: A comparison of experiences in Leeds, UK and in Sydney, Australia. *Sex Education*, 6(4), 415–428.

Walker, J., Archer, J., & Davies, M. (2005). Effects of rape on men: A descriptive analysis. *Archives of Sexual Behavior*, 34(1), 69–80.

Walker, K. E. (2002). Exploitation of children and young people through prostitution. *Journal of Child Health Care*, 6(3), 182–188.

Wallerstein, E. (1980). *Circumcision: An American health fallacy*. New York: Springer.

Wallerstein, J., Lewis, J., & Rosenthal, S. (2013). Mothers and their children after divorce: Report from a 25-year longitudinal study. *Psychoanalytic Psychology*, 30(2), 167–187.

Wallien, M., Cohen-Kettenis, P. (2008). Psychosexual outcomes of gender-dysphoric children. *Journal of the American Academy of Child and Adolescent Psychiatry*, 47(12), 1413–1423.

Walls, N., Wisneski, H., & Kane, S. (2013). School climate, individual support, or both? Gay-straight alliances and the mental health of sexual minority youth. *School Social Work Journal*, 37(2), 88–112.

Walters, J. (2005, January 2). No sex is safe sex for teens in America. Retrieved October 19, 2005, from http://observer.guardian.co.uk/international/story/0,6903,1382117,00.html.

Walters, M., Chen, J., & Breiding, M. (2013). The national intimate partner and sexual violence survey (NISVS): 2010 Findings on victimization by sexual orientation. Retrieved from https://www.cdc.gov/violenceprevention/pdf/nisvs_sofindings.pdf.

Wampler, S. M., & Llanes, M. (2010). Common scrotal and testicular problems. *Primary Care*, 37(3), 613–626.

Wang, H., & Amato, P. R. (2000). Predictors of divorce adjustment: Stressors, resources and definitions. *Journal of Marriage and Family*, 62(3), 655–669.

Wang, H., Lin, S., Leung,G., & Schooling, C. (2016). Age at onset of puberty and adolescent depression: "Children of 1997" birth cohort. *Pediatrics*, 137(6). Retrieved February 10, 2017, from http://pediatrics.aappublications.org/content/early/2016/05/24/peds.2015-3231.

Wang, M., Lv, Z., Shi, J., Hu, Y., & Xu, C. (2009a). Immunocontraceptive potential of the Ig-like domain of Izumo. *Molecular Reproduction and Development*, 76(8), 794–801.

Wang, W. (2012). The rise of intermarriage, Chapter 1: Overview. Pew Research Center. Retrieved March 6, 2017, from http://www.pewsocialtrends.org/2012/02/16/chapter-1-overview/.

Wang, W. (2015). Interracial marriage: Who is "marrying out"? Pew Research Center. Retrieved March 6, 2017, from http://www.pewresearch.org/fact-tank/2015/06/12/interracial-marriage-who-is-marrying-out/.

Wang, W., & Parker, K. (2014, September 24). Record share of Americans have never married. Pew Research Center, Social & Demographic Trends. Retrieved March 6, 2017, from http://www.pewsocialtrends.org/2014/09/24/record-share-of-americans-have-never-married/.

Wang, W., Parker, K., & Taylor, P. (2013, May 29). Breadwinner moms. *Pew Research, Social & Demographic Trends*. Retrieved February 14, 2014, from http://www.pewsocialtrends.org/2013/05/29/breadwinner-moms.

Wang, W., Zhao, Y., Qiu, L., & Zhu, Y. (2014). Effects of emoticons on the acceptance of negative feedback in computer-mediated communication. *Journal of the Association for Information Systems*, 15(8), 454–484.

Wanzer, M., Foster, S., Servoss, T., & Labelle, S. (2013). Educating young men about testicular cancer. *Journal of Health Communication*, 19(3), 303–320.

Ward-Ritacco, C., Poudevigne, M., & O'Connor, P. (2017). Muscle strengthening exercises during pregnancy are associated with increased energy and reduced fatigue. *Journal of Psychosomatic Obstetrics & Gynecology*, 37(2), 68–72.

Ward, B., Dahlhamer, J., Galinsky, A., & Joestl, S. (2014). *Sexual orientation and health among U.S. adults: National health interview survey, 2013*. National Health Statistics Reports, No. 77, Hyattsville, MD.

Ward, D., Carter, T., & Perrin, D. (1994). *Social deviance: Being, behaving, and branding*. Boston: Allyn & Bacon.

Wardle, L. D. (2001). Multiply and replenish: Considering same-sex marriage in light of state interests in marital procreation. *Harvard Journal of Law and Public Policy*, 24(3), 771–815.

Warin, J. (2000). The attainment of self-consistency through gender in young children. *Sex Roles*, 41, 209–232.

Warne, G. L., Grover, S., & Zajac, J. D. (2005). Hormonal therapies for individuals with intersex conditions: Protocol for use. *Treatments in Endocrinology*, 4(1), 19–29.

Warnock, M. (1988). *Report of the committee of inquiry into human fertilization and embryology*. Department of Health & Social Security, Her Majesty's Stationery Office, London. Retrieved May 24, 2014, from http://www.hfea.gov.uk/docs/Warnock_Report_of_the_Committee_of_Inquiry_into_Human_Fertilisation_and_Embryology_1984.pdf.

Warren, J., Harvey, S., & Henderson, J. (2010). Do depression and low self-esteem follow abortion among adolescents? Evidence from a national study. *Perspectives on Sexual and Reproductive Health*, 42(4), 230–235.

Wassersug, R. (2016). Maintaining intimacy for prostate cancer patients on androgen deprivation therapy. *Current Opinion in Supportive and Palliative Care, 10*(1), 55–65.

Watkins, J. (2003). Insolent and contemptuous carriages. Re-conceptualization of illegitimacy in colonial British America. Retrieved April 10, 2008, from http://etd.fcla.edu/SF/SFE0000137/Thesis.pdf.

Watson, C., & Calabretto, H. (2007). Comprehensive review of conventional and non-conventional methods of management of recurrent vulvovaginal candidiasis. *Australian and New Zealand Journal of Obstetrics and Gynaecology, 47*(4), 262–272.

Watson, W., Miller, R., Wax, J., Hansen, W., Yamamura, Y., & Polzin, W. (2008). Sonographic findings of trisomy 18 in the second trimester of pregnancy. *Journal of Ultrasound in Medicine, 27*, 1033–1038.

Waxman, H. (2004). Abstinence-only education. Retrieved September 17, 2005, from http://www.democrats.reform.house.gov/investigations.asp?Issue=Abstinence-Only+ Education.

Wdowiak, A., Wdowiak, L., & Wiktor, H. (2007). Evaluation of the effect of using mobile phones on male fertility. *Annals of Agricultural and Environmental Medicine, 14*, 169–172.

Weatherall, A. (2002). *Gender, language and discourse.* London: Hove Routledge.

Weaver, K., Campbell, R., Mermelstein, R., & Wakschlag, L. (2008). Pregnancy smoking in context: The influence of multiple levels of stress. *Nicotine and Tobacco Research, 10*, 1065–1073.

Weaver, T. L. (2009). Impact of rape on female sexuality: Review of selected literature. *Clinics in Obstetrics and Gynecology, 52*(4), 702–711.

Weed, S. E. (2008). Marginally successful results of abstinence-only program erased by dangerous errors in curriculum. *American Journal of Health Behavior, 32*, 60–73.

Weeks, G., Gambescia, N., & Hertlein, K. (2015). *A clinician's guide to systemic sex therapy* (2nd ed.). New York: Routledge.

Weger, H., Bell, G., Minei, E., & Robinson, M. (2014). The relative effectiveness of active listening in initial interactions. *The International Journal of Listening, 28*(1), 13–31.

Wei, E. H. (2000). Teenage fatherhood and pregnancy involvement among urban, adolescent males: Risk factors and consequences. *Dissertation Abstracts International: Section B, 61*(1-B), #0419–4217.

Wei, S., Li, Q., Li. S., Zhou. C., Li, F., & Zhou, Y. (2015). A new surgical technique of hymenoplasty. *International Journal of Gynaecology and Obstetrics, 130*(10), 14–18.

Weigel, D. J. (2007). Parental divorce and the types of commitment-related messages people gain from their families of origin. *Journal of Divorce and Remarriage, 47*, 15.

Weigold, A., Weigold, I., Russell, E. (2013). Examination of the equivalence of self-report survey-based paper-and-pencil and Internet data collection methods. *Psychological Methods, 18*(1), 53–70.

Weijing H., Neil, S., Kulkarni, H., Wright, E., Agan, B., Marconi, V., et al. (2008). Duffy antigen receptor for chemokines mediates trans-infection of HIV-1 from red blood cells to target cells and affects HIV-AIDS susceptibility. *Cell Host and Microbe, 4*, 52–62.

Weil, E. (2012, March 30). Puberty before age 10: A new 'normal'? *New York Times.* Retrieved February 19, 2014, from http://www.nytimes.com/2012/04/01/magazine/puberty-before-age-10-a-new-normal.html?pagewanted=all.

Weinberg, M. S., Williams, C. J., & Pryor, D. W. (1994). *Dual attraction: Understanding bisexuality.* New York: Oxford University Press.

Weinert, C., Hess, K., Rose, C., Balaji, A., Smith, J., Paz-Bailey, G. (2016). Specific race and ethnicity disparities in HIV infection and awareness among men who have sex with men—20 U.S. cities, 2008–2014. *Journal of Infectious Diseases, 213*(5), 776–783.

Weinrich, J. (2014). On the design, development, and testing of sexual identity questions: A discussion and analysis of Kristen Miller and J. Michael Ryans' work for the National Health Interview Survey. *Journal of Bisexuality, 14*(3–4), 502–523.

Weinstock, H., Berman, S., & Cates, W. (2004). Sexually transmitted diseases among American youth: Incidence and prevalence estimates, 2000. *Perspectives in Sex and Reproductive Health, 36*(1), 6–10.

Weisel, J. J., & King, P. E. (2007). Involvement in a conversation and attributions concerning excessive self-disclosure. *Southern Communication Journal, 72*, 345–354.

Weiss, H., Dickson, K., Agot, K., & Hankins, C. (2010). Male circumcision for HIV prevention: Current research and programmatic issues. *AIDS,* (Suppl. 4), S61–S69.

Wejnert, C., Hess, K., Rose, C., Balaji, A., Smith, J., & Paz-Bailey, G. (2016). Age-specific race and ethnicity disparities in HIV infection and awareness among men who have sex with men—20 cities, 2008–2014. *Journal of Infectious Disease, 231*(5), 776–783.

Welbourn, A. (2006). Sex, life and the female condom: Some views of HIV positive women. *Reproductive Health Matters, 14*(28), 32–40.

Welch, S., Klassen, C., Borisova, O., & Clothier, H. (2013). The DSM-5 controversies: How should psychologists respond? *Canadian Psychology, 54*(3), 166–175.

Weller, S., & Davis, K. (2002). Condom effectiveness in reducing heterosexual HIV transmission. *The Cochrane Database of Systematic Reviews, 1,* CD003255.

Wellings, K., Collumbien, M., Slaymaker, E., Singh, S., Hodges, Z., et al. (2006). Sexual behavior in context: A global perspective. *Lancet, 368*, 1706–1728.

Wellisch, M. (2010). Communicating love or fear: The role of attachment styles in pathways to giftedness. *Roeper Review, 32*, 116–126.

Wells, B., Starks, T., Robel, E., Kelly, B., Parsons, J., & Golub, S. (2016). From sexual assault to sexual risk: A relational pathway? *Journal of Interpersonal Violence, 31*(20), 3377–3395.

Welty, S. E. (2005). Critical issues with clinical research in children: The example of premature infants. *Toxicology and Applied Pharmacology,* Epub ahead of print. Retrieved July 19, 2005, from http://www.ncbi.nlm.nih.gov/entrez/query.fcgi?cmd=Retrieve&db=pubmed&dopt=Abstract&list_uids=16023161&query_hl=14.

Wentzell, E. (2013). Aging respectably by rejecting medicalization: Mexican men's reasons for not using erectile dysfunction drugs. *Medical Anthropology Quarterly, 27*(1), 3–22.

Wéry, A., Vogelaere, K., Challet-Bouju, G., Poudat, F., Caillon, J., Lever, D., Billieux, J., & Grall-Bronnec, M. (2016). Characteristics of self-identified sexual addicts in a behavioral addiction outpatient clinic. *Journal of Behavioral Addictions, 5*(4), 623–630.

Wespes, E., & Schulman, C. C. (2002). Male andropause: Myth, reality and treatment. *International Journal of Impotence Research, 14*(Suppl. 1), 593–598.

West, D. J. (1993). *Male prostitution.* Binghamton, NY: Haworth Press.

West, E., & Krychman, M. (2016). Natural aphrodisiacs—A review of selected sexual enhancers. *Sexual Medicine Review, 3*(4), 279–288.

West, L. (1989). Philippine feminist efforts to organize against sexual victimization. *Response to the Victimization of Women and Children, 12*, 11–14.

West, S., D'Aloisio, A., Agans, R., Kalsbeek, W., Borisov, N., Thorp, J. (2008). Prevalence of low sexual desire and hypoactive sexual desire disorder in a nationally representative sample of U.S. women. *Archives of Internal Medicine, 168*, 1441–1449.

West, S., Hatters-Friedman, S., & Knoll, S. (2010). Lessons to learn: Female educators who sexually abuse their students. *Psychiatric Times, 9–10*(27), 8–9.

Westermarck, E. (1972). *Marriage ceremonies in Morocco.* London, U.K.: Curzon Press.

Westley, E., Kapp, N., Palermo, T., & Bleck, J. (2013). A review of global access to emergency contraception. *International Journal of Gynecology and Obstetrics, 123*(1), 4–6.

Westley, E., Rich, S., & Lawton, H. (2014). New research in emergency and postcoital contraception. *Current Obstetrics and Gynecology Reports*, 3(2), 150–154.

Whalen, R. E., Geary, D. C., & Johnson, F. (1990). Models of sexuality. In D. P. McWhirter, S. A. Sanders, & J. M. Reinisch (Eds.), *Homosexuality/heterosexuality: Concepts of sexual orientation* (pp. 61–70). New York: Oxford University Press.

Whayne, T., & Mukherjee, D. (2015). Women, the menopause, hormone replacement therapy and coronary heart disease. *Current Opinion in Cardiology*, 30(4), 432–438.

Whipple, B. (2000). Beyond the G spot. *Scandinavian Journal of Sexology*, 3, 35–42.

Whipple, B., & Brash-McGreer, K. (1997). Management of female sexual dysfunction. In M. L. Sipski & C. Alexander (Eds.), *Maintaining sexuality with disability and chronic illness: A practitioner's guide* (pp. 509–534). Baltimore: Aspen.

Whitam, F. L., Daskalos, C., Sobolewski, C. G., & Padilla, P. (1999). The emergence of lesbian sexuality and identity cross-culturally. *Archives of Sexual Behavior*, 27(1), 31–57.

White, S. D., & DeBlassie, R. R. (1992). Adolescent sexual behavior. *Adolescence*, 27, 183–191.

Whiteman, M. K., Hillis, S. D., Jamieson, D. J., Morrow, B., Podgornik, M. N., Brett, K. M., & Marchbanks, P. A. (2008). Inpatient hysterectomy surveillance in the United States, 2000–2004. *American Journal of Obstetrics and Gynecology*, 198(1), 34.e1–34.e7.

Whiting, B. B., & Whiting, J. W. (1975). *Children of six cultures: A psycho-cultural analysis*. Cambridge, MA: Harvard University Press.

Whiting, B., & Edwards, C. P. (1988). A cross-cultural analysis of sex differences in the behavior of children aged 3 through 11. In G. Handel (Ed.), *Childhood socialization* (pp. 281–297). New York: Aldine De Gruyter.

Whittaker, P. G., Merkh, R. D., Henry-Moss, D., & Hock-Long, L. (2010). Withdrawal attitudes and experiences: A qualitative perspective among young urban adults. *Perspectives in Sex and Reproductive Health*, 42(2), 102–109.

Whitty, M. T., & Quigley, L. (2008). Emotional and sexual infidelity offline and in cyberspace. *Journal of Marital and Family Therapy*, 34(4), 461–468.

WHO/UNAIDS. (2011). Joint strategic action framework to accelerate the scale-up of voluntary medical male circumcision for HIV prevention in Eastern and Southern Africa. Retrieved April 29, 2017, from http://files.unaids.org/en/media/unaids/contentassets/documents/unaidspublication/2011/JC2251_Action_Framework_circumcision_en.pdf.

Widman, L., Choukas-Bradley, S., Noar, S., Nesi, J., & Garrett, K. (2016). Parents-adolescent sexual communication and adolescent safer sex behavior: A meta-analysis. *Journal of the American Medical Association: Pediatrics*, 170(1), 52–61.

Wiederman, M. W. (1999). Volunteer bias in sexuality research using college student participants. *Journal of Sex Research*, 36(1), 59–66.

Wiegerink, C., Roebroeck, M., Bender, J., Stam, H., & Cohen-Kettenis, P. (2011). Sexuality of young adults with cerebral palsy: Experienced limitations and needs. *Sexuality and Disability*, 19(2), 119–128.

Wiegerink, C., Stam, H., Ketelaar, M., Cohen-Kettenis, P., & Roebroeck, M. (2012). Personal and environmental factors contributing to participation in romantic relationships and sexual activity of young adults with cerebral palsy. *Disability and Rehabilitation*, 34(17), 1481–1487.

Wienke, C., & Hill, G. (2008). Does the "marriage benefit" extend to partners in gay and lesbian relationships? Evidence from a random sample of sexually active adults. *Journal of Family Issues*, 30(2), 259–289.

Wierckx, K., Caenegem, E., Schreiner, T., Haraldsen, I., Fisher, A., Toye, K, Kaufman, J., & T'Sjoen, G. (2014). Cross-sex hormone therapy in trans persons is safe and effective at short-time follow-up: Results from the European network for the investigation of gender incongruence. *Journal of Sexual Medicine*, 11(8), 1999–2011.

Wierckx, K., Elaut, E., VanHoorde, B., Heylens, G., DeCuypere, G., Monstrey, S., Weyers, S., Hoebeke, P., T'Sjoen, G. (2014) Sexual Desire in Trans Persons: Associations with Sex Reassignment Treatment. *Journal of Sexual Medicine*, 11(1), 107–118.

Wierckx, K., Stuyver, I., Weyers, S., Hamada, A., Agarwal, A., DeSutter, P., & T'Sjoen, G. (2012). Sperm freezing in transsexual women. *Archives of Sexual Behavior*, 41, 1069–1071.

Wierckx, K., Van Caenegem, E., Pennings, G., Elaut, E., Dedecker, D., Van de Peer F., et al. (2012). Reproductive wish in transsexual men. *Human Reproduction*, 27(2), 483–487.

Wiesemann, C., Ude-Koeller, S., Sinnecker, G., & Thyen, U. (2010). Ethical principles and recommendations for the medical management of differences of sex development (DSD)/intersex in children and adolescents. *European Journal of Pediatrics*, 169(6), 671–679.

Wight, R., LeBlanc, A., Meyer, I., & Harig, F. (2015). Internalized gay ageism, matering, and depressive symptoms among midlife and older gay-identified men. *Social Science & Medicine*, 147, 200–208.

Wikan, U. (1977). Man becomes woman: Transsexualism in Oman as a key to gender roles. *Man*, 12, 304–391.

Wilcox, A. J., Weinberg, C. R., & Baird, D. D. (1995). Timing of sexual intercourse in relation to ovulation. Effects on the probability of conception, survival of the pregnancy, and sex of the baby. *New England Journal of Medicine*, 333(23), 1517–1521.

Wildemeersch, D., & Andrade, A. (2010). Review of clinical experience with the frameless LNG-IUS for contraception and treatment of heavy menstrual bleeding. *Gynecological Endocrinology*, 26(5), 383–389.

Wilkinson, D., Tholandi, M., Ramjee, G., & Rutherford, G. W. (2002). Nonoxynol-9 spermicide for prevention of vaginally acquired HIV and other sexually transmitted infections: Systematic review and meta-analysis of randomised controlled trials including more than 5000 women. *Lancet Infectious Diseases*, 2, 613–617.

Williams, J. E., & Best, D. L. (1994). Cross-cultural views of women and men. In W. J. Lonner & R. Malpass (Eds.), *Psychology and culture.* Boston: Allyn & Bacon.

Williams, K., & Umberson, D. (2004). Marital status, marital transition, and health: A gendered life course approach. *Journal of Health and Social Behavior*, 45(1), 81–98.

Williams, W. L. (1986). *The spirit and the flesh: Sexual diversity in American Indian culture.* Boston: Beacon Press.

Williams, W. L. (1990). Book review: P. A. Jackson, Male homosexuality in Thailand: An interpretation of contemporary Thai sources. *Journal of Homosexuality*, 19, 126–138.

Williamson, H., Hanna, M., Lavner, J., Bradbury, T., & Karney, B. (2013). Discussion topic and observed behavior in couples' problem-solving conversations: Do problem severity and topic choice matter? *Journal of Family Psychology*, 27(2), 330–335.

Wilson, C. (2005). Recurrent vulvovaginitis candidiasis: An overview of traditional and alternative therapies. *Advanced Nurse Practitioner*, 13(2), 24–29.

Wilson, C. A., & Davies, D. C. (2007). The control of sexual differentiation of the reproductive system and brain. *Reproduction*, 133, 331–359.

Wilson, E., Dalberth, B., & Koo, H. (2010). "We're the heroes!": Fathers' perspectives on their role in protecting their preteenage children from sexual risk. *Perspectives on Sexual and Reproductive Health*, 42(2), 117–124.

Wilson, G. D. (1987). An ethological approach to sexual deviation. In G. D. Wilson (Ed.), *Variant sexuality: Research and theory* (pp. 84–115). Baltimore: Johns Hopkins University Press.

Wilson, J., & Young, S. (2014, March). Second baby possibly 'cured' of HIV. *Vital Signs*. Retrieved June 6, 2014, from http://www.cnn.com/2014/03/06/health/hiv-baby-cured.

Wilson, M. (2014). Hate crime victimization, 2004–2012: Statistical tables. Washington, DC: Bureau of Justice Statistics, U.S. Department of Justice. Retrieved May 14, 2014, from http://www.bjs.gov/content/pub/pdf/hcv0412st.pdf.

Wilson, P. (1994). Forming a partnership between parents and sexuality educators. *SIECUS Report, 22*, 1–5.

Wilson, R. F. (2008). Keeping women in business (and the family). (Washington Lee Legal Studies Paper No. 2008–34.) Retrieved December 18, 2008, from http://ssrn.com/abstract=1115468.

Wilson, S. K., Delk, J. R., 2nd, & Billups, K. L. (2001). Treating symptoms of female sexual arousal disorder with the Eros-Clitoral Therapy Device. *Journal of Gender Specific Medicine, 4*(2), 54–58.

Wimalawansa, S. J. (2008). Nitric oxide: New evidence for novel therapeutic indications. *Expert Opinions in Pharmacotherapy, 9*, 1935–1954.

Winder, K., Linker, R., Seifert, F., Deutsch, M., Engelhorn, T., Dörfler, A., Lee, D., Hösl, K., & Hilz, M. (2016). Neuroanatomic correlates of female sexual dysfunction in multiple sclerosis. *Annals of Neurology, 80*(4), 490–498.

Winer, R., Hughes, J., Feng, Q., O'Reilly, S., Kiviat, N., Holmes, K., Koutsky, L. (2006). Condom use and the risk of genital human papillomavirus infection in young women. *The New England Journal of Medicine, 354*(25), 2645–2654.

Winters, K. (2009). Transvestic disorder and policy dysfunction in the *DSM-V*. The Bilerico Project. Retrieved May 1, 2017, from http://bilerico.lgbtqnation.com/2009/04/transvestic_disorder_and_policy_dysfunct.php.

Winters, K. (2010). Ten reasons why the transvestic disorder diagnosis in the *DSM-5* has got to go. GID Reform. Retrieved May 1, 2017, from https://gidreform.wordpress.com/2010/10/16/ten-reasons-why-the-transvestic-fetishism-diagnosis-in-the-dsm-5-has-got-to-go/.

Wise, L. A., Cramer, D. W., Hornstein, M. D., Ashby, R. K., & Missmer, S. A. (2011). Physical activity and semen quality among men attending an infertility clinic. *Fertility and Sterility 95*(3), 1025–1030.

Wise, L., Palmer, J., Stewart, E., & Rosenberg, L. (2005). Age-specific incidence rates for self-reported uterine leiomyomata in the Black Women's Health Study. *Obstetrics and Gynecology, 105*(3), 563–568.

Wise, M., & Rodriguez, D. (2013). Detecting deceptive communication through computer-mediated technology: Applying interpersonal deception theory to texting behavior. *Communication Research Reports, 30*(4), 342–346.

Wiseman, J. (2000). *Jay Wiseman's Erotic Bondage Handbook*. Oakland, CA: Greenery Press.

Witchel, S. (2012). Management of CAH during pregnancy: Optimizing outcomes. *Current Opinion in Endocrinology, Diabetes, and Obesity, 19*(6), 489–496.

Witchel, S., & Azziz, R. (2011). Congenital adrenal hyperplasia. *Journal of Pediatric and Adolescent Gynecology, 24*(3), 116–126.

Witt, W., Mandell, K., Wisk, L., Cheng, E., Chatterjee, D., Wakeel, F., Park, H., & Zarak, D. (2015). Predictors of alcohol and tobacco use prior to and during pregnancy in the U.S.: The role of maternal stressors. *Archives of Women's Mental Health, 18*(3), 523–537.

Wittmann, D., Foley, S., & Balon, R. (2011). A biopsychosocial approach to sexual recovery after prostate cancer surgery: The role of grief and mourning. *Journal of Sex and Marital Therapy, 37*(2), 130–144.

Wiwanitkit, V. (2008). Sexuality and rehabilitation for individuals with cerebral palsy. *Sex and Disability, 26*(3), 175–177.

Wojnar, D. (2007). Miscarriage experiences of lesbian couples. *Journal of Midwifery Women's Health, 52*, 479–485.

Wolak, J., Finkelhor, D., & Mitchell, K. J. (2005). Child pornography possessors arrested in Internet-related crimes: Findings from the National Juvenile Online Victimization Study. Retrieved November 7, 2005, from http://www.missingkids.com/en_US/publications/NC144.pdf.

Wolf, N. (1991). *The beauty myth: How images of beauty are used against women*. New York: W. Morris.

Wolfe, J. (2005). Gesture and collaborative planning: A case study of a student writing group. *Written Communication, 22*(3), 298–332.

Wolfinger, N. H. (2000). Beyond the intergenerational transmission of divorce. *Journal of Family Issues, 21*, 1061–1086.

Wolitski, R. J., Valdiserri, R. O., Denning, P. H., & Levine, W. C. (2001). Are we headed for a resurgence of the HIV epidemic among men who have sex with men? *American Journal of Public Health, 91*(6), 883–888.

Wolitzky-Taylor, K., Resnick, H., McCauley, J., Amstadter, A., et al. (2011). Is reporting of rape on the rise? A comparison of women with reported versus unreported rape experiences in the National Women's Study-Replication. *Journal of Interpersonal Violence, 26*(4), 807–832.

Wong, E. W., & Cheng, C. Y. (2011). Impacts of environmental toxicants on male reproductive dysfunction. *Trends Pharmacological Science, 32*(5), 290–299.

Woo, J., Fine, P., & Goetzl, L. (2005). Abortion disclosure and the association with domestic violence. *Obstetrics & Gynecology, 105*(6), 1329–1334.

Wood, E., Desmarais, S., & Gugula, S. (2002). The impact of parenting experience on gender stereotyped toy play of children. *Sex Roles, 47*(1–2), 39–49.

Wood, J. (1999). Gendered lives: Communication, gender, and culture. Belmont, CA: Wadsworth.

Wood, J. (2013). *Gendered lives: Communication, gender, and culture* (10th ed.). Boston, MA: Wadsworth Cengage Learning.

Woolner, A., Bhattacharya, S., & Bhattacharya, S. (2014). The effect of method and gestational age at termination of pregnancy on future obstetric and perinatal outcomes. *British Journal of Gynecology, 121*(3), 309–318.

Wooltorton, E. (2006). Visual loss with erectile dysfunction medications. *Canadian Medical Association Journal, 175*, 355.

Workowski, K., & Berman, S. (2010). Sexually transmitted disease treatment guidelines, 2010. *Morbidity and Mortality Weekly Report, 59*(RR-12), 1–110.

Workowski, K., & Bolan, G. (2015). Sexually transmitted diseases treatment guidelines, 2015. *MMWR Recommendations and Reports, 64*(3). Retrieved April 23, 2017, from https://www.cdc.gov/std/tg2015/tg-2015-print.pdf.

"World Contraceptive Use 2009." (2009). New York: United Nations, Department of Economic and Social Affairs, Population Division. Retrieved from http://www.un.org/esa/population/publications/contraceptive2009/contraceptive2009.htm.

World Health Organization. (2006). Female genital mutilation: New knowledge spurs optimism. *Progress in Sexual and Reproductive Health Research, 72*, 1.

World Health Organization. (2008). *Eliminating female genital mutilation: An interagency statement*. Retrieved March 22, 2008, from http://data.unaids.org/pub/BaseDocument/2008/20080227_interagencystatement_eliminating_fgm_en.pdf.

World Health Organization. (2010). *Standards for sexuality education in Europe: A framework for policy makers, educational and health authorities and specialists*. Retrieved July 7, 2014, from http://www.euro.who.int/en/health-topics/Life-stages/sexual-and-reproductive-health/news/news/2010/12/standards-for-sexuality-education-in-europe-start-their-way-to-countries-of-eastern-europe-and-central-asia.

World Health Organization. (2013). Global and regional estimates of violence against women: Prevalence and health effects of intimate partner violence and non-partner sexual violence. Geneva, Switzerland: Author. Retrieved January 4, 2014, from http://apps.who.int/iris/bitstream/10665/85239/1/9789241564625_eng.pdf.

World Health Organization. (2016, February). Female genital mutilation: Fact sheet.

Retrieved January 20, 2017, from http://www
.who.int/mediacentre/factsheets/fs241/en/.

World Health Organization. (2016). HIV/AIDS
Online Q&A. Retrieved April 26, 2017, from
http://www.who.int/features/qa/71/en/.

World Professional Association for
Transgender Health. (2001). "The Harry
Benjamin International Gender Dysphoria
Association's Standards of Care for Gender
Identity Disorders, Sixth Version." Retrieved
April 17, 2011, from http://wpath.org
/Documents2/socv6.pdf.

World Professional Association for Transgender
Health. (2012). Standards of Care, Volume 7.
Retrieved February 17, 2017, from http://www
.wpath.org/site_page.cfm?pk_association
_webpage_menu=1351&pk_association
_webpage=3926.

Worth, H., Reid, A., & McMillan, K. (2002).
Somewhere over the rainbow: Love, trust,
and monogamy in gay relationships. *Journal
of Sociology*, *38*(3), 237–253.

Wright, K. (1994). The sniff of legend—human
pheromones. Chemical sex attractants? A
sixth sense organ in the nose? What are we
animals? *Discover*, *15*(4), 60.

Wright, L., Mulick, P., & Kincaid, S. (2006).
Fear of and discrimination against bisexuals,
homosexuals, and individuals with AIDS.
Journal of Bisexuality, *6*, 71–84.

Wright, P., & Bae, S. (2015). A national prospective
study of pornography consumption and
gendered attitudes toward women. *Sexuality
and Culture*, *19*(3), 444–463.

Wright, P., Tokunaga, R., & Bae, S. (2014). More
than a dalliance? Pornography consumption
and extramarital sex attitudes among
married U.S. adults. *Psychology of Popular
Media Culture*, *3*(2), 97–109.

Wright, P. J., Randall, A. K., Arroyo, A. (2013).
Father-daughter communication about sex
moderates the association between exposure
to MTV's 16 and pregnant/teen mom and
female students' pregnancy-risk behavior.
Sexuality & Culture, *17*(1), 50–66.

Wu, F., Tajar, A., Beynon, J., Pye, S., Phil, M.,
Silman, A., Finn, J., O'Neill, T., & Bartfai,
G. (2010). Identification of late-onset
hypogonadism in middle-aged and elderly
men. *New England Journal of Medicine*, *363*,
123–135.

Wu, J., McKee, M., McKee, K., Meade, M.,
Plegue, M., & Sen, A. (2017). Female
sterilization is more common among women
with physical and/or sensory disabilities than
women without disabilities in the United
States. *Disability and Health Journal*, *16*.
Retrieved April 8, 2017, from https://www
.ncbi.nlm.nih.gov/pubmed/28110980.

Wu, M. V., & Shah, N. M. (2011). Control of
masculinization of the brain and behavior.
Current Opinions in Neurobiology, *21*, 116–123.

Wu, S. C. (2010). Family planning technical
services in China. *Frontiers of Medicine in
China*, *4*(3), 285–289.

Wuthnow, R. (1998). Islam. In *Encyclopedia of
politics and religion* (pp. 383–393). Washington,
DC: Congressional Quarterly Books.

Wyatt, G. (1998). *Stolen women: Reclaiming our
sexuality, taking back our lives*. New York: Wiley.

Wyatt, K. (2008, May 13). Anonymous rape tests
are going nationwide. *ABC News*. Retrieved
October 7, 2008, from http://abcnews
.go.com/Health/Story?id=4847901&page=1.

Wylie, K., Wootton, E., & Carlson, S. (2016).
Sexual function in the transgender
population. In R. Ettner, S. Monstrey, & E.
Coleman (Eds.), *Principles of transgender
medicine and surgery* (pp. 159–166).
New York: Routledge.

Wylie, K., Wootton, E., & Carlson, S. (2016).
Sexual function in the transgender population.
In Randi Ettner, Stan Monstrey, & Eli Coleman
(Eds.), *Principles of transgender medicine and
surgery* (pp. 159–166). New York: Routledge.

Wynn, L. (2016). "Like a virgin": Hymenoplasty
and secret marriage in Egypt. *Medical
Anthropology*, 1–14.

Wysoczanski, M., Rachko, M., & Bergmann,
S. R. (2008, April 2). Acute myocardial-
infarction in a young man using anabolic-
steroids. *Angiology*, *59*(3), 376–378.

Xia, Y. (2011). Mobile phones' role following
China's 2008 earthquake. In J. Katz (Ed.),
*Mobile communication: New dimensions of
social policy* (pp. 87–102). Piscataway, NJ:
Transaction Publishers.

Xia, Y. (2012). Chinese use of mobile texting for
social interactions: Cultural implication in the
use of communication technology. *Intercultural
Communication Studies*, *21*(2), 131–150.

Xiang, P., Dai, X., Leng, P., Liu, L., & Hu, X.
(2013). SRY gene-testing in the diagnosis
of disorders of sex development among
children. *Chinese Journal of Contemporary
Pediatrics*, *15*(7), 555–558.

Xiao, M., Gao, H., Bai, H., & Zhang, Z. (2016).
Quality of life and sexuality in disease-free
survivors of cervical cancer after radical
hysterectomy along: A comparison between
total laparoscopy and laparotomy. *Medicine*,
95(36), e4787.

Xiaohe, X., & Whyte, M. (1990). Love matches
and arranged marriages: A Chinese
replication. *Journal of Marriage and the
Family*, *53*(3), 709–722.

Xiong, X., Dickey, R., Buekens, P., Shaffer, J., &
Pridjian, G. (2017). Use of intracytoplasmic
sperm injection and birth outcomes
in women conceiving through in vitro
fertilization. *Paediatric and Perinatal
Epidemiology*, *31*(2), 108–115.

Yamawaki, N., & Tschanz, B. T. (2005). Rape
perception differences between Japanese and

American college students: On the mediating
influence of gender role traditionality. *Sex
Roles*, *52*(5–6), 379–392.

Yan, Z., Chen, Q., & Yu, C. (2013). The science of
cell phone use: Its past, present, and future.
*International Journal of Cyber Behavior,
Psychology and Learning*, *3*(1), 7–18.

Yanagimachi, R. (2011). Problems of sperm
fertility: A reproductive biologist's view.
Systems in Biological Reproductive Medicine,
57(1–2), 102–114.

Yancey, G. (2007). Homogamy over the net:
Using Internet advertisements to discover
who interracially dates. *Journal of Social and
Personal Relationships*, *24*, 913–930.

Yasin, B., Al-Tawil, N., Shabile, N., & Al-Hadithi,
T. (2013). Female genital mutilation among
Iraqui Kurdish women. *BMC Public Health*,
113, 809.

Yates, P., Hucker, S., & Ingston, D. (2008).
Sexual sadism: Psychopathology and theory.
In D. Laws & W. O'Donohue (Eds.), *Sexual
deviance: Theory, assessment and treatment*
(2nd ed., pp. 213–230). New York: Guilford
Press.

Yeh, D., & Alam, H. (2014). Hernia emergencies.
Surgical Clinics of North America, *94*(1),
97–130.

Yehuda, R., Lehrner, A., & Rosenbaum, T. (2015).
PTSD and sexual dysfunction in men and
women. *Journal of Sexual Medicine*, *12*(5),
1107–1119.

Yen, H. (2011, February 3). Census: Number
of multiracial Americans tops 5 million.
Houston Chronicle. Retrieved May 11, 2011,
from http://www.chron.com/disp/story.mpl
/chronicle/7410810.html.

Yen, H. (2014, January 11). As cohabitation gains
favor, shotgun weddings fade. *Miami Herald*.
Retrieved April 12, 2014, from http://www
.miamiherald.com/2014/01/11/3861055/as
-cohabitation-gains-favor-shotgun.html.

Yen, J., Chang, S., Ko, C., Yen, C., Chen, C., Yeh,
Y., & Chen, C. (2010). The high-sweet-fat
food craving among women with PMDD:
Emotional response, implicit attitudes and
rewards sensitivity. *Psychoneuroendocrinology*,
35(8), 1203–1212.

Yllo, K., & Finkelhor, D. (1985). Marital rape. In
A. W. Burgess (Ed.), *Rape and sexual assault*
(pp. 146–158). New York: Garland.

Yoder, V. C., Virden, T. B., & Amin, K. (2005).
Internet pornography and loneliness:
An association? *Sexual Addiction &
Compulsivity*, *12*(1), 19–44.

Yoshida, H., Sakamoto, H., Leslie, A., Takahashi,
O., Tsuboi, S., & Kitamura, K. (2016).
Contraception in Japan: Current trends.
Science Direct, *93*(6), 475–477.

Yost, M. R. (2010). Development and validation
of the attitudes about sadomasochism scale.
Journal of Sex Research, *47*(1), 79–91.

Young, B., Desmarais, S., Baldwin, J., & Chandler, R. (2016). Sexual coercion practices among undergraduate male recreational athletes, intercollegiate athletes, and non-athletes. Violence Against Women. Retrieved May 8, 2017, from http://journals.sagepub.com/doi/abs/10.1177/1077801216651339.

Young, K. A., Liu, Y., & Wang, Z. (2008, March 2). The neurobiology of social attachment: A comparative approach to behavioral, neuroanatomical, and neurochemical studies. *Comparative Biochemistry and Physiology: Toxicology and Pharmacology*. Retrieved October 3, 2008, from http://www.ncbi.nlm.nih.gov/pubmed/18417423?ordinalpos=1&itool= EntrezSystem2.PEntrez.Pubmed.Pubmed_ResultsPanel.Pubmed_RVDocSum.

Young, K. S., Griffin-Shelley, E., Cooper, A., O'Mara, J., & Buchanan, J. (2000). Online infidelity. In A. Cooper (Ed.), *Cybersex: The dark side of the force* (pp. 59–74). Philadelphia, PA: Brunner Routledge.

Young, K., Griffin-Shelley, E., Cooper, A., O'Mara, J., & Buchanan, J. (2000). Online infidelity: A new dimension in couple relationships with implications for evaluation and treatment. *Sexual Addiction & Compulsivity: The Journal of Treatment and Prevention, 7*(1–2), 59–74.

Young, L. J., & Wang, Z. (2004). The neurobiology of pair bonding. *Nature, 7,* 1048–1054.

Young, R., Gore, N., & McCarthy, M. (2012). Staff attitudes towards sexuality in relation to gender of people with intellectual disability: A qualitative study. *Journal of Intellectual & Developmental Disability, 37*(4), 343–347.

Young, S. (2014). Marijuana may affect fertility in young men. *CNN Health*. Retrieved June 24, 2014, from http://thechart.blogs.cnn.com/2014/06/05/marijuana-may-affect-fertility-in-young-men.

Young, S., & Wilson, J. (2014, July). Virus detected in baby 'cured' of HIV. *CNN Health*. Retrieved August 14, 2014, from http://www.cnn.com/2014/07/10/health/baby-not-cured-hiv.

Younger, J., Aron, A., Parke, S., Chatterjee, N., & Mackey, S. (2010). Viewing pictures of a romantic partner reduces experimental pain: Involvement of neural reward systems. *PLoS One, 5*(10), E13309.

Youssry, M., Ozmen, B., Zohni, K., Diedrich, K., & Al-Hasani, S. (2008). Current aspects of blastocyst cryopreservation. *Reproductive Biomedicine Online, 16,* 311–320.

Yu, R. (2016, October 28). Jury awards more than $70M to woman in J&J baby powder cancer lawsuit. *USA Today*. Retrieved January 20, 2017, from http://www.usatoday.com/story/money/business/2016/10/28/johnson-jnj-talcum-baby-powder-ovarian-cancer/92878176/.

Yuan, S., Hussain, S., Hales, K., & Cotton, S. (2016). What do they like? Communication preferences and patterns of older adults in the United States: The role of technology. *Educational Gerontology, 42*(3), 163–174.

Yule, M., Brotto, L., & Gorzalka, B. (2016). Sexual fantasy and masturbation among asexual individuals: An in-depth exploration. *Archives of Sexual Behavior, 46*(1), 311–328.

Zablotska, I., Holt, M., & Prestage, G. (2012). Changes in gay men's participation in gay community life: Implications for HIV surveillance and research. *AIDS Behavior, 16*(3), 669–675.

Zacur, H. A., Hedon, B., Mansourt, D., Shangold, G. A., Fisher, A. C., & Creasy, G. W. (2002). Integrated summary of Ortho Evra contraceptive patch adhesion in varied climates and conditions. *Fertility and Sterility, 77*(2 Suppl. 2), 532–535.

Zak, A., Collins, C., & Harper, L. (1998). Self-reported control over decision-making and its relationship to intimate relationships. *Psychological Reports, 82*(2), 560–562.

Zandbergen, D., & Brown, S. (2015). Culture and gender differences in romantic jealousy. *Personality and Individual Differences, 72,* 122–127.

Zanetti-Dallenbach, R. A., Krause, E. M., Lapaire, O., Gueth, U., Holzgreve, W., Wight, E. (2008). Impact of hormone replacement therapy on the histologic subtype of breast cancer. Epub retrieved on March 18, 2008, from http://www.ncbi.nlm.nih.gov/pubmed/18335229?ordinalpos=1&itool=EntrezSystem2.PEntrez.Pubmed.Pubmed_ResultsPanel.Pubmed_RVDocSum.

Zhang, Y., Huang, Z., Ding, L., Yan, H., Wang, M., & Zhu, S. (2010). Simultaneous determination of yohimbine, sildenafil, vardenafil and tadalafil in dietary supplements using high-performance liquid chromatography-tandem mass spectrometry. *Journal of Separation Science, 33*(14), 2109–2114.

Zhao, Y., Garcia, J., Jarow, J., & Wallach, E. (2004). Successful management of infertility due to retrograde ejaculation using assisted reproductive technologies: A report of two cases. *Archives of Andrology, 50*(6), 391–394.

Zheng, L., Wang, H., Li, B., & Zeng, X. (2013). Sperm-specific ion channels: Targets holding the most potential for male contraceptives in development. *Contraception, 88*(4), 485–491.

Zieman, M., Guillebaud, J., Weisberg, E., Shangold, G., Fisher, A., & Creasy, G. (2002). Contraceptive efficacy and cycle control with the Ortho Evra transdermal system: The analysis of pooled data. *Fertility and Sterility, 77,* S13–18.

Zimmer-Gembeck, M. J., & Helfand, M. (2008). Ten years of longitudinal research on U.S. adolescent sexual behavior: Developmental correlates of sexual intercourse, and the importance of age, gender and ethnic background. *Developmental Review, 28,* 153–224.

Zimmerman, F., Christakis, D., & Meltzoff, A. (2007). Television and DVD/video viewing in children younger than 2 years. *Archives of Pediatrics and Adolescent Medicine, 161,* 473–479.

Zinaman, M. J., Clegg, E. D., Brown, C. C., O'Connor, J., & Selevan, S. G. (1996). Estimates of human fertility and pregnancy loss. *Journal of Fertility and Sterility, 65*(3), 503–509.

Zinzow, H., McCauley, J., & Ruggiero, K. (2012). Prevalence and risk of psychiatric disorders as a function of variant rape histories: Results from a national survey of women. *Social Psychiatry and Psychiatric Epidemiology, 47*(6), 893–902.

Zoroya, G. (2016, June 9). 'Honor killings': 5 things to know. *USA Today*. Retrieved August 23, 2017, from https://www.usatoday.com/story/news/world/2016/06/09/honor-killings-united-nations-pakistan/85642786/.

Zucker, K., & Lawrence, A. (2009). Epidemiology of gender identity disorder: Recommendations for the standards of care of the World Professional Association for Transgender Health. *International Journal of Transgenderism, 1,* 8–18.

Zucker, K. J. (1990). Psychosocial and erotic development in cross-gender identified children. *Canadian Journal of Psychiatry, 35,* 487–495.

Zukerman, Z., Weiss, D., & Orvieto, R. (2003). Short communication: Does preejaculatory penile secretion originating from Cowper's gland contain sperm? *Journal of Assisted Reproduction and Genetics, 20*(4), 157–159.

Zukov, I., Ptacek, R., Raboch, J., Domluvilova, D., Kuzelova, H., Fischer, S., & Kozelek, P. (2010). PMDD—Review of actual findings about mental disorders related to menstrual cycle and possibilities of their therapy. *Prague Medical Reports, 111*(1), 12–24.

Zurbriggen, E. L., & Yost, M. R. (2004). Power, desire, and pleasure in sexual fantasies. *Journal of Sex Research, 41*(3), 288–300.

Zverina, J. (2004). Czech Republic. In R. T. Francoeur & R. J. Noonan (Eds.), *The Continuum International Encyclopedia of Sexuality* (pp. 320–328). New York/London: Continuum International.

Name Index

Nicolson, S., 301
Nie, J., 304
Niekerk, A., 463
Nielsen Mobile Netview, 59
Nieschlag, E., 147
Nikodem, V. C., 319
Nilsson, L., 113, 300, 317
Nisenblat, V., 122
Nissen, E., 320
Niv, E., 383
Niwa, S., 305
Nizielski, S., 58
Njeuhmeli, E., 143
Noar, S., 192, 193
Noble, M., 386
Nocera, R., 467
Noe, M., 122
Noel-Weiss, J., 324
Nolan, T., 441, 443
Noller, P., 72, 164
Noonan, R. J., 352, 353, 435
Noorimotlagh, Z., 139
Nordahl, H. M., 89
Nordkap, L., 313
Nordling, N., 440
Nordtveit, T., 321
Norman, W., 366
Norouzinia, M., 118
Norrgren, H., 422
Norris, J., 389, 458
Northrup, J., 173
Norton, L., 317
Norton, M., 316
Norwitz, E. R., 317
Nosek, B., 219
Nosoognoen, W., 115
"Not Alone," 465
Notman, M. T., 288, 468
Nowicka, G., 124
Noyes, N., 308
Ntshebe, O., 337
Nucatola, D., 366
Nueten, J. V., 316
Nulsen, J., 305
Nunes, A., 141
Nutan, F., 142
Nuttall, F., 141
Nyamukapa, C., 424
Nyce, J., 335
Nyilas, R., 379

Oakes, M., 86
Obedin-Maliver, J., 305
O'Brien, C., 471, 472
O'Brien, J., 251
O'Brien, P. H., 464, 473
Occhipinti, A., 109
Ocfemia, M., 400
Ochs, E., 220
Ochsenkühn, R., 378
O'Cleirigh, C., 420
O'Connell, H. E., 108
O'Connell, T., 286
O'Connor, J., 299
O'Connor, K., 305
O'Connor, M., 109
O'Connor, P., 310
Odenweller, K. G., 58
O'Donohue, W., 432, 448, 449, 451
O'Donohue, W. T., 35
Oduncu, V., 345
Oertel, W., 89
Offen, K. M., 14

Offit, A., 374, 386
Ofir, K., 322
Ogilvie, G., 401
Ogletree, S. M., 181
O'Gorman, L., 289
O'Grady, R., 443, 444
Oh, C., 387
O'Halloran, R. L., 445
O'Hare, P., 389
Ohl, D. A., 386
Ojanen, T., 185, 186
Oka, M., 214
Okami, P., 181, 444
Okeowo, A., 227
Olafson, L., 14
Olariu, A., 354
O'Leary, A., 255
O'Leary, D., 210
Oleszkiewica, A., 441
Oliffe, J., 219, 392
Olin, L., 412
Oliver, C., 458
Ollen, E., 469, 474
Olmstead, R., 181
Olmstead, S., 234, 260, 504
Olovsson, M., 122
Olp, J. J., 162
Olsen, E., 43, 191, 192
Olsson, A., 320
Olsson, S. E., 97
O'Mara, J., 447
O'Mathúna, D. P., 301
O'Meara, E., 127
Onda, T., 364, 367
Onderdonk, A., 122
O'Neill, G., 216
O'Neill, N., 216
Oner, B., 167
Onyango, P., 224, 226
Opoku, J., 417, 419
O'Rand, M., 361
Orhan, I., 386
Orman, J., 383
Ormerod, A. J., 482
Ornish, D., 156
Orosz, B., 318
Orosz, G., 172
Orovecz, J., 182, 189
Orr, D. P., 189
Ortega, L., 92
Orth, U., 170
Ortigue, S., 162, 163
Ortiz, C., 384
Ortiz, C. A., 212
Ortman, J., 207
Orvieto, R., 140, 366
Osamu, I., 97
Oselin, S., 506, 511
O'Shaughnessy, P., 392
Osmond, C., 312
Osofsky, H. J., 508
Ost, L., 386
Osterberg, E., 114
Osterman, M., 193, 298, 299, 318, 321, 322
O'Sullivan, L., 156, 189, 456
O'Sullivan, L. F., 338
Oswald, R., 207
Othman, A., 139, 304
Otis, M. D., 289
Ouellette, G., 59
Owen, J., 208, 247, 260
Owens, A., 435
Owens, Z., 281
Oxkuvanci, U., 387

Ozdemir, O., 388
Özdemir, S., 187
Ozgor, F., 387
Ozkardes, S., 388
Ozmen, B., 308

Paavonen, J., 124
Pacey, A., 139
Pachankis, J. E., 217
Pacik, P., 389
Padgett, J., 209
Padilla-Walker, L. M., 193
Padmanabhan, V., 124
Padron, E., 220
Paek, H., 496
Page, J., 440, 441
Pagliaro, L., 150
Pagnier, J., 424
Paik, A., 48, 198, 375, 377, 381, 384, 386, 388
Pal, L., 298
Palacio, A., 390
Palaia, I., 389
Palan, K., 496
Palca, J., 299, 317
Palermo, T., 360
Palimeri, S., 124
Palioura, E., 124
Palit, V., 382
Pallotta, F., 481
Palmer, C. T., 461
Palmer, J., 115, 120
Palmiotto, R., 124
Pan, A., 122
Pan, S., 112
Panay, N., 119
Pandey, S., 96
Pang, R., 118
Pang, S., 305
Panici, P., 305
Panidis, D., 124
Panjari, M., 391
Pant, B., 361
Pantalone, D., 281
Panuzio, J., 467
Papa, A., 305
Papp, J., 409
Paquet, L., 375
"Paraphilic Disorders," 434
Pargament, K., 193
Parish, S.; Hahn, S., 378
Parish, W., 247
Parish Hahn, 2016, 377
Park, H., 286, 312
Parker, D., 89
Parker, H., 14
Parker, H. A., 478
Parker, K., 60, 212
Parker, R., 316
Parker, S., 120
Parker, S. E., 316
Parker, W. J., 358
Parker-Pope, T., 221
Parkhill, M.; Abbey, A., 459
Parks, K. A., 466
Parks, S., 92
Parlante, A., 401
Parrish, T., 240
Parrott, D., 286
Parsai, S., 323
Parsonnet, J., 122
Parsons, J., 216, 218, 257, 478
Paschall, M. J., 466
Pasley, K., 234, 260

Pasterski, V., 86
Pasterski, V. L., 86
Pastwa-Wojciechowska, B., 302
Pasupathy, D., 322
Patel, N., 162, 163, 457, 458, 464, 469, 471, 472, 480
Patel, S., 379
Pathela, P., 268
Pattatucci, A. M., 269
Patterson, C., 219, 284
Patton, G. C., 115
Paul, B., 447
Paul, J. P., 289
Paul, P., 221, 503
Paulose-Ram, R., 414
Pauls, R., 108
Paulsen, J., 483
Payer, P. J., 12
Payne, K., 211
Pearce, A., 166
Pearson, C., 331
Peck, S., 158
Peddie, D., 127
Pedersen, C. B., 366, 367
Pedersen, G., 86
Peele, S., 173
Peeples, E. H., 473
Peipert, J., 354
Pelentsov, L., 392
Pellegrini, M., 269
Peller, M., 270
Pembrey, G., 424
Pence, B., 332
Penke, L., 172
Penna-Firme, T., 509
Penney, G., 69
Pennington, C., 287
Pennington, J., 424
Peplau, A., 114
Peplau, L., 208, 220
Peplau, L. A., 213, 273, 288
Peragallo-Urrutia, R., 128
Perales, M., 311
Peralta, R. L., 466
Pereira, M., 319
Pereira, N., 393
Perelman, M., 380, 386
Perelman-Hall, T., 267
Perilloux, C., 208, 468
Perkins, R., 506, 507
Perlman, D., 228
Perniola, G., 389
Perovic, S., 96
Perovic, S. V., 146
Perper, K., 193
Perper, T., 171
Perrin, D., 509
Perrin, K., 127
Perry, H., 382
Perry, S., 207
Perry-Jenkins, M., 220
Perz, J., 392
Peter, J., 494
Peterman, T., 305
Peters, A., 234
Peters, P., 288
Peters, S., 391
Petersen, I., 323
Petersen, L., 413
Peterson, C. M., 315
Peterson, J., 286
Peterson, K., 193
Petignat, P., 127
Petraglia, F., 349

Petras, H., 458, 482
Petrow, S., 424
Pettersson, H., 122
Peverelli, M., 59
Pew Research Center, 59, 210, 211, 212, 213, 222, 227, 276, 281, 291, 292
Pexman, P. M., 59
Pezzi, C., 149
Pfaus, J., 270
Phan-Weston, S., 345
Philbin, J., 191, 193, 330
Philip, E., 391
Philip, K., 69
Philip, S., 402
Philipp, S., 100
Phillips, B., 463
Phillips, M., 207, 216
Phillips-Plummer, L., 506
Piacentino, D., 147
Piaget, J., 91
Picaud, S., 382
Piccinelli, A., 146
Piccinino, L. J., 251
Pickar, J., 121
Piercy, F., 60, 216
Pihlstrom, H., 322
Pilishvili, T., 168
Pillard, R. C., 269, 270, 272
Pilling, A. R., 225
Pillsworth, E. G., 162
Pilver, C., 119
Pinell-White, X., 391
Ping, W., 11
Pinheiro, A. P., 117
Pink, L., 380
Pinkerton, J., 120
Pinkerton, S., 473
Pinney, S., 115
Pinquart, M., 219
Pisanski, K., 441
Pisetsky, E. M., 188
Pistorio, J. M., 462
Pitkultang, S., 359
Pitts, S., 352
Piwko, C., 301
Piyamongkol, W., 316
Pjekny, S., 495
Placik, O., 110
Planned Parenthood Federation of America, 198
Plant, A., 128, 281
Plaud, J. J., 49
Plaut, A., 143
Pleak, R. R., 507
Plitea, L., 495
Plotonicov, K., 117
Plummer, K., 178, 275
Pocklington, R., 499
Poeppl, T., 445
Pogatchnik, S., 227
Polaris Project, 514
Policar M., 330, 332, 334, 335, 337, 341, 343, 344, 345, 348, 349, 350, 351, 351–352, 353, 354, 356, 357, 358, 359, 360, 361
Pollack, L. M., 46
Pollak, S., 61
Pollock, N. L., 445
Polonec, L., 406
Pomara, C., 147
Pomeroy, E. C., 462
Pomeroy, W., 39, 189, 374, 386, 438, 439

Subject Index

Male Survivor, 486
male-on-top intercourse position, 253
males
    abortion effect on, 367
    adolescent, research on, 42–43
    aged-associate changes, 258–259
    ancient, 7–11
    arousal problems in, 381–383
    breast cancer, 142, 149
    early ejaculation, 385–386
    forced penetration, age at time of, 458
    intimacy styles, 167
    manual sex on, 249
    maturation cycle, 142–144
    oral sex on, 251
    orgasmic disorder, 385–387
    physical development, 187
    pregnancy experience of, 311
    puberty, 142–143, 184
    rape, effects of, 472
    rape victims, 471–473
    reactions to abortion, 367
    resolution phase in, 241–242
    sex organs, 82–83
    sex therapy, 382–383
    sex workers, 507–508
    sexual arousal, 240
    sexual fantasies, 245
    sexual response cycle, 240–242
    sexual violence, 471–473
    sexual violence, prevalence of, 457
    spinal cord risk, 394
    stereotypes of, 92–93
    sterilization, 358–359
    steroid abuse, 147
    television images, 494
male-to-female transsexuals, 96–97
male-typical activities, 273
malignant, 126
mammography, 126
manic love, 158
manual sex, 247
    on men, 249
    popularity of, 247
    on women, 248–249
marijuana, 312, 313, 379
marital customs, in other cultures, 225–226
marital satisfaction, 213–214
marital sexual violence, 469. *see also* intimate partner violence (IPV)
marriage. *see also* divorce
    in 19th Century, 18
    arranged, 223–224
    consanguineous, 226
    covenant, 220
    cultural differences, 223–224
    current trends, 211
    forced, 224
    governance of, 211
    infidelity, 215–216
    in later life, 212–213

mixed, 211–212
    nonexclusive, 216–217
    in other cultures, 223–224
    overview of, 211
    procreation, 219–220
    Protestant Reformation and, 13–14
    Puritan, 16
    rape in, 469
    reasons for, 211
    same-sex, 220, 526
    satisfaction in, 213–214
    sexuality outside of, 215–217
    sexuality within, 214–215
    statistics, 211
    trends in, 211
Marriage Law of the People's Republic of China, 224
Martin, Chris, 221
masculine socialization, 92
masculinity, 88, 92–93
masochism, 438
mass media, 491. *see also* media; social media
    changes in, 495–496
    LGBT images in, 287–288
    sexual behavior and, 32
    sexual images, 5–6
    television, 492–496
mastectomy, 391
Masters, William, 19, 39–40, 524
Master's and Mistress' Handbook, 440
Masters of Sex, 40, 522
masturbation
    in adolescence, 189
    in adulthood, 246–247
    attitudes about, 8
    in childhood, 184
    mutual, 247–248
    in older adults, 259
    overview of, 246–247
    in sexual dysfunction treatment, 385
maternal immune hypothesis, 270
maternal-serum alpha-fetoprotein screening (MSAFP), 315, 316
Mattachine Society, 21
Matthew Shepard and James Byrd, Jr. Hate Crimes Prevention Act, 287
McCarthy, Joseph, 21
McCormick, Katharine Dexter, 20
Mead, Margaret, 89
Measure B, 504
meatus, 134
media, 491
    erotic literature, 492
    Generation M, 495
    homophobia and heterosexism, combating, 287–288
    impact on sexuality, 5–6
    movement against sexualization of, 495–496
    sexuality in, 491–494
    television and film, 492–496

medical model, 519
medical transition, 94, 95–97
medication abortions, 365–366
MedlinePlus Health Information, 152
Medved, Michael, 496
Meese, Edwin, 501
Meese Commission, 501–502
Megan's Law, 433, 444
Memoirs of a Woman of Pleasure (Cleland), 491
Men Can Stop Rape (MCSR), 486
menarche, 115
menopause, 80
    characterization of, 120–121
    hormone replacement therapy, 121
    HRT during, 121
    male, 80, 143–144
    onset of, 120
    overview of, 120–121
menorrhagia, 118
menses, 116
Mensinga, Wilhelm, 529
menstrual cramps, 117–118
menstrual manipulation, 119
menstrual phase, 116
menstrual suppression, 119
menstrual synchronicity, 116
menstrual toxic shock syndrome (mTSS), 122
menstruation
    characterization of, 116–120
    hormones released in, 113, 118
    lifetime incidence of, 119
    manipulation of, 119–120
    negative feedback loop, 116, 118
    ovarian cycle and, 116–117
    overview of, 116–117
    phases of, 116
    premenstrual dysphoric disorder, 118–119
    premenstrual syndrome, 118–119
    sexual behavior and, 120
    sexual response and, 240
    suppression of, 119–120
    variations, 117–118
mental illness, 394–395
Mentors in Violence Prevention (MVP), 462
message interpretation, 71
methamphetamine, 379
metoidioplasty, 96, 97
Metronidazole (Flagyl), 411
Metropolitan Community Church, 291
Mexico City Policy, 368
Michael, Robert, 41
Michaels, Stuart, 41
Michelangelo, 490, 492
microbicides, 340
microsorting, 303
Middle Ages
    homosexuality in, 274
    liberalization during, 519
    sexuality, 11–12
Middle East
    abortion, 368

forced marriage in, 224
    HIV/AIDS, 424–425
    homosexuality, 277
    sexuality, 7
midwife, 318
mifepristone, 365, 530
military injuries, 383
Millett, Kate, 21
minipills, 351
Minnesota Multiphasic Personality Inventory (MMPI), 448
minority homosexuality, 289–290
minority sexuality in television and film, 493–494
Mioplex, 243
Mirena IUD, 353, 354, 530
miscarriage, 300
misgender, 78
misoprostol, 365
missionary position, 253
mitosis, 80
mittelschmerz, 115
mixed marriages, 211–212, 221
mixed-age marriages, 212
MMPI. *see* Minnesota Multiphasic Personality Inventory
Modern Family, 207, 287, 493
Molkara, Maryann Khatoon, 95
Moll, Albert, 36, 523
Monistat, 125
monogamous relationship, 247
monophasic pill, 344, 345
monosexism, 289
monozygotic, 300
mons pubis, 107
mons veneris, 107
Moral Majority, 501
morality
    Christian, 10–12
    Crusades, 18
morning sickness, 301, 304
Morrow, Prince, 18
Mosher, Clelia, 37, 523
motherhood mandate, 303
Motion Picture Code, 495–496
"motionless intercourse," 380
"Mozart Effect," 42
MSAFP. *see* maternal-serum alpha-fetoprotein screening
mTSS. *see* menstrual toxic shock syndrome
mucus plug, 298
Muhammad, 12
Müllerian duct, 83
Müllerian inhibiting factor, 83
multimodal, 378
multiple orgasms, 240
multiple sclerosis, 393
Muppets, 494
Museum of Menstruation & Women's Health, 130
mutual masturbation, 247–248
myocardial infarction, 390
myometrium, 112
myotonia, 236

Paltrow, Gwyneth, 221
pangender, 94
pansexual, 266, 289
Papanicolaou (Pap) tests, 121, 406, 413
ParaGard IUD, 353, 354, 530
paraphilias, 432
  assessment of, 448–449
  behavioral theories, 436–437
  biological theories, 435
  developmental theories, 436
  erotophonophiliac, 446
  exhibitionistic, 440–441
  fetishistic disorder, 437
  globally, 435
  history of, 434
  labeling, 451
  necrophilia, 446
  obscene telephone callers, 445–446
  overview of, 434–435
  pedophilia, 443–445
  principles of, 28–29
  psychoanalytic theory of, 436
  scatolophilia, 445–446
  sexual addictions, 446–448
  sexual masochism disorder, 438–440
  sexual sadism disorder, 438–440
  sociological theories, 437
  theories about, 435–437
  transvestic disorder, 438
  treatment options, 449–451
  variations in, 445–448
  voyeuristic, 441, 443
  zoophilia, 446
paraphilic disorders
  assessment of, 448–449
  exhibitionistic disorder, 440–441
  fetishistic disorder, 437
  frotteuristic disorder, 443
  pedophilia, 442
  pedophilic disorder, 443–445
  sexual masochism disorder, 438–440
  sexual sadism disorder, 438–440
  transvestic disorder, 438
  treatment options, 449–451
  voyeuristic disorders, 440, 441, 443
paraplegia, 394
parental consent, 363
parental notification, 363
"parenting happiness gap," 219
parents
  anxiety of, 185
  childhood relationships with, 185
  LGB, 283–284, 297
  postpartum issues, 322–324
  relationship satisfaction of, 220
  sexuality for, 323
  teen relationship with, 192–193
Parents, Families, & Friends of Lesbians and Gays (PFLAG), 281, 283, 295

participant observation, 46
partnered sexual behavior
  anal intercourse, 255–256
  foreplay, 247
  manual sex, 247–249
  oral sex, 249–251
  overview of, 247
  same-sex sexual behavior, 256–258
  vaginal intercourse, 251–255
Party for Neighborly Love, Freedom, and Diversity, 442
Pasandide, Hassan, 95
passing women, 274–275
passion, 159
patient-centered model, 87
patriarchal, 8
Patterns of Sexual Behavior (Ford/Beach), 524
Paul VI, Pope, 529
PCOS. *see* Polycystic ovarian syndrome
PCP. *see* Pneumocystis carinii pneumonia
pederasty, 7
pedophilia, 443
  characteristics, 443–444
  in Netherlands, 442
  political party advocating, 442
  recidivism, 445
  risk factors, 445
  social media and, 445
peer group interaction, 272
peers
  adolescents, 192
  childhood relationships with, 185–186
Peg + Cat, 495
pelvic cancer, 392
pelvic inflammatory disease (PID), 125, 314, **348**, 402, 406, 409
penectomy, 96
penile cancer, 149–150, 392
penile plethysmography, 448
penile strain gauges, 39, 40
penis, 133, 134
  cancer of, 149–150, 392
  erection, 134, 136–137
  internal structure, 135
  root, 134
  size of, 136
  structure of, 135
penitents, 11
perceived sperm competition, 504
perfect use, 334
performance fears, 374
performance-enhancing drugs (PED), 147
perimenopause, 120, 350
perimetrium, 112
perinatal HIV infections, 417
perineum, 111
permanent methods of contraception, 357–359
persistent sexual arousal syndrome, 380
Peyronie's disease, 146

Pfizer Pharmaceuticals, 524
PFLAG. *see* Parents, Families & Friends of Lesbians and Gays
PGD. *see* preimplantation genetic diagnosis
phallic stage, 29
phalloplasty, 96
phallus, 6
pharmacotherapy, 449, 450
pheromones, 162
Philippines, 331
Phineas and Ferb, 494
PHO. *see* prostitution-helping organization
photoplethysmographs, 39, 40
phthalates, 139
physical development
  adolescent, 186–187
  childhood, 179, 180, 181–184
  coordination and, 180
  puberty, 181–184
physiological arousal theory, 162
physiology, sexual orientation and, 270
PID. *see* pelvic inflammatory disease
piercings, 113
pimps, 509
"pink ovaries" concept, 241
placebo pills, 345
placenta, 300, 320
placenta previa, 322
Plan B One-Step, 359, 530
Planned Parenthood Federation of America, 20, 330, 363, 366, 371, 529
plateau phase, 236, 238, 239, 240
Plato, 8
platonic, 8
Playboy magazine, 20
PMDD. *see* premenstrual dysphoric disorder
PMS. *see* premenstrual syndrome
Pneumocystis carinii pneumonia, **418**
police, 474–475
political ideologies, 239
politics, 35
polyamory, 216
The Polyamory Society, 230
polyandry, 226
polycystic ovarian syndrome (PCOS), 123–124
polygamy, 9, 18, 225
polygyny, 225, 226
polyurethane, 335, 337–338
poly-victimization, 482
Pornhub, 503
pornography, 490
  adolescents, 494
  adult entertainment industry, 504–505
  anticensorship arguments, 502–503
  antipornography arguments, 502
  attitudes about, 505
  career in, 500

  child, 442, 445, 498
  commissions on, 501–502
  community standards and, 500
  court decisions, 500–501
  court rulings, 500–501
  debates over, 502–503
  definition of, 499–502
  development of, 490–491
  harmful effects research, 503–504
  industry, 504–505
  in literature, 492
  masturbation, 246
  and partner sex, 381
  presidential commissions, 501–502
  public attitudes toward, 505
  studies on, 503–504
  vaginal intercourse, 252
  websites for, 516
  workers in, 500
possessiveness, 173
postcoital drip, 337
postnuptial agreements, 211
postpartum depression, 323
postpartum parenthood, 322–324
postpartum psychosis, 323
"post-sex blues," 252
posttraumatic stress disorder (PTSD), 119, 387
  in child sexual abuse victims, 478
  in rape victims, 467, 470
  in secondary victims, 470–471
power, 456. *see also* sexual violence
pragmatic love, 158
preeclampsia, 316
pregnancy
  adolescents, 193–194
  in biological men, 301
  birth defects, 315–316
  dating of, 309
  drugs and alcohol, 312
  early signs of, 301–302
  ectopic, 302, 314–315
  exercise and nutrition, 311–312
  fathers' role in, 311
  first trimester, 309
  health care during, 311–314
  length of, 317
  in older women, 312–313, 314
  partner's experience, 311
  physical changes after, 322–323
  postpartum parenthood, 322–324
  prenatal period, 309–311
  problems during, 314–317
  psychological changes after, 323
  Rh incompatibility, 316
  second trimester, 309–310
  sex during, 313–314
  sex selection, 303–304
  sexually transmitted infections, 402–403
  spontaneous abortion, 315
  substance abuse and, 312
  syphilis and, 403